EIGHTH EDITION

PRINCIPLES AND PRACTICE OF MARKETING

DAVID JOBBER AND
FIONA ELLIS-CHADWICK

EIGHTH EDITION

PRINCIPLES AND PRACTICE OF MARKETING

DAVID JOBBER AND FIONA ELLIS-CHADWICK

Mc
Graw
Hill
Education

London   Boston   Burr Ridge, IL   Dubuque, IA   Madison, WI   New York   San Francisco
St. Louis   Bangkok   Bogotá Caracas   Kuala Lumpur   Lisbon   Madrid   Mexico City
Milan   Montreal   New Delhi   Santiago   Seoul   Singapore   Sydney   Taipei   Toronto

Principles and Practice of Marketing

David Jobber and Fiona Ellis-Chadwick
ISBN-13 9780077174149
ISBN-10 0077174143

Published by McGraw-Hill Education
Shoppenhangers Road
Maidenhead
Berkshire
SL6 2QL
Telephone: 44 (0) 1628 502 500
Fax: 44 (0) 1628 770 224
Website: www.mheducation.co.uk

British Library Cataloguing in Publication Data
A catalogue record for this book is available from the British Library

Library of Congress Cataloguing in Publication Data
The Library of Congress data for this book has been applied for from the Library of Congress

Content Acquisitions Manager: Leiah Norcott
Product Developer: Alice Aldous
Content Product Manager: Ben King
Marketing Manager: Geeta Kumar

Text Design by Kamae Design
Cover design by Adam Renvoize
Printed and bound by APP, Lebanon.

ISBN-13 9780077174149
ISBN-10 0077174143
eISBN-13 9780077174156

Dedication

To Brian, Shirley and John.

Brief Table of Contents

Detailed Table of Contents

Vignettes

MINI CASES

Case Guide

This guide shows the key concepts covered in each of the cases in both the book and the Online Learning Centre so you can easily pick out which cases are relevant to a particular part of your course. Go to **www.mheducation.co.uk/textbooks/jobber8** to find a pdf of this guide, and search by company, industry or topic to find the ideal case to use.

Chapter	Case number	Case title and author	Key concepts covered
1	Case 1	Coca-Cola versus Pepsi *David Jobber, Emeritus Professor, University of Bradford*	Market orientation, competition, leading brands, positioning
	Case 2	H&M Gets Hotter *David Jobber, Emeritus Professor, University of Bradford*	Market orientation, effectiveness and efficiency, customer value, fashion industry
2	Case 3	Searching for Sony's Salvation *Conor Carroll, Lecturer in Marketing, University of Limerick*	Product innovation, SWOT, marketing environment, strategic options
	Case 4	SodaStream: Adapting itself to a Changing Market *Tom McNamara and Asha Moore-Mangin, the ESC Rennes School of Business, France*	Marketing environment, microenvironment and macroenvironment, political and legal, economic, ecological/physical environmental, social/cultural and technological forces, how companies respond to environmental change
3	Case 5	Cappuccino Hotshots *David Jobber, Emeritus Professor of Marketing, University of Bradford*	Market development, competitive positioning, consumer choice
	Case 6	Red Bull *David Cosgrove, Lecturer, University of Limerick*	Buying decision process, marketing communications, choice criteria, social influences on consumer behaviour
4	Case 7	Flying in Tandem: Organizational Purchasing in the Airline Industry *Adrian Pritchard, Senior Lecturer in Marketing, Coventry University*	Characteristics of organizational buyers, organizational market, consumer versus organizational buying, reverse marketing, buyer-seller relationships
	Case 8	AstraZeneca: Sweden and the UK Join Forces to Form a Production Power Base to Serve New Market Habitats in the Pharmaceutical Industry *Fiona Ellis-Chadwick, Senior Lecturer, Loughborough University*	Role of marketing in the pharmaceutical industry, buying process, choice criteria, B2B buying behaviour
5	Case 9	The Co-operative-Leading the Way in Corporate Social Responsibility *Brian Searle, Programme Director Marketing MSc, Loughborough University*	Ethical production, influences on industry standards
	Case 10	Coop Danmark's Anti Food Wastage Initiatives: Social Responsibility or Good Business? *Robert Ormrod, Associate Professor, Aarhus University*	Corporate social responsibility (CSR), drivers of social responsibility, CSR as part of marketing strategy, business ethics

12	Case 23	easyJet and Ryanair *David Jobber, Emeritus Professor of Marketing, University of Bradford*	Pricing strategies, marketing strategy, low price strategy, airline industry
	Case 24	The Surge of German Limited Range Discounters *Conor Carroll, Lecturer in Marketing, University of Limerick*	Everyday low pricing, limited range discounters, retail discounters, price wars, competitive strategy
13	Case 25	Coke Gets Personal: The Share a Coke Campaign *Marie O'Dwyer, Lecturer in Marketing, Waterford Institute of Technology*	Benefits of integrated marketing communications (IMC), factors leading to growth of IMC campaigns, benefits and risks of a mass personalization campaign, debranding
	Case 26	Comparethemarket.com: 'Simples' *David Cosgrave, Lecturer, University of Limerick*	Integrated marketing communications, off- and online communications, brand identity, promotional mix
14	Case 27	Toyota and Buddy *Adele Berndt, Associate Professor, Jönköping International Business School*	Marketing strategy, integrated marketing communications, rebuilding a brand
	Case 28	Volvo: Fundamentally Changing the Way Cars are Marketed and Sold *Tom McNamara and Asha Moore-Mangin, the ESC Rennes School of Business*	Mass marketing communication in a limited home market, elements of an effective mass marketing communication strategy, media selection, differentiation and competitive advantage
15	Case 29	Selling in China *David Jobber, Emeritus Professor of Marketing, University of Bradford*	International marketing, cultural issues, self-reference criteria
	Case 30	JCPenney and Direct Marketing: Using Something Old to Improve Something New? *Tom McNamara and Asha Moore-Mangin, the ESC Rennes School of Business*	Direct marketing communication tools, how to manage direct marketing campaigns
16	Case 31	To Google or not to Google, that is the Question *Fiona Ellis-Chadwick, Senior Lecturer, Loughborough University*	Competitive advantage, differentiation, online resources and competencies
	Case 32	Social Media and Real-Time Marketing *James Saker, Synergy Sponsorship London, and Jim Saker, Ford Professor in Retail Management, Loughborough University*	Social media, real time content and its potential for engaging customers, new approaches to brand personality development, how reactive marketing fits into a marketing plan
17	Case 33	ASOS *David Jobber, Emeritus Professor of Marketing, University of Bradford*	Online fashion retailing, customer service, promotion strategy, SWOT analysis
	Case 34	From 'Clicks to Bricks' *Kim Cassidy, Julie Lewis and Sheilagh Resnick, Nottingham Trent University*	Strategic approaches to retail, multichannel retailing, channel capabilities, future challenges for multichannel retailers

Preface

Marketing is constantly adapting to meet the demands of dynamic business environments. Exploring both theoretical principles and business practices is the key to understanding this highly dynamic and complex subject. The 8th edition aims to bring these aspects together and engage readers in an illuminating journey through the discipline of marketing. The book provides many illustrative examples from many different perspectives.

The Principles and Practice of Marketing supports marketing education for students and practitioners of the subject. Students can enjoy learning from applying the principles to real world marketing problems and, in doing so, gain a richer knowledge of marketing.

Becoming a successful marketing practitioner also requires understanding of the principles of marketing together with the practical experience of implementing marketing ideas, processes and techniques. This book provides a framework for understanding important marketing topics such as organizational and consumer behaviour, segmentation, targeting and positioning, brand building, innovation, pricing, communications and digital technology, and implementation – core subject areas within the discipline, which form the backbone of marketing.

Technology is changing the way we do business and communicate, which has profound implications for the way organizations operate. By understanding how to interpret the marketing environment, apply principal concepts and plan for the future, students and practitioners can benefit from developing their knowledge of marketing.

I am joined in the writing of the 8th edition by Fiona Ellis-Chadwick, who as co-author brings to the book her expert knowledge of digital and retail marketing and detailed insight into the practical application of marketing.

Marketing is a very strong discipline, and around Europe there are specialist conferences which present the latest research: for example, the European Marketing Academy, and the Academy of Marketing in the UK. Such conferences highlight the variety and extent of marketing and ensure that there is a growing community of academics, researchers and students who are prepared to take on the challenges of modern marketing and build rewarding careers in this field.

Most students and practitioners enjoy marketing and find it rewarding and relevant not only from an academic but also a practical perspective. We hope this book adds to your knowledge of the subject of marketing and enhances your skills and understanding.

How to study

This book has been designed to help you to learn and to understand the important principles behind successful marketing and how these are applied in practice. We hope that you find the book easy to use and that you are able to follow the ideas and concepts explained in each chapter. As soon as you don't grasp something, go back and read it again. Try to think of *other* examples to which the theory could be applied. To check you really understand the new concepts you are reading about, try completing the exercises and questions at the end of each chapter. You can also test your understanding and expand your knowledge by exploring the resources in Connect™ and LearnSmart™.

To assist you in working through this text, we have developed a number of distinctive study and design features. To familiarize yourself with these features, please turn to the Guided Tour on pages xix–xxi.

New to the 8th edition

As always, recent events are reflected throughout this book. Here is a brief summary of the **key content changes** for this edition:

- New chapter on **Relationship Marketing**. Developing relationships is central to marketing thinking and this chapter explores how to manage customer relationships, use of CRM systems and key account management.
- **New content:** in response to reviewers' feedback and changes in the practical application of technology within marketing practice, throughout the book there are new **digital technology examples**, **Mini Cases**, and **Marketing in Action** vignettes. The Marketing Research chapter has been extended to include **business intelligence** and has been significantly updated to reflect changes in the use of data analytics. **Digital coverage** has been increased throughout the text with content including e-procurement, SOE, mobile technologies, content marketing, new hardware such as smartphones and tablets, and more.

Other topics covered include **social marketing** issues such as anti-consumerism, ethical brand value over shareholder value, the social impact of social media marketing and antibranding. Also coverage of global sourcing, more qualitative market research techniques such as ethnographic research, service dominant logic and guerrilla and ambient marketing.

- **Revised structure:** in response to review feedback, this edition focuses on how each of the elements of the marketing mix adds value and the importance of relationship marketing. Additionally, the final part of the book brings together five chapters which focus on the strategic elements of marketing: marketing, planning and strategy.

- **Brand new vignettes, case studies and illustrations throughout the book:** the principles of marketing cannot be fully grasped without solid examples of how these apply in practice. That is why in every chapter you will find a wealth of examples to support the concepts presented. These include current advertisements, Marketing in Action vignettes and Mini Cases that ask you to apply the principles learnt for yourself. Two case studies at the end of each chapter provide more in-depth examples. These features will not only help you to absorb the key principles of marketing, but will also allow you to make links between the various topics and demonstrate the marketing mix at work in real-life situations.

- **An exciting new package of supporting online resources,** including new video resources and cases, as well as a rich choice of activities designed to help students develop and apply their understanding of marketing concepts. See pages xxii–xxv for further details.

Guided Tour

Real Marketing

Throughout the *Principles and Practice of Marketing* 8th edition product, marketing principles are illustrated with examples of real marketing practice. The following features encourage you to pause to consider the decisions taken by a rich variety of companies.

> **MARKETING IN ACTION 5.1**
> IKEA Delivers Sustainable Cotton and Timber Products to Millions of its Customers
>
> For marketing managers, sustainability is possibly the biggest challenge of the 21st century. Not only are there issues of what to reduce, but there is also the problem of understanding the real impact of any action. However, research by Trucost, a company that helps its clients understand the real cost of their organization's operations and helps them plan for a better-resourced future across the value chain, suggested in a report on green business that environmental sustainability is at the top of most companies' agendas. Trucost measures the financial impact of environmental issues for 4,300 of the world's largest companies, and this information helps them to understand which actions are likely to bring the greatest dividends and reduce the impact on the environment. Trucost has helped GreenBiz, a leading source of news, opinion and best practice, to provide clear and concise information for businesses that are developing their environmental and sustainability policies and business practices. GreenBiz analyzes data and information and then disseminates news of good practice through its website and blogs.
>
> IKEA is an example of a company constantly reviewing its practices across the supply chain in order to ensure it provides sustainability on a large scale. According to Steve Howard, IKEA's Chief Sustainability Officer, the company is 'using IWay, a code of conduct that specifies environmental and social requirements for sourcing and distributing products, which is bringing sustainable and affordable cotton and timber products to millions of consumers around the world'. He also said that IKEA is 'committed to future proofing' the company in advance of the many challenges it is likely to face in the future. IKEA owns wind turbines and has introduced nearly half a million solar panels. In the USA, it is the second largest private commercial solar power owner. The company is aiming to isolate itself from the volatilities of the energy markets and has reported significant savings on energy consumption across the business.
>
> Based on: Milman (2013); Trucost (2012); King (2012); Kelly-Detwiler (2014)

≪ **Marketing in Action** vignettes provide practical examples to highlight the application of concepts, and encourage you to critically analyse and discuss real-world issues.

> **MINI CASE 5.1**
> Hybrid and Electric Cars

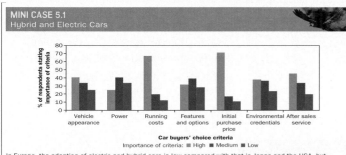

> In Europe, the adoption of electric and hybrid cars is low compared with that in Japan and the USA, but manufacturers are looking for new ways to boost sales. Toyota anticipates introducing 10 new models into Europe to boost sales to 1 million vehicles by 2014 (Kim, 2011). Research suggests there are important choice criteria consumers consider when buying new cars.
>
> The graph shows that initial outlay to buy the car and running costs are the two most influential criteria, followed by after-sales service and then vehicle appearance. Interestingly, features of the vehicle and power are much lower in terms of importance in the new car-buying decision.
>
> Therefore, while Toyota, Honda, Nissan and other manufacturers are introducing cars with new power options,

≪ **Mini Cases** provide further examples to encourage you to consider how key concepts work in practice, and have associated questions to help you critique the principles discussed in each chapter.

EXHIBIT 6.2
Loyalty cards are used by many different types of retailer and service provider as a source of continuous data

≪ **Exhibits** demonstrate how marketers have presented their products in real promotions and campaigns.

Mc Graw Hill Education connect®

≪ **Interactive Case Analysis Activities** encourage students to think analytically about real-world marketing situations. Two sets of multiple choice questions prompt them to critically asses the case and then test their understanding of core concepts covered.

Scan the QR code to see how EcoSwim is using the environment as part of its C...

≪ **AdInsight QR codes** provide links to specially selected YouTube videos showing official company adverts.

≪ **Case studies** Two are provided at the end of each chapter, based on up-to-date examples that encourage you to apply what you have learned in each chapter to a real-life marketing problem. Instructor's Teaching notes can be downloaded from the Online Learning Centre via Connect.

Marketing Ethics and Corporate Social Responsibility **CHAPTER 5**   **165**

Questions   connect   *This case study was written by Brian Searle, Programme Director Marketing MSc, Loughborough University.*

1. Using the key targets set out in the Co-operative plan as a benchmark, select one of the following supermarkets, Tesco, Asda, Sainsbury's or Morrisons, to use as a comparator. Use the Internet as a resource.

2. Companies have been accused of 'green washing', which is a light-touch approach for developing a corporate social responsibility (CSR) policy. Suggest the difficulties you may encounter when following a fully committed CSR plan like the Co-op.

3. Many organizations criticize CSR because

References

The Co-operative Group (2011), The Co-operative launches most radical corporate ethical plan and encourages customers to join the revolution, The Co-operative Group. Available at: http://www.co-operative.coop/corporate/Press/Pressreleases/Headline-news/Join-The-Revolution (accessed 7 June 2015); The Co-operative Group (2011), Setting New Sights: Our Ethical Plan 2012-14 (and beyond...), The Co-operative Group. http://www.co-operative.coop/Corporate/CSR/Our_Ethical_Plan_2012-2014.pdf (accessed 7 June 2015); The Co-operative Group (2013), The Co-operative Sustainability Report 2015, The Co-operative Group. http...

≪ **Questions** are provided at the end of each case study to allow you to test yourself on what you have read. Multiple Choice Questions are also available in Connect.

≪ **Videos** allow students to engage with how marketing professionals approach their day-to-day challenges through a series of interviews with marketing managers and directors from a broad range of companies.

Studying Effectively

Principles and Practice of Marketing is designed to make every study moment as efficient as possible. The following features will help you to focus your study, check your understanding and improve learning outcomes.

The marketing concept is a management philosophy which states that a firm's goals can be best achieved through identification and _____ of the customers' stated and unstated needs and wants.

Click the answer you think is right.

rejection

satisfaction

remediation

communication

Do you know the answer? Read about this

I know it   Think so   Unsure   No idea

≪ LearnSmart and SmartBook
LearnSmart is the most widely used and intelligent adaptive learning resource that is proven to strengthen memory recall, improve course retention and boost grades. Fuelled by LearnSmart, SmartBook is the first and only adaptive reading experience available today.

LEARNING OBJECTIVES

After reading this chapter, you should be able to:

1 explain the meaning of ethics, and business and marketing ethics
2 describe ethical issues in marketing
3 discuss business, societal, and legal and regulatory responses to ethical concerns
4 explain the stakeholder theory of the firm
5 discuss the nature of corporate social responsibility (CSR)
6 describe the dimensions of CSR
7 discuss the arguments for and against CSR programmes
8 discuss non-profit organizations' contribution to societal marketing

≪ Learning Objectives are listed at the beginning of each chapter to show you the topics covered. You should aim to attain each objective when you study the chapter.

Key Terms

business ethics the moral principles and values that guide a firm's behaviour
cause-related marketing a commercial activity by which businesses and charities or causes form a partnership with each other to market an image or product for mutual benefit
consumer movement an organized collection of groups and organizations whose objective it is to protect the rights of consumers
environmentalism the organized movement of groups and organizations to protect and improve the physical environment
ethical consumption the taking of purchase decisions

on the basis of the interests of society and the environment
ethics the moral principles and values that govern the actions and decisions of an individual or group
fair trade marketing the development, promotion and selling of fair trade brands and the positioning of organizations on the basis of a fair trade ethos
internal marketing training, motivating and communicating with staff to cause them to work effectively in providing customer satisfaction; more recently the term has been expanded to include marketing to all staff, with the aim of achieving the acceptance of marketing ideas

≪ Key Terms are provided at the end of each chapter—use the list to look up any unfamiliar words, and as a handy aid for quick revision and review.

Study Questions

1. What is big data and how is it used to help companies make marketing decisions?
2. What are the essential differences between a marketing information system and marketing research?
3. What are secondary and primary data? Why should secondary data be collected before primary data?
4. What is the difference between a research brief and proposal? What advice would you give a marketing research agency when making a research proposal?
5. Digital survey techniques offer the best solution for gathering data. Discuss this statement.
6. Discuss the problems facing market research as a method of generating information about consumer behaviour.
7. Why are marketing research reports more likely to be used if they conform to the prior beliefs of the client?

≪ Study Questions allow you to review and apply the knowledge you have acquired from each chapter. These questions can be undertaken either individually or as a focus for group discussion in seminars or tutorials.

References

Arthur, C. (2012) Search giant 'sneaking' citizens' privacy away warns EU justice chief, *The Guardian*, 2 March, 18–19.
BARB (2012) Television Measurement Service, http://www.barb. co.uk/about/tv-measurement?_s=4.
BBC (2015) News Technology, 9 February. http://www.bbc.co.uk/news/technology-31296188
Burrows, D. (2014) How to use ethnography for in-depth consumer insight, *Marketing Week*, 9 May. https://www.marketingweek.com/2014/05/09/how-to-use-ethnography-for-in-depth-consumer-insight (accessed 9 June 2015).
Chaffey, D. and F. E. Ellis-Chadwick (2016) *Digital Marketing: Strategy, Implementation and Practice*, 6th edn., Harlow: Pearson.
Clegg, A. (2001) Policy and Opinion, *Marketing Week*, 27 September, 63–5.
Costa, M. (2011) All roads to improvement start at insight, *Marketing Week*, 19 May, 31.
Cowlett, M. (2011) A Social Insight, *Marketing*, 31–3.
Crouch, S. and M. Housden (2003) *Marketing Research for Managers*,

Daniels, E., H. Wilson and M. McDonald (2003) Towards a map of marketing information systems: an inductive study, *European Journal of Marketing* 37(5/6), 821–47.
Denzin, N. K. and Y. S. Lincoln (eds) (2000) *The Handbook of Qualitative Research*, 2nd edn., Thousand Oaks CA: Sage Publications, 11.
Dye, P. (2008) Share The Knowledge, *Marketing*, 19 March, 33–4.
ESOMAR (2005) Industry Study on 2004, ESOMAR World Research Report.
ESOMAR (2015) Market Research Explained, ESOMAR, 8 March. http://www.esomar.org/knowledge-and-standards/market-research-explained.php
Fahy, J. and D. Jobber (2015) *Foundations of Marketing*, Maidenhead: McGraw-Hill Education.
Flack, J. (2002) Not So Honest Joe, *Marketing Week*, 26 September, 43.
Poleretzky, Z. (1999) Big Data: Friend or Foe of Digital Advertising?

≪ Further Reading at the end of each chapter can be used to research an idea in greater depth.

McGraw Hill Education connect®

McGraw-Hill Connect Marketing is a learning and teaching environment that improves student performance and outcomes whilst promoting engagement and comprehension of content.

You can utilize publisher-provided materials, or add your own content to design a complete course to help your students achieve higher outcomes.

PROVEN EFFECTIVE

With Connect ⬛ Without Connect

MORE As and Bs
WITH CONNECT

A   B   C   D

INSTRUCTORS

With McGraw-Hill Connect Marketing, instructors get:

- Simple **assignment management,** allowing you to spend more time teaching.
- **Auto-graded** assignments, quizzes and tests.
- **Detailed visual reporting** where students and section results can be viewed and analysed.
- Sophisticated **online testing** capability.
- A **filtering and reporting** function that allows you to easily assign and report on materials that are correlated to learning outcomes, topics, level of difficulty, and more. Reports can be accessed for individual students or the whole class, as well as offering the ability to drill into individual assignments, questions or categories.
- **Instructor materials** to help supplement your course.

Get Connected. Get Results.

Available online via Connect is a wealth of instructor support materials, including:

- Case study teaching notes
- Fully updated PowerPoint slides to use in lectures
- A solutions manual providing answers to the Mini Cases and the end of chapter questions in the textbook.
- Image library of artwork from the textbook.
- Additional case studies.
- Tutorial activities
- Further resources including Marketing Plan, Market Research Project and Marketing Accountability and Metrics

STUDENTS

With McGraw-Hill Connect Marketing, students get:

Assigned content

- Easy **online access** to homework, tests and quizzes.
- **Immediate feedback** and 24-hour tech support.

With McGraw-Hill SmartBook, students can:

- Take control of your own learning with a personalized and adaptive reading experience.

- Understand what you know and don't know; SmartBook takes you through the stages of reading and practice, prompting you to recharge your knowledge throughout the course for maximum retention.

- Achieve the most efficient and productive study time by adapting to what you do and don't know.

- Hone in on concepts you are most likely to forget, to ensure knowledge of key concepts is learnt and retained.

connect®

FEATURES

Is an online assignment and assessment solution that offers a number of powerful tools and features that make managing assignments easier, so faculty can spend more time teaching. With Connect marketing, students can engage with their coursework anytime and anywhere, making the learning process more accessible and efficient.

Videos

Videos featuring interviews with marketing managers and directors from a wide range of companies, along with advertising and promotional content, will engage students with the idea of marketing as a career and how the concepts they learn relate to a real world context. Autogradable questions encourage them to analyse and assess the content in the videos.

Case studies

A bank of case studies is available for assignment in Connect. Students read and assess a case before answering probing questions. Instructors can choose to assign multiple choice or short answer questions depending on the needs of the course.

Interactives

Assign interactive questions including case analysis, decision generator and drag and drop, to prompt students to make informed, analytical marketing decisions and fully comprehend marketing concepts.

Pre-built assignments

Assign all of the end of chapter or test bank material as a ready-made assignment with the simple click of a button.

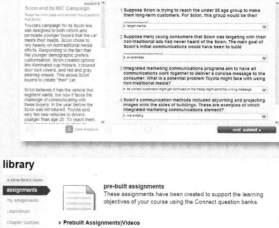

Get Connected. Get Results.

SmartBook™

Fuelled by LearnSmart—the most widely used and intelligent adaptive learning resource—SmartBook is the first and only adaptive reading experience available today. Distinguishing what a student knows from what they don't, and honing in on concepts they are most likely to forget, SmartBook personalizes content for each student in a continuously adapting reading experience. Valuable reports provide instructors insight as to how students are progressing through textbook content, and are useful for shaping in-class time or assessment.

LearnSmart™

McGraw-Hill LearnSmart is an adaptive learning program that identifies what an individual student knows and doesn't know. LearnSmart's adaptive learning path helps students learn faster, study more efficiently, and retain more knowledge. Now with integrated learning resources which present topics and concepts in different and engaging formats increases student engagement and promotes additional practice of key concepts. Reports available for both students and instructors indicate where students need to study more and assess their success rate in retaining knowledge.

Mc Graw Hill Education

create

<u>Let us help make our **content** your **solution**</u>

At McGraw-Hill Education our aim is to help lecturers to find the most suitable content for their needs, delivered to their students in the most appropriate way. Our **custom publishing solutions** offer the ideal combination of content delivered in the way which best suits lecturer and students.

Our custom publishing programme offers lecturers the opportunity to select just the chapters or sections of material they wish to deliver to their students from a database called CREATE™ at

http://create.mheducation.com/uk/

CREATE™ contains over two million pages of content from:

- textbooks
- professional books
- case books - Harvard Articles, Insead, Ivey, Darden, Thunderbird and BusinessWeek
- Taking Sides - debate materials

Across the following imprints:

- McGraw-Hill Education
- Open University Press
- Harvard Business Publishing
- US and European material

There is also the option to include additional material authored by lecturers in the custom product—this does not necessarily have to be in English.

We will take care of everything from start to finish in the process of developing and delivering a custom product to ensure that lecturers and students receive exactly the material needed in the most suitable way.

With a Custom Publishing Solution, students enjoy the best selection of material deemed to be the most suitable for learning everything they need for their courses – something of real value to support their learning. Teachers are able to use exactly the material they want, in the way they want, to support their teaching on the course.

Please contact your local McGraw-Hill Education representative with any questions or alternatively contact Warren Eels **e: warren.eels@mheducation.com.**

About the Authors

David Jobber is an internationally recognized marketing academic. He is Emeritus Professor of Marketing at the University of Bradford School of Management. He holds an honours degree in economics from the University of Manchester, a master's degree in business and management from the University of Warwick and a doctorate from the University of Bradford.

Before joining the faculty at the Bradford School of Management, David worked for the TI Group in marketing and sales, and was Senior Lecturer in Marketing at the University of Huddersfield. He has wide experience of teaching core marketing courses at undergraduate, postgraduate and post-experience levels with specialisms in business-to business marketing, sales management and marketing research. He has a proven, ratings-based record of teaching excellence at all levels. His competence in teaching is reflected in visiting appointments at the universities of Aston, Lancaster, Loughborough and Warwick in the UK, and the University of Wellington, New Zealand. He has taught marketing to executives of such international companies as BP, Allied Domecq, the BBC, Bass, Croda International, Rolls-Royce and Rio Tinto.

Supporting his teaching is a record of achievement in academic research. David has over 150 publications in the marketing area in such journals as the *International Journal of Research in Marketing, MIS Quarterly, Strategic Management Journal, Journal of International Business Studies, Journal of Management, Journal of Business Research, European Journal of Marketing, Journal of Product Innovation Management, Journal of Personal Selling and Sales Management* and *Journal of the Operational Research Society.* David has served on the editorial boards of the *International Journal of Research in Marketing, Journal of Personal Selling and Sales Management, European Journal of Marketing* and the *Journal of Marketing Management*.

He has acted as Special Adviser to the Research Assessment Exercise panel that rated research output from business and management schools throughout the UK. David has also received the Academy of Marketing's Life Achievement award for distinguished and extraordinary services to marketing.

Fiona Ellis-Chadwick has a successful professional business and academic career. She is a Senior Lecturer at Loughborough University School of Business & Economics, where she is the Director of the Institute of Consultancy and Research Application. As part of this role, Fiona is a very active researcher and innovative educator, and frequently leads the development of innovative multi-media teaching materials, bringing together research and business. Fiona has made many films for use in higher education on a variety of different topics, including retail marketing, digital technology and economic growth from the perspective of international business leaders. As an academic consultant for the Open University and BBC productions, she has worked on highly successful and award-winning series: *The Virtual Revolution, Foods That Make Billions, Evan's Business Challenges, Iceland Foods: Into the Freezer Cabinet, Business Boomers* and Radio 4's *The Bottom Line* programme. Fiona had a successful commercial career in retailing before becoming an academic and completing her PhD. Having made a significant contribution in the area of online retailing, she continues to focus her research and academic

publications on the strategic impact of the Internet and digital technologies on marketing and retailing. Her work on these topics has been widely published in the *Journal of Business Research, European Journal of Marketing, Internet Research, Industrial Marketing Management, International Journal of Retail Distribution and Management* plus additional textbooks and practitioner journals. Fiona is passionate about how technology and education can help business development in the future.

Acknowledgements

Authors' Acknowledgements

We would like to thank colleagues, contributors and the reviewers who have offered advice and helped develop this text. We would also like to thank our editors Alice Aldous, Natalie Jacobs, Leiah Norcott and Nina Smith, for their invaluable support and assistance.

Publisher's Acknowledgements

Our thanks go to the following reviewers for their comments at various stages in the text's development:

Sree Beg, University of Surrey
Christo Bisschoff, NWU Potchefstroom Business School
Margaret Cullen, Nelson Mandela Metropolitan University
Irute Daukseviciute, University of Reading
Andrea Davies, University of Leicester
Margaret Fletcher, University of Glasgow
Deborah Forbes, Newcastle University
Navid Ghannad, Halmstad University
Clare Halfpenny, Manchester Metropolitan University
Thomas Helgesson, Halmstad University
Monica Hope, University of Surrey
Helen McGrath, University College Cork
Patricia McHugh, National University of Ireland
Jan Mòller Jensen, University of Southern Denmark
Rene Moolenaar, University of Sussex
Devina Oodith, University of KwaZulu-Natal
Robert Ormrod, Aarhus University
Norman Peng, University of Westminster
Adrian Pritchard, Coventry University
Mariusz Soltanifar, Hanze University of Applied Sciences
Thorsten Strauss, University of Antwerp
Alex Thompson, University of Exeter

We would like to thank the following contributors for the case study material which they have provided for this textbook and its online resources:

Gillian Armstrong, Ulster University
Glyn Atwal, Burgundy School of Business
Adele Berndt, Jonkoping International Business School
Veronique Boulocher-Passet, University of Brighton
Douglas Bryson, ESC Rennes

Conor Carroll, University of Limerick
Kim Cassidy, Nottingham Trent University
David Cosgrave, University of Limerick
Clive Helm, University of Westminster
Lynn Kahle, Technical University of Denmark
Julie Lewis, Nottingham Trent University
Helen McGrath, University College Cork
Tom McNamara, ESC Rennes
Asha Moore-Mangin, ESC Rennes
Christina O'Connor, Maynooth University
Marie O'Dwyer, Waterford Institute of Technology
Robert Ormrod, Aarhus University
Adrian Pritchard, Coventry University
Sheilagh Resnick, Nottingham Trent University
Nina Reynolds, University of Wollongong
Jim Saker, Loughborough University
Brian Searle, Loughborough University
Fiona Whelan-Ryan, Waterford Institute of Technology

Finally, we would also like to thank the following contributors for their work on the material for this textbook in our Connect and LearnSmart platforms:

John Fahy, University of Limerick
Thomas Helgesson, Halmstad University
Nicole Gross, University College Dublin
Thomas Gulløv Longhi, University of Southern Denmark
Tom McNamara, ESC Rennes
Asha Moore-Mangin, ESC Rennes
Christina O'Connor, Maynooth University
Marie O'Dwyer, Waterford Institute of Technology
Lucia Walsh, University College Dublin
Fiona Whelan-Ryan, Waterford Institute of Technology

Picture Acknowledgements

The authors and publishers would like to extend thanks to the following for the reproduction of company advertising and/or logos:

Part and Chapter Opening Images
Part 1: Nutnarin Khetwong / iStock; Part 2: PeopleImages / iStock; Part 3: Izabela Habur / iStock; Part 4: Rawpixel Ltd / iStock

Exhibit
1.1: philipus / Alamy; 1.2: John Boud / Alamy; 2.1: Hans Engbers / Alamy; 2.2: studiomode / Alamy; 2.3: Izabela Habur / iStock; 2.4: Kumar Sriskandan / Alamy; 3.1: Courtney Keating / iStock; 3.2: The Advertising Archives / Alamy; 3.3: PackStock / Alamy; 3.4: Jeff Morgan 15 / Alamy; 4.1: Juice Images/Alamy; 4.2: Bernhard Classen / Alamy; 4.3: DenTak Oral Care, Inc; 5.1: Fedex; 5.2: "Too Young to drink" © Fabrica 2014; 5.3: Luke Miller / iStock; 6.1: Ingram publishing; 6.2: Erkan Mehmet / Alamy; 7.1: Bloomberg / Getty; 7.2: Fanny Karst; 7.3: Michelin Tyre Public Limited Company; 7.4: pengpeng / iStock; 7.5: Jeff Morgan 02 / Alamy; 8.1: Alex Hinds / Alamy; 8.2: Kia Motors Europe GmbH; 8.3: Newscast-online Limited / Alamy; 8.4: FilippoBacci / iStock; 8.5 Greenpeace / Lego; 9.1: horstgerlach / iStock 9.2: Singapore Airlines; 10.1: PeopleImages / iStock; 10.2: Burj Al Arab Jumeirah; 11.1: Jeffrey Blackler / Alamy; 12.1: geogphoto / Alamy; 12.2: imageBROKER / Alamy; 12.3: Kristoffer Tripplaar / Alamy; 13.1: Kumar Sriskandan / Alamy; 13.2: NetPhotos2 / Alamy; 13.3: NetPhotos / Alamy; 13.4: Copyright © by the United Nations Entity for Gender Equality and the Empowerment of Women. All worldwide rights reserved; 13.5: Thames Reach; 13.6: Alan Wilson / Alamy; 13.7: Lifestyle pictures / Alamy; 14.1: Tramino / iStock; 14.2: Ian Francis / Alamy; 14.3: Jeff Morgan 02 / Alamy; 14.4: jimkruger / iStock; 14.5: Reproduced with the permission of GSK group of companies; 15.1: Gyou Uni Kimchoe; 15.2: Alistair Laming / Alamy; 16.2: Hertz; 16.2: Net-a-Porter; 16.3: Global social media agency, We Are Social; 16.4: Dolf Veenvliet; 17.1: KPMG International Cooperativep; 17.2: Rentokil; 17.3: Waitrose.com; 17.4: Lifesizeimages / iStock; 17.5: Maxoidos / iStock; 17.6 Bloomberg / Getty; 18.1: Virgin Group; 18.2: Stuart Walker / Alamy; 18.3: Glasses Direct; 18.4: The Economist; 19.1: The Advertising Archives / Alamy; 19.2: FocusChina / Alamy; 19.3: Stringer / Getty; 19.4: keith morris / Cliff Hide Stock; 20.1: STANCA SANDA / Alamy; 20.2: Steve Stock / iStock; 20.3: imageBROKER / Alamy; 21.1: Porsche AG; 21.2: The McGraw-Hill Companies/Barry Barker, photographer; 21.3: Portland Press Herald / Getty; 22.1: AUTOGLASS® and the logo are registered trademarks of Belron S.A and its affiliated companies; 22.2: BMW; 22.3: Oli Scarff / Getty

Marketing in Action images
1.1: Peter Forsberg / Alamy; 1.3: Anatolii Babii / Alamy; 2.1: Greenpeace / Kennard Phillips; 2.4: Carsten Koall / Stringer; 2.5: Cathy Yeulet / iStock, IPG GutenbergUKLtd

/ iStock; 3.1: Groupon; 3.4: iStock; 4.1: Volvo Car Group 5.3: Change 4 Life; 6.3: Baona / iStock; 7.1: Fyndiq; 7.2: Global social media agency, We Are Social; 8.3: Colgate-Palmolive; 8.4: Sami Sert / iStock; 9.1: Mim Friday / Alamy; 10.1: Tupungato / iStock; 10.2: ACORN 1 / Alamy; 11.3: dpa picture alliance / Alamy; 11.4: BSIP SA / Alamy; 12.3: Reproduced by kind permission of Netto; 14.1: bizoo_n / iStock; 14.2: Saatchi & Saatchi; 14.4: The Advertising Archives / Alamy; 14.4: Pictorial Press Ltd / Alamy; 15.1: monsitj / iStock; 15.2: Fiona Ellis-Chadwick; 15.3: Butchers and Bicycles; 16.1: Newscast-online Limited / Alamy; 16.3: Shazam; 17.1: NoDerog / iStock; 17.2: Jeffrey Blackler / Alamy; 17.3: Jim Lane / Alamy; 18.1: David Ryder / Stringer; 18.3: Sean Gallup / Getty; 19.1: sydmsix / iStock; 19.2: Photo by Andrew Spear for The Washington Post via Getty Images; 20.4: M4OS Photos / Alamy; 21.2: Benedicte Desrus / Alamy; 22.1: Jan Mika / Alamy; 22.2: Unilever

Mini Case images

2.1: DON EMMERT / Getty; 4.1: David Askham / Alamy; 6.1: falcatraz / iStock; 8.1: Ingram Publishing/SuperStock; 9.1: courtesy of Sandals Resorts; 11.1: Milkos / iStock; 14.1: smontgom65; 15.1: David Williams / Alamy; 18.1: Kumar Sriskandan / Alamy; 20.1: age fotostock / Alamy; 22.1: Kumar Sriskandan / Alamy

Case images

1: The McGraw-Hill Companies/Mark Dierker, photographer; 2: George Clerk / iStock; 3: HotDuckZ / iStock; 4: WENN Ltd / Alamy Stock Photo; 5: frontpoint; 6: The McGraw-Hill Companies/Jill Braaten, photographer 7: frontpoint / iStock; 8: zoom-zoom / iStock; 9: Julie Edwards / Alamy Stock Photo; 10: Pixavril / iStock; 11: malerapaso / iStock; 12: franckreporter / iStock: 13: Ingram Publishing / SuperStock; 14: LanaDjuric / iStock; 15: Justin Sullivan / Getty; 16: zodebala / iStock; 17: Ian Dagnall / Alamy; 18: Kristoffer Tripplaar / Alamy; 19: Kumar Sriskandan / Alamy; 20: Paul Thomas / Getty; 21: Newscast-online Limited / Alamy; 22: Ryan McGinnis / Alamy; 23: fazon1 / iStock; 24: Bernd Wittelsbach / iStock; 25: mtreasure / iStock; 26: Ryan McGinnis / Alamy; 27: Toyota; 28: Volvo Car Group; 29: iStock; 30: The McGraw-Hill Companies/ Jill Braaten, photographer; 31: hillaryfox / iStock; 32: Kia Motors America; 33: Chris Ridley / Alamy; 34: M4OS Photos / Alamy; 35: Dixons Carphone; 36: Madecasse, Proudly Made in Africa, Value Added Africa; 37: shaunl / iStock; 38: Maurice Savage / Alamy; 39: Poulssen / iStock; 40: 4kodiak / iStock; 41: 200mm / iStock; 42 Moviestore collection Ltd / Richard Levine / Alamy; 43: tupungato / iStock; 44: digitallife / Alamy

Every effort has been made to trace and acknowledge ownership of copyright and to clear permission for material reproduced in this book. The publishers will be pleased to make suitable arrangements to clear permission with any copyright holders whom it has not been possible to contact.

PART 1
FUNDAMENTALS OF MARKETING

A number of videos featuring CEOs, CMOs, brand and PR managers related to the Chapters in this Part are available to lecturers for presentation and class discussion.

CHAPTER 1
Marketing and the Organization

Management must think of itself not as producing products, but as providing customer-creating value satisfactions. It must push this idea (and everything it means and requires) into every nook and cranny of the organization. It has to do this continuously and with the kind of flair that excites and stimulates the people in it.

THEODORE LEVITT

LEARNING OBJECTIVES

After reading this chapter, you should be able to:

1 explore the principles of marketing
2 define the marketing concept and its key components
3 compare a production orientation and a market orientation
4 differentiate between market-driven and internally driven businesses
5 compare the roles of efficiency and effectiveness in achieving corporate success
6 describe how to create customer value and satisfaction
7 describe how an effective marketing mix is designed
8 discuss the criticisms of the 4-Ps approach to marketing management
9 explain the relationship between marketing characteristics, market orientation and business performance
10 identify relevant business and research examples, which illustrate the principles of marketing in an organization

Introduction to Principles and Practice of Marketing

The principles of marketing have been influencing business practices for centuries, but the history of marketing as a distinct discipline can be traced back to the beginning of the 1990s (Sheth and Parvatiyar, 1995). Since then, marketing has developed into a guiding philosophy for firms of every shape, size and type.

At the heart of the principles of marketing is the customer. Over time, customers' needs and wants change; and as a result, marketing practices also change to reflect and accommodate new customer demands. The authors of this book recognize the importance of reflecting such developments and the shift in marketing teaching. Accordingly, the focus has changed. Whilst the 4-Ps are still important to teaching and remain a core part of the curriculum, the wider context of relationship marketing, value creation and other new approaches to marketing are integrated into the book.

The text is structured around four key dimensions of marketing:

Part 1: Fundamentals of Marketing—seven chapters that explore the essential elements of marketing.

Part 2: Creating Customer Value—five chapters that focus on main elements of delivering customer value.

Part 3: Communicating and Delivering Customer Value—five chapters concentrating on communications and distribution

Part 4: Marketing Planning and Strategy—five chapters that adopt a more strategic focus on marketing.

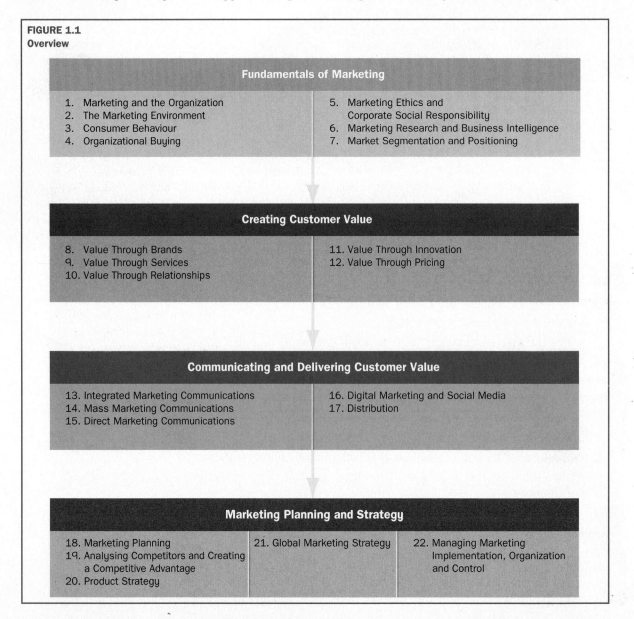

FIGURE 1.1
Overview

Fundamentals of Marketing

1. Marketing and the Organization
2. The Marketing Environment
3. Consumer Behaviour
4. Organizational Buying
5. Marketing Ethics and Corporate Social Responsibility
6. Marketing Research and Business Intelligence
7. Market Segmentation and Positioning

Creating Customer Value

8. Value Through Brands
9. Value Through Services
10. Value Through Relationships
11. Value Through Innovation
12. Value Through Pricing

Communicating and Delivering Customer Value

13. Integrated Marketing Communications
14. Mass Marketing Communications
15. Direct Marketing Communications
16. Digital Marketing and Social Media
17. Distribution

Marketing Planning and Strategy

18. Marketing Planning
19. Analysing Competitors and Creating a Competitive Advantage
20. Product Strategy
21. Global Marketing Strategy
22. Managing Marketing Implementation, Organization and Control

This chapter introduces the marketing concept and makes a case for adopting it as a guiding business philosophy for improving performance. However, to gain the potential advantages that marketing might bring, managers must make many decisions, for example: which customer groups to serve; how to create value-added products and services; which technology to use; and which marketing strategies are most likely to deliver competitive advantages. To add to these complex choices, managers must also consider the impact of the environment and determine how to get the best strategic fit between their organization's capabilities and resources and the market opportunities.

What is Marketing?

Marketing drives successful organizations but it is often misinterpreted and sometimes gets bad press. Critics use words like marketing 'gimmicks', 'ploys' and 'tricks' to undermine the valuable effect that marketing can deliver. This is unfortunate, because the essence of marketing is value creation not trickery. Successful companies rely on customers returning to repurchase, and the goal of marketing is long-term satisfaction not short-term deception. This theme is reinforced by the writings of top management consultant the late Peter Drucker, who stated (Drucker, 1999):

> Because the purpose of business is to create and keep customers, it has only two central functions—marketing and innovation. The basic function of marketing is to attract and retain customers at a profit.

What can we learn from this statement? First, it places marketing in a central role for business success and focuses managers' attention on attracting and keeping customers.

Second, it implies that the purpose of marketing is not to chase any customer at any price. Drucker used profit as a criterion. Please note that profit may be used by many commercial organizations, whereas in the non-profit sector other measures of success, such as reduction of social deprivation or hunger, are just as important as profit. Consequently, the concepts, principles and techniques described in this book are as applicable to Oxfam as to Apple.

Third, it is more expensive to attract new customers than to retain existing ones. Indeed, the costs of attracting a new customer have been found to be up to six times the costs of retaining old ones (Rosenberg and Czepeil, 1983). Companies that apply the principles of marketing recognize the importance of building relationships with customers by providing satisfaction, and attracting new customers by creating added value. Grönroos (1989) stressed the importance of relationship building in his definition of marketing, in which he describes the objective of marketing as to establish, develop and commercialize long-term customer relationships so that the objectives of the parties involved are met.

Finally, most markets—for example consumer, industrial and not-for-profit—are characterized by strong competition. This means organizations need not only to understand what their customers want, but also to understand what their competitors provide. If customers' needs are not met, they may switch to a rival supplier.

Marketing exists through exchanges. **Exchange** is the act or process of receiving something from someone by giving something in return. The something could be a physical good, a service, an idea or money. Money facilitates exchanges so that people can concentrate on working at things they are good at, earn money (itself an exchange) and spend it on products or services that someone else has supplied. The objective is for all parties in the exchange to feel satisfied and gain something of value. This is particularly important because satisfied customers are more likely than dissatisfied ones to return to buy more. Hence the notion of customer satisfaction as the central pillar of marketing is fundamental to the creation of a stream of exchanges upon which organizational success depends.

The rest of this chapter discusses the principles of marketing and provides an introduction to how marketing can create customer value and satisfaction.

The Marketing Concept

The above discussion introduces the notion of the marketing concept—that is, that companies achieve their profit and other objectives by satisfying (even delighting) customers (Houston, 1986). This is the traditional idea underlying marketing. However, it neglects a fundamental aspect of commercial life: competition. The traditional marketing concept is a necessary but not sufficient condition for corporate success. To achieve success, companies must go further than mere customer satisfaction; they must do better than the competition. British Airways (BA), an enduring brand that has led innovation in the airline industry, has built its reputation around

FIGURE 1.2
Key components of the marketing concept

its brand values, which are captured by the slogan 'To Fly, To Serve' (Superbrands, 2015). BA stays ahead of the competition by providing consistently good service and quality customer experiences. In 2014, BA was voted first, ahead of 1,500 companies in the annual Superbrand rankings in the UK (Winch, 2014).

The modern **marketing concept** can be expressed as:

> The achievement of corporate goals through meeting and exceeding customer needs and expectations better than the competition.

To apply this concept, three conditions should be met. 1) Company activities should focus on providing customer satisfaction rather than making things easier and better for the producer or manufacturer. This is not an easy condition to meet, but it is a necessity to place the customer at the centre of all activity. 2) The achievement of customer satisfaction relies on integrated effort. The responsibility for the implementation of the concept lies not just within the marketing department. The belief that customer needs are central to the operation of a company should run right through production, finance, research and development, engineering and other departments. The role of the marketing department is to play *champion* for the concept and to coordinate activities. But the concept is a business philosophy, not a departmental duty. 3) For integrated effort to work successfully, management must believe that corporate goals can be achieved through satisfied customers (see Figure 1.2).

Market Versus Production Orientation

There is no guarantee that all companies will adopt the marketing concept. However, research (e.g. Pulendran, Speed and Widing, 2003; Hooley and Lynch, 1985) has found evidence that the application of marketing and the adoption of a **market orientation** can lead to significant performance benefits. Research also suggests that the market orientation approach is an evolutionary process and companies can move from unawareness to complete acceptance of the importance of the marketing concept (Jaworski and Kohli, 1993; Hooley, Lynch and Shepherd, 1990) as a means of defining the orientation of a business. A competing philosophy is production orientation.[1] This is an inward-looking stance, where managers can become focused on the internal aspects of their business. This is particularly evident in manufacturing companies where employees spend their working day at the point of production, so it is easy to understand how this can happen.

Production orientation manifests itself in two ways. First, management becomes cost focused and believes that the central focus of its job is to attain economies of scale by producing a limited range of products (at the

---

[1]This, of course, is not the only alternative business philosophy. For example, companies can be financially or sales orientated. If financially orientated, companies focus on short-term returns, basing decisions more on financial ratios than customer value. Sales-orientated companies emphasize sales push rather than adaptation to customer needs. Some textbooks even allude to the existence of eras of business orientation—production, product, selling and marketing—each with its own time zone, and this has entered marketing folklore. However, research has shown that such a sequence is based on the flimsiest of evidence and is oversimplified and misleading (Lawson and Wooliscroft, 2004). We shall concentrate on the fundamental difference in corporate outlook: market versus production orientation.

FIGURE 1.3
Production orientation

```
Production        Manufacture        Aggressive
capabilities  →     product     →    sales effort   →    Customers
```

extreme, just one) in a form that minimizes production costs. Henry Ford is quoted as an example of a production-orientated manager because he built just one car in one colour—the black Model T—in order to minimize costs. However, this is unfair to Mr. Ford, since his objective was customer satisfaction—bringing the car to new market segments through low prices. The real production-orientated manager has no such virtues. The objective is cost reduction for its own sake, an objective at least partially fuelled by the greater comfort and convenience that comes from producing a narrow product range.

The second way in which production orientation is manifested is in the belief that the business should be defined in terms of its production facilities. Figure 1.3 illustrates production orientation in its crudest form. The focus is on current production capabilities that define the business mission. The purpose of the organization is to manufacture products and aggressively sell them to unsuspecting customers. A classic example of the catastrophe that can happen when this philosophy drives a company is that of Pollitt and Wigsell, a steam engine producer that sold its products to the textile industry. It made the finest steam engine available, and the company grew to employ over 1,000 people on a 30-acre (12-hectare) site. The company's focus was on steam engine production, so when the electric motor superseded the earlier technology, it failed to respond. The 30-acre site is now a housing estate. Contrast the fortunes of Pollitt and Wigsell with those of another company operating in the textile industry at about the same time. This company made looms and achieved great success when it launched the type G power loom, which allowed one person to oversee 50 machines. Rather than defining its business as a power loom producer, the company adopted a market orientation and sought new opportunities in emerging markets. In 1929, the type G power loom patent was sold to fund the creation of a car division. The company was Toyota (Morgan, 2006).

Tension between product and market orientation continues to define business success today. Kodak is a company that failed to adapt to the market and recognize changes in the film and photography industry. Consequently, it struggled to cope with the emergence of competitors who offered the market products more suited to their needs (Spector, Mattioli and Stech, 2012). Despite being the first company to introduce a digital camera (in 1991), Kodak lost market share to the smartphone—for example iPhones and other catch-all electronic devices that meet consumers' photographic and movie needs, on demand and on the move. There has been a significant shift in the needs of the consumer in the electronics industry and a merging of the boundaries between communications, photography and film.

Market-orientated companies focus on customer needs. Change is recognized as endemic, and adaptation considered a Darwinian condition for survival. Changing needs present potential market opportunities that drive the company. For example, the change towards ethical consumption has created opportunities for existing companies: for example M&S has taken actions across the supply chain to improve the ethical credentials of its products, from considering the cotton used in garment manufacture to water pollution (Moore, 2014). New companies have been created using ethical principles; for example One Water donates 100 per cent of its profits to life-saving projects in Africa, and Toms Shoes donates one pair of shoes every time a pair is sold. Within the boundaries of their distinctive competences, market-driven companies seek to adapt their product and service offerings to the demands of current and latent markets. Read more in Marketing in Action 1.1. This orientation is shown in Figure 1.4.

Market-orientated companies get close to their customers so that they can understand their needs and problems. For example, Dürr AG, the German paint and assembly systems manufacturer, gets close to its customers by assigning over half its workforce to the sites of its customers such as Ford and Audi. When personal contact is insufficient or not feasible, formal marketing research is commissioned to understand customer motivations and behaviour. Part of the success of German machine tool manufacturers can be attributed to their willingness to develop new products with lead customers—those companies that themselves are innovative (Parkinson, 1991). This contrasts sharply with the attitude of UK machine tool manufacturers, who saw marketing research as merely a tactic to delay new product proposals and who feared that involving customers in new

FIGURE 1.4
Market orientation

```
Customer        Potential         Marketing
 needs      →     market      →  products and   →    Customers
                opportunities       services
```

H&M is a retail organization that proactively searches for marketing opportunities and responds to the wider market. The company opened its first store in 1947 in Vasteras, Sweden, selling ladies' clothing. The brand expanded into other parts of Scandinavia before opening its first store in London in 1976. Throughout the 1980s and 90s, store openings continued, and by 2015 H&M was recognized as the world's second-largest fashion retailer, operating in Europe, Asia, North and South America, the Middle East and online. Previously, H&M's attempts at sustainability, for example its recycling events, were criticized for having little effect, as it sells 550 million items a year in the consumer-driven *fast*

fashion industry. But despite the strong development of the brand, H&M also concentrates on using its core competencies to drive positive change for people and communities. In partnership with DO School, Hamburg, Germany, H&M has launched the Green Store Challenge, which aims to encourage social entrepreneurs around the world to look for new and sustainable ways of doing business.

Based on: H&M (2015); The Guardian (2015); Balch (2013)

product design would have adverse effects on the sales of current products. Market orientation is related to the strategic aims of companies. Market-orientated firms adopt a proactive search for market opportunities, use market information as a base for analysis and organizational learning, and adopt a long-term strategic perspective on markets and brands (Morgan and Strong, 1998).

Understanding Market-driven Businesses

A deeper understanding of the marketing concept and orientation can be gained by contrasting a market-driven business with an internally focused business that focuses mainly on production-orientation. Table 1.1 summarizes the key differences.

TABLE 1.1 Contrasting businesses: market versus internal focus

Market focus	Internal focus
Customer concern throughout business	Convenience comes first
Knowledge of customer choice criteria enables matching with marketing mix	Assume price and product performance is key to generating sales
Segment by customer differences	Segment by product
Invest in market research (MR) and track market changes	Rely on anecdotes and received wisdom
Welcome change	Cherish status quo
Try to understand competition	Ignore competition
Marketing spend regarded as an investment	Regard marketing spend as a luxury
Innovation rewarded	Innovation punished
Search for latent markets	Stick with the same
Are fast	Think 'Why rush?'
Strive for competitive advantage	Are happy to be 'me too'
Are efficient and effective	Are efficient

EXHIBIT 1.1
The Toyota Yaris hybrid. Saatchi & Saatchi focuses on the positive emotions that are felt when driving and feeling good, to communicate the benefits of owning the car

 Scan the QR code to watch the Toyota Yaris hybrid advert to see how it communicates the car's benefits to customers.

Market-driven companies display customer concern throughout the business. All departments recognize the importance of the customer to the success of the business. Nestlé, for example, has placed the customer at the centre of its business philosophy by giving the company's head of marketing responsibility for the company's seven strategic business units. Marketers also control strategy, research and development, and production (Benady, 2005). For internally focused businesses, convenience comes first. If customer wants are inconvenient or expensive to produce, excuses are often used as avoidance tactics.

Market-driven businesses know how their products and services are being evaluated against those of the competition. They understand the choice criteria that customers are using and ensure that their **marketing mix** matches those criteria better than their competitors do.

Businesses that are driven by the market base their segmentation analyses on customer differences that have implications for marketing strategy. Businesses that are focused internally segment by product and, consequently, are vulnerable when customers' requirements change. Bombardier manufactures products for two industrial sectors: aerospace and rail transportation. However, this world-leading business also recognizes the importance of its customers, who have very specific needs.

A key feature of market-driven businesses is their recognition that marketing research expenditure is an investment that can yield rich rewards through better customer understanding. Toyota is a market-led company that uses market research extensively. The Yaris was specially designed to meet the needs of the European consumer, and Toyota's Optimal Drive technology was designed to provide its customers with the benefit of enhanced performance, lower emissions and better fuel economy.

Internally driven businesses see marketing research as a non-productive intangible and prefer to rely on anecdotes and received wisdom. Market-orientated businesses welcome the organizational changes that are bound to occur as an organization moves to maintain strategic fit between its environment and its strategies. In contrast, internally orientated businesses cherish the status quo and resist change.

Attitudes towards competition also differ. Market-driven businesses try to understand competitive objectives and strategies and anticipate competitive actions. Internally driven companies are content to ignore the competition. Marketing spend is regarded as an investment that has long-term consequences in market-driven businesses. The alternative view is that marketing expenditure is a luxury that never appears to produce benefits.

In market-orientated companies, those employees who take risks and are innovative are rewarded. Recognition of the fact that most new products fail is reflected in a reluctance to punish those people who risk their career championing a new product idea. Internally orientated businesses reward time-serving and the ability not to make mistakes. This results in risk avoidance and the continuance of the status quo. Market-driven businesses search for latent markets—markets that no other company has yet exploited. 3M's Post-it product filled a latent need for a quick, temporary attachment to documents, while eBay, the online auction site, exploited the latent market for individuals who wished to sell products directly to others. Nintendo identified a latent market for a new style of home entertainment with the launch of its Wii console and software. The new product targeted families, and the electronic games promised health and fitness for everyone who played. Internally driven businesses are happy to stick with their existing products and markets. Some companies have been quicker than others to tap into ethically driven markets, as Marketing in Action 1.2 discusses.

Test your knowledge about who owns who by matching the parent company with the brands it owns (answers below the table)			
A	Mondelēz International owns?	1	Rachel's Organic
B	PepsiCo owns?	2	Innocent
C	Groupe Lactalis owns?	3	Abel & Cole
D	Associated British Foods Plc owns?	4	Green & Black's
E	William Jackson Food Group owns?	5	Buxton
F	Unilever owns?	6	Tyrrell's
G	Coca-Cola owns?	7	Seeds of Change
H	Nestlé owns?	8	Dorset Cereals
I	Mars Foods owns?	9	Copella
J	Investcorp owns?	10	Ben & Jerry's

A 4   B 9   C 1   D 8   E 3   F 10   G 2   H 5   I 7   J 6

Intensive competition means market-driven companies should respond quickly to latent markets. They need to innovate and manufacture and distribute their products and services rapidly if they are to succeed before the *strategic window of opportunity* closes (Abell, 1978). In contrast, internally driven companies tend to take their time. An example of a company that was slow to respond to the opportunities in the mobile computer market is Microsoft. It introduced the tablet PC and carved a niche market in the health sector, but in 2010 Apple launched the iPad, widened market demand and now dominates this sector.

A key feature of market-orientated companies is that they strive for competitive advantage. They seek to serve customers better than the competition does. Internally orientated companies are happy to produce me-too copies of offerings already on the market.

Finally, market-orientated companies are both efficient and effective; internally orientated companies achieve only efficiency. The concepts of efficiency and effectiveness are discussed in the next section.

EXHIBIT 1.2
Volunteer knitters produced 800,000 hats and in return Innocent donated to Age UK to help vulnerable older people

MARKETING IN ACTION 1.2
Corporate Strategies to Access Niche Markets

Ethical spending in the UK 1999–2011, £bn

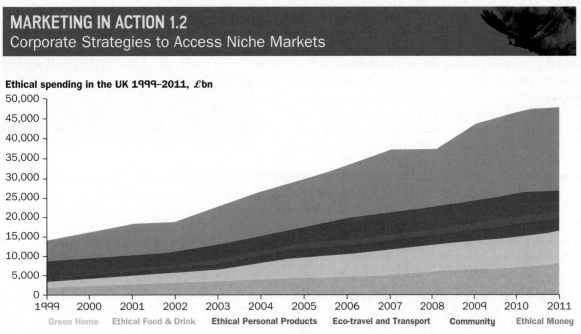

Green Home   Ethical Food & Drink   **Ethical Personal Products**   Eco-travel and Transport   **Community**   **Ethical Money**

Source: http://www.co-operative.coop/PageFiles/416561607/Ethical-Consumer-Markets-Report-2012.pdf

The Co-operative Group identified that markets for ethically sourced and produced food have grown almost three-fold in less than ten years, and demand is driving these markets towards becoming more mainstream. In the UK, 40 per cent of people are looking to buy ethically sourced products, and the market has grown in value to £47.2 billion. So it might come as no surprise that major corporate food manufacturers are seeking ways to access these emerging and potentially lucrative markets. According to a report by *Which?* magazine (2011), 'Wholesome-sounding brands have become household names, from Rachel's Organics to Green & Black's and many of us buy them partly because we like their principles and want to support small independents.' However, *Which?* magazine also discovered that multinational corporations have become parent companies of many niche organic and ethical brands and, while they may share their principles, the 'corporate parents often keep quiet about their ethical offspring'. Many ethical brands do not display the parent company's name on the product or on associated websites, and those that do tend to do so in very small print on an obscure part of the product packaging. According to academic experts, there are advantages to adopting this approach: access to target markets that are difficult to reach, and *off-the-shelf* products with ready-made branding and strong market positioning, giving easy access to the market.

Based on: Euromonitor International (2011); Which? magazine (2011); Fisher (2013); The Co-operative (2012)

 Scan the QR code to see how Innocent helps the community.

Efficiency Versus Effectiveness

Another perspective on business philosophy can be gained by understanding the distinction between efficiency and effectiveness (Brown, 1987). **Efficiency** is concerned with inputs and outputs. An efficient firm produces goods economically—it does things right. The benefit is that the cost per unit of output is low and, therefore, the potential for offering low prices to gain market share is present, or of charging medium to high prices and achieving high profit margins. For example, car companies attempt to achieve efficiency by gaining economies of scale and building several models on the same sub-frame and with the same components. However, to be successful, a company needs to be more than just efficient—it needs to be effective as well. **Effectiveness** means doing the right things. This implies operating in attractive markets and making products that customers want to buy. Conversely, companies that operate in unattractive markets or are not producing what customers want to buy will go out of business; the only question is one of timing.

The link between performance and combinations of efficiency and effectiveness can be conceived as shown in Figure 1.5. A company that is both inefficient and ineffective will go out of business quickly, because it is a high-cost producer of products that customers do not want to buy. One company that has suffered through a combination of inefficiency and ineffectiveness is General Motors. The inefficiency is the result of the legacy of paying healthcare costs to its current and retired workers—this adds $1,500 to the cost of each of its cars; the ineffectiveness stems from a history of making unreliable and undesirable cars (London, 2005).

A company that is efficient and ineffective may last a little longer because its low cost base may generate more profits from the dwindling sales volume it is achieving.

Kodak is an example of an efficient and ineffective company that has slowly died. It was an efficient producer of photographic film but has become ineffective as consumers have moved to digital photography (Teather, 2005).

Firms that are effective but inefficient are likely to survive, however, because they are operating in attractive markets and are marketing products that customers want to buy. Mercedes used to fall into this category, with its emphasis on over-engineering pushing up costs and lowering efficiency, while still making cars that people wanted to buy (driving an S500 has been likened to 'being wrapped in a freshly laundered silk sheet and blown up the road by a warm wind') (Smith, 2005) and so achieving effectiveness. The problem is that Mercedes' inefficiency is preventing the company from reaping the maximum profits from its endeavours.

Many small companies that operate in niche markets fall into the effective/inefficient category. One example is Morgan Motor Company, which manufactures bespoke, high-specification sports cars. Prices for the basic model start at less than £30,000 and, as a result, the company has a long waiting list of customer orders but the factory continues to manufacture fewer than 20 cars a week.

A combination of efficiency and effectiveness leads to optimum business success. Such firms do well and thrive because they are operating in attractive markets, are supplying products that consumers want to buy, and are benefiting from a low cost base.

Toyota is an example of an efficient and effective manufacturing company. Its investment in modern production practices ensures efficiency, while effectiveness is displayed by research and development investment into new products that consumers want to buy. Similarly, Dixons Carphone Group has streamlined the supply side of the business so it can focus on the changing demands of its multichannel retail operation efficiently. Dixons merged with Carphone Warehouse in 2014 to increase effectiveness by enabling customers to buy a wider range of consumer electronics (BBC News, 2014). These investments have put the company in a strong position in consumer electronic markets.

Inditex, owner of Zara, the Spanish fashion chain, has also thrived through a combination of efficiency and effectiveness by using its own highly efficient automated manufacturing and distribution facilities, clothing workers in 350 independently owned workshops in Spain and Portugal, and low advertising expenditures (its shops have always been its primary marketing tool). The company is highly effective, as it matches quickly changing fashion trends by means of an extremely fast and responsive supply chain. The result is that Zara has become the world's largest clothing retailer (Ruddick, 2014).

The essential difference between efficiency and effectiveness, then, is that the former is cost focused while the latter is customer focused. An effective company has the ability to attract and retain customers while remaining cost-efficient.

FIGURE 1.5
Efficiency and effectiveness

	Ineffective	Effective
Inefficient	Goes out of business quickly	Survives
Efficient	Dies slowly	Does well thrives

Benefits and Limitations of the Marketing Concept as a Guiding Business Philosophy

Academics have raised important questions regarding the value of the marketing concept. The four key issues are:

1   The marketing concept as an ideology
2   Marketing and society
3   Marketing as a constraint on innovation
4   Marketing as a source of dullness.

The marketing concept as an ideology

Brownlie and Saren (1992) argue the marketing concept has assumed many of the characteristics of an ideology or an article of faith that should dominate the thinking of organizations. They recognize the importance of a consumer orientation for companies but ask why, after 40 years of trying, the concept has not been fully implemented. They argue that there are other valid considerations that companies must take into account when making decisions (e.g. economies of scale), apart from giving customers exactly what they want. Marketers' attention should focus not only on propagation of the ideology but also on its integration with the demands of other core business functions in order to achieve a compromise between the satisfaction of consumers and the achievement of other company requirements.

Marketing and society

A second limitation of the marketing concept concerns its focus on individual market transactions. Since many individuals focus on personal benefits rather than the societal impact of their purchases, the adoption of the marketing concept will result in the production of goods and services that do not adequately correspond to societal welfare. Providing customer satisfaction is simply a means to achieve a company's profit objective and does not guarantee protection of the consumer's welfare. This view is supported by Wensley (1990), who regards consumerism as a challenge to the adequacy of the atomistic and individual view of market transactions. Bloom and Greyser present an alternative view. They regard consumerism as the ultimate expression of the marketing concept, compelling marketers to consider consumer needs and wants that hitherto may have been overlooked: 'The resourceful manager will look for the positive opportunities created by consumerism rather than brood over its restraints.'

Marketing as a constraint on innovation

Tauber (1974) presented a third criticism of marketing—that is, how marketing research discourages major innovation. The thrust of his argument was that relying on customers to guide the development of new products has severe limitations. This is because customers have difficulty articulating needs beyond the realm of their own experience. This suggests that the ideas gained from marketing research will be modest compared with those coming from the 'science push' of the research and development laboratory. Brownlie and Saren (1992) agree that, particularly for discontinuous innovations (e.g. Xerox, penicillin), the role of product development ought to be far more proactive than this. Indeed technological innovation is the process that 'realizes' market demands that were previously unknown—for example, search engines, social networks, cloud computing—are changing the very structure of society, and were unimaginable by most consumers less than two decades ago.

It is important to note that these criticisms are not actually directed at the marketing concept itself but towards its faulty implementation—an overdependence on customers as a source of new product ideas. The marketing concept does not suggest that companies must depend solely on the customer for new product ideas; rather the concept implies that new product development should be based on sound interfacing between perceived customer needs and technological research. For example, at Google innovation is encouraged and innovations are tested and launched—for example froogle (product search engine, launched November 2004, sidelined and renamed 2007), Google Sidewiki (web annotation tool launched 2009, discontinued December 2011), Google Buzz (social networking launched in September 2010), Google Glass (concept released 2012, mothballed 2015). However, innovations only succeed if they satisfy the user and there is widespread uptake. Google is very well informed about which of its innovations are effective and which need to be discontinued.

Marketing as a source of dullness

A fourth criticism of marketing is that its focus on analysing customers and developing offerings that reflect their needs leads to dull marketing campaigns, me-too products, copycat promotion and marketplace stagnation. Instead, marketing should create demand rather than simply reflect it.

Brown (1987) suggested that marketing should 'tease, tantalize and torment target markets to create insatiable desire'. He introduced 'retro marketing' as an approach built on five principles: exclusivity, secrecy, amplification, entertainment and 'tricksterism'.

1 *Exclusivity* is created by deliberately holding back supplies and delaying gratification. Consumers are encouraged to 'buy now while stocks last'. The lucky ones are happy in the knowledge that they are the select few, the discerning elite. Short supply of brands like Harley-Davidson (motorcycles), certain models of Mercedes cars and even the BMW Mini has created an aura of exclusivity.

2   *Secrecy* has the intention of teasing would-be purchasers, and was a tactic used by the Harry Potter marketing team. The pre-launch of the blockbuster *Harry Potter and the Goblet of Fire* involved a complete blackout of advance information, with the book's title, price and review copies being withheld prior to its launch.

3   *Amplification* is designed to get consumers talking about the new product or service. This can be achieved by controversial adverts—for example Benetton adverts, viral social media videos, Cadbury's gorilla playing the drums, Cravendale cats with thumbs. The growth in online advertising has facilitated wider use of such campaigns by many companies—for example Apple, Samsung and many other leading brands.

4   *Entertainment* ensures that marketing efforts are engaging target audiences. Brown (1987) claims 'modern marketing's greatest failure' is that it has lost its sense of fun in its quest to be rigorous and analytical.

5   *Tricksterism* means marketing with 'panache and audacity'. For example, Britvic made what appeared to be a public service announcement for television. Viewers were told that some rogue grocery stores were selling an imitation of its brand Tango. The difference could be detected because the drink was not fizzy, and viewers were asked to call a freephone number to name the outlets. Around 30,000 people rang, only to be informed that they had been tricked ('Tango'd') as part of the company's promotion for a new, non-carbonated version of the drink. Despite attracting censure for abusing the public information service format, the promotion had succeeded in amplifying the brand extension launch and reinforcing Tango's irreverent image.

These four emerging issues help prompt discussion about the value of the marketing concept, and together are useful for highlighting how aspects of the concept are evolving.

Creating Customer Value, Satisfaction and Loyalty

Creating value is a primary aim of market-orientated businesses. Four key benefits can be derived from adopting marketing as a guiding business philosophy:

1   Customer value
2   Customer satisfaction
3   Customer loyalty
4   Long-term customer relationships

Customer value

Market-orientated companies attempt to create **customer value** in order to attract and retain customers. Their aim is to deliver superior value to their target customers. In doing so, they implement the marketing concept by meeting and exceeding customer needs better than the competition does. For example, the global success of McDonald's has been based on creating added value for its customers, which is based not only on the food products it sells but on the complete delivery system that goes to make up a fast-food restaurant. It sets high standards in quality, service, cleanliness and value (termed QSCV). Customers can be sure that the same high standards will be found in all McDonald's outlets around the world. This example shows that customer value can be derived from many aspects of what the company delivers to its customers, not just the basic product.

 Scan the QR code to see how Cadbury focuses its multichannel advertising campaign on the value its brands deliver to customers.

Customer value is dependent on how the customer perceives the benefits of an offering and the sacrifice that is associated with its purchase. Therefore:

$$\text{Customer value} = \text{Perceived benefits} - \text{Perceived sacrifice}$$

Perceived benefits can be derived from the product (e.g. the taste of the hamburger), the associated service (e.g. how quickly customers are served and the cleanliness of the outlet) and the image of the company (e.g. whether the image of the company/product is favourable). If one of those factors—for example product benefits—changes then the perceived benefits and customer value also change. For instance, the downturn in the fortunes of McDonald's a few years ago was largely attributed to the trend towards healthier eating. This caused some consumers to regard the product benefits of its food to be less, resulting in lower perceived benefits and reduced customer value. In an attempt to redress the situation, McDonald's has introduced healthy-eating options including salad and fruit (Dickinson, 2005) and is developing allegiances with Weight Watchers and its popular weight-loss programme (Roberson, 2010).

A further source of perceived benefits is the relationship between customer and supplier. Customers may enjoy working with suppliers with whom they have developed close personal and professional friendships, and value the convenience of working with trusted partners.

Perceived sacrifice is the total cost associated with buying a product. This consists of not just monetary cost, but the time and energy involved in purchase. For example, with fast-food restaurants, good location can reduce the time and energy required to find a suitable eating place. But marketers need to be aware of another critical sacrifice in some buying situations. This is the potential psychological cost of not making the right decision. Uncertainty means that people perceive risk when purchasing; for example, McDonald's attempts to reduce perceived risk by standardizing its complete offer so that customers can be confident of what they will receive before entering its outlets. In organizational markets, companies offer guarantees to reduce the risk of purchase. Figure 1.6 illustrates how perceived benefits and sacrifice affect customer value. It provides a framework for considering ways of maximizing value. The objective is to find ways of raising perceived benefits and reducing perceived sacrifice.

Customer satisfaction

Exceeding the value offered by competitors is key to marketing success. Consumers decide upon purchases on the basis of judgements about the values offered by suppliers. Once a product has been bought, **customer satisfaction** depends upon the product's perceived performance compared with the buyer's expectations. Customer satisfaction occurs when perceived performance matches or exceeds expectations. Successful companies such as Canon, Toyota, Samsung, H&M, Waitrose, Apple and Virgin all place customer satisfaction at the heart of their business philosophy. Companies facing difficulties, such as General Motors, Chrysler, Gap and Kodak, have failed to do so as customers' needs and expectations have changed.

ASOS, a successful online fashion retailer, is succeeding by creating customer satisfaction. The company satisfies young women's desire to replicate the look of their favourite celebrities by offering affordable versions of celebrity styles and showing how to copy the designer looks of magazine favourites such as Victoria Beckham, Lindsay Lohan and Jennifer Lopez at a fraction of the cost (Finch, 2008).

Customer satisfaction is taken so seriously by some companies that they link satisfaction to financial bonuses. For example, two days after taking delivery of a new car, BMW (and Mini) customers receive a telephone call to check how well they were treated in the dealership. The customer is asked various questions, and their responses are measured. Dealerships have to be capable of achieving good performance scores, and existing dealerships that consistently fail to meet these standards are under threat of franchise termination. This approach makes a great deal of sense, as higher levels of customer satisfaction are associated with higher levels of customer retention, financial performance and shareholder value (see Mittal and Kamakura, 2001; Zeithaml, 2000; and Anderson, Fornell and Mazvancheryl, 2004).

In today's competitive climate, it is often not enough to match performance and expectations. For commercial success, expectations need to be exceeded so that customers are delighted with the outcome. In order to understand the concept of customer satisfaction, the so-called 'Kano model' (see Figure 1.7) helps to separate

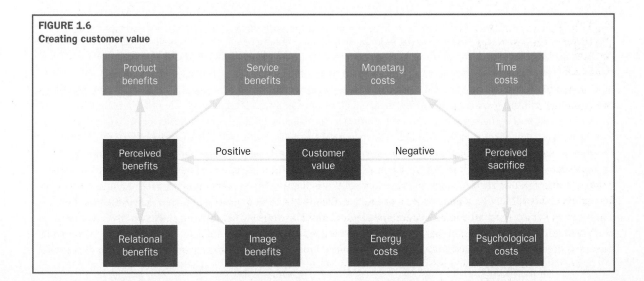

FIGURE 1.6
Creating customer value

characteristics that cause dissatisfaction, satisfaction and delight. Three characteristics underlie the model: 'must be', 'more is better' and 'delighters'.

'Must be' characteristics are expected to be present and are taken for granted. For example, in a hotel, customers expect service at reception and a clean room. The lack of these characteristics causes annoyance, but their presence only brings dissatisfaction up to a neutral level. 'More is better' characteristics can take satisfaction past neutral into the positive satisfaction range. For example, no response to a telephone call can cause dissatisfaction, but a fast response may cause positive satisfaction or even delight. 'Delighters' are the unexpected characteristics that surprise the customer. Their absence does not cause dissatisfaction but their presence delights the customer. For example, a UK hotel chain provides a free basket of fruit on arrival in visitors' rooms. This delights many of its customers, who were not expecting this treat. Another way to delight the customer is to under-promise and over-deliver (e.g., by saying that a repair will take about five hours, but getting it done in two) (White, 1999).

A problem for marketers is that, over time, delighters become expected. For example, some car manufacturers provided small unexpected delighters such as pen holders

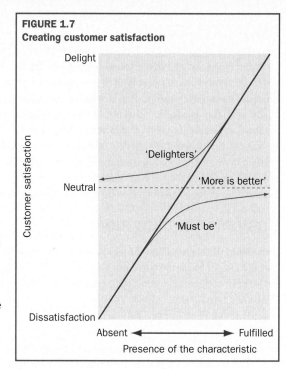

FIGURE 1.7
Creating customer satisfaction

and delay mechanisms on interior lights so that there is time to find the ignition socket at night. These are standard on most cars now and have become 'must be' characteristics, as customers expect them. This means that marketers must constantly strive to find new ways of delighting. Innovative thinking and listening to customers are key ingredients in this. Mini Case 1.1 explains how to listen to customers.

The importance of customer satisfaction is supported by studies which show that higher levels of customer satisfaction lead to higher financial (profits and sales) performance (see Anderson, Fornell and Lehmann, 1994; Anderson, Fornell and Rust, 1997; Reichheld and Sasser, 1990; and Rust and Zahorik, 1993), greater customer loyalty (Homberg, Koschate and Hoyer, 2005) and the willingness of customers to pay higher prices (see Anderson and Sullivan, 1997; and Bolton and Drew, 1991).

Customer loyalty

Customer satisfaction is linked to customer loyalty and profitability (Srinivasan, Anderson and Ponnavolu, 2002). It can cost up to five times more to attract a new customer than to serve an existing one (Strauss, El-Ansary and Frost, 2006).

In most situations, returning customers are beneficial to an organization, as they can increase sales volumes through repeat purchases. Loyalty is a response that a customer shows over time. Typically, customers will repeatedly return to the same supplier if they are satisfied with the products and services they receive (Christodoulides and Michaelidou, 2011). Customer loyalty can be built on convenience, quality of service and social interaction, for example. However, loyalty can take different forms and be triggered by different marketing initiatives. For example, Tesco uses sales promotions through its loyalty card programme to trigger repeat customer purchase behaviour. Arguably, this type of loyalty is driven by price, and the promotion acts as an incentive to trigger repeat purchases. Customer loyalty can be temporarily shaken when companies change their brand identity as Marketing in Action 1.3 explains.

At the other end of the scale is a form of loyalty that transcends emotional boundaries: brand love. Brand love is an extension of the concept of loyalty (Batra, Ahuvia and Bagozzi, 2012). Researchers have found that the connections between individuals and the brands they choose are closely associated with the concept of interpersonal physical love. However, while brand love has been found to involve passion, positive emotional connections, long-term relationships, positive attitudes, and distress at the thought of separation, it does not leave brand lovers as profoundly committed to a product as they might be to a personal partner. Nevertheless, there are consequences for marketing managers, and they should look for ways to turn *liked* brands into *loved* brands.

Looking for ways to maintain this high level of commitment to the relationship can be achieved by maximizing three key opportunities: 1) *Facilitate 'passion-driven behaviour'*, which is a strong commitment to use the brand,

The importance of listening to customers was emphasized by Sir Terry Leahy, former chief executive of Tesco Plc, the UK's largest supermarket chain: 'Let me tell you the secret of successful retailing,' he said to a group of business leaders. 'Are you ready? It's this: never stop listening to customers and giving them what they want. I'm sorry if that is a bit of an anticlimax…but it is that simple.' Kwik-Fit, the car repair group, also places listening to customers high on its list of priorities. Customer satisfaction is monitored by its customer survey unit, which telephones 5,000 customers a day within 72 hours of their visit to a Kwik-Fit centre.

Most leading companies recognize the importance of listening to their customers as part of their strategy to manage satisfaction. Customer satisfaction indices are based on surveys of customers, and the results plotted over time to reveal changes in satisfaction levels. The first stage is to identify those characteristics (choice criteria) that are important to customers when evaluating competing products. The second stage involves the development of measurement scales (often statements followed by 'strongly agree'/'strongly disagree' response boxes) to assess satisfaction quantitatively. Customer satisfaction data should be collected over a period of time to measure change. Only long-term measurement of satisfaction ratings will provide a clear picture of what is going on in the marketplace. However, the marketplace is changing and use of new data-capture methods and technologies means some customers are more aware of how their data are being used. Consequently, customers must see some benefit from the use of their data if an effective relationship is to develop, and both satisfied and dissatisfied customers are making themselves heard by using social media, for example Twitter. For marketers, understanding the digital arena is critical.

In this highly connected era, a strategy should be in place to manage customer complaints, comments and questions. A system needs to be set up that solicits feedback on product and service quality and feeds the information to the appropriate employees, who can respond in a timely fashion. To facilitate this process, frontline employees need training to ask questions, to listen effectively, to capture the information and to communicate it so that corrective action can be taken. Walmart used to believe that no response was the best policy for handling negative tweets but has changed its strategy; now the global grocery retailer proactively manages online communication and is a top brand in content engagement.

TripAdvisor is the world's largest online travel site, and it helps people plan their holiday and business trips by providing advice from over 60 million reviews and opinions from other travellers who have experience of services provided by hotels, restaurants and travel companies. Each service provider is ranked by a number of performance indicators, and this can make a big difference to future trade, as the opinions of other travellers can have a powerful influence.

Companies can also launch websites to solicit customers' new ideas. Dell did this after it received a flood of criticism over poor customer service, while also reaching out to online bloggers. The feedback led to a customer services overhaul and a fall in negative buzz.

Finally, Google listens to customers by releasing most products in 'beta' (which means they are not quite finished), allowing users to suggest improvements. This approach has led to the refinement of such products as Google News, Gmail and the Chrome browser.

Questions:
1 Explain why feedback from social media sites can be more accurate than surveys.
2 What strategy would you suggest for a business in handling customer complaints, comments and questions?

Based on: Jones and Sasser Jr (1995); Morgan (1996); White (1999); Roythorne (2003); Ryle (2003); Mitchell (2005); Wright (2006); Jarvis (2009); Hilpern (2011); Devaney and Stein (2014); Zhang (2014)

as in the case of luxury designer brands—for example, Gucci, Rolex, Porsche. 2) *Build brands that engender self-brand integration.* This is the way the brand connects to an individual's values and deeper thought processes. Rewards can be used effectively to emphasize the benefits of this higher-level commitment. Samsung is an example of a brand attempting to connect with customers by engendering self-identity through brand values associated with the environment. 3) *Create positive emotional connections.* Brands that succeed in being regarded as an 'old friend' and creating a strong bond with the customer benefit by finding a place in the customer's heart. Anita Roddick succeeded in making this type of connection with Body Shop customers (Batra, Ahuvia and Bagozzi (2012).

MARKETING IN ACTION 1.3
Brand Loyalty Wobbles when Starbucks Employs a Siren to Lead its Nameless Brand

Customer value is closely linked with perceptions of a brand. So when changes are made to a brand's identity they should be meaningful to customers in such a way that they will continue to make positive brand associations and buy the products and services offered. In 2011, Starbucks launched its new global brand identity as a mark of the company's 40 years in business.

According to Steve Barrett, the Starbucks global creative vice-president, the new look tested well with loyal consumers. However, the removal of the words *Starbucks* and *coffee* from the iconic green logo initially annoyed many of its customers, and they complained in their hundreds on the brand's official Facebook page, saying the new logo 'sucks'.

The company aimed to join the ranks of other companies with nameless identities, for example Nike and Apple. Another reason for the change was to give the brand a less corporate and more contemporary feel. The new identity also resonates with the introduction of new product lines, for example Tazo tea and Starbucks Refresha—cold drinks and ice cream that are not coffee based. In 2015, Starbucks made further product extensions by introducing beer and wine in thousands of outlets in the USA and a few selected stores in the UK.

The initial resistance to the change of identity did not last, and customers continue to flock to Starbucks' 22,000 outlets in 66 countries around the world.

Based on: Added Value (2011); Clark (2011); Wood (2011); Leroux (2014); Berr (2014); Spary (2015)

Long-term customer relationships

According to Sheth and Parvartiyar (1995), relationship marketing is a change in direction for marketing thinking and practices, and it places 'emphasis on relationships as opposed to transaction based exchanges'. The benefit of this redefinition of marketing is that a firm's activities become focused on attracting customers and seeking ways to retain them rather than just selling the products and services that customers might need and want. Relationship marketing enhances productivity and allows the firm and its customers to develop mutual cooperation. In the digital age, technology has become increasingly important in facilitating relationship development; social media has been used to understand and engage customers. Twitter, Facebook and Instagram provide platforms for interaction and information exchange between firms, employees and customers. Social platforms maximize customer engagement and create opportunities for marketers to react instantly when a customer tweets about a bad (or good) customer experience. Rapid response in the digital arena can also deliver relational benefits, as more than 70 per cent of customers are likely to spend more if a firm has a good service history (Sklar, 2013). The concept of relationship marketing is covered in greater detail in Chapter 10.

Making Marketing Work: Developing Plans and Application of the Marketing Mix

So far in this chapter we have discussed the conceptual meaning of marketing, adopting a market orientation, the importance of efficiency and effectiveness and the benefits and limitations of marketing as a guiding business philosophy. In this final section, we very briefly look at what is involved in developing marketing planning and strategy, and consider the implementation of the marketing mix. It is important to note that these are substantive topics, which are covered in detail in later chapters in the book.

Marketing planning

Making marketing work requires much planning and effort across an organization. Marketing planning is part of the overarching corporate strategic planning process and provides a range of insights from the trading environment to target markets and customer needs. But thinking about where marketing planning fits in the wider business-planning process is only part of the challenge managers encounter. They must also consider the core functions of the business and the key processes of marketing. Fundamentally, marketing planning functions at two levels:

1   At a business level—here the focus is strategic in nature and involves: setting a business mission; identifying the vision driving the firm forwards; carrying out a marketing audit (an analysis of a firm's current trading situation); conducting a SWOT (strengths, weaknesses, opportunities and threats) analysis to inform strategic direction; and setting high-level marketing objectives, which define the target markets and selection of goods and services offered by a firm.

2   At a product and or service level—here the focus is on the practical application of marketing. This level involves many decisions about how to use the product and service mix to create competitive advantage and then how these decisions are implemented.

At the heart of the planning process is the market strategy, which pulls together the planning process and defines the application of the marketing mix. For more details on marketing planning, see Chapter 18.

Application of the marketing mix

The original concept of the marketing mix consists of four major elements: product, price, promotion and place. These '4-Ps' are the four key decision areas that marketers must manage so that they satisfy or exceed customer needs better than the competition does.

The emphasis of each of the elements of the mix will vary depending on the products and services offered; for example, BMW cars and Rolex watches are market-orientated companies that focus primarily on the 4-Ps, as they are product manufacturers, but Starbucks and Burger King focus primarily on the elements of the extended mix, as service, process and the physical evidence are at the heart of their fast-food restaurants.

Decisions regarding the marketing mix therefore form a major aspect of marketing concept implementation. At this point, we briefly examine the 4-Ps and the service mix to provide an essence of marketing mix decision-making. Later in the book we look at the elements of the marketing mix in considerable detail.

Product

The **product** decision involves deciding what goods should be offered to a group of customers. As technology and tastes change, products become out of date and inferior to those of the competition, so companies must replace them with innovations: new products with features that add customer value and give greater benefits. Market leaders can change. For example, the Samsung MP3 player was the market leader in digital music players, but following its launch, the Apple iPod soon outsold the MP3 player.

Product decisions also involve choices regarding brand names, guarantees, packaging and the augmented aspects of products that accompany a product offering. For example, the operators of the AVE, Spain's high-speed train capable of travelling at 300 km/h, are so confident of its performance that they guarantee to give customers a full refund of their fare if they are more than 5 minutes late. See Chapters 11 and 20 for further discussion of the product element of the marketing mix.

Price

Price is a key element of the marketing mix, as it represents on a unit basis what the company receives for the goods being marketed. All the other elements of the marketing mix represent costs, for example expenditure on product design (product), advertising and sales people (promotion), and transportation and distribution (place). Marketers should be clear about pricing objectives and the factors that influence price setting, and also consider the necessity to discount and give allowances in some transactions. Pricing decisions can affect the perceived value of a product, as price affects the value that customers perceive they get from buying a product. Some companies attempt to position themselves as offering lower prices than their rivals. For example, supermarkets such as Asda (Walmart) in the UK, Aldi in Germany and Netto in Scandinavia employ a low-price positioning strategy. See Chapter 12 for more insight into how to develop value through pricing.

Promotion

Decisions about the **promotional mix**—advertising, personal selling, sales promotions, public relations, direct marketing and digital marketing—are critical to how a firm communicates with its target audience and engages a response. This element of the mix makes target audiences aware of products or services and the potential benefits (both economic and psychological).

Each element of the promotional mix has strengths and weaknesses. Advertising, for example, is able to reach wide audiences very quickly. Procter & Gamble used advertising to reach the emerging market of 290 million Russian consumers. It ran a 12-minute commercial on Russian television as its first promotional venture in order to introduce the company and its range of products (Charles, 2007). Sales promotions can be used to stimulate an immediate uplift in sales, but this effect can be short-term. Digital and social marketing now attract more advertising revenue than any other media. An advantage is that firms can reach consumers worldwide through websites and social media. Personal selling can be used to good effect, especially in business-to-business markets, as this promotional tool offers face-to-face interactions, which are an important part of sales negotiations. See Chapters 13, 14, 15 and 16 for detailed discussion of the tools and application of the promotional mix.

Place

Place concerns decisions about distribution channels. Key management decisions focus on the location of outlets, methods of transportation, and inventory levels held. The objective is to ensure products and services are available in required quantities, at the right time and in the right place. Distribution channels consist of organizations such as retailers or wholesalers through which goods pass on their way to customers. Producers need to manage their relationships with these organizations well, because they may provide the only cost-effective access to the marketplace. They also need to be aware of new methods of distribution that can create a competitive advantage. For example, Dell revolutionized the distribution of computers, selling direct to customers rather than using traditional computer outlets. Music and film are increasingly being distributed by downloading from the Internet rather than being bought at music shops.

Following this trend, Radiohead offered fans the opportunity to pay whatever they liked to download the group's new album, and the rock band Nine Inch Nails released its as a free download from the band's website (O'Flaherty, 2008).

The service mix

The growth of the service industries has given rise to an extended marketing mix of seven 'Ps'. The services marketing mix is an extension of the 4-Ps framework, with three further Ps *people*, *physical evidence* and *process* (Booms and Bitner, 1981). The need for the extension came about due to the high degree of direct contact between the firm and the customer, the highly visible nature of the service assembly process, and the simultaneity of production and consumption. Booms and Bitner (1981) argue for a 7-Ps approach to services marketing, as they suggest that the 4-Ps take no account of people, process and physical evidence. While it is possible to discuss people, physical evidence and process within the original 4-Ps framework (e.g., people could be considered part of the product offering), the extension allows a more thorough analysis of the marketing ingredients necessary for successful marketing planning and activities. In services, people often *are* the service itself, the process or how the service is delivered to the customer is usually a key part of the service, and the physical evidence—the décor of the restaurant or shop, for example—is so critical to success that it should be considered as a separate element in the services marketing mix.

See Chapter 9 for detailed discussion of services marketing.

Key Characteristics of an Effective Marketing Mix

There are four hallmarks of an effective marketing mix (see Figure 1.8).

The marketing mix matches customer needs

Sensible marketing mix decisions can be made only when the target customer is identified and understood. (Choosing customer groups, targeting, segmentation and positioning are explored in Chapter 7.) Once the target market(s) is identified, marketing management needs to understand how customers choose between rival offerings. Managers should consider the product or service through customers' eyes and understand, among other factors, the choice criteria they use.

Figure 1.9 illustrates the link between customer choice criteria and the marketing mix. The starting point is the realization that customers evaluate products on economic and psychological criteria. Economic criteria include factors such as performance, availability, reliability, durability and productivity gains to be made by using the product. Examples of psychological criteria are self-image, a desire for a quiet life, pleasure, convenience and risk reduction (see Chapter 3). The important point at this stage is to note that an analysis of customer choice criteria reveals a set of key customer requirements that must be met in order to succeed in the marketplace. Meeting or exceeding these requirements better than the competition leads to the creation of a competitive advantage.

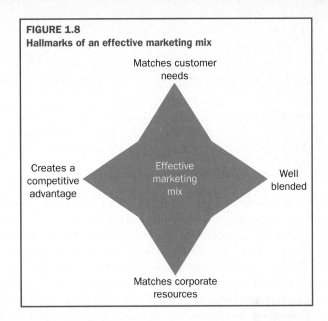

FIGURE 1.8
Hallmarks of an effective marketing mix

The marketing mix creates a competitive advantage

A **competitive advantage** is the achievement of superior performance through differentiation to provide superior customer value or by managing to achieve lowest delivered cost. Competitive advantage can be derived from decisions about the 4-Ps.

Apple's iPad is an example of a company using product features to convey customer benefits that exceed the competition's offerings. The iPad's portability, range of applications and its ability to download, display and store PDF documents, audio, music and films can, therefore, be regarded as the creation of competitive advantages over the previous market leader in the tablet computer market, Microsoft. Aldi, the German supermarket chain, achieves a competitive advantage by severely controlling costs, allowing it to make profits even though its prices are low, a strategy that is attractive to price-sensitive shoppers.

The strategy of using advertising as a tool for competitive advantage is often employed when product benefits are particularly subjective and amorphous in nature. Thus the advertising for perfumes such as those produced by Chanel, Givenchy and Yves St Laurent is critical in preserving the exclusive image established by such brands. The size and quality of the salesforce can act as a competitive advantage. A problem that a company such as Rolls-Royce, the aero engine manufacturer, faces is the relatively small size of its salesforce compared with those of its giant competitors Boeing and General Electric.

Finally, distribution decisions need to be made with the customer in mind, not only in terms of availability but also with respect to service levels, image and customer convenience. The Radisson SAS hotel at Manchester airport is an example of creating a competitive advantage through customer convenience. It is situated 5 minutes walk from the airport terminals, which are reached by covered walkways. Guests at rival hotels have to rely on taxis or transit buses to reach the airport.

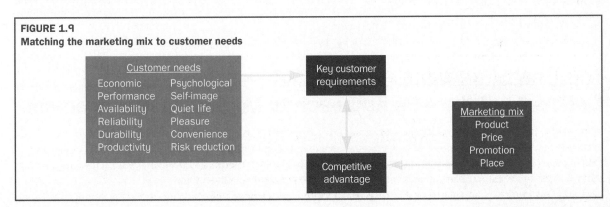

FIGURE 1.9
Matching the marketing mix to customer needs

The marketing mix should be well blended

The third characteristic of an effective marketing mix is that the four elements—product, price, promotion and place—should be well blended to form a consistent theme. If a product gives superior benefits to customers, price, which may send cues to customers regarding quality, should reflect those extra benefits. All of the promotional mix should be designed with the objective of communicating a consistent message to the target audience about these benefits, and distribution decisions should be consistent with the overall strategic position of the product in the marketplace. The use of exclusive outlets for upmarket fashion and cosmetics brands—Armani, Christian Dior and Calvin Klein, for example—is consistent with their strategic position.

The marketing mix should match corporate resources

The choice of marketing mix strategy may ultimately be down to the available financial resources of the company. For example, Amazon was only able to establish its global presence by massive financial investment in online advertising. Certain media—for example, television advertising—require a minimum threshold investment before they are regarded as feasible. In the UK, a rule of thumb is that at least £5 million per year is required to achieve impact in a national advertising campaign. Clearly those brands that cannot afford such a promotional budget must use other less expensive media—for example, digital marketing, posters or sales promotion—to attract and hold customers.

A second internal resource constraint may be the internal competences of the company. A marketing mix strategy may be too ambitious for the limited marketing skills of personnel to implement effectively. While an objective may be to reduce or eliminate this problem in the medium to long term, in the short term marketing management may have to heed the fact that strategy must take account of competences.

Marketing and Business Performance

The basic premise of the marketing concept is that its adoption will improve business performance. Marketing is not an abstract concept: its acid test is the effect that its use has on key corporate indices such as profitability and market share. Research in Europe and North America has examined the relationship between marketing and performance, and the results suggest that the relationship is positive.

Marketing characteristics and business performance

In a study of 1,700 senior marketing executives, Hooley and Lynch reported the marketing characteristics of high-versus low-performing companies (Hooley and Lynch, 1985). The approach that they adopted was to isolate the top 10 per cent of companies (based on such measures as profit margin, return on investment and market share) and to compare their marketing practices with those of the remainder of the sample. The 'high fliers' differed from the 'also rans' in that they:

- were more committed to marketing research
- were more likely to be found in new, emerging or growth markets
- adopted a more proactive approach to marketing planning
- were more likely to use strategic planning tools
- placed more emphasis on product performance and design, rather than price, for achieving a competitive advantage
- worked more closely with the finance department
- placed greater emphasis on market share as a method of evaluating marketing performance.

Criticisms of the 4-Ps Approach to Marketing Management

Some critics of the 4-Ps approach to the marketing mix argue that it oversimplifies the reality of marketing management. As mentioned earlier and discussed in some detail in Chapter 9 on services marketing, Booms and Bitner, for example, argue for a 7-Ps approach to services marketing (Bloom and Greyser, 1981). Their argument is that the 4-Ps do not take sufficient account of people, process and physical evidence.

Rafiq and Ahmed argue that this criticism of the 4-Ps can be extended to include industrial marketing (Rafiq and Ahmed (1992). The interaction approach to understanding industrial marketing stresses that success does not come solely from manipulation of the marketing mix components but from long-term relationship building, whereby the bond between buyer and seller becomes so strong that it effectively acts as a barrier to entry for out-suppliers (Ford, Håkansson and Johanson, 1986). This phenomenon undoubtedly exists to such an extent that industrial buyers are now increasingly seeking long-term supply relationships with suppliers. For example, car manufacturers have drawn up long-term contracts with preferred suppliers that provide stability in supply and improvements in new component development. Bosch, a German producer of industrial and consumer goods, conducts quality audits of its suppliers. These kinds of activities are not captured in the 4-Ps approach, it is claimed.

However, the strength of the 4-Ps approach is that it represents a memorable and practical framework for marketing decision-making and has proved useful for many years.

Market orientation and business performance

Narver and Slater studied the relationship between market orientation and business performance (Narver and Slater, 1990). Market orientation was based on three measures: customer orientation, competitor orientation, and degree of inter-functional coordination. They collected data from 113 strategic business units (SBUs) of a major US corporation. The businesses comprised 36 commodity businesses (forestry products) and 77 non-commodity businesses (speciality products and distribution businesses). They related each SBU's profitability, as measured by return on assets in relation to competitors' over the last year in the SBU's principal served market, to their three-component measure of market orientation.

Figure 1.10 shows the results of Narver and Slater's study. For commodity businesses the relationship was U-shaped, with low and high market orientation businesses showing higher profitability than the businesses in the mid range of market orientation. Businesses with the highest market orientation had the highest profitability, and those with the lowest market orientation had the second-highest profitability. Narver and Slater explained this result by suggesting that the businesses lowest in market orientation may achieve some profit success through a low-cost strategy, though not the profit levels of the high market orientation businesses, an explanation supported by the fact that they were the largest companies of the three groups.

For the non-commodity businesses the relationship was linear, with the businesses displaying the highest level of market orientation achieving the highest levels of profitability, and those with the lowest scores on market orientation having the lowest profitability figures. As the authors state, 'The findings give marketing scholars and practitioners a basis beyond mere intuition for recommending the superiority of a market orientation.'

Recent studies have found a positive relationship between market orientation and business performance. Market orientation has been found to have a positive effect on sales growth, market share and profitability (Pelham, 2000), sales growth (Narver, Jacobson and Slater, 1999), sales growth and new product success (Slater and Narver, 1994; Im and Workman, 2004), perception of product quality (Pelham and Wilson, 1996) and overall business performance (Pulendran, Speed and Wilding, 2003; for a review of the literature on market orientation and business performance see Cano, Carrillet and Jaramillo, 2004).

Finally, a study by Kirca, Jayachandran and Bearden (2005) analysed the empirical findings from a wide range of studies that sought to identify the antecedents and consequences of market orientation. Their findings showed

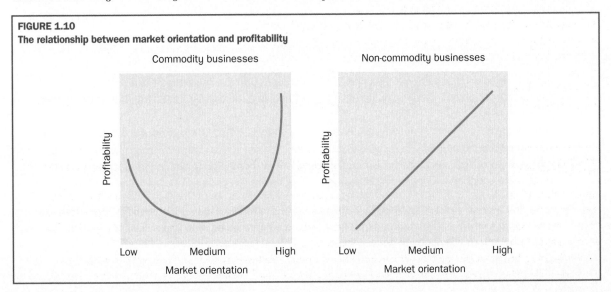

FIGURE 1.10
The relationship between market orientation and profitability

that a market orientation led to higher overall business performance (higher profits, sales and market share), better customer consequences (higher perceived quality, customer loyalty and customer satisfaction), better innovative consequences (higher innovativeness and better new product performance) and beneficial employee consequences (higher organizational commitment, team spirit, customer orientation and job satisfaction, and lower role conflict). Their analysis of the antecedents of the market orientation showed the importance of top management's emphasis on marketing, good communications between departments, and systems that reward employees for market success to the implementation of market orientation.

So, what overall conclusions can be drawn from these studies? In order to make a balanced judgement, limitations must be recognized. Most were cross-sectional studies based on self-reported data. With any such survey there is the question of the direction of causality. However, this clearly did not occur with the commodity sample in the Narver and Slater study (1990). What these studies have consistently and unambiguously shown is a strong association between marketing and business performance. As one condition for establishing causality, this is an encouraging result for those people concerned with promoting the marketing concept as a guiding philosophy for business.

The results of these pioneering studies have been supplemented with further empirical evidence showing a positive link between market orientation and business performance, e.g., Amazon, a company that focuses its efforts on creating a customer-centric culture throughout the business.

When you have read this chapter

Discover further resources and test your understanding: McGraw-Hill **Connect**™ is a digital teaching and learning environment that improves performance over a variety of critical outcomes; it can be tailored, is easy to use and is proven effective. **LearnSmart**™ is the most widely used and intelligent adaptive learning resource that is proven to strengthen memory recall, improve course retention and boost grades. Fuelled by **LearnSmart**™, **SmartBook**™ is the first and only adaptive reading experience available today.

Review

1   Identify the fundamental principles of marketing

- The marketing concept sets out the core ideas that underpin the nature of marketing and provides central planks on which to build a market-orientated organization.
- The market-orientation provides a guiding philosophy that enables an organization to concentrate its activities on its customers.
- Focusing on efficiency and effectiveness enables an organization to ensure that it is doing things *right* and doing the *right* things. Getting the balance correct between the two can mean the difference between success and failure.
- Customers are at the heart of marketing; consequently understanding how to create customer value and satisfaction is very important.
- Designing an effective marketing mix is an essential element of marketing and is the means by which customers are satisfied and marketing objectives are achieved.

2   The marketing concept: an understanding of the nature of marketing, its key components and limitations

- The marketing concept is the achievement of corporate goals through meeting and exceeding customer needs better than the competition does.
- It exists through exchanges where the objective is for all parties in the exchange to feel satisfied.

- Its key components are customer orientation, integrated effort and goal achievement (e.g. profits).
- The limitations of the concept are that the pursuit of customer satisfaction is only one objective companies should consider (others, such as achieving economies of scale, are equally valid), the adoption of the marketing concept may result in a focus on short-term personal satisfaction rather than longer-term societal welfare, the focus on customers to guide the development of new products will lead to only modest improvements compared to the innovations resulting from technological push, and the emphasis on reflecting rather than creating demand can lead to dull marketing campaigns and me-too products.

3 The difference between production orientation and market orientation
- Market orientation focuses on customer needs to identify potential market opportunities, leading to the creation of products that create customer satisfaction.
- Production orientation focuses on production capabilities, which defines the business mission and the products that are manufactured. These are then sold aggressively to customers.

4 The differences between market-driven and internally orientated businesses
- Customer concern versus convenience.
- Know customer choice criteria and match with marketing mix versus the assumption that price and performance are key.
- Segment by customer differences versus segment by product.
- Marketing research versus anecdotes and received wisdom.
- Welcome change versus cherish status quo.
- Understand competition versus ignore competition.
- Marketing spend is an investment versus marketing spend is a luxury.
- Innovation rewarded and reluctance to punish failure, versus avoidance of mistakes rewarded and a failure to innovate is conspicuously punished.
- Search for latent markets versus stick with the same.
- Recognize the importance of being fast versus content to move slowly.
- Strive for competitive advantage versus happy to be me-too.
- Efficiency and effectiveness versus efficiency.

5 The different roles of efficiency and effectiveness in achieving corporate success
- Efficiency is concerned with inputs and outputs. Business processes are managed to a high standard so that cost per unit of output is low. Its role is to 'do things right'—that is, use processes that result in low-cost production.
- Effectiveness is concerned with making the correct strategic choice regarding which products to make for which markets. Its role is to 'do the right things'—that is, make the right products for attractive markets.

6 How to create customer value and satisfaction
- Customer value is created by maximizing perceived benefits (e.g. product or image benefits) and minimizing perceived sacrifice (e.g. monetary or time costs).
- Customer satisfaction once a product is bought is created by maximizing perceived performance compared to the customer's expectations. Customer satisfaction occurs when perceived performance matches or exceeds expectations.

7 How an effective marketing mix is designed
- The classical marketing mix consists of product, price, promotion and place (the '4-Ps').
- An effective marketing mix is designed by ensuring that it matches customer needs, creates a competitive advantage, is well blended and matches corporate resources.

8 Criticisms of the 4-Ps approach to marketing management
- Criticisms of the 4-Ps approach to marketing management are that it oversimplifies reality. For example, for services marketing three further Ps—people, process and physical evidence—should be added and, for

industrial (business-to-business) marketing, the marketing mix approach neglects the importance of long-term relationship building.

9 The relationships between marketing characteristics, market orientation and business performance
- Research has shown a positive relationship between business performance, market orientation and marketing characteristics (although for commodity businesses the relationship was U-shaped).

10 Identify relevant business and research examples, which illustrate the principles of marketing in a modern organization
- This chapter has described marketing and demonstrated how the principles of marketing can be applied in the modern organization through the use of examples, marketing insights and case studies at the end of the chapter. For each of the key concepts it is possible to identify illustrative examples.

Key Terms

competitive advantage the achievement of superior performance through differentiation to provide superior customer value or by managing to achieve lowest delivered cost

customer satisfaction the fulfilment of customers' requirements or needs

customer value perceived benefits minus perceived sacrifice

effectiveness doing the right thing, making the correct strategic choice

efficiency a way of managing business processes to a high standard, usually concerned with cost reduction; also called 'doing things right'

exchange the act or process of receiving something from someone by giving something in return

marketing concept the achievement of corporate goals through meeting and exceeding customer needs better than the competition

marketing mix a framework for the tactical management of the customer relationship, including product, place,

price, promotion (the 4-Ps); in the case of services, three other elements to be taken into account are process, people and physical evidence

market orientation companies with a market orientation focus on customer needs as the primary drivers of organizational performance

place the distribution channels to be used, outlet locations, methods of transportation

price (1) the amount of money paid for a product; (2) the agreed value placed on the exchange by buyer and seller

product a good or service offered or performed by an organization or individual, which is capable of satisfying customer needs

production orientation a business approach that is inwardly focused either on costs or on a definition of a company in terms of its production facilities

promotional mix advertising, personal selling, sales promotions, public relations, direct marketing, and Internet and online promotion

Study Questions

1. What are the essential characteristics of a market-orientated company?

2. Are there any situations where market orientation is not the most appropriate business philosophy?

3. Explain how the desire to become efficient may conflict with being effective.

4. How far do you agree or disagree with the criticism that marketing is a source of dullness? Are there any ethical issues relevant to the five principles of 'retromarketing'?

5. To what extent do you agree with the criticisms of the marketing concept and the 4-Ps approach to marketing decision-making?

Recommended Reading

Bergkvist, L. and T. Bech-Larsen (2010) Two studies of consequences and actionable antecedents of brand love, *Journal of Brand Management* 17, 504–18.

Dewar, N. (2013) When marketing is strategy, *Harvard Business Review*, 91.

Dibb, S., C. Simoes and R. Wensley (2014) Establishing the scope of marketing practice: insights from practitioners. *European Journal of Marketing*, 48(1-2) 380–404.

Harvard Business School, Working Knowledge, Marketing http://hbswk.hbs.edu/topics/marketing.html

Ravald, A. and C. Grönroos (1996) The value concept and relationship marketing, *European Journal of Marketing*, 30(2), 19–30.

Rust, R., C. Moorman and G. Bhalla (2010) Rethinking marketing, *Harvard Business Review*, 88 (1/2), 94–101.

References

Abell, D. F. (1978) Strategic Windows, *Journal of Marketing*, July, 21–6.

Added Value (2011). The Starbucks Debate, January. http://added-value.com/the-starbucks-debate (accessed 14 February 2015).

Anderson, E. W., C. Fornell and D. R. Lehmann (1994) Customer Satisfaction, Market Share and Profitability: Findings From Sweden, *Journal of Marketing* 58 (July), 53–66.

Anderson, E. W., C. Fornell and R. T. Rust (1997) Customer Satisfaction, Productivity, and Profitability: Differences Between Goods and Services, *Marketing Science* 16 (Z), 129–45.

Anderson, E., C. Fornell and S. K. Mazvancheryl (2004) Customer Satisfaction and Shareholder Value, *Journal of Marketing* 68 (October), 172–85.

Anderson, E. W. and M. W. Sullivan (1997) The Antecedents and Consequences of Customer Satisfaction for Firms, *Marketing Science* 12 (Spring), 125–43.

Balch, O. (2013). H&M: can fast fashion and sustainability ever really mix? *The Guardian*, 3 May. http://www.theguardian.com/sustainable-business/h-and-m-fashion-sustainability-mix (accessed 30 January 2015).

Batra, R., A. Ahuvia and R. P. Bagozzi (2012) Brand Love, *Journal of Marketing* 76(2), 1–16.

BBC News (2014) Dixons Carphone unveils new stores, 7 August. http://www.bbc.co.uk/news/uk-28689236 (accessed 30 January 2015).

Benady, A. (2005) Nestlé's New Flavour of Strategy, *Financial Times*, 22 February, 13.

Berr, J. (2014) Starbucks' growth plans impress Wall Street, *CBS Money Watch*, 5 December. http://www.cbsnews.com/news/starbucks-ceos-growth-plans-impress-wall-street (accessed 14 January 2015).

Bloom, P. N. and S. A. Greyser (1981) The Maturity of Consumerism, *Harvard Business Review*, Nov–Dec, 130–9.

Booms, B. H. and M. J. Bitner (1981) Marketing Strategies and Organisation Structures for Service Firms, in Donnelly, J. H. and W. R. George (eds.) *Marketing of Services*, Chicago: American Marketing Association, 47–51.

Bolton, R. N. and J. H. Drew (1991) A Longitudinal Analysis of the Impact of Service Changes on Customer Attitudes, *Journal of Marketing* 55 (January), 1–9.

Booms, B. H. and M. J. Bitner (1981) Marketing Strategies and Organisation Structures for Service Firms, in Donnelly, J. H. and W. R. George (eds.) *Marketing of Services*, Chicago: American Marketing Association, 47–52.

Brown, R. J. (1987) Marketing: A Function and a Philosophy, *Quarterly Review of Marketing* 12(3), 25–30.

Brownlie, D. and M. Saren (1992) The Four Ps of the Marketing Concept: Prescriptive, Polemical, Permanent and Problematical, *European Journal of Marketing* 26(4), 34–47.

Cano, C. R., F. A. Carrillet and F. Jaramillo (2004) A Meta-Analysis of the Relationship between Market Orientation and Business Performance: Evidence from Five Continents, *International Journal of Research in Marketing* 21(2), 179–200.

Charles, J. (2007) Facebook Protest Forces Interest Rate Climbdown, Timesonline.co.uk, 31 August (retrieved from www.timesonline.co.uk/tol/money/student_finance/article2358640.ece).

Christodoulides, G. and N. Michaelidou (2011) Shopping motives as antecedents of e-satisfaction and e-loyalty, Journal of Marketing Management 27(1–2), 181–197.

Clark, A. (2011) Starbucks joins Nike and Apple in the big league of no-name logos, *The Guardian*, 9 January. http://www.theguardian.com/business/2011/jan/09/starbucks-new-logo-no-name (accessed 14 February 2015).

Devaney, T. and T. Stein (2014). Handling Haters: How To Respond To Negative Online Reviews, *Forbes*, 3 March. http://www.forbes.com/sites/sage/2014/03/03/handling-haters-how-to-respond-to-negative-online-reviews (accessed 2 February 2015).

Dickinson, H. (2005) Forget Supersizing, Think Downsizing, *Marketing*, 7 December, 13.

Drucker, P. F. (1999) *The Practice of Management*, London: Heinemann.

Euromonitor International (2011) Organics to continue to withstand downturn, http://www.just-food.com/analysis/organic-to-continueto-withstand-downturn_id117742.aspx, 20 December.

Finch, J. (2008) Nick Robertson: Wannabe Celebs Provide the Silver on Screen, *The Guardian*, 18 April, 31.

Fisher, J. (2013) The future of ethical retailing, *Retail Gazette*, 12 January. http://www.retailgazette.co.uk/articles/04032-the-future-of-ethical-retailing (accessed 8 February 2015).

Ford, D., H. Håkansson and J. Johanson (1986) How Do Companies Interact? *Industrial Marketing and Purchasing* 1(1), 26–41.

Grönroos, C. (1989) Defining Marketing: A Market-Oriented Approach, European *Journal of Marketing* 23(1), 52–60.

H&M (2015) H&M Conscious Foundation. http://about.hm.com/en/About/sustainability/hm-conscious/conscious-foundation.html (accessed 30 January 2015).

Hilpern, K. (2011) Does your marketing serve? *The Marketer*, March, 28–31. TripAdvisor, http://www.tripadvisor.co.uk/pages/about_us.html, accessed January 2012.

Homberg, C., N. Koschate and W. D. Hoyer (2005) Do Satisfied Customers Really Pay More? A Study of the Relationship Between Customer Satisfaction and Willingness to Pay, *Journal of Marketing* 69 (April), 84–96.

Hooley, G. and J. Lynch (1985) Marketing Lessons from UK's High-Flying Companies, *Journal of Marketing Management* 1(1), 65–74.

Hooley, G. J., J. E. Lynch and J. Shepherd (1990) The Marketing Concept—Putting the Theory into Practice, *European Journal of Marketing* 24, 7–23.

Houston, F. S. (1986) The Marketing Concept: What It Is and What It Is Not, *Journal of Marketing* 50, 81–7.

Im, S. and J. P. Workman Jr. (2004) Market Orientation, Creativity, and New Product Performance in High Technology Firms, *Journal of Marketing* 68 (April), 114–32.

Jarvis, J. (2009) How the Google Model Could Help Detroit, *Business Week*, 9 February, 33–6.

Jaworski, B. J. and A. K. Kohli (1993) Market Orientation: Antecedents and Consequences, *Journal of Marketing* 57(3), 53–70.

Jones, T. O. and W. E. Sasser Jr (1995) Why Satisfied Customers Defect, Harvard Business Review, Nov–Dec, 88–99.

Kirca, A. H., S. Jayachandran and W. O. Bearden (2005) Market Orientation: A Meta-Analytic Review and Assessment of its Antecedents and Impact on Performance, *Journal of Marketing* 69(2), 24–41.

Lawson, R. and B. Wooliscroft (2004) Human Nature and the Marketing Concept, *Marketing Theory* 4(4), 311–26.

Leroux, M. (2014). Starbucks wakes up and smells . . . beer and wine, *The Times*, 6 December. http://www.thetimes.co.uk/tto/business/industries/retailing/article4289417.ece (accessed 14 February 2015).

London, S. (2005) Rotten Cars, Not High Costs are Driving GM to Ruin, *Financial Times*, 23/24 April, 11.

Mitchell, A. (2005) The Path to Success is Simple—Why Do So Few Stay the Course? *Marketing Week*, 19 May, 20–1.

Mittal, V. and W. Kamakura (2001) Satisfaction, Repurchase Intent, and Repurchase Behaviour: Investigating the Moderating Effect of Customer Characteristics, *Journal of Marketing* 38 (February), 131–42.

Moore, B. (2014) How ethical are high street clothes? *The Guardian*, 17 June. http://www.theguardian.com/sustainable-business/sustainable-fashion-blog/how-ethical-high-street-clothes (accessed 30 January 2015).

Morgan, A. (1996) Relationship Marketing, *Admap*, October, 29–33.

Morgan, O. (2006) Toyota's Spin to Pole Position is Just a Start, *Observer*, 2 April, 4.

Morgan, R. E. and C. A. Strong (1998) Market Orientation and Dimensions of Strategic Orientation, *European Journal of Marketing* 32(11/12), 1051–73.

Narver, J. C. and S. F. Slater (1990) The Effect of a Market Orientation on Business Profitability, *Journal of Marketing* 54 (October), 20–35.

Narver, J. C., R. L. Jacobson and S. F. Slater (1999) Market Orientation and Business Performance: An Analysis of Panel Data, in R. Deshpande (ed.) *Developing a Market Orientation*, Thousand Oaks, CA: Sage Publications, 195–216.

O'Flaherty, K. (2008) Keeping a Fresh Spin On Things, *Marketing Week*, 22–3.

Parkinson, S. T. (1991) World Class Marketing: From Lost Empires to the Image Man, *Journal of Marketing Management* 7(3), 299–311.

Pelham, A. M. (2000) Market Orientation and Other Potential Influences on Performance in Small and Medium-Sized Manufacturing Firms, *Journal of Small Business Management* 38(1), 48–67.

Pelham, A. M. and D. T. Wilson (1996) A Longitudinal Study of the Impact of Market Structure, Firm Structure, and Market Orientation Culture of Dimensions of Small Firm Performances, *Journal of the Academy of Marketing Science* 24(1), 27–43.

Pulendran, S., R. Speed and R. E. Wilding (2003) Marketing Planning, Market Orientation and Business Performance, *European Journal of Marketing* 37(3/4), 476–97.

Rafiq, M. and P. K. Ahmed (1992) The Marketing Mix Reconsidered, *Proceedings of the Marketing Education Group Conference*, Salford, 439–51.

Reichheld, F. and E. W. Sasser Jr (1990) Zero Defections: Quality Comes to Services, *Harvard Business Review* 68 (September/October), 105–11.

Roberson, J. (2010) Anger over Weight Watchers' endorsement of McDonald's, http://www.guardian.co.uk/business/2010/mar/03/weight-watchers-mcdonalds-obesity, 3 March.

Rosenberg, L. J. and J. A. Czepeil (1983) A Marketing Approach to Customer Retention, *Journal of Consumer Marketing* 2, 45–51.

Roythorne, P. (2003) Under Surveillance, *Marketing Week*, 13 March, 31–2.

Ruddick, G. (2014) How Zara became the world's biggest fashion retailer, *The Telegragh*, 20 October. http://www.telegraph.co.uk/finance/newsbysector/retailandconsumer/11172562/How-Inditex-became-the-worlds-biggest-fashion-retailer.html (accessed 31 January 2015).

Rust, R. T. and A. J. Zahorik (1993) Customer Satisfaction, Customer Retention and Market Share, *Journal of Retailing* 69 (Summer), 193–215.

Ryle, S. (2003) Every Little Helps Leahy Tick, *Observer*, 13 April, 18.

Sheth, J. N. and A. Parvatiyar (1995) The Evolution of Relationship, *International Business Review*, 4(4), 397–418.

Sklar, C. (2013). How to use social media to understand and engage your customers, *The Guardian*, 13 March. http://www.theguardian.com/media-network/media-network-blog/2013/mar/13/social-media-customer-engagement (accessed 14 February 2015).

Slater, S. F. and J. C. Narver (1994) Does Competitive Environment Moderate the Market Orientation Performance Relationship, *Journal of Marketing* 58, January, 46–55.

Smith, G. (2005) Four Wheels, *The Guardian G2*, 15 March, 26–7.

Spary, S. (2015) Starbucks to sell wine and beer in premium food push, campaign, 20 February. http://www.campaignlive.co.uk/news/1334898/starbucks-sell-wine-beer-premium-food-push/?DCMP=ILC-SEARCH.

Spector, M., D. Mattioli and K. Stech (2012) Kodak files for bankruptcy protection, *The Wall Street Journal*, 19 January. http://online.wsj.com/article/SB10001424052970204555904577169920031456052.html (accessed 19 January 2012).

Srinivasan, S. S., R. Anderson and K. Ponnavolu (2002) Customer loyalty in e-commerce: An exploration of its antecedents and consequences, *Journal of Retailing* 78(1), 41–50.

Strauss, J., A. El-Ansary and R. Frost (2006) *E-marketing*, Upper Saddle River, NJ: Pearson Prentice Hall.

Superbrands (2015) British Airways. http://d3iixjhp5u37hr.cloudfront.net/files/2014/02/British-Airways-for-website-aemm11.pdf (accessed 30 January 2015).

Tauber, E. M. (1974) How Marketing Research Discourages Major Innovation, *Business Horizons* 17, 22–6.

Teather, D. (2005) Kodak Cuts 10,000 More Jobs as its Film Business Weakens, *The Guardian*, 21 July, 20.

The Co-operative (2012) Ethical consumer Market Report 2012. http://www.co-operative.coop/PageFiles/416561607/Ethical-Consumer-Markets-Report-2012.pdf (accessed 30 January 2015).

The Guardian (2015) H&M searching for innovation in sustainable fashion retail, *The Guardian*. http://www.theguardian.com/sustainable-business/hm-partner-zone/search-innovation-sustainable-fashion-retail (accessed 30 January 2015).

Wensley, R. (1990) The Voice of the Consumer? Speculations on the Limits to the Marketing Analogy, *European Journal of Marketing* 24(7), 49–60.

Which? (2011) Food and Drink: Brands Unwrapped, February, 28–31.

White, D. (1999) Delighting in a Superior Service, *Financial Times*, 25 November, 17.

Winch, J. (2014) British Airways tops UK brand rankings, *The Telegraph*, 24 February. http://www.telegraph.co.uk/finance/newsbysector/retailandconsumer/10656804/British-Airways-tops-UK-brand-rankings.html (accessed 30 January 2015).

Wood, Z. (2011) Starbucks gets a new face—and drops the mugs, *The Guardian*, 5 January. http://www.theguardian.com/business/2011/jan/05/starbucks-rebranding-new-face-drops-mugs (accessed 14 February 2015).

Wright, J. (2006) *Blog Marketing*, New York: McGraw-Hill.

Zeithaml, V. A. (2000) Service Quality, Profitability, and the Economic Worth of Customers: What We Know and What We Need to Learn, *Journal of the Academy of Marketing Science* 28 (Winter), 67–8.

Zhang, M. (2014) Wal-Mart Leads Social Media Engagement for Black Friday, *Social Times*, 28 November. http://www.adweek.com/socialtimes/wal-mart-leads-social-media-engagement-black-friday/208508 (accessed 8 February 2015).

Coca-Cola versus Pepsi

Competition in a Changing Marketing Environment

For most companies, owning the number one brand name in the world (valued at over $67 billion by the Interbrand consultancy), having global brand recognition and earning $4.8 billion profits on sales of $21.9 billion a year in 2005 would spell success on a huge scale. But Coca-Cola is not 'most companies'. In the face of strong competition and a changing marketing environment, the fortunes of Coca-Cola turned for the worse during the early 2000s.

Once a Wall Street favourite, Coca-Cola created a global brand by the expert marketing of something as humble as brown carbonated water laced with caffeine and vegetable extracts. For decades the company outperformed its arch rival PepsiCo such that in early 2000 Coca-Cola's market capitalization was $128 billion, almost three times that of PepsiCo, which was valued at $44 billion. By December 2005 all that had changed: PepsiCo had nudged ahead with a market capitalization of $98.4 billion against Coca-Cola's $97.9 billion. For the first time in the history of the two companies PepsiCo was valued more highly than its old enemy. Suddenly, the 'real thing' was second best.

Coke's problems

Many observers dated Coke's problems back to the death in 1997 of Roberto Goizueta, its charismatic and highly successful chief executive, who delivered double-digit annual profit growth. His success over PepsiCo led him to treat that company with contempt. He once said, 'As they become less relevant, I don't need to look at them any more.' Shortly after his death, however, the company's shares lost a third of their value, and profit growth collapsed to the low single digits. His successors reigned during a time of bungled takeovers, disastrous product launches, contamination scares, and constant feuding between factions within the management and boardroom. A classic illustration of Coke's problems was the scandal involving the launch of Dasani, a bottled mineral water that turned out to be distilled tap water. When the harmful chemical bromate was found in a batch the brand was withdrawn in the UK.

However, other people attributed the roots of Coke's failings to Goizueta's single-minded devotion to cola. His philosophy was that nothing could beat the low-cost, high profit-margin business of producing syrupy concentrate for bottlers, under licence, to transform into the world's favourite drink. While Coca-Cola focused on carbonated colas, PepsiCo diversified away from sugary fizzy drinks into a powerful portfolio of non-carbonated products. In 1998 it bought the fruit juice business Tropicana, which it has built to be the number one fruit juice brand in the USA. Three years later it bought Quaker Oats, thereby acquiring the energy drink Gatorade, which has also been built into a major brand. (Coca-Cola pulled out of the Quaker Oats bidding war believing its price to be too high.) PepsiCo also owns Aquafina, the leading bottled water brand in the USA. The fruit juice, energy drink and bottled water sectors all experienced double-digit growth in recent years. It continued its acquisition programme with the purchase of the South Beach Beverage Co, which manufactures the SoBe healthy drinking range, and has launched SoBe Lifewater, which it claims contains the full recommended daily amount of vitamin C together with vitamins E and B, and no preservatives or artificial flavourings. Its bottling partner Pepsi-Americas also bought Ardea Beverages, which markets the Nutrisoda range containing amino acids, vitamins, CoQ10, herbs and minerals. In contrast to Coke, the culture at PepsiCo was reported to be more dynamic and customer focused and less bureaucratic.

»

»

Where Coke focused on soft drinks, Pepsi has interests in the snack food business (it bought the Frito-Lay snack food business in 1965), owning such brands as Doritos, Walkers Crisps, Quavers, Lay's Potato Crisps and Wotsits (see Table C1.1). The result is that PepsiCo generates about 23 per cent of its worldwide profits from the stagnant carbonated drinks sector, while Coca-Cola relies on fizzy drinks for 80 per cent of profits. Coca-Cola always seemed to be playing catch-up, having launched Minute Maid fruit juice to challenge Tropicana, Dasani to take on Aquafina, and Powerade, an energy drink, following the success of Red Bull and Gatorade in this sector.

PepsiCo's diversification programme and its brand-building expertise has made it the world's fourth largest food and beverage company, ranking behind Nestlé, Kraft and Unilever. Its sales were more than $67 billion compared with Coke's $47 billion in 2014; it owns 6 of the 15 top-selling food and drink brands in US supermarkets—more than any other company, including Coke, which has two. Coke, on the other hand, is market leader in carbonated drinks (43 per cent versus 32 per cent).

Life since Mr Goizueta also saw Coke criticized for its fall in marketing investments, including advertising and marketing research, in an effort to maintain

short-term profits, and the lack of iconic brand-building advertising. Its culture was also questioned and its high-rise headquarters building in central Atlanta was known in the industry as 'the Kremlin', because of the political intrigue and bureaucratic culture that pervaded its corridors.

A new era?

In response to its problems, Coca-Cola brought an ex-employee, Neville Isdell, out of retirement to become chairman and chief executive in 2004. One of his first acts was to allocate an additional $400 million a year to marketing and innovation. This was in recognition of the under-investment in brands and product development. Emerging markets such as China and India were also targeted more aggressively. He also briefed advertising agencies around the world in an attempt to create new iconic campaigns to revive the core brand and reconnect with consumers. In the face of research that showed the proportion of Americans agreeing that cola is liked by everyone falling from 56 per cent in 2003 to 44 per cent in 2005, and those agreeing that the drink was 'too fattening' increasing from 48 per cent to 59 per cent, Coke increased investment in sugar-free brands such as Diet Coke and Sprite Zero. Sugar-free colas have also been launched, such as Coke Zero, which comes in black cans and bottles, and is targeted at calorie-conscious young males who have failed to connect with Diet Coke, believing that it lacks a masculine image. The brand is designed to compete with PepsiMax, which is also a diet cola targeted at men. Overall, marketing spend for the category doubled. Isdell also oversaw the acquisition of a number of small water and fruit juice companies in Europe. Isdell resisted the temptation to follow Pepsi with the acquisition of a snacks company. Instead, his strategy was to focus on building a portfolio of branded drinks. Following this strategy, Coca-Cola purchased the US firm Energy Brands, which owns Glacéau, a vitamin-enhanced water brand, and bought a stake of between 10 and 20 per cent of Innocent (increased to over 90 per cent in 2013), the market leader (68 per cent) of fruit smoothie drinks in the UK. Innocent has built a reputation for making only natural healthy products, and using only socially and environmentally aware products. At the time of the deal (2009), Innocent operated in the UK, Ireland, France, Scandinavia, Germany and Austria. Coca-Cola also launched an energy drink Relentless aimed at 18- to 40-year-old men.

Meanwhile, PepsiCo has introduced its own labelling system in the USA to identify healthier products, using criteria set by an independent board of health experts. Now 40 per cent of sales derive

TABLE C1.1 Cola wars: who owns what	
Coca-Cola brands	**PepsiCo brands**
Coca-Cola	Pepsi
Diet Coke	Diet Pepsi
Coca-Cola Zero	Gatorade
Coca-Cola Life	Tropicana
Powerade	Aquafina
Minute Maid	Lipton Iced Tea
Dasani	Frappuccino
Fanta	Mountain Dew
Lilt	Walkers crisps
Sprite	Lay's potato crisps
Calypso	Quaker Oats
Oasis	Quavers
Just Juice	Doritos
Kia Ora	Cheetos
Five Alive	Wotsits
Malvern water	Sugar Puffs
	7-Up

from products with the green 'Smart Spot' given to healthier brands such as sugar-free colas and baked rather than fried crisps. Most of its research and development is focused on healthier products such as Tropicana-branded fruit bars, which provide the nutritional equivalent to fresh fruit. Sales of Smart Spot products are growing at twice the rate of those without the designation, and account for over half of Pepsi's product portfolio.

Continuing its focus on healthy drinks, PepsiCo launched PurVia which uses Stevia, a South American herb used to create natural sugar substitutes, as a zero-calorie sweetener. It was first used in flavours in PepsiCo's water brand SoBe Life. Coca-Cola followed this launch with its own equivalent, Truvia. PepsiCo has continued its move into healthier fare with yoghurt drinks, hummus and oatmeal bars.

Both companies have also attempted to arrest the decline in the carbonated soft drinks sector by launching a flurry of new products such as lime- and cherry-flavoured colas. Nevertheless, colas have come under attack for their contribution to obesity with some schools banning the sale of all carbonated drinks on their premises.

Other ethical controversies have been encroaching upon Coca-Cola's global hold on the drinks market. Concern at American foreign policy and anti-American sentiment around the world has led to the launch of brands such as Mecca Cola to provide an alternative to US colas.

Under Mr Isdell Coca-Cola achieved steady international sales and profit growth. In 2008 he returned to retirement and was succeeded by Muhtar Kent, who has steadily built sales of Coke's brands globally. Falling sales of carbonated drinks in the USA have been offset by penetration in emerging overseas markets such as China, Brazil, Russia and India.

A new low calorie soft drink, Coca-Cola Life was launched in 2014 to expand its range of low-calorie offerings. The brand was positioned as being based on natural ingredients (stevia extract) rather than artificial sweeteners. The following year the company launched its own brand of milk, Fairlife, in the USA. Premium priced, it is designed to be a superior product to regular milk, tasting better with higher levels of protein and less sugar.

Questions

1. Compare Coca-Cola's response to the changing marketing environment before the arrival of Neville Isdell to that of PepsiCo.

2. Assess both companies in terms of their level of marketing orientation at that time.

3. How would you position Coca-Cola and PepsiCo on the efficiency–effectiveness matrix? Justify your answer.

4. What advantages, if any, does PepsiCo's greater diversification give the company over Coca-Cola?

5. Assess Coca-Cola's ownership of Innocent drinks from the point of view of both companies.

6. What future challenges is Coca-Cola likely to face?

This case study was written by David Jobber, Emeritus Professor of Marketing, University of Bradford.

References

Based on: Devaney, P. (2006) As US Tastes Change, Coca-Cola's Supremacy Drip, Drip, Drips Away, *Marketing Week*, 6 April, 30–1; Teather, D. (2005) Bubble Bursts for the Real Thing as PepsiCo Ousts Coke from Top Spot, *Guardian*, 27 December, 26; Ward, A. (2005) A Better Model? Diversified Pepsi Steals Some of Coke's Sparkle, *Financial Times*, 28 February, 21; Ward, A. (2005) Coke Gets Real: The World's Most Valuable Brand Wakes Up to a Waning Thirst for Cola, *Financial Times*, 22 September, 17; Sweeney, M. and C. Tryhorn (2009) The Day Innocent Lost Its Innocence, *Guardian*, 7 April, 3; Bokai, J. (2008) Soft Drinks Eye Herbal 'Sugar', *Marketing*, 6 August, 2; Bokai, J. (2008) Soft Drinks Eye Premium Boost, *Marketing*, 19 March, 2; Rappeport, A. (2011) China the Real Thing for Business rather than US, *Financial Times*, 27 September, 17; Anonymous (2012) At Pepsi a Renewed Focus on Pepsi, *Bloomberg BusinessWeek*, 6 January—12 February, 25; Eleftheriou-Smith, L.-M. (2011) Pepsi and Coke Fill War Chests, *Marketing*, 15 February, 7; Neate, R. (2013) Coca-Cola Takes Full Control of Innocent, www,theguardian.com/ business, 22 February; Neate, R. (2014) Coca-Cola Enters Dairy Market with 'Milka-Cola', *The Guardian*, 26 November, 14; Smithers, R. (2014) Coca-Cola Life: Coke with Fewer Calories and Less Sugar to Tackle Obesity, www.theguardian.com/business, 11 June; Arnett, G. (2015) How Coca-Cola Is Fighting against a US Public Losing the Taste for It, www.theguardian.com/business, 13 February.

CASE 2
H&M Gets Hotter

Stefan Persson, chairman of Swedish retailer Hennes & Mauritz (H&M), vividly remembers his company's first attempt at international expansion. It was 1976, the year H&M opened its London store in Oxford Circus. 'I stood outside trying to lure in customers by handing out Abba albums' he recalls with a wry laugh. Persson, then 29, son of the company's founder, waited for the crowds. And waited. 'I still have most of those albums,' he says.

But Stefan is not crying over that unsold vinyl. In a slowing global economy, with lacklustre consumer spending and retailers across Europe struggling to make a profit, H&M's pre-tax profits hit £2 billion in 2014 on sales of £14 billion. At current sales levels, the chain is the largest apparel retailer in Europe. This is not just a store chain; it is a money-making machine. Table C2.1 compares H&M with Gap and Zara, its closest rivals.

Marketing at H&M

If you stop by its Fifth Avenue location in New York or check out the mothership at the corner of Regeringsgatan and Hamngatan in Stockholm, it's easy to see what's powering H&M's success. The prices are as low as the fashion is trendy, turning each location into a temple of 'cheap chic'. At the Manhattan flagship store, mirrored disco balls hang from the ceiling, and banks of televisions broadcast videos of the body-pierced, belly-baring pop princesses of the moment. On a cool afternoon in October, teenage girls in flared jeans and with two-tone hair mill around the ground floor, hoisting piles of velour hoodies, Indian-print blouses and patchwork denim skirts— each £16 (€23) or under. (The average price of an H&M item is just £10 (€14).) This is not Gap's brand of classic casuals or the more grown-up Euro-chic of Zara. It's exuberant, it's over the top, and it's working. 'Everything is really nice—and cheap,' says Sabrina Farhi, 22, as she clutches a suede trenchcoat she has been eyeing for weeks.

The H&M approach also appeals to Erin Yuill, a 20-year-old part-time employee from New Jersey, USA, who explains, 'Things go out of style fast. Sometimes, I'll wear a dress or top a few times, and that's it. But

I'm still in school and I don't have a lot of money. For me this is heaven.'

H&M is also shrewdly tailoring its strategy to the US market. In Europe, H&M is more like a department store—selling a range of merchandise from edgy street fashion to casual basics for the whole family. Its US stores are geared to younger, more fashion-conscious females. H&M's menswear line, a strong seller in Europe, hasn't proved popular with the less-fashion-conscious American male. So a number of US outlets have either cut back the selection or eliminated the line. And while the pricing is cheap, the branding sure isn't. H&M spends a hefty 4 per cent of revenues on marketing.

Behind this stylish image is a company so frugal that you can't imagine its executives tuning into a soft-rock station, let alone getting inside a teenager's head. Stefan Persson, whose late father founded the company, looks and talks more like a financier than a merchant prince—a penny-pinching financier, at that. 'H&M is run on a shoestring' says Nathan Cockrell, a retail analyst at Credit Suisse First Boston in London. 'They buy as cheaply as possible and keep overheads low.' Fly business class? Only in emergencies. Taking cabs? Definitely frowned upon.

But that gimlet eye is just what a retailer needs to stay on its game—especially the kind of high-risk game H&M is playing. Not since IKEA set out to conquer the world one modular wall unit at a time has a Swedish retailer displayed such bold international ambition.

TABLE C2.1 The clash of the clothing titans				
Company	Style	Strategy	Global reach	Financials
H&M	Motto is 'fashion and quality at the best price'; translates into cutting-edge clothes.	Production outsourced to suppliers in Europe and Asia. Some lead times are just three weeks.	Has 3,500 stores in 55 countries. Largest sales are to Germany, the USA, the UK, Sweden and China.	Pre-tax profits were £2 billion (euro 2.8 billion) in 2014 on sales of £14 billion (euro 19.4 billion).
Gap	Built its name on wardrobe basics such as denim, khakis and T-shirts.	Outsources all production. Slower than H&M and Zara for turnaround.	Operates 3,300 stores in the USA, Europe, Japan and Canada, plus 400 franchises.	Pre-tax profits were £1.4 billion (euro 2 billion) in 2014 on sales of £11.1 billion (euro 15.3 billion).
Zara	Billed as 'Armani on a budget' for its Euro-style clothing for women and men.	Bulk of production is handled by company's own manufacturing facilities in Spain.	Runs 6,683 outlets in 88 countries.	Parent Inditex Group's pre-tax profits were £1.8 billion (euro 2.5 billion) on sales of £13.1 billion (euro 18.1 billion).

Source of data: company reports, Santander Central Hispano, BNP Paribas, Goldman Sachs & Co

H&M is pressing full-steam ahead on a programme that brought its total number of stores to 3500 in 55 countries by the end of 2014—a 40 per cent increase in the past three years. In addition, its online store is open in 22 countries.

Yet H&M is pursuing a strategy that has undone a number of rivals. Benetton tried to become the world's fashion retailer but retreated after a disastrous experience in the USA in the 1980s. Gap, once the hottest chain in the States, has lately been choking on its relatively slow reaction time to changing fashion trends and its failure to attract young shoppers, and has never taken off abroad. Body Shop and Sephora had similar misadventures.

Nevertheless, Persson and his crew are undaunted. 'When I joined in 1972, H&M was all about price,' he says. 'Then we added quality fashion to the equation, but everyone said you could never combine [them] successfully. But we were passionate that we could.' Persson is just as passionate that he can apply the H&M formula internationally.

What's that formula, exactly? Treat fashion as if it were perishable product: Keep it fresh, and keep it moving. That means spotting the trends even before the trendoids do, turning the ideas into affordable clothes, and making the apparel fly off the racks. 'We hate inventory,' says H&M's head of buying, Karl Gunnar Fagerlin, whose job it is to make sure the merchandise doesn't pile up at the company's warehouses. Not an easy task, considering H&M stores sell over 600 million items per year.

Although H&M sells a range of clothing for women, men and children, its cheap-chic formula goes down particularly well with the 15-to-30 set. Lusting after that Dolce & Gabbana corduroy trenchcoat but unwilling to cough up £600 (€900)-plus? At £32 (€46), H&M's version is too good to pass up. It's more Lycra than luxe and won't last for ever. But if you're trying to keep au courant, one season is sufficient. 'At least half my wardrobe comes from H&M,' says Emma Mackie, a 19-year-old student from London. 'It's really good value for money.'

H&M's high-fashion, low-price concept distinguishes it from Gap, Inc., with its all-basics-at-all-price-points, and chains such as bebe and Club Monaco, whose fashions are of the moment but by no means inexpensive. It offers an alternative for consumers who may be bored with chinos and cargo pants, but not able—or willing—to trade up for more fashion. H&M has seized on the fact that what's in today will not be in tomorrow. Shoppers at the flagship store agreed, particularly the younger ones that the retailer caters to.

In 2004, H&M commissioned Karl Lagerfeld, Chanel's designer, to create the limited-edition Lagerfeld range, which included a £70 (€102) sequinned jacket and cocktail dresses for under £55 (€80). The range, which was offered in the USA and 20 European countries, sold out within two hours in some stores. This was followed in 2005 by the Stella McCartney collection. McCartney, the British designer whose clothes normally retail for hundreds and sometimes thousands of pounds, designed 40 pieces for H&M, including camisoles,

»

skinny jeans and tailored waistcoats. The average price was £40 (€58) per item, around 15 times cheaper than her own prices. The limited edition was a resounding success, with customers queuing from as early as 6.30 am to get first pick of the clothes.

Since then, many other top names have lined up to work with H&M, including Kylie Minogue, Madonna and Beyoncé. In 2009, Matthew Williamson, who has designed dresses for Sienna Miller, Keira Knightley and Penélope Cruz, reworked his most popular designs—kaftan dresses, beaded cardigans and print frocks—for the retailing giant. His designs sold out within hours of hitting the stores. In 2011 and 2012, H&M ran highly successful collaborations with the Versace and Marni fashion labels and in 2014 with Alexander Wang.

H&M has invested heavily in social media to connect with its target audience. Fashion developments at H&M can be followed on Facebook, Twitter, Instagram, YouTube, Google+ and Pinterest, as well as on mobile phone apps for iPhone and Android. Fourteen million fans follow H&M on Facebook, where they can find updates on new products and promotions. Its growing presence in global markets is supported in China by way of the Youku and Sina Weibo social network sites and in Russia through VKontakte.

The company has also made strides to improve its sustainability credentials. It has launched an ethical fashion brand called Conscious Collection as part of its drive to become a more sustainable and ethical fashion retailer. The range is made from 'green' materials such as organic cotton and recycled polyester. Its commitments include using more organic and sustainable cotton, educating farmers and developing the Sustainable Apparel Coalition, an initiative aimed at measuring the environmental impact of and labour practices for clothing and footwear manufacture.

Design at H&M

H&M's design process is as dynamic as its clothes. The 95-person design group is encouraged to draw inspiration not from fashion runways but from real life. 'We travel a lot,' says designer Ann-Sofie Johansson, whose trip to Marrakech inspired a host of creations worthy of the bazaars. 'You need to get out, look at people, new places. See colours. Smell smells.' When at home, Johansson admits to following people off the subway in Stockholm to ask where they picked up a particular top or unusual scarf. Call it stalking for style's sake.

The team includes designers from Sweden, the Netherlands, Britain, South Africa and the USA. The average age is 30. Johansson is part of the design group for 15 to 25 year olds, and one style for the autumn they designed was Bohemian: long crinkled cotton skirts with matching blouses and sequinned sweaters for a bit of night-time glamour. Johansson and Emneryd were not pushing a whole look. They know H&M's customers ad-lib, pairing up one of its new off-the-shoulder chiffon tops with last year's khaki cargo pants for instance. The goal is to keep young shoppers coming into H&M's stores on a regular basis, even if they're spending less than £16 (€23) a pop. If they get hooked they'll stay loyal later on, when they become more affluent.

Not all designs are brand new: many are based on proven sellers such as washed denim and casual skirts, with a slight twist to freshen them up. The trick is striking the right balance between cutting-edge designs and commercially viable clothes.

To deliver 500 new designs to the stores for a typical season, designers may do twice as many finished sketches. H&M also has merchandise managers in each country, who talk with customers about the clothes and accessories on offer. When they travel, buyers and designers spend time with store managers to find out why certain items in each country have or haven't worked. In Stockholm, they stay close to the customers by working regularly in H&M's stores. Still, Johansson and her crew won't chase after every fad: 'There are some things I could never wear, no matter how trendy,' she says. Hot pants are high on that list. It's safe to say they won't be popping up at H&M anytime soon.

H&M's young designers find inspiration in everything from street trends to films to flea markets. Despite the similarity between haute couture and some of H&M's trendier pieces, copying the catwalk is not allowed, swears Margareta van den Bosch, who heads the H&M design team. 'Whether it's Donna Karan, Prada or H&M, we all work on the same time frames,' she says. 'But we can add garments during the season.'

Cutting lead times and costs

Working hand in glove with suppliers, H&M's 21 local production offices have compressed lead times—the time it takes for a garment to travel from design table to store floor—to as little as three weeks. Only Zara has a faster turnaround. Zara's parent company, Inditex, owns its own production facilities in Galicia, Spain, allowing Zara to shrink lead times to a mere two weeks. Gap, Inc. operates on a much longer cycle.

H&M's speed maximizes its ability to churn out more hot items during any season, while minimizing its fashion faux pas. Every day, Fagerlin and his team tap into the company's database for itemized sales reports by country, store and type of merchandise. Stores are restocked daily. Items that do not sell are quickly marked down in price to make room for the next styles. Faster turnaround means higher sales, which helps H&M charge low prices and still log gross profit margins of 58 per cent.

All major fashion retailers aim for fast turnaround these days, but H&M is one of the few in the winners' circle. To keep costs down, the company outsources all manufacturing to a huge network of 900 garment shops located in 21 mostly low-wage countries, primarily Bangladesh, China and Turkey. 'They are constantly shifting production to get the best deal,' says John Tisell, an analyst at Enskilda Securities in Stockholm.

Questions

1. To what extent is H&M marketing orientated? What evidence is there in the case to support your view?

2. Into which cell of the efficiency–effectiveness matrix does H&M fall? Justify your answer.

3. What is the basis of the customer value H&M provides for its customers?

4. What are the marketing benefits to H&M of commissioning Karl Lagerfeld, Stella McCartney and Matthew Williamson to design limited edition clothing ranges?

5. What challenges are likely to face H&M in the future?

6. Do you consider the marketing of disposable clothes contrary to societal welfare? Justify your opinion.

This case study was written by David Jobber, Emeritus Professor of Marketing, University of Bradford.

References

Based on: Capell, K., G. Khermouch and A. Sains (2002) How H&M Got Hot, *Business Week*, 11 November, 37–42. Additional material from: M. Wilson (2000) Disposable Chic at H&M, *Chain Store Age*, May, 64–6; Jones, A. and E. Rigby (2005) A Good Fit? Designers and Mass Market Chains Try to Stitch Their Fortunes Together, *The Financial Times*, 25 October, 17; Fisher, A. (2009) Woman Who Gave Us the A-List Look, *Observer*, 22 March, 21; Venkatraman, A. (2008) Basic Instinct, *Marketing Week*, 21 August, 27; Anonymous (2011) Global Stretch, *The Economist*, 12 March, 77; Arthurs, D. (2012) Sold Out Again? H&M Strike Gold Once More with Marni Collection, Daily Mail Online, 12 July, www.dailymail.co.uk; Baker, R. (2011) H & M Launches Ethical Fashion Brand, www.marketingweek.com, 15 April; Neville, S. (2013) H & M Goes R & B: Beyoncé's Fashion Role, *The Guardian*, 22 March, 4; Anonymous (2015) Five Year Summary—About H&M, www.about.hm.com/en/About.

CHAPTER 2
The Marketing Environment

> *When life gives you questions Google has the answers.*
>
> **A. J. CARPIO**

LEARNING OBJECTIVES

After reading this chapter, you should be able to:

1 describe the nature of the marketing environment

2 explain the distinction between the microenvironment and the macroenvironment

3 discuss the impact of political and legal, economic, ecological/physical environmental, social/cultural and technological forces on marketing decisions

4 explain how to conduct environmental scanning

5 discuss how companies respond to environmental change

A market-orientated firm looks outwards to the environment in which it operates, adapting to take advantage of emerging opportunities and to minimize potential threats. In this chapter we will examine how to monitor the marketing environment. In particular, we will look at some of the major forces acting on companies in their macro- and microenvironments.

The **marketing environment** consists of the actors and forces that affect a company's capability to operate effectively in providing products and services to its customers (see Figure 2.1). The **macroenvironment** consists of a number of broad forces that affect not only the company but also the other actors in the microenvironment. Traditionally four forces—political/legal, economic, social/cultural and technological—have been the focus of attention, with the result that the term 'PEST analysis' has been used to describe macroenvironmental analysis. However, the growing importance of ecological/physical environmental forces on companies has led to the acronym being expanded to **PEEST analysis**. The microenvironment consists of the actors in the firm's immediate environment that affect its capabilities to operate effectively in its chosen markets. The key actors are customers, competitors, distributors and suppliers. The macro- and microenvironments shape the character of the opportunities and threats facing a company and are largely uncontrollable.

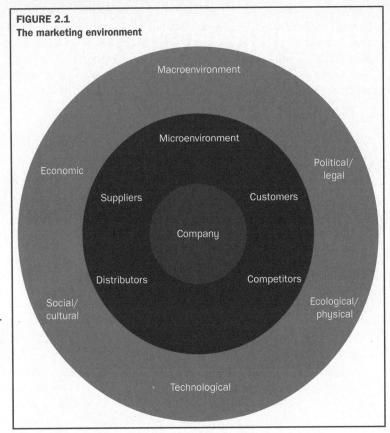

FIGURE 2.1
The marketing environment

Because of the changing nature of the marketing environment, decision-making is shrouded in uncertainty, with marketing managers sometimes unclear about what is happening and how to respond. This can delay exploitation of emerging needs and new markets, but it can also provide opportunities for the fleet-of-foot. For example, while larger companies dithered, changes in consumers' tastes towards healthy eating and ethical consumption led to the successful creation of such brands and companies as The Body Shop, Innocent drinks, Green & Black's chocolate and Ben & Jerry's ice cream (Ashill and Jobber, 2010, 2013, 2014).

This chapter focuses on the macroenvironmental forces—political/legal, economic, ecological/physical, social/cultural and technological—that affect marketing decisions. Later in the chapter the four dimensions of the microenvironment—customers, competitors, distributors and suppliers—are introduced and then examined in greater detail throughout the book. The influence of customers on marketing decisions is discussed in Chapters 3 and 4, and the changing nature of the supply chain examined in Chapter 17; competitive forces will be analysed in Chapter 19.

Political and Legal Forces

Political and legal forces can influence marketing decisions by setting the rules by which business is conducted. For example, smoking bans in public places can have dramatic short- and long-term effects on the demand for cigarettes. Because of politicians' power to affect business activities, companies try to cultivate close relationships with them, both to monitor political moods and also to influence them.

Political forces are complex to analyse, and the impact difficult to determine. However, unrest in the North African countries of Libya, Egypt and Tunisia has affected various industries, for example: the oil industry raised the price of a barrel of oil on the wholesale markets due to fear of loss of supply and in the travel and tourism industry there was reducing demand for holidays and travel in these regions. Thomas Cook is a company that has attributed some of its losses to these events. Mini Case 2.1 focuses on how campaigns to change society through political change have varying outcomes, Marketing in Action 2.2 discusses political and other forces which can affect company decision-making.

In Europe, companies are affected by legislation at European Union (EU) and national levels. We will first examine EU-wide laws before discussing the impact of national laws on business life.

EU-wide laws

EU laws exist at two levels: 1) those that are binding on all member states; 2) those that are enactments of a law within the member state. A major influence at the European level is EU competition, which is based on the belief that business competitiveness benefits from intense competition. The role of competition policy, then, is to encourage competition in the EU by removing restrictive practices, barriers to competition and other anti-competitive activities. The objectives of these legal rules are the prevention of:

- *Collusion* by price fixing, cartels and other collaborative activities. Competition is encouraged by preventing firms joining forces to act in a monopolistic way. The European Commission enforces EU rules, and has had considerable success in disbanding and fining cartels. For example, the Commission broke up a cartel between producers of cathode ray tube (CRT) glass used in televisions and computer screens (Asahi Glass (AGC), Nippon Electric Glass (NEG) and Germany's Schott AG). The producers were fined a total of a 128 million euros for operating a cartel that ultimately affected consumers in Europe (European Commission (2011). British Airways was also fined £270 million for conspiring with Virgin Airways (which escaped prosecution because it alerted the regulators to the price fixing) to fix the price of passenger fuel surcharges on transatlantic flights (Milmo, 2008). Some of Europe's biggest truck makers (DAF, Daimler, Scania, Volvo) have been accused of operating a cartel for over 14 years that has potentially held up developments in emission-reducing technology; Volvo had made provision of $490 million for the likely legal action (Sharman, 2014). The European Commission has succeeded in punishing firms that collude, often with severe fines.

- *Abuse of market dominance.* Monopoly and discriminatory pricing, which could harm small buyers with little bargaining power, is discouraged. Market dominance was successfully challenged when Italian cigarette producer and distributor AAMS was found guilty of such abuse in the wholesale distribution of cigarettes. AAMS was protecting its own sales by imposing restrictive distribution contracts on foreign manufacturers, limiting the access of foreign cigarettes to the Italian market (Mercado, Welford and Prescott, 2001). Possibly the most high-profile case occurred when Microsoft was fined £340 million for its alleged misuse of its near monopoly in operating systems, when trying to squeeze out rivals by bundling Media Player into the Windows operating system (Helmore, 2004). Microsoft was fined £650 million for failing to disclose technical information on 'reasonable terms' to allow rivals to develop products that would work with Windows (Tait and Allison, 2008). Systembolaget is an interesting example of a state-run monopoly, which controls the retail sales of alcohol in Sweden. In 2007, the European Court of Justice ruled against the Swedish regulations and declared that these policies were inhibiting free movement of goods. The ruling opened up the opportunities for direct importing by private consumers, which in turn stimulated the growth on online alcohol retailers. However, this has led to further challenges for Systembolaget, as Swedish food retailer CityGross has teamed up with Danish wine seller Winefinder, thereby creating a legal loophole for retailers and Swedish wine drinkers (Nilsson, 2014).

- *Acquisition of excessive market power.* The objective is to control the size that firms grow to through buying or merging with other firms. Actions to prevent the build-up of excess power include blocking mergers, as in the case of the Swedish truck and coach builders Volvo, which wanted to acquire Scania. The reason was that such a merger would create a near monopoly. Less severe action is to apply strict conditions to any merger such as the requirement that Nestlé sell a number of Perrier brands to encourage a third force to emerge in the French mineral water market to compete with Nestlé and BSN, the second major supplier of bottled water in France.

- *Reliance on state aid.* It can be in a nation's interest for its government to give state aid to ailing firms within its boundaries; on a broader scale this can give artificial competitive advantages to recipient firms, enabling them to charge lower prices than their unsupported rivals; recipients may also be unfairly shielded from the full force of the competitive pressures affecting their markets. European Commission approval of state aid is usually given as part of a restructuring or rescue package for ailing firms. The general principle is that such payments should be 'one-offs' to prevent uncompetitive firms being repeatedly bailed out by their governments. When the Icelandic volcano erupted, the ash cloud caused many European airlines to be grounded for several days, resulting in the loss of billions of pounds of revenue, lost travel and compensation

MINI CASE 2.1
Cascades of Activism Grab Headlines, but Do They Change the World?

For the last few decades, continuing economic growth has engendered a relatively peaceful life for financial districts around the world, for example New York, London, Athens and Rome. However, in 2008 a global economic downturn seemingly changed everything. A financial collapse began when the so-called credit crunch hit and credit became less available. The knock-on effect on the housing market was far-reaching: house prices collapsed, and banks lost vast sums of money. Eventually, leading banks started to fold as their losses made it very difficult to borrow on the international money markets. In the USA, UK and Ireland, major banks were bailed out by their governments. The outcome was global recession, which lasted into 2013, and changes in taxation and austerity measures introduced by national governments, designed to reduce national debts, made life difficult for citizens in developed economies.

There was an unexpected response to the economic downturn. In September 2011, protestors gathered and set up camp in New York's financial district to protest about social inequalities. This 'Occupy Wall Street' protest inspired others around the globe to follow suit. In Rome, the protests turned violent as demonstrators set cars alight and hurled rocks at police. Greek workers demonstrated against yet another set of austerity measures.

Public anger was fuelled by economic troubles, but the link between economic conditions and unrest is complex. UK politician Ken Livingstone suggested that an economic downturn and government cuts create unrest, as the combination of events intensifies social divisions. Service cuts tend to have more impact on those with lower incomes, and these people can easily become disenfranchised. This contrasts with tax increases, which tend to have a greater impact on those with higher incomes, while these people are less likely to protest. This means the greater the level of actual and perceived inequality between incomes, the greater the likelihood of unrest and civil disturbances.

The Occupy Wall Street demonstrators were adamant that they would initiate social change; their slogan was, 'We are the 99 per cent and want to end the regime.' They were referring to figures which estimate that 58 per cent of the real economic growth in the USA in the past 30 years was captured by the top 1 per cent of earners; this highlights the trend towards a polarization in the US labour force into high- and low-skilled segments, especially in technology industries.

Despite the intensity of feelings, 3 years later the protestors have dissipated, and the leaders who were inciting revolution have moved out of cities and parks. So what happened? Back in New York, the protestors dispersed and politicians regained a hold on negotiating peaceable change in financial dealings. Why? The attention of *social media*—which enabled the setting up of movements like Occupy Wall Street and facilitated instantaneous dispersion of campaign messages on a global scale—has moved on. Tufekci (2014) commented, 'These huge mobilisations of citizens inexplicably wither away without the impact on policy you might expect from their scale,' and suggested that, 'It's much easier to pull off spectacular events with digital technologies than to knit together lasting organizations.' In other words, Twitter, Facebook, Snapchat and the like are consuming the next 'deal of the day' on the global village menu rather than introducing a new cuisine.

Ultimately, changes in the macroenvironment tend to be incremental and occur over a lengthy period. They also require a steady build-up of momentum, which then leads to far-reaching implications that can reshape society. However, short-term protests have a more limited impact, as seen in the case of Occupy Wall Street.

Questions:

1   Arguably, political, economic and legal factors are shaping society.
    For a marketing manager, what does this case infer about the use of social media?
2   Suggest other examples of recent movements that have sought to achieve political changes, and discuss the extent to which they have succeeded.
3   Discuss the reasons why social media campaigns might be less influential in the long term than other forms of citizens' protests.

Based on: The Economist (2011); Alesina and Perotti (1966); Gitlin (2014); Tufekci (2014)

Norway's largest oil company, Statoil ASA, responded to opportunities to exploit untapped oil reserves in the Arctic. Statoil has invested billions of dollars exploring the remote and geographically challenging region in search of exploitable oil deposits. The outcome of the initial investment was major oil-field discoveries, for example the Johan Castberg field in the Barents Sea. The company estimates that these fields could yield in excess of 600 million barrels of oil. But so far no oil has been extracted, and this is largely due to market forces beyond the control of Statoil.

Oil extraction is an industry where the initial investment costs are exceedingly high; Statoil estimated that the required new infrastructure and bespoke technologies needed to exploit the Arctic field would cost over $15 billion. Statoil is no stranger to the vast wilderness of the Arctic region, yet in order to proceed with the investment the company needed to consider how market forces might affect the price of oil from these fields once it became available, in order to evaluate future investment.

Political changes proved to have negative influences on Statoil's investment evaluation, as the Norwegian Government introduced tax increases that affected the oil and gas industry. The changes mean that energy companies can only write off 22 per cent rather than 30 per cent of their capital investments against revenues from new oil fields.

Currently, economic influences are also negative. Changes in global oil prices have resulted in a fall in the price of crude oil, which has put significant pressure on the financial feasibility of huge capital investment projects like the ones proposed by Statoil. The plunge in the price of oil has been driven by a global glut in supply, shrinking demand and a strong US dollar (global commodity prices are usually quoted in dollars). The implications for Statoil are that production from the Johan Castberg field would not break even. Their breakeven point is at about $80 to $85 per barrel, but the economic changes—which are all forces beyond Statoil's control—saw the price of Brent crude fall from $116 in 2014 to below $50 in 2015.

Environmental influences are also fairly negative, as environmental pressure groups such as Greenpeace have campaigned vigorously against drilling in the Arctic, which is seen as an extremely fragile ecosystem. The threat of oil spills has enabled Greenpeace's efforts to gather global press coverage and support.

Whilst evaluation of the market environment suggests currently there is reduced potential for Statoil's investment in the oil fields in the Barents Sea, this situation is likely to be temporary. Statoil is not likely to be giving up on the Arctic completely, as future rises in the price of oil and ongoing innovation in cost-reducing technologies could once again make this region an attractive investment proposition. For the time being, Statoil has licences to explore the Sandino Basin off the Nicaraguan coast, which is under investigation as another potential site for future oil extraction.

Based on: Greenpeace (2014); Statoil (2015)

to passengers and, consequently, several airlines applied for state assistance. The European Commission's response was that Brussels would have to sanction national government bail-outs if they amounted to state aid. The European Commission cautioned that non-state aid would be allowed, but warned against providing 'unfair assistance' that could undermine competition (*London Evening Standard*, 2012). Generally, the level of state aid given to firms in most of the EU member states is declining.

Scan the QR code to find out how Greenpeace uses emotive issues to engage support for its 'Protect what you love' campaign aimed at stopping oil extraction in the Arctic.

Legal and Regulatory Responses to Ethical Issues in Marketing

European countries are bound by several layers of laws and by regulatory bodies that restrict company actions and encourage the use of ethical practices, as described below.

- EU competition laws and regulatory bodies that seek to ban anti-competitive practices: these regulations have teeth and have resulted in fines on companies such as Microsoft (product bundling), AstraZeneca (blocking generic copies of its ulcer drug), and Hoechst, Atofina and Akzo Nobel (price fixing), imposed by the European Commission, a body set up to enforce EU competition and consumer law.
- EU laws and regulatory bodies that aim to protect the rights of consumers: consumers' rights are also protected by EU regulatory bodies and regulations. For example, consumers' interests regarding food safety are protected by the European Food Standards Authority, and the right to compensation for air travellers whose flights are overbooked, cancelled or delayed is covered by EU rules.
- National laws covering consumer rights and protection, and competition regulation supported by government-backed regulatory bodies: legislation at national level is also designed to prevent marketing and business malpractice. For example, the Financial Services Authority fined Shell £17 million under UK market abuse laws, and the Securities and Exchange Commission (SEC) fined the same company $120 million for breaches of SEC rules and US laws.
- Voluntary bodies set up by industries to create and enforce codes of practice: industries often prefer self-regulation to the imposition of laws by government. For example, most European countries are self-regulating with regard to advertising standards, through the drawing up and enforcement of codes of practice.

Marketers in Europe have great freedom with which to practice their profession. Business-imposed, societal and legal constraints on their actions not only make good sense from a long-term social and environmental perspective, they make good long-run commercial sense, too.

Political and legal forces can exert constraints on marketing activities. Marketing managers should continually monitor and assess these forces and consider how they might influence their operations. Moreover, firms need to ensure that their activities are in accord with EU and national laws and codes of practice.

 Scan the QR code to check out how Weetos are using interactive advertising to promote products which happen to be high in fat, sugar and salt.

Economic Forces

The *economic environment* can have a critical impact on the success of companies through its effect on supply and demand. Companies must choose those economic influences that are relevant to their business and monitor them. We will examine four major economic influences on the marketing environment of companies: economic growth and unemployment, interest and exchange rates, the Eurozone, and the growth of the BRIC economies (Brazil, Russia, India, China) and G7 group of major advanced economies. For more discussion of emerging economies, see Marketing in Action 2.2.

Economic growth and unemployment

The general state of national and international economies can have a profound effect on a company's prosperity. Economies tend to fluctuate according to the business cycle, although more enlightened economic management has reduced the depth of the contraction in some countries. Most of the world's economies have gone through a period of significant growth since the mid 1990s, driven partly by productivity gains brought about by developments in computing and telecommunications technologies. This growth was followed by a period of economic slump which began in 2008 with a period referred to as the 'credit crunch'; this was followed by deepening recession and the Eurozone debt crisis (*Wall Street Journal*, 2012), which threatened to impact on the worldwide economy.

During periods of boom, well-managed companies experience an expansion in the demand for their products, while periods of slump may bring a decline in sales as consumers became wary of discretionary expenditures. A major marketing problem is predicting the next boom or slump. Investments made during periods of high growth can become massive cash drains when consumer spending falls suddenly. Retailers are often the first to be affected; Carrefour, Tesco and Walmart are only too aware that they must plan to manage their national and international operations in anticipation of rising and falling consumer demand. Derived demand also affects manufacturers because, as consumer demand falls, manufacturers are affected too.

Within an economy, different sectors experience varying growth rates, leading to changing degrees of market attractiveness. Undoubtedly, the services sector has experienced the fastest growth and become the dominant force in most western economies. For example, among the 28 EU countries, services account for over 70 per cent of gross domestic product, which is a measure of the total value of goods and services produced within an economy.

Low growth rates are reflected in high unemployment levels, which in turn affect consumer spending power. The 2008–13 recession caused unemployment rates to rise and consumer spending to fall in many European economies, for example in Greece, Portugal and Ireland. This has led to calls for state aid for ailing companies— for example, in the motor industry—to help them through the slump. However, this is not the case in emerging economies such as Brazil, China and India, where economic growth is positive and employment and spending on the increase. Indeed, the International Monetary Fund (IMF) has declared China the largest global economy (Carter, 2014).

Interest and exchange rates

A key monetary tool that governments use to manage the economy is interest rates. Interest rates represent the price that borrowers have to pay lenders for the use of their money over a specified period of time. Most western economies lowered interest rates during the credit crunch to encourage borrowing and lending, in an effort to avert a major slump in consumer and business demand.

An exchange rate is the price of one currency in terms of another (e.g. an exchange rate of £1 = €1.20 means that £1 buys €1.20). Fluctuations in exchange rates mean that the price a consumer in one country pays for a product and/or the money that a supplier in an overseas country receives for selling that product can change. For example, if the exchange rate between the pound sterling and the euro changes, such that a pound buys fewer euros, a German car manufacturer that receives payment in euros will receive fewer euros if the price of the car remains unchanged in the UK. In an attempt to maintain a constant euro price, the German car manufacturer may raise the UK pound sterling price to UK distributors and consumers. The following example illustrates these points.

At £1 = €1, a German car manufacturer would receive €10,000 for a £10,000 car. If the exchange rate changed to £1 = €0.5, the German car manufacturer's receipts would fall to €5000. To maintain euro receipts at €10,000 the UK price would have to rise to £20,000.

The exchange rates between most European countries are now fixed, thus avoiding such problems. However, the rates at which major currencies such as the US dollar, the euro, the pound sterling and the yen are traded are still variable. As seen in the example above, this can have significant implications for sales revenues and hence the profitability of a firm's international operations. For example, during the credit crunch, the pound fell against the dollar. This meant that UK goods and services exported to Eurozone countries could be sold cheaper, or, if sold at the same price, would realize higher sterling profit margins.

The EU and the Eurozone

The EU is a massive—largely deregulated—market, and it has far-reaching implications for marketing, as the barriers to the free flow of goods, services, capital and people among the member states are removed. A key objective of the EU is to lower the costs of operating throughout Europe and to create an enormous free market in which companies can flourish. As we have already seen, competition is encouraged through the enactment and enforcement of laws designed to remove restrictive practices and other anti-competitive activities. The EU currently consists of 28 member states and it is continually expanding. Table 2.1 shows the spread of the member states, when they joined and candidate countries that are likely to become members in the future.

As the EU has expanded, new member states have contributed to the development of the community and economic growth of the union. Expansion to include eastern European countries has brought a low-cost, technically skilled workforce that has proved to be competitive with those in China and India. The strengths of the economies of member states have been boosted by EU membership and have led to considerable inward

TABLE 2.1 EU member states

Membership year	Member states	Total population (in millions)
Founding members	France, Netherlands, Belgium, Luxembourg, Germany, Italy	235
	UK, Ireland, Denmark	72
1981–1990	Spain, Portugal, Greece	69
1991–2000	Austria, Sweden, Finland	23
2001–present	Poland, Estonia, Latvia, Lithuania, Czech Republic, Slovakia, Hungary, Slovenia, Romania, Bulgaria, Cyprus, Malta, Croatia	103 4
Candidate countries	Iceland, the former Yugoslav Republic of Macedonia, Turkey, Montenegro, Serbia	80
		586

Statistics source: http://europa.eu/about-eu/countries/member-countries

investment—for example the Korean firm LG Electronic, which is the world's second largest producer of televisions, committed to invest US$110 million to build a plant in Poland to produce plasma and LCD televisions (LG Electronics, nd).

The Eurozone is an economic and monetary union between 19 of the member states of the EU. Each state has adopted the euro (€) as a common currency, which is managed and controlled by the European Central Bank (ECB). A primary responsibility of the ECB is to control inflation and manage debt and economic reforms, and a common currency brings advantages through facilitating the flow of free trade within the community. However, turbulence in economic markets has exposed weaknesses in areas of the Eurozone, which potentially have far-reaching implications for economies around the world.

China and India

The economies of both China and India are growing at high and consistent rates, although both, like other major economies, have suffered a slowdown since 2010. Moreover, both nations possess considerable strengths in low-cost labour, but increasingly also in technical and managerial skills. China possesses strengths in mass manufacturing, and is currently building massive electronics and heavy industrial factories. India, on the other hand, is an emerging power in the software, design, services and precision industries. These complementary skills are persuading multinational firms to have their products built in China with software and circuitry designed in India.

China and India not only pose threats to western companies, they also provide opportunities for international firms. Chinese consumers are spending their growing incomes on all manner of consumer durables from cars to shampoo. The Chinese buy more cars than the Americans (13.5 million compared with 11.6 million), and western brands are becoming increasingly popular—from Burberry to Tesco, Bosch, Nestlé and Procter & Gamble (O'Neill, 2011). However, companies wishing to expand in these booming markets must do adequate research, as it is very important to get things right. M&S made a mistake on opening its stores in China, as it filled its rails with clothes of the wrong sizes. Chinese women are smaller and slimmer than European women and have smaller feet. In fact, many Chinese students studying in the UK buy their shoes in children's shoe shops (Muller, 2011).

In India, the consumer market is also growing rapidly. Nestlé operates factories making many dairy products and chocolates, and Hindustan Unilever is another European firm taking opportunities in India to create competitive advantage. In India preferences for soap and shampoo vary much less than their taste in food, so Unilever is doing even better than Nestlé, with an 18 per cent increase in profits.

China's and India's economies are not just booming in the physical world, but are also rapidly expanding online and in mobile markets. Read Marketing in Action 2.3 and find out more about online shopping and social networks in China.

In the Indian mobile phone industry there are over 600 million active mobile phone subscribers, which is about one phone per two heads of the population; the country also has the lowest prices anywhere in the world. Bharti Airtel is the main mobile network operator in India, and it is bringing phone access to everyone regardless of where they live.

MARKETING IN ACTION 2.2
Is there Life after BRIC?

Average annual growth rates for the BRICS and three developed economies		
Country	% Growth 2001–2011	% Growth 2010–2014
Brazil	3.75	1.5
Russia	4.75	2.5
India	7.5	5.5
China	10.5	8.0
South Africa	3.5	2.5
US	1.75	2.0
Japan	0.75	1.0
UK	1.5	1.75

Based on BBC.com. Calculated from IMF World Economic Outlook Database October 2014

Brazil, Russia, India and China (BRIC), were grouped together as an emerging economic force by Jim O'Neill of Goldman in 2001, when he was considering the performance of the world economy. The BRIC group represented a shift away from older economies (UK, Japan, USA) and highlighted where future economic growth was expected to originate. The premise on which this grouping is based is that these nations have similar economic characteristics. In 2011, South Africa was added, turning the acronym into BRICS.

Since then, BRICS countries have seen their overall economic growth slow down, but are still ahead of UK, Japan and USA. While China's economy is one and a half times the size of the others added together, Brazil and Russia are facing challenges which might affect their long-term economic performance. In 2015, there was further speculation about whether Brazil and Russia would retain their BRIC membership due to poor economic performance and political turbulence. But O'Neill claims that BRICS is still a credible grouping and that it will continue to grow to the size of the G7 by 2035. He also predicts that India will overtake France to become the world's fifth-largest economy by 2017.

BRICS are not the only economic grouping suggested by O'Neill. In 2013, he presented a new grouping of economies called MINT, which was made up of Mexico, Indonesia, Nigeria and Turkey. According to O'Neill, these are frontier markets and although their economies are smaller than the BRIC nations, they represent areas of considerable future growth in terms of markets. And whilst there are arguments against putting countries together, there appears to be a need to use such taxonomies to help simplify understanding of the world's economic performance.

Based on: O'Neill (2014); O'Neill (2001); Boeleser (2013); Hamlin (2015); Spence; Palmer and Oliver (2014)

However, for international competitors trying to operate in or enter the mobile market, there are limited profits to be made and massive investment required to improve network operations and services (*The Economist*, 2011b).

There are also major cultural and logistic barriers to overcome, although these apply to both on- and offline markets. The retail industry in both China and India is underdeveloped. There are potentially big opportunities for western retailers (especially supermarkets) to enter Asian markets. However, in the Indian subcontinent, 'there are 20 officially recognized languages, 14 main types of cuisines and countless religious and ethnic festivals as well as a passion for cricket' (*The Economist*, 2011c), which presents exhaustive challenges for developing a national retail operation. Western companies need to understand the importance of culture in both India and China if they are to succeed. In China, *guanxi* networks are important. *Guanxi* is a set of personal relationships/connections on which a person can draw to obtain resources or an advantage when doing business. *Guanxi* is one reason why working with a Chinese partner is usually better than going it alone. When entering into business relationships, the Chinese seek stability and trust more than intimacy. They want to feel comfortable that western companies will not spring surprises that may hurt them, but they do not need to feel that they are the company's best friend. It is claimed that the failure of Rupert Murdoch's News Corp. to penetrate China was largely because the company did not spend enough time and effort on building *guanxi*. See more discussion in the case study on selling in China in Chapter 15.

MARKETING IN ACTION 2.3
China: The Greatest Connected Market in the World?

Less than 10 years ago, fewer than 3 per cent of the Chinese population were online (about 33.7 million people). However, in the past four years China has seen an Internet boom. Around 145 million people shop online, and it is predicted that by 2015 each consumer will spend the equivalent of $1,000 a year (which is about what the Americans were spending in 2012). The boom is being driven by the Chinese government, which is heavily subsidizing the roll-out of high-speed Internet access, and, surprisingly, by the inefficiency of existing bricks-and-mortar retailers. Many shoppers go online because they cannot find the goods in the stores.

Taobao is a giant online retailer, and part of Alibaba. According to its founder, Jack Ma, 'In other countries, e-commerce is a way to shop, in China it is a lifestyle,' and Alibaba has become the largest e-commerce company in the world (PTL Group of Companies, 2013).

As well as shopping, the Chinese have taken to socializing and sharing information online, as shoppers are fearful of being tricked by fraudsters so they like to share their experiences. According to research, over 40 per cent of online shoppers read and post product reviews. Social networking, like e-commerce, started slowly, but there are now three large social networks in China: QQ, Weibo and RenRen. Weibo is the Chinese equivalent of Twitter, and its top stars have more fans than their celebrity counterparts on Twitter. Also, there are over 200 million people with a social network account. Facebook, Twitter and YouTube are banned in China, which has created an opportunity for these homegrown networks to emerge. Furthermore, Chinese society is being changed extensively by the Internet. Traditionally, families were reluctant to socialize with those outside their known circle of close friends and family, tending to be shy and reserved. However, now families use social networks to organize holidays and find families with similar interests from distant towns, arranging to meet, share car journeys and lots more.

Based on: Chaffey and Ellis-Chadwick (2012); The Economist (2011a); Muller (2011); PTL group of companies (2013); Stanley and Ritacca (2014)

Russia and Brazil

Russia and Brazil are emerging economies with market development potential. Russia's economy has changed dramatically since the collapse of the communist state, and its centrally planned economy has moved into a globally integrated economy (The World Facts Book, 2012). However, despite Russia becoming the world's largest exporter of natural gas, the second-largest in oil and third-largest in steel, in 2009 the Russian economy was hit hard by the recession caused by its reliance on such commodities. In an attempt to reduce this reliance, Russia has been investing in building up its high-tech industries but with limited success. High oil prices in 2011 helped economic recovery and put Russia back on a growth trajectory. However, it still faces long-term challenges in the form of a shrinking workforce, a high level of corruption, difficulty in accessing capital for smaller, non–energy companies, and poor infrastructure. Retail markets are also recovering, showing growth rates of around 13 per cent, but this is considerably slower than in the pre-recessionary period.

Russia is interesting for having one of the lowest income tax rates in the world: a flat rate of 13 per cent. Also all Russians own their own homes, having been given their own flat or house free as the Soviet era ended (most of these, however, are in a poor state of repair). Wealth tends to be centred around Moscow, and there are cash-rich consumers present, as the fact that Russia is the fourth biggest consumer of luxury goods after the USA, Japan and China testifies (European Commission Eurostat, 2012).

Brazil's was one of the first emerging markets to show signs of recovery from the global recession, with a 7.5 per cent growth in gross domestic product (GDP) in 2010, but it has since experienced a slowdown. However, high interest rates still make Brazil a destination for foreign investors, and in 2012 the country was ranked eighth in the world in terms of its GDP purchasing power parity (a measure used by economists to compare the living conditions and resources of different countries). Brazil's industry is linked to agribusiness and other primary products. Its main output comes from sugar, steel, oil and iron. It also has an important technological sector that ranges from submarines to aircraft, and it is involved in space research. Its economy has benefited from high levels of foreign investment by such companies as Procter

& Gamble, IBM, Ford, DuPont, Peugeot Citroën, Anheuser-Busch InBev and PepsiCo. Among its largest companies are Petrobas (energy) and Vale (material), ITau Unibanco Holding (finance) and BRF—Brazil Foods (consumables). The country is also a major producer of ethanol, a sugar-based biofuel. Growth in the economy has led to rising demand for cars, mobile phones, computers and televisions among the large population of 190 million. However, like the other BRIC nations, Brazil has not developed significant brand-building capabilities (*The Economist*, 2012).

Companies need to be aware of the economic forces that may affect their operations and be wary of assuming that the benign economic environment will last forever. Sudden changes in growth, interest and/or exchange rates can alter the economic climate quickly so that contingency plans are needed to cope with economy-induced downturns in demand. Firms also need to monitor the international economic environment, including the change to market-driven economies and the move into the EU by central and eastern European countries, and the opportunities and threats posed by the rise of China and India as major economic forces.

Ecological/Physical Environmental Forces

Ecology in a marketing context is concerned with the relationship between people and the physical environment. Environmentalists attempt to protect the physical environment; they are concerned with the environmental costs of consumption, not just the personal costs to the consumer. Five environmental issues are of particular concern: 1) climate change, 2) pollution control, 3) energy conservation, 4) use of environmentally friendly components, and 5) recycling and non-wasteful packaging.

Climate change

Concerns about climate change and the problems associated with global warming originate from a quadrupling of carbon dioxide emissions over the past 50 years, evidenced by more extreme weather conditions, such as hurricanes, storms and flooding. There is much discussion about whether or not climate change is caused by human activity and associated with carbon dioxide emissions. However, industries such as insurance, agriculture and oil have felt the impact from natural disasters like hurricane Katrina in the USA (Macalister, 2006). At the heart of the debate is the rate at which the planet is warming and the impact on global average temperature changes, which is different from the temperature changes we experience in our daily lives.

In 1992, countries joined in an international treaty to 'cooperatively consider what they could do to limit average global temperature increases and the resulting climate change and to cope with whatever impacts were, by then, inevitable' (UNFCCC, 2012). The United Nations Framework Convention on Climate Change (UNFCCC) realized that the measures in place to control climate change were insufficient. Accordingly, they developed the Kyoto Protocol (KP), which is an international agreement that focuses member countries on how to keep global temperature increases below 2 degrees Celsius. Thirty-seven industrialized nations and the European community which have signed up to the KP have committed themselves to the reduction by 2012 of four greenhouse gases, carbon dioxide, methane, nitrous oxide and sulphur hexafluoride, by 5 per cent (UNFCCC, 2012). This means consumers and organizations have to alter their behaviour, particularly as it has been found that sustainability strategies can lead to high returns on investment (Confino, 2014). In 2014, Kingfisher (Europe's largest home improvement retail chain), Hewlett Packard (technology industry) and Accenture (consulting and outsourcing) were recognized for their sustainability (Confino, 2014).

EXHIBIT 2.1
Smart car voted greenest and most energy-efficient car by the American Council for an Energy-Efficient Economy (ACEEE)

Pollution

The manufacture, use and disposal of products can have a harmful effect on the quality of the physical environment. The production of chemicals that pollute the atmosphere, the use of nitrates as a fertilizer that pollutes rivers, and the disposal of by-products into the sea have caused considerable public concern. For example, there is a garbage patch in the northern Pacific Ocean, which is an accumulation of plastics, chemical sludge and debris deposited by ocean currents. The 'trash vortex', as it is called by Greenpeace, is equivalent in size to the state of Texas in the USA, and is a major pollution problem for the marine environment. As the waste degrades, it is being ingested by marine animals, poisoning them and thereby entering the food chain (Greenpeace, n.d.). The list of manufactured products that have found their way to the vortex is extensive and includes plastic bottles, polystyrene packaging, traffic cones, disposable lighters, vehicle tyres and even toothbrushes.

 Scan the QR code to see how EDF communicates how the company is helping to preserve the planet.

In response to pollution issues, Denmark has introduced a series of anti-pollution measures, including a charge on pesticides and a chlorofluorocarbon (CFC) tax. The Netherlands has imposed higher taxes on pesticides, fertilizers and carbon monoxide emissions. The EU has made an agreement with car manufacturers to produce colour-coded labels to make it easier for car users to understand the environmental impact of the vehicle they choose to drive (Environmental Protection UK, n.d.). Not all initiatives mean adding costs, however. In Germany, for example, one of the marketing benefits of its involvement in green technology has been a thriving export business in pollution-control equipment.

Energy and scarce resource conservation

The finite nature of the world's resources is driving conservation. Energy conservation is reflected in the demand for energy-efficient housing and fuel-efficient cars. In Europe, Sweden has taken the lead in developing an energy policy based on renewable resources. The tax system penalizes the use of polluting energy sources such as coal and oil, while less polluting resources such as peat and woodchip receive favourable tax treatment. In addition, it is planning to become the world's first oil-free economy by 2020, not by building nuclear power stations but by utilizing renewable resources such as wind and wave power, geothermal energy and waste heat. The plan is a response to warnings that the world may be running out of oil, together with global climate change and rising petrol prices. (See Marketing in Action 2.4.) Companies are also making more energy-efficient products. Ikea installed over 150,000 solar panels in 2014 and aims to generate more energy than it uses by 2020.

Another concern of environmentalists is the consumption of wood. Forest depletion by the deforestation activities of companies and the effects of acid rain damage the ecosystem. Consumers' desire for soft- and hardwood furniture and window frames is at odds with the need to preserve forests. Trees' leaves absorb carbon dioxide and their roots help to stabilize slopes; a landslide in the Philippines that cost many lives was allegedly caused by illegal logging. A solution is the replanting of forests to maintain the long-term stock of trees. Ikea produces 100 million pieces of furniture each year and in doing so uses 1 per cent of the world's wood supply, 23 per cent of which comes from responsibly managed forests. IKEA's aim is that by 2017 the percentage will be 50 per cent (IKEA, 2012).

Environmentally friendly ingredients and components

Environmentalists favour the use of biodegradable and natural ingredients and components when practicable. Companies have responded to the challenge by launching products such as the Estée Lauder Origins skincare and cosmetics range of vegetable-based products containing no animal ingredients. PETA (People for the Ethical Treatment of Animals) campaigns relentlessly against cruelty to animals. In response, Massimo Dutti, Topshop, Primark, H&M and Inditex (owner of Zara) have banned the use of angora wool in its garments, in an attempt to curb appalling animal management practices in wool-producing countries (Kassam, 2015).

Angela Merkel has been described as Europe's most powerful politician. In her role as German Chancellor, she has taken on the challenge of dealing with climate change policies. But Merkel is not a left-wing *green* politician. She is the daughter of a Lutheran pastor from East Germany, a trained quantum chemistry researcher and currently leads the Christian Democratic Union, which is very pro-business. In 2011, she announced the phasing out of all of Germany's nuclear reactors, as it was her aim for her country to become the first to transform from nuclear and fossil fuels to renewable power.

But the costs of such laudable environmental aims are proving to be very high for the people of Germany and its industries. In terms of sources of energy, 23 per cent of electricity comes from renewable sources, with the figure set to rise to 65 per cent by 2035, but the cost of the government subsidies means that German domestic fuel bills are 48 per cent higher than the average in Europe. Also, closing the nuclear power stations has meant burning more coal and opening more coal-fired power stations to support the intermittent renewable solar and wind sources of power.

Based on: Schwagerl (2011); The Financial Times (2014)

Recycling and non-wasteful packaging

Germany took the lead in the recycling of packaging when it introduced the Verpackvo, a law that allows shoppers to return packaging to retailers and retailers to pass it back to suppliers. In response, suppliers promised to assume responsibility for the management of packaging waste. Over 400 companies have created a mechanism called the Dual System Deutschland (DSD). Consumers are asked to return glass bottles and waste paper to recycling bins and are also encouraged to separate other recyclable materials such as plastics, composite packaging and metals, and place them in yellow bags and bins supplied by the DSD. Collections take place every month and (together with the separating of the refuse) are paid for by the DSD; the cost is eventually absorbed by the packaging manufacturers.

Recycling is also important in Sweden, where industry has established a special company to organize the collection and sorting of waste for recycling, and in Finland where over 35 per cent of packaging is recycled. Clothing retailer H&M introduced a clothing recycle scheme, where it gathers its used products and then donates them to charitable organizations for resale. And further back along the supply chain, manufacturers are developing new fabrics for the fashion industry made from waste, for example Econyl made from abandoned fishing nets and old carpets. According to DutchAwearness (2015), these types of fabric can reduce the CO_2 impact by 73 per cent.

Marketing managers need to be aware of the environmental consequences of their decisions and activities, and recognize the possible impact of environmentally irresponsible actions on the reputation of their companies and brands. Managers should be alert to the opportunities created by a greater focus on the environment and should consider communicating their environmentally conscious credentials to their target markets. See Chapter 5 for further detailed discussion of marketing ethics and corporate social responsibility.

Social/Cultural Forces

Three key *social/cultural forces* that have implications for marketing are: 1) the changes in the demographic profile of the population, 2) cultural differences within and between nations, and 3) the influence of consumerism. Each will now be examined.

Demographic forces

Demographic forces concern changes in populations in terms of their size and characteristics. **Demography** is important to marketers, because it helps to predict the size and growth rates of markets and the need for products such as schools, one-person housing and homes for the elderly. Three major demographic forces are world population growth, the changing age distribution and the changing structure of households in western countries.

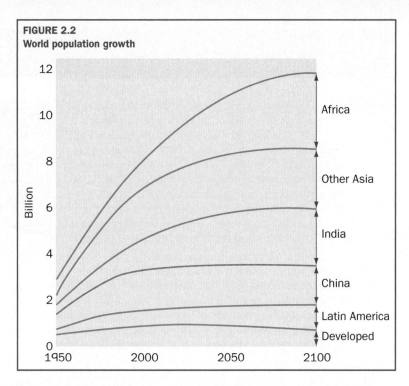

FIGURE 2.2
World population growth

World population growth

Overall, the global population is expanding at an increasing rate. However, the rate of growth is uneven across the world. In particular, the population in developed economies is expected to be stable or shrinking, whereas countries of Africa, India, 'other Asia' and Latin America are expected to account for over 90 per cent of the projected population increase during the 21st century (see Figure 2.2) (Brown, 1992). As these countries grow more youthful, the developed countries will play host to an ageing population. In 2025, half the population of Europe will be over 45 years old. For the next decade, the world population is expected to grow by an average of 97 million per year.

The changing world population distribution suggests that new markets outside the developed economies may provide attractive opportunities, although the extent to which this force progresses will depend on a rise in income levels in the less developed world. The problem is major population growth is predicted in countries that are already poor. In Niger, the poorest place on earth, lack of food but high fertility rate means that the average birth rate is over seven children per woman. Currently, the United Nations Population Fund is the only agency importing condoms and offering education in birth control (Economist, 2014), and the economic prospects and political interest remain low.

Age distribution

A major demographic change that will continue to affect the demand for products is the ageing population. In Europe, the share of the population that is over 65 is growing and life expectancy is increasing. Population pyramids, which show age distribution by sex and age group, are predicting growth of older age bands going forward to 2080. Furthermore, younger age bands are predicted to shrink relative to older groups (Eurostat, 2014).

The growth of older segments has significant implications for marketing. On the supply side, there will be an ageing workforce and a growing number of migrant workers who move according to labour demands. On the demand side, EU citizens over 45 represent substantial marketing opportunities because of their high level of per-capita income and higher disposable income and savings than younger people. With an older population who have higher disposable incomes and increased leisure time, the demand for holidays and recreational activities such as entertainment and sporting activities (e.g. golf) should increase. They also have different tastes and needs in terms of levels of service and style of products. As the palettes of older customers change, these people look to buy saltier and more spicy foods.

Similar ageing trends are evident in other parts of the globe, and businesses are already seeking to differentiate their offers for the lucrative ageing market. In Japan, retailers have designed a new retail concept: Funabashi. This is a shopping mall specially designed for elderly shoppers, who can access medical clinics, get discounts on pension day and enjoy leisure activities ranging from dancing to finding romantic partners (Lucas, 2014).

Household structure

Changes in household structure and behaviour that have marketing implications are the rise in one-person households and households with no children, and the growth in dual-income families.

More people are living alone by choice and through divorce or bereavement. This suggests that a key market segment is people who demand products that meet their particular needs, such as one-bedroom houses or apartments, and single-portion foods. However, households are also changing their behaviour regarding employment. In many European countries, there has been a growth in dual-earner families. In the UK, for example, over half of couples with dependent children are double-income families. The rise of two-income households means this market segment possibly has higher disposable income, which can lead to reduced price sensitivity and the capacity to buy luxury furniture and clothing products (e.g. upmarket furniture and clothing) and expensive services (e.g. foreign holidays, restaurant meals).

EXHIBIT 2.2
Walkers extends its Sensations range of snacks to include new spicy popcorn flavours which might tempt the palettes of old snackers as well as the young

Cultural forces

Culture is the combination of traditions, taboos, values and attitudes of the society in which an individual lives. A number of distinctive subcultures in the UK provide a rich tapestry of lifestyles and the creation of new markets. The Asian population, for example, has provided restaurants and stores supplying food from that part of the world. This influence is now seen in supermarkets, where Asian foods are readily available. The free movement of workers around the EU has also encouraged the growth of subcultures—for example, the flow of workers from central and eastern Europe to older established EU countries. To meet the needs of the Polish community in the UK, for example, Tesco now runs a groceries website in the Polish language (*The Economist*, 2008).

Subcultures can also span national boundaries. Youth subcultures provide cues for the development of brands, for example Levi's jeans, Coca-Cola, Pepsi and MTV. The generation of Facebook, Twitter, Google, etc., are different and don't gather together as hippies, punks and goths have in the past. The Internet doesn't inspire long-lived mass anti-fashion movements; instead it spawns brief microcosmic ones that have neither longevity nor time to pervade society. But social media does encourage sharing personal information, photographs, music and videos. A *haul video* (an example of a microcosmic Internet trend) is made after a shopping trip and then posted on YouTube to show what has been purchased. These videos are about showing not only what you have bought but also about showing the shopping experience in a highly creative manner (Petridis, 2014).

Attitudes towards food among some sections of society in Europe are also changing. Pressures towards healthy eating have prompted moves towards food with less fat, sugar and salt, and towards health labelling. For example, the Nestlé-branded cereal range targeted at children has been reformulated with 10 per cent less sugar. New brands focusing on their healthy credentials have emerged, like Innocent smoothies, and even McDonald's has a nutrition calculator which enables savvy consumers to check what they are eating (http://www.mcdonalds.ca/ca/en/food/nutrition_calculator.html#). Market segments have appeared, based on the concept of ethical consumption, and leading to demand for fair trade and organic products, together with avoidance of companies and brands that are associated with dubious labour practices. The growth in healthy eating and ethical consumption has prompted the acquisition of small ethical brands by larger corporates, for example Rachel's Organic yoghurts by Group Lactilis, a subsidiary of BSA international, and Ben & Jerry's by Unilever (*Which?*, 2011).

Successful marketing depends on knowing the cultural differences that exist between consumers.

Cultural differences also have implications for business-to-business marketing. Within Europe cultural variations affect the way business should be conducted. Humour in business life is acceptable in the UK, Italy, Greece, the Netherlands and Spain, but less commonplace in France and Germany. These facts of business life need to be recognized when interacting with European business customers. International culture is revisited in detail in Chapter 21.

EXHIBIT 2.3
Carlsberg embraces the subculture of the 'everyday beer drinker' to reinvigorate the brand in UK, Ireland, Sweden and Denmark

Consumerism

For decades there has been a debate about consumerism and whether it is driven by economic or social drivers, and what the implications are for marketing. Pinpointing the actual origins of consumerism is difficult, but, simply stated, the situation has been aggravated by 'marketing excesses, inflation, economic recession and questioning of mass-consumption society values has apparently pushed consumers to ever higher levels of dissatisfaction' (Straver, 1978). Arguably, marketing stands accused of creating opportunities for firms to sell more to the consumer, using tactical applications of the marketing mix. The response has been growing interest in **consumerism**, which takes the form of organized action against business practices that are not in the interests of consumers. The consumer movement has had notable successes, including improvements in car safety, the encouragement of fast-food restaurants to provide healthy-eating options, health labelling of food products, and the banning of smoking in public places in some European countries, including Ireland and the UK.

Consumers International (CI) is a worldwide federation of consumer groups that have joined together as an independent voice of the consumer (Consumers International, 2012). On 15 March every year, World Consumer Rights Day (WCRD) endorses solidarity of the consumer movement and is an opportunity to promote the basic rights of the consumer. CI tackles issues from around the world. For example, in Kenya there were problems with product safety and inappropriate use of labelling, which could cause serious harm to young consumers; in Asia there is a great deal of marketing of unhealthy food to children; in Latin America CI is working to protect consumers' right to a healthy environment. Globally, unhealthy diets are linked to four of the 10 major causes of early death: obesity and high blood pressure, glucose and cholesterol. CI is championing the consumer's rights to make healthy food choices, but one key issue is the mass availability of unhealthy options (Consumer International, 2014).

Marketing managers, however, should not consider the consumer movement a threat to business, but rather an opportunity to create new product offerings to meet the needs of emerging market segments. For example, in the detergent market, brands have been launched that are more environmentally friendly, while food companies have reduced the fat and salt content of some of their products and continue to introduce healthy option ranges. Pressure

British children are trapped in a cycle of compulsive consumption, according to UNICEF. But children in Sweden are different: they don't appear to crave products in the same way as UK children do, and have high levels of well-being compared with children in other European countries.

In both the UK and Sweden, the behaviour of parents is cited as a potential cause of children's behaviour. In the UK, parents are said to give their children gifts to compensate for their absence when working long hours, whereas in Sweden, where compulsive consumption is almost absent, parents spend time with their children, and families enjoy indoor and outdoor pastimes together. But research suggests there are reasons that contribute to well-being: health and safety, educational well-being, and family and peer relationships. A recent study found that when children in UK and Sweden said they had had a good day, it was always because of people not things. A child's view of a good day is simple: time with those they love (friends, family and even pets); creative or sporting activities; being outdoors and having fun. However, the study did reveal a desire for products, for example phones, tablet computers, laptops and game consoles were on the wanted lists of children from both nations and from a range of different social backgrounds. Also functional goods like footballs, creative art materials and musical instruments, which enabled the children to fulfil certain activities, were also high in the list of desired items.

In 2015, more firms are realizing the importance of children's rights and are seeking ways to use marketing and communications to not have an adverse impact. Through the web, companies are opening up the debate to explore how they can interact with children.

Based on: The Swedish Wire (2011); Nairn (2011); UNICEF (2015)

from the consumer movement, environmentalists, and individuals who engage in ethical consumption has resulted in most organizations adopting corporate social responsibility as a guide to their business practices. **Corporate social responsibility** (CSR) refers to the ethical principle that an organization should be accountable for how its behaviour might affect society and the environment. The importance of CSR is considered in detail in Chapter 5.

Going forward, changes in the social and cultural aspects of the marketing environment need to be monitored and understood, so that marketing management is aware of the changing tastes and behaviour of consumers. Such changes can create demand shifts that may act as either opportunities or threats. For further discussion of consumerism, see Marketing in Action 2.5.

Technological Forces

Technology can have a substantial impact on people's lives and companies' fortunes. Technological breakthroughs have given us body scanners, biotechnology, the Internet, mobile phones, computers and many other products. Many technological breakthroughs have changed the rules of the competitive game: the launch of the computer and word-processing software destroyed the market for typewriters; email largely replaced the fax machine; compact discs decimated the market for records and cassette tapes. Technological change can provide opportunities for new product development, create new markets, change marketing practices and communications, and revolutionize society.

Research and development

Technology investments require sound understanding of the market. Marketing and R&D staff should work closely together to ensure that investments are purposeful and not just for the sake of technology. The classic example of a high-technology initiative driven by technologists rather than by the market is Concorde. Although technologically sophisticated, management knew before launch that it never stood a chance of being commercially viable. By contrast, the development of the Airbus A380, the world's biggest passenger plane, has been market-based, taking into account the need for greater passenger comfort on long-haul flights, pressure to reduce carbon emissions and increasing demand for these flights. By using aircraft like the A380, the predicted increase in passenger demand can be accommodated using the same number of planes (Edemariam, 2006).

R&D in new technology can pay handsome dividends and secure market share. ICI, for example, invested heavily in the biotechnology area and became market leader in equipment used for genetic fingerprinting.

A lack of investment in high-potential technological areas can severely affect the fortunes of companies. For example, Sony—once regarded as a leader in high-tech product innovation—lost ground due to its lack of early investment in developing flat-screen television, liquid crystal display allowing Samsung to gain a competitive advantage in flat-screen televisions. Similarly, Nokia went through an era of complacency when it failed to monitor the competition effectively and respond accordingly; as a result, in 2013 the Finnish mobile phone company was bought out by Microsoft.

Information and data management

Technology also affects the way in which marketing is conducted. Developments in information technology have revolutionized marketing practices. Information technology describes the broad range of processes and products within the fields of computing and telecommunications. Accessibility of information has been found to be a source of competitive advantage and data warehouses are an important new technology that offers organizations the potential to leverage such advantage from their information resources effectively. Data warehouses facilitate sharing of information and enable information to be accessible at the point of need. Indeed, research has found that accessibility of strategic information can facilitate commercial benefits (Doherty and Doig, 2011). Using better quality information, managers can make more informed decisions, save time and make a greater contribution to corporate and marketing success.

Information systems and data warehouses are used in many areas of business. Salesforce automation is improving the efficiency of salesforces, and this is described and the implications examined in Chapter 15. Customer relationship management (CRM), founded on data technologies, has enabled companies to improve communications and relationships with customers and is discussed further in Chapter 10. Multichannel retailing is underpinned by information and data technology and is discussed in Chapter 17.

Communications

The Internet and mobile phone technology have allowed companies to use new channels of communication and distribution (e.g. music downloads) to reach consumers. New technology speeds up communications and enables multiple interactions using various media. In the multichannel world we communicate and gather information from multiple points—websites, apps, a multitude of television channels, printed publications and perhaps more importantly each other. Digital technologies have completely altered modes of communication but in so doing are eroding the boundaries between the message, the media, the channel and the product. The applications, issues and implications of digital communication technology are covered in detail in Chapters 13, 14, 15 and 16.

Society

Digital technologies are becoming increasingly important in most sectors of economic activity. The Internet has provided the impetus for many companies to rethink the role of technology and it has also had a significant effect on society. For its users, the Internet has not only provided the means to find, buy and sell products, but has also created an environment for building communities, where like-minded people can network, socialize and be entertained. The emergence of social networking sites such as Facebook, LinkedIn, Google and microblogging sites like Twitter have had a significant impact on global society. Social media have given a voice to masses of individuals, businesses and communities around the world, and their influence can be powerful. Social media have been used to communicate, organize protests and influence politics and governments. It has also been argued that 'Social media is reshaping human language through the unprecedented mixing of idioms, dialects, and alphabets,' and this is bringing into question whether the technology will have long-term effects on the way we speak, write and listen (Schillinger, 2011). The importance of such developments for marketing is considered in detail in Chapter 16.

In summary, marketing-led companies seek not only to monitor technological trends but also to pioneer technological breakthroughs that can transform markets and shift competitive advantage in their favour. They also seek to use technology to improve the efficiency and effectiveness of their marketing operations.

The Microenvironment

The **microenvironment** consists of the actors in the firm's immediate environment that affect its capabilities to operate effectively in its chosen markets. Those actors—customers, competitors, distributors and suppliers—will now be introduced and analyzed in more depth throughout the book.

Customers

As we saw in Chapter 1, customers are at the centre of the marketing philosophy and effort, and it is the task of marketing management to satisfy their needs and expectations better than the competition. The starting point is an understanding of them and this is considered in Chapters 3 and 4. The techniques for gathering and analyzing customer and other marketing information are discussed in Chapter 6, on marketing research. The grouping of consumers to form market segments that can be targeted with specific marketing mix offerings is the subject of Chapter 7.

Changing customer tastes, lifestyles, motivations and expectations need to be monitored so that companies supply the appropriate targeted marketing mix strategies that meet their needs. Changes in consumer behaviour also need to be monitored. For example, consumers are using social network sites like Twitter to communicate—a fact not lost on marketers.

Competitors

Competitors have a major bearing on the performance of companies. For example, when competitors price-cut, the attractiveness of the market can fall and their ability to innovate can ruin once highly profitable brands. Marketing history is littered with brands that were once successful but are now defunct (e.g. Nokia mobile phones, Amstrad computers and Lotus software) because rivals developed and marketed better alternatives. No longer is it sufficient to meet customer needs and expectations—success is dependent on doing it better than the competition.

Market-orientated companies not only monitor and seek to understand customers but also research competitors and their brands to understand their strengths, weaknesses, strategies and response patterns. In this book, the importance of these issues is reflected in a section being devoted to such analysis and the strategies that can be employed to anticipate and combat competitive moves. These matters are discussed in Chapter 19.

Distributors

Some companies, such as those providing services, dispense with the use of distributors, preferring to deal directly with end-user customers. The others use the services of distributors such as wholesalers and retailers to supply end users. As we shall see in Chapter 17, on distribution, these channel intermediaries perform many valuable services, including breaking bulk, making products available to customers where and when they want them, and providing specialist services such as maintenance and installation.

Distributors can reduce the profitability of suppliers by putting pressure on profit margins. For example, large retailers such as Walmart and Tesco have enormous buying power and can demand low prices from their suppliers, a fact that has been criticized in the media when applied to small farmers.

Distribution trends need to be monitored. For example, the trend towards downloading music has hit traditional music outlets that sell CDs, and the growth of the Internet-based sellers such as Amazon has impacted on traditional bricks-and-mortar booksellers. As the attractiveness of distribution channels changes so suppliers must alter their strategies to keep in touch with customers.

Suppliers

The fortunes of companies are not only dependent on customers, competitors and distributors, they are also influenced by their suppliers. Increases in supply costs can push up prices, making other alternatives more attractive. For example, increases in the price of aluminium make plastic more attractive. Also, as with distributors, powerful suppliers can force up prices. The rise in the price of gas has been blamed on powerful European suppliers who, it is alleged, restricted supply in order to force prices higher.

Companies need to monitor supply availability, such as shortages due to labour strikes or political factors, as these can cause customer dissatisfaction and lost sales. They also need to be sensitive to alternative input materials that can be substituted for those of existing suppliers if the latter's prices rise or availability diminishes significantly.

The importance of suppliers is reflected in discussion of their relationship with customers in Chapter 4, which focuses on organizational buying behaviour. Many customers are increasingly forming partnerships with selected suppliers in order to enhance value delivery.

All the elements of the microenvironment need to be monitored and assessed so that opportunities can be exploited and threats combated. This forms an essential ingredient in maintaining strategic fit between a company and its marketing environment.

Environmental Scanning

The process of monitoring and analysing the marketing environment of a company is called **environmental scanning**. Research has found that formal environmental scanning can deliver potential benefits (Dieffenbach, 1983):

- better general awareness of, and responsiveness to, environmental changes
- better strategic planning and decision-making
- greater effectiveness in dealing with government
- improved industry and market analysis
- better foreign investment and international marketing
- improved resource allocation and diversification decisions
- superior energy planning.

Additionally, environmental scanning provides the essential informational input to create strategic fit between a company's strategies, its organizational operations and the marketing environment (see Figure 2.3). Marketing strategy should reflect the environment even if this means a fundamental reorganization of operations.

The most appropriate organizational arrangement for scanning will depend on the unique circumstances facing a firm. A judgement needs to be made regarding the costs and benefits of each alternative approach. The size and profitability of the company and the perceived degree of environmental turbulence will be factors that impinge on this decision. Clearly, in theory, every event in the world has the potential to affect a company's operations, but to establish a scanning system that covers every conceivable force would be unmanageable. Consequently, there are two key questions for managers when establishing environmental scanning: 1) what to scan, and 2) how to organize the process. In order to answer these questions and develop an effective scanning system, action should be taken to:

1 *define a feasible range of forces that require monitoring*. These are the *potentially relevant environmental forces* that have the most likelihood of affecting future business prospects. Research suggests that companies should monitor and analyze trends, issues and

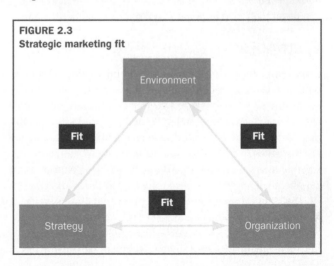

FIGURE 2.3
Strategic marketing fit

events which have implications for their company (Brownlie, 2002). Ansoff identified that environmental scanning monitors a company's environment for signals of the development of *strategic issues* which have an influence on company performance (Ansoff, 1991). For example, Google was slow to respond to the social media phenomenon, which could have been the result of not scanning the right forces. Not only has this allowed Facebook to develop a very powerful member base for its social network, but it is now also a potential threat to one of Google's core revenue streams, online advertising.

2 *design a system that provides a fast response* to events. Some events are only partially predictable, emerge as surprises and grow very rapidly. It is essential for companies to be informed if they are to manage in increasing turbulent marketing environments. Research (Brownlie, 2002) suggests environmental scanning should enable a company to:

- develop forecasts, scenarios and issues analysis as input to strategic decision-making
- provide a focal point for the interpretation and analysis of environmental information identified by other people in the company
- establish a library or database for environmental information
- provide expertise on environmental affairs
- disseminate information on the business environment through newsletters, reports and lectures
- evaluate and revise the scanning system itself by applying new tools and procedures.

In order to develop such a system for environmental scanning, four approaches are open to the organization (Brownlie, 2002):

1 *Line management*: functional managers (e.g. sales, marketing, procurement) can conduct environmental scanning in addition to their existing duties. The problem with this approach is that the scanning can suffer if employees are resistant to taking on additional duties. They may also lack the specialist research and analytical skills required for scanning.

2 *Strategic planner*: in this case environmental scanning is part of the strategic planner's job. The drawback is that a head office planner may not have the depth of understanding of a business unit's operations to be able to do the job effectively.

3 *Separate organizational unit*: sometimes regular and ad hoc scanning is conducted by a separate organizational unit which is then responsible for disseminating relevant information to managers. The advantage with this approach is a dedicated team concentrating its efforts on the scanning task. The disadvantage is that it is very costly and unlikely to be feasible except for large, profitable companies.

4 *Joint line/general management teams*: a temporary planning team consisting of line and general (corporate) management may be set up to identify trends and issues that may have an impact on the business. Alternatively, an environmental trend or issue may have emerged that requires closer scrutiny. A joint team may be set up to study its implications.

The benefits of environmental scanning appear straightforward: better understanding of the trading environment gives a company the knowledge to respond effectively to environmental changes. However, despite potential positive outcomes, companies respond differently to environmental change.

Responses to Environmental Change

Companies respond in various ways to environmental change (see Figure 2.4).

Ignorance

Because of poor environmental scanning, companies may not realize that salient forces are affecting their future prospects. They therefore continue as normal, ignorant of the environmental issues that are threatening their existence or of opportunities that could be seized. No change is made.

Scan the QR code to see how Carlsberg is using the heritage of its earlier advertising to reinvigorate the brand as part of its latest communications campaign.

Delay

The second response is to delay action once the force is understood. This can be caused by *bureaucratic decision processes* that stifle swift action. The slow response by Swiss watch manufacturers to the introduction of digital watches was thought, in part, to be caused by the bureaucratic nature of their decision-making.

Marketing myopia can slow response through management being product- rather than customer-focused. CompuServe and then America Online (AOL) created an online market by providing customized content and services as well as internet service providers (ISP) for their subscribers. In the 1990s when Internet access was relatively new, subscribers were prepared to pay to access the Internet through such custom portals. However, both companies failed to respond effectively to technological and market changes and the move to a more commoditized marketplace. In 2003 CompuServe became a division of AOL, and by 2009 it announced it would no longer operate as an ISP. AOL was rated as 'the worst tech product of all time' by *PC World* magazine (Tynan, 2006).

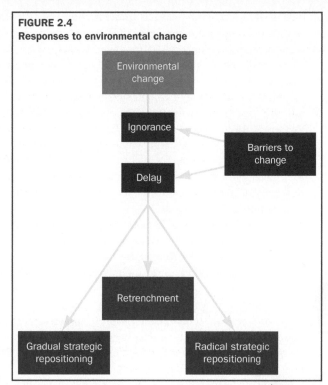

FIGURE 2.4
Responses to environmental change

A third source of delay is *technological myopia*, where a company fails to respond to technological change. An example is Kodak's slow response to the emergence of digital technology in cameras.

Finally, delay occurs as a result of *psychological recoil* by managers who see change as a threat and defend the status quo.

Retrenchment

This response tackles efficiency problems but ignores effectiveness issues. As sales and profits decline, management cuts costs; this leads to a period of higher profits but does nothing to stem declining sales. Costs (and capacity) are reduced once more but the fundamental strategic problems remain. Retrenchment policies only delay the inevitable.

Gradual strategic repositioning

This involves a gradual, planned and continuous adaptation to the changing marketing environment. Tesco is a company that has continually repositioned itself in response to changing social and economic trends. Originally a supermarket based on a 'pile it high, sell it cheap' philosophy, Tesco maintained its low price positioning while moving to higher-quality products. It has also expanded the range of products it sells (including CDs, electrical goods, financial services and clothing) to provide one-stop shopping, and has expanded into new market segments (Tesco Express convenience stores) and international markets including the Far East, the USA and central and eastern Europe.

Radical strategic repositioning

Radical strategic repositioning involves changing the direction of the entire business. Samsung has successfully repositioned itself, transferring from a copy-cat producer of consumer electronics into a technology company marketing mobile phones, flat-screen televisions, and flash memory technology. This is followed by a move away from electronics into energy technology and solar panels (*The Economist*, 2011d). Such radical strategic repositioning is much riskier than gradual strategic repositioning and could have dramatic consequences should such a venture fail.

This chapter has explored the major forces in the marketing environment at two levels—macro and micro—and has discussed methods of scanning for these forces and other changes that may fundamentally reshape the fortunes of companies. The chapter suggests that failure to respond to a changing environment can lead to poor business performance.

When you have read this chapter

Discover further resources and test your understanding: McGraw-Hill **Connect**™ is a
digital teaching and learning environment that improves performance over a variety of
critical outcomes; it can be tailored, is easy to use and is proven effective. **LearnSmart**™
is the most widely used and intelligent adaptive learning resource that is proven to strengthen
memory recall, improve course retention and boost grades. Fuelled by **LearnSmart**™,
SmartBook™ is the first and only adaptive reading experience available today.

Review

1 **The nature of the marketing environment**
   • The marketing environment consists of the microenvironment (customers, competitors, distributors and
     suppliers) and the macroenvironment (economic, social, political, legal, physical and technological forces).
     These shape the character of the opportunities and threats facing a company and yet are largely uncontrollable.

2 **The distinction between the microenvironment and the macroenvironment**
   • As can be seen above, the microenvironment consists of those actors in the firm's immediate environment
     that affect its capabilities to operate effectively in its chosen markets.
   • The macroenvironment consists of a number of broader forces that affect not only the company but also the
     other actors in the microenvironment.

3 **The impact of political and legal, economic, ecological/physical environmental, social/cultural and
   technological forces on marketing decisions**
   • Political and legal forces influence marketing decisions by determining the rules for conducting business. In
     Europe marketing decisions are affected by legislation at EU and national levels. EU laws seek to prevent
     collusion, prevent abuse of market dominance, control mergers and acquisitions, and restrict state aid to
     firms. National laws also affect marketing decisions by regulating anti-competitive practices.
   • Economic forces can impact marketing decisions through their effect on supply and demand. Key factors
     are economic growth, unemployment, interest and exchange rates and changes in the global economic
     environment such as growth of the EU and the Eurozone and the rise of the BRIC economies. Marketers need
     to have contingency plans in place to cope with economic turbulence and downturns, and to be aware of the
     opportunities and threats arising from changes in the global marketing environment.
   • Ecological/physical environmental forces are concerned with the environmental costs of consumption. Five
     issues that impact marketing decisions are combating global warming, pollution control, conservation of
     energy and other scarce resources, use of environmentally friendly ingredients and components, and the use
     of recyclable and non-wasteful packaging. Marketers need to be aware of the environmental consequences of
     their actions, and the opportunities and threats associated with ecological issues.
   • Social/cultural forces can have an impact on marketing decisions by changing demand patterns (e.g. the
     growth of the over-50s market) and creating new opportunities and threats. Three major influences are
     changes in the demographic profile of the population, cultural differences within and between nations, and
     the impact of consumerism.
   • Technological forces can impact marketing decisions by changing the rules of the competitive game.
     Technological change can provide major opportunities and also pose enormous threats to companies.
     Marketers need to monitor technological trends and pioneer technological breakthroughs.

4 How to conduct environmental scanning
- Two key decisions are what to scan and how to organize the activity.
- Four approaches to the organization of environmental scanning are to use line management, the strategic planner, a separate organizational unit and joint line/general management teams.
- The system should monitor trends, develop forecasts, interpret and analyze internally produced information, establish a database, provide environmental experts, disseminate information, and evaluate and revise the system.

5 How companies respond to environmental change
- Response comes in five forms: ignorance, delay, retrenchment, gradual strategic repositioning and radical strategic repositioning.

Key Terms

consumerism organized action against business practices that are not in the interests of consumers

corporate social responsibility the ethical principle that an organization should be accountable for how its behaviour might affect society and the environment

culture the combination of traditions, taboos, values and attitudes of the society in which an individual lives

demography changes in the population in terms of its size and characteristics

ecology the study of living things within their environment

environmental scanning the process of monitoring and analyzing the marketing environment of a company

macroenvironment a number of broader forces that affect not only the company but also the other actors in the microenvironment

marketing environment the actors and forces that affect a company's capability to operate effectively in providing products and services to its customers

microenvironment the actors in the firm's marketing environment: customers, suppliers, distributors and competitors

PEEST analysis the analysis of the political/legal, economic, ecological/physical, social/cultural and technological environments

Study Questions

1. Choose an organization and identify the major forces in the environment that are likely to affect its prospects in the next three to five years.

2. What are the major ecological/physical environmental forces acting on marketing? What are their implications for marketing management?

3. Imagine you are a marketing manager of a new web based company. Discuss how you would decide which of the environmental forces to monitor and why.

4. Generate two lists of products and services. The first list will identify those products and services that are likely to be associated with falling demand as a result of changes in the age structure in Europe. The second list will consist of those that are likely to see an increase in demand. What are the marketing implications for their providers?

5. How does technological change affect marketing? What should marketing management do to take account of technological forces?

6. Evaluate the marketing opportunities and threats posed by the growing importance of the socially conscious consumer.

Recommended Reading

Competition & Markets Authority: https://www.gov. uk/government/organisations/competition-and-markets-authority

European Union: How EU Decisions are made: http://europa.eu/eu-law/decision-making/procedures/index_en.htm

Eurostat Key to European Statistics: http://ec.europa.eu/eurostat

Lefebvre, C. (2013) *Social Marketing and Social Change*, London: Wiley.

Ormond, R., S. Henneberg and N. O'Shaughnessy (2013) *Political Marketing: Theory and Concepts*, London: Sage Publications Ltd.

Webster, F.E. and R.F. Lusch (2012) Elevating marketing. Marketing is dead! Long live marketing! *Journal of the Academy of Marketing Science* 41, 389–99.

References

Alesina, A. and R. Perotti (1966) Income distribution, political instability, and investment, *European Economic Review* 109, 465–89.

Ansoff, H. I. (1991) *Implementing Strategic Management*, Englewood Cliffs, NJ: Prentice-Hall.

Ashill, N. and D. Jobber (2010) Measuring State, Effect and Response Uncertainty, *Journal of Management* 36 (4), 1278–1308.

Ashill, N. and D. Jobber (2013) The Effects of Experience on Managerial Decision-Making, *Journal of General Management*, 39 (1), 81–110.

Ashill, N. and D. Jobber (2014) The Effects of the External Environment on Marketing Decision-Maker Uncertainty, *Journal of Marketing Management*, 30 (3–4), 268–94.

Boeleser, M. (2013) The Economist Who Invented The BRICs Just Invented A Whole New Group Of Countries: The MINTs, *Business Insider*, 13 November. http://www.businessinsider.com/jim-oneill-presents-the-mint-economies-2013-11?IR=T (accessed 20 February 2015).

Brown, P. (1992) Rise of Women Key to Population Curb, *The Guardian*, 30 April, 8.

Brownlie, D. (2002) Environmental Analysis, in Baker, M. J. (ed.) *The Marketing Book*, Oxford: Butterworth-Heinemann.

Carter, B. (2014) Is China's economy really the largest in the world? *BBC News Magazine*, 16 December. http://www.bbc.co.uk/news/magazine-30483762 (accessed 16 February 2015).

Chaffey, D. and F.E. Ellis-Chadwick (2012) *Digital Marketing: Strategy, Implementation and Practice*, 5th edn., Harlow: Pearson.

Confino, J. (2014) Sustainable corporations perform better financially, report finds, *The Guardian*, 23 September. http://www.theguardian.com/sustainable-business/2014/sep/23/business-companies-profit-cdp-report-climate-change-sustainability (accessed 20 February 2015).

Consumer International (2014). WCRD 2015 to focus on consumers' rights to healthy food, 1 December. http://www.consumersinternational.org/news-and-media/news/2014/12/wcrd-2015-theme-announcement (accessed 22 February 2015).

Consumers International (2012) Who we are, http://www.consumersinternational.org/who-we-are

Dieffenbach, J. (1983) Corporate Environmental Analysis in Large US Corporations, *Long-Range Planning* 16 (3), 107–16.

Doherty, N. F. and G. Doig (2011) The role of enhanced information accessibility in realizing the benefits from data warehousing investments, *Journal of Organisational Transformation and Social Change* 8(2), 163–82.

DutchAwearness.com (2015) Dutch Awareness and Sustainability. http://dutchawearness.com/ (accessed 20 February 2015).

Edemariam, A. (2006) Wings of Desire, *The Guardian*, 23 February, 6–17.

Environmental Protection UK (n.d.) http://www.environmental-protection.org.uk/transport/car-pollution

European Commission (2011) Antitrust: Commission fines producers of CRT glass a128 million in fourth cartel settlement. http://europa.eu/rapid/pressReleasesAction.do?reference=IP/11/1214&format=HT ML&aged=0&language=EN&guiLanguage=en (accessed January 2012).

European Commission Eurostat (2012) http://epp.eurostat.ec.europa.eu

Eurostat (2014) Population structure and ageing, Eurostat, May. http://ec.europa.eu/eurostat/statistics-explained/index.php/Population_structure_and_ageing (accessed 12 February 2015).

The Financial Times (2014) The costly muddle of German energy policy, *The Financial Times*, 6 October. http://www.ft.com/cms/s/0/ffa462f2-4d4b-11e4-bf60-00144feab7de.html#axzz3SUDkZ6rd (accessed 16 February 2015).

Gitlin, T. (2014) Where are the Occupy protesters now? *The Guardian*, 17 June. http://www.theguardian.com/cities/2014/jun/17/where-occupy-protesters-now-social-media (accessed 30 January 2015).

Greenpeace (n.d.) The Trash Vortex. http://www.greenpeace.org/international/en/campaigns/oceans/pollution/trash-vortex (accessed January 2012).

Greenpeace (2014) *Save the Artic*, Greenpeace, 14 March. http://www.greenpeace.org.uk/climate/arctic (accessed May 2015).

Hamlin, K. (2015) BRIC in Danger of Becoming 'IC,' Says Acronym Coiner O'Neill. *BloombergBusiness*, 8 January. http://www.bloomberg.com/news/articles/2015-01-08/bric-in-danger-of-becoming-ic-says-acronym-coiner-jim-o-neill8 (accessed 18 February 2015).

Helmore, E. (2004) Do Not Pass Go Says EC, *Observer*, 28 March, 3.

IKEA (2012) IKEA Group Sustainability Summary FY12. http://www.ikea.com/ms/en_US/pdf/sustainability_report/sustainability_summary_2012.pdf (accessed 22 February 2015).

Kassam, A. (2015) Inditex bans angora sales worldwide after animal welfare protests, *The Guardian*, 8 January. http://www.theguardian.com/business/2015/feb/09/inditex-bans-angora-sales-animal-rights-protests (accessed 20 February 2015).

LG Electronics Inc. (n.d.) http://www.lg.com/us/download/pressrelease/700339858050412PolandDTV.pdf (accessed January 2012).

London Evening Standard (2010) http://www.thisislondon.co.uk/standard-business/article-23828536-airlines-given-hope-for-state-aid-over-volcanic-ash-crisis.do, *London Evening Standard*, 27 April 2012.

Lucas, L. (2014) Retailers target grey spending power, *The Financial Times*, 14 August. http://www.ft.com/cms/s/0/bb60a5b2-e608-11e1-a430-00144feab49a.html#axzz3SUDkZ6rd (accessed 12 February 2015).

Macalister, T. (2006) BP to Make Biggest Profit in UK History, *The Guardian*, 12 January, 26.

Mercado, S., R. Welford and K. Prescott (2001) *European Business: An Issue-Based Approach*, Harlow: FT Pearson.

Milmo, D. (2008) British Airways executives charged over price-fixing scandal, *The Guardian*, 7 August, 26.

Muller, R. (2011) Target: China, *The Marketer*, 32–4.

Nairn, A. (2011) Children's Well-being in UK, Sweden and Spain, Ipsos MORI Social Research Institute. https://www.unicef.org.uk/

Documents/Publications/IPSOS_UNICEF_ChildWellBeingreport.pdf (accessed 20 February 2015).

Nilsson, D. (2014) *New proposal on the supervision of online retail of alcohol in Sweden*, Bird & Bird, 17 January. http://www.twobirds.com/en/news/articles/2014/global/food-law/sweden-online-retail-of-alcohol (accessed 26 February 2015).

O'Neill, J. (2001) Building Better Global Economic BRICs, Goldman Sachs, 30 November. http://www.goldmansachs.com/our-thinking/archive/archive-pdfs/build-better-brics.pdf (accessed 16 February 2015).

O'Neill, J. (2011) *The Growth Map: Economic Opportunity in the BRICs and Beyond*, London: Penguin.

O'Neill, J. (2014) Is the BRICS rise over? Bruegel, 26 July. http://www.bruegel.org/nc/blog/detail/article/1404-is-the-brics-rise-over (accessed 16 February).

Petridis, A. (2014) Youth subcultures: what are they now? *The Guardian*, 20 March. http://www.theguardian.com/culture/2014/mar/20/youth-subcultures-where-have-they-gone (accessed 20 February 2015).

PTL group of companies (2013) E-commerce in China: Gain entrance into a completely different world, 18 June. http://www.ptl-group.com/blogs/e-commerce-in-china-gain-entrance-into-a-completely-different-world (accessed 2 February 2015).

Schillinger, R (2011) Social Media and the Arab Spring: What Have We Learned? Huff Post: The Blog, 20 September. http://www.huffingtonpost.com/raymond-schillinger/arab-spring-social-media_b_970165.html

Schwagerl, C. (2011) How Angela Merkel became Germany's unlikely green energy champion, *The Guardian*, 9 May. http://www.theguardian.com/environment/2011/may/09/angela-merkel-green-energy (accessed 30 January 2015).

Sharman, A. (2014) Top truckmakers operated cartel for 14 years, says EU, *The Financial Times*, 23 December. http://www.ft.com/cms/s/0/da53eb98-8073-11e4-872b-00144feabdc0.html#axzz3SUDkZ6rd (accessed 22 February 2015).

Spence, P., D. Palmer and M. Oliver (2014) Beyond the BRICs: the guide to every emerging market acronym, *The Telegraph*, 13 October. http://www.telegraph.co.uk/finance/economics/11158386/Beyond-the-BRICs-the-guide-to-every-emerging-market-acronym.html (accessed 18 February 2015).

Stanley, T. and R. Ritacca (2014) E-commerce in China, China 360, January. http://www.kpmg.com/CN/en/IssuesAndInsights/ArticlesPublications/Newsletters/China-360/Documents/China-360-Issue15-201401-E-commerce-in-China.pdf (accessed 24 January 2015).

Statoil (2015) Statoil awarded licences offshore Nicaragua, Statoil.com, 29 May. http://www.statoil.com/en/newsandmedia/news/pages/default.aspx (accessed May 2015).

Straver, W. (1978) Consumerism in Europe: Challenges and Opportunities for Marketing Strategy, *European Journal of Marketing* 12 (4), 316–25.

Tait, N. and K. Allison (2008) Brussels Hits Microsoft with a899m Antitrust Fine, *The Financial Times*, 28 February, 27.

The Economist (2008) Poles Apart, 30 August, 33–4.

The Economist (2011) Unrest in peace: protestors in the West have roots beyond austerity. http://www.economist.com/node/21533365 (accessed January 2012).

The Economist (2011a) E-commerce from China: The great leap online, 26 November, 81.

The Economist (2011b) Happy Customers, no profits, 18 June, 71.

The Economist (2011c) Send for the supermarkets, 16 April, 69–70.

The Economist (2011d) The next big bet, 1 October, 73–5.

The Economist (2012) France goes soft-core, 14 January, http://www.economist.com/blogs/freeexchange/2012/01/euro-zone-crisis (accessed January 2012).

The Economist (2014) Population explosion, *The Economist*, 16 August.

The Swedish Wire (2011) Consumerism absent among Swedish children, 14 September. http://www.swedishwire.com/politics/11236-consumerism-absent-among-swedish-children (accessed 23 February).

The World Facts Book (2012) Russia, https://www.cia.gov/library/publications/the-world-factbook/geos/rs.html (accessed January 2012).

Tufekci, Z. (2014) After the Protests, *The New York Times*, 19 March. http://www.nytimes.com/2014/03/20/opinion/after-the-protests.html?smid=pl-share&_r=0 (accessed 30 January 30 2015).

Tynan, D. (2006) The worst tech products of all time, *PCWorld*, 26 May. UNFCCC (2012) Background on the UNFCCC. http://unfccc.int/essential_background/items/6031.php

UNICEF (2015) Respecting and supporting children's rights in marketing and advertising—webinar, *The Guardian*. http://www.theguardian.com/sustainable-business/2015/feb/16/respecting-and-supporting-childrens-rights-in-marketing-and-advertising-webinar (accessed 23 February 2015).

Wall Street Journal (2012) IMF: Without Action, Debt Crisis May Force 4% Euro-Area Contraction, *Wall Street Journal*, 12 January, http://online.wsj. com/article/BT-CO-20120124-709079.html

Which? Magazine (2011) Food & drink brands unwrapped, February, 28–31.

YouTube (2015) A Song of Oil, Ice and Fire, Greenpeace video, 26 May.

CASE 3
Searching for Sony's Salvation

The Turnaround Strategy of an Industrial Giant

All is not well in the Sony dynasty. The performance in recent years of this once global brand icon has been terrible. The Sony brand (www.sony. com) was once a byword for innovation, being a company known for firsts. In 2011 Sony had a traumatic year: the devastating Japanese tsunami, a strong Japanese yen, computer hackers stealing customers' personal information on Sony's online gaming network, and spiralling losses culminating in a loss of $6.7 billion for the year. Now the loss has narrowed to $1 billion in 2015. The company has failed to tap into new opportunities, and been criticized for being complacent and over-reliant on past successes. Its pioneering electronics division is struggling, with sales plummeting. Aggressive competitors are stealing market share in key markets where once it dominated. Now the company is being criticized for its lack of focus, and for failing to avail itself of strategic windows of opportunity that its competitors have rapidly exploited. Faced with intensification of price competition, a strong currency and the global economic slowdown, it is fighting for its very survival. The once-lauded technology brand powerhouse now has had to change focus and reverse this traumatic decline.

Following the ravages of the Second World War, Akito Morita and Masaru Ibuka joined together to form a small electronics firm that would become a global colossus. In the ramshackle remains of a bombed-out department store in Tokyo the pair started to make radio components and repair radios. Morita was the consummate salesman, while Ibuka was a technical expert, forming a perfect partnership. Both guided the firm for over 50 years. One of the company's first engineering forays was an electric rice cooker and electrically heated seat cushions. In the early years the company set upon an innovation focus, always looking for potentially lucrative markets, and exploiting new technology. The founders would frequently visit other countries with a view to exploiting new opportunities. Ibuka visited the USA in 1952, and brought back the idea of exploiting new transistor technology and developing radios. This became the launch pad for Sony's early success, when people

bought hundreds of thousands of transistor radios to listen to the new rock 'n' roll. The company went from strength to strength through a combination of leading-edge technology products and miniaturization. Sony became the embodiment of post-war Japanese industry: entrepreneurial, creative, pioneering and highly successful. The company was always at the forefront of technology, entering untested new markets, and creating one hit product after another. Table C3.1 presents some key facts about Sony.

From these humble origins, Sony has now become a highly respected global brand name, manufacturing audio, video, communications and information technology products for both consumer and industrial markets worldwide. The Sony brand has developed into a well-respected and sought-after brand, instantly recognizable the world over. Its products have the reputation of being highly innovative, extremely reliable, and possessing high-quality standards. The company has evolved to become more than just an electronics business. There are several key divisions within the group (see Table C3.2).

One of the biggest hopes was Sony mobile devices. However, these have failed as yet to capture the product allure of Sony's rival Apple with its iPhone success. Its hopes lie in its range of phones equipped with high-end camera capabilities and Walkman-branded capabilities, turning the mobile phones into portable digital music devices. It is hoped that these devices will be the future 'iPhone killer', and help Sony regain the portable music market which it once

»

»

TABLE C3.1 Sony at a glance

Headquarters in Tokyo, Japan.

Founded in 1946.

Employs over 131,700 people worldwide.

Annual sales expected to exceed over ¥7,900 billion (yen) or $66 billion (dollars).

Revenue down 3.8 per cent.

Loses ¥126 billion ($1.05 billion) in 2015 financial year.

Estimated to make profit of ¥320 billion ($2.7 billion) in 2016 financial year.

Nine main divisions: mobile communications; imaging products and solutions; home entertainment and sound; devices (includes semiconductors and components); Sony pictures, Sony music; game and network services; financial services; other (including PC business).

Pioneers of groundbreaking technology such as the Walkman, PlayStation, transistor radios, tape recorders, video recorders, CD players and video cameras.

Owns second-largest music company in the world.

Large investment in the motion picture and television industry, with Sony Pictures.

TABLE C3.2 The major divisions of Sony

Name	Details	Performance 2015
Sony Entertainment and Sound	Manufactures a wide variety of electronic products for both consumer and industrial markets. Products include DVD and Blu-Ray players, LED TV screens, digital audio players, audio headphones products and other consumer electronic products.	Sales of $10 billion Profit of $167 million
Sony Game and Network Services	Markets the Sony PlayStation family of products and produces gaming content for these devices. Over 22 million PlayStation 4s have been sold so far.	Sales of $11.5 billion Profit of $401 million
Sony Imaging Products and Solutions	Manufactures digital cameras, video cameras, professional broadcast products. Particularly strong component sales of CMOS image sensors within smartphones (e.g. image sensors within Apple iPhone).	Sales of $6 billion Profit of $456 million
Sony Mobile Communications	Formerly a 50:50 joint venture with Swedish firm Ericsson, focused on the mobile telephony industry. Joint venture established in October 2001, ended in 2012.	Sales of $11 billion Loss of $1.8 billion
Sony Pictures	Produces and distributes motion pictures and TV programmes worldwide. Films include the *Spiderman* series, *Spectre* (James Bond Series), and *Men in Black* series. TV shows include a variety of game shows, soap operas, comedies and drama. Owns several studios and a variety of TV stations. The company bought MGM Studios through a consortium bid, strengthening its position in the movie business. The MGM film library has over 4,000 films.	Sales of $7.3 billion Profit of $488 million
Sony Music Entertainment	Second-largest music publisher in the world. A music colossus owning several music labels in a variety of genres. Artists on roster include Adele, Beyoncé, Jennifer Lopez, One Direction, Bruce Springsteen, Meghan Trainor and Rod Stewart. Owns huge back catalogue of master works including Elvis Presley and Johnny Cash.	Sales of $4.5 billion Profit of $491 million
Sony/ATV Music Publishing	Joint venture with estate of the late Michael Jackson, which owns a treasure trove of a music back catalogue including music from the Beatles, Bob Dylan and Jimi Hendrix. The firm owns and administers the copyright of these songs.	N/A
All other (includes PC business)	Personal computing business	Sales of $4 billion Loss of $862 million

dominated. Similarly, it missed the boat when Apple successfully launched the iPad tablet device, which created a burgeoning category of its own. It now is seen as a follower within the technology sector. It needs to be seen as creating category-defining products. This mantle has been taken by companies such as Apple and Google.

The company has initiated a raft of changes to turn around its performance, including radical cost-saving initiatives to stop the haemorrhaging losses, but with little success. One of the biggest areas of concern for Sony is its electronics business, which was the cornerstone of the business. At present the firm is over-reliant on the success of the PlayStation games console business; it was a rare coup for the company when the PlayStation was outselling its Microsoft-rival console. Mobile games sales are burgeoning through sales on mobile phone and tablet devices. The company's sales of Cybershot digital cameras, Vaio laptops and Handycam camcorders are seeing decreased demand. The company is still yearning for a blockbuster product that will revitalize the company. Its Bravia television screens are finding it difficult to compete against low-priced competitors. Its iconic status as the world's leading electronics brand is losing its lustre; other firms have taken the lead, such as its Korean arch-rival Samsung and the Apple colossus. It has tried to take the lead in new platforms like e-readers only to be surprisingly trounced by Amazon. com with its Kindle Paperwhite device, thanks to wireless connectivity and abundance of content, while Apple's iPhone and iPad devices are dominating the smartphone and tablet computing categories. Both Amazon and Apple are thrashing Sony due to the sheer scale of digital content available on Amazon.com and the iTunes marketplace.

Table C3.3 shows some key Sony milestones

Some blame Sony's current problems on its past successes, making it complacent in the face of the changing needs of the market. The company is facing intense competition from several key competitors in the several diverse markets in which it operates. In televisions, where it was once so dominant, it has lost the impetus by failing to provide a viable LCD screen and plasma screen offering. Competitors like Samsung devoured the market, while Sony continued to focus on the traditional bulky televisions. Sony completely missed the market. In the mid-1990s it decided to stay out of the LCD market because it felt that the technology was simply not good enough. It failed to invest in LCD manufacturing capabilities. In trying to catch up with the market, Sony had to buy in LCD screen technology from competitors, as it didn't have the expertise or production capacity when the market's demand for flat screen televisions took off. Losing market leadership in the television

sector could have very serious consequences for the Sony brand and sales of other products. Typically a television in the home was the centrepiece, to which other electronics peripherals would be attached, such as camcorders and DVD players. Consumers bought devices that worked well with their televisions. Having a Sony-branded television had a knock-on effect for the sales of other peripherals. Now Sony is losing market share against aggressive Korean competition from LG and Samsung, coupled with the emergence of manufacturers from China and Taiwan, brands like Xiaomi and Huawei. Its television business had lost money for 11 straight years. Should it pull out? The firm has considered a spinoff of the division. All the big traditional Japanese television manufacturers are struggling, such as Panasonic, Sharp and Toshiba.

In other markets, they are feeling the pressure of intense competition on multiple fronts. Competitors are offering very good-quality technology products, at competitive price points. Apple iPods have become this generation's new Walkman. While Apple pioneered the market, Sony was more concerned with piracy and copyright issues associated with the digital music revolution. It was reluctant to manufacture devices that could impinge on its music business. The company has ultimately failed to rekindle the Walkman brand as a digital music device. It is fighting Dell, Acer, Lenovo, Toshiba and HP in its mobile computing business. Nikon and Canon have retaken their lead in the digital photography market. It faces strenuous competition in the games console market against Microsoft X-Box One and the online gaming platform Microsoft Live. Samsung and now Apple dominate the mobile telephone market. Traditionally Sony was regarded as a premium brand because of its reputation for quality, higher specifications, reliability and innovation. This strong reputation enabled it to charge consumers premium prices. Consumers are now being enticed by the competition's high quality and competitive pricing, leaving Sony unable to justify its higher prices. Sony needs to develop 'must have' consumer electronics gadgets that consumers want. However, these champion products aren't beating their competitors.

The company has diversified widely from being solely an electronics firm. The purchase of Columbia Pictures cost Sony $3.4 billion in 1989, and it purchased CBS Records for $2 billion, which were both bold moves for an electronics company. This was during the heady times of the Japanese bubble economy. Sony felt it wanted to create a global entertainment empire combining technology with the best entertainment content. The acquisition of CBS Records and Columbia Pictures garnered a mixed reception from industry commentators, with many casting doubt on the rationale of a technology firm, which specialized in gadgets, knowing anything about

»

»

TABLE C3.3 Sony milestones	
1946	Founded by Masaru Ibuka and Akito Morita in post-war Tokyo, using a bombed-out department store and employing 20 people. Called the company Tokyo Tsuchin Kogyo KK (Tokyo Telecommunications Engineering Corporation).
1954	Produces Japan's first transistor radio.
1958	Name changed to Sony (derived from *sonus*, Latin for 'sound').
1962	Releases the world's smallest transistor TV.
1968	Manufactures Trinitron colour TV.
1971	Sells the first videocassette recorder.
1975	Launches the ill-fated Betamax home video recorder, loses format war to VHS standard.
1979	Launches the Sony Walkman, the personal portable stereo that becomes a worldwide phenomenon.
1983	Releases the first consumer camcorder.
1988	Launches American acquisitions phase and diversifies by buying CBS Records.
1989	Acquires Columbia Pictures, which now forms Sony Pictures.
1995	Enters the games console market with the first Sony PlayStation.
1999	Founder, Akito Morita, dies, aged 78.
2000	PlayStation 2 launched.
2001	Sony Ericsson venture launched.
2004	Sony BMG Music Entertainment launched after successful merger.
2005	Launches the PlayStation Portable, the PSP.
2005	Welshman Sir Howard Stringer appointed as chairman and CEO of Sony.
2006	Launches the PlayStation 3.
2007	Cancels Sony Connect, music distribution platform.
2008	Announces a ¥95 billion (£590 million) loss.
2009	Demonstrates the motion-sensitive Sony PlayStation Move for the PlayStation 3.
2011	Japanese tsunami and flooding in Thailand disrupt supply chain.
2012	New Japanese CEO Kazuo Hirai takes the reins.
2012	Launches PlayStation Vita (portable handheld gaming device).
2013	Launches the PlayStation 4 games console.
2014	Heavily promotes 4K technology within TVs.
2014	Announces Project Morpheus—virtual reality system for gaming.
2014	Sony Pictures' confidential data is hacked.
2015	Forecasts profit for 2016 period with uplift in revenue projections.

the entertainment industry. The company decided to diversify into entertainment in the hope that synergies could emerge between both the hardware and software aspects of the business. Sony now has the opportunity to set the standard, and provide content which works on its devices. Convergence is seen as the 'Holy Grail'; however, the vision and successful integration of both Sony's hardware and entertainment division remain elusive. The entertainment divisions are providing a substantial contribution to the business. However, critics of the strategy see it as side-tracking the business, and losing focus on its central business—electronics. Also, success can be fickle in these sectors, dependent on notoriously unreliable blockbuster movies, and a new record superstar to emerge.

In the music arena the industry is consolidating even further. The Sony Music Entertainment division has an impressive roster of talent and is now the second largest music label behind Universal Music Group. The strategy of owning the content and the technology has yet to reap its full potential. Some question the logic behind the strategy, citing that Apple's success in becoming the dominant player in the digital music landscape was not due to it owning a record label. Some commentators view the entertainment division as an unnecessary distraction for Sony, and consider that it curtailed the development of digital technology because it was too concerned with the effects of piracy and the copyright of its entertainment division. Other rival electronics firms have no such qualms, trying to placate their entertainment divisions and developing hit products quickly. The music business itself is facing enormous challenges, as sales are falling and most revenue is generated through touring rather than sales of albums. Music streaming services are killing album sales. Furthermore, digital piracy is a huge concern.

One of the main challenges facing Sony is leveraging the content that it owns through its entertainment ventures with its hardware technology. Sony had to abandon its Sony Connect initiative as an alternative music distribution channel similar to iTunes. This was due to a lack of popularity in comparison with that of its rivals. The market wanted content that was digital rights management free, where consumers could transfer content with ease to multiple devices. Innovation within Sony remains the core challenge. For the company to maintain its product leadership status, and command price premium—developing products that are cutting edge, and that the market wants—is pivotal to its future. One big hope for Sony is the medical industry, where the company hopes to leverage its technology in the areas of diagnostic and surgical equipment. Furthermore, it is abandoning pet R&D projects, like robotic dogs.

A major element of its business is the PlayStation suite of products. The games industry is very cyclical with new consoles fighting for market dominance. Sales of the games console have been less than stellar due to strong competition from Microsoft and Nintendo. Although PlayStation 4 was the most technologically sophisticated, Sony's rivals exploited different gaps in the market to enormous success. Furthermore, the Microsoft Xbox One continues to thrive thanks to a strong games portfolio and online gaming capability (with over 12 million units sold and 50 million active online subscribers to Microsoft Live). In addition, the company faces strong competition from Nintendo and Apple in the handheld gaming market. The future of gaming relies on immersive games like the Grand Theft Auto series, addictive gameplay, games that cater for divergent markets (e.g. Nintendo sells 54 per cent of its DS consoles to females), and motion sensitive technology (where physical movement is captured on screen in gaming environments). The biggest threat to the category is the emergence of smartphones and tablet devices as a central gaming platform.

After several years in charge, the Sony president Sir Howard Stringer stepped down. The Welsh-born US citizen and former television producer who spoke little or no Japanese had the onerous task of turning around the fortunes at Sony. He tried to transform the core business. Sony was seen by many as top-heavy in terms of top management, too bureaucratic, and with not enough cohesion between divisions. The firm has undertaken several initiatives to turn around the business. These initiatives have focused on cutting costs, removing layers of management, greater coordination of expenditure on research and development, streamlining the business, and consolidating important business activities such as warehousing and information technology. The Sony chief bemoaned the fact that Apple has a higher market value based on a small handful of products, whereas Sony has thousands. His turnaround efforts failed to quell the problems at Sony. In 2012 a Japanese Sony insider, Kazuo Hirai, took over the reins. He has now deployed a five-pronged strategy of: focus on core business; leveraging the games business; concentration on burgeoning developing countries; more of an innovation focus; and optimizing resources across divisions.

The Sony brand still enjoys massive retailer support. Sony's brand status is being eroded by strong competition, with competitors such as Samsung, LG and HTC investing in high-profile global sponsorships and brand advertising. Therefore, the Sony brand is not as strong as it once was within the electronics sector. Sony may be tempted to sell off non-core activities, but ironically these businesses are contributing a healthy profit to the business. Now in 2015, the company has three refined central business strategies: 1) Focus on profitability, without necessarily pursing volume; 2) Give business units greater autonomy, with a focus on shareholder value; and 3) Develop clearly defined positioning for each business.

There are several growth drivers that the company may experience. Within smartphone/tablet devices it will see strong demand for its image sensors. The company is the world's largest supplier of image sensors in digital cameras. The four divisions of devices, game and network services, pictures and music are likely to be strong contributors to business performance. However, there are strong technological innovations such as the demand for streaming services for digital content that will provide both opportunities

>>

and challenges. Within the technological space, commoditization can occur if there is a failure to innovate and invest in high-value products. Utilizing its strong patent portfolio and expertise in technologies can help Sony to mitigate against this. The television market and mobile communications business are extremely volatile, subject to intense competition, posing a risk to the business in terms of cost competition and commoditization.

The company under a new management initiative wants greater cross-company collaboration, removing the silos that developed within the company and hindered the cross-fertilization of ideas, inhibiting growth and innovation. The new CEO has a number of challenges facing him at the helm of Sony. He has to stem the losses in Sony's electronics business, make a greater profit, improve the coordination between Sony's disparate divisions, renew the focus on research and development, and figure out where Sony is heading in the next five years.

Questions

1. Discuss the importance of product innovation to the future success of Sony, in regard to the changing marketing environment.

2. Conduct a SWOT analysis on Sony.

3. What are the strategic options available to Sony? Furthermore, recommend a course of action for Sony, giving reasons for your answer.

This case study was written by Conor Carroll, Lecturer in Marketing, University of Limerick.

References

The material in the case has been drawn from a variety of published sources.

SodaStream: Adapting Itself to a Changing Market

SodaStream, despite having Scarlett Johansson as a spokeswoman, is currently having difficulties. Previously, the company had experienced several years of solid double-digit growth in revenue. However, a slowdown in its performance in the US market, later spreading to Europe, resulted in weak customer demand, sales and earnings, with the company's stock price falling by over 60 per cent in 2014. What burst its bubble?

SodaStream has a long tradition and rich history. The company's origins go back to 1903, when it was one of the first providers of a system that allowed people to make carbonated water (otherwise known as 'sparkling water') at home. The company, constantly improving and updating its technology, now sells systems that allow people to add flavouring and produce their own soda, from regular tap water, whenever they want to. SodaStream claims that its machines are cost effective, allowing people to make sparkling water for only $0.20 per litre and traditional flavoured sodas for about $0.57 per litre. Their machines can be bought at more than 60,000 different retail locations, spread across 45 countries.

A reported 1 per cent of homes in the USA have a SodaStream machine, with the rate being an astounding one in four in Sweden. World consumption of soft drinks in 2012 was estimated to be 490 billion litres, and this is expected to grow to at least 595 billion litres by 2017. Asia is currently the largest market for carbonated soft drinks, based on total litres consumed, and is expected to remain so for the foreseeable future. So how could the self-proclaimed world's 'largest manufacturer, distributor and marketer of home carbonation systems' have such horrible performance? In SodaStream's defence, it says that the weakness in European performance is concentrated mostly in the countries where its operations are run by distributors, like France and the Czech Republic. Where the company has direct control over its operations, as it does in Germany and Switzerland, the performance is significantly better. Some analysts believe that if SodaStream could reorganize, simplify and take direct control of its distribution process, sales and revenue might improve.

The company realizes that it is having difficulties, and it is trying to turn things around, announcing major changes regarding its internal management structure, its production and operations, as well as the way it manages its distribution network. Details, many analysts argue, are lacking.

Unfortunately for the people who produce soft drinks (namely soda), there are fundamental changes going on in the operating environment. As consumers around the world become more health conscious and increasingly worried about obesity and diabetes, many are questioning the wisdom of drinking litres of water that contains the preservatives, artificial colouring and calories normally found in regular soda. In the USA, consumption of carbonated drinks has dropped over the five years to 2015. These market changes are also being felt by two of the biggest players in the industry, namely Coca-Cola and Pepsi. In response to these trends, SodaStream has increased its offering of healthier items, including a new line of fruit-flavoured syrups called 'Sparkling Naturals', which don't contain artificial preservatives or sweeteners.

The company has made it clear that it plans to revamp the way it markets its products, focusing less on the making of flavoured soda and putting more emphasis on just sparkling water. As a result, SodaStream recently changed its slogan from 'set the bubbles free' to 'water made exciting', in an effort to reposition itself in the carbonated drinks market and promote its brand as the healthier option. The boxes that the machines come in will also have the words 'sparkling water maker' instead of 'home soda maker'. To reinforce this healthy option, the company cites a recent study reportedly showing that having a SodaStream machine in your home can result in an increase in the amount of water and water-based drinks that a person consumes, as compared with classic (and somewhat less healthy) soft drinks. Daniel Birnbaum, Chief Executive at SodaStream, says that users of his company's systems are only using flavouring syrups to make soda 30 per cent of the time. The rest of the time, the machines are used to just make sparkling water.

>>

However, will this be enough to turn things around for the company and put it in a position to take advantage of ongoing developments in the carbonated drinks market? The global carbonated soft drinks and bottled water market generates about $247 billion in revenue annually. A survey of future trends in the beverage industry provides some helpful guidance. It found that drinks labelled as 'high protein' and 'natural' were most likely to be popular with consumers in 2015. If SodaStream can effectively communicate the 'naturalness' of some of its products, sales might see a boost.

In an example of 'if you can't beat them, join them', SodaStream announced a possible strategic alliance with Pepsi. The two companies are currently experimenting with using Pepsi flavouring in SodaStream machines. While this might undercut SodaStream's 'healthy option' communication efforts, the benefit is that its name and brand recognition should be impacted positively (overall) by being associated with Pepsi. There is also the possibility of cross-marketing initiatives with the PepsiCo line of snacks, like Lay's, Doritos, Cheetos and Tostitos, to name a few. The reality for SodaStream is that it appears that it really does not have the choice of going it alone. The other major player in the soft drinks industry, Coca-Cola, with a market capitalization almost 500 times greater than SodaStream's, has announced a $2 billion investment in Keurig Green Mountain, a competing maker of home beverage machines.

In addition to financial, marketing and strategic challenges, the company is also facing political challenges. SodaStream's corporate head office is located in Israel, and SodaStream has a production facility in a Jewish settlement called Mishor Adumim, which is considered to be (technically) in the occupied West Bank. The company is adamant that it is a responsible and model corporate citizen, stating that the roughly 500 Palestinians who work at the plant receive salaries four or five times the average wage in the territories controlled by Palestinian authorities. Nonetheless, the company has come under increasing criticism from an international boycott, divestment, and sanctions (BDS) campaign. The BDS campaign is calling for restrictions on Israeli products that help the country 'profit from the occupation' of the West Bank. In an example of the double-edged sword that is social media, between July and October of 2014, 29 per cent of the conversations on the Internet regarding SodaStream were about boycotting its products. In response, the company says that it will close the controversial facility by the end of 2015. Production will be replaced by a new plant in the Negev Desert, in southern Israel, which opened in May of 2014. Mr. Birnbaum says that he will try to secure Israeli work permits so that his Palestinian employees will be able to work at the new facility, which is about 60 miles from the old one.

Luckily for SodaStream, it has one element clearly in its favour: consumer psychology. The company's home systems sell for anywhere from roughly $80 to $200, and for many people who buy one, this registers mentally as a type of investment rather than a simple purchase. Customers have incurred a sunk cost, and as a result have a 'psychological incentive' to use the machine as many times as possible in order to recoup the purchase cost through the savings they receive by making soda more cheaply at home. Hopefully for SodaStream, people trying to save money is a trend that will never go out of style.

Questions

1. Do a SWOT analysis for Sodastream.
2. What marketing challenges face Sodastream?
3. Apart from marketing, what other challenges is the company facing?
4. What strategic action is Sodastream taking in reaction to its current challenges? Do you think they will be successful? Justify your answer.

This case study was written by Tom McNamara and Asha Moore-Mangin, the ESC Rennes School of Business, France.

References

Based on: Jacobsen, J. (2015) 2015 New Product Development Outlook Survey-takers report using nearly 12 flavors in 2014, Beverage Industry, January 12, 2015, http://www.bevindustry.com/articles/88120-new-product-development-outlook; IBIS (2014) Global Soft Drink & Bottled Water Manufacturing Market Research Report, IBIS World Market Research, September 2014, http://www.ibisworld.com/industry/global/global-soft-drink-bottled-water-manufacturing.html; Cardenal, A. (2015) Is SodaStream a Top Turnaround Candidate in 2015? The Motley Fool, 15 January 2015, http://www.fool.com/investing/general/2015/01/15/is-sodastream-a-top-turnaround-candidate-in-2015.aspx; Rudorenoct, J. (2014) Israeli Firm, Target of Boycott, to Shut West Bank Plant, NY Times, 30 October, 2014, http://www.nytimes.com/2014/10/31/world/middleeast/sodastream-to-close-factory-in-west-bank.html?_r=1; IBIS (2014) Soda Production in the US: Market Research Report, Soda Production Market Research Report, NAICS 31211a, November 2014, http://www.ibisworld.com/industry/default.aspx?indid=285; AFP (2014) Sodastream Is Closing Its Controversial West Bank Plant That Caused Its Ambassador Scarlett Johansson To Quit Her Role At Oxfam, AFP, through Business Insider, 30 October, 2014, http://www.businessinsider.com/afp-sodastream-to-close-controversial-west-bank-plant-2014-10#ixzz3P77YIoXy; Stanford, D. D. (2012) SodaStream Takes Marketing Tactic to Coca-Cola's Hometown, Bloomberg, 20 June, 2012, http://www.bloomberg.com/news/2012-06-20/sodastream-takes-marketing-tactic-to-coca-cola-s-hometown.html; Esterl, M. (2014) SodaStream to Close West Bank Factory By Mid-2015, The Wall Street Journal, 29 October 2014, http://www.wsj.com/articles/sodastream-to-close-controversial-west-bank-factory-by-mid-2015-1414599238; Statista (2015) Soft drink sales worldwide in 2012 and 2017, by region (in million litres), Statista, http://www.statista.com/statistics/232794/global-soft-drink-sales-by-region; Stock, K. (2013) The Secret of SodaStream's Success, Bloomberg Businessweek, 31 July 2013, http://www.businessweek.com/articles/2013-07-31/the-secret-of-sodastreams-success

CHAPTER 3
Consumer Behaviour

> "A brand isn't only made by the people who buy it, but also by the people who know about it."
>
> **JOHN HEGARTY (2011)**

LEARNING OBJECTIVES

After reading this chapter, you should be able to:

1. define the dimensions of consumer buyer behaviour
2. describe the role of the buying centre (who buys) and its implications
3. describe the consumer decision-making process (how people buy)
4. discuss the marketing implications of need recognition, information search, evaluation of alternatives, purchase and post-purchase stages
5. compare the differences in evaluation of high- versus low-involvement situations
6. describe the nature of choice criteria (what are used) and their implications
7. explain the influences on consumer behaviour—the buying situation, personal and social influences—and their marketing implications

I n Chapter 2 we looked at the macro environment and identified forces beyond the control of a firm that can influence decision-making. In this chapter and in Chapter 4 we will build an understanding of customers, which is a cornerstone of marketing. We will explore factors that influence decision-making in consumer and business markets. In this chapter our focus is on consumer behaviour, and in Chapter 4 on organizational buyer behaviour. You will find there are similarities and key differences between the types of purchaser (individual consumers and professional **buyers**), which have important implications for marketing. More specifically, this chapter examines three key areas that are important for understanding consumer behaviour and its implications for marketing: 1) the *dimensions*; 2) the *processes*; 3) the *influences*.

Understanding consumer behaviour is important because consumers are changing. While average incomes rise, income distribution is more uneven in most nations and household size is gradually decreasing. In all European Union (EU) nations, the consumption of services is rising at the expense of consumer durables, and demand for (and supply of) health, green (ecological), fun/luxury and convenience products is increasing. The marketing environment impacts on consumer behaviour and often leads to significant changes in what we buy. For example, children are losing interest in traditional toys like building bricks, dolls and toy cars at a younger age as these toys are being replaced by tablet computers, mobile phones and computer games. This trend has resulted in changes in demand and losses for companies like Mattell and Lego. To ensure survival, these companies have to adapt; for example, Mattel's best-selling doll Barbie comes with a range of modern attributes such as an inbuilt video camera and tattoos. Lego sells classic ranges as well as having multiple product themes that link closely to the lives of consumers, such as the blockbuster movies *The Hobbit, Star Wars*, seasonal themes such as Christmas and Valentine's day, and architectural themes such as the Eiffel Tower, the White House and the Sydney Opera House.

The lesson is that companies need to have a deep understanding of their customers and be alert to their changing behaviours. This chapter provides the foundations for developing such understanding and sensitivity.

The Dimensions of Buyer Behaviour

Consumers are individuals who buy products or services for personal consumption. Organizational buying, on the other hand, focuses on the purchase of products and services for use in an organization's activities. Sometimes it is difficult to classify a product as being either a consumer or an organizational good. Cars, for example, sell to consumers for personal consumption and to organizations for use in carrying out their activities (e.g. to provide transport for a sales executive). For both types of buyer, an understanding of customers can be gained by answering the following questions (see also Figure 3.1).

- *Who* is important in the buying decision?
- *How* do they buy?
- *What* are their choice criteria?
- *Where* do they buy?
- *When* do they buy?

These questions help define the key dimensions of behaviour (and are relevant to both consumer and organizational purchasers). In this chapter we focus on the consumer perspective, and in Chapter 4 on the organizational perspective. Understanding the dimensions identified by these questions is important and has implications for different levels of marketing planning. The structure of this chapter will be based on three questions: who, how and what. These are often the most difficult aspects of buyer behaviour to understand. Answering the questions of where and when do customers buy can be more straightforward, especially in the physical world. In the digital world, these questions become more of an issue for marketers, as the physical and temporal aspects of online consumer behaviour have more significant implications for marketers. The questions of where and when are considered in some detail in Chapter 16.

Additionally, the following discussion of consumer buying throws much light on a further question: *why* do they buy? For example, analysis of need recognition/problem awareness within the section on how consumers

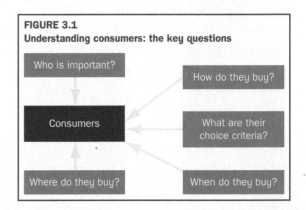

FIGURE 3.1
Understanding consumers: the key questions

Who is important?

How do they buy?

Consumers

What are their choice criteria?

Where do they buy?

When do they buy?

buy explains why consumers may decide a purchase should be made; discussion of choice criteria and **motivation** explains why one consumer may choose a Nissan car because of its (competitive) price, while another may choose a Mercedes for its perceived status; and coverage of the influence of personality may explain why an extrovert may choose a red sports car while an introvert may prefer a grey Skoda. Because the issue of *why* consumers buy bridges many of the following sections, it is not treated separately.

First, the dimensions of consumer behaviour (who, how and what) are analysed. Second, the key influences on those dimensions are discussed: buying situation; personal influences; motivation, beliefs and attitudes; personality; economic circumstances; lifestyle; lifecycle and age; and social influences.

Consumer Behaviour

Who buys?

Many consumer purchases are individual. When purchasing a Snickers (probably the bestselling chocolate bar in the world with sales of over $2 billion) a person may make an impulse purchase upon seeing an array of confectionery at a newsagent's counter. However, decision-making can also be made by a group such as a household. In such a situation, a number of individuals may interact to influence the purchase decision. Each person may assume a role in the decision-making process. Blackwell, Miniard and Engel (2005) describe five roles, as outlined below. Each may be taken by parents, children or other members of the **buying centre**.

1 *Initiator*: the person who begins the process of considering a purchase. Information may be gathered by this person to help the decision.
2 *Influencer*: the person who attempts to persuade others in the group concerning the outcome of the decision. Influencers typically gather information and attempt to impose their choice criteria on the decision.
3 *Decider*: the individual with the power and/or financial authority to make the ultimate choice regarding which product to buy.
4 *Buyer*: the person who conducts the transaction. The buyer calls the supplier, visits the store, makes the payment and effects delivery.
5 *User*: the actual consumer/user of the product.

One person may assume multiple roles in the buying group. In a laptop purchase, for example, a teenage girl may be the *initiator* and attempt to *influence* her parents, who are the *deciders*. The girl may be *influenced* by her brother to buy a different brand to the one she initially preferred. The *buyer* may be one of the parents, who visits the store to purchase the laptop and brings it back to the home. Finally, both sister and brother may be *users* of the laptop. Although the purchase was for one person, in this example marketers have four differing viewpoints—both of the parents and the two teenagers—to affect the outcome of the purchase decision. The respective roles in a buying group may change during the purchasing process. The Internet is also having an influence on consumer behaviour. Read Marketing in Action 3.1 to find out the influence of groups on the decision to purchase.

As roles and the marketing environment change, so does our purchasing behaviour; consumers are eating more convenience food than ever before and more working family members and single person households mean that convenience is a high priority for many people (Costa et al., 2007). Consumers are also getting heavier—Europe has the highest number of overweight people in the world (World Health Organization, 2010)—and this influences what they buy, that is the likelihood of buying healthy convenience food is affected by overall liking of the meal (Olsen et al., 2012), so chicken meals are favoured over salmon. Technology is enabling sophisticated analysis of consumer

EXHIBIT 3.1
See how WeightWatchers has focused on behavioural trends to show how fad dieting is not for everyone and to position the brand as being 'here to help'

The Internet is influencing how people buy in many different ways, from how they search for product alternatives, to comparing purchase options, to 365/24/7 any time, anywhere modes of purchasing. Another powerful effect on the changing of consumer

GROUPON®

behaviour comes from the idea that success breeds success. For example, online, people look for frequently downloaded music or YouTube videos and quickly join trending news feeds which may create a Twitter storm, i.e. a spike in activity surrounding a particular news topic. Research has suggested that the actions of others have a strong influence on individual behaviour, which implies that consumers can influence and be influenced by others on a mass scale via the Internet. Groupon is a web portal that offers consumers promotional deals on restaurants, entertainment, sporting events and other services on a mass scale. While offers are provided on a regional basis to individuals, they are based on 'collective' buying power. The popularity of such deals has been found to have a more profound effect on positive purchase intentions and be more influential than prior shopping experiences. Another compelling finding was that the size of the discount on the service offered is more of a motivating factor than the actual price offered.

Based on: Zhang (2010); Salganik, Sheridan and Watts (2006); Groupon (2015); Luo et al. (2014)

decision-making, which has implications for marketing initiatives. Research for Carlsberg Sweden, using spectacles that track exactly what consumers are looking at, found that point-of-sale materials are more important in influencing the purchase decision than previously thought (Barda, 2011).

The marketing implications of understanding who buys lie within the areas of marketing communications and segmentation.

An identification of the roles played within the buying centre is a prerequisite for targeting persuasive communications. As the previous discussion has demonstrated, the person who actually uses or consumes the product may not be the most influential member of the buying centre, nor the decision-maker. Even when the user does play the predominant role, communication with other members of the buying centre can make sense when their knowledge and opinions may act as persuasive forces during the decision-making process.

The second implication is that the changing roles and influences within the family buying centre are providing new opportunities to creatively segment hitherto stable markets (e.g. cars). Read Mini Case 3.1 to understand more about influences on consumer decision-making and fine-tuning marketing directed at the previously stable age 21–35 male segment.

How they buy

How consumers buy may be regarded as a decision-making process beginning with the recognition that a problem exists. For example, a personal computer may be bought to solve a perceived problem: for example, lack of access to the Internet. Problem-solving may thus be considered a thoughtful reasoned action undertaken to bring about need satisfaction. In this example, the need was for fast and accurate calculations. Blackwell, Miniard and Engel (2005) define a series of steps a consumer may pass through before choosing a brand. Figure 3.2 shows these stages, which form the **consumer decision-making process**.

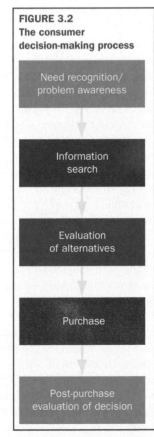

FIGURE 3.2
The consumer decision-making process

Need recognition/ problem awareness → Information search → Evaluation of alternatives → Purchase → Post-purchase evaluation of decision

Things you ought to know about pre-family man (PFM):

- 92 per cent are online across multiple devices.
- 67 per cent don't see their friends as much as they did.
- 75 per cent see love as a top priority (Microsoft, 2012).
- 92 per cent use email at least once a day.
- 55 per cent use social networks at least once a day.
- 91 per cent watch short videos online.
- 72 per cent of PFMs buy online at least once a month.

Microsoft has its eye on PFMs—young men aged between 21–35—as they make up a large market. In the seven largest countries in Europe, there are over 21 million PFM and this group is predicted to grow. Research has revealed that PFMs, who are between secondary education and having a family, should not be targeted as one group. According to Microsoft, PFM is evolving: he moves from living with parents, through living on his own or with a friend, to living with a partner. During this evolution, PFM has to achieve a balance between his desire for fun and the need to be responsible; he has to work out how to manage the things he wants to do and to set priorities, as there are always too many things he wants to do. PFM is *always switched on to digital technology* devices, and access to the Internet is critical for managing his busy life.

However, depending on where PFM is on the evolutionary track, his priorities will vary according to which country he lives in. For example, between the ages of 21 and 23 in Sweden, 20 per cent of PFMs are living with parents, whereas in Spain the figure is 80 per cent. Priorities are different too; in Germany, 35 per cent are looking for more money, while in Sweden the figure is only 15 per cent. Career aspirations appear to be higher in Sweden, with 31 per cent looking for a better job, whereas in the Netherlands the figure is 7 per cent.

As technology has enabled marketers to become more informed about consumer behaviour, a complex set of rules emerge, which could give more insight into how better to serve the needs of various customers. The study by Microsoft provides guidance on targeting PFMs and suggests four golden rules that marketers should adhere to when targeting them.

1 Life stages—if targeting by age, it is key to also factor in life stages; when PFM is living with parents, his focus is on fun and he is interested in flats to rent and sports events. For the marketer, in-game advertising is very important. When PFM is living alone or with friends, marketers should target money, fashion, health and fitness websites. PFM's priorities change when living with a partner. The focus is no longer on fun: he becomes more responsive to messages about DIY, holidays, property, cooking and money. Social media and review sites are good places to advertise to capture his attention.

2 Cultural differences—the PFM's evolution goes at a different speed depending on which country he lives in; he makes use of the Internet, social media and email to stay in touch through the evolution.

3 Priorities—PFM has many hurdles to overcome during his evolution. Advertisers should be aware of these and seek to give him the information he needs to achieve different priorities.

4 Information—marketers should always aim to give PFM the right type of information he needs at the point he wants it, whether that is online or on the move.

Questions:

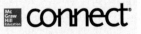

1 Suggest how you would advise a company manufacturing tablet computers to communicate with PFM.

2 Explain how the priorities of PFM change during his evolution and suggest what the implications are for marketing managers.

3 Using the available information, suggest which country (Sweden, Germany, the Netherlands or Spain) and which accompanying PFM life stage you might target if you were responsible for developing a communication campaign for:
    a) an international property company
    b) state-of-the-art gaming console
    c) a shopping app.

Based on: Microsoft (2012)

Need recognition/problem awareness

In the computer example, *need recognition* is essentially *functional*, and recognition may take place over a period of time. Other problems may occur as a result of routine depletion (e.g. petrol, food) or unpredictability (e.g. the breakdown of a television set or washing machine). In other situations consumer purchasing may be initiated by more *emotional* or *psychological* needs. For example, the purchase of Aqua Pour Homme Cologne for Men by Bulgari is likely to be motivated by status needs rather than any marginal functional superiority over other perfumes.

The degree to which the consumer intends to resolve the problem depends on two issues: the magnitude of the discrepancy between the desired and present situation, and the relative importance of the problem (Neal, Quester and Hawkins, 2007). A problem may be perceived, but if the difference between the *current and desired situation* is small, then the consumer may not be sufficiently motivated to move to the next step in the decision-making process. For example, a person considering upgrading their mobile phone from a basic handset to a smartphone model will only make the purchase if they consider the difference in benefits to be sufficient to incur the costs involved (even though they might desire the more sophisticated product).

Conversely, a large discrepancy may be perceived but the person may not proceed to information search because the *relative importance* of the problem is small. A person may feel that a smartphone has significant advantages over a mobile phone, but that the relative importance of the advantages compared with other purchase needs (e.g. the mortgage or a holiday) might be small.

The existence of a need, however, may not activate the decision-making process in all cases. This is due to the existence of *need inhibitors* (O'Shaughnessey, 1987). For example, someone may want to buy an item on Amazon Marketplace but may be inhibited by fear of paying online and not receiving the goods. In such circumstances, the need remains passive.

There are a number of marketing implications in the need-recognition stage, and marketing managers should be aware of:

1 *the needs* of consumers and the problems that they face. By being more attuned to customers' needs, companies have the opportunity to create a competitive advantage. This may be accomplished by intuition. For example, intuitively a marketing manager of a washing machine company may believe that consumers would value a silent machine. Alternatively, marketing research could be used to assess customer problems or needs. For example, group discussions could be carried out among people who use washing machines, to assess their dissatisfaction with current models, what problems they encountered and what their ideal machine would be. This could be followed by a large-scale survey to determine how representative the views of the group members were. The results of such research can have significant effects on product redesign.

2 *need inhibitors* which potentially stop a purchase. For example, eBay has recognized that overcoming the need inhibitor lack of trust in being sent the product is important. To overcome this need inhibitor, eBay introduced its PayPal system, which acts as financial insurance against non-receipt of goods, and has developed a feedback system that allows buyers to post information on their transactions and their experiences with particular vendors.

3 *need stimulation* which might encourage a purchase. Marketers' activities, such as developing advertising campaigns and training salespeople to sell product benefits, may act as cues to needs arousal. For example, an advertisement displaying the features and benefits of a smartphone may stimulate customers to regard their lack of a computer, or the limitations of their current model, to be a problem that warrants action.

As we have seen, activating problem recognition depends on the size of the discrepancy between the current and desired situation, and the relative importance of the problem. An advertiser could therefore focus on the advantages of a smartphone over a mobile phone, to create awareness of a larger discrepancy than originally perceived and/or stress the importance of owning a top-of-the-range model as a symbol of innovativeness and professionalism (thereby increasing the importance of the purchase relative to other products).

Not all consumer needs are obvious. Consumers often engage in exploratory behaviour such as being early adopters of new products, taking risks in making product choices, recreational shopping and seeking variety in purchasing products. Such activities can satisfy the need for novel purchase experiences, offer a change of pace and relief from boredom, and satisfy a thirst for knowledge and the urge of curiosity (Baumgartner, and Bem Steenkamp, 1996).

Information search

If problem recognition is sufficiently strong, the consumer decision-making process is likely to move to the second stage: **information search**. This involves the identification of alternative ways of problem solution. The search may be internal or external. *Internal search* involves a review of relevant information from memory. This review would include potential solutions, methods of comparing solutions, reference to personal experiences and marketing communications. If a satisfactory solution is not found, then *external search* begins. This involves *personal sources* such as, say, friends and family, and/or *commercial sources* such as advertisements, salespeople, websites and social media.

Third-party reports, such as product-testing reports in the press and on the Internet, may provide unbiased information, and *personal experiences* may be sought, such as asking for demonstrations and viewing, touching or tasting the product.

The objective of information search is to build up the **awareness set**—that is, the array of brands that may provide a solution to the problem. Using the smartphone example again, an advertisement may not only stimulate a search for more unbiased information regarding the advertised smartphone, but also stimulate an external search for information about rival brands.

Information search by consumers is facilitated by the growth of Internet usage and companies that provide search facilities, such as Yahoo! and Google. Consumers are increasingly using the Internet to gather information before buying a product. For example, many purchases only take place after consumers have researched brands online.

EXHIBIT 3.2
The Cool Water Night Dive advert uses emotional triggers to communicate with target audiences

Evaluation of alternatives and the purchase

The first step in *evaluation* is to reduce the awareness set to a smaller set of brands for serious consideration. The brands in the awareness set pass through a screening filter to produce an **evoked set**—those brands that the consumer seriously considers before making a purchase. In a sense, the evoked set is a shortlist of brands for careful evaluation. The screening process may use different choice criteria from those used when making the final choice, and the number of choice criteria used is often fewer (Kuusela, Spence and Kanto, 1998). One choice criterion used for screening may be price. Those smartphones priced below a certain level may form the evoked set. Final choice may then depend on such choice criteria as ease of use, speed of connection to the Internet and reliability. The range of choice criteria used by consumers will be examined in more detail later in this chapter.

Although brands may be perceived as similar, this does not necessarily mean they will be equally preferred. This is because different product attributes (e.g. benefits, imagery) may be used by people when making similarity and preference judgements. For example, two brands may be perceived as similar because they provide similar functional benefits, yet one may be preferred over the other because of distinctive imagery (Creusen and Schoormans, 1997).

A key determinant of the extent to which consumers evaluate a brand is their level of *involvement*. Involvement is the degree of perceived relevance and personal importance accompanying the brand choice (Blackwell, Miniard and Engel, 2005). When a purchase is highly involving, the consumer is more likely to carry out extensive evaluation. High-involvement purchases are likely to include those incurring high expenditure or personal risk, such as buying a car or a home. In contrast, low-involvement situations are characterized by simple evaluations about purchases. Consumers use simple choice tactics to reduce time and effort rather than maximize the consequences of the purchase (Elliott and Hamilton, 1991). For example, when purchasing bread, milk or breakfast cereal, consumers are likely to make quick choices rather than agonize over the decision.

This distinction between high- and low-involvement situations implies different evaluative processes. For high-involvement purchases, the Fishbein and Ajzen theory of reasoned action (Ajzen and Fishbein, 1980) provides a robust starting point for understanding purchase behaviour (see, for example: Budd and Spencer, 1984; Farley, Lehman and Ryan, 1981; Shimp and Kavas, 1984) in situations where individuals are in complete control of the buying situation. But there are situations where buyers have limits on the control they can exercise, for example limits on their mental and physical processing skills, emotions and compulsions. As a result, their intentions to buy can be moderated. So the degree to which individuals can make a reasoned decision affects their intentional behaviour (Ajzen, 1991). This issue of control has led Ajzen (Ajzen and Madden, 1985) to extend the theory of reasoned action model to include behavioural control. The extended model—the theory of planned behaviour (TPB) (Ajzen, 1985)—takes into account the degree of control individuals have over their behavioural intentions. Each of these models will now be examined.

Theory of reasoned action—Fishbein and Ajzen model   This model suggests that an attitude towards a brand is based upon a set of **beliefs** about the brand's attributes (e.g. value for money, durability). These are the perceived consequences resulting from buying the brand. Each attribute is weighted by how good or bad the consumer believes the attribute to be. Those attributes that are weighted highly will be that person's choice criteria and have a large influence in the formation of attitude.

Attitude is the degree to which someone likes or dislikes the brand overall. The link between personal beliefs and attitudes is shown in Figure 3.3. However, evaluation of a brand is not limited to personal beliefs about the consequences of buying a brand. Outside influences also play a part. Individuals will thus evaluate the extent to which *important others* believe that they should or should not buy the brand. These beliefs may conflict with their personal beliefs. People may personally believe that buying a sports car may have positive consequences (providing fun driving, being more attractive to other people) but refrain from doing so if they believe that important others (e.g. parents, boss) would disapprove of the purchase. This collection of *normative beliefs* forms an overall evaluation of the degree to which these outside influences approve or disapprove of the purchase (*subjective norms*).

The link between normative beliefs and subjective norms is shown in Figure 3.3. This is a *theory of reasoned action*. Consumers are highly involved in the purchase to the extent that they evaluate the consequences of the purchase *and* what others will think about it. Only after these considerations have taken place are purchase intentions formed and the ultimate purchase result. Purchase intentions are important, as they are a strong predictor of future behaviour—an intention is an indication of an individual's state of willingness to carry out a particular action.

Theory of planned behaviour   While the theory of reasoned action provides sound insight into how attitudes and beliefs shape intentions, it was found that an individual's behaviour is not always completely controlled and rational. So the theory of planned behaviour brings in the notion of control and suggests that the *extent* to which individuals freely make decisions will shape their intentions. In other words, our *actual shopping behaviour*, say of buying healthy foodstuffs, will be affected by *our intention to buy* healthy foodstuffs. But also our intentions can be changed by external influences over which we have limited control. So our healthy food purchase might be contingent on time available to make the purchase, money, and our skills of being able to identify genuine healthy option foodstuffs. Ajzen (2012, 1991) suggested that measuring *perceived behavioural control*, which is an individual's belief of how easy or difficult it is to make an intended purchase, could reveal insight into a person's motivations. The *control beliefs* are the existence of factors that might facilitate or impede a person's behavioural intentions and ultimately their purchase behaviour, for example social, cultural or religious factors. See Figure 3.4. Therefore, if our healthy food buyer is a nutritionist who can

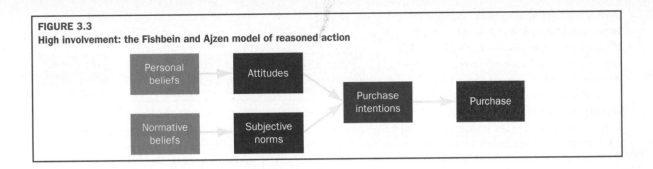

FIGURE 3.3
High involvement: the Fishbein and Ajzen model of reasoned action

readily identify healthy options, he or she is likely to be more in control and more likely to make a purchase of healthy foodstuffs based on scientific knowledge. A person who is less well-informed about nutrition might be more inclined to be influenced, say, by social factors and buy skimmed milk based on presumptions about the milk, without specific knowledge of the health benefits.

Ultimately, a person's intention to perform a particular behaviour is a strong indicator of whether they will carry out a certain act (e.g. buy healthy foodstuffs). However, obstacles can get in the way—for example, demands from family, and work, which can limit the time available—and so a person buys a fast-food ready meal, high in fat and sugar, instead of a healthier option.

Ehrenberg and Goodhart model   In low-involvement situations (Ehrenberg and Goodhart, 1980), the amount of information processing implicit in the earlier model may not be worthwhile or sensible. A typical low-involvement situation is the *repeat purchase* of fast-moving consumer goods. The work of Ehrenberg and Goodhart suggests that a very simple process may explain purchase behaviour (see Figure 3.5). According to this model, awareness precedes trial, which, if satisfactory, leads to repeat purchase. This is an example of a behavioural model of consumer behaviour: the behaviour becomes *habitual* with little conscious thought or formation of attitudes preceding behaviour. The limited importance of the purchase simply does not warrant the reasoned evaluation of alternatives implied in the Fishbein and Ajzen model. The notion of low involvement suggests that awareness precedes behaviour and behaviour precedes attitude. In this situation, the consumer does not actively seek information but is a passive recipient. Furthermore, since the decision is not inherently involving, the consumer is likely to satisfice (i.e. search for a satisfactory solution rather than the best one) (Wright, 1974). Consequently any of several brands that lie in the evoked set may be considered adequate.

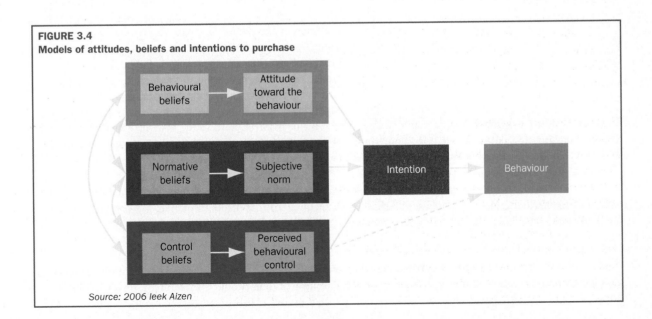

FIGURE 3.4
Models of attitudes, beliefs and intentions to purchase

Source: 2006 Ieek Aizen

Distinguishing between high- and low-involvement situations   The distinction between high- and low-involvement purchasing situations is important because the variations in how consumers evaluate products and brands leads to contrasting marketing implications. The complex

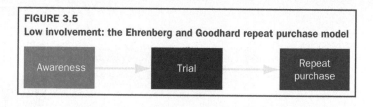

FIGURE 3.5
Low involvement: the Ehrenberg and Goodhard repeat purchase model

Awareness → Trial → Repeat purchase

evaluation outlined in the high-involvement situation suggests that marketing managers need to provide a good deal of information about the positive consequences of buying. Messages with *high information content* would enhance knowledge about the brand; because the consumer is actively seeking information, high levels of repetition are not needed (Rothschild, 1978). Print media and websites may be appropriate in the high-involvement case since they allow detailed and repeated scrutiny of information. Car advertisements often provide information about the comfort, reliability and performance of the model, and also appeal to status considerations. All of these appeals may influence the consumer's beliefs about the consequences of buying the model. However, persuasive communications should also focus on how the consumer views the influence of important others. This is an area that is underdeveloped in marketing and provides avenues for further development of communications for high-involvement products.

The salesforce also has an important role to play in the high-involvement situation by ensuring that the customer is aware of the important attributes of the product and correctly evaluates their consequences. For example, if the differential advantage of a particular model of a car is fuel economy the salesperson would raise fuel economy as a salient product attribute and explain the cost benefits of buying that model vis-à-vis the competition.

For low-involvement situations, as we have seen, the evaluation of alternatives is much more rudimentary, and attitude change is likely to follow purchase. In this case, attempting to gain *top-of-mind awareness* through advertising and providing positive *reinforcement* (e.g. through sales promotion) to gain trial may be more important than providing masses of information about the consequences of buying the brand. Furthermore, as this is of little interest, the consumer is not actively seeking information but is a passive receiver. Consequently advertising messages should be *short* with a small number of key points but with *high repetition* to enhance learning (Rothschild, 1978). In the past television has been seen as the best medium since it allows passive reception to messages while the medium actively transmits them. Also, it is ideal for the transmission of short, highly repetitive messages. Much soap powder advertising follows this format (for a discussion of the role of involvement in package labelling, see Davies and Wright, 1994). However, it is important to be aware that whilst these ideas are still valid, digital marketing and greater use of the Internet as an advertising medium has changed the format of communication messages and the way they are received. These issues are considered in detail in Chapters 13, 14 and 16.

Marketers must be aware of the role of emotion in consumer evaluation of alternatives. A major source of high emotion is when a product is high in symbolic meaning. Consumers believe that the product helps them to construct and maintain their self-concept and sense of identity. Furthermore, ownership of the product will help them communicate the desired image to other people. In such cases, non-rational preferences may form and information search is confined to providing objective justification for an emotionally based decision. Studies have shown the effects of emotion on judgement to be less thought, less information-seeking, less analytical reasoning and less attention to negative factors that might contradict the decision (Elliott, 1997). Instead, consumers consult their feelings for information about a decision: 'How do I feel about it?' Consequently, many marketers attempt to create a feeling of warmth about their brands. The mere exposure to a brand name over time, and the use of humour in advertisements, can create such feelings.

Impulse buying is another area that can be associated with emotions. Consumers have described a compelling feeling that is 'thrilling', 'wild', 'a tingling sensation', 'a surge of energy', and 'like turning up the volume' (see Elliott, 1998; Rook, 1987). See Marketing in Action 3.2.

Post-purchase evaluation of the decision

Effective marketing aims to create **customer** satisfaction in both high- and low-involvement situations. Marketing managers want to create positive experiences from the purchase of their products or services. Nevertheless, it is common for customers to experience some post-purchase concerns; this is called **cognitive dissonance**. These concerns arise because of uncertainty about making the right decision. This is because the choice of one product often means the rejection of the attractive features of the alternatives.

Dissonance is likely to increase in four ways: with the *expense* of purchase; when the decision is *difficult* (e.g. many alternatives, many choice criteria and each alternative offering benefits not available with the others); when the decision is *irrevocable*; and when the purchaser has a tendency *to experience anxiety* (Neal, Quester and Hawkins, 2007). Thus, it is often associated with high-involvement purchases. Shortly after purchase, car buyers may attempt to reduce dissonance by looking at advertisements, websites and brochures for their model, and seeking reassurance from owners of the same model. Volkswagen buyers are more likely to look at Volkswagen advertisements and avoid Renault or Ford advertisements. Clearly, advertisements can act as positive reinforcers in such situations, and follow-up sales efforts can act similarly. Car dealers can reduce *buyer remorse* by contacting recent purchasers by letter to reinforce the wisdom of their decision and to confirm the quality of their after-sales service.

However, the outcome of post-purchase evaluation is dependent on many factors besides this kind of reassurance. The quality of the product or service is obviously a key determinant, and the role of the salesperson acting as a problem-solver for the customer rather than simply pushing the highest-profit-margin product can also help create customer satisfaction, and thereby reduce cognitive dissonance.

MARKETING IN ACTION 3.2
Chocolate Shortages and Black Friday Promotions Cause Impulsive Behaviour and Panic Buying

Impulse purchasing and panic buying are characterized by highly charged emotions, limited cognitive control and reactive rather than planned behaviour. External factors appear to increase in importance in the consumer decision-making process and encourage shoppers to engage in frenzied bouts of buying. The following examples highlight how different external influences can stimulate emotionally charged purchasing.

Panic buying

Expat British consumers living in the USA reacted aggressively towards legal action taken by the American food producer Hershey's to stop the sale of Cadbury's chocolate bars due to an infringement of its trademark. Chocolate lovers started to buy up stocks of their favourite confectionery, and warehouses emptied quickly as panic about the future lack of availability of their beloved English-made chocolate bars increased.

The source of the argument was that Cadbury entered global markets through Mondelez International, and together the chocolate accounts for nearly a third of all the chocolate consumed in the UK; but when it comes to North America, Hershey's actually produces Dairy Milk under licence for the Cadbury brand, using a slightly different recipe. Cadbury has a long and illustrious history and chocolate with a distinctive taste to match; expat consumers were so attached to the Cadbury brand that emotions ran high and the threat of scarcity drove demand.

Impulse purchasing

Black Friday was introduced to online shoppers in the UK by Amazon in 2010. By 2014, it hit critical mass, and promotions moved to the physical High Street too. ASDA/Walmart ran flash promotions in its stores, which created chaos as consumers literally fought over LED televisions, electric drills and tablet computers at heavily discounted prices.

Originally, Black Friday was the Philadelphia police force's answer to the chaos that ensued in the 1950s and 60s after Thanksgiving (celebrated in USA on the fourth Thursday in November). The name came out of the effects of the frenzied shopping on the city's retailers, as they reportedly saw profits move out of the red and into the black. Whether true or not, Black Friday represented a kick start for Christmas shoppers, which seems set to continue.

Based on: Euromonitor (2014); McSherry (2015); Weinberg and Gottwald (1982); Ruddick (2014)

What are the choice criteria?

Choice criteria are the various attributes (and benefits) a consumer uses when evaluating products and services. They provide the grounds for deciding to purchase one brand or another. Different members of the buying centre may use different choice criteria. For example, a child may use the criterion of self-image when choosing shoes, whereas a parent may use price. The same criterion may be used differently. For example, a child may want the most expensive smartphone while the parent may want a less expensive alternative. Choice criteria can change over time due to changes in income through the family lifecycle. As disposable income rises, so price may no longer be the key criterion but is replaced by considerations of status or social belonging.

Table 3.1 lists four types of choice criteria and gives examples of each. *Technical criteria* are related to the performance of the product or service, and include reliability, durability, comfort and convenience. Convenience is often synonymous with ease of use.

 Scan the QR code to see how the advertising for Peugeot 208 uses technical performance criteria to celebrate the return of the GTi.

TABLE 3.1 Choice criteria used when evaluating alternatives

Type of criteria	Examples	Type of criteria	Examples
Technical	Reliability	Social	Status
	Durability		Social belonging
	Performance		Convention
	Style/looks		Fashion
	Comfort	Personal	Self-image
	Delivery		Risk reduction
	Convenience		Ethics
	Taste		Emotions
Economic	Price		
	Value for money		
	Running costs		
	Residual value		
	Lifecycle costs		

Economic criteria concern the cost aspects of purchase, and include price, running costs and residual values (e.g. the trade-in value of a car).

Social criteria concern the impact that the purchase makes on the person's perceived relationships with other people, and the influence of social norms on the person. The purchase of a BMW car may be based on status considerations as much as on any technical advantages over its rivals.

Social norms such as convention and fashion can also be important choice criteria, with some brands being rejected as too unconventional, although some advertisers do playfully use unconventional ideas to get their brands noticed. See Exhibit 3.3.

Personal criteria are to do with how the product or service relates to the individual psychologically. Self-image is our personal view of ourselves. Some people might view themselves as 'cool' and successful, and only buy fashion items such as Paul Smith, Superdry, Hugo Boss or Burberry clothes to reflect that perception of themselves. Risk reduction can affect choice decisions, since some people are risk averse and prefer to choose 'safe' brands; an example is the purchase of designer labels, which reduces the risk of being seen wearing unfashionable clothing. Ethical criteria can also be employed. For example, brands may be rejected because they are manufactured by companies that have offended a person's ethical code of behaviour.

Research has shown that consumers do consider ethical criteria and that a large majority enjoy buying products from companies that give something back to society (Confino and Muminova, 2011). The market for ethical products has grown in recent years. Some of the products currently deemed ethical include fairly traded foods and drinks that guarantee a fair deal to producers in developing countries. A company's *green credentials* can be confusing, though, and it is difficult for consumers to choose the 'best' products because, although organic may be seen as the greener and healthier food option, many scientific studies have cast doubts on such conclusions. Although ethical consumption is important in shaping and maintaining empowered ethical consumer identities and markets, there is much uncertainty about the choices to be made, and at times ethical trade-offs occur (e.g. products are not always organic as well as fair trade). This, in turn, generates much inconsistency with regard to what it is possible to achieve. Although people feel empowered and responsible for environmental issues at an individual level, this is coupled with the insecurity of not knowing what the 'right choices' are, and such contradictions pose huge challenges to policy-makers and marketers alike. Marketing ethics and corporate social responsibility are discussed in more detail in Chapter 5.

EXHIBIT 3.3
Snickers misspelt its advert to attract attention and drive social media impressions

EXHIBIT 3.4
Lurpak launches new product ranges using the intangible idea of new food adventures rather than the tangible product features

Emotional criteria can be important in decision-making. Many purchase decisions are experiential in that they evoke feelings such as fun, pride, or pleasure.

The importance of experiences to consumers has led to the growth in experiential consumption, as Marketing in Action 3.3 explains.

 Scan the QR code to see how Lurpak butter is using advertising creatively to promote its new product ranges in Europe.

Saab ran a two-page advertising campaign that combined technical and economic appeals with an emotional one. The first page was headlined '21 Logical Reasons to Buy a Saab'. The second page ran the headline 'One Emotional Reason'. The first page supported the headline with detailed body copy explaining the technical and economic rationale for purchase. The second page showed a Saab powering along a rain-drenched road. When a product scores well on a combination of choice criteria the outcome can be global success. For example, the success of the Apple smartphone derives from the convenience of being able to access emails and websites on the move (technical), and the status (social) and high self-image (personal) that is associated with owning one. The popularity of the iPod can also be understood by its high performance, access to a large library of music via iTunes, stylish looks (technical), affordability (economic), and the status (social) and high self-image (personal) associated with owning one.

Marketing managers need to understand the choice criteria that are being used by customers to evaluate their products and services. Such knowledge has implications for priorities in product design (e.g. are style/looks more

MARKETING IN ACTION 3.3
Experiences and Consumer Behaviour

What drives fans to pay excessive prices to see their favourite artists? Tickets for the Rolling Stones at Carnegie Hall New York were sold at $1,882 per seat; Pet Shop Boys tickets sold for £2,200 for two tickets to see the group perform live in London. Why did thousands of tickets for an Arctic Monkeys tour priced at £14 sell for over £60 each on eBay? What explains the demand for 112,000 Glastonbury Festival tickets, which took less than four hours to sell? And why did tickets for Led Zeppelin's gig at London's O2 arena sell for over £7,000 and the Rugby World Cup organizers see ticket prices rise to over 2,665 per cent more than the face value? The answer lies in the concept of experiential consumption.

A Rolling Stones or Pet Shop Boys CD can be bought for around £10, so what extra were those fans seeking that persuaded them to pay so much more for a ticket? We can imagine that the experience of seeing a favourite group play live engendered feelings of nostalgia, fun and pleasure at attending a rare event (especially as both bands only had two gigs in their tour). Fans may also have valued the experience of being with a crowd of like-minded fans, all of which would contribute to the feeling of excitement at being there.

In a world that can often seem bland, consumers are willing to pay premium prices for experiences that can arouse both positive feelings and emotions. The implications for marketers are that products that tap into this trend—such as music concerts, football matches, white-water rafting and piloting an aircraft—are likely to grow in demand in the future.

Based on: Mairs (2014); Smith (2005); Gibson (2008)

important than performance?) and the types of appeals to use in marketing communications, which should be linked to the key choice criteria used by buying centre members. Concern about store design and ambience at shops such as H&M and Zara reflects the importance of creating the right feeling or atmosphere when shopping for clothes.

Influences on Consumer Behaviour

Our discussion of *evaluation of alternatives* highlights that not all consumer decisions follow the same decision-making process, involve the same purchasers (buying centre) or use identical choice criteria. Neither do they occur at the same place or time. The consumer behaviour process, the buying centre, choice criteria, purchase situation and timing can be influenced by a number of factors: 1) the buying situation, 2) personal influences, 3) social influences (see Table 3.2).

TABLE 3.2 Influences on consumer purchasing behaviour

Areas of influence	Factors affecting decision-making	Examples of marketing implications/considerations
The buying situation	Extended problem-solving Limited problem-solving Habitual problem-solving	Level of information to provide for consumers to make informed decisions
Personal influences	Information processing Motivations Beliefs and attitudes Personality Lifestyle Lifecycle and age	Extent to which personal influences inform decision-making, e.g. an individual's perceptions can distort marketing messages; lifestyle can determine interest and opinions
Social influences	Culture Social class Geodemographics Reference groups	Extent to which social influences inform decision-making, e.g. culture can determine societal values, which might affect individual behaviour.

The buying situation

Three types of buying situation can be identified: extended problem-solving, limited problem-solving, and habitual problem-solving.

Extended problem-solving

Extended problem-solving involves a high degree of information search, and close examination of alternative solutions using many choice criteria (Neal, Quester and Hawkins, 2007). It is commonly seen in the purchase of cars, video and audio equipment, houses and expensive clothing, where it is important to make the right choice. Information search and evaluation may focus not only on which brand/model to buy but also on where to make the purchase. The potential for cognitive dissonance is greatest in this buying situation.

Extended problem-solving is usually associated with three conditions: the alternatives are differentiated and numerous; there is an adequate amount of time available for deliberation; and the purchase has a high degree of involvement (Blackwell, Miniard and Engel, 2005).

Figure 3.4 summarizes these relationships. High involvement means that the purchase is personally relevant and is seen as important with respect to basic motivations and needs (Bettman, 1982). Differentiation affects the extent of problem-solving because more comparisons need to be made and uncertainty is higher. Problem-solving is likely to be particularly extensive when all alternatives possess desirable features that others do not have. If alternatives are perceived as being similar, then less time is required in assessment.

Extended problem-solving is inhibited by time pressure. If the decision has to be made quickly, by definition the extent of problem-solving activity is curtailed. However, not all decisions follow extended problem-solving even though the alternatives may be differentiated and there is no time pressure. The decision-maker must also feel a high degree of involvement in the choice. Involvement—how personally relevant and important the choice is to the decision-maker—varies from person to person.

Research by Laurent and Kapferer (1985) identified four factors that affect involvement (Laurent and Kapferer, 1985).

1 *Self-image*: involvement is likely to be high when the decision potentially affects a person's self-image. Thus, purchase of jewellery, cars and clothing invokes more involvement than choosing a brand of soap or margarine.

2 *Perceived risk*: involvement is likely to be high when the perceived risk of making a mistake is high. The risk of buying the wrong house is much higher than that of buying the wrong chewing gum, because the potential negative consequences of the wrong decision are higher. Risk usually increases with the price of the purchase.

3 *Social factors*: when social acceptance is dependent upon making a correct choice, involvement is likely to be high. Buying of the *right* golf clubs may be highly involved, as making a *wrong* decision may affect social standing among fellow golfers; the principle may apply to clothes, trainers and other products that can affect the purchase's acceptance within a social group.

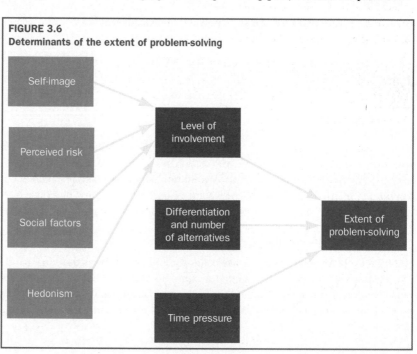

FIGURE 3.6
Determinants of the extent of problem-solving

4 *Hedonistic influences*: when the purchase is capable of providing a high degree of pleasure, involvement is usually high. The choice of restaurant when on holiday can be highly involving, since the difference between making the right or wrong choice can severely affect the amount of pleasure associated with the experience.

Marketers can help in this buying situation by providing information-rich communications—for example press advertisements, print media and websites, which are particularly suited to information-rich content—supported by a well-trained salesforce where appropriate. Increasingly, the Internet is providing consumers with more and more information, which can influence their purchase decisions. Two important sources of influence are *review* and *comparison*.

1 *Review*: this phenomenon has emerged as the role of personal recommendation and has become an integral part of the buying process. Person-to-person word of mouth has always been an important form of communication, but arguably the impact has been limited by the number of people reached by a person's review. However, it has been said that consumer review websites leverage the wisdom of the crowd (Dai et al. 2014), and this accumulated knowledge has significantly influenced buying decisions. There are now many review websites that provide aggregated consumer reviews, which increasingly play a central part in buying decisions. Such online sites include TripAdvisor (travel and tourism industry), Feefo and Epinions (retail industry), and other websites like eBay and Amazon have facilities for customers to provide feedback and comments on products and customer service.

2 *Comparison*: online consumers have the opportunity to visit websites designed to facilitate comparison. Price is often a key criterion used to influence the decision process. Comparison websites generate referrals for retailers and service providers—for example, comparethemarket.com enables consumers to compare home, car and life insurance. Comparison websites have been found to have a significant influence on consumer behaviour, both online and offline (Ong, 2011).

Table 3.3 shows how the consumer decision-making process changes between high- and low-involvement purchases.

TABLE 3.3 The consumer decision-making process and level of purchase involvement

Stage	Low involvement	High involvement
Need recognition/problem awareness	Minor	Major, *personally* important
Information search	*Limited* search	*Extensive* search
Evaluation of alternatives and the purchase	Few *alternatives* evaluated on few choice criteria	Many *alternatives* evaluated on many choice criteria
Post-purchase evaluation of the decision	*Limited* evaluation	*Extensive* evaluation including media search

Limited problem-solving

Many consumer purchases fall into the 'limited problem-solving' category. The consumer has some experience with the product in question, so an information search may be mainly internal, through memory. However, a certain amount of external search and evaluation may take place (e.g. checking prices) before purchase is made. This situation provides marketers with some opportunity to affect purchase by stimulating the need to conduct search (e.g. advertising) and reducing the risk of brand switching (e.g. warranties).

Habitual problem-solving

Habitual problem-solving occurs when a consumer repeat-buys the same product with little or no evaluation of alternatives—for example, buying the same breakfast cereal on a weekly shopping trip. The consumer may recall the satisfaction gained by purchasing a brand and automatically buy it again. Advertising may be effective in keeping the brand name in the consumer's mind and reinforcing already favourable attitudes towards it.

Personal influences

There are six personal influences on consumer behaviour: information processing, motivation, beliefs and attitudes, personality, lifestyle and lifecycle.

Information processing

Information processing refers to the process by which a stimulus is received, interpreted, stored in memory and later retrieved (Blackwell, Miniard and Engel, 2005). It is therefore the link between external influences, including marketing activities and the consumer's decision-making process. Two key aspects of information processing are perception and learning.

Perception is the complex process by which people select, organize and interpret sensory stimulation into a meaningful picture of the world (Williams, 1981). Three processes may be used to sort out the masses of stimuli that could be perceived into a manageable amount; these are selective attention, selective distortion and selective retention.

Selective attention is the process by which we screen out stimuli that are neither meaningful nor consistent with our experiences and beliefs. On entering a supermarket, there are thousands of potential stimuli (brands, point-of-sale displays, prices, etc.) to which we could pay attention. To do so would be unrealistic in terms of time and effort. Consequently we are selective in attending to these messages. Selective attention has obvious implications for advertising considering that studies have shown that consumers consciously attend to only 5–25 per cent of the advertisements to which they are exposed (Neal, Quester and Hawkins, 2007).

A number of factors influence attention. We pay more attention to stimuli that contrast with their background than to stimuli that blend with it. Computer and smartphone manufacturers use names of fruit to act as attention-grabbing brand names (e.g., Apple, BlackBerry, Raspberry Pi) because they contrast with the technologically orientated names usually associated with computers. The size, colour and movement of a stimulus also affect attention. Position is critical too. Objects placed near the centre of the visual range are more likely to be noticed than those on the periphery. This is why there is intense competition to obtain eye-level positions on supermarket shelves. We are also more likely to notice those messages that relate to our needs (benefits sought) (Ratneshwar et al., 1997) and those that provide surprises (e.g. large price reductions).

Selective distortion occurs when consumers distort the information they receive according to their existing beliefs and attitudes. We may distort information that is not in accord with our existing views. Methods of doing this include thinking that we misheard the message, and discounting the message source. Consequently, it is very important to present messages clearly without the possibility of ambiguity and to use a highly credible source, which reduces the scope for selective distortion of the message on the part of the recipient.

Distortion can occur because people interpret the same information differently. Interpretation is a process whereby messages are placed into existing categories of meaning. A cheaper price, for example, may be categorized not only as providing better value for money but also as implying lower quality. **Information framing** can affect interpretation. Framing refers to ways in which information is presented to people. Levin and Gaeth (1988) asked people to taste minced beef after telling half the sample that it was 70 per cent lean and the other half that it was 30 per cent fat. Despite the fact that the two statements are equivalent, the sample that had the information framed positively (70 per cent lean) recorded higher levels of taste satisfaction. The implications for marketing are that there is benefit in framing communication messages in a positive manner.

Words, images, colours and even smell can influence interpretations. For example, blue and green are viewed as cool, and evoke feelings of security. Red and yellow are regarded as warm and cheerful. Black is seen as an indication of strength. By using the appropriate colour in pack design it is possible to affect the consumer's feelings about the product. Marketers often base complete branding concepts on colour. The Virgin group uses 'red' throughout its branding. Smell can influence interpretation. For example, British Airways announced its intention to introduce a new fragrance and by doing so recreate a uniform experience for travellers, similar to walking into an expensive department store (Anon, 2011). Singapore Airlines has been using the aroma created by the infusion of Stefan Floridian Waters cologne into its hot towels and cabins for many years. The fragrance receives consistently positive feedback from passengers and is described as exotic and feminine. Singapore Airlines was the first airline to market itself through a sensory experience appealing to the emotions, as opposed to using the approach of its competitors, which emphasized price, food and comfort (Lindstrom, 2005).

Selective retention refers to the fact that only a selection of messages may be retained in memory. We tend to remember messages that are in line with existing beliefs and attitudes. In an experiment, 12 statements were given to a group of Labour and Conservative supporters. Six of the statements were favourable to Labour and six to the Conservatives. The group members were asked to remember the statements and to return after seven days. The result was that Labour supporters remembered the statements that were favourable to Labour and Conservative supporters remembered the pro-Conservative statements. Selective retention has a role to play in reducing cognitive dissonance: when reading reviews of a recently purchased car, positive messages are more likely to be remembered than negative ones.

Learning is any change in the content or organization of long-term memory, and is the result of information processing (Neal, Quester and Hawkins, 2007). There are numerous ways in which learning can take place. These include *conditioning* and *cognitive learning*. **Classical conditioning** is the process of using an established relationship between a stimulus and response to cause the learning of the same response to a different stimulus. Thus, in advertising, humour, which is known to elicit a pleasurable response, may be used in the belief that these favourable feelings will carry over to the product. Red Bull is a brand that benefits from such associations. The humour in its advertising conveys a fun image, and the promotion of Red Bull on the body of racing cars projects the feeling of excitement for the brand by association.

Operant conditioning differs from classical conditioning by way of the role and timing of the reinforcement. In this case, reinforcement results from rewards: the more rewarding the response, the stronger the likelihood of the purchase being repeated. Operant conditioning occurs as a result of product trial. The use of free samples is based on the principles of operant conditioning. For example, free samples of a new shampoo may be distributed to a large number of households. This means the shampoo can be used (desired response) without making an initial purchase. Olay introduced its body wash using this tactic. The rewards for the consumer are that they benefit by experiencing the desirable properties of the product at no cost. These experiences can then reinforce the likelihood of the consumer making a purchase. Thus, the sequence of events is different between classical and operant conditioning. In classic conditioning, liking precedes trial, whereas in operant conditioning, trial precedes liking.

For marketers, introducing a series of rewards (reinforcements) may encourage repeat buying of a product. A free sample may be accompanied by a coupon to buy the product at a discounted rate (reinforcement). On the pack may be another discount coupon to encourage repeat buying. After this purchase, the product relies on its own intrinsic reward—product performance—to encourage purchase. This process is known as *shaping*. Repeat purchase behaviour will have been shaped by the application of repeated reinforcers so that the consumer will have learned that buying the product is associated with pleasurable experiences.

Cognitive learning involves the learning of knowledge and development of beliefs and attitudes without direct reinforcement. **Rote learning** involves the learning of two or more concepts without conditioning. Having seen the headline 'Lemsip is for flu attacks' the consumer may remember that Lemsip is a remedy for flu attacks without the kinds of conditioning and reinforcement previously discussed.

Vicarious learning involves learning from others without direct experience or reward. It is the promise of the reward that motivates. Thus, we may learn the type of clothes that attract potential admirers by observing other people. In advertising, the 'admiring glance' can be used to signal approval of the type of clothing being worn. We imagine that the same may happen to us if we dress in a similar way.

Reasoning is a more complex form of cognitive learning and is usually associated with high-involvement situations. For example, some advertising messages rely on the recipient to draw their own conclusions through reasoning.

Whichever type of learning has taken place, the result of the learning process is the creation of *product positioning*. The market objective is to create a clear and favourable position in the mind of the consumer (Ries and Trout, 2001).

The ways in which consumers process information are highly complex, and whilst extensive research has been done in this field, the use of technology is creating opportunities for marketers to learn so much more about how consumers behave—and in a real-time basis. Online-tracking mechanisms such as super cookies, browser fingerprinting and behavioural tracking provide detailed information about what happens online. All a customer has to do is visit a retailer's e-commerce website, and the retailer has information about age, gender and physical location, and an estimation of income, without any input from the customer (O'Rourke, 2014). This monitoring of behaviour does not end online. Tracking through mobile phones and the use of Apple's iBeacon technology means that customers can be pinpointed within a few feet, and eye-tracking applications enable marketers to even know what we are looking at. Another technological technique that holds great potential for understanding how consumers process information is neuroscience, as Marketing in Action 3.4 discusses.

Motivation

An understanding of motivation lies in the relationship between needs, drives and goals (Luthans, 2001). The basic process involves needs (deprivations) that set drives in motion (deprivations with direction) to accomplish goals (anything that alleviates a need and reduces a drive). Maslow's hierarchy of needs model has been widely used in management education, but you should be aware that it was devised in the mid-20th century and centred on American society, where individualism was very important, especially to the *middle classes* (Bennet, 2011). Arguably, this is rather one-dimensional, as the model does not accommodate the influence of others—for example family, children, work colleagues, society—on an individual's motivation. According to Pinder (1998), 'Motivation is a force that prompts action and relates to conscious or unconscious decision involving how, when, and why to allocate effort to a task or activity' (Eysenck and Eysenck, 1985). The question of why people buy is complex; the discussion of choice criteria links to motivation and can explain why one consumer may choose a Nissan car because they are price conscious while another may choose a Mercedes because they are status conscious. The influence of personality may explain the motivations that underpin why an extrovert may choose a red sports car while an introvert may prefer a grey Skoda.

It is important to note that levels of motivation vary depending on the individual, the type of purchase and the purchase occasion. For example, the motivations for buying luxury goods focus on motives such as the desire to portray a specific social class, communicate a desired self-image and provide self-concept reinforcement, a visible proof that the consumer can afford higher priced products (Nwankwo, Hamelin and Khaled, 2014). So it is important to understand the motives that drive consumers in a wider context, particularly as motives can determine choice criteria and subsequently enable marketers get closer to their customers. For example, a consumer who is driven by the esteem and status motive may use self-image as a key choice criterion when considering the purchase of a car or clothes. Increasingly, technology is used to get inside the mind of the consumer and to develop more understanding of what drives consumer choice.

 Scan the QR code to see how Marmite 'lovers' are reminded not to neglect the brand.

Beliefs and attitudes

A *belief* is a thought that a person holds about something. In a marketing context, it is a thought about a product or service on one or more choice criteria. Beliefs about a Volvo car might be that it is safe, reliable and high status. Marketing people are very interested in consumer beliefs because they are related to attitudes. In particular, misconceptions about products can be harmful to brand sales. Duracell batteries were believed by consumers to last three times as long as Eveready batteries, but in continuous use they lasted over six times as long. This prompted Duracell to launch an advertising campaign to correct this misconception. The promotion for Marmite crisps recognizes that the beliefs of some consumers will be favourable towards the brand and others negative. By presenting the brand in this way, the advertisement is inviting consumers to try the crisps to discover which group they are in.

An *attitude* is an overall favourable or unfavourable evaluation of a product or service. The consequence of a set of beliefs may be a positive or negative attitude towards the product or service. Beliefs and attitudes play an important part in the evaluation of alternatives in the consumer decision-making process. They may be developed as part of the information search activity and/or as a result of product use, and play an important role in product design (matching product attributes to beliefs and attitudes); in persuasive communications (reinforcing existing positive beliefs and attitudes, correcting misconceptions and establishing new beliefs, for example 'Skoda is a quality car brand'); and in pricing (matching price with customers' beliefs about what a 'good' product would cost).

Personality

Our everyday dealings with people tell us that they differ enormously in their personalities. **Personality** is the inner psychological characteristics of individuals that lead to consistent responses to their environment (Kassarjan, 1971). A person may tend to be warm–cold, dominant–subservient, introvert–extrovert, sociable–loner, adaptable–inflexible, competitive–cooperative, etc. If we find from marketing research that our product is being purchased by people with a certain personality profile, then advertising could show people of the same type using the product.

MARKETING IN ACTION 3.4
Technology Delivers Consumer Insights, and Age of Neuromarketing is Here

Which image would you choose to sell milk?

According to one of the world's leading neuromarketing experts, Dr. A. K. Pradeep, when consumers are asked to choose 'the one that always wins out is the cow'. He suggests the underlying reasoning is that the source of a product hits a spot deep in the subconscious which is more evocative than any of the other associated images. Pradeep says that neuroscience allows marketers to find out what a brand means in the subconscious mind. One brand that he feels understands how to 'market to the buying brain' is Jo Malone. This perfume brand uses images of ingredients to trigger positive emotions, which he advocates are far more powerful than images of a man and woman in passionate embraces.

Dr. A. K. Pradeep is not the only advocate for using technology to understand consumer behaviour. Professor O'Rourke has made a stand, and his advice to marketers looking to determine insights into consumer behaviour is to 'ditch simplistic surveys' and use instead behavioural tracking and neuroscience. Increasingly, technology is providing insights into consumer behaviour using eyetracking and electroencephalography (EEG) tests, which involve measuring brains signals. For marketers, the key question is how consumers process information, because it sheds light on how they make purchasing choices—for example, what clothes we buy or what music we like to listen to. Potentially, neuroscience and the study of the brain and nervous system by means of functional magnetic resonance imaging (FMRI) scanning and EEG tests has all the answers. The brain is made up of networks of neurons. When these cell clusters are stimulated, they use more energy. These active areas light up on FMRI scans, allowing researchers to map emotion and cognition. The scanner produces a colour-coded image of the brain that is helpful in revealing a person's unconscious feelings about a brand, an advertisement, or even a media channel. For example, an understanding of the effects of different media channels (e.g. print versus the Internet) on brain stimulation have been found to be useful when making media decisions. This application of the techniques of neuroscience to marketing is called neuromarketing.

Neuromarketing advocates like O'Rouke and Pradeep argue that it is an objective tool that scientifically demonstrates and quantifies human reactions and provides new insights into how people process information. However, sceptics still counter that it has not revealed huge insights into human behaviour that are not already instinctively known and many brands still rely on surveys and focus group. As applications of neuromarketing develop, the truth about its worth to marketers will be revealed.

Based on: McCormick (2011); Lovell (2008); O'Rourke (2014); Hannaford (2013)

The concept of personality is also relevant to brands. *Brand personality* is their characterization as perceived by consumers. Brands may be characterized as 'for young people' (Tommy Hilfiger), 'for winners' (Nike), or 'intelligent' (Toyota iQ). This is a dimension over and above the physical (e.g. colour) or functional (e.g. taste) attributes of a brand. By creating a brand personality, a marketer may create appeal to people who value that characterization.

Economic circumstances

During periods of economic growth, consumer spending is fuelled by rising income levels and confidence in job security. Products that are the subject of discretionary spending, such as luxury brands, expensive holidays, restaurant meals and top-of-the-range consumer durables, thrive. However, changing economic circumstances—such as recession, deflation, inflation, and fears about employment prospects—drive many consumers to postpone purchases, become more price sensitive and change their shopping habits. Economic circumstances, therefore, can have a major effect on consumer behaviour.

Lifestyle

Lifestyle patterns have attracted much attention from marketing research practitioners. **Lifestyle** refers to the pattern of living as expressed in a person's activities, interests and opinions. Lifestyle analysis (psychographics) groups consumers according to their beliefs, activities, values, and demographic characteristics such as education and income. For example, the advertising agency Young & Rubicam has identified the following major lifestyle groups that can be found throughout Europe and the USA.

1 *The mainstreamers*: the largest group. Attitudes include conventional, trusting, cautious and family centred. Leisure activities include spectator sports and gardening; purchase behaviour is habitual, brand loyal and in approved stores.
2 *The aspirers*: members of this group tend to be ambitious, suspicious and unhappy. Leisure activities include trendy sports and fashion magazines; they buy fads, are impulse shoppers and engage in conspicuous consumption.
3 *The succeeders*: these people are leaders, industrious, confident and happy. Leisure activities include travel, sports, sailing and dining out. Purchase decisions are based on choice criteria such as quality, status and luxury.
4 *The transitionals*: members of this group are liberal, rebellious, self-expressive and intuitive. They have unconventional tastes in music, travel and movies; and enjoy cooking, and arts and crafts. Shopping behaviour tends to be impulsive and to involve unique products.
5 *The reformers*: these people are self-confident and involved, have broad interests and are issues orientated. They like reading, cultural events, intelligent games and educational TV. They have eclectic tastes, enjoy natural foods, and are concerned about authenticity and ecology.
6 *The struggling poor*: members of this group are unhappy, suspicious and feel left out. Their interests are in sports, music and television; their purchase behaviour tends to be price-based, and they are looking for instant gratification.
7 *The resigned poor*: people in this group are unhappy, isolated and insecure. Television is their main leisure activity and their shopping behaviour is price-based, although they also look for the reassurance of branded goods.

Lifestyle analysis has implications for marketing since lifestyles have been found to correlate with purchasing behaviour (O'Brien and Ford, 1988). A company may choose to target a particular lifestyle group (e.g. the succeeders) with a product offering, and use communications which reflect the values and beliefs of this group. An example of how changing lifestyles affect consumer behaviour is the popularity of on-the-go products with people who live very busy lives. On-the-go drinks, such as bottled water and takeaway coffee, and on-the-go food, such as cereal-based breakfast snack bars, have found favour among time-pressured consumers.

Lifecycle and age

Consumer behaviour might depend on the stages reached during their lives. A person's *lifecycle stage* (shown in Figure 3.7) is relevant since disposable income and purchase requirements may vary according to stage. For example, young couples with no children may have high disposable income if both work, and may be heavy purchasers of home furnishings and appliances since they may be setting up home. When they have children, disposable income may fall, particularly if they become a single-income family and the purchase of baby- and child-related products increases. At the empty-nester stage, disposable income may rise due to the absence of dependent children, low mortgage repayments and high personal income. This type of person may be a high-potential target for financial services and holidays. BMW uses lifecycle stage to segment consumers with its 4 × 4 X5 model targeted at young couples with children, and the 4 × 4 X6 model targeted at empty nesters. The

FIGURE 3.7
Lifecycle stages

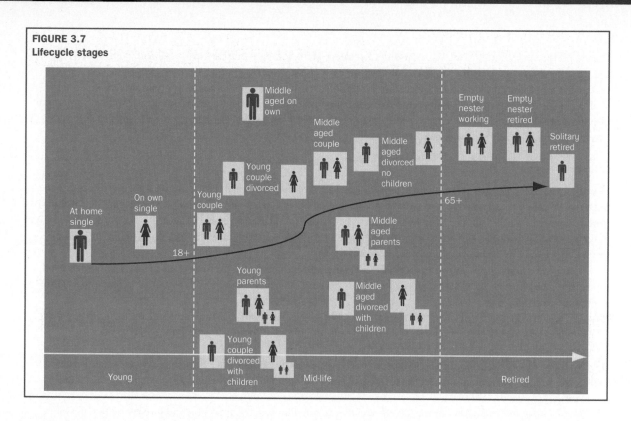

X6 is designed for someone who previously owned an X5 or something similar, but now is looking for an SUV that 'doesn't scream "family"' (Smith, 2008).

However, not all people follow the classic family lifecycle stages. Figure 3.7 also shows alternative paths that may have consumer behaviour and market segmentation implications.

Age is an effective discriminator of consumer behaviour. For example, young people have very different tastes in product categories such as clothing, drinks, holidays and television viewing compared to older people. The young have always been a prime target for marketers because of their capacity to spend.

Social influences

There are four social influences on consumer behaviour: culture, social class, geodemographics and reference groups.

Culture Culture refers to the traditions, taboos, values and basic attitudes of the whole society within which an individual lives. It provides the framework within which individuals and their lifestyles develop. Cultural norms are the rules that govern behaviour, and are based upon values: beliefs about what attitudes and behaviour are desirable. Conformity to norms is created by reward-giving (e.g. smiling) and sanctioning (e.g. criticism). Cultural values affect how business is conducted. Culture also affects consumption behaviour.

The spread of global communications technology and greater global mobility has led to a degree of social and cultural convergence. This does not mean that a global culture is replacing the diversity of local and national cultures in the world.

Social class Social class has long been regarded as an important determinant of consumer behaviour. In the UK it is largely based on occupation, and respondents to marketing research surveys are often classified in this way. Advertising media (e.g. newspapers) usually give readership/ viewership figures broken down by social class groupings. Every country has its own method of grouping and, in the UK, the National Statistics Socio-economic Classification system identifies eight categories based on occupation (see Table 3.4).

The implication is that social class is a predictive measure of consumption although consumption patterns are likely to vary within each of the groups (e.g. some people may be more inclined to spend their money on consumer durables, while others may have more hedonistic preferences). It is important to note that the influence of social class should be tempered by lifecycle, lifestyle and age.

TABLE 3.4 Social class categories		
Classification	**Descriptors**	**Occupations**
1	Higher managerial and professional occupations	Senior managers, directors and professionals
2	Traditional professional occupations	Higher technical and supervisory occupations, e.g. department managers
3	Modern professional Middle junior manager	Clerical/administrative, sales/service, technical/auxiliary and engineering occupations
4	Intermediate occupations	Non-professional and agricultural occupations, and self-employed sole traders
5	Technical craft worker	Technical craft and process operative occupations, e.g. shift manager in a factory
6	Semi-routine occupations	Service and technical operatives, agricultural, clerical and childcare occupations
7	Routine occupations	Production, technical, operative and agricultural occupations
8	Never worked	Never worked, long-term unemployed and students

Geodemographics   Another method of classifying households is based on geographic location. This analysis—called **geodemographics**—is based on population census data. Households are grouped into geographic clusters based on information such as type of accommodation, car ownership, age, occupation, number and age of children, and ethnicity. These clusters can be identified by postcodes, which makes targeting by mail easier. A number of systems are used in the UK, including MOSAIC and ACORN (A Classification Of Residential Neighbourhoods). The ACORN system identified 11 neighbourhood types (discussed in more detail in Chapter 7) which can be used for market segmentation and positioning. Geodemographics is an effective method of segmenting many markets

Reference groups   The term **reference group** indicates a group of people that influences an individual's attitude or behaviour. Where a product is conspicuous—for example, clothing or cars—the brand or model chosen may have been strongly influenced by what buyers perceive as acceptable to their reference group. This group may consist of family members, a group of friends or work colleagues. Some reference groups may be formal (e.g. members of a club or society), while others may be informal (friends with similar interests). Reference groups influence their members by the roles and norms expected of them. For example, students may have to play several roles: to lecturers, the student's role may be that of learner; to other students, their role may vary from peer to social companion. Depending on the role, various behaviours may be expected based upon group norms. To the extent that group norms influence values and attitudes, these reference groups may be seen as an important determinant of behaviour. Sometimes reference group norms can conflict, as when reference to the learning role suggests different patterns of behaviour from that of social companion. In terms of consumption, reference group influence can affect student purchasing of clothing, beverages, social events and textbooks, for example. The more conspicuous the choice is to the reference group, the stronger its influence.

There are two main types of reference group: membership and aspirant groups. *Membership groups* are the groups to which a person already belongs. What is believed to be suitable, acceptable and/or impressive to this group may play a major role in consumption behaviour. What other people think at a party, at work or generally socializing is of great importance. *Aspirant groups* are the groups to which the individual would like to belong. Stereotypically, men supposedly want to look/feel like their favourite sport stars and women want to look/feel like famous film stars or models. This motivates the purchase of football shirts with 'Ronaldo' on the back, and the buying of clothing seen to be worn by Adele or Kate Moss. ASOS, the online fashion retailer, bases its marketing strategy on aspirant group theory. It copies the style of clothing worn by film stars and models, and sells its clothes to aspirant women who wish to dress like them. Celebrities such as David Beckham, Ronaldo, Kate Moss and Angelina Jolie also act as opinion leaders to aspirant group members, influencing their consumption behaviour.

When you have read this chapter

Discover further resources and test your understanding: McGraw-Hill **Connect**™ is a digital teaching and learning environment that improves performance over a variety of critical outcomes; it can be tailored, is easy to use and is proven effective. **LearnSmart**™ is the most widely used and intelligent adaptive learning resource that is proven to strengthen memory recall, improve course retention and boost grades. Fuelled by **LearnSmart**™, **SmartBook**™ is the first and only adaptive reading experience available today.

Review

1 **The dimensions of buyer behaviour**
   - Looking at the dimensions of the buying decision: how they buy, what their choice criteria are, where they buy and when they buy, helps identify what is important and has implications for the marketing mix.

2 **The role of the buying centre (who buys) and its implications**
   - Some buying decisions are made individually, others by a group. A group decision may be in the hands of a buying centre with up to five roles: initiator, influencer, decider, buyer and user. The interaction between these roles determines whether a purchase is made.
   - Marketers need to understand the formulation of buying groups as this can be helpful in targeting and segmenting of markets, and planning the core strategy.

3 **The consumer decision-making process (how people buy)**
   - The decision to purchase a consumer product may pass through a number of stages: need recognition/problem awareness, information search, evaluation of alternatives, purchase, and post-purchase evaluation of the decision.

4 **The marketing implications of the consumer decision-making process**
   Each stage in the process potentially has implications for marketing managers:
   - *Need recognition*: awareness of consumer problems can create opportunities for building a competitive advantage and planning strategies to overcome any *need* inhibitors; stimulating need recognition through marketing communications might help initiate the decision-making process.
   - *Information search*: where consumers look for information to help solve their decision-making can aid marketing planning. Communication can direct consumers to suitable sources of information. One objective is to ensure that the company's brand appears in the consumer's awareness set.

- *Evaluation of alternatives*: when a consumer is highly involved, they might require much information about the positives of making a particular buying decision. In this situation it is important to provide sufficiently detailed information to aid decision-making. For low-involvement decisions, creating top-of-mind awareness through repetitive advertising and trial (e.g. through sales promotion) can aid the decision-making. For all consumer decisions, marketing managers must understand the choice criteria used to evaluate brands, including the importance of emotion.
- *Post-purchase evaluation*: consumers can experience cognitive dissonance after making a purchase and might need reassurance. Advertisements, direct mail or reviews and other communications can act as positive reinforcers.

5 **The differences in evaluation of high- versus low-involvement situations**
  - *High-involvement situations*: the consumer is more likely to carry out extensive evaluation and take into account beliefs about the perceived consequences of buying the brand, the extent to which important others believe they should or should not buy the brand, attitudes (which are the degree to which the consumer likes or dislikes the brand overall), and subjective norms (which form an overall evaluation of the degree to which important others approve or disapprove of the purchase).
  - *Low-involvement situations*: the consumer carries out a simple evaluation and uses simple choice tactics to reduce time and effort. Awareness precedes trial, which, if satisfactory, leads to repeat purchase. The behaviour may become habitual, with little conscious thought or formation of attitudes before purchase.

6 **The nature of choice criteria (what are used) and their implications**
  - Choice criteria are the various attributes (and benefits) a consumer uses when evaluating products and services. These may be technical (e.g. reliability), economic (e.g. price), social (e.g. status) or personal (e.g. self-image).
  - The implications are that knowledge of the choice criteria used by members of the buying centre aids product design (e.g. are style/looks more important than performance?) and the choice of the appeals to use in advertising and personal selling, which should be linked to the key choice criteria used by those members.

7 **The influences on consumer behaviour—the buying situation, personal and social influences—and implications for marketing**
  - *Buying situation*: the three types are extended problem-solving, limited problem-solving and habitual problem-solving. The marketing implications for each type are: extended problem-solving—provide information-rich communications; limited problem-solving—stimulate the need to conduct a search (when their brand is not currently bought) or reduce the risk of brand switching; habitual problem-solving—repetitive advertising should be used to create awareness and reinforce already favourable attitudes.
  - *Personal influences*: the six types are information processing, motivation, beliefs and attitudes, personality, lifestyle, and lifecycle and age, and have implications for marketing:
    1) *Information processing* involves perceptions and learning.
       Perceptions help consumers sort out the masses of stimuli into manageable amounts of information through processes called: i) *selective attention* (which implies that advertisements, logos and packaging need to be attention-getting); ii) *selective distortion* (which implies that messages should be presented clearly, using a credible source and with supporting evidence); iii) *selective retention* (which implies that messages that are in line with existing beliefs and attitudes are more likely to be remembered).
       Learning involves conditioning and cognitive learning. *Conditioning* suggests that associating a brand with humour (e.g. in advertisements) or excitement (e.g. motor racing sponsorship) will carry over to the brand, and also that the use of free samples and coupons (reinforcers) can encourage sales by inducing trial and repeat buying. Through the reinforcers the consumer will have learnt to associate the brand with pleasurable experiences.
       Cognitive learning suggests that statements in an advertisement may be remembered, the promise of a reward may influence behaviour, as may communications that allow the recipient to draw his/her own conclusions. The result of the learning process is the creation of product positioning.
    2) *Motives* influence choice criteria and include physiological, safety, belongingness and love, esteem and status, and self-actualization.

3) *Beliefs* and attitudes are linked in that the consequence of a set of beliefs may be a positive or negative attitude. Marketers attempt to match product attributes to desired beliefs and attitudes, and use communications to influence these and establish new beliefs.

4) *Personality* of the type of person who buys a brand may be reflected in the type of person used in its advertisements. Brand personality is used to appeal to people who identify with that characterization.

5) *Lifestyles* have been shown to be linked to purchase behaviour. Lifestyle groups can be used for market segmentation and targeting purposes.

6) *Lifecycle and age* stage may affect consumer behaviour as the level of disposable income and purchase requirements (needs) may depend on the stage that people have reached during their life. For similar reasons, age may affect consumer behaviour.

- There are four types of social influence: culture, social class, geodemographics and reference groups.

1) *Culture* affects how business is conducted and consumption behaviour. Marketers have to adjust their behaviour and the marketing mix to accommodate different cultures.

2) *Social class* can predict some consumption patterns, and so can be used for market segmentation and targeting purposes.

3) *Geodemographics* classifies consumers according to their location, and is used for market segmentation and targeting purposes.

4) *Reference groups* influence their members by the roles and norms expected of them. Marketers attempt to make their brands acceptable to reference groups, and target opinion leaders to gain brand acceptability.

Key Terms

attitude the degree to which a customer or prospect likes or dislikes a brand

awareness set the set of brands that the consumer is aware may provide a solution to the problem

beliefs descriptive thoughts that a person holds about something

buyers generally refers to professionals in procurement. A buyer makes business decisions on purchasing

buying centre a group that is involved in the buying decision (also known as a *decision-making unit*)

choice criteria the various attributes (and benefits) people use when evaluating products and services

classical conditioning the process of using an established relationship between a stimulus and a response to cause the learning of the same response to a different stimulus

cognitive dissonance post-purchase concerns of a consumer arising from uncertainty as to whether a decision to purchase was the correct one

cognitive learning the learning of knowledge and development of beliefs and attitudes without direct reinforcement

consumer a person who buys goods and services for personal use

consumer decision-making process the stages a consumer goes through when buying something—namely, problem awareness, information search,

evaluation of alternatives, purchase and post-purchase evaluation

customers a term used in both consumer and organizational purchasing situations. These are individuals and companies that have an established relationship with a seller (e.g. retailers, producers, manufacturers)

evoked set the set of brands that the consumer seriously evaluates before making a purchase

geodemographics the process of grouping households into geographic clusters based on information such as type of accommodation, occupation, number and age of children, and ethnic background

information framing the way in which information is presented to people

information processing the process by which a stimulus is received, interpreted, stored in memory and later retrieved

information search the identification of alternative ways of problem-solving

learning any change in the content or organization of long-term memory as the result of information processing

lifestyle the pattern of living as expressed in a person's activities, interests and opinions

motivation the process involving needs that set drives in motion to accomplish goals

operant conditioning the use of rewards to generate reinforcement of response

perception the process by which people select, organize and interpret sensory stimulation into a meaningful picture of the world

personality the inner psychological characteristics of individuals that lead to consistent responses to their environment

reasoning a more complex form of cognitive learning where conclusions are reached by connected thought

reference group a group of people that influences an individual's attitude or behaviour

rote learning the learning of two or more concepts without conditioning

selective attention the process by which people screen out those stimuli that are neither meaningful to them nor consistent with their experiences and beliefs

selective distortion the distortion of information received by people according to their existing beliefs and attitudes

selective retention the process by which people only retain a selection of messages in memory

vicarious learning learning from others without direct experience or reward

Study Questions

1. Choose a recent purchase which involved you and other people in the decision-making. Explain what role(s) you played in the buying centre. What roles did these other people play and how did they influence your choice?

2. What decision-making process did you go through? At each stage (need recognition, information search, etc.), try to remember what you were thinking about and what activities took place.

3. What choice criteria did you use? Did they change between drawing up a shortlist and making the final choice?

4. Think of the last time you made an impulse purchase. What stimulated you to buy? Have you bought the brand again? Why or why not? Did your thoughts and actions resemble those suggested by the Ehrenberg and Goodhart model?

5. Can you think of a brand that has used the principles of classical conditioning in its advertising?

6. Are there any brands that you buy (e.g. fragrances, fashion, cars) that have personalities that match your own?

7. To what kind of lifestyle do you aspire? How does this affect the types of product (particularly visible ones) you buy now and in the future?

8. Are you influenced by any reference groups? How do these groups influence what you buy?

Recommended Reading

Bridger, D. (2015) *Decoding the Irrational Consumer*, London: Kogan Page.

Harvard Business School: Thinking that leads, Marketing–consumer behaviour http://hbswk.hbs.edu/topics/marketing.html

Sheth, J. N., B. I. Newman and B. L. Gross (1991) Why we buy what we buy: a theory of consumption values, *Journal of Business Research* 22 (2), 159–70.

Solomon M. R., G. Bamossy, S. Askegaard and M. K. Hogg (2013) *Consumer Behaviour: A European Perspective*, 5th Edition, Prentice Hall.

Spenner, P. and K. Freeman (2012) To keep your customers, keep it simple, *Harvard Business Review* 90 (5), 108–14.

Wells, V. (2014) Behavioural psychology, marketing and consumer behaviour: a literature review and future research agenda, *Journal of Marketing Management* 30 (11–12), 1119–58.

References

Ajzen, I. (1985) From intentions to actions: A theory of planned behaviour, in Kuhl, J. B. J. (ed.) *Action-control: From cognition to behaviour*, Springer, 11–39.

Ajzen, I. (1991) The theory of planned behavior, *Organizational Behavior and Human Decision Processes* 50, 179–211.

Ajzen, I. (2012) The theory of planned behaviour, in Van Lange, P.A.M., A.W. Kruglanski and E.T. Higgins (eds.), *Handbook of theories of social psychology*, Vol. 1, 438–59, London, UK: Sage.

Ajzen, I. and M. Fishbein (1980) *Understanding Attitudes and Predicting Social Behaviour*, Englewood Cliffs, NJ: Prentice-Hall.

Ajzen, I. and T. Madden (1985) Prediction of Goal-Directed Behaviour: Attitudes, Intentions, *Journal of Experimental Social Psychology* 22, 453–74.

Anon (2011) Fragrance of flight planned to improve cabin experience. http://www.independent.co.uk/travel/news-and-advice/fragrance-of-flight-planned-to-improve-cabin-experience-2344095.html (accessed May 2015).

Barda, T. (2011) Beer Googles, *The Marketer*, April, 20–22.

Baumgartner, H. and J. Bem Steenkamp (1996) Exploratory Consumer Buying Behaviour: Conceptualisation and Measurement, *International Journal of Research in Marketing* 13, 121–37.

Bennet, B. (2011) Another criticism of Maslow's hierarchy of needs. http://billbennett.co.nz/2011/07/02/criticism-maslows-hierarchy

Bettman, J. R. (1982) A Functional Analysis of the Role of Overall Evaluation of Alternatives and Choice Processes, in Mitchell, A. (ed.) *Advances in Consumer Research 8*, Ann Arbor, Michigan: Association for Consumer Research, 87–93.

Blackwell, R. D., P. W. Miniard and J. F. Engel (2005) *Consumer Behaviour*, Orlando, FL: Dryden.

Budd, R. J. and C. P. Spencer (1984) Predicting Undergraduates' Intentions to Drink, *Journal of Studies on Alcohol* 45(2), 179–83

Confino, J., and O. Muminova (2011). What motivates consumers to make ethically conscious decisions? *The Guardian*, 11 August. http://www.theguardian.com/sustainable-business/motivates-consumers-environmental-ethical-decisions (accessed 23 February 2015).

Costa, A. I. A., D. Schoolmeester, M. Dekker and W. M. F. Jongen (2007) To cook or not to cook: A means-end study of motives for choice of meal solutions, *Food Quality and Preference* 18, 77–88.

Creusen, M. E. H. and J. P. L. Schoormans (1997) The Nature of Differences between Similarity and Preference Judgements: A Replication and Extension, *International Journal of Research in Marketing* 14, 81–7.

Dai, W., J. Lee, G. Lee and M. Luca (2014) *Optimal Aggregation of Consumer Ratings: An Application to Yelp.com.* http://www.people.hbs.edu/mluca/OptimalAggregation.pdf

Davies, M. A. P. and L. T. Wright (1994) The Importance of Labelling Examined in Food Marketing, *European Journal of Marketing* 28 (2), 57–67.

Ehrenberg, A. S. C. and G. J. Goodhart (1980) *How Advertising Works*, J. Walter Thompson/MRCA.

Elliott, R. (1997) Understanding Buyers: Implications for Selling, in D. Jobber (ed.) *The CIM Handbook of Selling and Sales Strategy*, Oxford: Butterworth-Heinemann.

Elliott, R. (1998) A Model of Emotion-Driven Choice, *Journal of Marketing Management* 14, 95–108.

Elliott, R. and E. Hamilton (1991) Consumer Choice Tactics and Leisure Activities, *International Journal of Advertising* 10, 325–32.

Euromonitor (2014) *Chocolate Confectionery in the United Kingdom*, Euromonitor International, September. http://www.euromonitor.com/chocolate-confectionery-in-the-united-kingdom/report (accessed 28 February 2015).

Eysenck, H. J. and M. W. Eysenck (1985) *Personality and individual differences*, New York: Plenum.

Farley, J., D. Lehman and M. Ryan (1981) Generalizing from 'Imperfect' Replication, *Journal of Business* 54(4), 597–610

Gibson, O. (2008) Led Zep Tickets Fetch £7425 as Online 'Touts' Strike Gold in £200m Bonanza, *The Guardian*, 8 January, 13.

Groupon (2015) About Groupon. http://www.groupon.co.uk/about (accessed 23 February 2015).

Hannaford, A. (2013). 'Neuromarketing': Can science predict what we'll buy? *The Telegraph*, 13 April. http://www.telegraph.co.uk/news/science/science-news/9984498/Neuromarketing-can-science-predict-what-well-buy.html (accessed 23 February 2015).

Hegarty, J. (2011) *Hegarty on Advertising: turning intelligence into magic*, London: Thames & Hudson, 43.

Kassarjan, H. H. (1971) Personality and Consumer Behaviour Economics: A Review, *Journal of Marketing Research*, November, 409–18.

Kuusela, H., M. T. Spence and A. J. Kanto (1998) Expertise Effects on Prechoice Decision Processes and Final Outcomes: A Protocol Analysis, *European Journal of Marketing* 32(5/6), 559–76.

Laurent, G. and J. N. Kapferer (1985) Measuring Consumer Involvement Profiles, *Journal of Marketing Research* 12 (February), 41–53.

Levin, L. P. and G. J. Gaeth (1988) Framing of Attribute Information Before and After Consuming the Product, *Journal of Consumer Research* 15 (December), 374–78.

Lindstrom, M. (2005) Sensing the Opportunity, *The Marketeer*, February, 4–17.

Lovell, C. (2008) Is Neuroscience Making a Difference?, *Campaign*, 3 October, 11.

Luo, X., M. Andrews, Y. Song and J. Aspara (2014). Group-Buying Deal Popularity, *Journal of Marketing* 78 (2), 20–33.

Luthans, F. (2001) *Organisational Behaviour*, San Francisco: McGraw-Hill.

Mairs, G. (2014) Rugby World Cup tickets: prices hit record levels amid fears touts will hold fans to ransome, *The Telegraph*, 27 October. http://www.telegraph.co.uk/sport/rugbyunion/rugby-world-cup/11189239/Rugby-World-Cup-tickets-Prices-hit-record-levels-amid-fears-touts-will-hold-fans-to-ransom.html (accessed 23 February 2015).

McCormick, A. (2011) Marketing on the brain, *Marketing*, 2 November, 24–5.

McSherry, M. (2015) Hershey's lawsuit sparks British revolt for 'superior' Cadbury chocolate, *The Guardian*, 27 January. http://www.theguardian.com/business/2015/jan/27/hersheys-lawsuit-ban-imported-cadbury-from-us (accessed 26 February 2015).

Microsoft (2012) The Evolution of Pre-family Man, http://advertising.microsoft.com/europe/WWDocs/User/Europe/ResearchLibrary/ResearchReport/8.%20The%20Evolution%20of%20Pre-family%20man.pdf

Neal, C., P. Quester and D. I. Hawkins (2007) *Consumer Behaviour: Implications for Marketing Strategy*, Boston, Mass: Irwin.

Nwankwo, S., N. Hamelin and M. Khaled (2014). Consumer values, motivation and purchase intention for luxury goods, *Journal of Retailing and Consumer Services* 21 (5), 735–44.

O'Brien, S. and R. Ford (1988) Can We at Last Say Goodbye to Social Class?, *Journal of the Market Research Society* 30(3), 289–332.

O'Rourke, D. (2014). Behavioural tracking and neuroscience are tools for sustainable innovation, *The Guardian*, 25 July. http://www.theguardian.com/sustainable-business/behavioural-insights/behavioural-tracking-neuroscience-tools-sustainable-innovation-advertising-marketing-consumers (accessed 23 February 2015).

O'Shaughnessey, J. (1987) *Why People Buy*, New York: Oxford University Press, 161.

Olsen, N. V., E. Menichelli, O. S rheim and T. Næs (2012) Likelihood of buying healthy convenience food: An at-home testing procedure for ready-to-heat meals, *Food Quality and Preference* 24(1), 171–8.

Ong, B.S. (2011) Online Shoppers' Perceptions and Use of Comparison-Shopping Sites: An Exploratory Study, *Journal of Promotion Management* 17 (2), 207–27.

Pinder C. C. (1998) *Work Motivation in Organizational Behavior*, Upper Saddle River, NJ: Prentice Hall.

Ratneshwar, S., L. Warlop, D. G. Mick and G. Seegar (1997) Benefit Salience and Consumers' Selective Attention to Product Features, *International Journal of Research in Marketing* 14, 245–9.

Ries, A. and J. Trout (2001) *Positioning: The Battle for Your Mind*, New York: Warner.

Rook, D. (1987) The Buying Impulse, *Journal of Consumer Research* 14(1), 89–99.

Rothschild, M. L. (1978) Advertising Strategies for High and Low Involvement Situations, *American Marketing Association Educator's Proceedings*, Chicago, 150–62.

Ruddick, G. (2014). Black Friday 2014 explained–retailers gearing up for day of deals, *The Telegraph*, 19 November. http://www.telegraph.co.uk/finance/newsbysector/retailandconsumer/11217839/Black-Friday-2014-Get-ready-for-the-biggest-online-shopping-day-in-history.HTML (accessed 26 February 2015).

Salganik, M., D. Sheridan and D. Watts (2006) Experimental Study of Inequality and Unpredictability, *Science* 311 (5762), 845–56.

Shimp, T. and A. Kavas (1984) The Theory of Reasoned Action Applied to Coupon Usage, *Journal of Consumer Research* 11, 795–809.

Smith, G. (2008) On the Road, *Guardian Weekend*, 21 June, 99.

Smith, L. (2005) Ten Sales a Second: Glastonbury Tickets Go in Record Rush, *The Guardian*, 4 April, 7.

Weinberg, P. and W. Gottwald (1982) Impulsive consumer buying as a result of emotions, *Journal of Business Research* 10 (1), 43–57.

Williams, K. C. (1981) *Behavioural Aspects of Marketing*, London: Heinemann.

World Health Organization (2010) 25–70% of adults in Europe are overweight. http://www.euro.who.int/en/who-we-are/regional-director/news/news/2010/12/2570-of-adults-in-europe-are-overweight

Wright, P. L. (1974) The Choice of a Choice Strategy: Simplifying vs Optimizing, Faculty Working Paper no. 163, Champaign, Ill: Department of Business Administration, University of Illinois.

Zhang, J. (2010). The Sound of Silence: Observational, *Marketing Science* 29 (2), 313–35.

CASE 5
Cappuccino Hotshots

The Battle of the Coffee Shops

The UK has come a long way from the days when a request for coffee would bring a cup of uniformly grey, unappealing liquid, sometimes served in polystyrene cups, which bore no relation to the rich, flavoursome coffee experienced on trips to continental Europe. The origin of this change was not Europe, however, but the USA, where the coffee bar culture was grounded.

Recent years have seen an explosion of coffee bars on UK high streets, with over 5 million lattés, cappuccinos and espressos served per week. The market is dominated by Costa Coffee (backed by Whitbread) with over 1,700 coffee shops, US-owned Starbucks with 750, and Caffè Nero with over 600 bars. In total, the UK has over 5,000 branded coffee shops, all charging over £2 (€2.90) for a small coffee. Often three or more bars will be located within 100 metres of each other.

The first US West Coast style coffee shop was opened in the UK in 1995 and was called the Seattle Coffee Company. The owners were Americans who saw an opportunity to serve the British with good-quality coffee in relaxed surroundings just like they experienced in the USA. The concept was a huge success, and by 1997 the company had 49 coffee outlets. It was joined by Coffee Republic and Caffè Nero, which also grew rapidly. In 1997, however, the coffee market in the UK was to change dramatically with the arrival of the US-based Starbucks coffee bar giant, which bought the Seattle Coffee Company.

Its strategy was to gain market share through fast rollout. For the first five years Starbucks opened an average of five shops a month in the UK: in 1999 it had 95 shops, by 2014 this had increased to 750. Today, Starbucks is in the Fortune Top 500 US companies and has over 20,000 coffee shops in more than 50 countries. Its approach is simple: blanket an area completely, even if the shops cannibalize one another's business. A new coffee bar will often capture about 30 per cent of the sales of a nearby Starbucks, but the company considered this was more than offset by lower delivery and management costs (per shop), shorter queues at individual shops and increased foot traffic for all the shops in an area as new shops take custom from competitors too. Over 20 million people

buy coffee at Starbucks every week, with the average Starbucks customer visiting 18 times a month.

One of its traditional strengths was the quality of its coffee. Starbucks has its own roasting plant, from which the media are banned lest its secrets are revealed. In its coffee shops, coffee is mixed with a lot of milk and offered in hundreds of flavours. Its Frappuccino is positioned as a midday break in advertisements where a narrator explains 'Starbucks Frappuccino coffee drink is a delicious blend of coffee and milk to smooth out your day.' The tag-line is 'Smooth out your day, everyday.'

A key problem was that Starbucks' major competitors—Costa Coffee and Caffè Nero—also followed a fast roll-out strategy, causing rental prices to spiral upwards. For example, Starbucks' Leicester Square coffee shop in London was part of a £1.5 million (€2.2 million) two-shop rental deal. Many coffee shops were not profitable; Starbucks, because it continued to operate them, was accused of unfairly trying to squeeze out the competition. However, the recession brought rental prices down, allowing the chains, especially Costa Coffee to expand rapidly. All three major players are now profitable.

The typical consumers at these coffee bars are young, single and high earners. They are likely to be professionals—senior or middle managers with company cars. Students also are an important part of the market. Coffee bars are seen as a 'little bit of heaven', a refuge where consumers can lounge on sofas, read broadsheet newspapers and view New Age poetry on the walls. They provide an oasis of calm for people between their homes and offices. They are regarded as a sign of social mobility for people who may be moving out of an ordinary café or low-end department store into something more classy. Even the language is important for these consumers: terms such as latté, cappuccino and espresso allow them to demonstrate connoisseurship. Consumers are offered a wide choice of combinations, including a sprinkling of marshmallow, syrup and an extra shot of espresso.

Coffee bars also cater for the different moods of consumers. For example, Sahar Hashemi, a founding partner of Coffee Republic, explains 'If I'm in my routine, I'll have a tall, skinny latté. But if I'm feeling in a celebratory mood or like spoiling myself, it's a grand vanilla mocha with whip and marshmallows.'

Starbucks has expanded the services it provides by offering a Wi-Fi service that allows laptop users to gain high-speed Internet access. This service has been copied by Costa Coffee and Caffè Nero.

Starbucks, Costa Coffee and Caffè Nero offer food alongside drinks. Starbucks targets breakfast, lunch and snack times with a limited range of both indulgent and healthy eating options. Costa Coffee has been offering hot foods and salads since 2002. Caffè Nero's food offer is integral to its Italian-style positioning, with most of the ingredients for its meals coming from Italy.

Many of the coffee shops have four zones. The first is at the front of the store, where customers can look outside and passers-by can see there are people inside. The second is an area containing perch seating, reminiscent of coffee houses in Italy. The third zone offers large community tables where groups or individuals can work on their laptops or read. Finally, softer seating creates a more intimate and relaxed zone.

The chains have also embraced the fair trade coffee idea, with Costa Coffee offering Cafédirect products since 2000, and Starbucks introducing fair trade coffee in 2002. The three chains almost entirely buy their coffee beans from sustainable sources, paying up to 12 per cent above average world prices. Low-calorie drinks are also offered.

Declining performance at Starbucks led to the reappointment in 2008 of Howard Schultz as chief executive, the man who grew the firm from just four outlets to 20,000 today. He identified Starbucks' problems as stemming from its outlets losing their

'romance and theatre'. He pointed out that the distinctive aroma of fresh coffee was less evident because of the advent of vacuum-sealed, flavour-locked packaging. Also, the use of new automated machines meant that customers could not see their drinks being prepared—eliminating an 'intimate experience' with the barista and impairing the spectacle of coffee-making. The result he concluded was that some customers found Starbucks coffee shops sterile places that no longer reflected a passion for coffee. The situation was made worse by the smell of sandwiches, which often overpowered the aroma of coffee. Some Starbucks staff were also criticized as being unfriendly.

The problems facing Starbucks were worsened by a strong challenge from McDonald's, which opened McCafés in some of its outlets, where customers can buy similar drinks at a cheaper price. Starbucks' woes continued with a report from the consumer magazine *Which*? that showed that Starbucks coffee was inferior to that of Costa Coffee and Caffè Nero, which won. It was also the most expensive.

Mr. Schultz began to address some of these problems by introducing new smaller expresso machines, so customers can once again see the baristas making their drinks. Coffee is once again being ground by hand, restoring the aroma, and a less potent-smelling cheese is being used in Starbucks' sandwiches. The baristas have all been retrained, not only in the art of making excellent coffee but also in connecting better with customers. The interiors of many of Starbucks' coffee shops have been renovated and redesigned.

To make the outlets more attractive during the recession, a new instant coffee brand, Via, was launched, which Starbucks claims tastes as good as ground coffee but at a much cheaper price. The company also introduced a loyalty card which allowed free extras such as a shot of whipped cream, syrup or soy in the coffee. Like Wi-Fi this innovation was copied by its rivals. A further change was the dropping of the 'Starbucks Coffee' logo from its mugs and changing the colour of its 'siren' figure from black to green.

Meanwhile, Costa Coffee has moved into the self-service market by buying Coffee Nation and its 900 vending machines. The offering carries the Costa Express branding and uses fresh milk and fresh coffee beans, roasted by Costa in London. While using the machine, the customer is treated to the gentle buzz of a coffee shop and the smell of pain au chocolat.

»

Questions

1. Why have coffee shops been so popular with consumers?

2. You are considering visiting a coffee shop for the first time. What would influence your choice of coffee shop to visit? Is this likely to be a high- or low-involvement decision?

3. Assess the coffee chains' moves to expand the offerings they provide for their customers.

4. Coffee shops are mainly located in the centres of towns and cities. Are there other locations where they could satisfy customer needs?

This case study was written by David Jobber, Emeritus Professor of Marketing, University of Bradford.

References

Based on: Cree, R. (2003) Sahar Hashemi, *The Director*, January, 44–7; Daniels, C. (2003) Mr Coffee, *Fortune*, 14 April, 139–40; Hedburg, A. and M. Rowe (2001) UK Goes Coffee House Crazy, *Marketing Week*, 4 January, 28–9; Sutter, S. (2003) Staff the Key to Marketing Success, *Marketing Magazine*, 19 May, 4; Bainbridge, J. (2005) Off the Boil, *Marketing*, 13 April, 28–9; Anonymous (2004) Starbucks to Offer 'Music to Go', *BBC News*, 12 March, http://news. bbc.co. uk.; Clark, A. (2008) Wall St Gets Palpitations Over Caffeine Fuelled Growth, *Guardian*, 7 January, 25; Anonymous (2008) Coffee Wars, *The Economist*, 12 January, 57–8; Fernandez, J. (2009) Back To Basics, *Marketing Week*, 26 February, 18–19; Charles, E. (2011) Change Brewing at Starbucks, *Marketing*, 12 January, 14–15; Reynolds, J. (2011) Costa Targets Tesco with Express Self-Service Offer, *Marketing*, 9 March, 9; Roberts, J. (2012) Quality Quest Keeps Sector Full of Beans, Marketing Week, 9 February, 22–3; Bolger, M. (2013) Café Culture, *The Marketeer*, July/August, 21–3; BBC (2014) Coffee Shop Hotspots, A BBC Open University Partnership Television programme.

CASE 6
Red Bull

'Gives you Wings'

Dietrich Mateschitz is probably not a name that most people are familiar with. However, he is one of the most successful entrepreneurs of our age, a man who single-handedly changed the landscape of the beverage industry by creating not just a new brand but a whole new category: the energy drink. Mateschitz is the founder and co-owner of Red Bull GmbH, a privately held energy beverages production and marketing firm based in Fuschl am See, Austria. Founded in 1984, Red Bull GmbH produces the energy drink named Red Bull and markets it all around the world. Red Bull GmbH has had high growth since its launch as a premium energy drink thanks to its innovative marketing strategies and innate ability to understand its customers and the market.

How It all Started

A chance trip to Thailand in 1982 would prove to be the turning point in Mateschitz's life. Here Mateschitz became aware of a local uncarbonated 'tonic drink' called Krating Daeng (Thai for water buffalo), which enjoyed widespread popularity throughout the Far East. Mateschitz was further intrigued when he read in a magazine that the top corporate taxpayer in Japan that year was a maker of such tonics. In 1984 Mateschitz approached Chaleo Yoovidhya, a Thai businessman who was selling the tonic in Southeast Asia, and suggested that the two introduce the drink to the rest of the world, with one crucial change: it would be carbonated. Yoovidhya liked the idea, and they agreed to invest $500,000 each to establish a 49/49 partnership, with the remaining 2 per cent going to Yoovidhya's son. (Yoovidhya remains a silent partner in the company.) Mateschitz then returned to Austria where he founded Red Bull establishing the company's headquarters in Fuschl am See, not far from Salzburg, and began to plan the all-important packaging and slogan. For help, he turned to his university friend Johannes Kastner, who owned his own ad agency in Frankfurt, finally deciding on the distinctive blue-and-silver can emblazoned with the logo of two muscular bulls about to smash heads in front of a yellow sun. A slogan

was harder to come by, with Kastner stating that the eventual slogan 'Gives you wings' came to him at 3 a.m. and was his last attempt after telling Mateschitz to find another agency. Mateschitz developed a unique marketing strategy to sell Red Bull as an ultra-premium drink in a category all its own by making it far-and-away the most expensive carbonated drink on the market. In 1987, Mateschitz started selling Red Bull Energy Drink on the Austrian market. This was not only the launch of a completely new product; it was in fact the birth of a totally new product category.

While the consumption was doubling year on year in Austria, Red Bull arrived in its first foreign markets, Singapore and Hungary in 1989 and 1992 respectively. The authorization for Germany was granted in 1994, the UK followed in 1995 and in 1997 Red Bull entered the US market over a five-year period starting in California.

As Red Bull is a privately held company, financial information is limited; however, the company reported net sales of €5 billion in 2013, and 5.4 billion cans sold, representing growth over 2012 of 2 per cent and 3 per cent respectively. This growth is down significantly from 2011–12 figures, dipping from 16 per cent and 13 per cent respectively. That said, Red Bull reported exceptionally strong net sales growth in India (+55 per cent), Japan (+32 per cent), Turkey (+18 per cent), Scandinavia (+16 per cent), Russia (+13 per cent) and Brazil (+12 per cent), to account for sales eclipsing the €5 billion mark for the first time. Despite

»

»

continuous growth in both volume and value, Red Bull has lost share each year over 2008–13. Red Bull's competitors Monster and Coca-Cola's focus on larger serving sizes, while Red Bull has stayed mainly with its smaller cans. This has kept Red Bull's shares below category growth. Both the category and Red Bull saw growth slow to under 10 per cent in 2012–13 as rivals outside the energy drinks category emerged in key markets. That said, Red Bull still dominates, with a 19 per cent share. In terms of absolute volume growth, the USA remained Red Bull's key growth engine in 2012–13, reflecting growth of 67 per cent over 2008–13. Brazil came second in terms of absolute volume growth, expanding by 313 per cent. The responsibility for the success of the world's number one energy drink is shared by the company's 8,294 employees around the world (compared with 7,758 in 2010) in 164 countries.

Understanding the Customer

Red Bull has been particularly successful in communicating its core brand values of individuality, humour, innovation and non-conformism. Red Bull actively describes its target market as a 'post-modern hedonistic group'. Mateschitz positioned Red Bull as the original energy drink with a believable and proven effect. Red Bull's positioning is a conscious decision by the company to differentiate the brand from other carbonates through premium pricing. However, Red Bull originally needed to secure food-and-drug authority approval of its contents and was delayed from entering a number of key markets (notably Germany, Norway, Denmark and France). While this was an initial source of frustration for Mateschitz, it turned out to provide exactly the marketing strategy he needed. Red Bull contains the active ingredients caffeine and taurine—the main reasons why drug approval was needed. However, because Red Bull was essentially illegal until approval was granted, rumours began circulating that the drink 'contained ecstasy', was 'made with bulls' testicles' and was 'liquid amphetamine'. These rumours spread among the clubbing community, a key target audience for the energy drink sector, and an audience for whom the idea of an illegal drink was distinctly inviting. Instead of attempting to quash the rumours, Red Bull added a 'rumours' section to its website to enhance the myth. This worked so well that when the drink was finally licensed, a group of worried mothers campaigned to have it banned, asserting that it led to drug use. Again, this just served to increase the attractiveness of the drink among its core market and Red Bull capitalized on this by launching guerrilla campaigns in bars and clubs. Red Bull affectionately became known as 'speed in a can' or even 'liquid cocaine'. Such health concerns simply reaffirmed Red Bull's reputation as an icon of the counter-culture,

and the flag-bearer of anti-brands. This initial mystique and intrigue drove Red Bull's brand in its early years. To enhance its attachment within the Generation Y community, Red Bull utilized regional marketing targeting trendy nightlife spots and student life, and specifically employed students as brand representatives.

Extreme Marketing

Marketing remains central to the brand's success, with 30–40 per cent of sales invested in marketing and promotion activity. Red Bull's marketing has historically been a three-pronged approach incorporating buzz marketing, sponsorship and television advertising.

The brand has engaged its core male 18-to-34 demographic and a broader mainstream audience through diverse platforms, third-party media, and, perhaps most important, its own channels. The central pillar of Red Bull's marketing campaign has always been its claim that it can improve athletic performance. In order to effectively communicate this message, Mateschitz zeroed in on the extreme-sports market. The first such involvement came in 1991, with the creation of the Red Bull Flugtag event, first hosted in Vienna, Austria. The Flugtag, which calls on participants to design and build flying contraptions to be launched off a 9.1-metre-high ramp, aligning perfectly with Red Bull's 'Gives you wings' slogan. Since the advent of the Flugtag event, Red Bull has been ever-present in adventure and 'New Age' sports, spending an estimated US$300 million per year on sports marketing, including sponsoring and heavily branding over 500 action sports events and athletes. Red Bull has even created its own sport known as Red Bull Crashed Ice. Red Bull's initial involvement in newly created sports and non-traditional adventure sports that were on the margins of mainstream popularity in the 1990s opened the door for Mateschitz to enter more traditional, high-profile sports with a degree of authority and authenticity. This is a key element of Red Bull's brand identity—to be considered both as an established drinks company and as a brand with a successful sporting history. Today Red Bull underwrites more than 500 athletes in 97 sports. Red Bull's place in sport, as well as positioning its energy drink as being beneficial for athletes and a driver of performance, has led to the creation both of new and innovative sports properties, and the sponsorship and eventual ownership of mainstream sports properties. Red Bull boasts an arguably unrivalled international sporting empire, including, among others: EC Red Bull Salzburg (Hockey League, Austria), FC Red Bull Salzburg (Austrian Bundesliga), F1 teams Red Bull Racing and Scuderia Toro Rosso, Major League Soccer's New York Red Bulls, NASCAR's Team Red Bull, Red Bull Brasil FC (Segunda Divisão Paulista, Brazilian second division). Each of Red Bull's properties, purchased or created, bears the Red Bull name in some way, and has been branded or rebranded to fit the company's colour scheme and identity. Mateschitz has used sport to further promote and grow the Red Bull brand and reach a broader audience of consumers internationally. By stressing authenticity and establishing the brand as an icon of the extreme sports subculture, the company has pioneered not only the energy drinks market, but also the use of sport as a brand extension.

Content is Key

The proliferation of new media channels and user-generated content has resulted in a frightening loss of control for many marketers. In keeping with its brand values 2011 saw an extremely dynamic expansion of Red Bull's media activities. Red Bull became an early adopter of Instagram, the photo-sharing app recently bought by Facebook for $1bn. It now has 2.8 million followers on this site. The visual images associated with the themes provided a more compelling call to action and structure for consumers to create on behalf of the brand versus a standard promotional call to action. Red Bull's business plan defies conventional advertising in favour of marketing through its own events, shows, and publications. Red Bull established its content arm, Red Bull Media House, in Europe in 2007 and expanded stateside last year. In 2011 alone it filmed movies, signed a partnership deal with NBC for a show called Red Bull Signature Series, developed reality-television ideas with big-time producer Bunim/Murray and MTV, honed its own web and mobile outlets, and became a partner in YouTube's new plan to publish original content among others. It also expanded its magazine Red Bulletin into the USA, giving it a global distribution of almost 5 million. The development of Media House demonstrates Red Bull's ambition to use all possible channels to capture the maximum young audience within the energy drinks market using original content to reinforce the core values of the brand. Red Bull Media is so adept at creating content that audiences value in its own right that its content isn't just used by Red Bull, but also commissioned and licensed by brands like Microsoft, Electronic Arts and DHL.

Red Bull continues to innovate through the creation of its content. The Red Bull campaign in 2012 highlighted the ambition of Red Bull to create superior and engaging content for customers. The campaign took sponsorship to new heights by sending Felix Baumgartner into space and helping him become the first person to break the sound barrier with a freefall jump from 128,000 feet above the earth—the Red Bull Stratos mission, heralded as the company's

greatest marketing stunt yet. The campaign achieved a record 8 million views on YouTube when it was live-streamed on 14 October 2012, easily beating the previous record of 500,000 set by Google during the 2012 Olympic Games. The jump was also broadcast on more than 40 television stations worldwide and 130 digital outlets. Half the global trending topics on Twitter were related to Stratos, and the video has since been watched over 10 million times on YouTube. This represents around £100 million in worldwide media value, and Red Bull Stratos will continue to be talked about and the video distributed socially for a long time. This represents extraordinary global reach. Felix Baumgartner's record-breaking supersonic freefall from the edges of space was expensive, unpredictable and dangerous, but fascinating, and perfectly aligned with Red Bull's brand. As well as generating a phenomenal amount of traditional and social media coverage globally, the stunt was incredibly effective. According to Red Bull, it sold 5.2 billion cans worldwide in 2012, and several markets saw double-digit growth, including a sales increase of 17 per cent in the USA.

In a further demonstration of the power of one-off videos to drive traffic for Red Bull, a skydiving version of the Harlem Shake, the dance craze, quickly racked up a total of 6.4 million hits in early 2013. Long-running series generate consistent involvement. The Sheckler Sessions, starring skateboarder Ryan Sheckler, for example, have accrued over 6 million views to date (in 2015). Red Bull's channel has 2.6 million YouTube subscribers. YouTube remains an important channel for the target demographic of the brand. Sponsorship agreements with brands such as GoPro have further enhanced the content-creation capabilities of Red Bull through extreme sports.

Conclusion

Red Bull continues to comfortably lead the global energy drinks market in both volume and value terms. However, the threat from The Coca-Cola Company and PepsiCo has been mounting following agreements with energy drinks such as Monster and Rockstar. The long-term focus for Red Bull is to remain relevant with the core audience and retain its edgy image with its consumer group, which may become increasingly difficult with the brand's status as a major global brand that has achieved mass-market success. New market entrants may become more attractive to the new generation of young consumers who want to be different and for whom the mass-market Red Bull may no longer be cool or trendy enough. In spite of this competition and the difficult financial and global economic climate, Red Bull's plans for growth and investment remain just as

»

»

ambitious. While it remains to be seen what future endeavours and extensions Mateschitz and Red Bull have planned, the foundations laid within youth culture leading to the company's market dominance have been thanks to an innate ability of Red Bull to understand its customers.

Questions

1. Using your understanding of who is important in the buying decision process, evaluate the significance of these roles in terms of creating marketing communications for Red Bull.

2. Discuss the potential choice criteria used by consumers when evaluating alternative energy drinks.

3. 'Red Bull actively describes its target market as a post-modern hedonistic group.' Critically evaluate the social influences on consumer behaviour with respect to the target market of Red Bull.

4. Discuss the potential benefits of sports marketing as a tool in the consumer decision-making process.

5. Evaluate the importance of Red Bull's content-generation strategy to the consumer decision-making process.

This case study was written by David Cosgrave, Lecturer, University of Limerick.

References

The material in the case has been drawn from a variety of published sources.

CHAPTER 4
Organizational Buying

> *People are people at work or at play.*
> **ANONYMOUS**

LEARNING OBJECTIVES

After reading this chapter, you should be able to:

1. discuss the characteristics of organizational buying
2. define the dimensions of organizational buying
3. discuss the nature and marketing implications of who buys, how organizations buy and the choice criteria used to evaluate products
4. explain the influences on organizational buying behaviour—the buy class, product type and purchase importance—and discuss their marketing implications
5. describe the developments in purchasing practice: just-in-time procurement, e-procurement, e-commerce, reverse marketing and leasing

Organizational buying involves purchasing products and services to meet the needs of manufacturers, resellers, government and public sector, and other types of organizations. There are three types of organizational market.

1   The *industrial market* consists of companies that buy products and services to help them produce other goods and services. Industrial goods include raw materials, components and capital goods such as machinery.

2   The *reseller market* comprises organizations that buy products and services to resell. Mail-order companies, retailers and online retailers are examples of resellers.

3   The *government market* consists of government agencies that buy products and services to help them carry out their activities—for example, that make purchases for local authorities and defence.

Whilst there are some similarities between consumer and organizational buying in terms of the stages of the buying process, organizational buying is different in terms of scale, risk, and complexity. The implications of making wrong decisions in an organizational setting are potentially far-reaching, as they could eventually lead to loss of market share, job losses and even company failure. Consequently, marketing managers need to develop an understanding of buyer behaviour and the structure of the buying group within the purchasing organization. This type of buying requires considerable and detailed information searching and methodical evaluation of alternatives. A key challenge for organizational buyers is to be able to satisfy diverse requirements in a single offering. A product that provides engineers the performance characteristics they demand, production managers the delivery reliability they need, purchasing managers the value for money they seek, and shop-floor workers the ease of installation they desire, is likely to be highly successful.

This chapter examines the characteristics of organizational buying and the implications for marketing, before examining some of the dimensions of buying: who buys, how they buy and what choice criteria they use. The chapter concludes by exploring developments in purchasing practice: just-in-time purchasing, centralized purchasing, e-commerce, e-procurement and reverse marketing.

Characteristics of Organizational Buying

Nature and size of customers

Typically the number of customers in organizational markets is smaller than in consumer markets. The Pareto rule often applies, with 80 per cent of output being sold to 20 per cent of customers, who may number fewer than 12.

The reseller market is a case in point, where, in Europe, most countries have a small number of supermarkets dominating the grocery trade.

In industrial manufacturing markets, the same situation is often found. For example, in the computer manufacturing industry, Apple, Sony, Hewlett Packard, Dell, Lenovo and Asus are the dominant global players and represent a large share of the market for computer components. As a result, the importance of key customers is significant. When Microsoft decided to move to IBM for the processor that drives the Xbox 360, this was a major blow to Intel, whose processors had powered almost everything that Microsoft had ever made (Naughton, 2005). The jet aircraft industry is even more concentrated, with only two key players: Airbus and Boeing.

The implications are that the importance of a small number of large customers makes it sensible for suppliers to invest heavily in developing long-term collaborative relationships. Dedicated sales and marketing teams under the title of 'key account management' (KAM) are usually employed to service such large accounts. (Relationship marketing and KAM are discussed in detail in Chapter 10.) Supply is usually direct, dispensing with the services of intermediaries, as large order sizes make it economical to deal directly with the manufacturer. Face-to-face meetings are important when negotiating large contracts, but the Internet is also widely used; Airbus has a supplier portal which it uses to support its purchasing processes (Airbus, 2012).

Complexity of buying

Often, organizational purchases, notably those that involve large sums of money and that are new to the company, involve many people at different levels of the organization. The managing director, product engineers, production managers, purchasing managers and operatives may influence the decision as to which expensive machine to purchase. The sales task may be to influence as many of these people as possible and may involve multilevel selling by means of a sales team, rather than an individual salesperson (Corey, 1991).

Economic and technical choice criteria

Although organizational buyers, being people, are affected by emotional factors such as liking or disliking a salesperson, organizational buying decisions are often made on economic and technical criteria. This is because organizational buyers have to justify their decisions to other members of their organization (Jobber and Lancaster, 2009). Also, the formalization of the buying function through the establishment of purchasing departments leads to the use of economic rather than emotional choice criteria. As purchasing becomes more sophisticated, economic criteria come to the fore, with techniques such as lifecycle cost, total cost of ownership and value-in-use analysis. Fleet buyers, for example, calculate lifecycle costs including purchase price, and running and maintenance costs when considering which company car to buy.

Risks

Industrial markets are characterized by a contract being agreed before the product is made. Further, the product itself may be highly technical and the seller may be faced with unforeseen problems once work has started. Thus, Scott-Lithgow won an order to build an oil rig for BP, but the price proved uneconomic given the nature of the problems associated with its construction. In the government market, the UK's National Health Service encountered major problems when the cost of its patient record system—with an estimated budget of £6.4 billion—rose significantly, to over £10 billion. Eventually, this major IT investment project had to be abandoned, with huge losses to the UK taxpayers. A commentator said, 'This saga is one of the worst and most expensive contracting fiascos in the history of the public sector' (Syal, 2013).

Buying to specific requirements

Because of the large sums of money involved, organizational buyers sometimes draw up product specifications and ask suppliers to design their products to meet them. Services, too, are often conducted to specific customer requirements, marketing research and advertising services being examples. This is much less a feature of consumer marketing, where a product offering may be developed to meet a need of a market segment but, beyond that, meeting individual needs would prove uneconomic.

Reciprocal buying

Because an industrial buyer may be in a powerful negotiating position with a seller, it may be possible to demand concessions in return for placing an order. In some situations, buyers may demand that sellers buy some of their products in return for securing the order. For example, in negotiating to buy computers, a company like Volvo might persuade a supplier to buy a fleet of Volvo company cars.

Derived demand

The demand for many organizational goods is derived from the demand for consumer goods. If the demand for compact discs increases, the demand for the raw materials and machinery used to make the discs will also expand. Clearly, raw material and machinery suppliers would be wise to monitor consumer trends and buying characteristics as well as their immediate organizational customers.

A further factor based upon the derived demand issue is the tendency for demand for some industrial goods and services to be more volatile than that for consumer goods and services. For example, a small fall in demand for compact discs may mean the complete cessation of orders for the machinery to make them. Similarly, a small increase in demand if manufacturers are working at full capacity may mean a massive increase in demand for machinery as investment to meet the extra demand is made. This is known as the *accelerator principle* (Bishop, Graham and Jones, 1984).

Negotiations

Because of the existence of professional buyers and sellers, and the size and complexity of organizational buying, negotiation is often important. Thus, supermarkets will negotiate with manufacturers about price, since their buying power allows them to obtain discounts. Car manufacturers will negotiate attractive prices from tyre manufacturers such as Pirelli and Michelin, since the replacement brand may be dependent upon the tyre fitted to the new car. The supplier's list price may be regarded as the starting point for negotiation and the profit margin ultimately achieved

MARKETING IN ACTION 4.1
From Sweden Not Hollywood

Sky Atlantic HD and Volvo signed a major sponsorship deal, and part of the package was a major creative media campaign centred on the television channel's programming, including its on-demand TV, Sky mobile TV service and SkyGo. The two organizations have come together as there is deemed to be synergy between their market positioning. Both are targeting premium markets where quality and added value are important. Volvo's core message is encapsulated in its advertising strapline, 'quality productions are made up of many parts'.

The sponsorship deal has been negotiated around opportunities for the two organizations to build long-term relationships both on and off screen. For Volvo, the benefits are extended reach for its brand messages, and opportunities to build understanding of the Volvo brand among a premium viewing audience and to showcase the quality of the car. For Sky Atlantic, the benefits are firmly centred on the relationship opportunities.

Whilst there are gains for both companies, this sponsorship deal was complex and was negotiated by an intermediary media agency, Mindshare. The deal involved multiple stakeholders across multiple media channels, television and digital, and with creative agency Grey London, which created the adverts (indents) and delivered a campaign that celebrates the art of filmmaking by playfully using a touch of Swedishness. The negotiators created a deal worth £5.3 million that involved Volvo sponsoring every programme on the Sky Atlantic Channel for two years and showing its 15-second indent adverts for 60 seconds every hour.

Based on: Advanced Television (2014); Skymedia (2014); Vizard (2013); Macleod (2014)

will be heavily influenced by the negotiating skills of the seller. The implication is that sales and marketing personnel need to be conversant with negotiating skills and tactics, and in many situations be aware of the complexities involved in the negotiation process, particularly when the products and services are also complicated, for example multichannel advertising deals, where both internal and media intermediaries can be involved in the negotiation. See Marketing in Action 4.1 for insight into the high stakes involved between Sky Atlantic and Volvo.

People and Process in Purchasing

Organizational buying behaviour involves the people who make the purchase decisions, the stages in the buying process, and the criteria used to inform the decision-making process. We will examine these issues in turn.

Who makes buying decisions?

Buyers are important people as they can influence many aspects of a firm's operation. They are responsible for sourcing and selecting products, which often involves complex decisions, but also for managing the buying process—decisions that can impact on company performance, suppliers and the workforce (Lewis and Arnold, 2012). However, it is important to understand in organizational buying that the buyer, or purchasing officer, is often not the only person that influences the decision or has the authority to make the ultimate decision. Rather, the decision is in the hands of a **decision-making unit** (DMU), or *buying centre* as it is sometimes called. This is not necessarily a fixed entity. Members of the DMU may change as the decision-making process continues. Thus, a managing director may be involved in the decision that new equipment should be purchased, but not in the decision as to which manufacturer to buy it from.

Six roles have been identified in the structure of the DMU, as follows (Webster and Wind, 1972).

1 *Initiators*: those who begin the purchase process, for example maintenance managers.
2 *Users*: those who actually use the product, for example welders.
3 *Deciders*: those who have authority to select the supplier/model, for example production managers.
4 *Influencers*: those who provide information and add decision criteria throughout the process, for example accountants.
5 *Buyers*: those who have authority to execute the contractual arrangements, for example purchasing officer.
6 *Gatekeepers*: those who control the flow of information, for example secretaries who may allow or prevent access to a DMU member, or a buyer whose agreement must be sought before a supplier can contact other members of the DMU.

 Scan the QR code to determine the messages that TomTom wants its corporate customers to receive about its online applications for managing mobile sales teams.

Conceptually, a DMU resides within the buying organization. Consequently, a decision-making unit is defined as a group of people within a buying organization who are involved in the buying decision. But, external influences do come from trade promotions and advertising messages from potential trade suppliers. Increasingly, the buying function is becoming a more collaborative process as organizations seek to develop mutually beneficial long-term relationships. Read more about relationship development in Chapter 10, and read about how suppliers get involved in the purchasing process in Mini Case 4.1. Distribution and channel management is also discussed in detail in Chapter 17.

For very important decisions, the structure of the DMU will be complex, involving numerous people within the buying organization. The marketing task is to identify and reach the key members in order to convince them of the product's worth. Often communicating only to the purchasing officer will be insufficient, as this person may be only a minor influence on supplier choice. Relationship management is of key importance in many organizational markets (discussed in detail in Chapter 10).

When the problem to be solved is highly technical, suppliers may work with engineers in the buying organization in order to solve problems and secure the order. One example where this approach was highly successful involved a small company that won a large order from a major car company thanks to its ability to work with the car company in solving the technical problems associated with the development of an exhaust gas recirculation valve (Cline and Shapiro, 1978). In this case, the small company's policy was to work with the major company's engineers and to keep the purchasing department out of the decision until the last possible moment, by which time it alone would be qualified to supply the part.

Often organizational purchases are made in committees where the salesperson will not be present. The salesperson's task is to identify a person from within the decision-making unit who is a positive advocate and champion of the supplier's product. This person (or 'coach') should be given all the information needed to win the arguments that may take place within the decision-making unit. For example, even though the advocate may be a technical person, he or she should be given the financial information that may be necessary to justify buying the most technologically superior product.

Where DMU members are inaccessible to salespeople, advertising, the Internet, social media or direct marketing tools may be used as alternatives.

The relatively low cost of direct mail and email campaigns makes them tempting alternatives to personal visits or telephone calls. Setting up a website can also be relatively inexpensive once the initial set-up costs have been met. However, wrongly targeted direct mail, a poorly designed website or a badly executed email campaign can cause customer annoyance and tarnish the image of the company and brand. Business-to-business companies are turning to integrated marketing communications as a means of using the strengths of a variety of media to target business customers. Integrated marketing communications is a concept that sees companies coordinate their marketing communications tools to deliver a clear, consistent, credible and competitive message about the organization and its products.

MINI CASE 4.1
Iceland Frozen Foods Made in Asia

Iceland Foods Ltd sources many of its products from South East Asia, where there are highly skilled production companies that can produce both the quality of foodstuff that the buying team requires but also at a price that enables Iceland to offer value to its customers in a highly competitive marketplace.

Iceland Foods Ltd has grown from a single retail store selling frozen foods in Oswestry in Shropshire, UK, in 1970, to a national retail chain with over 840 stores, 25,000 employees and a turnover in excess of £2.7 billion. The food retail marketplace is highly competitive, and Iceland has faced aggressive competition from major grocery retailers such as Tesco, Sainsbury and Morrisons, from limited-range discounters Aldi and Lidl, and from variety retailers such as Marks & Spencer. But Iceland has managed to withstand the attacks on its position by maintaining its competitive price proposition through its product ranges.

Part of Iceland's competitive armory is its innovative food ranges; sometimes over 120 new products are introduced each year. One of its most important ranges is its seasonal party food. Iceland was the first company to introduce large platters of Christmas party food, but its competitors have been quick to follow into this product territory. So each year, Iceland's buying team will work with suppliers to produce new products. Many of the party ranges include Chinese and Indian foods and snacks, and are sourced in China.

Annually, the buying team will set objectives for the producers so they can develop new product ranges. Once the products are ready, the buying team will visit suppliers in China to sample the new product ranges and test the extent to which their objectives have been met. Iceland's buyers taste the products, evaluate the actual look of the products and determine how many items of which foodstuffs might be offered. The buyers must also ensure that they can offer sufficient value to the retail customer at a profit. Once potential ranges have been selected, they are brought back to the UK and tested by in-house teams for ease of use, cooking instructions and taste. Sometimes Iceland's buyers go back to the producer to seek modifications to products, perhaps because they don't have the right appeal, flavour or cost base. Packaging design, the amount of content and promotional offers are also considered as part of the buying decision, as it is important to be able to offer the *right value* to the consumer. The final decision about which products make it into Iceland are made by the head buyer and following a final round of testing by the senior management team.

The buying team at Iceland plays a very important role in ensuring the retailer can stay ahead of the competition and retain its market share. But the buying team does not work alone; suppliers, packaging designers, taste-testers, users and the senior management team are all involved in putting together food ranges.

Questions:

1 Discuss the extent to which Iceland's buying team fits the conceptual model of a DMU.
2 Build a case report that shows the importance of the buying function at Iceland and highlight the potential impact of wrong buying decisions.

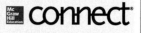

Based on: Iceland Foods Ltd (2014); Iceland Foods Ltd (2015); Pomeroy (2013)

Stages in the buying process: how they buy

Figure 4.1 describes the **decision-making process** for an organizational product (Robinson, Faris and Wind, 1967). The exact nature of the process will depend on the buying situation. In some situations some stages will be omitted. For example, in a routine rebuy situation the purchasing officer is unlikely to pass through the third, fourth and fifth stages (search for suppliers, and analysis and evaluation of their proposals). These stages will be bypassed, as the buyer, recognizing a need—perhaps shortage of stationery—routinely reorders from an existing supplier. In general, the more complex the decision and the more expensive the item, the more likely it is that each stage will be passed through and that the process will take more time.

The stages are:

1 Recognition of a problem (need)

   Needs and problems may be recognized through either *internal or external factors* (Jobber and Lancaster, 2015). An example of an internal factor would be the realization of under-capacity leading to the decision to purchase plant or equipment. Thus, internal recognition leads to active behaviour (internal/active). Some problems that are recognized internally may not be acted upon. This condition may be termed internal/passive. A production manager may realize that there is a problem with a machine but, given more pressing problems, decides to put up with it.

   Other potential problems may not be recognized internally, and become problems only because of external cues. Production managers may be quite satisfied with their production process until they are made aware of another, more efficient, method.

   Clearly, these different problems have important implications for marketing and sales. The internal/passive condition implies that there is an opportunity for a salesperson, having identified the condition, to highlight the problem by careful analysis of cost inefficiencies and other symptoms, so that the problem is perceived to be pressing and in need of solution (internal/active). The internal/active situation requires the supplier to demonstrate

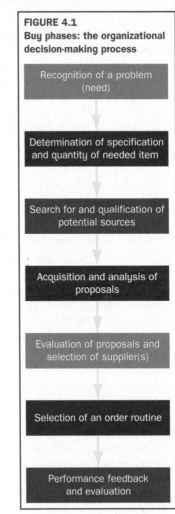

FIGURE 4.1
Buy phases: the organizational decision-making process

Recognition of a problem (need)

Determination of specification and quantity of needed item

Search for and qualification of potential sources

Acquisition and analysis of proposals

Evaluation of proposals and selection of supplier(s)

Selection of an order routine

Performance feedback and evaluation

EXHIBIT 4.1
Corporate customers such as bakeries are targeted by advertisers like E.On Energy

a differential advantage of its products over those of the competition. In this situation problem stimulation is unnecessary, but where internal recognition is absent, the marketer can provide the necessary external cues. A forklift truck sales representative might stimulate problem recognition by showing how the truck can save the customer money, due to lower maintenance costs, and lead to more efficient use of warehouse space through higher lifting capabilities. Advertising or direct mail could also be used to good effect.

2   Determination of specification and quantity of needed item
    At this stage of the decision-making process the DMU will draw up a description of what is required. For example, it might decide that five web servers are required to meet certain specifications. The ability of marketers to influence the specification can give their company an advantage at later stages of the process. By persuading the buying company to specify features that only the marketer's own product possesses, the sale may be virtually closed at this stage. This is the process of setting up *lock-out criteria*. Marketing in Action 4.2 explains the powerful effect a lock-out criterion has had on the market for diesel locomotives.

3   Search for and qualification of potential sources
    A great deal of variation in the degree of search takes place in industrial buying. Generally speaking, the cheaper and less important the item, and the more information the buyer possesses, the less search takes place. Marketers can use advertising to ensure that their brands are in the buyers' awareness set and are, therefore, considered when evaluating alternatives.

4   Acquisition and analysis of proposals
    Having found a number of companies that, perhaps through their technical expertise and general reputation, are considered to be qualified to supply the product, proposals will be called for and analysis of them undertaken.

5   Evaluation of proposals and selection of supplier(s)
    Each proposal will be evaluated in the light of the choice criteria deemed to be more important to each DMU member. It is important to realize that various members may use different criteria when judging proposals. Although this may cause problems, the outcome of this procedure is the selection of a supplier or suppliers.

6   Selection of an order routine
    Next, the details of payment and delivery are drawn up. Usually this is conducted by the purchasing officer. In some buying decisions—when delivery is an important consideration in selecting a supplier—this stage is merged into the acquisition and evaluation stages.

7   Performance feedback and evaluation
    This may be formal, where a purchasing department draws up an evaluation form for user departments to complete, or informal through everyday conversations.

MARKETING IN ACTION 4.2
Diesel Lock-out

The major player in the European diesel locomotive market is Electro-Motive Diesel (EMD), a former North American subsidiary of General Motors, which has sold 650 of its Class 66 diesel locomotives to European freight train operators since 1998. In the USA, however, General Electric (GE) is the market leader with about 70 per cent market share. This apparent paradox is explained by GE failing to meet a European lock-out criterion that does not apply in the USA. Until recently GE has not manufactured a locomotive small enough to pass under the low bridges and through the tunnels of the European rail system. EMD's Class 66 is able to fit on networks in nearly all of continental Europe and operates in 10 European countries.

This situation has now changed with the launch of GE's PowerHaul locomotive, which can fit the European system. Now that the lock-out criterion has been overcome, PowerHaul is threatening EMD's market share because, at the 'evaluation of proposals and selection of supplier(s)' decision-making stage, it possesses competitive advantages on key choice criteria. One is technical (an ability to accelerate freight trains faster than the Class 66) and the other economic (better fuel economy). GE is now winning orders from European operators such as Freightliner, the UK's second-largest freight operator. The PowerHaul has now enabled GE to enter not only European markets but also Turkey, the Middle East and North Africa.

This story demonstrates the importance of lock-out criteria and shows how the nature of choice criteria can differ between Stages 2 and 5 of the organizational decision-making process.

Based on: GE Transportation (2012); Wright (2008)

The implications of all this are that sales and marketing strategy can affect a sale through influencing need recognition, through the design of product specifications, and by clearly presenting the advantages of the product or service over those of the competition in terms that are relevant to DMU members. By early involvement, a company can benefit through the process of *creeping commitment*, whereby the buying organization becomes increasingly committed to one supplier through its involvement in the process and the technical assistance it provides.

Choice criteria

This aspect of industrial buyer behaviour refers to the criteria used by members of the DMU to evaluate supplier proposals. These criteria are likely to be determined by the performance criteria used to evaluate the members themselves (Draper, 1994). Thus, purchasing managers who are judged by the extent to which they reduce purchase expenditure are likely to be more cost conscious than production engineers, who are evaluated in terms of the technical efficiency of the production process they design.

In a similar manner to buying for consumers, organizational buying is characterized by *technical, economic, social* (organizational) and *personal criteria*. Key considerations may be, for plant and equipment, return on investment, while for materials and components parts they may be cost savings, together with delivery reliability, quality and technical assistance. Because of the high costs associated with production downtime, a key concern of many purchasing departments is the long-run development of the organization's supply system. Personal factors may also be important, particularly when suppliers' product offerings are essentially similar. In this situation the final decision may rest upon the relative liking for the supplier's salesperson.

Customers' choice criteria can change in different regions of the world. For example, Xerox is generally known as a company that provides solutions for creating documents—printers and copiers—and is so well known that it is a recognized household name. Xerox aims to shift the positioning of its brand to increase recognition of the service element of its global business (Snoad, 2012), as this creates around 50 per cent of the company's business. Therefore, the range of motives that key players in organizations use to compare supplier offerings are important to understand from a supplier perspective. For example, economic considerations play a part because commercial firms have profit objectives and work within budgetary constraints. Emotional factors should not be totally ignored, as decisions are made by people who do not suddenly lose their personalities, personal likes and dislikes and prejudices simply because they are at work. Let us examine a number of important technical and economic motives (quality, price and lifecycle costs, and continuity of supply) and then some organizational and personal factors (perceived risk, office politics, and personal liking/disliking).

Quality

The emergence of **total quality management** as a key aspect of organizational life reflects the importance of quality in evaluating suppliers' products and services. Many buying organizations are unwilling to trade quality for price. For example, the success of Intel was not based on price but reliable, ever-faster microprocessors for PCs and servers (Edwards, 2006). In particular, buyers are looking for consistency of product or service quality so that end products (e.g. motor cars) are reliable, inspection costs are reduced and production processes run smoothly. They are installing just-in-time delivery systems, which rely upon incoming supplies being quality guaranteed.

Price and lifecycle costs

For materials and components of similar specification and quality, price becomes a key consideration. For standard items—e.g., ball-bearings, transistors, carrier bags—price may be critical to making a sale given that a number of suppliers can meet delivery and specification requirements. The power of large buying organizations also means that they have the power to squeeze suppliers for tighter terms. For example, Marks & Spencer, in its drive to reduce costs, demanded a 10 per cent cut in all suppliers' prices (Walsh, 2006). To remain competitive when Tesco launched its 'Price Drop' initiative, many other supermarkets demanded reductions from their suppliers. Waitrose entered negotiations for a 5 per cent reduction from its ambient food suppliers to enable a new price-led marketing strategy '1000s of ways to great value' (Heagarty, 2011). However, it should not be forgotten that price is only one component of cost for many buying organizations. Increasingly buyers take into account **lifecycle costs**, which may include productivity savings, maintenance costs and residual values as well as initial purchase price when evaluating products. Marketers can use lifecycle costs analysis to break into an account. By calculating lifecycle costs with a buyer, new perceptions of value may be achieved.

Continuity of supply

Another major cost to a company is disruption of a production run. Delays of this kind can mean costly machine downtime and even lost sales. Continuity of supply is, therefore, a prime consideration in many purchase situations. Companies that perform badly on this criterion lose out even if the price is competitive because a small percentage price edge does not compare with the costs of unreliable delivery. Supplier companies that can guarantee deliveries and realize their promises can achieve a significant differential advantage in the marketplace. Organizational customers are demanding close relationships with *accredited suppliers* that can guarantee reliable supply, perhaps on a just-in-time basis.

Perceived risk

Perceived risk can come in two forms: *functional risk* such as uncertainty with respect to product or supplier performance, and *psychological risk* such as criticism from work colleagues. (For a discussion of the components of risk see Stone and Gronhaug, 1993.) This latter risk—fear of upsetting the boss, losing status, being ridiculed by others in the department, or, indeed, of losing one's job—can play a determining role in purchase decisions. Buyers often reduce uncertainty by gathering information about competing suppliers, checking the opinions of important others in the buying company, buying only from familiar and/or reputable suppliers and by spreading risk through multiple sourcing.

Office politics

Political factions within the buying company may also influence the outcome of a purchase decision. Interdepartmental conflict may manifest itself in the formation of competing camps over the purchase of a product or service. Because department X favours supplier 1, department Y automatically favours supplier 2. The outcome not only has purchasing implications but also political implications for the departments and individuals concerned.

Personal liking/disliking

A buyer may personally like one salesperson more than another and this may influence supplier choice, particularly when competing products are very similar. Obviously perception is important in all organizational purchases, since how someone behaves depends upon that person's perception of the situation. One buyer may perceive a salesperson as being honest, truthful and likeable, while another may not. However, analysis and managing of spending has become more closely monitored in recent years due to the widespread adoption of procurement and information systems related to e-commerce. So many firms have actively sought to introduce purchasing policies that reduce 'maverick spending'—that is, that reduce buying from non-preferred company suppliers. See Marketing in Action 4.3.

MARKETING IN ACTION 4.3
Is Eliminating the Mavericks a Good Thing?

Maverick spending is often referred to as the deals that are done outside an organization's procurement policy. This type of spending might occur when a powerful organizational buyer has a personal preference for a particular supplier (rather than the organization itself preferring a particular supplier). In this case, the company will be referred to as 'an off-contract supplier'. Furthermore, the practice is said to be widespread, with some firms experiencing up to 80 per cent of buying being uncontrolled and sourced from off-contract suppliers.

The difference between non-preferred and preferred suppliers is that the latter are established by determining their ability to comply with a buying firm's specification, for example agreed discount targets, delivery routines, and quality of goods. As a result, firms are increasingly investing in IT systems to gather data and analyze the efficiency of buying and selling with a view to reducing maverick spending, as this is seen as a source of budget cost savings.

However, sometimes the maverick spend is not about defying purchasing policies but about finding better purchasing solutions. Also, buying is a complex function, and implementing an IT system that effectively tracks all the nuances of purchasing agreements and deals can be costly and time-consuming and may not result in the ideal purchasing outcome. So, on one hand, reducing maverick spend can ensure compliance with purchasing policy, potentially reducing the overall budget spend and maximizing purchasing power. But on the other hand, this might lead to missed buying opportunities and increased cost through significant investment in sophisticated IT systems to manage the maverick spend.

Based on: Moretti (2013); Mitchell (2015); Batting (2014)

Implications of choice criteria

The implications of understanding the content of the decision are that appeals may need to change when communicating to different DMU members—discussion with a production engineer may centre on the technical superiority of the product offering, while much more emphasis on cost factors and the quality of goods to be supplied may prove effective when talking to the purchasing officer. Furthermore, the criteria used by buying organizations change over time as circumstances change. Price may be relatively unimportant to a company when trying to solve a highly visible technical problem, and the order will be placed with the supplier that provides the necessary technical assistance. Later, after the problem has been solved and other suppliers become qualified, price may be of crucial significance.

Influences on Buying Decisions

Figure 4.2 shows the three factors that influence how organizations buy, who buys and the choice criteria they use: the buy class, the product type and the importance of purchase (Cardozo, 1980).

The buy class

Organizational purchases may be distinguished between a new task, a straight rebuy and a modified rebuy (Robinson, Faris and Wind, 1967). A **new task** occurs when the need for the product has not arisen previously so that there is little or no relevant experience in the company, and a great deal of information is required. A **straight rebuy** occurs where an organization buys previously purchased items from suppliers already judged acceptable. Routine purchasing procedures are set up to facilitate straight rebuys. The **modified rebuy** lies between the two extremes. A regular requirement for the type of product exists, and the buying alternatives are known, but sufficient change (e.g. a delivery problem) has occurred to require some alteration to the normal supply procedure.

The buy classes affect organizational buying in the following ways. First, the membership of the DMU changes. For a straight rebuy possibly only the purchasing officer is involved, whereas for a new buy senior management, engineers, production managers and purchasing officers may be involved. Modified rebuys often involve engineers, production managers and purchasing officers, but senior management, except when the purchase is critical to the company, is unlikely to be involved. Second, the decision-making process may be much longer as the buy class changes from a straight rebuy to a modified rebuy and to a new task. Third, DMU members are likely to be much more receptive to new task and modified rebuy situations than to straight rebuys. In the latter case, the purchasing manager has already solved the purchasing problem and has other problems to deal with. So why make it a problem again?

The first implication of this buy class analysis is that there are big gains to be made if a company can enter the new task at the start of the decision-making process. By providing information and helping with any technical problems that can arise, the company may be able to create goodwill and creeping commitment, which secures the order when the final decision is made. The second implication is that since the decision process is likely to be long, and many people are involved in the new task, supplier companies need to invest heavily in sales personnel for a considerable period of time. Some firms employ missionary sales teams comprising their best salespeople, to help secure big new-task orders.

Companies in straight rebuy situations must ensure that no change occurs when they are in the position

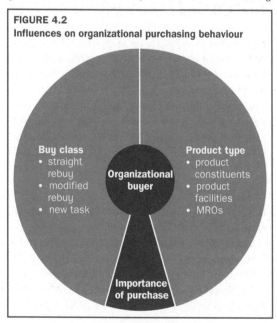

FIGURE 4.2
Influences on organizational purchasing behaviour

Buy class
- straight rebuy
- modified rebuy
- new task

Organizational buyer

Product type
- product constituents
- product facilities
- MROs

Importance of purchase

of the supplier. Regular contact to ensure that the customer has no complaints may be necessary, and the buyer may be encouraged to use automatic reordering systems. For the out-supplier (i.e. a new potential supplier), the task can be difficult unless poor service or some other factor has caused the buyer to become dissatisfied with the present supplier. The obvious objective of the out-supplier in this situation is to change the buy class from a straight rebuy to a modified rebuy. Price alone may not be enough since changing supplier represents a large personal risk to the purchasing officer. The new supplier's products might be less reliable, and delivery might be unpredictable. In order to reduce this risk, the company may offer delivery guarantees with penalty clauses and be very willing to accept a small (perhaps uneconomic) order at first in order to gain a foothold. Supplier acquisition of a total quality management (TQM) standard such as ISP9001:2000 or ISP9004 may also have the effect of reducing perceived buyer risk. Other tactics are the use of testimonials from satisfied customers, and demonstrations. Many straight rebuys are organized on a contract basis, and buyers may be more receptive to listening to non-suppliers prior to contract renewal.

Value analysis and lifecycle cost calculations are other methods of moving purchases from a straight rebuy to a modified rebuy situation. Value analysis, which can be conducted by either supplier or buyer, is a method of cost reduction in which components are examined to see if they can be made more cheaply. The items are studied to identify unnecessary

EXHIBIT 4.2
SAP emphasizes the speed and efficiency of its business management network solutions

costs that do not add to the reliability or functionality of the product. By redesigning, standardizing or manufacturing by less expensive means, a supplier may be able to offer a product of comparable quality at lower cost. Lifecycle cost analysis seeks to move the cost focus from the initial purchase price to the total cost of owning and using a product. There are three types of lifecycle costs: purchase price, start-up costs and post-purchase costs. (Forbis and Mehta, 1981) Start-up costs would include installation, lost production and training costs. Post-purchase costs include operating (e.g. fuel, operator wages), maintenance, repair and inventory costs. Against these costs would be placed residual values (e.g. trade-in values of cars). Lifecycle cost appeals can be powerful motivators. For example, if the out-supplier can convince the customer organization that its product has significantly lower post-purchase costs than the in-supplier's, despite a slightly higher purchase price, it may win the order. This is because it will be delivering a higher economic value to the customer. This can be a powerful competitive advantage and, at the same time, justify the premium price.

The product type

Products can be classified as four types: materials, components, plant and equipment, and MROs (maintenance, repair and operation), as follows:
1   materials to be used in the production process, such as aluminium
2   components to be incorporated in the finished product, such as headlights
3   plant and equipment, such as a bulldozer
4   products and services for maintenance, repair and operation (MRO), such as spanners, welding equipment and lubricants.

This classification is based upon a customer perspective—how the product is used—and may be employed to identify differences in organizational buyer behaviour. First, the people who take part in the decision-making process tend to change according to product type. For example, senior management tend to get involved in the purchase of plant and equipment or, occasionally, when new materials are purchased if the change is of fundamental importance to company operations—for example, if a move from aluminium to plastic is being considered. Rarely do they involve themselves in component or MRO supply. Similarly, design engineers tend to be involved in buying components and materials but not normally MRO and plant equipment. Second, the decision-making process tends to be slower and more complex as product type moves from:

$$MRO \rightarrow components \rightarrow materials \rightarrow plant\ and\ equipment$$

For MRO items, *blanket contracts* rather than periodic purchase orders are increasingly being used. The supplier agrees to resupply the buyer on agreed price terms over a period of time. Stock is held by the seller and orders are automatically printed out by the buyer's computer when stock falls below a minimum level. This has the advantage to the supplying company of effectively blocking the effort of the competitors for long periods of time.

Classification of suppliers' offerings by product type gives clues as to who is likely to be influenced in the purchase decision. The marketing task is then to confirm this in particular situations and attempt to reach those people involved. A company selling MROs is likely to be wasting effort attempting to communicate with design engineers, whereas attempts to reach operating management are likely to prove fruitful.

The importance of purchase

A purchase is likely to be perceived as being important to the buying organization when it involves large sums of money, when the cost of making the wrong decision—for example, in production downtime—is high, and when there is considerable uncertainty about the outcome of alternative offerings. In such situations, many people at different organizational levels are likely to be involved in the decision, and the process will be long, with extensive search and analysis of information. Extensive marketing effort is likely to be required, but great opportunities present themselves to those sales teams that work with buying organizations to convince them that their offering has the best payoff. This may involve acceptance trials; for example, private diesel manufacturers supply railway companies with prototypes for testing, engineering support and testimonials from other users. Additionally, guarantees of delivery dates and after-sales service may be necessary when buyer uncertainty regarding these factors is high.

An example of the time and effort that may be required to win very important purchases is the order secured by GEC to supply £250 million worth of equipment for China's largest nuclear power station. The contract was won after six years of negotiation, 33 GEC missions to China, and 4,000 person-days of work.

Developments in Purchasing Practice

Several trends have taken place within the purchasing function that have marketing implications for supplier firms. The advent of just-in-time purchasing and the increased tendency towards centralized purchasing, e-procurement, reverse marketing, leasing and outsourcing have all changed the nature of purchasing and altered the way in which suppliers compete.

Lean production and just-in-time purchasing

Lean production aims to ensure that manufacturing processes reduce waste, increase efficiency and improve financial performance (Hofer, Eriglu and Hofer, 2012). To achieve these aims, inventory leanness (streamlined stock holding and management) is also an important factor. Lean practices that facilitate improvement in financial performance include: Kanban and JIT and TQM. Each will now be briefly discussed:

Kanban and just-in-time

Kanban is a system for controlling logistics and managing the movement of stock through various stages in the supply chain. The Kanban scheduling system is used in lean and **just-in-time** (JIT) production.

The JIT concept aims to minimize stock by organizing a supply system that provides materials and components as they are required (Hutt and Speh, 2006). Stockholding costs are significantly reduced or eliminated, thus profits are increased. Furthermore, since the holding of stock is a hedge against machine breakdowns, faulty parts and human error, it may be seen as a cushion that acts as a disincentive to management to eliminate such inefficiencies.

JIT practices are also associated with improved quality. Suppliers are evaluated on their ability to provide high-quality products. The effect of this is that suppliers may place more emphasis on product quality. Buyers are encouraged to specify only essential product characteristics, which means that suppliers have more discretion in product design and manufacturing methods. Also, the emphasis is on the supplier certifying quality—which means that quality inspection at the buyer company is reduced and overall costs are minimized, since quality control at source is more effective than further down the supply chain.

The total effects of JIT can be enormous. Purchasing, inventory and inspection costs can be reduced, product design can be improved, delivery streamlined, production downtime reduced, and the quality of the finished item enhanced. Marketing in Action 4.4 discusses how Hitachi operates its JIT system.

However, the implementation of JIT requires integration into both purchasing and production operations. Since the system requires the delivery of the exact amount of materials or components to the production line as they are required, delivery schedules must be very reliable and suppliers must be prepared to make deliveries on a regular basis, perhaps even daily. Lead times for ordering must be short and the number of defects very low. An attraction for suppliers is that it is usual for long-term purchasing agreements to be drawn up.

The marketing implication of the JIT concept is that to be competitive in many industrial markets—for example, motor cars—suppliers must be able to meet the requirements of this fast-growing system.

An example of a company that employs the JIT concept is the Nissan car assembly plant at Sunderland in the UK. Nissan has adopted what it terms synchronous supply: parts are delivered only minutes before they are needed. For example, carpets are delivered by Sommer-Allibert, a French supplier, from its facility close to the Nissan assembly line, in sequence for fitting to the correct model. Only 42 minutes elapse between the carpet being ordered and fitted to the car. The stockholding of carpets for the Nissan Micra is now only 10 minutes. Just-in-time practices do carry risks, however, if labour stability cannot be guaranteed. Renault discovered this to its cost when a strike at its engine and gearbox plant caused its entire French and Belgian car production lines to close in only 10 days.

Total quality management

Total quality management (TQM) is a set of management principles and practices that seek to deliver improved performance throughout an organization. This can lead to improvements in management leadership, organizational culture, strategic planning, people, management product design, supplier management and customer focus, and lead to continuous improvement. TQM places an emphasis on looking at social and behavioural factors in an organization and technical factors such as design, implementation and the processes of management and control.

In order to achieve excellent results from TQM, it is essential for an organization to manage equally the social and the technical factors; for example, an open and flexible culture towards continuous improvement will require all stakeholders to be involved in the development of technical processes (Calvo-Mora et al., 2014).

Centralized purchasing

Where several operating units within a company have common requirements, and where there is an opportunity to strengthen a negotiating position by bulk buying, centralized purchasing is an attractive option. Centralization encourages purchasing specialists to concentrate their energies on a small group of products, thus enabling them to develop an extensive knowledge of cost factors and the operation of suppliers (Brierty, Eckles and Reeder, 1998).

The move from local to centralized buying has important marketing implications. Localized buying tends to focus on short-term cost and profit considerations, whereas centralized purchasing places more emphasis on long-term supply relationships. Outside influences—for example, engineers—play a greater role in supplier choice in local purchasing organizations since less specialized buyers often lack the expertise and status to question the recommendations of technical people. The type of purchasing organization can therefore give clues to suppliers regarding the important people in the decision-making unit and their respective power positions.

E-procurement

While many people relate the Internet with consumers shopping online, the reality is that the volume of trade carried out online between businesses through online e-procurements is much greater.

Modern **e-procurement** systems enable companies to fulfil a range of activities and processes associated with the purchasing function: tendering, awarding contracts, establishing contractual agreements, and ordering (Doherty, McConnell and Ellis-Chadwick, 2013). To action these processes, companies not only create their own websites but also develop extranets for buyers to send out requests for bids to suppliers. Online purchasing systems can take various formats.

- *Catalogue sites*: companies can order items through electronic catalogues.
- *Vertical markets*: companies buying industrial products such as steel, chemicals or plastic, or buying services such as logistics (distribution) or media can use specialized websites (called *e-hubs*). For instance, Plastics. com permits thousands of plastics buyers to search for the lowest prices from thousands of plastics sellers.
- *Auction sites*: suppliers can place industrial products on auction sites where purchasers can bid for them.
- *Exchange* (or spot) markets: many commodities are sold on electronic exchange markets where prices can change by the minute. For example, Title Transfer Facility provides an online marketplace where gas energy can be traded instantly.
- *Buying alliances*: companies in the same market for products join together to gain bigger discounts on higher volumes.

In government markets, the adoption of e-procurement systems has been slow in comparison with the adoption in industrial and reseller markets. Indeed, recent research (Doherty, McConnell and Ellis-Chadwick, 2013) has found that in the UK, government purchasing strategies involved less than 3 per cent of invoices being sent electronically despite the inefficiencies of the incumbent manual processing systems. The primary reasons cited for the slow rate of adoption in these markets are the complexity of the procurement processes and institutional policy restrictions.

E-commerce

E-commerce portals, hubs and marketplaces are creating information portals and purchasing ecosystems that are facilitating greater communication within and across industries and to the end consumer. Covisint (www.covisint.com) is such a system, which brings together companies in healthcare and manufacturing industries, streamlining processes and improving organizational performance. Alibaba.com is one of the leaders of e-commerce transactions in China. It provides a marketplace connecting small and medium-sized buyers and suppliers from China and around the world. Its web presence includes an international marketplace (www.alibaba. com) that focuses on global importers and exporters, and a China marketplace (www.alibaba.com.cn) that focuses on suppliers and buyers trading domestically in China (Chaffey and Ellis-Chadwick, 2015).

In the manufacturing industries, the benefits of such systems are: a reduction of procurement costs; more rapid supply; greater agility when responding to changes in marketing environment; better connectivity with

The supply chain has been transformed in the retail industry by digital technology. The movement of goods and the flow of information between retailers and their suppliers are critical to operational success and whereas retailers used to be 'passive recipients of products, allocated to stores by manufacturers in anticipation of demand', now they are in control and manage supplies in response to customer demand. ASOS sells over 20,000 branded and own-label products through its online e-commerce operation. Digital systems and bar code technologies are enabling ASOS to offer 'a much wider product range than its high-street competitors'. Lean and agile supply chains which support large retail operations manage the purchasing, processing and movement of vast quantities of products so that individual items are in the right place at the right time to satisfy customer needs. Online shopping is on the increase but it creates operational and logistical challenges, especially for grocery retailers. A typical online grocery order consists of '60–80 items, across three temperature regimes picking from a total range of 10,000–25,000 products within 12–24 hours for delivery to customers within one to two hour time slots'.

Supermarket retailers have made significant investment in technology to manage the complexities associated with receiving products from thousands of suppliers, picking and delivering orders to millions of consumer orders. Ocado, the online-only grocery retailer, makes extensive use of digital technology to enable its business to operate. To manage its complex online operations, Ocado has developed in-house software and uses state-of-the-art gaming software to visualize and identify problems with the aim of streamlining operations in its automated warehouse and national supply chain. The IT team is pushing the boundaries in every aspect of the business with online and mobile developing apps for all the latest platforms, for example Android and iPad.

To learn more about Ocado and its use of technology visit http://www.ocadotechnology.com

Based on: Ellis-Chadwick (2011); Fernie et al. (2010)

new suppliers; improvements in reliability; streamlined information processing; and closer working relationships between suppliers and customers. There are potential savings to be made. For example, United Technologies expected to pay around $25 million for an order for printed circuit boards. Through e-procurement, the company attracted 34 bids from suppliers and paid $14 million, a saving of $10 million, or 40 per cent. E-commerce is also benefiting resellers by opening up target markets, improving product ranges and availability, improving cost efficiencies and delivery, and ultimately enhancing customer relationships (Doherty and Ellis-Chadwick, 2010).

However, whilst e-commerce and e-procurement are improving the ability of companies to source large numbers of suppliers and handle large quantities of goods, there are further implications for logistics management. Read Marketing in Action 4.5 to find out more.

Reverse marketing

The traditional view of marketing is that supplier firms will actively seek the requirements of customers and attempt to meet those needs better than the competition. This model places the initiative with the supplier. Purchasers could assume a passive dimension relying on their suppliers' sensitivity to their needs, and on technological capabilities to provide them with solutions to their problems. However, this trusting relationship is at odds with a new corporate purchasing situation that developed during the 1980s and is becoming increasingly popular. Purchasing is taking on a more proactive, aggressive stance in acquiring the products and services needed to compete. This process, whereby the buyer attempts to persuade the supplier to provide exactly what the organization wants, is called **reverse marketing** (Blenkhorn and Banting, 1991). Figure 4.3 shows the difference between the traditional model and this new concept.

FIGURE 4.3
Reverse marketing

Supplier sells by taking the initiative

Traditional marketing

Supplier — Buyer

Reverse marketing

Buyer takes the initiative to persuade supplier to provide what the organization wants

The essence of reverse marketing is that the purchaser takes the initiative by approaching new or existing suppliers and persuading them to meet its supply requirements. The growth of reverse marketing presents two key benefits to those suppliers willing to listen to the buyer's proposition and carefully consider its merits. First, it provides the opportunity to develop a stronger and longer-lasting relationship with the customer. Second, it may be a source of new product opportunities that may be developed to a broader customer base later on.

This shift in the direction of marketing is also evident in reseller markets. Social media are facilitating the exchange of information between customer and the organization and creating opportunities for companies to become

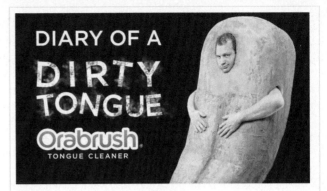

EXHIBIT 4.3
Orabrush—see how Dr. Bob Wagstaff used YouTube in an attempt to apply the principles of reverse marketing

more informed and better able to respond to customer requirements. Dr. Bob Wagstaff invented the Orabrush tongue cleaner early in 2000. The product was designed to help cure bad breath. But in the ensuing decade, he had fewer than 100 orders in total. So, with the help of a group of university students, he made a video starring Morgan the Orabrush tongue and based on 'the diary of a dirty tongue'. The aim was to drive demand for retail and e-commerce sales. The Orabrush tongue cleaner has become the number 1 brand in this category and is now sold in over 25 countries around the world (Orabrush, 2014).

Leasing

A lease is a contract by which the owner of an asset (e.g. a car) grants the right to another party to use the asset for a period of time in exchange for payment of rent (Anderson and Lazer, 1978). The benefits to the customer are that a leasing arrangement avoids the need to pay the cash purchase price of the product or service, is a hedge against fast product obsolescence, may have tax advantages, avoids the problem of equipment disposal and, with certain types of leasing contract, avoids some maintenance costs. These benefits need to be weighed against the costs of leasing, which may be higher than outright buying.

There are two main types of leases: financial (or full payment) leases and operating leases (sometimes called *rental agreements*). A *financial lease* is a longer-term arrangement that is fully amortized over the term of the contract. Lease payments, in total, usually exceed the purchase price of the item. The terms and conditions of the lease vary according to convention and competitive conditions. Sometimes the supplier will agree to pay maintenance costs over the leasing period. This is common when leasing photocopiers, for example. The lessee may also be given the option of buying the equipment at the end of the period. An *operating lease* is for a shorter period of time, is cancellable and is not completely amortized (Morris, 1988). Operating lease rates are usually higher than financial lease rates since they run for a shorter term. When equipment is required intermittently, this form of acquisition can be attractive because it avoids the need to let plant lie idle. Many types of equipment, such as diggers, bulldozers and skips, may be available for short-term hire, as may storage facilities.

Leasing may be advantageous to suppliers because it provides customer benefits that may differentiate product and service offerings. As such it may attract customers who might otherwise find the product unaffordable or uneconomic. The importance of leasing in such industries as cars, photocopiers and data processing has led an increasing number of companies to employ leasing consultants to work with customers on leasing arrangements and benefits. A crucial marketing decision is the setting of leasing rates. These should be set with the following factors in mind.

1 The desired relative attractiveness of leasing vs buying (the supplier may wish to promote/discourage buying compared with leasing)
2 The net present value of lease payments vs outright purchase
3 The tax advantages of leasing vs buying to the customer
4 The rates being charged by competitors
5 The perceived advantages of spreading payments to customers
6 Any other perceived customer benefits, for example maintenance and insurance costs being assumed by the supplier.

Outsourcing

Outsourcing is a booming business. From cleaning and Internet security to aircraft assembly, jobs are being outsourced. In the UK, about 10 per cent of the workforce is engaged in 'outsourced' jobs (*The Economist*, 2011).

As a business model, outsourcing can be very effective, as firms are contracted to do jobs they specialize in, leaving the business to get on with the core activities they are best at doing. Data centres and network computing are often outsourced to specialist providers. For example, E.ON contracted HP and T-Systems to take over its network and telecommunication services in a $1.4 billion deal that allowed E.ON to hand over the parts of the business it was struggling with in order to concentrate on its core business processes (Ovum, n.d.).

In Europe, IT and business processes outsourcing is on the increase (Heath, 2011) despite a global downturn. However, while outsourcing offers many potential benefits, contracts and specifications must be clearly defined at the outset as things can go wrong, and when they do there can be major problems. When Boeing, the USA's largest aircraft manufacturer, decided to outsource parts of the Dreamliner operation, major problems arose when subcontractors failed to deliver on time, and parts of the aircraft did not fit together. The result was an over-budget and over-schedule project that cost Boeing billions of dollars.

Whichever purchasing innovations firms use, central to success is the relationship between buyers and suppliers.

In this chapter we have considered the people, processes and practices involved in organizational buying. The issues raised in this chapter are relevant to Chapter 10, which discusses relationship management in detail.

When you have read this chapter

Discover further resources and test your understanding: McGraw-Hill **Connect**™ is a digital teaching and learning environment that improves performance over a variety of critical outcomes; it can be tailored, is easy to use and is proven effective. **LearnSmart**™ is the most widely used and intelligent adaptive learning resource that is proven to strengthen memory recall, improve course retention and boost grades. Fuelled by **LearnSmart**™, **SmartBook**™ is the first and only adaptive reading experience available today.

Review

1 **The characteristics of organizational buying**
   - The characteristics are based on the nature and size of customers, the complexity of buying, the use of economic and technical choice criteria, the risky nature of selling and buying, buying to specific requirements, reciprocal buying, derived demand and negotiations.

2 **The dimensions of organizational buying**
   - The dimensions are who buys, how they buy, the choice criteria used, and where and when they buy.

3 **The nature and marketing implications of the people: who buys, the processes involved in how organizations buy and the choice criteria used to evaluate products**
   - Who buys: there are six roles in the decision-making unit—initiators, users, deciders, influencers, buyers and gatekeepers. Marketers need to identify who plays each role, target communication at them and develop products to satisfy their needs.

- How organizations buy: the decision-making process has up to seven stages—recognition of problem (need), determination of specification and quantity of needed item, search for and qualification of potential sources, acquisition and analysis of proposals, evaluation of proposals and selection of supplier(s), selection of an order routine, and performance feedback and evaluation. Marketers can influence need recognition and gain competitive advantage by entering the process early.
- Choice criteria can be technical, economic, social (organizational) and personal. Marketers need to understand the choice criteria of the different members of the decision-making unit and target communications accordingly. Other marketing mix decisions such as product design will also depend on an understanding of choice criteria. Choice criteria can change over time necessitating a change in the marketing mix.

4 **The influences on organizational buying behaviour—the buy class, product type and purchase importance—and their marketing implications**
- The buy class consists of three types: new task, straight rebuy and modified rebuy. For new task, there can be large gains for suppliers entering the decision process early, but heavy investment is usually needed. For straight rebuys, the in-supplier should build a defensible position to keep out new potential suppliers. For out-suppliers, a key task is to reduce the risk of change for the buyers so that a modified rebuy will result.
- Product types consist of materials, components, plant and equipment, and maintenance items. Marketers need to recognize that the people who take part in the purchase decision usually change according to product type, and channel communications accordingly.
- The importance of purchase depends on the costs involved and the uncertainty (risk) regarding the decision. For very important decisions, heavy investment is likely to be required on the part of suppliers, and risk-reduction strategies (e.g. guarantees) may be needed to reduce uncertainty.

5 **The developments in purchasing practice: lean production, Kanban, just-in-time, TQM, e-procurement, e-commerce, centralized purchasing, reverse marketing and leasing**
- Kanban just-in-time practices and TQM aim to minimize stocks by organizing a supply system that provides materials and components as they are required. Potential gains are reduced purchasing, inventory and inspection costs, improved product design, streamlined delivery, reduced production downtime and improved quality.
- E-procurement and e-commerce are technology solutions for the purchasing functions. Platforms, gateways and hubs have been set up to facilitate electronic trading, and they have been widely adopted in industrial and reseller markets. The uptake in government markets has been much slower.
- Centralized purchasing encourages purchasing specialists to concentrate on a small group of products. This often increases the power of the purchasing department and results in a move to long-term relationships with suppliers.
- Reverse marketing places the initiative with the buyer, who attempts to persuade the supplier to produce exactly what the buyer wants. Suppliers need to be responsive to buyers and provide them with an opportunity to build long-term relationships and develop new products.
- Leasing may give financial benefits to customers and may attract customers that otherwise could not afford the product.
- Outsourcing enables firms to focus on their core business process while using contracted firms to provide peripheral services and support. Firms need to ensure that contracts and arrangements are correct to prevent mistakes.

Key Terms

decision-making process the stages that organizations and people pass through when purchasing a physical product or service

decision-making unit (DMU) a group of people within an organization who are involved in the buying decision (also known as the buying centre)

e-commerce involves all electronically mediated transactions between an organization and any third party it deals with, including exchange of information

e-procurement digital systems that facilitate the management of the procurement process; often integrates with e-commerce systems

just-in-time (JIT) this concept aims to minimize stocks by organizing a supply system that provides materials and components as they are required

lifecycle costs all the components of costs associated with buying, owning and using a physical product or service

modified rebuy where a regular requirement for the type of product exists and the buying alternatives are known but sufficient change (e.g. a delivery problem) has occurred to require some alteration to the normal supply procedure

new task refers to the first-time purchase of a product or input by an organization

reverse marketing the process whereby the buyer attempts to persuade the supplier to provide exactly what the organization wants

straight rebuy refers to a purchase by an organization from a previously approved supplier of a previously purchased item

total quality management the set of programmes designed to constantly improve the quality of physical products, services and processes

value analysis a method of cost reduction in which components are examined to see if they can be made more cheaply

Study Questions

1. What are the six roles that form the decision-making unit (DMU) for the purpose of an organizational purchase? What are the marketing implications of the DMU?

2. Why do the choice criteria used by different members of the DMU often change with the varying roles?

3. What are creeping commitment and lockout criteria? Why are they important factors in the choice of supplier?

4. Explain the difference between a straight rebuy, a modified rebuy and a new task purchasing situation. What implications do these concepts have for the marketing of industrial products?

5. Explain the meaning of reverse marketing. What implications does it have for suppliers?

Recommended Reading

Anderson, J. C., J. A. Narus and W. van Rossum (2006) Customer value propositions in business markets, *Harvard Business Review* 84(3) 90–9.

Arslanagic-Kalajdzic, M. and V. Zabkar (2015) The external effect of marketing accountability in business relationships: Exploring the role of customer perceived value, *Industrial Marketing Management* 46, April, 83–97.

Brennan, R., L. Canning and R. McDowell (2014) *Business to Business Marketing*, Sage Publications Ltd.

Ellis, N. (2010) *Business to Business Marketing*, Oxford, UK: Oxford University Press.

Ford, D., L.-E. Gadde, H. Hakansson and I. Snehota (2011) *Managing Business Relationships*, 3rd edn., UK: Wiley.

Grönroos, C. (2011) A Service perspective on business relationships: the value creation, interaction and marketing interface, *Industrial Marketing Management* 40 (2), 240–7.

O'Cass, A. and L. Ngo (2012) Creating superior customer value for B2B firms through supplier firm capabilities, *Industrial Marketing Management* 41(1), January 2012, 125–35.

References

Advanced Television (2014) Volvo Sponors Sky Atlantic. http://advanced-television.com/2014/01/02/volvo-sponsors-sky-atlantic (accessed 23 February 2015).

Airbus (2012) Airbus for suppliers, http://www.airbus.com/tools/airbusfor/suppliers/ (accessed February 2012).

Anderson, F. and W. Lazer (1978) Industrial Lease Marketing, *Journal of Marketing* 42 (January), 71–9.

Batting, J. (2014) *Five things you need to know to tackle maverick spend*, Supply Management, 7 October. http://www.supplymanagement.com/blog/2014/10/

five-things-you-need-to-know-to-tackle-maverick-spend (accessed 26 February 2015).

Bishop, W. S., J. L. Graham and M. H. Jones (1984) Volatility of Derived Demand in Industrial Markets and its Management Implications, *Journal of Marketing*, Fall, 95–103.

Blenkhorn, D. L. and P. M. Banting (1991) How Reverse Marketing Changes Buyer–Seller's Roles, *Industrial Marketing Management* 20, 185–91.

Brierty, E. G., R. W. Eckles and R. R. Reeder (1998) *Business Marketing*, Englewood Cliffs, NJ: Prentice-Hall, 105.

Calvo-Mora, A., C. Ruiz-Moreno, A. Picon-Berjoyo and L. Cauzo-Bottala (2014) Mediation effect of TQM technical factors in excellence management systems, *Journal of Business Research* 67(5), 769–74.

Cardozo, R. N. (1980) Situational Segmentation of Industrial Markets, *European Journal of Marketing* 14(5/6), 264–76.

Chaffey, D. and F. Ellis-Chadwick (2015) *Digital Marketing: Strategy, Implementation and Practice*, Pearson.

Cline, C. E. and B. P. Shapiro (1978) *Cumberland Metal Industries (A): Case Study*, Boston, Mass: Harvard Business School.

Corey, E. R. (1991) *Industrial Marketing: Cases and Concepts*, Englewood Cliffs, NJ: Prentice-Hall.

Doherty, N. and F. Ellis-Chadwick (2010) Evaluating the role of electronic commerce in transforming, *The International Review of Retail, Distribution and Consumer Research* 20(4), 375–8.

Doherty, N. F., D. McConnell and F. Ellis-Chadwick (2013) Institutional responses to electronic, *International Journal of Public Sector Management* 26(2), 495–515.

Draper, A. (1994) Organizational Buyers as Workers: The Key to their Behaviour, *European Journal of Marketing* 28(11), 50–62.

Edwards, C. (2006) Inside Intel, *Business Week*, 9 January, 43–8.

Ellis-Chadwick, F. E. (2011), *Retail Planning and Supply Chain Management*, Buckingham: The Open University, 5.

Fernie, J., L. Sparks and A. C. McKinnon (2010) Retail Logistics in the UK: Past present and Future, *International Journal of Retail Distribution & Management*, 38(11/12), 894–914.

Forbis, J. L. and N. T. Mehta (1981) Value-Based Strategies for Industrial Products, *Business Horizons*, May–June, 32–42.

GE Transportation (2012) Eco-minded PowerHaul leads the way into global markets, http://www.getransportation.com/rail/rail-blog/eco-minded-powerhaul-leads-the-way-into-global-markets.html.

Heagarty, R (2011) Waitrose demands a 5 per cent cut from suppliers, *The Grocer*, 10 October, http://www.thegrocer.co.uk/companies/waitrose-demands-a-5-cut-from-suppliers/221572.article.

Heath, N. (2011) Megadeals are out and multisourcing is in as Europe's outsourcing spend rises. *Silicon.com*, http://www.silicon.com/technology/it-services/2011/07/27/megadeals-are-out-and-multisourcing-is-in-as-europes-outsourcing-spend-rises-39747743/ (accessed February 2012).

Hitachi Transportation System (2012) Downsizing logistics space within factories and reduce parts/devices, http://www.hitachi-hb.co.jp/english/jirei/case_08.html (accessed 12 February 2012).

Hoer, A., C. Eriglu and A. Hofer (2012) The effect of lean production on financial performance: The mediating role of inventory leanness, *International Journal of Production Ecomonics* 138(2), 242–53.

Hutt, M. D. and T. W. Speh (2006) *Business Marketing Management*, New York: Dryden Press.

Iceland Foods Ltd (2014) A year of major investment for sustainable future growth. http://about.iceland.co.uk/_assets/files/Iceland-Foods-2014-results-FINAL.pdf (accessed 26 February 2015).

Iceland Foods Ltd (2015) Malcolm Walker's biography. http://about.iceland.co.uk/the-boss/malcolm-walkers-biography (accessed 26 February 2015).

Jobber, D. and G. Lancaster (2015) *Selling and Sales Management*, London: Pitman, 27.

Lewis, S. and J. Arnold (2012) Organisational career management in the UK retail buying and mrechandising community, *International Journal of Retail & Distribution Management* 40(6), 451–70.

Macleod, I. (2014) Volvo Cars suggests it is From Sweden Not Hollywood in Idents for Sky Atlantic, *The Drum*, 10 November. http://www.thedrum.com/news/2014/11/10/volvo-cars-suggests-it-sweden-not-hollywood-idents-sky-atlantic (accessed 23 February 2015).

Mitchell, P. (2015) How to use Mavericks to solve the maverick spending problem. *Spending Matters Network*, 26 January. http://spendmatters.com/cpo/use-mavericks-solve-maverick-spending-problem (accessed 26 February 2015).

Moretti, P. (2013) Spend Management: A Necessary Evil? My Purchasing Centre, 1 February. http://www.mypurchasingcenter.com/technology/technology-blogs/spend-management-a-necessary-evil (accessed 26 February 2015).

Morris, M. H. (1988) *Industrial and Organisation Marketing*, Columbus, OH: Merrill, 323.

Naughton, J. (2005) Is Apple Right to Cosy up to the Enemy?, *Observer*, 12 June, 6.

Orabrush. (2014) *The story of Orabrush*. Orabrush. https://www.orabrush.com/story

Ovum (n.d.) E.On's IT outsourcing deal augurs further activity in utilities in 2011, http://ovum.com/2010/12/22/e-ons-it-outsourcing-deal-augurs-further-activity-in-utilities-in-2011/.

Pomeroy, A. (producer) and Rogan, J. (director) (2013) *Iceland Frozen Foods: Life in the Freezer Cabinet* [Motion Picture], BBC Two.

Robinson, P. J., C. W. Faris and Y. Wind (1967) *Industrial Buying and Creative Marketing*, Boston, Mass: Allyn & Bacon.

Skymedia. (2014) Volvo becomes new Sky Atlantic Sponsor, Sky Media, 1 January. http://www.skymedia.co.uk/news/volvo-becomes-new-sky-atlantic-sponsor.aspx (accessed 23 February 2015).

Snoad, L. (2012) Taking personal control of the mission redefinition, *Marketing Week*, 26 January, 16–19.

Stone, R. N. and K. Gronhaug (1993) Perceived Risk: Further Considerations for the Marketing Discipline, *European Journal of Marketing* 27(3), 39–50.

Syal, R. (2013) Abandoned NHS IT system has cost £10bn so far, *The Guardian*. http://www.theguardian.com/society/2013/sep/18/nhs-records-system-10bn (accessed 23 February 2015).

The Economist (2011) Outsourcing is sometimes more hassle than its worth, 30 July, 62.

Vizard, S. (2013) Volvo signs 2-year Sky Atlantic sponsorship deal, *Marketing Week*. http://www.marketingweek.com/2013/12/19/volvo-signs-2-year-sky-atlantic-sponsorship-deal (accessed 23 February 2015).

Walsh, F. (2006) M&S Tightens Screw on Suppliers, *Guardian*, 4 March, 27.

Webster, F. E. and Y. Wind (1972) *Organizational Buying Behaviour*, Englewood Cliffs, NJ: Prentice-Hall, 78–80. The sixth role of initiator was added by Bonoma, T. V. (1982) Major Sales: Who Really does the Buying, *Harvard Business Review*, May–June, 111–19.

Wright, R. (2008) EMD Fighting to Regain Ground, *Financial Times*, Rail Industry Special Report, 23 September, 3.

Wright, R. (2008) GE Challenges EMD Dominance, *Financial Times*, 23 September, 29.

CASE 7
Flying in Tandem: Organizational Purchasing in the Airline Industry

Introduction

Thomas Cook is a tour operator known for selling good-quality package holidays for a wide range of tourist destinations; this forms the core of its business. The firm, which is a strong brand name in the UK travel industry, can trace its origins back to 1841, when its eponymous founder (Thomas Cook) began arranging day trips between Leicester and Loughborough. Currently, it sells into consumer markets online and through over 3,000 travel agents, providing holidays to destinations around the globe and flying passengers from over 20 airports in the UK. The company operates its own fleet of airplanes to facilitate this service.

However, the economic downturn of the late 2000s and changing consumer purchasing trends saw a significant fall in demand for traditional two-week holiday packages, which had a very negative effect on sales. Thomas Cook was plunged into financial crisis in November 2011 and had to turn to its lenders for help, sparking fears of a collapse. The company proved to be resilient, and as part of its recovery strategy set about reducing its £1 billion debt by selling assets. It sold part of its aircraft fleet, five Spanish hotels and its Indian travel operations. Since 2012, trade has improved and the Thomas Cook Group now includes Condor (Germany) together with Belgium and Scandinavian subsidiaries. The Chinese conglomerate Fosun purchased a 5 per cent stake in the company in 2015. Another part of easyJet's strategy was to find different low-cost ways to transport customers around the world, which meant working with other flight providers.

Flight Providers

The market for flights can be segmented in a number of ways. Traditionally, a distinction has been made between scheduled and charter flights. The former are planes that are scheduled to fly on a particular route at a particular time on a regular basis. A number of these operators have a long history, and many of those in Europe have been previously under state control, for example Aeroflot, Air France and BA. Charter flights are those whose main purpose is to transport holidaymakers to tourist destinations. Tickets for these are not sold directly to passengers but are bought

by holiday companies who have chartered the flight. At one time, Thomas Cook charter flights were only sold as part of a package holiday. However, this is no longer the case, and flights can be purchased without the need to buy a package holiday.

In the 1990s, the airline industry in Europe began to change as low-cost airlines opened out the market for flights by offering scheduled flights, which competed with those of the established carriers. Changes in legislation and the development of the Internet enabled these low-cost operators to grow rapidly by adopting a strategy that is similar to that pioneered by Herb Kelleher of Southwest Airlines in the USA. A low-cost airline is one that offers low fares but does not offer many of the services of the traditional airlines. Formed in 1995, easyJet has grown to be the second-largest low-cost airline in the UK (by number of passengers), just behind Ryanair. EasyJet operates domestic and international services on over 600 routes in 32 countries. Its head office is at Luton Airport.

EasyJet positions itself in the market as a no-frills airline that focuses on reducing costs and offering low prices. The key features of this strategy are:
- achieving high aircraft utilization and quick turnaround of flights at airports
- cutting costs by removing non-essential features from flights, such as reclining seats, food and drink, and baggage allowances; these services can be purchased at additional cost
- dealing directly with consumers to cut out the margin of travel agents and other distributors

- offering flights that can only be booked through the company website unless they are booked three months prior to the flight; in this case, telephone bookings are accepted
- offering short-haul flights, mainly in Europe, although Egypt, Morocco, Israel and Turkey are also served
- flying to major airports, unlike its main competitor, Ryanair, which often flies to secondary smaller airports on the outskirts of destinations as a cost-saving measure.

Company Cooperation

At Thomas Cook, senior buyers saw a potential opportunity to use low-cost carriers to service the company's holiday packages. As a result, in 2012 they negotiated an agreement to buy seats on easyJet flights. This allowed the tour operator to book seats for package holiday tourists only on easyJet scheduled flights. The agreement does not extend to selling seats only. It represents the first major move by easyJet into the marketing of its flights in bulk to another company, where previously its main focus was on the consumer market. In contrast, Thomas Cook has been used to buying in organizational markets and negotiating hard to secure the best deals on hotel rooms, cruises and entertainment to supply to its package holiday customers. When the agreement was signed, it was estimated that easyJet could cover up to 80,000 trips, about 3 per cent of Thomas Cook's capacity.

Whilst the move to partner with low-cost airlines was an innovative purchasing solution, Thomas Cook has regularly worked with other airlines such as Monarch and Thomson to provide its holidays. A spokesperson for flight planning and capacity confirmed the benefit of buying from easyJet as cost saving. In addition, it meant opportunities to broaden the product offer, as Thomas Cook can offer customers greater choice, convenience and flexibility. This is a result of the number of airports used and destinations served, and of increased departure times provided by easyJet. Since the summer of 2013, Thomas Cook customers have been able to choose package holidays from over 50 destinations on easyJet flights, including Spain, Greece, Turkey, Cyprus, Italy and Malta. Under the flying terms, passengers are allowed 15 kilograms of baggage; an extra allowance can be purchased, and 5 kilograms of hand luggage. Seats are not allocated and no meals are provided, although snacks can be purchased on board. This expansion of the product range has been welcomed by the high street travel agents, as it enables it to compete more effectively.

The first year of the partnership went well and was extended, but easyJet then announced that it would not be flying as many passengers. The reason for the reduction in capacity was due to the complexity of block-booking seats on flights. The number of flights that easyJet operates also acts as a constraint on its ability to supply seats. Summer, particularly the July and August period, which is the busiest season for package holidays, is also the peak time of the year for easyJet. For Thomas Cook, this arrangement is part of a set of flight solutions that help them serve the increasing demands of holiday travellers.

EasyJet and Organizational Markets

Partnerships like the one with Thomas Cook have helped easyJet recognize the opportunities and different requirements of its business customers, and consequently easyJet has begun to focus on the corporate market. To manage relationships with new types of customers, the company has set up a corporate sales team, mindful of the different requirements of organizational buyers. This meant dealing with agents as opposed to selling directly as in consumer markets. Since 2011, Thomas Cook has allowed business customers to use its booking system. This is linked to the Amadeus system that is used by a large number of airlines and allows users to check flight availability and change bookings.

Most business organizations that need their staff to work in different locations and travel as part of their job employ the services of a travel management company to administer arrangements. The professional body in the UK for this industry is the Guild of Travel Management Companies (GTMC); it represents most of the leading travel management companies, which account for about 80 per cent of the spending on business travel in the UK. The main remit of the GTMC is lobbying suppliers, government, opinion-formers and the media to provide a better deal for both companies and their employees.

In order to develop the travel management part of its business, easyJet became a member of the GTMC in 2010. This enabled it to discover more about the travel requirements of members of the GTMC. Membership may also be required to become an accredited supplier for certain organizations. The increased commitment to business passengers can be seen in the fact that the airline has become a listed supplier for members of the House of Parliament. As easyJet changed its policy to allow seat reservations to be made for a fee, it was added to the approved suppliers list of Hillard Travel, which has been responsible for making travel arrangements for MPs and members of the House of Lords. EasyJet also signed a deal in 2012 with the Scottish public sector to administer the flying arrangements of NHS staff, the police, members of the Scottish parliament (MSPs) and civil servants. Business travellers now

»

»

form a big part of easyJet's market; over 10 million passengers were carried in 2012, up from 9 million in 2011 and 8 million in 2010.

The airline industry presents challenges for organizational buyers, as there are many variables that can influence operating costs and are beyond the control of the flight operators—for example oil prices, exchange rates, legislation and political conflicts—so buyers in this industry have to be especially skilled in anticipating how the marketing environment can affect their negotiations.

Questions   ![McGraw Hill Education] **connect**

1. **Explain how easyJet's relationship with Thomas Cook may differ from that they have with individual buyers in terms of:**
   - **order size / number of seats purchased**
   - **economic and technical choice criteria**
   - **customer relationship**
   - **tailoring of service to buyers requirements**
   - **level of negotiation.**

2. **Explain what is meant by the decision making unit (DMU). How is the composition of the DMU likely to differ between individual buyers, Thomas Cook and government departments in the buying of easyJet airline seats?**

3. **The buyer-seller relationship between easyJet and Thomas Cook is in the development stage having been in operation for only two years. Explain the role of National Account Managers at both companies in developing the relationship over the long term.**

4. **Thomas Cook could be said to be employing a reverse marketing strategy with easyJet. Explain this term and why this is the case.**

5. **Demand from organizational buyers is often derived. Explain why the demand from Thomas Cook for seats on easyJet flights is likely to be derived.**

The case study was written by Adrian Pritchard, Senior Lecturer in Marketing, Coventry University.

Further reading

EasyJet www.easyJet.com; The Guild of Travel Management Companies www.gtmc.org.uk; Thomas Cook www.Thomascookairlines.com; YouTube (the first two videos look at easyJet's strategy in the business market; the third gives a good illustration of the Amadeus system): Business Travel Show 2014: easyJet targets business travellers, Business travel, Reuters, https://www.youtube.com/watch?v=IfGSTsPqoEs (2:23); EasyJet Sales Director Toby Joseph talks about the low cost carrier's focus on business travellers, https://www.youtube.com/watch?v=4uSrHOr9JXc (4:28); Amadeus upgrades easyJet to light ticketing booking flow, https://www.youtube.com/watch?v=DJUH9dKEEmY (3:58).

References

Based on: AirportWatch (2013) EasyJet had 10 million passengers in 2012, up from 9 million in 2011, AirportWatch, http://www.airportwatch.org.uk/2013/01/klm-and-world-wildlife-fund-pool-resources-to-reduce-co2-impact (accessed 7 July 2015); BBC (2015) Thomas Cook shares jump after Fosun buys 5% stake, BBC, http://www.bbc.co.uk/news/business-31761089 (accessed 7 July 2015); Belfast International Airport (2012) New Thomas Cook partnership with EasyJet from Belfast International Airport, Belfast International Airport, http://www.belfastairport.com/en/news/1/187/new-thomas-cook-partnership-with-easyJet-from-belfast-international-airport.html; Goodman, M. (2012) Thomas Cook books EasyJet seats, *The Sunday Times*, 9 September; Lea, R. (2012) It's easy MP as politicians leave business class behind, *The Times*, 18 September; McCosker, P. (2003) *EasyJet: The spectacular growth of low cost airlines*, ECCH Cranfield University; Russell, J. (2012) EasyJet signs up MPs for Parliamentary travel, *The Telegraph*, 18 September; This is Money (2013) Book with Thomas Cook, fly with EasyJet. . . Struggling package holiday giant 'to buy thousands of seats on budget airline', This is Money, http://www.thisismoney.co.uk/money/news/article-2200617/Thomas-Cook-buy-thousands-seats-easyJet.html#ixzz269fJBy6k (accessed 7 July 2015); Thomas Cook (2014)What's included, Thomas Cook, http:www.thomascook.com/airlines/easy-jet (accessed 7 July 2015); TravelMole (2014) EasyJet cools on deal with Thomas Cook, Travel Mole, www.travelmole.com/news_feature.php?id=2009144 (accessed 7 July 2015); Woods, D. (2012) Interview with Alita Benson, group director of people at EasyJet, *HR Magazine*, http://www.hrmagazine.co.uk/hr/features/1074277/interview-alita-benson-director-people-easyJet (accessed 7 July 2015)

CASE 8
AstraZeneca: Sweden and the UK Join Forces to Form a Production Power Base to Serve New Market Habitats in the Pharmaceutical Industry

AstraZeneca was developed following a merger between Astra AB of Sweden and Zeneca PLC of the UK. These two companies had similar organizational cultures and views of the pharmaceutical industry. The purpose of the merger was to take advantage of market growth opportunities, extend the reach of the business to global markets to create a more powerful innovation-led research and development platform and to improve financial flexibility. AstraZeneca became the fourth-largest pharmaceutical company in the world when the Swedish and UK companies merged. This created a challenge for the supply side of the business. This case explores the complexity of the buying process and associated issues in procurement in the pharmaceutical industry.

AstraZeneca is a manufacturer of drug treatments and specializes in cardiovascular, oncology and respiratory healthcare, which are the major areas of metabolic disease. The organization is involved in all stages of production and distribution, from the initial research and development required to find new drugs and

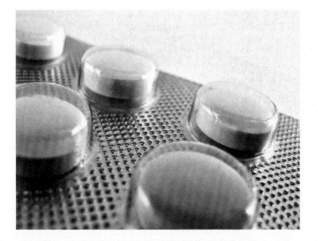

treatments, through manufacture, to delivery to its business customers.

Pharmaceuticals is a complex industry, especially when it comes to procurement. So companies in this industry need to be very clear about their buying objectives and product requirements and have strategies in place that can guide their purchasing. Over the last few decades there has been a seismic shift in the pharmaceuticals industry in terms of the way value is defined, and in the markets that products are created for. To understand this market sector we need to briefly delve into the history of its development.

Brief history of the evolution of pharmaceutical industry

Over the years, this industry has evolved and new business models have emerged. Until 1870, there was just one business model, and that was the apothecary shop; this was a robust approach to buying and selling drugs and is how Astra AB came into being with over 400 of these shops. This low-tech approach to medicine supply served the market demands well for over 600 years. But as the marketing environment changed through the period of the industrial revolution, social attitudes altered, populations grew, urbanization of living spaces was extended to a larger population, increased knowledge of technology opened up product-development opportunities, and the result was demand for different types of drug to treat a range of new and existing conditions. The pharmaceutical industry evolved to meet this new demand. There were then two types of approach to buying and selling drugs—prescription drugs, and over-the-counter drugs—and this became the module used for many decades.

»

Moving rapidly forward to the 1990s, the marketing environment again experienced major changes from social and technology perspectives, and there were major advances in medicines—for example antibiotics and beta blockers—which led to further and more sophisticated business models of buying and selling emerging. The evolution of the pharmaceutical industry, driven by technological and social change, has continued to intensify over the last 25 years. Now we have an even more complex set of business models guiding the way pharmaceutical products are bought and sold.

Figure C8.1 illustrates how there are different types of market emerging that are being shaped by: 1) the demand for fitness, 2) who defines the value, and 3) how the value is created. The habitats shown are potential markets for particular types of product. For example, the 'Lazarus and Narcissus' habitat is where there is demand for very innovative and expensive treatments that are highly personalized, for example gene therapy. Buyers of these types of product will be serving a target market of 'wealthy well' individuals who are seeking to maintain their health. In the centre of Figure C8.1 is the core state provision habitat. This is where government procurement processes define the value—which currently is to seek maximum efficiency from drugs at the lowest possible cost to serve a large state healthcare market. At the other end of the spectrum is the 'limited choice' habitat, which is similar to state provision but tends to occur more in emerging poorly served healthcare markets (Smith, 2011).

So, in summary, forces in the marketing environment are increasingly shaping demand, and the buying practices within the pharmaceutical industry and the emerging habitats (markets) are driving the market-based approach to purchasing.

Visit http://www.open.ac.uk/business-school/corporate/business-network/lessons-evolutionary-science to find out more about the evolution of business models in the pharmaceutical industry.

Market-based approach to purchasing

Drugs are specialized products made from chemical substances that interact with the human body to produce a biological response. These products are manufactured to a high specification by companies like AstraZeneca. Developing and clinical testing of new drugs can take many years before they are made available for sale, in order to ensure they are safe and effective. Finally, drugs must have regulatory approval and continuous monitoring. Once AstraZeneca has developed a new drug, it holds a patent, which gives the company protection for the production of the product for, say, 20 years. Once the patent runs out, then cheaper copies can be manufactured by other companies; these are called generics.

Buyers that are looking to purchase drugs from AstraZeneca have to navigate through a complex set of choice criteria. See Table C8.1 for definition of

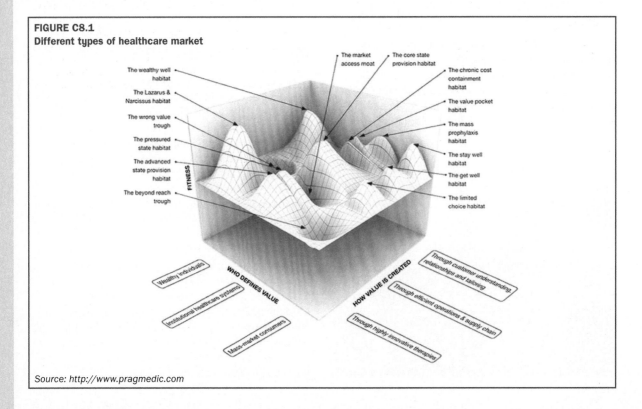

FIGURE C8.1
Different types of healthcare market

Source: http://www.pragmedic.com

TABLE C8.1 Drug types and example products

Drug type	Product examples	Description
Perception drugs Sold by the drug manufacturer who holds the patent	Pulmicort	Asthma treatment
Generics Made under licence, these are drugs that are no longer under a patent, and as a result the price is much lower	Nexium	Decreases the acid in the stomach and treats symptoms of reflux
Over the counter Sold by pharmacists without prescription	Ibuprofen	Anti-inflammatory, pain relief

the broad types of product bought and sold in the pharmaceutical industry.

Increasingly, buyers in this industry are under pressure to meet many different purchasing criteria, and determination of product specification and quality is very important. Berk et al. (2013) suggest it is important to consider all three of the broad types of product shown in Table C8.1 if a buying group is to meet its order requirements and the different routes to the emerging market segments, for example direct to consumer, direct to pharmacy. Berk et al. also suggest that manufacturers and buyers throughout the supply chain select a procurement model to guide their buying practices. The procurement models are based on the service requirement and demands for cost-effectiveness and value.

Questions

1. **Discuss the extent to which buyers in the pharmaceutical industry need to consider the marketing environment when making purchasing decisions.**

2. **Imagine you are a buyer of cardiovascular drugs and treatments for a large state healthcare provider. Identify a set of choice criteria you might use.**

3. **Explore the nature and size of manufacturers in the pharmaceutical industry and discuss the extent to which the Pareto rule applies.**

This Case study was written by Fiona Ellis-Chadwick, Senior Lecturer, Loughborough University

References

Berk, P., M. Gilbert, M. Herlant and G. Walter (2013) Rethinking the Pharma Supply Chain: New Models for a New Era, BCG Perspectives by the Boston Consulting group, https://www.bcgperspectives.com/content/articles/biopharma_supply_chain_management_rethinking_pharma_supply_chain_new_models_new_era/#chapter1 (accessed July 2015); AstraZenec (2015) About Us—History, http://www.astrazeneca.com/About-Us/History (accessed July 2015); Smith, B. (2011) *The Future of Pharma: evolutionary threats and opportunities*, Gower Publishing Ltd.

CHAPTER 5
Marketing Ethics and Corporate Social Responsibility

The premise of this Foundation is one life on this planet is no more valuable than the next.

MELINDA FRENCH GATES

LEARNING OBJECTIVES

After reading this chapter, you should be able to:

1 explain the meaning of ethics, and business and marketing ethics
2 describe ethical issues in marketing
3 discuss business, societal, and legal and regulatory responses to ethical concerns
4 explain the stakeholder theory of the firm
5 discuss the nature of corporate social responsibility (CSR)
6 describe the dimensions of CSR
7 discuss the arguments for and against CSR programmes
8 discuss non-profit organizations' contribution to societal marketing

The world has changed dramatically since the emergence of marketing as a business discipline, and as a result so have the principles and values which underpin modern marketing and management thinking. Companies are adopting environmental and social policies that fit with their organizational structure and stakeholder expectations. Concern for the physical environment has grown in significance in corporate and marketing planning in recent years and so sustainability—a company's survival into the future over say 10, 50 or 100 years—has become an important principle to many marketers. However, tension exists between the environmental, social and economic contexts, and the extent to which a company leans towards high or low sustainability policies and environmental credentials will determine where the emphasis is placed (see Figure 5.1). For example, high-sustainability companies pay attention to stakeholder relationships—for example, relationships with employees, customers and non-governmental organizations (NGOs) in the environment—engaging with them in a proactive way. Low-sustainability companies will concentrate on the traditional corporate model of profit maximization (Eccles, Ioannou and Serafin, 2011).

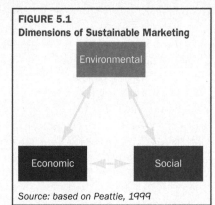

FIGURE 5.1
Dimensions of Sustainable Marketing

Source: based on Peattie, 1999

Environmental

Sustainability is at the heart of environmental marketing. To derive benefit from focusing on this dimension, companies should create marketing strategies that address issues facing the physical world. For example, Nestlé is considering how to maintain a sustainable water supply in its long-term strategic planning. Companies should consider the environmental costs of their corporate and marketing activities (Peattie, 1999). Green marketing is arguably an extreme form of environmental marketing; in its truest form the aim is to produce goods that do not negatively impact the physical environment. Furthermore, all the processes, packaging and distribution of these goods should conform to the highest environmental scrutiny. Problems can occur when companies only partially adopt this approach, as they could be accused of *greenwashing*—attempting to ride on the 'green tide' (Vandermerwe and Oliff, 1990; Peattie and Crane, 2006).

Social

Inequality and social deprivation is a global phenomenon; according to the World Bank, in 2011 over 2.2 billion people lived on less than $2 a day, and progress is very slow in moving them out of poverty (World Bank, 2015). The Poverty Index indicates there are over 91 countries where people are living with deprivations in health education and poor living standards, which can have devastating effects on life expectancy (United National Development Programme, 2015). The shift in focus towards how marketing might engage with the wider world began in the early 1970s and has since grown into a dimension of marketing that focuses on changing behaviour for individual and societal benefit. Social marketing is discussed in detail later in this chapter.

Economic

Strong economic performance is the bedrock of business activity, and economic growth is a strong force in the marketing environment. However, environmental issues have begun to impact on economic performance. For example, accessible reserves of oil and natural gas have dwindled, causing prices to rise across many raw materials and manufactured goods. Additionally, natural disasters such as the tsunami on the North Pacific coast of Japan have had a devastating economic impact: the Bank of Japan had to put billions of yen into its 'quake budget' to bolster the economy, and at the same time damage to factories caused major losses for Fuji Heavy Industries, GlaxoSmithKline and Nestlé (Webb, 2011). Moreover, extreme weather conditions, such as hurricane Sandy when it struck the Eastern Seaboard of the USA, have caused billions of dollars of damage.

Companies have responded in various ways to the dimensions of sustainable marketing.

Corporate social responsibility (CSR) and operating in an ethical way are becoming increasingly important in the modern world. Globally, companies are taking CSR seriously and responding positively; for example, TNT (Netherlands logistics firm) has 50 people on standby to respond within 48 hours to world emergencies; IBM's (USA computer corporation) philanthropic spending involves deploying staff to work on worthy projects in the developing world; Nestlé's answer to CSR is to look for ways of creating shared values. Nestlé's aim is to prosper as a business but in doing so to ensure that communities also prosper; it believes that having the ethos anchored so firmly makes the company more alert to both risks and opportunities.

Positive responses can benefit an organization's market position but, equally, unethical behaviour can lead to bad publicity and have a negative effect on customers' willingness to buy. Examples that have had a negative influence include: BA (price fixing), BAE Systems (bribery), BP and Shell (oil spills in USA and Nigeria), Walmart (allegations of poor employee relations), McDonald's (health concerns), Coca-Cola (marketing positioning of Dasani in the UK) and Procter & Gamble (Sunny D, the drink found to turn children yellow). These examples bear witness to the importance of business and marketing ethics, not only in their own right but also for the well-being of the organizations themselves.

Consequently, organizations are now reflecting on and defining their standards of ethical behaviour. They should also use these standards as the basis for designing CSR strategies that take account of how their actions might affect society and the environment. This requires an analysis of how decisions affect the wider community beyond the narrow interests of shareholders.

This chapter follows naturally from the discussion in Chapter 2 of the marketing environment (e.g. social/cultural, ecological/physical and technological) by discussing the meaning of marketing ethics and specific associated issues that might affect how organizations operate and respond. This chapter focuses on organizational responses in the shape of CSR programmes, the nature and dimensions of CSR, and an analysis of the arguments for and against the establishment of such programmes. Then social marketing and not-for-profit marketing are considered. Finally, the chapter concludes with a summary of some of the key issues in marketing ethics and CSR.

Marketing Ethics

Underpinning the idea of corporate social responsibility (CSR) and shaping its implementation is the concept of ethics. **Ethics** are the moral principles and values that govern the actions and decisions of an individual or group (Berkowitz et al., 2004). They involve *values* about right and wrong conduct. **Business ethics** are the moral principles and values that guide a firm's behaviour. Until recently, for many companies business ethics consisted mainly of compliance-based, legally driven codes and training that outlined in detail what employees could or could not do regarding such areas as conflicts of interest or improper use of company assets. Now, an increasing number of companies are designing value-based ethical programmes that are consistent across global operations. The aim is to provide employees with an in-depth understanding of ethical issues that will help them to make the correct decisions when faced with new ethical situations and challenges (Business for Social Responsibility Issue Briefs, 2003).

Marketing ethics are the moral principles and values that guide behaviour within the field of marketing, and cover issues such as product safety, truthfulness in marketing communications, honesty in relationships with customers and distributors, pricing issues, and the impact of marketing decisions on the environment and society. There can be a distinction between the legality and ethicality of marketing decisions. Ethics concern personal moral principles and values, while laws reflect society's principles and standards that are enforceable in the courts.

Not all unethical practices are illegal. For example, it is not illegal to include genetically modified (GM) ingredients in products sold in supermarkets. However, some organizations, such as Greenpeace, believe it is unethical to sell GM products when their effect on health has not been scientifically proven. Such concerns have led some supermarket chains to withdraw GM ingredients from their own-brand products. Nor was it illegal for Google to launch a self-censored search engine that prevents access to 'sensitive' subjects in China, yet the action has been criticized on ethical grounds (Naughton, 2006).

Ethical principles reflect the cultural values and norms of society. Norms guide what ought to be done in a particular situation. For example, being truthful is regarded as good. This societal norm may influence marketing behaviour. Hence—since it is good to be truthful—deceptive, untruthful advertising should be avoided. Often, unethical behaviour may be clear-cut but, in other cases, deciding what is ethical is highly debatable. Ethical dilemmas arise when two principles or values conflict. For example, Ben & Jerry's, the US ice cream firm, was a leading member of the Social Venture Network in San Francisco, a group that promotes ethical standards in business. A consortium, Meadowbrook Lane Capital, was part of this group and was formed to raise enough capital to make Ben & Jerry's a private company again. However, its bid was lower than that of Anglo–Dutch food multinational Unilever NV. Arguably, on the one hand, for Ben & Jerry's to stick to its ethical beliefs it should have accepted the Meadowbrook bid. On the other hand, the company also had to perform financially in the interests of its shareholders. Ben & Jerry's faced an ethical dilemma: one of its values and preferences inhibited the achievement of financial considerations. Ultimately, it accepted the Unilever bid (Reed, 2000).

Many ethical dilemmas derive from the conflict between the desire to increase profits and the wish to make decisions that are ethically justified. For example, the decision by Google to launch a self-censored search engine in China was driven by the need to be competitive in a huge market where it was lagging behind competitors. In order to secure a deal in China, Microsoft accepted censorship by the government in its agreement with Baidu (China's largest search engine) (Arthur, 2011). Companies do seek to address such conflicts: for example, Nike and Reebok monitor their overseas production of sports goods to ensure that no child labour is used, while still producing cost-efficient ranges.

Ethical Issues in Marketing

Marketing practices have been criticized by consumers, consumer groups and environmentalists, who complain that marketing managers have been guilty of harming the interests of consumers, society and the environment. In this section, these ethical concerns are analyzed by examining issues specific to the marketing mix; this is followed by consideration of general societal, environmental and political issues (see Figure 5.2).

Ethical issues relating to marketing mix effects on consumers

Ethical concerns impinge on all aspects of the marketing mix. The rest of this section gives examples for product, price, promotion and place. Further specific examples are given in later chapters.

Product: product safety

The tobacco, food and drinks industries have attracted criticism in recent years regarding the potential harm their products may cause to consumers. Tobacco companies have been criticized for marketing cigarettes, which cause lung cancer. The food industry has been criticized for marketing products that have high levels of fat, which can lead to obesity, and in the drinks industry concern has been expressed over the marketing to children of sugar-rich fizzy drinks, which cause tooth decay and can also lead to obesity. Concern over Sunny D's high level of sugar forced Procter & Gamble to withdraw the drink's original formulation from the market, and the lack of success of its relaunch persuaded Procter & Gamble to sell the brand six years after its original launch (Choveke, 2006). Pressure from consumers has prompted McDonald's, the world's largest fast-food retailer, to diversify its product ranges by adding healthier options to its menus.

On the other hand, the industry has also argued that businesses and government are taking steps to reduce the harmful effects of products, with bans on tobacco promotion escalating across Europe and the creation of bodies such as the Food Standards Agency (the independent food safety body set up to protect public health and consumer interests in relation to food in the UK) and the Portman Group

FIGURE 5.2
Ethical issues in marketing

(the industry-sponsored organization that oversees the UK's alcoholic drinks industry). Most European countries have similar organizations which are also able to provide advice to industry.

Pricing: price fixing

An anti-competitive practice associated with marketing is price fixing, where two or more companies collude to force up the price of products. European Union (EU) competition policy provides a legal framework that is designed to prevent companies from carrying out this practice. For example, the European Commission has fined three chemical groups (Hoechst, Atofina and Akzo-Nobel) £153 million for fixing the market for monochloroacetic acid, a widely used household and industrial chemical (Milner, 2005). National laws also ban price fixing, as is illustrated by BA's £121 million fine from the UK's Office of Fair Trading for fixing long-haul fuel surcharges, and its £148 million fine from the USA's Department of Justice for colluding over cargo and long-haul surcharges (Milmo, 2007). Price fixing is considered unethical because it interferes with the consumer's freedom of choice and raises prices artificially.

Supporters of marketing claim that price fixing is the exception rather than the rule, however, and that while it should not be conducted, most industries are highly competitive with prices reflecting what consumers are willing to pay.

Promotion

Misleading advertising can take the form of exaggerated claims or concealed facts. A claim that a diet product was capable of 1 kilogram of weight loss per week when in reality much less was the case is an example of an exaggerated claim. When Coca-Cola launched its bottled water brand Dasani in the UK, it concealed the fact that it was made from Sidcup tap water. Consumers were enraged and felt they had been cheated. A damaging media frenzy followed; even traces of bromate (a possible carcinogen) were found in the water. Coca-Cola withdrew tens of thousands of bottles, and shortly afterwards the brand was withdrawn from the UK altogether and the planned launch into Europe was scrapped. Advertising can conceal facts and may give a misleading impression to consumers, as when a food brand is advertised as healthy because it contains added vitamins without the advert pointing out its high sugar and fat content. Making such misleading claims is also known as 'greenwashing'.

Marketers argue that in most European countries advertising is tightly regulated, minimizing opportunities for advertisers to mislead. For example, the UK's Advertising Standards Authority censured GlaxoSmithKline for making the unfounded claim that drinking Horlicks could make children taller, stronger and more intelligent. EU law states that 'nutritional and health claims which encourage consumers to purchase a product, but are false, misleading, or not scientifically proven are prohibited' (O'Flaherty, 2008). Marketers also point out that high-profile scandals that meet with consumer and media disapproval are a major deterrent to marketers who may be contemplating making similar mistakes.

Salespeople can face great temptation to deceive in order to close a sale. Deceptive selling may take the form of exaggeration, lying or withholding important information. Examples of malpractice include financial services salespeople that mis-sold pension plans by exaggerating the expected returns, a media-driven scandal that resulted in millions of pounds worth of compensation being awarded to the victims. To counter this behaviour, an increasing number of companies provide ethical training in personal selling to communicate to staff how to behave appropriately.

The issue of the unethical practice of direct marketing companies entering names and addresses onto a database without the consumer's permission has caused concern. Some consumers fear that the act of subscribing to a magazine or a website or buying products by direct mail will result in the inconvenience of receiving streams of unsolicited direct mail or *spam* (the online equivalent to junk mail). Regulation in Europe by bodies such as the Direct Marketing Association (UK) and governments aims to ensure that consumers are protected and their data is only used and stored legally. Online consumers are given various options to opt in or opt out of non-essential data collection and subsequent promotional mailings.

Manufacturers promote their products and aim to outperform the competition. Consequently, they sometimes offer inducements to retailers to place special emphasis on particular products. A salesperson might try to sell a particular product to a consumer to earn extra bonuses. This practice is considered unethical by some groups as there can be overemphasis on the particular products. Defenders of the practice claim that consumers are able to determine their own needs and make informed decisions.

Place: slotting allowances

A slotting allowance is a fee paid by a manufacturer to a retailer in exchange for an agreement to place a product on the retailer's shelves. The importance of gaining distribution and the growing power of retailers means that slotting allowances are commonplace in the supermarket trade. They may be considered unethical since they distort competition, favouring large suppliers that can afford to pay them over small suppliers who may in reality be producing superior products. Marketers argue they are only responding to the realities of the marketplace (i.e. the immense power of some retailers) and claim the blame should rest with the purchasing practices of those retailers that demand payment for display space, rather than with the marketing profession who are often powerless to resist such pressures.

General societal, environmental and political issues

Broadly speaking, these issues focus on concerns that marketing practices promote too much materialism and put too much emphasis on the short term. Additionally, too little emphasis is placed on the long-term environmental consequences. A political concern is that the power of global companies fuelled by massive marketing budgets works against the interests of consumers and society.

Societal concerns

Two societal concerns are marketing's promotion of materialism and its emphasis on short-term issues.

Materialism is an ethical concern associated with an overemphasis on material possessions. Critics argue that people judge themselves and are judged by others not by who they are but by what they own and marketers use this trait to drive consumption. For example, status symbols such as expensive houses, cars, second homes, yachts, high-tech gadgets and designer clothing are marketed as representations of success and social worth. Such conspicuous consumption is fuelled by the advertising industry, which equates materialism and success with happiness, desirability and social worth. Materialism is not considered natural by the critics but a phenomenon created by business, to drive sales and deliver high profit margins. Such companies devote large marketing expenditures to these types of brands.

Supporters of marketing argue that sociological studies show that tribes in Africa that have never been influenced by marketing's pervasive and persuasive powers also display signs of materialism. For example, in some tribes people use the number of cows owned as a symbol of status and power. Some marketers argue that desire for status is a natural state of mind, with marketing simply promoting the kinds of possessions that may be regarded as indicators of status and success.

Marketing is accused of short-termism—putting the short-term interests of consumers before the consumers' and society's long-term interests. As we have seen when discussing product safety, marketers supply and promote products that can have long-term adverse health repercussions for consumers. Cigarettes may aid short-term relaxation, but they have harmful long-term health effects for both smokers and those people forced to breathe in their smoke. Fatty food may be tasty, but it may also lead to obesity and heart problems. Too much salt and sugar in food and drinks may enhance the taste but also lead to long-term health problems. Alcohol may remove inhibitions and help to create a convivial atmosphere, but may also lead to dependency and liver problems.

Marketers need to act responsibly in response to these issues. For example, Coca-Cola has reduced the sugar levels in some of its fizzy drinks and stopped advertising them in television programmes targeting the under-12s (Devaney, 2005). Marks & Spencer has also moved to reduce salt in its food, including a 15 per cent reduction of salt in its sandwiches (Milmo, 2006). Government and self-regulation is also required to limit individual companies' scope for neglecting the longer-term effects of their actions.

Environmental concerns

Marketers' desire to satisfy consumers' wants may also conflict with the interests of the environment. Businesses may want the cheapest ingredients and components in their products, whereas environmentalists favour more expensive materials that are biodegradable or recyclable. Marketers may favour large packaging that gains the attention of consumers in stores, whereas environmentalists favour smaller pack sizes and refill packs. As consumer awareness of the impact of climate change and use of non-renewable resources grows, perceptions are changing and companies that are seen to be taking a serious approach towards sustainability can gain commercial advantage over those that do not take positive action (Barnett, 2011).

Governments have also taken positive actions in an attempt to reconcile business and environmental interests—for example, with car scrappage schemes that aim to cut pollution and stimulate demand for new cars. The politically and economically desirable option would be to create incentive structures for the advancement of innovation in the area of energy-efficient cars, which could reduce emissions and maintain a healthy automotive industry. For example, the French government introduced a car scrappage scheme of €1,000 for consumers who exchange their old cars for fuel-efficient models; the result was improved sales. Prompted by European regulations, manufacturers in the automotive industry are continually fostering innovations that aim to meet carbon-reduction targets (Everitt, 2009). However, environmentalists have questioned the benefits of such schemes, saying new cars might be operationally greener but efficiency gains tend to be offset by the carbon footprint involved in the manufacture of a new car. They would prefer governments to invest in increasing access to and improving the efficiency of public transport. For different reasons, consumers are also yet to be convinced en masse to adopt fuel-efficient cars. Manufacturers have to work harder to counter consumer resistance to switch from their 'gas guzzling' vehicles to more fuel-efficient alternatives. Read Mini Case 5.1 to find out more.

Increasingly, marketing managers are developing CSR strategies that take account of the external impacts of their decisions on society and the environment. See Exhibit 5.1 for an example of how Fedex focuses on fuel-efficient and less polluting planes and fuels.

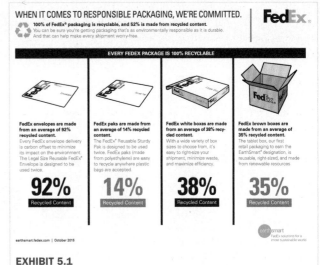

EXHIBIT 5.1
Fedex focuses on fuel efficiency when advertising its service

The politics of globalization

A third ethical concern is the growth of globalization. This is the move by companies to operate in more than one country, and is a term usually applied to large multinational corporations that exert considerable power in their host countries. It is the abuse of such power that is of ethical concern. Backed as large multinationals are by huge marketing expenditures and global mega brands, concern is expressed over their influence over consumers, governments and suppliers. Critics argue that their size and huge budgets mean that it is hard for smaller rivals to compete, thus reducing consumer choice. The impact on employment and the economy means that governments vie with each other to attract global organizations to their countries. Finally, their purchasing power means that they can negotiate very low prices from suppliers in the developing world.

Supporters of global companies argue that their size and global reach mean that they benefit from economies of scale in production and marketing (making them more efficient and, therefore, in a better position to charge low prices to consumers) and in R&D, enabling them to develop better-quality products and make technological breakthroughs—for example, in the area of healthcare. They further claim that their attraction to governments is evidence of the value they provide to host nations. Regarding their ability to negotiate down prices from developing-world suppliers, global organizations need to recognize their responsibilities to their supplier stakeholders. This is happening as more of them adopt corporate responsibility programmes and global corporations recognize the marketing potential of fair trade products (for example, Nestlé markets Partners' Blend, a fair trade coffee).

Having discussed the major ethical issues relating to marketing, in the next section we will explore business, societal, and legal and regulatory responses to these concerns (see Figure 5.3).

FIGURE 5.3
Responses to ethical issues in marketing

Business
Corporate social responsibility

Responses to ethical issues in marketing

Legal and regulatory
European and national laws and regulatory bodies

Societal
Consumerism
Environmentalism

MINI CASE 5.1
Hybrid and Electric Cars

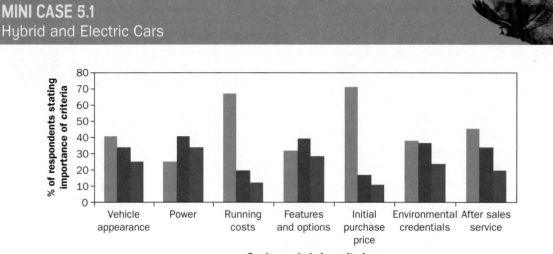

Car buyers' choice criteria

Importance of criteria: ■ High   ■ Medium   ■ Low

In Europe, the adoption of electric and hybrid cars is low compared with that in Japan and the USA, but manufacturers are looking for new ways to boost sales. Toyota anticipates introducing 10 new models into Europe to boost sales to 1 million vehicles by 2014 (Kim, 2011). Research suggests there are important choice criteria consumers consider when buying new cars.

The graph shows that initial outlay to buy the car and running costs are the two most influential criteria, followed by after-sales service and then vehicle appearance. Interestingly, features of the vehicle and power are much lower in terms of importance in the new car-buying decision.

Therefore, while Toyota, Honda, Nissan and other manufacturers are introducing cars with new power options, there are other issues to address to encourage the wider adoption of more fuel-efficient cars. The marketing director at Honda UK feels that electric and hybrid cars will have to have significantly lower prices to increase consumer uptake. He feels that even though consumers will benefit immediately from the lower running costs of hybrid and electric cars, it is still likely to take up to 10 years before they get any payback. The key trigger is lowering the price of the initial outlay.

Consequently, in order to increase the number of adopters of hybrid or electric cars, manufacturers will have to find ways to communicate the benefits to consumers and reduce the initial purchase price; governments will need to find ways to improve the quality of the road infrastructure, as electric cars in particular need very good road surfaces to run efficiently; consumers will have to achieve a greater understanding and ultimately willingness to adopt before there is likely to be a significant uplift in the number of more fuel-efficient cars on the roads of Europe.

Questions:

1   Price is often an indicator of quality and to lower the price can suggest an inferior product. However, the marketing director at Honda feels that the initial price of electric and hybrid cars should be low to encourage an increase in sales. Suggest other methods (apart from price) that you might use to market these cars.
2   Discuss what governments can do—apart from improving the roads—to ensure more 'environmentally friendly' motoring.

Based on: Barnett (2011)

Business responses to ethical issues in marketing: CSR

Business has taken action to address ethical concerns in marketing and other functional areas by adopting the philosophy of CSR. Over the past 10 years, CSR has become increasingly important and commands the attention of executives around the world. It would be difficult to find a recent annual report of any large multinational company that does not talk proudly of its efforts to improve society and safeguard the environment (Crook, 2005). We shall now examine the idea in depth by exploring the nature and dimensions of CSR and assessing the arguments for and against its adoption.

Corporate Social Responsibility

Corporate social irresponsibility can have painful consequences for organizations. The case of Siemens illustrates the negative fallout that can follow. Accused of paying bribes to win lucrative overseas telecoms and power contracts, Siemens was fined £523 million by the US Department of Justice, and £180 million by a court in its home town of Munich. A further £354 million was paid to settle a case in Munich over the failure of its former board to fulfil its supervisory duties. The total cost to Siemens, a symbol of German engineering excellence, was £2.25 billion, including lawyers' and accountants' fees, plus the loss of its reputation and that of former senior executives (Gow, 2008).

The fallout from this and other cases raises the issue of how harmful corporate social irresponsibility can be to companies and wider society. As a result companies are increasingly examining how their actions affect not only their profits but society and the environment. CSR refers to the ethical principle that an organization should be accountable for how its behaviour might affect society and the environment.

Commentators have claimed CSR is 'an idea whose time has come' (Moon, 2002), but CSR is not new. For many years companies have been aware of the obligations of being an employer and a consumer of natural resources. For example, the town of Bourneville was created by the founder of Cadbury to house the workers of that company (Moon, 2002). Nevertheless, there is little doubt that CSR is now higher on the agenda of many companies than it was in the past. Most multinational corporations now have a senior executive, often with staff at his/her disposal, specifically charged with developing and coordinating the CSR function (Crook, 2005). Furthermore, most large companies engage in corporate social reporting within their annual financial statements, as separate printed reports and/or on websites. The importance of CSR is also reflected in membership organizations, which offer services to members, such as providing information, lobbying and promoting the CSR cause. For example, the UK-based Business in the Community (www.bitc.org.uk) has a membership of over 700 companies, and includes in its activities cause-related marketing and the promotion of CSR internationally. Other notable organizations in Europe include Business and Society Belgium, Finnish Business and Society, Business in the Community Ireland, Samenleving and Bedrijf (Netherlands), CSR Europe (www.csreurope.org) and the European Business Ethics Network (www.eben-net.org). In the USA, Business for Social Responsibility (www.bsr.org) has grown into a major global organization (Moon, 2002). These, together with pressure groups such as Greenpeace and ASH (Action on Smoking and Health), highlight the belief that organizations should consider a wider perspective regarding their activities and objectives than a narrow focus on short-term profits. However, it is not straightforward to determine the best course of action for future sustainability. Read Marketing in Action 5.1 to find out more.

CSR is based on the **stakeholder theory** of the firm, which contends that companies are not managed purely in the interests of their shareholders alone. Rather, there is a range of groups (stakeholders) that have a legitimate interest in the company as well (Donaldson and Preston, 1995). Following this theory, a **stakeholder** of a company is an individual or group that either:

- is harmed by or benefits from the company *or*
- whose rights can be violated, or have to be respected, by the company (Crane and Matten, 2004).

Other stakeholder groups—besides shareholders, who typically would be considered stakeholders—are communities associated with the company, employees, customers of the company's products and suppliers (see Figure 5.4). The key point is that stakeholder theory holds that the company has obligations not only to shareholders but to other parties that are affected by its activities. We shall return to the notion of stakeholders when we explore the dimensions of CSR later in this chapter.

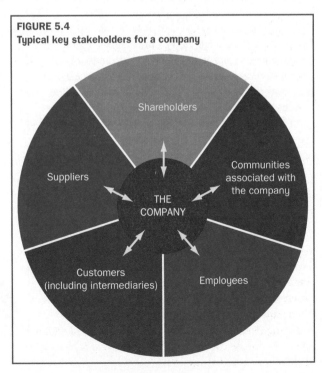

FIGURE 5.4
Typical key stakeholders for a company

For marketing managers, sustainability is possibly the biggest challenge of the 21st century. Not only are there issues of what to reduce, but there is also the problem of understanding the real impact of any action. However, research by Trucost, a company that helps its clients understand the real cost of their organization's operations and helps them plan for a better-resourced future across the value chain, suggested in a report on green business that environmental sustainability is at the top of most companies' agendas. Trucost measures the financial impact of environmental issues for 4,300 of the world's largest companies, and this information helps them to understand which actions are likely to bring the greatest dividends and reduce the impact on the environment. Trucost has helped GreenBiz, a leading source of news, opinion and best practice, to provide clear and concise information for businesses that are developing their environmental and sustainability policies and business practices. GreenBiz analyzes data and information and then disseminates news of good practice through its website and blogs.

IKEA is an example of a company constantly reviewing its practices across the supply chain in order to ensure it provides sustainability on a large scale. According to Steve Howard, IKEA's Chief Sustainability Officer, the company is 'using IWay, a code of conduct that specifies environmental and social requirements for sourcing and distributing products, which is bringing sustainable and affordable cotton and timber products to millions of consumers around the world'. He also said that IKEA is 'committed to future proofing' the company in advance of the many challenges it is likely to face in the future. IKEA owns wind turbines and has introduced nearly half a million solar panels. In the USA, it is the second largest private commercial solar power owner. The company is aiming to isolate itself from the volatilities of the energy markets and has reported significant savings on energy consumption across the business.

Based on: Jeffries (2011); Trucost (2012); King (2012); Kelly-Detwiler (2014)

The nature of CSR

A useful way of examining the nature of CSR is Carroll's four-part model of CSR (see Carroll and Buchholtz, 2000; Carroll, 1991). Carroll views CSR as a multilayered concept that can be divided into four interrelated responsibilities: economic, legal, ethical and philanthropic. The presentation of these responsibilities is in the form of layers within a pyramid, and the full achievement of CSR occurs only when all four layers are met consecutively (see Figure 5.5).

Economic responsibilities

Carroll recognized that the principal role of a firm was to produce goods and services that people wanted and to be as profitable as possible in so doing. Economic responsibilities include: maintaining a strong, competitive position; operating at high levels of efficiency and effectiveness; and aiming for consistently high levels of profitability. Without the achievement of economic responsibilities, the other three are redundant, since the firm would go out of business. Economic success is the *sine qua non* of CSR.

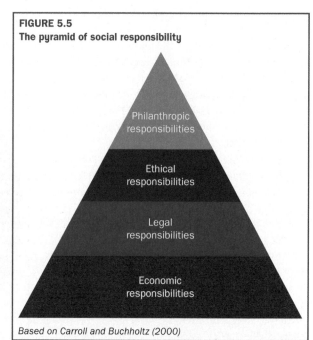

FIGURE 5.5
The pyramid of social responsibility

Philanthropic responsibilities

Ethical responsibilities

Legal responsibilities

Economic responsibilities

Based on Carroll and Buchholtz (2000)

Legal responsibilities

Companies must pursue their economic responsibilities within the framework of the law. Laws reflect society's principles and standards that are enforceable in the courts. Occasionally, the drive to maximize profits can conflict with the law—as with Microsoft, which has faced heavy financial penalties both in Europe and the USA for anti-competitive behaviour (e.g. bundling Media Player into the Windows operating system, thereby squeezing out competitors' software). Like economic responsibilities, the meeting of legal responsibilities is a requirement of CSR.

Ethical responsibilities

Although the establishment of laws may be founded on ethical considerations, as we have seen there can be important distinctions, as with the selling of genetically modified (GM) products, which may raise ethical questions and yet be lawful. The same could be said of the meat production industry, where 90 per cent of pork is produced by raising female pigs in metal cages so small that the pregnant sow can hardly move. This practice is not currently illegal, but thought by many to be inhumane (Gunther, 2012).

Ethical responsibilities mean that companies should perform in a manner consistent with the principles and values of society and prevent ethical norms being compromised in order to achieve corporate objectives. Companies such as BP draw up codes of ethical conduct and employ teams to govern legal compliance and business ethics (252 BP employees were dismissed in one year for unethical behaviour in a drive to weed out bribery and corruption) (Boxell and Harvey, 2005). Ethical responsibilities therefore comprise what is expected by society over and above economic and legal requirements.

Philanthropic responsibilities

At the top of the pyramid are the philanthropic responsibilities of companies—these are corporate actions that meet society's expectation that businesses be good corporate citizens. This includes promoting human welfare, or goodwill, such as making charitable donations, the building of leisure facilities or even homes for employees and their families, arts and sports sponsorship, and support for local schools (Crane and Matten, 2004). The key difference between philanthropic and complying with ethical responsibilities is that the former is not expected in an ethical sense. Communities may desire companies to contribute to their well-being, but do not consider them unethical if they do not. Philanthropic responsibilities are presented at the top of the pyramid, as they represent the 'icing on the cake'—actions that are desired by society but not expected or required. Warren Buffet, one of the world's richest men, made a record-breaking $37-billion donation to the Gates Foundation. The foundation, set up by former head of Microsoft—Bill Gates—and his wife, aims to give every life across the planet equal value, through philanthropic donations that support global, development and health programmes (Gates Foundation, 2012).

The dimensions of CSR

A strength of the four-part model of CSR is its realism in recognizing that without the fulfilment of economic responsibilities, a company would not have the capability to engage in ethical and/or philanthropic activities. However, to gain a deeper understanding of the scope of CSR activities it is necessary to explore its dimensions as well as its responsibilities.

CSR has four layers of responsibility: economic, legal, ethical and philanthropic. By examining the dimensions of CSR, an insight into where those responsibilities may be discharged can be gained. CSR dimensions are based on four key stakeholders—the individuals or groups affected by a company's activities—plus the physical environment, which, equally, can be affected by a company's activities such as pollution or usage of scarce natural resources (see Maignan and Ferrell, 2004; Fukukawa and Moon, 2004).

Table 5.1 outlines the CSR dimensions, lists associated key issues and describes marketing responses for each dimension. Please note that the key issues relating to each CSR dimension are not all exclusively marketing related. For example, pollution control at a chemical plant is a production-related issue, standard setting for supplies is a procurement-related topic, and the setting of fair pay is a human resources issue. Nevertheless, for most of the issues listed in Table 5.1, marketing practices can affect outcomes. For example, car design can affect pollution levels and the rate at which oil reserves are depleted, and the creation of healthy-eating brands can improve consumers' diets through the reduction in fat, sugar and salt levels.

TABLE 5.1 Dimensions of CSR

Dimension	Key issues	Marketing response
Physical environment	Combating global warming Pollution control Conservation of energy and scarce resources Use of environmentally friendly ingredients and components Recycling and non-wasteful packaging	Sustainable marketing
Social (community involvement)	Support for the local community Support for the wider community	Societal marketing Cause-related marketing
Consumer	Product safety (including the avoidance of harmful long-term effects) Avoidance of price fixing Honesty in communications Respecting privacy	Societal marketing
Supply chain	Fair trading standard-setting for supplies (e.g. human rights, labour standards and environmental responsibility)	Fair trade marketing
Employee relations	Fair pay Equal opportunities Training and motivation Information provision (e.g. on career paths, recruitment policies and training opportunities)	Internal marketing

Physical environment

Key issues in the physical environment, such as the use of environmentally friendly ingredients and components, recycling and non-wasteful packaging and pollution control, were introduced in Chapter 2. Marketers' response to these issues can be summarized under the term 'sustainable marketing'. Environmental sustainability means to maintain or prolong the physical environment. It involves action towards the use of renewable rather than finite raw materials, and the minimization and eventual elimination of polluting effluents and toxic or hazardous wastes. **Sustainable marketing** contributes to this goal by focusing on environmental issues and reducing environmental damage by creating, producing and delivering sustainable solutions while continuing to satisfy customers and other stakeholders. As 3M describes it: 'Business will need to accept a moral imperative towards planetary ecological problems' (Charter et al., 2002).

Since marketing operates at the interface between the organization and its environment, it is uniquely positioned to lead the move towards more sustainable products and strategies. Typically, companies move through several stages (see Figure 5.6). To facilitate the process, marketing as a function needs to address a range of questions from the strategic to the tactical. Key questions are as follows (Charter et al., 2002).

- Have the effects of sustainability issues on company activities been analyzed as part of the marketing planning process?
- Has the company conducted marketing research into the probable impacts on the organization of sustainability issues?
- Can the company modify existing products, services or processes to take account of sustainability considerations, or will innovations be required?
- Is the firm developing positive links with environmental groups?
- Do communications strategies accurately emphasize environmental considerations?

Responding positively to environmental issues is important in order to protect and sustain brands. Market-leading brands are always susceptible to attack by media and/or pressure groups following any environmental incident. It is, therefore, sensible to build into brand strategies sustainability issues to nurture and maintain brand trust.

Environmental issues can be a source of threats to organizations, but they can also provide opportunities. Toyota has responded to environmental trends by successfully launching the Toyota Prius hybrid car, which supplements normal fuel with an electric-powered engine. The electric engine starts the car and operates at low speeds using a battery. At higher speeds, the Prius automatically switches to a normal engine and fuel. This saves on fuel and is less polluting. The success of the Prius has led many of its rivals, including Honda, to launch similar hybrid cars, and to the development of electric cars powered by lithium-ion batteries. Renault has invested 4 billion euros in a range of 100 per cent electric vans and cars. According to Renault's marketing, the Kangoo Z.E. van puts an end to all the myths about driving electric cars and gives the motorist energy-efficient driving.

The production of biofuel has risen dramatically as companies have seized the opportunity to replace petrol. For example, BP has invested £284 million in biofuels. However, opposition from environmentalists may hamper further development. They fear that carbon-absorbing rainforests in countries such as Brazil are being depleted to make way for fuel crops such as soya and palm, and that such crops are displacing land use for food, forcing up prices (Macalister, 2008). Detergent companies like Unilever have also embraced sustainable marketing by producing concentrated soap powder that both helps the environment and improves profitability. Environmental damage is reduced because the product requires less plastic, less water, less space for transportation, fewer chemicals and less packaging (Skapinker, 2008). Procter & Gamble has also promoted the benefit of low-temperature washing with its award-winning Ariel 'Turn to 30' campaign, which raised awareness of the impact of washing temperatures on emissions (Murphy, 2008).

The giant US corporation GE has also embraced the environment as a source of opportunity, as Marketing in Action 5.2 describes.

Social and consumer dimensions

A social concern that businesses have sought to address is the need to support local and wider communities. Consumer concerns include the effect of business activities on product safety, including the avoidance of harmful long-term effects, the avoidance of price fixing, honesty in communications, and respecting privacy. Although social and consumer dimensions of CSR are distinct because their key issues differ, the two dimensions are analyzed together as marketing's major response—societal marketing—embraces both. Whereas sustainable marketing focuses on the physical environment, societal marketing relates to marketing's direct effect on people, both in the form of consumers and society in general.

Societal marketing takes into account consumers' and society's wider interests rather than their short-term consumption. One aim of societal marketing is to consider consumers' needs and long-term welfare and society's long-term welfare as keys to satisfying organizations' objectives and responsibilities. It aims to rectify potential conflicts between consumers' short-term needs—for example, for fast food, which may contain high levels of fat, sugar and salt—and their long-term needs—in this case, health.

In the face of intense media pressure, including the hit film *Super Size Me*, which records a film-maker's descent into serious illness while living on a McDonald's-only diet, McDonald's introduced healthy-eating options including salads and mineral water (instead of the ubiquitous cola). While cynics may view this as a public relations exercise, the response of McDonald's may be regarded as a move towards implementing societal marketing principles.

Kraft is another company responding to consumers' demands for healthier foods, by cutting fat in its Philadelphia Lite soft cheese and cutting salt in its Dairylea product line by over 30 per cent (Clarke, 2008).

Societal marketing also means that those activities that are not in consumers' or society's short- and long-term interests—such as price fixing, dishonest communications and invasions of privacy—are avoided and training is given to employees to lay out the boundaries of acceptable behaviour.

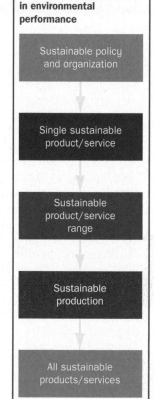

FIGURE 5.6
The stages in the move towards excellence in environmental performance

Sustainable policy and organization

Single sustainable product/service

Sustainable product/service range

Sustainable production

All sustainable products/services

Source: Charter, Peattie, Ottman and Polonsky (2002)

Scan the QR code to see how One makes a difference for people living in Africa.

MARKETING IN ACTION 5.2
GE Ecomagination and the Smart Grid: Saving Energy

GE, the US-based multinational, continues to develop its green credentials through its Ecomagination programme. The aim is to build innovative solutions for today's environmental challenges while driving economic growth. Since the start of the programme GE has invested $5 billion, and the resulting technology and products have generated over $160 billion in revenue. More specific examples of developments from the programme are compact fluorescent lighting, smart appliances, battery technology, wind turbines and fuel-efficient aircraft engines.

Jeffrey Immett, GE's chief executive, is so convinced that clean technologies are the future that he has made his new mantra 'green is green', equating the green of the environment with the green of the US dollar. Additionally, GE has benefited from a 32 per cent fall in greenhouse gases and a 45 per cent fall in use in freshwater, which has generated £300 million in cost reductions.

To qualify for Ecomagination branding, products must 'significantly and measurably' improve customers' environmental and operating performance. Already the company produces the GEnx aero engine, which powers the Airbus 350 and Boeing 787 and is 15 per cent more energy efficient than its predecessors, and the compact florescent light bulb that saves 70–80 per cent of energy compared with ordinary light bulbs. ClimateWell in Stockholm has developed energy-efficient solar hot water systems and is in partnership with GE to provide energy for GE home appliances (Clarke, 2008).

GE is not only aiming to cut its carbon emissions, but its investment in the smart grid is upgrading the existing energy infrastructure, making it more fuel efficient. The *smart grid* uses energy meters that are sensitive to times and temperatures and consequently can help reduce energy consumption in homes, businesses and on the road. GE's commitment to CO_2 reduction has enabled a massive saving of 52.4 billion pounds of CO_2 through the use of the smart technology.

Based on: GE Ecomagination (2015); The Economist (2005); Harvey (2005); Caulkin (2006); The Economist (2008)

A further aspect of societal marketing is in providing support for local and wider communities. One is a company that produces various products—from bottled water, eggs and toilet tissue, to condoms—and uses the profits to fund social projects in Africa that are improving health and welfare for communities (Costa, 2011). Other charitable donations (Walmart, for example, historically has made huge donations to charities) or partnerships with charities or causes are called **cause-related marketing**. This is a commercial activity in which businesses and charities or causes form a partnership with each other to market an image or product for their mutual benefit. As consumers increasingly demand accountability and responsibility from businesses, companies such as Procter & Gamble, Unilever, Tesco, IBM, British Gas and Orange have all incorporated major cause-related marketing programmes. Typical activities include sponsoring events such as Comic Relief (Procter & Gamble and Unilever), raising money and resources for schools (Tesco and IBM), tackling social problems such as fuel poverty (British Gas), and sponsoring the arts (Orange).

A set of cause-related marketing principles have been developed by Business in the Community, as listed below (Anderson, 1999).

1 Integrity: behave honestly and ethically.
2 Transparency: misleading information could cast doubt on the equity of the partnership.
3 Sincerity: consumers need to be convinced about the strength and depth of a cause-related marketing partnership.
4 Mutual respect: the partner and its values must be appreciated and respected.
5 Partnership: each partner needs to recognize the opportunities and threats the relationship presents.
6 Mutual benefit: for the relationship to be sustainable, both sides must benefit.

Cause-related marketing works well when the business and charity have a similar target audience. For example, Nambarrie tea company, a Northern Ireland winner of the annual Business in the Community award for excellence in cause-related marketing, chose to sponsor the breast cancer agency Action Cancer. The company and the charity targeted women aged 16–60. In a two-month period, Nambarrie released 100,000 specially designed packs promoting its sponsorship of Action Cancer and covered media costs for a TV advertising campaign. This generated income of over £200,000 (Anderson, 1999). Further societal marketing issues are discussed later in this chapter.

Critics of societal marketing view it as a short-term public relations exercise that cynically manipulates a company's stakeholders. Supporters argue that the stakeholder principle suggests that it is in a company's long-term interests to support the long-run concerns of consumers and society, resulting in a win–win situation.

By combining sustainable and societal marketing initiatives, organizations become better prepared to meet the requirements of triple bottom-line reporting, which takes into account not only financial matters but also environmental and social issues. In 2011, Electrolux was voted one of the world's most ethical companies, and sustainability is at the heart of the business strategy. The Ethisphere Institute (a think tank devoted to sharing of best practices in business ethics and CSR) publishes world rankings of the most ethical companies, and its director said in 2011 that, 'each year, the competition gets more intense' as companies vie to be the awarded the honour of being the most ethical.

Supply chain

Unfair trading arises when large buyers exert their power on small commodity producers to force prices to very low levels. This can bring severe economic hardship to the producers, who may be situated in countries of the developing world. Many of the growers of such products as coffee, tea and cocoa live in poverty and face hardship in the form of poor working conditions, health problems and prices that fail to provide a living wage. Fair trade seeks to improve the prospects of suppliers through ethical trading, including the guaranteeing of minimum prices.

 Scan the QR code to see how EcoSwim is using the environment as part of its CSR strategy.

Employee relations

Poor employee relations can have harmful marketing consequences. For example, Walmart has suffered from years of allegations regarding low pay and sexually discriminatory hiring and employment practices, a situation it is seeking to address (Devaney, 2005). Bad publicity can deter ethically aware consumers from buying from companies that suffer such criticism.

While most employee relations issues are the province of the human resources function, marketing can play a role through internal marketing programmes. **Internal marketing** is the development, training and motivation of employees designed to enhance their performance in providing customer satisfaction. The idea began in service organizations such as hotels and restaurants where staff are in daily communication with customers, but has spread to all sectors in reflection of the need for all employees who come into contact with customers to be trained in how to deal with such issues as giving help, dealing with complaints and treating customers respectfully. Such training avoids, as far as possible, employee–customer arguments and conflict, which not only improves customer satisfaction but is good for staff morale, reduces stress levels and aids staff retention. Marketing in Action 5.3 describes the importance of democracy and supportive working environments.

Arguments for and against CSR programmes

Not every observer believes that profit-orientated organizations should undertake CSR programmes.

There are also arguments *for* CSR programmes, which help explain their current popularity. Currently, the strengths of the arguments for CSR programmes are driving companies increasingly towards the adoption of socially and environmentally responsible strategies.

First, the arguments against CSR programmes will be examined, then those in favour of CSR.

CSR is misguided

In 1970, the Nobel Prize-winning economist Milton Friedman published a seminal article arguing that it was managers' responsibility to generate profits for their shareholders. To act in any other way was a betrayal of this special responsibility. He saw addressing social problems as being the province of governments not company managers. He did not believe, therefore, that managers should spend other people's money on some perceived social benefit, and thought that to do so was misguided (Friedman, 1970).

EXHIBIT 5.2
International campaign to raise awareness of the risks of drinking in pregnancy uses shock tactics

MARKETING IN ACTION 5.3
Employees Win Company Awards

CSR has many dimensions, one of which is employee relations: successful staff training programmes can have a significant impact on a company's overall effectiveness.

The Worldblu list of the most democratic places to work gives annual awards to companies that meet and exceed Worldblu's principles of organizational democracy.

AISEC International, the world's largest youth-run organization, based in Rotterdam, Netherlands, has regularly been featured in the list since 2007. This organization aims to unlock the potential of young people.

Dreamhost, a leading web hosting firm in Los Angeles, USA, enables its workforce to make choices based on team values.

Happy Computers is a company that has an enviable reputation and has won many industry and service excellence awards, including the Worldblu list Top Practice award in 2013.

Happy Ltd, a computer training company, believes that learning should be fun. The training programmes bring together technical expertise and excellent training skills. The training is based on the following ideas:

• Tell me and I will forget.
• Show me and I will remember.
• Involve me and I will understand.

Henry Stewart and Cathy Busani founded Happy Ltd in 1990 in response to their clients asking for help to create *great* workplaces. At Happy, there is a relatively small workforce of 45 employees, and a unique approach to CSR training. The company has won numerous awards for innovative approaches to training, customer service and the quality of the working environment. Cathy is Managing Director of Happy Ltd and is responsible for Happy employees. She has been rated one of the best bosses in the UK in two separate national awards programmes. She is passionate about valuing people and the role they play in creating truly great places to work.

The company achieves its success by applying some straightforward principles:

- Transparency is important throughout (e.g. employees at both the top and bottom of the scale are all aware of pay information).
- There is belief in the ability of the individual—members of the Happy team hold a fundamental belief that all people (with no exceptions) are born with enormous intelligence and tremendous eagerness to learn.
- Celebrate mistakes as part of the culture to engender learning and development—Happy believes that if you do not make mistakes you are not actively learning; it believes that you should enable an employee's natural learning abilities and delight in new possibilities to allow them to come to the fore.
- Create a feel-good environment, as individuals work to their best ability when they feel good about themselves. Happy has created a workplace where people are trusted to make the key decisions about their work.
- Share information—as Francis Bacon said, 'knowledge is power'. Happy's management team takes the view that information is required to make informed decisions and to enable individuals to take responsibility and full ownership of their jobs. As more companies turn to e-learning, Happy Computers has been finding additional ways to help. Learnfizz is one of Happy's products designed to 'find, organize and share the best free learning on the web'.

Applying these principles has enabled Happy to do more than win awards, and it has zero recruitment costs. This is due to its employee-focused working environment, high staff morale and demand from potential employees desiring to work for this unique organization.

Based on: www.happy.co.uk; Worldblu (2013)

CSR is too costly

Spending in the USA on CSR activities is in excess of $3 billion, and while Europe does not match this figure, spending there is vast too (Grow, Hamm and Lee, 2005). This brings with it the lost opportunity to spend the money on other priorities such as research and development.

CSR encourages consumer cynicism

Many consumers regard CSR initiatives as little more than public relations exercises. Corporate brands delegate tasks to 'ethics officers', who in turn outsource the task of delivering the organization's values to consultants (Plender and Persaud, 2005). Senior management then takes up the minimum number of initiatives that it believes places the company in an acceptable light among its stakeholders, without really embracing the ideas and ideals associated with those values.

CSR does not improve profitability

Accused of artificially upgrading its oil reserve figures by a fifth to help boost financial bonuses to staff, Shell was fined £84 million by the Securities and Exchange Commission in the USA and the Financial Services Authority (FSA) in the UK. The scandal led to the dismissal of Shell's chairman and two other senior executives. More damage to the company's image was done by the FSA's accusation that Shell had engaged in 'unprecedented misconduct', and by comments from oil experts that it was a corporate scandal of 'historic proportions' (Milner, 2004). Critics of CSR point out that, despite the bad publicity and tarnished corporate reputation, Shell's profitability was not harmed, since it generated record profits just a few years after the scandal.

Further, an academic review of 167 studies over 35 years concluded that although there was a positive association between companies' social and financial performance, the link was weak. It would seem that companies are not richly rewarded for CSR. However, neither does CSR appear to harm profits, and there is the potential for smarter forms of CSR to produce better returns in the future. (The results of the study were reported in Margolis, Elfenbein and Walsh (2007).

CSR leads to enhanced brand/corporate image and reputation

One argument *for* CSR is that a strong reputation in environmental and social responsibility can help a company build trust and enhance the image of its brands. For example, BP has taken steps to reduce harmful emissions. Orange has enhanced its image through sponsorship of the arts.

This approach can help when a company is faced with media criticism or regulatory scrutiny. Also if a company is moving to a new area or new market, or opening a new site such as a distribution centre, store or factory, it helps to be seen as trustworthy and a 'good neighbour' (Sclater, 2005).

CSR provides marketing opportunities

Environmental and social responsibility has created new markets for business-to-business and business-to-consumer goods and services. For example, GE is expanding its marketing of 'clean' technological goods to companies, and Cafédirect, Green & Black's, Innocent drinks and the Body Shop have built their businesses on CSR ideals.

Market segments have emerged based on 'green' credentials that provide targeting opportunities. One segment—known as ethical hard cores or dark greens—researches companies and their practices thoroughly before buying their products. These consumers view ethical consumerism as a way of life, whatever the sacrifice.

A second segment—known as ethical lites or light greens—do their bit but do not have the time to research products or companies thoroughly (Parkinson, 2005). They are happy to recycle newspapers, plastics and other material from their homes and buy ethical brands, provided there is not too much of a price premium.

CSR can reduce operating costs

Far from increasing operating costs, as is often assumed, better environmental management systems can improve efficiency by reducing waste, increasing energy efficiency and, in some cases, selling recycled materials (Sclater, 2005). For example, DuPont uses 7 per cent less energy than it did in 1990, despite producing 30 per cent more goods, thereby saving $2 billion, including savings of at least $10 million per year by using renewable sources (Aston and Helm, 2005).

CSR increases organizations' ability to attract and retain employees

Many employees are attracted to employers that are active in social issues. For example, membership of Netimpact.org, a network of socially conscious MBA graduates, rose from 4,000 in 2002 to over 10,000 in 2009. Some companies, such as salesforce.com (an Internet-based services company), have a policy of good corporate citizenship (staff are encouraged to devote time, at the company's expense, to charitable works) that they believe helps to attract, retain and motivate employees (see Grow, Hamm and Lee, 2005; *The Economist*, 2005).

CSR is a form of risk management

There are real penalties for companies that are not environmentally or socially responsible. The media criticisms of such companies as Nike (child labour in the developed world), BNFL (toxic discharges in the Irish Sea), Enron and Royal Bank of Scotland (financial scandals), and News of the World (phone hacking) have shown the harm that can arise from being perceived as irresponsible. CSR, then, can be employed as a form of risk management that reduces the chances of being the subject of the next corporate scandal to hit the headlines.

CSR improves access to capital

Organizations that are committed to CSR have access to socially responsible investment, whereby investors take into account considerations such as a company's environmental and socially responsible activities. These can be assessed using indices such as Business in the Community's Corporate Responsibility Index and the FTSE4Good Index (Sclater, 2005).

Societal Marketing

Societal marketing is nothing new; it was referred to as the applications of marketing to the solution of social and health problems early in 1970s by Kotler and Zaltman (1971). But this marked a departure point, whereby marketing began to evolve into more than just customer-focused strategies, tools and techniques to encourage people to buy more. Today, **social marketing** is a framework that involves changing behaviour in complex economic, social and political environments (Lefebvre and G, 1997). The development of this sub-discipline within marketing has passed through four key stages of development (Dibb and Carrigan, 2013):

Stage 1: Focusing on behaviour—this involves clarifying the objectives that social marketers should pursue. Such objectives focus on the actual behaviour that should change and not the attitudes towards the behaviour; for instance, the intention to eat a healthier diet is not the same as actually switching to healthy alternatives, as in the UK government's Change4Life eat well, move more, live longer campaign.

Stage 2: Modelling the planning process—taking the classic steps in the marketing planning process but redefining them in context of the social marketing framework.

Stage 3: Three levels of social marketing—downstream, mid-stream and upstream. This introduced the idea that just targeting behaviour change in an individual was only partially effective (downstream level). So the idea of also targeting peers of the individuals in the target market—friends, family acquaintances— was introduced in order to broaden the scope of the social marketing initiatives (mid-stream level); for example, mid-stream advocates can be targeted to encourage healthy eating behaviour. The final level (upstream) was to target organizations that could play a supporting role in the desired behaviour change. This extension of social marketing brings extra challenges—especially at the upstream level, which often involves bringing on side manufacturers that, say, produce sugary soft drinks and high fat content products.

Stage 4: Incorporating social media into social marketing—digital marketing and social media platforms have enabled the widespread distribution of social marketing messages. Also, it is possible for individuals to find information on how to change a particular behaviour, for example by adopting a healthier lifestyle.

Social marketing seeks to change behaviour for the benefit of the individual and society, and its applications come in many different guises. For example, cars are built with mechanisms to remind the driver to wear a seat belt; there are social movements for wider change, for example green and climate change organizations, the consumerism movement, the international campaign to raise awareness of the risks of drinking in pregnancy (see Exhibit 5.2), and social engineering (e.g. in Sweden, the government introduced into schools a 'say no to drugs initiative' (Dibb and Carrigan, 2013)).

Inevitably, laudable social issues have to be funded, and so there is an inevitable link between social and more traditional commercial marketing. Where the lines are drawn is not entirely clear, as some new commercial products clearly exhibit social marketing ideals—for example, hybrid cars designed to reduce fuel emissions and the consumption of carbon-based fuels, and fair trade products aimed at helping the producers earn a reasonable living. Marketing in Action 5.3 explores these ideas further. Non-profit organizations make significant contributions to societal marketing.

Non-profit organizations

Non-profit organizations attempt to achieve some objective other than profit. This does not mean they are uninterested in income, as they have to generate cash to survive. However, their primary goal is societal—for example, to provide cultural enrichment (an orchestra), to protect birds and animals (Royal Society for the Protection of Birds, Royal Society for the Prevention of Cruelty to Animals), to alleviate hunger (Oxfam), to provide education (schools and universities), to foster community activities (community association), and to supply healthcare (hospitals) and public services (local authorities). Their worth and standing are not dependent on the profits they generate.

EXHIBIT 5.3
Typical CSR activities include raising money and resources for schools

Overeating has become a pressing health issue in many developed countries. In the UK there are 9,000 premature deaths per year linked to obesity. Government data suggest that obesity-related illnesses will cost the taxpayer £50 billion by 2050, and up to 90 per cent of today's children will be obese or overweight by the same year if current trends continue.

In an attempt to raise public awareness of the link between obesity and life-threatening diseases such as coronary heart disease and diabetes, the UK government financed a £75 million social marketing campaign, which drew an additional £200 million-worth of services and marketing support from a variety of companies and organizations, including supermarkets, large food producers, health clubs, the London Marathon, voluntary groups and a wide-ranging media coalition. Rather than shocking people into healthier lifestyles, the Change4Life TV campaign used light-hearted animation to inform consumers of the threats posed by sedentary lifestyles, and drew particular attention to the need for children to eat more healthily and become more active.

The campaign was a social marketing effort aimed at employing the power of marketing tools and concepts to achieve specific behavioural goals for increased societal welfare.

Although the initiative was welcomed by most stakeholders, some have criticized the government's choice to engage in corporate partnerships, as food corporations and supermarkets are seen as part of the issue by selling junk food and pushing foods high in salt, fat and sugar as cheap and credit-crunch-friendly options for hard-pressed consumers. Critics have suggested that the use of legislation to protect children from junk food marketing, and effective nutritional labelling enforcement, would be far better investments than the Change4Life campaign.

However when the UK government reported on the Change4Life campaign, it found that, in its first year, the movement had become more widespread than expected and had many more supporters and partners, in business and government. The focus of the campaign widened and now includes Sugar Swap, Change4Life cooking guide, Change4Life healthy eating, Smart ReStart for the new school year, and Start4Life targeting pregnant women and families with very young children. The report stated that 'Over 1 million mums are already claiming to have made changes to their children's diets or activity levels as a result of Change4Life.' Change4Life has continued to have an impact, and its branding has become synonymous with improvement.

Based on: HM Government (2010); Boseley (2009); Sweeney (2009); Watts (2009); National Social Marketing Centre (2009); Public Health England (2015)

Marketing—**not-for-profit marketing**—is of growing importance to many non-profit organizations because of the need to generate funds in an increasingly competitive arena. Even organizations that rely on government-sponsored grants need to show how their work is of benefit to society: they must meet the needs of their customers. Many non-profit organizations rely on membership fees or donations, which means that communication to individuals and organizations is required, and they must be persuaded to join or make a donation. This requires marketing skills, which are increasingly being applied. Such is the case with political parties, which use marketing techniques to attract members (and the fees their allegiance brings) and votes at elections.

Non-profit characteristics

Despite the growing use of marketing in the non-profit sector, it is important to be aware of the characteristics that distinguish this form of marketing from that of profit-orientated marketing organizations (Bennett, 1988).

Education versus meeting current needs

Some non-profit organizations see their role as not only meeting the current needs of their customers but also educating them in terms of new ideas and issues, cultural development and social awareness.

Multiple publics

Most non-profit organizations serve several groups, or publics (discussed further in Chapter 14 under the topic of public relations). The two broad groups are *donors*, who may be individuals, trusts, companies or government bodies, and *clients*, who include audiences, patients and beneficiaries (Shapiro, 1992). Non-profit organizations need to adopt marketing as a coherent philosophy for managing multiple public relationships (Balabanis, Stables and Phillips, 1997), and in doing so satisfy the needs of donors and clients.

Measurement of success and conflicting objectives

Profit-orientated organizations' success is ultimately measured in financial terms. For non-profit organizations, measuring success is not so easy, and decision-making is therefore complex in non-profit-orientated organizations.

Public scrutiny

While all organizations are subject to public scrutiny, public-sector non-profit organizations are closely monitored. The reason is that they are publicly funded from taxes.

Marketing procedures for non-profit organizations

Despite non-profit organizations needing to take into account these characteristics, marketing procedures relevant to profit-orientated companies can largely be applied to non-profit organizations. Target marketing, differentiation and marketing-mix decisions need to be made. For example, when marketers are target marketing for political parties, potential voters are segmented according to their propensity to vote (obtainable from electoral registers) and the likelihood that they will vote for a particular party (obtainable from door-to-door canvassing returns). Resources can then be channelled to the segments most likely to switch votes in the forthcoming election, via direct mail and doorstep visits. (For an in-depth examination of political marketing, see Butler and Collins (1994).)

Developing a marketing mix

Non-profit organizations often use *event marketing*. Events including dinners, dances, coffee mornings, book sales, sponsored walks and theatrical shows, which are organized to raise funds. Not all events are designed to raise funds for the sponsoring organization. For example, the BBC hosts the Comic Relief and Children in Need telethons to raise money for worthy causes.

Like most services, distribution systems for many non-profit organizations are short, with production and consumption taking place almost simultaneously. Such organizations have to think carefully about how to deliver their services to accommodate the convenience that customers require. For example, the Hallé orchestra is based in Manchester, but over half of its performances are in other towns or cities. Some non-profit organizations have their own retail outlets. For example, Oxfam, an organization that seeks to reduce poverty and suffering around the world through fundraising and issue-awareness campaigns, has 750 shops around the UK that sell donated second-hand clothing, books, music and household items.

Many non-profit organizations are adept at using all aspects of the promotional mix to further their objectives. Print media and direct mail have been widely used to elicit donations for major disasters, for example for famine relief in Africa, and for victims of the tsunami in Japan. Advertising is widely used by charities such as Oxfam and Barnardo's to create awareness of issues and raise funds so they can continue to provide services. Public relations has an important role to play in generating positive word-of-mouth communications and to confirm the non-profit identity of the charity.

Fair trade marketing is the development, promotion and selling of fair trade brands and the positioning of organizations on the basis of a fair trade ethos.

Companies are increasingly realizing that many consumers care about how suppliers in countries of the developing world are treated, and wish to support them by buying fair trade brands, often at a price premium. For example, Cafédirect, a fair trade company and brand, was launched to protect coffee growers from the volatility in world coffee prices. Minimum prices for coffee beans are paid, which are pegged above market fluctuations, and business support and development programmes are provided. The popularity of fair trade brands has prompted Nestlé to launch its own fair trade coffee, Partners' Blend, and Marks & Spencer has launched a range of fair trade clothing, which benefits Indian cotton farmers through a price that includes a premium that can be invested in their communities (Milmo, 2006).

Supermarkets are supporting fair trade products, with the Co-op stocking only own-label fair trade tea, coffee and chocolates, and Sainsbury's selling only fair trade bananas. Coffee bar chains such as Costa Coffee and Pret A Manger offer fair trade varieties. Fast-moving consumer goods food manufacturers also support the spread of fair trade products, and they have been acquiring ethical brands to facilitate access to these markets—for example,

MARKETING IN ACTION 5.5
Commercial versus Not-for-Profit Marketing

Arguably, ethically orientated marketing faces commercial challenges, as the turnover of large corporations surpasses that of many national economies. For example, annually, Walmart ($476 billion total revenue) turns over more than the following countries produce—Denmark (GDP $347 billion), Finland (GDP $276 billion)—and nearly as much Sweden (GDP $560 billion) and Norway (GDP $512 billion). Indeed, if Walmart were a country, it would rank somewhere around the 28th largest economy in the world.

In the Nordic economies, social initiatives rank highly. Whilst Sweden is relatively small in terms of population, it tops the league tables in many things from economic competitiveness to social health and happiness. Indeed, along with the other Nordic nations (Denmark, Norway, Iceland and Finland), Sweden is seen as offering a blueprint for reform of the public sector and delivering societal well-being. This is a nation where social welfare is considered a priority. It is said that 'A Swede pays tax more willingly than a Californian because he gets decent schools and free healthcare.' Performance in schools and hospitals is measured in Sweden and the results are available to all, which creates an open culture that ensures transparency at government level (Anon, 2013). Soft factors such as equality and social cohesion are at the foundation of the Swedish economic model. Excessive drinking has been a problem in Sweden, and the response has been to invest in initiatives at all levels to change behaviour. Upstream, the government has set clear goals for behaviour change: alcohol-free childhood, postpone the age of first drink experiences, provide more alcohol-free environments, prevent drink-driving. Mid-stream, Systembolaget (the Swedish state-owned alcohol monopoly) trains its employees to be expert advisers on alcohol consumption, and downstream individual consumption of alcohol has reduced as many 15- to 16-year-olds change their behaviour and attitudes towards alcohol. (Hallgren, Leifman and Andréasson, 2012).

However, recently, the major shareholder of Walmart's global operations has been accused of being far less generous than other wealthy philanthropists and everyday donors. The Waltons are America's richest family, worth in excess of $140 billion, which is largely due to their shares in Walmart, the world's largest retailer. The Walton Family Foundation, a non-profit organization with assets of about $2 billion, regularly invests in education reform and the environment, but recently the family have been accused of using the foundation for its tax-saving efficiencies rather than as a way to channel some of their family's great wealth into benefiting society. This does not mean that Walmart is more or less inclined towards social endeavours than other large corporations, but serves to highlight the tensions that can arise when profits meet philanthropy.

Based on: Dibb and Carrigan (2013); Anon (2013); Milne (2014); Cheng, Kotler and Lee (2011); Walmart (2014); Knoema (2015); O'Connor (2014)

Unilever's acquisition of Ben & Jerry's, which is a brand that supports local farmers; all of the ingredients in its ice creams are certified as fair trade. Kraft Foods, the multinational food and beverage corporation, expanded its product portfolio with the acquisition of Green & Black's, the organic chocolate brand. From its independent origins this brand has taken a 95 per cent share of the organic chocolate market, and since 2009—with redesigned packaging—it is gaining market share in the mainstream chocolate market. Fair trade marketing can also be based on the positioning of companies on a fair trade ethos. The Body Shop has for many years operated its 'Trade Not Aid' programme, which assists small-scale, indigenous communities in improving their standard of living through fair prices to suppliers (Crane and Matten, 2004).

The success of fair trade marketing is based upon consumers being willing to try and repeat-buy fair trade brands, and organizations developing genuine fair trade programmes. Consumers will not put up with organizations that use such schemes as an ethical veneer. Corporate Watch (www.corporatewatch.org) and Greenpeace (www.greenpeace.org) provide examples of dubious practice by companies that consumers can boycott or campaign against in the press (CIM Insight Team, 2005).

Societal Responses to Ethical Issues in Marketing

Societal responses to ethical issues in marketing take three forms: consumerism, environmentalism and ethical consumption.

Consumerism

Consumerism takes the form of organized action against business practices that are not in the interests of consumers. Organized action is taken through the **consumer movement**, which is an organized collection of groups and organizations whose objective is to protect the rights of consumers.

The consumer movement seeks to protect consumers' rights, which include the right to expect the product to be safe, for it to perform as expected and for communications for the product to be truthful and not mislead. Pressure from consumer groups in Europe has resulted in prohibitions on tobacco advertising, improvements in car safety, reductions in the levels of fat, sugar and salt in foods, restrictions on advertising alcohol to teenagers and the forcing of financial services companies to display true interest charges (the annual percentage rate, or APR) on advertisements for credit facilities. Further successes include unit pricing (stating the cost per unit of a brand), and ingredient labelling (stating the ingredients that go into a brand).

The consumer movement often takes the form of consumer associations that campaign for consumers and provide product information on a comparative basis, allowing consumers to make informed choices. These have been very successful in establishing themselves as credible and authoritative organizations and are seen as trusted providers of information to help consumer choice. Their actions help to improve consumer power when dealing with organizations.

Environmentalism

While consumerism focuses on improving the balance between consumer and organizational power and protecting the rights of consumers in consumption decisions, environmentalism is broader in scope with its focus on the physical environment. **Environmentalism** is the organized movement of groups and organizations to protect and improve the physical environment. Their concerns are: production and consumption of products that lead to global warming, pollution, the destruction of natural resources such as oil and forests, and non-biodegradable waste. They believe producers and consumers should take account not only of short-term profits and satisfaction but the cost to the environment of their actions. They wish to maximize environmental quality, which is the satisfaction of individual needs in a manner that will yield the maximum benefits to the individual while minimizing the effects on people and natural resources (Charter et al., 2002).

Environmentalists support the concept of environmental sustainability, and pressure companies to adopt strategies that promote its objectives. Environmental sustainability means 'to maintain or prolong environmental health'. Pressure groups such as Greenpeace and Friends of the Earth have been successful in persuading organizations to produce 'greener' products such as cadmium-free batteries, ozone-safe aerosols, recycled toilet tissue and packaging, catalytic converters, lead-free petrol, unbleached tea bags and cruelty-free cosmetics. Other environmental groups have successfully changed company practices. For example, UPM-Kymmene, Finland's largest paper and pulp company, based in over 16 countries, has to ensure that the replanting of trees matches felling. This is the result of environmentalist action. Major electrical manufacturers like Philips and Electrolux incorporate environmental considerations systematically in new product development and have strict guidelines covering the integration of environmental considerations into product design and development (Charter et al., 2002).

Environmentalists have concerns about how business activity affects the environment. This means they constantly pressurize organizations to deal with issues like controlling carbon emissions, reducing global warming, eliminating harmful pollutants, and using recycled and recyclable materials in products. The overarching aim is to maintain a sustainable environment for future generations.

Ethical consumption

Consumerism and environmentalism are organized movements designed to protect society and the environment from the harmful effects of production and consumption. However, consumers also act in an individual way to protect society and the environment through engaging in ethical consumption. **Ethical consumption** occurs when individual consumers, when making purchase decisions, take into account not only personal interests but also the interests of society and the environment. Examples include the boycotting of products and companies that have poor records regarding social and environmental concerns, the buying of non-animal-tested products, choosing fair trade or organic products, avoiding products made by sweatshop or child labour, and purchasing products that are made from recycled materials (Crane and Matten, 2004).

As discussed earlier, consumers and businesses respond differently to ethical consumption. Some are very passionate about living and operating in a manner that does not impact on the environment, while others are not and many are somewhere in between these two extremes. Marketing managers must understand their target audiences, individual values, attitudes and motivations and align these with societal values if they are to develop successful marketing strategies.

When you have read this chapter

Discover further resources and test your understanding: McGraw-Hill **Connect**™ is a digital teaching and learning environment that improves performance over a variety of critical outcomes; it can be tailored, is easy to use and is proven effective. **LearnSmart**™ is the most widely used and intelligent adaptive learning resource that is proven to strengthen memory recall, improve course retention and boost grades. Fuelled by **LearnSmart**™, **SmartBook**™ is the first and only adaptive reading experience available today.

Review

1 **The meaning of ethics, and business and marketing ethics**
   - Ethics are the moral principles and values that govern the actions and decisions of an individual or group.
   - Business ethics are the moral principles and values that guide a firm's behaviour.
   - Marketing ethics are the moral principles and values that guide behaviour within the field of marketing.

2 **Ethical issues in marketing**
   - Ethical issues in marketing relate to concerns about how the marketing mix is applied to consumers, and more general societal, environmental and political issues. Specific examples include: product safety, price fixing, misleading advertising, deceptive selling, invasion of privacy through direct and Internet marketing activities, and the use of promotional and slotting allowances.
   - Societal concerns focus on materialism and short-termism; environmental concerns focus on the impact of marketing decisions on the environment; and political concerns focus on the power that global companies can exert on consumers, governments and suppliers.

3 **Business, societal, and legal and regulatory responses to ethical concerns**
   - The main response from businesses has been the adoption of CSR as a philosophy guiding decisions and actions.
   - Societal responses take the form of consumerism, environmentalism and ethical consumption.
   - Legal and regulatory responses are the enactment of laws at European and national levels to protect the consumer and to outlaw anti-competitive business practices, and the establishment of regulatory bodies to enforce those laws. Many industries have also established organizations to apply self-regulation through the drawing up and enforcement of codes of practice.

4 **The stakeholder theory of the company**
   - CSR is based on the stakeholder theory of the company, which contends that companies have multiple stakeholders, not just shareholders, to whom they hold a responsibility. These include communities associated with the company, employees, customers (including intermediaries) and suppliers.

5 The nature of CSR

- CSR refers to the ethical principle that an organization should be accountable for how its behaviour might affect society and the environment.
- Organizations have responsibilities to ensure: economic performance meets stakeholder requirements; operational practices do not break the law; ethical principles are consistent with values of society. Additionally, an organization has a responsibility to be a good corporate citizen: e.g. supporting good causes and making philanthropic donations.

6 The dimensions of CSR

- CSR involves five dimensions of organizational activity: the physical environment, social, consumer, supply chain, and employee relations.
- Marketing's response to each dimension involves responding to relevant issues, for example:
  - *physical environment issues*—combating global warming. By applying business practices which create, produce and deliver sustainable solutions to environmental problems while continuing to satisfy customers and other stakeholders.
  - *societal and consumer issues*—community support and attention to product safety. This is an example of societal marketing, as it takes account of consumers' and society's wider interests rather than just their short-term consumption. Societal welfare is also enhanced by cause-related marketing, which is the commercial activity by which businesses and charities form a partnership to market an image or product for mutual benefit.
  - *supply chain issues*—low prices to producers in the developing world, applying fair trade marketing, which is the development, promotion and selling of fair trade brands and the positioning of organizations on the basis of a fair trade ethos.
  - *employee relations issues*—training and motivation. This is referred to as internal marketing, which is the development, training and motivation of employees designed to enhance their performance in providing customer satisfaction.

7 Arguments for and against CSR

- Arguments against are that CSR is misguided and too costly.
- Arguments for are that CSR leads to enhanced brand/corporate image and reputation, provides marketing opportunities, reduces operating costs, increases an organization's ability to attract and retain employees, is a form of risk reduction, and improves access to capital.

8 The focus of social marketing and not-for-profit marketing

- The four stages of development of social marketing focusing on behaviour, modelling the planning process, the three levels of social marketing and incorporating social media into social marketing.
- Marketing procedures for non-profit organizations: target marketing, differentiation, developing a marketing mix.

Key Terms

business ethics the moral principles and values that guide a firm's behaviour

cause-related marketing a commercial activity by which businesses and charities or causes form a partnership with each other to market an image or product for mutual benefit

consumer movement an organized collection of groups and organizations whose objective it is to protect the rights of consumers

environmentalism the organized movement of groups and organizations to protect and improve the physical environment

ethical consumption the taking of purchase decisions not only on the basis of personal interests but also on the basis of the interests of society and the environment

ethics the moral principles and values that govern the actions and decisions of an individual or group

fair trade marketing the development, promotion and selling of fair trade brands and the positioning of organizations on the basis of a fair trade ethos

internal marketing training, motivating and communicating with staff to cause them to work effectively in providing customer satisfaction; more recently the term has been expanded to include marketing to all staff, with the aim of achieving the acceptance of marketing ideas and plans

not-for-profit marketing involves the use of marketing frameworks, concepts and ideas used by an organization that operates on a not-for-profit basis; this type of organization often employs a volunteer workforce and relies on donations and external funding

marketing ethics the moral principles and values that guide behaviour within the field of marketing

societal marketing focuses on consumers' needs and long-term welfare as keys to satisfying organizational objectives and responsibilities by taking into account consumers' and societies' wider interests rather than just their short-term consumption

social marketing seeks to change behaviour for the benefit of the individual and society and its applications come in many different guises.

stakeholder an individual or group that either (i) is harmed by or benefits from the company, or (ii) whose rights can be violated or have to be respected by the company

stakeholder theory this contends that companies are not managed purely in the interests of their shareholders alone but a broader group including communities associated with the company, employees, customers and suppliers

sustainable marketing focuses on reducing environmental damage by creating, producing and delivering sustainable solutions while continuing to satisfy customers and other stakeholders

Study Questions

1. What is 'marketing ethics'? To what extent do you believe marketing practices to be unethical and how might unethical practices in marketing be restricted?

2. What are the key responsibilities of CSR and to what extent do you believe businesses should accept them?

3. Describe the five dimensions of CSR. Evaluate marketing's response to the issues underlying each dimension.

4. What is meant by 'consumerism' and 'environmentalism'? To what extent do you believe these movements have achieved their goals of protecting consumers, society and the environment?

5. Evaluate the contention that if ethical consumption was the norm there would be no need to legislate to protect consumers.

6. Discuss the differences in meaning of sustainability and CSR.

7. Discuss the similarities and differences between social marketing and not-for-profit marketing.

Recommended Reading

Eagle, L. and S. Dahl (2015) *Marketing Ethics & Society*, London: Sage Publications Ltd.

Fryer, M. (2015) *Ethics Theory & Business Practice*, London: Sage Publications Ltd.

Horner, D. (2013) *Understanding Media Ethics*, London: Sage Publications Ltd.

Maignan, I. and O. C. Ferrell (2004) CSR and marketing; An integrated approach, *Journal of the Academy of Marketing Science* 32(1), 3–19.

Nill, A. and J. Schibrowsky (2007) Research on Marketing Ethics: A Systematic Review of the Literature, *Journal of Macromarketing* September 727, 256–73.

Rettie, R., K. Burchell and D. Riley (2012) Normalising green behaviour: A new Approach to sustainability marketing, *Journal of Marketing Management* 28(3), 420–44.

References

Anderson, P. (1999) Give and Take, *Marketing Week*, 26 August, 39–41.

Anon (2013) The Next Supermodel, *The Economist*, 2 February. http://www.economist.com/news/

leaders/21571136-politicians-both-right-and-left-could-learn-nordic-countries-next-supermodel (accessed 24 February 2015).

Arthur, C. (2011) Microsoft accepts censorship in Chinese search engine deal, *The Guardian*, 5 July, 16.

Aston, A. and B. Helm (2005) The Race Against Climate Change, *Business Week*, 12/19 December, 85–93.

Balabanis, G., R. E. Stables and H. C. Phillips (1997) Market Orientation in the Top 200 British Charity Organisations and its Impact on their Performance, *European Journal of Marketing* 31(8), 583–603.

Barnett, M. (2011) Driving home the benefits of green wheels, *Marketing Week*, 7 April, 24–6.

Bennett, P. D. (1988) *Marketing*, New York: McGraw-Hill, 690–2.

Berkowitz, E. N., R. A. Kerin, S. W. Hartley and W. Rudelius (2004) *Marketing*, Boston, MA: McGraw-Hill.

Boseley, S. (2009) Matter of Life and Death: Wallace and Gromit Makers get Animated over UK Obesity Crisis, Guardian.co.uk, 2 January (retrieved 6 April 2009 from www.guardian.co.uk/politics/2009/jan/02/wallace-gromitobesity-ad-health).

Boxell, J. and F. Harvey (2005) BP Sacked 252 in Corruption Drive, *The Financial Times*, 12 April, 22.

Business for Social Responsibility Issue Briefs (2003) Overview of Business Ethics, www.bsr.org

Butler, P. and N. Collins (1994) Political Marketing: Structure and Process, *European Journal of Marketing* 28(1), 19–34.

Carroll, A. B. (1991) The Pyramid of Corporate Social Responsibility: Toward the Moral Management of Organizational Stakeholders, *Business Horizons*, July/August, 39–48.

Carroll, A. B. and A. K. Buchholtz (2000) *Business and Society: Ethics and Stakeholder Management*, Cincinnati: South-Western College

Charter, M., K. Peattie, J. Ottman and M. J. Polonsky (2002) *Marketing and Sustainability*, Cardiff: Centre for Business Relationships, Accountability, Sustainability and Society (BRASS) in association with the Centre for Sustainable Design.

Cheng, H., P. Kotler and Lee. N., (2011) *Social Marketing for Public Health: Global Trends and Success Stories*, London, UK: Jones & Bartlett LLC.

Choveke, M. (2006) Can Anything Rescue Sunny D?, *Marketing Week*, 26 February, 7.

CIM Insight Team (2005) Fair Trade?, *The Marketer*, January, 6–8.

Clarke, B. (2008) Good Marketing Beats Regulation, *The Marketer*, March, 15.

Costa, M. L. (2011) One man's vision, *Marketing Week*, 5 May, 18–21.

Crane, A. and D. Matten (2004) *Business Ethics: A European Perspective*, Oxford: Oxford University Press.

Crook, C. (2005) The Good Company, *The Economist*, 22 January, 3–4.

Devaney, P. (2005) Who Cares Wins, But is There a Hidden Agenda?, *Marketing Week*, 28 April, 34–5.

Dibb, S. and M. Carrigan (2013) Social Marketing Transformed, *European Journal of Marketing* 47(9), 1376–98.

Donaldson, T. and L. E. Preston (1995) The Stakeholder Theory of the Corporation: Concepts, Evidence, and Implications, *Academy of Management Review* 20(1), 15–91.

Eccles, R., I. Ioannou and G. Serafeim (2011) The Impact of a Corporate Culture of Sustainability on Corporate Behaviour and Performance, *Harvard Business Review: Working Papers*, 14 November.

Everitt, P. (2009) Car Scrappage Schemes are Not a Motor Industry Green Scam, Guardian.co.uk, 19 March 2009, www.guardian.co.uk/commentisfree/2009/mar/19/paul-everitt-response (retrieved 3 April 2009)

Friedman, M. (1970) *The Social Responsibility of Business is to Increase the Profits*, New York Times Magazine, 13 September, 8.

Fukukawa, K. and J. Moon (2004) A Japanese Model of Corporate Social Responsibility: A Study of Online Reporting, *Journal of Corporate Citizenship* 16, Winter, 45–59.

Gates Foundation 2012 Programs and Partnerships, http://www.gatesfoundation.org/programs/Pages/overview.aspx.

Gow, D. (2008) Record US Fine Ends Siemens Bribery Scandal, *The Guardian*, 16 December, 24.

Grow, B., S. Hamm and L. Lee (2005) The Rebate Over Doing Good, *The Economist*, 5/12 September, 78–80.

Gunther, M. (2012) A big push to move meat production terrible to just bad, 23 February, http://www.greenbiz.com/topic/food–agriculture?page 2.

Hallgren, M., H. Leifman and S. Andréasson (2012,) Drinking Less But Greater Harm: Could Polarized Drinking Habits Explain the Divergence Between Alcohol Consumption and Harms among Youth? *Alcohol and Alcoholism*, 4 July, 47(5), 581–90. doi:http://dx.doi.org/10.1093/alcalc/ags071

HM Government (2010) Change4life, 17 February, http://www.dh.gov.uk/prod_consum_dh/groups/dh_digitalassets/@dh/@en/documents/digitalasset/dh_115511.pdf.

Jeffries, E. (2011) A clearer footprint, *Marketing*, 19 October, 26–27.

Kelly-Detwiler, P. (2014) IKEA's Aggressive Approach To Sustainability Creates Enormous Business Opportunities, *Forbes*, 7 February. http://www.forbes.com/sites/peterdetwiler/2014/02/07/ikeas-aggressive-approach-to-sustainability-creates-enormous-business-opportunities (accessed 3 March 2015).

Kim, C-R (2011) http://www.reuters.com/article/2011/02/28/us-autoshow-toyota-idUSTRE71R7GM20110228 (accessed February 2012).

King, H. (2012) Ikea's Steve Howard on bringing sustainability to the masses, Greenbiz.com, http://www.greenbiz.com/blog/2012/02/23/ikeas-cso-steve-howard-bringing-sustainability-masses.

Knoema (2015) World GDP Ranking 2014 | Data and Charts, Knoema. http://knoema.com/nwnfkne/world-gdp-ranking-2014-data-and-charts

Kotler, P. and G. Zaltman (1971) Social marketing: an approach to planned social change, *Journal of Marketing* 35, 3–12.

Lefebvre, D. and G, H. (1997) De-marketing: Putting Kotler and Levy's ideas into practice, *Journal of Marketing Management* 13(4), 315–25.

Macalister, T. (2008) Undercut and Under Fire: UK Biofuel Feels Heat From All Sides, *The Guardian*, 1 April, 28.

Maignan, I. and O. C. Ferrell (2004) Corporate Social Responsibility and Marketing: An Integrated Framework, *Journal of the Academy of Marketing Science* 32(1), 3–19.

Margolis, J., H.A. Elfenbein and J. Walsh (2007) *Does It Pay to be Good? A Meta-Analysis and Redirection of Research on the Relationship Between Corporate Social and Financial Performance*, Harvard Business School, Boston, MA: Mimeo.

Milmo, D. (2007) BA Fined £270m and Now Faces £300m Lawsuit, *The Guardian*, 2 August, 1.

Milmo, S. (2006) M&S Boosts Ethical Image With Fairtrade Clothing, *The Guardian*, 30 January, 21.

Milne, R. (2014) Scottish nationalists look to Nordic model for independence, *The Financial Times*, 2 February. http://www.ft.com/cms/s/0/57664dc2-8bf8-11e3-bcf2-00144feab7de.html#axzz3ToDmmcSK (accessed 2 March 2015).

Milner, M. (2004) Shell Fined £84m Over Reserves Scandal, *The Guardian*, 30 July, 16.

Milner, M. (2005) Brussels Inquiry Could Land BT with Huge Tax Bill, *The Guardian*, 20 January, 20.

Moon, J. (2002) Corporate Social Responsibility: An Overview, in *The International Directory of Corporate Philanthropy*, London: Europa Books.

Murphy, C. (2008) Green Gold, *The Marketer*, September, 30–3.

National Social Marketing Centre (2009) www.nsms.org.uk/public/default.aspx (accessed 6 April 2009).

Naughton, J. (2006) Google's Founding Principles Fall at Great Firewall of China, *The Observer*, Business and Media, 29 January, 10.

O'Flaherty, K. (2008) Brands Behaving Badly, *Marketing Week*, 30 October, 20–1.

O'Connor, C. (2014) Report: Walmart's Billionaire Waltons Give Almost None Of Own Cash To Foundation, Forbes, 3 June. http://www.forbes.com/sites/clareoconnor/2014/06/03/report-walmarts-billionaire-waltons-give-almost-none-of-own-cash-to-family-foundation (accessed 8 March 2015).

Parkinson, C. (2005) Make the Most of Your Ethics, *Marketing Week*, 9 June, 30–1.

Peattie, K. (1999). Trappings versus substance in the greening of marketing, *Journal of Strategic Marketing* 7(2), 131–48.

Peattie, K. and Crane, A. (2006) Green marketing: legend, myth, farce or prophesy? *Qualitative Market Research: An International Journal* 8(4), 357–70.

Plender, J. and A. Persaud (2005) Good Ethics Means More Than Ticking Boxes, *The Financial Times*, 23 August, 10.

Public Health England (2015) Campaign Resource Centre, Public Health England. http://campaigns.dh.gov.uk/category/change-4-life (accessed 8 March 2015).

Reed, C. (2000) Ethics Frozen Out in the Ben & Jerry Ice Cream War, *The Observer*, 13 February, 3; The Economist (2000) Slipping Slopes, 15 April, 85.

Sclater, I. (2005) Thank Goodness for Success, *The Marketer*, January, 11–13.

Shapiro, B. (1992) Marketing for Non-Profit Organisations, *Harvard Business Review*, Sept.–Oct., 123–32.

Skapinker, M. (2008) Taking a Hard Line On Soft Soap, *The Financial Times*, 7 July, 16.

Sweeney, M. (2009) Government in £275m Anti-obesity Drive, Guardian.co.uk, 2 January 2009 (retrieved 6 April 2009 from www. guardian.co.uk/media/2009/jan/02/change4life-obesity).

The Economist (2005) A Union of Concerned Executives, 22 January, 7–12.

Trucost (2012) State of Green Business 2012, http://www.trucost.com/ published-research/75/state-of-green-business-2012.

United National Development Programme (2015) Human Development reports, 8 March. http://hdr.undp.org/en/2014-report

Vandermerwe, S. and M. Oliff (1990) Customers drive corporations green, *Long Range Planning*, 23(6), 10–16.

Walmart (2014) Walmart 2014 Annual Report. http://cdn.corporate. walmart.com/66/e5/9ff9a87445949173fde56316ac5f/2014-annual-report.pdf (accessed 24 February 2015).

Watts, R. (2009) Taking a Wrong Turn in Tackling Obesity, Guardian. co.uk, 2 January 2009 (retrieved 6 April 2009 from www.guardian. co.uk/society/joepublic/2008/dec/31/change4lifecampaign-obesity).

Webb, T. (2011) Japan's economy heads into freefall after earthquake and tsunami, *The Guardian*, 13 March. http://www.theguardian. com/world/2011/mar/13/japan-economy-recession-earthquake-tsunami (accessed 8 March 2015).

World Bank (2015) Poverty, The World Bank. http://www.worldbank .org/en/topic/poverty/overview

Worldblu (2013) The Worldblu List 2013. http://www.worldblu.com/ awardee-profiles/2013.php

CASE 9
The Co-operative—Leading the Way in Corporate Social Responsibility

Niall FitzGerald, former chief executive of Unilever and current chairman of University College Dublin's Michael Smurfit Graduate Business School, once said:

'Corporate social responsibility is a hard-edged business decision. Not because it is a nice thing to do or because people are forcing us to do it . . . because it is good for our business.'

Corporate social responsibility is now at the forefront of many organizations' strategic thinking—none more so than the Co-op—and can be used as a differentiator from competitors. Over the past several years, Co-op has won numerous awards, from most responsible retailer four years in succession, to the *Which*? Energy award.

How did it all start? It was in Rochdale 168 years ago, when a group of everyday people founded a new kind of business. This revolution was called 'the Co-operative', based on democratic principles, owned by its customers and reinvesting in the community it served. Today it's grown to become a part of daily life, with over 5,000 stores and branches across the UK.

The Co-operative has always had a purpose beyond profit, going back to its founding fathers. It aims to be transparent and publishes 'warts and all' reports on topics from salt in food to animal welfare.

In 2011, it launched a groundbreaking new plan with one clear goal: to be the most socially responsible business in the UK. As former group chief executive Peter Marks said:

'Our ambition is to build a better society and this plan will stimulate and reinforce the unique benefit of the consumer co-operative model.

'At a time when UK society is picking up the pieces from a recession exacerbated by corporate greed and speculation, we are seeking to show that there is another way. The plc model is not the only game in town. It is possible for business to embrace the efficiencies of the market economy and also the need for robust legislation to ensure that progress is sustainable and just.'

Key targets set out in the plan include the following.

Democratic control and reward:

- Continue to set new standards for openness and honesty globally, and seek to utilize new technology to enhance consumers' abilities to make ethical choices
- Continue a profit-sharing scheme with its members that is amongst the broadest and most generous of any major UK business
- Aim to have 20 million members by 2020 and to be opened up to the under 16s as soon as legally possible
- Encourage ethical consumerism through engagement with members and extra share of profit.

Ethical finance:

The Co-operative Bank has withheld over £1 billion of funding from business activities that its customers say are unethical.

- Double financial support for renewable energy and energy efficiency projects from £400 million to £1 billion by 2013
- Continue to tackle global poverty via its £25 million microfinance fund support
- Continue to take a lead on financial inclusion and champion financial literacy among young people
- Encourage primary pension scheme to operate a responsible investment policy that is among the most comprehensive of private sector schemes in the UK.

»

Protecting the environment:

- Having reduced its own operational carbon emissions by 20 per cent since 2006, the target will now increase to 35 per cent by 2017—the most progressive of any major UK business
- It will enhance its pesticides policy further, and seek to ban chemicals such as endosulfan and paraquat
- Leading biodiversity work in areas such as wood and fish to be matched with new targets on palm oil and soya
- On top of the 15 per cent weight reductions achieved in packaging, they will reduce the environmental impact by a further 10 per cent by 2012 and increase carrier bag reduction target to 75 per cent by 2013
- The construction by 2012 of a head office that will set new standards in sustainable design, construction and operation in the UK.

Building a fairer and better society:

- Co-operative enterprise will be more heavily supported through the investment of £11 million by 2013 and the launch of a new £20 million international co-operative development loan fund
- The Co-operative's community investment, already among the most generous in the UK, will be expanded to include £5 million a year to help tackle poverty around its stores and branches
- The Co-operative will spearhead a cultural shift in youth perception and opportunity through a £30 million programme that will support an apprenticeship academy, a green schools programme and the creation of 200 Co-operative schools by 2013.

Tackling global poverty:

- Going forward, if it can be fair trade, it will be fair trade. By 2013, some 90 per cent of the primary commodities sourced from the developing world will be certified to Fairtrade standards; furthermore, the Co-operative will develop a unique range of projects and initiatives that benefit producers and take it beyond Fairtrade
- Invest £8 million per annum to help tackle global poverty through cooperative support initiatives.

Responsible retailing:

- Continue to target salt, saturated fat and sugar reductions in key products whilst maintaining food safety and product quality
- At least 30 per cent of own-brand food products that carry traffic lights will be healthy and a minimum of 30 per cent of food promotions will be for healthy offerings
- Ensure that Healthier Choice products are no more expensive than standard equivalent lines
- The nutritional content of Simply Value products will be at least as good as standard equivalent lines.

Respecting animal welfare:

- Continue to ensure that shoppers operating on a variety of budgets have the opportunity to support higher baseline animal welfare standards, and that all shell eggs and egg ingredients in own-brand products are at least free-range
- Continue to pursue higher welfare standards across our meat and fish, converting our own-brand salmon to Freedom Food standard in 2012
- Continue to take a lead on the issue of animal testing of cosmetic and household products.

The plan encourages all stakeholders to get involved in a variety of ways, from sending messages to the UK government to offer greater support for smallholder farmers and cooperatives, to offering a microloan of £15 and changing a life. The aim is to inspire more people to change the world.

Leading environmentalist Jonathan Porritt believes this is a new benchmark for others to measure against.

What's the advantage?

Building a reputation as an ethical and responsible business sets you apart from the competition. This differentiation appeals to more thoughtful customers and helps build loyalty, particularly among those who insist on ethical retailing.

Also, it helps in recruitment and employee retention, as well as generating positive publicity throughout the communications networks. However, that is not enough. The company must continue to make profits to enable it to carry out such an ambitious plan. So how is the Co-op doing?

Since Co-op launched its ethical plan, the journey hasn't been smooth. Now, in 2015, its most recent year, the Co-op doesn't fully own its banking division and some of the targets haven't been met. For example, the £1 billion support translated to only $1 billion, due to the difficulties the bank experienced during 2013–14. The problems have been with bad management and a sex scandal relating to the former bank chairman, undermining Co-op's previous good reputation. However, it is the number one convenience UK grocery store in 2015, voted for by customers, and number two by size.

Where next? New group chairman, Allan Leighton, stated that the business had strayed a long way: 'We lost the heart of what the Co-op was.' However, the Co-op still believes in its ethical policies, and recent television ads for the bank re-affirm this. Also, the changes at the top are starting to work, with the Co-op back in profit. Is this just the start of the Co-op getting back on track as Britain's most ethical retailer? Only time will tell.

Questions

1. Using the key targets set out in the Co-operative plan as a benchmark, select one of the following supermarkets, Tesco, Asda, Sainsbury's or Morrisons, to use as a comparator. Use the Internet as a resource.

2. Companies have been accused of 'green washing', which is a light-touch approach for developing a corporate social responsibility (CSR) policy. Suggest the difficulties you may encounter when following a fully committed CSR plan like the Co-op.

3. Many organizations criticize CSR because they don't see business delivering on its promises. Argue the case for the benefits of CSR.

This case study was written by Brian Searle, Programme Director Marketing MSc, Loughborough University.

References

The Co-operative Group (2011), The Co-operative launches most radical corporate ethical plan and encourages customers to join the revolution, The Co-operative Group. Available at: http://www.co-operative.coop/corporate/Press/Pressreleases/Headline-news/Join-The-Revolution (accessed 7 June 2015); The Co-operative Group (2011), Setting New Sights: Our Ethical Plan 2012-14 (and beyond…), The Co-operative Group. http://www.co-operative.coop/Corporate/CSR/Our_Ethical_Plan_2012-2014.pdf (accessed 7 June 2015); The Co-operative Group (2013), The Co-operative Sustainability Report 2013, The Co-operative Group, http://www.co-operative.coop/corporate/sustainability/Downloads (accessed 7 June 2015).

Coop Danmark's Anti Food Wastage Initiatives: Social Responsibility or Good Business?

Food wastage, and the efforts of supermarkets to combat this problem, is not a new phenomenon; in the UK, WRAP (Waste & Resources Action Programme) has estimated that there has been a 10 per cent reduction in food and drink waste by grocery retailers and manufacturers between 2007 and 2012. In 2013, the UK's seven major supermarkets contributed to just 1.3 per cent of all food waste, according to figures from the British Retail Consortium (BRC). The figures combine data from Asda, the Co-operative Food, M&S, Morrisons, Sainsbury's, Tesco and Waitrose, together making up 87.3 per cent of the UK grocery market. They reveal that, of the estimated 15 million tonnes of food thrown away in the UK each year, only 200,000 tonnes comes from these retailers. This is in stark contrast to domestic food waste, which constitutes more than half of all food waste generated.

In Denmark, households throw away food to the value of more than 16 billion Danish kroner (about £1.6 billion). However, in contrast to the UK, in Denmark supermarket retailers are not far behind consumers, throwing away around 150,000 tonnes of food annually with a value of around 8.4 billion Danish kroner. This case looks at the way in which the Danish supermarket retail cooperative Coop Danmark A/S (www.coop.dk) is attempting to reduce the amount of food that its supermarkets throw away and at the same time raising awareness among consumers about the problem of food wastage.

Coop's food wastage manifesto and in-store initiatives

Coop Danmark A/S (COOP) is the largest supermarket retailer in Denmark, employing around 40,000 people in over 1,200 retail outlets of varying sizes. Coop defines wasted food as 'food that could have been eaten by humans but for one reason or another ends up being thrown away'. Giving away unsold food

to food banks is not possible, as unlike in France, Danish law prohibits the donation of food that has passed its sell-by date. So how does Coop do its part to reduce the amount of food that is wasted? Coop acknowledges that the Danish food retail industry has a large influence over the food that is wasted by both producers and consumers, and so Coop has produced a 'food wastage manifesto' in conjunction with the Danish consumer movement Stop Wasting Food (www.stopspildafmad.dk). The manifesto spells out Coop's aims for reducing food waste in its supermarkets, by consumers and by producers. The Stop Wasting Food movement has been tasked with keeping track of the achievements of Coop's initiatives.

Coop states in its food wastage manifesto that the aims can be achieved through concrete in-store initiatives, such as reducing the price on food products as they get closer to their sell-by date, developing a visual concept that can help draw consumer attention to the need to reduce food waste, and through sharing knowledge about food waste among employees. Coop has also pledged in the food wastage manifesto to hold an annual campaign in all its stores that aims to increase awareness of the problem of food wastage, together with becoming an active participant in the public debate surrounding food wastage. So rather than simply passing the responsibility for reducing food wastage on to consumers, Coop has taken an active role.

Coop has long considered social responsibility to be part of the company's mission. Coop was the first company in Denmark to introduce a programme for improving consumer awareness and health, together with the production of educational materials for schools to encourage healthy eating. Today, Coop's corporate social responsibility initiatives focus on the avoidance of food wastage, thus continuing to support the company's social mission of changing consumer attitudes to consumption. These educational initiatives are supported by changes in pricing strategy and by highlighting the issue of food wastage; for example, Coop's discount format Fakta has stopped the 'buy one get one free' offers, instead offering lower prices on purchases of single products. When it was discovered that around 40,000 bananas were thrown away annually for the simple reason that the fruit was single rather than in a bunch of two or more, Coop then held an event in Copenhagen's Central Square where 40,000 single bananas were handed out to passers-by. Whilst the results of the event have yet to be measured in terms of bananas, there was wide coverage in the national media, thus fulfilling the pledge in Coop's food wastage manifesto to enter the public debate.

In a survey, Danish consumers were asked what would encourage them to purchase products close to the sell-by date. Given the high cost of food products in Denmark relative to other European countries, respondents answered that a lower price would make them more likely to purchase food products close to the sell-by date. In response to this, Coop has changed its pricing strategy by systematically reducing the price of food products that are approaching their sell-by date. For Coop, reduced prices leads to a lower profit margin on each item; however, unsold food that is just thrown away does not contribute anything to the costs associated with the production and warehousing of the products prior to them being put on the shelves of the supermarket, and the safe disposal of food items leads to other costs. In order to address consumer concerns about the quality of food that is near its sell-by date, the Kvickly chain has introduced a red label—in the same shade as Coop's brand logo—with the words 'buy today, eat today' and 'same good quality' in an effort to persuade consumers to buy food products near to their sell-by date. Whilst the intention of this labelling strategy is positive, one result may be

that food that the supermarket would have been forced to dispose of is actually thrown away at home.

Impact on the supply chain

In addition to the direct wastage that supermarkets are responsible for due to unsold food, supermarket retailers' power in the supply chain means that the impact of short-term demand fluctuations is passed back to farmers. Farmers are therefore forced to produce more than is necessary to ensure that they can supply the supermarkets. At the same time, the requirement for aesthetically pleasing produce to support a supermarket brand image focusing on quality leads to misshaped vegetables being thrown away by farmers before they even reach the supermarket shelves. By selling 'unorthodox'-shaped vegetables and fruit, Coop eases pressure on the supply chain, as farmers throw away less produce when demand is high.

Impact of the initiatives

So have Coop's initiatives had any impact on the purchasing behaviour of Danish consumers? The numbers speak for themselves: for example, in 2014 Coop destroyed 750,000 fewer loaves of bread and 300,000 fewer packets of meat compared with previous years (landbrugsavisen.dk). However, one problem that Coop and all supermarkets face is that customers expect full shelves at all times of the day; if the products are not available, consumers will shop elsewhere—maybe for good (Ritzau, 2014). So while consumers have become better at buying products that are closer to their sell-by date, consumers' purchase behaviour appears to be driven by lower prices rather than a change in social attitudes towards food wastage and an acceptance of the logistical challenges that lead to empty supermarket shelves. So the question remains: have social attitudes towards food wastage really changed, or is it just the impact of a change in price?

Questions ■ connect

1. **Coop Danmark A/S prides itself on its socially responsible business practices. Can Coop's pricing strategy be seen as a socially responsible business practice or just a way to pass on to consumers the responsibility of reducing food wastage?**

2. What do you think is the main reason for Coop Danmark's anti-food wastage initiatives: reducing Coop's costs, increasing Coop's income by selling food that would otherwise be wasted, or reinforcing Coop's socially responsible brand?

3. Do you think that Coop's initiatives will have an impact on consumers' purchasing behaviour?

This case study was written by Robert Ormrod, Associate Professor, Aarhus University.

Further reading

COOP Danmark A/S (www.coop.dk); Stop Spild af Mad (http://www.stopspildafmad.dk).

References

Based on: landbrugsavisen.dk (2015), COOP reducerer madspil. Available at: http://landbrugsavisen.dk/coop-reducerer-madspild (accessed 7 July 2015); Ritzau (2014), COOP om madspil: Kunder kræver fyldte hylder, http://www.msn.com/da-dk/finans/other/coop-om-madspild-kunder-kr%c3%a6ver-fyldte-hylder/ar-BB8isaf

CHAPTER 6
Marketing Research and Business Intelligence

> *Information is the oil of the 21st century, and analytics is the combustion engine.*
>
> **PETER SONDERGAARD, SENIOR VICE PRESIDENT, GARTNER RESEARCH (GARTNER, 2011)**

LEARNING OBJECTIVES

After reading this chapter, you should be able to:

1 define marketing research, marketing information systems and business intelligence
2 discuss the role of marketing research and the management of information
3 identify different types of marketing research
4 describe the stages in the marketing research process
5 explain how to prepare a research brief and proposal
6 discuss the role of different research methods
7 discuss approaches to research design decisions: sampling, survey method and questionnaire design issues
8 explain the processes involved with interpreting and presenting data and writing reports
9 distinguish between qualitative and quantitative research
10 discuss the ethical issues that arise in marketing research

Marketing research adds value to marketers and their organizations when they are faced with the following types of question. What kinds of people buy my products? What do they value? Where do they buy? What kinds of new products would they like to see on the market? How satisfied were they after they made a purchase? Answering such questions is the key to informed marketing decision-making, but marketing managers need to develop knowledge about their customers, the marketing environment and markets they operate in, in order to respond appropriately. Marketing research provides the solutions by listening to people, analyzing their data and producing information that can aid business decision-making. There are specialist skills involved in interpreting data in such a way that it becomes possible to accurately predict future events, actions and behaviours (ESOMAR, 2015).

In recent years, the marketing landscape has changed as the Internet, mobile phones and other devices have profoundly altered the way we communicate. Digital technologies have provided revolutionary new ways for researchers to operate. Data can be collected and analyzed instantaneously, and this enables analysts to measure real-time behaviour (Poynter, Williams and York, 2014). But whilst technology is changing, the methods of data collection and modes of analysis—the basic principles of marketing research—remain the same.

In this chapter, we begin by exploring the growth in business intelligence and how such data can form an important element in a company's marketing information system (MkIS). The components of an MkIS are then described, including the crucial role of marketing research in such systems. Then we look at the process of marketing research and its uses. Next, we will examine the influences of digital technologies and their impact on marketing research practices. The differences between qualitative and quantitative research are then explored before finally discussing ethical issues in marketing research.

Business Intelligence and Marketing Information Systems

Digital technology is creating opportunities to collect data from multiple sources in real time. As a result, the volume of data being generated has increased significantly and is now referred to as 'big data' (very large data sets). For marketing decisions to benefit from this glut of data, it has to be managed and analyzed correctly. **Business intelligence** is the actionable knowledge produced by the analysis of big data. Business intelligence techniques permit large data sets to be analyzed for the purpose of interpretation and decision-making.

Big data is not a new idea; since the linking of low-cost computing and scanners at the point of sale in shops, large quantities of data have been generated. This early form of big data improved understanding of shopper behaviour and enabled retailers to manage their stock more effectively. Retailers also had access to the information from their scanners almost immediately instead of waiting for weeks for the traditional accounting reports. Another major benefit of this new stream of information was more targeted sales promotions and advertising campaigns, and improved profitability (Fulgoni, 2013).

In the last few years the flow of big data has increased dramatically as use of the Internet has extended throughout the supply chain and even extended to include consumers as they shop online and via mobile devices. Big data is generated in volumes which it is difficult to comprehend, for example petabytes, zettabytes and yottabytes. These volumes of data are generated from many sources, from scanners to smartphone and cars. Forms of data include videos, documents, spreadsheets, online purchases, blogs and tweets. The list is becoming ever longer as the Internet of Things connects together more and more elements of human interaction (Kerschberg, 2014).

Moreover, the data is increasingly producing efficiency gains and creating opportunities to launch highly tailored and targeted promotional campaigns. Marketers still need to ensure that they use big data to design promotional campaigns that contribute to a well-planned marketing strategy rather than responding to every single 'click' made by the consumer (Fulgoni, 2013). For marketers, the capacity to interpret meaning from big data becomes more important as the sources of data increase. Online, vast stores of data are created every minute of the day, and the rate of data production is increasing significantly year on year. Between 2013 and 2014, there was a 197 per cent increase in the amount of content uploaded to YouTube, a 76 per cent increase in the number of photos uploaded to Instagram, and a 35 per cent increase in the apps downloaded from Apple (Hutchins, n.d.). The implications for brands are significant as customers begin to engage with products and services differently via digital platforms.

Moreover, the way consumers interact with digital technology, whether through Google searches, Facebook posts or tweets is being watched, and the data they generate analyzed. Supercookies, tiny pieces of data stored in web browsers, are used to record the websites visited and the dwell time on each site and page (Pagliery, 2015). Browser fingerprinting is used to provide behavioural advertisers (BA) with the information they need to develop highly targeted and personalized promotional offers. From watching browsing behaviour and analyzing the data, BAs are able to infer age, gender and personal interests without ever asking your permission (Truste, 2015). But data collection does not stop with web browsing; Samsung's Smart TV enabled the company to gather viewing behaviour directly from the television (BBC, 2015).

It is important to understand that big data is only of value once it is analyzed and turned into business intelligence (Kerschberg, 2014). Read Marketing in Action 6.1 to find out how GlaxoSmithKline (GSK) is using big data in this way.

Marketing information systems

In this section, we consider the information infrastructure that is used to support the gathering and analysis of data.

Marketing information system design is important, since the quality of a marketing information system has been shown to have an impact on the effectiveness of decision-making (Daniels, Wilson and McDonald, 2003). As use of these systems becomes more widespread, previous piecemeal systems are being replaced by integrated customer relationship management systems that are able to provide a unified view of the customer (Occam DM Ltd, 2012) and actionable business intelligence.

As we shall see, the analysis of large data sets may be an important part of a marketing information system for some companies, but for others their information systems will be based on other forms of data and information.

MARKETING IN ACTION 6.1
GSK Shares its Big Data

GlaxoSmithKline (GSK) is a company attempting to make use of big data by sharing its data with the world. This multinational pharmaceutical firm has a portfolio of brands stretching from prescription medicines like Amoxil and Betnovate cream to consumer healthcare brands including Aquafresh, Beechams and Sensodyne. Marketing research comes in many forms because of the nature of the business—carrying out clinical trials and research associated with bringing healthcare products to the market. However, when it comes to the analysis of consumer data, GSK has invested in its marketing research operation to ensure that collection and dissemination of findings happen at a company-wide level. The company has experts in every area of the business who concentrate on specific marketing research problems. They have taken the very bold step to share their data with outsiders and have posted over 450 studies online. This transparency and openness is a strategic move that aims to benefit the industry and humankind by enabling faster innovations through collaboration.

In the organization, it is felt that the most useful information is generated when experts work together on common goals, gathering data from large, complex data sources, including internal data and online sources, and weblogs, social media, web and smartphone analytics, through which consumers provide signals about what they are thinking at a given point in time. More specifically, GSK is working with Occam, a company that provides data management services to help its clients reach a better understanding of their own customers. Ultimately, GSK aims to build relationships with over a million of its customers through social media and to use these relationships as a base for market research and for multichannel marketing. Data collection takes place when customers are directed to targeted offers and promotions for particular brand websites, where external data are integrated with existing internal data. The process involves tracking a particular brand and analyzing what customers are saying and thinking specifically about the brand. The process also involves looking at everything else the customers are talking about (in areas of public access) in order to build a consumer profile. GSK then employs internal data management and processing analysts to make sense of the data, and uses the information to inform its marketing strategy and planning at both strategic and tactical levels.

Based on: Occam (2012); GlaxoSmithKline (2012); Hemsley (2011); Weintraub (2014)

A **marketing information system** has been defined as (Jobber and Rainbow, 1977):

A system in which marketing information is formally gathered, stored, analyzed and distributed to managers in accord with their informational needs on a regular planned basis.

The system is built on an understanding of the information needs of marketing management, and supplies that information when, where and how the manager requires it. Data are derived from the marketing environment and transferred into information that marketing managers can use in their decision-making. The difference between data and information is as follows.

- **Data** are the most basic form of knowledge, for example the brand of butter sold to a particular customer in a certain town; this statistic is of little worth in itself but may become meaningful when combined with other data.
- **Information** is a combination of data that provide decision-relevant knowledge, for example the brand preferences of customers in a certain age category in a particular geographic region.

An insight into the nature of marketing information systems (MkIS) is given in Figure 6.1. The MkIS comprises four elements: internal continuous data, internal ad-hoc data, environmental scanning, and marketing research.

Internal continuous data

Companies possess an enormous amount of marketing and financial data that can be used for marketing decision-making once organized by means of an MkIS. One advantage of setting up an MkIS is the conversion of financial data and a range of other data into a form usable by marketing management.

An MkIS may stimulate the provision of information that marketing managers can use, for example about the profitability of a particular product, customer or distribution channel, or even the profitability of a particular product to an individual customer. Widespread integration of information systems across businesses provides great insight into customers and provides more informed decision-making. An MkIS can incorporate big data and then provide opportunities to delve deeply into consumer behaviour, by monitoring consumers' profiles, attitudes, preferences and purchasing behaviour (Salvador and Ikeda, 2014). Internal data become more complex as information and data-collection points start to include websites, mobile apps and social media.

Read Marketing in Action 6.2 to find out how stationery distributor Viking was targeting the *wrong* customers.

Another application of the MkIS concept to internal continuous data is within the area of salesforce management. As part of the sales management function, many salesforces are monitored by means of recording sales achieved, number of calls made, size of orders, number of new accounts opened, and so on. This can be recorded in total or broken down by product or customer/customer type. The establishment of an MkIS where these data are stored and analyzed over time can provide information on salesforce effectiveness. For example, a fall-off in performance of a salesperson can quickly be identified and remedial action taken.

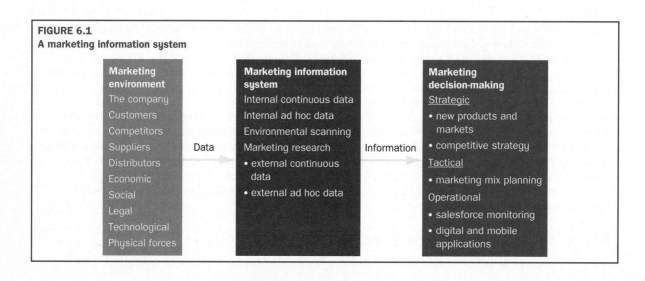

FIGURE 6.1
A marketing information system

Internal ad-hoc data

Company data can also be used for a specific (ad-hoc) purpose. For example, management may look at how sales have reacted to a price increase or a change in advertising copy. Although this could be part of a continuous monitoring programme, specific one-off analyses are inevitably required from time to time. Capturing the data on the MkIS allows specific analyses to be conducted when needed.

Environmental scanning

The environmental scanning procedures discussed in Chapter 2 also form part of the MkIS, and this includes environmental analysis—whereby the economic, social, political, legal, technological and ecological/physical forces are monitored. These forces can be difficult to monitor, due to their amorphous nature, but are important as they can shape the context within which the company, suppliers, distributors and the competition do business, as in the case of Viking Direct. Environmental scanning provides an early warning system for the forces that may impact on a company's products and markets in the future (Jain and Haley, 2009). In this way, scanning enables an organization to act on, rather than react to, opportunities and threats. The focus is on the longer-term perspective, allowing a company to be in the position to plan ahead and information from data analysis provides a major input into such strategic decisions as which future products to develop and market to enter, and the formulation of a competitive strategy (e.g. to attack or defend against competition).

Marketing research

While environmental scanning focuses on the longer term, **marketing research** considers the more immediate situation and is primarily concerned with providing information about markets and customer reactions to various product, price, distribution and promotion decisions (Moutinho and Evans, 1992). As such, marketing research is a key part of the MkIS because it makes a major contribution to marketing mix planning.

There are two main types of external marketing research:

1 *External continuous data sources* include television audience monitoring and **consumer panels** where household purchases are recorded over time. Loyalty cards are also a source of continuous data, providing information on customer purchasing patterns and responses to promotions. The growth of e-commerce has led to new forms of continuous data collection, as has the development of mobile apps. See Marketing in Action 6.3 to find out more about the power of apps as a source of data collection.

Nodes is a specialist agency, based in London and Copenhagen, which develops mobile apps for big brands such as Carlsberg, GSK, BMW, Unilever and Samsung, and aims to make strong connections with users. Its apps can be designed to meet various objectives, for example for social engagement, product demonstrations, tracking user experiences and proximity marketing campaigns. For example, Crowdit, which is a social bar finder app, was designed as a proximity marketing tool. The aim for Crowdit was to enable customers to generate a voucher on their mobile phones that could be used in a nearby bar. The app also included other features that enabled its users to order a cab, find a particular type of bar, and be informed of events and promotions.

The app was designed for Carlsberg, but there was none of the beer's branding on the app, so any bar was able to sign up to use the app. Bar owners in Denmark responded as quickly as their customers, with over 100,000 downloads soon after its launch.

Customers were offered a voucher that they could also share with their friends. iBeacons were used to send out notifications when a customer was within close proximity of a Crowdit bar. An iBeacon is a small Bluetooth device that transmits signals from a chosen location to smartphones that come within its range. Once the customer has the voucher, the bar redeems the voucher in exchange for a drink.

The bar owners benefit, as they are able to receive all of the information about each particular user of the voucher. Adopters of the app can view the analytics, which enables them to update their events based on customer adoption rates and engagement. Also data gathering does not end once the voucher is redeemed, because the voucher can then be sent to a friend. iBeacons also act as a bridge between the digital and the physical world and can keep track of how long a particular user is within range. This then enables bar owners to send highly targeted offers, for example a second drink notification. The second voucher is sent at the critical point at which the consumer decides whether to stay or move to a new location. The information provided by the app and the iBeacons devices can be used to develop customer loyalty and customer retention.

Based on: Nodes (2015); MobileMarketing (2014)

2   *External ad-hoc data* are often gathered by means of surveys into specific marketing issues, including usage and attitude studies, advertising and product testing, and corporate image research. More traditional forms of market research—telephone and face-to-face interviews—are being replaced by digital survey techniques. Digital platforms (web and mobile) are being used not only for gathering quantitative survey data, but also for gathering qualitative data through real-time audio and online video discussions. Social media are also providing access to an innovative form of digital discussion group, and companies are analyzing online conversations to find out what their consumers really think about their products (Manning, 2011).

The rest of this chapter will examine the process of marketing research and the factors that affect the use of research information.

Marketing research has been used by an increasing range of types of organization, from political parties to community groups. Some marketing research agencies specialize in particular types of marketing research. For example, Ipsos MORI specializes in brand loyalty, advertising, and political and social research; Sherbert Research focuses on qualitative research with children and teenagers.

Furthermore, not only are organizations making more use of technology, but the technology itself is also enabling more insightful analysis. The market research industry is penetrating deeper into the psyche of individual consumers.

 Scan the QR code to see how Morrisons aims to rediscover its identity after listening to its customers.

Types of Marketing Research

A major distinction is between **ad-hoc research** and **continuous research**.

Ad-hoc research

An *ad-hoc study* focuses on a specific marketing problem and collects data at one point in time from one sample of respondents. Examples of ad-hoc studies are usage and attitude surveys, product and concept tests, advertising development and evaluation studies, corporate image surveys, and customer satisfaction surveys. Ad-hoc surveys are either custom-designed or omnibus studies.

Custom-designed studies

Custom-designed studies are based on the specific needs of the client. The research design is based on the research brief given to the marketing research agency or internal marketing researcher. Because they are tailor-made, such surveys can be expensive.

Omnibus studies

The alternative is to use an **omnibus survey** in which space is bought on questionnaires for face-to-face or telephone interviews. The interview may cover many topics as the questionnaire space is bought by a number of clients who benefit from cost sharing. Usually the type of information sought is relatively simple (e.g. awareness levels and ownership data). Often the survey will be based on demographically balanced samples of 1,000–2,000 adults: for example, Ipsos UK, which covers Britain, France, Germany, Italy and Spain, takes a snapshot of consumer opinion using i-omnibus (online) capibus (weekly face-to-face survey). In the UK, YouGov promises next-day service on their omnibus surveys. See Exhibit 6.1 for an example of how YouGov carries out omnibus surveys.

Continuous research

Continuous research gathers information from external sources on an ongoing basis. Major types of continuous research are consumer panels, **retail audits**, television viewership panels, marketing databases, customer relationship management systems and website analysis.

Consumer panels

Consumer panels are formed by recruiting large numbers of households which provide information on their purchases over time. For example, a grocery panel would record the brands, pack sizes, prices and stores used for a wide range of supermarket brands. The most usual method of data collection is the use of diaries, which panel members fill in with details of purchases and return to the survey organization on a weekly basis. However,

EXHIBIT 6.1
Omnibus surveys are conducted through face-to-face or telephone interviews

nowadays more digital and online technology is involved in the data-collection process. By using the same households over a period, measures of brand loyalty and switching can be achieved, together with a demographic profile of the type of person who buys particular brands.

Taylor Nelson Sofres (TNS) specializes in consumer research and uses consumer panels in Europe, North and South America and Asia. TNS provides consumer insight with a network of consumer panels that use innovative methods of continuous data collection from households around the world, and which are equipped with the latest technology to record price, place of purchase and selected brand. Mobile and Online face-to-face sessions using webcams are set up to gather consumers' *top of the mind* data. What TNS has found is that different data-collection solutions lead to different results. So, if a company is looking for ideas on how to improve the performance of its marketing mix, ideation is a way to get inside the minds of the consumer.

Retail audits

Retail audits are a second type of continuous research. By gaining the cooperation of retail outlets (e.g. supermarkets), sales of brands can be measured by means of laser scans of barcodes on packaging, which are read at the checkout. Although brand loyalty and switching cannot be measured, retail audits can provide accurate assessment of sales achieved by store.

Nielsen produces retail trend information based on in-store scanning on a regular basis. From this research the company is able to produce vital information that can be used to predict future behaviour. For example, retailers globally are facing increasing challenges to get consumers to visit their stores. Private label brands are putting pressure on proprietary brands; for example, in the UK grocery sector 55 per cent of packaged grocery items are own-label (Nielsen, 2012).

Television viewership panels

Television viewership panels measure audience sizes. For example, Nielsen measure television viewership using panels. A television panel is selected from private homes and is made up of individuals who represent a cross-section of the homes in a particular country. All ages, demographics and lifestyles are included in the panel sample. Nielsen uses set-top boxes that provide real-time information on viewing behaviour. The company knows when viewers are watching and, importantly, not watching programmes and commercials.

The Broadcasters' Audience Research Board (BARB) also collects and collates (BARB, 2012) viewing data that show how particular television programmes have performed. The viewing figures provide data on the weekly share of programmes and channels as well as minute-by-minute analysis. This means that commercial breaks can be allocated *ratings points* (the proportion of the target audience watching), which are the currency by which television advertising is bought and judged.

Marketing databases

Companies collect data on customers on an ongoing basis. The data are stored on customer relationship databases, which contain each customer's name, address, telephone number, past transactions and, sometimes, demographic and lifestyle data. Information on the types of purchase, frequency of purchase, purchase value and responsiveness to promotional offers may be held. For further discussion of customer relationship management, see Chapter 10.

Retailers are encouraging the collection of such data by introducing loyalty card schemes such as the Nectar card, which allows customers to collect points that can be redeemed for cashback or gifts at various store groups, including Sainsbury's, Argos, Amazon and British Gas. Boots operates its own loyalty card, called Advantage, as do many other brands.

EXHIBIT 6.2
Loyalty cards are used by many different types of retailer and service provider as a source of continuous data

Operationally, a loyalty card is swiped through the cash machine at the checkout, and cardholder information is stored on the card with name and address, so that purchasing data including expenditure per visit, types of brands purchased, how often the customer shops and when, and at which branch, can be linked to individuals. Tesco's Clubcard is another example of a store loyalty card, which is used to gather consumer behaviour data, and this information is analyzed and used to produce personalized marketing and sales promotion initiatives.

See Exhibit 6.2 for examples of loyalty cards, and think about how the message on the card positions each card slightly differently; for example, Nectar's, Starbucks' and Boots' messages suggest a reward and/or a treat, but Tesco's message is about saving money.

Stages in the Marketing Research Process

This section presents a useful framework for understanding the main steps in the marketing research process, shown in Figure 6.2. This 'map' highlights what is involved in a major marketing research study covering both qualitative and quantitative research. This process is used by marketing research practitioners and can form the structure for a student marketing research project.

Research planning

Decisions made at the research planning stage will fundamentally affect what is done later so planning is required prior to any data collection. A commercial marketing research project is likely to involve marketing management at the client company, internal marketing research staff and, usually, research staff at an outside marketing research agency. The following discussion provides a generic view of the commercial marketing research process (see Figure 6.2).

Initial contact

The start of the process is usually the realization that a marketing problem (e.g. a new product or advertising decision) requires information to help find a solution. Marketing management may contact internal marketing research staff or an outside agency. Let us assume that the research requires the assistance of a marketing research agency. A meeting will be arranged to discuss the nature of the problem and the client's research needs.

Research brief

At the meeting with the marketing research agency, the client will explain the marketing problem and outline the research objectives. The marketing problem might be to attract new customers to a product line, and the research objectives could be to identify groups of customers (market segments) that might have a use for the product, and the characteristics of the product that appeal to them most (Crouch and Housden, 2003). The key point is that clients should not only tell research agencies what they want to understand but what the research will be used for (Dye, 2008).

Other information that should be provided for the research agency includes the following (Crouch and Housden, 2003).

1 *Background information*: the product's history and the competitive situation.
2 *Sources of information*: the client may have a list of industries that might be potential users of the product. This helps the researchers to define the scope of the research.

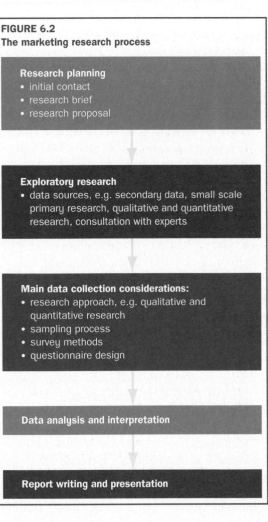

FIGURE 6.2
The marketing research process

Research planning
- initial contact
- research brief
- research proposal

Exploratory research
- data sources, e.g. secondary data, small scale primary research, qualitative and quantitative research, consultation with experts

Main data collection considerations:
- research approach, e.g. qualitative and quantitative research
- sampling process
- survey methods
- questionnaire design

Data analysis and interpretation

Report writing and presentation

3   *The scale of the project*: is the client looking for a 'cheap and cheerful' job or a major study? This has implications for the research design and survey costs.

4   *The timetable*: when is the information required?

The client should produce a specific written **research brief**. This may be given to the research agency prior to the meeting and perhaps modified as a result of it, but, without fail, should be in the hands of the agency before it produces its *research proposal*. The research brief should state the client's requirements and should be in written form to minimize misunderstandings. In the event of a dispute later in the process, the research brief (and proposal) form the benchmark against which any grievances can be settled.

Commissioning good research is similar to buying any other product or service. If marketing managers can agree on why the research is needed, what it will be used for, when it is needed and how much they are willing to pay for it, they are likely to make a good buy. Four suggestions for buying good research are as follows.

1   *Define terms clearly*. For example, if market share information is required, the term 'market' should clearly be defined.

2   *Beware of researchers who bend research problems* so that they can use their favourite technique. They may be specialists in a particular research-gathering method (e.g. group discussion) or statistical technique (e.g. factor or cluster analysis) and look for ways of using these methods no matter what research problem they face. This can lead to irrelevant information and unnecessary expense.

3   *Do not be put off by seemingly naïve researchers* who ask what appear to be simple questions, particularly if they are new to the client's industry.

4   *Brief two or three agencies*. The extra time involved should be rewarded by better feedback on how to tackle the research problem and a better priced quote.

Research proposal

The **research proposal** defines what the marketing research agency promises to do for its client, and how much it will cost. Like the research brief, the proposal should be written to avoid misunderstandings. A client should expect the following to be included:

1   *A statement of objectives*: to demonstrate an understanding of the client's marketing and research problems.

2   *What will be done*: an unambiguous description of the research design, including the survey method, the type of sample, the sample size and how the fieldwork will be controlled.

3   *Timetable*: if and when a report will be produced.

4   *Costs*: how much the research will cost and what, specifically, is/is not being included in those costs.

When assessing proposals a client might usefully check the following points.

1   *Beware of vagueness*: if the proposal is vague, assume that the report is also likely to be vague. If the agency does not state what is going to be done, why, who is doing it and when, assume that it is not clear in its own mind about these important issues.

2   *Beware of jargon*: there is no excuse for jargon-ridden proposals. Marketing research terminology can be explained in non-expert language, so it is the responsibility of the agency to make the proposal understandable to the client.

3   *Beware of what is missing*: assume that anything not specified will not be provided. For example, if no mention of a presentation is made in the proposal, assume it will not take place. Any doubts, ask the agency.

Exploratory research

Exploratory research involves the preliminary exploration of a research area prior to the main data-collection stage. The discussion that follows assumes that the initial proposal has been accepted and that exploratory research is to be carried out as the basis for survey design.

A major purpose of exploratory research is to guard against the sins of omission and admission (Wright and Crimp, 2003).

* *Sin of omission*: not researching a topic in enough detail, or failing to provide sufficient respondents in a group to allow meaningful analysis
* *Sin of admission*: collecting data that are irrelevant to the marketing problem, or using too many groups for analysis purposes and thereby unnecessarily increasing the sample size.

Exploratory research techniques allow the researcher to understand the people who are to be interviewed in the main data-collection stage, and the market that is being researched. The main survey stage can thus be designed with this knowledge in mind rather than being based on the researcher's ill-informed prejudices and guesswork.

Figure 6.3 displays the four exploratory research activities. An individual research project may involve all or some of them.

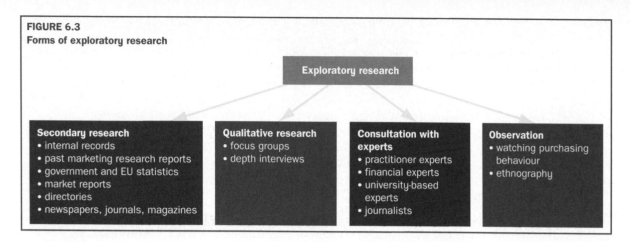

FIGURE 6.3
Forms of exploratory research

Exploratory research

Secondary research
- internal records
- past marketing research reports
- government and EU statistics
- market reports
- directories
- newspapers, journals, magazines

Qualitative research
- focus groups
- depth interviews

Consultation with experts
- practitioner experts
- financial experts
- university-based experts
- journalists

Observation
- watching purchasing behaviour
- ethnography

Please note that qualitative and quantitative research methods may be used at both the exploratory and main data-collection stage and it will be the market research project manager's responsibility to determine which methods will be the best methods to meet the research objectives.

Secondary research

Secondary research is so called because the data come to the researcher 'second-hand' (other people have compiled the data). When the researcher actively collects new data—for example, by interviewing respondents—this is called primary research (discussed in the next section).

Secondary data come from sources such as internal company records, reports and previous research carried out for the company. External sources of secondary data include: government and European Union (EU) statistics; publishers of reports and directories on markets, countries and industries; trade associations; banks; and newspapers, magazines and journals.

The Internet provides access to rich sources of secondary information. Websites like Trendwatching (www.trendwatching.com) specialize in identifying emerging global consumer and marketing trends. Some online sources are free to access, others are paid-for services; for example, IDC, Gartner and Experian have an Internet presence and provide both free and paid-for resources. Companies that specialize in providing secondary information also provide electronic content either by subscription or by selling individual reports. For example, a visit to Mintel (www.mintel.com) can provide hundreds of industry reports from the very specific, such as on innovations in German barbeques, to broader subjects such as personal health and beauty care. A word of caution when using online resources (especially free information): remember to verify the authenticity of the data; be critical of the findings and establish the origin of the data.

In the EU, there are many secondary sources of data. Table 6.1 lists some of the major sources of marketing information, classified by research questions, and provides examples of some of the main companies and online databases that supply information for specific industries, details of market competitors, economic trend statistics, and abstracts and indices.

Secondary research should be carried out before primary research. Without the former, an expensive primary research survey might be commissioned to provide information that is already available from secondary sources. Furthermore, directories such as *Kompass* can be invaluable when selecting a sample in a business-to-business marketing research project.

Primary research methods

Each ad-hoc marketing research project may be different. This is in order to fit the particular requirements and resources of various clients. For example, one study may focus on **qualitative research** using small numbers of respondents, while another may be largely **quantitative research**, involving interviewing hundreds or thousands of consumers. Therefore, it is important to take care to ensure that the data-collection method is suitable and best able to meet the objectives of the market research activity.

Qualitative research

Qualitative research has been defined as 'the analysis and understanding of patterned conduct and social process of society' (Denzin and Lincoln, 2000). The main forms of qualitative research used in market research which

TABLE 6.1 Sources of marketing information

Is there a survey of the industry?

Euromonitor International	http://www.euromonitor.com	Produces 17,000 reports each year on 27 industries and 200 sub-categories and thousands of company reports in 80 countries
Business Insight Reports	http://www.business-insights.com	Full text reports available online in the sectors of healthcare, financial services, consumer goods, energy, and e-commerce and technology
Keynote Reports	http://www.keynote.co.uk	Provides market intelligence in the UK including reports on market trends and company performance

How large is the market and where is it located?

WARC	http://www.warc.com	Comprehensive marketing information service, provides access to reports, forecasts, journal articles and case studies
Regional Trends	http://data.gov.uk/dataset/regional_trends	Economic and social statistics for UK regions

Who are the competitors?

Kompass	http://gb.kompass.com	Global business-to-business and product information database
Fame	http://www.bvdinfo.com	Comprehensive information on companies in the UK and Ireland For further international information services, see Amadeus, BankScope, Orbis and Isis

What are the trends?

Economic and Social Data Service	http://www.esds.ac.uk	Provides access to data collections showing economic and social trends data
Eurostat	http://epp.eurostat.ec.europa.eu/portal/page/portal/eurostat/home/	Provides access to European statistics and series of publications that provide a detailed picture of the EU

Abstracts and indices

Web of knowledge	http://wok.mimas.ac.uk/	Comprehensive research database including journals, article citations and conference papers
Science Direct	http://www.sciencedirect.com/	Full text scientific articles from journals and books
Zetoc	http://zetoc.mimas.ac.uk/	Comprehensive research database including journals, article citations and conference papers

Statistics

Eurostat	http://epp.eurostat.ec.europa.eu/portal/page/portal/eurostat/home/	Provides access to European statistics and series of publications that provide a detailed picture of the EU
ONS	http://www.ons.gov.uk/ons/index. html	Provides access to UK statistics and series of publications that provide a detailed picture of the EU

Note: some of these sites require passwords, which can be obtained from libraries.

Source: the author thanks Reshma Khan and Neil Jukes of Bradford University School of Management Library for their help in compiling this list.

help us to understand the complex patterns of human behaviour are: group discussions; **in-depth interviews and ethnography**, which involve bringing together personal encounters, life events and understandings into a more meaningful context (Tedlock, 2000). Qualitative research aims to establish customers' attitudes, values, behaviour and beliefs and aims to understand consumers in a way that traditional methods of interviewing people using questionnaires cannot. Qualitative research seeks to understand the 'why' and 'how' of consumer behaviour (Clegg, 2001). The key differences between qualitative and quantitative research are explored later in this chapter.

Focus groups involve unstructured or semi-structured discussions between a *moderator*, or group leader, who is often a psychologist, and a group of consumers. The moderator has a list of areas to cover within the topic but allows the group considerable freedom to discuss the issues that are important to them. The topics might be organic foods, men's cosmetics, motor sports or activity holiday pursuits. By arranging groups of 6–12 people to discuss their beliefs, attitudes, motivation, behaviour and preferences, a good deal of knowledge may be gained about the consumer. This can be helpful when planning questionnaires, which can then be designed to focus on what is important to the respondent (as opposed to the researcher) and worded in language that the respondent uses and understands.

A further advantage of the focus group is that the findings may provide rich insights into consumer motivations and behaviour because of the group dynamics where group members 'feed off' each other and reveal ideas that would not have arisen on a one-to-one basis. Such findings may be used as food for thought for marketers, without the need for quantitative follow-up.

The weaknesses of the focus group are that interpretation of the results is highly subjective, the quality of the results depends heavily on the skills of the moderator, sample size is usually small, making generalization to wider populations difficult, and there exists the danger that the results might be biased by the presence of 'research groupies', who enjoy taking part in focus groups and return again and again. Such people sometimes even take on different identities, skewing survey results, and have led the Association of Qualitative Research Practitioners to introduce a rule which says that focus group participants have to provide proof of identity each time they attend a group (Flack, 2002).

Technology is having an impact on such face-to-face discussion settings and high-tech labs can be used which allow participants to be observed through two-way glass, enabling the client organization to view the focus group session live. Online focus groups are also becoming popular and this method can reduce costs and create more opportunities to interact with customer groups. Also, research has found that, in some cases, participants are more honest in online discussion than when face to face in person.

Internet communities and social media sites can provide access to 'communities of interests', which can take the form of chat rooms or websites dedicated to specific interests or issues. These are useful forums for conducting focus groups, or at least identifying suitable participants. Questions can be posed to participants who are not under time pressure to respond. This can lead to richer insights since they can think deeply about questions put to them online. Another advantage is that they can comprise people located all over the world at minimal cost.

In-depth interviews involve the interviewing of consumers individually for perhaps one or two hours about a topic. The aims are broadly similar to those of group discussion but are used when the presence of other people could inhibit honest answers and viewpoints, when the topic requires individual treatment, as when discussing an individual's decision-making process, and where the organization of a group is not feasible (e.g., it might prove impossible to arrange for six busy purchasing managers to come together for a group discussion).

Care has to be taken when interpreting the results of qualitative research in that the findings are usually based on small sample sizes, and the more interesting or surprising viewpoints may be disproportionately reported. This is particularly significant when qualitative research is not followed by a quantitative study.

Qualitative research accounts for more than 10 per cent of all European expenditure on marketing research, of which the largest proportion is spent on group discussions, followed by in-depth interviews and then other qualitative techniques accounting for a small percentage of the spend (ESOMAR, 2005).

Consultation with experts

Qualitative research is based on discussions and interviews with actual and potential buyers of a brand or service. However, consultation with experts involves interviewing people who may not form part of the target market but who, nevertheless, can provide important marketing-related insights. Many industries have their experts in universities, financial institutions and the press, who may be willing to share their knowledge. They can provide invaluable background information, and can be useful for predicting future trends and developments.

Observation

Observation can also help in exploratory research when the product field is unfamiliar. Watching people buy wine in a supermarket or paint in a DIY store may provide useful background knowledge when planning a survey in these markets, for example. Another form of observational research that focuses on employee performance is *mystery shopping*. The 'shopper' acts like any other customer in visiting a store, but is trained to ask particular questions, and to assess performance on such criteria as service time, friendliness and product knowledge. The objective is to identify service weaknesses and strengths, and to provide input into staff training.

Ethnography Ethnography is a form of observation that involves detailed and prolonged observation of (in the context of this book) consumers. Its origins are in social anthropology, where researchers live in a studied society for months or years. Consumer researchers usually make their observations more quickly and use a range of methods, including direct observations, interviews and video and audio recordings (Peter, Olson and Grunert, 1999).

This method of data collection has become popular as it connects important personal experiences to specific contexts (Tedlock, 2000) and enables researchers to get closer to consumers in order to understand their behaviour in new and more detailed ways. Such research investigates how people behave in their own environment and interact with the world around them. Unlike focus groups, where consumers are brought to the researcher, ethnography takes the researcher to the consumer. Advocates of this form of research argue that focus groups only provide part of the story and do not yield the kinds of 'consumer insights' that ethnography can.

One company that has embraced ethnographic research is Procter & Gamble. 20 families in the UK and a further 20 in Italy were chosen to take part in a study that involved recording their daily household behaviour by video camera. The idea was that by studying people who buy Procter & Gamble products—such as Max Factor cosmetics, Ariel washing powder and Pampers nappies—the company could gain valuable insights into people's consumer habits. The findings have had implications for its approach to product design, packaging and promotion. For example, it was ethnographic research that revealed that the nappy was not as important as Procter & Gamble had previously thought. New mothers were more interested in information and knowledge than nappies. Using these consumer insights, Procter & Gamble launched Pampers.com, an online community for mothers that attracts over 650,000 users across Europe. Procter & Gamble has also used ethnographic research in China. It observed low-income consumers doing their washing and found that they were prepared to do the extra hand washing needed to compensate for water hardness. Procter & Gamble's response was to launch a cut-price version of its China Tide detergent without water softener (ESOMAR, 2005). A Procter & Gamble spokesman pointed out that ethnography will not replace other forms of research and that ethical issues concerning privacy are dealt with by getting full permission beforehand and giving the families complete editorial control over what is eventually shown to the marketing team.

The objective of ethnographic research is to bridge the gap between what people say they do and what they actually do. Its usefulness is reflected in the fact that companies such as Toyota, Land Rover, Intel, Adidas and Nike have used this genre of research.

The objective of the exploratory research stage in the marketing research process is not to form conclusions but to get better acquainted with the market and its customers. This allows the researcher to base the next stage, which involves wider data collection on *informed assumptions* rather than guesswork.

 Scan the QR code to find out more about how Shop Direct used ethnographic research and customer insights to improve profitability.

The main data-collection stage

Following careful exploratory research, the design of the main data-collection procedures will be made. In Figure 6.4, the assumption is that quantitative research methods are the most appropriate. However, in some situations, it may be better to extend the use of qualitative research methods used at the exploratory stage of a project. In either case it is important for the project manager to select the data-collection methods that are most likely to achieve the research objectives.

At the main data-collection stage two alternative approaches are descriptive and experimental research.

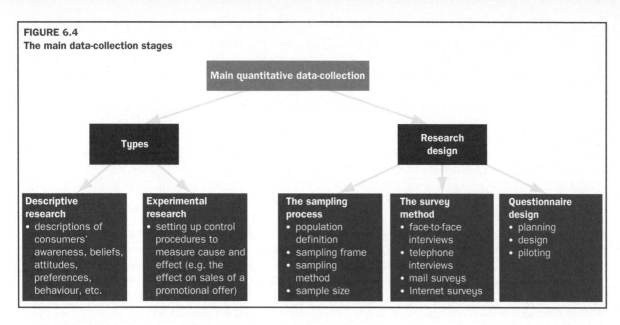

FIGURE 6.4
The main data-collection stages

Main quantitative data-collection

Types

Research design

Descriptive research
- descriptions of consumers' awareness, beliefs, attitudes, preferences, behaviour, etc.

Experimental research
- setting up control procedures to measure cause and effect (e.g. the effect on sales of a promotional offer)

The sampling process
- population definition
- sampling frame
- sampling method
- sample size

The survey method
- face-to-face interviews
- telephone interviews
- mail surveys
- Internet surveys

Questionnaire design
- planning
- design
- piloting

Assuming the main data-collection stage requires interviewing, the research design will be based on the following factors.

- Who and how many people to interview (the sampling process)
- How to interview them (the survey method)
- What questions to ask (questionnaire design).

Figure 6.4 displays the two types and three research design methods associated with the main quantitative data-collection stage. These research approaches and methods will now be examined.

Descriptive research

Descriptive research may be undertaken to describe consumers' beliefs, attitudes, preferences, behaviour, etc. For example, a survey into advertising effectiveness might measure awareness of the brand, recall of the advertisement and knowledge about its content.

Experimental research

The aim of experimental research is to establish cause and effect. **Experimental research** involves setting up control procedures to isolate the impact of a factor (e.g. a money-off sales promotion) on a dependent variable (e.g. sales).

The key to successful experimental design is the elimination of other explanations of changes in the dependent variable. One way of doing this is to use random sampling. For example, the sales promotion might be applied in a random selection of stores with the remaining stores selling the brand without the money-off offer. Statistical significance testing can be used to test whether differences in sales are likely to be caused by the sales promotion or are simply random variations. The effects of other influences on sales are assumed to impact randomly on both the sales promotion and the no-promotion alternatives.

The sampling process

Figure 6.5 outlines the **sampling process**. It begins by *defining the population*—that is, the group that forms the subject of study in a particular survey. The survey objective will be to provide results that are representative of this group. Sampling planners, for example, must ask questions like: 'Do we interview all people over the age of 18 or restrict it to those of the population aged 18–60?' and 'Do we interview purchasing managers in all textile companies or only those that employ more than 200 people?'

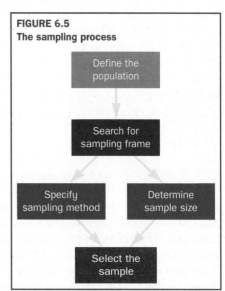

FIGURE 6.5
The sampling process

Define the population

Search for sampling frame

Specify sampling method

Determine sample size

Select the sample

Once the population has been defined, the next step is to search for a *sampling frame*—that is, a list or other record of the chosen population from which a sample can be selected. Examples include a register of electors, or the *Kompass* directory of companies. The result determines whether a random or non-random sample can be chosen. A random sample requires an accurate sampling frame; without one, the researcher is restricted to non-random methods.

Three major *sampling methods* are simple random sampling, stratified random sampling and quota sampling. It is also important to determine *sample size*.

- With simple random sampling, each individual (or company) in the sampling frame is given a number, and numbers are drawn at random (by chance) until the sample is complete. The sample is random because everyone on the list has an equal chance of selection.
- With stratified random sampling, the population is broken down into groups (e.g. by company size or industry) and a random sample is drawn (as above) for each group. This ensures that each group is represented in the sample.
- With quota sampling, a sampling frame does not exist but the percentage of the population that falls in various groupings (e.g. gender, social class, age) is known. The sample is constructed by asking interviewers to select individuals on the basis of these percentages, for example roughly 50:50 females to males. This is a non-random method since not everyone has an equal chance of selection, but it is much less expensive than random methods when the population is widely dispersed.
- Sample size is a further key consideration when attempting to generate a representative sample. Clearly, the larger the sample size the more likely it will represent the population. Statistical theory allows the calculation of sampling error (i.e. the error caused by not interviewing everyone in the population) for various sample sizes. In practice, the number of people interviewed is based on a balance between sampling error and cost considerations. Fortunately sample sizes of around 1,000 (or fewer) can provide measurements that have tolerable error levels when representing populations counted in their millions.

Data-collection methods: interviews and surveys

There are two basic *methods of gathering data*: personal interviews and non-personal surveys. Personal interviews, where there is direct contact between interviewer and interviewee, may be face to face, by telephone or through video. In contrast, with non-personal surveys contact is through impersonal media—that is, the Internet, mail or mobile phone. Each method has a number of different techniques which can be applied, and each has its own strengths and limitations.

Face-to-face, telephone and video interviews

A major advantage of *face-to-face interviews* is that response rates are generally higher than for telephone interviews (Yu and Cooper, 1983). Seemingly, the personal element in the contact makes refusal less likely. This is an important factor when considering how representative of the population the sample is and when using experimental designs. Testing the effectiveness of a stimulus would normally be conducted by face-to-face interview rather than a mail survey where high non-response rates and the lack of control over who completes the questionnaire would invalidate the results. Face-to-face interviews are more versatile than telephone.

The use of many open-ended questions can be used effectively when interviewing, although as time restrictions for a telephone interview can limit their use. Probing is easier with face-to-face interviews. Two types of probes are *clarifying probes* (e.g. 'Can you explain what you mean by . . . ?'), which help the interviewer understand exactly what the interviewee is saying, and *exploratory probes*, which stimulate the interviewee to give a full answer (e.g. 'Are there any other reasons why . . . ?'). A certain degree of probing can be achieved with a telephone interview, but time pressure and the less personalized situation will inevitably limit its use. Visual aids (e.g. a drawing of a new product concept) can be used where clearly they cannot with a telephone interview.

However, face-to-face interviews have their drawbacks. They are more expensive than telephone and mail questionnaires. Telephone interviews are cheaper because the cost of contacting respondents is much less expensive, unless the population is very concentrated (face-to-face interviewing of students on a business studies course, for instance, would be relatively inexpensive). The presence of an interviewer can cause bias (e.g. socially desirable answers) and lead to the misreporting of sensitive information. For example, O'Dell (1962) found that only 17 per cent of respondents admitted borrowing money from a bank in a face-to-face interview compared with 42 per cent in a comparable mail survey, which gave the respondent more privacy when answering questions.

In some ways *telephone interviews* are a halfway house between face-to-face and mail surveys. Telephone interviews generally have a higher response rate than mail questionnaires, but lower than face-to-face interviews; their cost is usually less than face-to-face, but higher than for mail surveys; and they allow a degree of flexibility when interviewing. However, the use of visual aids is not possible and there are limits to the number of questions that can be asked before respondents either terminate the interview or give quick (invalid) answers to speed up the process. The use of computer-aided telephone interviewing (CATI) is common. Centrally located interviewers read questions from a computer monitor and input answers via the keyboard. *Routing* through the questionnaire is computer-controlled, helping the process of interviewing.

Video interviews via the web and mobile phones offer a solution to get over some of the issues of face-to-face and telephone interviews. For example, offers mobile video interviews and focus groups (Mindswarms, 2015). Clients are able to set research objectives and then view the results, which can gather detailed behavioural data. Companies like Virgin America, Dell and Microsoft have used this form of interviewing to gain deep insight into their customers' needs when developing new products.

Internet, mail and mobile surveys

These are a widely used and robust means of gathering data, and there are some compelling reasons why a company might choose one of these data-collection methods. Surveys represent a lower cost option than interviewing, they can be used to reach a widely dispersed population, and can be delivered in a variety of ways, for example via the web and by mail and mobile phone. However, the major problem is the potential of low response rates and the accompanying danger of an unrepresentative sample.

In recent years there has been a significant shift away from mail surveys to using Internet-based approaches. Digital platforms (web and mobile) are increasingly used to conduct survey research. With **digital surveys**, the questionnaire is administered by email, on a website by registering key words, or appears in banner advertising on search engines such as Yahoo! or Google, which drive people to the questionnaire. Mobile devices can also be used. Digital surveys have grown in popularity to such an extent that they now account for a significant proportion of all the quantitative data collected in Europe and the USA. There are now many bespoke online survey and poll companies, for example Survey monkey (http://www.surveymonkey.com), eSurveysPro (http://www.esurveyspro .com) and EZpolls (http://www.ezpolls.com), which provide survey tools and methods of analysis.

Major advantages of digital marketing research platforms are:
- flexibility of content—visual aids such as video and graphics can be used, as well as audio input
- reach—there are no geographical limitations
- speed of delivery (Gigliotti, 2011)
- automated digital data collection—data sets are readily available in digital format for analysis
- potential cost saving.

However, the more complex the survey—for example, when it includes video and interactive experiments—the higher the cost of production. So while these digital techniques can be highly flexible, the size of the survey should be taken into consideration when evaluating the relative cost. Sampling problems are a potential disadvantage, as they can arise because of the skewed nature of Internet users (if the online target populations are from younger and more affluent groups in society), although this issue is becoming less important as the global Internet user population increases.

In summary, it is suggested that digital surveys are faster, easier, cheaper and better. However, research has found that the benefits do not come in equal quantities when compared with other survey tools. For example:
- *Faster* digital surveys are faster to distribute than mail surveys, but telephone surveys can provide the most instantaneous response.
- *Easier* digital surveys may be easier to compile and use, but this will be subjective as it depends on the technological literacy of those involved.
- Digital surveys may be *cheaper* in terms of sample size, as the larger the sample the greater the cost of the other methods of data collection, but there can be significant up-front costs involved in setting up a digital survey and accessing the desired target respondents.
- To be *better* than other survey tools, digital surveys need to ensure the validity of response.

An absence of accurate contact lists remains a problem when using email to survey populations. Even when lists can be found, researchers need to tread very carefully, as 'spamming'—sending junk mail—is seen as very offensive by most email users and messages may be blocked by firewalls and therefore never get to the recipient's mail box.

Mobile technology has brought innovation to ethnographic research and enables research teams to get even closer to peoples' lives by observing their actions in real time. For example, Mumsnet and Saatchi & Saatchi teamed up to study mothers to find out more about the roles they play in the family, the relationships they have with their children, and the implications for marketing. The mobile ethnographic study was conducted over a week with a representative sample of 1,022 mothers in the UK. The aim was to gain in-depth understanding about the mother's role and her home and personal environment.

The study revealed eight emotional roles that mothers assume when caring for their families. These roles were created from 35 emotions that were identified in the ethnographic study.

TABLE 6.2 Emotional roles adopted by mothers in their daily lives

Roles	Examples of raw emotions	Implications for the role of brands
Carer	Comforting, helpful, needed, loving, trusted	Help the mother feel great that she can be there for her children
Safe house	Safe, reliable, control, stability, strong, trusted	Help the mother be there when she's needed
Coach	Knowledgeable, experienced, impactful, important	Give support for mentoring
Fan	Proud, inspired, amazed	Help the mother have more time to enjoy her children's achievements
Partner in crime	Playful, creative, entertained	Focus on opportunities to create fun
Rule breaker	Rebellious, fun, silly	Give the mother permission to break her rules
Friend	Understanding, accepted, admired, cool	Focus on the balance between parent and friend
Hero	Encouraging, successful, impactful, confident	Help the role the mother wants for herself and her family

The marketing implications for the research are that if brands find ways to enable mothers to spend more time with their families, this is seen as an important potential benefit. Another finding from the study is that mothers would like to spend more time having fun with their children rather than just being providers of entertainment. While mothers are considered to be primary carers in the family unit, with 58 per cent saying they take on the majority of the parenting role, they would like more time to 'break the rules' and have the freedom to let go and have fun.

Based on: Vince, 2015; Saatchi & Saatchi (2015); Burrows (2014)

A possible way to reap the benefits and counter the problems associated with digital surveys is to use a mixed-method approach which allows for different modes of data collection to be used to address validity issues. The use of two methods will, however, slow the survey process and increase the costs, but it should ensure greater validity in the findings, which is one of the fundamentals when using survey data to make strategic and tactical marketing decisions (Gigliotti, 2011). Read Marketing in Action 6.4 to discover how digital mobile ethnography has been used to find out the emotional roles that mothers play in family lives.

Questionnaire design

Three conditions are necessary to get a true response to a question.
1 Respondents must *understand* the question.
2 Respondents must be *able to provide* the information.
3 Respondents must be *willing to answer*.

Researchers must remember these conditions when designing questionnaires. Questions need to be phrased in language the respondent understands and is able to interpret. Equally, researchers must not ask about issues that respondents cannot remember or that are outside their experience. For example, it would be invalid to ask about attitudes towards a brand of which the respondent is unaware. Finally, researchers need to consider the best way to elicit sensitive or personal information. As we have already seen, willingness to provide such information depends on the survey method employed.

Figure 6.6 shows the three stages in the development of the questionnaire: planning, design and pilot.

The *planning stage* involves the types of decision discussed so far in this chapter. It provides a firm foundation for designing a questionnaire that provides relevant information for the marketing problem that is being addressed.

The *design stage* involves a number of interrelated issues, as described below.

1 *Ordering of topics*: an effective questionnaire has a logical flow. It is sensible to start with easy-to-answer questions. This helps to build the confidence of respondents and allows them to relax. Respondents are often anxious at the beginning of an interview, concerned that they might show their ignorance. Other rules of thumb are simply common sense: for example, it would be logical to ask awareness questions before attitude measurement questions, and not vice versa. Unaided awareness questions must be asked before aided ones. Classificatory questions that ask for personal information such as age and occupation are usually asked last.

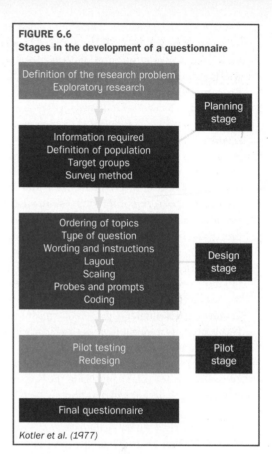

FIGURE 6.6
Stages in the development of a questionnaire

Kotler et al. (1977)

2 *Types of question*: closed-ended questions specify the range of answers that will be recorded. If there are only two possible answers (e.g. 'Did you visit a cinema within the last seven days?' YES/NO) the question is *dichotomous* (either/or). If there are more than two possible answers, then the question is *multiple choice* (e.g. 'Which, if any, of the following cinemas have you visited within the last seven days?' ODEON, SHOWCASE, CINEWORLD, NONE). *Open-ended questions* allow respondents to answer the question in their own words (e.g. 'What did you like about the cinema you visited?'). The interviewer then writes the answer in a space on the questionnaire.

3 *Wording and instructions*: great care needs to be taken in the wording of questions. Questionnaire designers need to guard against ambiguity, leading questions, asking two questions in one and using unfamiliar words. Table 6.3 gives some examples of poorly worded questions and suggests remedies. Instructions should be printed in capital letters or underlined so that they are easily distinguishable from questions.

TABLE 6.3 Poorly worded questions and how to avoid them	
Question	**Problem and solution**
What type of wine do you prefer?	'Type' is ambiguous; respondents could say 'French', 'red', 'claret', depending on their interpretation. Showing the respondent a list and asking 'from this list . . .' would avoid the problem.
Do you think that prices are cheaper at Asda than at Aldi?	Leading question favouring Asda; a better question would be 'Do you think that prices at Asda are higher, lower or about the same as at Aldi?' Names should be reversed for half of the sample.
Which is more powerful and kind to your hands: Ariel or Bold?	Two questions in one: Ariel may be more powerful, but Bold may be kinder to the hands. Ask the two questions separately.
Do you find it paradoxical that X lasts longer and yet is cheaper than Y?	Unfamiliar word: a study has shown that less than a quarter of the population understand such words as 'paradoxical', 'chronological' or 'facility'. Test understanding before use.

4 *Layout*: the questionnaire should not appear cluttered. In mail questionnaires, it is a mistake to squeeze too many questions on to one page so that the questionnaire length (in pages) is shortened. Response is more likely to be lower if the questionnaire appears heavy than if its page length is extended (Jobber, 1985).

5 *Scaling*: careful exploratory research may allow attitudes and beliefs to be measured by means of scales. Respondents are given lists of statements (e.g. 'My company's marketing information system allows me to make better decisions') followed by a choice of five positions on a scale ranging from 'strongly agree' to 'strongly disagree'. Furthermore, computer advances are enabling the measurement of emotions using avatars (pictorial representations of people).

6 *Probes and prompts*: probes seek to explore or clarify what a respondent has said. Following a question about awareness of brand names, the *exploratory probe* 'Any others?' would seek to identify further names. Sometimes respondents use vague words or phrases like, 'I like going on holiday because it is nice.' A *clarifying probe* such as, 'In what way is it nice?' would seek a more meaningful response. *Prompts*, on the other hand, aid responses to a question. For example, in an aided-recall question, a list of brand names would be provided for the respondent.

7 *Coding*: by using closed questions the interviewer merely has to ring the code number next to the respondent's choice of answer. In computer-assisted telephone interviewing and with the increasing use of laptop computers for face-to-face interviewing, the appropriate code number can be keyed directly into the computer's memory. Such questionnaires are *pre-coded*, making the process of interviewing and data analysis much simpler. Open-ended questions, however, require the interviewer to write down the answer verbatim. This necessitates *post-coding*, whereby answers are categorized after the interview. This can be a time-consuming and laborious task.

Once the preliminary questionnaire has been designed, it should be piloted with a representative sub-sample to test for faults. The *pilot stage* is not the same as exploratory research. Exploratory research helps to decide upon the research design whereas piloting tests the questionnaire design and helps to estimate costs. Face-to-face piloting, where respondents are asked to answer questions and comment on any problems concerning a questionnaire read out by an interviewer, is preferable to impersonal piloting, where the questionnaire is given to respondents for self-completion and they are asked to write down any problems found (Reynolds and Diamantopoulos, 1998). If desired, several kinds of question on the same topic can be asked in order to assess the effects of the wording on respondents (Sigman, 2001). Once the pilot work proves satisfactory, the final questionnaire can be administered to the chosen sample.

Data analysis and interpretation

Quantitative analysis of questionnaire data will invariably be carried out by computer. Basic marketing analyses can be carried out using such software-analysis packages as SNAP or more sophisticated analyses can be conducted using a package such as SPSS. Sophisticated software is being developed to enable better and more accurate analysis of increasingly complex data sets.

Basic analysis may be at the descriptive level (e.g. means, standard deviations and frequency tables) or on a comparative basis (e.g. cross-tabulations and t-tests). More sophisticated analysis may search for relationships (e.g. regression analysis), group respondents (e.g. cluster analysis) or establish cause and effect (e.g. analysis of variance techniques used on experimental data). Computer-aided analysis of marketing research data is not limited to quantitative data. The analysis of vast volumes of qualitative data can be aided by the use of software packages NVIVO or NUD*IST, where data can be filed, accessed and organized in more sophisticated ways than manual analysis.

Great care is required when interpreting marketing research results. One common failing is to infer cause and effect when only association has been established. For example, establishing a relationship that sales rise when advertising levels increase does not necessarily mean that raising advertising expenditure will lead to an increase in sales. Other marketing variables—for example, salesforce effect—may have increased at the same time as the increase in advertising, or the advertising budget may have been dependent on sales levels. Either explanation would invalidate the claim that advertising causes sales to rise.

A second cautionary note concerns the interpretation of means and percentages. Given that a sample has been taken, any mean or percentage is an estimate subject to *sampling error*—that is, the error in an estimate due to taking a sample rather than interviewing the entire population. A market research survey which estimates that 50 per cent of males but only 45 per cent of females smoke does not necessarily suggest that smoking is more prevalent among males. Given the sampling error associated with each estimate, the true conclusion might be that there is no difference between males and females. Statistical hypothesis testing allows sample differences to be evaluated in the light of sampling error to establish whether they are likely to be real differences (statistically significant) or likely to be a result of taking a sample (rather than interviewing the entire population).

Digital technology is now widely used in the research process but, as discussed at the beginning of the chapter, the difference is that big data is largely collected automatically and used to provide companies with business intelligence that is informing marketing decision-making online. A widely used term is 'web analytics', and this refers to measurement and analysis of how a website is performing in terms of visitor numbers, unique visitors, keyword search terms used to find a site, areas of the site most frequently visited, time spent on the site, responses to promotions, and, for online retailers, the proportion of visitors proceeding to the checkout (Fahy and Jobber, 2015). Further discussion of website analysis is provided in Chapter 16. On the web, Google has led the way in providing such data and information about how the web is used. Google Analytics is a suite of marketing research solutions that help companies track customer engagement and improve site visits. Read Mini Case 6.1 to find out more about how analytics can help and how data capture is changing.

MINI CASE 6.1
Does Google Track our Every Move?

Website analysis enables the assessment of site performance and helps to identify key areas for improvement such as web pages on a site which are rarely visited, or features on the home page which are rarely clicked. In other words, marketing managers can summarize the actions of visitors to their websites by statistically analyzing users' data. Google Analytics provides a range of statistics such as bounce rates, unique visitors, page views, and average time a user spends on a particular site.

Understanding website performance can be important for customer relationship management strategies by helping identify areas for improvement that might increase customer acquisition, conversion, retention and enjoyment during website visits. For example, a website might include personalized recommendations for loyal customers or introduce interactive tools to help with product selection.

Sophisticated analytical tools and software applications mean that all eyes are on the consumer, but marketing managers should be aware that consumers are becoming increasingly unwilling to hand over their personal data, especially online. In the past, retailers and consumer-facing brand websites have been able to entice consumers into signing up to newsletters, surveys and other data capture devices by offering a small incentive such as discount vouchers for handing over their personal details. However, some consumers are increasingly reluctant to knowingly hand over personal information. In fact, research has found that consumers now expect more free information from brand websites than ever before. Sectors yet to experience this trend are insurance, charities and some alcoholic drink brands, where consumers are signing up and handing over personal details in record numbers.

Paradoxically, it is perhaps the increase in our ability to analyze data and make more meaningful interpretations that is making collecting data from some consumers harder. Part of the problem is that consumers are concerned about online security and identity fraud. Google is doing little to alleviate these fears as it integrates more data-collection methods into its search engine and links together with social media, encouraging consumers to unwittingly divulge more and more personal details. As one of the Internet giants, Google provides a very efficient information search engine for 90 per cent of users in Europe. Nevertheless, it has been rebuked by the European Commissioner for Justice over what are seen as weak protection policies for personal data. Some EU member states were concerned because Google has made changes that mean it can pool data about registered users and how they use the web, make video searches, find map directions and browse the web, and which adverts they click. This pooling of data means no stone is left unturned and Google can capture data on every aspect of an individual's life and build personalized profiles which it can then use for its lucrative Adwords pay-for-search advertising.

»

The Market Research Society's (MRS's) code of conduct advocates maintaining anonymity for any opinions deduced from analyzing online content, but the tools that are facilitating the analyses are emerging faster than the MRS can produce control measures. This means that consumer profiles can become very transparent and this information can be used for marketing initiatives. For instance, before you receive your next email marketing message, the time of day you are most likely to open and respond to the message will have been analyzed, the contents of the mailing may have been personalized to suit your preferences, and sophisticated software will be ready to monitor your next move. If you access the web using a smartphone, someone somewhere may have read your electronic diary and know when you are free next week and already be planning which marketing initiatives you are going to receive.

Questions:

1   Give an example of an online marketing campaign that targets consumers.
2   Suggest the broad types of consumer data a digital marketer might need to carry out the campaign.
3   From your own experience provide detailed examples of companies which are using these types of campaigns.

Based on: Chaffey and Ellis-Chadwick (2016); Cowlett (2011); Arthur (2012); Costa (2011)

Report writing and presentation

Crouch suggests that the key elements in a research report are as follows (Crouch and Housden, 2003).

1   Title page
2   List of contents
3   Preface (outline of agreed brief, statement of objectives, scope and methods of research)
4   Summary of conclusions and recommendations
5   Previous related research (how previous research has had a bearing on this research)
6   Research method
7   Research findings
8   Conclusions
9   Appendices.

Sections 1–4 provide a concise description of the nature and outcomes of the research for busy managers. Sections 5–9 provide the level of detail necessary if any particular issue (e.g. the basis of a finding, or the analytical technique used) needs checking. The report should be written in language the reader will understand; jargon should be avoided.

Software packages such as PowerPoint considerably ease the production of pie charts, histograms, graphs, and so on, for use in the report or for presentational purposes (such as the production of acetates for overhead projection). Clients are increasingly asking for live discussions in which ideas are thought about and the implications for marketing decisions discussed. Some agencies recommend the use of workshops, following the presentation of results, to encourage this kind of discussion (Dye, 2008).

The Essential Differences between Qualitative and Quantitative Research

An important distinction in marketing research is that between qualitative and quantitative research. Earlier in this chapter we discussed qualitative and quantitative research as elements in the marketing research process. Qualitative research usually precedes quantitative research and forms the basis for an understanding of consumers that can aid planning questionnaires, which can then be designed to focus on what is important to the consumer, and worded in language that consumers use and understand. However, when the objectives of the research are to gain rich, in-depth insights into consumer motivations, attitudes and behaviour the study may be based on qualitative research alone without the quantitative follow-up.

Whichever approach is taken, there are a number of essential differences between these two key primary data-gathering methods that mean the skills required vary. Indeed many marketing research practitioners specialize in one or the other approach. These differences relate to the research purpose and whether it is to gather verbal or numerical data. Qualitative research can provide rich, in-depth insights into consumer behaviour, whereas the purpose of quantitative research tends to be to provide information that can be generalized across the study population.

Also, the methods used for data collection tend to be different. Qualitative data are often gathered through focus groups and in-depth interviews, whereas quantitative data is gathered using a structured questionnaire. Qualitative methods offer more flexibility than quantitative studies, as questions can be varied to some degree depending on the answers given by a respondent. Although a structured questionnaire can provide the means for varying questions through the use of filter questions (e.g. 'If the answer to question 6 is yes, go to question 7, if no go to question 10'), there is much less flexibility to vary the questions at the discretion of the interviewer.

It is also important to note that sample sizes differ. Qualitative methods such as in-depth interviews and focus groups have a higher cost per respondent and so tend to focus on insight rather than statistical precision, which means that qualitative studies are associated with smaller samples than quantitative research. Quantitative studies can involve thousands of people. For example, OnePoll conducts surveys on a local, national or international scale, using tailor-made surveys, teams of researchers and selected relevant participants. A typical qualitative study, however, may involve fewer that 30 people.

Analysis and presentation of results can also vary. Qualitative data is analyzed using content analysis, which can result in a report that provides summary statements and uses quotes from research respondents. Quantitative survey data is approached by statistical analysis, and reporting back is through the use of graphs, tables and other methods of statistical presentation. In both cases, careful interpretation is required.

Ethical Issues in Marketing Research

Despite these good intentions of benefiting customers and sellers, there are three ethical concerns about marketing research, discussed below.

Intrusion of privacy

Many consumers recognize the positive role marketing research plays in the provision of goods and services, but some resent the intrusive nature of marketing research surveys. Most consumer surveys ask for classificatory data such as age, occupation and income. While most surveys ask respondents to indicate an age and income band rather than requesting specific figures, some people feel that this is an intrusion of privacy. Other people object to receiving unsolicited telephone calls or mail surveys, dislike being stopped in the street to be asked to complete a face-to-face survey, and resent unsolicited online surveys and email questionnaires.

The right of individuals to privacy is incorporated in the guidelines of many research associations. For example, a code of conduct of the European Society for Opinion and Marketing Research (ESOMAR) states that 'No information which could be used to identify informants, either directly or indirectly, shall be revealed other than to research personnel within the researchers' own organization who require this knowledge for the administration and checking of interviews and data processing' (Schlegelmilch, 1998). Under no circumstances should the information from a survey combined with the address/telephone number of the respondent be supplied to a salesperson.

Misuse of marketing research findings

When marketing research findings are to be used in an advertising campaign or as part of a sales pitch, the results could be manipulated to show a bias in favour of the desired outcome. Respondents could be chosen who are more likely to give a favourable response. For example, a study comparing a domestic versus foreign brand of car could be biased by only choosing people that own domestic-made cars.

Another potential source of bias in the use of marketing research findings is where the client explicitly or implicitly communicates to the researcher the preferred research result. Most marketing researchers, however, accept the need for objective studies where there is room for more than one interpretation of study findings.

In the long term, it is in everyone's interest to produce *accurate* findings, as these are likely to be used for marketing planning decision-making. Using misinformation can prove to be very risky.

Selling under the guise of marketing research

This practice, commonly known as 'sugging', is a real danger to the reputation of marketing research. Despite the fact that it is usually practised by unscrupulous selling companies who use marketing research as a means of gaining compliance with their requests to ask people questions, rather than by bona fide marketing research agencies, the marketing research industry suffers from its aftermath. Usually, the questions begin innocently enough but quickly move on to the real purpose of the exercise. Often this is to qualify leads and ask whether they would be interested in buying the product or having a salesperson call. 'Fruging' is similar, but is fundraising under the *cover* of marketing research.

In Europe, ESOMAR encourages research agencies to adopt codes of practice to prevent this sort of behaviour, and national bodies such as the Market Research Society in the UK draw up strict guidelines. However, the problem remains that the organizations that practise sugging are unlikely to be members of such bodies. The ultimate deterrent is the realization on the part of 'suggers' that the method is no longer effective.

When you have read this chapter

Discover further resources and test your understanding: McGraw-Hill **Connect**™ is a digital teaching and learning environment that improves performance over a variety of critical outcomes; it can be tailored, is easy to use and is proven effective. **LearnSmart**™ is the most widely used and intelligent adaptive learning resource that is proven to strengthen memory recall, improve course retention and boost grades. Fuelled by **LearnSmart**™, **SmartBook**™ is the first and only adaptive reading experience available today.

Review

1 **The nature and purpose of marketing information systems, and the role of marketing research and business intelligence within such systems**
   - A marketing information system provides the information required for marketing decision-making and comprises internal continuous data, internal ad-hoc data, marketing research and environmental scanning.
   - Marketing research is one component of a marketing information system and is primarily concerned with the provision of information about markets and the reaction of these to various product, price, distribution and promotion decisions.
   - Business intelligence is the actionable knowledge produced by the analysis of 'big data' (very large data sets) that are often provided by digital outputs within a marketing information system.

2 **Types of marketing research**
   - There are two types of marketing research, which are ad-hoc research (custom-designed and omnibus studies) and continuous research (consumer panels, retail audits, television viewership panels, marketing databases, customer relationship management systems and website analysis).

3 **Approaches to conducting marketing research**
   - The options are to do it yourself personally, do it yourself using a marketing research department, do it yourself using a fieldwork agency, or use the full services of a marketing research agency.

4   Stages in the marketing research process

- The stages in the marketing research process are research planning (research brief and proposal), exploratory research (secondary research, qualitative research, consultation with experts, and observation), the main (quantitative) data-collection stage (descriptive and experimental research, sampling, survey method, questionnaire design), data analysis and interpretation, and report writing and presentation.

5   How to prepare a research brief and proposal

- A research brief should explain the marketing problem and outline the research objectives. Other useful information is background information, possible sources of information, the proposed scale of the project and a timetable.
- A research proposal should provide a statement of objectives, what will be done (research design), a timetable and costs.

6   The nature and role of exploratory research

- Exploratory research involves the preliminary exploration of a research area prior to the quantitative data-collection stage. Its major purpose is to avoid the sins of omission and admission. By providing an understanding of the people who are to be interviewed later, the quantitative survey is more likely to collect valid and reliable information.
- Exploratory research comprises secondary research, qualitative research, consultation with experts and observation.

7   Quantitative research design decisions: sampling, survey method and questionnaire design issues

- Sampling decisions cover who and how many people to interview. The stages are population definition, sampling frame search, sampling method specification, sample size determination and sample selection.
- Survey method decisions relate to how to interview people. The options are face-to-face, by telephone or mail, and over the Internet.
- Questionnaire design decisions cover what questions to ask. Questionnaires should be planned, designed and piloted before administering to the main sample.

8   Analysis and interpretation of data

- Qualitative data analysis can be facilitated by software packages such as NUD*IST.
- Quantitative data analysis is conducted by software packages such as SPSS.
- Care should be taken when interpreting marketing research results. One common failing is inferring cause and effect when only association has been established.

9   Report writing and presentation

- The contents of a marketing research report should be title page, list of contents, preface, summary, previous related research, research method, research findings, conclusions and appendices.
- Software packages such as PowerPoint can be used to make professional presentations.

10   The distinguishing features between qualitative and quantitative research

(*Qualitative research features precede those of quantitative research in the following list.*)

- *Focus*: verbal data versus numerical data.
- *Research purpose and outcome*: rich, in-depth insights versus broad generalizations.
- *Research means*: focus groups or depth interviews versus structured questionnaires.
- *Operation*: high flexibility in data collection versus low flexibility in data collection.
- *Data capture*: audio recording requiring post-coding versus pre-coded response categories on structured questionnaire.
- *Sampling*: small samples versus large samples.
- *Analysis*: content analysis of respondent statements from audio recording versus statistical analysis of pre-coded responses from a structured questionnaire.
- *Reporting*: underlying themes illustrated by quotes from respondents and summary statements versus statistical.

11 Factors that affect the usage of marketing information systems and marketing research reports

- Usage of marketing information systems has been shown to be higher when the system is sophisticated and confers prestige to its users, other departments view it as a threat, there is pressure from top management to use the system, and users are more involved.
- Usage of marketing research is higher if results conform to the client's prior beliefs, the research is technically competent, the presentation of results is clear, the findings are politically acceptable, and the status quo is not challenged.

12 Ethical issues in marketing research

- These are potential problems relating to intrusions on privacy, misuse of marketing research findings, and selling under the guise of marketing research.

Key Terms

ad-hoc research a research project that focuses on a specific problem, collecting data at one point in time with one sample of respondents

business intelligence the actionable knowledge produced by the analysis of 'big data' (very large data sets)

consumer panel household consumers who provide information on their purchases over time

continuous research repeated interviewing of the same sample of people

data the most basic form of knowledge, the result of observations

descriptive research research undertaken to describe customers' beliefs, attitudes, preferences and behaviour

digital surveys various methods of gathering qualitative (and in some cases quantitative) data using email or web-based surveys

ethnography a form of qualitative research which involves detailed and prolonged observation of consumers in the situations which inform their buying behaviour

experimental research research undertaken in order to establish cause and effect

exploratory research the preliminary exploration of a research area prior to the main data-collection stage

focus group a group normally of six to twelve consumers brought together for a discussion focusing on an aspect of a company's marketing

in-depth interviews the interviewing of consumers individually for perhaps one or two hours, with the aim of understanding their attitudes, values, behaviour and/or beliefs

information combinations of data that provide decision-relevant knowledge

marketing information system a system in which marketing information is formally gathered, stored, analyzed and distributed to managers in accordance with their informational needs on a regular, planned basis

marketing research the gathering of data and information on the market and consumer reactions to product, pricing, promotional and distribution decisions

omnibus survey a regular survey, usually operated by a marketing research specialist company, which asks questions of respondents for several clients on the same questionnaire

qualitative research exploratory research that aims to understand consumers' attitudes, values, behaviour and beliefs

quantitative research a structured study of small or large samples using a predetermined list of questions or criteria

research brief a written document stating the client's requirements

research proposal a document defining what the marketing research agency promises to do for its client and how much it will cost

retail audit a type of continuous research tracking the sales of products through retail outlets

sampling process a term used in research to denote the selection of a sub-set of the total population in order to interview them

secondary research data that have already been collected by another researcher for another purpose

Study Questions

1. What is big data and how is it used to help companies make marketing decisions?

2. What are the essential differences between a marketing information system and marketing research?

3. What are secondary and primary data? Why should secondary data be collected before primary data?

4. What is the difference between a research brief and proposal? What advice would you give a marketing research agency when making a research proposal?

5. Digital survey techniques offer the best solution for gathering data. Discuss this statement.

6. Discuss the problems facing market research as a method of generating information about consumer behaviour.

7. Why are marketing research reports more likely to be used if they conform to the prior beliefs of the client? Does this raise any ethical questions regarding the interpretation and presentation of findings?

8. What are the strengths and limitations of using the Internet as a data-collection instrument?

Recommended Reading

Carson, D., A. Gilmore and K. Gronhaug (2001) *Qualitative Marketing Research*, London: Sage Publications.

Easterby-Smith, M., R. Thorpe and P. Jackson (2015) *Management and Business Research*, London: Sage Publications Ltd.

Experian Mosaic (2015) http://www.experian.co.uk/marketing-services/products/mosaic/mosaic-resources.html

Hair, J., R. P. Bush and D. J. Ortinau (2012) *Essentials of Marketing Research*, London: McGraw Hill Higher Education.

Leventhal, B. (2016) *Geodemographic for Marketers*, London: Kogan Page.

McFee, A. and E. Brynjolfsson (2012) Big data: The management revolution, *Harvard Business Review* 90(10), 60–8.

References

Arthur, C. (2012) Search giant 'sneaking' citizens' privacy away warns EU justice chief, *The Guardian*, 2 March, 18–19.

BARB (2012) Television Measurement Service, http://www.barb. co.uk/about/tv-measurement?_s=4.

BBC (2015) News Technology, 9 February. http://www.bbc.co.uk/news/technology-31296188

Burrows, D. (2014) How to use ethnography for in-depth consumer insight, *Marketing Week*, 9 May. https://www.marketingweek.com/2014/05/09/how-to-use-ethnography-for-in-depth-consumer-insight (accessed 9 June 2015).

Chaffey, D. and F. E. Ellis-Chadwick (2016) *Digital Marketing: Strategy, Implementation and Practice*, 6th edn., Harlow: Pearson.

Clegg, A. (2001) Policy and Opinion, *Marketing Week*, 27 September, 63–5.

Costa, M. (2011) All roads to improvement start at insight, *Marketing Week*, 19 May, 31.

Cowlett, M. (2011) A Social Insight, Marketing, 31–3.

Crouch, S. and M. Housden (2003) *Marketing Research for Managers*, Oxford: Butterworth-Heinemann, 253.

Daniels, E., H. Wilson and M. McDonald (2003) Towards a map of marketing information systems: an inductive study, *European Journal of Marketing* 37(5/6), 821–47.

Denzin, N. K. and Y. S. Lincoln (eds) (2000) *The Handbook of Qualitative Research*, 2nd edn., Thousand Oaks CA: Sage Publications, 11.

Dye, P. (2008) Share The Knowledge, *Marketing*, 19 March, 33–4.

ESOMAR (2005) Industry Study on 2004, ESOMAR World Research Report.

ESOMAR (2015) Market Research Explained, ESOMAR, 8 March. http://www.esomar.org/knowledge-and-standards/market-research-explained.php

Fahy, J. and D. Jobber (2015) *Foundations of Marketing*, Maidenhead: McGraw-Hill Education.

Flack, J. (2002) Not So Honest Joe, *Marketing Week*, 26 September, 43.

Fulgoni, G. (2013) Big Data: Friend or Foe of Digital Advertising? *Journal of Advertising Research*, 1 December.

Gartner (2011) Gartner Says Worldwide Enterprise IT Spending to Reach $2.7 Trillion in 2012. http://www.gartner.com/newsroom/id/1824919

Gigliotti, L. M. (2011) Comparision of an Internet Versus Mail Survey: A Case Study, *Human Dimensions of Wildlife* 16(1), 55–62.

GlaxoSmithKline plc (2012) http://www.gsk.com

Hemsley, S. (2011) Embracing the elephant in the room, *Marketing Week*, October, 39–43.

Hutchins, B. (n.d.) How the World uses the Internet in 60 Seconds, NewsCred Publisher Network. http://blog.newscred.com/article/how-the-world-uses-the-internet-in-60-seconds-infographic/8b8efd786f9cc6165e9e95c8235722ba

Jain, S. C. and G. T. Haley (2009) *Marketing: Planning and Strategy*, USA: South Western Publishing.

Jobber, D. (1985) Questionnaire Design and Mail Survey Response Rates, *European Research* 13(3), 124–9.

Jobber, D. and C. Rainbow (1977) A Study of the Development and Implementation of Marketing Information Systems in British Industry, *Journal of the Marketing Research Society* 19(3), 104–11.

Kerschberg, B. (2014) How Big Data, Business Intelligence and Analytics Are Fueling Mobile Application Development, *Forbes*, 17 December. http://www.forbes.com/sites/benkerschberg/2014/12/17/how-big-data-business-intelligence-and-analytics-are-fueling-mobile-application-development (retrieved 9 June 2015).

Kotler, P., W. Gregor and W. Rodgers (1977) The Marketing Audit Comes of Age, *Sloan Management Review*, Winter, 25–42.

Manning, J. (2011) Online Research insights, The Marketer, June, 42–3.

Mindswarms (2015) How our mobile video Survey works, Mindswarms, 20 May. https://www.mindswarms.com/for-researchers/how-mobile-video-surveys-work

MobileMarketing (2014) Making Sense: watch Nodes Making sense of Proximity Marketing, Mobile Marketing Magazine, 23 July. http://mobilemarketingmagazine.com/tag/making-sense

Moutinho, L. and M. Evans (1992) *Applied Marketing Research*, Wokingham: Addison-Wesley, 5.

Nielsen (2012) Retailing, http://www.acnielsen.co.uk/industry/retailing.shtml

Nodes (2015) Voucher and proximity marketing. http://www.nodesagency.com/cases (accessed June 2015).

O'Dell, W. F. (1962) Personal Interviews or Mail Panels, *Journal of Marketing* 26, 34–9.

Occam DM Ltd (2012) http://www.occam-dm.com/how-we-help.

Pagliery, J. (2015) 'Super cookies' track you, even in privacy mode, CNN Money, 9 January. http://money.cnn.com/2015/01/09/technology/security/super-cookies

Peter, J. P., J. C. Olson, and K. G. Grunert (1999) *Consumer Behaviour and Marketing Strategy*, Maidenhead: McGraw-Hill.

Poynter, R., N. Williams and S. York (2014) *Handbook of Mobile Market Research*, ESOMAR. doi:978-1-118-93562-0

Reynolds, N. and A. Diamantopoulos (1998) The Effect of Pretest Method on Error Detection Rates: Experimental Evidence, *European Journal of Marketing* 32(5/6), 480–98.

Saatchi & Saatchi (2015) Less of a housekeeper, more of a rule breaker. http://saatchi.co.uk/en-gb/news/less-of-a-house-keeper-more-of-a-rule-breaker (accessed June 2015).

Salvador, A. and A. Ikeda (2014) Big Data Usage in the Marketing Information System, *Journal of Data Analysis and Information Processing* 2, 77–85. doi:http://dx.doi.org/10.4236/jdaip.2014.23010

Schlegelmilch, B. (1998) *Marketing Ethics: An International Perspective*, London: International Thomson Business Press.

Sigman, A. (2001) The Lie Detectors, *Campaign*, 15 June, 29.

Tedlock, B. (2000) Ethnography and ethnographic representation, in *The Handbook of Qualitative Research*, Denzin, N. K. and Y. S. Lincoln (eds), 2nd edn., Thousand Oaks CA: Sage Publications, 455–86.

Truste (2015) Understanding Online Behavioral Advertising (OBA), Truste, 6 March. http://www.truste.com/consumer-privacy/about-oba Viking Direct, http://www.viking-direct.co.uk/specialLinks.do;jsessionid=0000iLL4HvfFivp2SWXHkkxKk2P:130mjq8ku?ID=rb_company_info

Vince, L. (2015) Motherhood is not a job, London: Saatchi & Saatchi London. http://saatchi.co.uk/uploads/142676674036405/original.pdf (accessed 6 June 2015).

Weintraub, A. (2014) Big Pharma Opens Up Its Big Data, MIT Technology Review, 21 July. http://www.technologyreview.com/news/529046/big-pharma-opens-up-its-big-data

Wright, L. T. and M. Crimp (2003) *The Marketing Research Process*, London: Prentice-Hall.

Yu, J. and H. Cooper (1983) A Quantitative Review of Research Design Effects on Response Rates to Questionnaires, *Journal of Marketing Research* 20, February, 156–64.

Apple's MP3 players hardly need an introduction. The first version of the iPod (the classic) had the capacity to store thousands of music tracks thanks to its large memory (160 Gb), and a well-designed navigation system that allowed individual tracks to be accessed with ease. However in 2014, this version of the iPod was discontinued by Apple. The iPod shuffle, in contrast, has less memory (2 Gb) and limited features, but is the smallest and cheapest of Apple's MP3 players. Apple also offers the iPod nano, with a multi-touch display and more storage capacity (16 Gb) than the shuffle. Critically, Apple has squeezed the iPod nano into a business-card-sized package. A more recent addition to the range is the iPod touch, with a multi-touch display (16, 32 or 64 Gb of storage). The iPod 'package' also allows consumers to access Apple's iTunes, with a huge range of easily downloaded tracks. This site alone accounts for 70–80 per cent of legal music downloads. The elegant design of the iPod hardware and its navigation system, and access to iTunes, has resulted in Apple dominating the market for MP3 players.

A multitude of accessories increase the spending associated with the iPod. Some of these accessories protect the basic product (insurance and protective cases), some are aimed at increasing convenience to the consumer (worldwide chargers, cables that reduce music download times); others extend where the iPod can be used (car and home stereo connectors, armbands, volume booster); while yet others are aimed at increasing either the quality of the basic equipment (headphone upgrades and speakers) or the functionality of the iPod (digital camera connectors, equipment allowing dictation to be taken).

The iPod is not just important because of the revenue it generates for Apple; it is also important to Apple in other ways as 10–20 per cent of PC users who have an iPod go on to buy a Mac. This 'halo' effect has been noted by shareholders and has boosted Apple's share price. Yet, despite its current success, Apple cannot afford to count on the iPod's current phenomenal performance in the market. Consumers have questioned the value for money of the iPod shuffle, and the quality of the iPod nano's screen. Competitors are encroaching on iTunes by setting up alternative music download sites with extensive playlists. They also fear increased competition from mobile handset manufacturers.

Consequently, Apple is interested in learning more about how consumers view the iPod. In particular, it wants to know about three areas.

1 What are the ownership and usage patterns of the different iPod models? Do consumers own multiple models and use them on different occasions, or do they just have one? Which is bought first?
2 Which features do consumers find most useful? Do different age groups use different features? How are accessories used and when do consumers buy them?
3 What are consumers' attitudes towards the iPod? Do they see it as a style/image icon, or do they look at it as a functional product?

An initial draft of the questions to be included on a questionnaire has been written with these objectives in mind (see overleaf). Apple is considering two different ways to collect data. The first idea is to sample from its customer database. After dividing the database into owners of the iPod classic, the iPod nano, the iPod shuffle and the iPod touch, Apple would mail 500 questionnaires at a time to each group. When the responses were returned, it would look at who responded from each group, and then select more customers from each group to mail the questionnaires to. This process would be repeated until it managed to get 1,000 responses from each group that reflected the demographic characteristics of the owners of the iPod classic, nano, shuffle and touch. Owners of the classic would be included in the sample, even though

»

≫

it is no longer on sale, as they could become future buyers of the other iPod variants.

The second way Apple is considering collecting data is to set up an online questionnaire on the iTunes website. This would appear to every 25th visitor to the site, inviting them to contribute. The questionnaire would remain available until 3,000 responses had been achieved.

Proposed questions

1 Which of the following Apple products do you own? (tick all that apply)
iPod classic ☐
iPod nano ☐
iPod shuffle ☐
iPod touch ☐

2 When do you use your iPod? (tick all that apply)
When commuting/travelling ☐
When working/studying ☐
When shopping ☐
When at the gym ☐
When jogging ☐

3 Which accessories for the iPod do you own? (tick all that apply)
Protective case ☐
Insurance cover ☐
Worldwide charger ☐
Upgraded headphones ☐
Car stereo adaptor ☐
Digital camera connector ☐
Armbands ☐
Speakers ☐

Please indicate the extent to which you agree/disagree with each of the following statements.

4 The iPod's design is ahead of its time.
Strongly agree ☐
Agree ☐
Neither agree nor disagree ☐
Disagree ☐
Strongly disagree ☐

5 The technical features of the iPod are miles ahead of other companies' MP3 players.
Strongly agree ☐
Agree ☐
Neither agree nor disagree ☐
Disagree ☐
Strongly disagree ☐

6 iTunes makes it easy for me to find music I like.
Strongly agree ☐
Agree ☐
Neither agree nor disagree ☐
Disagree ☐
Strongly disagree ☐

7 I show off my iPod whenever I get the opportunity.
Strongly agree ☐
Agree ☐
Neither agree nor disagree ☐
Disagree ☐
Strongly disagree ☐

8 Music is a very important part of my life.
Strongly agree ☐
Agree ☐
Neither agree nor disagree ☐
Disagree ☐
Strongly disagree ☐

9 It is easy to find the track I want on my iPod.
Strongly agree ☐
Agree ☐
Neither agree nor disagree ☐
Disagree ☐
Strongly disagree ☐

10 I am able to find new artists I like using iTunes.
Strongly agree ☐
Agree ☐
Neither agree nor disagree ☐
Disagree ☐
Strongly disagree ☐

11 I talk about my iPod to anyone who will listen.
Strongly agree ☐
Agree ☐
Neither agree nor disagree ☐
Disagree ☐
Strongly disagree ☐

12 Having an iPod impresses people I meet.
Strongly agree ☐
Agree ☐
Neither agree nor disagree ☐
Disagree ☐
Strongly disagree ☐

13 I enjoy watching films a great deal.
Strongly agree ☐
Agree ☐
Neither agree nor disagree ☐
Disagree ☐
Strongly disagree ☐

14 The iPod has better memory than other MP3 players.
Strongly agree ☐
Agree ☐
Neither agree nor disagree ☐
Disagree ☐
Strongly disagree ☐

15 What is your income? _____

16 What is your occupation? _____

17 Gender (please circle): male/female

Questions

1. Will the proposed questions in the questionnaire answer Apple's questions? Outline any problems and suggest solutions.

2. Assess the expertise required, and costs associated with, the two proposed survey methods. Which design would you recommend and why?

3. Assess the strengths and weaknesses of the two proposed sampling methods. Which would you recommend and why?

This case study was written by Nina Reynolds, Professor and Marketing Discipline Leader, University of Wollongong, Sheena MacArthur, formerly of Glasgow Caledonian University, and David Jobber, Emeritus Professor of Marketing, University of Bradford.

References

The material in the case has been drawn from a variety of published sources.

TomTom: Helping Us Find Our Way Around the Planet

TomTom was founded in 1991 by a group of Dutch entrepreneurs. Harold Goddijn is a tenacious Dutchman, Peter-Frans Pauwles wanted to be his own boss, Corinne Vigreux knew about international selling and the importance of building business relationships, and Alexander Ribbink had an eye for technology innovations. All four went to the university, three to the University of Amsterdam and the fourth to ESSEC Business School in France. Harold studied economics, Peter-Frans studied business and computer science, Corinne studied international affairs, and Alexander studied law. Together, their skills and expertise gave them what they needed to bring an innovation to market: satellite navigation system TomTom. This case study explores how TomTom uses different types of data to ensure its satellite navigation system retains traction in the marketplace.

How Does TomTom Stay Ahead?

In the early days, the team realized that in order to make sure their product would sell, they needed to look at the target market carefully and sell directly to the users of the product. They initially developed a mobile-phone-based mapping system, with Ericsson as the mobile handset producer and digital navigation software supplied by TomTom. However, they soon realized that to make this into a product they could market effectively, they needed to build the hardware too.

Together, they researched the market and discovered that at the time car navigation devices cost around £3,000 and were too costly for most consumers. The aim for TomTom was to develop a good, simple and robust design that would be easy to use and an affordable price to consumers. The team realized that at the time this would be a small market, but they felt there was vast potential. Arguably, growth in the market came sooner than expected when Bill Clinton liberalized the Global Positioning System (GPS) for public use during his term as president of the USA and opened the way for the development of satellite navigation (satnav) that was more affordable for everyone.

TomTom is not the only satellite navigation system available in the market; Garmin is a US manufacturer of a competing brand that also serves the consumer car market, and there are now mobile phone apps, for example Google maps, many of which are freely available. TomTom is widely used in consumer markets as a means of navigation but also in business-to-business and government markets. TomTom aims to stay ahead by providing services for walkers, health monitoring and a range of other services. The brand's competitive advantage is based on providing up-to-date maps and real-time information.

Information and Traffic Updates

TomTom uses vast amounts of data to give accurate and up-to-the-minute maps of global road networks. It produces high-quality digital maps that provide a rich range of data, which can be used and analyzed to guide us around the planet. TomTom can analyze addresses and find places. To do this, it uses various sources of private and government data which enable the geo-navigation systems to pinpoint individual buildings.

Historical traffic data is used to factor in known hazards and difficulties that can be encountered. Satnavs can use this data to determine the effects of the school run and bank holidays, and can even anticipate the effect of changing weather conditions on our road journeys. Actual speed data from millions of users make calculations on actual journeys, rather than using permitted speed limits. Traffic flow data reveals what is happening in real time for every part of the road network. By combining these sources of data, TomTom is able to supply real-time navigation information.

TABLE C12.1 Sources of data used by TomTom					
Professional mapmaking			**Community input**		
Mobile mapping vans	Field survey	Authoritative sources	Probe data	Community input	Sensor data

Source: TomTom

The Technology

TomTom has built up years of innovation and geospatial expertise, which is available to the government and the public sector, and through continuous investment and a vast workforce it is able to provide the most accurate maps and navigation using satellite imagery, field surveys, mobile mapping vans and fleets with rigorously controlled community input. TomTom has a large number of live (community) input sources, which provides greater accuracy and increased consumer confidence, and gives it the ability to publish data on any road.

TomTom key data assets, available to government and public sector customers, are (TomTom, 2015):

- Millions of connected GPS devices, 80 million GSM probes, millions of government road sensors and thousands of journalists collecting incident information
- OpenLR technology (for dynamic location referencing); TomTom can describe incidents or congestion on any road, including secondary roads, on any map.
- Mature and proven fusion engine
- Class-leading traffic information. Frequency of data:
- Every second, new road data is received
- Every 30 seconds, the traffic status is updated
- Every minute (or less), all data is made available to customers.

Questions

1. Identify the sources of data that TomTom uses and explain how this becomes useful information.
2. Explain the different types of data TomTom uses to supply navigational information for drivers.
3. Visit the websites of TomTom and Garmin and identify the different criteria you might use if you were thinking of buying a satellite navigation system. Explain which you would choose to buy.
4. Imagine you are the marketing director for TomTom and you are responsible for new market development. Discuss how you would go about finding growth opportunities.

This case study was written by Fiona Ellis-Chadwick, Senior Lecturer, Loughborough University.

References

Garside, J. (2011) Harold Godijin: TomTom's founder needs his business to turn the corner, *The Guardian*, http://www.theguardian.com/business/2011/nov/24/harold-goddijn-tomtom; Bickerton, I. (2007) TomTom's Road Less Travelled, *The Financial Times*; http://www.ft.com/cms/s/1/99581e48-c1b3-11db-ae23-000b5df10621.html#axzz3fnUR01tf; TomTom (2015) http://www.tomtom.com/lib/doc/licensing/S-GOV.EN.pdf

CHAPTER 7
Market Segmentation and Positioning

Finding the most revealing way to segment a market is more an art than a science. . . . Any useful segmentation scheme will be based around the needs of customers and should be effective in revealing new business opportunities.

PETER DOYLE (2008)

LEARNING OBJECTIVES

After reading this chapter, you should be able to:

1 define the concepts of market segmentation and target marketing, and discuss their use in developing marketing strategy
2 discuss the methods of segmenting consumer and organizational markets
3 consider the rise of tribal marketing
4 identify the factors that can be used to evaluate market segments
5 distinguish between the four target marketing strategies—undifferentiated, differentiated, focused and customized marketing
6 discuss online target markets
7 define the concept of positioning and discuss the keys to successful positioning
8 discuss positioning and repositioning strategies

ew products or services satisfy all customers in a market. Not all customers want or are prepared to pay for the same things. British Airways, KLM and SAS are airlines which recognize different groups of travellers and cater for their needs accordingly. Business travellers and holidaymakers are different in terms of their price sensitivity and the level of service required. In jewellery markets the type of person who buys a Swatch fashion watch is different from the type of person who buys an 18-carat gold Rolex watch; the underlying reasons for their purchases are different (fashion versus status), and the type of watch they want is different in terms of appearance, design and quality of materials. Therefore, to implement the marketing concept and satisfy customer needs, product and service offerings need to be tailored to meet the diverse requirements of different customer groups.

The technique used by marketers to get to grips with the diverse nature of markets is called **market segmentation**. Market segmentation may be defined as 'the identification of individuals or organizations with similar characteristics that have significant implications for the determination of marketing strategy'. Market segmentation involves dividing a diverse market into a number of smaller, more similar, sub-markets. The objective is to identify groups of customers with similar requirements so that they can be served effectively while being of a sufficient size for the product or service to be supplied efficiently. Usually, in consumer markets, it is not possible to create a marketing mix that satisfies every individual's particular requirements exactly—although online, high levels of personalization are becoming increasingly possible (see Chapter 16). Market segmentation, by grouping together customers with *similar* needs, provides a commercially viable method of serving these customers and is at the heart of strategic marketing.

For the process of market segmentation and targeting to be implemented successfully, all relevant people in the organization should be made aware of the reasons for segmentation and its importance, and be involved in the process as much as is practicable. By gaining involvement, staff will be more committed to the results, leading to better implementation in the later stages.

Why Bother to Segment Markets?

Why go to the trouble of segmenting markets? What are the gains to be made? Figure 7.1 identifies four benefits, which will now be discussed.

Target market selection

Market segmentation provides the basis for the *selection of target markets*. A *target market* is a chosen segment of market that a company has decided to serve. As customers in the target market segment have similar characteristics, a single marketing mix strategy can be developed to match those requirements. Creative approaches towards segmentation may result in the identification of new segments that have not been served adequately and may form attractive target markets. For example, Google regularly introduces new product offers to serve the functional needs of different target markets, such as Google Wallet for shoppers who want to buy while on the move, Google+—a social network, providing an alternative to Facebook—and Google Maps for iPhone users.

Tailored marketing mix

Market segmentation allows the grouping of customers based upon similarities (e.g. benefits sought) that are important when designing marketing strategies. Consequently this allows marketers to understand in-depth the requirements of a segment, and *tailor a marketing mix package* that meets its needs. This is a fundamental step in the implementation of the marketing concept; segmentation

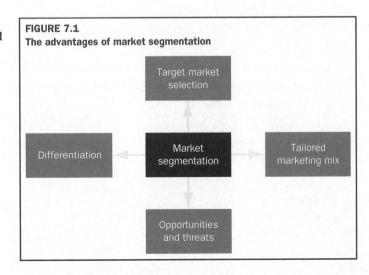

FIGURE 7.1
The advantages of market segmentation

Target market selection

Differentiation — Market segmentation — Tailored marketing mix

Opportunities and threats

promotes the notion of customer satisfaction by viewing markets as diverse sets of needs that suppliers must understand and meet.

For example, BMW has introduced the BMWi3, which is a high-performance but low-emission saloon car, to serve a target market that wants a more sustainable mode of transport than a conventional carbon-fuel car. See Exhibit 7.1 to discover how BMW uses psychographic segmentation focusing on lifestyle variables to target customers for the BMWi3.

Differentiation

Market segmentation allows the development of **differential marketing strategies**. By breaking a market into its constituent sub-segments, a company may differentiate its offerings between

EXHIBIT 7.1
The BMWi3

segments (if it chooses to target more than one segment), and within each segment it can differentiate its offering from the competition. By creating a differential advantage over the competition, a company is giving the customer a reason to buy from it rather than the competition. For example, Apple created the smartphone market with the launch of its first iPhone in 2007. Bundling a new set of applications and functionality into its mobile handset gave the iPhone the difference needed to attract a new generation of mobile users. For a while Apple led the way, but now competition in this market is intense. Nearest rival, Samsung, sells smartphones that are technically similar, and so both firms are seeking ways to differentiate their offer (Davis, 2014). Read Marketing in Action 7.1 to find out how Fyndiq is differentiating its business from Internet giants Amazon and eBay.

Opportunities and threats

Market segmentation is useful when attempting to spot *opportunities and threats*. Markets are rarely static. As customers become more affluent, seek new experiences and develop new values, new segments emerge. The company that first spots a new and underserved market segment and meets its needs better

than the competition can benefit from increasing sales and profit growth. Zara is a fashion brand built on a market opportunity—to supply fashionable clothing to the market quickly. Zara pioneered the concept of fast fashion, which means new designs are available in weeks rather than the fashion industry standard of six months. Spotting this opportunity has enabled Zara to develop into one of the world's largest fashion brands.

Similarly, the neglect of a market segment can pose a threat if the competition use it as a gateway to market entry. Gap, US fashion brand and rival to Zara, failed to spot the changing trends among fashion-conscious shoppers, so as Gap's core target market aged the brand failed to attract the younger fashion-hungry consumers and so lost its market lead to Zara; this remains a position that Gap has not been able to recapture (Keely and Clark, 2008; Bearne, 2015).

The point is that market segments need to be protected from competitors. Otherwise there is a threat that new entrants might establish a foothold and grow market share in the poorly served segment of a market.

The Process of Market Segmentation and Target Marketing

The selection of a target market or markets is a three-step process (see Figure 7.2).

1 *Understand the requirements and characteristics of the individuals and/or organizations* that comprise the market. Marketing research can be used here.

2 *Divide the market, according to these requirements and characteristics, into segments* that have implications for developing marketing strategies. Note a market can be segmented in various ways depending on the choice of criteria. For example, the market for cars could be segmented by: type of buyer (individual or organizational), major benefit sought in a car (e.g. functionality or status), and family size (empty nester versus family with children). There are no rules about how a market should be segmented. Using a new criterion or using a combination of well-known criteria in a novel way may give fresh insights into a market. For example, TomTom changed the way drivers navigate with the launch of its satellite navigation device: TomTom Go.

3 *Choose market segment(s) to target.* A marketing mix can then be developed, based on a deep understanding of target-market customers' needs and values. The aim is to design a mix that is distinctive from competitors' offerings. This theme of creating a *differential advantage* will be discussed in more detail when we examine how to position a product in the marketplace.

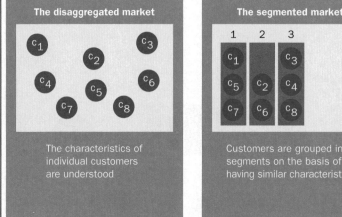

FIGURE 7.2
The process of market segmentation and target marketing

Segmenting Consumer Markets

Markets can be segmented in many ways. Segmentation variables are the criteria that are used for dividing a market into segments. When examining criteria, the marketer is trying to identify good predictors of differences in buyer behaviour. There are an array of options and no single prescribed way of segmenting a market (Wind, 1978). Now we look at possible ways of segmenting consumer markets before we explore how to segment organizational markets.

There are three broad groups of consumer segmentation criteria: 1) *behavioural*, 2) *psychographic* and 3) *profile* variables. Since the purpose of segmentation is to identify differences in behaviour that have implications for marketing decisions, *behavioural variables* such as benefits sought from the product and buying patterns may be considered the ultimate bases for segmentation. Psychographic variables are used when researchers believe that purchasing behaviour is correlated with the personality or lifestyle of consumers; consumers with different personalities or lifestyles have varying product or service preferences and may respond differently to marketing mix offerings. Having found these differences, the marketer needs to describe the people who exhibit them, and this is where profile variables such as socio-economic group or geographic location are valuable (Van Raaij and Verhallen, 1994). For example, a marketer may see whether there are groups of people who value low calories in soft drinks and then attempt to profile them in terms of their age, socio-economic groupings, and so on.

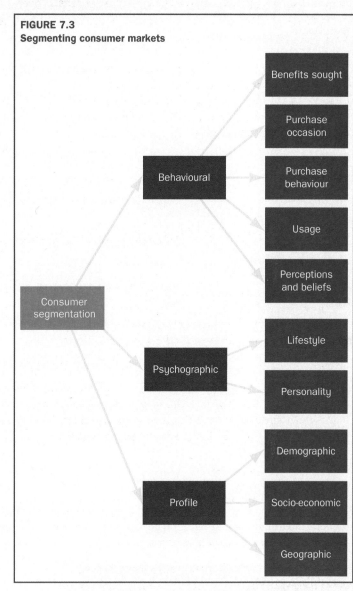

FIGURE 7.3
Segmenting consumer markets

In practice, however, segmentation may not follow this logical sequence. Often, profile variables will be identified first and then the segments so described will be examined to see if they show different behavioural responses. Age or income groups are frequently used as a basis for identifying market segments, and marketing managers examine groups of individuals to see if they show different attitudes and requirements towards particular products and initiatives. For example, Abercrombie & Fitch have found their market to be 25-year-olds with attitude (Ritson, 2011). Figure 7.3 shows the major segmentation variables used in consumer markets, and Table 7.1 describes each of these variables in greater detail.

Behavioural segmentation

The key behavioural bases for segmenting consumer markets are: benefits sought; purchase occasion; purchase behaviour; usage; and perceptions, attitudes beliefs and values. Each will now be discussed.

TABLE 7.1 Consumer segmentation methods	
Variable	**Examples**
Behavioural	
Benefits sought	Convenience, status, performance, price
Purchase occasion	Self-buy, gift, special occasions, eating occasions
Purchase behaviour	Solus buying, brand switching, innovators
Usage	Heavy, light
Perceptions, beliefs and values	Favourable, unfavourable
Psychographic	
Lifestyle	Trendsetters, conservatives, sophisticates
Personality	Extroverts, introverts, aggressive, submissive
Profile	
Age	Under 12, 12–18, 19–25, 26–35, 36–49, 50–64, 65+
Gender	Female, male
Lifecycle	Young single, young couples, young parents, middle-aged empty nesters, retired
Social class	Upper middle, middle, skilled working, unwaged
Terminal education age	16, 18, 21 years
Income	Income breakdown according to study objectives and income levels per country
Geographic	North versus south, urban versus rural, country
Geodemographic	Upwardly mobile young families living in larger owner-occupied houses; older people living in small houses; European regions based on language, income, age profile and location

Benefits sought

This segmentation criterion can be applied when the people in a market seek different benefits from a product. For example, the fruit drink market could be segmented by benefits sought. Table 7.2 shows such a breakdown with examples of the brands targeting each segment.

TABLE 7.2 Benefit segmentation in the fruit drink market	
Benefits sought	**Products favoured**
Extra energy	Lucozade Energy Orange
Vitamins	Ribena Blackcurrant juice drink
Natural	Innocent apple and mango
Low calorie	PLJ Lemon juice cordial
Convenience	Capri-Sun Orange sachets

Benefit segmentation provides an understanding of why people buy in a market and can aid the identification of opportunities. For example, previously the Lego Group focused predominantly on toys for boys, with its packs of building bricks designed to assemble helicopters, trains, rockets and 'warrior-themed' product ranges. However, after four years of research into how girls play, the company introduced a range called Lego Friends aimed at 6- to 12-year-old girls. Now, both boys and girls playing with Lego bricks can enjoy the products educational benefits—for example, developing spatial awareness, mathematical and fine motor skills through play (Weiners, 2011; Wachman, 2012).

Many markets are segmented on the basis of price sensitivity. Often a market will be characterized by a segment of customers who value the benefit of low price and another that values high quality or service and is prepared to pay more for that benefit. In the grocery market, the UK market leader, Tesco, has developed several product ranges, for example Tesco Everyday Value and Tesco Finest, to cater for different market segments, while Sainsbury's has over 1,000 products in its Taste the Difference range of premium quality products which have enabled the supermarket chain to capture market share and drive sales growth (Cattermole, 2012). In the travel industry, established national airlines missed an opportunity to cater for the price-sensitive market segment, which created and opportunity for the so-called 'no-frills' airlines EasyJet and Ryanair to grow rapidly.

 Scan the QR code to find out how Virgin Media uses lifecycle variables to promote its superfast fibre broadband services.

Benefit segmentation is a fundamental method of segmentation, because the objective of marketing is to provide customers with benefits they value. Knowing the various benefits people value is therefore a basic prerequisite of understanding markets. Benefit segmentation provides the framework for classifying individuals based upon this knowledge. Profile analyses can then be performed to identify the type of people (e.g. by age, gender, socioeconomic grouping) in each benefit segment so that targeting can take place.

Purchase occasion

Customers can be distinguished according to the occasions when they purchase a product. For example, a product (e.g. tyres) or service (e.g. plumbing) may be purchased as a result of an emergency or as a routine unpressurized buy. Price sensitivity, for example, is likely to be much lower in an emergency buying situation. Some products (e.g. mobile phones) may be bought as gifts or as self-purchases. These different occasions can have implications for marketing mix and targeting decisions. If it is found that the gift market is concentrated at Christmas, advertising budgets will be concentrated in the pre-Christmas period. Package design may differ for the gift versus personal-buy segment also. Many brands of chocolate are targeted at the gift segment of the confectionery market; for example, Thorntons (UK), Bonnat (France) and Ritter Sport (Germany).

Segmentation by purchase occasion is also relevant in the grocery market. Tesco, the UK's leading supermarket, has different store formats according to the occasions when consumers purchase groceries. For the weekly shop, there are Tesco superstores offering a wide range of food and non-food items; for convenience purchases, a more restricted range of food products are offered by Tesco Metro shops in central urban locations and Tesco Express shops next to petrol stations.

Often, special occasions such as Easter and Christmas are associated with higher prices. However, prices fall rapidly after the occasion; for example, chocolate eggs are discounted after Easter Sunday.

Purchase behaviour

Differences in purchase behaviour can be based on the time of purchase relative to the launch of the product or on patterns of purchase. When a new product is launched, a key task is to identify the innovator segment of the market. These people (or organizations) may have distinct characteristics that allow communication to be targeted specifically at them (e.g. young, middle class). Innovators are more likely to be willing to buy the product soon after launch. Other segments of the market may need more time to assess the benefits, and delay purchase until after the innovators have taken the early risks of purchase. Only when the credentials have been established among these 'innovators' is the brand moved to a wider target audience. For example, the number of electric cars is still relatively low and prices are typically high, and as yet this type of car still has to appeal to a wide audience.

The degree of *brand loyalty* in a market may also be a useful basis for segmenting customers. Solus buyers are totally brand loyal, buying only one brand in the product group, such as a person who buys only Ariel washing powder. Most customers brand-switch; some may have a tendency to buy Ariel but also buy two or three other brands (e.g. Persil, Fairy); others might show no loyalty to any individual brand but switch brands on the basis of special offers (e.g. money off) or because they are variety-seekers who look to buy a different brand each time.

By profiling the characteristics of each group, a company can target each segment accordingly. By knowing the type of person (e.g. by age, socio-economic group, media habits) who is brand-loyal, a company can channel persuasive communications to defend this segment. By knowing the characteristics and shopping habits of the offer-seekers, sales promotions can be targeted correctly.

In the consumer durables market, brand loyalty can be used as a segment variable to good purpose. For example, Volkswagen has divided its customers into first-time buyers, replacement buyers (model-loyal replacers and company-loyal replacers) and switch replacers. These segments are used to measure performance and market trends, and for forecasting purposes (Hooley et al., 2012).

A recent trend in consumer services sectors has been towards biographics. This is the linking of actual purchase behaviour to individuals. The growth in retailer loyalty schemes has provided a mechanism for gathering behavioural data. Customers are given cards that are swiped through an electronic machine at the checkout so that points can be accumulated towards discounts and vouchers. The more loyal the shopper, the higher the number of points gained. The retailer benefits by knowing the purchasing behaviour of named individuals. Online behavioural targeting and browser fingerprinting are discussed in Chapter 16.

Usage

Customers can also be segmented on the basis of heavy users, light users and non-users of a product category. The profiling of heavy users allows this group to receive most marketing attention (particularly promotion efforts) on the assumption that creating brand loyalty among these people will pay heavy dividends. Sometimes the 80:20 rule applies, where about 80 per cent of a product's sales come from 20 per cent of its customers.

However, information technology has increased access to and knowledge of niche markets, and the 'long tail' is a term used to reflect the increase in interest in niche products by marketers (Brynjolfsson et al., 2011). Brands are increasingly developed to target niche market segments. For example, as populations are ageing there is more demand for specialist healthcare products, and car manufacturers like Ford and BMW are adding healthcare technology to their cars so they can access niche segments—for example, the electrocardiogram (ECG) seat measures the heart rate of the driver automatically (Barnett, 2011).

Marketing managers need to be aware that selecting heavy-user segments can deliver benefits in terms of volume of potential sales, but analyzing the light-user segments can provide insights that can deliver advantages over the competition. Target Group Index Europa is a good source of consumer product usage information and provides actionable marketing information on adults (Kantar Media, 2012). An important point to note is that whilst *use* may prove helpful for identifying buyers of particular products, it may not necessarily give insight into an individual's 'shopping basket' of items. For example, luxury foods and drinks may be purchased for a special event like a birthday, but value groceries may be selected for everyday use.

The key issue to remember is that market segmentation concerns the grouping of individuals or organizations with similar characteristics that have implications for the determination of marketing strategy.

Perceptions, attitudes, beliefs and values

The final behavioural base for segmenting consumer markets is by studying perceptions, attitudes, beliefs and values. This is classified as a behaviour variable because perceptions, attitudes, beliefs and values are often strongly linked to behaviour. Consumers are grouped by identifying those people who view the products in a market in a similar way (perceptual segmentation) and have similar beliefs (belief segmentation). These kinds of segmentation analyses provide an understanding of how groups of customers view the marketplace. To the extent that the groups' perceptions and beliefs are different, opportunities to target specific groups more effectively may arise.

Attitudes towards products and services can prove fruitful as a basis for segmenting a market. Research in the UK found that 71 per cent of the population said they were middle class, but this very large section of the population represented a wide spectrum of incomes, wealth and attitudes. Six distinct *tribes* were identified, showing different attitudes towards brand preferences. For example: 'squeezed strugglers' liked Gillette and ITV but disliked the National Trust and Sainsbury's; 'bargain hunters' liked eBay and Muller but disliked John Lewis; 'Daily Mail disciplinarians' liked British Airways but disliked L'Oréal and Channel 4; 'comfortable greens' liked Fair Trade and Green & Black's but disliked Asda and Coca-Cola (Chorley and Rentoul, 2011). But there is more to being part of a tribe than liking or disliking a particular brand. See Marketing in Action 7.2 for further discussion of tribal marketing.

The concept of tribal marketing offers a new way of thinking about segmentation and target markets. From a marketing viewpoint, a tribe is made up of a network of individuals who are linked together by shared beliefs about a brand. A tribe can offer an innovative way to identify customers and to cut through the increasingly fragmented nature of society. Tribes are different to segments in that members share *feelings, passions* and *beliefs* rather than similar demographic variables. They form groups similar to 'clans', and these groupings are not defined by age or other demographic variables. Brand tribes can be built around a strong association with a particular product.

Over the past 3 years We Are Social has worked with Unilever to create a secret and exclusive society of Marmite lovers: The Marmarati

We Are Social

Unilever used the concept of tribalism and the medium of social media to create a tribe called the Marmarati—a group of consumers who were so passionate about Marmite XO (especially strong) that they were prepared to publicly demonstrate their love of the product through Facebook and Twitter. Their approach created excitement around the product both online and offline.

To create a successful tribe, marketers need to identify what it is that brings these individuals together. Tribes are not homogenous like segments; they are linked by passion for a brand and are capable of collective action. Tribes are fuzzy, more like societal sparkle than socio-economic certainty, and so can be difficult to identify.

Based on: Dixon (2005); Veloutsou and Moutinho (2009); Cova and Cova (2002)

Car manufacturers use belief segmentation to divide the market and target specific groups. For example, Toyota aimed to attract a new generation of car buyers in Europe with its Yaris model. In targeting 20- to 30-year-olds, Toyota used direct marketing to persuade this group that these cars are fun, entertaining and enjoyable to own. The new models have added attributes such as touch-screen multimedia systems and other gadgets to attract the attention of the target group (Brownsell, 2011).

Values-based segmentation is based on the principles and standards that people use to judge what is important in life. Values are relatively consistent and underpin behaviour. Values form the basis of attitudes and lifestyles, which in turn manifest as behaviour. Marketers have recognized the importance of identifying the values that trigger purchase for many years, but now it is possible to link value groups to profiling systems that make targeting feasible.

Psychographic segmentation

Psychographic segmentation involves grouping people according to their lifestyle and personality characteristics.

Lifestyle

This form of segmentation attempts to group people according to their way of living, as reflected in their activities, interests and opinions. As we saw in Chapter 3, marketing researchers attempt to identify groups of people with similar patterns of living. The question that arises with lifestyle segmentation is the extent to which general lifestyle patterns are predictive of purchasing behaviour in specific markets (Sampson, 1992). Nevertheless, **lifestyle segmentation** has proved popular among advertising agencies, which have attempted to relate brands (e.g. Hugo Boss) to a particular lifestyle (e.g. aspirational). In television, Sky has used lifestyle segmentation to target special interest groups including sports enthusiasts (Sky Sports), film lovers (Sky Movies) and news followers (Sky News).

Personality

The idea that brand choice may be related to personality is intuitively appealing. However, the usefulness of personality as a segmentation variable is likely to depend on the product category. Buyer and brand personalities are likely to match where brand choice is a direct manifestation of personal values, but for most fast-moving consumer goods (e.g. detergents, tea, cereals), the reality is that people buy a repertoire of brands (Lannon, 1991). Personality (and lifestyle) segmentation is more likely to work when brand choice is a reflection of self-expression; the brand becomes a *badge* that makes public an aspect of personality—'I choose this brand to say this about me and this is how I would like you to see me.' For example, Mercedes' brand personality is all about the brand's *assertiveness*, and is reflected in its strapline, 'the best or nothing', whereas BMW uses the phrase 'the ultimate driving machine' to reflect the desirable aspects of its more *sensuous* personality (Millward Brown, 2015).

Profile segmentation

Profile segmentation variables allow consumer groups to be classified in such a way that they can be reached by the communications media (e.g. advertising, Internet communications). Even if behaviour and/ or psychographic segmentation have successfully distinguished between buyer preferences, there is often a need to analyze the resulting segments in terms of profile variables such as age and socio-economic group to communicate to them. The reason is that readership and viewership profiles of newspapers, magazines and television programmes tend to be expressed in that way.

We shall now examine a number of demographic, socio-economic and geographic segmentation variables.

Demographic variables

The demographic variables we shall look at are age, gender and lifecycle.

- *Age* has been used to segment many consumer markets (Tynan and Drayton, 1987). For example, children receive their own television programmes; cereals, computer games and confectionery are other examples of markets where products are formulated with children in mind. The sweeter tooth of children is reflected in

EXHIBIT 7.2
Old Ladies' Rebellion range, created by Fanny Karst for women over 60

Personality-based profiles and ageist stereotyping are becoming less effective as a segmentation strategy as boundaries between segments blur and attitudes morph. For example, a rebellious person who is a keen media consumer and interested in the latest innovations could be a teenager, but these days this description more aptly fits the 'baby boomer'. Interestingly, baby boomers (born between 1946 and 1964) are the *original* teenagers and are equally as likely to use Skype as their 15- to 24-year-old counterparts; they feel more up to date than today's youngsters and very eager to use new communication technology. However, the boomers are often missed by marketers who prefer to use age to discriminate and so target the 18–34 market segment.

Perhaps it is not surprising that marketers are getting it wrong when using age as a segmentation variable. In Europe, young people seem to be different ages up to a point where they become 'old people', but even this distinction lacks precision. In the UK you are an old person at 59; youth ends at 35 and middle age spans the 24 years in between. In Greece, youth does not end until you are 52, and old age does not start until you reach 67, leaving just 15 years to be middle-aged. Moreover, stereotyped groupings of old and young have often been defined using measures of competence, with the 'old' regularly being placed in the low competence group.

However, wherever the lines are drawn between young and old, marketers need to take care not to alienate the 'old people', as they account for a rapidly growing and increasingly wealthy market segment. Furthermore, analysis suggests that the median age in Europe will increase from 37 to 52 by 2050. In Britain, the government is increasing the minimum retirement age (by 2046 it could be 68), so the trend is set to continue and grow in the future.

Marketers need to be aware that attitudes and preferences change as we age; for example, the desire for sweet tastes dwindles and is replaced by a preference for dryer, sharper and more sophisticated flavours, while responsibilities tend to increase with age as marriage, children and property ownership come along. Some new and existing brands are taking advantage of the potential opportunities afforded by targeting the 'old people'. Old Ladies' Rebellion is a new fashion label created by Fanny Karst for over-60 women. She developed the brand based on her knowledge of traditional tailoring skills and respect for 'the older generation'. Her designs reflect the age of the customers but also incorporate a sense of fun. More-established brands from Marks & Spencer to Aviva motor insurance specifically aim to develop their customer base among the 50-somethings.

How to communicate with the 'old people' is another consideration. New media are proving to be effective in communicating with this market segment; for example, women over 55 are the fastest-growing user segment on Facebook and they are the most unlikely to reply to direct mailing. More consumers (of all ages) are turning to the web to find pre-purchase information and compare what is on offer online before deciding where and from whom to buy.

The reality is that the world is changing rapidly, and using stereotypes and easily accessible demographic variables such as age is likely to prove ineffective as consumers grow older. A possible solution is to take a more rounded view by seeking to identify how customers interact with brands and examining the different channels through which they connect with a brand.

Questions:

Mc Graw Hill Education **connect**®

1 Think of a segmentation classification for 'old people' that would enable you to access this target group more precisely.
2 Discuss the implications for the lifecycle stage model discussed in Chapter 3.
3 Make a list of the brands that might profitably target 'old people'.

Based on Edwards (2011); Handley (2011); Hilpern (2011); Rochon (2014)

sugared cereal brands targeted at children (e.g. Kellogg's Frosties). L'Oréal targets the over-50s with its Age Perfect and Revitalift brands, while Vodafone targets 35- to 55-year-olds with an easy-to-use, no-frills mobile phone that offers the uncomplicated functionality that many in this segment group value (Simms, 2005).

Age is not only widely used for segmenting product markets, but is also used as a segmentation variable in services. The holiday market is heavily age segmented, with offerings targeted at the under-30s and the over-60s segments, for example. This reflects the different requirements of these age groups when on holiday. Mini Case 7.1 explores some of the issues associated with using age as a segmentation variable.

Despite the latest challenges raised by using age as a segmentation variable, many companies covet the youth segment, which comprises the major purchasers of items such as clothing, consumer electronics, drinks, personal care products and magazines. One popular way to communicate with these segments is through digital media communications. Marketing in Action 7.3 explores some of the issues related to understanding this key market segment.

- *Gender* also offers much for a marketing manager planning a segmentation strategy. The different tastes and customs of men and women are reflected in specialist products aimed at these market segments. Magazines, clothing, hairdressing and cosmetics are product categories that have used segmentation based on gender.
- The classic family *lifecycle* stages offer opportunities to segment by a range of related variables such as: disposable income; family responsibilities; consumption patterns based on family circumstances, for example single, married, divorced, living with or without children. Lifecycle stages are discussed in detail in Chapter 3.

 Scan the QR code to compare how Santander uses the concept of segmentation in the marketing of its 1|2|3 Credit Card.

Based upon population census data, 'People UK' is arranged in eight life stages: starting out, young with toddlers, young families, singles/couples/no kids, middle-aged families, empty nesters, retired couples, and older singles. Produced by CACI, the system is particularly useful for targeted mailing, because it can be applied to everyone on the UK electoral roll. People are classified according to the neighbourhood in which they live (Chisnall, 2005). The methodology is described a little later in this section, when we discuss the ACORN geodemographic system.

Socio-economic variables

Socio-economic variables include social class, terminal education age and income. Here we shall look at social class as a predictor of buyer behaviour.

Social class is measured in varying ways across Europe. In the UK occupation is used, whereas in other European centres a combination of variables are used. Like the demographic variables discussed earlier, social class is relatively easy to measure, and is used for creating media readership and viewership profiles. However, as shown in Table 7.1, social class can be multi-layered and consequently may be more difficult to identify. Furthermore, many people who hold similar occupations have very dissimilar lifestyles, values and purchasing patterns. Nevertheless, social class has proved useful in discriminating on the basis of owning a dishwasher, having central heating, and privatization share ownership, for example, and therefore should not be discounted as a segmentation variable (O'Brien and Ford, 1988).

Geographic variables

The final set of segmentation variables is based on geographic differences. A marketer can use pure geographic segmentation or a hybrid of geographic and demographic variables called *geodemographics*.

The *geographic* segmentation method is useful where there are geographic locational differences in consumption patterns and preferences. For example, variations in food preferences may form the basis of geographic segments; differences in national advertising expectations may also form geographic segments for communicational purposes. Germans expect a great deal more factual information in their advertisements than French or British audiences do. France, with its more relaxed attitude to nudity, broadcasts commercials that would be banned in the UK. In the highly competitive Asian car market, both Honda and Toyota have launched their first 'Asia-specific' cars, designed and marketed solely for Asian consumers, but they face emerging competitors—for example, Tata Motors in India, a company manufacturing cars specifically for the home market (e.g. Nano, a small, affordable, reliable car for Indian families (Tata Motors, 2009)).

Geodemographic: in countries that produce population census data, the potential for classifying consumers on the combined basis of location and certain demographic (and socio-economic) information exists. Households are classified into groups according to a wide range of factors, depending on what is asked for on census returns. In the UK variables such as age, social status, family size, ethnic background, joint income, type of housing and car

MARKETING IN ACTION 7.3
The A–Z of Digital Generations

During the last two decades, a generation of digitally informed new consumers have been born to shop online. But they are not the only generations who have learned how to function in the technology-enhanced world: others, too, are learning how to become digital natives. So marketers need to understand and be able to identify these consumers in order to engage with the generations. Here are just a few of the digitally able generations:

B is for baby boomers, 55 years old and over, who have no intention of retiring or opting for a quiet life. People in this group tend to be both mentally and physically active, and as a segment are likely to drive future growth in retail spending; they are high online spenders but spend a smaller percentage of their income online than the millennials. They are tech-savvy consumers and have taken to mobile commerce too.

C is for content. Generation C are the group of customers who, rather than being consumers of content, are in fact the creators of content, or prosumers as they have been called. Highly sophisticated digital devices enable consumers to produce content such as images, videos and audio tracks. There are individuals of all ages and backgrounds, so age is not a useful segmentation variable. For marketers, the commercial advantage of consumer-generated content is that it reveals hidden preferences; for example, the rise in popularity of 'unboxing', where a person films the unwrapping and the initial operation of a new purchase (invariably a newly released piece of technology), reveals what the buyer finds difficult and what he or she enjoys about a particular product. Increasingly, marketers are engaging consumers in the product development process, working together to produce finely tuned market offerings.

D is for digital natives—a broad term coined in 2001 to capture the group of people who were 'born digital'. This term has come to mean people born after 1980, who have been exposed to computer technology and digital communications.

M is for millennials, who are a key target group of online consumers because they spend more money online than any other group. Millennials are 18- to 34-year-olds. Their attitudes vary and millennials have been labelled the 'me, me, generation', but also the 'nice generation'. Arguably, those in this generation have grown up with more structure in their lives, and family values are important. During their early years there was a downturn in violence against children and an increase in child-friendly gadgets to promote their safe upbringing. Millennials are risk averse, aspire to stable careers, and are less likely to have a credit card than Generation Xers.

X is for Generation Xers. Born between 1965 and 1980, this is a generation of extremes: during childhood, they tended to experience indulgent parenting styles from their baby boomer parents, but as they got older, divorce, poor schooling and other social factors led to this group being called the 'baby bust generation'. The Xers were hit hard by the 2008 recession and tended to downsize and live a DIY lifestyle.

Y is for Generation Y, young boomers that followed the baby boomers. They tend to be 32 or younger and have unique product preferences and different attitudes to brands; multi-channel shopping particularly appeals to this group. They are accused of being selfish and love spending time online.

Z is for Generation Z. This group have a relatively low income but spend the largest percentage online. Born since the millennium and in their mid-teens, they have grown up in a world of political and financial turmoil. They care about the world they live in and see education as a thing to be treasured. They are more likely to volunteer than their Generation X parents and the millennials.

Based on: Kimmel (2010); Smith (2014); KPMG (2013); Prensky (2001); Howe (2014); Wallop (2014); Trendwatching.com (2004); Independent (2009)

ownership are used to group small geographic areas (known as *enumeration districts*) into segments that share similar characteristics. The two best-known geodemographic systems in the UK are ACORN and Mosaic. Both use census data and postcodes to produce categorisations of the population in the UK. See Table 7.3 for details of ACORN's system of classification.

TABLE 7.3 ACORN categories, groups and types (ACORN CACI, 2014)

Category	Traits	Group	Type—examples
1 Affluent achievers	Financially successful, middle-aged plus, mainly empty nesters; confident with new technology	Lavish life styles Executive wealth Mature money	Exclusive enclaves Asset rich families Upmarket downsizers
2 Rising prosperity	Highly educated younger singles and couples, living in modern flats, with good incomes; earlier adopters of the Internet	City sophisticates Career climbers	Socializing young renters Career-driven young families
3 Comfortable communities	Tend to live in suburbs or smaller towns, own their homes (average value for region), have average income and average education; professional, managerial and clerical jobs	Countryside communities Successful suburbs Steady neighbourhoods Comfortable seniors Starting out	Farms and cottages Large family homes, multi-ethnic Suburban semis, conventional attitudes Older people; neat and tidy neighbourhoods Smaller houses and starter homes
4 Financially stretched	Tend to live in terraced houses or semi-detached; more single separated and divorced than average; less likely to have a credit card; use the Internet to shop but will use it socially	Student life Modest means Striving families Poorer pensioners	Term-time terraces Fading owner-occupied terraces Families in right-to-buy estates Elderly people in social rented flats
5 Urban adversity	Deprived areas of large and small towns; low household incomes, refused credit; low levels of qualifications; higher levels of health problems than other areas	Young hardship Struggling estates Difficult circumstances	Young families in low cost private flats Low-income terraces Deprived areas and high-rise flats
6 Not private households	Communal establishments, e.g. military bases, hotels, other holiday accommodation	Not private households	Active communal Inactive communal

ACORN is a powerful consumer classification that segments the UK population. By analysing demographic data, social factors, population and consumer behaviour, it provides precise information and an understanding of different types of people.

Mosaic is a classification system that provides insight into demographics and lifestyles in the world's major economies. In the UK the system classifies individuals, household and/or postcodes into homogenous consumer segments. There are 141 Mosaic person types, which can be aggregated into 67 household types and 15 groups. For example, groups include: alpha territory; career and kids; claimant culture. The classification system can then be overlaid onto a map of an area to show the areas in relation to the person types, household types and groups (Experian, 2015).

A major strength of these geodemographics systems for marketers is the capacity to link buyer behaviour to customer groups and locations. There are a wide range of variables that can be used to segment consumer markets. Often a combination of variables will be used to identify groups of consumers that respond in the same way to marketing mix strategies.

Research companies are also combining lifestyle- and values-based segmentation schemes with geodemographic data. For example, CACI's Census Lifestyle system classifies segments using lifestyle and geodemographic data.

Influences of digital technology on segmentation variables

According to research (Doherty and Ellis-Chadwick, 2010a and b), online consumer markets can be identified by considering demographic variables and behavioural and psychographic variables, which have implications for segmentation. While there is a similarity between categories of variables online and offline, each group of variables has different characteristics in the virtual world. For example, research suggests that in terms of their personal profiles—age, gender, education, salary, and so on—Internet shoppers are likely to be similar to their offline counterparts (Jayawardhena, Wright and Dennis, 2007). However, it is still possible to distinguish the most enthusiastic and profitable Internet shoppers on the basis of their perceptions, beliefs and behaviours. For example, it has recently been found that the Internet is a favourite channel for the compulsive shopper, as consumers are able to 'buy unobserved', 'without contact with other shoppers', and in so doing, 'experience strong positive feelings during the purchase episode'.

Furthermore, the demographic variables which have significant implication for online targeting are those found to remain static throughout an individual's lifetime, or to evolve slowly over time—such as education, race, age (Hoffman, Novak and Schlosser, 2003), gender (Slyke, Comunale and Belanger, 2002) and lifestyle (Shui and Dawson, 2004).

Important psychographic and behavioural variables are those that shape the perceptions, beliefs and attitudes that might influence consumers' online behaviour, and in particular their intention to shop or engage with an online offer. Online behavioural characteristics—such as knowledge, attitude, innovativeness and risk aversion—have been found to have significant implications when segmenting online markets and when considering a consumer's likelihood to shop online. For example, it has been found that consumers who are primarily motivated by convenience were more likely to make purchases online, while those who value physical social interactions were found to be less interested (Swaminathan, Lepkowska-White and Rao, 1999; Kukar-Kinney, Ridgway and Monroe, 2009). Moreover, a study of Internet shoppers from six countries (developing and developed) found a surprisingly high degree of homogeneity in their characteristics and habits (Brashear et al., 2009). It concluded that Internet shoppers share 'their desire for convenience, are more impulsive, have more favourable attitudes towards direct marketing and advertising, are wealthier, and are heavier users of both email and the Internet'.

Segmenting Organizational Markets

While the consumer goods marketer is interested in grouping individuals into marketing-relevant segments, the business-to-business marketer profiles organizations and organizational buyers. The organizational market can be segmented on several factors broadly classified into two major categories: macrosegmentation and microsegmentation (see Wind and Cardozo, 1974; Plank, 1985).

Macrosegmentation focuses on the characteristics of the buying organization, such as size, industry and geographic location. **Microsegmentation** requires a more detailed level of market knowledge, as it concerns the characteristics of decision-making within each macrosegment, based on such factors as choice criteria, decision-making unit structure, decision-making process, buy class, purchasing organization and organizational innovativeness. Often organizational markets are first grouped on a macrosegment basis and then finer sub-segments are identified through microsegmentation (Wind and Cardozo, 1974).

Figure 7.4 shows how this two-stage process works. The choice of the appropriate macrosegmentation and microsegmentation criteria is based on the marketer's evaluation of which criteria are most useful in predicting buyer behaviour differences that have implications for developing marketing strategies. Figure 7.5 shows the criteria that can be used.

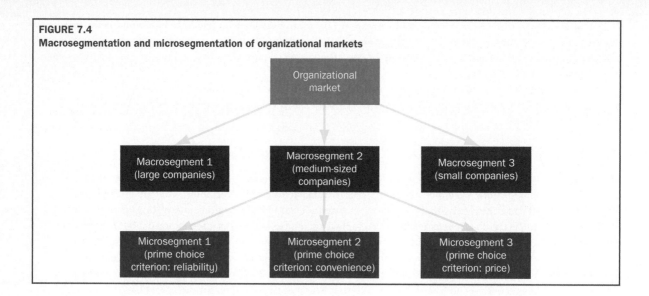

FIGURE 7.4
Macrosegmentation and microsegmentation of organizational markets

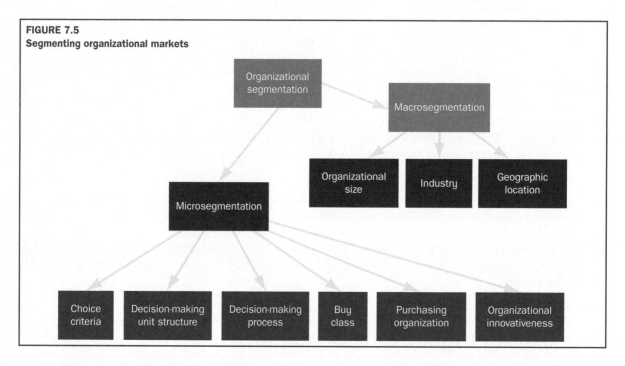

FIGURE 7.5
Segmenting organizational markets

Macrosegmentation

The key macrosegmentation criteria of organizational size, industry and geographic location will now be discussed.

Organizational size

The size of buying organizations may be used to segment markets. Large organizations differ from medium-sized and small organizations in having greater order potential, more formalized buying and management processes, increased specialization of function, and special needs (e.g. quantity discounts). The result is that they may form important target market segments and require tailored marketing mix strategies. For example, the salesforce may need to be organized on a key account basis, where a dedicated sales team is used to service important industrial accounts. List pricing of products and services may need to take into account the inevitable demand for volume discounts from large purchasers, and the salesforce team will need to be well versed in the art of negotiation.

Industry

Another common macrosegmentation variable is industry sector. Different industries may have unique requirements from products. For example, software application suppliers like Oracle and SAP can market their products to various sectors such as banking, manufacturing, healthcare and education, each of which has unique needs in terms of software programs, servicing, price and purchasing practice. By understanding each industry's needs in depth, a more effective marketing mix can be designed. In some instances further segmentation may be required. For example, the education sector may be further divided into primary, secondary and further education as their product and service requirements may differ.

Geographic location

Regional variations in purchasing practice and needs may imply the use of geographic location as a basis for differentiating marketing strategies. The purchasing practices and expectations of companies in central and eastern Europe are likely to differ markedly from those in western Europe. Their more bureaucratic structures may imply a fundamentally different approach to doing business that needs to be recognized by companies attempting to enter these emerging industrial markets. In Chapter 2, we saw how different cultural factors affect the purchasing practices in European countries. These differences, in effect, imply regional segments since marketing needs to reflect these variations.

Microsegmentation

Marketers may find it useful to divide each macrosegment into smaller microsegments on the basis of the buyer's choice criteria, decision-making unit structure, decision-making process, buy class, purchasing organization, and organizational innovativeness.

Choice criteria

This factor segments the organizational market on the basis of the key choice criteria used by buyers when evaluating supplier offering. One group of customers may rate price as the key choice criterion, another segment may favour productivity, while a third segment may be service orientated. These varying preferences mean that marketing and sales strategies need to be adapted to cater for each segment's needs. Three different marketing mixes would be needed to cover the three segments, and salespeople would have to stress different benefits when talking to customers in each segment. Variations in key choice criteria can be powerful predictors of buyer behaviour. An important choice criterion for business customers is economic value to the customer, which takes into account not only price, but also other costs. Michelin introduced Cross climate tyres targeting business people with the aim of improving safety and year-round care. For fleet users of these tyres, ATS Euromaster said they will be a 'game changer in the market place' (Fleet News, 2015).

Decision-making unit structure

Another way of segmenting organizational markets is based on decision-making unit (DMU) composition: members of the DMU and its size may vary between buying organizations. As discussed in Chapter 4, the DMU consists of all those people in a buying organization who have an effect on supplier choice. One segment might be characterized by the influence of top management on the decision, another by the role played by engineers, and a third segment might comprise organizations where the purchasing manager plays the key role. DMU size can also vary considerably: one segment might feature large, complex units, while another might comprise single members.

Decision-making process

As we saw in Chapter 4, the decision-making process can take a long time or be relatively short in duration. The length of time is often correlated with DMU composition. Long processes are associated with large DMUs. Where the decision time is long, high levels of marketing expenditure may be needed, with considerable effort placed on personal selling. Much less effort is needed when the buy process is relatively short and where, perhaps, only the purchasing manager is involved.

Buy class

Organizational purchases can be categorized into straight rebuy, modified rebuy and new task. As we discussed in Chapter 4, the buy class affects the length of the decision-making process, the complexity of the DMU and the number of choice criteria that are used in supplier selection. It can therefore be used as a predictor of different forms of buyer behaviour, and hence is useful as a segmentation variable.

Purchasing organization

Decentralized versus centralized purchasing is another microsegmentation variable because of its influence on the purchase decision (Corey, 1978). Centralized purchasing is associated with purchasing specialists who become experts in buying a range of products. Specialization means that they become more familiar with cost factors, and the strengths and weaknesses of suppliers, than decentralized generalists. Furthermore, the opportunity for volume buying means that their power base to demand price concessions from suppliers is enhanced. They have also been found to have greater power within the DMU vis-à-vis technical people like engineers, than decentralized buyers, who often lack the specialist expertise and status to challenge their preferences. For these reasons, the purchasing organization provides a good base for distinguishing between buyer behaviour and can have implications for marketing activities. For example, the centralized purchasing segment could be served by a national account salesforce, whereas the decentralized purchasing segment might be covered by territory representatives.

EXHIBIT 7.3
This advert explains how Michelin tyres offer better economic value and safety than those of its rivals

Organizational innovativeness

A key segmentation variable when launching new products is the degree of innovativeness of potential buyers. In Chapter 11 we discuss the characteristics of innovator firms. Marketers need to identify the specific characteristics of the innovator segment, since these companies should be targeted first when new products are launched. Follower firms may be willing to buy the product but only after the innovators have approved it. Although categorized here as a microsegmentation variable, it should be borne in mind that organizational size (a macrosegmentation variable) may be a predictor of innovativeness too.

Table 7.4 summarizes the methods of segmenting organizational markets and provides examples of how each variable can be used to form segments.

TABLE 7.4 Organizational segmentation methods	
Variable	**Examples**
Macrosegmentation	
Organizational size	Large, medium, small
Industry	Engineering, textiles, banking
Geographic location	Local, national, European, global
Microsegmentation	
Choice criteria	Economic value, delivery, price, service
Decision-making unit structure	Complex, simple
Decision-making process	Long, short
Buy class	Straight rebuy, modified rebuy, new task
Purchasing organization	Centralized, decentralized
Organizational innovativeness	Innovator, follower, laggard

Target Marketing

Market segmentation is a means to an end: *target marketing*. This is the choice of specific segments to serve and is a key element in marketing strategy. A company needs to evaluate the segments and decide which ones to serve. For example, CNN targets its news programmes to what are known as 'influentials'. This is why CNN has, globally, focused so much of its distribution effort into gaining access to hotel rooms. Business people know that wherever they are in the world, they can see international news on CNN in their hotel. Eurosport uses a similar targeting approach and provides plenty of coverage of upmarket sports such as golf and tennis for viewers in Europe. In high-tech markets, Apple's introduction of the iPad enabled the company to gain a stronghold in corporate markets for its multi-touch devices. When Coca-Cola targeted consumer markets in China, it gave its soft drinks brand a makeover, including a new name (see Exhibit 7.4) and a strapline which, when translated from Mandarin, becomes 'delicious happiness' (Muller, 2011).

EXHIBIT 7.4
Coca-Cola targeted consumer markets in China with a new image and strapline

Entering markets can be costly, especially when products need to be altered, so it is important to take care in selecting those target markets that will meet marketing objectives. Accordingly, first we examine how to evaluate potential market segments, and then consider how to make a balanced choice about which markets to serve.

Evaluating market segments

When evaluating market segments, a company should examine two broad issues: market attractiveness and the company's capability to compete in the segment. Market attractiveness can be assessed by looking at market factors, competitive factors, and political, social and environmental factors (see Abell and Hammond, 1979; Day, 1986; Hooley et al., 2012). Figures 7.6 and 7.7 illustrate the factors that need to be examined when evaluating market segments.

Market factors

Segment size: generally, large-sized segments are more attractive than small ones, since sales potential is greater, and the chance of achieving economies of scale is improved. However, large segments are often highly competitive since other companies are realizing their attraction, too. Furthermore, smaller companies may not have the resources to compete in large segments, and so may find smaller segments more attractive.

Segment growth rate: growing segments are usually regarded as more attractive than stagnant or declining segments, as new business opportunities will be greater. However, growth markets are often associated with heavy competition (e.g. in the mobile computing market, tablet computers, ultra netbooks and smartphones are three high-growth markets that are highly competitive). Therefore, an analysis of growth rate should always be accompanied by an examination of the state of competition.

Segment profitability: the potential to make profits is an important factor in market attractiveness.

Price sensitivity: in segments where customers are price sensitive, there is a danger of profit margins being eroded by price competition. Low price-sensitive segments are usually more attractive, since margins can be maintained. Competition may be based more on quality and other non-price factors.

Bargaining power of customers: both end and intermediate customers (e.g. distributors) can reduce the attraction of a market segment if they can exert high bargaining pressure on suppliers. The result is usually a reduction in profit margins as customers (e.g. supermarket chains) negotiate lower prices in return for placing large orders.

Bargaining power of suppliers: a company must assess not only the negotiating muscle of its customers but also its potential suppliers in the new segment. Where supply is in the hands of a few dominant companies, the segment will be less attractive than when served by a large number of competing suppliers.

Barriers to market segment entry: for companies considering entering a new segment there may be substantial entry barriers that reduce its attractiveness. Barriers can take the form of the high marketing expenditures

FIGURE 7.6
Factors used to assess market attractiveness

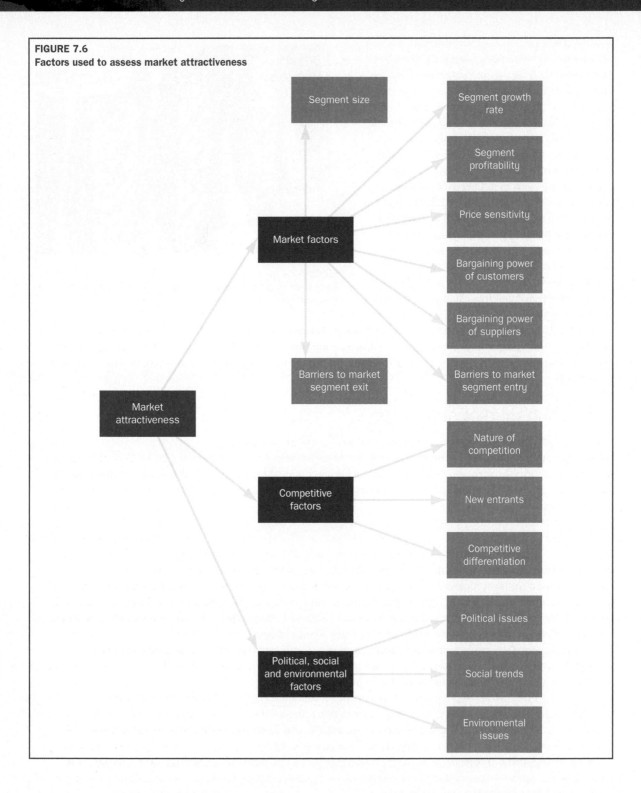

necessary to compete, patents, or high switching costs for customers. However, if a company judges that it can afford or overcome barriers to entry, its existence may raise segment attractiveness if the company judges that the barriers will deter new rivals from entering.

Barriers to market segment exit: a segment may be regarded as less attractive if there are high barriers to exit. Exit barriers may take the form of specialized production facilities that cannot easily be liquidated, or agreements to provide spare parts to customers. Their presence may make exit extremely expensive and therefore segment entry more risky.

Competitive factors

Nature of competition: segments that are characterized by strong aggressive competition are less attractive than where competition is weak. The weakness of European and North American car manufacturers made the Japanese entry into a seemingly highly competitive (in terms of number of manufacturers) market segment relatively easy. The quality of the competition is far more significant than the number of companies operating in a market segment.

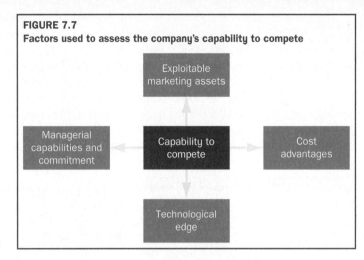

FIGURE 7.7
Factors used to assess the company's capability to compete

New entrants: a segment may seem superficially attractive because of the lack of current competition, but care must be taken to assess the dynamics of the market. A judgement must be made regarding the likelihood of new entrants, possibly with new technology, that might change the rules of the competitive game (e.g. Google changed the rules in the online advertising market with the introduction of AdWords.).

Competitive differentiation: segments will be more attractive if there is a real probability of creating a differentiated offering that customers value. This judgement is dependent on identifying unserved customer requirements, and the capability of the company to meet them.

Political, social and environmental factors

Political issues: political forces can open up new market segments (e.g. the deregulation of telecommunications in the UK paved the way for private companies to enter consumer and organizational segments of that market). Alternatively, the attraction of entering new geographic segments may be reduced if political instability exists or is forecast; for example, unrest in Tunisia, Egypt and Morocco caused a reduction in the number of tourists travelling to such regions and a downturn in sales for travel firms like Thomas Cook (Moore, 2011).

Social trends: changes in society need to be assessed to measure their likely impact on the market segment. Changes in society can give rise to latent market segments, under-served by current products and services. Big gains can be made by first entrants (e.g. Apple's entry into the mobile music market with iTunes).

Environmental issues: the trend towards more environmentally friendly products has affected market attractiveness both positively and negatively. The Body Shop took the opportunity afforded by the movement against animal testing of cosmetics and toiletries; conversely the market for CFCs has declined in the face of scientific evidence linking their emission with depletion of the ozone layer.

In organizational markets, individual customers may be evaluated on such criteria as sales volume, profitability, growth potential, financial strength and their fit with market and product strategy. Their allocation to a segment will be based on these factors.

Capability

Against the market attractiveness factors must be placed the company's *capability to serve the market segment*. The market segment may be attractive but outside the resources of the company. Capability may be assessed by analyzing exploitable marketing assets, cost advantages, technological edge, and managerial capabilities and commitment.

Exploitable marketing assets: does the market segment allow the firm to exploit its current marketing strengths? For example, is segment entry consonant with the image of its brands, or does it provide distribution synergies? However, where new segment entry is inconsistent with image, a new brand name may be created. For example, Toyota developed the Lexus model name when entering the upper-middle executive car segment.

Cost advantages: companies that can exploit cheaper material, labour or technological cost advantages to achieve a low cost position compared to the competition may be in a strong position, particularly if the segment is price sensitive.

Technological edge: strength may also be derived by superior technology, which is the source of differential advantage in the market segment. Patent protection (e.g. in pharmaceuticals) can form the basis of a strong defensible position, leading to high profitability. For some companies, segment entry may be deferred if they do not possess the resources to invest in technological leadership.

Managerial capabilities and commitment: a segment may look attractive, but a realistic assessment of managerial capabilities and skills may lead to rejection of entry. The technical and judgemental skills of management may be insufficient to compete against strong competitors. Furthermore, the segment needs to be assessed from the viewpoint of managerial objectives. Successful marketing depends on implementation. Without the commitment of management, segment entry will fail on the altar of neglect.

Target marketing strategies

The purpose of evaluating market segments is to choose one or more segments to enter. Target market selection is the choice of which and how many market segments in which to compete. There are four generic **target marketing** strategies from which to choose: undifferentiated marketing, differentiated marketing, focused marketing, and customized marketing (see Figure 7.8). Each option will now be examined.

Undifferentiated marketing

Occasionally, a market analysis will show no strong differences in customer characteristics that have implications for marketing strategy. Alternatively, the cost in developing a separate market mix for separate segments may outweigh the potential gains of meeting customer needs more exactly. Under these circumstances a company may decide to develop a single marketing mix for the whole market. This absence of segmentation is called **undifferentiated marketing**.

Unfortunately, this strategy can occur by default. For example, companies that lack a market orientation may practise undifferentiated marketing through lack of customer knowledge. Furthermore, undifferentiated marketing is more convenient for managers, since they have to develop only a single product. Finding out that customers have diverse needs that can be met only by products with different characteristics means that managers have to go to the trouble and expense of developing new products, designing new promotional campaigns, training the salesforce to sell the new products and developing new distribution channels. Moving into new segments also

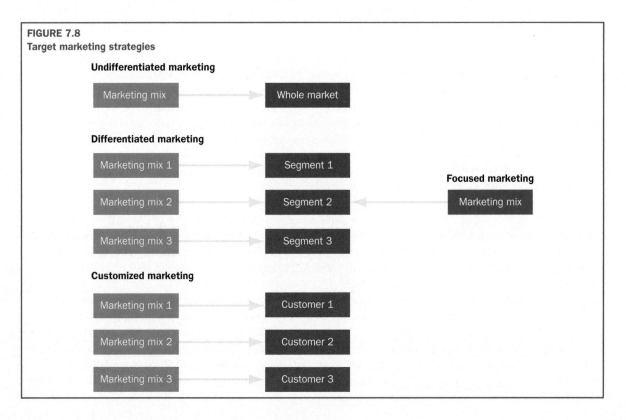

FIGURE 7.8
Target marketing strategies

Undifferentiated marketing

Marketing mix → Whole market

Differentiated marketing

Marketing mix 1 → Segment 1

Marketing mix 2 → Segment 2

Marketing mix 3 → Segment 3

Focused marketing

Marketing mix → Segment 2

Customized marketing

Marketing mix 1 → Customer 1

Marketing mix 2 → Customer 2

Marketing mix 3 → Customer 3

means that salespeople have to start prospecting for new customers. This is not such a pleasant activity as calling on existing customers who are well known and liked.

The process of market segmentation, then, is normally the motivator to move such companies from practising undifferentiated marketing to one of the next three target marketing strategies.

Differentiated marketing

When market segmentation reveals several potential targets, specific marketing mixes can be developed to appeal to all or some of the segments. This is called **differentiated marketing**. For example, airlines design different marketing mixes for first-class and economy passengers, including varying prices, service levels, quality of food, in-cabin comfort and waiting areas at airports. A differentiated target marketing strategy exploits the differences between marketing segments by designing a specific marketing mix for each segment. Marketing in Action 7.4 describes how Tesco and Sky have designed different products to cater for the segments that exist in their markets.

One potential disadvantage of a differentiated compared with an undifferentiated marketing strategy is the loss of cost economies. However, the use of flexible manufacturing systems can minimize such problems.

MARKETING IN ACTION 7.4
Companies Use Different Brands to Meet the Needs of their Various Target Markets

Market segmentation is a creative act that relies upon a clear understanding of the groups of customers that make up a particular target market. The actual basis of segmentation will vary by market sector. However, large corporations frequently aim to ensure their product portfolios offer a mix of product ranges and brands that meet the needs of different market segments. For example, Tesco differentiates its various offers by channel choice and store format. The weekly shopper tends to look for a store where they can purchase all of their needs in one location, while the convenience shopper is looking for a limited range of products and is prepared to pay a slightly higher price and select from a limited range of products as the store is very conveniently located, often within walking distance of the consumer's home. The online shopper often wants a mix of both convenience and range, but is prepared to wait for their shopping to be delivered. Each of these shoppers is looking for a different type of convenience.

By utilizing three distinct brands, Tesco is able to target different target segments, extend its reach and protect its market share from competitors:

Tesco Stores	→	targets weekly shoppers
Tesco Express	→	targets convenience shoppers
Tesco.com	→	targets online shoppers

Sky has also differentiated some of its product offerings to target specific segments:

Sky Sports	→	targets sports enthusiasts
Sky Movies	→	targets film lovers
Sky News	→	targets news followers
Sky Atlantic	→	targets drama lovers

Airlines apply similar principles. For example, United Airlines is based in North America and is one of the world's largest airlines, operating a fleet of over 700 aircraft. The airline serves many target markets, catering for domestic and commercial customers and operates internal, transcontinental, and transatlantic routes. On all United Airlines flights passengers are offered a choice of classes:

First class	→	targets top business executives
Business class	→	targets senior managers
Economy class	→	targets other business travellers, and domestic travellers

All of these companies—whether they be retail or broadcast orientated, or travel related—have recognized that market segmentation can lead to higher rates of satisfaction of consumer needs than producing a single offering and hoping it will meet it all the diverse expectations of a given market.

Based on: United Airlines (2012); Rose (2008); Smith (2008); Jack (2009)

Focused marketing

The identification of several segments in a market does not imply that a company should serve all of them. Some may be unattractive or out of line with business strengths. Perhaps the most sensible route is to serve just one of the market segments. When a company develops a single marketing mix aimed at one target market (*niche*) it is practising **focused marketing**.

This strategy is particularly appropriate for companies with limited resources. Small companies may stretch their resources too far by competing in more than one segment. Focused marketing allows research and development expenditure to be concentrated on meeting the needs of one set of customers, and managerial activities can be devoted to understanding and catering for their needs. Large organizations may not be interested in serving the needs of this one segment, or their energies may be so dissipated across the whole market that they pay insufficient attention to their requirements.

An example of focused marketing in the consumer market is given by Bang & Olufsen (B&O), the Danish audio electronics firm. It targets upmarket consumers who value self-development, pleasure and open-mindedness, with its stylish television and music systems. B&O describes its **positioning** as 'high quality but we are not Rolls-Royce—more BMW'. The company places emphasis on distinctive design, good quality and simplicity of use. Focused targeting means that B&O defies the conventional wisdom that a small manufacturer could not make profits marketing consumer electronics in Denmark (Gapper, 2005).

One form of focused marketing is to concentrate efforts on the relatively small percentage of customers that account for a disproportionately large share of sales of a product (the heavy buyers). For example, in some markets 20 per cent of customers account for 80 per cent of sales. Some companies aim at such a segment because it is so superficially attractive. Unfortunately, they may be committing the *majority fallacy* (Zikmund and D'Amico, 1999). The majority fallacy is the name given to the blind pursuit of the largest, most easily identified, market segment. It is a fallacy because that segment is the one that everyone in the past has recognized as the best segment and, therefore, it attracts the most intense competition. The result is likely to be high marketing expenditures, price cutting and low profitability. A more sensible strategy may be to target a small, seemingly less attractive, segment rather than choose the same customers that everyone else is after.

Customized marketing

In some markets, the requirements of individual customers are unique and their purchasing power sufficient to make designing a separate marketing mix for each customer viable. Segmentation at this disaggregated level leads to the use of **customized marketing**. Many service providers, such as advertising and marketing research agencies, architects and solicitors, vary their offerings on a customer-to-customer basis. They will discuss face-to-face with each customer their requirements and tailor their services accordingly. Customized marketing is also found within organizational markets, because of the high value of orders and the special needs of customers. Locomotive manufacturers design and build products to specifications given to them by individual rail transport providers. Customized marketing is often associated with close relationships between supplier and customer, in these circumstances because the value of the order justifies large marketing and sales efforts being focused on each buyer.

Positioning

So far our discussion has taken us through market segmentation and on to target market selection. The next step in developing an effective marketing strategy is to clearly position a product or service offering in the marketplace. Figure 7.9 summarizes the key tasks involved, and shows where **positioning** fits into the process.

Positioning is the choice of:

- *target market—where* we want to compete
- *differential advantage—how* we wish to compete.

Both of these elements of positioning should be considered in conjunction with customer needs. The objective is to create and maintain a distinctive place in the market for a company and/or its products.

Target market selection, then, has accomplished part of the positioning job already. But to compete successfully

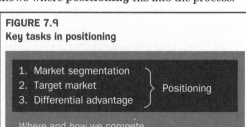

FIGURE 7.9
Key tasks in positioning

1. Market segmentation
2. Target market   } Positioning
3. Differential advantage

Where and *how* we compete

in a target market involves providing the customer with a differential advantage. This requires giving the target customer something better than the competition is offering. Creating a differential advantage is discussed in detail in Chapter 19. Briefly, it involves using the marketing mix to create something special for the customer. Product differentiation may result from added features that give customers benefits that rivals cannot match. Promotional differentiation may stem from unique, valued images created by advertising, or superior service provided by salespeople. Distribution differentiation may arise through making the buy situation more convenient for customers. Finally, price

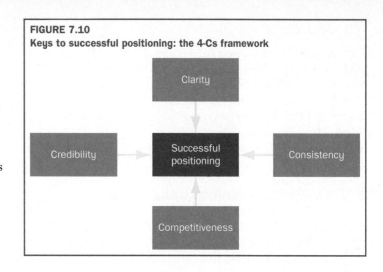

FIGURE 7.10
Keys to successful positioning: the 4-Cs framework

differentiation may involve giving superior value for money through lower prices.

A landmark book by Ries and Trout (2001) suggested that marketers are involved in a battle for the minds of target customers (Ries and Trout, 2001). Successful positioning is often associated with products possessing favourable connotations in the minds of customers. For example, Samsung is associated with high-technology, reliable and fashionable mobile phones. These add up to a differential advantage in the minds of its target customers whether they be in London, Amsterdam or Moscow. Similarly, the success of Cillit Bang has been based on its positioning of Cillit as the most powerful and versatile household cleaner on the market. Such positioning is hard won and relies on four factors, as shown in Figure 7.10 and listed below.

1 *Clarity*: the positioning idea must be clear in terms of both target market and differential advantage. Complicated positioning statements are unlikely to be remembered. Simple messages such as Walmart's 'always low prices' and Stella Artois' 'reassuringly expensive' are clear and memorable.

2 *Consistency*: people are bombarded with messages daily. To break through this noise a consistent message is required. Confusion will arise if this year marketers position on 'quality of service', then next year they change it to 'superior product performance'. Two examples of brands that have benefited from a consistent message being communicated to their target customers are Gillette ('the best a man can get') and L'Oréal ('because you're worth it'). Both receive high recall when consumers are researched because of the consistent use of a simple message over many years.

3 *Credibility*: the differential advantage that is chosen must be credible in the minds of the target customer. Nokia introduced the world to the smartphone and led the market with its Symbian series phones until 2007. But when Apple launched its iPhone with touch screen and app-based operating system, Nokia did not respond, and so the Symbian technology got older while the iPhone developed. The significant growth in demand for smartphones fuelled market growth, but Nokia lost credibility and market share due to its outdated technology platform (Chang, 2012).

4 *Competitiveness*: the differential advantage should have a competitive edge. It should offer something of value to the customer that the competition is failing to supply. For example, the success of the iPod was based on the differential advantage of seamless downloading of music from a dedicated music store, iTunes, to a mobile player that produced better sound quality than its rivals.

EXHIBIT 7.5
Glacéau appeals to members of its target audience by identifying their problems and providing solutions that match their preferences

Perceptual mapping

A useful tool for determining the position of a brand in the marketplace is the *perceptual map*—a visual representation of consumer perceptions of the brand and its competitors using attributes (dimensions) that are important to consumers. The key steps in developing a perceptual map are as follows.

1 Identify a set of competing brands.
2 Identify important attributes that consumers use when choosing between brands, using qualitative research (e.g. group discussions).
3 Conduct quantitative marketing research where consumers score each brand on all key attributes.
4 Plot brands on a two-dimensional map(s).

Figure 7.11 shows a perceptual map for seven supermarket chains. Qualitative marketing research has shown that consumers evaluate supermarkets on two key dimensions: price and width of product range. Quantitative marketing research is then carried out using scales that measure consumers' perception of each supermarket on these dimensions. Average scores are then plotted on a perceptual map.

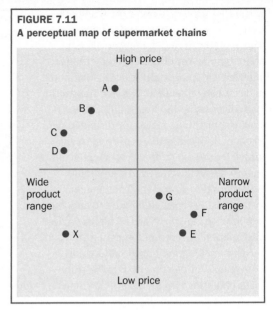

FIGURE 7.11
A perceptual map of supermarket chains

The results show that the supermarkets are grouped into two clusters: the high price, wide product range group, and the low price, narrow price range group. These are indicative of two market segments and show that supermarkets C and D are close rivals, as measured by consumers' perceptions, and have very distinct perceptual positions in the marketplace compared with E, F and G.

Perceptual maps are useful in considering strategic moves. For example, an opportunity may exist to create a differential advantage based on a combination of wide product range and low prices (as shown by the theoretical position at X).

Perceptual maps can also be valuable in identifying the strengths and weaknesses of brands as perceived by consumers. Such findings can be very revealing to managers, whose own perceptions may be very different from those of consumers. Consumers can also be asked to score their ideal position on each of the attributes so that actual and ideal positions can be compared.

Spidergram analysis

An alternative approach to perceptual mapping for understanding the position of a brand in the marketplace is spidergram analysis. (The author is indebted to Professor David Shipley, Trinity College, University of Dublin, for material used in the following description of spidergram analysis.) Like perceptual mapping, spidergram analysis provides a visual representation of consumer perceptions of the brand and its competitors using attributes (dimensions) that are important to consumers when evaluating those brands. However, spidergram analysis also asks consumers to rate the importance of the attributes, and their relative importance is represented visually by the length of the spoke on the spidergram.

The key steps are as follows.

1 Identify a set of competing brands.
2 Identify important attributes that consumers use when choosing between brands, using qualitative research (e.g. group discussions).
3 Conduct quantitative marketing research in which consumers:
   i) rate the importance of each attribute in their choice between brands on a 10-point scale
   ii) score each brand on all key attributes on a 10-point scale.
4 Plot brands on a spidergram.

Figure 7.12 shows a spidergram positioning map for the robotic systems market. The length of each spoke is proportional to the importance ratings of each attribute. Functionality is considered an essential attribute and has received a score of 10; the least important attribute is financing, scoring only 3. Each spoke is divided into 10 sections and each brand's score is plotted on each attribute. Our brand has received higher perceptual scores than its nearest competitor for functionality, customization, crisis help and delivery. Our brand and its nearest competitor are similarly rated for after-sales service, but for installation, price and financing, our nearest competitor is rated more highly. Since our company is rated more highly on those attributes that are more important to consumers, it is likely that our brand has a larger market share than its nearest competitor.

Like a perceptual map, spidergram analysis is valuable in identifying how consumers (as opposed to managers) perceive the strengths and weaknesses of competing brands. It provides a visual portrayal of the positions of brands along multiple dimensions. Spidergram software is available from the Aliah Corporation, USA, which permits the simultaneous analysis of up to six brands.

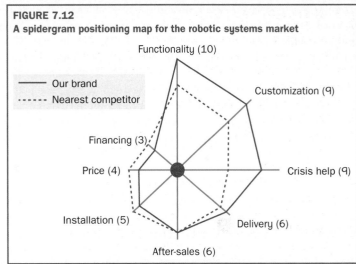

FIGURE 7.12
A spidergram positioning map for the robotic systems market

Functionality (10)

Customization (9)

—— Our brand
----- Nearest competitor

Financing (3)

Crisis help (9)

Price (4)

Installation (5)

Delivery (6)

After-sales (6)

Repositioning

Occasionally a product or service will need to be repositioned because of changing customer tastes or poor sales performance. **Repositioning** involves changing the target markets, the differential advantage, or both.

A useful framework for analyzing repositioning options is given in Figure 7.13. Using product differentiation and target market as the key variables, four generic repositioning strategies are shown.

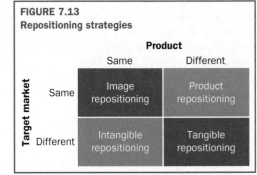

FIGURE 7.13
Repositioning strategies

	Product	
	Same	Different
Target market Same	Image repositioning	Product repositioning
Target market Different	Intangible repositioning	Tangible repositioning

Image repositioning

The first option is to keep product and target market the same but to change the image of the product. In markets where products act as a form of self-expression, the product may be acceptable in functional terms but fail because it lacks the required image. Many organizations—from McDonald's to low-cost airlines like Ryanair (Eletheriou-Smith, 2011) to giant industrial corporations like BASF, the German chemical company—have changed their image by altering business practices in order to be perceived as sustainable and environmentally friendly and better able to meet the needs of the target audience.

Product repositioning

With this strategy the product is changed while the target market remains the same. For example, IBM has used product repositioning very successfully by moving away from the manufacture of computers (IBM sold its PC division to Lenovo) to the provision of software and services to essentially the same type of business customers.

Intangible repositioning

This strategy involves targeting a different market segment with the same product. Beecham Foods initially targeted Lucozade, a carbonated drink, at sick children. But in the 1980s it was realized that the drink could become an everyday drink. So the strapline for its adverts changed from 'Lucozade aids recovery' to 'Lucozade replaces lost energy'. This shift allowed the product to be sold to new target markets. Since then Lucozade has successfully targeted the health drink and sports markets (Ward, 2009).

Tangible repositioning

When both product and target market are changed, a company is practising tangible repositioning. For example, a company may decide to move upmarket or downmarket by introducing a new range of products to meet the needs of the new target customers.

Highly successful tangible repositioning was undertaken by Samsung Electronics, which was once an unfocused manufacturer of cheap undifferentiated televisions and microwaves selling to all age groups and is now a premium-priced flat-screen television and mobile handset brand focused on, as we have seen, the 'high-life seeker' segment of the market—consumers who are willing to adopt technology early and pay a high price for it (Pesola, 2005).

Mercedes-Benz found it necessary to use tangible and product repositioning in the face of Japanese competition. Tangible repositioning took the form of developing new products (e.g. a city car) to appeal to new target customers. Product repositioning was also required in its current market segments to bring down the cost of development and manufacture in the face of lower-priced rivals such as Toyota's Lexus.

When you have read this chapter

Discover further resources and test your understanding: McGraw-Hill **Connect**™ is a digital teaching and learning environment that improves performance over a variety of critical outcomes; it can be tailored, is easy to use and is proven effective. **LearnSmart**™ is the most widely used and intelligent adaptive learning resource that is proven to strengthen memory recall, improve course retention and boost grades. Fuelled by **LearnSmart**™, **SmartBook**™ is the first and only adaptive reading experience available today.

Review

1 The concepts of market segmentation and target marketing and their use in developing marketing strategy
- Market segmentation is the identification of individuals or organizations with similar characteristics that have significant implications for the determination of marketing strategy.
- Its use aids target market selection, the ability to design a tailored marketing mix, the development of differential marketing strategies, and the identification of opportunities and threats.
- Target marketing is the choice of specific segment(s) to serve. It concerns the decision where to compete.
- Its use is focusing company resources on those segments it is best able to serve in terms of company resources and segment attractiveness. Once chosen, a tailored marketing mix that creates a differential advantage can be designed based on an in-depth understanding of target customers.

2 The methods of segmenting consumer and organizational markets
- Consumer markets can be segmented by behavioural (benefits sought, purchase occasion, purchase behaviour, usage, and perceptions and beliefs), psychographic (lifestyle and personality) and profile (demographic, socioeconomic and geographic) methods.
- Online markets are growing, and consideration of how demographic, behavioural and psychographic variables are affected by the online environment is required.
- Organizational markets can be segmented by macrosegmentation (organizational size, industry and geographic location) and microsegmentation (choice criteria, decision-making unit structure, decision-making process, buy class, purchasing organization, and organizational effectiveness) methods.

3 The factors that can be used to evaluate market segments
- Two broad issues should be used: market attractiveness and the company's capability to compete.
- Market attractiveness can be assessed by examining market factors (segment size, segment growth rate, price sensitivity, bargaining power of customers, bargaining power of suppliers, barriers to market segment

entry and barriers to market segment exit), competitive factors (nature of competition, the likelihood of new entrants, and competitive differentiation), and political, social and environmental factors (political issues, social trends and environmental issues).

- Capability to compete can be assessed by analyzing exploitable marketing assets, cost advantages, technological edge, and managerial capabilities and commitments.

4 Four target market strategies: undifferentiated, differentiated, focused and customized marketing
- Undifferentiated marketing occurs where a company does not segment but applies a single marketing mix to the whole market.
- Differentiated marketing occurs where a company segments the market and applies separate marketing mixes to appeal to all or some of the segments (target markets).
- Focused marketing occurs where a company segments the market and develops one specific marketing mix to one segment (target market).
- Customized marketing occurs where a company designs a separate marketing mix for each customer.

5 The concept of positioning and the keys to successful positioning
- There are two aspects of positioning: the choice of target market (where to compete) and the creation of a differential advantage (how to compete).
- The objective is to create and maintain a distinctive place in the market for a company and/or its products.
- The four keys to successful positioning are: clarity, consistency, credibility and competitiveness.

6 Positioning and repositioning strategies
- A useful tool for determining the position of a brand in the marketplace is the perceptual map.
- Positioning strategy should be based on a clear choice of target market based on market segment attractiveness and company capability, and the creation of a differential advantage (based on an understanding of the attributes—choice criteria—that consumers use when choosing between brands).
- Repositioning strategies can be based on changes to the product and/or target market. Four strategies are image repositioning, product repositioning, intangible repositioning and tangible repositioning.

Key Terms

benefit segmentation the grouping of people based on the different benefits they seek from a product

customized marketing the market coverage strategy where a company decides to target individual customers and develops separate marketing mixes for each

differential marketing strategies market coverage strategies where a company decides to target several market segments and develops separate marketing mixes for each

differentiated marketing a market coverage strategy where a company decides to target several market segments and develops separate marketing mixes for each

focused marketing a market coverage strategy where a company decides to target one market segment with a single marketing mix

lifestyle segmentation the grouping of people according to their pattern of living as expressed in their activities, interests and opinions

macrosegmentation the segmentation of organizational markets by size, industry and location

market segmentation the process of identifying individuals or organizations with similar characteristics that have significant implications for the determination of marketing strategy

microsegmentation segmentation according to choice criteria, DMU structure, decision-making process, buy class, purchasing structure and organizational innovativeness

positioning the choice of target market (where the company wishes to compete) and differential advantage (how the company wishes to compete)

profile segmentation the grouping of people in terms of profile variables, such as age and socio-economic group, so that marketers can communicate to them

psychographic segmentation the grouping of people according to their lifestyle and personality characteristics

repositioning changing the target market or differential advantage, or both

target marketing the choice of which market segment(s) to serve with a tailored marketing mix

undifferentiated marketing a market coverage strategy where a company decides to ignore market segment differences and develops a single marketing mix for the whole market

Study Questions

1. What are the advantages of market segmentation? Can you see any advantages of mass marketing, that is of treating a market as homogeneous and marketing to the whole market with one marketing mix?

2. Choose a market you are familiar with and use benefit segmentation to identify market segments. What are the likely profiles of the resulting segments?

3. In what kind of markets is psychographic segmentation likely to prove useful? Why?

4. How might age affect online market segmentation?

5. Explain how you might select segmentation variables when aiming to access online markets.

6. Discuss the difficulties you might encounter when segmenting organizational markets.

7. Why is buy class a potentially useful method of segmenting organizational markets? (Use both this chapter and Chapter 4 when answering this question.)

8. What is the majority fallacy? Why should it be taken into account when evaluating market segments?

9. What is the difference between positioning and repositioning? Choose three products and services and describe how they are positioned in the marketplace—that is, what is their target market and what is their differential advantage?

Recommended Reading

Cova, B. and V. Cova (2002) Tribal marketing: The tribalisation of society and its impact on the conduct of marketing, *European Journal of Marketing* 36(5/6), 595–620.

Experian fashion segments (2015) http://www.experian.co.uk/assets/business-strategies/brochures/fashion_segments_handbook_females_small[1].pdf

Experian Financial Segments (2015) http://www.experian.co.uk/assets/business-strategies/brochures/financial-strategy-segments-factsheet.pdf

Experian Mosaic (2015) http://www.experian.co.uk/marketing-services/products/mosaic/mosaic-resources.html

Fromm, J. and C. Garton (2013) *Marketing to Millennials*, London: McGraw Hill Higher Education.

Richardson, B. (2013) Tribal Marketing, *Tribal Branding: An Expert Guide to the Brand Co-creation Process*, UK: Palgrave Macmillan.

References

Abell, D. F. and J. S. Hammond (1979) *Strategic Market Planning: Problems and Analytical Approaches*, Hemel Hempstead: Prentice-Hall

ACORN CACI (2014) *The User Guide: The Consumer Classification*. London. http://acorn.caci.co.uk/downloads/Acorn-User-guide.pdf (accessed 17 March 2015).

Barnett, M. (2011) Hi-tech healthcare, *Marketing Week*, 30 June, 14–17.

Bearne, S. (2015) How Gap Failed to fill a gap in the fashion market, *Retail week*, 30 January. http://www.retail-week.com/sectors/fashion/analysis-how-gap-failed-to-fill-a-gap-in-the-fashion-market/5071599.article?blocktitle=Zara:-Latest-news-and-insight&contentID=9719 (accessed 28 February 2015).

Brashear, T. G., V. Kashyap, M. D. Musante and N. Donthu (2009) A profile of the internet shopper: evidence from six countries, *Journal of Marketing Theory and Practice* 17(3), 267–81.

Brownsell, A. (2011) Toyota targets young drivers in £7.5m push, *Marketing Magazine*, 10 August, 3.

Brynjolfsson, E., Y. J. Hu and D. Simester (2011) Goodbye Pareto Principle, Hello Long Tail: the effect of search costs on the concentration of product sales, *Management Science* 57(8), 1373–86.

Cattermole, G. (2012) Sainsbury's boosted by Christmas food sales growth, http://www.guardian.co.uk/business/2012/jan/11/sainsburys-christmas-food-sales.

Chang, A. (2012) *5 Reasons why Nokia Lost its Handset Sales Lead and Got Downgraded to 'Junk'*, Wired, 27 April. http://www.wired.com/2012/04/5-reasons-why-nokia-lost-its-handset-sales-lead-and-got-downgraded-to-junk (accessed 6 March 2015).

Chisnall, P. (2005) *Marketing Research*, Maidenhead: McGraw-Hill.

Chorley, M. and J. Rentoul (2011) Seven in 10 of us belong to middle class Britain, *The Independent on Sunday*, 20 March, 13–17.

Corey, R. (1978) *The Organisational Context of Industrial Buying Behavior*, Cambridge, MA: Marketing Science Institute, 6–12.

Cova, B. and V. Cova (2002) Tribal marketing: The tribalisation of society and its impact on the conduct of marketing. *European Journal of Marketing 36*(5), 595–620.

Davis, A. (2014) Cut-throat competition grips smartphone market, *The Telegraph*, 28 July. http://www.telegraph.co.uk/sponsored/finance/macroeconomics-investment/10995602/cutthroat-competition-grips-smartphone-market.html (accessed 10 March 2015).

Day, G. S. (1986) *Analysis for Strategic Market Decisions*, New York: West.

Dixon, P. (2005) Wake up to stronger tribes and longer life, *Financial Times*, 31 October http://www.globalchange.com/financialtimesdixonfeature31oct2005.pdf (accessed 7 April 2012).

Doherty, N. F. and F. Ellis-Chadwick (2010a) Evaluating the role of electronic commerce in transforming the retail sector, *The International Review of Retail, Distribution and Consumer Research* 20(4), 375–378.

Doherty, N. F. and F. Ellis-Chadwick (2010b) Internet retailing: the past, the present and the future, *International Journal of Retail & Distribution Management* 38, 11/12, 943–65.

Doyle, P. (2008) *Value-Based Marketing*, John Wiley & Sons.

Edwards, H. (2011) Sixty is the new old, *Marketing Magazine*, 9 November, 19.

Eletheriou-Smith, L.-M. (2011) Ryanair signal brand U-turn with eco-claims, *Marketing*, 27 July, 1.

Experian (2015) *Mosaic United Kingdom*, http://cld.bz/RUfDTGu

Fleet News (2015) *Michelin Cross Climate tyres will be a 'game-changer' for UK fleets, says ATS Euromaster*, FleetNews, 16 March. https://www.fleetnews.co.uk/news/2015/3/16/michelin-cross-climate-tyres-will-be-a-game-changer-for-uk-fleets-says-ats-euromaster/55157

Fyndiq (2014) *'Amazon for bargain products' Fyndiq reaches break-even, over 200 000 products sold in December*, Mynewsdesk, 30 January. http://www.mynewsdesk.com/se/fyndiq/pressreleases/amazon-for-bargain-products-fyndiq-reaches-break-even-over-200-000-products-sold-in-december-955282

Gapper, J. (2005) When High Fidelity Becomes High Fashion, *Financial Times*, 20 December, 11.

Handley, L. (2011) Original teenagers kick segmentation into touch, *Marketing Week*, 1 December, 18–19.

Hilpern, K. (2011) An ageless strategy, *The Marketer*, November/December, 28–31.

Hoffman, D. L., T. P. Novak and A. Schlosser (2003) The evolution of the digital divide: how gaps in internet access may impact electronic commerce, in C. Steinfield (ed.) *New Directions in Research on E-Commerce*, West Lafayette, IN: Purdue University Press, 245–292.

Hooley, G. J., J. Saunders, N. Piercy and B. Nicoulaud (2012) *Marketing Strategy and Competitive Positioning: The Key to Market Success*, Hemel Hempstead: Prentice-Hall, 148.

Howe, N. (2014) *Generation X: Once Xtreme, Now Exhausted*, 27 August. http://www.forbes.com/sites/neilhowe/2014/08/27/generation-x-once-xtreme-now-exhausted-part-5-of-7 (accessed 12 March 2015).

Jack, L. (2009) Cleaning Up Its Act, *Marketing Week*, 12 February, 21.

Jayawardhena, C., L. T. Wright and C. Dennis (2007) Consumers online: intentions, orientations and segmentation, *International Journal of Retail & Distribution Management* 35(6), 512–26.

Kantar Media (2012) TGI Europa, http://kantarmedia-tgigb.com/tgi-surveys/tgi-europa/.

Keely, G. and A. Clark (2008) Zara overtakes Gap to become world's largest clothing retailer, *The Guardian*, 11 August. http://www.theguardian.com/business/2008/aug/11/zara.gap.fashion (accessed 10 March 2015).

Kimmel, A. J. (2010) *Connecting with consumers: marketing for new marketplaces realties*, Oxford University Press, 15–19.

KPMG (2013) *How will demographic trends affect the retail sector?* KPMG http://www.kpmg.com/uk/en/issuesandinsights/articlespublications/newsreleases/pages/how-will-demographic-trends-in-the-uk-affect-the-retail-sector.aspx (accessed 23 February 2015).

Kukar-Kinney, M., N. M. Ridgway and K. B. Monroe (2009) The relationship between consumers' tendencies to buy compulsively and their motivations to shop and buy on the internet, *Journal of Retailing* 85(3), 298.

Lannon, J. (1991) Developing Brand Strategies across Borders, *Marketing and Research Today*, August, 160–8.

Lunden, I. (2014) *Fyndiq Raises $20M To Take Its Bargain Marketplace Beyond Sweden*, Techcrunch, 7 November. http://techcrunch.com/2014/11/07/fyndiq-raises-20m-to-take-its-bargain-marketplace-beyond-sweden (accessed 15 March 2015).

Millward Brown (2015) *Brand Personality*, MillwardBrown, 20 March. http://www.millwardbrown.com/mb-global/brand-strategy/brand-equity/brandz/top-global-brands/previous-years-results/2012-brandz-top-100/brand-personality

Moore, J. (2011) No fly-by-night firm but Thomas Cook can't afford to trip up in appeal to lenders, *The Independent*, 23 November, http://www.independent.co.uk/news/business/comment/jamesmoore-no-flybynight-firm-but-thomas-cook-cant-afford-to-trip-up-inappeal-to-lenders-6266321.html.

Muller, R. (2011) Target China, *The Marketer*, July/August, 32–5.

O'Brien, S. and R. Ford (1988) Can We at Last Say Goodbye to Social Class?, *Journal of the Market Research Society* 30(3), 289–332.

Pesola, M. (2005) Samsung plays to the young generation, *Financial Times*, 29 March, 11.

Plank, R. E. (1985) A Critical Review of Industrial Market Segmentation, *Industrial Marketing Management* 14, 79–91.

Prensky, M. (2001) Digital Natives, Digital Immigrants, *On the Horizon* 9(5), 1–6.

Ries, A. and J. Trout (2001) *Positioning: The Battle for your Mind*, New York: Warner.

Ritson, M. (2011) Know when to shut the door on your customer, *Marketing Week*, 25 August, 50.

Rochon, M.-E. (2014) Conversation with Fanny Karst, young designer but old lady at heart, La Passerelle, 6 May. http://lapasserellemontreal.com/2014/05/06/conversation-with-fanny-karst-young-designer-but-old-lady-at-heart/#sthash.6FrqL5ui.dpuf (accessed 12 March 2015).

Rose, S. (2008) There Are Plenty of Reasons Why Britain Still Loves M&S, *Guardian*, 25 January, 41.

Sampson, P. (1992) People are People the World Over: The Case for Psychological Market Segmentation, *Marketing and Research Today*, November, 236–44.

Shui, E. and J. Dawson (2004) Comparing the Impacts of Technology and National Culture on Online Usage and Purchase from a Four-Country Perspective, *Journal of Retailing and Consumer Services* 11(6), 385–94.

Simms, J. (2005) Strategising Simplicity, *Marketing*, 25 May, 15.

Slyke, C. V., C. L. Comunale and F. Belanger (2002) Gender differences in perceptions of Web-based shopping, *Communications of the ACM* 45(7), 82–86.

Smith, C. (2014) 7 Statistics About E-Commerce Shoppers That Reveal Why Many Consumer Stereotypes Don't Apply Online, Business Insider, 13 August. http://www.businessinsider.com/the-demographics-of-who-shops-online-and-on-mobile-2014-8?IR=T

Smith, G. (2008) On The Road, *Guardian Weekend*, 21 June, 99.

Swaminathan, V., E. Lepkowska-White and B. P. Rao (1999) Browsers or buyers in cyberspace? An investigation of factors influencing electronic exchange, *Journal of Computer-Mediated Communication* 5(2), 1–19.

Tata Motors (2009) The story of the Nano, http://www.tatanano.com.

Trendwatching.com (2004) 'Generation' [url] from p. 217 *Independent* (2009), Unboxing: The new geek porn [url]

Tynan, A. C. and J. Drayton (1987) Market Segmentation, *Journal of Marketing Management* 2(3), 301–35.

United Airlines (2012) www.united.com.

Van Raaij, W. F. and T. M. M. Verhallen (1994) Domain-specific Market Segmentation, *European Journal of Marketing* 28(10), 49–66.

Veloutsou, C. and Moutinho, L. (2009) Brand relationships through brand reputation and brand tribalism, *Journal of Business Research* 62(3), 314–22.

Wachman. (2012) Lego's profits rise as it thinks pink, *The Guardian*, 1 March. http://www.theguardian.com/business/2012/mar/01/lego-profits-rise-pink

Wallop, H. (2014) Gen Z, Gen Y, baby boomers—a guide to the generations, *The Telegraph*. http://www.telegraph.co.uk/news/features/11002767/Gen-Z-Gen-Y-baby-boomers-a-guide-to-the-generations.html (accessed 12 March 2015).

Ward, L. (2009) The history of Lucozade, TheFactSite. http://www.thefactsite.com/2009/03/history-of-lucozade.html

Wieners, B. (2011) Lego is for girls, *Bloomberg Business Week*, 19 December, 68–73.

Wind, Y. (1978) Issues and Advances in Segmentation Research, *Journal of Marketing Research*, August, 317–37.

Wind, Y. and R. N. Cardozo (1974) Industrial Market Segmentation, *Industrial Marketing Management* 3, 153–66.

Zikmund, W. G. and M. D'Amico (1999) *Marketing*, St Paul, MN: West, 249.

CASE 13
Utilization of Loyalty Card Data for Segmentation—Morelli's Story

With over 100 years of trading in Northern Ireland, selling ice cream is by no means new to the Morelli family (see Table C13.1). Morelli's award-winning ice cream business has a unique heritage, symbolizing a long history of migration, romance, war, and strong Italian family values. First established in 1911 with a café parlour in Coleraine, by 1914 the business had quickly blossomed, expanding to meet demand with similar premises opening in Portstewart and Portrush on the north coast of Ireland. The years of achievement rolled on, and by 2001 four generations of the Morelli family had successfully developed and passed on an ever-growing selection of their award-winning ice creams. However, Morelli's success was inextricably linked to the ice cream parlours, and the goal to develop the brand as a take-home ice cream was yet to be achieved.

TABLE C13.1 Overview of Morelli's ice cream business

Overview of Morelli's ice cream	
Category	• Artisan Italian ice cream specialist.
Established	• Morelli's has been making ice cream in Ireland since 1911.
History	• Originally from Frosinone, near Rome, Peter Morelli came to Northern Ireland at the end of the 19th century.
	• In 1911, six years after he began selling the ice cream from a handcart around the seaside town of Portstewart, County Londonderry, he opened the first Italian ice cream parlour.
	• Another branch of the family own and run a Morelli ice cream parlour in Broadstairs in Kent. The same family also franchise in the Middle East and have also recently opened a parlour at London's Covent Garden.
Unique selling proposition	• Family-owned and family-run business.
	• Secret family recipe.
	• Synonymous with high-quality scoop ice cream.
Wholesale and retail market outlets	• Family-owned ice cream parlours (Portrush, Portstewart, Cookstown & Ballycastle)
	• Franchise stores over Ireland (Portaferry, Garvagh, Belfast, Newcastle and Balbriggan, Co. Dublin)
	• Retail: Tesco, Sainsburys, Asda, Mace, Supervalu, Spar & Costcutter

»

≫

Overview of Morelli's ice cream	
Awards won	• National Ice Cream Competitions 2015: 1st Prize Gold medal and the Silver Challenge Cup in Ice Cream Open Class Dairy Vanilla • Great Taste Awards 2014: 2 Stars for Cherry Frozen Yogurt, 1 Star for Rhubarb & Custard and 1 Star for Sea Salty Caramel • National Ice Cream Competitions 2014: 1st Prize Gold medal and the Silver Challenge Cup in Ice Cream Open Class Dairy Vanilla • Champion of Champions status for Best Vanilla Ice Cream UK and Ireland 2012. • Great Taste Awards 2011: 1 Star for Morelli's Double Cream Vanilla Ice Cream; 1 Star for Morelli's Cheesecake Ice Cream with Blueberries and Biscuit Crumb. • 2009 National Ice Cream Competition: Silver Challenge Cup in the Dairy Artisan category; Diploma in the Champion of Champions for Vanilla flavour; Diplomas of Merit in the Ice Cream Open, Chocolate and Raspberry Ripple categories; Diploma in the Pistachio flavour category.
Product portfolio	• Over 80 sumptuous and innovative flavours using only the finest Italian natural flavours, pastes and fruit extracts. Additional ingredients are sourced from all over the world.

Source: http://www.morellisices.com

Retail to wholesale

In 1997 Arnaldo Morelli, the fourth generation of the Morelli family to run the business, saw an opportunity to develop the wholesale side of the business. The expansion of wholesale trade enabled Morelli's to maintain sales volume year round while appealing to consumers across Northern Ireland.

Morelli-branded take-home tubs were introduced into Tesco stores across Northern Ireland in 2006. With distinctive product attributes, a strong business heritage and the Italian family brand name, the scope for opportunity within the competitive take-home ice cream category at Tesco is relatively vast. Yet, the challenge faced by Arnaldo Morelli in 2006 was also vast, as Morelli's strived to meet the needs and wants of both the new customer, Tesco, and the new consumer, the Tesco shopper. Morelli's had to

re-evaluate its pricing strategy within Tesco, decide on core product flavours to stock and assess the appropriateness of promotions, all in order to build a strong awareness of the brand as a take-home product, and to gain a loyal consumer base, while trying to compete successfully for share of the consumer's wallet, and for maintenance of its shelf position within the retailer, with good sales and no product wastage.

In order to address these challenges, Morelli was among the first companies in Northern Ireland to gain free consumer insight into Tesco's loyalty card data. This data has been managed by leading marketing consultancy firm Dunnhumby Ltd since 1995 (Humby, Hunt and Phillips, 2007), who are responsible for translating billions of data points from Tesco customers' shopping baskets every week into detailed insight into shopper behaviour and lifestyles (Anstead, Samuel and Crofton, 2008) (see Table C13.2).

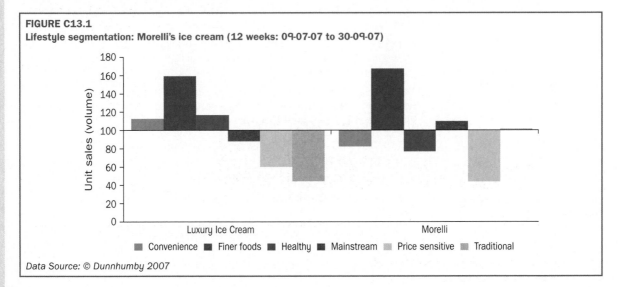

FIGURE C13.1
Lifestyle segmentation: Morelli's ice cream (12 weeks: 09-07-07 to 30-09-07)

Data Source: © Dunnhumby 2007

TABLE C13.2 Lifestyle segmentation (2007)		
Lifestyle Segment	**Shoppers (%)**	**Key characteristics**
Finer foods	16	Affluent shoppers who enjoy luxury products and premium brands and who typically like to cook from scratch.
Convenience	22	11% affluent shoppers who are time poor but food rich. 11% mid-market shoppers who can't cook and won't cook.
Mainstream	25	Mainstream shoppers typically purchase mid-price brands and driven by kids' choice.
Healthy	10	Mainstream shoppers who typically count the calories and make healthy choices.
Traditional	11	Less affluent shoppers who shop for value and who typically like to cook from scratch.
Price-sensitive	16	Price-conscious shoppers likely to be on a lower income, stretching the budget and in search of the cheapest products.

Source: Dunnhumby (2009)

Getting to Know the Consumer

In 2007, Dunnhumby data identified that the type of Tesco shopper most likely to buy Morelli's ice cream in a take-home pack fell into the older families and younger families life stages category. The data also identified that Morelli's had a stronger appeal amongst finer foods and traditional shoppers[1] than luxury ice cream and under-performed amongst healthy shoppers,[2] confirming indulgence status (see analysis below).

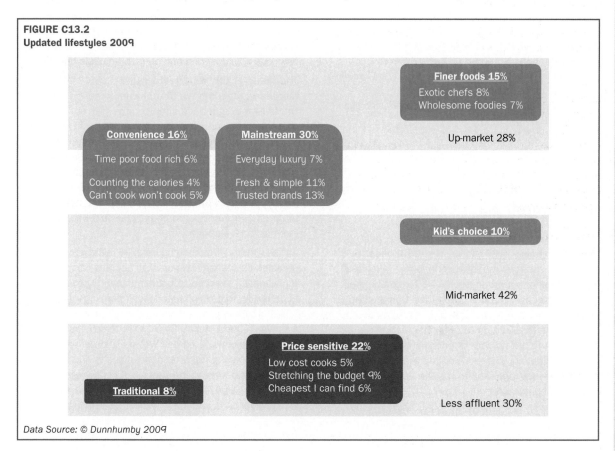

FIGURE C13.2
Updated lifestyles 2009

Finer foods 15%
Exotic chefs 8%
Wholesome foodies 7%

Up-market 28%

Convenience 16%
Time poor food rich 6%
Counting the calories 4%
Can't cook won't cook 5%

Mainstream 30%
Everyday luxury 7%
Fresh & simple 11%
Trusted brands 13%

Kid's choice 10%

Mid-market 42%

Price sensitive 22%
Low cost cooks 5%
Stretching the budget 9%
Cheapest I can find 6%

Traditional 8%

Less affluent 30%

Data Source: © Dunnhumby 2009

[1]Stronger appeal demonstrated on the Y-axis of 100 to 180.

[2]Under-performance demonstrated on the X-axis of 100 to 0.

»

»

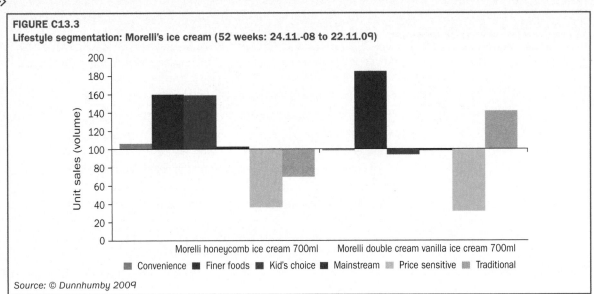

FIGURE C13.3
Lifestyle segmentation: Morelli's ice cream (52 weeks: 24.11.-08 to 22.11.09)

Source: © Dunnhumby 2009

On the strength of this lifestyle insight, Arnaldo decided to develop brand loyalty amongst the finer foods shopper, recognizing that this segment was a key target group for Morelli's to increase sales and maintain this in the long term.

> 'The more I looked at the dunnhumby data, it showed me that the people who are buying our ice cream aren't the people who want a bargain... so that really told me that I don't really want to be on promotion... I want to try and establish our ice cream with customers who will be loyal to our brand.'

(Arnaldo Morelli)

Evolving Nature of the Consumer

In 2009, the lifestyles segmentation was updated from the existing 2007 profile in order to meet the significant changes within the economy, Tesco and the Tesco shopper group itself. The Tesco shopper had changed over the five years, and Dunnhumby decided to replace less significant lifestyles and move certain lifestyles into more detailed lifestyle groups. The growth in the number of price-sensitive customers needed reflecting, and more detail was placed on the mainstream customer, as it was the largest proportion of Tesco's customers.

Comprising 10 per cent of the Tesco market, kids choice shoppers are strongly influenced by their children, shop frequently and take advantage of promotions. With this new change in lifestyle segmentation, Arnaldo required further insight into the Morelli products to remain in tune with the consumer lifestyle segmentation.

Insight into Morelli's Lifestyle Segmentation

Lifestyle segmentation analysis completed on the two types of Morelli offerings within Tesco Northern Ireland (after the update in lifestyle segmentation in 2009) revealed extremely informative insight as a result of the new kids choice segmentation (see analysis below).

The result of this report illustrated the demand for Morelli Honeycomb Ice Cream was driven by both the finer foods and kids choice lifestyle, but under-performed in traditional shoppers. Although the finer foods and traditional shopper over-performed in Morelli Double Cream Vanilla Ice Cream, the demand from kids choice shoppers was less significant. By understanding actual lifestyles for each product, Arnaldo Morelli received in-depth understanding of consumer lifestyle segmentation to aid further business developments.

Armed with this Dunnhumby data, Morelli's worked to redesign its packaging in order to address issues of functionality, to reinforce brand authenticity and, most importantly, to develop brand loyalty amongst its desired target group: finer foods and traditional shoppers. This was also an opportunity for Morelli's to develop new packaging alongside its new website in order to sell its amazing family story. After generations of successfully engaging and winning the support of consumers through its parlours, Morelli's wanted to be able to share its story with a wider consumer base within their family homes.

Successful Targeting of Morelli Ice Cream In Store

New packaging arrived in Tesco stores in late 2010. It took almost a year before Arnaldo could be sure

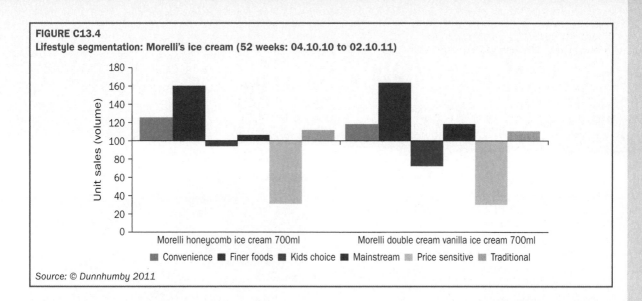

FIGURE C13.4
Lifestyle segmentation: Morelli's ice cream (52 weeks: 04.10.10 to 02.10.11)

Source: © Dunnhumby 2011

whether the new packaging and focused positioning of the product had successfully achieved in gaining loyalty amongst the finer foods and traditional shopper (see Figure C13.4).

This report illustrated the change in consumer purchasing for the Morelli Honeycomb Ice Cream from the kid's choice shopper to the traditional shopper. This change is aligned with the more focused targeting by Morelli's in developing brand loyalty amongst the finer foods and traditional shoppers who value heritage and quality over price.

Morelli's Continues to Innovate

Despite investing significant time and money on repackaging in 2010, Morelli's continues to listen to the market and embrace change. Market information continues to be a key business tool as Morelli's moves forward to meet new challenges in its 104th year in business. With insight and experience built on over a century of selling ice cream on the island of Ireland, and today gaining insight into real consumer purchasing behaviour, Morelli's continues to compete in a highly competitive ice cream market against all the big players, from Ben & Jerry's to Haagen Daaz. Change continues to bring new ideas and new offerings to the market.

Based on market information, Morelli's introduced a new offering of its best-selling flavours in two different sizes of eye-catchingly packaged, pre-filled cartons. These included individual-sized 140 millilitre spoon-in-lid pots and 750 millilitre take-home packs to address the needs of consumers today, who purchase

ice cream for different occasions. With a constant finger on the pulse of the current consumer, Arnaldo Morelli feels confident in the future of the business and in his role in ensuring that many more Morelli generations to come will continue in the ice cream business!

Questions

1. **What key challenges did Morelli's face in bringing its product to retail?**

2. **How does segmentation benefit the marketing strategy of Morelli's ice cream?**

3. **Develop a consumer segmentation basis for Morelli's ice cream.**

This case was written by Christina O'Connor, Lecturer in Marketing, Maynooth University and Gillian Armstrong, Head of Department of Accounting, Finance and Economics, University of Ulster.

References

Based on: Humby, C., T. Hunt and T. Phillips (2007) *Scoring Points: How Tesco continues to win customer loyalty*, 2nd edition, London & Philadelphia: Kogan Page, 51–6; Anstead, J., J. Samuel and A. Crofton (2008) dunnhumby—A Retailer's Secret Weapon, Citigroup Global Market, *Feeders Digest* 60, 6–25; Dunnhumby (2009) Quick Guide—What's Changing with Lifestyles? (December).

Segmentation and Product Lines: The LEGO Case

LEGO, the Danish toy manufacturer of plastic building bricks, has a large website that is translated into 17 languages across 23 different markets. Most of LEGO's 30 product lines have their own microsites with apps, games, downloads and even display sections for builders' own models—a good alignment with the needs of the digitally able generation. However, only one product line, LEGO Duplo, has external links to social media such as Facebook, Twitter and Pinterest on the product line microsite. At the other extreme, the LEGO Architecture microsite contains only images of the current range, and information about the original buildings. So why is LEGO moving its online presence away from an exclusive focus on Web 2.0 on most of the product line microsites to include the social media for one customer segment, and back to more traditional 'Web 1.0' marketing for another? This case looks at why demographic segmentation criteria are not enough; behavioural and psychological segmentation also have a role to play in reaching out to target consumers.

The LEGO Duplo and LEGO Architecture Product Lines

LEGO Duplo bricks are designed to be used by young children, in the age range two to five years. The LEGO Duplo bricks are only found in the range of sets that make up the LEGO Duplo product line, and focus on themes that pre-school children can relate to, such as animals, food and the circus. LEGO Duplo bricks are also much larger than the standard LEGO bricks, making it easier for the youngest children to build creatively without the need for the fine motor skills that older children have.

The LEGO Architecture product line, on the other hand, is primarily targeted towards the adult segment. Standard LEGO bricks are used to build scale models of famous buildings such as the Eiffel Tower, the White House and the Sydney Opera House. Only one LEGO Architecture product encourages independent creativity, containing white bricks and a booklet explaining the principles of modernist architecture, developed in conjunction with architectural design bureaus from around the world.

Target Segments

The majority of LEGO's main website focuses on reaching out to school children up to the age of about 14, and emphasizes interaction and the co-creation of content through the ability to upload the builder's own models to forums.

The LEGO Duplo and LEGO Architecture microsites are fundamentally different, as both of these microsites focus on adults. On entering the British LEGO Duplo microsite (http://www.lego.com/en-gb/duplo) of lego.com, a pop-up window displays the text:

'LEGO.com/DUPLO is a website for parents—moms and dads who want to know more about LEGO® DUPLO®. This website is made for grownups and contains links off LEGO.com to app stores and social media services.'

This pop-up window is unique to the LEGO Duplo microsite; for comparison, the microsite of LEGO Junior, a product line that targets the four- to seven-year-old segment, has no pop-up window and no offsite links to social media, despite being aimed mostly at parents. It makes sense to reach out to adults through the social media using mobile devices, as the majority of adults are constantly online and have a high consumption of social media, especially Facebook and Pinterest, using a variety of devices. Whilst pre-schoolers do not understand the Internet in the same way as their parents do and do not have the fine motor skills to use a mouse, they can use tablets and smartphones due to the intuitive user interface of these mobile devices which, coupled with the high level of consumption by parents, makes the mobile platform ideal.

In contrast, a key aim of the LEGO Architecture product line is to entice adults back to building with LEGO bricks, as LEGO tends to 'lose' builders after the age of about 14. Rather than focusing on themes that may be seen as childish by some, its aim is building a scale model of a famous structure. The target segment for LEGO Architecture understands the web in the same way as the LEGO Duplo target segment does; however, the value that needs to be provided by the LEGO Architecture microsite is different.

Segmentation, Value, and the LEGO Duplo and LEGO Architecture Microsites

From a market segmentation perspective, a key difference between the LEGO Duplo and LEGO Architecture product lines on the one hand, and LEGO's other product lines on the other, are the segmentation criteria that are used. Instead of targeting children, LEGO targets parents, with the core demographic characteristics being individuals who are middle class, middle income and between the ages of 25 and 40. Behavioural and psychological segmentation criteria are used to understand the needs of adults. The key value proposition that is provided by both the LEGO Duplo and LEGO Architecture microsites is information. The information on the LEGO Duplo microsite details how the building bricks can be used to support child development, with text boxes providing information to parents about general child development in the first five years of their child's life, and shows how LEGO Duplo can contribute to this development using colours, shapes and language. LEGO also underlines on the Duplo microsite how building with the bricks can improve fine motor skills and provide a way for children to express themselves and use their imagination. The value provided on the LEGO Architecture microsite for customers consists of information about the buildings themselves—the architect, the building and its history—together with details of the process through which a LEGO Architecture model is developed and realized.

Conclusion: Segmentation and Online Marketing

The LEGO Duplo and LEGO Architecture microsites have a different target segment to the other LEGO microsites: adults rather than children. This provides LEGO with a challenge: how can the product line microsites address the needs of adults rather than children? The answer lies in enabling those in the target segment to receive the most important content in the format that they gain the most value from. In the case of LEGO Duplo, this means optimizing content to focus on the social media through mobile devices; in the case of LEGO Architecture, information about the real-world building that inspired the model. So even though both microsites target the same demographic segment—adults—behavioural and psychological segmentation criteria enable LEGO to identify and add extra value on the product line microsites.

Questions

1. **Do you think that LEGO targets the right segment with its LEGO Duplo microsite? Can you think of any other segments that the focus on social media might miss? What about the LEGO Architecture microsite?**

2. **Look on the websites of other toy manufacturers. What do these toy manufacturers do to engage parents? Do they do anything at all?**

3. **How can LEGO ensure a smooth transition from how parents and children interact with the Duplo range to the LEGO ranges targeted to older children?**

4. **Marketing today focuses on the co-creation of value. Is LEGO right to take a more traditional approach to the online marketing of the LEGO Architecture product line? What is the added value of the LEGO Architecture microsite?**

This case study was written by Robert Ormrod, Associate Professor, Aarhus University.

References

The material in the case has been drawn from a variety of published sources.

PART 2
CREATING CUSTOMER VALUE

A number of videos featuring CEOs, CMOs, brand and PR managers related to the Chapters in this Part are available to lecturers for presentation and class discussion.

McGraw Hill Education **connect®**

CHAPTER 8
Value Through Brands

> *The first lesson of branding is memorability. It is very difficult to buy something you can't remember.*
> **JOHN HEGARTY, CREATIVE DIRECTOR, BBH (HEGARTY, 2011)**

LEARNING OBJECTIVES

After reading this chapter, you should be able to:

1 define the concepts of product, brand, product line and product mix

2 distinguish between manufacturer and own-label brands

3 distinguish between a core and augmented product (the brand)

4 explain why strong brands are important

5 define brand equity, the components of customer-based and proprietary-based brand equity and brand valuation

6 explain how to build strong brands

7 distinguish between family, individual and combined brand names, and discuss the characteristics of an effective brand name

8 discuss why companies rebrand and explain how to manage the process

9 discuss the concepts of brand extension and stretching, and their uses and limitations

10 describe the two major forms of co-branding, and their advantages and risks

11 discuss the arguments for and against global and pan-European branding, and the strategic options for building such brands

12 discuss ethical issues concerning products

M arketing success goes beyond merely satisfying customer needs. Brand manufacturers have to consider ways to focus market opportunities, using their customers' values. In this chapter we focus on value creation from the perspective of brands.

The core element in the marketing mix is the company's product because this provides the functional requirements sought by customers. Marketing managers develop their products into brands that help to create a unique position (see Chapter 7) in the minds of customers. Brand superiority leads to high sales, the ability to charge price premiums and the power to resist distributor power. Firms attempt to retain their current customers through brand loyalty. Loyal customers are typically less price sensitive, and the presence of a loyal customer base provides the firm with valuable time to respond to competitive actions (DeKimpe et al., 1997). The management of products and brands is therefore a key factor in marketing success.

This chapter will explore the nature and importance of branding, how successful brands are built and how brand equity is created. Then we explore a series of key branding decisions: brand name strategies and choices, rebranding, brand extension and stretching, and co-branding. The chapter then explores global and pan-European branding. The chapter concludes by exploring ethical issues associated with branding.

Products, Services and Brands

A product is anything that is capable of satisfying customer needs. For example, a Belvita breakfast biscuit, a pair of Nike trainers, a Ford Focus car, or a haircut by Toni & Guy are all capable of satisfying different needs from hunger, through clothing, transportation and self-image. However, we often distinguish between products and services, with products being tangible (e.g. a can of Heinz soup) and services mainly intangible (e.g. a haircut). Consequently, it is logical to include services within the definition of the product but to be aware there are differences. Hence, there are *physical products* (goods) such as a watch, a car or a wind turbine, or *service products* such as insurance or banking.

All of these products satisfy customer needs; for example, a wind turbine provides sustainable power and insurance reduces financial risk. The principles discussed in this chapter apply equally to physical and service products. However, because there are special considerations associated with service products (e.g. intangibility), and as service industries (e.g. restaurants, tourism, banking, and the public sector) are an important and growing sector in most developed countries, Chapter 9 is dedicated to examining service products and services marketing in detail.

Branding is the process by which companies distinguish their product offerings from the competition. By developing a distinctive name, packaging and design, a **brand** is created. Most brands are supported by logos— for example, the Nike 'swoosh' and the prancing horse of Ferrari. By developing an individual identity, branding permits customers to develop associations with the brand (e.g. prestige, style, low cost) and eases the purchase decision (De Chernatony, 1991). The marketing task is to ensure positive associations between the chosen positioning objectives (see Chapter 7), the product and the brand.

Branding affects perceptions. In blind product testing, consumers often fail to distinguish between brands in each product category and often cannot correctly identify what they perceive to be their favourite brand. For example, the Pepsi Challenge used a series of taste tests and blind tests (i.e. the brand identities were concealed) to determine preferred brand. The results showed that while more people bought Coca-Cola, they preferred the taste of Pepsi when blindfolded. Advances in neuroscience may go some way to explaining the results. A re-creation of the test produced identical results, but when the tasters were wired to a brain scanner, there was a flurry of activity in the part of the brain that is stimulated by taste in the blind test. However, when the consumers were told which brand they were drinking, the part of the brain associated with higher thinking was activated during tasting (Valantine, 2009).

The word 'brand' is derived from the Old Norse word 'brandr', which means 'to burn' as brands were and still are the means by which livestock owners mark their animals to identify ownership (Keller, 2008). This definition is still pertinent today, as modern branding aims to permanently capture a part of the buyer's mind (Hegarty, 2011), with the aim that buyers always choose a particular brand.

The Product Line and Product Mix

Brands are not often developed in isolation. They normally fall within a company's product line and mix. A **product line** is a group of brands that are closely related in terms of their functions and the benefits they provide (e.g. Dell's range of personal computers; Samsung's or Philips Consumer Lifestyle's line of television sets).

The *depth* of the product line depends upon the pattern of customer requirements (e.g. the number of segments to be found in the market), the product depth being offered by competitors, and company resources. For example, although customers may require wide product variations, a small company may decide to focus on a narrow product line serving only sub-segments of the market.

A **product mix** is the total set of brands marketed in a company: the sum of the product lines offered. Thus, the *width* of the product mix can be gauged by the number of product lines an organization offers. Royal Philips of the Netherlands has a diversified product mix offer, from healthcare ranges for business markets to consumer electronics and lighting. But the company has a consistent brand message for this diverse range of products, which is 'improving people's lives through meaningful innovation' (Phillip, 2015). Other companies have a much narrower product mix comprising just one product line—such as Aston Martin, which produces high-performance cars.

The management of brands and product lines is a key element of product strategy. First, we shall examine the major decisions involved in managing brands: the type of brand to market (manufacturer versus own-label), how to build brands, brand name strategies, brand extension and stretching, and the brand acquisition decision. Then we look at how to manage brands and product lines over time using the product life-cycle concept. Finally, we discuss managing brand and product line portfolios.

Brand Types

The two alternatives regarding brand type are manufacturer and own-label brands. **Manufacturer brands** are created by producers and bear their own chosen brand name. The responsibility for marketing the brand lies in the hands of the producer. Examples include Kellogg's Cornflakes, Gillette Sensor razors and Norton Securities anti-virus software. The value of the brand lies with the producer and, by building major brands, producers can gain distribution and customer loyalty.

A fundamental distinction that needs to be made is between category, brands and variants (see Figure 8.1). A category (or product field) is divided into brands, which in turn may be divided into variants based on flavour, formulation or other feature (East, 1997). For example, Heinz tomato soup is the tomato variant of the Heinz brand of the category 'soup'. In recent years several products have emerged which have become category-creating products: for example, the iPod, Yakult probiotic drinks, Spanx body-shaping underwear and Twitter (Carter, 2011).

Own-label brands (sometimes called *distributor brands*) are created and owned by distributors. Own-label branding, if associated with tight quality control of suppliers, can provide consistent high value for customers,

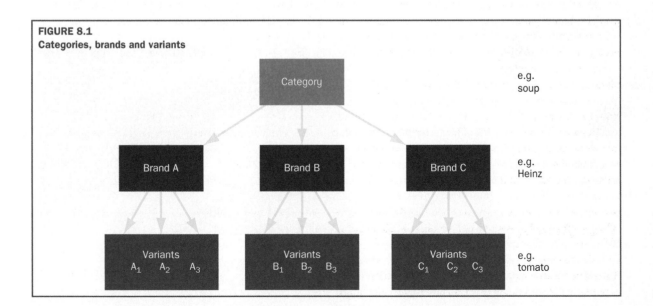

FIGURE 8.1
Categories, brands and variants

and be a source of retail power as suppliers vie to fill excess productive capacity with manufacturing products for own-label branding. The power of low-price supermarket own-label brands has focused many producers of manufacturer brands to introduce so-called **fighter brands** (i.e. their own low-price alternative). Not all own-label brands come with a low price tag, however. An example is Tesco Finest, a premium-priced own-label brand that has overtaken Kellogg's as the UK's biggest grocery brand (Bokaie, 2007).

Fighter brands are not just low-price alternatives, but are generally developed as part of a competitive strategy to protect market share from predatory competitors. Examples include Qantas launching Jetstar to fight the entry of Virgin Australia Airlines into Australian airspace. Intel introduced the Intel Celeron both to protect its premium market produce, the Pentium, and to fight off its cheaper competitors.

A major decision that producers have to face is whether to agree to supply own-label products for distributors. The danger is that, should customers find out, they may believe that there is no difference between the manufacturer's brand and its own-label equivalent. This led some companies, such as Kellogg's, to refuse to supply own-label products; indeed, this global food manufacturer has developed secret recipes for its Special K brand to fight against the rise of supermarket own brands (Reynolds, 2015). For other producers, supplying own-label goods is a means of generating income from the high sales volumes contracted with distributors. Bokomo Foods is a leading cereal maker and produces branded own-label foods for the UK and Scandinavia. For example, it produces cereals for Sainsbury's, Tesco and Morrisons in the UK, and makes Belso exclusively for Danish stores Netto, Fotex and Bilka (Bokomo Foods Ltd, 2015).

Why Strong Brands are Important

Apple, Google, IBM, China Mobile and General Electric are world-leading brands valued at over $50 billion (Costa, 2011) and customers are prepared to pay for the assurances they offer. Strong brands, typically product category leaders, are important to both companies and consumers. Companies benefit because strong brands add value to companies, positively affect consumer perceptions of brands, act as a barrier to competition, improve profits and provide a base for brand extensions. Strong brand names also have positive effects on consumer perceptions and preferences. See Mini Case 8.1 to find out how Douwe Egberts is more than just coffee to its consumer. Consumers gain because strong brands act as a form of quality certification and create trust. We now look at these factors.

Company value

The financial value of companies can be greatly enhanced by the possession of strong brands. For example, Nestlé paid £2.5 billion for Rowntree, a UK confectionery manufacturer, a sum that was six times its balance sheet value. Nestlé was not so much interested in Rowntree's manufacturing base as its brands—such as Kit Kat, Quality Street, After Eight and Fruit Pastilles—which were major brands with brand-building potential.

Strong branding enhances company value and brand makeovers can seriously affect valuations. For example, ghd, manufacturer of haircare equipment, more than doubled its profits from £16 million to £32 million when its CEO, Paul Stoneham, gave the brand a makeover (White, 2014); see Exhibit 8.1. eBay increased its brand value by 15 per cent ($10.7 billion) by undergoing a transformation driven by launching its online outlet dedicated to fashion. Amazon is another very successful brand, valued at over $64 billion (three times more than eBay). In emerging markets, China Mobile (valued at $50 billion) and Baidu search engine (valued at $30 billion) (Brandz, 2015) are growing rapidly. Brands can also lose market share for various reaons; for example, Angry Birds, produced by Finnish firm Rovio Entertainment experienced a significant drop in sales due to declining

EXHIBIT 8.1
ghd has developed the brand so that it has become synonymous with hair straighteners

interest in its merchandise (Dregde, 2015). German power group E.ON reported difficulties in its fossil fuel businesses as wholesale electricity prices plummeted (Macalister, 2015).

Barrier to competition

The impact of the strong, positive perceptions held by consumers about top brands means it is difficult for new brands to compete (even if the new brand performs well on blind taste testing). As we have seen, this may be insufficient to knock the market leader off the top spot. This is one of the reasons Virgin Coke failed to dent Coca-Cola's domination of the cola market. The reputation of strong brands, then, may be a powerful barrier to competition. However, in technology markets the top spot is not so assured. Digital brands can grow quickly, as they spread like infectious diseases across the Internet, but they can fall out of favour in the same manner. Research has predicted that Facebook will lose a significant number of its users by 2017, following the path of MySpace (Cannarella and Spechler, 2014) and Friends Reunited.

High profits

Strong, market-leading brands are rarely the cheapest. Brands such as Heinz, Kellogg's, Mercedes, Apple, Michelin, L'Oréal and Microsoft are all associated with premium prices. This is because their superior brand equity means that consumers receive added value over their less powerful rivals. Strong brands also achieve distribution more readily, gain economies of scale, and are in a better position to resist retailer demands for price discounts. These forces feed through to profitability.

Base for brand extensions

A strong brand provides the foundation for leveraging positive perceptions and goodwill from the core brand to brand extensions. Examples include Diet Coke, Dove Visible Care body wash, Baileys Chocolat Luxe and H&M's Modern Essentials. The new brand benefits from the added value that the brand equity of the core brand bestows on the extension. There is a full discussion of brand extensions later in this chapter.

Quality certification

Strong brands also benefit consumers in that they provide quality certification, which can aid decision-making. The following example illustrates the lengths consumers will go to when using strong brands as a form of quality certification.

Hyundai cars were not noted for their quality. Chung Ju-Yung, founder of the car company in South Korea, used to count clapped-out deserted cars as a measure of his brand's performance. So long as there were more Hyundais abandoned on the roadside than his competitors' cars, he was convinced the company was doing well. Things are very different today, and the launch of the Prada Genesis cars from the Hyundai stable shows how the brand has changed. Hyundai joined with the Italian designer fashion house Prada to produce an exclusive, high-quality version of its Genesis range. Buyers in the Gulf and China are the main target audience. While this model will not significantly increase annual revenues, it is a clear indication and informal certification of the quality of the brand. For online brands, consumer trust is paramount (Oliver, 2011). VeriSign produces formal certification for online brands to indicate security of an e-commerce website. In the case of Hyundai, Prada is acting as an intangible form of quality certification, whereas VeriSign certificates are highly tangible.

Trust

Consumers tend to trust strong brands and are making greater use of the web and comparison sites to gather information about their favoured brands. Ultimately, the belief that a brand will deliver on its promises is a deal breaker when everything else is equal. For example, Aviva and the AA both offer motor insurance in this highly competitive consumer market. Price is still a strong discriminating factor in this market, but motorists are looking for something extra. Market research found that if all motor insurance companies were offering exactly the same rate and terms, consumers' favourite brand would be the AA as it is most trusted to deliver on its brand promises (Barnett, 2012). Arguably, the AA has risen to this position in the minds of its target audiences by increasing its media spend and subsequently improving brand awareness.

Examples of trusted European brands are Volkswagen (cars), Samsung (mobile phones), Cannon (cameras) and Nivea (cosmetics) (Readers Digest, n.d.).

When consumers stop trusting a brand, the fallout can be catastrophic; history has revealed many notable examples. Gerald Ratner destroyed his chain of high street jewellery stores when he repeatedly spoke about the poor quality of the merchandise at public speaking engagements; Sunny Delight, Procter & Gamble's highly successful children's fruit drink, fell from grace instantly once it was revealed that drinking too much could turn children yellow; when Coca-Cola launched its Dasani bottled water in the UK, all went well until consumers were made aware it was actually bottled tap water. In each of these examples, consumers lost trust in the brands because they felt they had been cheated and, while the brands made every attempt to recover, consumers were not willing to forget.

Brand Equity

Strong brands are rich in a property called brand equity. **Brand equity** is a measure of the strength of a brand in the marketplace by adding tangible value to a company through the resulting sales and profits. There are two types of brand equity: customer-based and proprietary-based brand equity. Customer-based brand equity resides in the minds of consumers and consists of brand awareness and brand image. Proprietary-based brand equity is based on assets that are attributable to the company, and consists of patents and channel relationships.

Customer-based brand equity

Mini Case 8.1 discusses how Douwe Egberts has reinforced the value of its brand in the minds of its customers. The type of brand equity that resides in the minds of consumers who hold more favourable perceptions and associations towards the brand than towards its rivals is called *customer-based brand equity*. Brands with customer-based brand equity include Douwe Egberts, Diet Coke and Toyota.

Customer-based brand equity is defined as the differential effect that brand knowledge has on consumer response to the marketing of that brand (Keller, 2008). A brand has positive customer-based brand equity when consumers react more favourably to a product when the brand is identified than when it is not (e.g. the Diet Coke versus Diet Pepsi product tests discussed in the section 'Products, Services and Brands'). Positive, customer-based brand equity is likely to result in high customer loyalty, low price sensitivity, a high willingness for customers to visit more than one outlet in order to purchase the brand, and a strong base for brand extensions. On the other hand, negative customer-based brand equity occurs when consumers react less favourably towards the brand when it is identified than when it is not.

There are two sources of customer-based brand equity: brand awareness and brand image (see Figure 8.2).

Brand awareness

Brand awareness is related to brand equity in two ways. First, by raising brand awareness, the likelihood that the brand will enter a consumer's evoked set (those brands that a consumer seriously considers before making a purchase) is increased since awareness is a pre-condition of evaluation of a brand. Second, in low-involvement situations, as we saw in Chapter 3 on understanding consumer behaviour, a purchase may follow awareness of a brand with little information processing since the purchase is of low importance or low price. In both these cases, increasing brand awareness can lead to higher sales and profits and hence increased brand equity. The global brand awareness of brands like Coca-Cola, Philips, Google, Facebook, Apple, Samsung and IKEA is a major contributor to their brand equity.

Brand image

Brand equity can also be increased by creating a strong brand image. A positive brand image is formed by generating strong, favourable and unique associations to the brand in the memory (Keller, 2008). A brand image is created through the use of all elements of the marketing mix.

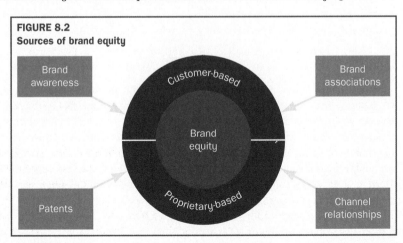

FIGURE 8.2
Sources of brand equity

Customer-based

Brand awareness

Brand associations

Brand equity

Proprietary-based

Patents

Channel relationships

Egbert Douwes opened his first coffee shop in Joure, Netherlands, in 1753 with his wife Akke. Together they laid the foundations for what was to become a powerful global mega brand. Their mission was simple: to sell products that could deliver 'the pleasure of daily living'. As a result, the coffee they produced was very popular and the business continued to grow. The brand strength was built around the taste and functionality of the coffee.

The company was always keen to adapt to the changing needs of its coffee-drinking customers. For example, in 1954 Douwe Egberts instant coffee was introduced, and later instant cappuccino. Then Douwe Egberts started to notice changes in coffee drinking habits; it found this

meant brewed coffee needed to provide customers with a more personalized, individual and luxury feel. So they worked with Dutch technology company Phillips to produce a coffee machine that could be used with their coffee to make an expresso-like foamy coffee in an instant. In 2001, the launch of the Senseo was a revolution in coffee drinking and provided a way for individual customers to have freshly brewed coffee. The Senseo got a positive reaction and was bought by millions of customers around the world.

Despite being a major player in the global coffee market, in 2010 Douwe Egberts was in danger of falling behind its competitors. As a result, it set about refreshing its identity, drawing on the heritage of the brand and using its 250 years of history and craftsmanship to reinforce the brand's position and be perceived positively by its customers. This action significantly boosted the brand's popularity and sales, enabling further growth. Recently, Douwe Egberts joined forces with Modelèz International in a mega merger, bringing it together with the US group's Carte Noire, Kenco and Tassimo brands. This move meant the newly named Jacobs Douwe Egberts held a market-leading position in many countries.

In spite of the size of this powerful global brand, it constantly aims to be in touch with its customers and responds to the ever-changing market environment. In 2014, it partnered with Prostate Cancer; Douwe Egberts encouraged its customers to drink a cup of its coffee and post a selfie on Facebook showing foamy moustaches to raise the profile of the global Movember fundraising campaign. In 2015, Douwe Egberts joined forces with Actimel yoghurt, Bonne Maman preserves, HP sauce, Nestlé cereal and other leading brands in the 'A Better Breakfast' campaign designed to encourage the population of the UK not to skip breakfast, because it is a very important meal.

Since opening a single store in the Netherlands, Douwe Egberts has built its reputation and its business around being first in the minds of its customers when they think about drinking coffee. With this in mind, consider the following questions.

Questions:

1 Explain how Douwe Egberts has extended the brand and how this has enabled the brand to reach more customers.
2 Discuss the extent to which Douwe Egberts has built customer-based brand equity for its brand.
3 From a branding perspective, suggest why Douwe Egberts has become involved with Prostate Cancer and the 'A Better Breakfast' campaign.

Based on: Douwe Egberts Coffee Company (2015); Hilpern (2010); Armstrong (2014); Kimberly (2014); Cassidy (2012)

The brand image of a car, for example, is influenced by product quality (associating it with perceptions of comfort, reliability, durability, and so on), promotion (an integrated marketing communications campaign may imbue the car with high-status connotations), price (a competitive price may confer associations with value for money), and place (a smart modern dealership may associate the car with efficient after-sales service). Advertising is often employed to create a brand image. A positive brand image, then, increases the likelihood of purchase and hence brand equity. Brands like Johnson & Johnson, Dulux and Colgate gain equity through their image of being trustworthy.

Proprietary-based brand equity

Proprietary-based brand equity is derived from company attributes that deliver value to the brand. These can be found in many aspects of corporate activity but the two main sources are patents and channel relationships.

Patents

As we shall see later when discussing brand valuation, a common method is to calculate the value of a brand by taking into account future profits and discounting them to the present day. Patents give greater certainty to future revenue streams by protecting a brand from competitive threat over the lifetime of the patent. Brand equity, therefore, falls towards the end of this period. For example, the value of many pharmaceutical brands falls as their patents expire, because of the launch of low-priced generic competitors. As we have seen, the value of Gillette's patents when the company was acquired by Procter & Gamble was estimated at £7 billion (Fisk, 2005).

Channel relationships

Experience, knowledge and close relationships with distributors and suppliers can enhance the value of company brands. For example, one of the attractions of Gillette to Procter & Gamble was its complementary global distribution strengths. Gillette has strengths in India and Brazil, whereas Procter & Gamble is strong in China, Russia, Japan and Turkey. This allows Gillette to push Procter & Gamble brands in India and Brazil, and Procter & Gamble to use its existing strong channel relationships in China, Russia, Japan and Turkey to distribute Gillette brands (Mitchell, 2005). It is reported that the value to Procter & Gamble of Gillette's channel relationships was estimated at £10 billion (Fisk, 2005).

Brand valuation is a difficult task. It is the process of estimating the financial value of an individual or corporate brand. A widely cited list of the top 100 global brands by financial value is produced by the Interbrand Corporation. Interbrand bases its calculations on a brand's financial performance (profits on products and services, earnings attributable to the brand), its influence on customer choice, and the strength of the brand relative to the competition (Interbrand, 2014).

Although Interbrand's approach does not give estimates of the value of brands in the future (something that would be useful to investors), it does provide a picture of the value of brands in any one year. Calculating the value of brand equity is an important task since it indicates the rewards that can be reaped from marketing investments. Apple and Google are valued at being worth in excess of $100 billion and are at the top of the list of 100 global brands; Amazon ranks 15th, Volkswagen 31st, Audi 45th, Fedex 92nd, and a new entrant, Huawei, the Chinese telecoms corporation, has entered at 94th (Interbrand, 2014).

Brand Building

The importance of strong brands means that brand building is an essential marketing activity. Successful brand building can reap benefits in terms of premium prices, achieving distribution more readily, and sustaining high and stable sales and profits through brand loyalty (Ehrenberg, Goodhardt and Barwise, 1990). Strong brands are also better able to withstand external market forces such as economic recessions and financial downturns (Millward Brown, 2014).

A brand is created by augmenting a **core product** with distinctive values that distinguish it from the competition. To understand the notion of brand values we first need to understand the difference between features and benefits. A feature is an aspect of a brand that may or may not confer a customer benefit. For example, adding fluoride (*feature*) to a toothpaste confers the customer *benefits* of added protection against tooth decay and decreased dental charges. Not all features necessarily confer benefits to all users. For example, Microsoft Office is a bundle of software programs. However, for a user who only wishes to use the word processor, the spreadsheet and PowerPoint software confer no benefits.

Core-benefits derive from the core product (see Figure 8.3). Toothpaste, for example, cleans teeth and therefore protects against tooth decay. But all toothpastes achieve that. Branding allows marketers to create added values that distinguish one brand from another. Successful brands are those that create a set of brand values that are superior to other rival brands. So brand building involves a deep understanding of both the functional (e.g. ease of use) and emotional (e.g. confidence) values that customers use when choosing between brands, and the ability to combine them in a unique way to create an augmented *product* that customers prefer. This unique, **augmented product** is what marketers call the *brand*. The success of the Swatch brand was founded on the recognition that watches could be marketed as fashion items to younger age groups. By using colour and design, Swatch successfully augmented a basic product—a watch—to create appeal for its target market. Swatch combined functional and emotional values to create a

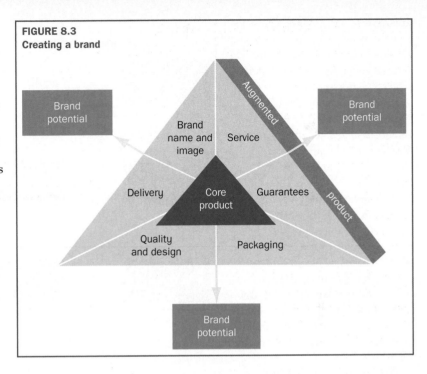

FIGURE 8.3
Creating a brand

successful brand. Focusing on functional values alone is rarely sufficient. Once Blackberry set itself apart from other mobile devices by offering email on the go, but when the iPhone entered the marketplace with touchscreen phones, the benefits of Blackberry's phone with a keyboard were eroded it was no longer seen as the phone for business professionals.

Figure 8.3 shows how products can be augmented. Singapore Airlines has augmented its brand by providing superior *service*. Kia has differentiated its cars by offering seven-year *guarantees* (warranties) when most of its competitors offer only three years (see Exhibit 8.2 and how Kia conveys the extent to which it offers benefits to its customers). Nivea was the first to differentiate its sunblock brand by the use of innovative *packaging* that allowed it to be sprayed onto the body. The iPod has created a differential advantage by augmenting its brand through *delivery* by creating a highly efficient means of downloading music from Apple's iTunes music store.

EXHIBIT 8.2
Kia conveys the extent to which it offers its benefits to customers

Apple has followed this success by creating its app store for its iPhone, which allows anyone to create and sell an application, providing efficient *delivery* of extra *services* to customers. Finally, BMW has augmented its brand by its *image*, embodied in its 'the ultimate driving machine' strapline, which differentiates it from the competition.

Managing brands involves a constant search for ways of achieving the full brand potential. To do so usually means the creation of major global brands. Leading brands such as Apple, Google, Coca-Cola, Microsoft, IBM, General Electric, AT&T and China Mobile have achieved this. But how are successful brands built? A combination of some or all of seven factors can be important (see King, 1991; Doyle, 1989). These are shown in Figure 8.4 and described below.

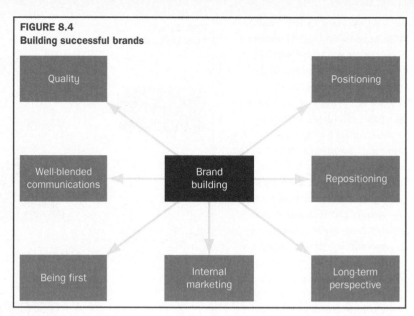

FIGURE 8.4
Building successful brands

Quality

It is vital to build quality into the core product; a major reason for brand failure is the inability to get the basics right. Marketing a computer that overheats, a vacuum cleaner that does not pick up dirt effectively or a garden fork that breaks is courting disaster. The core product must achieve the basic functional requirements expected of it. A major study of factors that affect success has shown statistically that higher quality brands achieve greater market share and higher profitability than their inferior rivals (Buzzell and Gale, 1987). Total quality management techniques (see Chapter 4) are increasingly being employed to raise quality standards. Product quality improvements have been shown to be driven mainly by market pull (changing customer tastes and expectations), organizational push (changes in the technical potential and resources of a company) and competitor actions (Lemmink and Kaspar, 1994).

Top companies such as Canon, BBC, Apple, Guinness, FedEx, Siemens, Intel, Toyota and Google understand the importance of quality in the brand-building process. Their success has been based on high-quality foundations. Once a brand is associated with quality, it forms a formidable barrier for competitors to overcome.

Positioning

Creating a unique position in the marketplace involves a careful choice of target market and establishing a clear differential advantage in the minds of those people. This can be achieved through brand names and image, service, design, guarantees, packaging and delivery. In today's highly competitive global marketplace, unique positioning normally relies on combinations of these factors. For example, the success of BMW is founded on a high-quality, well-designed product, targeted at distinct customer segments and supported by a carefully nurtured exclusive brand name and image. No matter which factors are given highest priority, positioning should be founded on the 4-Cs framework discussed in Chapter 7, on market segmentation and positioning. These are clarity, consistency, credibility and competitiveness. Often the essence of the 4-Cs is used in a brand's positioning statement. For example, Mercedes' 'precision engineered luxury' or DHL's 'Excellence. Simply Delivered.'

An analytical framework that can be used to dissect the current position of a brand in the marketplace and form the basis of a new brand positioning strategy is given in Figure 8.5. The strength of a brand's position in the marketplace is built on six elements: **brand domain**, **brand heritage**, **brand values**, **brand assets**,

brand personality and **brand reflection**. The first element, brand domain, corresponds to the choice of target market (where the brand competes); the other five elements provide avenues for creating a clear differential advantage with these target consumers. Each will now be explained.

1 *Brand domain*: the brand's target market: that is, where it competes in the marketplace. For example, the brand domain for Innocent drinks is the general consumer, whereas Innocent Kids are fruit smoothies and fruit tubes that are designed especially for children.

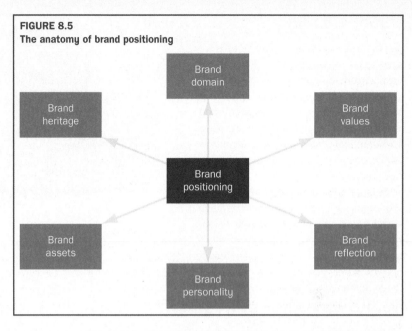

FIGURE 8.5
The anatomy of brand positioning

2 *Brand heritage*: the background to the brand and its culture. How it has achieved success (and failure) over its life. Brand heritage can form an extremely useful platform to build on, and some brands have long histories to help them stand out. For example, the foundations of Wolsey (knitwear, hosiery and underwear for men) stretch back to 1755 and the company has built its reputation on a longstanding history of quality design and fabrics and its Britishness. Burberry is another fashion brand that has gained from its history; founded in 1856, its reputation has been built on producing hard-wearing coats and outerwear, even for polar explorers and pilots. The Burberry trench coat designed in the 1940s remains a popular choice for men and women. Exhibit 8.3 shows how Kerrygold butter uses its heritage to convey the richness and pureness of the brand—an approach that it uses around the world.

3 *Brand values*: the core *values* and characteristics of the brand. For example, the brand values of Berghaus are high-performance outdoor clothing and the spirit of adventure, for Lycra they are comfort and fit, for Absolut Vodka purity and fun, and for Audi sophistication and progression. Ethical values for brands and companies are important. For example, Ecover, Innocent smoothies, Green & Black's chocolate and Café Direct coffee all combine strong brand values with ethical credentials.

4 *Brand assets*: what makes the brand distinctive from other competing brands, such as symbols, features, images and relationships. For example, Puma uses its namesake as its symbol that distinguishes it from other brands; IKEA's blue and yellow underpins its Swedishness and relates to being full of light and yet restrained, which reflects the country's culture, and the Dyson bagless vacuum cleaner is distinguished from traditional vacuum cleaners. Nivea's 'feeling closer' strapline and distinctive blue colour captures the image of the brand, and the close relationship with customers developed by IBM over many years is a major brand asset for the company.

5 *Brand personality*: the character of the brand described in terms of other entities, such as people, animals or objects. Marketing researchers ask consumers to describe brands in these terms. For example, consumers might be asked, 'If brand X were a person, what kind of person would it be?', 'If brand X were an animal, what kind of animal would it be?' or 'If brand X were a car, what kind of car would it be?' See Marketing in Action 8.1 for further details of the personality of brands.

6 *Brand reflection*: how the brand relates to self-identity; how the customer perceives him/herself as a result of buying/using the brand. The branding illustration visualizes how people use brands to reflect and project their self-identity. The importance of brand reflection is apparent in the demand for aspirational brands such as Gucci handbags, Cartier or Rolex watches, and Mercedes cars.

By analysing each element, brand managers can form an accurate portrait of how brands are positioned in the marketplace. From there, thought can be given to whether and how the brand can be repositioned to improve performance.

Repositioning

As markets change and opportunities arise, repositioning may be needed to build brands from their initial base. Skoda was repositioned from a downmarket car brand of dubious quality to a mid-market brand whose quality has led to several awards, and significant sales and profit growth. Samsung successfully repositioned from being perceived as a producer of cheap televisions and microwave ovens to being regarded as a 'cool' youth brand producing mobile phones and flat-screen televisions for the 'techno savvy'. Nokia also built its brand by repositioning from being a paper manufacturer to market leader in terms of its volume of mobile phone sales. See Mini Case 8.1 to find out more about repositioning a brand.

EXHIBIT 8.3
Heritage can be used in advertisements to position brands, in the marketplace, Irish Brand Kerrygold uses its heritage to position the brand in the minds of consumers

Integrated marketing communications

Brand positioning is based on customer perception. To create a clear position in the minds of a target audience requires considerable thought and effort regarding the tools (e.g. advertising, sales promotions) and media (e.g. broadcast, Internet) used to communicate brand messages. Awareness needs to be built, the brand personality projected and favourable attitudes reinforced. Integrated marketing communications, combining the strengths of traditional and digital media, are often used to promote such successful brands as Coca-Cola, Virgin Atlantic, Hertz car hire, Marmite and Birds Eye.

Marketers can make their brands more noticeable through attractive display or package design, and also through generating customer familiarity with brand names, brand logos and a brand's visual appearance. All

MARKETING IN ACTION 8.1
The Personality of a Brand

A brand's personality is an intangible but important part of the market position of goods and services. Like individuals, brands aspire to conveying their uniqueness and the characteristics of their personalities as this can help both in terms of a customer's understanding of the brand but also from the company's perspective when selecting appropriate messages and media to use to communicate a brand's position.

According to Millward Brown (2012), to understand a brand personality it is important to consider the personality characteristics and archetypes. For example, generous and caring characteristics could be combined with the archetype 'mother' in a similar way as adventurous and brave could be combined with a 'hero' archetype. The next step is to consider what the archetype represents; for example a 'mother' archetype could relate to stability and well-being. To be successful, a brand personality should link to archetypes that interest a brand's target audience. For example, the 'wise' archetype, with its characteristics of trustworthiness, has been attributed to Google, China Mobile and Visa. L'Oreal has been classified as fitting the 'seductress' archetype (with characteristics of being sexy and desirable); its Age Perfect campaign featuring Dame Helen Mirren added to the list of characteristics using the words 'outrageous' and 'bold' in its advertising message. Some archetypes are less likely to deliver success; having a *friendly* personality (like Airtel, Home Depot and KFC) might be straightforward and easy to understand but is less likely to stand out from the crowd.

Based on: Millward Brown (2012)

Traditionally, retailers have played the role in the supply chain of breaking bulk; this means they enable consumers to buy in the small quantities they require for their own use. As a consequence, marketing messages often focus on promotions designed to encourage action, for example buy one get one free offers. But large retailers have realized the need to clearly differentiate their offers in order to survive in highly competitive markets. This means paying more attention to branding than shifting products.

For some retailers, the solution has been to go into the *movie business* and produce high-budget films to differentiate their brands at Christmas time. UK retailers John Lewis Partnership (JLP), Sainsbury's and Tesco have produced movies not adverts to promote their brands, often aiming to create strong attachments between the retailer and the customer. Emotional attachment and likability are physiological factors that can evoke positive reactions towards a brand and enhance loyalty.

Tesco successfully got closer to its customers by focusing on nostalgia and effectively used real-life video cams to produce a movie showing six decades of family Christmases. JLP aimed to create an emotional attachment with its customers using a young boy and Monty the penguin, and wanted its customers to trust JLP 'to help deliver a perfect Christmas'. The advert was launched on TV but was also a hit on social media where it received 22 million hits over the Christmas period and produced strong positive emotions towards this retailer's brand. The total cost of the Monty the penguin campaign (including the movie, in-store advertising, print and digital) was £7 million.

Based on: Reynolds (2013); Quinn (2013); Wallop (2014); Reysen (2005)

of the considerations for developing well-blended and integrated communication campaigns are discussed in detail in Chapter 13.

Being first

Research has shown that pioneer brands are more likely to be successful than follower brands. For example, Urban et al. (1986) showed that for frequently purchased consumer goods, the second firm in the market could expect only 71 per cent of the market share of the pioneer, and the third only 58 per cent of the pioneer's share. Also Lambkin (1992) found that those pioneers that invest heavily from the start in building large production scale, in securing wide distribution and in promoting their products achieve the strongest competitive position and earn the highest long-term returns. (For a useful summary and further evidence see Denstadli, Lines and Grønhaug (2005).) Being first gives a brand the opportunity to create a clear position in the minds of target customers before the competition enters the market. It also gives the pioneer the opportunity to build customer and distributor loyalty (Bainbridge, 2013). Nevertheless, being first into a market with a unique marketing proposition does not guarantee success; it requires sustained marketing effort and the strength to withstand competitor attacks. For example, Blackberry failed to retain its position, once Apple entered the market with its iPhone.

Being first does not necessarily mean pioneering the technology. Bigger returns may come to those who are first to enter the mass market: for example, the Apple iPad. Microsoft had introduced the tablet PC in 2000 but did not successfully launch the product in the mass market, whereas Apple seized the opportunity in 2010 to capture and develop the market. Indeed, some of the world's most successful brands have benefited from following rather than leading, as they have gained important insights from first movers. For example, Google followed Alta Vista in the search engine marketplace as it realized the importance of a clean, clear user interface not cluttered with adverts; Facebook followed Myspace in the social media market and succeeded with its more subtle approach to connecting people (McWilians, 2009). Gillette is often considered to have invented the safety razor, but it was not the first brand to sell this product. Gillette made an important change by adding the disposable blade to the earlier design, and this enabled it to dominate the market.

Long-term perspective

Brand building is a long-term activity and can take many years to achieve. There are many demands on people's attention so generating awareness, communicating brand values and building customer loyalty requires significant commitment. Management should constantly evaluate brand investment to ensure they establish and maintain the desired position of a brand in the marketplace. Unfortunately, it can be tempting to cut back on expenditure in the short term. Cutting the marketing communication spend by half a million euros may immediately cut costs and increase profits. Conversely, for a well-established brand, sales are unlikely to fall substantially in the short term because of the effects of past advertising. The result is higher short-term profits. This may be an attractive proposition for managers who are often in charge of a brand for less than two years. One way of overcoming this danger is to measure brand manager (and brand) performance by measuring brand equity in terms of awareness levels, brand associations and intentions to buy, and being vigilant in resisting short-term actions which may cause harm.

Companies also need to be prepared to suffer losses when marketing brands in entirely new markets. For example BSkyB was prepared to incur losses while building its Sky satellite television brand for several years before recording its current high profits. Perhaps the most significant new market investment was Amazon. Jeff Bezos launched Amazon in 1995, and continued to invest in building the brand for a further six years before his online bookstore made a profit (Gale Encyclopedia of E-commerce, 2002).

Internal marketing

Many brands are corporate in the sense that the marketing focus is on building the company brand (King, 1991). This is particularly the case in services, with banks, supermarkets, insurance companies, airlines and restaurant chains attempting to build awareness and loyalty to the services they offer. A key feature in the success of such efforts is internal marketing—that is, training and communicating with internal staff. Training of staff is crucial because service companies rely on face-to-face contact between service provider (e.g. waiter) and service user (e.g. diner). Also, brand strategies must be communicated to staff so that they understand the company ethos on which the company brand is built. Investment in staff training is required to achieve the service levels required for the brand strategy. Top service companies like Federal Express, IBM and Singapore Airlines make training a central element of their company brand-building plans.

Besides incorporating the above factors into brand-building plans, it can be useful to examine the reasons for brand failure so that they can be avoided. Marking in Action 8.3 discusses some of the reasons for failure.

Key Branding Decisions

Besides the branding decisions so far discussed, marketers face four further key branding decisions: brand name strategies and choices, rebranding, brand extension and stretching, and co-branding.

Brand name strategies and choices

Another key decision area is the choice of brand name. Three brand name strategies can be identified: family, individual and combination.

Family brand names

A **family brand name** is used for all products (e.g. Philips, Microsoft, Heinz, Procter & Gamble, Samsung and Apple—see Exhibit 8.4). The goodwill attached to the family brand name benefits all brands, and the use of the name in advertising helps the promotion of all of the brands carrying the family name. The risk is that if one of the brands receives unfavourable publicity or is unsuccessful, the reputation of the whole range of brands can be tarnished. This is also called *umbrella branding*. Some companies create umbrella brands for part of their brand portfolios to give coherence to their range of products. For example, Lego created the umbrella brand of Duplo for its range of bricks and toys targeting small children.

Brands live in an unforgiving, harsh environment. Their survival depends on many factors, and their demise can be swift when they are not met. Here are some suggestions why brands fall out of favour and lose their place in the market.

1   Leading brands are more likely to fail than to persist as leaders over time.
    Hoover used to dominate the vacuum cleaner market but was knocked off the top spot when Dyson's bagless cleaner gained popularity. The Co-op was the UK's leading grocery retailer, but over the years its dominance has been eroded by Tesco, Sainsbury's and more recently discounters Lidl and Aldi. Toyota, Mercedes and BMW have been top-performing brands in the car market for some years, but Volkswagen, Audi and Nissan are rising stars that could challenge the market leaders, especially as demands for fuel efficiency and non-carbon fuel substitutes become more important to car buyers.

2   Once brand leadership is lost, it is likely to be gone forever.
    In 2000, Gap was 29th in the 100 global brands list, but by 2014 had fallen to 99th place. It was a leader in the youth fashion market but has been overtaken by new fashion brands like Zara and H&M. The newcomers battle it out in the fast-fashion market. H&M offers its customers a larger range and tends to achieve a lower average price over all its merchandise than Zara. H&M frequently offers discounts, but this is rarely the case for Zara. But Zara has an extremely efficient supply side, which supports the 'catwalk-inspired' fashion ranges. The demand for fast fashion helped the rapid growth of these brands, but both will need to monitor external market trends for fundamental shifts in buying behaviour that might affect their brands' prominence in the future.

3   Difficult economic circumstances are good for leading brands.
    Whilst consumers might be inclined to turn to private labels and own brands during difficult economic trading conditions, leading brands tend to be robust and maintain market share. Nestlé, Kraft and Kellogg's performed well in the recent economic crises as more consumers turned to eating at home and the brands they knew.

4   Brand leadership can be dependent on category.
    Some product categories offer better long-term brand leadership than others; fashion apparel and consumer electronics are the most difficult to stay ahead in, as fashion tastes change and technological advances can springboard new entrants such as Google and Amazon to the top of the list. Foods and household supplies tend to be more durable, as consumers can seek familiarity and avoid risk—for example, Heinz, Colgate and Danone. Such brands tend to constantly remind their customers about the benefits the brands offer in their communication messages, for example see how Colgate reminds us about how its toothpaste can aid oral health.

Based on: Golder, Irwin and Mitra (2013); Interbrand (2014); Anon (2009)

Individual brand names

An **individual brand name** does not identify a brand with a particular company (e.g. Procter & Gamble does not use the company name on brands such as Ariel, Fairy Liquid, Daz and Pampers). This may be necessary when it is believed that each brand requires a separate, unrelated identity. Toyota also abandoned its family brand name when it launched its upmarket executive car, which was simply called the Lexus. In some instances the use of a family brand name when moving into a new market segment may harm the image of the new product line. The same can be true when brands make acquisitions. For example, when Coca-Cola acquired Innocent, the reputation of the latter was damaged as it was viewed as selling out to a large corporation (Barda, 2010) and setting aside its ethical brand principles. BMW also chose not to attach its family brand name to the Mini, since it would have detracted from the car's sense of 'Britishness'.

Combination brand names

A **combination brand name** combines family and individual brand names to capitalize on the reputation of the company, while allowing the individual brands to be distinguished and identified. For example, in the Apple family there are the iPad, iPhone, iPod, MacBook, iTunes and the latest Apple Watch.

Criteria for choosing brand names

The choice of brand name should be carefully thought out, since names convey images. For example, the brand name Pepsi Max was chosen for Pepsi's diet cola targeted at men, as it conveyed a masculine image in a product category that was associated with women. So, one criterion for deciding on a good brand name is that it evokes *positive associations*.

A second criterion is that the brand name should be easy to *pronounce and remember*. Short names such as Esso, Shell, Daz, Ariel, Orange and Mini fall into this category. There are exceptions to this general rule, as in the case of Häagen-Dazs, which was designed to sound European in the USA where it was first launched. A brand name may suggest *product benefits*, such as with Right Guard (deodorant), Head & Shoulders (anti-dandruff shampoo) and MacBook Air (light computer), or express what the brand is offering in a *distinctive way*, such as Toys 'Я' Us. Technological products may benefit from *numerical* brand naming (e.g. Airbus 380, Aston Martin DB9) or *alphanumeric* brand names (e.g. Audi A4, Samsung Galaxy S6). This also overcomes the need to change brand names when marketing in different countries.

The question of brand *transferability* is another brand name consideration. With the growth of global brands, names increasingly need to be able to cross geographical boundaries. Companies that do not check the meaning of a brand name in other languages can be caught out, as when General Motors launched its Nova car in Spain only to discover later that the word meant 'it does not go' in Spanish. The lesson is that brand names must be researched for cultural meaning before being introduced into a new geographic market. One advantage of non-meaningful names such as Diageo and Exxon is that they transfer well across national boundaries.

Specialist companies have established themselves as brand name consultants. Market research is used to test associations, memorability, pronunciation and preferences. Legal advice is important so that a brand name *does not infringe an existing brand name*. Table 8.1 summarizes the issues that are important when choosing a brand name.

EXHIBIT 8.4
Apple uses family brand symbols for all its products including its new watch

TABLE 8.1 Brand name considerations
A good brand name should:
1. evoke positive associations
2. be easy to pronounce and remember
3. suggest product benefits
4. be distinctive
5. use numerals or alphanumerics when emphasizing technology
6. be transferable
7. not infringe an existing registered brand name

Brand names can also be categorized, as shown in Table 8.2.

TABLE 8.2 Brand name categories	
People	Adidas, McDonald's, Chanel, Heinz, Marriott, Louis Vuitton
Places	Singapore Airlines, Deutsche Bank, Air France
Descriptive	China Mobile, Body Shop, Federal Express, Airbus, Weetabix
Abstract	KitKat, Kodak, Prozac, IKEA
Evocative	iPod, Orange, Apple, Häagen-Dazs, Dove
Brand extensions	Diet Coke, Pepsi Max, Lucozade Sport
Foreign meanings	Lego (from 'play well' in Danish)

Rebranding

The act of changing a brand name is called **rebranding**. It can occur at the product level (e.g. Treets to M&Ms) and the corporate level (e.g. Orange and T-Mobile merged and were rebranded as Everything Everywhere (EE); Microsoft bought Nokia in 2013 and renamed its mobile phone brands as Lumia; and TNT Post has rebranded as Whistl and announced that its postmen will deliver mail on electric unicycles (Mortimer, 2014)).

Rebranding is risky and the decision should not be taken lightly, as potentially a rebranding exercise can cause a loss of sales of between 5 and 20 per cent (Klara, 2015). Abandoning a well-known and, for some, favourite brand runs the risk of customer confusion and resentment and loss of market share. When Coca-Cola was rebranded (and reformulated) as New Coke, negative customer reaction forced the company to withdraw the new brand and reinstate the original one (Benady, 2002). When Italo Suisse chocolates decided to rebrand, it came up with a new name: ISIS. But this name change ended up getting the chocolates removed from retailers' shelves in 2014 when the Islamic State of Iraq and Syria (ISIS) began releasing its terror videos. The chocolate-maker quickly rebranded again using the name of the founder, Libeert (Klara, 2015).

 Scan the QR code to see the how Whistl is delivering something different.

Why rebrand?

Despite such well-publicized problems, rebranding is a common activity. The reasons are as follows (see Keller, 2008; Riezebos, 2003).

Merger or acquisition

When a merger or acquisition takes place a new name may be chosen to identify the new company. Sometimes a combination of the original corporate names may be chosen (e.g. when Glaxo Wellcome and SmithKline Beecham formed GlaxoSmithKline), a completely new name may be preferred (e.g. when Grand Metropolitan and Guinness became Diageo) or the stronger corporate brand name may be chosen (e.g. when Nestlé acquired Rowntree Mackintosh).

Desire to create a new image/position in the marketplace

Some brand names are associated with negative or old-fashioned images. The move by BT Wireless to drop its corporate brand name was because it had acquired an old-fashioned, bureaucratic image. The new brand name, O_2, was chosen because it sounded scientific and modern, and because focus groups saw their mobile phones as an essential part of their lives (like oxygen) (Thurtle, 2002). The negative image of the cable television company ntl, caused by poor service, was part of the reason for buying Virgin Mobile, which allows it to use the Virgin brand under licence across its consumer businesses (Wray, 2006). Similar motivations were behind the rebranding of Andersen Consulting to Accenture. Image considerations were also prominent when the negative association of the word 'fried' in Kentucky Fried Chicken stimulated the move to change the name to KFC.

The sale or acquisition of parts of a business

The sale of the agricultural equipment operations of the farm equipment maker International Harvester prompted the need to change its name to Navistar. The acquisition of the Virgin One financial services brand by the Royal Bank of Scotland from the Virgin Group necessitated the dropping of the Virgin name. The new brand is called The One Account.

Corporate strategy changes

When a company diversifies out of its original product category, the original corporate brand name may be considered too limiting. Esso (Standard Oil) changed its name to Exxon as its product portfolio extended beyond oil. Also Dixons Retail has become Dixons Carphone, because the company has widened its product range strategically to place more emphasis on mobile technology.

Brand familiarity

Sometimes the name of a major product brand owned by a company becomes so familiar to customers that it supersedes the corporate brand. In these circumstances the company may decide to discard the unfamiliar name in favour of the familiar. That is why Consolidated Foods became Sara Lee, and Boussois-Souchon-Neuvesel (BSN) became Danone.

International marketing considerations

A major driver for rebranding is the desire to harmonize a brand name across national boundaries in order to create a global brand. This was the motivation for the change of the Marathon chocolate bar name in the UK to Snickers, which was used in continental Europe, the dropping of the Treets and Bonitos names in favour of M&Ms, the move from Raider to Twix chocolate bars, the consolidation of the Unilever cleaning agent Jif/Cif/Vif/Vim to Cif, and the changing of Norwich Union to Aviva. Companies may also change brand names to discourage parallel importing. When sales of a premium-priced brand in some countries are threatened by reimports of the same brand from countries where the brand is sold at lower prices, rebranding may be used to differentiate the product. This is why the Italian cleaning agent Viakal was rebranded in some European countries as Antikal.

Legal problems

A brand name may contravene an existing legal restriction on its use. For example, the Yves St Laurent perfume brand Champagne required a name change because the brand name was protected for use only with the sparkling wine from the Champagne region of France.

Managing the rebranding process

Rebranding is usually an expensive, time-consuming and risky activity, and should only be undertaken when there is a clear marketing and financial case in its favour and a strong marketing plan in place to support its implementation (Keller, 2008). Management should recognize that a rebranding exercise cannot of itself rectify more deep-seated marketing problems.

Once the decision to rebrand has been made, two key decisions remain: choosing the new name and implementing the name change.

Choosing the new brand name

The issues discussed earlier in this chapter regarding choosing brand names are relevant when changing an existing name. These are that the new brand name should evoke positive associations, be easy to pronounce and remember, suggest positive benefits, be distinctive, be transferable, not infringe an existing registered brand name, and consideration should be given to the use of numerals when emphasizing technology. These issues should form the basis of the first step, setting the rebranding objectives (see Figure 8.6). For example, a key objective of the new name might be that it should be easily remembered, evoke positive associations and be transferable across national boundaries.

The second step is to generate as many brand names as possible. Potential sources of names include consumers, employees, distributors, specialist brand name consultants and advertising agencies.

The third step is to screen the names to remove any with obvious flaws, such as those that are difficult to pronounce, too close to an existing name, have adverse

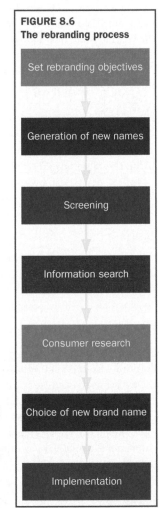

FIGURE 8.6
The rebranding process

Set rebranding objectives

↓

Generation of new names

↓

Screening

↓

Information search

↓

Consumer research

↓

Choice of new brand name

↓

Implementation

double meanings and do not fit with the rebranding objectives. The objective is to reduce the names to a shortlist of around 6–12. For the fourth step, an information search is carried out to check that each name does not infringe on an existing registered brand name in each country where the brand is, or may be, marketed.

The fifth step is to test the remaining names through consumer research. The key criteria, such as memorability, associations and distinctiveness, chosen in step one (rebranding objectives), will be used to assess the performance of the new names.

Finally, management will assess the virtues of each of the shortlisted brand names and come to a conclusion about which one should be chosen and registered.

Implementing the name change

Name changes can meet considerable resistance from consumers, employees and distributors. All three groups can feel that their loyalty to a brand has been betrayed. Attention also has to be paid to the media and financial institutions, particularly for corporate name changes. Careful consideration is required to change a name and all interested parties should be involved in the process and understand the logic underlying the change. Implementing a brand name change requires attention to five key issues (Kapferer, 2008).

1 *Coordination*: name change requires harmonious working between the company departments and those groups most involved—marketing, production, the salesforce, logistics and general management. All must work together to avoid problems and solve any that may arise.

2 *Communication*: all stakeholders—for example, customers, employees and investors—need to be targeted with communications that notify them early and with a full explanation. When the chocolate bar known as Raider in continental Europe changed its name to Twix, which was the name used everywhere else, consumers in Europe were informed by a massive advertising campaign (two years' advertising budget was spent in three weeks). Retailers were told of the name change well in advance by a salesforce whose top priority was the Twix brand. Trial was encouraged by promotional activities at retail outlets. The result was a highly successful name change and the creation of a global brand.

3 *Understanding what the consumer identifies with the brand*: consumer research is required to understand what consumers identify as the key characteristics of the brand. Shell made the mistake of failing to include the new colour (yellow) of the rebranded Shell Helix Standard (from Puissance 7) in its advertising, which stressed only the name change from Puissance 7 in France. Unfortunately, customers, when looking for their favourite brand of oil, paid most attention to the colour of the can, so they could not find their usual brown can of Puissance 7 and did not realize it was now in a yellow can and had a new and unfamiliar name. The lesson is that rebranding means making sure target audiences are informed of all of the brand changes.

4 *Providing assistance to distributors/retailers*: to avoid confusion at distributors/retailers, manufacturers should avoid double-stocking of the old and new brand and ensure barcodes and product management systems are updated. Mars management took great care to ensure that on the day of the transfer from Raider to Twix, no stocks of Raider would be found in the shops, even if this meant buying back stock.

5 *Speed of change*: consideration should be given to whether the change should be immediate (as with Twix) or subject to a transitional phase where, for example, the old name is retained (perhaps in small letters) on the packaging after the rebrand. Old names are retained during a transitional period when the old name has high awareness and positive associations among consumers. Retaining an old brand name following a takeover may be wise for political reasons, as when Nestlé retained the Rowntree name on its brands for a few years after its takeover of the UK confectionery company.

Brand Extension and Stretching

A **brand extension** is the use of an established brand name on a new brand within the same broad market or product category. For example, the Anadin brand name has been extended to related brands Anadin Extra, Maximum Strength, Soluble, Paracetamol and Ibuprofen. The Lucozade brand has undergone a very successful brand extension with the introduction of Lucozade Sport, with isotonic properties that help to rehydrate people more quickly than other drinks, and replace the minerals lost through perspiration. Coca-Cola has extended its Coke brand into Diet Coke, and its variant form: Diet Coke with cherry. Google has also extended its core brand with many variants including Google Plus, Google Answers, Google Maps, Google Street View, Google Book Search, Google Scholar. These are examples of *line* extensions.

An extreme form of brand extension is known as brand stretching. **Brand stretching** is when an established brand name is used for brands in unrelated markets or product categories, such as the use of the Yamaha pianos brand name on hi-fi equipment, skis and motorcycles. Menswear designer fashion brands like Paul Smith, Ted Baker and Tommy Hilfiger have also been extended from clothing to fragrances, footwear and home furnishings. Table 8.3 gives some examples of brand extensions and stretching.

 Scan the QR code to see how Kia is using brand stretching.

TABLE 8.3 Brand extensions and stretching	
Brand (line) extensions	**Brand stretching**
Anadin brand name used for Anadin Extra, Maximum Strength, Soluble, Paracetamol and Ibuprofen	Dyson, from vacuum cleaners to hand dryers and bladeless room fans
McDonald's launched McCafé, a coffee house style food chain	Yamaha (pianos) brand name used on motor cycles, hi-fi, skis, pianos and summerhouses
Lucozade extends to Lucozade Sport, Energy, Hydroactive and Carbo Gel	Jimmy Choo, the luxury shoemaker, has moved into bags, men's fragrances, jewellery and clothing
McCain Chips extended its range with Home Chips (Authentic), Oven Chips (Healthier), French Fries, ready baked jacket potatoes, micro chips	Mont Blanc (pen specialist) has moved into watches, jewellery and glasses

Some companies have used brand extensions and stretching very successfully. Richard Branson's Virgin company is a classic example. Beginning in 1970 as Virgin Records, the company grew through Virgin Music (music publishing), Megastores (music retailing), Radio, Vodka, Cola, Atlantic Airways (long-haul routes), Express (short-haul routes), Rail, Money (insurance, credit cards, mortgages etc.), One (one-stop online banking), Media (digital TV, broadband, phone and mobile), Healthcare and many more. The Virgin Group has over 400 subsidiaries.

Another spectacular success was when Gabrielle Coco Chanel stretched her clothing brand to perfume. Chanel No. 5 became the world's best-selling perfume, allowing women who could not afford Chanel fashion clothing to share the aura of the brand (BBC4, 2009).

Brand extension is an important marketing tactic. Two key advantages of brand extension in releasing new products are that it reduces risk and is less costly than alternative launch strategies (Sharp, 1990). Both distributors and consumers may perceive less risk if the new brand comes with an established brand name. Distributors may be reassured about the 'saleability' of the new brand and therefore be more willing to stock it. Consumers appear to attribute the quality associations they have of the original brand to the new one (Aaker and Keller, 1990). An established name enhances consumer interest and willingness to try the new brand (Aaker, 1990). Consumer attitudes towards brand extensions are more favourable when the perceived quality of the parent brand is high (Bottomley and Doyle, 1996). For example, Yakult Light is an extension of the Yakult brand.

Launch costs can also be reduced by using brand extension. Since the established brand name is already well known, the task of building awareness of the new brand is eased. Consequently, advertising, selling and promotional costs are reduced. Furthermore, there is the likelihood of achieving advertising economies of scale since advertisements for the original brand and its extensions reinforce each other (Roberts and McDonald, 1989).

A further advantage of brand extensions is that the introduction of the extension can benefit the core brand because of the effects of the accompanying marketing expenditure. Sales of the core brand can rise due to the enhancement of consumers' perception of brand values and image through increased communication (Grime, Diamantopoulos and Smith, 2002).

However, these arguments can be taken too far. Brand extensions that offer no functional, psychological or price advantage over rival brands often fail (Saunders, 1990). Consumers shop around, and brand extensions that fail to meet expectations will be rejected. *Cannibalization*, which refers to a situation where the new brand gains sales at the expense of the established brand, can also occur. For example, additional flavour extensions of the Absolut Vodka brand were found to cannibalize sales of existing ones, leading to a refocus on the original brand (Bokaie, 2008). Further, brand extension has been criticized as leading to a managerial focus on minor modifications, packaging changes and advertising rather than the development of real innovations (Bennett and Cooper, 1981).

There is also the danger that bad publicity for one brand affects the reputation of other brands under the same name. The Virgin brand name was in danger of being tarnished at one time by the poor punctuality of its trains under the Virgin Trains brand. Massive investment in new locomotives and rolling stock cured the problem (Sharp, 1990). However, research has shown that the danger of the brand extension damaging the reputation of the core brand is much greater when the brand is extended within its original line (as in the Anadin example) than when the brand is stretched into new product categories. A major test of any brand extension opportunity is to ask whether the new brand concept is compatible with the values inherent in the core brand. Brand extensions, therefore, are not viable when a new brand is being developed for a target group that holds different values and aspirations from those in the original market segment. When this occurs, the use of the brand extension tactic would detract from the new brand. The answer is to develop a separate brand name, as with Toyota's Lexus, and Seiko with its Pulsar brand developed for the lower-priced mass market for watches.

MARKETING IN ACTION 8.4
Developing the Lotus Bakeries Brand of Caramelized Biscuit

Caramelized biscuits are an original Belgian specialty. Lotus Bakeries, family owned since 1932, has acquired international exposure thanks to this flagship product. This Belgian company is very small compared with Mondelèz International or United Biscuits, but it has succeeded in cornering a growing share of a niche market. The market in question is the speculoos market, which consists of suppliers of a type of spiced shortcrust biscuit. In Belgium, Lotus's version of speculoos is a top product across the biscuit market. The biscuits are also proving increasingly popular internationally, so that today more than 75 per cent of sales are realized outside Belgium. Lotus Bakeries annually manufactures 6 billion of the lightly  spiced, thin and crunchy biscuits for export to 40 countries. With its modern rectangular shape, the Lotus biscuit has been widely adopted by bars and quality restaurants around the world.

Speculoos is the name used to market Lotus original caramelized biscuits in Belgium and France. However, Biscoff (a fusion of 'biscuits for coffee', a shorter, snappier name) was chosen as a product brand name for the USA, quickly replacing the original caramelized biscuit brand in other international markets, including the UK, where the Biscoff brand name was introduced in March 2014. Speculoos is Lotus Bakeries' largest and most important product group, and has driven the group's growth in recent years, especially outside Belgium. Given its strategic importance, major sales and marketing efforts have been made to stimulate the product's further development and growth.

Brand line extensions

Alongside family packs and pocket-size formats of the Original Speculoos, developed in most countries, as well as a chocolate version, Lotus Bakeries is testing, in its traditional markets of Belgium and France, other line extensions, among which are Original Speculoos Crumbs, Rolls and Minis.

Brand stretching

After launching a Lotus Speculoos ice-cream, Lotus Bakeries innovated in 2008 and conquered a new market with its spreadable version of the Original Lotus Speculoos. Introduced year by year to many countries, including the UK in 2013, it has become a firm favourite, creatively used in a range of recipes shared by customers. Retail giants Sainsbury's and Waitrose saw sales of Biscoff Spread (smooth and crunchy versions) rocket in 2014. Following its successful debut, the product was launched in 20g packs for catering and food services. A chocolate version of the spread can also be found in Quebec, Canada.

Lotus Bakeries is looking for the next development strategy to undertake to promote Original Speculoos. Should it stretch the brand further? Should it co-brand? Should Biscoff become its unique global brand for caramelized biscuits?

Based on: Flambard-Ruaud and Daly (2012)

Finally, management needs to guard against the loss of credibility if a brand name is extended too far. This is particularly relevant when brand stretching. The use of the Pierre Cardin name for such disparate products as clothing, toiletries and cosmetics has diluted the brand name's credibility (Aaker, 1990).

Brand extensions are likely to be successful if they make sense to the consumer. If the values and aspirations of the new target segment(s) match those of the original segment, and the qualities of the brand name are likewise highly prized, then success is likely. The prime example is Marks & Spencer, which successfully extended from clothing to food based on its core values of quality and reliability.

Co-branding

There are two major forms of co-branding: **product-based co-branding** and **communications-based co-branding** (see Figure 8.7).

Product-based co-branding

Product-based co-branding involves the linking of two or more existing brands from different companies or business units to form a product in which the brand names are visible to consumers. There are two variants: parallel and ingredient co-branding. **Parallel co-branding** occurs when two or more independent brands join forces to produce a combined brand. An example is Häagen-Dazs ice cream and Baileys liqueur combining to form Häagen-Dazs with Baileys flavour ice cream. For example, BlackBerry (RIM) partnered with Sky in the Sky Atlantic channel, and both brand names appear together on the channel communications; Siemens and Porsche Design, which produce a range of kettles, toasters and coffee machines under the Siemens Porsche co-brand (Tomkins, 2005).

Ingredient co-branding is found when one supplier explicitly chooses to position its brand as an ingredient of a product. Intel is an ingredient brand. It markets itself as a key component (ingredient) of computers. The ingredient co-brand is formed by the combination of the ingredient brand and the manufacturer brand—for example, Hewlett-Packard or Sony. Usually the names and logos of both brands appear on the computer. Although Baileys liqueur may at first sight seem to be an ingredient brand, it is not since its main market positioning is as an independent brand (a liqueur) not as an ingredient of ice cream (Riezebos, 2003). Figure 8.8 shows the distinction between parallel and ingredient co-branding.

Advantages

The advantages of product-based co-branding are as follows.

Added value and differentiation   The co-branding alliance of two or more brands can capture multiple sources of brand equity, and therefore add value and provide a point of differentiation. For example, Disney has launched a service called Disney Movies Anywhere; it has expanded its alliance with Apple to include Google's Android to allow the unlimited streaming of Disney movies (Nieva, 2014). Target (mass-market USA retailer) has joined with the Italian designer Missoni to introduce a range of 400 fashion garments (Ritson, 2011).

If co-branding is going to work, there needs to be certain contrasts between the brands so that joining together brings synergistic benefits. In the case of Target the Missoni design flare adds value and enables the retailer to associate more closely with premium brands. For Missoni, the biggest benefit is creating brand awareness in North America. Both companies cater for different audiences, so strong co-branding can again deliver added benefits by giving access to

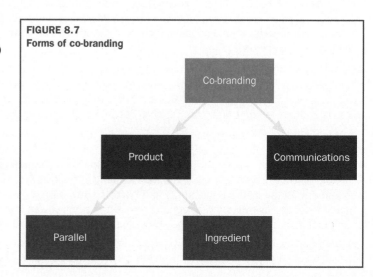

FIGURE 8.7
Forms of co-branding

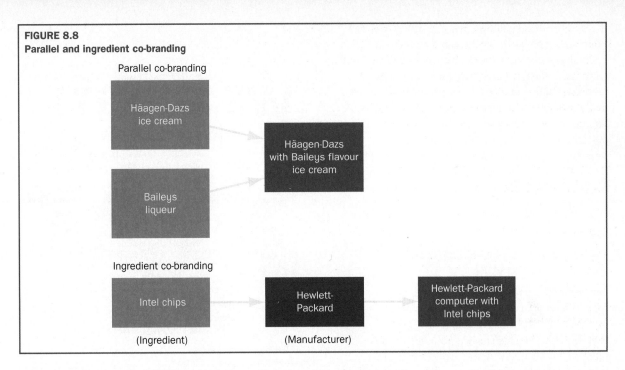

FIGURE 8.8
Parallel and ingredient co-branding

Parallel co-branding

Häagen-Dazs ice cream

Baileys liqueur

Häagen-Dazs with Baileys flavour ice cream

Ingredient co-branding

Intel chips

Hewlett-Packard

Hewlett-Packard computer with Intel chips

(Ingredient)

(Manufacturer)

new customers. The potential benefits of successful co-branding are better integrated communication, organizational learning, increased brand equity and improved profits.

Positioning   A co-brand can position a product for a particular target market. Best Western International hotel group and Harley Davidson Motor Company entered into partnership to promote Rider Friendly hotels. The deal brought advantages for both companies and the customers: Best Western gained access to motorcycling enthusiasts who like to travel; Harley Davidson demonstrated its commitment to getting the best for its customers, who on arrival at the hotel could enjoy selected benefits (PRNewswire, 2013). Apple and Volkswagen joined forces, bringing together the Beetle and iPhone to produce a new car called the iBeetle.

Reduction of cost of product introduction   Co-branding can reduce the cost of product introduction since two well-known brands are combined, accelerating awareness, acceptance and adoption (Keller, 2008). Consumer technology manufacturer LG and Google joined forces and agreed to share their patent portfolios in a deal that aims to reduce costs and create opportunities for the development of future innovative products and services (Boxall, 2014).

Risks

There are also risks involved in product-based co-branding, as with other co-branding exercises.

Loss of control   Given that the co-brand is managed by two different companies (or at the very least different strategic business units of the same company), each company loses a degree of control over decision-making. There is potential for disagreement, misunderstanding and conflict. For example, American Express decided to end its co-branding relationship with Costco Wholesale because the two corporations could not agree to acceptable terms. The credit card company has seen its stock price fall significantly over the break-up of this unusual partnership, in which Costco exclusively accepted AMEX cards (Sidel, 2015).

Loss of brand equity   Poor performance of the co-brand could have negative effects on the original brands. In particular, each or either of the original brands' images could be tarnished.

Communications-based co-branding

Communications-based co-branding involves the linking of two or more existing brands from different companies or business units for the purposes of joint communication. This type of co-branding can take the form of recommendation. For example, Ariel and Whirlpool launched a co-branded advertising campaign where Ariel was endorsed by Whirlpool (Kapferer, 2008). In a separate co-branding campaign Whirlpool endorsed Finish Powerball dishwasher tablets. A second variant is when an alliance is formed to stimulate awareness and interest, and to provide promotional opportunities. An example is Shell's sponsorship of the Ferrari Formula One motor racing team. As part of the deal the Shell brand name appears on Ferrari cars.

EXHIBIT 8.5
Greenpeace, Lego and Shell Oil

Advantages

The advantages of communications-based co-branding are as follows.

Endorsement opportunities   As we have seen, Whirlpool and Ariel engaged in mutual endorsement in their advertising campaign. Endorsement may also be one-way: Shell gains by being associated with the highly successful international motor racing brand, Ferrari.

Cost benefits   One of the parties in the co-brand may provide resources to the other. Shell's deal with Ferrari demands that Shell pays huge sums of money, which helps Ferrari support the costs of motor racing. Also, joint advertising alliances mean that costs can be shared.

Awareness and interest gains   The McDonald's/Disney alliance means that new Disney movies are promoted in McDonald's outlets, enhancing awareness and interest.

Promotional opportunities   As we have discussed, McDonald's gained by the in-store promotional opportunities afforded by its co-branding alliance with Disney.

Risks

The risks involved in communications-based co-branding are similar to those of product-based co-branding.

Loss of control   Each party to the co-branding activity loses some of its control to the partner. For example, in joint advertising there could be conflicts arising from differences of opinion regarding creative content and the emphasis given to each brand in the advertising. For example, Lego ended its partnership with Shell Oil because Greenpeace campaigned against the oil company's plans to start drilling for oil in the Arctic. Lego felt that it should not be drawn into this dispute, and so to protect the brand it withdrew (Trangbaek, 2014).

 Scan the QR code to see how Greenpeace used Lego to attack Shell oil.

Brand equity loss   No one wants to be associated with failure. Poor performance of one brand could tarnish the image of the other. For example, an unsuccessful Disney movie prominently promoted in McDonald's outlets could rebound on the latter. Conversely, bad publicity for McDonald's might harm the Disney brand by association. Indeed, the Disney/McDonald's partnership was terminated by Disney, amid rumours that it did not want to be associated with a brand that had received unfavourable publicity about unhealthy eating (Hickman, 2006).

Global and Pan-European Branding

Global branding is the achievement of brand penetration worldwide. Table 8.4 lists the brands that have achieved this to become top global brands. The USA dominates the world market by owning the top ten global brands.

TABLE 8.4 Top global brands		
Brand	**Brand value ($ millions)**	**Country of ownership**
Apple	118,863	USA
Google	107,439	USA
Coca-Cola	81,563	USA
IBM	72,244	USA
Microsoft	61,154	USA
GE	45,480	USA
Samsung	45,462	USA
Toyota	42,392	USA
McDonalds	42,254	USA
Mercedes-Benz	34,338	USA

Based on Interbrand Report Top Global Brand Rankings http://www.bestglobalbrands.com/2014/ranking/

Europe, too, is home to other highly respected and well-known brands (see Table 8.5).

TABLE 8.5 Top brands in Europe		
Brand	**Brand value ($ millions)**	**Country of origin**
Mercedes-Benz (world rank 10)	34,338	Germany
BMW1	34,214	Germany
Louis Vuitton (world rank 19)	22,552	France
H&M (world rank 21)	21,083	Sweden
SAP (world rank, 25)	17,340	European
IKEA (world rank 26)	15,885	Sweden
Volkswagen (world Rank 31)	13,761	Germany
HSBC (World rank 33)	13,142	UK
Zara (world rank 36)	12,126	Spain
Nescafe (world rank 38)	11,406	Switzerland
Gucci (world rank 41)	110,385	Italy

Based on Interbrand Report (2014) Top Global Brands http://www.bestglobalbrands.com/2014/ranking/#?filter=Europe%20%26%20Africa

Levitt, a champion of global branding, argues that intensified competition and technological developments will force companies to operate globally, ignoring superficial national differences. Globally consumers seek reliable, quality products at a low price, and the marketing task is to offer the same products and services in the same way, thereby achieving enormous global economies of scale. Levitt's position is that the new commercial reality is the emergence of global markets for standardized products and services on a previously unimagined scale. The engine behind this trend are the twin forces of customer convergence of tastes and needs, and the prospect of global efficiencies in production, procurement, marketing, and research and development. Asian economies are being successful in achieving these kinds of economies to produce high-quality, competitively priced global brands (e.g. Japan: Toyota, Honda, Sony and Canon).

The creation of global brands also speeds up a brand's time to market by reducing time-consuming local modifications. The perception that a brand is global has also been found to affect positively consumers' belief that the brand is prestigious and of high quality (Steenkamp, Batra and Alden, 2003).

In Europe, the promise of pan-European branding has caused leading manufacturers to seek to extend their market coverage and to build their portfolio of brands. Nestlé has widened its brand portfolio by the acquisition of such companies as Rowntree (confectionery) and Buitoni-Perugina (pasta and chocolate), and has formed a joint venture (Cereal Partners) with the US giant General Mills to challenge Kellogg's in the European breakfast cereal market. Mars has replaced its Treets and Bonitos brands with M&Ms and changed the name of its third-largest UK brand, Marathon, to the Snickers name used in the rest of Europe.

Some global successes, such as Coca-Cola, BMW, Gucci and McDonald's, can be noted, but national varieties in taste and consumption patterns will ensure that such achievements in the future will be limited. For example, the fact that the French eat four times more yoghurt than the British, and the British buy eight times more chocolate than the Italians reflects the kinds of national differences that will affect the marketing strategies of manufacturers (Barwise and Robertson, 1992). Indeed, many so-called global brands are not standardized, claim the 'local' marketers. For example, Coca-Cola in Scandinavia tastes different from that in Greece, and Nescafé has many different varieties of its classic instant coffee blend, the aim being to suit local tastes.

When entering international markets, brands should consider which parts of the brand can be standardized and which must be varied across countries. A useful way of looking at this decision is to separate out the elements that comprise the brand, as shown in Figure 8.9. Can brand name and image, advertising, service, guarantees, packaging, quality and design, and delivery be standardized?

Gillette's global success with its Sensor, Fusion and Mach 3 razors was based on a highly standardized approach: the product, brand name, the message 'the best a man can get', advertising visuals and packaging were standardized; only the voice-overs in the advertisement were changed to cater for 26 languages across Europe, the USA and Japan.

Lever Brothers found that, for detergent products, brand image and packaging could be standardized but the brand name, communications execution and brand formulation needed to vary across countries (Halliburton and Hünerberg, 1993). Brand image and packaging were the same but the name and formulation (fragrance, phosphate levels and additives) differed between countries.

In other circumstances, the brand form and additions may remain the same across countries but the brand communications may need to be modified. Consequently, differing advertising appeals would be needed to communicate the concept of exclusiveness in these countries.

Much activity has taken place over recent years to achieve global and pan-European brand positions. There are three major ways of doing this, as outlined below (Barwise and Robertson, 1992).

1 *Geographic extension:* taking present brands into the geographic markets
2 *Brand acquisition:* purchasing brands
3 *Brand alliance:* joint venture or partnerships to market brands in national or cross-national markets

Managers need to evaluate the strengths and weaknesses of each option, and Figure 9.10 summarizes these using as criteria speed of market penetration, control of operations and the level of investment required.

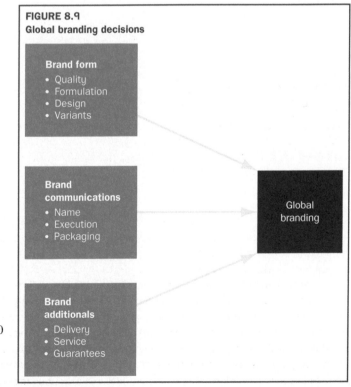

FIGURE 8.9
Global branding decisions

Brand form
- Quality
- Formulation
- Design
- Variants

Brand communications
- Name
- Execution
- Packaging

Brand additionals
- Delivery
- Service
- Guarantees

Global branding

Brand acquisition gives the fastest method of developing global brands. For example, Unilever's acquisition of Fabergé, Elizabeth Arden and Calvin Klein immediately made it a major player in fragrances, cosmetics and skincare.

Brand alliance usually gives moderate speed. For example, the use of the Nestlé name for the Cereal Partners (General Mills and Nestlé) alliance's breakfast cereals (e.g. Cheerios, Shreddies and Shredded Wheat) in Europe helped retailer and consumer acceptance.

Geographic extension is likely to be the slowest unless the company is already a major global player with massive resources, as brand building from scratch is a time-consuming process. Many brands are attempting to enter the rapidly expanding markets in China, with varying success. For example, B&Q and Best Buy have opened and then closed stores but Tesco and Bosch are succeeding. Bosch attributes its success to understanding the needs of the market. The company has been trading in China for over a century using the name Bo Shi and develops specific products for the local markets, such as power tools (Costa, 2011).

However, geographic extension provides a high degree of control since companies can choose which brands to globalize, and plan their global extensions. Brand acquisition gives a moderate degree of control although many may prove hard to integrate with in-house brands. Brand alliance fosters the lowest degree of control, as strategy and resource allocation will need to be negotiated with the partner.

Finally, brand acquisitions are likely to incur the highest level of investment. For example, Nestlé paid £2.5 billion for Rowntree, a figure that was over five times its net asset value and Procter & Gamble paid £10 billion for brands owned by Gillette (Gillette, Duracell, Oral B and Braun). Geographic extension is likely to be more expensive than brand alliance since, in the latter case, costs are shared, and one partner may benefit from the expertise and distribution capabilities of the other. For example, in the Cereal Partners' alliance, General Mills gained access to Nestlé's expertise and distribution system in Europe. Figure 8.10 provides a framework for assessing the strategic alternatives when developing global and pan-European brands.

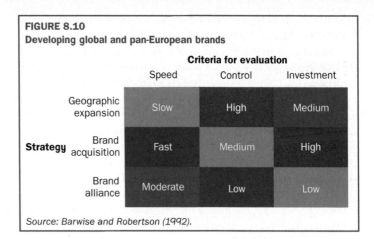

FIGURE 8.10
Developing global and pan-European brands

	Criteria for evaluation		
Strategy	Speed	Control	Investment
Geographic expansion	Slow	High	Medium
Brand acquisition	Fast	Medium	High
Brand alliance	Moderate	Low	Low

Source: Barwise and Robertson (1992).

Ethical Issues and Anti-branding

Three major ethical issues relate to products.

1 *Product safety* is a major concern particularly in relation to consumables. Genetically modified (GM) products have attracted the attention of pressure groups such as Greenpeace, who have spoken out about the dangers of genetic modification. People are sharply divided as to whether GM products are safe. Although plant breeders have for thousands of years been tampering with the genes of plants through traditional cross-pollination of plants of the same species, genetic modification goes one step further as it allows scientists to cross the species barrier.

Concerns about product safety also relate to tobacco (lung cancer), the levels of fat, sugar and salt in foods (obesity and heart problems), and sugar in soft drinks (obesity and tooth decay). Such issues have led to bans on tobacco advertising, the setting up of independent bodies to protect consumers' interests in the food and drinks industries, and reductions in the levels of fat, sugar and salt in many food and drink brands, particularly the level of sugar in food and soft drinks consumed by children. For example, Nestlé has reduced the level of sugar in its cereals targeted at children and reformulated its Rowntree range of children's sweets to make them free from artificial flavours and colours (Sweenier, 2005).

2 *Planned obsolescence.* Many products are not designed to last a long time. From the producer's point of view this is sensible as it creates a repeat-purchase situation. Hence cars rust, clothes wear out, and fashion items are replaced by the latest styles. Consumers accept that nothing lasts forever, but the issue concerns what is an acceptable length of time before replacement is necessary. One driving force is competition. To quell the

Japanese invasion, car manufacturers such as Ford and Volkswagen have made the body shells of their cars much more rust-resistant than before. Furthermore, it has to be recognized that many consumers welcome the chance to buy new clothes, new appliances with the latest features and the latest model of car. Critics argue that planned obsolescence reduces consumers' 'right to choose', since some consumers may be quite content to drive an old car so long as its body shell is free from rust and the car functions well. As we have noted, the forces of competition may act to deter the excesses of planned obsolescence.

3 *Deceptive packaging.* This can occur when a product appears in an oversized package to create the impression that the consumer is buying more than is the case. This is known as 'slack' packaging (Smith, 1995) and has the potential to deceive when the packaging is opaque. Products such as soap powders and breakfast cereals have the potential to suffer from slack packaging.

A second area where packaging may be deceptive is through misleading labelling, for example the failure of a package to state that the product contains genetically modified soya beans. This relates to the consumer's 'right to be informed', and can include the stating on labels of ingredients (including flavouring and colourants), nutritional content and country of origin. Nevertheless, labelling can be misleading. For example, in the UK, 'country of origin' is only the last country where the product was 'significantly changed'. So oil pressed from Greek olives in France can be labelled 'French', and foreign imports that are packed in the UK can be labelled 'produce of the UK'.

Consumers should also be wary of loose terminology. For example, smoked bacon may well have received its 'smoked flavour' from a synthetic liquid solution, 'farm fresh eggs' are likely to be un-date-marked eggs of indeterminate age laid by battery hens, and 'farmhouse cheese' may not come from farmhouses but from industrial factories (Young, 1999). The use of loose language and meaningless terms in the UK food and drink industry has been criticized by the Food Standards Agency (FSA). A list of offending words has been drawn up that includes 'fresh', 'natural', 'pure', 'traditional' and 'original'. Recommendations regarding when it is reasonable to use certain words have also been drawn up. For example, 'authentic' should only be used to emphasize the geographic origin of a product, and 'homemade' should be restricted to the preparation of the recipe on the premises and must involve 'some degree of fundamental culinary preparation'. The FSA has also expressed concern about the use of meaningless phrases such as 'natural goodness' and 'country-style', and recommended that they should not be used (*Marketing Week*, 2001).

Anti-branding and developing economies

Critics of branding accuse the practice of concentrating power and wealth in the hands of companies and economies that are already rich and powerful, whereas poor countries have to compete on price. A vociferous critic of branding is Naomi Klein (Klein, 2000), who claims that branding concentrates power in the hands of the already rich and powerful, who exploit the labour force of developing countries by supporting the paying of low wages while charging high prices for their products (Klein, 2000).

Supporters of branding claim that it is not branding's fault that poor countries suffer from low wages and that by sourcing from those countries their economies benefit. They also point out that the companies accused of being the worst offenders, such as Nike and Gap, have taken steps to introduce ethical sourcing policies that apply when dealing with the developing world.

Arguably, such anti-brand feelings are on the increase. Powerful brands are being deconstructed by vociferous online consumers, who are voicing their opinions about brands and brand meaning via social networks, blogs and other online forums. The Internet is liberating consumers by giving them power through debate and discourse.

Consumers are making more and more use of the Internet, and instead of being passive consumers they are becoming increasingly active participants. Anti-branding websites appear high up in search listings and such sites are surviving. Expert brand-haters (rather than just moaners and complainers) are being viewed as serious sources of information for the discerning customer who likes to review and evaluate many sources of information before making a purchase decision. Websites, blogs and social media are proving to be ideal platforms for such communications.

Research has also found that there is an increasingly significant relationship between 'consumer-generated anti-branding activities' and 'brand value'. Furthermore, there has been a rise in the amount of anti-brand online content. Consequently, 'Consumers have total control of branding messages most of the time in such anti-branding spaces. Online anti-branding spaces, where the anti-branders deliver their messages in ways that conform to the consumers' points of view, gain more sympathy and credibility with most consumers' (Kucuk, 2010).

From the brand perspective, there is value in understanding consumer/buyer concerns and issues and seeking to identify ways to address the criticism from the increasingly powerful consumer (Kucuk, 2010).

When you have read this chapter

Discover further resources and test your understanding: McGraw-Hill **Connect**™ is a digital teaching and learning environment that improves performance over a variety of critical outcomes; it can be tailored, is easy to use and is proven effective. **LearnSmart**™ is the most widely used and intelligent adaptive learning resource that is proven to strengthen memory recall, improve course retention and boost grades. Fuelled by **LearnSmart**™, **SmartBook**™ is the first and only adaptive reading experience available today.

Review

1 **The concept of a product, brand, product line and product mix**
  - A product is anything that is capable of satisfying customer needs.
  - A brand is a distinctive product offering created by the use of a name, symbol, design, packaging, or some combination of these, intended to differentiate it from its competitors.
  - A product line is a group of brands that are closely related in terms of the functions and benefits they provide.
  - A product mix is the total set of products marketed by a company.

2 **The difference between manufacturer and own-label brands**
  - Manufacturer brands are created by producers and bear their chosen brand name, whereas own-label brands are created and owned by distributors (e.g. supermarkets).

3 **The difference between a core and an augmented product (the brand)**
  - A core product is anything that provides the central benefits required by customers (e.g. toothpaste cleans teeth). The augmented product is produced by adding extra functional and/or emotional values to the core product, and combining them in a unique way to form a brand.

4 **Why strong brands are important**
  Strong brands are important because they:
  - enhance company value
  - positively affect consumer perceptions and preferences
  - act as a barrier to competition because of their impact on consumer perceptions and preferences
  - produce high profits through premium prices and high market share
  - provide the foundation for brand extensions
  - act as a form of quality certification, which aids consumers' decision-making process
  - build trust among consumers.

5 **Brand equity, its components and the concept of brand valuation**
  - Brand equity is a measure of the strength of a brand in the marketplace by adding tangible value to a company through the resulting sales and profits.
  - It is composed of customer-based brand equity, which is the differential effect that brand knowledge has on consumer response to the marketing of that brand, and proprietary-based brand equity, which is derived from company attributes that deliver value to the brand.

- Sources of customer-based brand equity are brand awareness and brand image.
- Sources of proprietary-based brand equity are patents and channel relationships.
- Brand valuation is the process of estimating the financial value of an individual or corporate brand.

6 How to build strong brands

Strong brands can be built by:

- building quality into the core product
- creating a unique position in the marketplace based on an analysis of brand domain, brand heritage, brand values, brand assets, brand personality and brand reflection
- repositioning to take advantage of new opportunities
- using well-blended communications to create a clear position in the minds of the target audience
- being first into the market with a unique marketing proposition
- taking a long-term perspective
- using internal marketing to train staff

7 The differences between family, individual and combined brand names, and the characteristics of an effective brand name

- A family brand name is one that is used for all products in a range (e.g. Nescafé); an individual brand name does not identify a brand with a particular company (e.g. Procter & Gamble does not appear with Daz); a *combination brand name* combines family and individual brand names (e.g. Microsoft Windows).
- The characteristics of an effective brand name are that it should evoke positive associations, be easy to pronounce and remember, suggest product benefits, be distinctive, use numerics or alphanumerics when emphasizing technology, be transferable, and not infringe on existing registered brand names.

8 Why companies rebrand, and how to manage the process

- Companies rebrand: to create a new identity after merger or acquisition; to create a new image/position in the marketplace; following the sale or acquisition of parts of a business where the old name is no longer appropriate; following corporate strategy changes where the old name is considered too limiting; to reflect the fact that a major product brand is more familiar to consumers than the old corporate brand; for international marketing reasons (e.g. name harmonization across national borders); for consolidation of brands within a national boundary; in response to legal problems (e.g. restrictions on its use).
- Managing the rebranding process involves choosing the new brand name and implementing the name change.
- Choosing the new brand name has six stages: setting rebranding objectives, generation of new names, screening to remove any with obvious flaws, information search to identify any infringements of existing brand names, consumer research, and choice of new brand name.
- Implementing the name change requires attention to five key issues: coordination among departments and groups; communication to consumers, employees and distributors; discovering what consumers identify with the brand so that communications can incorporate all relevant aspects of the brand; provision of assistance to distributors/retailers so that the change takes place smoothly; and care over the speed of changeover.

9 The concepts of brand extension and stretching, their uses and limitations

- A brand extension is the use of an established brand name on a new brand within the same broad market or product category; brand stretching occurs when an established brand is used for brands in unrelated markets or product categories.
- Their advantages are that: they reduce perceived risk of purchase on the part of distributors and consumers; the use of the established brand name raises consumers' willingness to try the new brand; the positive associations of the core brand should rub off onto the brand extension; the awareness of the core brand lowers advertising and other marketing costs; and the introduction of the extension can raise sales of the core brand due to the enhancement of consumers' perception of brand values and image through increased communication.
- The limitations are that poor performance of the brand extension could rebound on the core brand, the brand may lose credibility if stretched too far, sales of the extension may cannibalize sales of the core brand and the use of a brand extension strategy may encourage a focus on minor brand modifications rather than true innovation.

10 The two major forms of co-branding, and their advantages and risks

- The two major forms are product-based (parallel and ingredient) co-branding and communications-based co-branding.
- The advantages of product-based co-branding are added value and differentiation, the enhanced ability to position a brand for a particular target market, and the reduction of the cost of product introduction.
- The risks of product-based co-branding are loss of control and potential brand equity loss if poor performance of the co-brand rebounds on the original brands.
- The advantages of communications-based co-branding are endorsement opportunities, cost benefits, awareness and interest gains, and promotional opportunities.
- The risks of communications-based co-branding are loss of control, and potential brand equity loss.

11 The arguments for and against global and pan-European branding, and the strategic options for building such brands

- The arguments 'for' are that intensified global competition and technological developments, customer convergence of tastes and needs, and the prospect of global efficiencies of scale will encourage companies to create global brands.
- The arguments 'against' are that national varieties in taste and consumption patterns will limit the development of global brands.
- The strategic options are geographic extension, brand acquisition and brand alliances.

12 Ethical issues concerning ethics and anti-branding

- Ethical issues concern product safety, planned obsolescence, deceptive packaging and beliefs that branding confers power to rich nations to the detriment of developing countries.

Key Terms

augmented product the core product plus extra functional and/or emotional values combined in a unique way to form a brand

brand a distinctive product offering created by the use of a name, symbol, design, packaging, or some combination of these, intended to differentiate it from its competitors

brand assets the distinctive features of a brand

brand domain the brand's target market

brand equity a measure of the strength of a brand in the marketplace by adding tangible value to a company through the resulting sales and profits

brand extension the use of an established brand name on a new brand within the same broad market or product category

brand heritage the background to the brand and its culture

brand personality the character of a brand described in terms of other entities such as people, animals and objects

brand reflection the relationship of the brand to self-identity

brand stretching the use of an established brand name for brands in unrelated markets or product categories

brand valuation the process of estimating the financial value of an individual or corporate brand

brand values the core values and characteristics of a brand

combination brand name a combination of family and individual brand names

communications-based co-branding the linking of two or more existing brands from different companies or business units for the purposes of joint communication

core product anything that provides the central benefits required by customers

customer-based brand equity the differential effect that brand knowledge has on consumer response to the marketing of that brand

family brand name a brand name used for all products in a range

fighter brands low-cost manufacturers' brands introduced to combat own-label brands

global branding achievement of brand penetration worldwide

individual brand name a brand name that does not identify a brand with a particular company

ingredient co-branding the explicit positioning of a supplier's brand as an ingredient of a product

manufacturer brands brands that are created by producers and bear their chosen brand name

own-label brands brands created and owned by distributors or retailers

parallel co-branding the joining of two or more independent brands to produce a combined brand

product-based co-branding the linking of two or more existing brands from different companies or

business units to form a product in which the brand names are visible to consumers

product line a group of brands that are closely related in terms of the functions and benefits they provide

product mix the total set of products marketed by a company

proprietary-based brand equity is derived from company attributes that deliver value to the brand

rebranding the changing of a brand or corporate name

Study Questions

1. **Why do companies develop core products into brands?**

2. **Suppose you were the marketing director of a medium-sized bank. How would you tackle the job of building the company brand?**

3. **Think of five brand names. To what extent do they meet the criteria of good brand naming as laid out in Table 8.1?**

4. **What are the strategic options for pan-European brand building? What are the advantages and disadvantages of each option?**

5. **Why do companies rebrand product and corporate names? What is necessary for successful implementation of the rebranding process?**

6. **What are the two main forms of co-branding? What are their advantages and risks?**

Recommended Reading

Christodoulides, G. G. and L. de Chernatony (2010) Consumer-based brand equity conceptualisation and measurement, *International Journal of Market Research* 52(1), 43–66.

Harvard Business School, Thinking that leads, Marketing: Brand management http://hbswk.hbs.edu/topics/marketing.html

Keller, K.L., T. Aperia and M. Georgson (2012) Strategic brand management: a European perspective, *Financial Times*, Prentice Hall.

Merz, M. A. and S. L. Vargo (2009) The evolving brand logic: a service-dominant logic perspective, *Journal of the Academy of Marketing Science* 37(3), 328–44.

Thompson, C., A. Rindfleisch and Z. Arsel (*2006*) Emotional Branding and the Strategic Value of the Doppelgänger Brand Image, *Journal of Marketing*, January 2006, 70(1), 50–64.

References

Aaker, D. A. (1990) Brand Extensions: The Good, the Bad and the Ugly, *Sloan Management Review*, Summer, 47–56.

Aaker, D. A. and K. L. Keller (1990) Consumer Evaluation of Brand Extensions, *Journal of Marketing* 54 (January), 27–41.

Anon (2009) The game has changed, *The Economist*, 20 August. http://www.economist.com/node/14259150 (accessed 15 February 2015).

Armstrong, A. (2014) Mondelez and Douwe Egberts maker in coffee mega-merger, *The Telegraph*. http://www.telegraph.co.uk/finance/newsbysector/retailandconsumer/10814141/Mondelez-and-Douwe-Egberts-maker-in-coffee-mega-merger.html (accessed 22 March 2015).

Bainbridge, J. (2013) Last-mover advantage: when brands should avoid taking the lead. *Marketing Magazine*. http://www.marketingmagazine.co.uk/article/1167648/last-mover-advantage-when-brands-avoid-taking-lead (accessed 20 January 2015).

Barda, T. (2010) Reforming reputation, *The Marketer*, November, 32.

Barnett, M. (2012) Brands build trust through media spend, *Marketing Week*, 23 February, 14–16.

Barwise, P. and T. Robertson (1992) Brand Portfolios, *European Management Journal* 10(3), 277–85.

BBC4 (2009) *Reputations: The Life of Gabrielle Coco Chanel*, 29 January.

Benady, D. (2002) The Trouble with Facelifts, *Marketing Week*, 6 June, 21–3.

Bennett, R. C. and R. G. Cooper (1981) The Misuse of the Marketing Concept: An American Tragedy, *Business Horizons*, Nov.–Dec., 51–61.

Bokaie, J. (2007) Too Much of a Good Thing, *Marketing*, 30 April, 15.

Bokaie, J. (2008) Absolut Scales Back Flavoured Roll-Outs, *Marketing*, 13 August, 8.

Bokomo Foods Ltd. (2015) *WE LOVE OUR CUSTOMERS*, Bokoma. http://www.bokomo.co.uk/about/our-customers

Bottomley, P. A. and J. R. Doyle (1996) The Formation of Attitudes towards Brand Extensions: Testing and Generalising Aaker and Keller's Model, *International Journal of Research in Marketing* 13, 365–77.

Boxall, A. (2014) LG and Google hope more innovative products will come from new patent sharing deal, Digital Trends, 6 November. http://www.digitaltrends.com/mobile/lg-google-sign-patent-sharing-deal

Brandz. (2015) Brandz Top 100 Global, Brandz. http://www.brandz100.com/#/tabbed/global-100/149?tab_id=150&tab_url=%2Ftop-table%2Ftop-100-48673d91-a201-4477-aefd-86db2db2b656%2F150 (accessed 20 March 2015).

Buzzell, R. and B. Gale (1987) *The PIMS Principles*, London: Collier Macmillan

Cannarella, J. and J. Spechler (2014) Epidemiological modeling of online social network dynamics. http://arxiv.org/abs/1401.4208 (accessed 22 March 2015).

Carter, M. (2011) 21st century alchemy, *The Marketer*, April, 28–32.

Cassidy, A. (2012) Ad agencies vie for £4m Douwe Egberts brief, *Campaign*, 30 August.

Costa, M. (2011) Brand value is jewel in the crown for marketers, *Marketing Week*, 12 May, 12–14.

De Chernatony, L. (1991) Formulating Brand Strategy, *European Management Journal* 9(2), 194–200.

DeKimpe, M. C., J.-B. E. M. Steenkamp, M. Mellens and P. Vanden Abeele (1997) Decline and Variability in Brand Loyalty, *International Journal of Research in Marketing* 14, 405–20.

Denstadli, J. M., R. Lines and K. Grønhaug (2005) First Mover Advantage in the Discount Grocery Industry, *European Journal of Marketing* 39(7/8), 872–84.

Douwe Egberts Coffee Company (2015) DE Coffee Company, History of Douwe Egberts. http://www.decoffeecompany.com/History_of_Douwe_Egberts_s/31.htm

Doyle, P. (1989) Building Successful Brands: The Strategic Options, *Journal of Marketing Management* 5(1), 77–95.

Dregde, S. (2015) Angry Birds revenues fell in 2014 due to sharp decline in merchandise sales, *The Guardian*, 19 March. http://www.theguardian.com/technology/2015/mar/19/angry-birds-revenues-2014-rovio

East, R. (1997) *Consumer Behaviour*, Hemel Hempstead: Prentice-Hall Europe.

Ehrenberg, A. S. C., G. J. Goodhardt and T. P. Barwise (1990) Double Jeopardy Revisited, *Journal of Marketing* 54 (July), 82–91.

Fisk, P. (2005) Proving Marketing's Worth, *Marketing*, 31 March, 27.

Flambard-Ruaud, S. and P. Daly (2012) Which Growth Strategy for Lotus Original Speculoos on the French market: Focusing on the core market or diversifying into new ones?, Case study M1783(GB), Paris: CCMP.

Gale Encyclopedia of E-commerce (2002), http://www.encyclopedia.com/topic/Jeffrey_Bezos.aspx.

Golder, P., J. Irwin and D. Mitra, (2013) Four Insights On How Great Brands Fail, *Forbes*, 12 July. http://www.forbes.com/sites/onmarketing/2013/07/12/four-insights-on-how-great-brands-fail (accessed 30 March 2015).

Grime, I., A. Diamantopoulos and G. Smith (2002) Consumer Evaluations of Extensions and their Effects on the Core Brand:

Key Issues and Research Propositions, *European Journal of Marketing* 36(11/12), 1415–38.

Halliburton, C. and R. Hünerberg (1993) Pan-European Marketing—Myth or Reality, *Proceedings of the European Marketing Academy Conference*, Barcelona, May, 490–518.

Hegarty, J. (2011) *Hegarty on advertising: turning intelligence into magic*, London: Thames & Hudson, 21.

Hegarty, J. (2011) *Hegarty on advertising: turning intelligence into magic*, London: Thames & Hudson, 39.

Hickman, M. (2006) Disney Drops McDonald's Amid Health Fears, *Independent*, 10 May, 24.

Hilpern, K. (2010) Douwe Egberts bagged a bigger share of the luxury coffee market with its master blend, *The Marketer*. http://www.themarketer.co.uk/archives/case-studies/brand-blend (accessed 22 March 2015).

Interbrand (2014) Interbrand's 15th annual Best Global Brands Report, Interbrand, October. http://interbrand.com/en/newsroom/15/interbrands-th-annual-best-global-brands-report

Interbrand (2014) Methodology, Interbrand. http://www.bestglobalbrands.com/2014/methodology

Kapferer, J.N. (2008) *The New Strategic Brand Management*, London: Kogan Page.

Keller, K. L. (2008) *Strategic Brand Management*, New Jersey: Pearson.

Kimberly, S. (2014) Douwe Egberts launches selfie campaign for Prostate Cancer, *Campaign*, 27 October. http://www.campaignlive.co.uk/news/1319010/douwe-egberts-launches-selfie-campaign-prostate-cancer (accessed 24 March 2015).

King, S. (1991) Brand Building in the 1990s, *Journal of Marketing Management* 7(1), 3–14

Klara, R. (2015) 11 Brand Names That Simply Couldn't Survive the Times Ayds diet candy and Isis Chocolates were doomed, *Adweek*, 18 March. http://www.adweek.com/news-gallery/advertising-branding/11-brand-names-simply-couldnt-survive-times-163440 (accessed 30 March 2015).

Klein, N. (2000) *No Logo. Taking Aim at the Brand Bullies*, London: HarperCollins.

Kucuk, S. U. (2010) Negative Double Jeopardy revisited: A longitudinal analysis, *Journal of Brand Management* 18(2), 150–8.

Lambkin, M. (1992) Pioneering New Markets: A Comparison of Market Share Winners and Losers, *International Journal of Research in Marketing* 9(1), 5–22.

Lemmink, J. and H. Kaspar (1994) Competitive Reactions to Product Quality Improvements in Industrial Markets, *European Journal of Marketing* 28(12), 50–68.

Macalister, T. (2015) E.On reports group losses as prepares to hive off fossil fuel business, *The Guardian*, 11 March. http://www.theguardian.com/business/2015/mar/11/eon-reports-record-group-losses-hive-off-fossil-fuel-business-german (accessed 27 March 2015).

Marketing Week (2001) An End to the Packet Racket, 2 August, 3; and Benady, D. (2001) Will They Eat Their Words? *Marketing Week*, 2 August, 24–6.

McWilians, J. (2009) How Facebook beats MySpace, *The Guardian*, 23 June. http://www.theguardian.com/commentisfree/cifamerica/2009/jun/23/facebook-myspace-social-networks (accessed 10 February 2015).

Millward Brown (2012) *Brand Personality*, Millward Brown. http://www.millwardbrown.com/mb-global/brand-strategy/brand-equity/brandz/top-global-brands/2012/brand-personality (accessed 31 July 2015).

Millward Brown (2014) *Most Valuable Brands 2014*, MillwardBrown.com. https://www.millwardbrown.com/brandz/2014/Top100/Docs/2014_BrandZ_Top100_Chart.pdf (accessed 31 July 2015).

Mitchell, A. (2005) P&G Scales Up Global Ambitions, *Marketing Week*, 3 February, 24–7.

Mortimer, N. (2014) Royal Mail challenger TNT Post rebrands as Whistl and trials electric unicycle deliveries, *The Drum*, 15 September. http://www.thedrum.com/news/2014/09/15/royal-mail-challenger-tnt-post-rebrands-whistl-and-trials-electric-unicycle (accessed 20 March 2015).

Nieva, R. (2014) Google partnership with Disney streams its catalog to Android, 4 November. http://www.cnet.com/uk/news/google-partnership-with-disney-streams-its-catalog-to-android

Oliver, C. (2011) Hyundai shifts gear with move to quality, *Financial Times*, 19 May, 22.

Phillip. (2015) Company Profile, Phillips, 20 March. http://www.philips.co.uk/about/company/companyprofile.page

PRNewswire. (2013) Best Western And Harley-Davidson Partnership Goes Global, PRNewswire, 20 February. http://www.prnewswire.com/news-releases/best-western-and-harley-davidson-partnership-goes-global-192015471.html

Quinn, I. (2013) Tesco strikes nostalgic note with Christmas advert, *The Grocer*, 8 November. http://www.thegrocer.co.uk/channels/supermarkets/tesco/tesco-strikes-nostalgic-note-with-christmas-advert/351464.article (accessed 18 March 2015).

Readers Digest (n.d.) Trusted Brands 2015—Winners, Trusted brands. http://www.rdtrustedbrands.com/tables/Winners%2520by%2520country.country.Portugal.shtml

Reynolds, J. (2013) Tesco to launch Christmas TV ad early to beat rivals, *The Guardian*, 7 November. http://www.theguardian.com/media/2013/nov/07/tesco-christmas-tv-ad-early-x-factor (accessed 18 March 2015).

Reynolds, J. (2015) Kellogg's hits back at own-label with top secret Special K recipe, *Marketing*, 17 May. http://www.marketingmagazine.co.uk/article/1182787/kelloggs-hits-back-own-label-top-secret-special-k-recipe (accessed 20 March 2015).

Reysen, S. (2005) Construction of a new scale: the Reysen likeability scale, *Social Behavior and Personality* 33, 201–8.

Riezebos, R. (2003) *Brand Management*, Harlow: Pearson Education.

Ritson, M. (2011) Opposites attract higher brand equity, *Marketing Week*, 22 September, 62.

Roberts, C. J. and G. M. McDonald (1989) Alternative Naming Strategies: Family versus Individual Brand Names, *Management Decision* 27(6), 31–7.

Saunders, J. (1990) Brands and Valuations, *International Journal of Advertising* 9, 95–110.

Sharp, B. M. (1990) The Marketing Value of Brand Extension, *Marketing Intelligence and Planning* 9(7), 9–13.

Sidel, R. (2015) AmEx-Costco Divorce Shakes Up Card Industry, *The Wall Street Journal*, 12 February. http://www.wsj.com/articles/american-express-to-lose-costco-exclusivity-1423746408 (accessed 16 March 2015).

Smith, N. C. (1995) Marketing Strategies for the Ethics Era, *Sloan Management Review*, Summer, 85–97. See also T. W. Dunfee, N. C. Smith and W. T. Ross Jr (1999) Social Contracts and Marketing Ethics, *Journal of Marketing* 63 (July), 14–32.

Steenkamp, J.-B. E. M., R. Batra and D. L. Alden (2003) How Perceived Brand Globalness Creates Brand Value, *Journal of International Business Studies* 34(1), 53–65.

Sweenier, M. (2005) Nestlé Takes 'Healthier' Line in Rowntree Revamp, *Marketing*, 21 March, 1.

Thurtle, G. (2002) Papering Over the Cracks, *Marketing Week*, 7 March, 25–7.

Tomkins, R. (2005) A Desire for Pairings Leads Brands on a Wild Goose Chase, *Financial Times*, 29 November, 13.

Trangbaek, R. (2014) About Us, Lego, 8 October. http://www.lego.com/en-GB/aboutus/news-room/2014/october/comment-on-the-greenpeace-campaign-and-the-lego-brand (accessed 30 March 2015).

Urban, G. L., T. Carter, S. Gaskin and Z. Mucha (1986) Market Share Rewards to Pioneering Brands: An Empirical Analysis and Strategic Implications, *Management Science* 32 (June), 645–59.

Valantine, M. (2009) It's All in the Mind, *Marketing Week*, 2 April, 29.

Wallop, H. (2014) 7 things you need to know about the John Lewis Christmas advert 2014, *The Telegraph*, 6 November. http://www.telegraph.co.uk/finance/newsbysector/retailandconsumer/11210848/7-things-you-need-to-know-about-the-John-Lewis-Christmas-advert-2014.html (accessed 14 December 2015).

White, A. (2014) How ghd is getting ahead, *The Telegraph*, 4 January. http://www.telegraph.co.uk/finance/newsbysector/retailandconsumer/10549768/How-ghd-is-getting-ahead.html (accessed 18 March 2015).

Wray, R. (2006) NTL Buys Virgin Mobile and Prepares to Battle with BSkyB, *The Guardian*, 5 April, 23.

Young, R. (1999) First Read the Label, Then Add a Pinch of Salt, *The Times*, 30 November, 2–4.

Lessons in Co-Branding: The Apple/U2 Experience

Introduction

On 9 September 2014, Irish rock band U2 pulled off the largest album release in history at Apple's event to launch its latest versions of the iPhone and its new smartwatch (Burke and Reuters, 2014). Amid much fanfare, Apple's chief executive, Tim Cook, announced that U2's latest album—Songs of Innocence—would be automatically loaded onto the music libraries of about 500 million iTunes customers in 119 countries at no charge (Matthews, 2014). To release U2's free album, Apple paid the band and Universal an unspecified fee as a blanket royalty and committed to a marketing campaign for the band worth up to $100 million (£62 million). That marketing campaign included a global television advertising campaign, the first piece of which was a commercial that was shown during the event (Sisario, 2014). Expecting excitement, gratitude and an increase in signups for their iTunes service, Apple was dismayed when fury erupted over the announcement. As it turns out, users were less than thrilled at the prospect of the U2 album being loaded onto their devices without their permission (Matthews, 2014).

The Use of Co-Branding

Co-branding is being increasingly used by companies large and small to raise awareness and generate sales. U2 and Apple first ignited the flame of celebrity–corporate co-creation in 2004, when they collaborated on the launch of the iPod U2 Special Edition (Deal and Dupri, 2013). Both brands may be seen as a good match as they have both thrived on constant reinvention, retaining a loyal audience through the delivery of pioneering leisure products—the iPhone and U2's ever-more-spectacular live shows (Sherwi, 2014). The recent Apple–U2 co-promotion brought together two very powerful superbrands in a co-branding arrangement that was envisaged as being beneficial to both brands. Apple's deal with U2 meant that the Songs of Innocence album would be exclusive to iTunes, iTunes Radio and Apple's Beats sharing music service for five weeks (Jurgensen, 2014).

Although U2's album release seemed to have little to do with the new iPhone and smartwatch that Apple introduced, U2's appearance closed the launch event

with celebrity power and also underscored Apple's continuing importance to the music industry (Sisario, 2014). Apple also knew that iTunes sales were dropping and were likely to plummet as music continues to morph into a streaming experience (Wallace, 2014). Apple's U2 giveaway may be seen as a last-ditch attempt at making iTunes downloads relevant. In addition, the deal also enabled Apple to boast about being part of the biggest album release in history (Hodgkins, 2014).

For U2 and its label, the deal satisfied what has become a requirement for any major album release in an era of falling sales: a big attention-grabbing media event to advertise the album and create online conversations (Hodgkins, 2014). U2 wanted to remain relevant in our Internet-driven culture (Wallace, 2014). U2's collaboration with Apple has been described by some as an original, compelling and attention-grabbing way of promoting the new album by making the content available for free. They succeeded in building buzz, both on social media and in the offline world. The hope was that this buzz would translate into more albums sold and more concert tickets purchased as new listeners discovered the pleasures of U2 through this new album giveaway (Clark, 2014). Since the giveaway began, more than 26 million people have downloaded Songs of Innocence in its entirety, and more than 81 million people have listened to at least one of the songs from the album on iTunes (Newman, 2014). The hope was that the album giveaway would also act as a promotional tool for the group's next global tour (Sherwi, 2014).

»

»

The Critics

There were complaints from some iTunes users that Songs of Innocence had essentially been forced on them without their permission. While it may seem ungrateful to complain about a free product, it is nevertheless legitimate to criticize the shoehorned nature of this product launch (Clark, 2014). The Apple–U2 promotion was embarrassing for both parties because of the public backlash that ensued. Instead of making the band's album an opt-in freebie, Apple was perceived by many as jamming it down the throats of half a billion iTunes store customers. Apple was giving away something free to its customers, but some argued that it may have been a more sensible approach for Apple to make the album download optional instead (Wallace, 2014).

This Apple–U2 fiasco illustrates the importance of consumer choice. There was no sense of choice for the consumer in this co-promotion. The band and Apple left no room for consumers to play a part or to feel like they contributed to this process. Users felt as though the product was forced upon them (Clark, 2014). The key lesson for marketers here is to avoid forcing anything onto consumers. In general, it is better to let consumers find their way to a brand by giving them enough information so that they can make the choice on their own (Clark, 2014).

Traditional media outlets like the Washington Post labelled the marketing stunt 'rock-and-roll dystopian junk mail' (Wallace, 2014). The New Yorker's pop music critic Sasha Frere-Jones also compared the stunt to junk mail, stating 'Don't shove your music into people's homes.' He wrote, 'A U2 album that some would have taken seriously was instead turned into an album that seemed as pointless as it probably is. Lack of consent is not the future.' Iggy Pop, the so-called 'godfather of punk' criticized the stunt also stating, 'The people who don't want the free U2 download are trying to say "Don't try to force me," and they've got a point' (Booth, 2014).

Other critics of the stunt argued that giving away digital music, particularly whole albums is damaging to the value of recorded music. Paul Quirke, Chairman of the Entertainment Retailers Association, argued that 'the U2 stunt vindicates our view that giving away hundreds of millions of albums, simply devalues music and runs the risk of alienating the 60 per cent of the population who are not customers of iTunes. Dumping an album on hundreds of millions of iTunes libraries whether people want it or not, reduces music to the level of a software update or a bug-fix or just plain spam' (Williams, 2014). Others argued that giving away songs for free had somewhat devalued a record that cost six years of the band members' lives and a lot of money to make (Kelion, 2014).

Conclusion

In response to the many consumer complaints that it wasn't immediately obvious how to delete the tracks, six days after the album's release Apple released a tool to remove the album from its customers' iTunes accounts and established a dedicated web page providing step-by-step instructions on how to do this. For Apple, there are important lessons to be learned from this co-branding exercise. Apple learned an important yet expensive lesson that brands should pay attention. No potential customers want to be told what to do or to be forced into action that is not of their choosing, or to feel as though their privacy is being invaded (Matthews, 2014).

Questions   ![Mc Graw Hill Education] **connect**

1. **Both Apple and U2 are world-leading brands. Describe the main benefits of strong brands for both the companies involved and their consumers.**

2. **The Apple–U2 promotion is an example of a co-branding exercise. Which type of co-branding was being used here and what are the advantages and risks of this co-branding approach?**

3. **What are the main lessons to be learned from the Apple–U2 fiasco?**

4. **What other options could Apple have taken to ensure that customers felt that they were part of the process and had a choice?**

This case was written by Marie O'Dwyer, Lecturer in Marketing, Waterford Institute of Technology.

References

Based on: Burke, M. and A. P. T. N. Reuters (2014) Apple iPhone launch: U2 announces surprise album free for all iTunes users, The Telegraph, http://www.telegraph.co.uk/technology/apple/11086213/Apple-iPhone-launch-U2-announces-surprise-album-free-for-all-iTunes-users.html; Matthews, K. (2014) '3 lessons from Apple's U2 fiasco, PR Daily, http://www.prdaily.com/Main/Articles/3_lessons_from_Apples_U2_fiasco_17288.aspx; Sisario, B. (2014) For U2 and Apple, a Shrewd Marketing Partnership, NY Times, http://www.nytimes.com/2014/09/10/business/media/u2-appears-at-apple-event-and-songs-of-innocence-appears-free-on-itunes.html?_r=0; Deal, D. and J. Dupri (2013) 4 lessons on using co-branding to co-crush the competition, FastCompany.com, http://www.fastcompany.com/3009372/4-lessons-on-using-co-branding-to-co-crush-the-competition; Sherwi, A. (2014) Free U2 album: How the most generous giveaway in music history turned PR disaster, The Independent, http://

www.independent.co.uk/arts-entertainment/music/features/free-u2
-album-how-the-most-generous-giveaway-in-music-history-turned-into
-a-pr-disaster-9745028.html; Jurgensen, J. (2014) U2, Apple and the
Deal Behind Getting 'Songs of Innocence' Free of Charge, Wall Street
Journal, http://blogs.wsj.com/speakeasy/2014/09/09/u2-apple-and
-the-deal-behind-getting-songs-of-innocence-free-of-charge; Wallace, L.
(2014) U2 and Apple crank marketing debacle up to 11, Cult of Mac,
http://www.cultofmac.com/295576/u2-apple-marketing-debacle;
Hodgkins, K. (2014) Business side of Apple's exclusive launch of
U2's 'Songs of Innocence' album, Engadget.com, http://www.tuaw.
com/2014/09/10/business-side-of-apples-exclusive-launch-of-u2s
-songs-of-inno; Clark, A. (2014) Content marketing lessons learned
from U2, Digitalist, http://blogs.sap.com/innovation/sales-marketing/
content-marketing-lessons-learned-from-u2-01431354; Newman, J.
(2014) 81 million people listed to U2's iTunes giveaway, Macworld,
http://www.macworld.com/article/2824569/81-million-people
-listened-to-u2s-itunes-giveaway.html; Booth, R. (2014) U2's Bono
issues apology for automatic Apple iTunes album download, The
Guardian, http://www.theguardian.com/music/2014/oct/15/u2-bono
-issues-apology-for-apple-itunes-album-download Williams, C. (2014)
Apple tie-up with U2 branded a 'dismal failure' by music retailers,
The Telegraph, http://www.telegraph.co.uk/finance/newsbysector/
mediatechnologyandtelecoms/digital-media/11098907/Apple-tie
-up-with-U2-branded-a-dismal-failure-by-music-retailers.html Kelion, L.
(2014) Apple releases U2 album removal tool, BBC, http://www.bbc
.com/news/technology-29208540

CASE 16
Burberry

Reinventing the Brand

It is called 'doing a Gucci' after Domenico De Sole and Tom Ford's stunning success at turning nearly bankrupt Gucci Group into a £7 billion (€10 billion) (market capitalization) fashion powerhouse. Since 1997, when she took over, Rose Marie Bravo's makeover of the 143-year-old Burberry brand followed the same path.

The Burberry story began in 1856 when Thomas Burberry opened his first gentlemen's outfitters. By the First World War business was booming as Burberry won the contract to supply trenchcoats to the British army. Its reputation grew when it proved its contribution to the national cause. The Burberry check was introduced in the 1920s and became fashionable among the British middle to upper classes. Later, when it was worn by Humphrey Bogart in Casablanca and Audrey Hepburn in Breakfast at Tiffany's, the Burberry trenchcoat gained widespread appeal.

Bought by Great Universal Stores in 1955, the brand's huge popularity from the 1940s to the 1970s had waned by the 1980s. A less deferential society no longer yearned to dress like the upper classes, and the Burberry brand's cachet fell in the UK. This was partially offset by a surge in sales to the newly rich Japanese and other Asians after they discovered its famous (and trademarked) tan, black/red and white check pattern. By the mid-1990s the Far East accounted for an unbalanced 75 per cent of Burberry sales. British and American consumers began to regard it as an Asian brand and rather staid. Furthermore, distribution was focused on small shops with few big fashion chains and upmarket stores like Harrods stocking the brand. In the USA, stores like Barney's, Neiman Marcus and Saks only sold Burberry raincoats, not the higher-profit-margin accessories (e.g. handbags, belts, scarves and wraps).

Change of strategy

These problems resulted in profit falls in the 1990s culminating in a £37 million (€53 million) drop in profits to £25 million (€36 million) in 1997. This prompted some serious managerial rethinking and

the recruitment of American Rose Marie Bravo as a new chief executive. Responsible for the turnaround of the US store chain Saks Fifth Avenue, she had the necessary experience to make the radical changes required at Burberry.

One of her first moves was to appoint young designer Roberto Menichetti to overhaul the clothes range. His challenge was to redesign Burberry's raincoats and other traditional products to keep them fresh and attractive to new generations of younger consumers. Furthermore, he sought to extend the Burberry image to a new range of products. The Burberry brand name began to appear on such products as children's clothes, personal products, watches, blue jeans, bikinis, home-wares and shoes in order to attract new customers and broaden the company's sales base. Commenting on Menichetti, Bravo said, 'Coming in, I had studied Hermes and Gucci and other great brands, and it struck me that even during the periods when they had dipped a bit, they never lost the essence of whatever made those brands sing. And I thought, "This man will retain what's good and move us forward".'

Design was further strengthened in 2001 with the appointment of Christopher Bailey (from Gucci) as Burberry's creative director. He created Burberry 'classics with a twist' (for example, recasting the classic trenchcoat in hot pink). Bailey's job was to design clothes that met Bravo's vision of heritage and classic, but young, modern, hip and fashionable.

A second element of her strategy was to bring in advertising agency Baron & Baron and celebrity photographer Mario Testino to shoot ads featuring models Kate Moss and Stella Tennant. Other celebrities, such as the Beckhams, Callum Best, Elizabeth Jagger, Nicole Appleton and Jarvis Cocker, also featured in Burberry advertising. The focus was to emphasize the new credentials of the Burberry brand without casting off its classic roots. Getting key celebrities to don the Burberry check in its advertising was highly important in achieving this. Bravo once remarked that the famous picture of Kate Moss in a Burberry check bra cut the average age of its customers by 30 years.

A third strand in Bravo's strategy was to sort out distribution. Unprofitable shops were closed and an emphasis placed on flagship stores in cosmopolitan cities. Prestige UK retailers including Harvey Nichols were selected to stock exclusive ranges. Bravo commented, 'We were selling in 20 small shops in Knightsbridge alone, but we weren't in Harrods.' Also, stores that were selling only raincoats were persuaded to stock high-margin accessories as well. Burberry accessories increased from 20 per cent to 25 per cent of turnover. This was part of a wider focus on gifts—the more affordable side of luxury that can drive heavy footfall through the stores. As Bravo said, 'Burberry has to be thought of as a gift store. Customers have to feel they can go into Burberry and buy gifts at various price points.'

International expansion was also high on Bravo's priority list. A succession of new stores were opened, including flagship stores in London, New York and Barcelona. The New York store on 57th Street was the realization of a personal dream for Bravo, whose vision was to replace the store the company had been running in Manhattan for almost 25 years with one that was bigger, better and far more profitable. It is the biggest Burberry store worldwide and has a number of Burberry 'firsts': a lavish gift department, a large area for accessories, private shopping and an in-store Mad Hatters tea room. It also offers a service called Art of the Trench where customers can get made-to-measure trenchcoats customized by allowing them to pick their own lining, collar, checks and tartan. The Barcelona store was regarded as vital in helping to reposition the Burberry brand in Spain. Prior to its opening the brand was slightly less fashionable and sold at slightly lower prices than in the UK. The opening of the Barcelona store saw the London product being displayed for the first time as Burberry moved towards one global offering. Besides the USA and Spain, Burberry's third priority country was Japan since it was an enormous market for the company already.

The results of this activity were astonishing. Profits soared to £162 million (€227 million) by 2005, a six-fold increase since she took over, and in 2002 Great Universal Stores floated one-third of Burberry, its subsidiary, on the stock market, raising £275 million (€396 million). Then, in December 2005 it demerged Burberry completely, allocating Burberry stores to GUS shareholders in proportion to their holdings in a deal worth £1.4 billion (€2.0 billion).

Burberry did face problems, however. One was the weeding-out of grey-market goods, which were offered cheaply in Asia only to be diverted back to western markets at discounts. Not only were sales affected but brand image was tarnished. Like Dior before it, Burberry was willing to spend the necessary money to try to eliminate this activity. Another problem was that of copycats which infringed its trademark. Burberry claim to spend about £2 million (€2.8 million) a year fighting counterfeits, running advertisements in trade publications and sending letters to trade groups, textile manufacturers and retailers reminding them about its trademark rights. It uses an Internet-monitoring service to help pick up online discussion about counterfeits. It also works with Customs officials and local police forces to seize fakes and sue infringers.

The fondness with which so-called 'chavs' regarded the Burberry check was a third problem. One observer defined a chav as a young, white, under-educated underclass obsessed with brands and unsuitable jewellery. One product with which chavs became particularly associated was the Burberry baseball cap. They were also associated with violence, particularly at football matches. The sight of football hooligans appearing in the media adorned in beige and black check was not one appreciated at Burberry HQ. In response, the company stopped producing the infamous cap and shifted emphasis to other non-check lines, including its Prorsum line of luxury clothing designed by creative director, Christopher Bailey.

A fourth problem arose in 2005 with the announcement that Bravo had decided to step down as chief executive. The woman who had built Burberry into an ultra-fashionable major global brand would need to be replaced. Her successor was Angela Ahrendts, who was recruited from the US clothing company Liz Claiborne, which owns such brands as DKNY jeans and Juicy Couture. After a period of working together, Ahrendts took the helm in July 2006 with Bravo taking the newly created role of vice-chairperson, a part-time executive position.

A New Era

Ms Ahrendts made changes to the Burberry product line by making the check more subtle and using it mainly in linings and discreet areas of garments. She also placed greater emphasis on higher margin

»

accessories such as handbags and perfumes, and top-of-the-range fashion. She continued to use British celebrities such as Agnes Deyne and Emma Watson to represent the brand. Burberry also opened stores in emerging markets such as China, India, Russia, the Middle East and eastern Europe. In 2008 Burberry's first standalone children's-wear store in Hong Kong was opened, and in 2011 the company bought out its Chinese franchise partner in order to tighten its rein on its global image. It also built up its presence in the USA with the opening of its new headquarters in New York and further store openings.

Ms Ahrendts also improved efficiency by installing new IT systems and replacing 21 scattered distribution centres with three regional hubs in the USA. Her attention was also placed on better sourcing in an effort to improve margins.

Another major focus was to revive Burberry's heritage to the digital generation. Where once luxury brands were reluctant to use the Internet, believing it would cheapen their image, Burberry embraced digital. Now digital represents 60 per cent of the marketing budget. Burberry live-streams seasonal shows online and in stores, allowing customers to order products for early delivery with a personalized touch, such as an engraved nameplate in a coat or bag. Pictures of the latest designs are posted on Twitter before they are released to traditional media. Burberry has over 8 million Facebook fans, who can watch most of its catwalk shows live and purchase Burberry products direct from its virtual store.

Burberry's digital presence extends to China, where sales have soared. The brand features on Chinese sites such as Sina Weibo (China's equivalent to Twitter) and Youku (similar to YouTube), helping the brand to outperform its rivals in the country. Asia now accounts for over 40 per cent of Burberry's revenues.

As well as global and digital expansion, Ms Ahrendts saw menswear and male accessories such as bags and scarves as key to Burberry's continuing success. In 2012 its first standalone menswear store, next to its branch in Knightsbridge, London, was opened. By 2014 menswear accounted for a quarter of Burberry's sales.

The expansion of fragrance and beauty products has also driven sales growth. In 2014 its first dedicated makeup and perfume shop was opened in Covent Garden, London.

By 2014, Burberry sales had soared to £2.33 billion with profits of £461 million. However, in the same year, Ms Ahrendts was tempted by an offer to join Apple and

was succeeded by creative director Christopher Bailey, who had received much of the credit for the success of Burberry's digital marketing operations. His aims were to continue global expansion, particularly in Japan, where Burberry has underperformed, expansion of its beauty business, including entering the £26 billion skincare market in 2015, and to continue to penetrate the menswear market.

Questions

1. How were the clothes bearing the Burberry name augmented to create a brand before the 1980s?

2. What elements of the brand-building factors discussed in this chapter have been used by Burberry to rebuild its brand?

3. What problems might arise in trying to build Burberry into a global brand?

4. What are the dangers inherent in Burberry's strategy since 1997?

This case was written by David Jobber, Emeritus Professor of Marketing, University of Bradford.

References

Based on: Heller, R. (2000) A British Gucci, Forbes, 3 April, 84–6; ; White, E. (2003) Protecting the Real Plaid from a Lineup of Fakes, Wall Street Journal, 7 May; Barns, E. (2005) Are Advertisers Wise to Chase the Chav Pound?, Campaign, 24 March, 18; ;Walsh, F. (2006) Burberry Chief Turns on Charm with 19 per cent Growth in Retail Sales, The Guardian, 13 July, 28; Kollewe, J. and G. Wearden (2008) Burberry Sees Profits Rise While Laura Ashley Suffers, The Guardian, 29 May, 26; Gumbel, P. (2008) The Luxury Market Loses Its Lustre, Fortune, 22 August, 27; Wardell, J. (2009) Burberry Makes Loss For Year, Business Week, 19 May, 64; Wood, Z. (2010) Burberry Buys Out Chinese Partner to Unify the Brand, The Guardian, 17 July, 33; Ritson, M. (2011) Burberry Offers a Lesson in Consistency, Marketing Week, 2 June, 54; Barrett, C. and T. Bradshaw (2011) Burberry in Step with Digital Age, The Financial Times, 1 September, 16; Leroux, M. and S. Thompson (2012) Burberry Banks on the Ascent of (Fashionable) Man, The Times, 24 May, 43; Butler, S. (2013) Chilly Spring Warms Hearts at Burberry, The Guardian, 11 July, 26; Butler, S. and J. Rankin (2014) Doubt Over Leaving Date for Outgoing Boss at Burberry, The Guardian, 17 April,31; Rankin, J. (2014) Bailey Outlines His Design for Burberry Seamless Move, The Guardian, 22 May, 29; Vizard, S. (2015) 'Commitment to Customer Experience' Helps Burberry to Festive Sales Boost, marketingweek.com, 14 January.

CHAPTER 9
Value Through Services

> *It is not so much the products you sell that guarantee success but the service you provide to customers.*
>
> **LUKE JOHNSON, ENTREPRENEUR**

LEARNING OBJECTIVES

After reading this chapter, you should be able to:

1. describe the nature and special characteristics of services
2. describe the activity sectors in the services industry
3. explain how customer relationships should be managed
4. explain how to manage service quality, productivity and staff
5. explain how to position a service organization and brand
6. discuss the services marketing mix
7. describe the nature and special characteristics of non-profit marketing

T his chapter discusses the marketing of services and how they deliver value. Throughout this text we adopt the stance that physical products and service products are equally important in terms of the marketing requirements. It is also essential to be aware of how principles of marketing apply to services. In addition to the 4-Ps the marketing of services requires understanding of the services marketing mix. Furthermore, it is important to be aware of how superior value is created in the service industries by bringing together a company and its customers in the value creation process (Karpen, Bove and Lukas, 2012). This approach has been called service *dominant logic* and it focuses marketers' attention on the creation of value and the importance of relationships in contrast to the traditional model of marketing, which has the exchange of manufactured goods as its dominant logic. From this point of view, marketers should think about how best to manage and co-create value with customers. This means developing long-term relationships that are mutually beneficial (Karpen, Bove and Lukas, 2012). The management of customer relationships is discussed in detail in Chapter 10.

Services become increasingly valuable to industrialized economies as advances in technology lead to the development of sophisticated products that require more design, production and maintenance services. Other reasons for the rising contribution of services to the global economy are growth in per capita income. This gives citizens a greater percentage of their income to spend on non-essentials such as restaurant meals, national and international travel, which are all service-intensive products. Greater discretionary income increases demand for financial services such as investment trusts and personal pensions. It is not just in the consumer sector where there is an increase in demand for services. In industrial sectors, the trend towards outsourcing means that manufacturers are buying in services. Often it is more efficient for a company to use external expertise to manage distribution, warehousing and catering, leaving time to focus on its core competencies. Deregulation has also increased the level of competition in certain service industries (e.g. telecommunications, television, airlines) and this has also been a driver of expansion of services.

To give you an idea of the growing significance of the services industry, in Europe it accounts for over 73 per cent of GDP compared to 25 per cent from industrial manufacturing and 2 per cent from agriculture. Moreover, the dominance of services can be seen globally. See Table 9.1.

TABLE 9.1 Contribution of industrial, agricultural and service industry sectors to GDP can be divided into sectors				
Country	GDP (purchasing power parity)	Industrial sector (%)	Agricultural sector (%)	Services sector (%)
USA	$17.01 trillion	20.7	1.6	77.4
China	$16.4 trillion	42.6	9.2	48.2
India	$7.3 trillion	31.0	20.0	49.0
Japan	$4.7 trillion	24.5	1.2	74.3
Russia	$3.5 trillion	36.3	4.0	59.7
Germany	$3.2 trillion	30.8	0.9	68.4
Brazil	$3.2 trillion	23.8	5.8	70.4
United Kingdom	$2.5 trillion	20.6	0.6	78.8
France	$2.5 trillion	21.3	3.0	75.7
Italy	$2.1 trillion	23.9	2.2	73.9

Source: CIA World Facts Book (2015)

The service sector in the UK dominates the economy, contributing nearly 79 per cent of GDP. There are discretely different sub-sectors within the sector (see Table 9.2).

In addition, public administration, and other services industries, which include work carried out in private households, and employed persons contribute to the service economy.

The Service Industries

The sectors that make up the service industries vary considerably and are constantly evolving as new service concepts are developed, for example web developers and social media engagement analysts. Various forces are driving the changes, such as technological innovations and changing patterns of ownership. For example, privatization of parts of the UK National Health Service opened up opportunities for private service providers to perform medical scans and carry out diagnostic tests and X-rays on patients (Campbell, 2015).

TABLE 9.2 The UK service industry sectors		
Sector	**Areas of activity**	**Leading companies**
Creative industries	Advertising, software design, web services, film industry, theatres, TV and radio, publishing, music	BBC, Tiger Aspect, Sky, Channel 4
Government services	Education, health and social work	NHS Direct
Financial and business services	Banking	HSBC, Barclays Bank, Admiral insurance, Aviva
Hotels and restaurants	Tourism, fast food, pubs, leisure clubs	Intercontinental Hotels, Thomas Cook, Whitbread, Greene King
Property management	Real estate, renting, computer related	
Transport, storage and communications	Land, air transport, business services, post and telecoms	Vodafone, Virgin, EE, British Airways
Retailing	Motor, wholesale, supermarkets	Tesco, Morrisons, Marks & Spencer, Asda, Next, Costco
Non-profit	Alleviation of hunger, protection of animals	Oxfam, RSPCA

In this section we briefly consider each of the areas of activity highlighted in Table 9.2. The basic premise in each of the sectors is that businesses engage in economic activity, which involves using particular knowledge, skills and expertise in the production of specialist services, as opposed to manufacturing products (e.g. car production), growing produce (e.g. farming) or extracting minerals (e.g. mining). We will explore this idea in more detail in the next section when discussing the physical goods–service continuum model.

Creative industries

This sector relies on developing services based on creative skills; for example creatives (advertising), writers, fashion designers, artists, musicians and television producers. Creative industries are enjoying a period of growth, and in the UK around 2.2 million people work in this sector (DCMS, 2010). Software development and electronic publishing are the most active parts of the sector—in economic terms—followed by publishing, advertising, architecture, music and the visual arts, film, television and radio and design. Creative industries generate distinctive and authentic 'products' which are difficult to replicate, for example Electronic Arts (video game publisher) *Need for Speed* and *Battlefield* games. So creative labour 'is geared to the production of original or distinctive commodities that are primarily aesthetic and/or symbolic—expressive rather than utilitarian and functional' (Hirsch, 1972). Nick Park (creator, animator and director, perhaps best known for Wallace and Gromit and Shaun the Sheep), J. K. Rowling (writer, best known for Harry Potter) and First Aid Kit (international singer/songwriters best known for 'My Silver Lining') are all examples of successful individuals who began and developed their careers in the creative industries. Increasingly, creative people understand the importance of leveraging market advantage from their skills and talents. In the past, commercial values and artistic autonomy were seen as being in opposition. But now 'the very best artists are also some of the most effective entrepreneurs' (Arts Council, 2004).

See Marketing in Action 9.1 to learn more about how Nordic film makers and production companies have influenced the global creative industry.

Furthermore, it is important to remember that creative skills are also at the centre of product

EXHIBIT 9.1
Canary Wharf financial services centre in London, UK

MARKETING IN ACTION 9.1
Nordic Noir Changes the Mood in the Creative Industry

Moody, brooding epic productions like *Fortitude*, produced by UK production company Fifty Fathoms/Tiger Aspect demonstrated the extent to which 'Nordic noir' has percolated through the creative industries' psyche. Filmed in Reydarfjordur on the eastern Fjords of Iceland, *Fortitude* used the appeal of the Nordic landscape and the fresh, clean environment, entwined with complex, dark undertones of social deviation to create a blockbuster drama series shown on Sky Atlantic (pan-European satellite broadcaster). But this is literally the tip of the iceberg of the Nordic creative industry, as there are hundreds of writers, film producers and drama series that have emerged from Sweden, Denmark, Finland and Iceland and associated territories such as the Hebrides.

Furthermore, this powerhouse of creative development has become an important source of economic growth. The distinctive and authentic nature of these creative products has captured the hearts and minds of readers, television viewers and film goers globally.

For example, *Wallander* (adapted from Henning Mankell's novels) was a series of crime drama novels (published in Swedish in 1991) that arguably began the popularization of Nordic noir in the UK and unwittingly helped to nudged this emerging genre into the mainstream. Initially, European crime dramas were in the bargain basement for broadcasters looking for cheap, watchable alternatives to the high-cost USA productions. As well as price, demand has driven growth: due to the proliferation of television channels, there was the need to find new drama to attract viewers. The Swedish version of *Wallander* was aired in the UK with English subtitles on BBC 4 (new satellite channel). But the UK's BBC 1 also produced its own version of the series, with leading actor Sir Kenneth Branagh; this version was aired on BBC 1 at prime viewing times. Although critically acclaimed, the English version is said to have been outpaced by the Swedish language version, which proved very popular with viewers and created demand for similar foreign language drama productions, paving the way to success for other series such as *Borgen*, *The Killing* and *The Bridge*.

In a similar vein, the work of author Stieg Larsson, writer and creator of the best-selling *Millennium* trilogy, which included *The Girl with the Dragon Tattoo*, has become internationally acclaimed. The books, which were published after Larsson's death, topped best-seller lists around the world and inspired film makers in Scandinavia and the USA.

Nordic noir has become so popular that producers and broadcasters are seeking every opportunity to partner with the individuals and businesses in the Nordic creative industry to secure an opportunity to find the next best-selling blockbuster.

Based on: Booth (2014); Gallagher (2009); Jodelka (2015)

---

innovation, and a company's innovation in the design area can contribute significantly to its overall level of performance (Rubera and Kirca, 2012).

Government services

The public sector in many countries around the world involves the provision and delivery of services by the government for the country's citizens. The sector typically includes education, health, social care, police, defence and transport. This is a highly complex part of the service industry, and processes are central to much of the activity that takes place. For example, maintaining relationships with suppliers is important to ongoing success of procurement processes.

E-procurement has been widely adopted as a means of reducing operational cost while maintaining organizational standards. However, while it is arguably easy to measure the performance of the process of procurement (especially since the advent of e-procurement systems), it is more difficult to monitor the process of, say, a patient being taken into hospital, as the individual circumstances can vary considerably—as can the outcome, depending on the patient's health at presentation at the hospital (or point of care).

This sector also tends to have less clear goals, which makes setting objectives complex. Another complexity that is arguably unique to this sector is the involvement of politics. In the UK, the National Health Service is often subject to public scrutiny through the media (Collinson, 2012).

Nevertheless, marketing has an important role to play, and organizations from councils to hospitals can use the marketing mix in their strategy and planning. For example, Gov.uk is a digital service provided to help UK citizens find helpful information and access services. It is important to note that much of the marketing activity in this sector is concerned with customer satisfaction, despite the lack of direct competition.

Financial services

In this sector of the industry, banking and insurance are the key areas of activity. The focus of the industry is financial management, which includes investment, and the lending of money, insurance issues, and pensions. This industry sector serves both large corporations and individuals. Investment banking typically provides services to corporate clients. We have mentioned mergers and acquisitions and takeovers earlier, and these activities are likely to be handled by investment banks that provide the required skill sets to handle the moves. Commercial banks handle deposits and loans for companies and individuals. In the UK, the financial services sector employs 1 million people and contributes around 12 per cent to GDP. The City of London is a centre of excellence for financial expertise and has attracted many leading financial organizations to locate part of their businesses there. This sector of the services industry plays a significant part in the economic well-being of local and global economies.

Hospitality, travel and tourism

This part of the sector is very diverse. Under this heading we are primarily thinking about the providers of travel and hospitality services rather than the transportation element, which is covered separately. Hospitality is made up of many facets, from pubs, restaurants and hotels, to theme parks and special-interest activities like wine-tasting events. The hospitality industry caters for the needs of business and individuals alike.

From a marketing perspective, an important point to be aware of is that many of the services offered in this part of the sector are highly perishable. In other words, the vacancy rate in a hotel is an important determinant of its likely success. If the rate is high and there are many empty rooms, the business is performing poorly. The same is true of the travel industry. Service suppliers such as travel agents and operators both online and offline are constantly aiming to fill their holidays and tours. Sales promotions are widely used to sell available places. Travelling for pleasure has been on the increase for many years. While travel used to be an activity associated with the rich, package holidays and more recently low-cost air travel have made foreign travel accessible to more consumers. This sector also includes business travel.

Property management

As with other parts of the sectors, a range of activities are involved and, although provided primarily for business-to-business markets, there is a part of the sector which provides services for the individual. Property management includes handling day-to-day management of clients, maintenance and repairs, and this can mean handling residential or commercial properties.

Transport, storage and communications

This part of the sector covers rail, road, water and air transportation, and communications services for both individuals and businesses. Communication services include postal and telecommunications services.

Retailing

Retailing is an important element of the service industry: it is the activity involved in the sale of products to the ultimate consumer. Retailing is a major employer of the European Union's workforce. Again this is a very diverse industry, and retailers make use of every aspect of the product and services marketing mix. In order to deliver the service expectations of their customers, retailers have to ensure they have the right products in the right place and at the right time, which has implications for purchasing and logistics (discussed in detail in Chapter 17). One of the key functions of retailing is to 'break-bulk so that consumers can buy goods in small quantities to satisfy their needs' (Ellis-Chadwick, 2011).

Consumer decision-making involves not only the choice of product and brand, but also of retail outlet. Most retailing is conducted in stores such as supermarkets, catalogue shops and departmental stores, but non-store retailing such as mail order and automatic vending also accounts for a large amount of sales. Retailing provides an important service to customers, making products available when and where customers want to buy them.

Many large retailers exert enormous power in the distribution chain because of the vast quantities of goods they buy from manufacturers. The purchasing power of retailers has meant that manufacturers have to maintain high service levels and good buyer–supplier relationships.

Non-profit organizations

Non-profit organizations contribute to service sector activity but are not driven by the profit motive to satisfy their stakeholders. This sector is discussed in some detail in Chapter 5.

The Nature of Services

In the previous section, we briefly introduced different areas of activity in the services industry. Next we shall examine the nature of services, as these principles guide much of the management activity in all of the above.

Cowell states that 'what is significant about services is the relative dominance of *intangible attributes* in the make-up of the 'service product'. Services are a special kind of product. They may require special understanding and special marketing efforts (Cowell, 1995). Services often involve the use of something without ever gaining ownership, for example renting an apartment, a car or a hotel room. However, whilst pure services do not result in ownership, they may be linked to a physical good. For example, a machine (physical good) may be sold with a one-year maintenance contract (service).

Many offerings, however, contain a combination of the tangible and intangible. For example, a marketing research study would provide a report (physical good) that represents the outcome of a number of service activities (discussions with client, designing the research strategy, interviewing respondents and analysing the results). In the creative industries, the service is the generation of the ideas and concepts, which are then delivered in a tangible form; for example, an author writes a manuscript, and the publisher then produces a book or a production company a film.

This distinction between physical and service offerings can, therefore, best be understood as a matter of degree rather than in absolute terms. Figure 9.1 shows a physical goods–service continuum, with the position of each offering dependent upon its ratio of tangible/intangible elements. At the pure goods end of the scale is

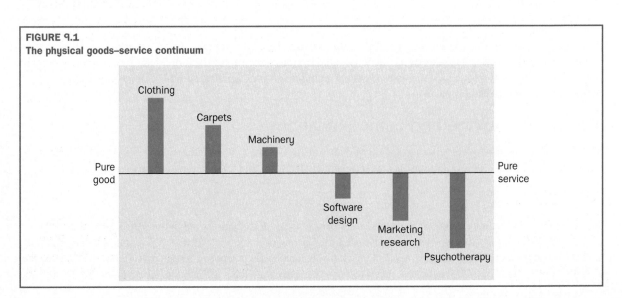

FIGURE 9.1
The physical goods–service continuum

clothing, as the purchase of a skirt or socks is not normally accompanied by a service. Carpet purchases may involve an element of service if they require professional laying. Machinery purchase may involve more service elements in the form of installation and maintenance. Software design is positioned on the service side of the continuum since the value of the product is dependent on design expertise rather than the cost of the physical product (disk). Marketing research is similarly services based, as discussed earlier. Finally, Internet banking (management of digital assets) or psychotherapy (treatment of a mental health issue) may be regarded as a pure service since the client receives nothing tangible from the transaction.

Drawing a line between goods and services is difficult. Indeed, it has been argued that any such attempt to do so misses the point. Vargo and Lusch (2006) suggest the marketers' 'love affair' with products is over and has been superseded by a new 'service-aligned ethos'. This means that managers should make services central to their activities rather than the product. Ultimately, in this model the product becomes a 'keepsake' of the service experience and the customer is a 'co-creator of value'. The paper by Vargo and Lusch's (2006) has been influential in the marketing literature, but the terminology has been hotly debated by academics (Brown and Patterson, 2009) (O'Shaughnessy and O'Shaughnessy, 2009). Nevertheless there is a growing body of work that supports the notion that marketing now extends well beyond the 4-Ps framework. Indeed, services have been defined in the marketing literature as: 'the application of specialized competences (knowledge and skills) through deeds, processes, and performances for the benefit of another entity or the entity itself' (Lusch and Vargo, 2011; Vargo and Lusch, 2004).

Furthermore, services are everyday occurrences or acts (in a commercial setting) that provide assistance or help to a customer. This action entails activities, tasks and processes to be performed, and they can be carried out directly or indirectly; for example, 'I have received excellent service from my hairdresser' (directly) or 'I received excellent service through my bank account' (indirectly) (Vargo and Lusch, 2011).

Ultimately, service-dominant logic sets out a model that suggests that marketing can serve as a framework for integrating marketing and supply chain management (SCM) practices in a manner that enables the 'target user/ consumer' to take part in the creation process (Lusch, Vargo and Tanniru, 2010). According to Wirtz and Chew (2003) and Wirtz, Chew and Lovelock (2012), there are different categories of services which can be defined by looking at service users and their possessions and the extent to which the services provided are tangible or intangible.

- People processing, where the services are directed at the individual, as in the case of a manicurist, a barber and an optician. In this situation, the service user visits the service provider in order to receive the services on offer.
- Possession processing, where the services are directed at physical possessions, for example dry cleaners, a shoe repairer and a cleaner. Here the service user is less involved in the actual process, and to a certain extent the production of the services (repairing the shoes) can be separated from the consumption of the service (enjoyment of wearing the shoes with a newly replaced heel).
- Mental stimulus processing, where the services aimed at the mind of the individual, for example education. In this case, the service is information based.
- Information processing, where services are associated with an intangible asset, for example accounting, banking and insurance. This is the most intangible type of service production, whereby intangible assets are processed to produce intangible outputs for the user, for example insurance cover for a car driver. Until the point at which the driver needs the insurance cover, there is limited physical evidence of its existence. Should the driver be involved in an accident, then tangible features of the product might increase, for example a courtesy car and medical healthcare. If the driver never needs to use his or her insurance cover, then the only tangible evidence of its existence is the payment for the service and a policy number.

The first two categories focus on tangible actions associated with people and possessions, whereas the last two focus on intangible actions with people and possessions—and each has different implications for the way the service users and the service provider interact.

We have already touched on one characteristic of services that distinguishes them from physical goods—intangibility—and how this concept might relate to service delivery. But there are, in fact, four key distinguishing characteristics: intangibility, inseparability, variability and perishability (see Figure 9.2).

Intangibility

Pure services cannot be seen, tasted, touched, or smelled before they are bought—that is, they are intangible. Rather a **service** is *a deed, performance or effort*, not an object, device or thing (Berry, 1980). This may mean that a customer finds difficulty in evaluating a service before purchase. For example, it is virtually impossible to judge how enjoyable a holiday will be before taking it because the holiday cannot be shown to a customer before consumption.

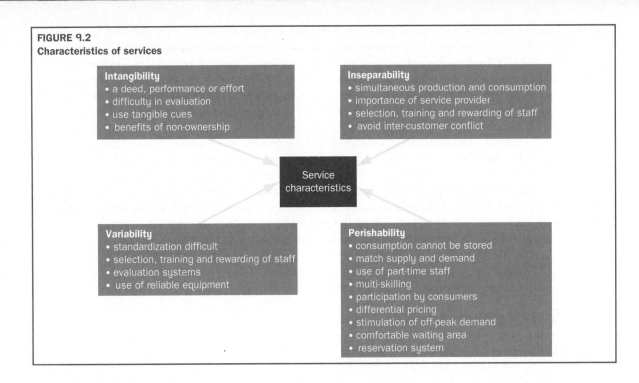

FIGURE 9.2
Characteristics of services

Intangibility
- a deed, performance or effort
- difficulty in evaluation
- use tangible cues
- benefits of non-ownership

Inseparability
- simultaneous production and consumption
- importance of service provider
- selection, training and rewarding of staff
- avoid inter-customer conflict

Service characteristics

Variability
- standardization difficult
- selection, training and rewarding of staff
- evaluation systems
- use of reliable equipment

Perishability
- consumption cannot be stored
- match supply and demand
- use of part-time staff
- multi-skilling
- participation by consumers
- differential pricing
- stimulation of off-peak demand
- comfortable waiting area
- reservation system

For some services, their **intangibility** leads to *difficulty in evaluation* after consumption. For example, it is not easy to judge how thorough a car service has been immediately afterwards: there is no way of telling if everything that should have been checked has been checked.

The challenge for the service provider is to *use tangible cues* to service quality. For example, a holiday firm may show pictures of the holiday destination, display testimonials from satisfied holidaymakers and provide details in a brochure of the kinds of entertainment available. A garage may provide a checklist of items that are required to be carried out in a service, and an indication that they have been completed.

The task is to provide evidence of service quality. McDonald's does this by controlling the physical settings of its restaurants and by using its 'golden arches' as a branding cue. By having a consistent offering, the company has effectively dealt with the difficulties that consumers have in evaluating the quality of a service. Standard menus and ordering procedures have also ensured uniform and easy access for customers, while allowing quality control (Edgett and Parkinson, 1993).

Intangibility also means that the customer cannot own a service. Payment is for use or performance. For example, a car may be hired or a medical operation performed. Service organizations sometimes stress the *benefits of non-ownership* such as lower capital costs and the spreading of payment charges.

Inseparability

Unlike physical goods, services have **inseparability**—that is, they have *simultaneous production and consumption*. For example, a haircut, a holiday and a rock concert are produced and consumed at the same time. This contrasts with a physical good, which is produced, stored and distributed through intermediaries before being bought and consumed. This illustrates the *importance of the service provider*, which is an integral part of the satisfaction gained by the consumer. How service providers conduct themselves may have a crucial bearing on repeat business over and above the technical efficiency of the service task. For example, how courteous and friendly the service provider is may play a large part in the customer's perception of the service experience. The service must be provided not only at the right time and in the right place, but also in the right way (Berry, 1980).

Often, in the customer's eyes, the airline cabin crew member *is* the company. Consequently, the *selection, training and rewarding of staff* who are the frontline service people are of fundamental importance in the achievement of high standards of service quality. This notion of the inseparability of production and consumption gave rise to the idea of relationship marketing in services. In such circumstances, managing buyer–seller interaction is central to effective marketing and can only be fulfilled in a relationship with the customer (Aijo, 1996).

Furthermore, the consumption of the service may take place in the presence of other consumers. This is apparent with restaurant meals, air, rail or coach travel, and many forms of entertainment, for example. Consequently, enjoyment of the service is dependent not only on the service provided, but also on other consumers. Therefore service providers need to identify possible sources of nuisance (e.g. noise, smoke, queue jumping) and make adequate provision to *avoid inter-customer conflict*. For example, a restaurant layout should provide reasonable space between tables so that the potential for conflict is minimized.

Marketing managers should not underestimate the role played by customers in aiding other customers in their decision-making. A study into service interactions in IKEA stores found that almost all customer–employee exchanges related to customer concerns about 'place' (e.g. 'Can you direct me to the pick-up point?') and 'function' (e.g. 'How does this chair work?'). However, interactions between customers took the form of opinions on the quality of materials used in products, advice on bed sizes and how to move around the in-store restaurant. Many customers appeared to display a degree of product knowledge or expertise bordering on that of contact personnel (Baron, Harris and Davies, 1996).

Variability

Service quality may be subject to considerable **variability**, which makes standardization difficult. Two restaurants within the same chain may have variable service owing to the capabilities of their respective managers and staff. Quality variations among physical products may be subject to tighter controls through centralized production, automation and quality checking before dispatch. Services, however, are often conducted at multiple locations, by people who may vary in their attitudes (and tiredness), and are subject to simultaneous production and consumption. The last characteristic means that a service fault (e.g. rudeness) cannot be quality checked and corrected between production and consumption, unlike a physical product such as misaligned car windscreen wipers.

The potential for variability in service quality emphasizes the need for rigorous selection, training, and rewarding of staff in service organizations. Training should emphasize the standards expected of personnel when dealing with customers. *Evaluation systems* should be developed that allow customers to report on their experiences with staff.

Service standardization is a related method of tackling the variability problem. The *use of reliable equipment* rather than people can also help in standardization—for example, the supply of drinks via vending machines or cash through bank machines. However, great care needs to be taken regarding equipment reliability and efficiency. For example, bank cash machines have been heavily criticized for being unreliable and running out of money at weekends.

Perishability

The fourth characteristic of services is their **perishability** in the sense that *consumption cannot be stored* for the future. A hotel room or an airline seat that is not occupied today represents lost income that cannot be gained tomorrow. If a physical good is not sold, it can be stored for sale later. Therefore it is important to *match supply and demand* for services. For example, if a hotel has high weekday occupancy but is virtually empty at weekends, a key marketing task is to provide incentives for weekend use. This might involve offering weekend discounts, or linking hotel use with leisure activities such as golf, fishing or hiking.

Service providers also have the problem of catering for peak demand when supply may be insufficient. A physical goods provider may build up inventory in slack periods for sale during peak demand. Service providers do not have this option. Consequently, alternative methods need to be considered. For example, supply flexibility can be varied through the *use of part-time staff* during peak periods. *Multi-skilling* means that employees may be trained in many tasks. Supermarket staff can be trained to fill shelves and work at the checkout at peak periods. *Participation by consumers* may be encouraged in production (e.g. self-service breakfasts in hotels) and in avoiding queues (e.g. self-service checkouts in supermarkets). Demand may be smoothed through *differential pricing* to encourage customers to visit during off-peak periods (e.g. lower-priced cinema and theatre seats for afternoon performances). *Stimulation of off-peak demand* can be achieved by special events (e.g. spa breaks or gourmet weekends for hotels). If delay is unavoidable, then another option is to make it more acceptable—for example, by providing a comfortable waiting area with seating and free refreshments. Finally, a *reservation system*, as commonly used in restaurants, hair salons and theatres, can be used to control peak demand and assist time substitution.

Managing Services

In order to manage services effectively the service provider should understand the whole of the customer journey, which involves five key aspects: managing customer relationships, managing service quality, managing service productivity, managing service staff and positioning services. Customer relationship management is covered in Chapter 10. Read Mini Case 9.1 to consider how Sandals Resorts manages its service offering.

MINI CASE 9.1
Sandals Resorts: Knowing your Customers is the Key to their Hearts and a Way to Stand Out in a Crowded Marketplace

The hospitality and tourism industry offers many opportunities for service providers to devise highly targeted offers. This is an industry where competition is intense and opportunities to create a differentiated offer are hard to find. But, at the Sandals Resorts International (SRI), success has been built on providing very specialized services.

The first Sandals resort was established in Montego Bay, Jamaica. Largely due to the reputation built on excellent personalized service, the business has grown and now employs over 10,000 people and operates 13 couples-only and 6 family-oriented resorts under the brand names Sandals and Beaches. These all-inclusive resorts are located close to some of the best beaches in the Caribbean. The business has been built around the idea of 'giving customers more than they expect or think they need'. Sandals are classified in the industry as all-inclusive resorts, but they have successfully differentiated themselves in this sector too by offering 'Ultra All-inclusive' offers, which include special packages for weddings and honeymoons, with features such as access to private offshore islands and themed gourmet restaurants, and some holiday packages even include personal butler services.

At the heart of the company's operation is a business intelligence system, which enables the marketing team at Sandals resorts to have the right tools to carry out the analysis needed to not only ensure that customers are completely satisfied but also ensure that the company operates profitably. The system gathers data on a daily basis, and close attention is paid to key performance indicators such as occupancy rates, staffing levels, food costs and spend per room. Daily management updates enable the team to monitor performance and take immediate action if any issues are detected.

In addition to the emphasis on exceeding guests' expectations, SRI invests substantially in its employees, who they call 'team members', through the Sandals Corporate University (SCU). Each team member is specially selected and trained to carry out his/her role, and continually encouraged to develop personally. The SCU ensures that team members understand that they are as important as their guests, which is fundamental to a successful service organization, because happy team members give excellent service, resulting in happy, loyal guests.

SRI does not stop with its customers; it is also a commitment to society. The Sandals Foundation makes investments to support the development of local communities. There are three core elements to the foundation: the community, education and the environment. By working with the community, the foundation tackles social issues relating to violence, poverty, unemployment and healthcare, and community programmes have succeeded in 'giving people chance to change their lives'. Education initiatives have provided scholarship and learning for thousands of students in the Caribbean of all ages and across all aspects of life. For example, in Montego Bay, parenting workshops raise awareness of the importance of education and lifelong learning. Preserving the environment is very important, and the foundation increasingly is taking a leadership role in environmental programmes in both the public and private sector. At the Boscobel marine sanctuary, ecologists are working to protect coral and fish stocks and also engage local community fishermen to raise awareness of behaviour that is damaging the fragile underwater environment.

Over the past 30 years, SRI has been consistently rewarded for its emphasis on people. It receives high satisfaction levels from guests, and more than half return; SRI's employees are happy and remain loyal, and SRI holds numerous awards from the hospitality sector. Furthermore, Gordon 'Butch' Stewart, the founder of the Sandals vision, has shown how a successful hospitality brand can foster wide economic and social development that has made a significant contribution to helping communities in the Caribbean have a more sustainable way of living.

Questions:

1 Customer retention is at the centre of relationship management. Suggest why Sandals Resorts has been successful in encouraging over half its customers to return.
2 Imagine you are the customer service manager for one of the Sandals Resorts and there has been a serious incident of food poisoning that has resulted in several guests becoming ill. Suggest how you are going to manage this situation.

Based on: Brown, Hassan and Teare (2011); Pike (2011); Sandals Resorts International Websites—sandals. com and beaches.com; Aptech Computer Systems (2014); http://www.aptech-inc.com/index.php/2014/11/ sandals-upgrades-bi-to-latest-aptech-execuvue-with-dashboards-for-21-resorts

Managing service quality

Intuitively, it makes sense to suggest that improving service quality will increase customer satisfaction, leading to higher sales and profits. Indeed, it has been shown that companies that are rated higher on service quality perform better in terms of market share growth and profitability (Buzzell and Gale, 1987). Yet, for many companies, high standards of service quality remain elusive. There are four causes of poor perceived quality (see Figure 9.3). These are the barriers that separate the perception of service quality from what customers expect (Parasuraman, Zeithaml and Berry, 1985).

Misconception barrier: this arises from management's misunderstanding of what the customer expects. Lack of marketing research may lead managers to misconceive the important service attributes that customers use when evaluating a service, and the way in which customers use attributes in evaluation. For example, a restaurant manager may believe that shortening the gap between courses may improve customer satisfaction, when the customer actually values a pause between eating.

Inadequate resources barrier: managers may understand customer expectations but are unwilling to provide the resources necessary to meet them. This may arise because of a cost reduction or productivity focus, or simply because of the inconvenience it may cause.

Inadequate delivery barrier: managers may understand customer expectations and supply adequate resources but fail to select, train and reward staff adequately, resulting in poor or inconsistent service. This may manifest itself in poor communication skills, inappropriate dress, and unwillingness to solve customer problems.

Exaggerated promises barrier: even when customer understanding, resources and staff management are in place, a gap between customer expectations and perceptions can still arise through exaggerated promises. Advertising and selling messages that build expectations to a pitch that cannot be fulfilled may leave customers disappointed even when receiving good service. For example, a tourist brochure that claims a hotel is 'just a few minutes from the sea' may lead to disappointment if the walk takes 10 minutes.

Meeting customer expectations

A key to providing service quality is the understanding and meeting of *customer expectations*. To do so requires a clear picture of the criteria used to form these expectations, recognizing that consumers of services value not only the *outcome* of the service encounter but also the *experience* of taking part in it. For example,

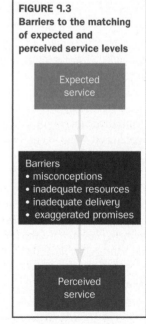

FIGURE 9.3
Barriers to the matching of expected and perceived service levels

Expected service

Barriers
- misconceptions
- inadequate resources
- inadequate delivery
- exaggerated promises

Perceived service

an evaluation of a haircut depends not only on the quality of the cut but also the experience of having a haircut. Clearly, a hairdresser needs not only technical skills but also the ability to communicate in an interesting and polite manner. Meeting and exceeding customers' expectations is even more important as good and bad experiences can easily be shared via social media such as Twitter and Instagram.

Ten criteria may be used when evaluating the outcome and experience of a service encounter, and form a checklist for service providers to monitor performance (Parasuraman, Zeithaml and Berry, 1985).

1 *Access*: is the service provided at convenient locations and times with little waiting?
2 *Reliability*: is the service consistent and dependable?
3 *Credibility*: can customers trust the service company and its staff?
4 *Security*: can the service be used without risk?
5 *Understanding the customer*: does it appear that the service provider understands customer expectations?
6 *Responsiveness*: how quickly do service staff respond to customer problems, requests and questions?
7 *Courtesy*: do service staff act in a friendly and polite manner?
8 *Competence*: do service staff have the required skills and knowledge?
9 *Communication*: is the service described clearly and accurately?
10 *Tangibles*: how well managed is the tangible evidence of the service (e.g. staff appearance, décor, layout)?

Where service quality is dependent on a succession of service encounters (e.g., a hotel stay may encompass the check-in, the room itself, the restaurant, breakfast and check-out), each should be measured in terms of their impact on total satisfaction so that corrective actions can be taken (Danaher and Mattson, 1994). Customer service questionnaires are widely used in the service industry to gather feedback on customer experiences. Social media are also widely used in the same context.

Measuring service quality

A scale called SERVQUAL was developed to aid the measurement of *service quality* (Zeithaml, Parasuraman and Berry, 1988). Based on five criteria—reliability, responsiveness, courtesy, competence and tangibles—it aims to measure customer perceptions and expectations so that gaps can be identified and, where necessary, service providers can improve their offer. The scale is simple to administer with respondents indicating their strength of agreement or disagreement with a series of statements about service quality. Service quality can also be measured by *mystery shoppers*, who visit retail outlets as normal consumers. Their job is to assess and report the quality of the service they receive (Sherwood, 2008).

Managing service productivity

Productivity is a measure of the relationship between an input and an output. For example, if more people can be served (output) using the same number of staff (input), productivity per employee has risen. Clearly there can be conflict between improving service productivity (efficiency) and raising service quality (effectiveness). For example, a beauty therapist who reduces time spent with a client may increase the number of clients per day, but the reduction in quality of service may affect the quality of service and customer retention.

Clearly a balance must be struck between productivity and service quality. At some point quality gains become so expensive that they are not worthwhile. However, there are ways of improving productivity without compromising quality. Technology, obtaining customer involvement in production of the service, and balancing supply and demand are three methods of achieving this.

Technology

Technology can be used to improve productivity and service quality. For example, airport X-ray surveillance equipment raises the throughput of passengers (productivity) and speeds the process of checking-in (service quality). Automatic cash dispensers in banks increase the number of transactions per period (productivity) while reducing customer waiting time (service quality). Automatic vending machines increase the number of drinks sold per establishment (productivity) while improving accessibility for customers (service quality).

Retailers have benefited from barcodes and electronic fund transfer at point of sale (EFTPOS). Timely and detailed sales information can aid buying decisions and provide retail buyers with a negotiating advantage over suppliers. Other benefits from this technology include better labour scheduling, stock management and distribution systems. Read Marketing in Action 9.2 to discover how the humble hashtag has been transformed into a marketing tool.

MARKETING IN ACTION 9.2
Social Media Transformed the Hashtag into a Marketing Tool

Social media have provided popular platforms on which to engage with customers, and the hashtag has enabled messages to be found and shared.

The hashtag # was just a simple symbol used in the IT industry to highlight a special meaning for computer coders, but now it has been transformed into a powerful marketing tool. Twitter started using hashtags in 2007, and a bush fire in the same year proved the usefulness of the hashtag, as messages tagged #sandiegofire were shared across California. Twitter then began linking anything preceded by # so that its users could share their experiences and find other tweets with similar things to say. Instagram and Flickr followed suit, and then leading brands began making use of the hashtag in their marketing campaigns.

Marketers realized that tweets containing hashtags were more likely to be shared and retweeted and could be used to build different types of powerful communications campaigns. For example, the #IceBucketChallenge was used by the Motor Neurone Disease charity. The challenge encouraged people to throw a bucket of icy water over their heads, and exceeded expectations by raising in excess of $100 million.

British Airways wanted to remind its customers about the 'magic of flying', so the company used #Lookup as part of its campaign. It used interactive digital advertising boards that tracked aircraft using sophisticated surveillance technology and interrupted other advertisers' displays with a child pointing to the sky every time a plane flew overhead.

The beer industry in the UK wanted to change behaviour and to urge consumers to drink differently (cutting down on alcohol consumption) during the month of January rather than completely abstain from visiting bars and pubs. Its campaign was #DryJanuary.

The hashtag symbol is widely used by marketers to build interest in a brand and to create successful campaign-specific hashtags to generate genuine user content. Hashtags can also be used to follow trends and create campaigns to manage customer expectations.

Based on: Offerpop (2013); Milington (2015); Tesseras (2014)

Customer involvement in production

The inseparability between production and consumption provides an opportunity to raise both productivity and service quality. For example, self-service breakfast bars and petrol stations improve productivity per employee and reduce customer waiting time (service quality). The effectiveness of this tactic relies heavily on customer expectations, and on managing transition periods. It should be used when there is a clear advantage to customers in their involvement in production. In other instances, reducing customer service may reduce satisfaction. For example, a hotel that expected its customers to service their own rooms would need a persuasive communications programme to convince customers that the lack of service was reflected in cheaper rates.

Balancing supply and demand

Because services cannot be stored, balancing supply and demand is a key determinant of productivity. Hotels or aircraft that are less than half full incur low productivity. If in the next period, the hotel or airline is faced with excess demand, the unused space in the previous period cannot be used to meet it. The combined result is low productivity and customer dissatisfaction (low service quality). By smoothing demand or increasing the flexibility of supply, both productivity and service quality can be achieved.

Smoothing demand can be achieved through differential pricing and stimulating off-peak demand (e.g. weekend breaks). Increasing supply flexibility may be increased by using part-time employees, multi-skilling and encouraging customers to service themselves.

Managing service staff

Many services involve a high degree of contact between service staff and customers. This is true for such service industries as healthcare, banking, catering and education. The quality of the service experience is therefore heavily dependent on staff–customer interpersonal relationships. John Carlzon, the head of Scandinavian Airlines

System (SAS), called these meetings *moments of truth*. He explained that SAS faced 65,000 moments of truth per day, and that the outcomes determined the success of the company.

Research on customer loyalty in the service industry showed that only 14 per cent of customers who stopped patronizing service businesses did so because they were dissatisfied with the quality of what they had bought. More than two-thirds stopped buying because they found service staff indifferent or unhelpful (Schlesinger and Heskett, 1991). Clearly, the way in which service personnel treat their customers is fundamental to success in the service industry.

Also, frontline staff are important sources of customer and competitor information and, if properly motivated, can provide crucial inputs in the development of new service products (Lievens and Moenaert, 2000). For example, discussions with customers may generate ideas for new services that customers would value if available on the market.

In order for service employees to be in the frame of mind to treat customers well, they need to feel that their company is treating them well. In companies where staff have a high regard for the human resources policy, customers also have a positive opinion of the service they receive.

The *selection of suitable people* is the starting point of the process. Personality differences mean that it is not everyone who can fill a service role. The nature of the job needs to be defined and the appropriate personality characteristics needed to perform effectively outlined. Once selected, training is required to familiarize recruits with the job requirements and the culture of the organization. *Socialization* allows the recruit to experience the culture and tasks of the organization. Usually, the aim is creative individualism, whereby the recruit accepts all of the key behavioural norms but is encouraged to display initiative and innovation in dealing with problems. Thus, standards of behaviour are internalized, but the creative abilities of the individual are not subjugated to the need to conform.

Service quality may also be affected by the degree to which staff are *empowered*, or given the authority to satisfy customers and deal with their problems. Google is a business that empowers its staff to be creative. Google cafés are an initiative designed to encourage interaction and innovation among employees. However, empowerment programmes need to recognize the increased responsibility thrust on employees. Not everyone will welcome this, and reward systems (e.g. higher pay or status) need to be thought through. At the luxury hotel chain Ritz-Carlton, customer service is of paramount importance, and as a result the frontline staff are given the *right* be involved with the work they are doing and make decision on how to best serve the hotel guests. The company empowers its employees through training and trusting in them to make accurate decisions that will wow their customers (Solomon, 2014).

Maintaining a motivated workforce in the face of irate customers, faulty support systems and the boredom that accompanies some service jobs is a demanding task. The motivational factors include recognition of achievement, role clarity, opportunities for advancement, the interest value of the job, monetary rewards, and setting challenging but achievable targets. A key factor in avoiding demotivation is to monitor support systems so that staff work with efficient equipment and facilities to help them carry out their job.

Service evaluation is also important in managing staff. Customer feedback is essential to maintaining high standards of service quality. McDonald's continually monitors quality, service, cleanliness and value, and if a franchisee fails to meet these standards they are dropped. The results of customer research should be fed back to employees so that they can relate their performance standards to customer satisfaction. Enlightened companies tie financial incentives to the results of such surveys.

Positioning services

Positioning is the process of establishing and keeping a distinctive place in the market for a company and its products. Most successful service companies differentiate themselves from the competition on attributes that their target customers value highly. They develop service concepts that are highly valued, and communicate to target customers so that they accurately perceive the position of the service.

The positioning task entails two decisions:

1   Choice of target market (where to compete)
2   Creation of a differential advantage (how to compete)

These decisions are common to both physical products and services. Creating a differential advantage is based on understanding the target customers' requirements better than the competition. Figure 9.4 shows the relationship between *target customer needs* and the *services marketing mix*. On the left of the figure is an array of factors (choice criteria) that customers may use to judge a service. How well a service company satisfies

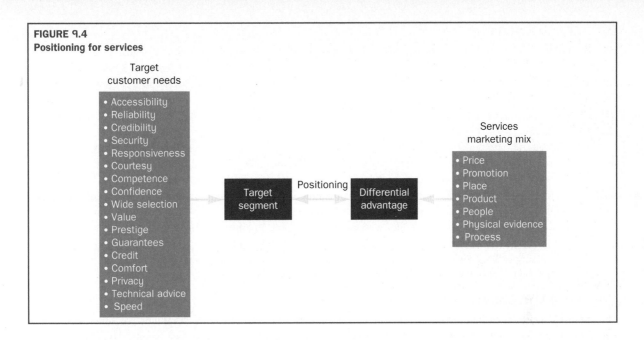

FIGURE 9.4
Positioning for services

Target
customer needs

- Accessibility
- Reliability
- Credibility
- Security
- Responsiveness
- Courtesy
- Competence
- Confidence
- Wide selection
- Value
- Prestige
- Guarantees
- Credit
- Comfort
- Privacy
- Technical advice
- Speed

Target
segment

Positioning

Differential
advantage

Services
marketing mix

- Price
- Promotion
- Place
- Product
- People
- Physical evidence
- Process

those criteria depends on its marketing mix (on the right of the figure). Marketing research can be useful in identifying important choice criteria but care needs to be taken in such studies. Asking customers which are the most important factors when buying a service may give misleading results. For example, the most important factor when travelling by air may be safety. However, this does not mean that customers use safety as a choice criterion when deciding which airline to use. If all major airlines are perceived as being similar in terms of safety, other less important factors like the quality of in-flight meals and service may be the crucial attributes used in decision-making.

Target marketing

The basis of target marketing is market segmentation. A market is analysed to identify groups of potential customers with similar needs and price sensitivities. The potential of each of these segments is assessed on such factors as size, growth rate, degree of competition, price sensitivity, and the fit between its requirements and the company's capabilities.

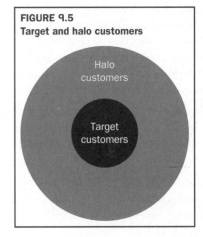

FIGURE 9.5
Target and halo customers

Halo customers

Target customers

The most attractive markets are often not the biggest (as discussed in Mini Case 9.1 on Sandals Resorts International), as saturated markets often confer high levels of competition. So a service organization should apply segmentation and target marketing analysis to determine a suitable marketing mix for the specific groups of customers, thereby creating an opportunity to differentiate its offer. For example, Southwest Airlines uses this strapline to differentiateitself in the crowded airline industry: 'We like to think of ourselves as a Customer Service company that happens to fly airplanes' (Southwest Airlines, 2015).

Marketing managers also need to consider those potential customers who are not directly targeted but may find the service mix attractive. Those customers that are at the periphery of the target market are called **halo customers** and can make a substantial difference between success and failure (see Figure 9.5). Launching into a new target market may require trials to test the innovation and refine the concept. For example, when KFC was considering moving into the breakfast segment of the fast-food market it ran trials in selected outlets before the full launch (Charles, 2008).

Scan the QR code to see how Southwest Airlines differentiates its flight services.

Differential advantage

Understanding customer needs will be the basis of the design of a new service concept that is different from competitive offerings, is highly valued by target customers, and therefore creates a differential advantage. It will be based on the creative use of marketing-mix elements, resulting in such benefits as more reliable or faster delivery, greater convenience, more comfort, higher-quality work, higher prestige or other issues (listed on the left of Figure 9.4). Mini Case 9.1 describes how the Sandals luxury hotel chain has differentiated itself from larger chains through the use of service excellence.

Research can indicate which choice criteria are more or less valued by customers, and how customers rate the service provider's performance on each (Christopher and Yallop, 1990). For marketers, it is important to achieve a balance between what is valued by the customer as important and how the customer perceives the service provider's performance. For both the service provider and its customers, there is no point in going too far to provide quality service. FedEx, the international shipping company, has guidelines on how to avoid customer *overkill*. It suggests avoiding: too much contact (hotel guest constantly contacted by front desk); asking too many questions; providing excessive perks (e.g, lavish baskets of fruit in a hotel room; private boxes at sporting events). Furthermore, it suggests that listening to what the customer wants and making appropriate decisions about when to say no is the key to providing a balanced and highly regarded service (FedEx, 2015).

The services marketing mix

The **services marketing mix** is an extension of the 4-Ps framework introduced in Chapter 1. The essential elements of *product, promotion, price* and *place* remain, but three additional variables—*people, physical evidence* and *process*—are included to produce a 7-Ps mix (Booms and Bitner, 1981). The need for the extension is due to the high degree of direct contact between the company and the customer, the highly visible nature of the service assembly process, and the simultaneity of production and consumption. While it is possible to discuss people, physical evidence and process within the original 4-Ps framework (e.g. people could be considered part of the product offering) the extension allows a more thorough analysis of the marketing ingredients necessary for successful services marketing. Each element of the marketing mix will now be examined.

Product   Physical products can be inspected and tried before buying, but pure services are intangible; you cannot go to a showroom to see a marketing research report or medical operation that you are considering. This means that service customers suffer higher perceived risk in their decision-making and that the three elements of the extended marketing mix—people, physical evidence and process—are crucial in influencing the customer's perception of service quality. These will be discussed later.

 Scan the QR code to see how Visa advertises its services.

The *brand name* of a service can also influence the perception of a service. Four characteristics of successful brand names are as follows (Berry, Lefkowith and Clark, 1980).
1   *Distinctiveness*: it immediately identifies the services provider and differentiates it from the competition.
2   *Relevance*: it communicates the nature of the service and the service benefit.
3   *Memorability*: it is easily understood and remembered.
4   *Flexibility*: it not only expresses the service organization's current business but is also broad enough to cover foreseeable new ventures.

Examples of effective brand names are: Visa, which suggests internationality; Travelodge, which implies travel accommodation; and Virgin Atlantic, which associates the airline with flights to and from North America.

Service providers such as hotels are constantly seeking ways of differentiating themselves from their competitors. For example, Marriott has invested heavily in new super-comfortable beds and bedding to gain an advantage over its competitors.

The quality of the physical product is also used as a differentiator by airlines—for example, stainless steel rather than plastic cutlery, more leg room, personal television screens showing up-to-date movies and, for first-class long-haul passengers, more comfortable beds. Service companies need to reassess their product offerings to keep up with changing consumer tastes. For example, to appeal to a generation of young people who spend a lot of time playing computer games, Disneyland has designed attractions that offer theme park guests the chance to 'get interactive', and is experimenting with mobile phones and other handheld electronic devices to add interactive appeal (Garrahan, 2005).

Promotion   The intangible element of a service may be difficult to communicate. For example, it may be difficult to represent courtesy, hard work and customer care in an advertisement. Once again, the answer is to use *tangible cues* that will help customers understand and judge the service. A hotel can show its buildings, swimming pool, friendly staff and happy customers. An investment company can provide tangible evidence of past performance. Testimonials from satisfied customers can also be used to communicate services benefits. Netto, the Danish-based supermarket chain, used testimonials from six customers in its UK advertising to explain the advantages of shopping there.

Advertising can be used to communicate and reinforce the image of a service. For example, store image can enhance customer satisfaction and build store loyalty (Bloemer and de Ruyter, 1998). Advertising can also be used to create awareness of the benefits consumers can expect from the service provider, as the advertisement for HSBC shows.

 Scan the QR code to see how HSBC's advert makes its services tangible.

Digital marketing is widely used to encourage engagement with service brands. Marks & Spencer spent 25 per cent of its marketing budget on digital communications. Personal selling can also be effective in services marketing because of the high perceived risk inherent in many service purchases. For example, a salesperson can explain the details of a personal pension plan or investment opportunity, answer questions and provide reassurance.

Because of the high perceived risk inherent in buying services, salespeople should develop lists of satisfied customers to use in reference selling. Also salespeople need to be trained to ask for referrals. Customers should be asked if they know of other people or organizations that might benefit from the service. The customer can then be used as an entrée and point of reference when approaching and selling to the new prospect.

Word of mouth is critical to success for services because of their experiential nature. For example, talking to people that have visited a resort or hotel is more convincing than reading holiday brochures. Social media are playing an increasingly important part in this form of communications; for example, the Four Seasons hotel group used Facebook and Twitter to share both guest and staff messages about what the hotels had on offer, things to do at particular destinations, and local tips and deals.

Communication should also be targeted at employees because of their importance in creating and maintaining service quality. Internal communications can define management expectations of staff, reinforce the need to delight the customer and explain the rewards that follow from giving excellent service. External communications that depict service quality can also influence internal staff if they include employees and show how they take exceptional care of their customers.

Care should be taken not to exaggerate promises in promotional material since this may build up unachievable expectations. For example, Delta Airlines used the advertising slogan 'Delta is ready when you are'. This caused problems because it built up customers' expectations that the airline would always be ready—an impossible task. This led Delta to change its slogan to the more realistic 'We love to fly and it shows' (Sellers, 1988).

Price   Price is a key marketing tool, for three reasons. First, as it is often difficult to evaluate a service before purchase, price may act as an indicator of perceived quality. For example, in a travel brochure the price charged by hotels may be used to indicate their quality. Some companies expect a management consultant to charge high fees, otherwise they cannot be particularly good. Second, price is an important tool in controlling demand: matching demand and supply is critical in services because they cannot be stored. Creative use of pricing can help to smooth demand. Third, a key segmentation variable with services is price sensitivity. Some customers may be willing to pay a much higher price than others.

Time is often used to segment price-sensitive and price-insensitive customers. For example, the price of international air travel is often dependent on length of stay. Travellers from Europe to the USA will pay a lot less if they stay a minimum of six nights (including Saturday). Airlines know that customers who stay for less than that are likely to be business people who are willing and able to pay a higher price. An exception is the budget hotel chain Travelodge. The company has adopted a demand-led online pricing system similar to that pioneered by easyJet and Ryanair. Rooms are often priced cheaply to begin with, but the price rises as the hotel becomes fully booked (Fernandez, 2009).

 Scan the QR code to see how Virgin Airlines claims to lead the way for Business travellers.

Some services, such as accounting and management consultancy, charge their customers fees. A strategy needs to be thought out concerning fees. How far can fees be flexible to secure or retain particular customers? How will the fee level compare to that of the competition? Will there be an incentive built in to the fee structure for continuity, forward commitment or the use of the full range of services on offer? Five pricing techniques may be used when setting fee levels.

1 *Offset*: low fee for core service but recouping with add-ons.
2 *Inducement*: low fee to attract new customers or to help retain existing customers.
3 *Diversionary*: low basic fees on selected services to develop the image of value for money across the whole range of services.
4 *Guarantee*: full fee payable on achievement of agreed results.
5 *Predatory*: competition's fees undercut to remove them from the market; high fees charged later.

The Internet is making price transparency a reality. This has caused problems for premium-price service companies such as Avis. In the face of online holiday companies offering cheap holidays and car rental deals, and the ease with which consumers can compare prices, Avis has had to reduce prices, thereby depressing profitability (Davoudi, 2005).

Place   Distribution channels for services are usually more direct than for many physical goods. Because services are intangible, the services marketer is less concerned with storage, the production and consumption is often simultaneous, and the personal nature of services means that direct contact with the service provider (or at best its agent) is desirable. Agents are used when the individual service provider cannot offer a sufficiently wide selection for customers. Consequently, agents are often used for the marketing of travel, insurance and entertainment. However, the advent of the Internet means that direct dealings with the service provider are becoming more frequent.

Growth for many service companies means opening new facilities in new locations. Whereas producers of physical goods can expand production at one site to serve the needs of a geographically spread market, the simultaneous production and consumption of hotel, banking, catering, retailing and accounting services, for example, means that expansion often means following a multi-site strategy. The evaluation of store locations is therefore a critical skill for services marketers. Much of the success of top European supermarket chains has been due to their ability to choose profitable new sites for their retailing operations.

People   Because of the simultaneity of production and consumption in services, the company's personnel occupy a key position in influencing customer perceptions of product quality (Rafiq and Ahmed, 1992). In fact, service quality is inseparable from the quality of the service provider. Without courteous, efficient and motivated staff, service organizations will lose customers. A survey has shown that one in six consumers have been put off making a purchase because of the way they were treated by staff (Wilkinson, 2002). An important marketing task, then, is to set standards to improve the quality of service provided by employees and monitor their performance. Without training and control, employees tend to be variable in their performance, leading to variable service quality.

Service providers need to adopt a customer-first attitude rather than putting their own convenience and enjoyment before that of their customers.

Marketing should also examine the role played by customers in the service environment and seek to eliminate harmful interactions. For example, the enjoyment of a restaurant meal or air travel will very much depend on the actions of other customers. At Christmas, restaurants are often in demand by groups of work colleagues for staff parties. These can be rowdy affairs that can detract from the pleasure of regular patrons. This situation needs to be managed, perhaps by segregating the two types of customer in some way.

EXHIBIT 9.2
The iconic Singapore girl is used in Singapore Airlines' advertising to illustrate the company's passion for service quality

Physical evidence Physical evidence is the environment in which the service is delivered, and any tangible goods that facilitate the performance and communication of the service. Customers look for clues to the likely quality of a service by inspecting the tangible evidence. For example, prospective customers may gaze through a restaurant window to check the appearance of the waiters, the décor and furnishings. The ambience of a retail store is highly dependent on décor, and colour can play an important role in establishing mood because colour has meaning. For example, black signifies strength and power, whereas green suggests mildness. The interior of jet aircraft is pastel-coloured to promote a feeling of calmness, whereas many nightclubs are brightly coloured, with flashing lights to give a sense of excitement.

The layout of a service operation can be a compromise between operations' need for efficiency, and marketing's desire to serve the customer effectively. For example, the temptation to squeeze in an extra table at a restaurant or extra seating in an aircraft may be at the expense of customer comfort.

Process This describes the procedures, mechanisms and flow of activities by which a service is acquired. Process decisions radically affect how a service is delivered to customers. For example, a self-service cafeteria is very different from a restaurant. Marketing managers need to know whether self-service is acceptable (or indeed desirable). Queuing may provide an opportunity to create a differential advantage by reduction/elimination, or making the time spent waiting more enjoyable. Certainly, waiting for service is a common experience for customers and is a strong determinant of overall satisfaction with the service and customer loyalty. Research has shown that an attractive waiting environment can prevent customers becoming irritated or bored very quickly, even though they may have to wait a long time. Both appraisal of the wait and satisfaction with the service improved when the attractiveness of the waiting environment (measured by atmosphere, cleanliness, spaciousness and climate) was rated higher (Pruyn and Smidts, 1998). Providing a more effective service (shorter queues) may be at odds with operations, as the remedy may be to employ more staff.

Reducing delivery time—for example, the time between ordering a meal and receiving it—can also improve service quality. As discussed earlier, this need not necessarily cost more if customers can be persuaded to become involved in the production process, as successfully reflected in the growth of self-service breakfast bars in hotels.

When you have read this chapter

Discover further resources and test your understanding: McGraw-Hill **Connect**™ is a digital teaching and learning environment that improves performance over a variety of critical outcomes; it can be tailored, is easy to use and is proven effective. **LearnSmart**™ is the most widely used and intelligent adaptive learning resource that is proven to strengthen memory recall, improve course retention and boost grades. Fuelled by **LearnSmart**™, **SmartBook**™ is the first and only adaptive reading experience available today.

Review

1 **The nature and special characteristics of services**
   - Services are a special kind of product that may require special understanding and special marketing efforts because of their special characteristics.
   - The key characteristics of pure services are intangibility (they cannot be touched, tasted or smelled); inseparability (production and consumption takes place at the same time, e.g. a haircut); variability (service quality may vary, making standardization difficult); and perishability (consumption cannot be stored, e.g. a hotel room).

2 **Managing service quality, productivity and staff**
   - Two key service quality concepts are customer expectations and perceptions. Customers may be disappointed with service quality if their service perceptions fail to meet their expectations. This may result because of four barriers: the misconception barrier (management's misunderstanding of what the customer expects); the inadequate resources barrier (management provides inadequate resources); inadequate delivery barrier (management fails to select, train and adequately reward staff); and the exaggerated promises barrier (management causes expectations to be too high because of exaggerated promises).
   - Service quality can be measured using a scale called SERVQUAL, which is based on five criteria: reliability, responsiveness, courtesy, competence and tangibles (e.g. quality of restaurant décor).
   - Service productivity can be improved without reducing service quality by using technology (e.g. automatic cash dispensers); customer involvement in production (e.g. self-service petrol stations); and balancing supply and demand (e.g. differential pricing to smooth demand).
   - Staff are critical in service operations because they are often in contact with customers. The starting point is the selection of suitable people, socialization allows the recruit to experience the culture and tasks of the organization, empowerment gives them the authority to solve customer problems, they need to be trained and motivated, and evaluation is required so that staff understand how their performance standards relate to customer satisfaction.

3 **How to position a service organization or brand**
   - Positioning involves the choice of target market (where to compete) and the creation of a differential advantage (how to compete). These decisions are common to both physical products and services. However, because of the special characteristics of services, it is useful for the services marketer to consider not only the classical 4-Ps marketing mix but also an additional 3-Ps—people, physical evidence and process—when deciding how to meet customer needs and create a differential advantage.

4 **The services marketing mix**
   - The services marketing mix consists of 7-Ps: product, price, place, promotion, people (important because of the high customer contact characteristic of services), physical evidence (important because customers look for cues to the likely quality of a service by inspecting the physical evidence, e.g. décor), and process (because the process of supplying a service affects perceived service quality).

Key Terms

exaggerated promises barrier a barrier to the matching of expected and perceived service levels caused by the unwarranted building up of expectations by exaggerated promises

halo customers customers that are not directly targeted but may find the product attractive

inadequate delivery barrier a barrier to the matching of expected and perceived service levels caused by the failure of the service provider to select, train and reward staff adequately, resulting in poor or inconsistent delivery of service

inadequate resources barrier a barrier to the matching of expected and perceived service levels caused by the unwillingness of service providers to provide the necessary resources

inseparability a characteristic of services, namely that their production cannot be separated from their consumption

intangibility a characteristic of services, namely that they cannot be touched, seen, tasted or smelled

misconception barrier a failure by marketers to understand what customers really value about their service

perishability a characteristic of services, namely that the capacity of a service business, such as a hotel room, cannot be stored—if it is not occupied, this is lost income that cannot be recovered

service any deed, performance or effort carried out for the customer

services marketing mix product, place, price, promotion, people, process and physical evidence (the '7-Ps')

variability a characteristic of services, namely that, being delivered by people, the standard of their performance is open to variation

Study Questions

1. To what extent is the marketing of services the same as the marketing of physical goods? Discuss.

2. What are the barriers that can separate expected from perceived service? What must service providers do to eliminate these barriers?

3. Discuss the role of service staff in the creation of a quality service. Can you give examples from your own experience of good and bad service encounters?

4. Identify and evaluate how hotels can differentiate themselves from their competitors. Choose three hotel groups and evaluate their success at differentiation.

5. Discuss the problems of providing high-quality service in retailing in central and eastern Europe.

6. Discuss the benefits to organizations and customers of developing and maintaining strong customer relationships.

Recommended Reading

Anker, T., L. Sparks, L. Moutinho, L. and C. Gronroos (2015) Consumer dominant value creation: A theoretical response to the recent call for a consumer dominant logic for marketing, *European Journal of Marketing* 49(3/4), 532–60.

Golder, P. N., D. Mitra and C. Moorman (2012) What Is Quality? An Integrative Framework of Processes and States, *Journal of Marketing* 76(4), 1–23.

Gummesson, E. and C. Grönroos (2012) The emergence of the new service marketing: Nordic School perspectives, *Journal of Service Management* 23(4), 479–97.

Palmer, A. (2014) *Principles of Services Marketing*, 7th edn., Maidenhead: McGraw Hill.

Vargo, S. L. and R. F. Lusch (2004) The Four Service Marketing Myths, *Journal of Service Research* 6(4), 324–35.

Wilson, A., V. A. Zeithaml, M. J. Bitner and D. D. Gremler (2012) *Services Marketing—Integrating Customer Focus Across the Firm*, 2nd European edition, Maidenhead: McGraw Hill.

References

Aijo, T. S. (1996) The Theoretical and Philosophical Underpinnings of Relationship Marketing, *European Journal of Marketing* 30(2), 8–18; Grönroos, C. (1990) *Services Management and Marketing: Managing the Moments of Truth in Service Competition*, Lexington, MA: Lexington Books.

Aptech Computer Systems (2014) Sandals Upgrades BI to Latest Aptech Execuvue with Dashboards for 21 Resorts, Aptech. http://www.aptech-inc.com/index.php/2014/11/sandals-upgrades-bi-to-latest-aptech-execuvue-with-dashboards-for-21-resorts (accessed 11 November 2014).

Arts Council (2004) Market matters: the dynamics of the contemporary art market, London: Arts Council.

Baron, S., K. Harris and B. J. Davies (1996) Oral Participation in Retail Service Delivery: A Comparison of the Roles of Contact Personnel and Customers, *European Journal of Marketing* 30 (9), 75–90.

Berry, L. L. (1980) Services Marketing is Different, *Business Horizons*, May–June, 24–9.

Berry, L. L., E. E. Lefkowith and T. Clark (1980) In Services: What's in a Name?, *Harvard Business Review*, Sept.–Oct., 28–30.

Bloemer, J. and K. de Ruyter (1998) On the Relationship Between Store Image, Store Satisfaction and Store Loyalty, *European Journal of Marketing* 32(5/6), 499–513.

Booms, B. H. and M. J. Bitner (1981) Marketing Strategies and Organisation Structures for Service Firms, in Donnelly, J. H. and W. R. George (eds.) *Marketing of Services*, Chicago: American Marketing Association, 47–51.

Booth, M. (2014) Dark lands: the grim truth behind the 'Scandinavian miracle', *The Guardian*, 27 January. http://www.theguardian.com/world/2014/jan/27/scandinavian-miracle-brutal-truth-denmark-norway-sweden (accessed 22 March 2015).

Brown, P., S. Hassan and R. Teare (2011) The Sandals philosophy: exceeding guest expectations—now and in the future, *Worldwide Hospitality and Tourism Themes* 3(1), 8–13.

Brown, S. and A. Patterson (2009) Harry Potter and the Service-Dominant Logic of marketing: a cautionary tale, *Journal of Marketing Management* 25(5–6), 519–33.

Buzzell, R. D. and B. T. Gale (1987) *The PIMS Principles: Linking Strategy to Performance*, New York: Free Press, 103–34.

Campbell, D. (2015) NHS agrees largest-ever privatisation deal to tackle backlog, *The Guardian*, 12 March. http://www.theguardian.com/society/2015/mar/12/nhs-agrees-largest-ever-privatisation-deal-to-tackle-backlog (accessed 18 March 2015).

Charles, G. (2008) KFC Launches Breakfast Menu, *Marketing*, 7 May, 1.

Christopher, M. and R. Yallop (1990) Audit your Customer Service Quality, *Focus*, June–July, 1–6.

CIA World Facts Book (2014) https://www.cia.gov/library/publications/the-world-factbook

Collinson, S. (2012) Why is the public sector so complex? http://flipchartfairytales.wordpress.com/2012/03/19/why-is-thepublic-sector-so-complex

Cowell, D. (1995) *The Marketing of Services*, London: Heinemann, 35.

Danaher, P. J. and J. Mattson (1994) Customer Satisfaction during the Service Delivery Process, *European Journal of Marketing* 28(5), 5–16.

Davoudi, S. (2005) From Brand Leader to Struggler in Eight Years, *Financial Times*, 17 June, 24.

DCMS (2010) *Creative industries economic estimates statistical bulletin*, London: DCMS, http://www.culture.gov.uk/images/research/CIEE_Full_Release_Dec2010.pdf

Edgett, S. and S. Parkinson (1993) Marketing for Services Industries: A Review, *Service Industries Journal* 13(3), 19–39.

Ellis-Chadwick, F. (2011) *B22 An introduction to retail management and marketing: Book 1 What is retailing?* The Open University, 7.

FedEx (2015) Customer Service Overkill, Fedex, 30 March. https://getahead.fedex.ca/customer-service-overkill

Fernandez, J. (2009) Sparking a Hotel Price War, *Marketing Week*, 12 March, 22–3.

Gallagher, P. (2009) Henning Mankell creates a 'female Wallander' following star's suicide, *The Observer*, 27 December. http://www.theguardian.com/uk/2009/dec/27/wallandar-hemming-mankell-tv-books-detective (accessed 21 March 2015).

Garrahan, M. (2005) The Ride of a Lifetime, *Financial Times*, 18 August, 19.

Hirsch, P. (1972) Processing fads and fashions: an organization set analysis of culture industry systems, *American Journal of Sociology*, 77, 639–659. In M. Banksa and D. Hesmondhalgh (2009) Looking for work in creative industries policy, *International Journal of Cultural Policy* 15(4), 415–430.

Jodelka, F. (2015) Fortitude: 'not another chunk of Nordic noir', *The Guardian*, 29 January. http://www.theguardian.com/tv-and-radio/2015/jan/29/fortitude-sky-atlantic (accessed 21 March 2015).

Karpen, I., L. Bove and B. Lukas (2012) Linking service-dominant logic and strategic business practice: A conceptual model of a service-dominant orientation, *Journal of Service Research* 15(1), 21–38; DOI: 10.1177/1094670511425697.

Lievens, A. and R. K. Moenaert (2000) Communication Flows During Financial Service Innovation, *European Journal of Marketing* 34(9/10), 1078–110.

Lusch, R. F. and Vargo, S. L. (2011) Service-dominant logic: a necessary step, *European Journal of Marketing* 45(7/8), 1298–1309.

Lusch, R. F., S. L. Vargo and M. Tanniru (2010) Service, value networks and learning, *Journal of the Academy of Marketing Science* 38, 19–31.

Milington, A. (2015) Pubs and bars hit back at New Year health campaigns with 'Try January' push, *Marketing Week*, 6 January. http://www.marketingweek.com/2015/01/06/pubs-and-bars-hit-back-at-new-year-health-campaigns-with-try-january-push (accessed 22 March 2015).

O'Shaughnessy, J. and O'Shaughnessy, N. (2009) The service-dominant perspective: a backward step? *European Journal of Marketing* 43(5/6), 784–93.

Offerpop (2013) *History of the Hashtag*, Offerpop, 6 November. http://www.offerpop.com/resources/blog/history-hashtags

Parasuraman, A., V. A. Zeithaml and L. L. Berry (1985) A Conceptual Model of Service Quality and its Implications for Future Research, *Journal of Marketing*, Fall, 41–50.

Pike, J. (2011) Sandals' Success Story, Travel Agent, Questex Media Group, 25 July, 19–21.

Pruyn, A. and A. Smidts (1998) Effects of Waiting on the Satisfaction with the Service: Beyond Objective Times Measures, *International Journal of Research in Marketing* 15, 321–34.

Rafiq, M. and P. K. Ahmed (1992) The Marketing Mix Reconsidered, *Proceedings of the Annual Conference of the Marketing Education Group*, Salford, 439–51.

Rubera, G. and A. Kirca (2012) Firm Innovativeness and Its Performance Outcomes: A Meta-Analytic Review and Theoretical Integration *Journal of Marketing* 76(May), 130–47.

Schlesinger, L. A. and J. L. Heskett (1991) The Service-Driven Service Company, *Harvard Business Review*, Sept.–Oct., 71–81.

Sellers, P. (1988) How to Handle Customers' Gripes, *Fortune* 118 (October), 100.

Sherwood, B. (2008) An Eye For The Next Opportunity, *Financial Times*, 17 September, 16.

Solomon, M. (2014) Self-Leadership The Best Leadership? Ritz-Carlton's Employee Empowerment, *Forbes*, 13 May. http://www.forbes.com/sites/micahsolomon/2014/05/13/ritz-carltons-corporate-culture (accessed 20 March 2015).

Southwest Airlines. (2015) Customer Service, Southwest Airlines. https://www.southwest.com/html/customer-service

Tesseras, L. (2014) The Marketing Year: The top campaigns of 2014, *Marketing Week*, 8 December. http://www.marketingweek.com/2014/12/08/the-marketing-year-the-top-campaigns-of-2014 (accessed 12 December 2014).

Vargo, S. L. and R. F. Lusch (2004) Evolving to a new dominant logic for marketing, *Journal of Marketing*, 68(January), 1–17.

Vargo, S. L. and R. F. Lusch (2006) 'Service-Dominant Logic: What It Is, What It Is Not, What It Might Be', in R. F. Lusch and S. L. Vargo (eds), *The Service-Dominant Logic of Marketing: Dialog, Debate, and Directions*, Armonk: M.E. Sharpe, 43–56.

Wilkinson, A. (2002) Employees can get the Message Across, *Marketing Week*, 3 October, 20.

Wirtz, J. and P. L. Chew (2003) *Essentials of Services Marketing*, Pearson Education.

Wirtz, J., P. L. Chew and C. Lovelock (2012) *Essentials of Services Marketing*, 2nd edn., Pearson Education.

Zeithaml, V. A., A. Parasuraman and L. L. Berry (1988) SERVQUAL: A Multiple Item Scale for Measuring Consumer Perceptions of Service Quality, *Journal of Retailing* 64(1), 13–37.

CASE 17
Pret A Manger: 'Passionate About Food'

Introduction

Pret a Manger (French for 'ready to eat') is a chain of coffee shops that sell a range of high-quality sandwiches, salads, sushi, desserts and coffee to an increasingly discerning set of lunchtime customers. Started in London, England, in 1986 by two university graduates, Pret now has more than 350 stores across the UK and in several US cities including New York and Boston, as well as in Paris, Hong Kong and Shanghai. Pret has reportedly made regular deliveries of sandwiches to Buckingham Palace, home of the British royal family, and to number 10 Downing Street, the office of the British Prime Minister, for working lunches.

Background and Company History

Pret was founded with a single shop in central London by two property law graduates, Julian Metcalf and Sinclair Beecham, who had been students together in the early 1980s. At that time, the choice of lunchtime eating in London and other British cities was much more limited than it is today. Some chose restaurants or those well-known British institutions, pubs. However, lunchtime habits were changing. There was a growing awareness of the benefits of healthier eating, and also a trend among office workers towards taking shorter lunch breaks and eating at their desks. The choice in carry-out food was dominated by fast-food chains such as McDonald's, Burger King and KFC. Sandwiches also played an important part in lunchtime eating. Prior to Pret's arrival, sandwiches had been sold mainly pre-packed in supermarkets and high street chain stores or made to order in the many small, owner-run sandwich bars found in city centres and business districts.

Dissatisfied with both the food and service from traditional sandwich bars –Metcalf described the food as 'soggy sandwiches and mush'—Metcalf and Beecham were determined that Pret should offer something different and much better. They wanted Pret's food to be not only high quality, but also preservative- and additive-free, using natural ingredients. According to Metcalf, this proved to be a lot harder than it looked. In the beginning with only one store, they shopped for the food themselves at local markets and then returned to the shop where they made the sandwiches each morning. Metcalf would go in on Sunday evenings to cook 25 chickens ready to make sandwiches for the following day. As he recalls,

> 'Half the battle was getting preservative-free, chemical-free food. And it was an immense logistical challenge to get the ingredients delivered each morning.'

Pret's offer was based around premium quality sandwiches, other food and coffee, all priced higher than existing sandwich bars, sold in attractive packaging ready to carry out or eat in a comfortable store environment, with a focus on best quality natural ingredients and high quality service.

The Pret Vision—'Passionate About What We Do'

From the very outset, Pret strongly focused on the quality of its food and ingredients in line with its own distinctive set of values. On its website, Pret claims to be: 'Passionate about food. Our mission is to create, handmade, natural food, avoiding the obscure chemicals, additives and preservatives common to so much of the 'prepared' and 'fast' food on the market today. Using natural ingredients is sacred to Pret.'

Great importance is placed on freshness. Uniquely, unlike those sold in other coffee chains, shops or supermarkets, Pret's sandwiches are all made and pre-packed for sale by hand in the kitchens of most Pret shops, starting at 6.30 each morning, rather than being prepared by a supplier or at a central location. No sandwiches or salads are kept overnight—any that aren't sold by the end of the day are offered free to local charities or disposed of. This means that store managers have the difficult logistical balancing act of keeping the shelves sufficiently full while at the same time not ordering or making too much food which has to be disposed of at the end of the day. If a store runs out of a particular sandwich during the day, customers can ask to have one made especially for them.

Careful sourcing of supplies has also always been critical, and Pret has taken time to build relationships with a number of suppliers it can trust to provide food of the quality and standard it requires. The organic coffee, for example, is supplied by small growers that operate as co-operatives and follow sustainable growing policies under the Fairtrade banner. (Fairtrade is a scheme that tries to ensure that sellers of agricultural products in developing countries receive a fair price for their products.) The milk, which is also organic, is from British farms where cows are allowed to graze and eat naturally. Genetically modified ingredients are banned, and the tuna used in Pret sandwiches has to be 'dolphin friendly'. The eggs in the egg mayonnaise are free range, and the ham comes from pigs fed on a strictly vegetarian diet on Farm Assured farms.

At the same time, Pret is also continually searching for new supplies of ingredients of the quality and standard it requires. There is also a drive for constant product improvement and innovation—Pret claims that its chocolate brownie has been improved more than 30 times over the years. New product ideas meetings are held in the company head office every Wednesday, and on average a new product is tried out every four days. There is also a sustainability strategy in place to reduce energy usage, waste and build long-term partnerships with other suppliers in developing countries. Pret has a charitable foundation, set up in 1995, which contributes to charities that help homeless people in the UK.

Pret is aware that some of its customers are increasingly health conscious. Its website menu carefully lists all the ingredients and nutritional values of every menu item in terms of energy, protein, fat and dietary fibre.

Although the stores are mainly self-service, the quality of service provided by staff in the few moments that a customer spends buying coffee and paying at the counter is also critical in providing an experience that can differentiate Pret and build loyalty with customers who are usually in a hurry and buying on impulse. The service in Pret is friendly and efficient, in contrast to that in many restaurants and retailers in Britain, where historically service quality has not always been high. Customer-facing store staff are young, enthusiastic and motivated, and they are often given discretion to offer customers a free replacement for any item that is out of stock. There is a strong emphasis on staff recruitment and training to achieve this service quality—Pret claims it takes 12 weeks to fully train a coffee barista to the standard it needs—pay is above the industry average, and there are opportunities for career development into management. While staff turnover at 98 per cent a year may seem high, it is low against the fast-food industry average of around 150 per cent. As many Pret stores open early for breakfast, depending on customer demand, staff may be required to work on rotas that begin early in the morning. Advertised jobs are many times oversubscribed by applicants, and Pret has been voted by *Fortune Magazine* as one of the top 10 companies to work for in Europe. According to Pret, it offers an attractive and fun place to work: 'We wear jeans, and twice a year we throw a massive party. Some have passed into Pret legend. Everyone at Pret is invited!'

Monitoring the quality of the service in the stores is important, and quality is checked regularly by using mystery shoppers. If a shop receives a good report, then all the staff there receive an hourly bonus for the week of the visit. Managers also regularly visit and work as buddies for a week in stores every few months to help them keep in touch with how things are working on the shop floor. Store staff work in teams and are briefed daily, often on the basis of customer feedback, which Pret actively encourages through its website, in-store reply cards or by phone. Pret takes this very seriously and places great importance on this customer feedback, both positive and negative, which is discussed at weekly management meetings.

The design of the store environment is also distinctive. Shops are fitted out in a light and airy style featuring walls in bare and white-painted brick, Pret's trademark dark red, and furniture and fittings with natural wood finishes. Some stores play music, which helps to create a lively, fast-moving environment. Pret does not advertise, but attractive point-of-sale promotional material and graphics are on the walls of most shops, explaining Pret's values and philosophy and announcing new products. The paper napkins are made from unbleached paper, while packaging, cutlery and paper cups are simply and attractively designed and recyclable. Pret also offers an online delivery service for businesses.

Competition

As Pret's chain expanded throughout the 1990s and 2000s into city centres, business and shopping areas as well as airports and railway stations throughout

»

the UK, so did the competition. Rivals such as Caffè Nero, Costa Coffee and USA-based Starbucks all entered the market, as well as a number of smaller independent chains. All offered a choice of coffees but with varying offerings in terms of sandwiches and food. In a London shopping street, it is not uncommon to see three or four rival coffee shops next door to or within a few metres of each other. Prices in each chain are roughly comparable. Pret, however, currently sees its main competitor as Eat, a chain of around 120 outlets throughout the UK, founded in 1996, with a similar offering of coffee, sandwiches and other hot and cold food. Eat describes its food as, 'made from scratch and served fresh', but does not claim that it is made in the store, nor that its ingredients are natural or organic.

The Future

As work and lifestyles get busier, the demand for convenience and fast food continues to grow. But while the growth in sales of some types of fast food like burgers are showing signs of slowing down, sandwiches continue to increase in popularity. Customers are also generally getting more health-conscious and choosy about what they eat, particularly about the levels of fat, sugar and additives in food. They are also getting increasingly concerned about finding nutritional information from food labelling.

After a long run of success, Pret has plans for further growth. It hopes to open more new stores in the UK, but as Pret owns and manages all its stores and does not franchise their format, its plan is, as always, to expand carefully and cautiously. It also aims to open more stores internationally, particularly in New York and Hong Kong, where the brand has already been successful.

Questions

Go to Pret's website at http://www.pret.com and use it in conjunction with the case study to answer the following questions:

1. How would you define the market and product category that Pret a Manger operates in?

2. Which companies do you think are Pret a Manger's competitors?

3. How does Pret a Manger differentiate its brand from its competitors in this market? In a few key words or phrases, define what you think is the defining positioning or 'essence' of the Pret a Manger brand.

4. Discuss how Pret a Manger manages each of the elements of its services marketing mix, below, to deliver a distinctive customer experience and build its brand equity.
   - Products and merchandise
   - Store locations
   - Pricing
   - Marketing communications
   - Processes and systems
   - Store environment
   - People

This case study was written by Clive Helm, Senior Lecturer, University of Westminster.

References

The material in the case has been drawn from a variety of published sources.

CASE 18
Nordstrom: A Shining Example of Service Excellence

'Use your best judgement in all situations. There will be no additional rules.' That is all the guidance that Nordstrom, the famous Seattle-based upscale fashion retailer, gives its employees regarding how to handle all customer service interactions. The company, famous for its 'no-questions-asked' returns policy, is also well known for providing some of the highest levels of customer service in the retail industry. Nordstrom's reputation for service is so great that a book was actually written about it, *The Nordstrom Way to Customer Service Excellence*. It offers a guideline for managers who are looking to emulate best practices and improve the levels of service at their companies.

Nordstrom, founded in 1901, has always had a strong presence in the Pacific Northwest of the USA. Currently, it has 118 full-service stores spread out over 38 states. From the very beginning, providing the best customer service as well as the best service experience was at the heart of everything that Nordstrom did. The company says that it has a 'relentless drive to exceed expectations'.

Analysts believe that Nordstrom's exemplary levels of customer service are based on two key factors: 1) the increased level of attention to detail regarding the customer's experience when shopping (regardless of the channel), and 2) the high degree to which employees are empowered to take decisions and solve problems autonomously.

Examples of Nordstrom's commitment to service are legendary. A former employee, Ambra Benjamin, explained in an interview some of the policies and expectations regarding behaviour that workers were required to adhere to. The most important was the company's returns policy. It doesn't matter how long ago an item was bought, what condition it is in, or whether the customer does not have the receipt. As an employee, you are expected to accept the item without question.

Nordstrom also provides its customers a better experience by not consolidating checkout counters into endless rows near the exit, like other retailers do. Every department has its own cashier dedicated to helping customers who are looking to buy a certain category of item. The company also offers personal shoppers and concierges to give an even higher level of personalized service and a customized shopping experience. Other in-store amenities are comfortable

and clean toilets as well as nursing and changing rooms for mothers with infants.

Realizing that its employees are the 'face' of the company, Nordstrom tends to provide good pay and benefits, with commission running as high as 10 per cent and salaries going into the six figures for high performers. The company even has something called the 'million-dollar club'. This is a select group of salespeople who bring in more than $1 million in sales per year. This 'elite of the elite' go out of their way to cultivate personal relationships with Nordstrom's customers, contacting them directly about certain events and promotions that might be of interest, as well as sending hand-written thank-you cards.

As you would expect from a company demanding service excellence, courtesy and politeness are paramount. That is why Nordstrom employees do not point you in the right direction when you ask where something is. Instead, they walk you there themselves. They do not hand you your purchased items over the counter. They walk around and place the items into your hands. Also, customers are never rushed, even when it is closing time.

Nordstrom is also obsessed with using the latest technology, starting in the late 1990s with trying to find new ways to improve customer service and the overall shopping experience by incorporating the latest IT developments into its operations. Its goal is to become the world's best 'omni-channel' retailer— that is to say, provide as many different ways for customers to shop as possible (both online and offline) and making all the channels perform seamlessly from

»

»

a service experience point of view. Analysts say that Nordstrom is 'at the forefront of e-commerce and omni-channel retail', having reportedly spent at least $1 billion developing its technological capabilities.

An example of Nordstrom's commitment to IT is the introduction of an inventory system as far back as 2002 that provided customers with a 'consistent multi-channel experience'. Nordstrom was one of the first retailers to have a point-of-sale system that allowed salespeople to track an individual customer's order and service needs through the Internet. Nordstrom was also an early innovator and adopter of apps and social media, as well as mobile checkout systems that allow people to purchase an item in a store without having to wait in a checkout line and see a cashier. The company recently made it possible to buy items posted on Instagram immediately through a link. Nordstrom also analyzes marketing and fashion trends, using information it receives from its Pinterest page to help it identify items that it should display more prominently in its stores. This results in higher service by more effectively providing customers with the items that they themselves believe are popular. The company also acquired the 'flash-sale' site Hautelook in an effort to provide high fashion at lower prices. All these innovations have helped Nordstrom to provide a personalized and superior customer experience to shoppers in the USA and 96 countries worldwide through its website.

In 2014, Nordstrom decided to spread its excellence north, expanding into Canada. The company opened its first store in Calgary, with a second store opening in Ottawa in March in 2015, followed by a third store in Vancouver around September 2015. The company plans to have three Toronto locations by 2016 or 2017.

In a further sign of its commitment to service excellence, Nordstrom said that it plans 'to stay focused on serving customers one at a time and getting to know and understand our customers in each city in which we are opening'. As an example of perhaps learning from the mistakes of others, Nordstrom's market entry plan appears to be on a much smaller and cautious scale than that of another US retailer, Target. At the end of 2014, Target announced that it would be leaving Canada due to poor performance (the company reportedly lost $2 billion on its venture in the 'great white north'). Unfortunately, in business, sometimes when a weak competitor leaves a market a stronger one enters. Saks Fifth Avenue, another US luxury retailer known for high levels of customer service, announced plans to open two stores in Toronto in 2016. Analysts believe that many Canadians are familiar with, and have shopped, at both Nordstrom and Saks Fifth Avenue. This is good news for the competing companies and their respective expansion plans. The challenge is that Canadian customers will most likely have extremely high expectations regarding customer service and their overall shopping experience. If disappointed, it will probably be a long time before they return again, if they ever do.

Questions

1. What kind of services does Nordstrom offer its customers?
2. What role do employees play in providing excellent customer service?
3. How does Nordstrom use technology to improve its customer service?
4. What steps can Nordstrom take to be successful in its expansion abroad, maintain its excellent customer service and keep its competitive advantage?

This case study was written by Tom McNamara and Asha Moore-Mangin, The ESC Rennes School of Business, France.

References

Based on: Lutz, A. (2014) How Nordstrom Became The Most Successful Retailer, Business Insider, December 30, 2014, http://www.businessinsider.com/nordstroms-business-strategy-is-working-2014-12#ixzz3PAx3pRKo; Khan, H. (2014) How Nordstrom Made Its Brand Synonymous With Customer Service (and How You Can Too), Shopify, 2 October, http://www.shopify.com/blog/15517012-how-nordstrom-made-its-brand-synonymous-with-customer-service-and-how-you-can-too; Janus, A. (2015) Nordstrom take note, here's what Target's Canadian failure can teach you, CTVNews, 15 January, http://www.ctvnews.ca/business/nordstrom-take-note-here-s-what-target-s-canadian-failure-can-teach-you-1.2190662#ixzz3P7eeR6IT; Solomon, M. (2014) Take These Two Steps To Rival Nordstrom's Customer Service Experience, Forbes, 15 March, http://www.forbes.com/sites/micahsolomon/2014/03/15/the-nordstrom-two-part-customer-experience-formula-lessons-for-your-business; Martinez, A. (2011) Tale of lost diamond adds glitter to Nordstrom's customer service, The Seattle Times, May 11, http://seattletimes.com/html/businesstechnology/2015028167_nordstrom12.html; Udland, M. (2015) Target Is Leaving Canada, Business Insider, 15 January, http://www.businessinsider.com/target-shuts-down-canada-operations-2015-1#ixzz3PBURMzRa; Quora (2014) Why is Nordstrom known for their good customer service? Quora, 19 February, http://www.quora.com/Why-is-Nordstrom-known-for-their-good-customer-service; Ross, J.W., C. M. Beath and I. Sebastian (2015) Why Nordstrom's Digital Strategy Works (and Yours Probably Doesn't), Harvard Business Review, 14 January, https://hbr.org/2015/01/why-nordstroms-digital-strategy-works-and-yours-probably-doesnt

CHAPTER 10
Value Through Relationships

LEARNING OBJECTIVES

After reading this chapter, you should be able to:

1 define the concept of relationship marketing
2 discuss the nature of relationship marketing and how to build customer relationships
3 explain how customer relationships should be managed
4 suggest ways of developing customer relationship strategies
5 explain the significance and benefits of customer retention
6 discuss approaches towards customer loyalty programmes
7 explain and discuss the function of customer relationship management (CRM) systems
8 explain the main stages of key account management (KAM)

M arketers are increasingly considering societal as well as economic factors when developing their strategies so they can deliver value not only for customers but also for employees, their families and many other stakeholders. The benefits that can be derived from a value-driven approach are many. In this chapter we examine how value can be created through relationship marketing.

Relationship marketing is a philosophy (Berry, 2008) that involves 'marketing based on relationships, networks and interaction, recognizing that marketing is embedded in the total management of the networks of the selling organization, the market and society' (Gummesson, 2002). Hence, developing successful relationships between buyer and supplier becomes an organization's ultimate goal, which arguably can deliver value for all involved.

The principles of relationship marketing are nothing new (McGarry, 1953) but do represent a fundamental change in marketing practice. Since the 1990s, the shift in marketing research and practice (Grönroos, 1994) away from the 4-Ps which had dominated marketing thinking since 1960 occurred in response to growing customer demands and an ever more complex business environment (Singh, Agrariya and Deepali, 2011). The significance of relationship marketing has continued to gather momentum as companies have moved away from developing short-term transactional relationships towards building long-term relationships (Kotler, 1991). At the heart of relationship building theory is the idea of value creation by managing customer expectations and experiences within social networks. In this chapter, we build on earlier discussions of customer value (Chapter 1) to explore relationship marketing and associated management practices. Throughout the chapter, illustrative examples are provided from both business-to-business and business-to-consumer contexts. More specifically, this chapter examines the concepts of value creation, relationship marketing and relational networks, before considering building and managing relationships, the benefits of developing organizational and consumer relationships, developing customer retention strategies, customer loyalty programmes, customer relationship management (CRM) systems and key account management (KAM).

Value Creation

Value creation companies engage in value creation when they enter into exchanges with their customers, and this is central to building relationships. Exchange relationships happen when an arrangement is established between trading partners, and can occur in business-to-business or a business-to-consumer setting. Value is created through the use of the resources and management structures that the exchange partners control (Hammervoll, 2012). Various types of value creation initiative can be established depending on the extent of the interaction between the trading partners and the aims for the value creation interaction (Grönroos and Voima, 2012). For example:

Information sharing to aid supplier learning: a buyer might supply market intelligence about market demand and competitors in a new market to its supplier, in order to aid learning that might deliver future improvements in the seller's offer. In this situation, the success of the interaction is dependent on the quality of the information provided by the buyer and the supplier's ability to use the intelligence effectively (Ciborra, 1991).

Supplier development: a supplier improves the quality of its products through insights derived from discussion and consultation with buyers. In this case, there is a shared initiative that focuses on improvements that can contribute to creating a competitive advantage, which will ultimately benefit both companies. Such initiatives might result in better quality service achieved through improved training, reduced costs, and more innovative product design (Hammervoll, 2012).

Strategic knowledge sharing: a supplier improves its production processes by engaging in joint projects with a buyer. Both companies (buyer and supplier) participate in such ventures by contributing ideas, suggestions and feedback to gain mutual benefit (Hammervoll, 2009). For this level of interaction to be successful, both parties need to be willing to share sensitive strategic information, utilise their company's capabilities and fully engage in the co-creation of value.

As a result, relationship management plays an essential role in value creation, because both buyer and supplier need to work together in the pursuit of mutual gains. Managers in all markets can consider the idea of value creation, as it may be a way to identify new opportunities to differentiate a company's offer. In order to benefit, managers should allocate time and resources to learning about their customers' requirements and then considering how to improve their products and services. In consumer markets, service providers need to demonstrate their commitment not only towards their customers but also towards employees, suppliers and other stakeholders, in order to create trusting relationships and excellent customer experiences. For example, the coffee shop sector has focused on how to create customer experiences that matter. See Marketing in Action 10.1 for discussion of how Starbucks created the third place concept and in doing so revolutionised the coffee shop industry.

MARKETING IN ACTION 10.1
The Third Place; Creating Customer Value in the Coffee Shop Industry

Howard Shultz joined Starbucks when it had just four coffee shops. Then he went on a trip to Italy and came back with an idea that would change coffee drinking behaviour and stimulate the development of a multi-billion dollar industry. Schultz wanted to give Americans the Italian coffee experience, but realised that he needed to adapt the product and the service offer to suit the needs of his customers, as they would not want the strong, bitter espresso coffee drunk by Italians. So he invented a version of coffee to entice young adults away from sugary drinks like Coke and sought to change their beverage-drinking behaviour. He added milk and sugary syrups to strong black coffee so his customers could get their caffeine 'kick' in a different way. Shultz encouraged people to drink frothy cappuccinos and milky lattés, and their response was overwhelming: they queued in their hundreds outside the company's coffee shops in Seattle.

Adapting the product was only part of Schultz's strategy; he also realised the importance to the customers of creating a unique environment in which to experience their coffee drinking. Schultz conceived *the third place*—a place between work and home, a place to meet friends. The coffee shops were designed to provide a warm and convivial atmosphere to appeal to customers, a principle that has remained important to the company throughout its development into a global mega-brand. The third place idea was so successful that it is a model that has been used by all the world's successful coffee shop brands, such as Costa Coffee and Caffé Nero.

Each Starbucks store is designed to be as unique as possible, even though the company operates over 22,000 stores globally. But as well as the look and feel, distinct zones within many stores aim to provide different customer experiences. For example: seating by windows allows customers to watch passers-by while they sip their macchiatos; stylish bars to stand at to drink frothy espressos and then go aim to create an experience reminiscent of traditional coffee houses in Italy; communal tables, for groups of customers or individuals, have space to drink, eat, socialise, read or work on a laptop; softer seating areas offer more 'intimate' coffee drinking experiences.

Also the heart of Starbucks' success is a set of core principles that focus on value creation and the development of relational capital. Relationships with customers, employees, suppliers and alliance partners are considered so valuable that they form a central part of the company's activities.

>>

For customers, it is important to understand the service operation from the perspective of the person the service exists for, so Starbucks works with its customers to get ideas on how to improve its service. For example, the My Starbucks Idea website invites customers to submit ideas and suggestions. Many new product ideas and service improvements have been introduced from customer ideas, for example 'buy 10 get one free', reduced fat cinnamon swirl coffee cake, Evolution Fresh (fruit and veg) smoothies, and Teavana, premium loose leaf tea.

For employees, learning is an important part of the value creation process at Starbucks. For example, Starbucks and the Schultz Family Foundation work with disengaged young adults to help them find employment; they also provide job training programmes as well as life skills coaching to support young people throughout their lives, not only at work. Mutual benefits are generated: for the company, happier and more satisfied employees mean genuine good service experiences for Starbucks customers, and for the individual, there is a sense of purpose and belonging.

For suppliers and alliance partners, supplier development and knowledge sharing for strategic development is vital to the company's ongoing success. Starbucks works with its suppliers and farmers to ensure that its coffee beans are grown in a sustainable manner, for example through the Coffee And Farmer Equity Practices; this not only provides high quality beans but also ensures the livelihoods of the farmers and their families.

Based on: Hammervoll (2012); Centrum för Tjänsteforskning (2015); Starbucks (2015a and b); Wilson (2014)

Scan the QR code to find out more about Starbucks' coffee shop design.

Key Concepts of Relationship Marketing

The term 'relationship marketing' was coined by Berry, Shostak and Upah (1983), who defined it in terms of the marketing strategies that companies need to apply to retain customers over a longer time. Much of the logic that underpins the core elements of relationship marketing come from the marketing of services rather than physical products. This is due to the majority of costs being incurred when setting up a service, as opposed to the situation for a product, where the associated costs are offset by the revenue generated by purchases (Harker and Egan, 2010). There are two important elements of relationship marketing to consider).

- **Core service:**
  A core service can be developed around a company's offer that meets customers' needs in a distinctive manner. Retail banks have developed tailored financial products that enable customers to choose the level of service that is wrapped around their personal bank account; for example, HSBC plc offers a Basic account, an Advanced account and a Premier account.

- **Relationship quality:**
  Customers develop relationships with companies by engaging in the exchange process, and are motivated to do so by the potential value that might be gained. But from a relationship marketing perspective the ongoing interaction between parties is of primary importance. In other words, companies seek to build relationships that develop customer **loyalty** and in doing so encourage customers to engage in repeated purchasing. Ultimately, the quality of a relationship is likely to affect customer loyalty and determine whether a company is able to retain its customers (Vize et al., 2013).

  Relationship quality is a complex subject, but there are several key factors to consider (Vize, 2012) which potentially affect the outcome of a relationship:
  - **Service quality**—this involves the experience a customer has of a company's offer. Services vary in complexity and in the investment and risk a customer makes in the purchase—for example, having a haircut or buying a cup of coffee. Service quality is discussed in detail in Chapter 9, but it is important to

note that service quality plays an important part in the development of relationships, especially in service industries (Chenet, Dagger and O'Sullivan, 2010).

- **Trust**—this refers to a customer's level of confidence in a company's ability to supply the required goods, and its reliability and integrity (Hunt, Morgan and Shelby, 1994). Trust is developed over time as customers base their perceptions and expectations on past purchase experiences. Trust plays a very important role in relationships, especially in an online setting. Building trust is a very effective way to increase satisfaction and subsequently develop commitment to long-term relationships (Geyskens, Steenkamp and Kumar, 1998; Selnes, 1998; Vlaga and Eggert, 2006; Hunt et al., 1994). It can also help weaker partners in a business relationship to gain power over time in their dealings with more powerful companies (Narayandas and Rangan, 2004). As a relationship develops, a customer may develop positive feelings about a company as he or she comes to rely on the credibility of a brand and the competency with which the goods and services are provided. When customers trust a brand they are more likely to recommend it to others and also to continue to use the brand themselves (Adams, 2014).

- **Commitment**—this involves the extent to which customers seek to develop an enduring relationship with a company (Moorman, Zaltman and Deshpande, 1992), and is likely to affect their loyalty to a company. Commitment is a driver of loyalty, as some of the benefits of a committed relationship are reduced uncertainty, greater satisfaction and enhanced performance, through the synergies of an effective relationship. There are different types of commitment. Some customers can form emotional attachments to a brand, and this forms the basis of their commitment to a brand. For example, when food manufacturer Heinz used the slogan 'Beanz, Meanz, Heinz' to promote its baked beans in 1967, little did it realise that this would become one of the most enduring and long-lasting advertising slogans of all time (Gerges, 2012), and arguably it still acts as a mantra for committed loyal customers of the brand. Other customers base their commitment on more rational calculations; for example, some mobile phone companies offer contracts that bundle together benefits including handsets, Internet services and telephone services, which provide an overall discount.

- **Satisfaction**—once customers have engaged in the exchange process, they are likely to reflect on their experiences and evaluate the extent to which their choice has generated the results they wanted. There are many influences which might determine a customer's level of satisfaction, for example level of knowledge, prior experience, economic requirements and social influences (Geyskens, Steenkamp and Kumar, 1999).

From a buyer's (business and consumer) point of view, the proliferation of *choice* and the development of the online marketplace has made moving between competitors easier than ever before. When customers are faced with many alternatives while making purchasing decisions, they have the opportunity to switch between suppliers (Singh, Agrariya and Deepali, 2011), so the greater the number of suppliers and the more product choice there is, the easier it becomes to change. Mobile phone operators use this knowledge and often develop *relational price incentives* (Berry, 2008) to encourage customers to move to a new network operator. European phone carrier EE, for example, includes unlimited calls, inclusive cloud storage, free music, a television service, and a bundle of other services in an attempt to retain its customers and also attract new customers. In this dynamic marketing environment it becomes increasingly important for companies to seek ways to develop lasting relationships with their customers. In response to these changes, companies have begun to focus on how to develop long-term relationships.

Value and Relational Networks

Value and relational networks involve people and the roles they play within the networks. 'Network' is a term used to describe a set of connections among people, which from a marketing perspective might be used as a resource to solve problems, share knowledge and extend the network by adding new connections (Wenger, Trayner and de Latt, 2011). Networks are highly complex and intangible entities but are formed to co-produce service offerings, exchange service offerings and facilitate the co-creation of value (Lusch, Vargo and Tanniru, 2010). LinkedIn is an example of an online network that connects professional workers together. However, it is important to note that the roles people assume within a network can be highly complex and an individual may assume different identities in social situations (Edvardsson, Tronvall and Gruber, 2011). For example, a software company may be made up of a number of individuals who play various roles, for example leader, problem-solver, designer or service provider. A role within a value network is different from a job title. So at the software company, the leader may have the job title senior developer but may also act as a problem solver.

Networks are important, especially as all markets are now electronically connected through the Internet. A network relationship should facilitate the sharing of competencies and aid the development of relationships in order to enable companies to perform better ((Lusch, Vargo and Tanniru, 2010). For example, eBay is an electronic marketplace made up of buyers and sellers that has created new opportunities for different types of seller (hobbyists and collectors) who previously did not have access to a commercial platform. As eBay has grown, so have the connections and number of buyers and sellers that use the marketplace. Working together, eBay and its participants have created a highly successful value network that is clearly differentiated from its competitors.

Having briefly considered some of the core concepts and ideas that form the basis of relationship marketing, the next section looks at managerial issues and the practical implication of adopting a relationship marketing approach.

Types of Relationship Management

Relationships can take different forms and achieve different levels of success for all parties concerned.

At a very basic level, buyers and suppliers can engage in simple transactional relationships that centre on a single purchase, and neither party makes contact again after a sale is completed. For example, a business passenger at an international airport who needs road transportation will probably never meet the taxi driver again, and the choice of taxi supplier depend on the passenger's position in the queue rather than free choice. In this case, the exchange—cash for the journey—is a pure transaction; the driver knows that it is unlikely that there will ever be a repeat purchase (Egan, 1997; see also Coviello et al., 2002). Nowadays, this limited level of involvement is relatively rare, as most companies look for opportunities to begin to build a relationship.

In the most light-touch relationships, there is usually a means of seeking redress in the case where the buyer wishes to complain about their purchase experience. Building on this approach, a company may actually contact the buyer to find out about the purchase experience in order to determine whether the customer expectation has been meet. Online sellers like Ebuyer send post-purchase surveys to poll customer views and seek customers' reviews of the product and service. The more a seller commits to the notion of a *relationship* with its customers (in both business and consumer markets), the more inclined it is towards being proactive about the development of the relationship.

Ultimately, at the most engaged level of relationship building, buyer and supplier develop a partnership approach, and this results in working together for mutual benefit (McDaniel, 1998). Therefore, the nature of the relationship can increase the complexity of the task of managing relationships. No longer is it sufficient to just focus on the transactional element of a sale. New approaches are needed that move on from market-mix-based solutions towards those that are built on relationship development and the specific types of relationship (Harker and Egan, 2010).

Four types of relationship have been identified (Gummesson, 1996).

The first two are market relationships between suppliers and customers. They make up the core of relationship marketing and are externally orientated. The first type is classic market relationships concerning supplier–customer, supplier–customer–competitor and the physical distribution network. These types of relationship are discussed in this chapter.

The second type is special market relationships such as between the customer as a member of a loyalty programme and the interaction in the service encounter. These concepts are examined further in the services marketing and direct marketing communications chapters (Chapters 9 and 15).

The third type of relationship concerns the economy and society in general. Examples of such relationships are mega-marketing (lobbying, public opinion and political power), mega-alliances (the European Union, which forms a stage for marketing) and social relationships (friendships and ethnic bonds). These issues are covered in the marketing environment and consumer behaviour chapters (Chapters 2 and 3).

Finally, nano-relationships concern the internal operations of an organization, such as relationships between internal customers, internal markets, divisions and business areas inside organizations. Such relationships are discussed within managing physical products (portfolio planning) and marketing implementation organization and control chapters (Chapters 20 and 22).

Managing relationships is a key ingredient in successful organizational marketing. In practical terms, **relationship marketing** concerns the shifting from activities focusing on attracting customers to activities concerned with current customers and how to retain them. Customer retention is critical, since small changes in retention rates have significant effects on future revenues (Andreassen, 1995). At its core is the maintenance of relations between a company and its suppliers, channel intermediaries, the public and its customers.

Ultimately, the key idea is for companies to take action to create customer loyalty so that a stable, mutually profitable and long-term relationship is developed (Ravald and Grönroos, 1996). Furthermore, loyal customers are likely to spend more than non-loyal customers and recommend a company to others. So for relationship marketing to be successful, two essential conditions should be met:

1   A relationship should be a mutually rewarding connection between two or more parties.
2   The parties involved in the relationship should commit to the relationship over time and be willing to make adaptations to their own behaviour to maintain its continuity (Takala and Uusitalo, 1996).

As discussed earlier, service quality, trust and commitment feature strongly in the creation of satisfaction between parties in the relationship. Read Marketing in Action 10.2 to find out more about how UK supermarket Morrisons took action to win back consumer trust in the face of German discounters Aldi and Lidl.

MARKETING IN ACTION 10.2
Strategies for Winning Back Customer Trust: Morrisons 'Match & More' Card

Loyalty cards have been used widely by retailers, particularly supermarkets, as part of a strategy for retaining customers, gathering customer data and developing targeted promotions. Recently, Morrisons, a leading UK supermarket retailer, launched a new loyalty card, Match & More, in an attempt to regain market share and to win back customer trust. The supermarket chain was losing market share to discounters, which had benefited from shoppers trading down in order to reduce the cost of their weekly shopping baskets. Morrisons have invested over £1 billion in price cuts over a three-year period to establish and consistently deliver everyday low pricing.

The Match & More card aimed to regain shoppers' trust by matching the prices of discounters Aldi and Lidl. These German discount chains had gained market share and seen double-digit growth in sales, while the 'big four'—Tesco, Asda, Sainsbury's and Morrisons—had been reporting losses. But the bigger problem Morrisons had to face is that since the global economic recession, consumers had started to shop for their favourite products in a range of different stores, based on which retailer offered the greatest discount. Furthermore, the so-called investment in price cutting was not delivering significant savings to consumers and was a high-cost strategy for Morrisons. The supermarket may need to look for a more substantive way of developing trusting relationships with its shoppers in the future, if it is to retain and grow its customer base.

Based on: Chesters (2015); Eales (2014); Christie (2014); Anon (2015); Harker and Egan (2010)

Managing Customer Relationships

Relationship marketing in services has attracted much attention in recent years as organizations focus their efforts on retaining existing customers rather than just attracting new ones. It is not a new concept, however, since the idea of a company earning customer loyalty was well known to the earliest merchants, who had the following saying: 'As a merchant, you'd better have a friend in every town.' (Grönroos, 1994). From a marketing viewpoint, it is important to recognise that relationship marketing involves shifting away from activities concerned with attracting customers to activities that focus on current customers and how to retain them and convert them into loyal advocates of the brand (and/or company). Although the idea of relationship marketing can be applied to many industries, it is particularly important in services, where there is often direct contact between service provider and customer—for example, the client–agency relationship in the advertising industry, the relationship between a web service provider and its clients, and that between hotel staff and guests. See Marketing in Action 10.3 for further discussion of building communities in the web service industry.

The quality of the relationship is likely to determine the length of a relationship, levels of satisfaction and loyalty. Companies therefore need to decide when the practice of relationship marketing is most applicable. The following conditions suggest potential areas for the use of relationship marketing activities (Berry, 1995):

- where there is an ongoing or periodic desire for the service by the customer; for example insurance, banking, telephone, Internet services
- where the customer controls the selection of a service provider; for example selecting a hotel, a restaurant, an entertainment provider or an airline

There are situations where the supplier may have few competitors, and in these circumstances may feel it is less important to develop strong customer relationships—for example utility providers such as gas, water and electricity companies, and health services. While there is some competition in these markets, the suppliers tend to hold the power and it is not always easy, affordable or viable for customers to switch suppliers.

We will now explore how to build a relationship and then the benefits of relationship marketing to organizations and customers, and the customer retention strategies used to build relationships and tie customers closer to companies.

How to Build Relationships

Once marketers have made the decision that it is appropriate to invest resources into building a relationship, they should also consider the degree of effort to put into relationship building (Jackson, 1985). In most exchange relationships there is some potential benefit to be gained from relationship development. The section on value creation highlighted some of the important features of close partnership relationships and highlighted how parties engaged in relationship development adapt their processes and products to achieve a better match with each other, and how they share information and experience, which reduces insecurity and uncertainty. Sharing information is a good start point for the development of a relationship and for building a better atmosphere for future business (Zineldin, 1998). Many companies are using the Internet to encourage their customers to share information. For example, John Deere, business-to-business supplier of agricultural machinery, uses social media sites (e.g. Facebook and Twitter) to communicate with farmers with similar interests around the world.

Effective relationship building can create opportunities to develop competitive advantage and is especially powerful if embedded within the culture of the organization. This makes it more difficult for competitors to copy (see O'Driscoll, 2006; Winklhofer, Pressey and Tzokas, 2006). Exchanging information is potentially a low-level approach to relationship building, so to create a more involved relationship-orientated culture a company needs to identify aspects of its business that could be considered part of a relationship-building strategy. There are a number of potential sources a company might consider; these are discussed below.

Technical support

Technical support can take the form of research and development cooperation, before-sales or after-sales service, and providing training to the customer's staff. The supplier is thus enhancing the customer's know-how and productivity.

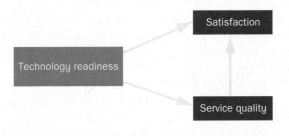
For example, leading European retailer of consumer electronics Dixons Carphone has developed strong relationships with its suppliers, and consequently suppliers trust Dixons Carphone to carry out repairs on high-tech equipment. Much learning, training and sharing of information has taken place so that the retailer and manufacturers can ensure better service for the end consumer. So retail customers with faulty goods can have repairs carried out through the retailer, and in doing so enjoy better service and faster turnaround times on repairs. This is an example of how strong relationships can benefit many companies in the supply chain.

Expertise

Suppliers can look for opportunities to provide expertise for their customers, which enable them to improve their service quality. The customer can benefit through acquiring extra skills at a minimal cost, the benefits of which they can pass on to their own customers.

For example, French cosmetics and beauty company L'Oreal Professionnel (Paris) develops specialist haircare products for salons and beauty specialist businesses. This business-to-business division provides specialist training for stylists and salon owners and shares the expertise it has built up over years of researching and developing new haircare products. L'Oreal has an extensive range of educational programmes which it offers to its customers, from learning about how to apply new hair care products to how to build and run a successful business in the beauty industry (see Exhibit 10.1).

Resource support

Suppliers can support the resource base of customers, for example by extending credit facilities, giving low-interest loans, agreeing to cooperative promotion and accepting reciprocal buying practices where the supplier agrees to buy goods from the customer. The overall effect of these activities is a reduced financial burden for the customer.

Service levels

Suppliers can improve their relationships with customers by improving the level of service offered to them. This can involve providing more reliable delivery, fast or just-in-time delivery, setting up

EXHIBIT 10.1
L'Oreal provides training for stylists and salon owners.

computerized reorder systems, offering fast, accurate quotes and reducing defect levels. In so doing, the customer gains by lower inventory costs, smoother production runs and lower warranty costs. By creating systems that link the customer to the supplier—for example, through recorder systems or just-in-time delivery—*switching costs* may be built in, making it more expensive to change supplier (Jackson, 1985). Advances in technology are providing opportunities to improve service levels. For example, BMW is using IBM's big data analytics technology to improve its repair and maintenance services as well as its products. IBM's predictive analytics are able to detect and fix potentially faulty elements of new cars (Savvas, 2014).

Risk reduction

If a company is looking to acquire new customers, it may encounter resistance as target customers are familiar with their existing suppliers. So to use risk reduction as part of a relationship-building strategy a company should identify initiatives that enable it to show there are low levels of risk in switching suppliers. This may involve free demonstrations, the offer of products for trial at zero or low cost to the customer, product and delivery guarantees, preventative maintenance contracts, swift complaint handling and proactive follow-ups. These activities are designed to provide customers with reassurance. Birds Eye, a European manufacturer of frozen foods, launched a new range of pasta and rice dishes called Stir Your Senses. To launch the product range, it ran a 'try me for free' campaign, giving away 1.6 million packs through leading UK supermarkets (IPM, 2015). Additionally, this product range has been developed by working with consumers to understand how the frozen food manufacturer can best cater for the changing needs of its customers. These products were developed to provide a hassle-free meal solution for busy consumers. See Exhibit 10.1.

Benefits for the Organization

Ultimately, building a successful relationship can bring a range of benefits to both the supplier and the buyer. There are six major benefits to service companies in developing and maintaining strong customer relationships (Zeithaml, Bitner and Gremier, 2005).

1 *Increased purchases*: which help to develop trust between the company and the customer as they become more and more satisfied with the quality of services provided by the supplier.

2 *Lower cost*: the start-up costs associated with attracting new customers are likely to be far higher than the cost of retaining existing customers. Start-up costs include the time for making repeat calls in an effort to persuade a prospect to open an account, the advertising and promotional costs associated with making prospects aware of the company and its service offering, the operating costs of setting up accounts and systems, and

According to Sinomson and Rosen (2014), 'In the past, buyers typically made relative comparisons ("Is Brand A better than Brand B?") or went by the maxim "You get what you pay for."' Buyers largely had to rely on information provided by suppliers, media reports and/or word of mouth from individuals who had personal experience of a particular brand.

But the rules of the game have changed in the last decade. Before 2004, there was limited scope for gathering independent information on product performance, quality and customer experiences, which could then inform purchase decisions. But the launch of Facebook helped consolidate the social media revolution started by Friends Reunited and Myspace and paved the way for online reviews. People now consult social media for information about physical products, brand experiences and service quality. Social media provide a rich tapestry of reviews of customer experiences. Also peer-to-peer reviews on products and services give potential buyers the opportunity to get a sense of what it's like to own or use the goods they're considering.

As a result of the growth and availability of information, marketers have begun to change their marketing strategies to account for the increased influence of customer opinions. Asus is an example of a business in the computing industry that has risen to be the fifth-best-selling brand of PCs and third in the tablet market, largely as a result of good customer reviews. The rise of this brand that was largely unknown in 1989 to world-leading brand in 2013 demonstrates the relative power of reviews. Indeed, this raises questions about the future significance of brand names.

From a marketer's perspective, the three best places to capture online reviews are:
1 Google+ local account, as these posts often appear in Google's organic search results
2 industry-specific review sites—for example, TripAdvisor in the hotel industry; Feefo.com in the global consumer industry
3 company website, where customer testimonials and reviews can show satisfaction ratings

Questions:
1 How might social media affect the value of a brand name?
2 How can brands use social media to support brand development?
3 To what extent is the rise of an unknown brand, for example ASUS, sufficient to suggest this is a strategy that might be adopted by other new companies?

Based on: Sinomson and Rosen (2014); Able (2014); Ellis-Chadwick (2013)

the time costs of establishing bonds between the supplier and customer in the early stages of the relationship. Furthermore, costs associated with solving early teething problems and queries are likely to fall as the customer becomes accustomed to using the service.

3 *Lifetime value of a customer*: the lifetime value of a customer is the profit made on a customer's purchases over the lifetime of that customer. If a customer spends £80 in a supermarket per week, resulting in £8 profit, and uses the supermarket 45 times a year over 30 years, the lifetime value of that customer is £10,800. Thus, a bad service experience early on in this relationship which results in the customer defecting to the competition would be very expensive to the supermarket, especially when the costs of bad word of mouth are added, as this may deter other customers from using the store.

4 *Sustainable competitive advantage*: the intangible aspects of a relationship are not easily copied by the competition. For example, the friendships and high levels of trust that can develop as the relationship matures can be extremely difficult for competitors to replicate. This means that the extra value to customers that derives from the relationship can be a source of sustainable competitive advantage for suppliers (Roberts, Varki and Brodie, 2003).

5 *Word of mouth*: word of mouth is very important in services due to their intangible nature which makes them difficult to evaluate prior to purchase. In these circumstances, potential purchasers often look to

others who have experienced the service (e.g. a hotel, financial service) for personal recommendation. See Mini Case 10.1 for further discussion of the growing importance of online reviews. A company that has a large number of loyal customers is more likely to benefit from word of mouth than another without such a resource.

6 *Employee satisfaction and retention*: satisfied, loyal customers benefit employees in providing a set of mutually beneficial relationships and less hassle. This raises employees' job satisfaction and lowers job turnover. Employees can spend time improving existing relationships rather than desperately seeking new customers. This sets up a virtuous circle of satisfied customers leading to happy employees, which raises customer satisfaction even higher.

The net result of these six benefits of developing customer relationships is high profits. A study has shown across a variety of service industries that profits climb steeply when a company lowers its customer defection rate (Reichheld and Sasser Jr, 1990). Companies could improve profits from 25 to 85 per cent (depending on the industry) by reducing customer defections by just 5 per cent. The reasons are that loyal customers generate more revenue for more years, and the costs of maintaining existing customers are lower than the costs of acquiring new ones. An analysis of a credit card company revealed that improving the defection rate from 10 to 20 years increased the lifetime value of a customer from $135 to $300.

Benefits for the Customer

Entering into a long-term relationship can also reap the following four benefits for the customer.

1 *Risk and stress reduction*: since the intangible nature of services makes them difficult to evaluate before purchase, relationship marketing can benefit the customer as well as the company. This is particularly so for services, which are personally important, variable in quality, complex and/or subject to high-involvement buying (Berry, 1995). Such purchases are potentially high risk in that making the wrong choice has severe negative consequences for the buyer. Banking, insurance, motor servicing and hairstyling are examples of services that exhibit some or all of the characteristics—importance, variability, complexity and high involvement—that would cause many customers to seek an ongoing relationship with a trusted service provider. Such a relationship reduces consumer stress, as the relationship becomes predictable, initial problems are solved, special needs are accommodated and the consumer learns what to expect. After a period of time, the consumer begins to trust the service provider, can count on a consistent level of quality service and feels comfortable in the relationship (Bitner, 1995).

2 *Higher-quality service*: experiencing a long-term relationship with a service provider can also result in higher levels of service. This is because the service provider becomes knowledgeable about the customer's requirements. For example, beauticians and hairstylists learn about the preferences of their clients. Knowledge of the customer built up over a series of service encounters facilitates the tailoring or customizing of the service to each customer's special needs.

3 *Avoidance of switching costs*: maintaining a relationship with a service supplier avoids the costs associated with switching to a new provider. Once a service provider knows a customer's preferences and special needs, and has tailored services to suit them, to change would mean educating a new provider and accepting the possibility of mistakes being made until the new provider has learnt to accommodate them. This results in both time and psychological costs to the customer. Bitner (1995) suggests that a major cost of relocating to a new geographic location is the need to establish relationships with unfamiliar service providers such as banks, schools, doctors and hairdressers.

4 *Social and status benefits*: customers can also reap social and status benefits from a continuing relationship with a supplier. Since many service encounters are also social encounters, repeated contact can assume personal as well as professional dimensions. In such circumstances, service customers may develop relationships resembling personal friendships. For example, hairdressers often serve as personal confidantes, and restaurant managers may get to know some of their customers personally. Such personal relationships can feed a person's ego (status); for example, a hotel customer commented, 'When employees remember and recognize you as a regular customer, you feel really good.' (Parasuraman, Berry and Zeithaml, 1991). Read Mini Case 10.1 to understand how peer-to-peer reviews empower customers in their relationships with organizations.

Developing Customer Retention Strategies

The potential benefits of developing long-term relationships with customers mean that it is worthwhile for organizations to consider designing customer retention strategies. This involves targeting customers for retention, bonding, internal marketing, promise fulfilment, building of trust and service recovery (see Figure 10.1).

Whilst these retention strategies are important in both business-to-business and consumer markets, the following discussion gives examples from the consumer perspective.

Targeting customers for retention

Not all customers deliver benefit from relationship building—for example, habitual brand switchers who respond to the lowest priced deal available regardless of the brand, and low spenders, who may not generate sufficient revenue to justify the expense of acquiring them and maintaining the relationship; and disruptive customers who may be so troublesome, and whose attitudes and behaviour may cause so much disruption to the service provider, that the costs of servicing them outweigh the benefits. Consequently, companies need to analyse their customers and identify those customers that they wish to engage in a long-term relationship, those for whom a transactional marketing approach is better suited, and those with whom they would prefer not to do business. This is the classical market segmentation and targeting approach discussed in Chapter 7. The characteristics of those customers that are candidates for a relationship marketing approach are high-value, frequent-use, loyalty-prone customers for whom the actual and potential service offerings that can be supplied by the company have high utility.

Targeting customers for retention involves the analysis of loyalty- and defection-prone customers. Service suppliers need to understand why customers stay or leave, what creates value for them, and their profile. Decisions can then be made regarding which types of customer defector they wish to try to save (e.g. price or service defectors) and the nature of the value-adding strategy that meets their needs, while at the same time maintaining bonds with loyalty-prone customers (Berry, 1995).

Bonding

Retention strategies vary in the degree to which they bond the parties together. One framework that illustrates this idea distinguishes between three levels of retention strategy based on the types of bond used to cement the relationship (Berry and Parasuraman, 1991).

- *Level 1*: at this level the bond is primarily through financial incentives, for example higher discounts on prices for larger-volume purchases, or loyalty points and associated tailored promotions which can result in lower future prices. The problem is that the potential for a sustainable competitive advantage is low, because price incentives are easy for competitors to copy even if they take the guise of frequent-flyer or loyalty points. Most airlines and retailers compete in this way, and consumers have learnt to join more than one scheme, thus negating the desired effect.

- *Level 2*: this higher level of bonding relies on more than just price incentives, and consequently raises the potential for a sustainable competitive advantage. Level 2 retention strategies build long-term relationships through social as well as financial bonds, capitalizing on the fact that many service encounters are also social encounters. Customers become clients, the relationship becomes personalized and the service customized. Characteristics of this

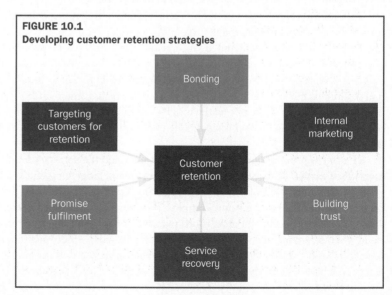

FIGURE 10.1
Developing customer retention strategies

type of relationship include frequent communication with customers, providing continuity of service through the same person or people employed by the service provider, providing personal treatment like sending cards, and enhancing the core service with educational or entertainment activities such as seminars or visits to sporting events. Often hotels keep records of their guests' personal preferences, such as food allergies and requirements for non-smoking rooms. This builds a special bond between the hotel and its customers, who feel they are being treated as individuals. Increasingly, social media and other forms of digital communication are used to develop such relationships.

- *Level 3*: this top level of bonding is formed by financial, social and structural bonds. Structural bonds tie service providers to their customers through providing solutions to customers' problems that are designed into the service delivery system. For example, logistics companies often supply their clients with equipment that ties them into their systems. When combined with financial and social bonds, structural bonds can create a formidable barrier against competitor inroads and provide the basis for a sustainable competitive advantage.

Internal marketing

A fundamental basis for customer retention is high-quality service delivery. This depends on high-quality performance from employees, since the service product is a performance and the performers are employees (Berry, 1995). Internal marketing concerns training, communicating with and motivating internal staff. Staff need to be trained to be technically competent at their jobs as well as to handle service encounters with customers. To do this well, they must be motivated and understand what is expected of them. Service staff act as 'part-time marketers', since their actions can directly affect customer satisfaction and retention (Gummesson, 1987). Staff are critical in the 'moments of truth' when they and customers come into contact in a service situation.

A key focus of an internal marketing programme should be employee selection and retention. Service companies that suffer high rates of job turnover are continually employing new, inexperienced staff to handle customer service encounters. Employees that have worked for the company for years know more about the business and have had the opportunity to build relationships with customers. By selecting the right people and managing them in such a way that they stay loyal to the service organization, higher levels of customer retention can be achieved through the build-up of trust and personal knowledge gained through long-term contact with customers.

Promise fulfilment

The fulfilment of promises is a cornerstone for maintaining service relationships. This implies three key activities: *making* realistic promises initially, and *keeping* those promises during service delivery by *enabling* staff and service systems to deliver on promises made (Bitner, 1995).

Making promises is done through marketing communications channels, for example the web, and more traditional advertising, selling and promotion, as well as the specific service cues that set expectations, such as the dress of the service staff and the design and décor of the establishment. It is important not to over-promise with marketing communications or the result will be disappointment and consequently customer dissatisfaction and defection. The promise should be credible and realistic. Some companies adhere to the adage 'under-promise and over-deliver'. For example, UK retailer John Lewis has made an enduring commitment to its customers that they can shop with confidence as the retailer operates a 'never knowingly undersold' policy. If a customer buys a product from John Lewis and finds that he or she could have bought it cheaper elsewhere, the retailer will refund the difference.

Keeping of promises occurs when the customer and the service provider interact—the 'moment of truth' mentioned earlier. Research has shown that customers judge employees on their ability to deliver the service right the first time, their ability to recover if things go wrong, how well they deal with special requests, and on their spontaneous actions and attitudes (see Bitner, Booms and Tetreault, 1990; Bitner, Booms and Mohr, 1994). These are clearly key dimensions that must play a part in a training programme and should be borne in mind when selecting and rewarding service staff. Not all service encounters are equal in importance, however. Research conducted on behalf of Marriott hotels has shown that events occurring early in a service encounter affect customer loyalty the most. On the basis of these findings, Marriott developed its 'first 10 minutes' strategy.

It is hardly surprising that first impressions are so important, since before then the customer has had no direct contact with the service provider and is uncertain of the outcome.

Enabling staff is a necessary condition for promises to be kept. This means staff must have the skills, competences, tools, systems and enthusiasm to deliver. Some of these issues have been looked at in the earlier discussion of internal marketing, and are dependent on the correct recruitment, training and rewarding of staff, and on providing them with the right equipment and systems to do their jobs. Finally, we need to recognize that the keeping of promises does not depend solely on service staff and technology. Because service delivery is often in a group setting (e.g. a meal with friends or family in a restaurant, watching a film

EXHIBIT 10.2
Burj Al Arab delivers a seven-star customer experience

or travelling by air), the quality of the experience can be as dependent on the behaviour of other customers as on that of the service provider. Lovelock, Vandermerwe and Lewis (1999) label the problem customers 'jaycustomers'. These are people who act in a thoughtless or abusive way, causing problems for the organization, its employees and other customers. One particular kind of jaycustomer is the belligerent person who shouts abuse and threats at service staff because of some service malfunction. Staff need to be trained to develop the self-confidence and assertiveness required to deal with such situations and to know what to do if the situation escalates beyond their control and more senior staff are required to be involved. Ultimately, the jaycustomer should be moved away from contact with other customers to minimize the discomfort of the latter.

See Exhibit 10.2 to see how the world's most luxurious hotel delivers on its promises of service excellence.

Building trust

Customer relationships *per se* depend on building trust. But trust is also a very important aspect of customer retention, particularly where the intangible nature of a service means the customer can find it difficult to evaluate prior to purchase. Buying a service for the first time can leave the customer with a feeling of uncertainty and vulnerability, particularly when the service is personally important (see Chapter 9 for more detailed discussion of the impact of the characteristics of services). Consequently, when customers have developed trust in a supplier they are often reluctant to switch to a new supplier and experience the uncomfortable feelings of uncertainty and vulnerability all over again.

Companies that wish to build up their trustworthiness should keep in touch with their customers by regular two-way communication to develop feelings of closeness and openness, provide guarantees to symbolize the confidence they feel in their service delivery as well as reduce their customers' perceived risk of purchase, and operate a policy of fairness and high standards of conduct with their customers (Berry, 1995).

Service recovery

Service recovery strategies should aim to solve problems and restore customers' trust in the company, and also improve the service system so that the problem does not recur (Kasper, van Helsdingen and Gabbott, 2006). Recovery is crucial, because if carried out effectively it can encourage customers to become advocates for a company and will reduce the likelihood of dissatisfied customers telling others of their negative experiences.

There are three important considerations when establishing a service recovery strategy.

1 *Set up a tracking system to identify system failures.* Customers should be encouraged to report service problems, since those customers that do not complain are the least likely to purchase again. Systems should be established to monitor complaints, follow up on service experiences (e.g. through the web, using feedback surveys, by phone) and provide opportunities for both service staff and customers to feed back on their experiences.

2 *Train and empower staff* to respond to service complaints. This is important, because research has shown that the successful resolution of a complaint can cause customers to feel more positive about the company than before the service failure.

The first response from a service provider to a genuine complaint is to apologize. Often this will take the heat out of the situation and lead to a spirit of cooperation rather than recrimination.

The next step is to attempt to solve the problem quickly. Marriott hotels facilitate this process by empowering frontline employees to solve customers' problems quickly, even though this may mean expense to the hotel, and without recourse to seeking approval from higher authority.

Other key elements in service recovery are to appear pleasant, helpful and attentive, show concern for the customer and be flexible. Regarding problem resolution, service staff should provide information about the problem, take action and appear to put themselves out to solve the problem (Johnson, 1995).

It is important to note that whilst careful and appropriate handling of a complaint can result in a customer developing a positive attitude, if a second problem occurs, this effect (called the 'recovery paradox') disappears (Maxham and Netemeyer, 2002).

3 *Encourage learning among staff* so that service recovery problems are identified and corrected. Service staff should be motivated to report problems and solutions so that recurrent failures are identified and fixed. In this way, an effective service recovery system can lead to improved customer service, satisfaction and higher customer retention levels.

Customer retention is a fundamental to the success of a modern company, and technology is now widely used to gather customer feedback and manage the whole of the customer experience. The remaining part of this chapter examines customer relationship management, focusing on relationship development in both consumer and business markets, and then on key account management (KAM), specifically looking at relationship development in business-to-business markets, where the importance of strong relationships can mean the difference between success and failure in highly competitive markets.

Technology-enhanced Customer Relationship Management

Customer relationships are increasingly managed through the use of technology in consumer and business-to-business markets. Effective **customer relationship management (CRM)** begins by understanding the value, attitudes and behaviour of various customers and future prospects, which might form part of a relationship marketing strategy. Rapid development of digital, mobile and remote computer technologies has enabled the development of highly sophisticated CRM systems that can manage relationships, interactions and customer journeys. These journeys include all the touchpoints where a customer interacts with a business and then creates a data collection point. CRM is seen by many marketers as the practical implementation of relationship marketing (Harker and Egan, 2010). 'CRM' is a term for the methodologies, technologies and e-commerce capabilities used by companies to manage customer relationships. In particular, CRM software packages aid the interaction between the customer and the company, enabling the company to coordinate all of the communication effort so that the customer is presented with a unified message and image.

CRM companies offer a range of IT-based services such as call centres, data analysis and website management. The basic principle behind CRM is that company staff have a single-customer point of view of each client. As customers are now using multiple channels more frequently, they may buy one product from a salesperson and another from a website. A website may provide product information, which is used to buy the product from a distributor. Interactions between a customer and a company may take place through the salesforce, call centres, websites, email and social media. However, it is important to ensure that data is gathered and shared effectively.

For example, Volvo Construction Equipment (Volvo CE) has built its reputation on producing high quality market-leading equipment and excellent customer support (Volvo Construction Equipment, 2015). In this business, relationships are very important and sales are primarily through local dealers. The company has been proactive about using the web as a way for customers to interact with the brand and submit enquiries through online forms on the website. But there was an issue that Volvo was only receiving limited feedback and a limited number of leads collected from the website; also, customers completing the online form merely received a simple 'thank you' message. It was decided that the company should try to make better use of Internet technology to interact with customers, provide more dynamic information, automate the customer communication process and gather more data about customer interactions. Volvo CE had to devise a cost-efficient system to achieve its goals. The team's response was to create a process that evaluated the customer lifecycles and their online interactions using the newly implemented CRM system. Using customer data, the system was able to send relevant information to customers and up-to-date reports to dealers and internal staff.

Although the term 'CRM' is seen as referring to a recent management technology, the ideas and principles behind CRM are not new. Businesses have long practised some form of CRM. What sets present-day CRM apart is that companies now have an increased opportunity to use technology and manage one-to-one relationships with huge numbers of consumers. This is facilitated by companies such as Salesforce.com, IBM, SAP and Oracle.

Therefore, it is crucial that no matter how a customer contacts a company, all staff have instant access to the same data about the customer, such as his/her details and past purchases. This usually means the consolidation of the many databases held by individual departments in a company into one centralized database that can be accessed by all relevant staff on a computer screen. CRM is much more than simply the technology, as demonstrated by the E.ON CRM update in Marketing in Action 10.4.

Success factors in CRM

CRM projects have met with mixed success. As the customer journeys and experiences become a more important feature in marketing initiatives, so does the successful deployment of CRM systems and associated technologies. It has been found that nearly half of CRM projects fail due to insufficient attention being paid to the *processes* involved and the function the system was designed to achieve. *People* can also create issues in the adoption of new CRM systems by resisting the use of the new technology or having a lack of adequate training. Many CRM systems

---

MARKETING IN ACTION 10.4
E.ON, European Energy Supplier Updates its CRM Systems

E.ON is a brand that supplies energy to residential and corporate clients in Europe. The brand was created with the merger of VEBA and VIAG—two large German corporations—in 2000 and it quickly entered the US, UK and Swedish markets. Through a number of large acquisitions of Powergen (UK), Enel (Italy) and Endesa (Spain), E.ON was able to expand its operation significantly.

However, whilst E.ON was committed to providing 'cleaner and better energy' to its corporate and domestic clients, the technology it was using to facilitate the relationships was not delivering. Whilst CRM systems can deliver technology-enhanced relationships by managing the relationship at every touchpoint across a company, there are many aspects involved in effective customer management. E.ON faced difficulties, particularly in Scandinavia, as its CRM systems were out of date and difficult for employees to use. When selling energy in business-to-business markets the stakes are high, the volumes are large and the agreements placed between supplier and buyer are highly complex. The problems facing E.ON salespeople in Sweden was that they could not develop a clear picture of customers' needs, due to the antiquated CRM system.

As a result, E.ON started to look for solution providers who could deliver a CRM technology solution. Stratiteq, an IT solution provider in Sweden, provided a CRM solution based on the Microsoft platform, which required a change in working practices at E.ON. Employees had to adapt to new ways of working and in doing so also realise the benefits offered from the new system. At the heart of the success of the implementation was the commitment and support provided by Stratiteq. The collaborative nature of the relationship enabled a successful roll-out of the technology, and as a result E.ON was able to link together all aspects of its engagement with customers. The sales process is now streamlined and sales managers are able to review all the customer data in one place, which has significantly improved levels of service and customer relationships.

Based on: E.ON (2015); Stratiteq (2015)

have been found to fail due to lack of planning and clear objectives. Finally, about a third of CRM systems fail due to lack of suitable technology (Band, 2013).

Research has revealed that the following factors are associated with successful CRM implementations:

- having a customer orientation and organizing the CRM system around customers
- taking a single view of customers across departments, and designing an integrated system so that all customer-facing staff can draw information from a common database
- having the ability to manage cultural change issues that arise as a result of system development and implementation
- involving users in the CRM design process
- designing the system in such a way that it can readily be changed to meet future requirements
- having a board-level champion of the CRM project, commitment within each of the affected departments to the benefits of taking a single view of the customer, and an understanding of the need for common strategies—for example, prioritizing resources on profitable customers
- creating 'quick wins' to provide positive feedback on the project programmes
- ensuring face-to-face contact (rather than by paper or email) between marketing and IT staff
- piloting the new system before full launch.

Much of the development of CRM systems and solutions is being driven through digital marketing and customer experience initiatives, as customers expect to have instantaneous access to information. Consequently, it has become more of an imperative to ensure that CRM systems perform effectively, especially as they are being used in all business sectors. For example: in the not-for-profit sector, donations are increasingly being given by mobile phone and through social media platforms; retailers are selling more online; airlines and other transport companies use mobile phones to supply travel updates (Frost and Sullivan, 2011). Social media are also taking a more important role as individuals share their experiences on everything from grocery shopping and eating out to engagement in large-scale fundraising campaigns such as #icebucketchallenge.

CRM systems are becoming progressively more complex as the number of potential touchpoints where a customer can interact with a company increases (see Figure 10.2). **Touchpoints** are where customers interact with a company, and that data about their interactions can be gathered. Interactions with customers can be through physical human interactions, for example with customer service staff or sales representatives, or where customers interact virtually, for example through loyalty schemes, online reviews and search enquiries. Interactions can also occur at any stage in a customer journey and give rise to opportunities for companies to use the touchpoint productively. For example, a retailer might offer existing customers a future discount if they refer

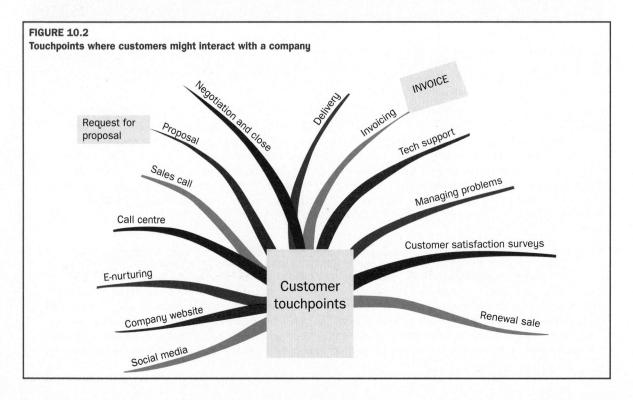

FIGURE 10.2
Touchpoints where customers might interact with a company

a friend through the company website, or on receipt of a delivery a customer might be encouraged to comment on the quality of the product and the delivery service.

As customers engage with companies through a variety of touchpoints it becomes increasingly challenging to ensure the quality of the customer experience. Figure 10.3 shows a potential cross-channel touchpoint customer experience (Gill, 2014). Initially, customers may become aware of a new product or service through traditional channels, for example broadcast media, TV and radio. As they begin to consider, evaluate and move toward selecting a particular product, then they may move over to digital channels, for example online reviews and blogs. Once customers are ready to make a purchase, they may choose from various channels, for example online, in store or through a direct mail catalogue. After the sale is complete, customers may seek advice about how to use their product, for example through an online FAQs database, or comment on their experience in a forum. Finally, they might become an advocate for their chosen product and make future purchases, read newsletters, and even write a blog post about their experiences.

Cross-channel touchpoints test companies who wish to manage their customers' journeys to ensure a uniform experience. Many brands struggle to provide a seamless customer experience. For example, Gap offers its customers a flexible click-and-collect service to pick up their online orders through any of the group's stores, for example Gap, Old Navy and Banana Republic. But when it comes to returning goods, customers must take the returns back to the specific store selling the brand they have purchased. The problem for retailers is reverse logistics—in other words, getting the goods back where the stock was originally held, especially if a retailer manages online and offline stock through different locations (Gill, 2014), and customers are left struggling to work out where to return their goods.

Air Canada is another example where there are breaks in the cross-channel customer experience: its customers can book flights via mobile devices but cannot amend the details or change flights via any digital touchpoints. Customers wishing to make changes must use the telephone. As a result, the cross-channel experience can be frustrating rather than rewarding.

So how can companies manage multiple cross-channel touchpoints and use their CRM systems effectively? According to research (Gill, 2014), companies should consider the overall customer experience and aim to 'identify, design, implement and optimise end-to-end customer journeys'. In order to do this, they should aim to follow three rules (Gill, 2014).

1 **Do not try to please everyone**. Marketing managers should aim to concentrate on creating high-value experiences which involve touchpoints that create meaningful journeys for target customers. They should also identify tasks that add value to the experience.

    For example, Starbucks has developed a cross-touchpoint experience for its tech-savvy customers. It uses sophisticated software and GPS positioning to push time-specific offers to its customers in particular locations. The aim is to increase footfall in Starbucks coffee shops. The My Starbucks app enables pre-payment and acts as a point of sale using QR codes and also links to individual's loyalty data to be used for future promotions.

    Finally, the focus should also be on a frequently occurring task, as it is not viable to try to streamline every customer journey. For example, Debenhams has integrated its mobile app with its e-commerce site so it can ensure a seamless mobile-to-store-to-web customer shopping journey.

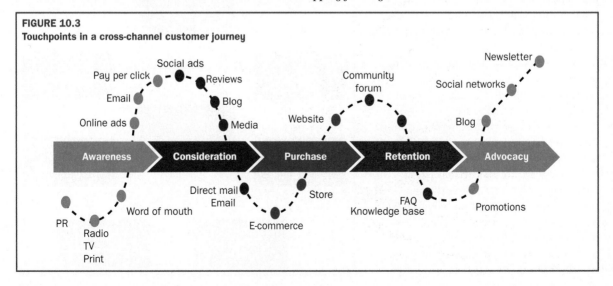

FIGURE 10.3
Touchpoints in a cross-channel customer journey

2 **Optimise the journey, not the touchpoint**. Marketing managers responsible for mapping customer journeys have to decide which channels and technologies will provide the best customer journey. They should also ensure that each touchpoint is deemed important.

Prisma, one of Finland's most advanced online retailers, designed its customer journey by mapping out a series of common touchpoints shoppers wanted to use. The journey maps showed how customers used mobile phones, the web and physical stores; when the maps were combined with historical customer data, the retailer was able to improve the customer experience.

Ultimately, the marketer should aim to understand how an individual touchpoint contributes to the total customer journey.

3 **Manage the transitions**. Marketing managers should look for innovative ways to move customers from one touchpoint to another and across channels. One way to achieve this is to make sure that the customer is in control. So if customers need to move from the digital to physical space, for example in getting their eyes tested and buying a pair of glasses, the online appointment system should ensure there is sufficient choice of appointment times. The earlier Starbucks example demonstrates how to link the digital and physical space using a mobile device.

As customers become more connected and more familiar with using multiple touchpoints, it will become increasingly important for all companies to manage their customer journeys effectively in order to deliver a seamless customer experience.

Business-to-Business Relationship Development Strategies

Customer relationships are becoming increasingly important in both business-to-consumer and business-to-business markets. A key tool for implementing relationship marketing is **key account management (KAM)**. In many industries there is a trend towards the use of KAM, which reflects the increasing concentration of buying power into fewer but larger customers. Developing relationships with key accounts is often crucial to the survival of a business, for example E.ON and Volvo CE. Key accounts are serviced by a key account salesforce comprising senior salespeople who develop close personal relationships with customers, can handle sophisticated sales arguments and are skilled at negotiation.

A number of advantages may be derived from adopting a key-account-structured approach towards relationship development; see Figure 10.4.

A potential advantage of the KAM approach is that it can lead to the development of close connective relationships. For example, the salesperson can get to know who the decision-makers are in a company and who influences the buying decision. This creates opportunities to gain greater penetration of the decision-making unit (DMU) and cultivate relationships within the key account. Salespeople can *pull* the buying decision through the organization from the users, deciders and influencers to the buyer, rather than the more difficult task of pushing it through the buyer into the organization, as is done with more traditional sales approaches. Closer relationships can foster better communication, as the buyer becomes familiar with a dedicated salesperson or sales team and know who to contact for information or if a problem occurs. The selling company can devote

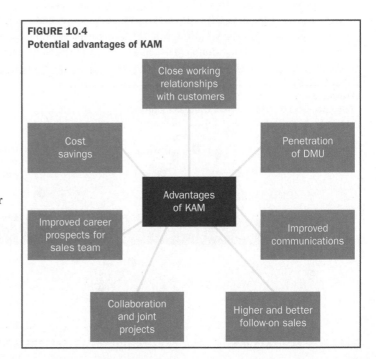

FIGURE 10.4
Potential advantages of KAM

Close working relationships with customers

Cost savings

Penetration of DMU

Improved career prospects for sales team

Advantages of KAM

Improved communications

Collaboration and joint projects

Higher and better follow-on sales

extra resources to the key account, which can result in higher sales and better follow-up and after-sales service. Effective KAM can also benefit the selling team. As the KAM relationship develops, the sales team may have the opportunity for career development: a tiered salesforce system with key (or national) account selling at the top provides promotional opportunities for salespeople who wish to advance within the salesforce rather than enter a traditional sales-management position. Lower costs can be achieved through joint agreement of optimum production and delivery schedules, and demand forecasting. And finally, there may be cooperation on research and development for new products and joint promotions (e.g. within the fast-moving consumer goods/retail sector).

The development and management of a key account can be understood as a process that takes place over time between buyers and sellers. The KAM relational development model plots the typical progression of a buyer–seller relationship based on the nature of the customer relationship (transactional–collaborative) and the level of involvement with customers (simple–complex) (Wilson et al., 2000). Figure 10.5 shows the five stages: pre KAM, early KAM, mid KAM, partnership KAM and synergistic KAM. A sixth stage (uncoupling KAM) represents the breakdown of the relationship, which can happen at any point during the process.

Pre KAM: this describes preparation for KAM, or 'prospecting'. The task is to identify accounts with potential that can be developed and opportunities for developing closer relationships.

Early KAM: involves the exploration of opportunities for closer collaboration by identifying the motives, culture and concerns of the customer. The selling company needs to convince the buyer company of the benefits of being a preferred supplier. The seller seeks to understand the buyer's decision-making unit and processes and the problems and opportunities that relate to the value-adding activities. An objective of the sales effort is to build trust based on consistent performance and open communications. The account manager seeks to create a more attractive offering than any competing supplier and attempts to establish credibility and deepen personal relationships.

Mid KAM: by now, trust has been established and the supplier is one of a small number of preferred sources of the product. The number and range of contacts increases. These may include social events, which help to deepen relationships across the two organizations. The account-review process carried out at the selling organization tends to move upwards to involve senior management because of the importance of the customer and the level of resource allocation. Since the account is not yet exclusive, the activities of competitors require constant monitoring.

Partnership KAM: at this stage, the buying organization regards the supplier as an important strategic resource. The level of trust is sufficient for both parties to be willing to share sensitive information. The focus of activities moves to joint problem solving, collaborative product development and mutual training of the other company's staff. The buying company is now channelling nearly all of its business in the relevant product group(s) to the one supplier. The arrangement is formalized in a partnership agreement, which has a timeframe that can ensure stability. Performance is monitored and contacts between departments of the two organizations are extensive. The buying organization expects guaranteed continuity of supply, excellent service and top-quality products. A key task of the account manager is to reinforce the high levels of trust to form a barrier against potential competitors.

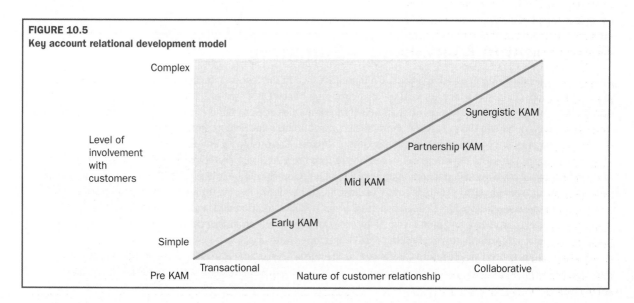

FIGURE 10.5
Key account relational development model

Synergistic KAM: this is the ultimate stage of the relational development model. Buyer and seller see one another not as two separate organizations but as part of a larger entity. Top management commitment manifests itself in joint board meetings. Joint business planning, research and development, and marketing research take place. Costing systems become transparent, unnecessary costs are removed, and process improvements are mutually achieved. For example, a logistics company together with one of its retail key accounts has six cross-boundary teams working on process improvements at any one time (Wilson and Millman, 2003).

Uncoupling KAM: this is when transactions and interaction cease. The causes of uncoupling need to be understood so that it can be avoided.

Breakdowns are more often attributable to changes in key personnel and relationship problems than price conflicts. The danger of uncoupling is particularly acute in early KAM when the single point of contact prevails. If, for example, the key account manager leaves to be replaced by someone who, in the buyer's eyes, is less skilled, or there is a personality clash, the relationship may end.

A second cause of uncoupling is breach of trust; for example, the breaking of a promise over a delivery deadline, product improvement or equipment repair can weaken or kill a business relationship. The key to handling such problems is to reduce the impact of surprise. The supplier should let the buying organization know immediately a problem becomes apparent. It should also show humility when discussing the problem with a customer.

Companies also uncouple through neglect. Long-term relationships can foster complacency, and customers can perceive themselves as being taken for granted. Cultural mismatches can occur—for example, when the customer stresses price, whereas the supplier focuses on lifecycle costs. Difficulties can also occur between bureaucratic and entrepreneurial styles of management. Product or service quality problems can also provoke uncoupling. Any kind of performance problem, or the perception that rivals now offer superior performance, can trigger a breakdown in relations. 'In' suppliers must build entry barriers by ensuring that product quality is constantly improved and any problems dealt with speedily and professionally.

Not all uncoupling is instigated by the buying company. A key account may be de-rated or terminated because of loss of market share or the onset of financial problems that impair the attractiveness of the account.

The importance of KAM on a worldwide scale is reflected in the employment of global account managers by many multinational organizations. **Global account management (GAM)** is the process of coordinating and developing mutually beneficial long-term relationships with a select group of strategically important customers (accounts) operating in globalized industries (Montgomery and Yip, 1999). Global account managers perform two key roles: (i) managing the internal interface between global and national account management, which is often embedded in a headquarters/subsidiary relationship; (ii) managing the external interface between the supplier and the dispersed activities of its global accounts (Wilson and Millman, 2003). Multinational customers are increasingly buying on a centralized or coordinated basis and seek suppliers who are able to provide consistent and seamless service across countries (Montgomery and Yip, 1999). Consequently, suppliers are developing and implementing GAM and are creating global account managers to manage the interface between seller and buyer on a global basis.

Relationship Marketing—Summary

In summary, relationship marketing has grown in importance in the last two decades, largely as a result of increased competition and wider application of technology-based CRM systems and growing user acceptance of digital technologies. The implication of change is that companies seek to build closer long-term relationships with their customers, unlike in the past when short-term transactional relationships sufficed.

For a company to become successful in its application of relationship marketing, it must be able to manage customer expectations and experiences in such a way that there are opportunities to deliver added value. There are various types of relationship management which a company should be aware of if it is to successfully shift attention away from physical products towards customers. Furthermore, customer retention is important in creating a long-term relationship. From a practical point of view, relationships can be built through use of technical support, expertise and high levels of service, and can result in long-term benefits for a company, for example a sustainable competitive advantage and lower operating costs.

Technology is central to CRM, and CRM systems are often seen as the practical application of relationship marketing. CRM systems are used in both consumer- and business-facing industries and as part of the process of KAM.

Review

1 Value creation

- Companies engage in value creation when they enter into exchanges with their customers and this is central to building relationships. Co-creation of value involves: Information sharing to aid supplier learning, Supplier development and Strategic knowledge sharing.

2 The key concepts of relationship marketing

- The concepts are: relationship quality, service quality trust, satisfaction commitment, and loyalty.

3 The nature of relationship marketing and how to build customer relationships

- Relationship marketing concerns the shift from activities associated with attracting customers to activities concerned with current customers and how to retain them. A key element is the building of trust between buyers and sellers.
- Relationship building can be enhanced by the provision of customer services including giving technical support, expertise, resource support, improving service levels and using risk-reduction strategies.

4 Value and relational networks

- People and the roles they play within the network.
- A network is a term used to describe a set of connections among people, which from a marketing perspective might be used as a resource to solve problems, share knowledge and extend the network.

5 Types of relationship management

- Relationships can take different forms. There are four key types of relationship.
  1. Classic market relationships: supplier–customer, supplier–customer–competitor and the physical distribution network.
  2. Special market relationships, such as between the customer as a member of a loyalty programme and the interaction in the service encounter.
  3. Relationships with the economy and society in general.
  4. Nano-relationships concern the internal operations of an organization, such as relationships between internal customers, internal markets, divisions and business areas inside organizations.

6 The management of customer relationships

- Concerns focusing a company's activities on building long-term relationships and identifying opportunities for relationship development, for example where there is a desire from the customer for delivery of an ongoing service, where the customer makes a choice of service provider, or where the customer has many alternative suppliers to choose from.

7 Building customer relationships

- Effective relationships can be a source of competitive advantage and are developed through a number of different operational aspects of a business: technical support, expertise, resource support, service levels, risk reduction.

8 Benefits to the organization

- Engaging in relationship management can deliver a number of benefits to the organization: increased purchases, lower costs, lifetime value of a customer, sustainable competitive advantage, employee satisfaction and retention.

9 Benefits to the customer

- For relationships to work there should be mutual benefits for all parties involved in the relationship.
- For the customer, potential benefits are: stress reduction, higher quality service, avoidance of switching costs, social and status benefits.

10 Customer retention strategies are central to the marketing effort of relationship marketing

- Customer retention involves the targeting of customers for retention, bonding, internal marketing, promise fulfilment, building of trust and service recovery.

11 Technology-enhanced customer relationship management (CRM)

- Technology is key to the development of successful relationships.
- CRM systems are technology-based solutions that facilitate interactions between the customer and the company, enabling the company to coordinate all of the communication effort so that the customer is presented with a unified message and image.
- Cross-channel customer journeys occur when customers interact with different channels during the purchasing process.

12 Key account management

- Key accounts are serviced by a key account salesforce comprising senior salespeople who develop close personal relationships with customers, can handle sophisticated sales arguments and are skilled at negotiation.
- KAM is a five-stage process: pre KAM, early KAM, mid KAM, partnership KAM and synergistic KAM. A sixth stage (uncoupling KAM) represents the breakdown of the relationship, which can happen at any point during the process.

Key Terms

commitment a process whereby individuals (and companies) establish a bond to reduce negative aspects of a relationship

customer relationship management (CRM) a term for the methodologies, technologies and e-commerce capabilities used by companies to manage customer relationships

global account management (GAM) the process of coordinating and developing mutually beneficial long-term relationships with a select group of strategically important customers (accounts) operating in globalized industries

key account management (KAM) an approach to selling that focuses resources on major customers and uses a team selling approach

loyalty a term used to explain repeated purchasing behaviour

relationship marketing the process of creating, maintaining and enhancing strong relationships with customers and other stakeholders

satisfaction an indicator of the extent to which customer expectations have been met. As a concept it is important to long-term relationship building

service quality involves the experience a customer has of a company's offer. Services vary in complexity and the investment and risk a customer makes in the purchase

touchpoints points at which a customer interacts with a company across a customer journey and where data can be collected

trust a customer's level of confidence in a company's ability to supply the required goods, its reliability and integrity

Study Questions

1. Explain the concept of value from a relationship marketing perspective.

2. Why is relationship management important in many supplier–customer interactions?

3. How can suppliers build close relationships with organizational customers?

4. What are the benefits derived from engaging in a relationship for a) the organization, b) the customer?

5. To what extent is technology involved in the development of successful relationships?

6. Is social media a tool which can be harnessed to facilitate relationships? Discuss the pros and cons.

7. Why is customer retention important in relationship marketing?

8. Suggest how CRM can be used to develop customer relationships.

9. Discuss the importance of touchpoints in a cross-channel customer journey.

10. Justify the adoption of a KAM approach to selling.

Recommended Reading

Egan, J. (2011), *Relationship Marketing: exploring relationship strategies in marketing 4E*, London: Pearson Education.

Flint, D., C. Blocker and P. Boutin (2011), Customer value anticipation, customer satisfaction and loyalty: An empirical examination, *Industrial Marketing Management* 40(11), 219–30.

Gronroos, C. (2011) A service perspective on business relationships: The value creation, interaction and marketing interface, *Industrial Marketing Management* 40(11), 240–7.

Vargo, S. and R. Lusch (2010) It's all B2B . . . and beyond: toward a system perspective of markets, *Industrial Marketing Management* 40(11), 181–7.

Peelen, E. and R. Beltman (2013) *Customer Relationship Management*, London: Pearson Education.

Vargo, S. L. and R.F. Lusch (2008) Service-dominant logic: Continuing the evolution, *Journal of the Academy of Marketing Science* 36, 1–10.

References

Able, J. (2014) The 3 Best places Online to capture customer reviews.

Adams, M. (2014) Three ways to build customer trust, *Forbes*, 22 April.

Andreassen, T. W. (1995) Small, High Cost Countries' Strategy for Attracting MNC's Global Investments, *International Journal of Public Sector Management* 8(3), 110–18.

Anon (2015) Match & More. https://www.morrisons.com/matchandmore

Band, W. (2013) How to succeed with CRM: The Critical Success Factors. http://blogs.forrester.com/william_band/13-07-31-how_to_succeed_with_crm_the_critical_success_factors (accessed 20 April 2015).

Berry, L. L. (1995) Relationship Marketing of Services—Growing Interest, Emerging Perspectives, *Journal of the Academy of Marketing Science* 23(4), 236–45.

Berry, L. L. (1995) Relationship Marketing, in Payne, A., M. Christopher, M. Clark and H. Peck (eds) Relationship Marketing for Competitive Advantage, Oxford: Butterworth-Heinemann, 65–74.

Berry, L. L. (2008) Relationship Marketing Perspectives 1983 and 2000, *Journal of Relationship Marketing* 1(1), 59–77.

Berry, L. L. and A. Parasuraman (1991) Marketing Services, New York: Free Press, 136–42.

Berry, L. L., G. L. Shostak and G. D. Upah (eds.) (1983) Emerging Perspectives on Services Marketing, Chicago, IL: American Marketing Association.

Bitner, M. J. (1995) Building Service Relationships: It's All About Promises, *Journal of the Academy of Marketing Science* 23(4), 246–51.

Bitner, M. J., B. H. Booms and L. A. Mohr (1994) Critical Service Encounters: The Employee's View, *Journal of Marketing* 58, October, 95–106.

Bitner, M. J., B. H. Booms and M. S. Tetreault (1990) The Service Encounter: Diagnosing Favourable and Unfavourable Incidents, *Journal of Marketing* 43, January, 71–84.

Centrum för Tjänsteforskning (2015) Value Creation Through Service, Sweden: Karlstad University.

Chenet, P., T. Dagger and D. O'Sullivan (2010) Service quality, trust, commitment and service differentiation, *Journal of Services Marketing* 24, 336–46.

Chesters, L. (2015) Morrisons in the firing line, *Scottish Daily Mail*, 10 January, 101.

Christie, S. (2014) Can you get Lidl pricing at Morrisons with its new card? The Daily Telegraph, 18 October, 12.

Ciborra, C. (1991) Alliances as learning experiments: cooperation, competition and change in high-tech industries, in Mytelka, L. K. (ed.), Strategic partnerships and the world economy, 51–77.

Coviello, N. E., R. J. Brodie, P. J. Danaker and W. J. Johnson (2002) How Firms Relate to Their Markets: An Empirical Examination of Contemporary Marketing Practices, *Journal of Marketing* 66, July, 33–46.

Eales, T. (2014) Investing in price is an oxymoron, The Grocer, 29 November, 20.

Edvardsson, B., B. Tronvall and T. Gruber (2011) Expanding understanding of service exchange and value co-creation: a social construction approach, *Journal of the Academy of Marketing Science* 39(2), 327–39.

Egan, C. (1997) Relationship Management, in Jobber, D. (ed.) The CIM Handbook of Selling and Sales Strategy, Oxford: Butterworth-Heinemann, 55–88.

Ellis-Chadwick, F. (2013) *History of Online Retail*, Open University.

E-ON (2015) E-On History 2000–2014. http://www.eon.com/en/about-us/profile/history/2000-2015.html

Frost & Sullivan (2011) A smarter approach to CRM, IBM. https://www-935.ibm.com/services/uk/gbs/pdf/SMW03042WWEN.PDF

Gerges, D. (2012) Beanz Meanz Heinz beats out Nike's Just Do It to be named top advertising slogan of all time, *The Daily Mail*, 26 January.

Geyskens, I., J. Steenkamp and K. Kumar (1999) A meta-analysis of Satisfaction in Marketing Channel Relationships, *Journal of Marketing Research* 36, 223–38.

Geyskens, I., J.-B. E. M. Steenkamp and N. Kumar (1998) Generalizations About Trust in Marketing Channel Relationships Using Meta-Analysis, *International Journal of Research in Marketing* 15, 223–48.

Gill, M. (2014) Manage The Cross-Touchpoint Customer Journey. http://www.genesys.com/resources/Manage_The_Cross_Touchpoint_Customer_Journey.pdf (accessed 20 April 2015).

Grönroos, C. (1994) From Marketing Mix to Relationship Marketing: Towards a Paradigm Shift in Marketing, *Management Decision* 32(2), 4–20.

Grönroos, C. and P. Voima (2012) Critical service logic: making sense of value creation and co-creation, *Journal of Academy of Marketing Science* 41(1), 133–50.

Gummesson, E. (1996) Relationship Marketing and Imaginary Organizations: A Synthesis, *European Journal of Marketing* 30(2), 33–44.

Gummesson, E. (1987) The New Marketing–Developing Long-term Interactive Relationships, *Long Range Planning* 20, 10–20.

Gummesson, E. (2002) Relationship Marketing in the New Economy, *Journal of Relationship Marketing* 1(1), 37–57.

Hammervoll, T. (2009) Value-creation logic in supply chain relationships, *Journal of Business to Business Marketing* 16(3), 220–41.

Hammervoll, T. (2012) Managing interaction for learning and value creation in exchange relationships, *Journal of Business Research* 65(2), 128–36.

Harker, M. and J. Egan (2010) The past, present and future of relationship marketing, *Journal of Marketing Management* 2(1), 215–42.

Hunt, R., M. Morgan and D. Shelby (1994) The Commitment-Trust Theory of Relationship Marketing, *Journal of Marketing*, July, 58(3), 20–39.

IPM (2015) Birds Eye runs 'Try Me Free' on 1.6m 'Stir Your Senses' packs. http://www.theipm.org.uk/news/2015/02/birds-eye-runs-try-me-free-on-16m-stir-your-senses-packs (accessed 14 April 2015).

Jackson, B. B. (1985) Build Customer Relationships that Last, *Harvard Business Review*, Nov–Dec, 120–5.

Johnson, R. (1995), R. (1995) Service Failure and Recovery: Impact, Attributes and Process, in Swartz, T. A., D. E. Bowen and S. W. Brown (eds.) *Advances in Services Marketing and Management* 4, 52–65.

Kasper, H., P. van Helsdingen and M. Gabbott (2006) *Services Marketing Management*, Chichester: Wiley, 528.

Kotler, P. (1991) Philip Kotler Explores the New Marketing Paradigm, Marketing Science Institute Review, Spring, 1, 4–5.

Lovelock, C. H., S. Vandermerwe and B. Lewis (1999) *Services Marketing—A European Perspective*, New York: Prentice-Hall, 176.

Lusch, R., S. Vargo and M. Tanniru (2010) Service, value networks and learning, *Journal of the Academy of Marketing Science*, 38, 19–31.

Maxham III, J. G. and R. G. Netemeyer (2002) A Longitudinal Study of Complaining Customers' Evaluations of Multiple Service Failures and Recovery Efforts, *Journal of Marketing* 66, October, 57–71.

McDaniel, S. W. (1998) The Seven Habits of highly effective marketers, *Federal Highway Administration*, Nov/Dec, 62 (3).

McGarry, E. (1953) Some viewpoints in marketing, *Journal of Marketing* 17(3), 36–43.

Montgomery, G. and P. Yip (1999) Statistical Evidence on Global Account Management Programs, *Fachzeitschrift Für Marketing THEXIS* 16(4), 10–13.

Moorman, C., G. Zaltman and R. Deshpande (1992) Relationships between providers and users of market research: The dynamics of trust within and between organizations, *Journal of Marketing Research*, 29, 314–29.

Narayandas, D. and V. K. Rangan (2004) Building and Sustaining Buyer–Seller Relationships in Mature Industrial Markets, *Journal of Marketing*, 68 (July), 63–77.

O'Driscoll, A. (2006) Reflection on Contemporary Issues in Relationship Marketing: Evidence from a Longitudinal Case Study in the Building Materials Industry, *Journal of Marketing Management* 22(1/2), 111–34.

Parasuraman, A., L. L. Berry and V. A. Zeithaml (1991) Understanding Customer Expectations of Service, *Sloan Management Review*, Spring, 39–48.

Ravald, A. and C. Grönroos (1996) The Value Concept and Relationship Marketing, *European Journal of Marketing* 30(2), 19–30.

Reichheld, F. F. and W. E. Sasser Jr (1990) Zero Defections: Quality Comes to Services, Sept.–Oct., 105–11.

Roberts, K., S. Varki and R. Brodie (2003) Measuring the Quality of Relationships in Consumer Services: An Empirical Study, *European Journal of Marketing* 37(1/2), 169–96.

Savvas, A. (2014) BMW deploys IBM big data analytics to improve car performance, 11 March.

Selnes, F. (1998) Antecedents and Consequences of Trust and Satisfaction in Buyer–Seller Relationships, *European Journal of Marketing* 32(3/4), 305–22.

Singh, A., K. Agrariya and Deepali (2011) What Really Defines Relationship Marketing? A Review of Definitions and General and Sector-Specific defining Constructs, *Journal of Relationship Marketing* 10(4), 203–37.

Sinomson, I. and E. Rosen (2014) What Marketers Must Understand about Online reviews, *Harvard Business Review*.

Starbucks (2015a) C.A.F.E Practices. http://gr.starbucks.com/en-US/_Social+Responsibility/_Social+Responsibilities/C.A.F.E+Practices.htm (accessed 18 April 2015).

Starbucks (2015b) Starbucks and the Schultz Family Foundation Give Young Job Seekers a Roadmap to Opportunity. https://news.starbucks.com/news/starbucks-and-schultz-family-foundation-give-young-job-seekers-a-roadmap (accessed 18 April 2015).

Stratiteq (2015) Corporate home page. http://www.stratiteq.com

Takala, T. and O. Uusitalo (1996) An Alternative View of Relationship Marketing: A Framework for Ethical Analysis, *European Journal of Marketing* 30(2), 45–60.

Umbraco (n.d.) http://umbraco.com/about-us/history

Vize, R. (2012) *Exploring Relationship Quality (RQ) in an online B2B retail context: A Structural Equation Modelling Approach*, Dublin: Dublin Institute of Technology.

Vize, R., J. Coughlan, A. Kennedy and F. Ellis-Chadwick (2013) Technology readiness in a b2B online retail context: an examination of antecedents and outcomes, *Industrial Marketing Management* 42(6), 909–18.

Vlaga, W. and A. Eggert (2006) Relationship Value and Relationship Quality, *European Journal of Marketing* 40(3/4), 311–27.

Volvo Construction Equipment (2015) Volvo CE shortlisted for prestigious innovation award. http://www.volvoce.com/CONSTRUCTIONEQUIPMENT/CORPORATE/EN-GB/PRESS_ROOM/ARTICLES/COMPANY_STORIES/PAGES/INNOVATION_AWARD.ASPX

Wenger, E., B. Trayner and M. de Latt (2011) *Promoting and assessing, value creation in communities and networks: a conceptual framework*, Dutch Ministry of Education.

Wilson, K., S. Croom, T. Millman and D. Weilbaker (2000) The SRT-SAMA Global Account Management Study, *Journal of Selling and Major Account Management* 2(3), 63–84.

Wilson, K. and T. Millman (2003) The Global Account Manager as Political Entrepreneur, *Industrial Marketing Management* 32, 151–8.

Wilson, M. (2014) Can Starbucks Make 23,000 Coffee Shops Feel Unique? http://www.fastcodesign.com/3034441/starbucks-secrets-to-make-every-store-feel-unique (accessed 18 April 2015).

Winklhofer, H., A. Pressey and N. Tzokas (2006) A Cultural Perspective of Relationship Orientation: Using Organizational Culture to Support a Supply Relationship Orientation, *Journal of Marketing Management* 22(1/2), 169–94.

Zeithaml, V. A., M. J. Bitner, and D. D. Gremier (2005) *Services Marketing*, New York: McGraw-Hill, 174–8.

Zineldin, M. (1998) Towards an Ecological Collaborative Relationship Management: A 'Co-operative Perspective', *European Journal of Marketing* 32(11/12), 1138–64.

CASE 19
Starbucks: Managing Customer Relationships One Cup at a Time

Starbucks is on a roll. The company, which has over 21,000 stores in 65 different countries, reported record net revenue of $16.4 billion for fiscal year 2014 (an increase of 11 per cent from the previous year). The company that provides you with delicious (if pricey) coffee as well as free Wi-Fi is trying to provide you with something else—a personal relationship. So far, it seems to be succeeding.

Starbucks famously described its vision of reaching its customers as 'one neighborhood, one person and one cup at a time'. And thanks to its effective use of digital marketing, social media, customer relationships and technology management, the company is doing just that.

Starbucks appears to be one of the few companies that truly understands the intricate triangulation between consumers, a product and social media, and how the three, when successfully managed, can increase a brand's profile and develop a relationship between that brand and a customer (while at the same time, generating higher sales). As proof of Starbucks getting its customer relationship management right, a reported nine out of ten people who use Facebook are either fans of Starbucks or know somebody who is.

Starbucks, for quite some time now, has been at the cutting edge of incorporating the latest technological developments into its operations, allowing it to almost seamlessly merge its brick and mortar stores with the numerous digital marketing channels available. The company has also been adept at developing relationships with its customers, using the latest online innovations and social media platforms. Starbucks is adamant when it says that the purpose of new technology is not just to improve its website or to process payments more quickly for people who are queueing up. It is really about getting in touch with its customers and trying to better understand them so as to improve service levels and their experience with the brand. As a sign of its commitment, the company has reportedly taken all the money that it used to spend on traditional media outlets and shifted it into digital and social media marketing in an effort to deepen and consolidate its relationship with its customers.

Experts believe that when trying to build or protect customer relationships, there are certain rules of etiquette that should be respected. One important principle is to engage with customers on their own terms and to the degree that they want to be engaged with. 'Pushing' an ad in this always-connected age really does not work, especially with the generation known as millennials, who were basically born into a world of social media. Today, the expectation for many is that they will 'invite' a brand or product into their lives, while at the same time actively resisting something that was 'forced' upon them. As with any relationship, 'desperation' is the world's worst cologne.

An example of a company getting both its relationship management and social media etiquette wrong is Facebook, ironically the company that basically invented social media. In June 2014 it became known that the company had engaged in a massive experiment, manipulating the news feeds of hundreds of thousands of Facebook users and then observing their behaviour. (Some people were shown stories with fewer positive phrases, while others were shown stories with fewer negative phrases.) There was only one problem. The company never got the participants' permission. Many users were in uproar over what they perceived to be a personal violation of their privacy, with experts questioning the ethics, if not the outright legality, of the company's actions. Facebook, for its part, later admitted that it had 'communicated poorly' when carrying out the experiment.

Starbucks, however, is extremely adept at engaging with its customers and fans, making sure that it first gets 'permission' before interacting with them. One way it has done this is by developing a huge social media presence involving 50 million people who have agreed to join the Starbucks community on such sites as Facebook, as well as YouTube, Twitter, Google+ and Instagram. Another way that Starbucks has managed to get invited into people's lives is through its mobile payment app (which people must download). This ingenious little app allows people to order and pay for their favourite Chestnut Praline Frappuccino without having to queue. It is currently the most popular wallet app in the USA, with higher usage levels than even PayPal. Once again, in all of the above cases, Starbucks has permission, and has even been asked, to interact with an audience.

One example of how Starbucks engages with its customers, strengthening its relationship with them while also building brand recognition, is through a competition that it ran. The company put up new advertising posters in six major cities in the USA, and people had to take a picture of each poster and tweet it, with winners receiving a store gift card worth $20. The success of the campaign allowed Starbucks to amplify its message through social media, since the value of the interest that it generated was far greater than the actual cost of the promotion. Starbucks stated that the impact of the marketing campaign was 'the difference between launching with millions of dollars versus millions of fans'.

Another way that Starbucks actively engages with its customers is through its MyStarbucksIdea.com site. Here, people can leave their thoughts, ideas and opinions as to how Starbucks can improve its business. (A reported 500,000 people have done just that.) The site summarizes all the ideas and then ranks and clearly presents them according to different categories. As a sign that the company truly listens to its customers, it then tells people which ideas are seriously being thought about and which ideas have already been implemented.

A criticism from some quarters, oddly, is that Starbucks does not interact with its customers enough, that is to say, that the company does not update the content of its various social media platforms quickly enough. This is countered with the argument that the company is more concerned with the quality of its content rather than with the quantity or frequency of posts, adding an air of authenticity to Starbucks' attempts to engage its customers in a relationship that is genuine.

Another key element in Starbucks' successful relationship development is the quality of recruitment of new employees and the emphasis that it puts on training and excellence. If you were to ask top management at Starbucks, 'What is your main product?', the answer

would not be fine coffee. Rather, Starbucks sees itself as a purveyor of a unique 'experience' (much like McDonald's, which sees itself as not just providing hamburgers but rather a service experience). And that experience (and by extension, the relationship with the customer) is built on employees 'creating meaningful moments of connection more than 70 million times every week' with the people who visit Starbucks. The company says that it is committed to developing 'new choices and experiences that surprise and delight our customers at every interaction' in an effort to better serve them as well as develop a relationship with them.

One cup of coffee at a time.

Questions

1. What are some of the ways that Starbucks 'engages' its consumers in customer relationships?

2. How can an understanding of digital marketing and social media help companies gain a competitive advantage when it comes to customer relationship management?

3. Analyze the methods used by Starbucks and explain how the company has been successful in increasing its brand recognition while at the same time improving its customer relationship management.

This case study was written by Tom McNamara and Asha Moore-Mangin, The ESC Rennes School of Business.

References

Based on: Wharton (2014) Brand Challenge: Is There a 'Recipe' for Going Viral?, Knowledge@Wharton, Opinion North America, 19 September, http://knowledge.wharton.upenn.edu/article/is-there-a-recipe-for-going-viral; Divol, R., D. Edelman and H. Sarrazin (2012) Demystifying social media, *McKinsey Quarterly,* April, http://www.mckinsey.com/insights/marketing_sales/demystifying_social_media; Moth, D. (2014) Eight awesome social campaigns from Starbucks, Econsultancy, 13 February, https://econsultancy.com/blog/64328-eight-awesome-social-campaigns-from-starbucks; Digital Strategy Consulting (2014) Facebook investigated for secret experiment, Digital Strategy Consulting, July 3, http://www.digitalstrategyconsulting.com/intelligence/2014/07/facebook_investigated_for_secret_experiment.php; Fitgerald, M. (2013) How Starbucks Has Gone Digital, MIT Sloan Management Review, 4 April, http://sloanreview.mit.edu/article/how-starbucks-has-gone-digital; Sivitz, L. and M. Holup (2012) Inside Starbucks Digital Marketing—Going 'Beyond The Big, Seattle 24x7, 23 November, http://www

»

»

.seattle24x7.com/community/shoptalk/2012/11/23/starbucks-digital-marketing-going-beyond-the-big-idea; Bold, B. (2014) Starbucks admits opening brand to social media is 'doubled-edged sword', *Marketing Magazine* UK, 7 February, http://www.marketingmagazine.co.uk/article/1301515/starbucks-admits-opening-brand-social-media-doubled-edged-sword; Starbucks (2013) Starbucks Names Matthew Ryan Global Chief Strategy Officer, Starbucks Investor Relations Financial Release, 4 April, http://investor.starbucks.com/phoenix.zhtml?c=99518&p=irol-newsArticle&ID=1803454; Allison, M. (2013) Starbucks presses social media onward, *The Seattle Times*, 27 April, http://seattletimes.com/html/businesstechnology/2020862483_starbuckssocialxml.html

CASE 20
Sunderland Football Club and Bidvest Foodservice: Building a Beneficial Partnership

Bidvest is a company with a clear service-orientated mission. It states its aims to be to 'deliver service excellence, make life easier and help our customers to grow'. Bidvest is an international company, based in South Africa but trading in 26 countries in Europe, Asia-Pacific and other parts of Africa. Its operations span many industries, for example electrical products, automotive, freight, office products, travel and aviation services and food services. Working in the business-to-business sector means that developing customer relationships is especially important to Bidvest. The company believes in using local expertise and enabling its staff to grow and develop their divisions, and this is one of the values at the heart of the business. In Europe, the company concentrates its energies in the hospitality, catering, leisure and food-processing industries, where customer service and customer value is particularly important.

This case study explores how and why Bidvest decided to build a relationship with Sunderland Football Club in order to develop its profile in the UK.

Seeking Value for Bidvest

Bidvest engages in value creation when it enters into trading exchanges with its customers, which enables it to build strong relationships. It does this by looking for ways to create benefits for both partners. An opportunity for Bidvest arose in 2013 when Sunderland AFC was looking for a new sponsor. At the time, Bidvest wanted to raise its profile in the UK and Europe, and there was an increased appetite from European investors for shares in African companies. Indeed, at one point, the London Stock Exchange was actively looking to increase the number of African stocks for institutional investors. Bidvest saw this as a potential opportunity to strengthen its business in this part of the world.

The company was not just interested in securing investors; it was also interested in finding a partner that fitted the company's ethos, aims and aspirations. Sunderland FC was already a customer of Bidvest's Child Company Foodservice (formerly 3663), so the sponsorship deal created an opportunity to significantly extend the relationship with the brand.

Why Was There a Good Fit with Sunderland AFC?

Relationships are central to the development of successful sponsorships deals. But there are some important considerations when seeking to develop value in a partnership deal. For example, sponsorship deals should focus on the benefits for both sides. So to get to the root of what is likely to make a good sponsorship deal, it is vital for a sponsor to understand its target company and to find a fit that is right for both parties.

In this case, Brian Joffee, Chief Executive of Bidvest, loved sport, particularly football, and the company was looking to sponsor a premiership football club that shared its values. This interest in 'the beautiful game' was not just a whim of the CEO, however, as the UK premiership was an important global brand property and offered tremendous opportunities for raising awareness of the Bidvest brand among its target audience of business owners in the UK. Additionally, Sunderland AFC was already actively investing in trying to make a difference in Africa through the Invest in Africa programme and a partnership with the Nelson Mandela Foundation, which meant it was visible to Joffee, who is quoted as saying, 'Sunderland AFC is the perfect partner for us in the UK where we deliver food and drink to over 50,000 businesses each week.'

»

»

Bidvest decided to sponsor Sunderland AFC, in part because the club was looking for a new sponsor but also because there was a strong fit between the organizations. The support for local businesses was very important to Bidvest, which is a value which is at the heart of the organization. Sunderland also had wider business activities and a management focus that could deliver benefits. For example, in its charter, Sunderland AFC set out its values regarding the importance of its customers, providing the highest standards of service, acting as equal opportunities employer, celebrating cultural diversity and giving opportunities to all. The club reaches out to local communities through its charity work, empowering young people by encouraging them to have healthier lifestyles, improve their self-confidence and increase their employability skills through its training programmes.

Partner Benefits

Bidvest and Sunderland derived a significant amount of value from the sponsorship deal. For example, raising brand awareness for Bidvest through having the brand on the Sunderland shirts, branding at the Stadium of Light (Sunderland's ground), player appearances and signed merchandise, partner events, advertising in the fanzine *A Love Supreme*, and developing important links to local businesses. It also benefited from high-profile media events, which helped to enhance the brand and the corporate image.

Another unanticipated boon for the sponsors and the club came when club chaplain Father Marc Lyden-Smith went on a pilgrimage to Rome and presented the Pope with a Sunderland shirt. Much to the delight of Bidvest and Sunderland supporters around the world, Papa Francesco held up the shirt to the world's media. There was widespread global media coverage of this event, which would arguably have cost millions of dollars to create through traditional planned marketing communications.

Enhanced customer relations were also a key benefit for both sides: international involvement from a large global player enhanced Sunderland's reputation and also exposed Bidvest to local businesses and investors. The involvement that Sunderland had with both the local community and businesses enhanced relationships and created opportunities for the sponsor to engage with local business to derive further commercial value through its core business. Of course Sunderland also had the additional benefit of the financial support provided by Bidvest, for example £10 million for a two-year shirt sponsorship deal.

Questions

1. Discuss why Bidvest (B2B) chose to sponsor a football club.

2. Explain the key reasons why it is important for there to be a good fit between sponsorship partners like Sunderland AFC and Bidvest.

3. Use the concept of relationship quality as a lens to explain why Bidvest chose to sponsor Sunderland AFC.

4. Imagine that it is your job to find a new sponsor for Sunderland AFC when Bidvest's deal comes to an end. Make a list of your key priorities for identifying sponsorship opportunities.

This case study was written by Fiona Ellis-Chadwick, Senior Lecturer, in Marketing and Retailing Loughborough University.

References

Bidvest Group (2015) http://www.bidvest.com/downloads/pdf/Bidvest%20Group%20PAIA%20Manual%20updated%20Dec%202011.pdf (accessed July 2015); Blas, J. (2014) London Stock exchange to pursue African company listing, *The Financial Times*, 28 September; Harper, N. (2003) Stuart Hall, *The Guardian* (London), 2 May, http://www.theguardian.com/football/2003/may/02/newsstory.sport11 (accessed July 2015); Miller, A. (2013) Premier League shirt sponsors pour record £166m into top-flight bank accounts—with Arsenal seeing the biggest rise, *The Independent*, http://blogs.independent.co.uk/2013/08/26/premier-league-shirt-sponsors-pour-record-166m-into-top-flight-bank-accounts-with-arsenal-seeing-the-biggest-rise (accessed 10 July 2015); Sunderland Football Association Football Club (2013) *New Principal Partner Announced*, http://www.safc.com/the-club/safc-global/business/new-principal-partner-announced (accessed 10 July 2015); Sunderland Football Association Football Club (2015) Sunderland AFC Charter Report http://www.safc.com/the-club/about-us/customer-charter (accessed 10 July 2015).

Endnotes

1 Late in 2014, Bidvest decided not to go for listing on the Stock Exchange.

2 Bidvest refers to BFS Group. BFS Group owns but acts as a separate company to Bidvest Foodservice and Bidvest Logistics.

3 The deal between BFS Group and Sunderland ended in June 2015. The new sponsor of Sunderland Football Club is Dafabet. This case is intended to illustrate the motivations for entering into sponsor partnerships.

CHAPTER 11
Value Through Innovation

LEARNING OBJECTIVES

After reading this chapter, you should be able to:

1 define the different types of new products that can be launched
2 describe how to create and nurture an innovative culture
3 discuss the organizational options that apply to new product development
4 identify the methods of reducing time to market
5 explain how marketing and R&D staff can work together effectively
6 describe the stages in the new product development process
7 explain how to stimulate the corporate imagination
8 discuss the six key principles of managing product teams
9 describe the innovation categories and their marketing implications
10 discuss the key ingredients in commercializing technology quickly and effectively

A rguably, innovation is the lifeblood of corporate success, but it is increasingly important to consider how new products can add value. Changing customer tastes, technological advances and competitive pressures mean that companies cannot afford to rely on past product success. Companies must look closely at the needs of customers and other stakeholders and the impact on the wider environment if they are to develop new products that add value.

New product development is a risky activity as most new products fail. But new product development should not be judged in terms of the percentage of failures, as this could stifle the spirit of innovation. The acid test is the number of successes. Failure has to be tolerated.

To fully understand new product development, we need to distinguish between invention and innovation. **Invention** is the discovery of new ideas and methods. **Innovation** occurs when an invention is commercialized by bringing it to market. Not all countries have the same capacity for invention. The UK has a history of being inventive from the steam engine, the bicycle, to the television, the computer, and the jet engine. The Japanese are equally inventive but also have the ability to successfully market products by constantly seeking to improve and develop using a process called *Kaizen* (sometimes *Kaisan*) (Pearson, 1993). The classic example is the Sony Walkman, which was not an invention in the sense that it was fundamentally new; rather its success (over 75 million have been sold worldwide) was based on the innovative marketing of existing technologies. In Scandinavia many businesses were built on a local invention. For example, Tetra Pak was founded by a person who conceived of 'pouring milk into a paper bag'. Lego bricks revolutionized toys, and IKEA's invention of a new way to deliver furniture was central to its phenomenal growth. In these cases, the key was not just the invention, but the capability to innovate by bringing the product successfully to market (Richard, 1996).

The USA is a major source of innovation. The Internet is dominated by US companies such as Microsoft, Apple, Amazon, Google and eBay. Table 11.1 shows the world's most innovative companies and their country of origin (McGregor, 2006).

A key point to remember is that the focus of innovation should be on providing new solutions that better meet customer needs. Innovative solutions often do not require major breakthroughs in technology. For example, the growth of Starbucks was not fuelled by technological breakthroughs but by redefining what city-centre coffee drinking meant, and Ryanair has built its success by creating a different consumer appeal from that of traditional airlines, based on low prices and strict cost control (Doyle, 1997).

Because many innovations fail, it is important to understand the key success factors. Research into the key success factors in innovation identified the following (Kashami and Clayton, 2000).

- *Creating and delivering added value is important.* Innovations that produce large improvements in value perform much better than those that fail to deliver improved benefits. Radical innovation has greater potential for enhancing marketing performance but is inherently more risky than incremental innovations that deliver small improvements.
- *Speed to market counts.* The most successful new products tend to be those that are launched quickly. There are two reasons for this. First, delay increases the risk of others getting to market first; second, consumer priorities may change.
- A *product's inferior perceived value cannot be compensated for with high communications spending.* High expenditures on advertising and promotion only have a significant effect on performance where the product is already perceived to have high consumer value. High expenditures for inferior products actually worsen the performance: advertising makes bad products fail more quickly.

In this chapter we shall ask the question 'What is a new product?' and examine three key issues in new product development: 1) organization, 2) developing an innovation culture, 3) new product development process. Then we examine the strategies involved in product replacement and the most common form of new product development. Finally, we look at the consumer adoption process, which is how people learn about new products, try them, and adopt or reject them. Throughout this chapter reference will be made to research that highlights the success factors in new product development.

TABLE 11.1 The top 10 most innovative companies		
Company	**Headquarters—industrial sector**	**Innovative products**
Apple	USA—technology and telecommunication	iPad, iPhone, MacBook Air, iWatch
Google	USA—technology and telecommunication	Google search, Google Maps, Google+, Gmail
Samsung	S. Korea—technology and telecoms	Galaxy S6, Smart Camera, virtual reality headsets, Smart televisions

Company	Headquarters—industrial sector	Innovative products
Microsoft Facebook	USA—technology and telecommunication USA—technology and telecommunication	Microsoft Office, Windows 10 operating system, Bing, Microsoft SQL, Xbox Social network, social marketplace, customized advertising; the 'Like' button
IBM Sony Haier	USA—technology and telecommunication Japan—technology and telecommunication China—consumer and retail products	PureSystems, SmartCloud computing, Watson Analytics LCD televisions; SmartWear-wearable technology 3D refrigerators, Smart Home products and domestic appliances
Amazon.com Hyundai	USA—consumer and retail S. Korea—automotive	Online retail store, Kindle, MP3 player Blue Drive carbon reduction; eco-friendly cars; electric vehicles

Source: a 2012 survey of 2,700 senior executives by the Boston Consulting Group (Boston Consulting Group, 2012)

What is a New Product?

Some new products are so fundamentally different from products that already exist that they reshape markets and competition; for example satellite navigation systems, which have created a new market for digital navigation devices and reduced the sale of printed road maps significantly. Publisher HarperCollins said sales of maps and atlases declined from £13.5 million in 2006 to £9.7 million in 2010 (Geoghegan, 2011).

At the other extreme, a shampoo that is different from existing products only by means of its brand name, fragrance, packaging and colour is also a new product. In fact, four broad categories of new product exist (Booz, Allen and Hamilton, 1982).

1 *Product replacements*: these account for about 45 per cent of all new product launches, and include revisions and improvements to existing products, for example repositioning (existing products such as Lucozade Sport being positioned as a 'body fuel' to access new market segments) and cost reductions (existing products being reformulated or redesigned to cost less to produce). Dyson releases new products based on improvement to an existing product. Its new vacuum cleaner has an innovative ball to improve manoeuvrability, and is smaller and more flexible than previous models.

2 *Additions to existing lines*: these account for about 25 per cent of new product launches and take the form of new products that add to a company's existing product lines. This produces greater product depth. Chocolate Weetabix is an extension that enables the well-known cereal brand to compete with chocolate cereals. Another example is the addition to the Crest toothpaste brand of Crest Pro-health whitening toothpaste.

3 *New product lines*: these total around 20 per cent of new product launches, and represent a move into a new market. For example, in Europe Volvic introduced the 'Touch of Fruit' range of bottled waters, and Evian brought out a facial spray—both targeted at different audiences. This strategy widens a company's product mix.

4 *New-to-the-world products*: these total around 10 per cent of new product launches, and create entirely new markets. For example, netbooks, tablet computers and smartphones have created new markets because of the highly valued customer benefits they provide.

Clearly, the degree of risk and reward varies according to the new product category. New-to-the-world products normally carry the highest risk since it is often very difficult to predict consumer reaction. Effective new product development is based on creating and nurturing an innovative culture, organizing effectively for new product development and managing the new product development process. We shall now examine these three issues.

Creating and Nurturing an Innovative Culture

The foundation for successful new product development is the creation of a corporate culture that promotes and rewards innovation. Unfortunately, many marketing managers regard their company's corporate culture as a key constraint to innovation (Matthews, 2002). Managers, therefore, need to pay more attention to creating a culture

FIGURE 11.1
Creating and nurturing an innovative culture

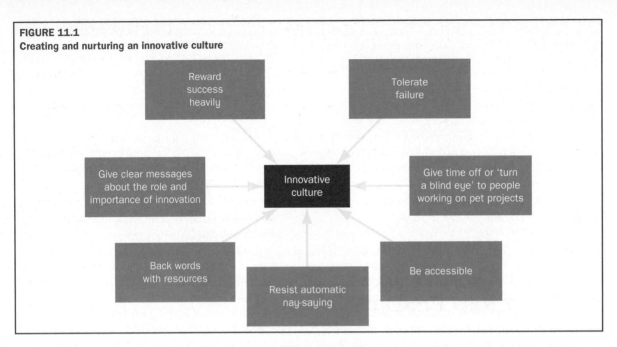

that encourages innovation. Figure 11.1 shows the kinds of attitudes and actions that can foster an innovative culture. People in organizations observe those actions that are likely to lead to success or punishment. The surest way to kill innovative spirit is to conspicuously punish those people who are prepared to create and champion new product ideas through to communication when things go wrong, and to reward those people who are content to manage the status quo. Such actions breed the attitude 'Why should I take the risk of failing when by carrying on as before I will probably be rewarded?' Research has shown that those companies that have supportive attitudes to rewards and risk, and a tolerant attitude towards failure, are more likely to innovate successfully (see Gupta and Wileman, 1990; Koshler, 1991; Shrivastava and Souder, 1987). Read Marketing in Action 11.1 to find out more.

MARKETING IN ACTION 11.1
Investing in Innovation at 3M

3M produces innovative products for many different industrial sectors, from healthcare to transport. With over $30 billion in global sales and operations in more than 65 countries the company has had a constant stream of innovation in its 100-year history. Innovations that have helped the company grow are: waterproof sandpaper, Scotch pressure-sensitive tape, Cellophane tape, Scotchgard fabric protector, Post-it notes, Privacy Plus filter, optical film for LCD televisions and Scotch-Brite cleaning products. Indeed, there are over 55,000 products in the company's portfolio.

3M has an innovative culture, set in place by former CEO William McKnight. He believed that if the company was going to continue to grow and make the innovative products then it needed to employ the right employees and then give them freedom to explore and to get things wrong. 3M has a programme known as '15 Percent Time', which allows employees to use part of their time at work to develop their own ideas. Although it may take years for this approach to bear fruit, the results of this programme have been some of the company's most innovative products, including the Scotch® Brand tapes, Post-it® notes, Scotchgard™ Fabric Protector and silicon adhesive systems for transdermal drug delivery. The firm also has a policy that each of its divisions must bring in 30 per cent of its revenues from products that are less than four years old.

Innovation development is well organized across the world. 3M has a global science and technical community which fosters a culture of cooperation, communication and cross-pollination of ideas. There are rewards for innovators and scientists and managers alike can progress up the career ladder. 3M also invests in supporting education and development beyond the walls of the business in order to promote industry standards and develop national workforces.

Based on: 3M (2012); Kovacs (2012); Govindarajan and Srinivas (2013)

An innovation culture can also be nurtured by senior management visibly supporting new product development in general and high-profile projects in particular (see Booz, Allen and Hamilton, 1982; Maidique and Zirger, 1984). Besides sending clear messages about the role and importance of new product development, senior management should reinforce their words by allowing time off from their usual duties to people who wish to develop their own ideas, make available funds and resources for projects, and make themselves accessible when difficult decisions need to be taken (see Bergen, Miyajima and McLaughlin, 1988; Hegarty and Hoffman, 1990; Cooper, 1979; Johne and Snelson, 1988).

Finally, management at all levels should resist the temptation of automatic 'nay-saying'—that is, whenever a new idea is suggested, there is a tendency for doubters in a firm to make negative comments and question the feasibility of the new idea. This does not mean that all ideas should immediately be developed as each will be scrutinized and have to pass through many stages of development before becoming a reality. The point is that stifling new ideas at conception only serves as a constraint on innovation. Managers need to seek ways to create an innovative culture.

Creative leadership is required to release the passions, imagination and energy needed for outstanding innovation. Such leadership encourages staff to reject the status quo and operate in a productive discomfort zone, has a clear vision of the future, and provides support for exploration (e.g. Apple, Google, Haier, 3M, Hyundai).

Arguably, there is an underlying assumption that all innovation by commercial profit-based businesses is for affluent markets, where customers will eventually pay for the research, development and marketing of new products and deliver surplus profits by paying high prices for such goods and services. On the one hand, perhaps this is a reasonable assumption as over half the world's population survives on less than $2.50 dollars a day and therefore are deemed to be uninterested in or unable to purchase innovative products (Shah, 2012). On the other hand, is it a classic example of marketing myopia as suggested by Theodore Levitt in the 1960s (Levitt, 1960), whereby companies are short-sighted about growth opportunities in the market? Read Mini Case 11.1 to find out more about how a shift towards frugal innovation is creating innovative products for billions of under-served consumers.

MINI CASE 11.1
Frugal Innovations: From Clay Fridges to Cardboard Splints

Historically, over half the world's population has been ignored by global corporations as a segment capable of being interested in innovation. However, Eric von Hippel, a professor of technological innovation, has argued for many years that the key to innovation comes from customers, not corporate thinking, and that everyone has *needs* that can be satisfied by new products and services.

Sustained global recession has affected many areas of business, and governments around the world have taken to using austerity as a watchword for managing national and regional affairs. This shift in emphasis has profound implications for marketers. For example, the engineers in India won the day with the Tata Nano

when Renault-Nissan asked its engineers in France, India and Japan to come up with some cost-saving ideas. The Haier Group, a Chinese consumer electronics manufacturer, has undercut western competitors by producing goods from air conditioners and washing machines to wine coolers, often at half the usual cost. The result has been that Haier has taken significant percentages of US and European markets. However, the shift towards frugal innovation is more far-reaching than just producing goods for western markets more cheaply. According to Prahalad and Mashelkar (2010), a form of new product development called *frugal innovation* or *reverse innovation* specifically engineers products to meet the needs of developing countries—for example, a rough-terrain wheelchair, or a $20 prosthetic knee that can be assembled in an hour.

In the developing world the various champions of frugal innovations include Anil Gupta, who is an academic at one of India's top business schools, the Indian Institute of Management. Anil is a champion of individuals who are deemed to be 'knowledge-rich yet economically poor'. Anil believes that there is a solution to world poverty, but it requires a different approach: a bottom-up one. He established the Honey Bee Network in the

1980s with the aim of nurturing innovation, knowledge and creativity at a grassroots level. This initiative led to the development of a village-to-government approach towards innovation. Innovation scouts go to rural villages in India looking for potential products to develop. Mansukhbhai Prajapati is an example of a successful entrepreneur who has emerged from this initiative. He developed the Mitti cool brands, which include clay pans, pressure cookers and non-electric refrigerators, which are making a difference to local communities' health through better-kept and better-cooked food.

Jugaad is an example of a company that began creating products from recycled material in 1997 through a Delhi-based children's home that organized work for disadvantaged children. *'Jugaad'* is a unique Hindi word that refers to the practice of getting required results by using whatever limited resources are available. People Tree (a retailer) provided outlets and supported Jugaad until it became an independent brand in 2004. This creative manufacturer now provides employment and training and helps members of its workforce to become independent entrepreneurs.

The Tata Nano may not have changed the world, but frugal innovation will!

Questions:

1   What are 'frugal' innovations and how might they change the world?
2   If you worked for a large multinational, suggest how you would incorporate frugal innovations into your marketing strategy.

Based on: Day (2012); The Economist (2012); Jugaad (2012); Kadri (2010); Duggan (2012); Honey Bee (n.d.); Prahalad and Mashelkar (2010)

Organizing Effectively for New Product Development

The second building block of successful innovation is an appropriate organization structure. Most companies use one or a combination of the following methods: project teams, product and brand managers, new product departments and new product committees.

Project teams

Project teams involve the bringing together of staff from such areas as research and development (R&D), engineering, manufacturing, finance and marketing to work on a new product development project. Research has shown that assigning the responsibility of new product development to such cross-functional teams has a positive effect on new product performance (Joshi and Sharma, 2004). Specialized skills are combined to form an effective team to develop the new product concept. Furthermore, if the members of the team remain stable for the duration of a project there is greater potential to foster better decision-making, engender shared responsibility, and leverage advantage from the collective expertise. Ultimately, this approach helps develop better new product advantage. Working together in stable teams can also help to avoid 'tunnel vision and inflexibility in problem solving', up to a point.

Slotegraaf and Atuahene-Gima (2011) discuss how stable teams benefit from better decision-making. However, a key challenge associated with developing a new product is that innovation requires the conversion of knowledge into something tangible, and the stability of a product team can help the process. However, there is a certain point where the benefits begin to diminish. So, long-term stability beyond a particular project may be less successful. Google supported new product development by allowing employees 20 per cent of their work time to spend on innovative projects. Gmail, AdSense and Google+ have all been developed in this manner (*The Marketers*, 2008). However, ensuring the productivity of this approach for everyone in the company has proved challenging.

Product and brand managers

Product and brand management entails the assignment of product managers to product lines (or groups of brands within a product line) and/or brand managers to individual brands. These managers are then responsible for their success and have the task of coordinating functional areas (e.g. production, sales, advertising and marketing research). They are also often responsible for new product development, including the creation of new product ideas, improving existing products and designing brand extensions. Product managers may be supported by a team of assistant brand managers and a dedicated marketing researcher. In some companies, a new product development manager may help product and brand managers in the task of generating and testing new product concepts. This form of organization is common for high-volume, relatively low-value products such as groceries and toiletries, and in the drinks industries.

New product departments and committees

The review of new product projects is normally in the hands of high-ranking functional managers, who listen to progress reports and decide whether further funds should be assigned to a project. They may also be charged with deciding new product strategies and priorities. No matter whether the underlying structure is venture team, product and brand management or new product department, a new products committee often oversees the process and services to give projects a high corporate profile through the stature of its membership.

The importance of teamwork

Whichever method (or combination of methods) is used, effective cross-functional teamwork is crucial for success (see Hise, O'Neal, Parasuraman and McNeal, 1990; Johne and Snelson, 1988; Walsh, 1990) and there has to be effective communication and teamwork between R&D and marketing (Fred, 1991). Although all functional relationships are important during new product development, the cultural differences between R&D and marketing are potentially the most harmful and difficult to resolve. The challenge is to prevent technical people developing only things that interest them professionally, and to get them to understand the realities of the marketplace.

The role of marketing directors

A study by Gupta and Wileman (1991) asked marketing directors of technology-based companies what they believed they could do to improve their relationship with R&D and achieve greater integration of effort. Six major suggestions were made by the marketing directors.

1 *Encourage teamwork*: marketing should work with R&D to establish clear, mutually agreed project priorities to reduce the incidence of pet projects. Marketing, R&D and senior management should hold regular joint project review meetings.

2 *Improve the provision of marketing information to R&D*: one of the major causes of R&D rejecting input from marketing was the lack of quality and timely information. Many marketing directors admitted that they could do a better job of providing such information to R&D. They also believed that the use of information would be enhanced if R&D personnel were made part of the marketing research team so that the questions on their minds could be incorporated into studies. They also felt that such a move would improve the credibility and trust between marketing and R&D.

3 *Take R&D people out of the lab*: marketing should encourage R&D staff to be more customer aware by inviting them to attend trade shows, take part in customer visits and prepare customer materials.

4 *Develop informal relationships with R&D*: they noted that there were often important personality and value differences between the two groups, which could cause conflict as well as being a stimulus to creativity. More effort could be made to break down these barriers by greater socializing, going to lunch together, and sitting with each other at seminars and presentations.

5 *Learn about technology*: the marketing directors believed that improving their 'technological savvy' would help them communicate more effectively with R&D people, understand various product design trade-offs, and comprehend the capabilities and limits of technology to create competitive advantages and provide solutions to customer problems.

6 *Formalize the product development process*: they noted that marketing people were often preoccupied with present products to the neglect of new products, and that the new product development process was far too unstructured. They advocated a more formal process, including formal new project initiation, status reports and review procedures, and a formal requirement that involvement in the process was an important part of marketing personnel's jobs.

The role of senior management

The study also focused on marketing directors' opinions of what senior management could do to help improve the marketing/R&D relationship. We have already noted, when discussing how to create an innovative culture, the crucial role that senior management staff play in creating the conditions for a thriving new product programme. Marketing directors mentioned six major ways in which senior management could play a part in fostering better relations.

1 *Make organizational design changes*: senior management should locate marketing and R&D near to each other to encourage communication and the development of informal relationships. They should clarify the roles of marketing and R&D in developing new products and reduce the number of approvals required for small changes in a project, which would give both R&D and marketing greater authority and responsibility.

2 *Show a personal interest in new product development*: organizational design changes should be backed up by more overt commitment and interest in innovation through early involvement in the product development process, attending product planning and review meetings, and helping to coordinate product development plans.

3 *Provide strategic direction*: many marketing directors felt that senior management could provide more strategic vision regarding new product/market priorities. They also needed to be more long term with their strategic thinking.

4 *Encourage teamwork*: senior management should encourage, or even demand, teamwork between marketing and R&D. Specifically, they should require joint R&D/marketing discussions, joint planning and budgeting, joint marketing research and joint reporting to them.

5 *Increase resources*: *some* marketing directors pointed to the need to increase resources to foster product development activities. The alternative was to reduce the number of projects. Resources should also be provided for seminars, workshops and training programmes for R&D and marketing people. The objective of these programmes would be to develop a better understanding of the roles, constraints and pressures of each group.

6 *Understand marketing's importance*: marketing directors complained of senior management's lack of understanding of marketing's role in new product development and the value of marketing in general. They felt that senior management should insist that marketing becomes involved with R&D in product development much earlier in the process so that the needs of customers are more prominent.

This research has provided valuable insights into how companies should manage the marketing/R&D relationship. It is important that companies organize themselves effectively since cross-functional teamwork and communication has proved to be a significant predictor of successful innovation in a number of studies (see Dwyer, 1990; Gupta and Wileman, 1990; Adler, Riggs and Wheelwright, 1989).

Managing the New Product Development Process

There are three inescapable facts about new product development: it is expensive, risky and time-consuming. For example, Gillette spent in excess of £100 million over more than 10 years developing its Sensor razor brand. The new product concept was to develop a non-disposable shaver that would use new technology to produce a shaver that would follow the contours of a man's face, giving an excellent shave (through two spring-mounted, platinum-hardened, chromium blades) with fewer cuts. This made commercial sense, since shaving systems are more profitable than disposable razors and allow more opportunity for creating a differential advantage. Had the brand failed, Gillette's position in the shaving market could have been damaged irreparably. Nike is another company that invests heavily in new product development to maintain its lead in the specialist sports shoe market. Read Marketing in Action 11.2 to discover how innovation drives the Decathlon service brand.

Managing the process of new product development is an important factor in reducing cost, time and risk. Studies have shown that having a formal process with review points, clear new product goals and a strong marketing orientation underlying the process leads to greater success, whether the product is a physical good or a service (Brentani, 1991; Johne and Storey, 1998).

An eight-step new product development process to provide these characteristics is shown in Figure 11.2 and consists of setting new product strategy, idea generation, screening, concept testing, business analysis, product development, market testing and commercialization. Although the reality of new product development may resemble organizational chaos, the discipline imposed by the activities carried out at each stage leads to a greater likelihood of developing a product that not only works, but also confers customer benefits. We should note, however, that new products pass through each stage at varying speeds; some may dwell at a stage for a long period, while others may pass through very quickly (Cooper and Kleinschmidt, 1986).

New product strategy

As we have already seen, marketing directors value strategic guidance from senior management about their vision and priorities for new product development. By providing clear guidelines about which products/markets the company is interested in serving, senior management staff can provide a focus for the areas in which idea generation should take place. Also, by outlining their objectives (e.g. market share gain, profitability, technological leadership) for new products they can provide indicators for the screening criteria that should be used to evaluate those ideas. A key issue in new product strategy is where to allocate resources. A company may have several divisions and a multitude of product lines so the company has to decide where funds should be invested.

Idea generation

One of the benefits of developing an innovative corporate culture is that it sparks the imagination (see Marketing in Action 11.2). The objective is to motivate the search for ideas so that salespeople, engineers, top management, marketers and other employees are all alert to new opportunities. Interestingly, questioning Nobel Prize winners about the time and circumstances when they had the important germ of an idea that led them to great scientific discovery revealed that it can occur at the most unexpected time: just before going to sleep, on waking up in the morning, at a place of worship. The common factor seems to be a period of quiet contemplation, uninterrupted by the bustle of everyday life and work.

Successful new product ideas are not necessarily based on technological innovation. Often they are based on novel applications of existing technology (e.g. Velcro poppers on disposable nappies). The iPhone created a need for a place to buy 'portable music' which led to the development of the iTunes store.

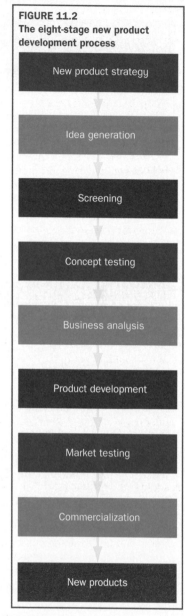

FIGURE 11.2
The eight-stage new product development process

New product strategy → Idea generation → Screening → Concept testing → Business analysis → Product development → Market testing → Commercialization → New products

Scan the QR code to find out how the mobile provider EE is launching its new product EE TV.

The sources of new product ideas can be internal to the company: scientists, engineers, marketers, salespeople and designers (as at 3M). Some companies use **brainstorming** as a technique to stimulate the creation of ideas, and use financial incentives to persuade people to put forward the ideas they have had. At Royal Dutch Shell, virtual teams meet via the Internet to share ideas. These sessions have generated many ideas for ways to reduce paperwork to using sophisticated laser sensors to find oil (Viklund, 2015).

The prediction by Hamel and Prahalad (1991) that global competitive battles will be won by those companies that have the corporate imagination to build and dominate fundamentally new markets has been proved right, especially in high-tech markets.

Often, fundamentally new products/markets are created by small businesses that are willing to invent new business models or radically redesign existing models. Sources of new product ideas can also be external to the company. Examining competitors' products may provide clues to product improvements. Competitors' new product plans can

MARKETING IN ACTION 11.2
Innovation Drives Passion Brands and Builds Sporting Universes at Decathlon

'*Create the need and make the pleasure and the benefits of sport accessible to as many people as possible*', is the promise that Decathlon has offered its clients since 1976. The idea of 'sport for all' enabled this French company to differentiate from other major brands focusing on competition and performance. This led it to the innovative concept to bring together all sports under one roof (from cycling to fishing) and to offer a large range of self-service sport products at the best price. Decathlon continued to develop the business and in 1999 opened its first store in the UK and its first Oxylane Village in France—an innovative sports environment based around a Decathlon store. By 2015, Decathlon had 285 shops and 9 Oxylane Villages in France and over 580 stores in more than 20 different countries. Worldwide sales are important to the company as they account for 58 per cent of sales. Central to the Decathlon offer are the 'Passion' brands. Each Passion brand represents a sporting universe, and collectively they accounted for more than 60 per cent of Decathlon's turnover in 2015. See Table 11.2 for examples.

TABLE 11.2 Examples of Passions, sporting universes and innovative products

Passion Brand	Sporting universe	Examples of products
Geologic	Darts, archery and boules	Soft archery kit, totally safe to use anywhere T-light, a safe dartboard
Newfeel	Walking	Propulse Walk 400, shoes that aid fitness Fullwalk 540 design shoes, with lightness in mind
Oxelo	Urban skate sport	Town 7 Easyfold scooter – easy to assemble anywhere Sneak-in inline skates to be worn with own shoes
Tribord	Nautical water sports	Easybreathe full-face snorkel; see and breathe underwater Izeber 50 floating system lifejacket to aid buoyancy

Each Passion brand conceives the products, exclusively distributed by Decathlon stores. The own-brand offer is due to Decathlon placing innovation at the heart of its activities. With a very advanced internal R&D department composed of researchers, engineers and designers, Decathlon's international design network is prolific, producing about 40 patents and nearly 3,000 products each year. Decathlon rewards excellence in innovation at an annual award-giving event, the Oxylane Awards.

Domyos is another Passion brand (dedicated to fitness) and is the best example of the firm's willingness to immerse the employees amongst its customers. Who better than sportspeople know what they need to improve their game? Decathlon provides them with a website, Openoxylane (http://www.openoxylane.com), dedicated to the co-creation of new products. Anyone can put forward ideas and participate in projects submitted by members of the community. At each stage of the creative process – from defining functions to selecting materials or colours and choosing a name and even the price—users can submit proposals, interact and give their opinion. Prototype workshops are also available for teams to observe the behaviour and test the components of finished products; they help speed up the design process. Organising this innovation culture allows the group to compete with major brands such as Nike and Adidas, who traditionally highlight their innovation and design.

Based on: http://www.decathlon.co.uk

be gleaned by training the salesforce to ask distributors about new activities. Distributors can also be a source of new product ideas directly, since they deal with customers and have an interest in selling improved products.

Another source of externally generated new product ideas is the millions of scientists, engineers and other companies globally. By collaborating with them, a firm can gain access to innovative solutions. Procter & Gamble leads the way by using online networks to get in touch with thousands of experts, as Marketing in Action 11.3 explains.

Anyone anywhere can connect with Procter & Gamble (P&G) through the web and share ideas. P&G taps into a vast well of expertise through its Connect + Develop programme. It practises open innovation, which is a means of accessing externally developed intellectual property while allowing its internally developed assets and know-how to be used by others. This two-way process has led to innovation in such areas as technology, engineering, marketing, packaging, design and business services. For example, Bounce, the world's first dryer-aided softener, was created by an independent Canadian inventor. By P&G and the inventor working together, this innovative product was patented and licensed and sold throughout the world. The Internet has enabled the creation of Connect + Develop hubs, joining together innovators as far and wide as China, Japan, Europe and North and South America. Febreze, which has become a billion-dollar brand for P&G, is another example of an innovation developed through the Connect + Develop programme.

The consumer is at the heart of innovation, and Bruce Brown, Chief Technology Officer for P&G, invites all innovators to submit their ideas. Through Connect + Develop, P&G actively seeks collaboration with external partners to generate and develop new product ideas. As Nabil Sakkab, global leader of its fabric and homecare research and development, commented, 'I pay 7,000 scientists to work for me at P&G but there are 1.5 million scientists out there who do not work for P&G. I want to make my R&D department 1,507,000 strong.' This attempt to 'unsource' ideas is working: 45 per cent of the new ideas he is working on have come from outside the company. Across P&G as a whole, external collaboration plays a key role in nearly 50 per cent of its products.

An example of external collaboration is the launch of Pringle Prints in North America. The product is a line of potato crisps printed with entertaining pictures and words, and was developed in record time and at a fraction of the usual cost. Instead of looking internally for solutions to the problem of how to print images on crisps, P&G searched its global networks of individuals and institutions. It discovered a small bakery in Italy, owned by a university professor who had invented an ink-jet method of printing edible images on cakes and biscuits. P&G adapted the method for crisps, and the result was double-digit growth for its North American Pringles business.

Based on: Procter & Gamble (2012); Huston and Sakkab (2006); Mitchell (2005)

A major source of good ideas is consumers themselves. Their needs may not be satisfied by existing products and they may be genuinely interested in providing ideas that lead to product improvement. Sometimes, traditional marketing research techniques such as focus groups can be useful. Other companies require a less traditional approach. Procter & Gamble, for example, has used ethnographic research to observe consumers using its products, in order to develop new and improved products. Philips has employed anthropologists and cognitive psychologists to gather insights into the needs and expectations of consumers around the world. Online, researching blogs and social community sites can reveal ideas for new products and give insights into the strengths and weaknesses of existing products, which can lead to improved product replacements.

 Scan the QR code to see the approach used by Kenco Coffee to product innovation.

In organizational markets, keeping in close contact with customers who are innovators and market leaders in their own marketplace is likely to be a fruitful source of new product ideas (Parkinson, 1982). These *lead customers* are likely to recognize required improvements ahead of other customers as they have advanced needs and are likely to face problems before other product users. For example, GE's healthcare division researches 'luminaries', who tend to be well-published doctors and research scientists from leading medical institutions. Up to 25 luminaries are brought together at regular medical advisory board sessions to discuss developments in GE's technology. GE then shares some of its advanced technology with a subset of these people. The result is a stream of new products that emerge from collaboration with these groups. Marketing research can play a role in providing feedback when the product line is familiar to customers. However, for radically new products customers may be unable to articulate their requirements and so conventional marketing research may be ineffective as a source of ideas. In this situation, as can be seen in Marketing in Action 11.4, companies need to be proactive in their search for new markets rather than rely on customer suggestions (Johne, 1992).

MARKETING IN ACTION 11.4
Creating Radical Innovation

Many new products are incremental, such as Diet Coke from Coca-Cola, or Persil Bio Action laundry capsules from Unilever; others fundamentally change the nature of a market and may be based on technological breakthroughs such as the wearable technologies like the iWatch from Apple, or the invention of new business models such as that of Google, which freely gives away its core search product for free, or Starbucks' reinvention of city-centre coffee drinking. Radical innovation is risky but can bring huge rewards, creating new markets and destroying old ones. The focus is on making the competition irrelevant by creating a leap in value for customers, and entry into new and uncontested market space.

Avoiding an incremental approach to new product development involves a sharpening of the corporate imagination to become more alive to new market opportunities. Five factors can aid this development.

1 *Escaping the tyranny of served markets*: looking outside markets that are currently served can be assisted by defining core competences and looking at products/markets that lie between existing business units. For example, Motorola's core competences in wireless technology led it to look beyond current products/markets (e.g. mobile phones) and towards global positioning satellite receivers.

2 *Searching for innovative product concepts*: this can be aided by viewing markets as a set of customer needs and product functionalities. This has led to adding an important function to an existing product (e.g. Yamaha's electronic piano), creating a new way to deliver an existing function (e.g. electronic notepads), or creating a new functionality (e.g. web browsers, search engines).

3 *Weakening traditional price–performance assumptions*: traditional price–performance assumptions should be questioned. For example, the price of drone technology, or unmanned aerial vehicles (UAVs), used to provide satellite signals to inaccessible parts, has fallen dramatically. Originally, this highly sophisticated technology cost thousands of dollars, but firms like Google and Facebook have been developing low-flying solar-powered drones to widen Internet access in remote locations, and in doing so have significantly reduced the cost. 3D Robotics is selling UAVs at less than $700.

4 *Leading customers*: a problem with developing truly innovative products is that customers rarely ask for them. Successful innovating companies lead customers by imagining unarticulated needs rather than simply following them. They gain insights into incipient needs by talking in-depth to and observing closely a market's most sophisticated and demanding customers. For example, Gillette held focus groups with female customers to find out how often they used their razors. In their focus groups, the women said they changed their razor blades regularly. However, Gillette carried out an ethnographic study by going to the homes of the women in the survey. The researchers found that the women regularly forgot to keep a supply of spare blades close to their shower. The outcome was the launch of the Venus razor with an in-shower blade dispenser making it more convenient for consumers. This also sold many more razor blades to women.

5 *Building a radical innovation hub*: a hub is a group of people who encourage and oversee innovation. It includes idea hunters, idea gatherers, internal venture capitalists, members of project evaluation committees, members of overseeing boards and experienced entrepreneurs. The hub's prime function is to nurture hunters and gatherers from all over the company to foster a stream of innovative ideas. Innovation hubs, which foster innovation and enterprise, have developed across the globe from Silicon Valley to Zurich and Helsinki.

The attitudes and practices within innovative firms are also important and help create a culture that assists in driving radical innovation. Attitudes include a tolerance for risk-taking and a future market focus that encourages managers to seek customer needs through strategic futures research. Key practices are the empowerment of product champions, which encourages them (supported by resources) to explore research and build on promising, but uncertain, future technologies, and the use of generous financial and non-financial (e.g. recognition and autonomy) rewards for innovative employees.

Based on: Belton (2015); Nadworny (2014); Moules (2013); Moosmayer and Koehn (2011); Tellis, Prabhu and Chandy (2009)

Screening

Having developed new product ideas, they need to be screened to evaluate their commercial worth. Some companies use formal checklists to help them judge whether the product idea should be rejected or accepted for further evaluation. This ensures that no important criterion is overlooked. Criteria may be used that measure the attractiveness of the market for the proposed product, the fit between the product and company objectives, and the capability of the company to produce and market the product.

Concept testing

Once the product idea has been accepted as worthy of further investigation, it can be framed into a specific concept for testing with potential customers. In many instances the basic product idea will be expanded into several product concepts, each of which can be compared by testing with target customers. For example, a study into the acceptability of a new service—a proposed audit of software development procedures that would lead to the award of a quality assurance certificate—was expressed in eight service concepts depending on which parts of the development procedure would be audited (e.g. understanding customer needs, documentation, benchmarking, and so on). Each concept was evaluated by potential buyers of the software to gauge which were the most important aspects of software development that should be audited (Jobber et al., 1989). **Concept testing** thus allows the views of customers to enter the new product development process at an early stage.

Group discussion can also be used to develop and test product concepts. The concept may be described verbally or pictorially so that the major features are understood. Potential customers can then state whether they perceive any benefits accruing from the features. A questionnaire is used to ascertain the extent of liking/disliking what is liked/disliked, the kind of person/organization that might buy the product, how/where/when/how often the product would be used, its price acceptability, and how likely they would be to buy the product.

Online marketing research is being used increasingly to test concepts, partly because of its relatively low cost. Companies such as Lego, BA, Philips and P&G have set up their own digital communities where they can test consumers' reactions to new product concepts. Considerable ingenuity is needed to research new product concepts. Some companies, such as Diageo, have developed their own highly innovative centres for concept testing. Shop Direct's user experience lab (UX lab) has been designed to help develop better understanding of online shoppers at its websites; for example very.co.uk, isme.co.uk and littlewoods.co.uk. Many innovations have emerged and contributed to Shop Direct's online success.

Often a consideration of buying intentions is a key factor in judging whether any of the concepts are worth pursuing further. In the grocery and toiletries industries, for example, companies (and their marketing research agencies) often use *action standards* (e.g. more than 70 per cent of respondents must say they intend to buy) based on past experience to judge new product concepts. Concept testing allows a relatively inexpensive judgement to be made by customers before embarking on a costly product development programme. Although concept testing is not foolproof, obvious non-starters can be eliminated early on in the process.

Business analysis

Based on the results of the concept test and considerable managerial judgement, estimates of sales, costs and profits will be made. This is the **business analysis** stage. In order to produce sensible figures a marketing analysis will need to be undertaken. This will identify the target market, its size and projected product acceptance over a number of years. Consideration will be given to various prices and the implications for sales revenue (and profits) discussed. By setting a tentative price this analysis will provide sales revenue estimates.

Costs will also need to be estimated. If the new product is similar to existing products (e.g. a brand extension) it should be fairly easy to produce accurate cost estimates. For radical product concepts, costings may be nothing more than informal 'guesstimates'.

Break-even analysis, where the quantity needed to be sold to cover costs is calculated, may be used to establish whether the project is financially feasible. *Sensitivity analysis*, in which variations from given assumptions about price, cost and customer acceptance, for example, are checked to see how they impact on sales revenue and profits, can also prove useful at this stage. Optimistic, most likely and pessimistic scenarios can be drawn up to estimate the degree of risk attached to the project.

If the product concept appears commercially feasible, this process will result in marketing and product development budgets being established based on what appears to be necessary to gain customer awareness and trial, and the work required to turn the concept into a marketable product.

Read Marketing in Action 11.5 to find out how 3D printers can turn ideas into reality.

Product development

At this stage, the new product concept is developed into a physical product. As we have seen, the trend is to move from a situation where this is the sole responsibility of the R&D and/or engineering department. Multi-disciplinary project teams are established with the task of bringing the product to the marketplace. A study by Wheelwright and Clark (1992) lays out six key principles for the effective management of such teams.

1 *Mission*: senior management must agree to a clear mission through a project charter that lays out broad objectives.
2 *Organization*: the appointment of a heavyweight project leader and a core team consisting of one member from each primary function in the company. Core members should not occupy a similar position on another team.
3 *Project plan*: creation by the project leader and core team of a contract book, which includes a work plan, resource requirements and objectives against which it is willing to be evaluated.
4 *Project leadership*: heavyweight leaders not only lead, manage and evaluate other members of the core team, they also act as product champions. They spend time talking to project contributors inside and outside the company, as well as customers and distributors, so that the team keeps in touch with the market.
5 *Responsibilities*: all core members share responsibility for the overall success of the project as well as their own functional responsibilities.
6 *Executive sponsorship*: an executive sponsor in senior management is required to act as a channel for communication with top management and to act as coach and mentor for the project and its leader.

MARKETING IN ACTION 11.5
3D Printers

3D technology is now widely available commercially. 3D printing brings manufacturing to your desktop.
3D printers create physical replicas of images from computer screens. A 3D form can be created layer by layer.

Globally, it is estimated that by 2018 the market for 3D printers will be approaching $20 billion. But this is just the beginning as more and more practical applications for this new technology emerge. According to Lisa Harouni (2011), we are witnessing 'an industrial revolution in the digital age'. This type of technology is not new; it has been around for about 20 years, but it is only now that the bespoke products built on demand are beginning to find a niche

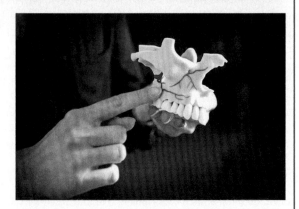

(but growing) market. There are advantages to this form of bespoke manufacturing: it is very localized and significantly reduces carbon footprints, and there is less waste too.

Currently, this technology is being increasingly used to produce body parts and medical devices. 3D printing is improving efficiency and significantly lowering the cost of production in the area of medical health. Additionally, the printers produce high quality products and have even been used to form face replicas and soft tissue used in bone grafts.

The car industry is also using 3D printer technology. Fiat Chrysler has developed models that can be used in engine testing. So, in the future we may be able to download physical goods like car parts, jewellery, phone covers and even chocolates in a similar way to which we download music, software and movies today.

Based on: Rowan (2011); Wheeler (2015)

The aim is to integrate the skills of designers, engineers and production, finance and marketing specialists so that product development is quicker, less costly and results in a high-quality product that delights customers. For example, the practice of **simultaneous engineering** means that designers and production engineers work together rather than passing the project from one stage of development to another once the first department's work is finished. Costs are controlled by a method called *target costing*. Target costs are worked out on the basis of target prices in the marketplace, and given as engineering/design and production targets.

Cutting time to market by reducing the length of the product development stage is a key marketing factor in many industries. This process, known as *virtual engineering*, has been used by Fiat, which, when designing its Bravo and 500, chose to rely solely on computer simulations rather than take the traditional route of making prototypes. This cut design-to-production time from 26 to 18 months (*The Economist*, 2008). In addition, three-dimensional CAD system designs can be shared with suppliers and customers. For example, Boeing engages customers such as British Airways and United Airlines in an online design process that allows them to engage in debates over alternative cabin layouts.

There are two reasons why product development is being accelerated. First, markets such as personal computers, digital cameras, laptops and cars change so fast that to be slow means running the risk of being out of date before the product is launched. Second, cutting time to market can lead to competitive advantage. This may be short-lived but is still valuable while it lasts. For example, Zara being consistently the fastest to market gives the company a competitive advantage in the fashion industry.

Marketing has an important role to play in the product development stage. R&D and engineering may focus on the functional aspects of the product, whereas seemingly trivial factors may have an important bearing on customer choice. For example, the foam that appears when washing-up liquid is added to water has no functional value—a washing-up liquid could be produced that cleans just as effectively but does not produce bubbles. However, the customer sees the foam as a visual cue that indicates the power of the washing-up liquid. Therefore, to market a brand that did not produce bubbles would have a negative outcome. Marketing needs to keep the project team aware of such psychological factors when developing the new product. Marketing staff need to make sure that the project team members understand and communicate the important attributes that customers are looking for in the product.

In the grocery market, marketing will usually brief R&D staff on the product concept, and the latter will be charged with the job of turning the concept into reality. For example, Yoplait, the French dairy cooperative and market leader in fruit yoghurts, found through marketing research that a yoghurt concept based on the following attributes could be a winner.

- Top-of-the-range dessert
- Position on a health–leisure scale at the far end of the pleasure range—the ultimate taste sensation
- A fruit yoghurt that is extremely thick and creamy

This was the brief given to the Yoplait research and development team that had the task of coming up with recipes for the new yoghurt and the best way of manufacturing it. Its job was to experiment with different cream/fruit combinations to produce the right product—one that matched the product concept—and to do it quickly. Time to market was crucial in this fast-moving industry. To help them, Yoplait employed a panel of expert tasters to try out the new recipes and evaluate them in terms of texture, sweetness, acidity, colour, smell, consistency and size of the fruit.

Product testing focuses on the functional aspects of the product and on consumer acceptance. Functional tests are carried out in the laboratory and out in the field to check such aspects as safety, performance and shelf life. For example, a car's braking system must be efficient, a jet engine must be capable of generating a certain level of thrust and a food package must be capable of keeping its contents fresh. Product testing of software products by users is crucially important in removing any 'bugs' that have not been picked up by internal testers. For example, Google releases new products as 'betas' (unfinished versions) so that users can check for problems and suggest improvements (Jarvis, 2009).

Market testing

So far in the development process, potential customers have been asked if they intend to buy the product but have never been placed in the position of having to pay for it. **Market testing** takes measurement of customer acceptance one crucial step further than product testing by forcing consumers to 'put their money where their mouth is'. The basic idea is to launch the new product in a limited way so that consumer response in the marketplace can be assessed. Two major methods are used: the simulated market test and test marketing.

The *simulated market test* can take a number of forms, but the principle is to set up a realistic market situation in which a sample of consumers chooses to buy goods from a range provided by the organizing company, usually a marketing research company. For example, a sample of consumers may be recruited to buy their groceries from a mobile supermarket that visits them once a week. They are provided with a magazine in which advertisements and sales promotions for the new product can appear. This method allows measurement of key success indicators such as *penetration* (the proportion of consumers that buy the new product at least once) and *repeat purchase* (the rate at which purchasers buy again) to be made. If penetration is high but repeat purchase low, buyers can be asked why they rejected the product after trial. Simulated market tests are therefore useful as a preliminary to test marketing by spotting problems, such as in packaging and product formulation, that can be rectified before test market launch. They can also be useful in eliminating new products that perform so badly compared to competition in the marketplace that test marketing is not justified. Indeed, as techniques associated with simulated market tests become more sophisticated and distributors increasingly refuse to cooperate in test marketing, they have become an attractive alternative to a full test market (Chisnall, 2005).

Test marketing involves the launch of the new product in one or a few geographical areas chosen to be representative of its intended market. Towns or television areas are chosen in which the new product is sold into distribution outlets so that performance can be gauged face to face with rival products. Test marketing is the acid test of new product development since the product is being promoted as it would during a national launch, and consumers are being asked to choose it against competitor products as they would if the new product went national. It is a more realistic test than the simulated market test and therefore gives more accurate sales penetration and repeat purchasing estimates. By projecting test marketing results to the full market, an assessment of the new product's likely success can be made.

Test marketing does have a number of potential problems. Test towns and areas may not be representative of the national market, and thus sales projections may be inaccurate. Competitors may invalidate the test market by giving distributors incentives to stock their product, thereby denying the new product shelf space. Also, test marketing needs to run over a long enough period to measure the repeat purchase rate for the product, since this is a crucial indicator of success for many products (e.g. groceries and toiletries). This can mean a delay in national launch stretching to many months or even years. In the meantime, more aggressive competitors can launch a rival product nationally and therefore gain market pioneer advantages. A final practical problem is gaining the cooperation of distributors. In some instances, supermarket chains refuse to take part in test marketing activities or charge a hefty fee for the service.

The advantages of test marketing are that the information it provides facilitates the 'go/no go' national launch decision, and the effectiveness of the marketing mix elements—price, product formulation/packaging, promotion and distribution—can be checked for effectiveness. Sometimes, a number of test areas are used with different marketing mix combinations to predict the most successful launch strategy. Its purpose therefore is to reduce the risk of a costly and embarrassing national launch mistake.

Although test marketing is commonly associated with fast-moving consumer goods, service companies use test marketing to check new service offerings. Indeed, when they control the supply chain, as is the case with banks and restaurants, they are in an ideal situation to do so. Companies selling to organizations can also benefit from test marketing when their products have short repeat purchase periods (e.g. adhesives and abrasives). For very expensive equipment, however, test marketing is usually impractical, although as we have seen product development with lead users is to be recommended.

On a global scale, many international companies roll out products (e.g. cars and consumer electronics) from one country to another. In so doing they are gaining some of the benefits of test marketing in that lessons learned early on can be applied to later launches.

Commercialization

In this section we shall examine four issues: a general approach to developing a commercialization strategy for a new product, specific options for product replacement strategies, success factors when commercializing technology, and reacting to competitors' new product introductions.

Developing a commercialization strategy for a new product

An effective commercialization strategy relies upon marketing management making clear choices regarding the target market (where it wishes to compete), and the development of a marketing strategy that provides a differential advantage (how it wishes to compete). These two factors define the new product positioning strategy, as discussed in Chapter 20.

A useful starting point for choosing a target market is an understanding of the **diffusion of innovation process** (Rogers, 2003). This explains how a new product spreads throughout a market over time. Particularly important is the notion that not all people or organizations who make up the market will be in the same state of readiness to buy the new product when it is launched. In other words, different actors in the market will have varying degrees of innovativeness— that is, their willingness to try something new. Figure 11.3 shows the *diffusion of innovation* curve which categorizes people or organizations according to how soon they are willing to adopt the innovation.

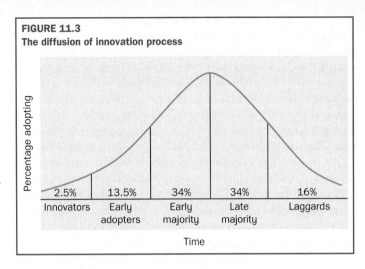

FIGURE 11.3
The diffusion of innovation process

| 2.5% | 13.5% | 34% | 34% | 16% |
| Innovators | Early adopters | Early majority | Late majority | Laggards |

Time

The curve shows that those actors (*innovators* and *early adopters*) who were willing to buy the new product soon after launch are likely to form a minor part of the total number of actors who will eventually be willing to buy it. As the new product is accepted and approved by these customers, and the decision to buy the new product therefore becomes less risky, so the people that make up the bulk of the market, comprising the *early and late majority*, begin to try the product themselves. Finally, after the product has gained full market acceptance, a group suitably described as the *laggards* adopt the product. By the time the laggards have begun buying the product, the innovators and early adopters have probably moved on to something new.

This diffusion of innovation categories has a crucial role to play in the choice of target market. The key is to understand the characteristics of the innovator and early adopter categories and target them at launch. Simply thinking about the kinds of people or organizations that are more likely to buy a new product early after launch may suffice. If not, marketing research can help. To stimulate the thinking process, Rogers suggests the following broad characteristics for each category (Rogers, 2003).

- *Innovators:* these are often venturesome and like to be different; they are willing to take a chance with an untried product. In consumer markets they tend to be younger, better educated, more confident and more financially affluent, and consequently can afford to take a chance on buying something new. In organizational markets, they tend to be larger and more profitable companies if the innovation is costly, and have more progressive, better-educated management. They may themselves have a good track record in bringing out new products and may have been the first to adopt innovations in the past. As such they may be easy to identify.
- *Early adopters:* these are not quite so venturesome; they need the comfort of knowing someone else has taken the early risk. But they soon follow their lead. They still tend to have similar characteristics to the innovator group, since they need affluence and self-confidence to buy a product that has not yet gained market acceptance. They, together with the innovators, can be seen as opinion leaders who strongly influence other people's views on the product. As such, they have a major bearing on the success of the product. One way of looking at the early adopters is that they filter the products accepted by the innovator group and popularize them, leading to acceptance by the majority of buyers in the market (Zikmund and D'Amico, 1999).
- *Early and late majorities:* these form the bulk of the customers in the market. The early majority are usually deliberate and cautious in their approach to buying products. They like to see products prove themselves on the market before they are willing to part with cash for them. The late majority are even more cautious, and possibly sceptical of new products. They are willing to adopt only after the majority of people or organizations have tried the products. Social pressure may be the driving force moving them to purchase.
- *Laggards:* these are tradition-bound people. The innovation needs to be perceived almost as a traditional product before they will consider buying it. In consumer markets they are often the older and less well-educated members of the population.

Scan the QR code to see how Samsung's Galaxy S6 smartphone advert targets early adopters.

These categories, then, can provide a basis for segmenting the market for an innovative product (see Chapter 20) and for target market selection (Easingwood and Beard, 1989). For example, Samsung Electronics directs much of its marketing effort towards the innovator/early adopter segments by targeting what it calls 'high-life seekers'—consumers who adopt technology early and are prepared to pay a premium price for it (Pesola, 2005). Note that the diffusion curve can be linked to the product lifecycle, which is discussed in Chapter 20. At introduction, innovators buy the product, followed by early adopters as the product enters the growth phase. Growth is fuelled by the early and late majority, and stable sales during the maturity phase may be due to repurchasing by these groups. Laggards may enter the market during late maturity or even decline. Thus promotion designed to stimulate trial may need to be modified as the nature of new buyers changes over time.

The second key decision for commercialization is the choice of marketing strategy to establish a differential advantage. Understanding the requirements of customers (in particular, the innovator and early adopter groups) is crucial to this process and should have taken place earlier in the new product development process. The design of the marketing mix will depend on this understanding and the rate of adoption will be affected by such decisions. For example, advertising, promotion and sales efforts can generate awareness and reduce the customer's search costs, sales promotional incentives can encourage trial, and educating users in product benefits and applications has been found to speed the adoption process (see Mahajan, Muller and Kerin, 1987; Robertson and Gatignon, 1986; Tzokas and Saren, 1992). The innovative Philips MRI scanner is an example of a company tapping in to the needs of customers in an attempt to create a differential advantage.

As we have seen, the characteristics of customers affect the rate of adoption of an innovation, and marketing's job is to identify and target those with a high willingness to adopt upon launch. The characteristics of the product being launched also affect the diffusion rate and have marketing strategy implications (see Figure 11.4).

First, its differential advantage compared to existing products affects the speed of adoption. The more added customer benefits a product gives to a customer the more customers will be willing to buy. The high differential advantage of a fax machine over sending telegrams (e.g. convenience) or letters (e.g. speed) meant fast adoption. In turn, the convenience of email over fax has meant rapid adoption. The differential advantage can be psychological. More recently, the adoption of the iPad can be explained by high functional (mobile email and Internet access) and psychological (status symbol among business people) benefits.

Second, there is the innovation's *compatibility* with consumers' values, experiences, lifestyles and behaviours. The congruence between mobile phones and the lifestyles of many young people helped their diffusion. The iPhone's rapid diffusion was also aided by such compatibility. The new product also needs to be compatible with consumers' behaviour. If its adoption depends on significant behaviour change, failure or prolonged diffusion may result. For example, the unsuccessful Dvorak typing keyboard was supposed to modestly increase typing speed, but at the behavioural cost of having to 'unlearn' the QWERTY keyboard. Although the telephone is now part of our everyday lives, diffusion was slow because its adoption required significant behaviour change (Gourville,

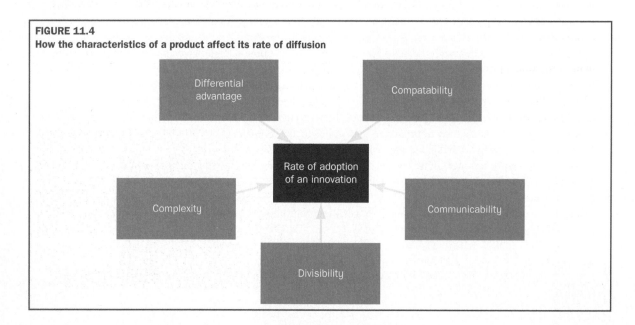

FIGURE 11.4
How the characteristics of a product affect its rate of diffusion

Differential advantage

Compatability

Complexity

Rate of adoption of an innovation

Communicability

Divisibility

2006). The diffusion of e-books has also been slow, partly because people value the tactility and aesthetics of books rather than reading from an electronic screen.

A third factor affecting diffusion rate is the innovation's *complexity*. Products that are difficult to understand or use may take longer to be adopted. For example, Apple launched its Macintosh computer backed by the proposition that existing computers were too complex to gain widespread adoption. By making its model more user friendly, it gained fast adoption among the large segment of the population that was repelled by the complexity of using computers.

Fourth, an innovation's *divisibility* also affects its speed of diffusion. Divisibility refers to the degree to which the product can be tried on a limited basis. Inexpensive products can be tried without risk of heavy financial loss. The rapid diffusion of Google was aided by the fact that its functionality could be accessed free of charge.

The final product characteristic that affects the rate of diffusion of an innovation is its *communicability*. Adoption is likely to be faster if the benefits and applications of the innovation can be readily observed or described to target customers. If product benefits are long term or difficult to quantify, then diffusion may take longer. For example, Skoda's attempt to produce more reliable cars took time to communicate, as buyers' acceptance of this claim depended on their long-term experience of driving the cars. In service industries, marketing innovations like providing more staff to improve the quality of service are hard to quantify in financial terms (i.e. extra revenue generated) and therefore have a low adoption rate by the management of some companies. The marketing implications are that marketing management must not assume that what is obvious to them will be clear to customers. They need to devise a communications strategy that allows potential customers to become aware of the innovation, and understand and be convinced of its benefits.

Product replacement strategies

As we found at the start of this chapter, product replacement is the most common form of new product introduction. A study of the marketing strategies used to position *product replacements* in the marketplace found eight approaches based on a combination of product change and other marketing modifications (i.e. marketing mix and target market changes) (Saunders and Jobber, 1994a). Figure 11.5 shows the eight replacement strategies used by companies.

1 *Facelift*: minor product change with little or no change to the rest of the marketing mix or target market. Cars are often given facelifts midway through their lifecycle by undergoing minor styling alterations; for example, Chinese and Japanese companies constantly facelift current electronic products such as cameras, LCD screen and smart televisions, tablet and laptop computers and smartphones by changing product features, a process known as **product churning**.

2 *Inconspicuous technological substitution*: a major technological change with little or no alteration of the other elements of the marketing mix. The technological change is not brought to the consumer's attention, a strategy often used by washing powder manufacturers, where the improved performance rather than the technological change is brought to the consumers' attention (e.g. Skip intelligent liquid detergent, which has Fibre Protect technology).

3 *Remerchandising*: a modification of name, promotion, price, packaging and/ or distribution, while maintaining the basic product. For example, Danone's Bio yoghurt changed to Activia; Jif cleaning products were rebranded as Cif; Orange mobile became Everything Everywhere (EE) in the UK when it merged with T-Mobile.

4 *Relaunch*: both the product and other marketing mix elements are changed. Relaunches are common in the car industry where, every four to five years, a model is replaced with an upgraded version. Sky has relaunched Sky 1, 2 and 3 channels as Sky Atlantic, Sky Living and Sky HD.

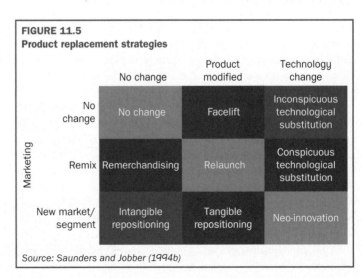

FIGURE 11.5
Product replacement strategies

	No change	Product modified	Technology change
No change	No change	Facelift	Inconspicuous technological substitution
Remix	Remerchandising	Relaunch	Conspicuous technological substitution
New market/ segment	Intangible repositioning	Tangible repositioning	Neo-innovation

(Marketing)

Source: Saunders and Jobber (1994b)

5 *Conspicuous technological substitution*: a major technological change is accompanied by heavy promotional and other mix changes to stimulate awareness and trial. An example is the replacement of the Rover Mini with the BMW Mini, which, despite remaining faithful to the character of the original, is technologically a fundamentally different car.

6 *Intangible repositioning*: the basic product is retained but other mix elements and target customers change. Diageo has retained the product (Piat D'Or wine) but is targeting a new audience of 45–50-year-old female wine drinkers. New packaging is designed to give clearer branding and shelf appeal (Fox, 2010).

7 *Tangible repositioning*: both the product and target market change. Skoda is an example of the product being significantly improved to appeal to a more upmarket, wealthier target market.

EXHIBIT 11.1
Orange mobile became Everything Everywhere (EE) in the UK when it merged with T-Mobile

8 *Neo-innovation*: a fundamental technology change accompanied by target market and mix changes. For example, Samsung's move into the sustainable energy market has seen the development of new technology for new target customers.

Companies, therefore, face an array of replacement options with varying degrees of risk. Figure 11.5 categorizes these options and provides an aid to strategic thinking when considering how to replace products in the marketplace.

Commercializing technology

Superior commercialization of technology has been, and will continue to be, a key success factor in many industries. Some companies make a significant commitment to developing the capability to bring sophisticated high-tech products to market faster than other companies that treat the commercialization process in a less disciplined manner. For example, Volkswagen spends around $13.5 billion on R&D, which is approximately 5.2 per cent of its revenue. Much of its recent investment has been on highbred vehicles and semi-autonomous features. Samsung spent a similar amount investing in smart televisions and other advanced projection devices. Intel has spent over 20 per cent of is revenue on R&D to keep pace with the demands for ever-increasing computing power. Its latest 14 nm Intel Core M processor is much smaller in size than the previous processor and has 20 per cent longer battery life and 60 per cent less energy consumption (Casey and Hackett, 2014).

Marketing's input in such situations is to provide the insight as to how the technology may provide customer benefits within a prescribed target market. For example, as we have already discussed, traditional marketing research techniques have only a limited role to play when using technology to create new markets; people find it difficult to articulate their views on subjects that are unfamiliar, and acceptance may come only over time (the diffusion of innovation). Indeed, the price the customer will be asked to pay is usually unclear during the early stage of technological development. A combination of these factors may have been responsible for the first-ever forecast for computers, which predicted worldwide sales of 10 units.

The marketing of technological innovations, therefore, calls for a blend of technology and marketing. The basic marketing question, 'What potential benefits over existing products is this product likely to provide?', needs to be asked constantly during product development.

Furthermore, the following lessons from the diffusion of innovation curve need to be remembered.

• The innovator/early adopter segments need to be identified and targeted initially.

• Initial sales are likely to be low; these groups are relatively small.

• Patience is required as the diffusion of an innovation takes time as people/organizations originally resistant to it learn of its benefits and begin to adopt it.

• The target group and message will need to be modified over time as new categories of customer enter the market.

Competitive Reaction to New Product Introductions

New product launches may be in response to new product entries by competitors. Research suggests that when confronted with a new product entry by a competitor, incumbent firms should respond quickly with a limited set of marketing mix elements. Managers should rapidly decide which ones (product, promotion, price and place) are likely to have the most impact, and concentrate their efforts on them (Gatignon, Robertson and Fein, 1997).

Competitors' reaction times to the introduction of a new product have been found to depend on four factors (Bowman and Gatignon, 1995). First, response is faster in high-growth markets. Given the importance of such markets, competitors will feel the need to take action speedily in response to a new entrant. Second, response is dependent on the market shares held by the introducing firm and its competitors. Response time is slower when the introducing firm has higher market share and faster for those competitors who have higher market share. Third, response time is faster in markets characterized by frequent product changes. Finally, it is not surprising to find that response time is related to the time needed to develop the new product.

 Scan the QR code to see how Samsung promoted its smart TV and learn about the creative ideas behind the advert.

When you have read this chapter

Discover further resources and test your understanding: McGraw-Hill **Connect**™ is a digital teaching and learning environment that improves performance over a variety of critical outcomes; it can be tailored, is easy to use and is proven effective. **LearnSmart**™ is the most widely used and intelligent adaptive learning resource that is proven to strengthen memory recall, improve course retention and boost grades. Fuelled by **LearnSmart**™, **SmartBook**™ is the first and only adaptive reading experience available today.

Review

1 **The different types of new product that can be launched**
   - There are four types of new product that can be launched: product replacements, additions to existing lines, new product lines and new-to-the-world products.

2 **How to create and nurture an innovative culture**
   - Creating and nurturing an innovative culture can be achieved by rewarding success heavily, tolerating a certain degree of failure, senior management sending clear messages about the role and importance of innovation, their words being supported by allowing staff time off to develop their own ideas, making available resources and being accessible when difficult decisions need to be taken, and resisting automatic nay-saying.

3 **The organizational options applying to new product development**
   - The options are project teams, product and brand managers, and new product departments and committees. Whichever method is used, effective cross-functional teamwork is essential for success.

4 Methods of reducing time to market

- A key method of reducing time to market is the process of simultaneous engineering. Design and production engineers, together with other staff, work together as a team rather than sequentially.
- Consumer goods companies are bringing together teams of brand and marketing managers, external design, advertising and research agency staff to develop simultaneously the brand and launch strategies.

5 How marketing and R&D staff can work together effectively

- A study by Gupta and Wileman suggests that marketing and R&D can better work together when teamwork is encouraged, there is an improvement in the provision of marketing information to R&D, R&D people are encouraged to be more customer aware, informal relationships between marketing and R&D are developed, marketing is encouraged to learn about technology, and a formal process of product development is implemented. Senior management staff have an important role to play by locating marketing and R&D close to each other, showing a personal interest in new product development, providing strategic direction, encouraging teamwork, increasing the resources devoted to new product development and enhancing their understanding of the importance of marketing in new product development.

6 The stages in the new product development process

- A formal process with review points, clear new product goals and a strong marketing orientation underlying the process leads to greater success.
- The stages are new product strategy (senior management should set objectives and priorities), idea generation (sources include customers, competitors, distributors, salespeople, engineers and marketers), screening (to evaluate their commercial worth), concept testing (to allow the views of target customers to enter the process early), product development (where the concept is developed into a physical product for testing), market testing (where the new product is tested in the marketplace) and commercialization (where the new product is launched).

7 How to stimulate the corporate imagination

- Four ways of stimulating the corporate imagination are: to encourage management to escape the tyranny of served markets by exploring how core competences can be exploited in new markets; to search for innovative product concepts—for example, by creating a new way to deliver an existing function (e.g. the electronic notepad); questioning traditional price–performance assumptions and giving engineers the resources to develop cheaper new products; and gaining insights by observing closely the market's most sophisticated and demanding customers.

8 The six key principles of managing product teams

- These are the agreement of the mission, effective organization, development of a project plan, strong leadership, shared responsibilities, and the establishment of an executive sponsor in senior management.

9 The diffusion of innovation categories and their marketing implications

- The categories are innovators, early adopters, early and late majorities, and laggards.
- The marketing implications are that the categories can be used as a basis for segmentation and targeting (initially the innovator/early adopters should be targeted). As the product is bought by different categories, so the marketing mix may need to change.
- The speed of adoption can be affected by marketing activities—for example, advertising to create awareness, sales promotion to stimulate trial, and educating users in product benefits and applications.
- The nature of the innovation itself can also affect adoption—that is, the strength of its differential advantage, its compatibility with people's values, experiences, lifestyles and behaviours, its complexity, its divisibility and its communicability.

10 The key ingredients in commercializing technology quickly and effectively

- The key ingredients are the ability of technologists and marketing people to work together effectively, simultaneous engineering, constantly asking the question 'What benefits over existing products is this new product likely to provide?', and remembering lessons from the diffusion of innovation curve (i.e. target the innovator/early adopter segments first).

Key Terms

brainstorming the technique where a group of people generate ideas without initial evaluation; only when the list of ideas is complete is each idea then evaluated

business analysis a review of the projected sales, costs and profits for a new product to establish whether these factors satisfy company objectives

concept testing testing new product ideas with potential customers

diffusion of innovation process the process by which a new product spreads throughout a market over time

innovation the commercialization of an invention by bringing it to market

invention the discovery of new methods and ideas

market testing the limited launch of a new product to test sales potential

product churning a continuous and rapid spiral of new product introductions

project teams the bringing together of staff from such areas as R&D, engineering, manufacturing, finance and marketing to work on a project such as new product development

simultaneous engineering the involvement of manufacturing and product development engineers in the same development team in an effort to reduce development time

test marketing the launch of a new product in one or a few geographic areas chosen to be representative of the intended market

Study Questions

1. Try to think of an unsatisfied need that you feel could be solved by the introduction of a new product. How would you set about testing your idea to examine its commercial potential?

2. How would you go about evaluating the idea?

3. What are the advantages and disadvantages of test marketing? In what circumstances should you be reluctant to use test marketing?

4. Your company has developed a new range of Thai curry sauce, intended to compete with the market leader. How would you conduct product tests for your new line?

5. What are the particular problems associated with commercializing technology? What are the key factors for success?

6. Discuss how marketing and R&D can form effective teams to develop new products.

Recommended Reading

Atuahene-Gima, K. (1996) Market orientation and innovation, *Journal of Business Research* 35(2) 93–103.

Fossas-Olalla, M., B. Minguela-Rata, J. López-Sánchez and J. Fernández-Menénde (2015) Product Innovation: when should suppliers begin to collaborate? *Journal of Business Research* 68(7), July, 1404–06.

Holman, R., H. Kaas and D. Keeling (2003) The future of product development, *McKinsey Quarterly* 3, 28–40.

Manu, F. and V. Sriram (1996) Innovation, marketing strategy, environment and performance, *Journal of Business Research* 35(1), January, 79–91.

Rogers, E. M. (2010) *Diffusion of innovations*, Simon and Schuster.

Tellis, G. (2013) *Unrelenting Innovation*, John Wiley & Sons Inc.

References

3M (2012) Who we are, http://solutions.3m.co.uk/wps/portal/3M/en_GB/about-3M/information/about/us.

Adler, P. S., H. E. Riggs and S. C. Wheelwright (1989) Product Development Know-How, *Sloan Management Review* 4, 7–17.

Belton, P. (2015). Game of drones: As prices plummet drones are taking off, BBC.co.uk, 16 January. http://www.bbc.co.uk/news/business-30820399

Bergen, S. A., R. Miyajima and C. P. McLaughlin (1988) The R&D/Production Interface in Four Developed Countries, *R&D Management* 18(3), 201–16.

Booz, Allen and Hamilton (1982) *New Products Management for the 1980s*, New York: Booz, Allen and Hamilton, Inc.

Boston Consulting Group (2012) The Most Innovative Companies 2012, Boston Consulting Group. https://www.bcgperspectives.com/content/articles/growth_innovation_the_most_innovative_companies_2012/?chapter=4 (accessed 20 April 2015).

Bowman, D. and H. Gatignon (1995) Determinants of Competitor Response Time to a New Product Introduction, *Journal of Marketing Research* 33, February, 42–53. Brentani, U. de (1991) Success Factors in Developing New Business Services, *European Journal of Marketing* 15(2), 33–59

Casey, M. and R. Hackett (2014) The 10 biggest R&D spenders worldwide, *Fortune*, 17 November. http://fortune.com/2014/11/17/top-10-research-development (accessed 20 April 2015).

Chisnall, P. (2005) *Marketing Research*, Maidenhead: McGraw-Hill.

Cooper, R. G. (1979) The Dimensions of Industrial New Product Success and Failure, *Journal of Marketing* 43 (Summer), 93–103;

Cooper, R. G. and E. J. Kleinschmidt (1986) An Investigation into the New Product Process: Steps, Deficiencies and Impact, *Journal of Product Innovation Management*, June, 71–85.

Day, P. (2012), http://www.bbc.co.uk/programmes/b01gvtjj.

Doyle, P. (1997) From the Top, *Guardian*, 2 August, 17.

Duggan, M. (2012) Frugal innovation, http://knowinnovation.com/frugal-innovation/

Dwyer, L. M. (1990) Factors Affecting the Proficient Management of Product Innovation, *International Journal of Technological Management* 5(6), 721–30.

Easingwood, C. and C. Beard (1989) High Technology Launch Strategies in the UK, *Industrial Marketing Management* 18, 125–38.

Fox, P. (2010) Piat d'Or launches first Sauvignon Blanc, http://www.talkingretail.com/products/drinks-news/piat-dor-launches-first-sauvignon-blanc, 1 July.

Fred, D. (1991) Learning the Ropes: My Life as a Product Champion, *Harvard Business Review*, Sept.–Oct, 46–56.

Gatignon, H., T. S. Robertson and A. J. Fein (1997) Incumbent Defence Strategies Against New Product Entry, *International Journal of Research in Marketing* 14, 163–76.

Geoghegan, J. (2011) Satnavs and smartphones put traditional maps on the road to nowhere as sales drop massively, The Mail online, http://www.dailymail.co.uk/sciencetech/article-2033227/Satnavs-smart-phones-traditional-maps-road-sales-drop-massively.html#ixzz1rwFKziSX, 3 September.

Gourville, J. (2006) The Curse of Innovation: Why Innovative Products Fail, MSI Report No. 05-117.

Govindarajan, V. and S. Srinivas (2013) The Innovation Mindset in Action: 3M Corporation, *Harvard Business review*, 6 August. https://hbr.org/2013/08/the-innovation-mindset-in-acti-3 (accessed 20 April 2015).

Gupta, A. K. and D. Wileman (1990) Improving R&D/Marketing Relations: R&D Perspective, *R&D Management* 20(4), 277–90.

Gupta, A. K. and D. Wileman (1991) Improving R&D/Marketing Relations in Technology Based Companies: Marketing's Perspective, *Journal of Marketing Management* 7(1), 25–46.

Hamel, G. and C. K. Prahalad (1991) Corporate Imagination and Expeditionary Marketing, *Harvard Business Review*, July–August, 81–92.

Harouni, L. (2011) A Primer on 3d Printing https://www.ted.com/talks/lisa_harouni_a_primer_on_3d_printing?language=en (accessed August 2015).

Hegarty, W. H. and R. C. Hoffman (1990) Product/Market Innovations: A Study of Top Management Involvement among Four Cultures, *Journal of Product Innovation Management* 7, 186–99.

Hise, R. T., L. O'Neal, A. Parasuraman and J. U. McNeal (1990) Marketing/R&D Interaction in New Product Development: Implications for New Product Success Rates, *Journal of Product Innovation Management* 7, 142–55.

Honey Bee (n.d.) http://www.sristi.org/hbnew

Huston, L. and N. Sakkab (2006) Connect and Develop: Inside Procter & Gamble's New Model for Innovation, *Harvard Business Review* 84(3), 58–72.

Jarvis, J. (2009) The Foresight of Google, *Media Guardian*, 9 February, 8.

Jobber, D., J. Saunders, G. Hooley, B. Gilding and J. Hatton-Smooker (1989) Assessing the Value of a Quality Assurance Certificate for Software: An Exploratory Investigation, *MIS Quarterly*, March, 19–31.

Johne, A. (1992) Don't Let Your Customers Lead You Astray in Developing New Products, *European Management Journal* 10(1), 80–4.

Johne, A. and C. Storey (1998) New Source Development: A Review of the Literature and Annotated Bibliography, *European Journal of Marketing* 32(3/4), 184–251.

Johne, A. and P. Snelson (1988) Auditing Product Innovation Activities in Manufacturing Firms, *R&D Management* 18(3), 227–33.

Joshi, A. W. and S. Sharma (2004) Customer Knowledge Development: Antecedents and Impact on New Product Performance, *Journal of Marketing*, 68 (October), 47–9.

Jugaad (2012) http://www.jugaad.org/?page_id=2.

Kadri, M. (2010) Finding innovation in every corner, http://changeobserver.designobserver.com/feature/findinginnovation-in-every-corner/12691/, 2 August.

Kashami, K. and T. Clayton (2000)—study reported in Murphy, D. Innovate or Die, *Marketing Business*, May, 16–18.

Koshler, R. (1991) Produkt—Innovation as management als Erfolgsfaktor, in Mueller-Boehling, D. *et al.* (eds) *Innovations— und Technologiemanagement*, Stuttgart: C. E. Poeschel Verlagi.

Kovacs, J. (2012) 3M and NJATC Join Forces to Develop Online Curriculum for All IBEW/NECA Electrical Workers, press release, 10 April, Market Watch, *Wall Street Journal*.

Levitt, T. (1960) Marketing Myopia, *Harvard Business Review*, July–August.

Mahajan, V., E. Muller and R. Kerin (1987) Introduction Strategy for New Product with Positive and Negative Word-of-Mouth, *Management Science* 30, 1389–404.

Maidique, M. A. and B. J. Zirger (1984) A Study of Success and Failure in Product Innovation: The Case of the US Electronics Industry, *IEEE Transactions in Engineering Management*, EM-31 (November), 192–203.

Matthews, V. (2002) Caution Versus Creativity, *Financial Times*, 17 June, 12.

McGregor, J. (2006) The World's Most Innovative Companies, *Business Week*, 24 April, 63–76.

Mitchell, A. (2005) After Some Innovation? Perhaps You Just Need to Ask Around, *Marketing Week*, 16 June, 28–9.

Moosmayer, D. C. and A. Koehn (2011) The moderating role of managers' uncertainty avoidance values on the performance impact of radical and incremental innovation, *International Journal of Business Research* 11(6), 32–39.

Moules, J. (2013) Tech start-ups: Innovation hubs all over world seek to follow Silicon Valley lead, *The Financial Times*, 11 June. http://www.ft.com/cms/s/2/e357a258-b3d2-11e2-b5a5-00144feabdc0.html#axzz3YdUGITLb (accessed 20 April 2015).

Nadworny, R. (2014) Observe your cusomters to unlock innovation, Burlington Free press, 18 December. http://www.burlingtonfreepress.com/story/money/industries/2014/12/18/nadworny-observe-customers-unlock-innovation/20554685

Parkinson, S. T. (1982) The Role of the User in Successful New Product Development, *R&D Management* 12, 123–31.

Pearson, D. (1993) Invent, Innovate and Improve, *Marketing*, 8 April, 15.

Pesola, M. (2005) Samsung Plays to the Young Generation, *Financial Times*, 29 March, 11.

Prahalad, C. K. and R. A. Mashelkar (2010) Innovation's Holy Grail, *Harvard Business Review*, July–August.

Procter & Gamble (2012) Connect + develop, http://www.pg.com/connect_develop/index.shtml.

Richard, H. (1996) Why Competitiveness is a Dirty Word in Scandinavia, *European*, 6–12 June, 24.

Robertson, T. S. and H. Gatignon (1986) Competitive Effects on Technology Diffusion, *Journal of Marketing* 50 (July), 1–12.

Rogers, E. M. (2003) *Diffusion of Innovations*, New York: Free Press.

Rowan, D. (2011) 3D printing—an industrial revolution in the digital age? *IWired*, 9 May, http://www.wired.com/epicenter/2011/05/3d-printing-an-industrial-revolution-in-the-digital-age.

Saunders, J. and D. Jobber (1994a) Product Replacement Strategies: Occurrence and Concurrence, *Journal of Product Innovation Management* (November).

Saunders, J. and D. Jobber (1994b) Strategies for Product Launch and Deletion, in Saunders, J. (ed.) *The Marketing Initiative*, Hemel Hempstead: Prentice-Hall, 227.

Shah, A. (2012) Causes of poverty, http://www.globalissues.org/issue/2/causes-of-poverty, 8 April.

Shrivastava, P. and W. E. Souder (1987) The Strategic Management of Technological Innovation: A Review and a Model, *Journal of Management Studies* 24(1), 24–41.

Slotegraaf, R. J. and K. Atuahene-Gima (2011) Product Development Team Stability and New Product Advantage: The Role of Decision-Making Processes, *Journal of Marketing* 75(1), 96–108.

Tellis, G., J. C. Prabhu and R. K. Chandy (2009) Radical Innovation Across Nations: The Preeminence of Corporate Culture, *Journal of Marketing* 73(1), 3–23.

The Economist (2008) Rebirth of a Carmaker, 26 April, 91–3.

The Economist (2012) Asian Innovation, http://www.economist.com/node/21551028, 24 March.

The Marketers (2008) Marketing Greats, May, 7.

Tzokas, N. and M. Saren (1992) Innovation Diffusion: The Emerging Role of Suppliers Versus the Traditional Dominance of Buyers, *Journal of Marketing Management* 8(1), 69–80.

Viklund, A. (2015) Brainstorming, http://teamvirtute.wordpress.com/promotingcreativity/brainstorming/.

Walsh, W. J. (1990) Get the Whole Organisation Behind New Product Development, *Research in Technological Management*, Nov.–Dec., 32–6.

Wheeler, A. (2015) 3D Printing Industry, *3D Printing Industry*, 23 April. http://3dprintingindustry.com/3dp-applications

Wheelwright, S. and K. Clark (1992) *Revolutionizing Product Development*, New York: Free Press.

Zikmund, W. G. and M. D'Amico (1999) *Marketing*, St Paul, MN: West.

CASE 21
In the Dragons' Den

New product development is a risky business and most new products fail. To succeed, innovations not only need to provide better solutions but must also deliver improved benefits to users and profits to the manufacturers. Successful innovations can secure a company's future. Business legend, Steve Jobs, is said to have saved Apple from bankruptcy with a new computer: iMac. This was an innovation in computing, which provided straightforward access to the Internet for the individual. At the time desktop computers were not specially designed to provide easy access to the Internet, so the iMac occupied a unique market position, offering better solutions and benefits than competing products. Apple invested heavily in this new design and the risk paid off as the iMac sold millions of units. Apple has continued to use innovation as a central part of its marketing strategy, and the iPod, iPhone and iPad are innovative products that have enabled the company to become a world-leading brand. The company continues to produce new products and services such as the iWatch and Apple Pay (which enables contactless payments through iPhone) to sustain its market growth strategy. However, such investment is not for the faint-hearted. New product development is expensive and risky and requires management time and commitment.

The new product development process (discussed in Chapter 11) highlights the stages a product is likely to pass through before eventually reaching its intended markets. Large corporations tend to have formal organizational structures designed to facilitate and support the innovation development process. However, in small and medium-sized enterprises such structures often do not exist, and the resources and capabilities required to make such investment work are often not readily available. Sometimes entrepreneurial innovators need to find financial investors and management expertise from outside the business to help support, develop and commercialize their ideas.

The Dragons

Dragons' Den is a BBC television series which gives real entrepreneurs and inventors three minutes to pitch their ideas, with the aim of attracting financial investment and management expertise from the multimillionaire Dragons.

Potential investors (Dragons) include: Peter Jones, who founded the Phones International Group, a multimillion-pound telecoms company; Deborah Meaden, formally Director of Weststar Holidays and now full-time investor; and Nick Jenkins, founder of Moonpig.com, the online greetings card business. Nick is no stranger to the struggles and challenges an entrepreneur faces when establishing a new business; it took him five years and many rounds of fundraising to build Moonpig into a successful brand that is recognized worldwide. Nick now uses his knowledge and expertise to invest in technology start-ups and enjoys helping new entrepreneurs to manage the risks they face in the early days of developing their businesses.

Together, the Dragons have a wealth of experience spanning many industrial sectors and the business experience and financial resources to offer to entrepreneurs who enter the Den with a convincing business proposition. However, budding entrepreneurs must be ready to show they know a great deal about their innovation, what they aim to achieve with their business idea, and why their idea will be a success, and to exhibit personal passion and commitment.

The Entrepreneurs

Many entrepreneurs have entered the Den. Some have successfully secured investment, of which perhaps the most notable example is Levi Roots, who attracted the attention of the Dragons by entering the Den and singing his way to success with his innovative recipe for hot, spicy barbecue sauce called 'Reggae Reggae Sauce'. Levi secured £50,000 of investment from two Dragons in return for a 40 per cent share of his business. The brand has subsequently developed and expanded. New product ranges include soft drinks, snacks and chilled ready meals such as Levi Roots Curried Chicken Noodles and Reggae Reggae Pasta, which is even part of Birds Eye's new range of frozen foods. Additionally, Levi has written several cookery books, which offer different ways to use his products. (Find out more about Reggae Reggae Sauce at http://www.reggae-reggae.co.uk.)

However, others have failed to secure funding in the Den but still gone on to develop their products and grow their businesses:

- Shaun Pulfrey had a problem—how to deal with tangled wet hair—and so he invented the Tangle Teezer. He went to the Dragons' Den and wanted around £80,000 for a 15 per cent investment in his business, but was unsuccessful. His idea was in the form of a brush, which worked differently—by 'flicking and teasing hair apart' rather than by pulling the bristles through the hair. Nevertheless, this proved to be a successful idea and from a small manufacturing base in Oxford (with much publicity from Shaun's appearance on the show) Shaun was able to grow his business and make the Tangle Teezer into a top-selling hair brush. (Find out more about the Tangle Teezer at http://www.tangleteezer.com).

- Rob Law created a product called Trunki, which is a rideable suitcase for under-6s. The Dragons rejected the pitch for help to produce and market this innovative new product. After the rejection, Rob battled ahead, using his knowledge from his earlier successes in design innovations. He believed in this product, and by 2011 over 20 per cent of three- to six-year-olds in the UK owned one of the ride-on, pull-along suitcases. (Find out more about Rob's inspiration for developing Trunki and the challenges he faced along the way at http://www.designcouncil.org.uk/news-opinion/how-i-created-successful-brand-rob-law-trunki.)

Developing a Commercialization Strategy

Before making an investment, the Dragons intensely question the entrepreneurs about why they need the money, how it will be spent and why the idea is going to work. Many of the entrepreneurs fail to convince the Dragons to invest, sometimes due to lack of market potential, lack of compatibility with potential customer values, or the presence of high risk. Ultimately, the success of an innovation relies heavily on developing a commercialization strategy that identifies the right target market and marketing strategy that can monetize

the differential advantage offered by the product. The diffusion of the innovation process helps to explain how innovative products spread through market over time, and this model highlights the importance of the concept 'readiness'. In other words, if sufficient customers in a particular target market are not willing to try a product, then it is likely to fail. So, innovative entrepreneurs need to understand the extent to which their target customers are willing to try something new. Their willingness is also likely to be affected by the characteristics of the product and the extent to which it offers advantage over existing market offers. Ultimately, the characteristics of the product affect its rate of diffusion over time.

Questions

1. Reggae Reggae Sauce, Tangle Teezer and Trunki are three examples of innovations which have successfully been commercialized. Imagine you are responsible for new product development and wish to seek investment in the Den for a new product idea but you want to get some ideas of how other innovations have been successful before developing your own commercialization strategy and the pitch for the Dragons.

2. Use the characteristics of a product which are likely to affect its rate of diffusion (see Figure 11.4 earlier in the chapter) to determine why Reggae Reggae Sauce, Tangle Teezer and Trunki have been successfully accepted by their target markets.

3. Select one of these products and then suggest which of its characteristics offer the greatest potential for communicating the benefits of the product to the target audience.

4. Sketch out a new product idea and then write an executive summary, which gives an outline of the product, the problem(s) it will solve and explain your passion and commitment to making this innovation work.

This case study was written by Fiona Ellis-Chadwick, Senior Lecturer, Loughborough University.

References

Based on: BBC Media Centre (2015) Three New Dragons enter The Den for Series 13, http://www.bbc.co.uk/mediacentre/latestnews/2015/new-dragons-s13 (accessed July 2015); Design Council (2015) How I created a successful brand: Rob Law of Trunki, http://www.designcouncil.org.uk/news-opinion/how-i-created-successful-brand-rob-law-trunki

CASE 22
Clorox: Bringing Innovation to Everyday Products

Clorox, the century-old consumer goods maker, has done the impossible: it has found a way to make bleach and other home cleaning products exciting. The company produces some of the most well-known, and best-selling, brands on the market: Clorox, Glad, Hidden Valley, Kingsford and Brita are just a few of the names that you can find on the shelves of your local store worldwide. (A reported 80 per cent of Clorox's brands are ranked as either first or second according to market share.) It has achieved its current level of marketing success due in no small part to its focus on innovation and product development, as well as brand management.

Meeting and surpassing consumer expectations is a key element to Clorox's success, which it achieves thanks to effective marketing research initiatives. Selling products in over 100 countries, the company is constantly looking to improve the performance of its consumer goods as well as identify niche markets or markets that are currently underserved. One example is the company's line of products that claims to be 'sustainable' or 'environmentally friendly'. Growth in this one sector alone accounted for a 40 per cent increase in sales between 2007 and 2012. Clorox also practises what it preaches, boasting that improvements to its facilities resulted in a $15 million decrease in annual operating costs and a reduction in energy and water usage. In an effort to be a more responsible and transparent corporate citizen, the company recently released a smart phone app that shows the ingredients of some of its products.

An example of the company developing innovative ways to better serve previously ignored markets is its 2012 creation of the Clorox Fragancia marketing platform. This incorporated items from the Floor, Toilets and Bathrooms and Air Care lines into one cohesive ad campaign aimed at Hispanics in the US market. Commercials were aired on two major television channels serving the Hispanic community in the USA (Telemundo and Univision). The campaign also included the use of radio, digital media and coupon mailings. All communication was in Spanish. This was reportedly the first time that a line of home cleaning products was specifically designed and marketed to Hispanics living in the USA.

Clorox sees the future business environment as being defined by four different trends or dimensions

(the company refers to them as 'megatrends'): health and wellness, affordability, sustainability and multicultural. Rest assured that Clorox plans on developing new products or adapting existing products to take advantage of the expected evolution that its markets will undergo. Not content to just rely on creativity to drive new growth, the company reportedly plans on increasing the amount of money it spends on marketing as well. In a drive to make its product line more cohesive, Clorox has also got rid of brands that were not seen as being essential or well integrated with other products, like the Armor All line of car cleaning products, which the company sold off a few years ago.

Traditionally, companies making products for use in the home have done everything possible to improve supply chain efficiencies in an effort to reduce costs, and then reinvested those savings into increased spending on research and development (R&D) and new marketing initiatives. Clorox has said that it would eventually like spending on marketing to equal 10–11 per cent of sales. Unfortunately, a lot of the 'low hanging fruit' regarding savings has most likely already been picked, and demand in the consumer goods market in the USA is expected to be soft in the immediate future (an estimated 80 per cent of Clorox's profits come from the USA). The negative effects of this should be mitigated by the fact that the vast majority of the company's brands are either number one or number two in their markets, giving

Clorox some leverage with regard to maintaining prices or even slightly increasing them (a strong competitive advantage).

Clorox has another advantage which might not be obvious at first. Its headquarters is located in the San Francisco Bay Area, in Oakland, not too far from the high-tech centre of the universe known as Silicon Valley. While the company does not make smartphones or digital music players, Clorox says that it benefits from its close proximity to companies that do. The Bay Area is a vibrant, culturally diverse region, with highly skilled and highly educated workers and consumers. This makes recruitment, as well as carrying out informed market research to discover new trends and possible new products, much easier. To promote creativity and new ideas even more, Clorox has its own in-house consumer learning centre, as well as an innovation centre. The company spends a reported $130 million a year on R&D (over 2 per cent of annual sales) and has a dedicated team of 300 scientists and engineers trying to come up with new ideas. All of this should hopefully keep the company at the cutting edge of developing new consumer goods products.

One example of this commitment to innovation is the company's popular Glad brand of garbage bags. A person would be forgiven for thinking that there is only so much that could be done to improve a plastic bag, but the people who work in product development at Clorox do not think this. Designers there figured out a way to make trash bags more flexible or 'stretchy'. They also added deodorants in order to reduce the unpleasant odour associated with garbage and garbage bags. Not exactly the technical equivalent of sending a man to the moon, but a creative innovation none the less that could give Clorox an advantage over rivals.

An area that is expected to see somewhat robust growth is the market for bacteria-killing disinfectant, a product that was no doubt aided by the massive amounts of media coverage given to the ebola epidemic of 2014 in West Africa. An estimated 100,000 Americans die each year from infections that they pick up during a hospital stay. This is a serious problem that hospitals, the government and insurance providers are looking to address. In a rare misstep, Clorox has been found to be a bit slow off the mark in relation to its main (and much larger) competitor, Procter & Gamble, whose new product line of disinfectants already meets rigorous European Union standards for use in the areas of hygiene and sanitation. In the short term, Clorox plans to address falling sales in this sector through the better promotion and marketing of its disinfecting wipes. Longer term,

the company is working with an outside partner to develop ultraviolet lighting systems to better help identify and kill infections.

When it comes to ingenuity in marketing campaigns, Clorox has developed what it calls its '3D demand-creation model'. This involves creating a 'desire' (making the consumer aware of and interested in its products), making people decide (influencing the consumer at the point of purchase) and providing delight (a positive experience using the product). The company believes that this focused and methodical way of interacting with customers is critical, given the explosive growth in the number of channels through which consumers can be reached. Digital communication and e-commerce capabilities are seen as being key elements in providing higher levels of customer satisfaction, as well as giving the company the ability to better adapt and personalize its products for a given market.

Clorox even talks of creativity and product improvement in terms of 'cost-o-vation'—that is to say, in terms of reducing costs while at the same time making a product better. An example of this was the decision to make Clorox bleach 33 per cent more concentrated, which resulted in using less raw material, lower transportation costs, lower greenhouse gas emissions, improved product performance and an increase in sales. Not bad for a company that was founded at the turn of the last century with an initial capital investment of only $500 and a dream of making liquid bleach.

Questions   ![Mc Graw Hill Education] **connect**

1. **How has Clorox achieved its current level of marketing success and how does it plan to maintain this success?**

2. **How has the company developed innovative products to serve the market and how has this given the company a competitive advantage? Give examples.**

3. **How does Clorox manage innovation?**

4. **Explain why the company's '3D demand-creation model' is innovative and how the company believes that it will reach and serve consumers better?**

This case study was written by Tom McNamara and Asha Moore-Mangin, the ESC Rennes School of Business.

»

References

Based on: Calvey, M. (2014) Clorox: Innovation is one of its brands, *San Francisco Business Times, 28 March,* http://www.bizjournals .com/sanfrancisco/print-edition/2014/03/28/clorox-innovation -wayne-delker-pleasanton.html; Equity Watch (2014) Clorox Company Making All The Right Moves To Keep Its Future Secured, Equity Watch, through Seeking Alpha, July 1, http://seekingalpha.com/ article/2295125-clorox-company-making-all-the-right-moves-to -keep-its-future-secured; Portada (2012) Clorox Introduces Clorox Fragancia Marketing Platform / Ad Campaign, Portada, 16 July, http://www.portada-online.com/2012/07/16/clorox-introduces -clorox-fragancia-marketing-platform-ad-campaign/#ixzz3PwzYTrjo; Willow Street Investments (2015) Clorox: Strong Brands, Product Innovation And Pricing Power Will Reward Shareholders,Willow Street Investments, through Seeking Alpha, 2 January, http://seekingalpha. com/article/2792845-clorox-strong-brands-product-innovation- and-pricing-power-will-reward-shareholders; Neff, J. (2014) Despite Sluggish Value-Focused Market, Dorer Sees Room for Growth, Ad Age, 24 September, 2014, http://adage.com/article/cmo-strategy/ clorox-ceo-follow-p-g-marketing-cuts/295112; Portada (2012)

Marketer Interview- Clorox's David Cardona: 'Research guides our Innovation Strategy', Portada, 17 July, http://www.portada-online. com/2012/07/17/marketer-interview-cloroxs-david-cardona-research -guides-our-innovation-strategy/#ixzz3Q2kv35vW; Kaye, L. (2014) New Clorox App Allows Consumers to See More Ingredients Inside, Triple Pundit, 13 October, http://www.triplepundit.com/2014/10/ new-clorox-app-allows-consumers-see-ingredients-inside; Market Watch (2013) The Clorox Company Introduces 2020 Strategy to Drive Long-Term Growth, Market Watch, 3 October, http://www.marketwatch .com/story/the-clorox-company-introduces-2020-strategy-to-drive -long-term-growth-2013-10-03/print; Neff, J. (2014) 'We're Not Your Father's Clorox': CEO Don Knauss Talks Marketing, Ad Age,March 24, http://adage.com/article/cmo-strategy/clorox-ceo-don-knauss -talks-marketing/292209; Ferry, D. (2013) What Makes Clorox One of America's Best Companies, The Motley Fool, 27 February, http:// www.fool.com/investing/general/2013/02/27/what-makes-clorox -one-of-americas-best-companies.aspx; Neff, J. (2014) Why New Clorox CEO Won't Mimic Alma Mater P&G's Marketing Cuts Despite Sluggish Value-Focused Market, Dorer Sees Room for Growth, Ad Age, 24 September, http://adage.com/article/cmo-strategy/ clorox-ceo-follow-p-g-marketing-cuts/295112

CHAPTER 12
Value Through Pricing

LEARNING OBJECTIVES

After reading this chapter, you should be able to:

1 explain the economist's approach to price determination

2 distinguish between full-cost and direct-cost pricing

3 discuss your understanding of going-rate pricing and competitive bidding

4 explain the advantages of market-orientated pricing over cost and competitor-orientated pricing

5 discuss the factors that affect price setting when using a market-orientated approach

6 identify when and how to initiate price increases and cuts

7 identify when and when not to follow competitor-initiated price increases and cuts; when to follow quickly and when to follow slowly

8 discuss ethical issues in pricing

P rice is the odd-one-out of the marketing mix, because it is the revenue earner. The price of a product is what the company gets back in return for all the effort that is put into producing and marketing the product. The other three elements of the marketing mix—product, promotion and place—are costs. Therefore, no matter how good the product, how creative the promotion or how efficient the distribution, unless price covers costs the company will make a loss. Therefore, managers need to understand how to set prices, because both undercharging (lost margin) and overcharging (lost sales) can have dramatic effects on profitability.

The obvious way of adding value to an offering is to cut price. However, this can be a dangerous tactic since it can lead to price wars and can damage perceptions of the brand. In this chapter, we will consider how pricing can be used as a strategic weapon to achieve corporate and brand objectives without necessarily cutting price.

One of the key factors that marketing managers need to remember is that price is just one element of the marketing mix. Price should not be set in isolation; it should be blended with product, promotion and place to form a coherent mix that provides superior customer value. The sales of many products, particularly those that are a form of self-expression—such as drinks, cars, perfume and clothing—could suffer from prices that are too low. As we shall see, price is an important part of positioning strategy since it often sends quality cues to customers.

Understanding how to set prices is an important aspect of marketing decision-making, not least because of changes in the competitive arena that many believe will act to drive down prices in many countries. One major force is technological change, as Marketing in Action 12.1 explains. Since price is a major determinant of profitability, developing a coherent pricing strategy assumes major significance.

Many people's introduction to the issue of pricing is a course in economics. We will now consider, very briefly, some of the ideas discussed by economists when considering price.

Economists' Approach to Pricing

Although a full discussion of the approach taken by economists to pricing is beyond the scope of this chapter, the following gives a flavour of some of the important concepts relating to price. The discussion will focus on demand since this is of fundamental importance in pricing. Economists talk of the *demand curve* to conceptualize the relationship between the quantity demanded and different price levels. Figure 12.1 shows a typical demand curve.

MARKETING IN ACTION 12.1
Technology Drivers of Price

Technology is having a major impact on prices. First, the Internet has spawned price-comparison sites such as Kelkoo and PriceRunner that allow consumers, at the click of a button, to check prices to find bargains. Before the Internet, consumers often needed to spend time and money searching retail outlets for the best offers. Auction houses, the most successful of which is eBay, have allowed the creation of virtual marketplaces where sellers and buyers can trade products and arrive at prices by competitive bidding.

The Internet has also facilitated the growth of yield management systems that allow price to change according to supply and demand. American Airlines was the pioneer in developing yield management, and the system has been adopted by other airlines such as easyJet, hotel chains such as Premier Inn, and intercity bus companies such as Megabus in the UK and Onnibus in Finland. Using hotels as an example, when a room is first offered on the market, the price is typically set low to attract customers. As the hotel moves closer to full capacity, the price rises by an amount that is dependent on demand. If demand is low, the price rise will be small or the price could even fall, but if demand is high, meaning that there are very few rooms available, the price will rise sharply. Customers are never told how soon or by how much the price will be changed. The objective is to maximize occupancy and thereby revenue (yield), because when selling airline or bus seats or hotel rooms, vacancies cannot be stored; if seats or rooms are not occupied, the revenue from them is lost. The system is based on sophisticated statistical modelling with the key variable being the number of seats/rooms unsold, but other factors, such as the number of clicks on the website, also have an effect on price, as a high number of clicks is often indicative of forthcoming sales.

Technological forces are also driving down the cost of manufacture, with consequent price reductions. For example, the prices of DVD players, camcorders and mobile phones have fallen over recent years as advances in technology and economies of scale have driven down costs.

At a price of P_1, demand is Q_1. As price drops so demand rises. Thus at P_2 demand increases to Q_2. For some products, a given fall in price leads to a large increase in demand. The demand for such products is said to be *price elastic*. For other products, a given fall in price leads to only a small increase in demand. The demand for these products is described as *price inelastic*. Clearly it is useful to know the price elasticity of demand. When faced with elastic demand, marketers know that a price drop may stimulate much greater demand for their products. Conversely, when faced with inelastic demand, marketers know that a price drop will not increase demand appreciably.

An obvious practical problem facing marketers who wish to use demand curve analysis is plotting demand curves accurately. There is no one demand curve that relates price to demand in real life. Each demand curve is based on a set of assumptions regarding other factors such as advertising expenditure, salesforce effectiveness, distribution intensity and the price of competing products, which also affect demand. For the purposes of Figure 12.1, these have been held constant at a particular level so that one unique curve can be plotted. A second problem regarding the demand curve relates to the estimation of the position of the curve even when other influences are held constant. Some companies conduct experiments to estimate likely demand at various price levels. However, it is not always feasible to do so since they may rely on the cooperation of retailers who may refuse or demand unrealistically high fees. Second, it is very difficult to implement a fully controlled field experiment. Where different regions of the country are involved, differences in income levels, variations in local tastes and preferences, and differences in the level of competitor activities may confound the results. The reality is that while the demand curve is a useful conceptual tool for thinking about pricing issues, in practice its application is limited. In truth, traditional economic theory was not developed as a management tool but as an explanation of market behaviour. Managers therefore turn to other methods of setting prices and it is these methods we shall discuss in this chapter.

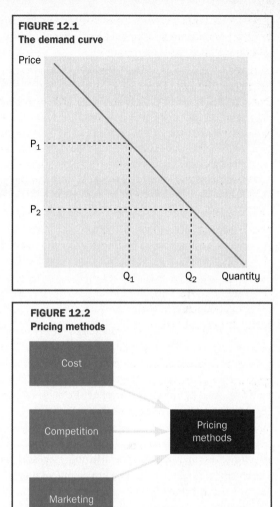

FIGURE 12.1
The demand curve

FIGURE 12.2
Pricing methods

Shapiro and Jackson (1978) identified three methods used by managers to set prices (see Figure 12.2). The first reflects a strong internal orientation and is based on costs. The second is to use competitor-orientated pricing where the major emphasis is on competitor activities. The final approach is called market-orientated pricing, as it focuses on the value that customers place on a product in the marketplace and its marketing strategy. In this chapter we shall examine each of these approaches and draw out their strengths and limitations. We shall also discuss how to initiate and respond to price changes.

Cost-orientated Pricing

Companies often use cost-orientated methods when setting prices (see Shipley, 1981; Jobber and Hooley, 1987). Two methods are normally used: full-cost pricing and direct- (or marginal-) cost pricing.

Full-cost pricing

Full-cost pricing can best be explained by using a simple example (see Table 12.1). Imagine that you are given the task of pricing a new product (a memory card) and the cost figures given in Table 12.1 apply. Direct costs such as labour and materials work out at £10 per unit. As output increases, more people and materials will be needed and so total costs increase. Fixed costs (or overheads) per year are calculated at £1,000,000. These costs (such as office and manufacturing facilities) do not change as output increases. They have to be paid whether 10 or 1 million memory cards are produced.

TABLE 12.1 Full-cost pricing

Year 1			Year 2		
Direct costs (per unit)	=	£10	Expected sales		=50,000
Fixed costs	= £1,000,000				
Expected sales	=	100,000			
Cost per unit			**Cost per unit**		
Direct costs	=	£10	Direct costs	=	£10
Fixed costs (1,000,000 ÷ 100,000)	=	£10	Fixed costs (1,000,000 ÷ 50,000)	=	£20
Full costs	=	£20	Full costs	=	£30
Mark-up (10%)	=	£2	Mark-up (10%)	=	£3
Price (cost plus mark-up)	=	£22	**Price** (cost plus mark-up)	=	£33

Having calculated the relevant costs, the next step is to estimate how many memory cards we are likely to sell. We believe that we produce good-quality memory cards and therefore sales should be 100,000 in the first year. Therefore, total (full) cost per unit is £20 and, using the company's traditional 10 per cent mark-up, a price of £22 is set.

In order to appreciate the problem of using full-cost pricing, let us assume that the sales estimate of 100,000 is not reached by the end of the year. Because of poor economic conditions or as a result of setting the price too high, only 50,000 units are sold. The company believes that this level of sales is likely to be achieved next year. What happens to price? Table 12.1 gives the answer: it is raised because cost per unit goes up. This is because fixed costs (£1,000,000) are divided by a smaller expected sales volume (50,000). The result is a price rise in response to poor sales figures. This is clearly nonsense and yet can happen if full-cost pricing is followed blindly. A major European technology company priced one of its main product lines in this way, and suffered a downward spiral of sales as prices were raised each year with disastrous consequences.

The first problem with full-cost pricing, then, is that it leads to an increase in price as sales fall. Second, the procedure is illogical because a sales estimate is made *before* a price is set. Third, it focuses on internal costs rather than customers' willingness to pay. Finally, there may be a technical problem in allocating overheads in multi-product firms (Christopher, 1982).

However, inasmuch as the method forces managers to calculate costs, it does give an indication of the minimum price necessary to make a profit. Once direct and fixed costs have been measured *break-even analysis* can be used to estimate the sales volume needed to balance revenue and costs at different price levels. Therefore, the procedure of calculating full costs is useful when other pricing methods are used since full costs may act as a constraint. If they cannot be covered then it may not be worthwhile launching the product.

Direct-cost pricing

In certain circumstances, companies may use **direct-cost pricing** (sometimes called *marginal cost pricing*). This involves the calculation of only those costs that are likely to rise as output increases. In the example shown in Table 12.1 direct cost per unit is £10. As output increases, so total costs will increase by £10 per unit. Like full-cost pricing, direct-cost pricing includes a mark-up (in this case 10 per cent) giving a price of £11.

The obvious problem is that this price does not cover full costs and so the company would be making a loss selling a product at this low price. However, there are situations where selling at a price above direct costs but below full cost makes sense. Suppose a company is operating at below capacity and the sales director receives a call from a buyer who is willing to place an order for 50,000 memory cards but will pay only £11 per unit. If, in management's judgement, to refuse the order will mean machinery lying idle, a strong case for accepting the order can be made since the £1 per unit (£50,000) over direct costs is making a contribution to fixed costs that would not be made if the order was turned down. The decision is not without risk, however. The danger is that customers who are paying a higher price become aware of the £11 price and demand a similar deal.

Direct-cost pricing is useful for services marketing—for example, where seats in aircraft or rooms in hotels cannot be stored; if they are unused at any time the revenue is lost. In such situations, pricing to cover direct costs plus a contribution to overheads can make sense. As with the previous example, the risk is that customers who have paid the higher price find out and complain.

Direct costs, then, indicate the lowest price at which it is sensible to take business if the alternative is to let machinery (or seats or rooms) lie idle. Also, direct-cost pricing does not suffer from the 'price up as demand down' problem that was found with full-cost pricing, as it does not take account of fixed costs in the price calculation. Finally, it avoids the problem of allocating overhead charges found with full-cost pricing for the same reason. However, when business is buoyant it gives no indication of the correct price because it does not take into account customers' willingness to pay. Nor can it be used in the long term as, at some point, fixed costs must be covered to make a profit. Nevertheless, as a short-term expedient or tactical device, direct-cost pricing does have a role to play in reducing the impact of excess capacity.

Competitor-orientated Pricing

A second approach to pricing is to focus on competitors rather than costs when setting prices. This can take two forms: **going-rate pricing** and **competitive bidding**.

Going-rate pricing

In situations where there is no product differentiation—for example, a certain grade of coffee bean—a producer may have to take the going rate for the product. This accords most directly to the economist's notion of perfect competition. To the marketing manager it is anathema. A fundamental marketing principle is the creation of a differential advantage, which enables companies to build monopoly positions around their products. This allows a degree of price discretion dependent upon how much customers value the differential advantage. Even for what appear to be commodity markets, creative thinking can lead to the formation of a differential advantage on which a premium price can be built. A case in point was Austin-Trumans, a steel stockholder, which stocked the same kind of basic steels held by many other stockholders. Faced with a commodity product, Austin-Trumans attempted to differentiate on delivery. It guaranteed that it would deliver on time or pay back 10 per cent of the price to the buyer. So important was delivery to buyers (and so unreliable were many of Austin-Trumans' rivals) that buyers were willing to pay a 5 per cent price premium for this guarantee. The result was that Austin-Trumans were consistently the most profitable company in its sector for a number of years. This example shows how companies can use the creation of a differential advantage to move away from going-rate pricing.

Competitive bidding

Many contracts are won or lost on the basis of competitive bidding. The most usual process is the drawing up of detailed specifications for a product and putting the contract out to tender. Potential suppliers quote a price that is confidential to themselves and the buyer (sealed bids). All other things being equal, the buyer will select the supplier that quotes the lowest price. A major focus for suppliers, therefore, is the likely bid prices of competitors.

Statistical models have been developed by management scientists to add a little science to the art of competitive bidding (Edelman, 1965). Most use the concept of *expected profit* where:

$$\text{Expected profit} = \text{Profit} \times \text{Probability of winning}$$

It is clearly a notional figure based on actual profit (bid price—costs) and the probability of the bid price being successful. Table 12.2 gives a simple example of how such a competitive bidding model might be used. Based on past experience the bidder believes that the successful bid will fall in the range of £2,000–£2,500. As price is increased so profits will rise (full costs = £2,000) and the probability of winning will fall. The bidder uses past experience to estimate the probability of each price level being successful. In this example the probability ranges from 0.10 to 0.99. By multiplying profit and probability an expected profit figure can be calculated for each bid price. Expected profit peaks at £160, which corresponds to a bid price of £2,200. Consequently this is the price at which the bid will be made.

Bid price (£)	Profit	Probability	Expected profit
2,000	0	0.99	0
2,100	100	0.90	90
2,200	200	0.80	160*
2,300	300	0.40	120
2,400	400	0.20	80
2,500	500	0.10	50

TABLE 12.2 Competitive bidding using the expected profit criterion

*Based on the expected profit criterion, recommended bid price is £2,200.

Unfortunately this simple model suffers from a number of limitations. First, it may be difficult, if not impossible, for managers to express their views on the likelihood of a price being successful in precise statistical probability terms. Note that if the probability of the £2,200 bid was recorded as 0.70 rather than 0.80, and likewise the £2,300 bid was recorded as 0.50 rather than 0.40, the recommended bid price would move from £2,200 (expected profit £140) to £2,300 (expected profit £150). Clearly the outcome of the analysis can be dependent on small changes in the probability figures. Second, use of the expected profit criterion is limited to situations where the bidder can play the percentage game over the medium to long term. In circumstances where companies are desperate to win an order, they may decide to trade off profit for an improved chance of winning. In the extreme case of a company fighting for survival, a more sensible bid strategy might be to price at below full cost (£2,000) and simply make a contribution to fixed costs, as we discussed above under direct-cost pricing.

Clearly the use of competitive bidding models is restricted in practice. However, successful bidding depends on having an efficient competitor information system. One Scandinavian ball-bearing manufacturer, which relied heavily on effective bid pricing, installed a system that was dependent on salespeople feeding into its computer-based information system details of past successful and unsuccessful bids. The salespeople were trained to elicit successful bid prices from buyers, and then to enter them into a customer database that recorded order specifications, quantities and the successful bid price.

Because not all buyers were reliable when giving their salespeople information (sometimes it was in their interest to quote a lower successful bid price than actually occurred), competitors' successful bid prices were graded as category A (totally reliable—the salesperson had seen documentation supporting the bid price or it came from a totally trustworthy source), category B (probably reliable—no documentary evidence but the source was normally reliable) or category C (slightly dubious—the source may be reporting a lower than actual price to persuade us to bid very low next time). Although not as scientific as the competitive bidding model, this system, built up over time, provided a very effective database that salespeople could use as a starting point when they were next asked to bid by a customer.

Market-orientated Pricing

Market-orientated pricing is more difficult than cost-orientated or competitor-orientated pricing because it takes a much wider range of factors into account. In all, 10 factors need to be considered when adopting a market-orientated approach—these are shown in Figure 12.3.

Marketing strategy

The price of a product should be set in line with *marketing strategy*. The danger is that price is viewed in isolation (as with full-cost pricing) with no reference to other marketing decisions such as positioning, strategic objectives,

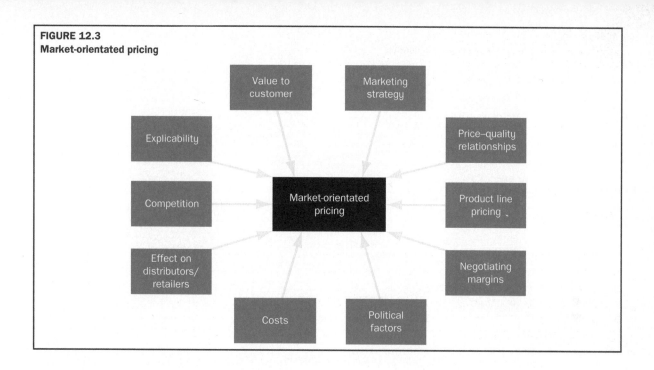

FIGURE 12.3
Market-orientated pricing

- Value to customer
- Marketing strategy
- Explicability
- Price–quality relationships
- Competition
- **Market-orientated pricing**
- Product line pricing
- Effect on distributors/ retailers
- Negotiating margins
- Costs
- Political factors

promotion, distribution and product benefits. The result is an inconsistent mess that makes no sense in the marketplace and causes customer confusion.

The way around this problem is to recognize that the pricing decision is dependent on other earlier decisions in the marketing planning process (see Chapter 18). For new products, price will depend on positioning strategy, and for existing products price will be affected by strategic objectives. First, we shall examine the setting of prices for new products. Second, we shall consider the pricing of existing products.

Pricing new products

The usual pricing objective for new products is to gain profitable market penetration. However, occasionally organizations will sacrifice short-term profits in order to achieve long-term goals. For example, BSkyB priced its set-top boxes below cost in order to encourage consumers to subscribe to its television channels. In this section we explore the way in which positioning strategy affects price, launch strategies based upon skimming and penetration pricing, and the factors that affect the decision to charge a high or low price.

Positioning strategy: a key decision that marketing management faces when launching new products is **positioning strategy**. This in turn will have a major influence on price. As discussed in Chapter 7, product positioning involves the choice of target market and the creation of a differential advantage. Each of these factors can have an enormous impact on price.

When strategy is being set for a new product, marketing management is often faced with an array of potential target markets. In each, the product's differential advantage (value) may differ. For example, when calculators were developed commercially for the first time, three distinct segments existed: S1 (engineers and scientists who placed a high value on calculators because their jobs involved a lot of complex calculations); S2 (accountants and bankers who also placed a high value on a calculator because of the nature of their jobs, although not as high as S1); and S3 (the general public, who made up the largest segment but placed a much lower value on the benefits of calculators) (Brown, 1991).

Clearly the choice of target market had a massive impact on the price that could be charged. If engineers/ scientists were targeted, a high price could be set, reflecting the large differential advantage of the calculator to them. For accountants/bankers the price would have to be slightly lower, and for the general public a much lower price would be needed. In the event, the S1 segment was chosen and the price set high (around £250/€360). Over time, price was reduced to draw into the market segments S2 and S3 (and a further segment,

FIGURE 12.4
Adoption of innovations by segments: calculators

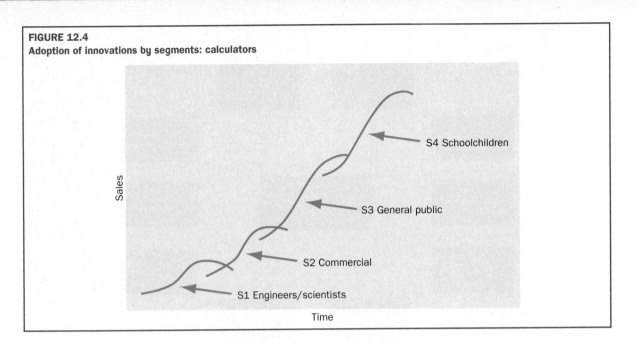

S4, when exam regulations were changed to allow schoolchildren to use calculators). Much later, when Casio entered the market, it targeted the general public with calculators priced at less than £10. The development of the market for calculators, based upon targeting increasingly price-sensitive market segments, is shown in Figure 12.4.

Two implications follow from this discussion. First, for new products, marketing management must decide on a target market and on the value that people in that segment place on the product (the extent of its differential advantage): only then can a market-based price be set which reflects that value. Second, where multiple segments appear attractive, modified versions of the product should be designed and priced differently, not according to differences in costs, but in line with the respective values that each target market places on the product.

Launch strategies: price should also be blended with other elements of the marketing mix. Figure 12.5 shows four marketing strategies based on combinations of price and promotion. Similar matrices could also be developed for product and distribution, but for illustrative purposes promotion will be used here.

A combination of high price and high promotion expenditure is called a *rapid skimming strategy*. The high price provides high margin returns on investment and the heavy promotion creates high levels of product awareness and knowledge. Nike usually employs a rapid skimming strategy when it launches new ranges of trainers. Coca-Cola also employs rapid skimming strategies. A *slow skimming strategy* combines high price with low levels of promotional expenditure. High prices mean big profit margins, but high levels of promotion are believed to be unnecessary, perhaps because word of mouth is more important and the product is already well known (e.g. Rolls-Royce) or because heavy promotion is thought to be incompatible with product image.

Companies that combine low prices with heavy promotional expenditure are practising a *rapid penetration strategy*. The aim is to gain market share rapidly, perhaps at the expense of a rapid skimmer. For example, no-frills airlines such as easyJet and Ryanair have successfully attacked British Airways by adopting a rapid penetration strategy. Direct Line is an example of a company that challenged traditional UK insurance companies with great success by using heavy promotion and a low charge for its insurance policies. Supermarkets also use a rapid penetration strategy with low prices heavily promoted. For example, Tesco uses the strapline 'Every little helps'; Asda uses 'Permanently low prices forever', 'Price guarantee 10 per cent lower than other supermarkets'; Aldi uses 'Like brands, only cheaper'.

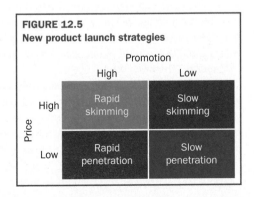

FIGURE 12.5
New product launch strategies

Finally, a *slow penetration strategy* combines a low price with low promotional expenditure. Own-label brands use this strategy: promotion is not necessary to gain distribution, and low promotional expenditure helps to maintain high profit margins for these brands. The supermarket chains Netto and Lidl adopted a slow penetration strategy in their early years in the UK. The low promotional expenditures help to promote the low cost base necessary to support their low prices. This price/promotion framework is useful in thinking about marketing strategies at launch.

A major question remains, however: when is it sensible to use a *high price (skimming) strategy* and when should a *low price (penetration)* strategy be used (Jobber and Shipley, 1998)? To answer this question we need to understand the characteristics of market segments that can bear a high price. These characteristics are shown in Table 12.3. The more that each of these characteristics is present, the more likely that a high price can be charged (Jobber and Shipley, 2012).

EXHIBIT 12.1
Chanel confers high psychological value to customers where its brand image is reinforced by its high price

 Scan the QR code to see how Aldi uses humour to promote its pricing strategy.

TABLE 12.3 Characteristics of high-price market segments
1   Product provides high value
2   Customers have high ability to pay
3   Consumer and bill payer are different
4   Lack of competition
5   Excess demand
6   High pressure to buy
7   Switching costs

The first characteristic is that the market segment should place a *high value on the product*, based on the customer benefits it provides. Calculators provided high functional value to engineers and scientists, other products (e.g. perfumes and clothing) may rely more on psychological value where brand image is crucial (e.g. Chanel perfume or Gucci shoes). Second, high prices are more likely to be viable where *customers have a high ability to pay. Cash rich segments* in organizational markets often correlate with profitability. For example, the financial services sector and the textile industry in Europe may place similar values on marketing consultancy skills but in general the former has more ability to pay.

In certain markets the *consumer of the product is different from the bill payer*. This distinction may form the basis of a high-price market segment. Rail travel is often segmented by price sensitivity. Early-morning, long-distance trips are more expensive than midday journeys since the former are usually made by business people and often the company they are working for will pay for their travel.

The fourth characteristic of high-price segments is *lack of competition* among supplying companies. The extreme case is a monopoly where customers have only one supplier from which to buy. When customers have no, or very little, choice of supply, the power to determine price is largely in the hands of suppliers. This means that high prices can be charged if suppliers so wish.

During the latter part of 2014, the price of oil more than halved from $116 a barrel in June to around $50 in December. Such an immense price drop could only be caused by powerful forces. These were the classic economists' drivers of supply and demand.

Supplies boomed as the USA increased oil production by investing in fracking projects. Between 2008 and 2014, US oil companies increased production by 70 per cent, or 3.5 million barrels per day. While US output soared, the Organization of the Petroleum Exporting Countries (OPEC), led by Saudi Arabia, refused to cut production, leading to a glut of oil on the international market.

The supply effect could have been offset by growing demand, but this did not happen. Consumption in Europe and Japan fell in 2014 as economies struggled to cope with stagnation. In the USA, tighter fuel economy standards for vehicles and the closure of petrochemical plants reduced demand. These demand issues were compounded by a marked slowdown in the Chinese economy.

The combined effects of a glut in supply, not compensated for by a rise in demand, were the underlying causes of the dramatic oil price fall. This example provides evidence of how powerful the forces of supply and demand can be on prices.

Based on: Associated Press (2014); Rankin (2015)

The fifth characteristic of high price segments is *excess demand*. When demand exceeds supply there is the potential to charge high prices. For example, when the demand for gold/petrol/cocoa exceeds supply the price of gold/petrol/cocoa usually rises. Conversely when there is excess supply, prices usually fall. The power of supply and demand in affecting prices is discussed in Marketing in Action 12.2.

The next situation where customers are likely to be less price sensitive is where there is *high pressure to buy*. For example, in an emergency situation where a vital part is required to repair a machine that is needed to fulfil a major order, the customer may be willing to pay a high price if a supplier can guarantee quick delivery.

The final situation where high prices can be charged is where there are high *switching costs*. Buyers may have made investments in dealing with a supplier that they would have to make again if they switched suppliers. Production, logistical or marketing operations may be geared to using the equipment of a particular supplier (e.g. computer systems). Customers may have invested heavily in product-specific training that would have to be repeated if they chose to switch. These factors are likely to make customers less sensitive to the price charged by existing suppliers in such circumstances.

The task of the marketing manager is to evaluate the chosen target market for a new product using the checklist provided in Table 12.3. It is unlikely that all seven conditions will apply and so judgement is still required. But the more these characteristics are found in the target market, the greater the chances that a high price can be charged.

Table 12.4 lists the conditions when a *low price (penetration) strategy* should be used. The first situation is when an analysis of the market segment using the previous checklist reveals that a low price is the *only feasible alternative*. For example, a product that has no differential advantage launched on to a market where customers are not cash rich, pay for themselves, have little pressure to buy and have many suppliers to choose from has no basis for charging a price premium. At best it could take the going-rate price but, more likely, would be launched using a penetration (low-price) strategy, otherwise there would be no incentive for consumers to switch from their usual brand. The power of consumers to force down prices is nowhere greater than on the Internet as it improves price transparency.

TABLE 12.4 Conditions for charging a low price
1 Only feasible alternative
2 Market penetration or domination
3 Experience curve effect/low costs
4 Make money later
5 Make money elsewhere
6 Barrier to entry
7 Predation

There are, however, more positive reasons for using a low-price strategy. A company may wish to gain *market penetration* or *domination* by pricing its products aggressively. This requires a market containing at least one segment of price-sensitive consumers. Direct Line priced its insurance policies aggressively to challenge traditional insurance companies and is now market leader for home and motor insurance in the UK. Tesco, the UK supermarket chain, has also become the market leader through charging low prices for good-quality products, although its position is being eroded by Aldi and Lidl, who offer even lower prices.

Penetration pricing for market presence is sometimes followed by price increases once market share has reached a satisfactory level. Tata cars has followed this approach with the Nano, partly as a strategic move and partly in response to increased production costs.

EXHIBIT 12.2
Intel is a low cost supplier

Low prices may also be charged to increase output and so bring down costs through the *experience curve effect*. Research has shown that, for many products, costs decline by around 20 per cent when production doubles (Abell and Hammond, 1979). Cost economies are achieved by learning how to produce the product more effectively through better production processes and improvements in skill levels. Economies of scale through, for example, the use of more cost-effective machines at higher output levels also act to lower costs as production rises. Marketing costs per unit of output may also fall as production rises. For example, an advertising expenditure of £1 million represents 1 per cent of revenue when sales are £100 million, but rises to 10 per cent of revenue when sales are only £10 million.

Therefore, a company may choose to price aggressively to become the largest producer and, if the experience curve holds, the lowest-cost supplier. Intel has taken full advantage of the cost economies that come with being the dominant market leader in the microprocessor market, with over 80 per cent share and the investment of billions of dollars in hyper-productive plants that can produce more processors in a day than some of its rivals can produce in a year (Edwards, 2006). This has given it the option of achieving higher profit margins than its competitors or charging low prices, as it did with its top-performing Pentium processor; prices dropped by 57 per cent in a six-week period in a move designed to hurt its major rival AMD (Popovich, 2002). Indeed, *low costs* through ruthless cost-cutting may be necessary to achieve profits using low-price strategies. For example, the German supermarket chain Lidl keeps costs low by displaying products on racks and in the packaging in which they are delivered.

 Scan the QR code to see how Asda uses pricing strategies to promote its brand.

A low-price strategy can also make sense when the objective is to *make money later*. Two circumstances can provoke this action. First, the sale of the basic product may be followed by profitable after-sales service and/or spare parts. For example, the sale of an aero-engine at cost may be worthwhile if substantial profits can be made on the later sale of spare parts.

Two companies that have successfully applied this strategy are Hewlett-Packard and Gillette. Hewlett-Packard printers are sold at a low price to consumers but replacement ink cartridges are expensive, which is where it makes large profits. Gillette follows a similar strategy, pricing its razors competitively but charging a high price for replacement blades. Its razors account for 5 per cent of the razor division's profits, while blades account for 95 per cent (Nagle and Hogan, 2006). Sony and Microsoft have also sold their games consoles at a loss, making money on the subsequent sales of games.

Second, the price sensitivity of customers may change over time as circumstances change. For example digital cameras were highly priced initially, then prices began to fall as more competitors entered the market. Prices then fell further as mobile phones and smartphones incorporated highly sophisticated cameras as part of a bundle of features.

Marketers also charge low prices to *make money elsewhere*. For example, retailers often use loss leaders, which are advertised in an attempt to attract customers into their stores and to create a low-cost image. Supermarkets, much to the annoyance of traditional petrol retailers, use petrol as a loss leader to attract motorists to their stores (Eastham, 2002). Manufacturers selling a range of products to organizations may accept low prices on some goods in order to be perceived by customers as a full-range supplier. In both cases, sales of other higher-priced and more profitable products benefit.

Low prices can also act as a *barrier to entry*. A company may weigh the longer-term benefits of deterring competition by accepting low margins to be greater than the short-term advantages of a high-price, high-margin strategy, which may attract rivals into its market.

EXHIBIT 12.3
Gillette razors are priced competitively. Most profits are made on its high priced replacement blades

Finally, low prices may be charged in an attempt to put other companies out of business; this is known as *predation*. However, this approach is rarely used because it can cause harmful price wars and in many countries is considered as an anti-competitive practice.

Pricing existing products

For new products, the pricing objective is usually straightforward: to build profitable sales and market share. However for existing products, the choice is not so clear-cut. The pricing of existing products should be set within the context of strategy. Specifically, the *strategic objective* for each product has a major bearing on pricing objectives and actions. As with new products, price should not be set in isolation, but should be consistent with strategic objectives. Three strategic objectives are relevant to pricing: build, hold, and harvest. These will impact on pricing objectives and actions (see Table 12.5).

TABLE 12.5 Strategic objectives, pricing objectives and pricing actions		
Strategic objectives	**Typical pricing objectives**	**Pricing actions**
Build	Market penetration	Low price relative to rivals
	Market share leadership	Value leadership
	Long-term profit maximization	Slow/fast to match rivals' price increases/decreases
		Positioning strategy
Hold	Maintain sales/market share	Maintain or match price relative to competition
		Value parity
		Fast to match rivals' price falls and rises
Harvest	Maintain or raise profit margins	Premium prices
	Short-term profit maximization	Reluctance to match price cuts
		Fast matching of price rises

- *Build objective*: relevant pricing objectives would be *market penetration* and *market share leadership*. Achieving these goals should result in long-term profit maximization. For price-sensitive markets, an appropriate pricing action would be to *price lower than the competition* or use *value leadership*, where the customer benefit-to-price ratio is kept higher than that of the competition. If the competition raises its prices we would be *slow to match* it, whereas for prices falls we would be *fast to match*. For price-insensitive markets, the best pricing strategy becomes less clear-cut. Price in these circumstances are dependent on the overall *positioning strategy* thought appropriate for the product.

- *Hold objective*: the corresponding pricing objective is to maintain sales and/or market share. Appropriate pricing actions are to *maintain or match price relative to the competition* or to use *value parity*, where the customer benefit-to-price ratio is maintained vis-à-vis the competition. The response to competitors' price changes is to match them quickly.
- *Harvest objective*: appropriate pricing objectives are to *maintain or raise profit margins* for the purposes of *short-term profit maximization*, even if the result is long-term falling sales and/or market share. Pricing actions are to *set or maintain premium prices*. For products that are being harvested, there would be much greater reluctance to match price cuts than for products that are being built or held. On the other hand, price increases would swiftly be matched consistent with raising profit margins. Examples of brands that are being harvested (high price/low promotion) are Bovril, Horlicks, Ovaltine and Vaseline.

The above examples show how developing clear strategic objectives helps the setting of price and clarifies appropriate reaction to competitive price changes. Price setting, then, is much more sophisticated than simply asking 'How much can I get for this product?' The process starts by asking more fundamental questions like 'How is this product going to be positioned in the marketplace?' and 'What is the appropriate strategic objective for this product?' Only after these questions have been answered can price sensibly be determined.

Value to the customer

A second marketing consideration when setting prices is estimating a product's value to the customer. Already when discussing marketing strategy its importance has been outlined: price should be accurately keyed to the value to the customer. In brief, the more value a product gives compared to that of the competition, the higher the price that can be charged. In this section we shall explore a number of ways of estimating value to the customer. This is critical because of the close relationship between value and price. Three methods of estimating value will now be discussed: trade-off analysis, experimentation and economic value to the customer analysis.

Trade-off analysis

Trade-off analysis (otherwise known as *conjoint analysis*) measures the trade-off between price and other product features so that their effects on product preference can be established (Kucher and Simon, 1987). Respondents are not asked direct questions about price; instead product profiles consisting of product features and price are described and respondents are asked to name their preferred profile. From their answers, the effect of price and other product features can be measured using a computer model. The following is a brief description of the procedure.

The first step is to identify the most important product features (attributes) and benefits that are expected to be gained as a result of buying the product. Product profiles are then built using these attributes (including price) and respondents are asked to choose which product they would buy from pairs of product profiles. Statistical analysis allows the computation of *preference contributions* that permit the preference for attributes to be compared. For example, if the analysis was for a business-to-business product, trade-off analysis might show that improving delivery time from one week to one day is worth a price increase of 5 per cent. In addition, the relative importance of each of the product attributes, including price, can be calculated. By translating these results into market share and profit figures for the proposed new product the optimal price can be found.

This technique has been used to price a wide range of industrial and consumer products and services, and can be used to answer such questions as the following (Cattin and Wittink, 1989).

1 What is the value of a product feature including improving service levels in price terms?
2 What happens to market share if price changes?
3 What is the value of a brand name in terms of price?
4 What is the effect on our market share of competitive price changes?
5 How do these effects vary across European countries?

Experimentation

A limitation of trade-off analysis is that respondents are not asked to back up their preferences with cash expenditure. Consequently, what they say they prefer may not be reflected in actual purchase when they are asked to part with their money. *Experimental pricing research* attempts to overcome this drawback by placing a product on sale at different locations with varying prices.

The major alternatives are to use a controlled store experiment or test marketing. In a *controlled store experiment* a number of stores are paid to vary the price levels of the product under test. Suppose 100 supermarkets are being used to test two price levels of a brand of coffee; 50 stores would be chosen at random (perhaps after controlling for region and size) and allocated the lower price, the rest would use the higher price. By comparing sales levels and profit contributions between the two groups of stores the most profitable price would be established. A variant of this procedure would test price differences between the test brand and major rival brands. For example, in half the stores a price differential of 2p may be compared with 4p. In practice, considerable sums need to be paid to supermarkets to obtain approval to run such tests, and the implementation of the price levels needs to be monitored carefully to ensure that the stores do sell at the specified prices.

Test marketing can be used to compare the effectiveness of varying prices so long as more than one area is chosen. For example, the same product could be sold in two areas using an identical promotional campaign but with different prices between areas. A more sophisticated design could measure the four combinations of high/low price and high/low promotional expenditure if four areas were chosen. Obviously, the areas would need to be matched (or differences allowed for) in terms of target customer profile so that the result would be comparable. The test needs to be long enough so that trial and repeat purchase at each price can be measured. This is likely to be between 6 and 12 months for products whose purchase cycle lasts more than a few weeks.

A potential problem of using test marketing to measure price effects is competitor activity designed to invalidate the test results. For example, competitors could run special promotions in the test areas to make sales levels atypical if they discovered the purpose and location of the test marketing activities. Alternatively, they may decide not to react at all. If they know that a pricing experiment is taking place and that syndicated consumer panel data are being used to measure the results they may simply monitor the results since competitors will be receiving the same data as the testing company (Moutinho and Evans, 1992). By estimating how successful each price has been, they are in a good position to know how to react when a price is set nationally.

Economic value to the customer analysis

Experimentation is more usual when pricing consumer products. However, industrial markets have a powerful tool at their disposal when setting the price of their products: **economic value to the customer (EVC)** analysis. Many organizational purchases are motivated by economic value considerations since reducing costs and increasing revenue are prime objectives of many companies. If a company can produce an offering that has a high EVC, it can set a high price and yet still offer superior value compared to the competition. A high EVC may be because the product generates more revenue for the buyer than competition or because its operating costs (such as maintenance, operation or start-up costs) are lower over its lifetime. The Lexus was marketed using the latter approach, with the tag-line 'Lowest Cost of Ownership' based on its decent fuel economy, durability and resale value. Lexus salespeople were trained to provide the financial evidence to justify the claim (Helm, 2008). Microsoft also used EVC analysis to defend its Windows platform against the threat from the lower-cost Linux operating system. Microsoft commissioned independent tests that showed how the total lifetime cost of open-source operating systems could exceed the costs of Windows despite their lower purchase price (Nagle and Hogan, 2006). EVC analysis is usually particularly revealing when applied to products whose purchase price represents a small proportion of the lifetime costs to the customer (Forbis and Mehta, 1979).

Figure 12.6 illustrates the calculation of EVC and how it can be used in price setting.

A reference product is chosen (often the market leader) with which to compare costs. In the example, the market leader is selling a machine tool for £50,000. However, this is only part of a customer's lifecycle costs. In addition, £30,000 start-up costs (installation, lost production and operator training) and £120,000 post-purchase costs (operator, power and maintenance) are incurred. The total lifecycle costs are, therefore, £200,000.

Our new machine tool (product X) has a different customer cost profile. Technological advances have reduced start-up costs to £20,000 and post-purchase costs to £100,000. Therefore, total costs are reduced by £30,000 and the EVC our new product offers is £80,000 (£200,000 − £120,000). Thus, the EVC figure is the amount a customer would have to pay to make the total lifecycle costs of the new and reference products the same. If the new machine tool was priced at £80,000 this would be the case. Below this price there would be an economic incentive for customers to buy the new machine tool.

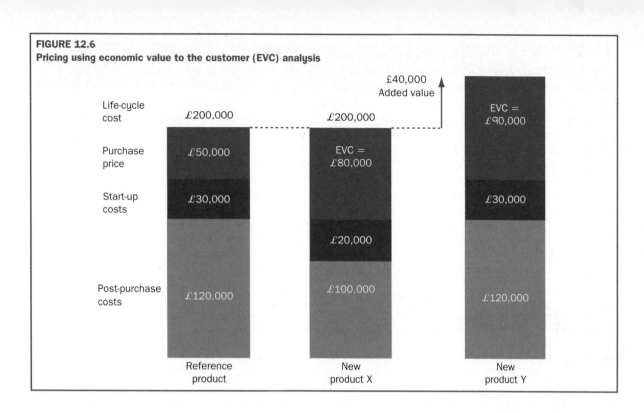

FIGURE 12.6
Pricing using economic value to the customer (EVC) analysis

EVC analysis is clearly a powerful tool for price setting since it establishes the upper economic limit for price. Management then has to use judgement regarding how much incentive to give the customer to buy the new product and how much of a price premium to charge. A price of £60,000 would give customers a £20,000 lifetime cost saving incentive while establishing a £10,000 price premium over the reference product. In general, the more entrenched the market leader, the more loyal its customer base and the less well known the newcomer, the higher the cost saving incentive needs to be.

 Scan the QR code to see the creative approach used by American Airlines to differentiate its business and first class services.

In the second example shown in Figure 12.6, the new machine tool (product Y) does not affect costs but raises the customer's revenues. For example, faster operation may result in more output, or greater precision may enhance product quality leading to higher prices. This product is estimated to give £40,000 extra profit contribution over the reference product because of higher revenues. Its EVC is, therefore, £90,000 indicating the highest price the customer should be willing to pay. Once more, marketing management has to decide how much incentive to give to customers and how much of a price premium to charge.

EVC analysis can be useful in target market selection since different customers may have varying EVC levels. A decision may be made to target the market segment that has the highest EVC figure since for these customers the product has the greatest differential advantage. The implementation of an EVC-based pricing strategy relies on a well-trained salesforce that is capable of explaining sophisticated economic value calculations to customers, and field-based evidence that the estimates of cost savings and revenue increases will occur in practice.

Price–quality relationships

A third consideration when adopting a market-orientated approach to pricing is the relationship between price and perceived quality. Many people use price as an indicator of quality. This is particularly the case for products where objective measurement of quality is not possible, such as drinks and perfume. But the effect is also to be found with consumer durables and industrial products. A study of price and quality perceptions of cars, for example, found that higher-priced cars were perceived to possess (unjustified) high quality (Erickson and Johansson, 1985). For example, the Seat Leon is built using many of the same components as the Audi A3, but the two cars are perceived differently, with the latter often being perceived to be of higher quality. Also sales of a branded agricultural fertilizer rose after the price was raised above that of its generic competitors despite the fact that it was the same compound. Interviews with farmers revealed that they believed the fertilizer to improve crop yield compared with rival products. Clearly price had influenced quality perceptions.

Mini Case 12.1 discusses some interesting results of experiments conducted to investigate the influence of price on quality perceptions. A potential problem, therefore, is that, by charging a low price, brand image may be tarnished.

Product line pricing

Market-orientated companies also need to take account of where the price of a new product fits into its existing product line. For example, when Apple developed the iPod nano it had to carefully price-position the device against the original iPod mobile music player. Given that some potential buyers of the original iPod might now buy the nano, pricing it too cheaply could have resulted in lower overall profits for Apple.

Some companies prefer to extend their product lines rather than reduce the price of existing brands in the face of price competition. They launch cut-price fighter brands to compete with the low-price rivals. This has the advantage of maintaining the image and profit margins of existing brands. For example, Apple found itself being attacked by low-priced competitors in the mobile music player market. The company chose a fighter brand strategy to compete. The iPod shuffle, originally retailing at £49 compared with £219 for the iPod, was launched to compete with low-price MP3 players. Sainsbury's has formed an alliance with Netto to provide a fighter brand to compete with limited range discounters, as Marketing in Action 12.3 explains.

By producing a range of brands at different price points, companies can cover the varying price sensitivities of customers and encourage them to trade up to the more expensive, higher-margin brands.

Explicability

The capability of salespeople to explain a high price to customers may constrain price flexibility. In markets where customers demand economic justification of prices, the inability to produce cost and/or revenue arguments may mean that high prices cannot be set. In other circumstances the customer may reject a price that does not seem to reflect the cost of producing the product. For example, sales of an industrial chemical compound that repaired grooves in drive-shafts suffered because many customers believed that the price of £500 did not reflect

Some supermarkets use fighter branding to minimize the impact of heavy discounters like Aldi and Lidl. For example, Tesco created its Value brand for this purpose. However, Sainsbury's went one step further by relaunching the Netto chain in the UK to fight back against the discount stores. Sainsbury's joined forces with Denmark's biggest retailer, Dansk Supermarked, to build a new Netto business. For Netto, the Sainsbury's joint venture represents a return to UK retailing. The business traded in the UK until 2010, when Dansk sold its 200 outlets to the UK supermarket Asda. Since then the discount market has boomed as shoppers have looked for bargains.

Like Aldi and Lidl, Netto stores carry around 2,200 products, most of which are own label, such as Kat cat food, which sells in Netto stores around Europe, and Snaxter crisps and Bell's cereals, both created especially for the British market. Also following the German discounters, Netto is targeting more affluent shoppers with bargains on champagne, wine and chocolates, as well as cheap basics.

The partnership is a bold move to take on the discounters, which are stealing customers from Britain's largest supermarkets. Sainsbury's has repeatedly claimed it will not join the supermarket price war led by Tesco and Asda. Instead, by joining forces with Netto, itself a discounter, it is competing against Aldi and Lidl by using a fighter brand that can compete on price against the German discounters without the need to enter a damaging price war itself.

Based on: Butler and Farrell (2014); Butler (2014)

the cost of producing the compound. Only when the salesforce explained that the premium price was needed to cover high research and development expenditure did customers accept that the price was not exploitative.

Competition

Competition factors are important determinants of price. At the very least, competitive prices should be taken into account; yet it is a fact of commercial life that many companies do not know what the competition is charging for its products.

Care has to be taken when defining competition. When asked to name competitors, many marketing managers list companies that supply technically similar products. For example, a paint manufacturer will name other paint manufacturers. However, as Figure 12.7 illustrates, this is only one layer of competition. A second layer consists of dissimilar products solving the

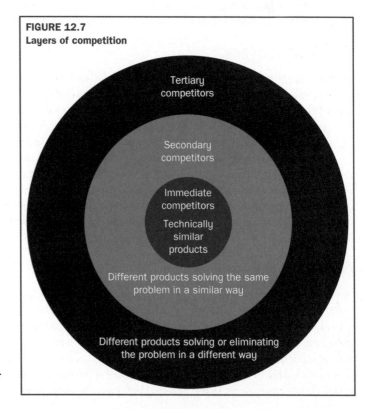

FIGURE 12.7
Layers of competition

same problem in a similar way. Polyurethane varnish manufacturers would fall into this category. A third level of competition would come from products solving the problem (or eliminating it) in a dissimilar way. Since window frames are often painted, PVC double glazing manufacturers would form competition at this level.

This analysis is not simply academic, as the effects of price changes can be misleading if these three layers of competition are not taken into consideration. For example, if all paint manufacturers raised their prices simultaneously, they might believe that overall sales would not be dramatically affected if they mistakenly defined competition as technically similar products. The reality is, however, that such price collusion would make polyurethane varnish and, over a longer period, PVC double glazing more attractive to customers. The implication is that companies must take into account all three levels of competition when setting and changing prices.

Negotiating margins

In some markets customers expect a price reduction. Price paid is therefore very different from list price. In the car market, for example, customers expect to pay less than the asking price . For organizational customers, Marn and Rosiello describe the difference between list price and realized or transaction price as the **price waterfall** (Marn and Rosiello, 1992). The difference can be accounted for by order-size discounts, competitive discounts (a discretionary discount negotiated before the order is taken), a fast payment discount, an annual volume bonus and promotional allowances.

Managing this price waterfall is a key element in achieving a satisfactory transaction price. Market-orientated companies recognize that such discounting may be a fact of commercial life and build in *negotiating margins* that allow prices to fall from list price levels but still permit profitable transaction prices to be achieved.

Effect on distributors/retailers

When products are sold through intermediaries such as distributors or retailers, the list price to the customer must reflect the margins required by them. When Müller yoghurt was first launched in the UK, a major factor in gaining distribution in a mature market was the fact that its high price allowed attractive profit margins for the supermarket chains. Conversely, the implementation of a penetration pricing strategy may be hampered if distributors refuse to stock the product because the profit per unit sold is less than that for competitive products.

The implication is that pricing strategy is dependent on understanding not only the ultimate customer but also the needs of the distributors and retailers who form the link between them and the manufacturer. If their needs cannot be accommodated, product launch may not be viable or a different distribution system (e.g. direct selling) may be required.

Political factors

High prices can be a contentious public issue and may invoke government intervention. Where price is out of line with manufacturing costs, political pressure may act to force down prices. The European Commission and national bodies such as the Competition Commission have been active in discouraging anti-competitive practices such as price-fixing. Indeed, the establishment of the single European market was a result of the desire to raise competitive pressures and thereby reduce prices throughout the European Union.

Companies need to take great care that their pricing strategies are not seen to be against the public interest. For example, in the UK sharp increases in energy prices have brought much adverse publicity and threats from politicians to curb further increases. Ofcom, the independent regulator for the UK communications industries, provides advice to help consumers and businesses make informed choices when selecting communication products. Exploitation of a monopoly position or collusion between firms may bring short-term profits but incur the backlash of a public inquiry into pricing practices.

Costs

The final consideration that should be borne in mind when setting prices is costs. This may seem in contradiction to the outward-looking market-orientated approach but, in reality, costs do enter the pricing equation. The secret is to consider costs alongside all of the other considerations discussed under market-orientated price setting rather than in isolation. In this way costs act as a constraint: if the market will not bear the full cost of producing and marketing the product it should not be launched.

What should be avoided is the blind reference to costs when setting prices. Simply because one product costs less to make than another does not imply that its price should be less.

Initiating Price Changes

Our discussion of pricing strategy so far has looked at the factors that affect it. By taking into account the 10 market-orientated factors, managers can judge the correct level at which to set prices. But in a highly competitive world, pricing is dynamic: managers need to know when and how to raise or lower prices, and whether or not to react to competitors' price moves. First, we shall discuss initiating price changes, before analysing how to react to competitors' price changes.

Three key issues associated with initiating price changes are the *circumstances* that may lead a company to raise or lower prices, the *tactics* that can be used, and *estimating competitor reaction*. Table 12.6 illustrates the major points relevant to each of these considerations.

TABLE 12.6 Initiating price changes

	Increases	Cuts
Circumstances	Value greater than price	Value less than price
	Rising costs	Excess supply
	Excess demand	Build objective
	Harvest objective	Price war unlikely
Tactics	Price jump	Price fall
	Staged price increases	Staged price reductions
	Escalator clauses	Fighter brands
	Price unbundling	Price bundling
	Lower discounts	Higher discounts
Estimating competitor reaction	Strategic objectives	
	Self-interest	
	Competitive situation	
	Past experience	
	Statements of intent	

Circumstances

A price increase may be justified as a result of marketing research (e.g. trade-off analysis or experimentation) which reveals that customers place a higher *value* on the product than is reflected in its price. *Rising costs*, and hence reduced profit margins, may also stimulate price rises. Another factor that leads to price increases is *excess demand*. A company that cannot supply the demand created by its customers may choose to raise prices in an effort to balance demand and supply. This can be an attractive option as profit margins are automatically widened. The final circumstance when companies may decide to raise prices is when embarking on a *harvest objective*. Prices are raised to increase margins even though sales may fall.

Correspondingly, price cuts may be provoked by the discovery that price is high compared to the *value* that customers place on the product, *falling costs* (and the desire to bring down costs further through the experience curve effect), and where there is *excess supply* leading to excess capacity. As we have seen, excess supply in the oil industry in 2014 led to a dramatic fall in the price of oil. A further circumstance that may lead to price falls is the adoption of a *build objective*. When customers are thought to be price sensitive, price cutting may be used to build sales and market share. The final circumstance that might lead to price cuts is the desire to *pre-empt competitive entry* into a market. Proactive price cuts—before the new competitor enters—are painful to implement because they incur short-term profit sacrifices but immediately reduce the attractiveness of the market to the potential entrant and reduce the risk of customer annoyance if prices are reduced only after competitive entry.

Tactics

Price increases and cuts can be implemented in many ways. The most direct is the *price jump* or *fall*, which increases or decreases the price by the full amount in one go. A price jump avoids prolonging the pain of a price increase over a long period but may raise the visibility of the price increase to customers. Using *staged price increases* might make the price rise more palatable but runs the risk of a company being charged with 'always raising its prices'. A *one-stage price fall* can have a high-impact dramatic effect that can be heavily promoted, but also has an immediate impact on profit margins. *Staged price reductions* have a less dramatic effect but may be used when a price cut is believed to be necessary but the amount necessary to stimulate sales is unclear. Small cuts may be initiated as a learning process that proceeds until the desired effect on sales has been achieved.

Price can also be raised by using *escalator clauses*. The contracts for some organizational purchases are drawn up before the product has been made. Constructing the product—for example, a new defence system or motorway—may take a number of years. An escalator clause in the contract allows the supplier to stipulate price increases in line with a specified index—for example, increases in industry wage rates or the cost of living.

Price unbundling is another tactic that effectively raises prices. Many product offerings actually consist of a set of products for which an overall price is set (e.g. computer hardware and software). Price unbundling allows each element in the offering to be priced separately in such a way that the total price is raised. A variant on this process is charging for services that were previously included in the product's price. For example, manufacturers of mainframe computers have the option of unbundling installation and training services, and charging for them separately.

A final tactic is to maintain the list price but *lower discounts* to customers. In periods of heavy demand for new cars, dealers lower the cash discount given to customers, for example. Quantity discounts can also be manipulated to raise the transaction price to customers. The percentage discount per quantity can be lowered, or the quantity that qualifies for a particular percentage discount can be raised.

Companies that are contemplating a price cut have three options besides a direct price fall. A company defending a premium-priced brand that is under attack from a cut-price competitor may choose to maintain its price while introducing a *fighter brand*. The established brand keeps its premium-price position while the fighter brand competes with the rival for price-sensitive customers. Where a number of products and services that tend to be bought together are priced separately, *price bundling* can be used to effectively lower price. For example, televisions can be offered with 'free three-year repair warranties' or cars offered with 'free labour at first service'. Finally, *discount terms* can be made more attractive by increasing the percentage or lowering the qualifying levels. However, giving higher discounts over too long a period of time can be risky, as General Motors found to disastrous effect. By pursuing a four-year price discounting strategy in the USA in the face of poor sales, it provoked a price war with Ford and Chrysler, caused consumers to focus on price rather than value offered by the product, and reduced profits (Simon, 2005).

Estimating competitor reaction

A key factor in the price change decision is the extent of competitor reaction. A price rise that no competitor follows may turn customers away, while a price cut that is met by the competition may reduce industry profitability. Four factors affect the extent of competitor reaction: their strategic objectives, what is in their self-interest, the competitive situation at the time of the price change, and past experience.

Companies should try to gauge their *competitors' strategic objectives* for their products. By observing pricing and promotional behaviour, talking to distributors and even hiring their personnel, estimates of whether competitor products are being built, held or harvested can be made. This is crucial information: the competitors' response to our price increase or cut will depend upon it. They are more likely to follow our price increase if their strategic objective is to hold or harvest. If they are intent on building market share, they are more likely to resist following our price increase. Conversely, they are more likely to follow our price cuts if they are building or holding, and more likely to ignore our price cuts if they are harvesting.

Self-interest is also important when estimating competitor reactions. Managers initiating price changes should try to place themselves in the position of their competitors. What reaction is in their best interests? This may depend on the circumstances of the price change. For example, if price is raised in response to a general rise in cost inflation, the competition is more likely to follow than if price is raised because of the implementation of a harvest objective. Price may also depend upon the *competitive situation*. For example, if the competition has excess capacity, a price cut is more likely to be matched than if this is not the case. Similarly, a price rise is more likely to be followed if the competition is faced with excess demand.

Competitor reaction can also be judged by looking at their reactions to previous price changes. While *past experience* is not always a reliable guide, it may provide insights into the way in which competitors view price changes and the likely responses they might make. Past experience may be supplemented by *statements of intent*. For example, when T-Mobile dropped the price of its Flext brand, Vodafone immediately responded to prevent T-Mobile gaining market share, and its chief executive stated publicly, 'If anyone thinks that just by dropping prices they will take share from us, I will respond. I will compete, so they won't be getting an advantage on pure price.' Such declarations leave competitors in no doubt about Vodafone's reaction to further price falls (Ritson, 2008b).

Reacting to Competitors' Price Changes

When competitors initiate price changes, companies need to analyse their appropriate reactions. Three issues are relevant here: when to follow, when to ignore, and the tactics required if the price change is to be followed. Table 12.7 summarizes the main considerations.

TABLE 12.7 Reacting to competitors' price changes		
	Increases	**Cuts**
When to follow	Rising costs	Falling costs
	Excess demand	Excess supply
	Price-insensitive customers	Price-sensitive customers
	Price rise compatible with brand image	Price fall compatible with brand image
	Harvest or hold objective	Build or hold objective
When to ignore	Stable or falling costs	Rising costs
	Excess supply	Excess demand
	Price-sensitive customers	Price-insensitive customers
	Price rise incompatible with brand image	Price fall incompatible with brand image
	Build objective	Harvest objective
Tactics:	Margin improvement urgent	Offset competitive threat
– quick response	Gains to be made by being customer's friend	High customer loyalty
– slow response		

When to follow

Competitive price increases are more likely to be followed when they are due to general *rising cost* levels, or industry-wide *excess demand*. In these circumstances the initial pressure to raise prices is the same on all parties. Following a price rise is also more likely when customers are relatively *price insensitive*, which means that the follower will not gain much advantage by resisting the price increase. Where *brand image is consistent* with high prices, a company is more likely to follow a competitor's price rise as to do so would be consistent with the brand's positioning strategy. Finally, a price rise is more likely to be followed when a company is pursuing a *harvest or hold objective* because, in both cases, the emphasis is more on profit margin than sales/market share gain.

Price cuts are likely to be followed when they are stimulated by general *falling costs* or *excess supply*. Falling costs allow all companies to cut prices while maintaining margins, and excess supply means that a company is unlikely to allow a rival to make sales gains at its expense. Price cuts will also be followed in *price-sensitive markets* since allowing one company to cut price without retaliation would mean large sales gains for the price cutter. The image of the company can also affect reaction to price cuts. Some companies position themselves as low-price manufacturers or retail outlets. In such circumstances they would be less likely to allow a price reduction by a competitor to go unchallenged for to do so would be *incompatible with their brand image*. Finally, price cuts are likely to be followed when the company has a *build* or *hold strategic objective*. In such circumstances an aggressive price move by a competitor would be followed to prevent sales/market share loss. In the case of a build objective, response may be more dramatic with a price fall exceeding the initial competitive move.

When to ignore

The circumstances associated with companies not reacting to a competitive price move are in most cases simply the opposite of the above. Price increases are likely to be ignored when *costs are stable or falling*, which means that there are no cost pressures forcing a general price rise. In the situation of *excess supply* companies may view a price rise as making the initiator less competitive, and therefore allow the price rise to take place unchallenged, particularly when customers are *price sensitive*. Companies occupying low-price positions may regard a price rise in response to a price increase from a rival to be *incompatible with their brand image*. Finally, companies pursuing a *build objective* may allow a competitor's price rise to go unmatched in order to gain sales and market share.

Price cuts are likely to be ignored in conditions of *rising costs*, *excess demand* and when servicing *price-insensitive customers*. Premium price positioners may be reluctant to follow competitors' price cuts for to do so would be *incompatible with brand image*. Lastly, price cuts may be resisted by companies using a *harvest objective*.

Tactics

When a company decides to follow a price change it can do so quickly or slowly. A *quick price reaction* is likely when there is an urgent need to *improve profit margins*. Here the competitor's price increase will be welcomed as an opportunity to achieve this objective.

Conversely, a *slow reaction* may be desirable when an *image of being the customer's friend* is being sought. The first company to announce a price increase is often seen as the high-price supplier. Some companies have mastered the art of playing the low-cost supplier by never initiating price increases and following competitors' increases slowly (Ross, 1984). The key to this tactic is timing the response: too quickly and customers do not notice; too slowly and profit is foregone. The optimum period can be found only by experience but, during it, salespeople should be told to stress to customers that the company is doing everything it can to hold prices for as long as possible.

A *quick response* to a competitor's price fall will happen to ward off a *competitive threat*. In the face of undesirable sales/market share erosion, fast action is needed to nullify potential competitor gains. However, reaction will be slow when a company has a *loyal customer base* willing to accept higher prices for a period so long as they can rely on price parity over the longer term.

Ethical Issues in Pricing

Key issues regarding ethical issues in pricing are price fixing, predatory pricing, deceptive pricing, penetration pricing and obesity, price discrimination and product dumping.

Price fixing

One of the driving forces towards lower prices is competition. Therefore, it can be in the interests of producers to agree among themselves not to compete on price. Groups of companies that collude are said to be acting as a cartel. If discovered, there can be heavy fines. For example, some of the world's largest consumer products companies, including Unilever, Proctor & Gamble, Gillette and Reckitt Benckiser, were fined a combined €951 million by the French competition authorities for price fixing in supermarkets (Kollewe, 2014).

Opponents of price fixing claim that it is unethical because it restrains the consumer's freedom of choice and interferes with each firm's interest in offering high-quality products at the best price. Proponents argue that under harsh economic conditions price fixing is necessary to ensure a fair profit for the industry and to avoid price wars that might lead to bankruptcies and unemployment.

Predatory pricing

This refers to the situation where a firm cuts its prices with the aim of driving out the competition. The firm is content to incur losses with the intent that high profits will be generated through higher prices once the competition is eliminated.

Deceptive pricing

This occurs when consumers are misled by the price deals offered by companies. Two examples are misleading price comparisons. Misleading price comparisons occur when a store sets artificially high prices for a short time so that much lower 'sale' prices can be claimed later. The purpose is to deceive the customer into believing they are being offered bargains. Some countries, such as the UK and Germany, have laws that state the minimum period over which the regular price should be charged before it can be used as a reference price in a sale.

Penetration pricing and obesity

A controversial issue is the question of the ethics of charging low prices for fatty food targeting young people. Critics claim that, by doing so, fast-food companies encourage obesity. Others claim that such companies cannot be blamed when consumers are made well aware by the media of the consequences of eating fatty foods.

Price discrimination

This occurs when a supplier offers a better price for the same product to one buyer and not to another, resulting in an unfair competitive advantage. Price discrimination can be justified when the cost of supplying different customers varies, where the price differences reflect differences in the level of competition and where different volumes are purchased.

Product dumping

This involves the export of products at much lower prices than charged in the domestic market, sometimes below the cost of production. Products are 'dumped' for a variety of reasons. First, unsold stocks may be exported at a low price rather than risk lowering prices in the home market. Second, products may be manufactured for sale overseas at low prices to fill otherwise unused production capacity. Finally, products that are regarded as unsafe at home may be dumped in countries that do not have such stringent safety rules. For example, the US Consumer Product Safety Commission ruled that three-wheel cycles were dangerous. Many companies responded by selling their inventories at low prices in other countries (Schlegelmilch, 1998).

When you have read this chapter

Discover further resources and test your understanding: McGraw-Hill **Connect**™ is a digital teaching and learning environment that improves performance over a variety of critical outcomes; it can be tailored, is easy to use and is proven effective. **LearnSmart**™ is the most widely used and intelligent adaptive learning resource that is proven to strengthen memory recall, improve course retention and boost grades. Fuelled by **LearnSmart**™, **SmartBook**™ is the first and only adaptive reading experience available today.

Review

1 **The economist's approach to price determination**
   - The economist's approach to pricing was developed as an explanation of market behaviour and focuses on demand and supply. There are limitations in applying this approach in practice, which means that marketers turn to other methods in business.

2 The differences between full-cost and direct-cost pricing

- Full-cost pricing takes into account both fixed and direct costs. Direct-cost pricing takes into account only direct costs such as labour and materials.
- Both methods suffer from the problem that they are internally orientated methods. Direct-cost pricing can be useful when the corporate objective is survival and there is a desperate need to fill capacity.

3 An understanding of going-rate pricing and competitive bidding

- Going-rate pricing is setting price levels at the rate generally applicable in the market, focusing on competitors' offerings and prices rather than on company costs. Marketers try to avoid going-rate pricing by creating a differential advantage.
- Competitive bidding involves the drawing up of detailed specifications for a product and putting the contract out to tender. Potential suppliers bid for the order with price an important choice criterion. Competitive bidding models have been developed to help the bidding process but they have severe limitations.

4 The advantages of market-orientated pricing over cost-orientated and competitor-orientated pricing methods

- Market-orientated pricing takes into account a much wider range of factors that are relevant to the setting of prices. Although costs and competition are still taken into account, marketers will take a much more customer-orientated view of pricing, including customers' willingness to pay as reflected in the perceived value of the product. Marketers will also evaluate the target market of the product to establish the price sensitivity of customers. This will be affected by such factors as the degree of competition, the degree of excess demand, and the ability of target customers to pay a high price. A full list of factors that marketers take into account is given in point 5 below.

5 The factors that affect price setting when using a market-orientated approach

- A market-orientated approach involves the analysis of marketing strategy, value to the customer, price–quality relationships, explicability, product line pricing, competition, negotiating margins, effect on distributors/retailers, political factors and costs.

6 When and how to initiate price increases and cuts

- Initiating price increases is likely to be carried out when value is greater than price, in the face of rising costs, when there is excess demand and where a harvest objective is being followed.
- Tactics are a price jump, staged price increases, escalator clauses, price unbundling and lower discounts.
- Initiating price cuts is likely to be carried out when value is less than price, when there is excess supply, where a build objective is being followed, where a price war is unlikely and when there is a desire to pre-empt competitive entry.
- Tactics are a price fall, staged price reductions, the use of fighter brands, price bundling and higher discounts.

7 When and when not to follow competitor-initiated price increases and cuts; when to follow quickly and when to follow slowly

- Competitor-initiated price increases should be followed when there are rising costs, excess demand, price-insensitive customers, where the price rise is compatible with brand image and where a harvest or hold objective is being followed.
- Competitor-initiated price increases should not be followed when costs are stable or falling, with excess supply, with price-sensitive customers, where the price rise is incompatible with brand image and where a build objective is being followed.
- The price increase should be followed quickly when the need for margin improvement is urgent, and slowly when there are gains to be made by being seen to be the customer's friend.
- Competitor-initiated price cuts should be followed when there are falling costs, excess supply, price-sensitive customers, where the price cut is compatible with brand image, and where a build or hold objective is being followed.

- Competitor-initiated price cuts should not be followed when there are rising costs, excess demand, price-insensitive customers, where the price fall is incompatible with brand image and where a harvest objective is being followed.
- The price cut should be followed quickly when there is a need to offset a competitive threat, and slowly where there is high customer loyalty.

8 Ethical issues in pricing

- There are potential problems relating to price fixing, predatory pricing, deceptive pricing, price discrimination and product dumping.

Key Terms

competitive bidding drawing up detailed specifications for a product and putting the contract out to tender

direct-cost pricing the calculation of only those costs that are likely to rise as output increases

economic value to the customer (EVC) the amount a customer would have to pay to make the total lifecycle costs of a new and a reference product the same

full-cost pricing pricing so as to include all costs and based on certain sales volume assumptions

going-rate pricing pricing at the rate generally applicable in the market, focusing on competitors' offerings rather than on company costs

market-orientated pricing an approach to pricing that takes a range of marketing factors into account when setting prices

positioning strategy the choice of target market (*where* the company wishes to compete) and differential advantage (*how* the company wishes to compete)

price unbundling pricing each element in the offering so that the price of the total product package is raised

price waterfall the difference between list price and realized or transaction price

trade-off analysis a measure of the trade-off customers make between price and other product features so that their effects on product preference can be established

Study Questions

1. Accountants are always interested in profit margins; sales managers want low prices to help promote sales; and marketing managers are interested in high prices to establish premium positions in the marketplace. To what extent do you agree with this statement in relation to the setting of prices?

2. You are the marketing manager of a company that is about to launch an electric car. What factors should you take into consideration when pricing this product?

3. Why is value to the customer a more logical approach to setting prices than cost of production? What role can costs play in the setting of prices?

4. Discuss the advantages and disadvantages of experimentation in assessing customers' willingness to pay.

5. What is economic value to the customer analysis? Under what conditions can it play an important role in price setting?

6. Under intense cost-inflationary pressure you are considering a price increase. What other considerations would you take into account before initiating the price rise?

7. You are the marketing manager of a range of premium-priced all-weather tyres. A competitor has launched a cut-price alternative that possesses 90 per cent of the effectiveness of your product. If you do not react, you estimate that you will lose 30 per cent of sales. What are your strategic pricing options? What would you do?

8. The only reason that companies set low prices is that their products are undifferentiated. Discuss.

Recommended Reading

Baker, W., M. Marn and Zawada (2010) Do You Have a Long-Term Pricing Strategy? *McKinsey Quarterly*, October, 1–7.

Bertini, M. and J. Gourville (2012) Pricing to Create Shared Value, *Harvard Business Review* 90(6), 96–104.

Cross, R. G. and A. Dixit (2005) Consumer centric pricing: The surprising secret for pricing, *Business Horizons* 48, 483–91.

Jobber, D. and D. Shipley (2012) Marketing-orientated Pricing: Understanding and Applying Factors that

Discriminate Between Successful High and Low Pricing Strategies, *European Journal of Marketing* 46(11/12), 1647–70.

Nagle, T. T. and J. E. Hogan (2006) *The strategy and tactics of pricing*, Upper Saddle River, USA: Pearson International.

Shipley, D. and D. Jobber (2001) Integrated Pricing Via the Pricing Wheel, *Industrial Marketing Management* 30(3), 301–14.

References

Abell, D. F. and J. S. Hammond (1979) *Strategic Marketing Planning*, Englewood Cliffs, NJ: Prentice-Hall.

Associated Press (2014) Collapse in Oil Prices: Producers Howl, Consumers Cheer, Economists Fret, *The Guardian*, 16 December. www.the guardian.com/business

Brown, R. (1991) The S-Curves of Innovation, *Journal of Marketing Management* 7(2), 189–202.

Butler S. (2014) Venture with Sainsbury's has Less than a Year to Work, *The Guardian*, 6 November. www.the guardian.com/business

Butler, S. and S. Farrell (2014) Sainsbury's Links Up with Discounter, *The Guardian*, 21 June, 35.

Cattin, P. and D. R. Wittink (1989) Commercial Use of Conjoint Analysis: An Update, *Journal of Marketing*, July, 91–6.

Christopher, M. (1982) Value-in-Use Pricing, *European Journal of Marketing* 16(5), 35–46.

Eastham, J. (2002) Prices Down, Numbers Up, *Marketing Week*, 20 June, 22–5.

Edelman, F. (1965) Art and Science of Competitive Bidding, *Harvard Business Review*, July–August, 53–66.

Edwards, C. (2006) Inside Intel, *Business Week*, 9 January, 43–8.

Erickson, G. M. and J. K. Johansson (1985) The Role of Price in Multi-Attribute Product Evaluations, *Journal of Consumer Research*, September, 195–9.

Forbis, J. L. and N. T. Mehta (1979) *Economic Value to the Customer*, McKinsey Staff Paper, Chicago: McKinsey & Co., Inc., February, 1–10.

Helm, B. (2008) How to Sell Luxury to Penny-Pinchers, *Business Week*, 10 November, 60.

Jobber, D. and D. Shipley (1998) Marketing-orientated Pricing Strategies, *Journal of General Management* 23(4), 19–34.

Jobber, D. and D. Shipley (2012) Marketing-orientated Pricing: Understanding and Applying Factors that Discriminate Between Successful High and Low Pricing Strategies, *European Journal of Marketing* 46(11/12).

Kollewe, J. (2014) France Fines Thirteen Consumer Goods Firms Euro951m for Price Fixing, *The Guardian*, 18 December. www.theguardian.com/business

Kucher, E. and H. Simon (1987) Durchbruch bei der Preisentscheidung: Conjoint-Measurement, eine neue Technik zur Gewinnoptimierung, *Harvard Manager* 3, 36–60.

Marn, M. V. and R. L. Rosiello (1992) Managing Price, Gaining Profit, *Harvard Business Review*, Sept.–Oct., 84–94.

Moutinho, L. and M. Evans (1992) *Applied Marketing Research*, Wokingham: Addison-Wesley, 161.

Nagle, T. T. and J. E. Hogan (2006) *The Strategy and Tactics of Pricing*, New Jersey: Pearson Education.

Popovich, K. (2002) Intel to Cut Chip Pricing by 57 per cent, *eWeek*, 4 January, 16.

Rangel, A., J. O'Doherty and B. Shiv (2008) *Marketing Actions Can Modulate Neural Representations of Experienced Pleasantness*, Stanford University Working Paper.

Rankin, J. (2015) Oil Prices: Why Are They Falling And Who Are the Winners and Losers, *The Guardian*, 6 January. http://www.theguardian.com/business/2015/jan/06/why-are-oil-prices-falling

Ritson, M. (2008a) Why Brands Are at a Premium, *Marketing*, 30 April, 19.

Ritson, M. (2008b) Mobile Brands Make Poor Call on Value, *Marketing*, 23 January, 21.

Ross, E. B. (1984) Making Money with Proactive Pricing, *Harvard Business Review*, Nov.–Dec., 145–55.

Schlegelmilch, B. (1998) *Marketing Ethics: An International Perspective*, London: International Thomson Business Press.

Shapiro, B. P. and B. B. Jackson (1978) Industrial Pricing to Meet Customer Needs, *Harvard Business Review*, Nov.–Dec., 119–27.

Shipley, D. (1981) Pricing Objectives in British Manufacturing Industry, *Journal of Industrial Economics* 29 (June), 429–43; Jobber, D. and G. J. Hooley (1987) Pricing Behaviour in the UK Manufacturing and Service Industries, *Managerial and Decision Economics* 8, 167–71.

Simon, B. (2005) Detroit Giants Count Cost of Four Year Price War, *Financial Times*, 19 March, 29.

The Guardian (2008) In Praise of Placebos, 5 March, 36.

CASE 23
easyJet and Ryanair

Flying High with Low Prices

The story behind the success of Europe's no-frills airlines began in the USA. Southwest Airlines, a Texas-based carrier, was the first to benefit from the deregulation of American skies in 1978. The airline began the operation of a no-frills, low-fare business model, involving no free meals or coffee, only peanuts. The attraction was fares set at about one-fifth of those of the mainstream airlines. Its fleet was made up entirely of one type of aircraft, the Boeing 737, to keep costs down by reducing pilot training and maintenance costs. It flew between secondary airports, which were sometimes over an hour's drive from city centres.

An essential component in the Southwest Airlines approach was fast turnaround times from uncongested airports, which could be as short as 20 minutes. This meant that aircraft could be used for 15 hours per day. In comparison, conventional airlines that ran a 'hub and spoke' network flew aircraft for only half that length of time, as aircraft must wait to connect with incoming flights. Southwest Airlines embraced Internet transactions to cut paperwork and administrative costs, and rejected corporate acquisitions in favour of organic growth. The result has been a continual stream of profits (unlike for other American airlines) and a business that attracts around 65 million passengers a year.

In Europe, Southwest Airlines' approach and success has been mirrored by easyJet and Ryanair, who have pioneered low-fare, no-frills flying. Growth has been spectacular with both airlines consistently recording annual increases in passenger numbers of 15–20 per cent although this has slowed in recent years.

The growth in the low-cost sector has been fuelled by the burgeoning market for short-haul city breaks, the desire of more adventurous holidaymakers to arrange their own vacation packages, and their wish to own holiday homes in warm, sunny climates. These factors, together with the drive by business to trim back on travel costs, have fuelled growth in passenger numbers.

Marketing Strategy at easyJet

A key element in the success of easyJet has been its approach to pricing. The conventional method of selling airline seats was to start selling at a certain

price and then lower it if sales were too low. What Stelios Haji-Ioannou, owner of easyJet, pioneered was the opposite: the start was a low headline price that grabbed attention, then it was raised according to demand. Customers are never told how soon or by how much the price will be changed. This system, called *yield management*, is designed to allow airline seats to be priced according to supply and demand, and achieve high seat occupancy. This reflects the fact that a particular seat on a specific flight cannot be stored for resale: if it is empty, the revenue is lost.

For the customer the result has been fares much lower than those offered by conventional airlines such as BA and Lufthansa, and, to be profitable, easyJet has needed to control costs strictly. Following the example of Southwest Airlines, it has achieved this through simplicity (using one aircraft type), productivity (fast turnaround times to achieve high aircraft use) and direct distribution (using the Internet for upfront payment and low administrative charges). Also, onboard costs are reduced by not providing free drinks or meals to passengers.

Although easyJet operates out of secondary airports such as Luton in the UK, it is increasingly using mainstream airports such as Gatwick in a direct attempt to take passengers from more conventional rivals such as BA. Its approach is to fly to relatively few destinations but with a higher frequency on each route. This provides a barrier to entry, and the higher frequency attracts high-volume business travellers

»

»

who prize schedule over price and are, therefore, willing to pay a little more for the service (the average easyJet seat price is reported to be higher than that of Ryanair). EasyJet also offers flexible fares that are attractive to business travellers as they allow free date changes. One in five of easyJet's passengers are business customers. The airline also derives revenue from the sale of onboard food and drinks, check-in charges, priority boarding fees, car hire and hotel bookings.

In 2002 easyJet bought the rival Go airline for £374 million (€523.6 million), a price lower than expected by many analysts. For easyJet, the deal was about creating a route network that stretched across Europe. With the exception of domestic routes, the two airlines had few destinations in common. EasyJet's top routes include Amsterdam, Geneva and Paris, while Go took holidaymakers to Faro, Bologna and Bilbao. There was overlap on only a handful of destinations, both flying to Barcelona, Nice, Majorca and Malaga. Furthermore, the UK bases of the two airlines were complementary, with easyJet operating from Luton, Gatwick and Liverpool, while Go operated from Stansted, Bristol and East Midlands airports. At the time the combined companies were about the same size as Ryanair in terms of passenger numbers. The takeover alone gave easyJet scale and increased buying power, a factor that was important when it decided to abandon its policy of using only Boeing 737s by buying a fleet of aircraft from Airbus in 2002 at a knockdown price.

In 2007 easyJet bought GB Airways in a £103 million deal that allowed easyJet to expand operations at London Gatwick airport and also establish a base at Manchester airport.

Under its entrepreneurial leader, Stelios, the easyJet group moved into other areas, such as car hire, Internet cafés and cruises, using the same low-price model. Another venture was the setting up of easyCinema to challenge the established cinema chains. The motivation was the half-empty cinema auditoria Stelios saw when visiting conventional cinemas. He could not understand why price was not varied according to demand (by day and by film). Although some cinemas did reduce prices midweek, their pricing policies were not considered flexible enough compared to pricing using yield management. Also, he argued, why pay the same to see a blockbuster as a flop? And why is the price of the blockbuster the same on the opening night as it is six weeks later? What he proposed was an infinite number of prices depending on supply and demand, following his success in the airline business.

The easyCinema formula worked as follows. The pricing structure began at 20 pence (less than €0.30). People logged on to easyCinema.com where they found three options. First, they could select the movie they most wanted to see, the dates when they could see it and at what prices; second, they could select the day on which they wanted to visit the cinema, what films were showing and at what prices; and third they could come to the site with a budget of, say, £1 (€1.44), and find all the movies that could be seen for £1 or less. Bookings could be made up to two weeks in advance. As with aircraft seats, the likelihood was that, the earlier the booking was made, the cheaper the seat would be. Also, after examining costs, Stelios decided not to install food and drink stands, saying, 'If ya want popcorn, go to a popcorn vendor. For movies come to easyCinema'. Staff costs were also reduced since there were no tickets. Booking was done through the website, and a membership card was printed out that admitted visitors to the cinema via a turnstile. Finally, no advertising for unrelated products (e.g. the local curry house) prior to the movie showing was allowed. The first easyCinema was opened in Milton Keynes with a view to expanding the business across the UK. In 2006, however, three years after its opening, it closed, and the plan to transform the movie business was abandoned in the face of meagre audiences.

In 2002 Mr. Haji-Ioannou stood down as chairman to take on the role of non-executive director. He remains the largest shareholder, and in 2008 became embroiled in a dispute with the board, believing that their plans for expansion were too ambitious in the light of a looming recession. Nevertheless, in 2013 easyJet ordered 135 Airbus A320s for delivery between 2015 and 2022, and in 2014 added a further 27 aircraft to its order. The A320s were more fuel efficient and were 15 per cent larger than easyJet's previous aircraft, the A319.

Marketing Strategy at Ryanair

Ryanair is run by Michael O'Leary, who is famous for his outspoken views and controversial advertising campaigns. Like easyJet, Ryanair has followed the Southwest Airlines business model but, if anything, has been more ruthless on cost-cutting. It provides cheap point-to-point flying from secondary airports, rather than shadowing and undercutting the major carriers as easyJet increasingly does. Sometimes the airports can be 60 miles from the real destination: for Frankfurt read Hahn, for Hamburg read Lübeck, for Stockholm read Vesteraas or Skavsta, and for Brussels read Charleroi. Ryanair has kept to its single-aircraft policy, the Boeing 737, which it bought second-hand and cheaply, reducing maintenance, spares and crew training. Its fleet of 737–800s were purchased at record low prices at the bottom of the market. They offer 45 per cent more seats at lower operating costs and the same number of crew. Ryanair has continued this policy with the purchase of a further 70 Boeings in 2005 at an even lower price. In 2009 it entered negotiations with Boeing and Airbus over the purchase of up to 300 short-haul jets and announced plans to become a transatlantic carrier. In the event, Ryanair continued its policy of buying only one type of aircraft. By 2011 it operated over 300 Boeing 737s, and in 2013 ordered 200 Boeing 737 Max 200s, which provided more passenger legroom than its existing fleet while increasing capacity by nine seats.

Turnaround times at airports are fast, to keep more aircraft in the air, and online booking has slashed sales and distribution costs. Ryanair.com has become the largest travel website in Europe, selling more than 2 million seats per month. Ryanair's focus on cost reduction has resulted in profit margins about double those of easyJet despite the latter's higher prices. Some of the cost savings are passed on to the customers in the form of lower fares (the plan is an average fall in fare levels of 5 per cent per year) to make Ryanair even more attractive to its target market: the leisure customer. By contrast, easyJet has increasingly targeted business passengers. Ryanair is the only European airline to record profits for each of the last 16 years. Even during the recession it continued to make a small operating profit despite soaring fuel prices. An important part of its revenue comes from the sale of onboard food and drinks, charges for passengers checking in rather than doing so online, priority boarding and for putting luggage in the hold, and income from car hire and hotel bookings.

Ryanair has also been on the acquisition trail by buying Buzz, the budget division of KLM Royal Dutch Airlines, for £15.8 million (€23 million). Loss-making Buzz was immediately given the Ryanair cost-cutting treatment, including the loss of 440 jobs and new contracts for pilots, which raised pay but meant longer flying hours. Half of Buzz's routes were axed, but Ryanair still intended to increase passenger load from 2 million to 3 million through lower prices—£31.50 (€45) versus £56 (€81) previously—and more frequent flying along the retained routes.

Competitive Response

The stellar growth in low-cost flying has attracted new entrants such as Flybe, bmibaby and Jet2 in the UK, and TUIfly, Goodjet and Transavia elsewhere in western Europe. There are now over 50 no-frills airlines operating in Europe. Traditional airlines have also responded. For example, Air France, Lufthansa and BA have cut prices on many of their European flights in an attempt to stem the flow to the low-price carriers.

BA has embarked on an aggressive strategy of slashing prices from Heathrow and Gatwick to almost all its European short-haul destinations. Fares to places such as Berlin, Paris and Barcelona have been cut by up to 50 per cent. Unlike the low-cost carriers, BA still offers its traditional service benefits, including free food and drinks, on all flights and, unlike Ryanair, which charges £6, there are no charges for checking in luggage. The strategy of competitive fares, inflight extras and the convenience and flight transfers offered by Heathrow and Gatwick is designed to win large numbers of passengers from no-frills operators. In support of the strategy, BA's former chief executive, Willie Walsh, whose nickname—The Slasher—was earned during his time at Aer Lingus, cut 600 managerial jobs and announced a further 1000 job losses at the airline's call centres and travel shops in 2006.

Ryanair's reaction was to claim that BA's prices were still more expensive than its own after the cuts, and pointed out that, unlike BA and many other carriers, it had not introduced a fuel surcharge. It also claimed better punctuality—90 per cent flights arriving on time compared to BA's 74 per cent—and a significantly lower missing bags ratio: 0.5 per 1000 passengers against 17.7 for BA.

Customer service

The need to trim costs to the bone has meant that some customers have been dissatisfied with the service provided by both no-frills airlines. For example, the need for fast turnaround times at airports has meant that customers who check in late are usually refused entry. Where lateness is the fault of another travel provider, such as a rail company, customers have been known to complain bitterly about entry refusal. Fast turnaround times also mean that there is little slack should a flight be delayed, with a knock-on effect on other flights.

Another problem is the reluctance of the no-frills airlines to pay compensation. For example, when easyJet cancelled a flight after it admitted it had no crew to fly the aircraft, it offered a refund of the ticket price but no compensation for the other costs, such as the lost hotel deposit and car parking fees incurred by one of its customers. Ryanair, similarly, was reported to have said, 'We never offer compensation, food or hotel vouchers'. Ryanair also experienced teething problems with lost and delayed luggage after switching baggage contractors, and in the past has appeared reluctant to pay compensation with respect to lost luggage.

Of particular concern to customers was the lack of pre-booking of seats, leading to a rush to board a plane. EasyJet was the first to respond to customer complaints and introduced an allocated seating policy in 2012. No longer would families need to worry about

»

»

being split up, and passengers were spared the mad rush across the tarmac. EasyJet also invested in its website, making booking easier than when using the Ryanair website, which was criticized for its poor user-friendliness. A fare-finder app was launched that allowed budget-conscious travellers to find the lowest fares across a month. These innovations saw easyJet's performance outstrip that of Ryanair.

In the face of falling sales and profits and a survey by the consumer magazine *Which?* that placed Ryanair in the worst of 100 biggest brands serving the UK market, Ryanair changed tack and sought to improve customer service. In 2014, the company introduced allocated seating along with a series of measures that were designed to quell the flow of complaints from customers. These included a more flexible baggage allowance, lighter penalties for reissuing boarding cards (a passenger had complained that she had been charged several hundred euros, resulting in half a million people on Facebook backing her complaint), reduced baggage fees and the curbing of in-flight sales announcements. It also invested in upgrading its website to make booking quicker and easier, and followed easyJet by introducing a fare-finder tool. A new staff training programme was designed to improve the customer experience.

Ryanair also began to improve its marketing to business customers. It introduced a flexible business fare that allowed passengers to change their flights, and business-plus fares that provided premium seats at the front of the plane for quick boarding, or on exit rows with extra legroom. Flight schedules to locations like Madrid, Milan and Barcelona, which are popular with business people, were improved to three daily returns so that passengers could travel there and back in a day. Ryanair also began targeting more primary airports around Europe, rather than out-of-the-way secondary airports.

Questions

1. How do easyJet and Ryanair achieve success using low-price strategies?

2. What are the advantages and risks associated with low-price strategies?

3. To what extent do the conditions for charging low prices discussed in this chapter hold for easyJet and Ryanair?

4. Why did the low-price, no-frills business model fail with easyCinema?

This case was prepared by David Jobber, Emeritus Professor of Marketing, University of Bradford. It is based on a large number of published sources.

References

The material in the case has been drawn from a variety of published sources.

The Surge of German Limited Range Discounters

Business is Booming, Leading to a Shift in the Retail Landscape

In the wake of the credit crisis, discount retailers have been surging ahead. Grocery retailers like Aldi and Lidl are proving formidable competitors. Non-grocery retailers like fixed-price stores (e.g. Poundland, Poundstretcher) are reaping rich dividends through their focus on frugality. Value fashion brands like New Look and Primark are booming, while online buying clubs (e.g. Vente Privée) and daily deal sites (e.g. Groupon) are garnering larger customer bases. There is a huge appetite among customers for value for money. Discounters are powering ahead with their expansion plans throughout Europe and beyond. Their formula of low prices and offering a limited assortment of products on their shelves appears to be a winning pan-European formula for retailing. The retailing concept was pioneered by German hard discounter Aldi, and has now been successfully duplicated by other discounters such as the German Lidl, Italian Eurospin and Danish Netto chains. In Germany over 90 per cent of the German population lives within 15 minutes of an Aldi store. The discounter has control of 40 per cent of the German market.

These limited-range discounters (LRDs) believe that success can be achieved through offering good-quality products at low prices, and stocking minimal assortments that match consumers' basic needs, such as staple items that consumers buy regularly. Success is achieved through the generation of high volumes, their ability to communicate to consumers, their price gaps with traditional retailers, and placing costs at the forefront of all their business activities. Their continued success has led to dramatic changes within the retail sector, leaving manufacturers with difficult decisions as to how to supply these LRDs effectively, while not damaging their brands, and relations with other retailers. So who are these LRDs, and how do they operate?

In the UK, the discounters are experiencing huge year-on-year growth, triple the growth rates of traditional stores. Aldi alone achieved 16.8 per cent growth thanks to new store openings. Even the average basket sizes of Aldi shoppers have grown by 6 per cent. It has now

become the sixth-largest supermarket the UK, with 5.3 per cent of the market. Lidl has grown by 12.1 per cent in the UK. Countries like Norway (40 per cent) and Germany (38 per cent) have high levels of discounter activity, whereas countries like the UK (9 per cent) and Ireland (17 per cent) have very low levels. Hard discounters have four central planks in their operating philosophies. First, they stock a very limited product assortment (around 1,000 stock-keeping units), whereas a traditional store may have 25,000 different product variants. These are typically fast-moving, high stock rotation items. Usually, a shopper is offered only one type of brand from a category. Second, these stores are very simple in layout, design and operation. They require lean management and very few employees to operate. A hard discounter will typically have longer queues, which people bear for greater savings. Third, the retailers have a low-cost and highly efficient supply chain infrastructure, utilising large regional distribution centres to service their retail outlets. Last and most importantly, these stores operate on the principle of EDLP, or 'every day low prices'.

Competition between discounters is rife. Price wars are common between these retailers. However, if they stock similar products they typically stock different size variants and at different prices, to avoid direct confrontation where possible. Their success has led traditional supermarkets to introduce cheaper brand ranges such as Tesco Value in an attempt to deter

»

customers from switching. Some consumers view these discounters as too frugal and downmarket to give them their custom. LRDs' decision to locate in socially deprived areas has contributed to this image even further, although this is changing. Open pallets, lack of assortment, and lack of extra value added services alienate some shoppers. However in Germany, where many of these discounters initially emerged, wealthy Mercedes' drivers typically frequent these retailers. Their appeal spans across different socio-economic groups.

Aldi is completely privately owned by the secretive Albrecht family. Its owners are now one of Europe's wealthiest families. The name originated from Albrecht Discount. It pioneered the hard discounter market. The Aldi Group from its German base has two main divisions: Aldi Nord and Aldi Sud. Both operate independently and have clearly defined operating markets and different own-label brands, but both cooperate in terms of pricing and assortment decisions. Aldi Sud is responsible for Southern Germany, and Austria, and English-speaking countries, while Aldi Nord is responsible for all other non-German-speaking European countries. Aldi has saturation coverage within the German market, and possesses limited growth opportunities. Every German is within a 15–20-minute drive to an Aldi outlet. As a result the chain has grown aggressively abroad. It aims to open up to 1,000 Aldi stores in the UK by 2021.

The emphasis within Aldi is on efficiency and productivity. Each store is responsible for its own revenues and cost base. Costs are kept to an absolute minimum. By having a basic store layout and design, low staff numbers, non-expensive in-store storage displays, and a limited number of products on shelves, it keeps costs to an absolute minimum, which other retailers find hard to compete against. It has built up

a reputation among its loyal consumer based on the strength of the quality of its product offering. Products are strenuously tested for quality and are only allocated to stores once they are proved to be fast movers. The company has also moved into selling an organic range of produce. Aldi sources products from leading food manufacturers, and sells them under the Aldi own-label brand. Indeed, the discounters now have two-tier private label strategies offering both standard and premium variants of their own-label brands. Its sheer size enables Aldi to save through bulk buys, and through strong price negotiation with suppliers. The company now sells products that are specific to a particular country in a bid to attract local customers. Through its scale it can then source country-specific products suitable for market needs. If it still does not have the necessary scale, it will import brands into that country. Aldi utilizes huge regional distribution centres to service up to 50 outlets at a time. Goods are brought into the store on pallets, and are gradually emptied by consumers before being replenished with another new pallet. The company is famous for its frugality and thriftiness at all levels of its operations, utilizing a strong, decentralized operation with the focus on simplicity.

The first Lidl discount outlet opened in 1973. It originated as a clone of the successful Aldi format, but has since evolved into having its own strong brand identity. Like Aldi, Lidl has grown rapidly by expanding its international operations. It is privately owned by the Schwarz Group, who are notoriously secretive about its operations. The group owns a suite of different retailing divisions such as hypermarkets, traditional supermarkets, and discounters. The company is still number 2 in its domestic German market, but it has been pursuing a rapid internationalization strategy, hoping to achieve over 70 per cent of its revenues from overseas markets. Its scope of operations is limited

TABLE C26.1 LRDs: A profile—A comparison of Lidl and Aldi

Lidl	Aldi
Owned by Schwarz Group, privately owned	Owned by Albrecht family, privately owned
Stores in the UK—635	Stores in the UK—510
Stores in Sweden—167	Stores in Denmark—232
Stores in Germany—3,256	Stores in Germany—4,250
Stores in France—1,520	Stores in USA—1,375
Stores in Ireland—170	Stores in Ireland—106
Total no. of stores—10,230	Total no. of stores—9,802
Estimated sales by 2018 of over €79.23 billion	Estimated sales by 2018 of over €76.12 billion
Stocks up to 1,600 products	Stocks around 1,000 products
A third of products are branded items	Over 90 per cent are private label
Typical store size—1,000 sq. metres	Typical store size—900 sq. metres

to Europe, unlike Aldi which also owns stores in the USA and Australia. The company uses a rapid property acquisition programme, and establishes large regional distribution centres to service these new markets. The majority of its stores in international markets are non-unionized; however, in some markets it has appeased local interests by allowing trade union activity.

One of the biggest weapons in the armoury of discounters is their 'one-off' specials. These promotions typically entail the sale at substantial discount of a non-food item (e.g. ski, gardening or DIY equipment, etc.). These specials are promoted on a weekly basis through local press advertising, and leaflet drops. They act as a major inducement and increase footfall to these stores. These heavily discounted items are allocated to stores, where there are only a handful of units per store. This creates a weekly sale frenzy at these stores. The biggest problem with 'one-off specials' is that it is very hard to estimate demand and, if a special proves unpopular, the stores are left with unsold stock, which can create logistical difficulties and contributes to costs.

One of the main reasons behind their success and apparent unstoppable growth is their store location strategy. Each of these discounter stores is substantially smaller in size than a typical traditional supermarket. In addition, they require smaller property sites, and ancillary works such as car parking and special entry and exit points. This has allowed the LRDs to obtain planning permission at a much faster rate than typical retailers and with enhanced likelihood of success. In France, Lidl achieved rapid growth rates through store adaptation of their business formula, which overcame strict planning laws, through having higher shelves, smaller aisles, and lower product assortments.

The LRDs are continually evolving with some offering in-store bakeries, fresh produce and premium regional products to bolster their brand. In addition, Aldi has signed up several celebrity chefs as endorsers for their brands. In essence, they are moving away from the imagery of a pure hard discounter. The middle tier of supermarkets are under pressure from the discounters, as their operating philosophies of large assortments places them at a cost disadvantage. The discounters themselves are facing a number of new challenges with the likes of Tesco testing discount outlets in Eastern Europe, and Asda testing discount store concepts. This is a similar strategy to that carried out by continental retailers in response to the threat of discounters.

In the wake of the discounters' onslaught, leading UK supermarket chain Sainsbury's has formed a joint venture with Danish discounter chain Netto.

Both are investing £12.5 million each in a joint venture to relaunch Netto in the UK. Netto had originally sold its UK stores to Asda in 2010, but is now planning to roll out 15 new discount stores. The discounter market is expected to double in the UK in the next five years. This strategy does have inherent risks for Sainsbury's. The chain is primarily seen as middle market, with a focus on the south of England. Its thinking is to launch the Netto concept in northern areas, thereby mitigating against possible cannibalisation. Surprisingly, however, some of these new stores are located right beside those of their co-owner. These stores will stock typically 2,000 products, combining own-label and some popular branded best-selling goods. Two-thirds are own-label goods, 20 per cent are less well known brands, with the remaining 10 per cent popular brand staples. The stores will also promote the regular one-off weekly specials, to act as inducements.

In some overseas markets, market share has plateaued after the initial success of the discounters. Shoppers are still drawn to their traditional supermarket retailers because of the attraction of wide choice, one-stop shopping and the availability of low-price product ranges. However, LRDs are here to stay, and leave both retailers and suppliers with difficult decisions to face—how do we compete? And how do we supply?

Questions

1. Discuss the strengths and weaknesses associated with the LRD format.

2. What are the advantages associated with the EDLP concept versus Hi-Lo pricing for retailers?

3. How should branded manufacturers respond with their pricing strategies if they want to supply an LRD while simultaneously supplying traditional retailers?

This case was written by Dr. Conor Carroll, Lecturer in Marketing, University of Limerick. Copyright © Conor Carroll (2015). The material in the case has been drawn from a variety of published sources.

References

The material in the case has been drawn from a variety of published sources.

PART 3
COMMUNICATING AND DELIVERING CUSTOMER VALUE

A number of videos featuring CEOs, CMOs, brand and PR managers related to the Chapters in this Part are available to lecturers for presentation and class discussion.

CHAPTER 13
Integrated Marketing Communications

Probably the most powerful form of communication we have at our disposal is story telling. It has been incorporated by virtually every civilization into their culture. It is the simplest, most memorable device we have for engaging, learning, entertaining and persuading.

JOHN HEGARTY (2011), WORLDWIDE CREATIVE DIRECTOR AND FOUNDER OF BARTLE BOGLE HEGARTY

LEARNING OBJECTIVES

After reading this chapter, you should be able to:

1　explain how to develop an IMC strategy and set relevant communication objectives
2　describe the elements of integrated marketing communications
3　explain the distinction between mass and direct communications
4　discuss the promotional communication mix
5　explain the key characteristics of each of the main media channels
6　consider the implications for planning communications for different audiences and contexts

G ood communications are the lifeblood of successful market-orientated companies and their brands, but creating good communications presents many challenges. As discussed in Chapter 8, all companies need to communicate what they stand for and the benefits they have on offer if they are to earn their customers' trust. Trust is at the core of a brand's very existence (Hegarty, 2011). However, the way businesses communicate with their audiences is constantly evolving. Currently, digital technology is reshaping both the tools and the media through which we communicate. There are also more channels and opportunities for a customer to engage with a brand. In the UK alone over 500 television channels compete to catch the attention of consumers; around the world tens of millions of company websites provide product and marketing information to stimulate buyer behaviour. Social media are used by individuals and companies as a means of extending their communication networks. This increase in the number of opportunities to engage and interact with customers has created a need for better coordination of all of an organization's communications activities. Additionally, to manage these challenges of the changing communication environment and the proliferation of channels, organizations wishing to promote themselves also have to understand which communications tools to use in which situations. They must also consider operational issues associated with the management of promotional campaigns and assess whether to place responsibility for campaigns with an internal department or to employ external specialist communication agencies. For example, large manufacturing organizations producing fast-moving consumer goods (FMCG) (e.g. Kraft Foods, Unilever, Procter & Gamble), promotional activity might involve various types of communication tools, such as digital marketing, advertising, sales promotion and public relations.

Organizations of this size tend to have the resources for all these activities to be controlled internally under the umbrella of the marketing function. For example, personal selling strategies can be decided by the sales management team, advertising and sales promotion initiatives by the marketing communications team, and a publicity event by the public relations department. However, the danger of a piecemeal approach to communication planning is that messages sent to the target audience are all slightly different, which means overall they can become blurred at best and conflicting at worst. This can happen if the advertising department creates messages that aim to convey a brand as high quality, while at the same time the sales team are using heavy discounting and money-off sales promotions to sell their products. The result can be that customers do not know what to think about the brand. Mixed messages can seriously damage the public's perception of a brand.

Consequently, leading brand manufacturers usually employ external specialists, as they have the talent to bring fresh creativity and the organizational skills needed to deliver highly effective and coordinated communication campaigns. For example, Bartle Bogle Hegarty (BBH) devised the 'Keep walking' campaign for drinks manufacturer Diageo. Not only did BBH revive the brand, but it also delivered a 7 per cent increase in sales (McMains, 2014). Procter & Gamble is another large manufacturer that employs external specialists to handle its marketing communications campaigns. Its approach is to appoint a brand agency leader that acts as a single point of contact for all the agencies working on brands in its portfolio.

Finding communication solutions to these challenges has been a driver of change in the communication environment and has led to the **integrated marketing communications (IMC)** school of thought. This approach delivers many benefits through integration, but as the use of digital communications increases, there are many challenges for marketing managers to consider.

This chapter will focus on IMC, and how brand message, the tools and the media channels can be managed to develop coordinated communication strategies which maximize the efficiency and effectiveness of the promotional element of the marketing mix.

The chapter begins with a consideration of the drivers of IMC, then looks at the planning process and how to develop a communication strategy. Next we explore the elements of IMC including the principles of communication and the importance of the message, the communication tools and their characteristics, and then we briefly introduce the media channels, touch on the people involved in communications and finally consider communication contexts: business to business (B2B) and business to consumer (B2C). Chapter 14 focuses in detail on mass communications tools by examining advertising, the media, sales promotions and public relations (PR). Chapter 15 discusses direct communications tools: personal selling and sales management, direct marketing, and customer relationship management, while Chapter 16 explores the tools and channels of digital marketing and social media.

Integrated Marketing Communications Approach

The IMC school of thought aims to move the emphasis of communications away from a step-by-step, linear, transactional process to an ongoing relational dialogue. Another fundamental shift is to move away from transactional communications to make communications customer-centered by capturing and using the reality of how individuals and businesses engage and come into contact with communications.

The transactional approach means promotional campaigns are designed to meet specific communication objectives such as creating awareness or stimulating action, using separate communications tools. Rarely are there any linkages between the messages carried by each tool. For example, in the past Heinz had a long-running television advertising campaign for its baked beans that aimed to position the product as a quality brand. However, at times it also used sales promotions techniques (e.g. multipack of four cans for the price of three) to combat supermarket value brands being sold at a few pence per can, although there were no explicit links between the television advertising campaign and the sales promotion initiatives. Now Heinz takes a very different approach. Its highly successful 'Grow your own' campaign, currently implemented for the third year running, seeks to remind sauce lovers across Europe about the quality of the brand and encourage engagement. Shoppers are encouraged to grow their own tasty tomatoes. This IMC campaign was activated via a mobile app, has its own Facebook page and is supported by a £1 million television campaign. Additionally, there is also in-store activation of the campaign, with on-pack labelling featuring the 'Grow your own' message, and at selected stores shoppers can also pick up a free pack of seeds. The campaign encourages the whole family to take part.

IMC campaigns seek to rationalize the approach to communications. By focusing on developing relational and coordinated communication strategies, it becomes possible to bring together communication tools, techniques, messages and media channels favoured by a particular target audience (Fill, 2011). It is difficult to pinpoint exactly when this change in communication planning took place. However, IMC began to be accepted as a valid approach for communications in the early 1990s. Duncan and Everett (1993) commented that the new customer-focused, technology-driven communications were an *orchestration, whole egg, seamless communication* approach, and Schultz referred to it as 'the process of developing and implementing various forms of persuasive communication programs with customers and prospects over time' (Schultz, 1993). From the mid 1990s, IMC adoption has become increasingly widespread and now IMC means integrating all useable promotional tools and appropriate media to deliver synergistic communication campaigns. In other, words, promotional campaigns select the most appropriate tools and channels which can be used in harmony with one another to maximize communication effectiveness so that the sum is greater than the individual parts.

The principles of IMC are that organizations coordinate their use of marketing communications tools, branding, images, logos and CRM strategies to deliver a clear, consistent, credible and competitive message about the organization and its products. The objective is to position products and organizations clearly and distinctively in the marketplace by providing target audiences with multiple opportunities to see, hear, read and/or interact with consistent marketing messages. As we discussed in Chapter 7, successful positioning is associated with products and services being favourably positioned in the minds of target audiences. 'A brand is the most valuable piece of real estate in the world: a corner of someone's mind' (Hegarty, 2011). IMC facilitates the positioning process by sending out consistent messages through all of the components of the promotional mix, and in doing so reinforces the core message.

EXHIBIT 13.1
O2's creative IMC campaign featuring cats grabs attention using the slogan, 'Be more dog'

Scan the QR code to see O2's £3 million IMC campaign 'Be More Dog'.

Drivers of IMC

Currently, advances in communication technology account for many changes taking place in the industry, but there are other key drivers that help to explain why more organizations are adopting the IMC approach:

- *Organizational drivers* focus on the benefits IMC can bring from an operational perspective—for example, streamlining communications activities, creating opportunities for increased profits through efficiency gains. Many organizations are faced with having to show greater accountability in the communication budget, and more measurable outcomes. IMC creates opportunities to create competitive advantage through coordinated brand development, and across an organization can deliver improved productivity and greater focus.
- *Target-market-based drivers* focus on changes which are affecting the delivery of communication messages. For example, the cost and availability of media channels is changing. Audiences are becoming more fragmented, and organizations are using different media and different timings to grab the attention of their audiences. Technology-enabled communications are used more frequently as target audiences' skills and communication literacy are increasing.
- *Communication drivers* focus on the potential benefits associated with the delivery of the message: for example, increased effectiveness of the message, through constant reinforcement of the core ideas, consistent product and brand communication across a range of touchpoints; less confusion over the meaning of the message; opportunities to build brand reputation and position clearly a product, brand or firm (based on Fill, 2011).

For marketing managers, achieving high levels of consistency across a range of communications is challenging. On the one hand, well-planned IMC campaigns can contribute to the development of competitive advantage, building stronger relationships between a brand and its stakeholders, improved consistency and clearer positioning of brands in the minds of customer. This approach can also be a source of further advantages insofar as there are opportunities to:

- *reduce costs* by standardizing communication messages across a selected promotional mix
- *create synergies* between the use of communication tools: for example, television advertising can be linked to in-store sales promotions and social media. So, members of a target audience receive a consistent message wherever they 'touch' an IMC campaign
- *reinforce competitive advantage* by creating a more consistent communication experience for customers. IMC campaigns potentially garner greater advantage than isolated campaigns. Following the global economic recession and subsequent changes in consumer buying patterns, some retail brands have found they need to reclaim market share by emphasizing the value of buying the brand. Marks & Spencer has increased its market spend as part of a relaunch; see Exhibit 13.2. The aim of the company's campaign is to communicate 'improved style and quality in general merchandising and innovation in food' (Vizard, 2015) through a range of communication channels.

On the other hand, however, organizations might have to change management structures and organizational culture to accommodate IMC, and creativity can be stifled if campaigns go wrong, they can do on a grander scale and have greater potential to damage a brand's reputation. Increased use of digital channels and social media is intensifying the demands on both creating and controlling campaigns. There are now many more opportunities to 'touch' a brand. Marketers have to consider the multiple touchpoints in a customer journey if they are to bridge the gap between the physical and digital world (Bylykbashi, 2015). Furthermore, other potential disadvantages of adopting an IMC approach are:

- *requires greater management commitment* throughout the development and implementation of an IMC campaign.

EXHIBIT 13.2
M&S revitalizes its market positioning with a new look

- *requires increased agency commitment* with the integration of all of the stages across a number of platforms, media and promotional tools, leading to a need for more involvement from all agencies involved.
- *encourages uniformity* since increased commitment from management and agencies can lead to demand for uniformity and might stifle creativity (Fill, 2011).

Managers should consider the advantages and disadvantages when planning and developing an IMC approach to campaigns (Fill, 2011).

Planning for Integrated Marketing Communications

So far, we have discovered there are many drivers which are now encouraging wider uptake of IMC as a framework for planning and managing communication campaigns and initiatives. We have, however, also identified a number of management considerations and challenges to be taken up if a brand is to maximize the potential advantages and avoid the disadvantages of adopting an IMC approach. A framework for applying an integrated marketing communications approach is given in Figure 13.1.

Marketing strategy and situation analysis

IMC is a framework for planning the use of the promotional mix. Therefore, it is important to remember that the objectives, the brand positioning statement, and more come from the marketing strategy (see Chapter 18 for more details). Opportunities identified from the marketing situation analysis and the target market analysis should be captured in order to enable use of promotions to contribute to the creation of differential advantage. This initial stage in the planning framework serves to ensure integration between the marketing strategy and promotional mix selection. The

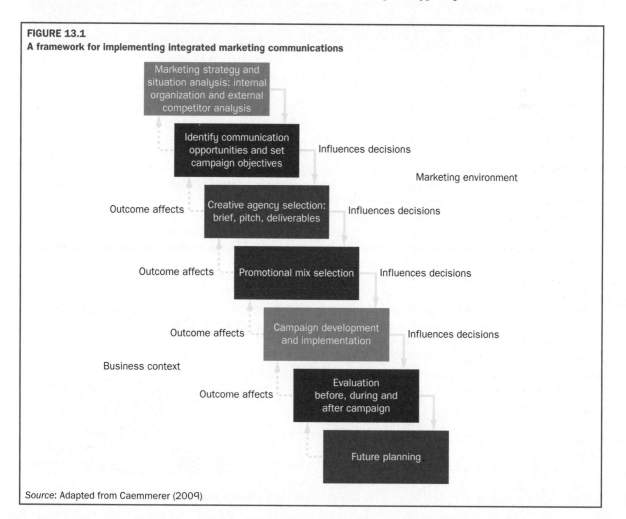

FIGURE 13.1
A framework for implementing integrated marketing communications

Source: Adapted from Caemmerer (2009)

analysis should also clarify the overarching objectives which guide the campaign, in the manner of Renault, wishing to enter new markets in Germany and position its products as the safest cars available. The promotional mix decisions depend on the marketing strategy, competitive positioning and the target market. For example, target market definition will lead to an understanding of the needs of the target audiences and how they can be reached by different promotional tools and media channels. Furthermore, differential advantage will affect message decisions.

IMC campaign objectives

Once issues from the marketing strategy and situation analysis have been decided, communication objectives will be set and promotional options selected (e.g. advertising,

EXHIBIT 13.3
Virgin Media's new mascot is an owl

direct marketing and personal selling) to form a brand-led approach. However, it should be noted that among practitioners there is some debate over which comes first—the marketing and brand strategy or the objectives for

---

MARKETING IN ACTION 13.1
Nike Attracts Creative Talent to Communicate its Global Messages

Harry Kane joined Wayne Rooney, Omar Abdulrahman and other top footballers in the launch of the Hypervenom II boots. The boots are positioned as 'crafted for a new breed of attacker'.

Nike is a brand that creative agencies want to work for, and it is seen as an innovative and thought-provoking brand. Nike's clothing and digital sport divisions are constantly conducting research and development so the brand can lead the way in wearable sport technologies. An example of a product is the FuelBand, which measures the wearer's movements throughout the day and produces reports on calorie intake, distance covered and total NikeFuel points accumulated. R/GA picked up the Fuelband business from Nike due to is prowess as a digital agency. In 2014 it won industry awards for its cross-platform campaigns, bringing together television and digital channels. The success of this agency in meeting Nike's communication goals has enabled it to be retained for European football events in 2016.

Nike is constantly developing and improving its product offerings such as the Hypervenom football boot, and this means plenty of opportunities for creative agencies to engage with the brand. Agencies are very keen to work with innovative companies, as it gives them an opportunity to develop highly differentiated communication campaigns. The Man vs machine, an award-winning agency, developed the creative solutions for Nike's Hypervenom II campaign. The creative theme was used at every stage of the campaign: film, in print, in stores and online.

Wieden + Kennedy is another highly creative global communications agency, which has worked with Nike since creating the brand's first-ever national television advert, aired in 1982 during the New York City Marathon. Since then, the agency has worked on Nike's outdoor, television and digital interactive campaigns, including the iconic 'Just do it' 'Write the future' and 'Endless possibilities' campaigns.

AKQA is a digital agency that is happy to collaborate with Nike to ensure its products are truly integrated into people's lives. The agency launched Nike Presto, which encouraged people to engage with the brand through arts and sounds. More recently, it developed the Ice Kings campaign, which aimed to ensure that Nike's customers could talk to its fans in the Moscow winter street soccer tournament.

Even though Nike is an attractive brand from a creative agency's perspective, both client and agency must build foundations to ensure a good working relationship is established. Setting clear and measurable goals, working collaboratively and choosing an agency with exploitable skills are some of the key areas that need to be right for a successful working partnership to develop.

Based on: Carr (2013); Anon (2015a); Beltrone (2014); Swift (2015); Manvsmachine (2015)

the communication campaign (further discussion of these issues and specific communication objectives appears in Chapters 14, 15 and 16; also see Marketing in Action 13.1).

So how do companies decide on communication objectives for integrated campaigns?

There are benefits to following the top-down, market-strategy-driven, brand-led approach as it means the marketing team are aware of what is required to position the brand and can tailor communications accordingly. This approach means that campaigns are coordinated and efficient. See Exhibit 13.3 for how Virgin Media uses its film *Birds behind bars* to promote a new season of the Netflix hit *Orange is the New Black*. This multi-platform campaign uses social media, retail channels and video on demand. However, sometimes marketing managers actually use (Ritson, 2011) their large IMC budgets to determine the shape of the campaign. In other words, they select promotional tools which are affordable, desirable or in-vogue with only a limited consideration of what the IMC campaign objectives actually are. This approach means that campaigns can become disjointed and inefficient, and the outcome can be that they perform poorly and achieve little for the brand when driven by the promotional tools rather than the marketing and branding strategy.

The key point to be aware of is this: clear objectives are imperative for IMC if it is to be considered as a valid and achievable framework for planning communications. (Specific communication objectives for each of the tools are discussed in Chapters 14, 15 and 16.)

Creative agency selection

Once the objectives are set, the next step is to select creative **agencies** (which includes using internal teams and departments) to develop a communication brief and determine the deliverables. Once the creative brief has been developed, creative agencies will be selected to pitch for the campaign. It should be noted that often communications are developed by the internal marketing team, but there should still be a briefing document, as this sets down on a single page the core requirement of the campaign, which acts as a guide for everyone in terms of the message, target audiences, the tone, the budget and the deliverables. Agencies and/or internal departments will prepare a pitch for the client that will show how their ideas and use of the communication budget will meet the client's requirements. Marketing managers must decide how to determine whether an agency can deliver on its promises. This has always been an issue, but it is a problem that has become increasingly difficult to solve in the digital age. Agencies are not opposed to claiming they offer a full range of services when, in fact, they are not able to deliver seamless integration across all of the communication tools (Bendaby, 2011) (the issue of agency selection is revisited in Chapters 14 and 16). See Marketing in Action 13.1 to find out how Nike works with creative agencies to produce innovative IMC campaigns.

 Scan the QR code to find out where the inspiration came from for the Wieden & Kennedy 'Just do it' campaign for Nike.

In the past, selection of the agencies that will produce the required elements of the campaign was considered to be in the advertising domain. This is no longer the case as a full service agency should offer the capacity to provide all of the promotional tools. Some agencies (e.g. BBH advertising agency) do offer a complete service across all of the communication tools. However, there are specialist agencies with particular expertise (e.g. Fever PR, an agency specializing in public relations online and offline) or an internal company team. Once the agency selection is complete the creative teams, account managers and other service providers will work together to produce each of the elements of the campaign. Media schedulers will be involved in making sure that any media requirements are available and fulfilled. A Gantt chart or similar project management timetable will be set out as a guide to make sure that each of the elements of the campaign is ready at the prescribed time. Timing is very important to IMC campaigns, especially as different tools might be required to fulfil different functions, and digital technology is enabling brands to communicate with their supporters in real time. The Lawn Tennis Association has always been positioned as a quintessentially English, and its approaches to communication have fitted this stance. However, the Lawn Tennis Association teamed up with IBM to use the latest technology to capture and engage tennis fans in real time via social media, iBeacons, television and websites (Bernard, 2014).

 Scan the QR code to see how IBM is communicating with tennis fans at Wimbledon.

MARKETING IN ACTION 13.2
Digital Platforms, Managed Content and Customer Journeys Move IMC to a New Level

Some commentators argue that manufacturers have to go beyond *just* integrating their brand communications across a number of different media. In the digital space, it is suggested that communications are synchronized to ensure that a company's campaigns allow everyone who touches a product from *cradle to grave* to get the communication messages. This approach requires collaborative cross-stakeholder involvement to produce a seamless brand experience.

Arguably, an IMC campaign uses communication tools sequentially and the core communication message is translated into a format that is appropriate for the media channel. For example, Tesco spends over £110 million a year on its brand communications, which is key to it retaining is market leadership position; for example, its 'Every little helps' campaign, along with the introduction of its Tesco Value range and the Tesco Clubcard, helped the brand move into number one spot in the UK grocery market by 1995, overtaking its rival Sainsbury's. The 'Every Little Helps' campaign message was used first in the 1990s and was launched first on television, followed by sales promotions in print media and in store and through the Tesco Clubcard. The initial campaign attracted 1.3 million new customers to Tesco. Since then, the message has been consistently applied through various communication tools as a fully integrated series of campaigns. But as Tesco moves forward, its new communications agency BBH will have to consider how to engage customers simultaneously across multiple platforms.

Arguably, synchronized campaigns change the emphasis by focusing on the strengths of each communication technique and identifying each step of the customer journey and the touchpoints where customers will engage with a brand. This allows creatives to plan how to manage the execution of the campaign in real time and respond to engagement from the target audience. The reason for the shift in emphasis is that previously, choosing the message and then controlling how it was received by the target audience was more straightforward. Today, a customer's first encounter with a brand could be a Twitter feed, a shared Facebook message or a mobile app.

Another consideration is the content that is developed in conjunction with communication campaigns. Brands are increasingly aiming to tell an enduring story which will foster engagement and customer loyalty. Content management also needs to be planned around campaign objectives, the target audience and the targeting opportunities. Content marketing enables a brand to focus on its core values and reflect on customers' needs. But it is important that the content does not become a rambling dialogue that dilutes the meaning of a brand. According to Hertz Europe, 'The secret is to ensure the content focuses on what a product enables someone to do or the experiences it opens up for them.' Taking this approach enables Hertz to ensure the content is constantly refreshed and on-message.

Consequently, companies have new challenges if they wish to take IMC campaigns to a new level. They have to consider their customers' journeys and where, when and how customers encounter various communication tools and digital platforms, before developing specific communication messages. Companies also have to devise a strategy for managing content that might support the campaign to ensure that the brand positioning is not diluted by an *off-topic* digital conversation.

Based on: Magee (2015); Anon (n.d.); DeSantis Breindel (2015); Hill (2015); Hemsley (2015); Clark and Chan (2014)

The advantage of using one agency is better communication and specialist expertise but using several agencies gives clients more flexibility regarding the choice of the best agencies to handle each media type (Weissberg, 2008). However, using several agencies can lead to conflict regarding who is paid for what and who takes charge. Suppose an integrated campaign is mainly direct marketing, but includes an online game, created by a digital specialist who also thinks of the main campaign strap-line. Which agency has contributed more to the campaign and which deserves the greater financial reward (Bidlake, 2008)? Such questions can create conflict between agencies, and problems for clients. The chosen integrated communication strategy will be executed and subsequently evaluated in the light of the set objectives. At the NSPCC, communication messages are often informative and aim to change behaviour. In a thought-provoking campaign, 'Alex's willy', this leading children's charity in the UK used prime-time television, social media and digital spaces to deliver messages to achieve its new brand objectives for its Share Aware campaign, aimed at helping parents keep their children safe on social media and teach them not to share inappropriate content (West, 2015).

Please note, integrated marketing communications is not restricted to consumer markets. Furthermore, relationships between clients and agencies are fundamental to the success of communication initiatives. (Client–agency relationships are covered in detail in Chapter 14.) Read Marketing in Action 13.2 to find out how the IMC concept is developing in the digital space and helping businesses communicate.

 Scan the QR code to see how the NSPCC used animated film in its informative IMC 'Share Aware' campaign.

The promotional mix

The communication objectives can help to determine which communication tools to include in a campaign (Caemmerer, 2009). Furthermore, the creative pitch enables an agency to make suggestions about which tools are the most likely to achieve the campaign objectives set by the client. Ultimately, the client (the company commissioning the campaign) decides which tools to use, which creative message and combination of agencies represent the best value, and which are likely to achieve their communication aims.

Campaign development and implementation

At this stage the promotional mix decision is finalized and the message and creative execution confirmed. Other major decisions taken at this stage are the media channel selection, planning and scheduling. The media decision will affect the budget. For example, television advertising reaches a large television audience but can be expensive, whereas print media advertising using regional newspapers can be a relatively low-cost option but will not have the same reach, and digital platforms offer scope for interactive campaigns, which can foster high levels of engagement. The relative merits of media channels are discussed later in the chapter and in Chapter 14.

Evaluation

Following the implementation, each of the elements of the campaign will be evaluated to assess overall effectiveness. Evaluation should take place at all stages of the campaign, including pre-testing, tracking studies and post-testing. This approach can help to assess the effectiveness and efficiency of the IMC campaign (Sherwood, Stevens and Warren, 1989). Measurements are taken to determine the extent to which campaigns have achieved communication objectives, and whether it is moving target audiences in the planned direction. Evaluation also feeds into future planning.

Future planning

After the implementation of an IMC campaign each of the elements should be reviewed. Findings from the review should be fed back and recorded to inform the development of future campaigns. Throughout the campaign information should be fed back. While the planning framework shows a linear process which moves from one stage to another, in reality the process is rather more iterative with information and learning influencing and informing developments at every stage of the process.

This section has examined the IMC planning process. The next section looks at the elements which underpin the IMC planning process and are fundamental to its successful application: the message, the tools, the media channels, and the contexts.

Elements of Integrated Marketing Communications

To survive, organizations need to communicate with their customers; marketing messages tell buyers about the meaning of a brand and the benefits it can deliver. Arguably, 50 years ago delivering a message to a particular target audience was relatively straightforward; there were a small number of commercial television and radio channels and a few well-known printed publications, which a marketer might use to get the messages across. Now the communications environment has changed, however; it is more complex, integrated and universal. There are more interconnections between the core elements of communications to consider when planning an IMC campaign. The core elements are: the message, which is used to position a product, brand and/or an organization in the minds of the customer; the tools, the six key methods which provide the means of achieving communication objectives; the media, which are the channels that carry the message to the audience; the people, who collectively are responsible for creating, planning, managing and implementing the communication campaign; and the context, the setting in which communication takes place (see Table 13.1).

TABLE 13.1 Core elements of IMC

Elements	Examples
The message	Rational, emotional
The tools	Advertising, personal selling, sales promotions, digital marketing, direct marketing, public relations
The media channels	Broadcast, print, Internet, mobile, outdoor
The people	Account managers, clients, agencies, schedulers, planners, web service providers
The context	Industrial, consumer, public sector

The message

In this section we explore the function of the **message** and how it might be communicated to target audiences using both simple and complex processes.

At the heart of communications is the message. Messages are very important as they not only transfer information from a message sender to its recipient but can also determine the nature of a relationship, establish credibility (Fill, 2011), set the tone for a *conversation* and cross tangible and intangible boundaries. Effective messages can become so powerful that they can be heard around the globe, when used with suitable media channels. For example, when Bob Geldof, the Irish rock star, wanted to communicate the message that millions of people in Africa were dying of starvation, he decided to use a rock concert to get the message across to young audiences around the world. His core message was famine relief for Africa. The rock concert was Live Aid. This concert was transmitted from the UK and the USA on live television. Bob's message brought together a global audience, united music and youth and spread the message of famine relief to a 400 million television viewers, in over 50 countries (Hegarty, 2011).

In marketing, messages take on a special meaning—they are not mercurial asides between individuals, or unplanned, off-the-cuff remarks, but are carefully planned and crafted. Messages play an important role in positioning. To create effective messages, marketers need to consider the credibility of the message and its source (Kelman, 1961). For a target audience to engage with a marketing message, it has to be attractive and interesting, the source (the sender of the message) has to be perceived as credible and believable to have the power to deliver the message promise. The next step is to establish suitable brand messages to communicate with target audiences.

As discussed earlier, product (Chapter 8) and service (Chapter 9) brands are distinctive market offerings which can be easily identified by target audiences for whom they deliver a parcel of benefits. During the development of a brand, its quality, value, features, name, design, packaging are determined. These features of the brand can then be used in crafting marketing messages.

Marketing messages take many forms: for example, emotional and rational appeals that are designed to stimulate different responses such as fear, humour, action. In Chapters 4 and 5 we discovered how consumers react to both emotional and factual stimuli, whereas business buyers respond to more rational, information-based messages.

 Scan the QR code to see how e-harmony is using humour to attract customers.

Information-based messages

Sometimes companies wish to provide their customers with information that will enable them to make an informed decision about the brands they choose.

Increasingly, brands are using digital platforms to provide their customers with the information they need to make their choices, as well as more traditional print and broadcast channels. For example, DW Fitness Clubs use inspirational stories from the members of their gyms to communicate the benefits of becoming a member. DW's website has detailed information about its membership, its clubs and personal trainers, but it also uses outdoor billboards and television adverts.

Information-based messages use different formats, for example Weetabix's 'incredible inside', a £10-million campaign, reached out to all its customers with a television advert that aimed to remind them how important their bodies are, and in doing so deliver hard facts. This style of message delivery is sometimes referred to as a *slice of life*.

 Scan the QR code to see Weetabix's 'incredible inside' television advert.

Emotional messages

Sometimes messages are designed to stimulate a response and possibly connect with the target audience through a particular emotion. For example, Procter & Gamble's 'Like a girl' campaign focused on a girl's life to promote its Always brand, and used male/female perceptions, relationships and music to create a highly emotional appeal.

Messages that shock are often used to attract not only the attention of the target audiences but also of the wider media. See Exhibit 13.4 for how the United Nations used shock tactics in its campaign against sexism and discrimination against women. To accompany the poster campaign it ran a YouTube animation that sought to demonstrate the level of sexism within society using a global Google autofill study. Whilst not necessarily accurate in the inference of its finding of the levels of discrimination against women (as autofill searches make many bizarre suggestions), this campaign raised awareness of the injustices against women on a global scale (Mahdawi, 2013).

 Scan the QR code to see Procter & Gamble's 'Like a girl' campaign and see how it used a slice of life to convey a complex message.

In Chapter 14 we explore messages in more detail and look at how to create different types of message appeal—informative, interactive or actionable. Now we are going to consider how the message is delivered through the communication process.

The communication process: simple and complex

While messages are at the heart of the process, the actual way we communicate is also very important. In this section we examine the elements of the simple communication model which shows how a message is transferred from one person to another. Then we consider how messages are spread within and across communities.

A simple model of the *communication process* is shown in Figure 13.2.

The *source* (or communicator) *encodes* a message by translating the idea to be communicated into a symbol consisting of words, pictures and numbers. Some advertisements attempt to encode a message using the minimum of words, while others provide extensive detail. We explore message content later in this section.

The message is *transmitted* through media such as television or posters, which are selected for their ability to reach the desired target audience in the desired way. Communication requirements may affect the choice of media. For example, if the

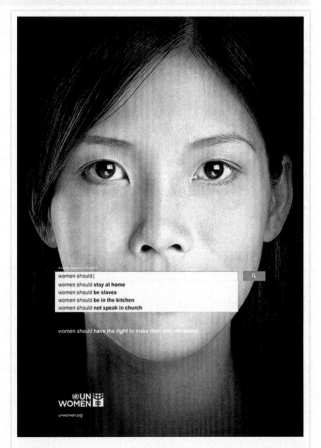

EXHIBIT 13.4
The United Nations used Google search behaviour to communicate its messages about sexual discrimination

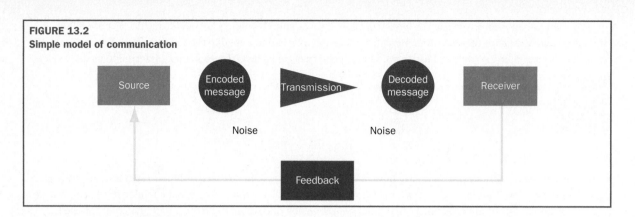

FIGURE 13.2
Simple model of communication

encoded message requires the product to be demonstrated, the Internet, television and cinema may be preferred to posters and the printed publications.

Noise—distractions and distortions during the communication process—may prevent transmission to some of the target audience. A television advertisement may not reach a member of the household because of conversation or the telephone ringing. Similarly, a press advertisement may not be noticed because of editorial competing for attention.

When a *receiver* sees or hears the message, it is *decoded*. This is the process by which the receiver interprets the symbols transmitted by the source. The aim is for the receiver's decoding to coincide with the source's encoding process. The receiver thus interprets the message in the way intended by the source. Messages that rely on words more than pictures can also be decoded differently. For example, a message such as 'the most advanced washing machine in the world' may be accepted by some receivers but rejected by others.

Communicators need to understand their targets before encoding messages so that they are credible. Otherwise the response may be disbelief and rejection. In a personal selling situation, *feedback* from buyer to salesperson may be immediate, as when objections are raised or a sale is concluded. For other types of marketing such as advertising and sales promotion, feedback may rely on marketing research to estimate reactions to commercials, and increases in sales due to incentives.

An important point to recognize in the communication process is the sophistication of receivers and how they can play different roles in the wider dissemination of the message.

The simple model of communication explains the basic concepts and transmission of a message from sender to receiver, but the communication of a message rarely takes place in such isolation. Message receivers interact with one another and consequently they can act as a conduit to spread messages further afield.

There are also other levels of complexity to consider; different message recipients play different roles in the wider diffusion of messages. Katz and Lazarfield (1955) found that some individuals were able to exert greater influence than others. These opinion leaders (Rogers, 1983)—as they have become known—enjoy higher status within social groups and their views are considered more highly by other members of the social/peer group. Opinion leaders play an important role in the communication process as 'they are receptive to new ideas' and are happy to try and buy new products and services (Fill, 2011). Opinion formers are individuals who are able to exert personal influence because of authority, education or status associated with the objects of the communication process (Fill, 2011). The influence of opinion formers is also important in the communication process. A theatre critic writing reviews in a local or national newspaper or blogging online has also become an important form of opinion former. For example, Elin Kling is a Swedish fashion blogger who collaborated with H&M and then became a fashion designer; Pete Cashmore, the Scottish founder of the famous blog site Mashable, is a highly influential voice in technology, business, social media and entertainment.

The simple model of communication suggests that communications are unidirectional, passing from sender to receiver, and in the past this model has been used to explain the spread of many mass-marketing campaigns. But the world of communications has become highly complicated. There are many different ways for individuals and companies to communicate and interact. Indeed, the boundaries between the pillars of the marketing mix are becoming eroded as products and communications come closer together.

In a multichannel world, where message receivers gather information from multiple points such as websites, apps, a multitude of television channels, printed publications and, perhaps more importantly, each other, a more complex model is needed to understand how communication messages are disseminated. Figure 13.3 shows the complexity of communication networks.

FIGURE 13.3
Complex model of communication

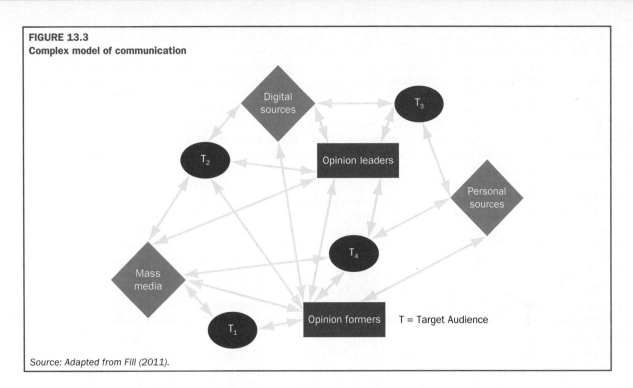

Source: Adapted from Fill (2011).

Figure 13.3 shows how complex two-way linkages can form between target audiences, opinion formers and leaders, the media (television, radio, Internet), digital sources of influence (e.g. websites, social media), and personal sources of information (experiences). The implications for developing IMC campaigns are that multiple two-way integrated communications become formal and informal. This means message senders need to use multiple methods and channels to ensure messages are being received by the intended target audience. For instance, a website selling innovative products (digital source) may provide information that may then be picked up by a journalist (opinion former) who does a review for a special interest magazine (mass media) which is read by the local computer expert (opinion leader) who informs her friends (target audience). The communication message potentially is the central core of a conversation between multiple participants. Read more about how conversations and storytelling can help to spread a message in Mini Case 13.1.

MINI CASE 13.1
Conversations, Storytelling and Happy Endings

Conversations

When Owen Baxter and Geoffrey Lewis (executives of the then failing Hush Puppy brand of shoes) had a conversation with a New York stylist, they were told that Hush Puppies had suddenly become hip in the clubs and downtown bars of Manhattan and that there were resale shops in the Village in Soho where the shoes (Hush Puppies) were being sold (Gladwell, 2000). Reportedly, what followed was that the shoes were chosen by fashion buyers to feature in their new ranges, and the basset hound (symbol for the brand) was used by a Los Angeles designer on his store in Hollywood. The sales of Hush Puppies quadrupled year on year, and so the brand that was on its way out was not only saved but became a staple item in every young trendy American's wardrobe. In this tale, the informal communication network enabled the message to be filtered back from the target audience (young people in East Village Manhattan), to the opinion leaders (fashion designers and stylists), and eventually to more formal traditional mass media communication channels.

Storytelling

Storytelling is part of our daily lives and helps us to make sense of the complex world around us. Often we become part of the story, and brands utilize storytelling as a platform for developing meaning. John

»

Hegarty, Creative Director of Bartle Bogle Hegarty (BBH), is one of the world's advertising aficionados, and he advocates that storytelling is probably the most powerful form of communication as it can be used very effectively to make brands memorable (see quote at opening of chapter). However, he suggests that messages and stories need to be created for the screen-based culture (television, computers, mobile phones) that is now so prevalent in modern society. To be successful in the screen-based world of communications, it is important to get the balance right between visuals and words. In many of the highly successful Levi's 501 jeans commercials the story is a visual narrative. For example, in the 1985 classic advert, set in a 1950s launderette, Nick Kamen (the leading character) walks into the launderette wearing sunglasses, which he proceeds to remove. He then fills the washing machine with soap powder, removes his top and Levi's and then, wearing just his boxer shorts, sits down to read a magazine while he waits for his jeans to be washed. The slogan shown on screen at the end of the commercial 'Levi's 501 the original shrink-to-fit jeans' neatly brings the tale to an end.

Another tip, from William Goldman, award-winning novelist and screenwriter, is 'Come in late, leave early.' What this means is that the scriptwriter should leave space for the target audience to fill in some of the gaps and should not over-explain. Scripts for commercials do tend to be brief and give the creative director space to tell the story visually. According to John Hegarty, 'Great writing and storytelling also has to understand the principle of input and out-take. For example, "If I want to make you think I'm funny, I don't tell you that I'm really funny, I tell you a joke. You laugh and think, Wow, that guy is really funny." He also explains that communicators should inspire people to do something rather than merely give them instructions and should never forget that 'a brand is an agglomeration of stories linked together by a vision.'

Happy endings

Creating successful communication messages is a challenge for marketing managers and identifying opportunities to stimulate meaningful conversations or create a story that *captures the hearts and minds* of the target audience is difficult. Furthermore, the attitude of the recipient will be influenced by whether they are favourably disposed towards advertising in general or not, as this will affect the effectiveness of the communication message. Despite these challenges, manufactures of generic products like butter, milk, tea and toilet rolls have frequently been successful in ticking all the boxes and creating messages with the best happy endings in the communication industry by developing stories involving animals and children.

In 1972, the likeable Labrador puppy first appeared in Andrex toilet-roll commercials and proved so successful that it has since appeared in over 130 campaigns. The puppies feature on the products and the website, and over the years the slogans have evolved from 'soft strong and very long' through 'tuggable, huggable softness' to 'Be kind to your behind'. The loveable puppies continue to make the brand memorable, and deliver happy endings all round for Andrex and its customers. More recently, Budweiser is another brand to use 'puppy love' to produce highly emotional adverts with happy endings.

There are many other examples of products that have successfully used animals in their campaign stories: Kerrygold butter with its cows; PG Tips tea and its chimpanzees; Cesar dog food with a white west highland terrier; and the Felix cat food brand that uses the iconic black and white cartoon cat. From shoes to car commercials, animals score highly on the likeability scale and are usually a safe bet for delivering a happy ending that captures the imagination of the target audience and delivers a good return on investment for the brand.

But not all happy endings are born out of cuteness and likeability. Social media and video on demand have opened new routes to follow Hegarty's principles. In a viral campaign, #epicstrut, Moneysupermarket.com arguably applied the general principles of the Levi's classic advert to capture attention and drive engagement. In the advert, which features the Pussycat Dolls hit 'Don't Cha', Dave expresses his satisfaction at the saving on his car insurance by strutting in a combination of suit, hot pants and black patent high heels, much to the surprise of passers-by. Within the first few days this campaign went viral.

Questions:

1 How does the interactional model of communication work for Hush Puppies?
2 Explain more fully why coming in late might be a valid approach for developing communication messages. Give examples of commercials which take this approach.
3 Why do certain brands use animals in their campaigns?

Based on: Anon (2015b); Gladwell (2000); Hegarty (2011); Mehta (2000); Fill (2011); Cordiner (2009)

The increasing complexity of communications channels, the shift towards informal away from formal lines of communications and the growing importance of digital and mobile channels and media are blurring the divisions between communication tools, sales channels and the media. Research (Doherty, Ellis-Chadwick and Hart, 1999) into the use of digital technology in the retail sector has highlighted that for this industry the Internet is a channel which facilitates communications, interactions and sales. For example, Dixons Carphone uses SMS to send messages to its customers, informing them of the latest offers but also uses this channel to provide product delivery information. Additionally, the firm's brand websites are used for sales, communications and aftersales care. For the customer, the message, the media and the channel work seamlessly together, while for the firm the main point is that the basic premise of their messages has not changed but the opportunities to leverage advantage through greater functionality and extended touchpoints of the message have increased significantly.

The tools

In this section we explore the promotional communication tools which deliver the message to the target audiences. We also examine their key characteristics and the impact on selection of tools to use for IMC campaigns. In addition to this brief section introducing the tools, each element of the promotional communication mix, and how they can be used in campaigns, is covered in more detail in the following chapters. Three chapters cover specific tools: Chapter 14 mass communications, which are those tools that reach wide audiences using non-personal communication techniques, such as advertising, public relations, sales promotions; Chapter 15 direct communications, the tools that communicate with specific members of the target audience, such as direct marketing, and personal selling; Chapter 16 digital promotions and social media, tools that connect with target audiences through digital and mobile channels, such as buzz marketing and email marketing.

Before looking at the specific tools we briefly consider the division of tools into the groups: mass, direct and digital.

Mass, direct and digital communications

As explored earlier, messages can take many forms and be communicated to various audiences. Because of the volume of marketing messages that are currently aimed at consumers and businesses there is a likelihood that many of these messages will not reach the target recipients in the way that might be intended. This fact makes the study of marketing communications a fascinating aspect of marketing. Currently, there are three major groups of tools available to the marketer.

1 *Mass marketing communications* include advertising, sales promotions and public relations. These are methods of communication which can be styled to meet IMC campaign objectives. Mass communications methods are those which primarily involve sending non-personal messages to wide target audiences. The main media for mass communications are broadcast, print and digital. Mass communications are sometimes criticized because their impart is difficult to measure—particularly advertising and PR—therefore it can be difficult to value the return on investment.

2 *Direct marketing communications* include personal selling, exhibitions and direct marketing. These are also methods of communications which can be styled to meet IMC campaign objectives, but the main difference is that direct communications can be personalized, highly specific and tend to be used to target narrow or niche audiences. These tools rarely use broadcast or print media to deliver the message. Direct communications are also easier to measure than mass communications. The measurement aspect has been a key driver in the increase in the use of these tools in recent years.

3 *Digital promotions and social media communications* include, websites, email marketing, buzz marketing and social media. Digital communications can also be styled to meet IMC campaign objectives, but are more difficult to categorize because of their flexibility. For example, a company website can accommodate many aspects and elements of IMC (Chaffey and Ellis-Chadwick, 2012). The BBC uses its websites as a communication channel, an information resource, a media player and a sales channel. Digital communications can reach wide, narrow and individual target audiences. These forms of communication are the most measurable: sophisticated analytics and metric programs provide a wealth of data ranging from what a website user downloads to the time of day they open and read their email messages. Digital marketing and social media are explored in detail in Chapter 16.

The rest of this section introduces the individual tools that make up the promotional mix and considers their impact for IMC campaigns.

The challenge for marketing managers responsible for communications is selecting the *right* mix of tools and then the media channels to deliver the message. The promotional communication mix is a key element in any IMC campaign. The reason is that the mix provides the means by which the message achieves campaign objectives and determines the style used to craft the message. There are six major components of the mix: advertising, personal selling, direct marketing, digital promotions, sales promotion and public relations.

1 **Advertising**: any paid form of non-personal communication of ideas or products in the prime media: i.e. television, the press, outdoor, cinema, radio and the Internet.
2 **Personal selling**: oral communication with prospective purchasers with the intention of making a sale.
3 **Direct marketing**: the distribution of products, information and promotional benefits to target consumers through interactive communication in a way that allows response to be measured.
4 **Digital promotions**: the promotion of products to consumers and businesses through digital media channels.
5 **Sales promotion**: incentives to consumers or the trade that are designed to stimulate purchases.
6 **Public relations**: to educate and inform an organization's publics through the media without paying for the time or space directly.

In addition, product placement, sponsorship and exhibitions are also used to communicate with target audiences, and branding.

These tools are covered in Chapters 14 and 15 respectively.

In order to develop an IMC campaign, the marketing manager must make a choice of the promotional blend needed to communicate to the target audience. Each of the six major promotional tools has its own strengths and limitations and these are summarized in Table 13.2. Marketers will carefully weigh these factors against communication objectives to decide the amount of resources to channel into each tool. Usually, five considerations will have a major impact on the choice of the promotional mix.

1 *Resource availability and the cost of promotional tools*: to conduct a national advertising campaign may require several million pounds. If resources are not available, cheaper tools such as sales promotion or public relations may have to be used.
2 *Market size and concentration*: if a market is small and concentrated then personal selling may be feasible, but for mass markets that are geographically dispersed selling to the ultimate customer would not be cost effective. In such circumstances advertising, digital promotion or direct marketing may be the correct choice.
3 *Customer information needs*: if a complex technical argument is required, personal selling may be preferred. If all that is required is the appropriate brand image, advertising may be more sensible.
4 *Product characteristics*: because of the above arguments, business-to-business companies tend to spend more on personal selling than advertising, whereas consumer goods companies tend to do the reverse.
5 *Push versus pull strategies*: a push strategy involves an attempt to sell into channel intermediaries (e.g. retailers) and is dependent on personal selling and trade promotions. A pull strategy bypasses intermediaries to communicate to consumers directly. The resultant consumer demand persuades intermediaries to stock the product. Advertising and consumer promotions are more likely to be used.

TABLE 13.2 Key characteristics of the core tools of the promotional mix
Advertising
• Good for awareness building because it can reach a wide audience quickly • Repetition means that a brand positioning concept can be communicated effectively; television is particularly strong, but the level of use is changing due to the Internet • Can be used to aid the sales effort, to legitimize a firm and its products • Impersonal, lacks flexibility and questions cannot be answered • Limited capability to close the sale
Personal selling
• Interactive: questions can be answered and objectives overcome • Adaptable: presentations can be changed depending on customer needs • Complex arguments can be developed • Relationships can be built because of its personal nature • Provides the opportunity to close the sale • Sales calls are costly

Direct marketing

- Individual targeting of consumers most likely to respond to an appeal
- Communication can be personalized
- Short-term effectiveness can easily be measured
- A continuous relationship can be built through periodic contact
- Activities are less visible to competitors
- Response rates are often low
- Poorly targeted direct marketing activities cause consumer annoyance

Digital promotions

- Global reach to consumers and businesses at a comparatively low cost
- Highly measurable
- Interactive enables a dialogue between companies and their customers and suppliers
- Highly adaptable as messages, prices, products and content can be changed rapidly
- Highly flexible, can be used to create sales and communication channel
- Highly targeted and can be personalized
- Convenient form of access to product and firm information and purchasing
- Avoids the necessity of negotiating and arguing with salespeople
- High cost of development of websites and mobile content
- Poses security issues and risk of intrusion

Sales promotion

- Incentives provide a quick boost to sales
- Effects may be only short-term
- Excessive use of some incentives (e.g. money off) may damage brand image

Public relations

- Highly credible as message comes from a third party
- Higher readership than advertisements in trade and technical publications
- Loss of control: a press release may or may not be used, and its content may be distorted

Two points need to be stressed. First, marketing communications is not the exclusive province of the promotional mix. All of the marketing mix communicates to target customers. The product itself communicates quality; price may be used by consumers as an indicator of quality, and the choice of distribution channel will affect customer exposure to the product. Secondly, effective communication is not a one-way producer-to-consumer flow. Producers need to understand the needs and motivation of their target audience before they can talk to them in a meaningful way. For example, marketing research may be used to understand large consumer segments before designing an IMC campaign, and salespeople may ask questions of buyers to unfold their particular circumstances, problems and needs before making a sales presentation. Furthermore, through the Internet and the web, members of the target audience can freely express their views and opinions through customer feedback, reviews, blogs and social media.

Developing a successful IMC campaign involves careful planning and implementation, topics which are discussed in more detail later in the chapter. However, at the start of a campaign, companies should ensure they have completed a situation analysis and have identified communication opportunities before selecting the communication mix. Read Marketing in Action 13.3 to find out how Renault used an IMC campaign to enter German markets.

Furthermore, communication mix decisions should not be taken in isolation. Marketers need to consider the complete communication package by selecting tools which create a suitable blend with other components of the promotional campaign mix. The aim is to ensure that a clear and consistent message is received by target audiences. The media channel which carries the message is a further consideration. In the past media decisions were mainly associated with advertising, but now other tools can be involved in media selection. For example, sales promotions can appear on broadcast, outdoor media, in store, or delivered via email. Direct marketing uses the Internet, mail services, mobile, and even personal selling is now possible via the web. Public relations messages can also involve similar media selection as they can be sent via the Internet and through mobile messaging.

The Renault IMC campaign highlights how combining tools and media to deliver a consistent message can be effective in generating the interest of a wide audience and eventually changing the attitudes of target consumers.

MARKETING IN ACTION 13.3
What do Sausage, Sushi and Crispbreads have in Common?
Renault's IMC Campaign has the Answer

When Renault was looking to expand its market share into Germany, the director of marketing communications and his team took advantage of primary and secondary data. They used tracking studies carried out by GfK (www.gfk.com), and readership surveys in leading car magazines such as *Auto* and *Motor und Sport* (Caemmerer, 2009), to capture changing consumer attitudes towards car brands. Following this analysis, the Renault communications director decided to attack the main German competitors directly by positioning Renault's cars closer to Mercedes, Audi and BMW, improving perceptions of safety and desirability of the Renault products.

The objective of the IMC campaign was to raise awareness, so one of the key challenges was to decide on the promotional mix. The core message for the campaign was '*Die sichersten Autos kommen aus Frankreich*' ('The safest cars come from France'). Renault sent the brief (outline of the communication details) to various communication agencies—advertising, public relations and direct marketing—for them to suggest creative ideas that could communicate the message. German agency Nordpol + Hamburg (http://www.nordpol.com) suggested a mix of cinema and television advertising supported by a viral marketing initiative and a new website, as well as print media. These tools were chosen to give widespread reach, grab attention and provide a source of detailed information to enable potential customers to find out about the safety record of Renault cars against other leading German, Japanese and Swedish manufacturers. To reinforce the central message of safety, a television commercial showed national food items (rather than cars) being tested in a crash test situation. To represent Germany, a huge frankfurter squashed into the barrier and exploded, an enormous sushi roll (Japan) and giant crispbread (Sweden) suffered the same fate, but when it was the turn of the French bread, it bounced back from the barrier with very limited damage, as it was able to absorb the impact of the crash. The message was reinforced with the slogan '*Die sichersten Autos kommen aus Frankreich Renault*' appearing at the end of the commercial.

Once the creative side was decided on, the media channels were selected—cinema, radio and the Internet— as a good media mix whose elements would complement each other. The cinema advert was supported by a viral email marketing campaign. Post-campaign evaluation and analysis revealed that consumer attitudes were changing as a result of seeing the campaign.

The crash concept proved very successful, and Renault continued to use the idea in follow-up commercials for a number of years including creating a ballet with eight different Renault models.

Based on: Caemmerer (2009)

Media channels

This section introduces the channels which carry the message using the selected communication tool to the target audience. There used to be a joke among media people that the client's attitude to its part in advertising was, '10 minutes to go before lunch. Just enough time to discuss media' (Syedain, 1992). However, as media costs have risen and brands become more targeted, and the choice of media channels has increased, this attitude has disappeared. Table 13.3 shows the different media channels available to marketing communication managers.

TABLE 13.3 Media channels

Media channel	Type
Broadcast	Television, radio
Print	Newspapers, magazines, fanzines
Digital	Websites, intranets, portals, email, interactive TV, mobile
Social	Online communities, blogs
Outdoor	Billboards, street furniture, transport, guerrilla
Indoor	Point of sale, in-store posters, window and shelf displays, ambient
Cinema	Multiplex, Imax, outdoor

Arguably, before the Internet was available commercially (pre-1989), media decisions were clear cut. They involved deciding which **media class** (e.g. broadcast, print), and which media vehicle (the specific newspaper) would carry the message. Print was the most widely used media, followed by television. However, since the commercialization of the Internet the whole media world has changed. The Internet now accounts for more of the communication budget spend than any other single media (e.g. television, newspapers, radio, outdoor). The reason for its increasing popularity is bound up in its flexibility. The Internet (the web and associated technology) can act not only as a multimedia channel, offering marketing communication managers the opportunity to send video, audio and text-based messages, but also creates an environment for advertising, sales promotions, direct marketing, personal selling and public relations. Consequently, digital technologies now accommodate almost every aspect of the communication and media mix. The technology also adds innovative ways to communicate with messages to a target audience, for example animation, interaction, social communities and crowd-sourcing (discussed further in Chapter 16).

Currently, organizations use various media channels to carry their message. Probably the key media decision is which forms of **media channel** to use (e.g. broadcast, print, digital).

Media channel choice

When considering which media channel the media planner faces the choice of using television, press, cinema, outdoor, radio, digital platforms and channels or some combination of media classes. Various considerations will be taken into account: *creative factors* may have a major bearing on the decision. The key question that needs to be addressed is 'Does the medium allow the communication objectives to be realized?' For example, if the objective is to position the brand as having a high-status aspirational personality, television would be better than posters. However, if the communication objective is to remind the target audience of a brand's existence, a poster campaign may suffice. Each medium possesses its own set of creative qualities and limitations, as described below.

Broadcast television: advertisers can demonstrate the product in action. For example, a lawnmower can be shown to cut grass efficiently, or the ease of application of a paint can be demonstrated. The capability of television to combine colour, movement and sound (unlike the press, posters and radio) means that it is often used when building brand image and introducing new products. It is easier to create an atmosphere using television than other media that lack its versatility. Traditionally, viewers could not refer back to the advertisement once it has been broadcast (unlike the press); however, with the advent of YouTube and other online video platforms adverts can be viewed repeatedly. Indeed, adverts are often launched through YouTube and social media. John Lewis's highly successful Christmas adverts were shown first online in recent years.

Despite the increase in popularity of television commercials online, a potential threat to mainstream television advertising is digital recording devices (e.g. DVD recorders, digi-boxes like Sky, FreeSat), which can store over 100 hours of programmes, allowing viewers to record their choice of programmes, watch them when convenient and skip through the adverts, potentially reducing television advertising effectiveness. But in response, some advertisers have been producing their adverts as mini movies and creating a buzz online. In 2014, Sainsbury's used the 100-year anniversary of the World War I football match between English and German soldiers to deliver its 'Christmas is for sharing' message. The advert was a highly emotional appeal, and at an unprecedented 3.18 minutes in length, it took up the whole of the commercial break when it was launched. Television companies have also been taking actions to encourage more viewer engagement. See Marketing in Action 13.4 to find out how Sky is providing advertisers with precision targeting opportunities.

Digital television technology means that signals can be compressed, allowing more to be sent to the viewer. The result is the escalation of the number of channels that can be received. The extra 'bandwidth' created by digital technology is likely to reduce costs, enabling small players to broadcast to small target audiences such as small geographical areas and special interest groups (e.g. shoppers). Also, digital technology allows the development of interactive services, promoting the potential for home shopping (Ellis-Chadwick, Doherty and Anastasakis, 2007).

Television programmes can now be watched via a computer and mobile phone, with the development of such online services as the BBC's iPlayer and ITVPlayer. Following the success of YouTube companies have found that setting up their own-brand television channel is proving to be very successful for fostering consumer engagement. Many companies have taken advantage of this opportunity to communicate with their target audiences, for example Apple, Coca-Cola, and fashion retailers H&M and New Look. Audi has found that potential car buyers return 12 times during the decision-making process and the channel features several streams of video-on-demand

MARKETING IN ACTION 13.4
Sky Adsmart: Clas Ohlson uses Precision Advertising to Penetrate the UK High Street

Sky Adsmart gives advertisers the opportunity to use highly sophisticated targeting techniques to deliver specific adverts at specific times to individual homes. Advertisers can set highly specific variables for the viewing audience they want to communicate to, for example by age, region and demographic profile. This means that companies can develop specific adverts for particular target audiences; for example, young families with children may receive one version of an advert, whereas older households without children another.

Audi has used Adsmart to advertise its top quality A6 and RS6 cars by targeting highly affluent viewers, cherry-picking the time slots when its target group are most likely to be watching television.

Clas Ohlson is a large Swedish retailer that used precision television advertising to promote its hardware stores in the UK, where currently it has 12 stores. Its Adsmart campaigns aimed to raise awareness and drive traffic to specific metropolitan regions where their stores are situated. Adsmart not only allowed Clas Ohlson to distribute its adverts geographically, they also made sure it was targeting 'young and mature home sharers and families of mid to very high affluence'. It had a relatively low budget of £57,000, but the precision approach resulted in reaching 219,000 Sky households and delivered millions of impressions. The results were that brand awareness of Clas Ohlson was increased, and the brand was also put into the purchase consideration set of a new set of customers.

Based on: SkyAdsmart (2015)

content: sport, lifestyle, behind the scenes, on the road, adventure, people, culture, places. (Press and media vehicles are discussed in more detail in Chapter 14, in the section on advertising.)

 Scan the QR code to see how Sainsbury's produced an emotional mini movie in partnership with the Royal British Legion to convey its seasonal campaign message.

Broadcast radio: this is creatively limited to sound and thus may be better suited to communicating factual information (e.g. a special price reduction) than attempting to create a brand image. The nature of the audience changes during the day (e.g. motorists during rush hours) and so a measure of targeting is possible. Production costs are relatively low. The arrival of digital radio has increased the number of radio stations available, and marginally improved sound quality. Digital radios have screen displays, which allow websites and telephone numbers to be run at the same time as an advertisement is being played (Hicks, 2005). Radio listening may rise with the growth of the Internet as people listen to the radio while surfing and because radio listening through web browsers is fast becoming a reality (Croft, 1999).

Press: factual information can be presented in a press advertisement (e.g. specific features of a washing machine, car or computer) and the readers are in control of how long they take to absorb the information. Allied to this advantage is the possibility of re-examination of the advertisement at a later date. But print media lacks movement and sound, and advertisements in newspapers and magazines compete with editorial for the reader's attention. However, the boundaries are blurring and the introduction of the iPad and other tablet computers is enabling print publications to be delivered digitally and in doing so they are able to carry multimedia content. (Press and media vehicles are discussed in more detail in Chapter 14, in the section on advertising.)

Digital: this medium allows global reach at relatively low cost. The number of website visits, clicks on advertisements and products purchased can be measured. Interactivity between supplier and consumer is possible either by website-based communication or email. Direct sales are possible, which is driving the growth of e-business in such areas as hotels, travel and information technology. Advertising content can be changed quickly and easily. Catalogues and price lists can be amended rapidly, and a dialogue between companies and their customers and suppliers can be established. The fastest form of advertising is the placing of sponsored links to websites on search engines. Google and Yahoo! are the market leaders in so-called 'paid search' or 'pay-per-click' advertising. The basic idea is that advertisers bid in an online auction for the right to have their link displayed next to the results for specific search terms, such as 'used cars' or 'digital cameras', and then pay only when an Internet surfer actually clicks on that link (hence 'pay-per-click'). An advantage to the advertiser is that the consumer has already expressed interest and intent—first by typing in the search term and then by clicking on the advertiser's link—and, therefore, is more likely to make a purchase than someone passively watching an advertisement on television or looking at one in a newspaper (*The Economist*, 2005). Internet-based advertising is on the increase and now accounts for more of the media spend than any other form of media-based advertising. (Digital marketing, social media and the Internet are discussed in greater detail in Chapter 16.)

Social media: messages can be straightforward and direct but the way messages are transmitted through social media communities can be highly complex and multilayered. To make creative use of this media, it is important to understand the concept of social capital and how power is attached to particular members of the online community (Coleman, 1988). Such communities provide an area for digital conversations, where members of the community can feel a sense of belonging (Tuten and Solomon, 2013). For example, Facebook enables its millions of users to start conversations with their friends, and share thoughts, pictures and conversations with likeminded people around most parts of the globe. This type of media can act as a conduit to access homogeneous groups of individuals, but commercial organizations which use this type of space to carry their messages should be aware that social media can be many things to many people—from a community to a publishing space to entertainment and social commerce arena—and consequently great care needs to be taken to ensure the content and tone of the message is in keeping with the expectations of the chosen target community (Tuten and Solomon, 2013). For example, Mumsnet.com is an online community for parents seeking help and advice on bringing up children. Many issues have been debated within this community from the sexualization of children to the growth in occurrence of childhood diabetes. (Social media is discussed in greater detail in Chapter 16.)

Outdoor: simplicity is required in the creative work associated with outdoor advertising because many people (e.g. car drivers) will have the opportunity only to glance at a poster. Like the press, it is largely a visual medium and is often used as a support medium alongside television, Internet or press campaign because of its creative limitations. However, it is an effective medium for carrying messages which remind target audiences of issues and products (see Exhibit 13.5 which was used in a campaign for a homelessness charity). In conjunction with its poster campaigns, Thames Reach's communication director also used print media. Poster campaigns can be created with a limited promotions budget but can be used to good effect. Probably the most effective use of outdoor advertising was done by Bennetton's creative director, Olivera Toscani. With a series of highly controversial poster campaigns Toscani led the brand from being a medium-sized European brand into a global one. In 2011, to gain attention for its 'Unhate campaign'—which aims to break down cultural barriers—a series of thought-provoking images carrying the Benetton logo have appeared on billboards around the world. Often outdoor advertising sites are sold as a package targeting specific audiences. For example, targeting supermarket shoppers can be realized by buying a retail package where advertisers can buy space close to supermarket stores; if business people are the target, it is possible to buy a package of sites at major airports (Tomkins, 1999).

Technology is helping outdoor advertising to gain a bigger share of advertising in the prime media. Backlit and scrolling sites are gradually replacing more traditional glued posters. Digital technology is allowing animated posters, whose content alters during the day, and high-definition-quality moving images. For outdoor advertising the keyword is simplicity. An ad has, on average, just six seconds to get a message across, which has led to the golden rule 'no more than seven words on a poster' (Fitzsimmonds, 2008). Piccadilly Circus in London is an ideal place for outdoor messages as millions of pedestrians and drivers pass by every week. The Piccadilly Lights complex carries static and animated adverts, and messages can be changed according to the time of day.

Guerrilla is potentially a controversial way to use outdoor media. The aim is often to deliver

EXHIBIT 13.5
Thames Reach makes use of thought-provoking posters as part of an IMC campaign

communication messages through unexpected means and in ways that almost 'ambush' the consumer to gain attention (Fahy and Jobber, 2015). One of the most effective guerrilla marketing campaigns was that used by Carlsberg in the UK, which also employed its well-known positioning slogan, 'Carlsberg don't do . . . but if they did it would probably be the best . . . in the world'. The company dropped £50,000 worth of £5 and £10 notes all over London on which were stickers containing the slogan—'Carlsberg don't do litter but if they did, it would probably be the best litter in the world'. For a small investment, the brand received enormous publicity. Another example is when DSL55 launched its first London store aimed at young skateboarders. It employed people to place stickers showing the firm's winged angel at locations where the target audience might be, for example, close to skateboard parks, on street furniture,

EXHIBIT 13.6
Costa Coffee uses lenticular advertising to attract customers away from the competition

lamp posts, etc. To use this form of media, communicators must be prepared to connect with their target audience in a very unusual, unconventional, surprising and often illegal manner. This is not mainstream media and is often used when the communication budget is small.

Indoor media include in-store point-of-purchase materials, packaging, window display signs and the on-shelf display. This form of media is used predominantly by retailers and consumer-facing service providers, but may also be used at transit stations, within shopping malls, at entertainment and sports arenas. This type of media is increasingly using digital technology to deliver highly creative messages. For example, East Midlands Airport has a cut-out figure of a member of the airport service staff, and a moving image is projected on to the face of the model, informing passengers how to streamline their journey through the airport.

In addition, both outdoor and indoor media can apply techniques called *ambient media*. This is a non-traditional form of media and is often used to take the target audience by surprise. Ambient advertising generally refers to the established outdoor categories such as billboards (Fahy and Jobber, 2012), bus signs, or the point-of-sale or in-store posters found at checkouts. Advertising that appears on shopping bags, on petrol pump nozzles, on balloons or on banners towed by airplanes, on street pavements, on overhead lockers on an aircraft, and so on are also classed as ambient. Ambient media are only limited by the advertiser's imagination.

Cinema: advertisements can benefit from colour, movement and sound, and exposure is high, due to the captive nature of the audience. Repetition may be difficult to achieve given the fact that people visit cinemas intermittently. In the past, cinema-goers tended to be between 15 and 25 years of age. Brands like BMW Mini, Volkswagen, Toyota, Citroën and Ford have used the cinema to target young audiences (Donnelly, 2008). However, the demographic of cinema-goers has changed; there are many young families and 45-plus ABC1s going to the movies on a regular basis. Family films such as the *Lego Movie, Muppets Most Wanted* and *Paddington* continue to attract the younger audience, and this has led companies to invest in longer adverts for delivery through cinemas; for example, Disney purchased 60-second slots before family feature films. Older audiences are attracted by comedy dramas; for example, *The Best Exotic Marigold Hotel* series and Marks & Spencer have been attracted by this target market. Marks & Spencer offered its first movie-related promotion, offering a buy one get one free film ticket deal on Mother's Day (Durrani, 2015).

The creative opportunities afforded by the media channel can add to the richness of the message. Other considerations when selecting media are the **media type** (newspaper, website, poster, mobile), the **media vehicle decision**

EXHIBIT 13.7
Movies for under-12s attract more families to the cinema

(e.g. a particular newspaper, *The Times, Le Monde*) and **media planning** (the media buying, scheduling, timing, frequency). These issues are covered in detail in Chapter 14.

The people

Managing communications involves complex decision-making. There are also many challenges involved in bringing together teams and departments in an integrated manner to satisfy the marketing objectives of the audiences, while engaging the attention of target audiences. Research proposes a two-stage approach: the first stage is the client / agency level, the second stage is target audience level (Mishra and Muralie, 2010)). Consequently, there are three types of people to consider: the customer, the client and the agency.

Customers vary from single individuals, to families and groups to business customers and global corporations. Consequently, their motivations, interests, spending power and needs vary considerably. Nevertheless, it is becoming increasingly important to ensure that any firm (the client) wishing to communicate does so by understanding its customers' needs and how they engage with communications.

Clients can come in many different shapes and sizes from large corporate clients, with multimillion-dollar communication budgets to spend in promoting a wide portfolio of products and building brands (e.g. Unilever, Kraft Foods, GE, Mercedes) to small independent companies planning their first website.

Agencies which develop communications also vary considerably in terms of what they have to offer. Agencies generally provide account management and liaison with the client, the creative teams and production of the communication campaigns. They also plan the media and can be responsible for research. Types of agencies include: full service, creative boutiques, specialized agencies, digital agencies and web service providers.

The client is generally the originator of communication initiatives and is also likely to make key decisions, and ultimately be responsible for the planning approach—target market selection (the customer), financial resources and agency selection. Corporate marketing is where decisions are made about a firm's image and corporate identity. Again the client (the firm) will strongly influence communication decisions. Selection of the marketing communication mix and media coordination is where the agency can become much more influential in the decision-making process and is likely to be responsible for the management of these elements of IMC. Ensuring consistency of the message is really the responsibility of both the client and the agency and they need to ensure that, whatever form the IMC campaign takes, it should deliver a consistent message throughout to the target audiences (the customer).

Office politics can occur, especially when there are clashes between advertising creatives who, say, have radical ideas to take a brand forward with the latest of a series of television commercials, and brand executives with very conservative values, who want to protect a brand's traditional target markets. Other difficult situations can arise when IMC strategies call for a shift in expenditure from advertising to direct or digital promotion. Other problems surround the specialist nature of different communication disciplines that can narrow people's minds to such an extent that they fail to understand how some marketing objectives can be better achieved by using a different communications technique (Murgatroyd, 2004).

However, to be successful, issues and problems must be overcome and this is often achieved by appointing a senior level communications officer to oversee all of the firm's communications activities. A director of marketing communications is likely to be responsible for deciding the extent to which each of the components of the promotional mix is used to achieve business and marketing objectives. The person needs to be a visionary and someone with passion, who has the communications ability to persuade everyone of the benefits of an integrated approach to marketing communications (Eagle and Kitchen, (2000).

Client and agency relationships are discussed in more detail in Chapter 14 and types of digital agencies and web service providers in Chapter 16. Figure 13.4 shows the core tasks that people must manage to create an integrated campaign.

The contexts

In this chapter we have explored the changing nature of the communication environment, looked at the drivers for the adoption of an IMC approach, considered the processes associated with developing a campaign, and examined important elements which form the core constituents of an IMC campaign. In this final section we look at the different contexts for IMC campaigns: namely, business-to-consumer, business-to-business settings and corporate profile.

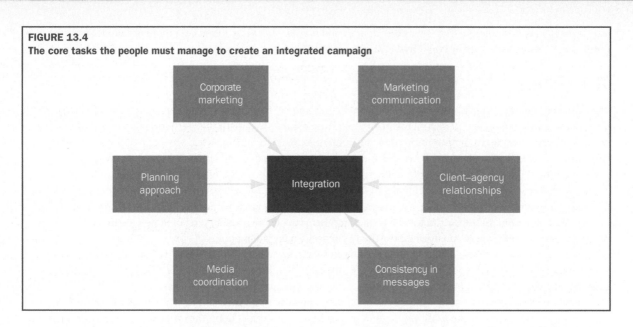

FIGURE 13.4
The core tasks the people must manage to create an integrated campaign

There are three main contexts which define the target audience and nature of IMC campaigns. These contexts determine the focus, strategy and the actions which a campaign aims to achieve. The three contexts are:

1   Pull-positioning strategies aim to encourage consumers and end-user business customers to make a purchase, thereby pulling goods through the supply chain from the manufacturer to the retailer (or final purchase point in the supply chain) (see Figure 13.5).

   In a pull-positioning strategy messages tend to be designed to create awareness, and *stimulate action among members of the target audience*. The underlying idea is that target audiences expect the product to be available when they wish to make a purchase. Many consumer brands use pre-announcement, and give launch dates to stimulate interest and excitement. For example, Apple gives launch dates for its new products and latest versions of existing products. This raises anticipation, excitement and creates pre-sale demand. High-tech shoppers and Apple aficionados form queues at Apple stores and stockists on the launch date hoping to be able to make a purchase of the latest iPhone or iPad. The pull strategy also enables Apple to encourage its stockists (e.g. PC World, Giganten, Ledfal, Electro World) to have stock available in store to meet consumer demand.

2   Push-positioning strategies aim to *move goods through the supply chain*. The target audiences for this type of communications initiatives are channel intermediaries. Often communication objectives aim to build relationships between channel intermediaries and influence trade partners to take stock, allocate shelf space and also help to develop trade partners' awareness of product features and benefits (Fill, 2011). Push communications also tend to take place in a channel network moving goods from one point to another (see Figure 13.6).

   This strategy is widely used between businesses, and the most prevalent communication tools are personal selling and trade promotions (see Chapter 14

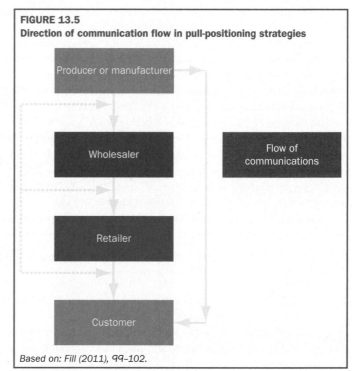

FIGURE 13.5
Direction of communication flow in pull-positioning strategies

Based on: Fill (2011), 99–102.

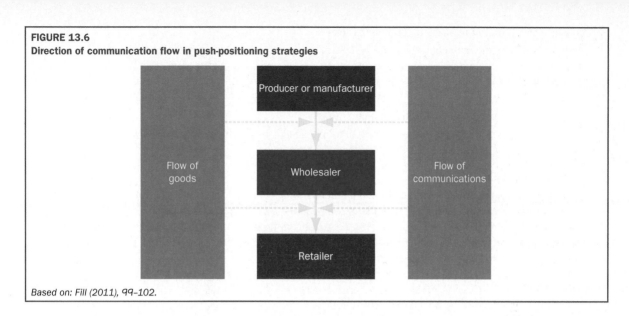

FIGURE 13.6
Direction of communication flow in push-positioning strategies

Producer or manufacturer

Flow of goods

Wholesaler

Flow of communications

Retailer

Based on: Fill (2011), 99–102.

for further details). For example, Costco is a large intermediary in the retail supply chain. It supplies both trade and retail customers with FMCG top brands (e.g. Heinz, Coca-Cola, Gillette, Colgate), white goods (e.g. Beko, Bosch), small electrical (e.g. Breville), electric kettles and fresh foods from various producers. Each of the suppliers engages in push communications designed to ensure that Costco continues to stock its ranges. Manufacturers also work together with Costco to increase purchases using a range of techniques from tastings to bonus packs.

3 Profile-positioning strategies aim to *develop the image and identity of an organization*. In addition to consumer and business target audiences there are many other stakeholders that might be interested in an organization: for example, investors, the local community, the media, trade unions, pressure groups, employees. Perceptions and views of such stakeholders are increasingly important, and this has given rise to greater use of IMC campaigns to raise corporate reputations. Public relations, sponsorship, lobbying, **media relations** and internal communications are examples of the methods which are used in this instance to develop a corporate profile (further discussion of these methods is in Chapters 15 and 22).

When you have read this chapter

Discover further resources and test your understanding: McGraw-Hill **Connect**™ is a digital teaching and learning environment that improves performance over a variety of critical outcomes; it can be tailored, is easy to use and is proven effective. **LearnSmart**™ is the most widely used and intelligent adaptive learning resource that is proven to strengthen memory recall, improve course retention and boost grades. Fuelled by **LearnSmart**™, **SmartBook**™ is the first and only adaptive reading experience available today.

Review

1. **The elements of integrated marketing communication campaigns**
   - These include the message, the tools, the media channel and the context applied in a coordinated campaign designed to create multiple opportunities to engage with the target audience.

2. **The value of integrated marketing communications**
   - Integrated marketing communications is the concept by which companies coordinate their marketing communications tools to deliver a clear, consistent, credible and competitive message about the organization and its products.
   - Its achievement can be hampered by office politics, and a high-ranking communications officer may be needed to see through its successful implementation.
   - Its philosophy has led to the rise in media-neutral planning, which is the process of solving communications problems through an unbiased evaluation of all media.

3. **How IMC campaigns are organized**
   - Planning campaigns develop from a situation analysis, which should aid a firm in identifying communication opportunities. Following on from this is agency selection, the briefing process and setting out the deliverables that an agency will produce. The next stage in the process is the development of the campaign and its implementation. The penultimate stage is evaluation of the effectiveness of all of the elements of the campaign. The final stage is future planning.

4. **Elements of IMC**
   - The core elements are: the messages, which are used to position a product, brand and/or an organization in the minds of the customer; the tools, the six key methods which provide the methods of achieving communication objectives; the media, which are the channels that carry the message to the audience; the people, who collectively are responsible for creating, planning, managing and implementing the communication campaign; and the context, the setting in which communication takes place.

5. **The message**
   - At the heart of communications is the message. Messages are very important as they not only transfer information from a message sender to its recipient, but can also determine the nature of a relationship, establish credibility (Fill, 2011), set the tone for a *conversation* and cross tangible and intangible boundaries. Effective messages can become so powerful that they can be heard around the globe, when used with suitable media channels.

6. **The communication process**
   - The communication process begins with the source encoding a message that is transmitted through media to the receiver who decodes. Noise (e.g. distractions) may prevent the message reaching the receiver. Feedback may be direct when talking to a salesperson or through marketing research. The communication process: the simple model explains the basic elements of the communication model whereas the complex model explains how communication messages pass by formal and informal messages between message senders and different types of message recipients.

7. **The factors that affect the choice of the promotional mix for IMC campaigns**
   - These are resource availability and the cost of promotional tools, market size and concentration, customer information needs, product characteristics and push versus pull strategies.

8. **The key characteristics of the major promotional tools**
   - Advertising: strong for awareness building, brand positioning, firm and brand legitimization, but it is impersonal and inflexible, and has only a limited ability to close a sale.
   - Personal selling: strong for interactivity, adaptability, the delivery of complex arguments, relationship building and the closing of the sale, but is costly.
   - Direct marketing: strong for individual targeting, personalization, measurement, relationship building through periodic contact, low visibility to competitors, but response rates are often low and can cause annoyance.
   - Digital marketing: strong for global reach, measurement, establishing a dialogue, quick changes to catalogues and prices, convenience and avoids arguments with salespeople, but impersonal and requires consumers to visit website.

- Sales promotion: strong on providing immediate incentive to buy but effects may be short-term and can damage brand image.
- Public relations: strong on credibility, high readership but loss of control.

9. The media channels

- When considering which media channel the media planner faces the choice of using television, the press, cinema, outdoor, radio, the Internet or some combination of media classes. Various considerations will be taken into account: *creative factors* may have a major bearing on the decision. The key question that needs to be addressed is 'Does the medium allow the communication objectives to be realized?'

10. The people

- Managing communications involves complex decision-making. There are also many challenges involved in bringing together teams and departments in an integrated manner to satisfy the marketing objectives of the audiences, while engaging the attention of target audiences.
- Research proposes a two-stage approach: the first stage is the client/agency level, the second stage is target audience level (Mishra and Muralie, 2010). Consequently, there are three types of people to consider: the customer, the client and the agency.

11. The contexts

- There are three main contexts that define the target audience and nature of IMC campaigns. These contexts determine the focus, strategy and the actions which a campaign aims to achieve.

Key Terms

advertising any paid form of non-personal communication of ideas or products in the prime media: i.e. television, the press, posters, cinema and radio, the Internet and direct marketing

agency an organization that specializes in providing services such as media selection, creative work, production and campaign planning to clients

digital promotion the promotion of products to consumers and businesses through electronic media

direct marketing (1) acquiring and retaining customers without the use of an intermediary; (2) the distribution of products, information and promotional benefits to target consumers through interactive communication in a way that allows response to be measured

integrated marketing communications (IMC) the concept that companies coordinate their marketing communications tools to deliver a clear, consistent, credible and competitive message about the organization and its products

media channel the means used to transmit a message, including spoken words, print, radio, television or the Internet. Also called the *medium*

media class the press, cinema, television, posters, radio, or some combination of these

media planning an advertising strategy most commonly employed to target consumers using a variety of informational outlets. Media planning is generally conducted by a professional media planning or advertising agency and typically finds the most appropriate media outlets to reach the target market

media relations the communication of a product or business by placing information about it in the media without paying for time or space directly

media type (also referred to as a *content type*) is a general category of data content, such as: application (executable program), audio content, an image, a text message, a video stream, and so forth

media vehicle decision the choice of the particular newspaper, magazine, television spot, poster site, etc.

message the use of words, symbols and illustrations to communicate to a target audience using prime media

personal selling oral communication with prospective purchasers with the intention of making a sale

public relations the management of communications and relationships to establish goodwill and mutual understanding between an organization and its public

sales promotion incentives to customers or the trade that are designed to stimulate purchase

target audience the group of people at which an advertisement or message is aimed

Study Questions

1. **Compare the possible use of advertising and personal selling in an IMC campaign.**

2. **Discuss how communication messages can be used to build a brand.**

3. **Explain how digital media and platforms are changing the focus of IMC campaigns.**

4. **Explain when a company might use different elements of the promotional mix.**

5. **Suggest why media channel choice is increasingly important in the digital age.**

6. **Outline the stages in the IMC planning framework.**

7. **Discuss the drivers of an IMC and suggest possible limitations when developing a pan-European campaign.**

8. **Discuss the advantages and disadvantages of adopting an IMC approach towards communication planning.**

Recommended Reading

Belch, G. and M. Belch (2014) *Advertising and promotions: an integrated marketing communication perspective*, Global edition, London: McGraw Hill Higher Education.

Finne, A. and C. Gronroos (2009) Rethinking marketing communication: From integrated marketing communication to relationship communication, *Journal of Marketing Communications* 15 (2–3), 179–95.

Harvard Business School: Thinking that leads, Marketing: Marketing strategy; http://hbswk.hbs.edu/topics/marketing.html

Mulhern, F. (2009) Integrated marketing communications: From media channels to digital connectivity, *Journal of Marketing Communications* 15 (2–3), 85–101.

Schultz, D. and C. Patti (2009) The evolution of IMC: IMC in a customer-driven marketplace, *Journal of Marketing Communications* 15 (2–3), 75–84.

Zook, Z. and P. R. Smith (2016) *Marketing Communications Offline and Online Integration, Engagement and Analytics*, London: Kogan Page.

References

Anon (2015a) Nike to crown its football 'Ice Kings', The 12ethman, 27 January. http://12elfthman.com/2015/01/27/nike-to-crown-its-football-ice-kings

Anon (2015b) Why Moneysupermarket's #EpicStrut is a viral hit, *Marketing*, 23 January. http://www.marketingmagazine.co.uk/article/1330549/why-moneysupermarkets-epicstrut-viral-hit (accessed 10 June 2015).

Anon (n.d.) Tesco—how 'Every little helps' was a big help to Tesco, Thinkbox. http://www.thinkbox.tv/server/show/ConCaseStudy.1642 (accessed 10 June 2015).

Beltrone, G. (2014) How R/GA Dominated Digital by Finding Its TV Groove, *AdWeek*, 15 December. http://www.adweek.com/news/advertising-branding/agency-year-how-rga-dominated-digital-finding-its-tv-groove-161925 (accessed 8 June 2015).

Bendaby, D. (2011) Marketers divided on the merits of integration, *Pitch Agency Reputation Survey*, 40.

Bernard, G. (2014) This Tech Company is the Real Winner of Wimbledon 2014, Bostinno, 7 July. http://bostinno.streetwise.co/2014/07/06/wimbledon-2014-tech-partnership-with-ibm-wimbledon-2014-championship-winner

Bidlake, S. (2008) Goodwill to All Agencies, *Campaign*, 5 December, 3.

Bylykbashi, K. (2015) Brands are struggling to join up multichannel customer journeys', *Marketing Week*, 14

April. https://www.marketingweek.com/2015/04/14/brands-are-struggling-to-join-up-multichannel-customer-journeys

Caemmerer, B. (2009) The planning and implementation of integrated marketing communications, *Marketing Intelligence & Planning* 27(9), 524–38.

Carr, A. (2013) *NIKE: THE NO. 1 MOST INNOVATIVE COMPANY OF 2013*, Fastcompany, 11 February. http://www.fastcompany.com/most-innovative-companies/2013/nike

Chaffey, D. and F. E. Ellis-Chadwick (2012) *Digital Marketing: Strategy, Implementation and Practice*, 5th edn, Harlow: Pearson.

Clark, T. and S. P. Chan (2014) A history of Tesco: The rise of Britain's biggest supermarket, *The Telegraph*, 14 October.

Coleman, S. (1988) Social capital in the creation of human capital, *The American Journal of Sociology* 94, 95–120.

Cordiner R. (2009) Set free your core native: the brand as a storyteller, *Admap*, October.

Croft, M. (1999) Listeners Keep Radio On Air, *Marketing Week*, 8 July, 30–1.

DeSantis Breindel (2015) Integrated Marketing is No Longer Enough: Why B2B Brands Need to be Synchronized, DeSantis Breindel.com, 10 June. http://www.desantisbreindel.com/integrated-marketing-is-no-longer-enough

Doherty, N. F., F. E. Ellis-Chadwick and C. A. Hart (1999) Cyber retailing: the potential in the UK: the potential of the Internet as a retail channel, *International Journal of Retail & Distribution Management* 27(1).

Donnelly, A. (2008) Big Screen Draw, *Marketing*, 9 July, 19.

Duncan, T. and S. Everett (1993) Client perceptions of integrated communications, *Journal of Advertising Research*, 3(3), 30–39.

Durrani, A. (2015) M&S makes debut film promotion for The Second Best Exotic Marigold Hotel, *Media Week*, 5 March. http://www.mediaweek.co.uk/article/1336864/m-s-makes-debut-film-promotion-second-best-exotic-marigold-hotel

Eagle, L. and P. J. Kitchen (2000) Brand Communications and Corporate Cultures, *European Journal of Marketing*, 35(5/6), 667–86.

Ellis-Chadwick, F., N. F. Doherty and L. Anastasakis (2007) E-strategy in the UK retail grocery sector: a resource-based analysis, *Managing Service Quality* 17(6), 702–27.

Fahy, J. and D. Jobber (2015) *Foundations of Marketing*, London: McGraw-Hill Education, 242–3.

Fill, C. (2011) *Essentials of Marketing Communications*, London: Prentice Hall, 7–8.

Fitzsimmonds, C. (2008) Outdoor's Digital Future, *Campaign*, 18 July, 24–5.

Gladwell, M. (2000) *The Tipping Point*, London: Abacus, 3–5.

Hegarty, J. (2011) *Hegarty on advertising: turning intelligence into magic*, London: Thames & Hudson, 95.

Hemsley, S. (2015) How to create content relevant to your business, *Marketing Week*, 12 June. http://www.marketingweek.com/2015/06/12/how-to-create-content-relevant-to-your-business

Hicks, R. (2005) Special Report: Radio, *Campaign*, 4 November, 26.

Hill, C. (2015) 10 steps to an effective content strategy, *The Guardian*, 10 June. http://www.theguardian.com/media-network-outbrain-partner-zone/content-strategy-marketing-customer-engagement

Katz, E. and P. F. Lazarfield (1955) *Personal Influence*, Glencoe, Il: Free Press.

Kelman, H. (1961) Process of opinion change, *Public Opinion Quarterly*, 25(spring), 57–78.

Magee, K. (2015) Tesco shifts trade and tactical ad work to BBH, *Brand Republic*, 12 June. http://www.brandrepublic.com/article/1351209/tesco-shifts-trade-tactical-ad-work-bbh

Mahdawi, A. (2013) Google's autocomplete spells out our darkest thoughts. *The Guardian*, 22 October. http://www.theguardian.com/commentisfree/2013/oct/22/google-autocomplete-un-women-ad-discrimination-algorithms (accessed 10 June 2015).

Manvsmachine (2015) Hypervenom case study. http://manvsmachine.co.uk/project/hypervenom-2

McMains, A. (2014) Even BBH's Rivals Wonder Why Johnnie Walker Is in Review After all, the shop's 'Keep walking' campaign has delivered results, *ADweek*, 10 November. http://www.adweek.com/news/advertising-branding/even-bbhs-rivals-wonder-why-johnnie-walker-review-161311 (accessed 10 May 2015).

Mehta, A. (2000) Advertising Attitudes and Advertising Effectiveness, *Journal of Advertising Research*, May/June, 67–72.

Mishra, S. and S. Muralie (2010) Managing dynamism of IMC Anarchy to order, *Journal of Marketing & Communications*, 6(2), 29–37.

Murgatroyd, L. (2004) All together now, *Marketing Business*, March, 39.

Ritson, M. (2011) What if your customers are silent? *Marketing Week*, 14 April, 70.

Rogers, E. (1983) *Diffusion of innovations*, 3rd edn, New York: Free Press.

Schultz, D. (1993) Integrated marketing communications: maybe definition is in the point of view, *Marketing News*, 18 January, 17.

Sherwood, P. K., R. E. Stevens and W. E. Warren (1989) Periodic and continuous tracking studies: matching methodology with objectives, *Marketing Intelligence and Planning*, 7(1/2), 11–14.

SkyAdsmart (2015) *Clas Ohlson & Sky AdSmart*, Skymedia, 10 June. http://www.skymedia.co.uk/sky-adsmart/Case-Studies/clas-ohlson-&-sky-adsmart.aspx

Swift, J. (2015) R/GA and Dare win Nike football brief, *Campaign*, 28 May. http://www.campaignlive.co.uk/news/1348941

Syedain, H. (1992) Taking the Expert Approach to Media, *Marketing*, 4 June, 20–1.

The Economist (2005) Pay Per Sale, 1 October, 73.

Tomkins, R. (1999) Reaching New Heights of Success, *Financial Times*, 28 May, 16.

Tuten, T. L. and M. R. Solomon (2013) *Social media marketing*, Harlow: Pearson, 86.

Vizard, S. (2015) M&S promises personalisation push to boost online sales. *Marketing Week*, 20 May. http://www.marketingweek.com/2015/05/20/ms-promises-personalisation-push-to-boost-online-a-sales (accessed 10 June 2015).

Weissberg, T. (2008) One Message, Many Media, *Marketing Week*, 18 September, 31–4.

West, G. (2015) Ad of the Day: NSPCC—Share Aware. *The Drum*, 12 January. http://www.thedrum.com/news/2015/01/12/ad-day-nspcc-share-aware (accessed 10 June 2015).

Youde, K. (2011) Case Study: Thames Reach—A persistent campaign that worked, Third Sector, 25 January. http://www.thirdsector.co.uk/news/1050651/Case-Study-Thames-Reach--persistent-campaign-worked/?DCMP=ILC-SEARCH

Coke Gets Personal: The Share a Coke Campaign

Introduction

In recent years, the Coca-Cola company has been faced with declining sales as it battles concerns over links between soft drinks consumption and obesity. Faced with this setback, the company wanted to develop an advertising campaign that would inject new life into the brand, engage the public and ultimately reverse the declining sales trend. This led to the birth of the Share a Coke campaign, which was launched in Britain and Ireland on 29 April 2013. The integrated multimedia campaign has seen the soft drinks giant replace its usual branding on its bottles and cans with 250 of the UK and Ireland's most popular names. TV adverts, billboards, experiential marketing and social media were used to inform the public of the campaign and to encourage engagement (The Drum, 2014).

The 2013 campaign saw a sales increase of 10 per cent on immediate consumption formats across Coca-Cola's portfolio in Great Britain (Talking Retail, 2014). Following on from this initial success, the campaign was run once again in the summer of 2014. More names were added and selected nicknames – for example mate, bestie – were included on bottles and cans to make every pack shareable. Coke's innovative use of personalization and successful use of an integrated multimedia campaign ensured that the Share a Coke campaign emerged as one of the most compelling campaigns of recent years (Talking Retail, 2014).

Mass Personalization

The Coca-Cola Share a Coke campaign cleverly played to the fact that people love anything personalized, particularly from major marketers. Everyone loves something that's personal and unique to him or her, even if it's just a drink (Grimes, 2013). Coca-Cola's campaign captured the public's attention by featuring the top 250 most popular names in Ireland and the UK. The campaign gave people a very personal reason to engage with the brand and a sense of ownership of the brand. Through the use of personalized bottles, the brand made people feel special and appreciated and spoke to Coke's consumers as individuals. Consumers have taken extra steps to seek out products featuring

The Share a Coke campaign

their names and also the names of their family and friends (Incitrio, 2014).

Beyond the obvious attempt at personalization, the campaign was also about sharing. Coca-Cola wanted people not just to find bottles with their own names on, but to surprise someone they love by seeking out a bottle with their name on it (Fisher, 2013). The campaign created a gift-giving dynamic which further encouraged the collectability of Coke products. People have been scouring retail locations and even resorting to eBay in the hope of finding their name or a friend's name on a Coke bottle (Incitrio, 2014). As the campaign progressed, the public nominated and voted on which names they wanted to appear on the next round of Coke cans and bottles (Chill, 2012).

The Coke brand is so ubiquitous that it can engage in such a de-branding exercise by replacing its logo with individual names. Even with the removal of its traditional logo, the Coca-Cola script is still iconic, and the red and white is immediately recognizable the world over. Coca-Cola's efforts at de-branding appear to have been successful. By dropping its logo, the company made itself appear more forward-thinking, bold and less corporate. It worked because its brand already had so much brand equity behind it (Fisher, 2013).

An Integrated Approach

The Share a Coke campaign went beyond customized Coke bottles. Coke used a multi-faceted integrated marketing campaign with a strong social media arm to raise awareness of the campaign and to encourage consumer engagement (Setaysha, 2014). The integrated campaign took a holistic approach and created a cohesive message that was available on multiple channels.

Coke recently breathed new life into its successful campaign with a new TV ad featuring Bobby the dog hunting for his name. The commercial followed the story of a loveable dog as he interacted with lots of people during his search for his own name up in lights. The ad featured music from the UK band the Ting Ting's ('That's Not My Name') and aired on digital platforms, on television and on out-of-home media (Fisher, 2014).

This TV campaign was supported by an outdoor advertising campaign. Coca-Cola wanted to keep the campaign fresh and give people new reasons to Share a Coke. It pulled on its huge resource of Facebook fans and Twitter followers and asked the public who they would share a Coke with next. The responses were broadcast across billboards and real-time activated digital panels, bringing consumer interaction with the promotion to the streets (Outdoor Media Centre, n.d.).

Recently, Coke also held a four-day 'party pod' outdoor Share a Coke domination campaign in London's Covent Garden. After getting a bottle of Coke or Coke Zero personalized with their name or the name of a loved one, passers-by were invited to drop into a special Share a Coke selfie kiosk. Here they could capture a picture of themselves along with their personalized bottle. Afterwards people could listen to music and share a Coke with friends in the rooftop party pod, set up especially for the campaign (Wearebulletproof.com, 2014). In Ireland, Coca-Cola and JCDecaux Ireland created a fully branded tram in Dublin. All the seats had red covers on them, each cover being embroidered with a popular name, bringing a personal touch to the commuters' journeys. The interior was also covered with domination stickers and posters, from panels, strap-lines and window strips to complete ceiling branding (JCDecaux, 2014).

Social media also plays a huge role in the success of the campaign. When people are successful in finding their name on a bottle, they are encouraged to share their find on social media using the hashtag #shareacoke. This sharing behavior acts as a means of spreading brand awareness throughout social media platforms. Friends see each other finding their names, enjoying a Coke product, and they are inclined to interact with the brand (Incitrio, 2014). Coke also created a Facebook app that allows people to share a virtual Coke bottle with friends or download personalized bottles. Key media and celebrity influencers with a large social media footprint were identified and sent personalized seeding kits with a Coke product bearing their name, including campaign messaging, to share with their network of fans (Chill, 2012). One man went so far as to use his Coke personalized bottle to propose to his girlfriend. Their happy announcement received more than one million likes on Facebook within 48 hours (Coca-Cola, 2014)!

In addition, for those who cannot find their names on Coke bottles and cans on the shelves, an online personalization site with more than 500,000 names to choose from was introduced. This offers consumers the chance to purchase Coca-Cola glass bottles featuring their own, their friends or their families' names (Talking Retail, 2014). There are also chances for consumers to get personalized products at pop-up events in major cities across Ireland and the UK and in stores via shopper activation, which allows customers to instantly print labels featuring their surname on Coke sharing products (Talking Retail, 2014).

The campaign has also extended to the retail environment and in response to feedback from retailers, Coke have begun using improved displays in store and transparent dump bins that make it easier for shoppers to locate the specific personalized bottles they want (Waqas, 2014). The campaign's simple concept has encouraged vast numbers of people to buy and share the brand in both the real and the virtual world (Grimes, 2013).

Conclusion

The Share a Coke campaign has helped bring a whole new meaning to mass personalization (Saul, 2014). It speaks to consumers as individuals, while making them feel more connected to the brand and to one another and this is what makes this integrated campaign a huge success (The Drum, 2014). It reiterates the importance of brand perception, along with the use of an integrated campaign that uses advertising and social media to influence and alter consumer experiences (Grimes, 2013).

Coke has significantly altered its IMC strategies in recent years to target younger consumers in particular. The Share a Coke campaign illustrates how the company's focus has moved to creating content which can be disseminated easily and unexpectedly via social media rather than via traditional advertising media. Coca-Cola realize that interactivity is extremely important for communicating to a younger audience. They are a group that is not satisfied with just being told a story, but want to help tell the story, affect the brand and see themselves in the brand's story. In order to build on the Share a Coke campaign's success, Coke's future IMC and advertising will still need to be all about engaging the public, not only emotionally,

»

but also through action and interaction. Coke hopes that by doing so, it can continue to tackle the declining sales trend that has threatened its soft drinks brand (Russell, 2014).

Questions

1. Evaluate Coke's integrated campaign for Share a Coke. What are the key objectives of this campaign?

2. What factors are driving the growth of integrated campaigns such as the Share a Coke campaign? What advantages does integrated marketing communications (IMC) offer?

3. What are the benefits associated with the use of a mass personalization campaign, such as the Share a Coke campaign? Are there any dangers associated with using such an approach?

4. Coca-Cola's efforts at de-branding appear to have been a success. Why do companies engage in de-branding? Does de-branding present any risks for brands?

This case study was written by Marie O'Dwyer, Lecturers in Marketing, Waterford Institute of Technology.

References

Based on: The Drum (2014) What brands can learn from the integrated Share a Coke campaign of 2013, The Drum, http://www.thedrum.com/news/2014/01/28/case-study-what-share-coke-campaign-can-teach-other-brands; Talking Retail (2014) Coca-cola's Share a Coke campaign returns, Talking Retail, http://www.talkingretail.com/products-news/soft-drinks/coca-colas-share-coke-campaign-returns; Grimes, T. (2013) What the Share a Coke campaign can teach other brands, *The Guardian*, http://www.theguardian.com/media-network/media-network-blog/2013/jul/24/share-coke-teach-brands; Incitrio (2014) Coke's 'Share a Coke campaign: an integrated marketing success, Incitrio, http://incitrio.com/cokes-share-a-coke-campaign-an-integrated-marketing-success; Fisher, L. (2013) Debranding: why Coca-Cola's decision to drop its name worked, *The Guardian*, http://www.theguardian.com/media-network/media-network-blog/2013/aug/06/coke-debranding-name-dropping; Chill (2012) Top experiential campaigns – What made the cut! Chill, http://www.chill.com.au/2012/11/top-experiential-campaigns-what-made-the-cut; Setaysha, O. (2014) Coca-Cola 'Share A Coke' Campaign Rolls Out In The United States, creativeguerillamarketing.com, http://www.creativeguerillamarketing.com/guerrilla-marketing/coca-cola-share-coke-campaign-rolls-united-states; Fisher, L. (2014) Has Coca-Cola's Share a Coke campaign passed its sell-by date? *The Guardian*, http://www.theguardian.com/media-network/media-network-blog/2014/aug/14/coca-cola-share-coke-marketing; Outdoor Media Centre (n.d.) New outdoor campaigns in August, http://www.outdoormediacentre.org.uk/outdoor_advertising_info/news/Latest_News/item/5406; Wearebulletproof.com (2014) Share a Coke comes to Covent Garden, wearebulletproof.com, http://www.wearebulletproof.com/share-coke-comes-covent-garden; JCDecaux (2014) Campaign Showcase – Coca-Cola's Share a Coke, JCDecaux, http://www.jcdecaux-oneworld.com/2014/09/coca-cola-share-a-coke-best-of-outdoor-advertising-compilation; Coca-Cola (2014) #ShareaCoke Marriage Proposal Goes Viral, Coca Cola, http://www.coca-colacompany.com/stories/shareacoke-marriage-proposal-goes-viral; Waqas, Q. (2014) Coca-Cola 'Share a Coke' campaign returns, Packaging News, http://www.packagingnews.co.uk/news/coca-cola-share-a-coke-campaign-returns; Saul, H. (2014) Coca-Cola 'Share a Coke' campaign boosts US sales for first time in a decade, *The Independent*, http://www.independent.co.uk/news/business/cocacola-share-a-coke-campaign-boosts-us-sales-for-first-time-in-a-decade-9759739.html; Grimes, T. (2013) What Coke's New Campaign Says About the Future of Advertising, *Media Post*, http://www.mediapost.com/publications/article/226491/what-cokes-new-campaign-says-about-the-future-of.html

Comparethemarket.com: 'Simples'

In 2009, Comparethemarket.com revolutionized the scope of marketing in the insurance industry forever. The price comparison website embraced a totally integrated and symbiotic communications plan that linked above-the-line media (television and radio), digital (Comparethemeerkat.com and search) and social media (Twitter and Facebook) and was completely different from any campaign ever produced in that industry. The success of this integrated marketing communication campaign was due to a modern day cult advertising hero – Aleksandr Orlov, a meerkat from Russia. Six years on from the creation of this campaign, this case study examines the success of Comparethemeerkat.com and discusses how Comparethemarket.com has maintained the effectiveness of Aleksandr Orlov.

Background to the Campaign

Comparethemarket.com is a price comparison website operating in the insurance industry in the UK since 2006. The insurance comparison market in the UK was notoriously crowded, competitive and undifferentiated. It was also a very low-interest category, even though consumers could save hundreds of pounds on insurance costs by switching providers. Comparethemarket.com was a small player in this category where market share is king. In a category where market share is determined by spend, Comparethemarket.com were fourth in a category of four. Comparethemarket.com were being heavily outspent on generic Google search terms, such as 'car insurance' and 'compare insurance'. Similarly, they were one of the last entrants to an already crowded market, had no clear point of difference and a cumbersome brand name that no one could remember. In a market where name familiarity is key, research demonstrated that Comparethemarket. com had a long unmemorable name and that its identity and name were very similar to those of its nearest (bigger spending) competitor, GoCompare. In research, Compare.com (which doesn't exist) was as well remembered as Comparethemarket.com. People would describe GoCompare's ads and site and attribute them to those of Comparethemarket.com (and vice versa). This similarity enhanced the challenge faced

by Comparethemarket.com in having no single feature on which they could build a point of differentiation to capture market share.

A good summary of the battle within the category was 'to spend more than the competition on communicating the generic benefit'. Not surprisingly the ads were perceived by consumers to all be the same – computer screens, cars with stars and price-saving claims. The four major players shared around 1,500 spots a day. The benefits being communicated to consumers were the same. By increasingly focusing on 'differentiating' claims in advertising, all the sites increasingly blended into one. As a result, despite what this new category did for consumers, few seemed to like it much and consumers couldn't differentiate rationally between them. This lack of differentiation reinforced the necessity to spend heavily on search terms. If comparison sites want to keep costs down, they have to get people to type in their brand name directly. Google charges less if people search by brand name; it charges more if they search for something generic, such as 'car insurance'. In order to close the gap on the market leaders – Moneysupermarketcom, Confused.com and GoCompare.com – creating affection for Comparethemarket.com was crucial. To create affection for a price comparison site would require Comparethemarket.com to shatter the conventions of marketing communications within the industry.

>>

Outmanoeuvred in a crowded market overflowing with rational messages Comparethemarket.com recognized the need to create love for the brand. The only thing that distinguished Comparethemarket.com from the competition was the word 'market'. It was felt that by drawing attention to the word 'market', Comparethemarket.com would be able to create space between its site and the competition. Comparethemarket.com turned to the agency VCCP to deliver such a campaign. VCCP's planning process started with an insight about the way people use Google. The majority of consumers find a price comparison site through Google, so it was essential for VCCP to think about the key words consumers were typing in if they wanted them to come to Comparethemarket.com, rather than any of its competitors.

The footnote of the creative brief from Comparethemarket.com asked the creatives if they could find a way of sidestepping the high cost per click on the word 'market' (which is over £5). It asked the creatives if they might be able to find a way of introducing a cheaper term or phrase into their advertising that could exist alongside the word 'market'. The emphasis was to make the word 'market' famous, as many other companies used the word 'compare' in their brand names. In exploring this idea it found that cost per click on the word 'meerkat' was in the region of 5p (market was £5). By learning from other communication successes (Cadbury's gorilla) and applying this to the forgotten rules of the insurance market (a brand icon), it was possible to create affection for the differentiated part of their name (market) and make it stand out. This discovery was the starting point for the creation of Aleksandr Orlov, a loveable but complex character who is desperately frustrated by the confusion between Comparethemarket.com and Comparethemeerkat.com. For Aleksandr to be successful Comparethemarket.com needed to create layers to his character, in order to generate continued warmth and affection towards the brand.

Comparethemeerkat.com

Aleksandr Orlov is a very successful business meerkat. He is the founder of Comparethemeerkat.com, the world's premier meerkat comparison website. Aleksandr's website allows his customers to key in a few details, such as the size of meerkat you are looking for, your hobbies and your preferred meerkat location. The bane of Aleksandr's life is a company called Comparethemarket.com, a UK-based insurance price comparison website. The problem is that its name sounds very much like that of Aleksandr's site, so people come to his website wanting to compare cheap car insurance instead of wanting to compare meerkats. It is taking up his time and valuable bandwidth and distracting him from his everyday business. Aleksandr decided to launch an advertising campaign to clear up 'meerkat/market' confusion once and for all. You see, it is really quite simple. Or, as Aleksandr would say, 'simples'. The Comparethemeerkat.com website (where you can compare thousands of meerkats) built by Aleksandr, Sergei (his trusty IT manager) and the integrated team at VCCP captured the imagination of consumers in initial research. Historically, many great insurance brands had been built on affection and salience embodied in an icon. Admiral, Churchill, Hastings all developed warm iconic personalities with which to become famous. The comparison site category however, had been slow to embrace this type of marketing communications. Instead marketers in this category seemed keen to communicate a revolutionary product and moved away from unfashionable conventions. Comparethemarket.com recognized that Aleksandr's character was the key to capture market share and developed an integrated marketing communications plan.

Each communications platform was carefully considered and used for a specific purpose within the advertising campaign strategy for Comparethemarket.com. Traditional communication allowed mass reach and awareness, developing the lovable character of Aleksandr. Television advertising was the catalyst, without which the other components would not have worked as effectively. The digital focus was spent on developing Aleksandr's official comparison website, Comparethemeerkat.com, and ensuring that engagement levels were high. Social media were at the very heart of the campaign in order to create and facilitate conversations about Aleksandr Orlov, Comparethemeerkat.com and Comparethemarket.com, primarily on Facebook and Twitter. Facebook was designed to be the place for Aleksandr's community to engage, create and connect together. Comparethemarket.com used the space to upload content, pictures, videos and notes on a weekly basis. They use Facebook to encourage consumer uploads of meerkat suggestions (which are being fed into version two of the website), meerkat photos and ideas for new marketing launches (toys, ringtones etc). Aleksandr is the first UK advertising character to have his own Twitter account. He is an active and engaged participant in the Twittersphere, sharing links, photos and his daily thoughts. He is also committed to answering specific questions that his fans tweet him. Twitter was also used to find real people to appear as part of his new Testimonials page on his website. Social media was also used to introduce the campaign's second execution where Comparethemeerkat's bespectacled IT manager Sergei was created and discussed through posts on Twitter and Facebook.

Initial Campaign Results

The love for Aleksandr Orlov has had an outstanding impact on the fortunes of the brand. Return on investment for this integrated communications campaign can be proven by robust figures. The campaign achieved all of its 12-month objectives in nine weeks. In the first five months, there was a 100 per cent increase in traffic to Comparethemarket.com. Cost per visit reduced by 75 per cent. The campaign also saw a 100 per cent increase in insurance quotes. Market share tripled and 5.5 million people visited Comparethemeerkat.com in 2009, of which 21 per cent clicked through to Comparethemarket.com. Softer metrics, such as spontaneous brand awareness, saw the brand rise from fourth to first in the sector. Social media conversations about car insurance were monitored before the campaign broke, and 15 per cent were about Comparethemarket.com. Now the firm accounts for 55 per cent of UK conversations about car insurance. Aleksandr now has 839,000 fans on Facebook, making his the most popular branded fan site in the UK. Aleksandr is being followed by 67,000 people on Twitter. This number of followers to a branded advertising campaign is unprecedented. A Twitter influence model developed by *Marketing* magazine/JCPR in 2009 discovered that Aleksandr was more influential on Twitter than the London Mayor, Boris Johnson, and US Secretary of State, Hillary Clinton. For Comparethemarket.com, the campaign has significantly impacted on its human resources. Job applications increased dramatically and staff morale is at an all-time high. Finally, the campaign has also brought about a major change for competitors in terms of their search strategies: the success of the campaign means that competitors of Comparethemarket.com are now forced to actively target the keyword 'meerkat'.

Keeping the Campaign Fresh

Comparethemarket.com, which is owned by the BGL Group, has grown rapidly since the creation of Aleksandr Orlov in 2009, and is now one of the UK's leading price comparison websites. The challenge for the brand moving forward from the initial success of the campaign in 2009 was how to maintain the effectiveness of Aleksandr and Comparethemeerkat.com in attracting potential customers.

Comparethemarket.com has adopted a number of strategies as part of the campaign's evolution. For example, 2011 saw the launch of its rewards campaign. Customers who purchased car, home, van, pet, life and bike insurance, switched energy supplier or got a credit card or loan through comparethemarket.com could collect one of eight exclusive meerkat toys. After just one year, Comparethemarket.com had delivered over 1 million toys to customers. In September 2012, comparethemarket.com.au was launched to give customers in Australia the same opportunity to compare insurance prices. In November 2012, Comparethemarket.com became proud sponsors of the UK's best loved soap, *Coronation Street*. This £30 million exclusive three-year partnership included broadcast, online, mobile and licensing elements, bringing both brands to as many fans as possible. The sponsorship advertising was focused on Aleksandr Orlov and his pals visiting the famous street. In November 2013, the singer Gary Barlow appeared in two Comparethemarket.com commercials ahead of the release of his new album. In 2014, Comparethemarket.com launched Meerkat Movies, offering two for one cinema tickets every Tuesday or Wednesday for a year. This campaign was fronted by Aleksandr along with legendary movie star Arnold Schwarzenegger.

However, the biggest evolution in the campaign has been the introduction and development of new characters. Most famously, the campaign saw Aleksandr meet his rival, Maurice Wigglethorpe-Throom, for the first time. The characters, who have been at odds because they both run comparison sites, decide to make peace and sing a version of Paul McCartney and Stevie Wonder's 'Ebony And Ivory'. But, just when the pair seem to have settled their differences, a falcon released by Orlov attacks Wigglethorpe-Throom's dove. The television ad was preceded by an online spot, also created by VCCP, which showed the two characters confronting each other in Aleksandr's mansion. More recently, the Comparethemarket.com campaign shows Aleksandr Orlov and his sidekick Sergei getting to grips with parenthood after a baby meerkat called Oleg is dumped on their doorstep. The introduction and development of these characters has added a new dimension to an already phenomenally successful campaign.

Conclusion

Comparethemarket.com and VCCP have been heralded as modern communications visionaries for the success of the current campaign. Comparethemeerkat.com is a very good example of modern integrated marketing communications planning. The idea at the heart of the campaign is totally consistent, but they have incorporated dispersed fragments of the brand narratives across multiple platforms. Comparethemarket.com have revolutionized the conventions of the marketing communications in the insurance comparison industry. The challenge now for Comparethemarket.com is to keep Aleksandr Orlov relevant and maintain the character's effectiveness for the brand into the future.

Questions

1. Discuss the potential advantages and disadvantages of implementing an integrated marketing communications campaign. What were the key success factors for the Comparethemarket.com campaign?

2. Outline the factors that would have impacted on the choice of promotional mix used by Comparethemarket.com.

3. Evaluate the importance of the meerkat character to the brand's identity. Discuss the importance of social media as a tool in the creation of Aleksandr's message.

4. Discuss the risks associated with Aleksandr's character becoming stale for Comparethemarket. com. As a marketer, what steps could you take to ensure that the campaign continues to maintain its effectiveness?

This case study was written by David Cosgrave, Lecturer, University of Limerick.

References

The material in the case has been drawn from a variety of published sources.

CHAPTER 14
Mass Marketing Communications

> *All of us professionally who use the mass media are the shapers of society. We can vulgarize that society. We can brutalize it. Or we can help lift it on to a higher level.*
> **WILLIAM BERNBACH (SEE REINHARD, 2006)**

LEARNING OBJECTIVES

After reading this chapter, you should be able to:

1. explain the role of each of the tools in the mass communication promotional mix
2. discuss how advertising works and how to develop an advertising strategy
3. discuss the reasons for the growth of product placement
4. define public relations, key objectives, targets and characteristics
5. describe the guidelines to use when writing a press release
6. discuss the objectives and methods of sponsorship
7. explain how to select and evaluate a potential sponsored event
8. identify the major sales promotion types, including objectives
9. explain how to evaluate sales promotion
10. describe trade promotions
11. discuss ethical issues in mass marketing communications

W ider use of communications has placed the emphasis on developing integrated communications campaigns, using different communication methods. As discussed in Chapter 13, mass marketing communications primarily involve sending non-personal messages to wide target audiences. These key tools are the focus of this chapter and are discussed in the following order: advertising and product placement, public relations and sponsorship, and sales promotions. The chapter also explores the main media channels, building on coverage of the topics in the previous chapter and looking specifically at media vehicle selection.

Introduction

Mass communication methods enable wide dispersion of product, brand and company messages. The simple and complex communication processes explain how messages spread. Mass communication tools provide the focus, style and tone of the message. This is then delivered to the target audience by a variety of media channels. Each aspect shapes the communication message and impacts on how it might be received. For example, television commercials sometimes seek to irritate the target audience to get their attention. Gocompare.com, webuyanycar.com and Cillit Bang are some of the most irritating, according to the latest survey (Burn-Callander, 2015). Conversely, print adverts usually present rational and logical arguments to encourage target audiences to make a buying decision. For

EXHIBIT 14.1
Nissan award-winning family cars

example, according to car manufacturer Nissan, the company offers customers *innovation that excites* with its award-winning family cars. Nissan's print media adverts provide details of financing and free servicing offers, plus information about the Nissan Pulsar's performance and fuel consumption. See Exhibit 14.1.

Other mass communication tools also add more opportunities to vary and shape the message. For instance, in the case of public relations (PR), stories in the media and events provide a source of public information and experience, which can raise awareness and educate various publics (target audiences) about a brand and its corporate image. It should be noted that the use of PR is on the increase as corporate reputations are increasingly at the heart of a company's competitive advantage. Sales promotions are often used to elicit action and this technique is used widely from selling fast-moving consumer goods (FMCGs) to car finance. For example, PC World regularly offers promotional discounts to encourage purchases of consumer electronics; typical promotions offer customers the opportunity to save up to £150 on selected laptops or claim £250 when trading in their old televisions. Digital advertising offers scope to engage target audiences and create communities using social media platforms. For example, Purina used a mix of slice of life and likeability in its digital advert 'puppyhood' as a call to action. The pet-food brand has used the web advert as '*a sales pitch with a servicey content play*' (Pathak, 2015). The website Puppyhood is a magazine-style site which is a resource of information for pet owners. Using the web in this way is transcending the divide between television and print media. Digital marketing is covered in detail in Chapter 16. These examples help to highlight various theories that seek to explain how mass communications might work.

Scan the QR code to see some of the most irritating adverts from the last 15 years.

Broadly speaking, advertising and PR raise awareness, while sales promotion is used to stimulate action. But each tool has much more to offer a marketing manager planning an integrated marketing communications campaign. These tools are now explored in more detail.

Advertising

What is advertising? How does it work? When should it be used and how can we evaluate its effectiveness? These questions, asked about advertising, have tormented academics and practitioners alike and filled thousands of pages of hundreds of publications. Yet still there are no definitive answers. Hegarty (2011) says success comes from the big idea. For Sorrell, it is all about the capacity to deliver ROI (Sweney, 2012). Jones (1991) explains how it can persuade, while Ehrenberg (1992) suggests a weaker response. And just when you think you might have some answers, throw into the debate *disruptive* technology like the Internet. Here, newcomers to the world of business, like college students Page and Brin (Google) and Zuckerberg (Facebook), have created new environments that are part of the networks that encase the planet and operate at the speed of light.

Furthermore, digital channels and social networks are rapidly changing the way we communicate and the content of the messages we use to influence others. Also, more information is available on how customers respond to messages delivered through digital channels. For example, Weetabix used Skyview as a research tool to evaluate the effectiveness of its intensive television advertising campaigns. Skyview is a panel of over 30,000 viewers that have Sky boxes to record their watching behaviour, and this is linked to TNS's Worldpanel, which gathers data on purchasing habits. Weetabix was able to confirm the effectiveness of its television campaign and saw an over 10 per cent increase in sales. Weetabix was also able to determine the frequency needed to get the best results; one exposure to the advert prompted purchasing, but two to four exposures were needed to achieve sales; any more was a waste, which was a very important finding for Weetabix (SkyMedia, 2015).

So, what can we achieve in this short section on advertising? We start with the basics: strong and weak theories of advertising, which seek to explain the principle of how advertising works. Then we look at the practicalities: identify the different objectives which create a platform for using advertising, look at campaign planning, media decisions, and client–agency relationships. Furthermore, throughout this section, we use practitioner examples to provide evidence of the difficulties and possible solutions for the simple questions raised at the start.

Advertising: the basics

Advertising messages rely on mass media to deliver communications messages. Uses and gratifications theory suggests that the mass media constitute a resource on which audiences draw to satisfy various needs. Its assumptions are as follows.

- The audience is active and their consumption of mass media is largely directed by its needs.
- The initiative in linking need satisfaction with media choice lies mainly with the individual.
- The media compete with other sources of need satisfaction.
- The gratifications sought from the media include diversion and entertainment, as well as information (Katz, Gurevitch and Haas, 1973).

Scan the QR code to see how Scandinavian brands are using Nordic stoicism to communicate with their target audiences.

Research suggests that people use advertising for at least seven kinds of satisfaction, namely product information, entertainment, risk reduction, added value, past purchase reassurance, vicarious experience and involvement (Crosier, 1983). Indirect experiences are an opportunity to experience situations or lifestyles to which an individual would not otherwise have access. 'Involvement' refers to the pleasure derived from participation in the brand messages that are delivered through advertising. Research among a group of young adults found such participation uses various forms of advertising appeals, including escapism, ego enhancement (demonstrating their intelligence by understanding the advertisement) and checking out the opposite sex (O'Donohoe, 1994).

Uses and gratifications theory (UGT) identifies the link between advertising, the media and the motivations of message receivers. Marketing in Action 14.1 explores this concept by exploring the harsh, sometimes melancholic, adverts produced by Nordic brands. In essence, television commercials support the UGT research, as they deliver

MARKETING IN ACTION 14.1
Nordic Brands Invite Audiences to Experience the Benefits of a Brutal Landscape

Arguably, Volvo cars, Arla yoghurt and Finlandia vodka share a common message theme with their adverts: they want their customers to know how the harsh Nordic environment and the strength needed to survive builds better brands. But why might the brooding, melancholy film produced by Volvo attract more car buyers? And how does Arla's journey of a young boy across Iceland's desolate landscapes help sell yoghurt? Why might spending over two minutes viewing snippets of Nordic wisdom encourage us to drink more vodka?

Gratification researchers offer some insight into why such approaches might work. UGT suggests that audiences voluntarily engage with media, motivated by their own needs and goals. And their reward for actively participating in the communication process (e.g. viewing adverts on television, downloading video on demand, sharing via social media) is the gratification that results. UGT hangs on the premise that it is different to mass communication theories, because it endows the consumer of the media with the power to determine which media they engage with rather than being passively captivated by powerful brand messages. Researchers in this field suggest various ways in which audiences achieve gratification and satisfy their needs. For example, utility is seen as using the media to achieve certain tasks; selectivity as audiences using the media to support their own interests and beliefs; personal interest as serving psychological needs through reassurance and self-understanding.

So when Volvo decided to adopt a global approach to communications, it produced its Nordic noir film as a centrepiece for the campaign. In the advert (a four-minute film), a Volvo car was shown traversing the tough Nordic landscape accompanied by emotive music and lyrics to match. Viewers were invited to experience and gain insights into how these extremes ensure that Volvo cars are able to deal with all eventualities. Engaging with this advert arguably reassures car buyers that a car *made by Sweden* offers performance and safety for the precious things in life.

For Arla Icelandic yogurt, there are also gains for those who engage with this advert. The personal benefits are said to be the offer of a healthy alternative and giving health-conscious consumers *'a great treat after exercise, since protein contributes to maintaining and growing muscle mass'*. In the advert, the journey of a boy named Orri, seen delivering an important message, seeks to convey that nothing is too difficult once you've eaten Arla, a product with 1,000 years' worth of heritage.

With Finlandia, audiences are offered insight and wisdom from quirky individuals. If they engage this *knowledge collective*, amassed from 1,000 years (combined age of the knowledge providers in the advert) of insight, it offers a guide to vodka drinkers on how they might live a 'life less ordinary'.

Possibly these and other brands do look for ways to engage their audiences and give something back. As media channels become more fragmented and digital platforms more widely used, there are more opportunities to deliver benefits that go beyond the simple message of 'buy more product'.

Based on: Levy and Windahl (1985); Oster (2015); Gilbert (2015); Magee (2015); Elihu, Blumer and Gurevitch (1974); West and Turner (2010)

entertainment as a reward for engaging with the media. Through the web, target audiences can derive further satisfaction by engaging directly with adverts. The brand message provides further gratification by telling its users what to expect when they buy the brand.

These linkages give us some clues to why advertising appears on different media and also why the Internet has become such a popular medium for messages that invite engagement. But we need to know more about how advertising works.

Strong and Weak Theories of How Advertising Works

For many years, there has been considerable debate about how advertising works. The consensus is that there can be no single all-embracing theory that explains how all advertising works because it has varied tasks (Wright and Crimp, 2003). For example, advertising that attempts to make an instant sale by incorporating a return coupon that can be used to order a product is very different from corporate image advertising that is designed to reinforce attitudes.

The competing views on how advertising works have been termed the **strong theory of advertising** and the **weak theory of advertising** (Jones, 1991). The strong theory has its base in the USA and is shown on the left-hand side of Figure 14.1. A person passes through the stages of awareness, interest, desire and action (AIDA). According to this theory, advertising is strong enough to increase people's knowledge and change people's attitudes, and as a consequence is capable of persuading people who had not previously bought a brand to buy it. It is therefore a conversion theory of advertising: non-buyers are converted to buyers. Advertising is assumed to be a powerful influence on consumers.

This model has been criticized on two grounds (Ehrenberg, 1992). First, for many types of product there is little evidence that consumers experience a strong desire before action (buying the brand). For example, in the case of an inexpensive product, a brand might be bought on a trial basis without any strong conviction that it is superior to competing brands. Second, the model is criticized because it is limited to the conversion of a non-buyer to a buyer. It ignores what happens after action (i.e. first purchase). Yet in most mature markets advertising is designed to affect people who have already bought the brand at least once.

The major alternative to the strong advertising theory is shown on the right-hand side of Figure 14.1. The steps in this model are awareness, trial and reinforcement (ATR). The ATR model, which has received support in Europe, suggests that advertising is a much less powerful influence than the strong theory would suggest. As Ehrenberg explains, 'advertising can first arouse awareness and interest, nudge some customers towards a doubting first trial purchase (with the emphasis on trial, as in "maybe I'll try it") and then provide some reassurance and reinforcement after that first purchase. I see no need for any strong AIDA-like Desire or Conviction before the first purchase is made' (Ehrenberg, 1992). His work in fast-moving consumer goods (FMCG) markets has shown that loyalty to one brand is rare. Most consumers purchase a selection of brands. The proportions of total purchases represented by the different brands show little variation over time, and new brands join the selection only in exceptional circumstances. A major objective of advertising in such circumstances is to defend brands. It does not work to increase sales by bringing new buyers to the brand advertised. Its main function is to retain existing buyers, and sometimes to increase the frequency with which they buy the brand (Jones, 1991). Therefore, the target is existing buyers who are fairly well disposed to the brand (otherwise they would not buy it), and advertising is designed to reinforce these favourable perceptions so they continue to buy it (Dall'Olmo Riley et al., 1997).

As we saw when discussing consumer behaviour, level of involvement has an important role in determining how people make purchasing decisions. Jones (1991) suggests that involvement may also explain when the strong and weak theories apply. For high-involvement decisions such as the purchase of expensive consumer durables, mail order or financial services, the decision-making process is studied with many alternatives considered and an extensive information search undertaken. Advertising, therefore, is more likely to follow the strong theory either by creating a strong desire to purchase (as with mail order) or by convincing people that they should find out more about the brand (e.g. by visiting a showroom). Since the purchase is expensive it is likely that a strong desire (or conviction) is required before purchase takes place.

However, for low-involvement purchase decisions (such as low-cost packaged goods) people are less likely to consider a wide range of brands thoroughly before purchase and it is here that

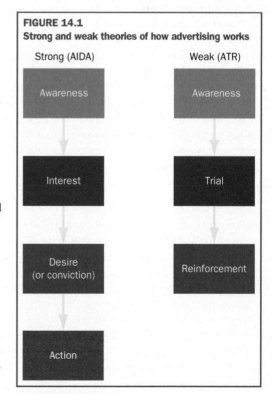

FIGURE 14.1
Strong and weak theories of how advertising works

Strong (AIDA)

Awareness

Interest

Desire
(or conviction)

Action

Weak (ATR)

Awareness

Trial

Reinforcement

the weak theory of advertising almost certainly applies. Advertising is mainly intended to keep consumers doing what they already do by providing reassurance and reinforcement. Advertising repetition will be important in maintaining awareness and keeping the brand on the consumer's selection of brands from which individual purchases will be chosen.

Advertising: the Practicalities of Developing a Strategy

Advertising is one element of the marketing mix and decisions regarding advertising expenditure should not be taken in isolation. Marketing strategy needs to be taken into account. In particular, competitive positioning needs to be considered: what is the target market and what differential advantage does the product possess? Target market definition allows the *details of the audience* to be identified through segmentation variables: both in consumer and industrial markets (e.g. 16- to 19-year-old women, or fashion buyers in the retail industry). More specifically, for example, Asus is a leading manufacturer of computer hardware, such as high-performance motherboards. It targets gamers (age 20-plus males) who are looking for intense action from their selected products, and Asus uses knowledge of its customers to develop advertising which grabs the attention of its target audiences. The target selection process also helps focus on the differential advantage and the features and benefits of the product to stress in the advertising. Figure 14.2 shows the major decisions that need to be taken when developing advertising strategy.

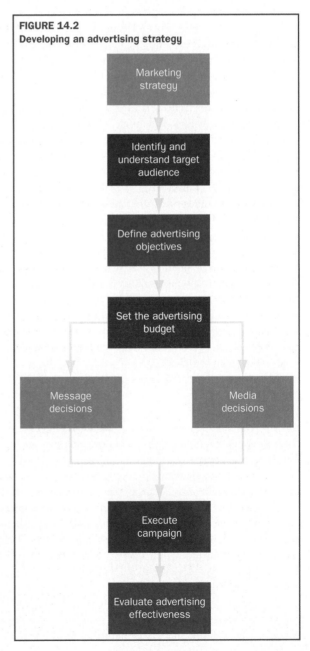

FIGURE 14.2
Developing an advertising strategy

Identify and understand the target audience

The **target audience** is the group of people at which the advertisement is aimed. In consumer markets it may be defined in terms of socio-economic group, age, gender, location, buying frequency (e.g. heavy versus light buyers) and/or lifestyle. In organizational markets, it may be defined in terms of role (e.g. purchasing manager, managing director) and industry type.

Once the target audience has been identified, it needs to be understood. Buyer motives and choice criteria need to be analyzed. Choice criteria are those factors buyers use to evaluate competing products. Understanding criteria in line with the needs of the target audience is vital: it has fundamental implications for message and media decisions.

Define advertising objectives

Advertising is used to achieve various objectives including stimulating sales and increasing profits. To deliver operational value from using advertising it is important to set clear communication *objectives*. Advertising can create awareness, stimulate trial, position products in customers' minds, correct misconceptions, remind and reinforce, and provide support for the salesforce. Each objective will now be discussed. Read Marketing in Action 14.2 to find out about the advice that Saatchi & Saatchi global creative agency gives its clients when setting advertising objectives.

MARKETING IN ACTION 14.2
Saatchi & Saatchi Advocates Love and Respect When Planning Communication Objectives

Advertising is a way that brands set themselves apart from their competitors. Today, most goods *work* in the way they are expected to, as the ramifications of a customer revolt through social media can destroy a brand's reputation very quickly. So how do marketers make their cars, chocolates, wine or clothing stand out from the crowd? Saatchi & Saatchi suggests that is it a matter of love and respect. Lovemarks are brands that are *'owned by the people (customers) who love them, and they (brand owners) use their respect equity to build new mysterious, sensual and intimate relationships'*.

Creators of the love–respect axis at Saatchi & Saatchi suggest that if a brand has high respect and high love, it is considered a *'Lovemark'*. However, if it has high respect and low love, then it is merely a *brand*. High love and low respect is the domain of fads, and low love and low respect is where commodities (products) reside on the matrix. The purpose of the matrix is to inspire companies to shift the positioning of their market offers until they achieve the high status of a *Lovemark*. And in order to help, Saatchi & Saatchi has a *'Lovemarker'*, which is an index

Source of image: http://www.saatchi.be/ lovemarks

that allows it to score companies on levels of: *respect*, which is made up of the three constructs performance, trust and reputation; and *love*, which is similarly made up of mystery, sensuality and intimacy.

In total, 14 respect and 13 love variables are used to determine a score. The Lovemarker allows companies to determine whether they are hot (2 points), warm (1 point) or cold (0 points) against each variable, and they must score over 41 points to be a Lovemark. Examples of Lovemarks are McDonald's and Harley Davidson.

Achieving the Lovemark status is done by not only getting the story-telling right and connecting it in a logical and coherent way from the past to the future, but also by tapping into customer emotions in order to inspire and excite. However, some goods have a head start. For example, we might know that green beans are better for us than sweets and are something we need to eat, but the sugar boost from confectionary is more likely to be a heart pumping *want* than is a plate of healthy vegetables, which means it is easier for us to love a bag M&Ms than a packet of Florette salad mix.

According to Dina Howell, Worldwide CEO Saatchi & Saatchi, a want is more powerful than a need, and she advocates three ways for companies to unlock positive emotions:

1 ***Know the market, understanding the culture and triggers that might prompt emotion and excitement***. When Cadbury's Dairy Milk sought to enter Arabian markets by targeting young single adults, the company had to find a way to make its products more exciting than market leader Galaxy. Its solution was to invite young shoppers to sample the 'Joy Elevator'. Saatchi & Saatchi devised the campaign, which was delivered through store experiences, online and using traditional media channels.
2 ***Know the channel and what it has to offer***. When Swiffer mops set out to revive its sales, the Saatchi & Saatchi team identified a *lovegap* between the manufacturer (Procter & Gamble) and potential new customers. The problem was that whilst customers were aware of the brand, when they got to the store to buy the product, they often could not find it, touch it or see how it worked, as the Swiffer mop was sealed in a box. The solution was to supply the mop ready assembled, so customers could see in store how easy it would be to use. Adapting the product to the channel and promoting the brand through media channels raised its profile and moved it into Lovemark territory.
3 ***Know the shopper***. In the USA, 86 per cent of purchases are made in the store by women. So when Quaker Oats asked Saatchi & Saatchi for help, together they devised the 'power their potential' campaign. The challenge was how to get children to concentrate more at school (by eating breakfast and heathy snacks) and at the same time how to give parents an easy solution for providing children with the 'fuel' they needed to get them through to lunch time. The solution was a combination of brands of hot cereals and ready-to-eat healthy snacks and cookies that were highly visible when parents went shopping. Using in-store displays and online media, this campaign enabled Quaker to increase its market share.

Based on: Saatchi & Saatchi (2015); Roberts (2015a and b); Howells (2015); http://www.lovemarks.com

Create awareness

Advertising can create awareness of a company, a brand, a website, an event, or something of interest to target audiences. It can even alert buyers to a solution to a problem. For example, Colgate toothpaste can stop plaque, bad breath, tooth and gum decay. Discount supermarket Lidl aimed to help its customers deal with the problem of the cost of shopping with its 'shop a Lidl smarter' campaign. It is widely agreed (in principle) that advertising can help to legitimize a company, its products, brands and sales teams in the minds of the target audience. In doing so it can also improve acceptance of what a company has on offer. Brand awareness is considered as a precondition of purchase and can be achieved through advertising.

 Scan the QR code to see how Lidl used taste tests to promote saving and encourage customers to buy its own-label brands.

Stimulate trial

Advertising can create interest and stimulate trial. The sale of some products suffers because of lack of trial. Perhaps marketing research has shown that, once consumers try the product, acceptance is high but for some reason only a small proportion of the target group has actually bought the product. In such circumstances, advertising focuses on stimulating trial, and increasingly digital technology is being used. For example, Tesco has joined with Unilever to promote the Magnum brands using iBeacons. At 270 stores, shoppers who had downloaded the mPulse app were able to receive exclusive offers and discounts to encourage them to try Magnum's Black and Pink varieties of ice-cream bar (Spary, 2015).

Position products in customers' minds

Advertising copy and visuals have a major role to play in positioning brands in the minds of the target audience (Ries and Trout, 2001). Creative positioning involves the development or reinforcement of an image or set of associations for a brand, see Exhibit 14.2. There are seven ways in which this objective can be achieved (Aaker, Batra and Myers, 1996).

1 *Product characteristics and customer benefits*: this is a common positioning strategy. For example, Ryanair launched its first television adverts in 25 years to let its customers know about changes to its previously restrictive baggage rules, the introduction of seating allocation, and improvements to its online booking website. Headphone manufacturer Dre positioned its products as offering top-quality sound and reliability. Ford Focus uses its high-tech features and characteristics—for example, voice-control navigation and entertainment system, active parking assistance, EcoBoost, low-speed safety system, traffic sign recognition—to portray its car's benefits to the user, and this is summed up in the statement 'Ford Focus goes further'.

EXHIBIT 14.2
The Beats advert aims to communicate product characteristics and benefits to position the brand in the minds of consumers

 Scan the QR code to see Ryanair's TV advert which aims to make customers aware of changes at the airline.

Another tactic used for positioning is being first; for example, Sky News claims the number one position with its claim to be 'first for breaking news'. Occasionally two or more attributes are used, as with Ecover laundry liquid (cleans clothes with its non-biological ingredients, and is good for the environment as it uses less packaging and fewer transport miles). L'Oréal Men Expert Pure Power helps improve impurities in the skin, making it cleaner (see Exhibit 14.3).

EXHIBIT 14.3
L'Oréal appeals to its target audience by identifying their problems and providing solutions which match consumer preferences

2 *Price*: this positioning approach focuses on price as a weapon to deliver higher value to consumers. Many airlines use price as a differentiator: for example, low-cost airlines like easyJet, Jet2, Wizz Air. Sainsbury's promotes low-price lines branded under its 'basics' range, and Morrisons has its M Saver range. Price positioning is not always focused on low prices, however. Occasionally a brand is positioned based on its high price, as is the case with Stella Artois ('reassuringly expensive').

3 *Product use*: another positioning method is to associate the product with a use. An example is Cillit Bang, with its 'power to wow' cleaning products, which is easy to use and shifts dirt and grime easily; Elnett Satin, L'Oréal hairspray, 'Nothing holds you like Elnett'; the Co-operative Bank is 'Good with money'.

4 *Product user*: another way of positioning is to associate a brand with a user or user type. Polo by Ralph Lauren portrays its users to be bohemian romantics who live on the edge of the city, with an interest in antiques, art and music (Stubbs, 2014). Celebrity endorsements are often used, such as by David Beckham (Adidas, H&M, Breitling), Michael Jordan (Nike), Helen Mirren (L'Oréal), Nicole Kidman (Chanel No 5). Positioning by user type has been successfully used by *The Economist* (intelligent, knowledgeable).

 Scan the QR code to see how St John's Ambulance uses celebrities and animations to raise awareness of the dangers to babies of choking.

5 *Product class*: some products can benefit by positioning themselves within a product class. For example, Red Mountain coffee positioned itself within the ground coffee class with the tagline 'Ground coffee taste without the grind', and a margarine called 'I Can't Believe It's Not Butter' was positioned within the butter class by virtue of its name and advertising; and, of course, there is the enduring classic 'Beanz Meanz Heinz'.

6 *Symbols*: the use of symbols to position brands in the marketplace has been achieved by Michelin (Michelin Man), McDonald's (golden arches) and Apple (white apple logo). The use of symbols is particularly effective when the symbol reflects a quality desired in the brand, as with the Andrex puppy (softness).

7 *Competition*: positioning against well-entrenched competitors can be effective since their image in the marketplace can be used as a reference point. For example, Subaru positioned against Volvo by claiming 'Volvo has built a reputation for surviving accidents. Subaru has built a reputation for avoiding them', based on ABS for better braking and four-wheel drive for better traction. Dyson positions itself against the competition by claiming that, unlike those of its rivals, its vacuum cleaners do not lose suction thanks to Dyson's patented technology. Adidas positions its products against other brands of trainers (e.g. Nike). In the Steadicam campaign, a runner in the desert is wearing Nike trainers but the cameraman, carrying a heavy camera and filming the event, is wearing Adidas. The message is that Adidas trainers offer better performance and enable users to remain fresh and lively even after an extreme run. Positioning against competitors can be effective when consumers base their purchase decision on facts. Hence, a well-adjusted

statement claiming a factual advantage against a key competitor can be highly successful. However, research has shown that, if used inappropriately, it can tarnish the image of the brand that is using the technique. There is also the risk of legal action. Aldi upset Tesco with its 'Swap & Save' campaign. Aldi claimed that 84 out of 98 people had saved money by switching to shopping with the discount supermarket. Tesco disagreed, and the Advertising Standards Authority (ASA) banned Aldi's advert on the grounds that is was misleading to customers. (In the UK, the ASA is an independent regulator that controls advertising standards across all media.)

 Scan the QR code to find out about advertising standards and codes of practice.

Not all slogans are used for their intended purpose. Read Marketing in Action 14.3 to find how to 'Keep Calm and Carry On'.

Correct misconceptions

A fourth objective of advertising can be to correct misconceptions that consumers hold against brands. For example, McCain's, the market leader in the UK for oven chips, ran a successful advertising campaign claiming that oven chips contained 40 per cent less fat than home-cooked chips. However, marketing research showed that consumers still believed that their oven chips contained 30 per cent fat. A new campaign was designed to correct this misconception by stating that they contained only 5 per cent fat. Advertising cosmetic surgery has become increasingly commonplace. Service providers are keen to dispel fears, and often use advertising as a way of conveying the message that cosmetic procedures and treatments are safe. However, in the UK, the ASA has often ruled against such advertising, on the grounds of it being misleading, exaggerated or breaching social responsibility.

Remind and reinforce

Once a clear position in the minds of the target audience has been established, the objective of advertising may be to remind consumers of the brand's existence and to reinforce its image. For many leading brands in mature markets, such as Coca-Cola, Heinz Beans or Nestlé's Kit Kat, the objective of their advertising is to maintain top-of-mind awareness and favourable associations. Given their strong market position, a major advertising task is to defend against competitive inroads, thus maintaining high sales, market share and profits. Guinness has managed to maintain its brand for over 250 years making it one of the world's most successful alcoholic drink brands, see Exhibit 14.4.

Provide support for the salesforce

Advertising can provide invaluable support for the salesforce by identifying warm prospects and communicating with otherwise unreachable members of a decision-making unit. Some business-to-business advertising contains return coupons that potential customers can send to the advertiser indicating a degree of interest in the product.

EXHIBIT 14.4
Guinness uses a thought-provoking campaign to maintain top-of-mind awareness among its target audiences

Set the advertising budget

The achievement of any of the previous objectives will depend upon the size of the budget and how effectively it is spent. There are various methods of setting budgets which are discussed in more detail later in this section. These are the percentage of sales, affordability, matching competition, and the objective and task methods.

Message decisions

This section builds on our earlier discussion of the message (see Chapter 13) and explores how messages can be tailored to suit the advertiser's need and the target audience's behaviour. Advertising messages should clearly communicate with the target audience, be important to them, communicate benefits and aim to secure competitive advantage. This is why an understanding of the motives and choice criteria of the target audience is essential for effective advertising. Without this knowledge a campaign could be built upon an advertising platform that is irrelevant to its audience.

An **advertising message** translates the platform into words, symbols and illustrations that are attractive and meaningful to the target audience (see Marketing in Action 14.3).

Humour is another powerful weapon in

EXHIBIT 14.5
Aquafresh uses a humorous visual appeal to demonstrate the flexibility and movement of its Flexigel toothbrush

advertising, associating the brand with a feeling of warmth. Humour can be used in various media, see Exhibit 14.5.

 Scan the QR code to see how the Accor hotel group uses humour to promote the brand.

Television messages also need to be built on a strong advertising platform. Because television commercials are usually 30 seconds or less in duration, most communicate only one major selling appeal—sometimes called the *single-minded proposition*—which is the single most motivating and differentiating thing that can be said about the brand (Saatchi & Saatchi Compton, 1985).

Television advertising often uses one of three creative approaches (Hall, 1992). First, the *benefits* approach, where the advertisement suggests a reason for the customer to buy (customer benefit). For example, WeightWatchers warns of the dangers of overeating, to promote the benefits of taking control of weight loss.

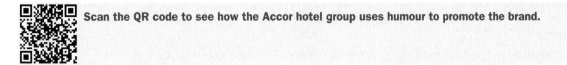 Scan the QR code to see how WeightWatchers uses reverse psychology and fear in its 'Big Game' advert.

The second approach is more subtle: no overt benefit is mentioned. Instead, the intention is to *involve* the viewer. An example of involvement advertising was the commercial for Heinz Spaghetti in which a young couple's son tells them that the tomato on his plate is the sun, the triangles of toast are the mountains, and the Heinz Spaghetti is the sea. When the father enters into the game and asks 'So that's the boat then?', the boy responds witheringly 'No, it's a sausage'.

MARKETING IN ACTION 14.3
Keep Calm and Carry On

Successful advertising slogans (sometimes referred to as straplines) are short, memorable phrases. They can focus on a particular aspect of a product or service and can be long lasting. Or they may be created for a single campaign. They are not a new phenomenon. The iconic Keep Calm and Carry On poster was originally designed for the British government to be used in the advent of an invasion, and the message aimed to encourage the nation to be positive and to boost morale. However, the poster was never used officially. The 2.5 million copies were held in reserve and remained largely unseen by the British public until 2000.

Stuart Manley, owner of Barter Books (www.barterbooks.co.uk), a second-hand book shop in Alnwick, Northumberland, found a copy of the poster and had it framed for his wife, who liked it so much she displayed it by the side of the shop checkout. The bookshop is unusual insofar as it allows its customers to *barter* for goods as well as making cash purchases. But more notably, it has become famous for finding the poster. Since their discovery of the 'Keep Calm and Carry On' poster, millions of copies have been sold worldwide. The posters can be seen in places far and wide, from Buckingham Palace, the US Embassy in Belgium, to David Beckham's chest (on a T-shirt). The slogan appears on mugs, jewellery, baby clothes, T-shirts, travel bags and screen savers.

Simple, timeless and succinct, this slogan has longevity. Although not used for its intended purpose, the slogan eschews common values and brings people together in a common goal and, according to Alain Samson (social psychologist at the London School of Economics), 'The words are also particularly positive, reassuring, in a period of uncertainty, anxiety, even perhaps of cynicism.' The number of uses of the slogan have been expanded and it has appeared on products around the world. The Keep Calm and Carry On website has a product creator that enables shoppers to make their own products using this iconic logo.

Based on: Wikipedia (2012); Barter Books (2012); Henley (2009); Keep Calm and Carry On (n.d.)

The third type of creative approach attempts to register the brand as significant in the market, and is called *salience advertising*. The assumption is that advertising that stands out as being different will cause the brand to stand out as different. For example, Cillit Bang uses the name of the brand, the colours associated with the brand and the style of its television adverts to stand out. Shock advertising is arguably an extreme form of salient advertising. Research by Dahl, Frankenberger and Manchanda (2003) suggests that shock adverts take the audience by surprise because they do not conform to social norms. For example: FCUK (connotation of vulgar language); Pot Noodle ran an advertising campaign called the 'slag of all snacks', which was ultimately banned (sexual innuendo) (Whitehead, 2002). Advertisers using shock advertising should take extra care to ensure that the messages do not alienate the target audience. Benetton's Death campaign resulted in a social outcry culminating in the loss of its coveted franchise with the leading US department store chain Sears. Barnardo's, the children's charity, is known for its use of shock advertising to stimulate a response from its target audiences. In one campaign the life story of Michael, a vulnerable child, is told in reverse. The reasonable, smiling face of the 25-yearold Michael regresses as the viewer hears about what he has been through since a very early age. The strapline 'It doesn't have to end how it began'

MARKETING IN ACTION 14.4
Pioneering Messages Can Create Meaningful Campaigns

According to John Caples (a top direct response copywriter), using the right message is important. He suggested there can be significant benefits: 'I have seen one ad actually sell not twice as much, not three times as much but 19 times as much as another. Both ads occupied the same space. Both were run in the same publication. Both had photographic illustrations. Both had carefully written copy. The difference was that one used the *right* appeal and the other used the *wrong* appeal.'

In the 1970s, the Health Education Council ran a poster campaign (see http://www.fpa.org.uk/aboutus/fpahistory/ourfirst80years) that got the message and balances *right* between the images and the copy and achieved great impact. The campaign brief was to raise awareness of the issues of contraception and get young men to accept greater responsibility. The poster of the pregnant man was highly successful: it not only changed attitudes towards contraception among the target audience of young men, but it also helped to change wider societal attitudes towards sex education.

The HEC poster proved to be particularly powerful, and its success lies in the dramatization of reality, the message and the copywriting. So, the key challenge is how to get the entire element right. Here are some useful pointers for print advertisements based on guidance from David Ogilvy (anonymously quoted as the 'father of advertising'):

The message:

The appeal (benefit) should be important to the target audience, written in language it can understand, be specific to the target audience's needs and should provide supporting evidence (as required).

The advert (complete, with image, headline and body copy) should contain:
- a *headline* which aims to achieve one of the following: promise a benefit; deliver news; tell a significant story; identify a problem; cite a satisfied customer review.
- *body copy* (if required—additional copy supporting and flowing from the headline) should adhere to the following rules.
  - only use long copy if it is relevant to the needs of the target audience
  - avoid long paragraphs and sentences
  - maximize the use of white space, break up text to avoid it looking heavy to read
  - use coupons as a device for providing company contact details. Alternatively, website and other contact details should appear at the end of the body copy.
- *images* These can affect comprehension and add to the complexity of developing messages which the target audience can understand. Therefore it is important to get the *right* balance between the emotional content and the informational content.

Increasingly, adverts that can be interpreted by a global target audience are becoming important. Images can provide instant access to the message idea. But it is important to ensure that the visual imagery is as clear and uncluttered as the headline and the body copy.

Remember, most people when reading a press advertisement read the headline but not the body copy and then use associated imagery to help with their interpretation of the message. Simple visuals can convey powerful messages and reinforce brand identity.

Based on: Hegarty (2011); Ogilvy (1987); Pieters, Wedel and Batra (2010)

is the trigger to encourage the target audience to make a donation and support the charity so that more vulnerable children may benefit.

Television advertising is also often used to build a brand personality. The *brand personality* is the message that the advertisement seeks to convey.

Media decisions

Media planning has changed significantly in recent years, as digital platforms, mobile and the web e.g., account for a much larger part of a communication budget. The UK is the first nation globally to see digital media overtake the traditional channels (see Figure 14.3), with a spend of close to £8 billion. This includes search engines, mobile apps, newspaper websites and video on demand. This increase in digital spend has mainly affected print media, which are experiencing a sharp decline overall.

In Chapter 13, we discuss media channels and the implications of channel choice. In this section, we build on the discussions in the previous chapter by exploring further decisions affecting the media planner's decision. Each of the media can be used to carry different types of message; for example, television advertising is often used to convey the desired emotional response and the print media to supply objective information. In low-involvement situations, such as with the choice of drinks and convenience foods, humour is sometimes used to create a feeling of warmth about a brand and even regular exposure to a brand name over time can generate the desired feeling of warmth (Elliott, 1997). Interestingly, different media are perceived with different levels of 'trustworthiness': for example, television, print and cinema advertising is generally seen as more trusted than outdoor, online and direct mail (Barnett, 2011). Consequently, selecting media can be complex and there are five considerations to be taken into account.

1   *Creative factors.* The key question that needs to be addressed is 'Does the medium allow the communication objectives to be realized?' For example, if the objective is to position the brand as having a high-status aspirational personality, television would be better than posters. However, if the communication objective is to remind the target audience of a brand's existence, a poster campaign may suffice. Outdoor media are becoming more dynamic thanks to technological advancements that mean many of the benefits of television can be conveyed to outdoor adverts. J. C. Decaux is an example of a company making use of new technology to bring outdoor advertising to life (see http://www. jcdecaux.co.uk). Cinema advertising is also gaining popularity as it delivers highly targeted audiences.

2   *Size of the advertising budget.* Some media are naturally more expensive than others. For example, £500,000 may be sufficient for a national poster campaign but woefully inadequate for national television. However, the shift towards online has created opportunities for smaller companies that cannot afford to advertise on national television (Glennie, 2015).

3   *Relative cost per opportunity to see.* The target audience may be reached much more cheaply using one medium rather than another. However, the calculation of opportunity to see differs according to media class, making comparisons difficult. For example, in the UK an opportunity to see for the press is defined as 'read or looked at any issue of the publication for at least two minutes', whereas for posters it is 'traffic past site' and online it is the number unique visits or downloads. Mobile devices are also subject to measurement, and ad impressions are a method of tracking exposure. See Table 14.1 for definition of opportunity to see.

4   *Competitive activity.* The key decision is whether to compete in the same medium or to seek to dominate an alternative medium. Deciding to compete in the same medium may be appropriate if it is seen as the most effective one by the competition, so that to ignore it would be to hand the competition a massive communication advantage. Domination of an alternative medium may be sensible for third or fourth players in a product market who cannot match the advertising budgets of the big two competitors. Supposing the major players were using television, the third or fourth competitor might choose the press or the Internet where it could dominate, achieving higher impact than if it followed the competition into television.

5   *Views of the retail trade* (e.g. supermarket buyers). These may influence the choice of media class. Advertising expenditure is often used by

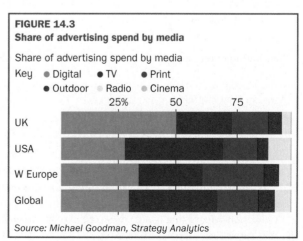

FIGURE 14.3
Share of advertising spend by media

Source: Michael Goodman, Strategy Analytics

salespeople to convince the retail trade to increase shelf space for existing brands and to stock new brands. Since distribution is a key success factor in these markets, the views of retailers will be important. For example, if it is known that supermarkets favour television advertising in a certain product market, the selling impact on the trade of £3 million spent on television may be viewed as greater than the equivalent spend of 50:50 between television and the press.

Media vehicles

This refers to the choice of the particular newspaper, magazine, television spot, poster site, and so on. Although creative considerations still play a part, *cost per thousand calculations* is more important. This requires readership and viewership figures. In the UK, readership figures are produced by the National Readership Survey, based on over 36,000 interviews per year. Viewership is measured by the Broadcasters' Audience Research Board (BARB), which produces weekly reports based on a panel of 5,100 households equipped with metered television sets. Poster research is conducted by an organization called Route. It provides information on not only the number of people who pass each poster, but also on the number of people who are likely to see a particular site.

TABLE 14.1 Definition of an opportunity to see (OTS)	
Television	Presence in room with set switched on at turn of clock minute to relevant channel, provided that presence in room with set on is for at least 15 consecutive seconds
Press	Read or looked at any issue (for at least two minutes) within the publication period (e.g. for weeklies, within the last seven days)
Posters	Traffic past site (including pedestrians)
Cinema	Actual cinema admissions
Mobile	Ad impressions

Sometimes a combination of media classes is used in an advertising campaign to take advantage of their relative strengths and weaknesses. For example, a new car launch might use television to gain awareness and project the desired image, the Internet to foster engagement, the press to supply more technical information and later in the campaign outdoor media posters may be used as a support medium to remind and reinforce earlier messages.

Execute campaign

Once the advertisements have been produced and the media selected, they are sent to the relevant media for publication, transmission or launch online. A key organizational issue is to ensure that the right advertisements reach the right media at the right time. Each media vehicle has its own deadlines after which publication or transmission may not be possible.

Evaluate advertising effectiveness

All marketing communications, not just advertising, should be evaluated to determine a) whether the message and the tools that are to be used to deliver the campaign are likely to be effective; and b) the impact and effectiveness of the campaign once it has been released (Fill, 2009). This means pre-testing (before the campaign) and post-testing (during and after the campaign).

What should be measured depends on whatever the advertising is trying to achieve. As we have already seen, advertising objectives include gaining awareness, trial, positioning, correcting misconceptions, reminding and providing support for the salesforce (e.g. by identifying warm prospects). By setting targets for each objective, advertising research can assess whether objectives have been achieved. For example, a campaign might have the objective of increasing awareness from 10 to 20 per cent, or of raising beliefs that the product is the 'best value brand on the market' from 15 to 25 per cent of the target consumers. If advertising objectives are couched in sales or market share terms, campaign evaluation methods should monitor the sales or market share effects of the advertising. If trade objectives are important, distribution and stock levels of wholesalers and/or retailers, and perhaps their awareness and attitudes, could be measured. Each tool has different methods of evaluation. In the rest of this section we focus on advertising research methods by looking at pre- and post-testing.

Pre-testing before the campaign is part of the creative process. Adverts can be tested at various stages of development from testing the concept to finished adverts (before they are released). For example:

- *Concept testing* is part of the development of the advertising campaign and helps the creative team to identify the ideas that are most likely to be effective. This method works by showing the target audience a rough outline of the ideas, for example storyboards, photographs. The advantages are that a variety of ideas can be tested prior to further development. Limitations of this approach are that it takes place in an artificial setting and this must be considered when evaluating the results.

- *Focus groups*—a small number of target audience members are brought together to discuss ideas and relevant topics. There will be a moderator who is experienced in interviewing who uses the gathering to probe thoughts and emotions. The advantages are that this is a relatively low-cost approach that can reveal in-depth information about target audience preferences, but the results can lack objectivity and be potentially biased.

- *Readability tests* are used for testing finished print-based adverts. This method enables testing comprehension of the words used in the copy.

- *Post-testing* is carried out after the release of the advert and can be used to assess its effectiveness throughout and when the campaign is over. Checking how well an advertising campaign has performed provides information for future campaigns. A key advantage of post-testing is that it is carried out in the 'live' environment. Methods of post-testing include:

- *Inquiry tests* that measure the number of direct inquiries and responses resulting from the advertising, which may include completed coupons or requests for more information. This method has become more widely used with the rise in the use of direct marketing.

- *Recall tests* are designed to measure the impact of adverts on the target audience. Recall tests usually rely on responses from many members of the target audience who are interviewed within a short time after seeing the advert. This form of measurement is considered to be reasonably accurate (e.g. each time an advert is tested, the results are the same). However, the ability of recall tests to predict sales is generally considered to be low (bringing the validity of this method into question). Despite these issues recall testing is widely used especially to evaluate television advertising and can also be used for press advertisements.

- *Recognition tests* are based on memory and the ability of members of the target audience to reprocess information in an advert. This is one of the main methods used for measuring magazine readership. The reliability of the recognition test is high and much better than recall tests (Fill, 2009: 453–9).

- *Likeability* has been found to be a very powerful predictor of sales (Gordon, 1992). The problem with likeability is it is difficult to measure. For example, if one person says 'I like the advert a lot' how does this compare with a person who says 'I like the advert a little'? For each person the evaluation will have a different meaning and relevance, and will stimulate different levels of interest.

- *Financial analysis* requires the cost of the resources to be evaluated, which includes the media spend. This is usually carried out continuously and acts as an early warning system if costs are spiralling out of control. Financial control and accountability of the advertising spend have become increasingly important in recent years.

In Chapter 16 we discuss web analytics and other forms of technological testing which are responding to the changing ways that audiences receive communication methods.

Organizing for Campaign Development

There are various options when developing an advertising campaign and this will be largely dependent on the resources, skills and capabilities of the company wishing to develop the campaign. In principle, campaigns may be developed:

- *in cooperation* with people from the media. For example, advertising copy may be written by company staff but the artwork and layout of the advertisement may be done by the newspaper or magazine.
- *in-house* by the advertising department staffed with copy-writers, media buyers and production personnel.
- *in cooperation with an **advertising agency***. Larger agencies offer a full service, comprising creative, media planning and buying, planning and strategy development, market research and production.

In reality, given the growing complexity of communication campaigns and wider use of media platforms, companies wishing to advertise use a combination of approaches. Central to the success of any campaign is the relationship between clients and agencies. Key figures in the development of a campaign are account directors and executives, who liaise with client companies and coordinate the work of the other departments on behalf of their clients. Because agencies work for many clients, they have a wide range of experience and can provide an objective outsider's view of what is required, and how problems can be solved.

When an advertiser uses an agency, managing the relationship is of critical importance. Therefore, a company should aim to find the type of agency which best suits its needs. Types of agency include: *full service agencies*, which offer strategic planning, research, creative development, brand building, media buying and scheduling and a full range of expertise across all of the communication tools; *boutiques or creative shops*, which provide specialist services, for example copywriting and creative content development expertise; smaller agencies, often chosen for their ability to develop specialist creative ideas; digital agencies (and/or web service providers), which can offer an extensive range for web-based and mobile services such as content development, blogging, online PR, buzz marketing, social media, and search engine optimization (SEO). The Internet and mobile and digital marketing have extended the range of choice of agencies, and these issues are discussed in more detail in Chapter 16.

The formal part of an agency selection is the pitching process, where the client produces a creative brief and the agency prepares a pitch to demonstrate how it will meet that brief. However, the communication industry is a 'people' business and therefore it is critically important to get the relationships right, in order to develop trust and commitment that will see the campaign through to a successful conclusion.

Managing the Client–Agency Relationship

Strong relationships between clients (advertisers) and their agencies can provide the platform for effective advertising. A survey of clients and agencies focused on those issues that were causing problems in achieving this desired state (Rauyruen and Miller, 2007; Morgan and Hunt, 1994).

Many clients demanded that agencies become more involved in their business, with comments like 'they need to spend more time understanding our challenges and goals' and 'they need to take more notice of the client's view with regard to creative work'. Clearly, clients were looking for agencies to spend more time and attention on understanding their business objectives before beginning the creative process (Curtis, 2002a and b).

The importance of the early stages of the advertising development process was also emphasized by agencies. Some complained about having to deal with junior people at the briefing stage who had not been trained to write a clear brief. This was critical, because unless clients get the briefing stage right, things will inevitably go wrong further down the line. This problem was connected to the lack of accessibility of senior marketing staff because they have too much other work to do. This means that briefing is left in the hands of junior staff, who have the power to say 'no' but not 'yes'. This can be very frustrating for agencies. One agency complained about not enough 'ear time' with a senior member of his client's marketing team: 'he is too busy and there is too big an experience gap between him and his team'. Two further consequences of this were insufficient access to business objectives and strategy and an inability to provide constructive feedback on their proposals.

One issue that can spoil client–agency relationships is client conflict. This occurs when an advertising agency wins a new account from a rival to an existing client, or when an agency is taken over by an agency that holds the account of a rival. Both of these scenarios have happened to Procter & Gamble. Media planning agency Zenith Optimedia won the L'Oréal account, causing potential client conflict with its existing Procter & Gamble account. Procter & Gamble was also concerned when its advertising agency Grey Global was acquired by the WPP Group, which counts arch-rival Unilever among its client base. Such situations can end relationships or, as was the case with WPP, the client's fears may be assuaged if it is satisfied that separate agency networks will be working for the two clients (Singh, 2005).

Research into relationships with web and Internet agencies indicates that firms will be more successful if they build long-term, mutually supportive relationships with their customers. However, in order to work together, both parties rely on making agreements that are dependent on high levels of trust and commitment. Furthermore, the need for understanding how to build successful relationships in highly complex and challenging online trading environments is not only important but critical for the success of digital campaigns (Vize et al., 2011).

Three key factors are critical in managing client relationships. First, the agency should be client-centric. This means understanding the client's market and business, and how both are changing. There can be a tendency for such an understanding to dwindle over time. To combat this, agencies should invite clients to talk about their business. Second, agencies should not neglect personal contact. With digital communication the easy option, it can be tempting to communicate remotely. However, face-to-face contact is critical as it is difficult to build and maintain a business relationship purely through email. Finally, the strength of the relationship needs to be checked regularly. The presumption that everything is fine because nobody has complained is a dangerous path to follow. (Rhind-Tutt (2009).

Agency selection

As with buying any product, agency selection begins by defining requirements, which can vary considerably depending on whether the advertising is for a discount grocery store, a new car or a luxury designer fashion brand, for example. While grocery retailer Lidl might communicate clear messages about pricing, BMW and Gucci are brands that give great priority to the creative talents of prospective agencies.

Consequently, agency selection involves: defining advertising objectives and creative message requirements in order to brief potential agencies; creating a list of possible agencies; arranging for agencies to pitch their creative ideas; analyzing each agency's offer; selecting and contracting the preferred agency.

Once an agency has been selected and the contract agreed, it is important to brief the agency carefully, giving much relevant information about the company developing the campaign: for example, product history in terms of past sales, market share, previous campaigns; product features and benefits; target audiences—who they are, their motives and choice criteria. In addition, communication objectives and timetable for delivery and launch of the campaign should be clearly stated and agreed, and the budget set, as this might affect choice of media.

Agency remuneration (payment) systems

According to the IPA, the changing media environment, digital technologies and the multiple service requirements of clients has had an impact on the way agencies are paid. The rest of this section discusses the industry guidelines on agency remunerations in the UK (IPA, 2012).

Before deciding how to pay its chosen agency(ies) the client should follow these 10 steps.

1 negotiate the scope of the work (which the client determines)
2 agree on the tenure—in other words the period the agency is to be employed
3 establish the territory—regional, national, global
4 set out a work plan showing the scope of the costs, people hours and how the client and agency will work together
5 compare the work plan with the available budget from the client's marketing plan. If there is a shortfall, revise the work plan for the agency
6 agree on the level of remuneration (and desired profit margins)
7 client and agency to determine the goals, and the key performance indicators
8 determine how much the client will pay the agency
9 determine how performance is to be evaluated and the timing of the review
10 finalize the terms of the contract.

This may seem a rather long list but client–agency relationships often break down over some of these details. Therefore, if the terms and details are agreed in advance there is less opportunity for conflict.

Product Placement

Product placement is the deliberate placing of products and/or their logos in movies, television programmes, songs and video games, usually in return for money, and is sometimes referred to as 'embedded marketing'. This form of marketing is lucrative, and placement opportunities often command high prices from brand owners. For example, Heineken struck a 15-year multi-picture deal for product placement in the James Bond movies. It paid a reported $45 million for its products to appear in *Skyfall*, which included a 30-second commercial and an online game featuring Daniel Craig in the Bond role (Nathanson, 2013). According to research, placements can be particularly effective if the respective brand is also advertised during the television show or movie.

Product placement has been used in the USA for some time. However, in Europe there have been restrictions preventing product placement until now when the rules are being gradually relaxed. Since 2011, paid-for product placement has been allowed in UK television programmes. The new rules for product placement are more stringent than in the USA. Tobacco, alcohol, gambling, medicines, baby milk and any foods which are high in fat, salt or sugar are not permitted. Furthermore, the product is not allowed to distort the editorial content or affect its independence. On the plus side, UK broadcasters are now able to access the revenue generated by the product placement. In the future many interesting relationships/issues may develop between advertisers and programme makers (Williams, 2011).

Product placement has grown significantly in recent years, for the following reasons: media fragmentation means it is increasingly hard to reach mass markets; the brand can benefit from the positive associations it gains from being in a film or television show; many consumers do not realize that the brand has been product-placed; repetition of the movie or television show means that the brand is seen again and again; careful choice of movie or television show means that certain segments can be targeted; and promotional and merchandising opportunities can be generated on the show's website. For example, the clothes and accessories worn by actresses in popular television shows like *Sex and the City* and *Desperate Housewives* have been in great demand from viewers and some have quickly sold out. Show producers are increasingly looking at the merchandising opportunities that their shows can present, and manufacturers are happy to pay handsomely. Reportedly, the company that makes the the Nescafé Dolce Gusto Melody II coffeemaker, which retails for about $130 in the United States, paid £100,000 ($162,000) to feature on *This Morning*, the UK breakfast-time programme, for a three-month period (Twilley, 2011).

Technological developments in the online gaming sector allow for different products to be placed in games at different times of the day or in different geographic locations, expanding the marketing possibilities available to companies. For example, Blizzard Entertainment, a video game developer, is looking to recruit a specialist who can work with consumer brands so real products can be licensed and then appear in Blizzard's next generation of games (Dumitrescu, 2012).

While product placement is becoming very popular, it is important to remember that there are risks involved. If the movie or television show fails to take off, it can tarnish the image of the brand and reduce its potential exposure. Even when a movie is highly successful, there may still be issues which prevent brands from wanting to be involved. For example, Danny Boyle in his film *Slumdog Millionaire* was not allowed to use Mercedes-Benz products in a slum setting (Wikipedia, 2012) and all images of the brand had to be removed from the film.

Furthermore, audiences can become annoyed by blatant product placement, damaging the image, and brand owners may not have complete control over how their brand is portrayed. Also, the popularity of product placement is fast giving rise to claims that it constitutes deceptive advertising. Lobby groups in the USA claim that one of the difficulties with product placement is that it can't be controlled by the consumer in the way the traditional advertising breaks can, through zapping, and they want it restricted.

Product placement is subject to the same kinds of analysis as all the other promotional techniques described in this chapter. For example, in the James Bond movie *Die Another Day*, the Ford Motor Company had three of its car brands 'starring' in the film: an Aston Martin Vanquish, a Thunderbird and a Jaguar XKR. Movie-goers were interviewed both before and after seeing the film to see if their opinions of the brands had changed. In addition, the product placement was part of an integrated campaign including public relations and advertising, which ensured that even people who had not seen the film were aware of Ford's association with it. During the film's peak viewing periods in the USA and UK, Ford's research found that the number of times its name appeared in the media increased by 34 per cent and that Ford corporate messages appeared in 29 per cent of the Bond-related coverage (*Campaign*, 2002; Tomkins, 2003; Armstrong, 2005; Silverman, 2005; Dowdy, 2003).

Public Relations and Sponsorship

In a 365-day, 24/7 interconnected global society, every move a company makes can be shared. Intended and unintended messages about a product, a brand or a company can appear online. This means corporate reputation is constantly in the spotlight and this change in emphasis has meant a rise in importance of public relations (PR) (Roper and Fill, 2012).

A company is dependent on many groups if it is to be successful. The marketing concept focuses on customers and distributors, but the needs and interests of other groups are also important, such as employees, shareholders, the local community, the media, government and pressure groups. **Public relations** is concerned with all of these groups and may be defined as:

> . . . the management of communications and relationships to establish goodwill and mutual understanding between an organization and its public.

Public relations is therefore wider ranging than marketing, which focuses on markets, distribution channels and customers. By communicating to other groups, public relations creates an environment in which it is easier to conduct marketing (White, 1991). These publics are shown in Figure 14.4.

Public relations activities include media relations, lobbying, corporate advertising and sponsorship (Fill, 2009: 256–72). PR can accomplish many objectives, as outlined below (Lesly, 1998).

1 *Prestige and reputation*: it can foster prestige and reputation, which can help companies to sell products, attract and keep good employees, and promote favourable community and government relations.
2 *Promotion of products*: the desire to buy a product can be helped by the unobtrusive things that people read and see in the press, radio and television. Awareness and interest in products and companies can be generated.
3 *Dealing with issues and opportunities*: the ability to handle social and environmental issues to the mutual benefit of all parties involved.
4 *Goodwill of customers*: ensuring that customers are presented with useful information, are treated well and have their complaints dealt with fairly and speedily.
5 *Goodwill of employees*: promoting the sense of identification and satisfaction of employees with their company. Activities such as internal newsletters, recreation activities, and awards for service and achievement can be used.
6 *Overcoming misconceptions*: managing misconceptions about a company so that unfounded opinions do not damage its operations.
7 *Goodwill of suppliers and distributors*: building a reputation as a good customer (for suppliers) and a reliable supplier (for distributors).
8 *Goodwill of government*: influencing the opinions of public officials and politicians so that they feel the company operates in the public interest.
9 *Dealing with unfavourable press coverage*: responding quickly, accurately and effectively to negative publicity such as an oil spill or an air disaster.

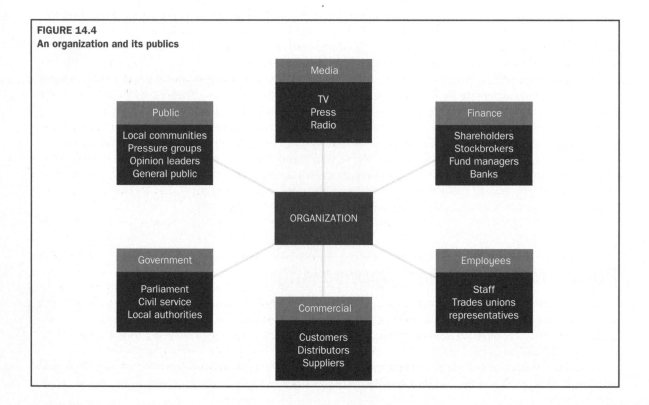

FIGURE 14.4
An organization and its publics

10 *Attracting and keeping good employees*: creating and maintaining respectability in the eyes of the public so that the best personnel are attracted to work for the company.

Public relations can take two basic models. In the first model communication messages flow one way—for example, a company's press agent produces favourable information in the form of press releases and media events. A variation of this approach is to disseminate information which presents a more balanced view (including positive and negative information). This is sometimes referred to as a *public information model* (Fill, 2009: 55).

The second model focuses on two-way communications so feedback from target audiences is of paramount importance. There are a further two derivations of this model:

• *Two-way asymmetric*. In this model power is not equally distributed between the stakeholders and the organization. The purpose of this form of PR is to influence attitudes and behaviour through persuasion (Fill, 2009: 256).

• *Two-way symmetric*. This model aims to be mutually rewarding as power is dispersed equally between the organization and its stakeholders. Communication flow is reciprocal. Some organizations use PR as a means of mediating relationships between the organization and its various stakeholders.

In the highly connected, multichannel media world it is difficult to isolate the various forms of PR and therefore there is a tendency for these models to coexist (Grunig, 1997). The remainder of this section on PR examines the different methods and techniques including: media relations, lobbying, corporate advertising, crisis communications, and sponsorship.

Media relations

A major element of public relations is media relations, which includes press releases, press conferences and interviews, and publicity. Media relations can be defined as communication about a product or organization by the placing of news about it in the media without paying for the time or space directly.

Three key tasks of a media relations department are (Lesly, 1998):

1 responding to requests from the media—although a passive service function, it requires well-organized information and prompt responses to media requests

2 supplying the media with information on events and occurrences relevant to the organization—this requires general internal communication channels and knowledge of the media

3 stimulating the media to carry the information and viewpoint of the organization—this requires creative development of ideas, developing close relationships with media people and understanding their needs and motivations.

The characteristics of media relations

Information dissemination may be through the web, news releases, news conferences, interviews, feature articles, photo calls and public speaking (at conferences and seminars, for example). No matter which method is used to carry the information, media relations has five important characteristics.

1 *The message has high credibility*: the message has higher credibility than advertising because it appears to the reader to have been written independently (by a media person) rather than by an advertiser.

2 *No direct media costs*: since space or time in the media is not bought, there is no direct media cost. However, this is not to say that it is cost-free. Someone has to write the news release, take part in the interview or organize the news conference. This may be organized internally, by a press officer or media relations department, or externally, by a public relations agency.

3 *Lose control of publication*: unlike advertising, there is no guarantee that the news item will be published. This decision is taken out of the control of the organization and into the hands of an editor. A key factor in this decision is whether the item is judged to be newsworthy. Table 14.2 lists a number of potentially newsworthy topics.

4 *Lose control of content*: there is no way of ensuring that the viewpoint expressed by the news supplier is reflected in the published article. For example, a news release might point to an increase in capital expenditure to deal with pollution, but this might be used negatively (e.g. saying the increase is inadequate).

5 *Lose control of timing*: an advertising campaign can be coordinated to achieve maximum impact. The timing of the publication of news items, however, cannot be controlled. For example, a news item publicizing a forthcoming conference to encourage attendance could appear in a publication after the event has taken place or, at least, too late to have any practical effect on attendance.

TABLE 14.2 Potentially newsworthy topics
Being or doing something first
Marketing issues
New products
Innovative research
Large orders/export contracts
Changes to the marketing mix, e.g. price
Rebranding
Production issues
Productivity achievements
Employment changes
Capital investments
Financial issues
Financial statements
Acquisitions
Sales/profit achievements
Personal issues
Training awards
Winners of company contests
Promotions/new appointments
Success stories
Visits by famous people
General issues
Conferences/seminars/exhibitions
Anniversaries of significant events

Writing news releases

Perhaps the most popular method of disseminating information to the media is through the news release. By following a few simple guidelines (as outlined below), the writer can produce news releases that please editors and therefore stand a greater chance of being used (Jefkins, 1985).

- *The headline*: make the headline factual and avoid the use of flamboyant, flowery language that might irritate editors. The headline should briefly introduce the story: 'HSBC to rebrand its high street banking offer'; 'Apple launch the iWatch'.
- *Opening paragraph*: this should be a brief summary of the whole release. If this is the only part of the news release that is published the writer will have succeeded in getting across the essential message.
- *Organizing the copy*: the less important ideas should be placed towards the end of the news release. The further down the paragraph, the more chance of its being cut by an editor.
- *Copy content*: like headlines, copy should be factual not fanciful. An example of bad copy would be 'We are proud to announce that Virgin Airlines, the world's most innovative airline, will fly exotic and exciting new routes in India'. Instead, this should read 'New routes to India will be flown by Virgin Airlines'. Whenever possible, statements should be backed up by facts.
- *Length*: news releases should be as short as possible. Most are written on one page, some are merely one paragraph. The viewpoint that long releases should be sent to editors so that they can cut out the parts they do not want is a fallacy. Editors' self-interest is that their job should be made as easy as possible; the less work they have to do amending copy the greater the chances of its publication.
- *Layout*: the release should contain short paragraphs with plenty of *white space* to make it appear easy to read. There should be good-sized margins on both sides, and the copy should be double-spaced so that amendments and printing instructions can be inserted by the editor. When a story runs to a second or third page, 'more' should be typed in the bottom right-hand corner and succeeding pages numbered with the headline repeated in the top left-hand corner.
- *Embargoes* must be clearly stated for date of release of sensitive information.

Media relations can be a powerful tool for creating awareness and strengthening the reputation of organizations. The trick is to motivate everyone in an organization to look for newsworthy stories and events, not simply to rely on the media relations department to initiate them. All forms of public relations should be part of an integrated communications strategy so that they reinforce the messages consumers receive from other communication methods.

To counter negative press and also build confidence among stakeholders, companies can engage in different forms of publicity events. Such events may focus on:

- *the product* and take the form of demonstrations, book signings and product launch events; for example, the *Harry Potter* and *Fifty Shades of Grey* series of books were used in conjunction with film launch dates to create a sense of anticipation and excitement.
- *corporate profile events*—open days, factory visits, donations, educational events.
- *community events*—activities, events and contributions that benefit local communities, such as funding development of facilities that benefit local people (play areas, gardens, computers for schools).
- *social media events*—Universal Studios used social media to create a buzz around the latest in the *Jurassic Park* movie series. A year before its launch date, *Jurassic World* had a Twitter account and shared pictures showing rides at the park and new dinosaurs (Powell, 2014). When the movie was launched in 2015, it grossed over $511 million in the first weekend, which was a record.

 Scan the QR code to see the Co-operative's new plan for becoming the most socially responsible business in the UK.

Sponsorship

Sponsorship has been defined by Sleight as (Sleight, 1989):

> '... a business relationship between a provider of funds, resources or services and an individual, event or organization which offers in return some rights and association that may be used for commercial advantage'.

Potential sponsors have a wide range of entities and activities from which to choose, including sports, arts, community activities, teams, tournaments, individual personalities or events, competitions, fairs and shows. Sports sponsorship is by far the most popular sponsorship medium as it can offer high visibility through extensive television press coverage, the ability to attract a broad cross-section of the community and to service specific niches, and the capacity to break down cultural barriers (Bennett, 1999).

Sponsorship can achieve a number of communicational objectives—but there are also risks, as follows (Barrand, 2005). Highly publicized arrests of senior officials and allegations of financial corruption at FIFA have caused its major partners and sponsors—for example, Visa, Coca-Cola, Kia and Adidas—to consider withdrawing (Wilson, 2015). Vodafone ended its sponsorship deal with McLaren Formula 1 racing to concentrate on partnerships that foster customer engagement (McCabe, 2013).

Companies should be clear about their reasons for spending money on sponsorship. The four principal objectives of sponsorship are to gain publicity, create entertainment opportunities, improve community relations and create promotional opportunities.

Gaining publicity

Sponsorship provides ample opportunities to create publicity in the news media. Worldwide events such as major golf, football and tennis tournaments supply the platform for global media coverage. Sponsorship of such events can provide brand exposure to millions of people. Some events, such as athletics championships, have mass audience appeal, while others such as golf have a more upmarket profile. Rolex supports more than 150 sporting events around the world exposing the brand name to its more upmarket customer segment. Budweiser's sponsorship of the FA cup has given it exposure to the young male demographic (Reynolds and Charles, 2011). Many companies sponsor large events like the Olympic Games; for example, Rio 2016 sponsors include Coca-Cola, Omega, Panasonic, Samsung, Bridgestone.

The publicity opportunities of sponsorship can produce major *awareness* shifts. For example, Sunglass Hut has taken over the sponsorship of London Fashion Week from Vodafone from 2016, with the aim of increasing awareness of the glasses brand. Together with the British Fashion Council, the aim is to promote the prominent role of the London fashion industry globally (Kilcooley-O'Halloran, 2015). Brands carefully select activities to sponsor that align with their values, such as WWF (environment), European Red Cross (social responsibility) and the Canon Foundation (education).

Sponsorship can also be used to position brands in the marketplace. Tag Heuer's sponsorship of the McLaren motor racing team was designed to position the watch brand as exciting, sporty and international (De Burton, 2004).

Creating entertainment opportunities

A major objective of much sponsorship is to create entertainment opportunities for customers and the trade. Sponsorship of music, the performing arts and sports events can be particularly effective. For example, Rolex supports classical concerts and the arts (e.g. the Vienna Philharmonic Orchestra's New Year's Concert; the Royal Opera House in London). Waitrose sponsored the England Cricket team. Often sports personalities are invited to join the sponsor's guests. Attendance at sponsored events can also be used to reward successful employees.

Figure 14.5 shows some broad values conferred on the sponsor from five sponsorship categories. They point out that these are composite views. Values may depend on a specific activity or event—for example, football versus tennis.

Improving community relations

Sponsorship of schools—for example, by providing low-cost personal computers—and supporting community programmes can foster a socially responsible, caring reputation for a company For examples, Lloyds bank's Social Entrepreneurs programme sponsors young adults in community and environmental projects.

Creating promotional opportunities

Sponsored events provide an ideal opportunity to promote company brands. Sweatshirts, bags, pens, etc., carrying the company logo and the name of the event can be sold to a captive audience. Where the brand can be consumed during the event (e.g. Nestlé at the Cannes Film Festival), this provides an opportunity for customers to sample the brand.

Sponsorship can also improve the effectiveness of other promotional vehicles. For example, responses to the direct marketing materials issued by the Visa credit card organization and featuring its sponsorship of the Olympic Games were 17 per cent higher than for a control group to whom the sponsorship images were not transmitted (Crowley, 1991).

Expenditure on sponsorship

Six factors account for the growth of sponsorship.
1 restrictive government policies on tobacco and alcohol advertising
2 escalating costs of media advertising
3 increased leisure activities and sporting events
4 the proven record of sponsorship
5 greater media coverage of sponsored events
6 the reduced efficiencies of traditional media advertising (e.g. clutter, and zapping between television programmes).

Although most money is spent on **event sponsorship**, such as a sports or arts event, of increasing importance is **broadcast sponsorship** where a television or radio programme is the focus. An example of event sponsorship is the sponsorship of music designed to target the youth market, as Figure 14.5 illustrates.

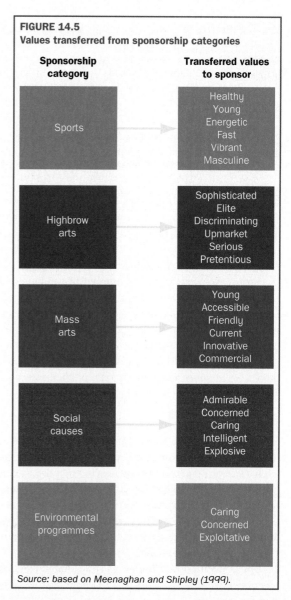

FIGURE 14.5
Values transferred from sponsorship categories

Source: based on Meenaghan and Shipley (1999).

MINI CASE 14.1
What do Sharp Electronics, Vodafone and Chevrolet have in common?

Manchester United Football Club (MUFC) has a long history of Premiership football and is reported to be amongst the top earning clubs in the world, with an income of £233 million. During the last decade it has become a brand that has global recognition. This means that MUFC is potentially an attractive sponsorship proposition for companies that are prepared to offer financial investment, e.g. in the club's ground at Old Trafford in Manchester or the team's football kit. Sharp Electronics was the first company to invest around half

a million pounds in the kit in 1982, a partnership which lasted 17 years. Vodafone replaced them in 1999, making an investment of £36 million. In 2012, Chevrolet put together a seven year deal worth in excess of £362 million. The size of the investment has increased significantly, but why are companies prepared to invest such significant sums in MUFC?

Firstly, MUFC eschews a number of values that could be transferred to sponsors, e.g. sporting achievements; winners; energetic; masculinity. These are values shared by current shirt sponsor Chevrolet – an American car brand – a company looking for opportunities to build its global presence. MUFC is an interesting sponsorship partner as it is not only a point of entry into the UK domestic market, as the club also has strong international connections. The global fan base for MUFC is over 700 million, over half of whom live in emerging markets in China and other parts of Asia, making it one of the world's most popular football clubs.

When the partnership with shirt sponsors Chevrolet was announced in 2012, there were over a billion page impressions downloaded from the car manufacturer's web site within two weeks. This news and subsequent online activity exceeded previous (similar scale) marketing campaigns by Chevrolet in the USA Super Bowl, making this a valuable communication and brand awareness campaign. The MUFC management team realize the importance of collaborative communications with their supporting partner to the club's global presence, and engages in many entertainment activities to ensure the club remains in the forefront of the minds of its fans, e.g. during the summer pre-season when there are no domestic league matches, the team goes on extensive tours to help develop the brand globally. There is a plan for MUFC to tour China in 2016, despite the many challenges surrounding the physical demands players will face due to the climate and availability of training facilities.

Other partners with MUFC have included: Aon (principal partner), DHL (logistics partner), Aeroflot (carrier), Bulova (timekeeping partner) and Adidas (official supplier of the team's football kit).

Questions:

1 Explain what should be considered when selecting an event to sponsor.
2 Identify and discuss the potential challenges for Chevrolet and other partners when sponsoring Manchester United.
3 Select a leading European football team, identify their main sponsors and then suggest the benefits of the partnership for both sponsor and team.

Source: Based on: manutd.com; Flanagan (2015); Gibson (2015); O'Leary (2015); Telegraph Sport (2012); Ogden (2015)

Broadcast sponsorship of programmes can extend into the sharing of production costs. This is attractive to broadcasters, who face increasing costs of programming, and sponsors, who gain a greater degree of influence in negotiations with broadcasters. Volvo signed up for a two-year deal as sponsor for a whole channel: Sky Atlantic. In this exclusive deal no other brand can sponsor content on the channel. Casillero del Diablo entered into a major sponsorship deal with Sky movies. There are key benefits for both companies: the wine producer will be able to reach an estimated 44 million individuals during the 12-month campaign and will in return promote Sky on over 4 million bottles of wine using promotional offers of free Sky subscriptions and competitions (The UK Sponsorship Database, 2015). Another growth area is that of **team sponsorship**, such as the sponsorship of a football, cricket or motor racing team. For example, Emirates, Europcar and Citroen are among the sponsors of Arsenal Football Club.

Selection and evaluation of an event or programme to sponsor

Selection of an event or programme to sponsor should be undertaken by answering a series of questions.

- *Communications objectives*: What are we trying to achieve? Are we looking for awareness or image, improvement in community relations or entertainment opportunities? Does the personality of the event match the desired brand image?
- *Target market*: Who are we trying to reach? Is it the trade or final customers? How does the profile of our customer base match the likely audience of the sponsored event or programme?
- *Risk*: What are the associated risks? What are the chances that the event or programme might attract adverse publicity (e.g. football hooliganism tainting the image of the sport and, by implication, the sponsor)? To what extent would termination of the sponsorship contract attract bad publicity (e.g. mean the closing of a theatre)?
- *Promotional opportunities*: What are the potential sales promotion and publicity opportunities?
- *Past record*: If the event or programme has been sponsored before, what were the results? Why did the previous sponsor withdraw?
- *Cost*: Does the sponsorship opportunity represent value for money?

The evaluation process should lead to a clear idea of why an event or programme is being sponsored. Understanding *sponsorship objectives* is the first step in evaluating sponsorship's success. For major sponsorship deals, evaluation is likely to be more formal and involve the measurement of *media coverage and name mentions/sightings* using a specialist monitoring agency. However, the reality is that evaluation of this tool is often neglected. A survey into the evaluation of football sponsorship found that while two-thirds of companies evaluated their sponsorship activities few went beyond the basic measurement of media coverage (Thwaites, 1995).

Sales Promotion

Sales promotions are incentives to consumers or the trade that are designed to stimulate purchase. Examples include money off and free gifts (consumer promotions), discounts and salesforce competitions (trade promotions).

A vast amount of money is spent on sales promotion. Peattie and Peattie explain the growth in sales promotion as follows (Peattie and Peattie, 1993).

- *Increased impulse purchasing*: the retail response to greater consumer impulse purchasing is to demand more sales promotions from manufacturers.
- *Sales promotions are becoming respectable*: through the use of promotions by market leaders and the increasing professionalism of the sales promotion agencies.
- *The rising cost of advertising and advertising clutter*: these factors erode advertising's cost effectiveness.
- *Shortening time horizons*: the attraction of the fast sales boost of a sales promotion is raised by greater rivalry and shortening product life-cycles.
- *Competitor activities*: in some markets, sales promotions are used so often that all competitors are forced to follow suit (Lal, 1990).
- *Measurability*: measuring the impact of sales promotions is easier than for advertising since their effect is more direct and, usually, short term. The use of electronic point-of-sale (EPOS) scanner information makes measurement easier.

The effects of sales promotion

Sales promotion is often used to provide a short, sharp shock to sales. In this sense it may be regarded as a short-term tactical device. Figure 14.6 shows a typical sales pattern. The sales promotion boosts sales during the promotion period because of the incentive effect. This is followed by a small fall in sales to below normal level because some consumers will have stocked up on the product during the promotion. The long-term sales effect of the promotion could be positive, neutral or negative. If the promotion has attracted new buyers, who find that they like the brand, repeat purchases from them may give rise to a positive long-term effect (Rothschild and Gaidis, 1981). Alternatively, if the promotion (e.g. money off) has devalued the brand in the eyes of consumers, the effect may be negative (Tuck and Harvey, 1972). Where the promotion has caused consumers to buy the brand only because of its incentive value, with no effect on underlying preferences, the long-term effect may be neutral (Brown, 1974). An international study of leading grocery brands has shown

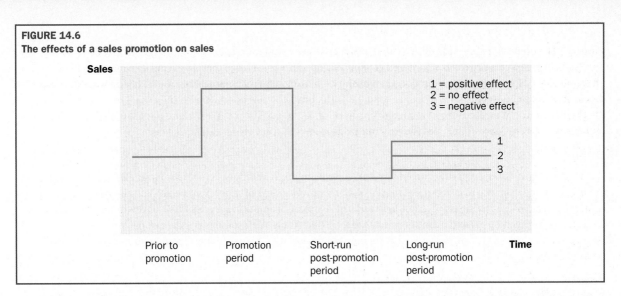

FIGURE 14.6
The effects of a sales promotion on sales

1 = positive effect
2 = no effect
3 = negative effect

that the most likely long-term effect of a price promotion for an existing brand is neutral. Such promotions tend to attract existing buyers of the brand rather than new buyers during the promotional period (Ehrenberg, Hammond and Goodhardt, 1994).

Major sales promotion types

Sales promotions can be directed at the consumer or the trade (see Figure 14.7). Major consumer sales promotion types are money off, bonus packs, premiums, free samples, coupons, prize promotions and loyalty cards. A sizeable proportion of sales promotions are directed at the trade, including price discounts, free goods, competitions, allowances, promotional price support, and in-store display and promotional support.

The following sections examine the main types of *consumer promotions*.

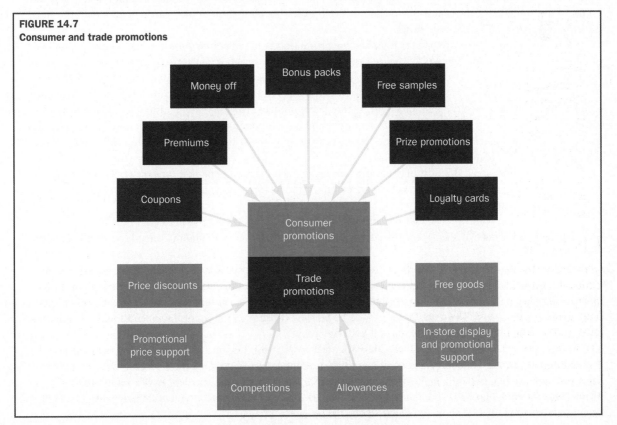

FIGURE 14.7
Consumer and trade promotions

Money off

Money-off promotions provide direct value to the customer, and therefore an unambiguous incentive to purchase. They have a proven track record of stimulating short-term sales increases and encouraging trial (Wilson, 2005). However, price reductions can easily be matched by the competition and if used frequently can devalue brand image. Consumer response may be 'If the brand is that good why do they need to keep reducing the price?' A variant on the normal money-off promotion is the *value pack*. With value packs, the consumer pays a higher price for the larger pack, but the per-unit price (e.g. per gram or per tablet) is less.

Bonus packs

These give *added value* by giving consumers extra quantity at no additional cost. **Bonus packs** are often used in the drinks, confectionery and detergent markets. For example, cans of lager may be sold on the basis of '12.5 per cent extra free!' Because the price is not lowered, this form of promotion runs less risk of devaluing brand image. Extra value is given by raising quantity rather than cutting price. With some product groups, this encourages buyers to consume more. For example, a Mars bar will be eaten or a can of lager drunk whether there is extra quantity or not.

Premiums

Premiums are any merchandise offered free or at low cost as an incentive to purchase a brand. There are four major forms: free in- or on-pack gifts; free-in-the-mail offers; self-liquidating offers; buy-one-get-one-free offers.

Free in- or on-pack gifts: gifts may be given away free with brands. For example, Innocent offered free seeds, linked to a series of competitions.

FMCG manufacturer brands from Lucozade and PG Tips to Garnier deodorants use premiums to promote sales. This technique is widely used in the cosmetics industry as an incentive to purchase more high-priced items. Clinique, Estee Lauder and L'Occitane frequently have offers which provide free gifts when the customer spends over a certain amount of money.

Occasionally, the gift is a free sample of one brand that is banded to another brand (*branded pack offer*). The free sample may be a new variety or flavour that benefits by getting trial. In other cases the brands are linked, as when Nestlé promoted its Cappuccino brand by offering a free KitKat to be eaten while drinking the coffee, and Cadbury ran a similar promotion with a packet of Cadbury's Chocolate Chip Cookies attached to its Cadbury's Chocolate Break, a milk chocolate drink.

When two or more items are banded together the promotion is called a *multibuy* and can involve a number of items of the same brand being offered together. Multibuys are a very popular form of promotion. They are frequently used to protect market share by encouraging consumers to stock up on a particular brand when two or more items of the same brand are packaged together. However, unlike price reductions, they do not encourage trial because consumers do not bulk buy a brand they have not tried before. When multibuys take the form of two different brands, range trial can be generated. For example, a manufacturer of a branded coffee launching a new brand of tea could band the two brands together, thus leveraging the strength of the coffee brand to gain trial of the new tea brand (Killigran and Cook, 1999).

Free-in-the-mail offers: this sort of promotion involves the collection of packet tops or labels, which are sent in the mail as proof of purchase to claim a free gift or money-off voucher: Kellogg's Fruit 'n Fibre has been promoted by such an offer.

Gifts can be quite valuable because redemption rates can be low (less than 10 per cent redemption is not unusual). This is because of *slippage*: consumers collect labels with a view to mailing them but never collect the requisite number.

Self-liquidating offers: these are similar to free-in-the-mail offers except that consumers are asked to pay a sum of money to cover the costs of the merchandise plus administration and postage charges. The consumer benefits by getting the goods at below normal cost because the manufacturer passes on the advantage of bulk buying and prices at cost. The manufacturer benefits by the self-funding nature of the promotion, although there is a danger of being left with surplus stocks of the merchandise.

Buy-one-get-one-free offers: sometimes known as a BOGOF, with this type of promotion the consumer is in effect getting two items for the price of one. Wine is sometimes offered as a BOGOF promotion so that the consumer can buy two bottles of a particular brand for the price of one. The danger of running BOGOF promotions for heavily advertised brands is that they lose their premium positioning and are seen as just another brand available in bulk at discount prices (Ritson, 2005).

Free samples

Free samples of a brand may be delivered to the home or given out in a store. The idea is that having tried the sample a proportion of consumers will begin to buy it. For new brands or brand extensions (e.g. a new shampoo or fabric conditioner) this form of promotion is an effective if expensive way of gaining consumer trial. However, sampling may be ineffective if the brand has nothing extra to offer the consumer but there may be other incentives a brand may add for free. For existing brands that have a low trial but high purchasing rate, sampling may be effective. As it would appear that many of those who try the brand like it and buy it again, raising the trial rate through free samples could have a beneficial long-term effect.

Coupons

There are three ways of couponing. Coupons can be delivered to the home, appear in magazines or newspapers, or appear on packs. *Home couponing*, after home sampling, is the best way to achieve trial for new brands (Davidson, 2003). *Magazine or newspaper couponing* is much cheaper than home delivery and can be used to stimulate trial, but redemption rates are much lower at around 5 per cent on average. The purpose of *on-pack couponing* is to encourage initial and repeat purchasing of the same brand, or trial of a different brand. A brand carries an on-pack coupon redeemable against the consumer's next purchase, usually for the same brand. Redemption rate is high; averaging around 40 per cent (Cummins and Mullin, 2008). The coupon can offer a higher face value than the equivalent cost of a money-off pack since the effect of the coupon is on both initial and repeat sales. However, it is usually less effective in raising initial sales than money off because there is no immediate saving and its appeal is almost exclusively to existing consumers (Davidson, 2003).

Prize promotions

There are three main types of *prize promotion*: competitions, draws and games. Unlike other promotions, the cost can be established in advance and does not depend on the number of participants. *Competitions* require participants to exercise a certain degree of skill and judgement. For example, a competition to win free cinema seats might require entrants to name five films based upon stills from each. Entry is usually dependent on at least one purchase. Compared to premiums and money off, competitions offer a less immediate incentive to buy, and one that requires time and effort on the part of entrants. However, they can attract attention and interest in a brand. *Draws* make no demands on skill or judgement: the result depends on chance. For example, a supermarket may run an out-of-the-hat draw, where customers fill in their name and address on an entry card and on a certain day a draw is made. Another example of a draw is when direct mail recipients are asked to return a card on which there is a set of numbers. These are then compared against a set of winning numbers.

An example of a *game promotion* is where a newspaper encloses a series of bingo cards and customers are told that, over a period of time, sets of bingo numbers will be published. If these numbers form a line or full house on a bingo card a prize is won. Such a game encourages repeat purchase of the newspaper.

The national laws governing sales promotions in Europe vary tremendously and local legal advice should be taken before implementing a sales promotion. The UK, Ireland, Spain, Portugal, Greece, Russia and the Czech Republic have fairly relaxed laws about what can be done. Germany, Luxembourg, Austria, Norway, Switzerland and Sweden are much more restrictive. For example, in Sweden free mail-ins, free draws and money-off-next-purchase promotions, and in Norway self-liquidating offers, free draws, money-off vouchers and money-off-next-purchase, are not allowed (PromoWatch, 2012).

We will now go on to look at *trade promotions*.

Price discounts

The trade may be offered (or may demand) *discounts* in return for purchase. The concentration of buying into fewer trade outlets has placed increasing power with these organizations. This power is often translated into discounts from manufacturers. The discount may be part of a joint promotion, whereby the retailer agrees to devote extra shelf space, buy larger quantities, engage in a joint competition and/or allow in-store demonstrations. Volume discounts are given to retailers that hit sales targets (Quilter, 2005).

Free goods

An alternative to a price discount is to offer more merchandise at the same price. For example, the *baker's dozen* technique involves offering 13 items (or cases) for the price of 12.

Competitions

This involves a manufacturer offering financial inducements or prizes to distributors' salesforces in return for achieving sales targets for their products. Alternatively, a prize may be given to the salesforce with the best sales figures.

Allowances

A manufacturer may offer an *allowance* (a sum of money) in return for retailers providing promotional facilities in-store (*display allowance*). For example, an allowance would be needed to persuade a supermarket to display cards on its shelves indicating that a brand was being sold at a special low price. An *advertising allowance* would be paid by a manufacturer to a retailer for featuring its brands in the retailer's advertising. *Listing allowances* are paid by the manufacturer to have a brand stocked.

Promotional price support

Promotional price support occurs when the manufacturer/supplier of particular goods or services works with the retailer to give money-off deals. For example, HSBC Bank had an introductory offer for its customers offering a £50 wine voucher to spend with Laithwaites Wine. This technique is often used by manufacturers and retailers.

In-store display and promotional support

Another form of trade promotion is when the manufacturer pays for in-store display and promotion. For example, a supplier could pay for a gondola-end display or a 10-second advertisement on the retailer's in-store television network (Quilter, 2005).

Sales promotion objectives

The most basic objective of any sales promotion is to provide extra value that encourages purchase. When targeted at consumers the intention is to stimulate **consumer pull**; when the trade is targeted **distribution push** is the objective. We will now look at specific sales promotion objectives.

Fast sales boost

Sales promotions deliver short-term sales increases, which may be required for a number of reasons: needing to reduce inventories or meet budgets prior to the end of the financial year, moving old stocks, or increasing stockholding by distributors in advance of the launch of a competitor's product (Cummins and Mullin, 2008). Promotions that give large immediate benefits, such as money off or bonus packs, have bigger effects on sales volume than more distant promotions such as competitions or self-liquidators. However, whatever the objective for the sales promotion, it should not be used as a means of patching up more fundamental inadequacies such as inferior product performance or poor positioning.

A classic sales promotion that went seriously wrong was Hoover's attempt to boost sales of its washing machines, vacuum cleaners, refrigerators and tumble driers by offering two free US flight tickets for every Hoover product purchased over £100. The company was the target of much bad publicity as buyers discovered that the offer was wreathed in difficult conditions (found in the promotion's small print) and complained bitterly to Hoover and the media. In an attempt to limit the danger done to its reputation, the company announced that it would honour its offer to its customers, at an estimated cost of £20 million.

Encourage trial

Sales promotions can be highly successful by encouraging trial. If new buyers like the brand, the long-term effect of the promotion may be positive. Home sampling and home couponing are particularly effective methods of inducing trial. Promotions that simply give more product (e.g. bonus packs) are likely to be less successful since consumers will not place much value on the extra quantity until they have decided they like it.

Encourage repeat purchase

Certain promotions, by their nature, encourage repeat purchase of a brand over a period of time. Any offer that requires the collection of packet tops or labels (e.g. free mail-ins and promotions such as bingo games) is attempting to raise repeat purchase during the promotional period. Loyalty cards are designed to offer consumers an incentive to repeat purchase at a store.

Stimulate purchase of larger or more expensive packs

Promotions that are specifically linked to larger pack sizes may persuade consumers to switch from the less economical smaller packs. However, there has been a trend within the FMCG market for more concentrated products, which come in smaller packages, are more expensive but last longer and give better value for money (e.g. Ecover, 40 washes; Fairy liquid concentrated lasts 50 per cent longer). Even own-label value brands offer concentrated versions of their products (Tesco Value Bio Concentrated Liquid Wash).

Gain distribution and shelf space

Trade promotions are designed to gain distribution and shelf space. These are major promotional objectives since there is a strong relationship between sales and these two factors. Discounts, free gifts and joint promotions are methods used to encourage distributors to stock brands. Also, consumer promotions that provide sizeable extra value may also persuade distributors to stock or give extra shelf space.

Traditionally, sales promotions have been associated with achieving objectives for supermarket brands. However, their presence has spread to other sectors such as financial services, cars, IT and telecoms. There is a trend towards integrated media campaigns. For example, the Royal Mail postal service in the UK launched a major direct mail campaign called Mail Men in a bid to tempt advertisers away from digital channels (Ghosh, 2015).

Evaluating sales promotion

There are two types of research that can be used to evaluate sales promotions: *pre-testing research* is used to select, from a number of alternative promotional concepts, the most effective in achieving objectives; *post-testing research* is carried out to assess whether or not promotional objectives have been achieved.

Ethical Issues in Advertising

As suggested by the quote at the start of the chapter advertising has an influence on society and subsequent behaviours. There are many controversial issues:

Advertising to children

Critics argue children are especially susceptible to persuasion and therefore need special protection from advertising. Others claim children are remarkably streetwise and can look after themselves. However, many European countries have regulations which control advertising to children. For example, in Germany advertising specific types of toys is banned and in the UK alcohol advertising is controlled (Schlegelmilch, 1998). In Sweden, advertising to under-12s on terrestrial television stations is banned, and in Belgium and Australia advertising within children's programmes is limited.

The UK has a code of practice to control advertisements aimed at children, which is designed to make sure advertisers avoid the misleading presentation of product information. For example, when advertising toys, accurate information about their size, price and operation should be included (Oates, Blades and Gunter, 2003). Pepsi and McDonald's have also introduced voluntary restrictions on their advertising to children in response to rising levels of obesity in the USA and western Europe (Ward and Grant, 2005).

Misleading advertising

This takes the form of exaggerated claims and concealed facts. For example, it would be unethical to claim that a car achieved 50 miles to the gallon when in reality it was only 30 miles. Nevertheless, most countries accept a certain amount of *puffery*, recognizing that consumers are intelligent and interpret the claims in such a way that they are not deceptive. In the UK the advertising slogan 'Carlsberg: probably the best lager in the world' is acceptable because of this. However, in Europe advertisers should be aware that a European directive on misleading advertising states that the burden of proof lies with the advertiser should the claims be challenged. Many industrialized countries have their own codes of practice that protect the consumer from deceptive advertising. For example, in the UK the Advertising Standards Authority (ASA) administers the British Code of

Advertising Practice. It insists that advertising should be 'legal, decent, honest and truthful' (discussed earlier in the chapter).

This means that advertisers need to be very careful about the claims they make. For example, supermarket retailer Waitrose claimed in a television and cinema advert that 'Everyone who works for Waitrose owns Waitrose.' However, cleaning services are outsourced, so this precluded certain workers. The supermarket and the ASA agreed that the case could be closed if Waitrose amended the advert. VIP Electronic cigarettes was accused of glamourizing e-cigarettes in its television adverts. This complaint was upheld, and as a result the adverts were banned (ASA, 2015).

Advertising's influence on society's values

Critics argue that advertising images have a profound effect on society. They claim that advertising promotes materialism and takes advantage of human frailties. Advertising is accused of stressing the importance of material possessions, such as the ownership of an expensive car or the latest in consumer electronics. Critics argue that this promotes the wrong values in society.

The ASA takes very seriously any campaigns that might bring advertising into disrepute. For example Paddy Power, an Irish bookmaker, launched a series of adverts offering incentives to bet on the outcome of the Oscar Pistorius murder trial. The ASA received 5,525 complaints, which were upheld as it ruled that '*The ad caused serious offence by trivializing the issues surrounding a murder trial, the death of a woman and disability.*' It also concluded that these adverts brought advertising into disrepute.

When you have read this chapter

Discover further resources and test your understanding: McGraw-Hill **Connect**™ is a digital teaching and learning environment that improves performance over a variety of critical outcomes; it can be tailored, is easy to use and is proven effective. **LearnSmart**™ is the most widely used and intelligent adaptive learning resource that is proven to strengthen memory recall, improve course retention and boost grades. Fuelled by **LearnSmart**™, **SmartBook**™ is the first and only adaptive reading experience available today.

Review

1 **The role of advertising in the promotional mix**
   - Advertising is any paid form of non-personal communication of ideas or products in the prime media: i.e. digital, television, the press, posters, cinema and radio.
   - It possesses strengths and limitations, and should be combined with other promotional tools to form an integrated marketing communications campaign.

2 **The differences between strong and weak theories of how advertising works**
   - The strong theory of advertising considers advertising to be a powerful influence on consumers, increasing knowledge, changing attitudes, and creating desire and conviction, and as a consequence persuading people to buy brands.
   - The weak theory of advertising considers advertising to be a much less powerful influence on consumers. It suggests that advertising may arouse awareness and interest, nudge some consumers towards trial, and then provide some reassurance and reinforcement after the trial.

3   How to develop advertising strategy: target audience analysis, objective setting, budgeting, message and media decisions, execution, and advertising evaluation

- Advertising decisions should not be taken in isolation but should be based on a clear understanding of marketing strategy, in particular positioning. Then the steps are as follows.
- Identify and understand the target audience: the audience needs to be defined and understood in terms of its motives and choice criteria.
- Define advertising objectives: communicational objectives are to create awareness, stimulate trial, position products in consumer's minds, correct misconceptions, remind and reinforce, and provide support for the salesforce.
- Set the advertising budget: options are the percentage of sales, affordability, matching competition, and objective and task methods.
- Message decisions: messages should be important to the target audience and communicate competitive advantages.
- Media decisions
- Execution: care should be taken to meet publication deadlines.
- Evaluation of advertising: three key questions are what, when and how to evaluate.

4   How campaigns are organized, including advertising agency selection and payment systems

- An advertiser has four organizational options:
  1 advertising can be developed directly in cooperation with the media
  2 an in-house advertising department can be created
  3 a full-service advertising agency can be used
  4 a combination of in-house staff (or the full service agency) can be used for some functions and a specialist agency (media or creative) for others.
- Agency selection should begin with a clear definition of requirements. A shortlist of agencies should be drawn up and each briefed on the product and campaign. Selection will take place after each has made a presentation to the client.
- Agency payment can be by commission, fee or payment by results.

5   The reasons for the growth in product placement and its risks

- Product placement activity is growing because of its mass-market reach, ability to confer positive associations to brands, high credibility, message repetition, its ability to avoid advertising bans, its targeting capabilities, the opportunities it provides for new linked brands and promotions, and the ability to measure its impact on audiences.
- Its risks are that the movie or television programme may fail, tarnishing brand image; there is the possibility that the placement may not get noticed or may cause annoyance; and there is also the reduction in control, compared to advertisements, concerning how the brand will be portrayed in the movie or television programme.

6   The objectives and targets of public relations

- The objectives of public relations are to foster prestige and reputation, promote products, deal with issues and opportunities, enhance the goodwill of customers and employees, correct misconceptions, improve the goodwill of suppliers, distributors and government, deal with unfavourable publicity, and attract and keep good employees.
- The targets of public relations are the general public, the media, the financial community, government, commerce (including customers) and employees.

7   The key tasks and characteristics of media relations

- Three key tasks are: responding to requests from the media; supplying the media with information on events relevant to the organization; stimulating the media to carry the information and the viewpoint of the organization.
- The characteristics of publicity are that the message has higher credibility than advertising, there are no direct media costs and no control over what is published (content), whether the item will be published or when it will be published.

8 The guidelines to use when writing a news release

- The guidelines are: make the headline factual and briefly introduce the story; the opening paragraph should be a summary of the whole release; the copy should be organized by placing the less important messages towards the end; copy should be factual and backed up by evidence; the release should be short; the layout should contain short paragraphs with plenty of white space.

9 The objectives and methods of sponsorship

- The objectives of sponsorship are to gain publicity, create entertainment opportunities, foster favourable brand and company associations, improve community relations and create promotional opportunities.
- The two key methods of sponsorship are event sponsorship (such as a sports or arts event) and broadcast sponsorship (where a television or radio programme is sponsored).

10 How to select and evaluate a potential sponsored event or programme

- Selection should be based on asking what we are trying to achieve (communication objectives), who we are trying to reach (target market), what are the associated risks (e.g. adverse publicity), what are the potential promotional opportunities, what is the past record of sponsorship of the event or programme, and what are the costs.
- Evaluation should be based on measuring results in terms of sponsorship objectives (e.g. changes in awareness and attitudes). Formal evaluation involves measurement of media coverage and name mentions/sightings using a specialist monitoring agency.

11 The growth in sales promotion

- The reasons for growth are increased impulse purchasing, the growing respectability of sales promotions, the rising costs of advertising and advertising clutter, shortening time horizons for goal achievement, competitor activities and the fact that their sales impact is easier to measure than that of advertising.

12 The major sales promotion types

- Major consumer promotions are money off, bonus packs, premiums (free in- or on-pack gifts, free-in-the-mail offers, self-liquidating offers and buy-one-get-one-free offers), free samples, coupons, prize promotions (competitions, draws and games), and loyalty cards; major trade promotions are price discounts, free goods, competitions, allowances, promotional price support, and in-store display and promotional support.

13 The objectives of sales promotion

- The objectives of sales promotion are to provide a fast sales boost, encourage trial, encourage repeat purchase, stimulate purchase of larger packs, and gain distribution and shelf space.

14 Ethical issues in mass marketing communication

- There are potential problems relating to misleading advertising, advertising's influence on society's values and advertising to children.
- There are potential problems relating to the use of trade inducements and the promotion of anti-social behaviour.

Key Terms

advertising any paid form of non-personal communication of ideas or products in the prime media, i.e. television, the press, posters, cinema and radio, the Internet and direct marketing

advertising agency an organization that specializes in providing services such as media selection, creative work, production and campaign planning to clients

advertising message the use of words, symbols and illustrations to communicate to a target audience using prime media

bonus pack giving a customer extra quantity at no additional cost

broadcast sponsorship a form of sponsorship where a television or radio programme is the focus

consumer pull the targeting of consumers with communications (e.g. promotions) designed to create demand that will pull the product into the distribution chain

distribution push the targeting of channel intermediaries with communications (e.g. promotions) to push the product into the distribution chain

event sponsorship sponsorship of a sporting or other event

media vehicle the choice of the particular newspaper, magazine, television spot, poster site, etc.

money-off promotions sales promotions that discount the normal price

premiums any merchandise offered free or at low cost as an incentive to purchase

product placement the deliberate placing of products and/or their logos in movies and television, usually in return for money

public relations (PR) the management of communications and relationships to establish goodwill and mutual understanding between an organization and its public

sales promotion incentives to customers or the trade that are designed to stimulate purchase

sponsorship a business relationship between a provider of funds, resources or services and an individual, event or organization that offers in return some rights and association that may be used for commercial advantage

strong theory of advertising the notion that advertising can change people's attitudes sufficiently to persuade people who have not previously bought a brand to buy it; desire and conviction precede purchase

target audience the group of people at which an advertisement or message is aimed

team sponsorship sponsorship of a team—for example, a football, cricket or motor racing team

weak theory of advertising the notion that advertising can first arouse awareness and interest, nudge some consumers towards a doubting first trial purchase and then provide some reassurance and reinforcement; desire and conviction do not precede purchase

Study Questions

1. Compare the situations where advertising and PR are more likely to feature strongly in the promotional mix.

2. Describe the strong and weak theories of how advertising works. Consider the extent to which each theory is more likely to apply to the purchase of a car, and the purchase of a bottle of water.

3. Media class decisions should always be based on creative considerations, while media vehicle decisions should be determined solely by cost per thousand calculations. Do you agree?

4. Describe the structure of a large advertising agency. Why should an advertiser prefer to use an agency rather than set up a full-service internal advertising department?

5. As a highly visible communication tool, advertising has its share of critics. What are their key concerns? How far do you agree or disagree with their arguments?

6. When you next visit a supermarket, examine three sales promotions. What types of promotion are they? What are their likely objectives?

7. Why would it be wrong to measure the sales effect of a promotion only during the promotional period? What are the likely long-term effects of a promotion?

8. Explain the difference between public relations and media relations.

9. Discuss the extent to which PR provides free advertising.

10. Discuss the main reasons for an organization becoming involved in event sponsorship.

Recommended Reading

Arens. W., et al. (2014) *Advertising*, London: McGraw Hill Higher Education.

Ewing, M. T. (2013) The Good News About Television: Attitudes Aren't Getting Worse: Tracking Public Attitudes toward TV Advertising, *Journal Of Advertising Research* 53(1), 83–9.

Fransena, M. L., P. W. J. Verleghb, A. Kirmanic and E. G. Smita (2014) A typology of consumer strategies for resisting advertising, and a review of mechanisms for countering them, *International Journal of Advertising: The Review of Marketing Communications* 34(1), 6–16.

Gregory, A. (2015) *Planning and Managing Public Relations Campaigns*, London: Kogan Page.

Pieters, R., M. Wedel and R. Batra (2010) The stopping power of advertising: measures and effects of visual complexity, *Journal of Marketing* 74(5), 48–60.

Zook, Z. and P. R. Smith (2016) *Marketing Communications Offline and Online Integration, Engagement and Analytics*, London: Kogan Page.

References

Aaker, D. A., R. Batra and J. G. Myers (1996) *Advertising Management*, New York: Prentice-Hall.

Armstrong, S. (2005) How to Put Some Bling into Your Brand, *Irish Times, Weekend*, 30 July, 7.

ASA (2015) *2014 most complained about adverts*, ASA, 20 February. https://www.asa.org.uk/News-resources/Media-Centre/2015/2014-most-complained-about-ads.aspx#.VX3tEPlVhBc

Barnett, M. (2011) In advertising we've a broad level of trust, *Marketing Week*, 2 May, 28–30.

Barrand, D. (2005) When Disaster Strikes, *Marketing*, 9 March, 35–6.

Barter Books (2012) http://www.keepcalmhome.com/about.htm

Bennett, R. (1999) Sports Sponsorship, Spectator Recall and False Consensus, *European Journal of Marketing* 33(3/4), 291–313.

Brown, R. G. (1974) Sales Response to Promotions and Advertising, *Journal of Advertising Research* 14(4), 33–9.

Burn-Callander, R. (2015) The most annoying adverts from the past 15 years, *The Telegraph*, 22 January. http://www.telegraph.co.uk/finance/newsbysector/retailandconsumer/11359924/The-most-annoying-adverts-from-the-past-15-years.html

Campaign (2002) The Top Ten Product Placements in Features, 17 December, 36.

Crosier, K. (1983) Towards a Praxiology of Advertising, *International Journal of Advertising* 2, 215–32.

Crowley, M. G. (1991) Prioritising the Sponsorship Audience, *European Journal of Marketing* 25(11), 11–21.

Cummins, J. and R. Mullin (2008) *Sales Promotion*, London: Kogan Page, 79.

Curtis, J. (2002a) Clients Speak Out on Agencies, *Marketing*, 28 March, 22–3.

Curtis, J. (2002b) Agencies Speak Out on Clients, *Marketing*, 4 April, 20–1.

Dahl, D. W., K. D. Frankenberger and R. V. Manchanda (2003) Does it pay to shock? *Journal of Advertising Research* 43, 3 September, 268–81.

Dall'Olmo Riley, F., A. S. C. Ehrenberg, S. B. Castleberry, T. P. Barwise and N. R. Barnard (1997) The Variability of Attitudinal Repeat-Rates, *International Journal of Research in Marketing* 14, 437–50.

Davidson, J. H. (2003) *Offensive Marketing*, Harmondsworth: Penguin, 249–71.

De Burton, S. (2004) Fancy a Touch of Star Status?, *Financial Times*, 13/14 November, 7–8.

Dowdy, C. (2003) Thunderbirds Are Go, *Financial Times*, Creative Business, 24 June, 10.

Dumitrescu, A. (2012) Blizzard's Project Titan Will Have Product Placement, 25 January, *Softpedia*, http://news.softpedia.com/news/Blizzard-s-Project-Titan-Will-Have-Product-Placement-248355.shtml.

Ehrenberg, A. S. C. (1992) Comments on How Advertising Works, *Marketing and Research Today*, August, 167–9.

Ehrenberg, A. S. C., K. Hammond and G. J. Goodhardt (1994) The After-Effects of Price-Related Consumer Promotions, *Journal of Advertising Research* 34(4), 1–10.

Elihu, K., G. Blumer and M. Gurevitch (1974) Uses and Gratifications Research, *The Public Opinion Quarterly 4th* 37(4), 509–23.

Elliott, R. (1997) Understanding Buyer Behaviour: Implications for Selling, in D. Jobber (ed.) *The CIM Handbook of Selling and Sales Strategy*, Oxford: Butterworth-Heinemann.

Fill, C. (2009) *Marketing Communications: Interactivity, communication and content*, Prentice Hall, 153.

Flanagan (2015), Ron Atkinson, Bryan Robson and the Sharp vertical record player: How Manchester United did kit launches in 1982, Manchester Evening News, 7th Jan http://www.manchestereveningnews.co.uk/sport/football/pictured-manchester-united-kit-launch-7388441

Gibson (2015), Manchester United fall behind Barcelona on Deloitte rich list, The Guardian, 2nd March 2015 http://www.theguardian.com/football/2010/mar/02/manchester-united-barcelona-deloitte-rich-list

Ghosh, S. (2015) Royal Mail launches 'Mail Men' campaign to boost direct mail, *Campaign*, 28 January. http://www.campaignlive.co.uk/news/1331384/royal-mail-launches-mail-men-campaign-boost-direct-mail/?HAYILC=RELATED (accessed 10 June 2015).

Gilbert, H. (2015) Arla makes new play for UK yogurt market with high protien quark products, *The Grocer*, 19 January. http://www.thegrocer.co.uk/buying-and-supplying/new-product-development/arla-makes-new-play-for-uk-yoghurt-market-with-high-protein-quark-product/512227.article

Glennie, A. (2015) UK's digital advertising spend set to outstrip all other forms, *The Guardian*, 18 February. http://www.theguardian.com/media/2015/feb/18/digital-advertising-spend-set-to-outstrip-all-other-forms (accessed 10 June 2015).

Gordon, W. (1992) Ad pre-testing—hidden maps, *Admap* (June) 23–7.

Grunig, J. E. (1997) A situational theory of publics: conceptual history, recent challenges and new research, in D. Moss, T. MacManus and D. Vercic (eds), *Public Relations Research: An International Perspective*, London: International Thomson Business, 3–48.

Hall, M. (1992) Using Advertising Frameworks: Different Research Models for Different Campaigns, *Admap*, March, 17–21.

Hegarty, J. (2011) *Hegarty on Advertising: Turning Intelligence into Magic*, London: Thames & Hudson, 23–4.

Henley, J. (2009) What crisis? *The Guardian*, 18 March, http://www.guardian.co.uk/lifeandstyle/2009/mar/18/keep-calmcarry-on-poster.

Howells, D. (2015) Love and Respect, key note, Academy of Marketing Science Annual Conference, Denver, Colorado .

IPA (2012) *Agency remuneration: A best practice guide on how to pay agencies*, IPA/ISBA/MCCA/PRCA Joint Industry Guidelines.

Jefkins, F. (1985) Timing and Handling of Material, in W. Howard (ed.) *The Practice of Public Relations*, Oxford: Heinemann, 86–104.

Jones, J. P. (1991) Over-Promise and Under-Delivery, *Marketing and Research Today*, November, 195–203.

Katz, E., M. Gurevitch and H. Haas (1973) On the Use of the Mass Media for Important Things, *American Sociological Review* 38, 164–81.

Keep Calm and Carry On (n.d.) http://www.keepcalmandcarryon.com/

Kilcooley-O'Halloran, S. (2015) LFW Announces New Sponsor, *Vogue*, 18 March. http://www.vogue.co.uk/news/2015/03/18/lfw-announces-new-sponsor-sunglass-hut assessed 21/6/2015.

Killigran, L. and R. Cook (1999) Multibuy Push May Backfire, *Marketing Week*, 16 September, 44–5.

Lal, R. (1990) Manufacturer Trade Deals and Retail Price Promotion, *Journal of Marketing Research* 27(6), 428–44.

Lesly, P. (1998) *The Handbook of Public Relations and Communications*, Maidenhead: McGraw-Hill, 13–19.

Levy, M. W. and S. Windahl (1985) The concept of audience activity, *Media Gratification Research*, 109–22.

Magee, K. (2015) Volvo shifts global creative account out of Grey London, *Campaign*, 11 June. http://www.campaignlive.co.uk/news/1351070/

McCabe, M. (2013) Vodafone ends McLaren F1 sponsorship in favour of owned marketing platform, *Marketing Magazine*, 14 March. http://www.marketingmagazine.co.uk/article/1174633/vodafone-ends-mclaren-f1-sponsorship-favour-owned-marketing-platform (accessed 10 June 2015).

Meenaghan, T. and D. Shipley (1999) Media Effect in Commercial Sponsorship, *European Journal of Marketing* 33(3/4), 432.

Morgan, M. R. and S. D. Hunt (1994) The Commitment-Trust Theory of Relationship Marketing, *Journal of Marketing* 58(July), 20–38.

Nathanson, J. (2013) *The Economics of Product Placements*, priceonomics, 4 December. http://priceonomics.com/the-economics-of-product-placements/

O'Donohoe, S. (1994) Advertising Uses and Gratifications, *European Journal of Marketing* 28(8/9), 52–75.

Oates, C., M. Blades and B. Gunter (2003) Marketing to Children, *Journal of Marketing Management* 19(4), 401–10.

Ogden, M (2015) Manchester United face pre-season tour to China in 2016, The Telegraph, 29th July http://www.telegraph.co.uk/sport/football/teams/manchester-united/11771517/Manchester-United-face-pre-season-tour-to-China-in-2016.html

Ogilvy, D. (1987) *Ogilvy on Advertising*, London: Pan.

O'Leary, N (2015), Chevy Paid $560 Millian to sponsor Manchester United, Adweek, 2nd Feb 2014 http://www.adweek.com/news/advertising-branding/chevy-paid-560-million-sponsor-manchester-united-and-now-its-pulling-out-europe-155399

Oster, E. (2015) W+K London Shares '1,000 Years of Less Ordinary Wisdom' for Finlandia, AdWeek, 12 June. http://www.adweek.com/agencyspy/wk-london-shares-1000-years-of-less-ordinary-wisdom-for-finlandia/88040

Pathak, S. (2015) Purina turns pet research into content with 'Puppyhood', Puppyhood, 10 June. http://digiday.com/brands/purina-turns-pet-research-content-puppyhood

Peattie, K. and S. Peattie (1993) Sales Promotion: Playing to Win?, *Journal of Marketing Management* 9, 255–69.

Pieters, R., M. Wedel and R. Batra (2010) The Stopping Power of Advertising: Measures and Effects of Visual Complexity, *Journal of Marketing* 74(5), 48–60.

Powell, S. (2014) Jurassic world's viral marketing campaign–modern techniques for a prehistoric promotion, Inbound Educators, 25 August. http://info.tmrdirect.com/inbound-marketing-agency-blog/jurassic-world%E2%80%99s-viral-marketing-campaign-%E2%80%93-modern-techniques-for-a-prehistoric-promotion

PromoWatch (2012) Shreddies Win 1 of 75 summer holidays with Eurocamp, 5 April. http://www.mosaicmarketing.co.uk/promowatch/2012/april/shreddies-win-1-of-75-summer-holidays-with-eurocamp.aspx

Quilter, J. (2005) Aisles of Plenty, *Marketing*, 10 August, 15.

Rauyruen, P. and K. E. Miller (2007) Relationship Quality as a Predictor of B2B Customer Loyalty, *Journal of Business Research* 60(1), 21–31.

Reinhard, K. (2006) *Response to 'Distinguished Communicator' Award*, California State University, Fullerton, http://communications.fullerton.edu/news/Faculty_news/May06_Reinhard.htm (accessed August 2006).

Reynolds, J. and G. Charles (2011) A game of four brands, *Marketing*, 29 June, 14–15.

Ries, A. and J. Trout (2001) *Positioning: The Battle for your Mind*, New York: McGraw-Hill.

Ritson, M. (2005) Cadbury's Decision to BOGOF is a Strategic Error, *Marketing*, 25 May, 24.

Roberts, K. (2015a) *Love/Respect Axis*, Saatchi & Saatchi, 10 June. http://www.saatchikevin.com/lovemarks/loverespect-axis

Roberts, K. (2015b) *Brand Loyalty Reloaded*, red paper, Saatchi & Saatchi. http://www.saatchikevin.com/wp-content/uploads/2014/09/Loyalty-Beyond-Reason-Red-Paper-Jan-2015.pdf

Roper, S. and C. Fill (2012) *Corporate Reputation: Brand and communication*, London: Pearson, 5.

Rothschild, M. L. and W. C. Gaidis (1981) Behavioural Learning Theory: Its Relevance to Marketing and Promotions, *Journal of Marketing* 45, Spring, 70–8.

Saatchi & Saatchi (2015) Lovemarks. http://www.saatchi.be/lovemarks (accessed 10 May 2015).

Saatchi & Saatchi Compton (1985) *Preparing the Advertising Brief*, 9.

Schlegelmilch, B. (1998) *Marketing Ethics: An International Perspective*, London: International Thomson Business Press.

Silverman, G. (2005) After the Break: The 'Wild West' Quest to Bring the Consumers to the Advertising, *Financial Times*, 18 May, 17.

Singh, S. (2005) P&G Reads the Riot Act Over Client Conflict, *Marketing Week*, 4 August, 9.

SkyMedia. (2015) Weetabix–SkyView TV Effectiveness, Skymedia, 10 June. http://www.skymedia.co.uk/Insight/Case-Studies/weetabix.aspx

Sleight, S. (1989) *Sponsorship: What It Is and How to Use It*, Maidenhead: McGraw-Hill, 4.

Spary, S. (2015) Tesco and Unilever partner on iBeacon Magnum ice cream app, *Marketing Magazine*, 12 June. http://www.marketingmagazine.co.uk/article/1351292/tesco-unilever-partner-ibeacon-magnum-ice-cream-app

Stubbs, D. (2014) The new Ralph Lauren Polo advert, *The Guardian*, 27 September. http://www.theguardian.com/tv-and-radio/2014/sep/27/ralph-lauren-polo-advert-hard-sell (accessed 10 June 2015).

Sweney, M. (2012) WPP breaks £1bn profit barrier, *Guardian*, 1 March.

Telegraph Sport (2012), Manchester United survey reveals they have doubled their global fan base to 659 million over five years, Telgraph, 29th May 2012 http://www.telegraph.co.uk/sport/football/teams/manchester-united/9298384/Manchester-United-survey-reveals-they-have-doubled-their-global-fan-base-to-659-million-over-five-years.html

The UK Sponsorship database (2015) Casillero del Diablo announces Sky Movies partnership, The UK Sponsorship database, March. http://www.uksponsorship.com/ukjan15-Casillero-del-Diablo-announces-Sky-Movies-partnership.htm#.VX3mxPIVhBc

Thwaites, D. (1995) Professional Football Sponsorship—Profitable or Profligate?, *International Journal of Advertising* 14, 149–64.

Tomkins, R. (2003) The Hidden Message: Life's a Pitch, and Then You Die, *Financial Times*, 24 October, 14.

Tuck, R. T. J. and W. G. B. Harvey (1972) Do Promotions Undermine the Brand?, *Admap*, January, 30–3.

Twilley, N. (2011) The Dawn of Product Placement: Morgan Spurlock on What the United Kingdom Can Expect Next, *Good Magazine: Lifestyle*, http://www.good.is/post/the-dawn-of-productplacement-morgan-spurlock-on-what-the-united-kingdom-canexpect-next/ 10 March.

Vize, R. J. Coughlan, A. Kennedy and F. Ellis-Chadwick (2011) 'B2B Relationship Quality: Conceptualisation of Relationship Quality in online B2B Retail services', *18th Recent Advances in Retailing and Services Science Conference*, The European Institute of Retailing and Services Science, San Diego USA, 12–18 July.

Ward, A. and J. Grant (2005) PepsiCo Admits Curbing Adverts to Children, *Financial Times*, 28 February, 23; J. Simms (2008) From Light Touch to Iron Fist, *Marketing*, 30 July, 30–3.

West, R. and L. Turner (2010) *Uses and Gratifications Theory, Introducing Communication Theory: Analysis and Application*, Boston USA: McGraw-Hill.

White, J. (1991) *How to Understand and Manage Public Relations*, London: Business Books.

Whitehead, J. (2002) Pot noodle banned for calling itself the 'slag of all snacks', *Brand Republic*, http://www.brandrepublic.com/news/155509/Pot-Noodle-banned-calling-itself-slag-snacks/.

Wikipedia (2012) Product placement, http://en.wikipedia.org/wiki/Product_placement.

Williams, A. (2011) TV product placement is here, *The Marketer*, April, 17.

Wilson, B. (2015) Fifa scandal 'a disaster' for sponsors, BBC News, 28 May. http://www.bbc.co.uk/news/business-32912445

Wilson, R. (2005) Brands Need Not Pay the Price, *Marketing Week*, 7 July, 39–41.

Wright, L. T. and M. Crimp (2003) *The Marketing Research Process*, London: Prentice-Hall, 180.

Steve Campbell was about to retire. As he went through his paperwork, he thought about all the previous experiences and challenges he had faced as the marketing communication director of Toyota Motors South Africa (TMSA). He had many memories. Some were good (such as healthy sales figures), while others were not so good. And then there was Buddy, his favourite character in Toyota advertising. He thought about the events of that time, and was drawn back into those events.

Steve had received the newspaper report from his American colleagues. 'Toyota recall: reports of runaway cars' was the headline provided by ABC News. Others were more dramatic: '"There's no brakes. . . hold on and pray": Last words of man before he and his family died in Toyota Lexus crash'. He imagined how his colleagues would be feeling, or even the families of those affected by the situation. He thought of how it would feel if this were *his* family that had been involved. As marketing communication director at Toyota, he knew he had to do something. Fortunately, no tragic events had been reported, but Steve was worried about how the news reports would affect Toyota owners and the general public. Toyota was such a reliable and trustworthy name in South Africa (as it was in many other parts of the world). As he travelled home, he made a decision. A marketing communication campaign was needed. But what type of campaign? What should the message be at a time like this? What did he want to achieve with the marketing campaign? What would be the best way to compile such a programme?

Background Information

Based in Japan, Toyota is an international manufacturer of passenger and commercial vehicles throughout the world. Manufacturing takes places via 54 manufacturing companies in 27 countries. Toyota vehicles are sold in 170 countries.

One country where Toyota has a manufacturing company is South Africa, where the motor vehicle industry is important to the local economy. Currently, the industry accounts for 6 per cent of the country's GDP, and the total industry (including associated industries) creates approximately 28,000 direct jobs and another 65,000 in the component industry. Yet another 200,000 are employed in retail and after-market vehicle-related

sectors. Toyota South Africa has a reputation in South Africa of producing and selling reliable, good quality motor vehicles. Toyota has consistently been the top selling motor vehicle manufacturer in South Africa, despite strong competition from Volkswagen South Africa.

In the midst of this positive situation for Toyota, technical problems were identified in November 2009 with the accelerator of various models. Initially the problem was identified in the United States, but by January 2010, the necessity for a recall of Toyota vehicles in South Africa was identified. This situation had the potential to affect the trust in the brand, as well as the perceptions of quality associated with the brand, if not managed well.

The Objectives of the Campaign

Steve knew that building trust in a brand is part of the task of any marketing manager, and once it has been built, it is important to keep the trust. This was important with existing customers, but also with people who may be customers in the future. This would have to be one of the goals of the campaign. Not only was it a question of maintaining trust, it was also to create an emotional connection with the viewer (both existing and potential Toyota owners). That gave him another idea.

Why a dog? Why Buddy?

Underpinning the campaign that was developed to rebuild the brand and prevent brand erosion was the use of a dog ('Buddy') in an integrated marketing communication campaign. The purpose of using the dog was to 'break through the advertising clutter' which was identified in the mass media. Further, Buddy (as all dogs) showed 'reliability, honesty, loyalty and warm-heartedness', and he was the symbol selected to appeal to people from various ages and races.

Selecting the type of dog was important, as each breed has characteristics with which it is associated. It is suggested that boxers are 'a combination of all dogs' while still being 'careful and cautious'. Buddy is a boxer in all ways, except in his lips, which are 'human', thus use is made of anthropomorphism. The breed of dog selected was required to have a flat snout so that the creative team could incorporate human lips. The campaign used both print and broadcast media, and advertised all Toyota brands (Corolla, Hi-Lux, as well as the used-vehicle division). The campaign commenced on 23 September 2009, and consisted of different versions that reflected different components of the Toyota business and brands (such as the used vehicles).

Components of the Campaign

Use of social media   When the problems with the motor cars were identified, Toyota published an open letter to the public which indicated the impact of the recall on customers and in so doing, attempted to address customer concerns and apologize for the situation. This was placed in the mass media as well as on the website. The Toyota website was also used so that customers could determine whether they were affected by the recall, and the actions necessary in this situation. Toyota owners could also access the official website and supply their vehicle's details. This would enable the owner to check whether the specific vehicle was affected by the recall, and Toyota could advise the owner on what the appropriate steps were to be. Blogs managed by Toyota SA were also used to discuss the situation and advise customers. An address from the managing director of Toyota South Africa was also placed on YouTube.

Use of mass media   Use was made of a print and television campaign in the national media. Magazines selected included those that focused on the motor enthusiast, as well as other popular magazines. The advertising was positively perceived, and in the case of the television campaign, Buddy and the Corolla were number 2 on the most liked advertising list for 2010, while Buddy and the Hilux were at number 10.

What Effect did Buddy have on the Toyota Brand?

Research was conducted among both Toyota and non-Toyota owners. They were shown the storyboard for the advertisement and asked a number of questions. These included:

- How did the advertisement make you feel about Toyota?
  Among Toyota owners, 85 per cent found Toyota much more appealing (in contrast with 51 per cent of owners of other vehicles). By contrast, 31 per cent of owners of other vehicles felt that the

advertisement made Toyota a little more appealing, while a further 18 per cent indicated that it didn't change their feelings about Toyota. Toyota owners were exceedingly positive towards Toyota after having seen the storyboard. Non-Toyota owners were also positive towards the brand, but not as positive as Toyota owners. The advertisement was positively perceived by all those who viewed the advertisement, affecting the perception of the brand.

- Has the advertisement improved your perceptions of the brand?
  Among Toyota owners, 93 per cent agreed strongly that the advertisement had improved their perceptions of the brand, compared with 62 per cent of owners of other vehicles. In the case of 'agree slightly', 25 per cent of owners of other cars responded in this way compared with 5 per cent of Toyota owners. This increase shows the effect of the advertisement on changes in brand perception. The effect was more pronounced among Toyota owners.

- Thinking about this advertisement, if you were to change/replace your current vehicle, how would this advertisement affect your consideration of Toyota?
  Among Toyota owners, 89 per cent indicated it would make them much more likely to consider Toyota, while 42 per cent of owners of other vehicles were much more likely to consider Toyota. A further 36 per cent of owners of other vehicles indicated that the advertisement would make them a little more likely to consider Toyota. This indicates the ability of the advertisement to change not only perceptions, but also the actions of customers.

- Thinking about the recalling of Toyota vehicles, if you were to change/replace your current vehicle, how would this recall issue affect your consideration of Toyota?
  This question was relevant as the campaign was associated with the attempt to limit any potential damage associated with the recall of Toyota motor vehicles. Among Toyota owners, 49 per cent indicated that it would make them much more likely to consider Toyota, while in the case of owners of other vehicles, 21 per cent indicated it would make them much more likely to consider Toyota. Among both groups, 12 per cent indicated that they would be a little more likely to consider Toyota. For 37 per cent of Toyota owners and 57 per cent of non-owners, the recall issue made no difference to their considering buying a Toyota.

Conclusion

Steve recalled Buddy fondly. The campaign had been a great success. It had built connection and trust, and opinions of consumers were reflected in the research and the statistics. It had been just what was needed. Toyota owed much to a dog!

»

»

Questions

1. Do you think Buddy was able to connect with Toyota owners and the general public?

2. What suggestions do you have for Steve concerning a follow-up campaign?

3. Was this the best way to deal with the situation facing Toyota South Africa?

4. What other strategies could also have been considered?

5. Watch the follow-up advertisement for the Toyota Corolla (https://www.youtube.com/watch?v=AI9nExRqmPY). Contrast the message with those in the advertisements featuring Buddy.

This case study was written by Adele Bendt, Associate Professor, Jonkoping International Business School.

References

Based on: Kruger, C. (2010) Personal interview with the author; Kruger, C. (2010) Presentation at Southern African Institute of Management Scientists Conference 2010 Mpekweni Sun, 12–15 September; Toyota http://www.toyota-global.com/company/profile/facilities/worldwide_operations.html (accessed 2 April 2015); Connor, M. (2010) Toyota Recall: Five Critical Lessons http://business-ethics.com/2010/01/31/2123-toyota-recall-five-critical-lessons/ (accessed 14 April 2015); ABC News (2010) Toyota recall: Reports of runaway cars http://abcnews.go.com/Blotter/RunawayToyotas/runaway-toyotas-problem-persists-recall/story?id=9618735&page=2 (accessed 14 April 2015); Mail Online (2010) 'There's no brakes. . . hold on and pray': Last words of man before he and his family died in Toyota Lexus crash, http://www.dailymail.co.uk/news/article-1248177/Toyota-recall-Last-words-father-family-died-Lexus-crash.html#ixzz1YaJKrtWw (accessed 21 September 2011); SouthAfrica.info (2012) South Africa's automotive industry; http://www.southafrica.info/business/economy/sectors/automotive-overview.htm#.VTUYhiGeDGc (accessed 2 April 2015).

CASE 28
Volvo: Fundamentally Changing the Way Cars are Marketed and Sold

Volvo, the 87-year-old Swedish car company, is in a delicate situation. In 2010 it was bought by the Chinese company Zhejiang Geely Holding Group, normally referred to just as Geely. (Previously, Volvo was owned by the US carmaker Ford.) Since then, the company has been walking a fine line, trying to stay true to its Scandinavian values of safety, environmental concern and classic understated design, while at the same time trying to appeal to affluent Chinese buyers who demand more luxury and performance from their cars. In August of 2014, Volvo launched a stylish new sport utility vehicle (SUV), the XC90, in an effort to bring these two worlds together.

The XC90 is Volvo's attempt to break into the premium car market, an area normally dominated by its much bigger German rivals. The company said that prices will be similar to what people would expect to pay for an Audi. In 2015, Volvo plans on releasing a sedan version, tentatively labelled the S90 sedan, which will be primarily aimed at the US and Chinese markets. Volvo needs to make some radical changes to its marketing and communication strategy, because although it is a market leader in Sweden, it has had stagnant sales for years in the rest of Europe and the USA. Encouragingly, at the moment it is experiencing significant growth and increased market share in China.

In addition to its attempts to blend Scandinavian sensibilities with Chinese demands for luxury while at the same time trying to move upmarket, Volvo recently made another announcement: it would like to completely change the way cars are marketed and sold, as well as redefining the concept of customer service and customer relations. Not bad for a company that used to be mocked for making money by 'selling schoolteachers cars shaped like bricks'.

Volvo's new marketing and communication strategy is called the 'Volvo Way to Market' and it is nothing if not ambitious. 'For decades, car marketing has been following a certain pattern which has been too conservative and lacking in imagination,' says Alain Visser, Senior Vice President of Marketing at Volvo. He believes that this new plan will finally allow the

Swedish company to 'implement a strategy that is geared towards its own needs'. It immediately calls for a doubling of the amount of money that the company will spend on marketing over the next five years; but even with this, the company's marketing budget is still no match for its largest rivals. These initiatives follow on the heels of Volvo's decision to restructure its marketing activities by merging its global media buying and planning business under one ad agency's roof—namely 'Mindshare', WPP's global media agency network. The company hopes that this consolidation will encourage more collaboration between Volvo's US marketing team and the global marketing team located at the company's headquarters in Sweden.

Volvo plans on highlighting its Scandinavian roots in all its mass marketing and communication efforts, and will focus more on developing its brand. As part of its new marketing initiative, the company also announced that it will be extensively renovating its dealerships to give them a true Scandinavian feel. This means that all waiting areas will be fitted out with Swedish furnishings as well as offering Swedish refreshments and snacks. It will be curious to see how this will play out with Li Shufu, the chairman of Geely and the ultimate owner of Volvo. He is known for making regular trips to Sweden to visit the local headquarters. In the past he has complained about how the interiors and design of the

>>

cars were 'too Scandinavian' and offered advice about what he thought his rich Chinese friends were looking for in a car.

In a radical departure from traditional marketing strategy, Volvo also announced that it would be cutting back drastically on corporate sponsorship activity and will basically remove itself from auto shows, something that, until now, was unheard of. Previously, the company sponsored equestrian events, theatre, golf tournaments and symphonies, to name just a few, as part of its coordinated mass marketing and communications strategy. But no more. Volvo still wants to communicate and engage with a large audience, it just wants to do it in a more controlled and rational manner. 'We are totally reshaping what we are doing and reinventing the way we go to market. We are a small but well-differentiated player and I wanted to think about, if I was starting from scratch, how I would get my message across,' says Mr. Visser.

One example of Mr. Visser's new vision of marketing and communication at Volvo is that instead of following the annual car show circuit, visiting the same cities year after year mixed in with every other car brand in the world, the company plans on striking out on its own. Volvo said it will focus on just one auto show in each major region once a year, namely Detroit in the USA, Geneva in Europe and Shanghai/Beijing in China. This reduced number of events will then be complemented and supported by additional mass communication and branding activities in other important markets. Also apparently on the chopping block is Volvo's participation in car racing, with Mr. Visser insisting that 'Motorsport does not conform with our brand.' Oddly enough, fans of yachting need not worry. The company still plans on sponsoring the Volvo Ocean Race, a triennial event in which boats race across four oceans and around six continents, covering 30,000 miles over nine months. The strategy behind limiting the number of corporate events but focusing more intensely on the ones that remain,is to differentiate Volvo from other car companies and allow it to get its message out more clearly.

The company also announced that it will improve its digital platform in an effort to better communicate with, engage and serve its customers. Volvo believes that 80–90 per cent of car buyers first shop online before going to a showroom. The company is upgrading its online platform in order to better integrate the online brand experience with the in-showroom brand experience. Customers who go online will be given a standard choice model which they then can personalize and upgrade, designing the eventual car they would like to buy. They will even receive a short video showing what the car will look like when finally delivered. Volvo does not see online purchasing as a replacement for car dealerships, but rather as a complement, since cars bought online will still have to 'pass through the dealer network', says Mr. Visser.

According to Mr. Visser, the company is looking beyond the traditional ways of marketing cars through print, television, billboards and corporate sponsorship events, and plans on increasing the amount of money it spends on digital advertising. Volvo said that it will focus on messages that develop its brand, and tailor the types of media that it uses, and how it will use them, according to the nature of the local markets that it operates in. 'TV is best for some markets, but in southern Europe, for example, billboards are very efficient,' said Mr. Visser. It is hoped that through these innovative changes in the way Volvo markets its cars, sales will double in the next five years.

Questions

1. **What factors are pushing Volvo to change its marketing communication strategy?**

2. **Identify and evaluate the different elements of Volvo's marketing communication strategy. How can it differentiate itself from other car makers and give the company a competitive edge?**

3. **How does Volvo plan to use digital marketing in its communication strategy and improve its relationship with customers?**

This case study was written by Tom McNamara and Asha Moore-Mangin, the ESC Rennes School of Business.

References

Based on: Groves, E. (2011) 3 ways to create unique customer experiences, American Express, 27 April, https://www.americanexpress.com/us/small-business/openforum/articles/3-ways-to-create-unique-customer-experiences; Taylor III, A. (2000) Ford's Mr. Continental WOLFGANG REITZLE, once BMW's enfant terrible, wants to make Ford a luxury-car superpower. Can he love a Lincoln?, *Fortune Magazine*, 16 October, http://archive.fortune.com/magazines/fortune/fortune_archive/2000/10/16/289641/index.htm; Hudson, N. (2014) Volvo boss says motorsport 'does not conform with our brand', *Touring Car Times*, 15 December, http://www.touringcartimes.com/2014/12/15/volvo-boss-says-motorsport-does-not-conform-with-our-brand; Volvo (2014) Volvo Cars announces new global marketing strategy Volvo Press release, 15 December, https://www.media.volvocars.com/global/en-gb/media/pressreleases/155208/volvo

-cars-announces-new-global-marketing-strategy; Bruell, A. (2014) Volvo Consolidates Global Media with Mindshare, *Ad Age*, 24 February, http://adage.com/article/agency-news/volvo-consolidates-global-media-mindshare/291822; Scrutton, A. (2014) Volvo's Make Or Break Moment For $11 Billion In China Plan Happens, 26 August, edited by Will Waterman, *Reuters*, 18 August, http://www.businessinsider.com/r-with-cigars-and-crystal-volvo-makes-eyes-at-chinese-rich-2014-18#ixzz3MN7tufZV; Edelstein, S. (2014) Volvo may swap auto shows for online sales and more digital marketing, *Digital Trends*, 17 December, http://www.digitaltrends.com/cars/volvo-may-swap-auto-shows-online-sales-digital-marketing/#ixzz3MORNGQBe; Hall, E. (2014) Volvo Will Try to Reinvent Auto Marketing With New Strategy, *Ad Age*, 16 December, http://adage.com/article/global-news/volvo-reinvent-auto-marketing-strategy/296222

CHAPTER 15
Direct Marketing Communications

> *Understand the power of asking.* 99
> **DRAYTON BIRD**

LEARNING OBJECTIVES

After reading this chapter, you should be able to:

1. discuss the key direct communication tools: personal selling, exhibitions, direct marketing
2. discuss the characteristics of modern selling and the stages in the selling process
3. consider the key issues involved in sales management
4. discuss exhibitions and trade shows in a business-to-business context
5. explain the concept of direct marketing and how to manage campaigns
6. describe the reasons for the growth in direct marketing communication activity
7. discuss the importance of database marketing and how this creates a foundation for customer relationship management
8. describe the media used in direct marketing
9. discuss the ethical issues in direct communications

The world of communications is changing rapidly. Digital and mobile communication platforms are blurring the boundaries between communication tools and media. Websites (potentially) carry text, audio, video messages as well as acting as information sources, means of data collection and sales channels (Chaffey and Ellis-Chadwick, 2012). In this chapter we are going to explore elements of the promotional mix that are direct forms of communication and generally do not require media scheduling, but do offer a level of personalization not afforded by the mass communication tools discussed in Chapter 14. The chapter begins with personal selling and sales management as this is the oldest, most direct and interactive form of direct communications. This is followed by exhibitions and trade fairs, and finally we explore direct marketing and the importance of **database marketing**. The chapter provides more detailed investigation of each tool, building on the foundations set down in Chapter 13 and, in doing so, provides more insight into how each of the direct communication methods might contribute to an Integrated Marketing Communication (IMC) campaign strategy.

Personal Selling and Sales Management

Personal selling is the marketing task that involves face-to-face contact with a customer. Unlike advertising, promotion, sponsorship and other forms of non-personal communication, personal selling permits a direct interaction between buyer and seller. This two-way communication means that the seller can identify the specific needs and problems of the buyer and tailor the sales presentation in the light of this knowledge. The particular concerns of the buyer can also be dealt with on a one-to-one basis.

This flexibility comes only at a cost. The cost of a car, travel expenses and sales office overheads can mean that the total annual bill for a field salesperson is often twice the level of their salary. In business-to-business marketing over 70 per cent of the marketing budget is usually spent on the salesforce. This is because of the technical nature of the products being sold, and the need to maintain close personal relationships between the selling and buying organizations.

However, the nature of the personal selling function is changing. Organizations are reducing the size of their salesforces in the face of greater buyer concentration, moves towards centralized buying, and recognition of the high costs of maintaining a field sales team. The concentration of buying power into fewer hands has also fuelled the move towards relationship management, often through key account selling. This involves the use of dedicated sales teams that service the accounts of major buyers.

According to research (Agarwal, Harmon and Viertier, 2009), a key challenge for marketers who manage sales teams is how to achieve a balance between the cost of sales generation and the revenue such activity generates. For example, when a large telecoms company wanted to reduce the cost of its salesforce while maintaining revenues, it reduced back-office support so it could protect the frontline sales staff. But the outcome was that the forward-facing sales representatives started doing the administrative support tasks, so reducing the time they had to concentrate on selling. Eventually, more junior sales staff were employed in the support role, but this forced costs up as they were more expensive than the original back-office staff. A good principle to use when looking at cost reductions in this area is to plan strategies that 'do no harm'; this is best achieved by systematically considering marketing systems and business practices in the light of customer needs and behaviour (Agarwal, Harmon and Viertier, 2009).

The changing marketing environment is affecting selling and sales management, and many companies are looking for ways to optimize the performance of their sales teams. The next section explores the characteristics of selling that are required to cope with the changing and challenging marketing environment.

Characteristics of Modern Selling

In today's competitive environment, a salesforce must have a wide range of skills to compete successfully. Gone are the days when salespeople required simple presentational and closing skills to be successful. The characteristics of the job today (illustrated in Figure 15.1) require a wide array of skills; these will be identified in the next section. In this part of the book we discuss the characteristics of modern selling. Without such an understanding salespeople will be ill-equipped to tackle the job.

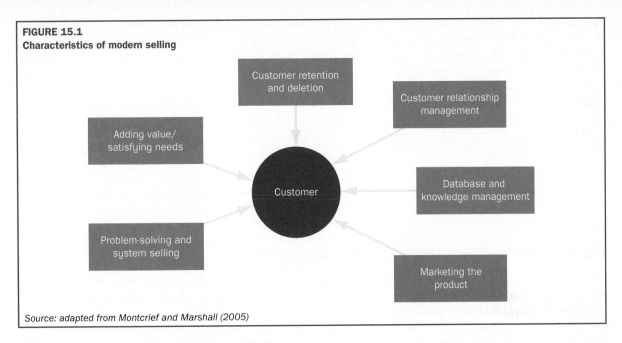

FIGURE 15.1
Characteristics of modern selling

Source: adapted from Montcrief and Marshall (2005)

Customer retention and deletion

Many companies find that 80 per cent of their sales come from 20 per cent of their customers. This means that it is vital to devote considerable resources to retaining existing high-volume, high-potential and highly profitable customers. **Key account management** (see Chapter 10) has become an important form of sales organization as it means a salesperson or sales team can focus their efforts on fewer major customers.

At the other end of the spectrum, companies are finding that some small customers actually cost the organization money. This is because servicing and distribution of products to these customers may push costs beyond the revenue generated but technology-driven solutions, for example **telemarketing** and **e-commerce** systems, are providing ways to service smaller accounts and control costs.

Customer relationship management

The emphasis on customer retention has led to an increasing focus on **customer relationship management** (see Chapter 10). Customer relationship management requires that the salesforce focuses on the long term and not simply on closing the next sale. The emphasis should be on creating win/win situations with customers so that both parties to the interaction gain and want to continue the relationship. For major customers, relationship management may involve setting up dedicated teams to service the account and maintain all aspects of the business relationship, but for smaller customers, social media, the web and the cloud offer solutions.

The focus moves from order taking and order making to strategic customer management (Lane and Piercy, 2004). The challenge is to reposition sales as a core element of a company's competitiveness, where the sales organization is closely integrated into marketing strategy and planning (Stephens, 2003). This process places the customer at the centre of the company's focus, with the sales organization charged with taking a strategic view of designing and implementing superior customer relationships (Lane and Piercy, 2004). This requires sales management to work towards the total integration of how customer relationships are designed, established, managed and sustained. For example, companies like Cisco Systems have developed sales strategies that use personal selling when the purchase is important and complicated, and the decision uncertain—usually the first sale to a customer or a new application—leaving subsequent purchases to be made via the Internet (Royal, 2004).

Database and knowledge management

Knowing your customers and how they want to interact is becoming increasingly important. The modern salesforce can use customer databases, the web and social media to aid the sales task (e.g. finding customer and competitor information). In the past, salespeople recorded customer information on cards and sent orders through the post to head office. Today, technological advances such as email, mobile phones and videoconferencing have transformed the way knowledge is transferred. Mobile computing devices mean that salespeople can store customer and competitor information, make presentations and communicate with head office electronically. Furthermore, all the information needed to make a sale, such as price lists, product availability and delivery times, can be held electronically so that it is readily available anywhere.

Marketing the product

Today, salespeople are involved in a broader range of activities, which go beyond simply planning and making sales presentations. Indeed, face-to-face presentations are often substituted by information presented on web pages and email attachments that can give the customer up-to-date information in a convenient and accessible format (Moncrief and Marshall, 2005). The role of the salesperson is expanding to participation in marketing activities such as product development, market development and the segmentation of markets, as well as other tasks that support or complement marketing activities, such as database management, provision and analysis of information, and assessing market segments (Leigh and Marshall, 2001).

Problem-solving and system selling

Much of modern selling, particularly in business-to-business situations, is based upon the salesperson acting as a consultant, who works with the customer to identify problems, determine needs, and propose and implement effective solutions (Rackham and DeVincentis, 1999). This approach is fundamentally different from the traditional view of the salesperson as a smooth, fast talker who breezes in to see a customer, persuades them to buy and walks away with an order. Selling often involves multiple calls, the use of a team-selling approach and considerable analytical skills. Further, customers are increasingly looking for a systems solution rather than the buying of an individual product. This means, for example, that to sell door handles to a firm like Ford Motor Company, a supplier must be able to sell a door *system* that includes door handles, locking and opening devices, as well as having a thorough knowledge of door technology, and the ability to suggest to Ford solutions to problems that may arise.

Satisfying needs and adding value

The modern salesperson must have the ability to identify and satisfy customer needs. Some customers do not recognize that they have a need. It is the salesperson's job in such situations to stimulate need recognition. For example, a customer may not realize that a machine in the production process has low productivity compared to newer, more technologically advanced machines. The salesperson's job will be to make the customer aware of the problem in order to convince him/her that they have a need to modernize the production process. In so doing, the salesperson will have added value to the customer's business by reducing costs, and created a win/win situation for both his/her company and the customer.

Personal Selling Skills

Success in selling comes from implementing the marketing concept when face to face with customers; increasingly this involves building long-term relationships, which means more emphasis on customer needs and wants and less on short-term sales transactions. The sales interview offers an unparalleled opportunity to identify individual customer needs and match behaviour to the specific customer that is encountered (Weitz, 1981). Salespeople have an opportunity to implement unique sales presentations tailored to individual customers and rapidly adjust messages in response to customer reactions. Indeed, research has shown that such customer-orientated selling is associated with higher levels of salesforce performance (Román, Ruiz and Munuera, 2002). Research has shown that making the customer central to the selling activity can deliver greater success than high-pressure selling tactics. Potential approaches are (Schuster and Danes, 1986; Sujan, Sujan and Bettman, 1998; Szymanski, 1988); Weitz, Sujan and Sujan, 1986; Krishnan, Netemeyer and Boles, 2002):

- asking questions
- providing product information, making comparisons and offering evidence to support claims
- acknowledging the viewpoint of the customer
- agreeing with the customer's perceptions
- supporting the customer

- releasing tension
- having a richer, more detailed knowledge of customers
- increased effort
- having confidence in one's own abilities.

In order to develop personal selling skills it is useful to distinguish seven phases of the selling process (see Figure 15.2). These phases need not occur in the order shown. Objections may be raised during the presentation or negotiation, and a trial close may be attempted at any point during the presentation if buyer interest is high. Furthermore, negotiation may or may not take place, or may occur during any of the stages. As Moncrief and Marshall (2005) report:

> The evolved selling process assumes that the salesperson typically will perform the various steps of the process in some form, but the steps (phases) do not occur for each sales call. Rather, they occur over time, accomplished by multiple people within the selling company, and not necessarily in any sequence.'

Each of these phases will now be discussed.

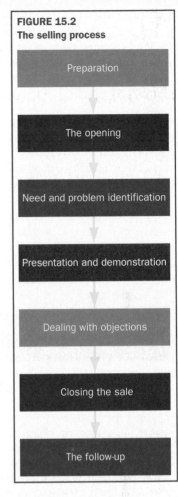

FIGURE 15.2
The selling process

- Preparation
- The opening
- Need and problem identification
- Presentation and demonstration
- Dealing with objections
- Closing the sale
- The follow-up

Preparation

Preparation before a sales visit can reap dividends by enhancing confidence and performance when face to face with the customer. Some situations cannot be prepared for—the unexpected question or unusual objection, for example—but many customers face similar situations, and certain questions and objections will be raised repeatedly. Preparation can help the salesperson respond to these recurring situations.

Salespeople will benefit from gaining knowledge of their own products and competitors' products, sales presentation planning, setting call objectives and understanding buyer behaviour.

Product knowledge

Product knowledge means understanding both **product features** and the customer benefits that they confer. Understanding product features alone is not enough to convince customers to buy because they buy products for the benefits that the features provide, not the features in themselves. Salespeople need to ask themselves what are the benefits a certain feature provides for customers. For example, a computer mouse (product feature) provides a more convenient way of issuing commands (customer benefit) than using the keyboard. The way to turn features into benefits is to view products from the customer's angle. A by-product of this is the realization that some features may provide no customer benefit whatsoever.

Competitors' products

Knowledge of competitors' products allows their strengths to be offset against their weaknesses. For example, if a buyer claims that a competitor's product has a cost advantage, this may be offset against the superior productivity advantage of the salesperson's product. Similarly, inaccuracies in a buyer's claims can be countered. Finally, competitive knowledge allows salespeople to stress the differential advantage of their products compared to those of the competition.

Sales presentation planning

Preparation here builds confidence, raises the chances that important benefits are not forgotten, allows visual aids and demonstrations to be built into the presentation, and permits the anticipation of objections and the preparation of convincing counter-arguments. Although preparation is vital there should be room left for flexibility in approach since customers have different needs. The salesperson has to be aware that the features and benefits that should be stressed with one customer may have much less emphasis placed on them for another.

Setting call objectives

The key to setting call objectives is to phrase them in terms of what the salesperson wants the customer to do rather than what the salesperson should do. For example:

- for the customer to define what his or her needs are
- for the customer to visit a showroom

- for the customer to try the product, for example test-drive a car
- for the customer to be convinced of the cost saving of 'our' product compared with that of the competition.

This is because the success of the sales interview is customer-dependent. The end is to convince the customer; what the salesperson does is simply a means to that end.

Understanding buyer behaviour

Thought should also be given to understanding *buyer behaviour* (see Chapters 3 & 4). Questions should be asked, such as 'Who are the likely key people to talk to?' 'What are their probable choice criteria?' 'Are there any gatekeepers preventing access to some people, who need to be circumvented?' 'What are the likely opportunities and threats that may arise in the selling situation?' All of the answers to these questions need to be verified when in the actual selling situation but prior consideration can help salespeople to be clear in their own minds about the important issues.

The Internet can provide a wealth of information about the buying organization. The buyer's website, online product catalogues and blogs are useful sources of information. Customer relationship management (CRM) systems allow salespeople to access customer information held by their company, via the Internet. But herein lies a potential problem: as customers expect more, sales teams need to be more informed and more able to search vast stores of information to find out about their customers' needs. See Marketing in Action 15.1 to find out more about how technology is changing the rules of the selling game.

MARKETING IN ACTION 15.1
Technology Rules, Online and on the Road

Technology is enabling sales teams to be more informed about their customers' behaviour, and is providing better and more responsive sales experiences. Mobile apps, analytics, cloud computing and mobile peripherals mean that sales representatives can have a wealth of information at their fingertips. From the software industry, through the financial sector and pharmaceuticals to the toy industry, companies are increasingly using sophisticated technology to enhance the selling process. For example, sales representatives who work for French toy manufacturer Juratoys use iPads and mobile phones to take orders, check stock availability and show their customers new lines and back-catalogue items.

The key technology trends that marketers in direct selling should be aware of are:

1 The Internet of Things (IoT) is enabling communications between people, between people and things, and between things communicating with things. This concept is not new, but it has become significant in recent years because there are now more interactions and communications between an ever-growing number of people and things. And when these interactions occur, data is created which can be collected and analyzed. So the challenge is for companies to be able to set up systems that ensure their sales teams have access to such information.
2 Data analytics are providing greater insight into opportunities and customer behaviour. By linking CRM systems to other forms of data capture device linked to the IoT, salespeople can provide decisions and sales solutions. But companies must ensure that all their information systems are connected if they are to gain the most benefit.
3 Cloud computing is creating opportunities to link up all the way through the sales process. This is improving the *richness* of available information and improving flexibility. For example, iPads are widely used in pharmaceutical sales; in this setting, technology is providing both sales representatives and doctors with access to extensive information and other collaborative sales tools such as web conferencing.

The impact of these trends is that buyers and sellers can collaborate in real time, negotiations can be handled and supported anywhere in the world, and the speed of selling is increasing.

Based on: Vongsingthong and Smanchat (2014); Zoltners, Sinha and Lorimer (2015); Movahhed (2014)

The opening

Initial impressions often affect later perceptions, and so it is important for salespeople to consider how to create a favourable initial response from customers. The following factors can positively shape first impressions.

- Be businesslike in appearance and behaviour.
- Be friendly but not over-familiar.
- Be attentive to detail, such as holding a briefcase in the hand that is not used for handshaking.
- Observe common courtesies like waiting to be asked to sit down.
- Ask if it is convenient for the customer to see you. This signals an appreciation of their needs (they may be too busy to be seen). It automatically creates a favourable impression from which to develop the sales call, but also a long-term relationship because the salesperson has earned the right to proceed to the next stage in selling: need and problem identification.
- Do not take the sales interview for granted: thank the customer for spending time with you and stress that you believe it will be worthwhile for them.
  Using the new digital technologies can help to create favourable first impressions and facilitate relationship development.

Need and problem identification

People buy products because they have problems that give rise to needs. For example, a machine's unreliability (problem) causes the need to replace it with a new one (purchase). Therefore the first task is to identify the needs and problems of each customer. Only by doing so can the salesperson connect with each customer's situation. Having done so, the salesperson can select the product that best fits the customer's need and sell the appropriate benefits. It is benefits that link customer needs to product features, as in:

$$\text{Customer need} \rightarrow \text{Benefit} \leftarrow \text{Product feature}$$

In the previous example, it would be essential to convince the customer that the salesperson's machine possessed features that guaranteed machine reliability. Knowledge of competitors' products would allow salespeople to show how their machine possessed features that gave added reliability. In this way, salespeople are in an ideal situation to convince customers of a product's differential advantage. Whenever possible, factual evidence of product superiority should be shown to customers. This is much more convincing than mere claims by the salesperson.

Effective needs and problem identification requires the development of questioning and listening skills. The problem is that people are more used to making statements than asking questions. Therefore the art of asking sensible questions that produce a clear understanding of the customer's situation requires training and considerable experience. The hallmark of inexperienced salespeople is that they do all the talking; successful salespeople know how to get the customer to do most of the talking. In this way they gain the information necessary to make a sale. Best Buy is a consumer electronics company that has struggled in recent years due to aggressive competition, especially from online retailers like Amazon. However, the business has been turned around by finding out about its end consumers and sharing this information with its suppliers. Best Buy began listening to its customers through the web and looking at online reviews, and has been able to tailor its product offer to better suit customer needs (Reid, 2015).

Presentation and demonstration

The presentation and demonstration provides the opportunity for the salesperson to convince the customer that his or her company can supply the solution to the customer's problem. It should focus on **customer benefits** rather than product features. These can be linked using the following phrases:

- which means that
- which results in
- which enables you to.

For example, the machine salesperson might say that the machine possesses proven technology (product feature), *which means that* the reliability of the machine (customer benefit) is guaranteed. Evidence should then be supplied to support this sales argument. Perhaps scientific tests have proved the reliability of the machine (these should be shown to the customer), satisfied customers' testimonials could be produced or a visit to a satisfied customer arranged.

In business-to-business markets, some salespeople are guilty of presenting features and failing to communicate the benefit to the business customer. For example, in telecommunications it is not enough to say how fast the line speed is. The benefit derives from the impact that the extra speed has on the customer. It could be that faster speed means reduced call costs, reduced number of lines or increased customer satisfaction (Brooke, 2002).

The salesperson should continue asking questions during the presentation to ensure that the customer has understood what the salesperson has said and to check that what the salesperson has mentioned really is of importance to the customer. This can be achieved by asking, say, 'Is that the kind of thing you are looking for?'

Technological advances have greatly assisted the presentation. For example, laptops allow the use of online resources such as video material, and the ability to get a response from a sales office during a presentation (Picaville, 2004). Access to company websites permits the carrying of masses of product information, including sound and animation.

Demonstrations allow the customer to see the product in operation. As such, some of the claims made for the product by the salesperson can be verified. Demonstrations allow the customer to be involved in the selling process through participation. They can, therefore, be instrumental in reducing the *perceived risk* of a purchase and moving the customer towards purchase.

Information technology can allow multimedia demonstrations of industrial products in the buyer's office. No longer is it always necessary for buyers to visit the supplier's site or to provide facilities to act as 'video show rooms' for salespeople wishing to demonstrate their product using video projectors (Long, Tellefsen and Lichtenthal, 2007).

Dealing with objections

It is unusual for salespeople to close a sale without the need to overcome objections. Objections are any concerns or questions raised by the buyer (see Hunt and Bashaw, 1999). While some objections are an expression of confusion, doubt or disagreement with the statements or information presented by the salesperson, objections should not always be viewed negatively since they highlight the issues that are important to the buyer.

The secret of *dealing with objections* is to handle both the substantive and emotional aspects. The substantive part is to do with the objection itself. If the customer objects to the product's price, the salesperson needs to use convincing arguments to show that the price is not too high. But it is a fact of human personality that the argument that is supported by the greater weight of evidence does not always win, since people resent being proved wrong. Therefore, salespeople need to recognize the emotional aspects of objection handling. Under no circumstances should the buyer lose face or be antagonized during this process. Two ways of minimizing this risk are to listen to the objection without interruption, and to employ the agree-and-counter technique.

The Internet can aid the creation of convincing answers to objections. The salesperson can guide buyers to the company's website, where frequently answered questions and testimonials may be found. Potential customers might also be directed to favourable online reviews at independent websites. This improved dialogue between sellers and buyers can improve the chances of a successful sale (Long, Tellefsen and Lichtenthal, 2007).

Listen and do not interrupt

Experienced salespeople know that the impression given to buyers by salespeople who interrupt buyers when they are raising an objection is that the salesperson believes that:
* the objection is obviously wrong
* the objection is trivial
* it is not worth the salesperson's time to let the buyer finish.

Interruption denies buyers the kind of respect they are entitled to receive and may lead to a misunderstanding of the real substance behind the objection.

The correct approach is to listen carefully, attentively and respectfully. The buyer will appreciate the fact that the salesperson is taking the problem seriously, and the salesperson will gain through having a clear and full understanding of what the problem really is.

Agree and counter

The salesperson agrees with the buyer's viewpoint before putting forward an alternative point of view. The objective is to create a climate of agreement rather than conflict, and shows that the salesperson respects the buyer's opinion, thus avoiding loss of face. For example:

Buyer: The problem with your bulldozer is that it costs more than the competition.

Salesperson: You are right, the initial cost is a little higher, but I should like to show you how the full lifetime costs of the bulldozer are much lower than the competition.

Closing the sale

Inexperienced salespeople sometimes think that an effective presentation followed by convincing objection handling should mean that the buyer will ask for the product without the seller needing to close the sale. This does occasionally happen, but more often it is necessary for the salesperson to take the initiative. This is because many buyers still have doubts in their mind that may cause them to wish to delay the decision to purchase.

If the customer puts off buying, the decision may be made when a competitor's salesperson is present, resulting in a lost sale.

Buying signals

The key to closing a sale is to look for **buying signals**. These are statements by buyers that indicate they are interested in buying. For example:

- 'That looks fine.'
- 'I like that one.'
- 'When could the product be delivered?'
- 'I think that product meets my requirements.'

These all indicate a very positive intention to buy without actually asking for the order. They provide excellent opportunities for the salesperson to ask the buyer to make a decision without appearing pushy.

Closing techniques

A variety of closing techniques can be used.

- *Simply ask for the order*: a direct question, such as 'Would you like that one?', may be all that is needed.
- *Summarize and then ask for the order*: with this approach, the salesperson reminds the buyer of the main points of the sales discussion in a manner which implies that the time for decision-making has arrived and that buying is the natural next step: 'Well, Ms Jones, we have agreed that the ZX4 model best meets your requirements of low noise and high productivity at an economical price. Would you like to place an order for this machine?'
- *Concession close*: by keeping a concession back to use in the close, a salesperson may convince an indecisive buyer to place an order: 'I am in a position to offer an extra 10 per cent discount on price if you are willing to place an order now.'
- *Action agreement*: in some situations it is inappropriate to try to close the sale. To do so would annoy the buyer because the sale is not in the hands of one person but a decision-making unit. Many organizational purchasing decisions are of this kind, and the decision may be made in committee without any salesperson being present. Alternatively, the salesperson may be talking to a specifier (such as a doctor or architect) who does not buy directly. In such circumstances, the close may be substituted by an action agreement: instead of closing the sale the salesperson attempts to achieve an action agreement with the customer. For example, in the selling of prescription drugs, either the salesperson or the doctor agrees to do something before the next meeting. The salesperson might agree to bring details of a new drug or attempt to get agreement from the doctor to read a leaflet on a drug before the next meeting. This technique has the effect of maintaining the relationship between the parties and can be used as the starting point of the discussion when they next meet.

The follow-up

Once the order is placed there could be a temptation for the salesperson to move on to other customers, neglecting the follow-up visit. However, this can be a great mistake since most companies rely on repeat business. If problems arise, customers have every right to believe that the salesperson was interested only in the order and not their complete satisfaction. By checking that there are no problems with delivery, installation, product use and training (where applicable), the follow-up can show that the salesperson really cares about the customer.

The follow-up can also be used to provide reassurance that the purchase was the right thing to do. As we discussed when analyzing consumer behaviour, people often feel tense after deciding to buy an expensive product. Doubts can materialize about the wisdom of spending so much money, or whether the product best meets their needs. This anxiety, known as *cognitive dissonance*, can be minimized by the salesperson reassuring the customer about the purchase during the follow-up phase.

Websites can be helpful following the order, reminding buyers about post-purchase support resources, and salespeople can maintain an open dialogue with buyers through online user newsletters. Companies such as Dell and Xerox allow customers to log in to a secure buyer website to track the status of their orders, order products online or pay invoices (Long, Tellefsen and Lichtenthal, 2007).

Salespeople operating in overseas markets need to be aware of the cultural nuances that shape business relationships. For example, in the West a deadline is acceptable, whereas in many Middle Eastern cultures, it would be taken as an insult. In China, salespeople need to acknowledge the importance of personalized and close business relationships, known as *guanxi*. *Guanxi* is a set of personal relationships/connections on which a person can draw to secure resources or advantage when doing business. *Guanxi* can lead to preferential treatment in the form of easy access to limited resources, increased accessibility to information and preferential credit terms. For foreigners, this means having as part of their *guanxi* network an influential person in an organization or government position. Another key issue in Chinese culture is the avoidance of 'loss of face'. Visiting salespeople should avoid creating a situation where a Chinese person might 'lose face' by finding themselves in an embarrassing situation (e.g. by displaying lack of knowledge or understanding).

Many salespeople make the mistake of using 'self-reference' criteria when selling abroad. They assume that the values and behavioural norms that apply in their own country are equally applicable abroad. To avoid this failing, they need training in the special skills required to sell to people of different cultures.

Sales Management

In many respects, the functions of the sales manager are similar to those of other managers. Sales managers, like their production, marketing and finance counterparts, need to recruit, train, motivate and evaluate their staff. However, there are several peculiarities of the job that make effective sales management difficult and the job considerably demanding.

Problems of sales management

Geographic separation

The geographic separation between sales managers and their field salesforce creates problems of motivation, communication and control.

Repeated rejections

Salespeople may suffer repeated rejections when trying to close sales. This may cause attrition of their enthusiasm, attitudes and skills. A major role for sales managers is to provide support and renew motivation in such adverse circumstances.

The salesperson's personality versus the realities of the job

Most people who go into sales are outgoing and gregarious. These are desirable characteristics for people who are selling to customers. However, the reality of the job is that, typically, only 30 per cent of a salesperson's time is spent face to face with customers, with travelling (50 per cent) and administration (20 per cent) contributing the rest (McDonald, 2002). This means that over half of the salesperson's time is spent alone, which can cause frustration in people who enjoy the company of others.

Oversimplification of the task

Some sales managers cope with the difficulties of management by oversimplifying the task. They take the attitude that they are interested only in results. It is their job to reward those who meet sales targets and severely punish those who fail. Such an attitude ignores the contribution that sales management can make to the successful achievement of objectives. Figure 15.3 shows the functions of a sales manager and the relationship between marketing strategy and the personal selling function.

Marketing strategy

As with all parts of the marketing mix, the personal selling function is not a stand-alone element, but one that must be considered in the light of overall marketing strategy. At the product level, two major marketing considerations are choice of target market and the creation of a differential advantage. Both of these decisions affect personal selling.

Target market choice

The definition of the target market has clear implications for sales management because of its relationship to **target accounts**. Once the target market has been defined (e.g. organizations in a particular industry over a certain size), sales management can translate that specification into individual accounts to target. Salesforce resources can, therefore, be deployed to maximum effect.

Differential advantage

The creation of a differential advantage is the starting point of successful marketing strategy, but this needs to be communicated to the salesforce and embedded in a sales plan which ensures that the salesforce is able to articulate it convincingly to customers.

Two common dangers

First, the salesforce undermines the differential advantage by repeatedly giving in to customer demands for price concessions. Second, the features that underlie the differential advantage are communicated but the customer benefits are neglected. Customer benefits need to be communicated in terms that are meaningful to customers. This means, for example, that advantages such as higher productivity may require translation into cash savings or higher revenue for financially minded customers.

Four strategic objectives

Marketing strategy also affects the personal selling function through strategic objectives. Each objective—build, hold, harvest and divest—has implications for *sales objectives* and strategy; these are outlined in Table 15.1. Linking business or product area strategic objectives with functional area strategies is essential for the efficient allocation of resources, and effective implementation in the marketplace (Strahle and Spiro, 1986).

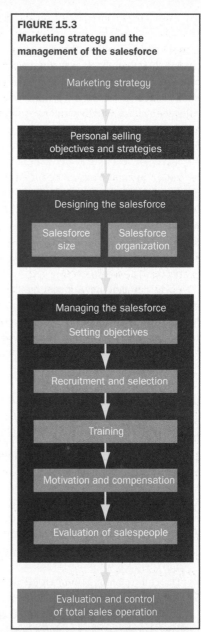

FIGURE 15.3
Marketing strategy and the management of the salesforce

TABLE 15.1 Marketing strategy and sales management

Strategic marketing objective	Sales objective	Sales strategy
Build	Build sales volume	High call rates on existing accounts
	Increase distribution	High focus during call
	Provide high service levels	Call on new accounts (prospecting)
Hold	Maintain sales volume	Continue present call rates on current accounts
	Maintain distribution	Medium focus during call
	Maintain service levels	Call on new outlets when they appear
Harvest	Reduce selling costs	Call only on profitable accounts
	Target profitable accounts	Consider telemarketing or dropping the rest
	Reduce service costs and inventories	No prospecting
Divest	Clear inventory quickly	Quantity discounts to targeted accounts

Source: adapted from Strahle and Spiro (1986).

Personal selling objectives and strategies

As we have seen, selling objectives and strategies are derived from marketing strategy decisions, and should be consistent with other elements of the marketing mix. Indeed, marketing strategy will determine if there is a need for a salesforce at all, or whether the selling role can be accomplished better by using some other medium, such as **direct mail**. Objectives define what the selling function is expected to achieve. Objectives are typically defined in terms of:

- sales volume (e.g. 5 per cent growth in sales volume)
- market share (e.g. 1 per cent increase in market share)
- profitability (e.g. maintenance of gross profit margin)
- service levels (e.g. 20 per cent increase in number of customers regarding salesperson assistance as 'good or better' in annual customer survey)
- salesforce costs (e.g. 5 per cent reduction in expenses).

Salesforce strategy defines how those objectives will be achieved. The following may be considered:

- call rates
- percentage of calls on existing vs potential accounts
- discount policy (the extent to which reductions from list prices allowed)
- percentage of resources
  - targeted at new vs existing products
  - targeted at selling vs providing after-sales service
  - targeted at field selling vs telemarketing
  - targeted at different types of customers (e.g. high vs low potential)
- improving customer and market feedback from the salesforce
- improving customer relationships.

Once sales managers have a clear idea of what they hope to achieve, and how best to set about accomplishing these objectives, they can make sensible decisions regarding salesforce design.

Designing the salesforce

Two critical design decisions are those of determining salesforce size and salesforce organization.

Salesforce size

The most practical method for deciding the number of salespeople is called the *workload approach*. It is based on the calculation of the total annual calls required per year divided by the average calls per year that can be expected from one salesperson (Talley, 1961). The procedure follows seven steps, as outlined below.

1 Customers are grouped into categories according to the value of goods bought, their potential for the future, and the need for prospecting.
2 The call frequency (number of calls per year to an account) is assessed for each category of customer.
3 The total required workload per year is calculated by multiplying the call frequency by the number of customers in each category and then summing for all categories.
4 The average number of calls that can be expected per salesperson per week is estimated.
5 The number of working weeks per year is calculated.
6 The average number of calls a salesperson can make per year is calculated by multiplying (4) and (5).
7 The number of salespeople required is determined by dividing the total annual calls required by the average number of calls one salesperson can make per year.

Salesforce organization

There are three basic forms of *salesforce organization*: geographic, product and customer-based structures. The strengths and weakness of each are as follows.

Geographic: the sales area is broken down into territories based on workload and potential, and a salesperson is assigned to each one to sell all of the product range. This provides a simple, unambiguous, definition of each salesperson's sales territory, and proximity to customers encourages the development of personal relationships. It is also a more cost-efficient method of organization than product- or customer-based systems. However, when products are technically different and sell in a number of diverse markets, it may be unreasonable to expect a salesperson to be knowledgeable about all products and their applications. Under such circumstances a company is likely to move to a product- or customer-based structure.

Product: product specialization is effective where a company has a diverse product range selling to different customers (or at least different people within a given organization). However, if the products sell essentially to the same customers, problems of route duplication (and, consequently, higher travel costs) and multiple calls on the same customer can arise. When applicable, product specialization allows each salesperson to be well informed about a product line, its applications and customer benefits. Hewlett-Packard uses a product-based system because of its wide product range. The salespeople are assigned to one of its three divisions: PCs, laptops and handheld devices; printers and printing; or IT solutions for large enterprises.

Customer-based: the problem of the same customer being served by product divisions of the same supplier, the complexity of buyer behaviour that requires input not only from the sales function but from other functional groups (such as engineering, finance, logistics and marketing), centralization of purchasing, and the immense value of some customers, have led many suppliers to rethink how they organize their salesforces. Companies are increasingly organizing around customers and shifting resources from product or regional divisions to customer-focused business units (Homburg, Workman and Jensen, 2000). Salesforces can be organized along market segment, account size, or new versus existing accounts lines. Firstly, computer firms have traditionally organized their salesforce on the basis of industry served (e.g. banking, retailing, manufacturing) in recognition of their varying needs, problems and potential applications. Specialization by these *market segments* allows salespeople to gain in-depth knowledge of customers and to be able to monitor trends in the industry that may affect demand for their products. In some industries, the applications knowledge of market-based salespeople has led them to be known as *fraternity brothers* by their customers (Magrath, 1989). Second, an increasing trend in many industries is towards key account management, which reflects the increasing concentration of buying power into fewer but larger customers. These are serviced by a key account salesforce comprising senior salespeople who develop close personal relationships with customers, can handle sophisticated sales arguments and are skilled in the art of negotiation. For more detailed discussion of KAM, see Chapter 10. Table 15.2 illustrates some important distinctions between traditional (transactional selling) and key account management.

TABLE 15.2 Distinctions between transactional selling and key account management

	Transactional selling	Key account management
Overall objective	Sales	Preferred supplier status
Sales skills	Asking questions	Building trust
	Handling objections	Negotiation
	Closing	Providing excellent service
Nature of relationship	Short, intermittent	Long, more intensive interaction
Salesperson goal	Closed sale	Relationship management
Nature of salesforce	One or two salespeople per customer	Many sales people, often involving multifunctional teams

Managing the salesforce

Besides deciding personal selling objectives and strategies, and designing the salesforce, the company has to manage the salesforce. This requires setting specific salesperson objectives, recruitment and selection, training, motivation and compensation, and evaluation of salespeople. These activities have been shown to improve salesperson performance, indicating the key role sales managers play as facilitators helping salespeople to perform better (Piercy, Cravens and Morgan, 1998).

Setting objectives

In order to achieve aggregate sales objectives, individual salespeople need to have their own sales targets to achieve. Usually, targets are set in sales terms (sales quotas) but, increasingly, profit targets are being used, reflecting the need to guard against sales being bought cheaply by excessive discounting. To gain commitment to targets, consultation with individual salespeople is recommended but in the final analysis it is the sales manager's responsibility to set targets. Payment may be linked to their achievement.

Sales management may also wish to set input objectives such as the proportion of time spent developing new accounts, and the time spent introducing new products. They may also specify the number of calls expected per day, and the precise customers who should be called upon.

Recruitment and selection

The importance of recruiting high-calibre salespeople cannot be overestimated. A study into salesforce practice asked sales managers the following question: 'If you were to put your most successful salesperson into the territory of one of your average salespeople, and made no other changes, what increase in sales would you expect after, say, two years?'(PA Consultants, 1979). The most commonly stated increase was 16–20 per cent, and one-fifth of all sales managers said they would expect an increase of over 30 per cent. Clearly the quality of salespeople that sales managers recruit has a substantial effect on performance.

The recruitment and selection process follows five stages:

1   preparation of the job description and personnel specification
2   identification of sources of recruitment and methods of communication
3   design of the application form and preparation of a shortlist
4   the interview
5   use of supplementary selection aids.

Training

Sometimes, more traditional sales managers believe that their salespeople can best train themselves by doing the job. This approach ignores the value of a training programme that provides a frame of reference in which learning can take place, and also ignores potential benefits such as enhanced skill levels, improved motivation, and greater confidence in the ability to perform well at selling, a factor that has been shown to be related to improved sales performance (Krishnan, Netemeyer and Boles, 2002).

A training programme should include knowledge about the company (its objectives, strategies and organization), its products (features and benefits), its competitors and their products, selling procedures and techniques, work organization (including report preparation), and relationship management. Salespeople need to be trained in the management of long-term customer relationships as well as context-specific selling skills (Wilson, 1993). For example, the IBM consultative sales training programme emphasizes working with clients as consultants to build close relationships and to work jointly to solve problems. The core components of the programme involve people and communication skills (Cron et al., 2005).

Lectures, films, role-playing and case studies can be used in a classroom situation to give knowledge and understanding and to develop competences. These should be followed up with in-the-field training, where skills can be practised face-to-face with customers. Both approaches have to be managed within the busy working lives of a sales team, and as a result companies are including web-based training and teleconferencing that can deliver effective alternatives to traditional face-to-face programmes. Additionally, sales managers and trainers should provide feedback to encourage on-the-job learning. In particular, the sales manager needs to:

- analyze each salesperson's performance
- identify strengths and weaknesses
- communicate strengths
- gain agreement that a weakness exists
- train the salesperson in how to overcome the weakness
- monitor progress.

Training should not end with the field sales team; it should include everyone involved in the sales process.

Motivation and compensation

Effective motivation is based on a deep understanding of salespeople as individuals, their personalities and value systems. In one sense, sales managers do not motivate salespeople—they provide the enabling conditions in which salespeople motivate themselves. Motivation can be understood through the relationship between needs, drives and goals. Luthans stated that, 'the basic process involves needs (deprivations) which set drives in motion (deprivations with direction) to accomplish goals (anything which alleviates a need and reduces a drive)' (Luthans, 1997). For example, the need for more money may result in a drive to work harder in order to receive increased pay. Improving motivation is important to sales success; research has shown that high levels of motivation lead to (see Pullins, 2001; Holmes and Srivastava, 2002):

- increased creativity
- working smarter and a more adaptive selling approach
- working harder

- increased use of win/win negotiation tactics
- higher self-esteem
- a more relaxed attitude and a less negative emotional tone
- enhancement of relationships.

It is important to note that motivation needs to encourage the types of behaviour that contribute to a company's marketing strategy and success. Therefore any reward schemes should benefit those who exhibit the correct behaviour.

Motivation has been the subject of much research over many years. Maslow, Herzberg, Vroom, Adams and Likert, among others, have produced theories that have implications for the motivation of salespeople (see Maslow, 1954; Herzberg, 1966; Vroom, 1964; Adams, 1965; Likert, 1961). Some of their important findings are summarized in the list below.

- Once a need is satisfied it no longer motivates.
- Different people have different needs and values.
- Increasing the level of responsibility/job enrichment, giving recognition of achievement and providing monetary incentives work to increase motivation for some people.
- People tend to be motivated if they believe that effort will bring results, results will be rewarded and the rewards are valued.
- Elimination of disincentives (such as injustices or unfair treatment) raises motivational levels.
- There is a relationship between the performance goals of sales managers and those of the salespeople they lead. The implication of these findings is that sales managers should:
- get to know what each salesperson values and what each one is striving for (unrealized needs)
- be willing to increase the responsibility given to salespeople in mundane jobs
- realize that training can improve motivation as well as capabilities by strengthening the link between effort and performance
- provide targets that are believed to be attainable yet provide a challenge to salespeople
- link rewards to the performance they want improved
- recognize that rewards can be both financial and non-financial (e.g. praise).

For many companies their market is the world, which means that they are faced with motivating international salesforces.

Evaluation of salespeople

Salesforce evaluation provides the information necessary to check if targets are being achieved, and provides the raw information to guide training and motivation. By identifying the strengths and weaknesses of individual salespeople, training can be focused on the areas in need of development, and incentives can be aimed at weak spots such as poor prospecting performance.

Often performance will be compared to standards of performance such as sales or profit quotas, although other comparisons such as salesperson-to-salesperson or current-to-past sales are also used. Two types of performance measures are used, based on quantitative and qualitative criteria.

Quantitative measures of performance: salespeople can be assessed on input, output and hybrid criteria. Output criteria include:
- sales revenue
- profits generated
- gross profit margin
- sales per active account
- number of new accounts opened.

Input criteria include:
- number of calls
- calls per active account
- calls on new accounts (prospects)
- number of prospects visited.

Hybrid criteria are formed by combining output and input criteria, for example:
- sales revenue per call
- profit per call
- prospecting success ratio = number of new accounts opened ÷ number of prospects visited.

These quantitative measures can be compared against target figures to identify strengths and weaknesses. Many of the measures are diagnostic, pointing to reasons why a target is not being reached. For example, a poor call rate might be a cause of low sales achievement. Measuring call rate is important as call frequency has been found to have a positive effect on sales volume and customer satisfaction. Some results will merit further investigation. For example, a low prospecting success ratio should prompt an examination of why new accounts are not being opened despite the high number of prospects visited. A survey of evaluation metrics has shown that there is an increasing tendency to use profit-orientated criteria.

Qualitative measures of performance: whereas quantitative criteria will be measured with hard figures, qualitative measures rely on soft data. They are intrinsically more subjective and include assessment of:

- sales skills, e.g. questioning, making presentations
- customer relationships, e.g. how much confidence do customers have in the salesperson, and whether rapport is good
- product knowledge; for example, how well informed the salesperson is regarding company and competitor products
- self-management, e.g. how well are calls prepared, routes organized
- cooperation and attitudes, e.g. to what extent does the salesperson show initiative, follow instructions?

An increasing number of companies are measuring their salespeople on the basis of the achievement of customer satisfaction. The use of quantitative and qualitative measures is interrelated. For example, a poor sales per call ratio will mean a close qualitative assessment of sales skills, customer relationships and product knowledge.

A final form of qualitative assessment does not focus on the salesperson directly but the likelihood of *winning or losing an order*. Particularly for major sales, a sales manager needs to be able to assess the chances of an order being concluded successfully in time to rectify the situation if things seem to be going astray. Unfortunately, asking salespeople directly will rarely result in an accurate answer. This is not because they are trying to deceive but because they may be deluding themselves. The answer is to ask a series of who, when, where, why and how questions to probe deeper into the situation. It also means working out acceptable and unacceptable responses. Table 15.3 provides an illustration of how such questions could be employed in connection with a major computer sale.

TABLE 15.3 Winning and losing major orders

Question	Poor (losing answer)	Good (winning answer)
Who will authorize the purchase?	The director of MIS	The director of MIS, but it requires an executive director's authorization, and we've talked it over with this person
When will they buy?	Right away. They love the new model	Before the peak processing load at the year end
Where will they be when the decision is made: in the office alone, in their boss's office, in a meeting?	What difference does that make? I think they have already decided	At a board meeting. But don't worry, the in-supplier has no one on its board and we have two good customers on it
Why will they buy from us? Why not their usual supplier?	They and I go way back. They love our new model	The next upgrade from the in-supplier is a big price increase, and ours fits right between its models. They are quite unhappy with the in-supplier about that
How will the purchase be funded?	They've lots of money, haven't they?	The payback period on reduced costs will be about 14 months and we've a leasing company willing to take part of the deal

The losing answers are thin and unconvincing. The salesperson may be convinced that the sale will be achieved, but the answers show that this is unlikely. The winning answers are much more assured and credible. The sales manager can be confident that there is no need to take action. When weaker—losing—answers are given, the salesperson may need to be counselled, and the sales manager works with the salesperson to improve performance. With very important orders, the sales manager may need to step in to secure the order. Also, the sales manager may need to monitor members of the sales team who are repeatedly losing orders, especially if they are with high value and/or important accounts. Ultimately, if this sequence continues, the salesperson may need to be moved to a more suitable job.

Evaluation and control of the total sales operation

Evaluation of the total personal selling function is necessary to assess its overall contribution to marketing strategy. The results of this assessment may lead to more cost-efficient means of servicing accounts being introduced (e.g. direct mail or telemarketing), the realization that the selling function is under-resourced, or the conclusion that the traditional form of sales organization is in need of reform. One company that suspected its salesforce had become complacent moved every salesperson to a different territory. Despite having to forge new customer relationships, sales increased by a quarter in the following year.

Evaluation of the personal selling function should also include assessing the quality of its relationship with marketing and other organizational units. Salespeople that manage the external relationship with distributors (e.g. retailers) must collaborate internally with their colleagues in marketing to agree joint business objectives and to develop marketing programmes (for example, new products and promotions) that meet the needs of distributors, as well as consumers, so that they are readily adopted by them. This means that close collaboration and good working relations are essential (Dewsnap and Jobber, 2002).

Personal selling enables individuals to interact and form bonds which can develop into long-term relationships that are beneficial for all parties concerned. Another element of the promotional mix which comes under the banner of direct communications is trade fairs and exhibitions, which are a platform for personal selling as well as other communication tools. Trade fairs and exhibitions are the topic in the next section.

Exhibitions and Trade Shows

Trade shows and **exhibitions** offer marketing managers a unique opportunity to engage with buyers, sellers and the competitors under one roof. These types of events are used in both industrial and consumer markets but are considered to be highly effective in the industrial buying process, second only to personal selling and ahead of direct mail and print advertising (Parasuraman, 1981). Indeed, exhibitions have been shown to increase the effectiveness of personal selling activities directly after the event (Smith, Gopalakrishna and Smith, 2004). A key role of trade fairs and exhibitions is to enable manufacturers, buyers, distributors, agents, present and future customers and media representatives to meet at a live event in a specific location (Fill, 2011).

The remainder of this section will focus on business-to-business trade shows and exhibitions as this element of the promotional mix is most frequently used in this context.

Why choose exhibitions and trade shows as part of the communication mix?

Good relationships are essential in industrial trade situations and these types of events have been found to be very useful for developing strong buyer–seller relationships (Geigenmüller, 2010).

Trade shows and exhibitions generally bring together all the major players in an industry, and in doing so provide an opportunity for buyers and sellers to engage across an industrial sector. There are many potential advantages; for example, buyers may spot new products; companies can interact with other companies working in the same industry, discuss issues and save money, as all companies are exhibiting in one place. Other potential benefits are: gathering market intelligence (Shipley and Wong, 1993) about competitors and industry trends (Hansen, 2004), and exchanging information and news about products, innovations, promotions and new marketing strategies. Exhibitions and trade shows are an ideal arena in which to demonstrate a company's new products, and despite the high cost associated with exhibiting, this is a widely used approach.

Events vary in style depending on the industry; for example, in the clothing industry a week-long series of events are held in leading fashion capitals around the world, such as New York, Paris, Milan and London. These events act as a showcase for designers, highlight new trends and present new product ranges. Buyers from around the world join the designers and media representatives in visiting runway shows. These events reveal cutting-edge designs that will shape what's in and what's out for the coming season. For many designers, a key aim is to be outstanding in order to maximize press coverage. See Exhibit 15.1 to see how Korean designers Gyo Kim and Yuni Choe used Nordic-style horned warrior helmets as inspiration for their designs shown at London Fashion Week.

Trade fair and exhibition objectives

There are various objectives that this element of the promotional mix can achieve and in doing so contribute to an IMC strategy:

- reach an audience with a distinct interest in the market and the products on display
- create awareness and develop relationships with new prospects
- strengthen existing customer relationships
- provide product demonstrations
- determine and stimulate needs of customers
- gather competitive intelligence
- introduce a new product
- recruit dealers or distributors
- maintain/improve company image
- deal with service and other customer problems
- generate a mailing list
- make a sale.

Research suggests that it is important to consider whether objectives are selling or non-selling oriented and whether they are aimed at new or existing customers (Bonoma, 1985). Despite the many possible objectives it has been found that the major objectives are:

- to generate leads/enquiries
- to introduce a new product or service
- because competitors are exhibiting
- to recruit dealers or distributors.

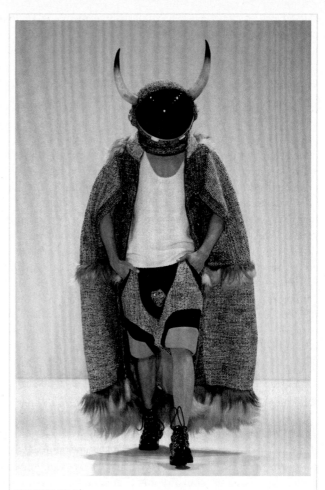

EXHIBIT 15.1
Designing with a '*respect of life and nature*'—Gyo Kim and Yuni Choe use a Nordic theme to stand out from the crowd

Planning for an exhibition

Success at an exhibition involves considerable pre-event planning. Clear objectives should be set, selection criteria for evaluating exhibition attendance determined, and design and promotional strategies decided. Pre-show promotions to attract visitors to the stand include direct mail, telephoning, a personal sales call before the event and an advertisement in the trade or technical press.

A high degree of professionalism is required by the staff who attend the exhibition stand. The characteristics of a good exhibitor have been found to be (Lancaster and Baron, 1977):

- exhibiting a wider range of products, particularly large items that cannot be demonstrated on a sales call
- staff always in attendance at the stand—visitors should never be told 'the person who covers that product is not here right now'
- well-informed staff
- informative literature available
- seating area or office provided on the stand
- refreshments provided.

Trade shows and exhibitions tend to be located where there are large conference facilities with the necessary prestige to attract industry leaders. For example, leading international auto shows are held in major cities such as Beijing, Chicago and Berlin. Events can also be located close to the centre of economic activity; for example, Slush is a fair that aims to bring together technology entrepreneurs, start-ups and technology innovators from across the world. It is held annually in Helsinki, Finland, because the Nordic region is known for being a hotbed of technology innovation, and many innovative products have emerged from this region, for example Rovio, Supercell, MySQL (Slush, 2015).

In order for an event to be successful, organizers have to ensure the location will be suitable and sufficiently attractive to potential attendees. For example, the organizers of the Spielwarenmesse international toy fair (Spielwarenmesse, n.d.) in Nüremberg, Germany, invest heavily to ensure that at the end of January each year over 2,800 exhibitors and 76,000 trade visitors from 120 nations visit 12 exhibition halls (each dedicated to a different type of toy-related product, such as dolls, hobbies, action toys, games, educational) at the fair to see over a million different products. Each company exhibiting at the fair then has to put together its own event plan, set objectives and decide how to allocate the budget to get best value. But there are many benefits, according to Pascal Bernard, CEO of Juratoys, France: '*Nuremberg is the place to be, since everyone is here. It is the only trade fair where you meet everyone from everywhere. Our company is represented with sales representatives from 50 countries here.*'

Trade fairs and exhibitions also need to be at a time in the calendar when buyers are considering new products and suppliers are able to attend. So the Nüremberg toy fair and others in this industry tend to be in the winter and spring after the busy end-of-year trading period around the festive season.

 Scan the QR code to see what is on offer at the World Travel Catering & Onboard Services EXPO.

Evaluating an exhibition

Post-show evaluation will examine performance against objectives. This is a learning exercise that will help to judge whether the objectives were realistic, how valuable the exhibition appears to have been and how well the company was represented.

Quantitative measures include:
- the number of visitors to the stand
- the number of key influencers/decision-makers who visited the stand
- how many leads/enquiries were generated
- the cost per lead/enquiry
- the number and value of orders
- the cost per order
- the number of new distributorships opened/likely to be opened.

Other more subjective, qualitative criteria include:
- the worth of competitive intelligence
- interest generated in the new products
- the cultivation of new/existing relationships
- the value of customer query and complaint handling
- the promotion of brand values.

Sales and marketing may not always agree on the key evaluation criteria to use. For example, sales may judge the exhibition on the number of leads while marketing may prefer to judge the show on the longer-term issue of the promotion of brand values (Blaskey, 1999).

Finally, since a major objective of many exhibitors is to stimulate leads and enquiries, mechanisms must be in place to ensure that these are followed up promptly. Furthermore, the leads generated at an exhibition can be used to build a marketing database for future direct mail campaigns. In the next section we examine direct marketing.

Direct Marketing

Direct marketing is a major component of the promotional mix and uses various media and technologies to precisely target consumers and request an immediate direct response. Originally, this communication method mainly involved **direct mail** and mail-order catalogues, but today's direct marketers use a wide range of media, including telemarketing, **direct response advertising**, the Internet and mobile devices. This section of the chapter links to discussion of 'big data' in Chapter 6 and digital marketing techniques in Chapter 16. Also see Marketing in Action 15.2 for further discussion of the challenges of the distinction between direct and digital marketing.

Direct marketing is no longer synonymous with 'junk mail', as it is a suite of communication techniques that are an integral part of the relationship marketing concept, where companies attempt to establish ongoing direct and profitable relationships with customers. As with all marketing communications, direct marketing campaigns should be integrated both within themselves and with other communication tools such as advertising, publicity and personal selling. Uncoordinated communication leads to blurred brand images, low impact and customer confusion.

Direct marketing attempts to acquire and retain customers by contacting them without the use of an intermediary and is usually designed to stimulate an immediate response from the recipient. A key advantage of direct marketing is it is easier to measure than mass-communication tools to determine the effectiveness of campaigns.

MARKETING IN ACTION 15.2
Has Direct Marketing been Given a One-way Ticket to Extinction?

Marketing is in flux as the use of digital technology intrudes into every aspect of marketing activity and every nook and cranny of human activity. Digital thinking has been heralded as an essential part of marketing strategy development and central to the mindset of marketers. Indeed, Ashley Friedlein, founder of Econsultancy, reported that *'if you don't "get digital" then you cannot be a modern marketer'*. Consequently, direct marketers are constantly wrestling with decisions about which media and which technology should be used to deliver which style of message in order to ensure the best *reach* and generate the highest level of returns. Marketers also have to contend with increasingly detailed information about the transient whims of the customers in their target markets, who are increasingly willing to publically parade the most intimate details of their daily lives online. So the

'Food Selfies' reveal digital behaviour

database that was at the heart of their campaigns is now overloaded with data, and the Internet holds a further vast store; anecdotally, there is more than a terabyte of information on the millennials alone.

There is no strong lead from industry bodies, either, to help beleaguered direct marketers choose between the old and the new approaches. For several years, the Direct Marketing Association (DMA) and the Institute of Direct and Digital Marketing (IDM) have been discussing whether to merge in order to form Europe's largest trade body in marketing. And while they have finally taken the plunge and merged, they will still serve the industry using their separate identities.

Confusion appears to reign, but before direct marketers abandon everything physical and move over completely to the digital world they should consider their capacity for being creative. Analysis of digital behaviour can be insular and inward facing; arguably selfies, pictures of food and pet videos reveal more about consumers than can currently be captured by machine code. So for the time being at least, the view of marketing of Giles Hedger (CSO, Leo Burnett) is likely to pervade: *'Marketing, however efficiently it runs, will never be about reductive computation . . . it will continue to be a test of the imagination, and there is no algorithm or app for that.'* Which in turn suggests that the principles of direct marketing are still very valid.

Based on: Friedlein (2013); Milington (2015); Hedger (2015)

A definition of direct marketing is:

The distribution of products, information and promotional benefits to target consumers through interactive communication in a way that allows response to be measured.

Direct marketing campaigns are not necessarily short-term, response-driven activities. More and more companies are using direct marketing to develop ongoing direct relationships with customers. Some marketers believe that the cost of attracting a new customer is five times that of retaining existing customers. Direct marketing techniques can be used effectively as part of an IMC campaign and also create further opportunities for selling more products using cross-selling and up-selling, which encourage the purchase of a wider range of products and higher value products respectively. Direct marketing covers a wide array of techniques, sometimes referred to as *media*. Each offers a marketing manager a set of potential benefits and limitations that need to be considered when planning to incorporate these techniques into an IMC campaign strategy.

Table 15.4 shows the main techniques/media used for direct marketing. The Internet and mobile are important platforms for direct marketing campaigns. How these techniques are used online and in mobile environments is discussed in more detail in Chapter 16.

TABLE 15.4 Benefits and limitations of direct communications techniques

Techniques/ media	Description	Benefits	Limitations
Direct mailing	Material sent via postal services direct to the recipient's home or business address, with the purpose of promoting a product and/or maintaining an ongoing relationship	– Relatively low cost; e.g. in business-to-business marketing, it might cost £50 to visit potential customers, and £5 to telephone them, but less than £1 to send out a mailing – Enables specific targeting of individuals and businesses	– Poor quality mailing lists, which can quickly become outdated by changes, e.g. moving location – Cost of creating, organizing and maintaining database
Email marketing	Material sent to the recipient's email address for the purpose of promoting a product and/or maintaining an ongoing relationship, linked directly to a company's website to foster further engagement with the brand and also the making of purchases	– Relatively low cost – Enables specific targeting of individuals and businesses – Global reach facilitates inclusion of multimedia and interactive features (Ellis-Chadwick and Doherty, 2012) – Highly flexible – Permission emails can help build relationships	– Poor quality mailing lists, email address changes – Reaching the recipient, as often treated as unsolicited junk mail
Telemarketing	Makes use of telecommunications and information technologies to conduct marketing and sales activities via telephone. Can be inbound telemarketing when a prospect contacts the company by telephone, or outbound when the company calls the prospect	– Versatility; e.g. telemarketing can support direct marketing, follow up sales leads, establish customer contact, validate information – Cost-effective – Accountable – Relative low cost – Less time-intensive than personal sales calls – Technology can automate and manage campaigns	– Intrusive and is often seen as an annoyance by customers – Lacks visual impact and stimulation – Cost per contact greater than direct mail

»

Techniques/ media	Description	Benefits	Limitations
Direct response advertising	Appears in the prime media—e.g. the web, TV, print media—but differs from standard advertising as it is designed to elicit a direct response such as an order, enquiry or request for a visit. Often a freephone telephone number is included in the advertisement and a website address	– Highly measurable in terms of performance of a campaign. e.g. Macmillan Cancer Support ran a direct-response campaign to drive more callers to use its financial and emotional support services; its 'Good Day, Bad Day' campaign significantly increased calls to its helplines (Fahy and Jobber, 2012)	– Application to certain product types can be perceived as difficult – Response rates can be low
Catalogue marketing	The sale of products through catalogues distributed to agents and customers, by mail, at stores or online	– Convenient way of selecting products at home – Accessibility to remote rural locations; provides valuable services; removes long distance travel to stores – Unlimited displays of product, as catalogues do not have any physical space restrictions – Distribution can be centralized, lowering costs	– Cost of catalogue production – Inflexible: print versions of catalogues require regular updating, particularly when selling fashion items; this issue has been circumvented to an extent by online catalogues – Costs associated with managing the flow of goods and return products

Direct Marketing Campaigns

Overall, direct marketing is growing in popularity as a communication tool in both consumer and industrial markets. However, there is wide variation in use of the different direct marketing techniques set out in Table 15.4.

Drivers of direct marketing are:

- *Market and media fragmentation* has meant the effectiveness of mass-marketing techniques (e.g. using television and other broadcast media) has declined, as the requirement to reach target segments with highly individualized needs has increased. Consequently, the importance of direct marketing media which can not only target specialized niche targets but also distribute highly personalized appeals has grown. Direct response advertising is more effective since market niches can be tightly targeted.

- *Technology advances* have led to the increasing sophistication of software, allowing the generation of personalized letters and telephone scripts, and enabling direct marketers to develop highly targeted and sophisticated campaigns. Databases and data warehouses hold detailed information on individuals and businesses and, once analyzed, this enhances targeting. Customer relationship management software has enabled companies to manage one-to-one relationships with huge numbers of consumers. Automated telephone systems make it possible to handle dozens of calls simultaneously, reducing the risk of losing potential customers. Furthermore, developments in technology in telephone, cable and satellite television and the Internet have triggered the rise in home-based electronic shopping.

- *Emerging analytical techniques* mean that by using geodemographic analysis, households can be classified into a neighbourhood type—for example, 'modern private housing, young families' or 'private flats, single people'. These, in turn, can be cross-referenced with product usage, media usage and lifestyle statements to create market segments that can be targeted by direct mail (see Chapter 7 for more detailed discussion).

Marketing database

The **marketing database** is central to direct marketing, as activities depend on customer information. A marketing database holds customer data—for example, names, addresses, telephone numbers, and lifestyle and transactional data. Information such as the types of purchase, frequency of purchase, purchase value and responsiveness to promotional offers may be held. By using the marketing database companies can take an interactive approach towards developing highly targeted direct communication campaigns using individually addressable marketing media and channels (such as mail, telephone and the salesforce) to provide information to a target audience.

Some key characteristics of marketing databases are that, first, they allow direct communication with customers through a variety of media, including direct mail, telemarketing and direct response advertising. Second, it usually requires the customer to respond in a way that allows the company to take action (such as contact by telephone, sending out literature or arranging sales visits). Third, it must be possible to trace the response back to the original communication (Fletcher, Wheeler and Wright, 1990). Sophisticated databases provide the capability of storing and analyzing large quantities of data from diverse sources and presenting information in a convenient, accessible and useful format (Linton, 1995). The creation of a database relies on the systematic collection and storage of information. Table 15.5 shows examples of basic sources and types of data.

TABLE 15.5 Basic Sources and types of data	
Data source	**Examples of data type**
Company records	Purchase behaviour, name, address, telephone number
Warranty and guarantee cards	Product types
Enquiries	Clarifications of data held; e.g. an account holder at HSBC bank might enquire about a new loan, at which point credit and personal finance data will be updated
Exchanging data with other companies	Loyalty cards like Nectar gather and share information between companies in the group (e.g. American Express, Sainsbury's, BP, Ford Hertz, Viking Direct)
Salesforce records	Account details, customer leads, past sales data
Application forms	Personal or business data
Complaints	Reasons for returns, outcomes
Responses to direct marketing activities	Sales promotions, direct marketing: e.g. timing, frequency, purchase activity
Organized events	At corporate events/conferences, business cards are often collected
Website registrations	Personal data, email addresses
Emails	Requirements, requests, qualitative data

Businesses across the globe have benefited from the use and management of data but as information technology has continued to expand the collection and distribution of data, companies also have to deal with the information overload. See Chapter 6 for further discussion.

 Scan the QR code and identify the different situations in which American Express promises that 'the journey never stops'.

Typical information stored in a database

Perhaps the most important thing to acknowledge about a marketing database is that it is a systematic way of gathering data that can be collated and analyzed to provide information that has implications for marketing campaigns. Figure 15.4 shows typical information that is recorded in a database. This is described in more detail below (Stone, Davies and Bond (1995).

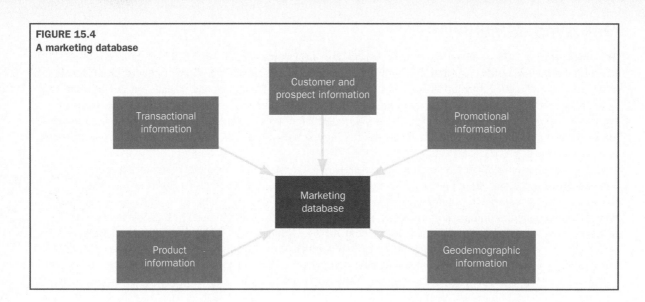

FIGURE 15.4
A marketing database

Customer and prospect information

This provides the basic data required to access customers and prospects (e.g. name, home and email addresses, telephone number) and contains their general behavioural characteristics (e.g. psychographic and behavioural data). For organizational markets, information on key decision-makers and influencers, and the choice criteria they use would also be stored.

Transactional information

Past transactions are a key indicator of likely future transactions. Transactional data must be sufficiently detailed to allow FRAC (frequency, recency, amount and category) information to be extracted for each customer. *Frequency* refers to how often a customer buys. Both the average frequency and the trend (is the customer tending to buy more or less frequently?) is of use to the direct marketer. *Recency* measures when the customer last bought. If customers are waiting longer before they rebuy (i.e. recency is increasing) the reasons for this (e.g. less attractive offers or service problems) need to be explored. *Amount* measures how much a customer has bought and is usually recorded in value terms. Analysis of this data may reveal that 20 per cent of customers are accounting for 80 per cent of the value of transactions. Finally, *category* defines the type of product being bought. Cross-analyzing category data with type of customer (e.g. geodemographics or lifestyle data) can reveal the customer profile most likely to buy a particular product. Also, promotions can be targeted at those individuals known to be interested in buying from a particular product category.

Promotional information

This covers information on what promotional campaigns have been run, who has responded to them and what the overall results were in terms of contacts, sales and profits. The database will contain information on which customers were targeted, and the media and contact strategy employed.

Product information

This information would include which products have been promoted, who responded, when and from where.

EXHIBIT 15.2
Ryman's stationers gathers detailed information when opening business accounts

Geodemographic information

Information about the geographic areas of customers and prospects, and the social, lifestyle or business category they belong to would be stored. By including postcodes in the address of customers and employing the services of an agency that conducts geodemographic analysis (such as ACORN) a customer profile would be built up. Direct mail could then be targeted at people with similar geodemographic profiles.

The main application of marketing databases

Marketing databases have the following uses.

- Developing targeted direct marketing campaigns: for example, a special offer on garden tools from a mail-order company could be targeted at those people who have purchased gardening products in the past. Another example would be a car dealer which, by holding a database of customers' names and addresses and dates of car purchase, could use direct mail to promote service offers and new model launches.
- Strengthening relationships with customers: for example, direct marketing techniques can be used strategically to improve customer retention with long-term programmes established to maximize customer lifetime value. Mini Case 15.1 shows how a database could be used by a retailer to develop customer loyalty.

MINI CASE 15.1
Using a Marketing Database in Retailing

Marketing databases offer great potential for planning and developing integrated marketing communications campaigns. Suppose a retailer wanted to increase sales and profits using a database. How might this happen? First, the retailer analyses its database to find distinct groups of customers for whom the retailer has the potential to offer superior value. The identification of these target market segments allows tailored products, services and communications to be aimed at them.

The purchasing patterns of individuals are established by means of a loyalty card programme, which enables companies to use the data generated to work out patterns of shopper behaviour at a very detailed level.

Retailers might argue their loyalty schemes' aim is to improve customer loyalty by rewarding various shopping behaviours, but the reality is that such schemes allow customers to be tracked by frequency of visit, expenditure per visit and expenditure per product category. Loyalty schemes are less about garnering customer allegiance to a particular brand and more about creating an opportunity for companies to capture data that can be used for future marketing initiatives. Retailers can gain an understanding of the types of products that are purchased together. For example, Boots, the UK retailer, uses its Advantage card loyalty scheme (which has 15 million active members) to conduct these kinds of analysis. For example, analysis of Advantage card data revealed a link between the purchase of digital photo frames and new-baby products. Because its products are organized along category lines, it never occurred to the retailer to create a special offer linked to picture frames for the baby products buyer, yet these are the kinds of products new parents are likely to want.

If a retailer's customers are classified into market segments based on their potential, their degree of loyalty, and whether they are predominantly price- or promotion-sensitive, analysis of loyalty data means it is possible to tailor the marketing strategy at a very personal level. For example, to trade up high-potential, promotion-sensitive, low-loyalty shoppers who do their main shopping elsewhere, high-value manufacturers' coupons for main shopping products are mailed every two months until the consumer is traded up to a different group. Also, high-loyalty customers can be targeted for special treatment such as receiving a customer magazine.

»

The Tesco Clubcard gathers a rich stream of information from many millions of Clubcard members in the UK and overseas, which is then used, for example, to: define segments—for example, discount-driven 'price sensitives', 'foodies', 'heavy category users' and 'brand loyalists'; test consumer response to promotions; test the effects of different prices and use of different media; and communicate more effectively with consumers. Product assortments in stores can also be fine-tuned according to the buying habits of customers. Both schemes have worked hard to tailor their rewards offered to consumers. For example, Boots launched a Health Club and a Parenting Club to offer card holders rewards relevant to their lifestyles and interests. Tesco Clubcard enables its users to collect green Clubcard points when customers use their own shopping bags.

The success of the Boots Advantage card and the Tesco Clubcard continues to prompt other retailers to launch loyalty cards: for example, Waitrose, the high-quality UK supermarket, has invested in developing a loyalty card as part of its strategy to reward customers and Morrisons' Match & More card. Rewarding customers has been found to be a highly successful strategy for improving ROI. Staples, the office and business stationery supplier, has introduced a reward card for targeting small businesses and uses the data on purchasing patterns to drive online promotional offers. Nectar is Britain's biggest loyalty card with over 18 million subscribers. It started as a joint initiative launched by its founders (Sainsbury's, BP, Barclaycard and Debenhams) and is constantly expanding its company membership in order to extend the rewards it can offer to signed-up shoppers. For example, Nectar points can be collected from Sainsbury's, eBay, Amazon, Sky and other Nectar member companies and then be used to buy goods (e.g. easyJet flights). In the early days when the technology needed to set up loyalty schemes was expensive, only the largest retailers offered loyalty cards but implementation costs have fallen dramatically, which has meant that more companies in different industries are developing such schemes. For example, Tata Group, which is India's biggest family conglomerate, has set up a loyalty scheme modelled on Nectar.

Questions:

1   Why do companies launch loyalty cards?
2   Explain the type of data you might need to gather if you are wishing to improve customer retention.

Based on: Mitchell (2002); James (2003); Barnes (2005); McCawley (2006); Murphy (2008); Finch (2009); Charles (2011); Clews (2011); The Economist (2011)

- Developing an information resource for use in direct marketing campaigns. For this various techniques are employed:
  - *Direct mail*: a database can be used to select customers for mailings.
  - *Telemarketing*: a database can store telephone numbers so that customers and prospects can be contacted. Also when customers contact the company by telephone, relevant information can be stored, including when the next contact should be made.
  - *Distributor management systems*: a database can be the foundation on which information is provided to distributors and their performance monitored.
  - *Loyalty marketing*: highly loyal customers can be selected from the database for special treatment as a reward for their loyalty.
  - *Target marketing*: other groups of individuals or businesses can be targeted as a result of analyzing the database. For example, buyer behaviour information stored by supermarkets can be used to target special promotions to those individuals likely to be receptive to them. For example, a consumer promotion for organic baby foods could be sent exclusively to mothers with young babies.
  - *Campaign planning*: using the database as a foundation for sending consistent and coordinated campaigns and messages to individuals and market segments.
  - *Marketing evaluation*: by recording responses to marketing mix inputs (e.g. price promotions, advertising messages and product offers), it is possible to assess how effective different approaches are to varying individuals and market segments.

The marketing database is at the heart of the customer relationship management systems that use databases as the foundation for managing customer relationships. (See Chapter 10 for further discussion of CRM.)

Managing a Direct Marketing Campaign

Direct marketing can be very effective when integrated with other elements of the promotional mix and used to support a coherent *marketing strategy*. In Chapter 13 on integrated marketing communications it was stressed that all of the communication tools should send a consistent message and reinforce other elements of the marketing mix (product, place and price). Following this logic, messages sent out using various direct marketing media should also form a coherent whole. For example, information disseminated through advertising should be consistent with that sent out via a direct mail campaign. In the past there was sometimes a tendency for direct marketing campaigns not to use multiple contacts or multiple media. However, increased use of digital channels gives direct marketers the opportunity to use a combination of media in sequence to achieve their objectives. For example, a business-to-business company marketing a new adhesive might place a direct response advertisement in trade magazines to stimulate trial and orders. A response coupon, freephone telephone number and email address would be provided, and prospects invited to choose their most convenient method of contact. An inbound telemarketing team would be trained to receive calls and take either orders or requests for samples for trial. Another team would deal with mail and email correspondence. An outbound telemarketing team would follow up prospects judged to be of small and medium potential and the salesforce targeted at large potential customers and prospects.

Accordingly direct marketers need to understand how a product is positioned and its target market as it is crucial that messages sent out as part of a direct marketing campaign do not conflict with those communicated by other channels such as advertising or the salesforce. The integrating mechanism is a clear definition of marketing strategy. Figure 15.5 shows the steps in the management of a direct marketing campaign.

In essence, the key stages in a direct marketing campaign are similar to those in a mass communication plan (as discussed in Chapter 14). However, there are certain differences at each of the stages.

Identify and understand target audience

These are the groups of people at whom the direct marketing campaign is aimed (targeting strategies are described in Chapter 7). Lifestyle is often targeted, but a particularly useful method of segmentation for direct marketing purposes involves considering the following groups:

- *Competitors' customers*: all people who buy the types of product our company produces but from our competitors.
- *Prospects*: people who have not bought from our company before but qualify as potential purchasers (e.g. our customers are large companies, therefore other large companies should be targeted).
- *Enquirers*: people who have contacted the organization and shown interest in one or more products but, as yet, have not bought.
- *Lapsed customers*: people who have purchased in the past but appear to have ceased buying.
- *Referrals*: people who have been recommended to the organization as potential customers.
- *Existing customers*: people who are continuing to buy.

Read Marketing in Action 15.3 to appreciate the usefulness of target audience identification to Butchers & Bicycles.

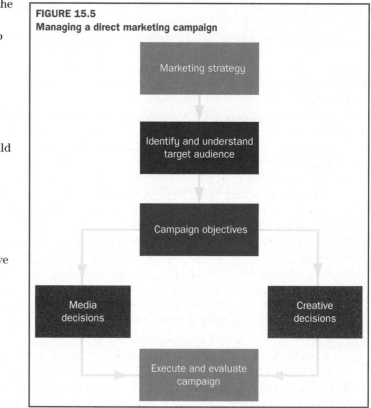

FIGURE 15.5
Managing a direct marketing campaign

- Marketing strategy
- Identify and understand target audience
- Campaign objectives
- Media decisions
- Creative decisions
- Execute and evaluate campaign

MARKETING IN ACTION 15.3
Society Profits from Cyclists, but Who is Doing the Driving?

Morten Wagener, Morten Mogensen and Jakob Munk are Danish designers and innovators who founded the cargo and personal transportation bicycle company, Butchers & Bicycles. They identified a business opportunity to improve the future of urban transport. The idea was that most of the trikes (three-wheeled bikes) on the market lacked good design, manoeuvrability and styling. With their backgrounds in engineering, the partners set out to design a new trike that would meet the needs of the target market, which their research identified as well-educated individuals who were very interested in aesthetics. The team was convinced that trikes were one of the answers to future urban transportation problems. So they decided to develop the best trike they could in

terms of quality, style, design, manoeuvrability, safety and a great riding experience. Each trike is hand made, and there is a waiting time of up to two months between order and delivery.

From a marketing perspective, one of the differentiating factors of the Butchers & Bicycles product is the quality of the ride (compared with that of competing products). The team coined the slogan 'built-to-tilt', because even though the vehicle is a trike, it feels like a two-wheeled bicycle to ride. The challenge was how to go to market with a marketing budget close to zero?

The target group had been clear from the beginning: consumers who were lifestyle oriented, such as readers of *Monocle* and *Wallpaper* magazines—first movers who appreciate quality and are willing to pay for it. Many of these customers were young urban families that might buy a Butchers & Bicycles trike as an alternative to a second car. Also, Copenhagen (Denmark's capital city) is number one in investment in cycling infrastructure, which makes it easier for families to adopt this form of transport.

How to reach the target market was initially a challenge, but the team at Butchers & Bicycles invested in the design of the website and a professional promotional video, which has reached 170,000 people since its launch. It also has Facebook and Instagram pages, which are used to build and develop customer relationships. This approach is rather organic insofar as the company has built a reputation through word of mouth and social media, but it has proved to be highly effective.

Based On: Butchers & Bicycles (n.d.); Colville-Andersen (2015)

Once a target group is identified, the marketing manager has to consider how to access the group. This may be done through existing Internet information from the CRM system and marketing database, which will provide a list of existing contacts, or may come from an external list broker. Experian is a global provider of individual and company information for direct marketing initiatives. Understanding current trends and changes in buying behaviour is important. For example, consumers have become increasingly in favour of opening direct mail letters, if they perceive the offer is relevant to them. In fact, consumers seem to have become less cynical about this form of communication and are often prompted to open the mailing to see if there are any reward vouchers or coupons (Handley, 2011).

Scan the QR code to see how Butchers & Bicycles created a low-budget promotional film to convey the benefits of buying one of its trikes.

Campaign objectives

Campaign objectives vary and may focus on financial goals—sales, profits and return on investment; marketing goals—acquire or retain customers, or to generate enquiries; communication goals—create awareness or change beliefs. However, one of the benefits of direct marketing is its capacity to deliver against short-term objectives, which are easily measured and evaluated. For example, the Spanish car maker, Seat, targeted a select list of UK companies in an effort to break into the lucrative fleet car business. A combined direct mail and press campaign generated a 44 per cent increase in new car sales (Fahy and Jobber, 2012).

Acquisition objectives can be costly as it is more expensive to attract new customers than develop and keep existing customers. So, a consideration when setting this type of campaign objectives is the concept of *lifetime value*. This measures the profits that can be expected from customers over their expected life with a company. Banks know, for example, that gaining student accounts has very high lifetime value since switching between banks is unusual. This means that the allowable marketing cost per acquisition (or how much a company can afford to spend to acquire a new customer) can be quite high. If the calculation was based on potential profits while a student, the figure would be much lower. The establishment of a marketing database can, over time, provide valuable information on buying patterns, which aids the calculation of lifetime value.

Retention objectives focus on keeping customers and can have a direct impact on profitability. A study conducted by PricewaterhouseCoopers showed that a 2 per cent increase in customer retention has the same profit impact as a 10 per cent reduction in overhead costs (Murphy, 1997). Customer loyalty programmes have blossomed as a result, with direct marketing playing a key role. Retention programmes are aimed at maximizing a customer's lifetime value to the company. Maintaining a long-term relationship with a customer provides the opportunity to up-sell, cross-sell and renew business. Up-selling involves the promotion of higher-value products—for example, a more expensive car. Cross-selling entails the switching of customers to other product categories, as when a music club promotes a book collection. Renewal involves the timing of communication to existing customers when they are about to repurchase. For example, car dealers often send direct mail promotional material two years after the purchase of a car, since many people change cars after that period.

Media decisions

Direct marketers have a large number of techniques and media which they can use to reach customers and prospects. Table 15.4 earlier in this chapter shows the main techniques/media used for direct marketing and the benefits and problems of using each of them.

Creative decisions

Most direct marketing campaigns have different objectives from those of advertising. Whereas advertising usually attempts to create awareness and position the image of a brand in prospects' minds, the aim of most direct marketing is to make a sale. It is more orientated to immediate action than advertising. Recipients of direct marketing messages (particularly through direct mail) need to see a clear benefit in responding. Costa Coffee Club offers its members (in return for signing up via the website and providing personal data) five points per pound on purchases. The Costa Coffee Club has worked very well and has a positive impact on customers' frequency of consumption (Baker, 2012).

Creative decisions will be captured using a creative brief, which is a document that usually contains details of specific communications objectives, product benefits, target market analysis, details of the offer being made, the message that is to be communicated and the action plan (i.e. how the campaign will be run).

Executing and evaluating the campaign

Execution of the campaign may be in-house or through the use of a specialist agency. Direct marketing activity usually has clearly defined short-term objectives against which performance can be measured. Some of the most frequently used measurements are:
- response rate (the proportion of contacts responding)
- total sales (volume and value)
- number of contacts purchasing
- sales rate (percentage of contacts purchasing)
- number of enquiries
- enquiry rate

- cost per contact
- cost per enquiry
- cost per sale
- conversion rate from enquiry to sale
- average order value
- renewal rate
- repeat purchase rate.

Direct marketers should bear in mind the longer-term effects of their activities. A campaign may seemingly be unprofitable in the short term, but when renewals and repeat purchases are taken into account the long-term value of the campaign may be highly positive.

Ethical Issues in Direct Communications

Personal selling and direct marketing methods are increasingly subject to scrutiny by industry bodies, consumer groups, governments and ultimately the national and international legal systems. Under the heading of personal selling deception, the hard sell, bribery and reciprocal buying are issues which marketing managers should plan to avoid. The implications of each of these issues are:

- *Deception.* A dilemma that, sooner or later, faces most salespeople is the choice of telling the customer the whole truth and risk losing the sale, or misleading the customer to clinch it. The deception may take the form of exaggeration, lying or withholding important information that significantly reduces the appeal of the product. Such actions should be avoided by influencing salespersons' behaviour by training, by sales management encouraging ethical behaviour, by their own actions and words, and by establishing codes of conduct for their salespeople. Nevertheless, sometimes evidence of malpractice in selling is discovered, and action taken to recompense the injured party; for example, UK banks Barclays, HSBC, Lloyds and Royal Bank of Scotland have set aside billions of pounds in order to compensate customers for mis-selling loan insurance (Gard, 2015).
- *The hard sell.* Personal selling is criticized for employing high-pressure sales tactics to close a sale. Car dealerships and the timeshare industry have been deemed unethical in using hard-sell tactics to pressure customers into making a quick decision on a complicated purchase that may involve expensive credit facilities.
- *Bribery.* This is the act of giving payment, gifts or other inducements to secure a sale. Bribes are considered unethical as they violate the principle of fairness in commercial negotiations. A major problem is that in some countries bribes are an accepted part of business life: to compete, bribes are necessary. So, organizations in such a situation face an ethical dilemma. On the one hand they will be castigated in their home country if they use bribes and this becomes public knowledge. On the other hand, without the bribe the organization could be operating at a commercial disadvantage. Taking an ethical stance may cause difficulties in the short term but in the long run the positive publicity that can follow is likely to be of greater benefit.

Direct marketing methods also face different types of ethical issues associated with consumer concerns:

- *Poorly targeted direct mail.* Although designed to foster closer relationships in targeting of consumers, some direct mail is of little relevance to the recipient and can be a clear source of irritation and distress. As more attention is paid to the natural environment, the waste of natural resources caused by poorly directed mailshots is a questionable practice (Reed, 2008).
- *Intrusive nature of telemarketing calls.* Consumers complain about the annoyance caused by unsolicited telephone calls pressuring them to buy products at inconvenient times. Technological development has engineered the capacity to take this to a new level—for example with robo calls (via computerized auto-diallers)—and whilst some countries legislate against this style of communication, there are still some types of call that manage to circumvent these controls.
- *Invasion of privacy.* Many consumers fear that every time they subscribe to a website, club, society or magazine, apply for a credit card, or buy anything by telephone or direct mail, their names, addresses and other information will be entered on to a database that will guarantee a flood of mail from the supplier.

The direct marketing industry and governments are responding to the public concerns noted above.

When you have read this chapter

Discover further resources and test your understanding: McGraw-Hill **Connect**™ is a digital teaching and learning environment that improves performance over a variety of critical outcomes; it can be tailored, is easy to use and is proven effective. **LearnSmart**™ is the most widely used and intelligent adaptive learning resource that is proven to strengthen memory recall, improve course retention and boost grades. Fuelled by **LearnSmart**™, **SmartBook**™ is the first and only adaptive reading experience available today.

Review

1 **The key direct marketing communication tools: personal selling, exhibitions, direct marketing**
   - Direct communications enable a direct dialogue between buyers and sellers; moreover they do not involve the purchase of media space.
   - Personal selling allows buyers and seller to communicate in a face-to-face manner, which facilitates relationship development but from a marketing management perspective is relatively costly.
   - Exhibitions are an opportunity to bring together all of the buyers and sellers in a particular market under one roof and create an environment for furthering customer relationships, enhancing corporate ideas and gathering competitive information.
   - Direct marketing is a means of creating a dialogue between buyers and sellers, using various techniques, such as direct mail, digital marketing, telemarketing and catalogue marketing.

2 **Characteristics of modern selling**
   - The characteristics are customer acquisition, retention and deletion, customer relationship management, adding value and satisfying customer needs.

3 **The stages in the selling process**
   - Salespeople should prepare for selling by gaining knowledge of their own and competitors' products, planning sales presentations, setting up call objectives and seeking to understand buyer behaviour.

4 **The key tasks of sales management**
   - The tasks of a sales manager are to understand marketing strategy; set personal selling objectives and strategies; design the salesforce; manage the salesforce by setting objectives, organizing recruitment and training, setting reward structures and performance measures for salespeople; and evaluation and control of the total sales operation.

5 **The objectives, conduct and evaluation of exhibitions**
   - Objectives of exhibitions can be classified as selling objectives to current customers (e.g. stimulate extra sales), selling objectives to potential customers (e.g. determine needs and transmit benefits), non-selling objectives to current customers (e.g. maintain image and gather competitive intelligence) and non-selling objectives to potential customers (e.g. foster image building and gather competitive intelligence).

- Staff conduct at an exhibition should ensure that there is always someone in attendance to talk to visitors, staff should be well-informed, provide informative literature and a seating area/office, and refreshments should be provided.
- Evaluation of an exhibition includes number of visitors/key influencers/decision-makers who visit the stand, number of leads/enquiries/orders/new dealerships generated and cost per lead/enquiry/order. Qualitative evaluation includes the worth of competitive intelligence, and interest generated in new products.

6 The meaning of direct marketing

- Direct marketing is the distribution of products, information and promotional benefits to target customers through interactive communication in a way that allows response to be measured.
- It includes such methods as direct mail, telemarketing, direct response advertising, catalogue marketing and digital media.

7 The reasons for the growth of direct marketing activity

- Direct marketing activity has grown because of market and media fragmentation, developments in technology, the list explosion, sophisticated analytical techniques, and coordinated marketing systems.

8 The importance of database marketing

- Database marketing is an approach to marketing communications that targets individuals using various media channels.
- Databases are central to all forms of direct marketing activity as they store customer contact and behavioural data which helps marketing strategy and planning; for example, when planning promotional campaigns designed to target very loyal customers who are to receive special treatment. Databases are useful for planning campaigns as they hold details of past customer behaviour, e.g. responses to price promotions.

9 How to manage a direct marketing campaign

- A direct marketing campaign should not be designed in isolation but based on a clear understanding of marketing strategy in particular positioning. Then the steps are as follows.
- Identify and understand the target audience: never sell to a stranger. Who is to be reached, their motives and choice criteria need to be understood.
- Campaign objectives: these can be expressed in financial (e.g. sales), in marketing (e.g. acquire or retain customers) or communication (e.g. change beliefs) terms.
- Media decisions: major media options are direct mail, telemarketing, mobile marketing, direct response advertising, catalogue marketing and the Internet
- Creative decisions: a creative brief will include a statement of communication objectives, product benefits (and weaknesses), target market analysis, development of the offer, communication of the message, and an action plan.
- Execute and evaluate the campaign: execution of the campaign may be in-house or through the use of a specialist agency. Evaluation should be taken against defined objectives such as total sales, number of enquiries, cost per sale and repeat purchase rate.

10 Ethical issues in direct communications

- Using direct communication tools can mean marketing managers face difficult choices. Personal selling has been criticized for using deception, bribery, and the hard sell in order to secure sales orders. Direct marketing tools can be seen by customers as poorly targeted, a waste of natural resources and an intrusion of privacy.

Key Terms

buying signals statements by a buyer that indicate s/he is interested in buying

campaign objectives goals set by an organization in terms of, for example, sales, profits, customers won or retained, or awareness creation

customer benefits those things that a customer values in a product; customer benefits derive from product features

customer relationship management the methodologies, technologies and e-commerce capabilities used by companies to manage customer relationships

direct mail material sent through the postal service to the recipient's house or business address promoting a product and/or maintaining an ongoing relationship

direct response advertising the use of the prime advertising media such as television, newspapers and magazines to elicit an order, enquiry or request for a visit

e-commerce involves all electronically mediated transactions between an organization and any third party it deals with, including exchange of information

exhibition an event that brings buyers and sellers together in a commercial setting

key account management an approach to selling that focuses resources on major customers and uses a team selling approach

marketing database an interactive approach to marketing that uses individually addressable marketing media and channels to provide information to a target audience, stimulate demand and stay close to customers

product features the characteristics of a product that may or may not convey a customer benefit

salesforce evaluation the measurement of salesperson performance so that strengths and weaknesses can be identified

target accounts organizations or individuals whose custom the company wishes to obtain

telemarketing a marketing communications system whereby trained specialists use telecommunications and information technologies to conduct marketing and sales activities

trade show similar to an exhibition as it brings together buyers, sellers and competitors under one roof, but is not open to the public

Study Questions

1. Select a car with which you are familiar. Identify its features and translate them into customer benefits.

2. Imagine you are face-to-face with a customer for that car. Write down five objections to purchase and prepare convincing responses to them.

3. You are the new sales manager of a company selling natural ingredients to the pharmaceutical industry. Discuss how you would motivate and manage your salesforce.

4. From your own personal experience, do you consider salespeople to be unethical? Can you remember any sales encounters when you have been subject to unethical behaviour?

5. Explain the benefits of using exhibitions for buyers and sellers.

6. Discuss the importance of setting clear marketing objectives for trade fairs and exhibitions.

7. Discuss the challenges a direct marketer might face while trying to distinguish between direct and digital marketing.

8. Define direct marketing. Identify the different forms of direct marketing. Give an example of how at least three of them can be integrated into a marketing communications campaign.

9. Discuss why databases are important for marketing communication campaigns and why. Explain the types of information that are recorded in a database.

10. What are the stages of managing a direct marketing campaign? Why is the concept of lifetime value of a customer important when designing a campaign?

Recommended Reading

Dewsnap, B. and D. Jobber (2009) An exploratory study of sales-marketing integrative devices, *European Journal of Marketing* 43 (7/8), 985–1007.

Hillebrand, B., J. Nijholt and E. Nijssen, E. (2011) Exploring CRM effectiveness: An institutional theory perspective, *Journal of the Academy of Marketing Science* 39, 592–608.

Jobber, D. and G. Lancaster (2015) *Selling and Sales Management*, Pearson.

Johnston, M. and G. Marshall (2013) *Sales Force Management: Leadership, Innovation, Technology*, 11th edn., Routledge.

Marshall, G., W. Moncrief, J. Rudd and N. Lee (2012), Revolution in Sales: The Impact of Social Media and Related Technology on the Selling Environment, *Journal of Personal Selling & Sales Management* 32(3), 349–363.

Wilson, H., E. Daniel and M. McDonald (2002) Factors for success in customer relationship management systems, *Journal of Marketing Management* 18(1/2), 193–200.

References

Adams, J. S. (1965) Inequity in Social Exchange, in Berkowitz, L. (ed.) *Advances in Experimental Social Psychology 2*, New York: Academic Press.

Agarwal, A., E. Harmon and M. Viertier (2009) *Cutting Sales Costs, not revenues*, McKinsey & Company. http://www.mckinsey.com/insights/marketing_sales/cutting_sales_costs_not_revenues (accessed 10 May 2015).

Baker, R. (2012) Costa eyes loyalty scheme for vending business, *Marketing Week*, 10 January.

Barnes, R. (2005) Nectar Readies B2B Loyalty Card Launch, *Marketing*, 19 January, 14.

Blaskey, J. (1999) Proving Your Worth, *Marketing*, 25 February, 35–6.

Bonoma, T. V. (1985) Get more out of your trade show, in Gumpert, D. E. (ed.) *The Marketing Renaissance*, New York: Wiley.

Brooke, K. (2002) B2B and B2C Marketing is not so Different, *Marketing Business*, July/August, 39.

Butchers & Bicycles (n.d.) About, http://www.butchersandbicycles.com

Chaffey, D. and F. E. Ellis-Chadwick (2012) *Digital Marketing: Strategy, Implementation and Practice*, 5th edn, Harlow: Pearson.

Charles, G. (2011) Waitrose unveils loyalty-card programme in strategic shift, *Marketing*, 26 October, 1.

Clews, M.-L. (2011) The evolution of loyalty, *Marketing Week*, August, 42–3.

Colville-Andersen, M. (2015) The Most Bike-Friendly Cities on the planet, *Wired*, 6 February.

Cron, W. L., G. Marshall, J. Singh, R. L. Spiro and H. Sujan (2005) Salesperson Selection, Training and Development: Trends, Implications and Research Opportunities, *Journal of Personal Selling and Sales Management* 25(2), 123–36.

Dewsnap, B. and D. Jobber (2002) A Social Psychological Model of Relations Between Marketing and Sales, *European Journal of Marketing* 36(7/8), 874–94.

Ellis-Chadwick, F. E. and N. F. Doherty (2012) Web advertising: the role of e-mail marketing, *Journal of Business Research* 65(6), 843–848.

Fahy, J. and D. Jobber (2012) *Foundations of Marketing*, Maidenhead: McGraw-Hill, 262.

Fill, C. (2011) *Essentials of Marketing Communications*, Harlow: FT/Prentice Hall, 312.

Finch, J. (2009) Tesco Sales Top £1 billion a Week, *The Guardian*, 22 April, 22.

Fletcher, K., C. Wheeler and J. Wright (1990) The Role and Status of UK Database Marketing, *Quarterly Review of Marketing*, Autumn, 7–14.

Friedlein, A. (2013) Our Modern Marketing Manifesto: will you sign? Econsultancy, 8 May. https://econsultancy.com/blog/62668-our-modern-marketing-manifesto-will-you-sign

Gard, S. (2015) New Mis-Selling Scandal set to Rock Barclays, HSbC Holdings plc, Lloyds Banking group & Royal Bank of Scotland Plc, The Motely Fool, 2 February. http://www.fool.co.uk/investing/2015/02/02/

new-mis-selling-scandal-set-to-rock-barclays-plc-hsbc-holdings-plc-lloyds-banking-group-plc-royal-bank-of-scotland-group-plc

Geigenmüller, A. (2010) The role of virtual trade fairs in relationship value creation, *Journal of Business and Industrial Marketing*, 25(4), 282–92.

Handley, L. (2011) Do you want to know an open secret? *Marketing Week*, 20 October, 25.

Hansen, K. (2004) Measuring Performance at Trade Shows: Scale Development and Validation, *Journal of Business Research* 54, 1–13.

Hedger, G. (2015) The fallacy of our time, *Brand Republic*, 23 April. http://www.brandrepublic.com/article/1343640/fallacy-time

Herzberg, F. (1966) *Work and the Nature of Man*, Cleveland: W. Collins.

Holmes, T. L. and R. Srivastava (2002) Effects of Job Perceptions on Job Behaviours: Implications for Sales Performance, *Industrial Marketing Management* 31, 421–8.

Homburg, C., J. P. Workman Jr and O. Jensen (2000) Fundamental Changes in Marketing Organization: the Movement Toward a Customer-Focused Organizational Structure, *Journal of the Academy of Marketing Science* 28, 459–78.

Hunt, K. A. and R. Bashaw (1999) A New Classification of Sales Resistance, *Industrial Marketing Management* 28, 109–18.

James, M. (2003) The Quest for Fidelity, *Marketing Business*, January, 20–2.

Krishnan, B. C., R. G. Netemeyer and J. S. Boles (2002) Self-efficacy, Competitiveness, and Effort as Antecedents of Salesperson Performances, *Journal of Personal Selling and Sales Management* 20(4), 285–95.

Lancaster, G. and H. Baron (1977) Exhibiting for Profit, *Industrial Management*, November, 24–7.

Lane, N. and N. Piercy (2004) Strategic Customer Management: Designing a Profitable Future for Your Sales Organization, *European Management Journal* 22(6), 659–68.

Leigh, T. H. and G. W. Marshall (2001) Research Priorities in Sales Strategy and Performance, *Journal of Personal Selling and Sales Management* 21, 83–93.

Likert, R. (1961) *New Patterns of Sales Management*, New York: McGraw-Hill.

Linton, I. (1995) *Database Marketing: Know What Your Customer Wants*, London: Pitman.

Long, M. M., T. Tellefsen and J. D. Lichtenthal (2007) Internet Integration into the Industrial Selling Process: A Step-by-Step Approach, *Industrial Marketing Management* 36, 676–89.

Luthans, F. (1997) *Organizational Behaviour*, New York: McGraw-Hill.

Magrath, A. J. (1989) To Specialise or Not to Specialise?, *Sales and Marketing Management* 14(7), 62–8.

Maslow, A. H. (1954) *Motivation and Personality*, New York: Harper & Row.

McCawley, I. (2006) Nectar Loyalty Card Set for Global Roll-out, *Marketing Week*, 19 January, 3.

McDonald, M. H. B. (2002) *Marketing Plans*, London: Heinemann.

Milington, A. (2015) DMA merger with IDM will create all-inclusive direct marketing organisation, *Marketing Week*, 22 May. http://www.marketingweek.com/2015/05/22/dma-merger-with-idm-will-create-all-inclusive-direct-marketing-organisation

Mitchell, A. (2002) Consumer Power Is on the Cards in Tesco Plan, *Marketing Week*, 2 May, 30–1.

Moncrief, W. C. and G. W. Marshall (2005) The Evolution of the Seven Steps of Selling, *Industrial Marketing Management* 34, 13–22.

Movahhed, M. (2014) Tales for a Road Warrior, Handshake, 12 September. https://www.handshake.com/blog/wholesale-selling-strategies-toys (accessed 10 May 2015).

Murphy, C. (2008) No Such Thing as a Freebie, *The Marketer*, May, 28–31.

Murphy, J. (1997) The Art of Satisfaction, *Financial Times*, 23 April, 14.

PA Consultants (1979) *Salesforce Practice Today: A Basis for Improving Performance*, Cookham: Institute of Marketing.

Parasuraman, A. (1981) The Relative Importance of Industrial Promotional Tools, *Industrial Marketing Management* 10, 277–81.

Picaville, L. (2004) Mobile CRM Helps Smith and Nephew Reps Give Hands-On Service, *CRM Magazine* 8(5), 53.

Piercy, N., D. W. Cravens and N. A. Morgan (1998) Salesforce Performance and Behaviour Based Management Processes in Business-to-Business Sales Organisations, *European Journal of Marketing* 32(1/2), 79–100.

Pullins, E. B. (2001) An Exploratory Investigation of the Relationship of Sales Force Compensation and Intrinsic Motivation, *Industrial Marketing Management* 30, 403–13.

Rackham, N. and J. DeVincentis (1999) *Rethinking the Sales Force: Redefining Selling to Create and Capture Customer Value*, New York: McGraw-Hill.

Reed, D. (2008) Making a Visible Difference, *Marketing Week*, 14 August, 27.

Reid, A. (2015) 3 BRANDS THAT PROVE LISTENING TO CUSTOMERS IS KEY TO COMPANY COMEBACKS, www.fastcompany.com, 2 September. http://www.fastcompany.com/3035054/hit-the-ground-running/3-brands-that-prove-listening-to-customers-is-key-to-company-comeback (accessed 14 May 2015).

Román, S., S. Ruiz and J. L. Munuera (2002) The Effects of Sales Training on Salesforce Activity, *European Journal of Marketing* 36(11/12), 1344–66.

Royal, W. (2004) Death of Salesmen, *Industry Week*, 21 December.

Schuster, C. P. and J. E. Danes (1986) Asking Questions: Some Characteristics of Successful Sales Encounters, *Journal of Personal Selling and Sales Management*, May, 17–27.

Shipley, D. and K. S. Wong (1993) Exhibiting, strategy and implementation, *International Journal of Advertising*, 12(2), 117–30.

Slush (2015) About, Slush. http://www.slush.org/about/media (accessed 10 May 2015).

Smith, T. M., S. Gopalakrishna and P. M. Smith (2004) The Complementary Effect of Trade Shows on Personal Selling, *International Journal of Research in Marketing* 21(1), 61–76.

Spielwarenmesse (n.d.) Fair Profile. http://www.spielwarenmesse.de/about-the-fair/fair-profile/?L=1 (accessed 10 May 2015).

Stephens, H. (2003) 'CEO', American Marketing Association Summer Educators' Conference, The H. R. Challey Group, August, Chicago.

Stone, M., D. Davies and A. Bond (1995) *Direct Hit: Direct Marketing with a Winning Edge*, London: Pitman.

Strahle, W. and R. L. Spiro (1986) Linking Market Share Strategies to Salesforce Objectives, Activities and Compensation Policies, *Journal of Personal Selling and Sales Management*, August, 11–18.

Sujan, H., M. Sujan and J. Bettman (1998) Knowledge Structure Differences Between Effective and Less Effective Salespeople, *Journal of Marketing Research* 25, 81–6.

Szymanski, D. (1988) Determinants of Selling Effectiveness: the Importance of Declarative Knowledge to the Personal Selling Concept, *Journal of Marketing* 52, 64–77.

Talley, W. J. (1961) How to Design Sales Territories, *Journal of Marketing* 25(3), 16–28.

The Economist (2011) Spies in your wallet, 5 November.

Vongsingthong, S. and S. Smanchat (2014) Internet of Things: A Review of Applications & Technologies, *Journal of Science and Technology*.

Vroom, V. H. (1964) *Work and Motivation*, New York: Wiley.

Weitz, B. A. (1981) Effectiveness in Sales Interactions: A Contingency Framework, *Journal of Marketing* 45, 85–103.

Weitz, B. A., H. Sujan and M. Sujan (1986) Knowledge, Motivation and Adaptive Behaviour: a Framework for Improving Selling Effectiveness, *Journal of Marketing* 50, 174–91.

Wilson, K. (1993) Managing the Industrial Salesforce in the 1990s, *Journal of Marketing Management* 9(2), 123–40.

Zoltners, A., P. Sinha and S. Lorimer (2015) The Technology Trends That Matter to Sales Teams, *Harvard Business Review*, 7 May. https://hbr.org/2015/05/the-technology-trends-that-matter-to-sales-teams (accessed 10 May 2015).

Selling in China

Harnessing the Power of the *Guanxi*

China's economy has been growing at an average of 9 per cent over the past 20 years. The country possesses considerable strengths in mass manufacturing and is currently building large electronics and heavy industrial factories. The country is also investing heavily in education and training, especially in the development of engineers and scientists. While these advances mean that China poses new threats to western companies, the country also provides opportunities. China has a population of over 1.3 billion people and they are spending their growing incomes on consumer durables such as cars, a market that has reached 3 million, mobile phones where China has the world's biggest subscriber base of over 500 million, and computers where over 200 million people browse the Internet on broadband connections. Western companies such as Microsoft, Procter & Gamble, Coca-Cola, BP and Siemens have already seen the Chinese market as an opportunity and entered it, usually with the aid of local joint-venture partners.

Although the Chinese economy undoubtedly possesses many strengths, it also has several weaknesses. First, it lacks major global brands. When business people around the world were asked to rank Chinese brands, Haier, a white-goods (refrigerators, washing machines, etc.) and home appliance manufacturer was ranked first, and Lenovo, a computer company, famous for buying IBM's personal computer division, second. Neither company is a major global player in their respective markets. Second, China suffers from the risk of social unrest—resulting from the widening gap between rich and poor, as well as from corruption. Third, the country has paid a heavy ecological price for rapid industrial and population growth, with thousands of deaths attributed to air and water pollution. Fourth, while still a low-labour cost economy, wage levels are rising fast, particularly in skilled areas, reducing its competitive advantage in this area. Finally, bureaucracy can make doing business in China difficult.

Although western companies have made successful entries to the Chinese market, some such as Whirlpool,

a US whitegoods manufacturer, and Kraft, the food multinational, have made heavy losses. Overseas companies hoping to sell successfully in China need to understand a number of realities of the market there. First, the country is very diverse: 1.3 billion people speak 100 dialects, and covering such a large geographic area the climate is very different across regions. For example, parts of the south are humid, while the north is more temperate. Also, income levels vary considerably between less affluent rural districts and richer cities.

Many western companies enter China by means of a joint venture, but they need to be aware of the different business conditions there. In China there is no effective rule of law governing business. Bureaucracy and governmental interference can also bring difficulties. For example, Thames Water pulled out of a 20-year water treatment project in Shanghai after the government ruled that the guaranteed rate of return to investors was illegal.

A key element in Chinese business dealings is the existence of *guanxi* networks. *Guanxi* is a set of personal connections on which a person can draw to obtain resources or an advantage when doing business. *Guan* means a gate or a hurdle, and *xi* refers to a tie, relationship or connection. Therefore *guanxi* literally means 'pass the gate and get connected'. The existence of *guanxi* or personal relationships is global, but *guanxi*'s ubiquitous nature makes it unique and distinctive to China. Intermediaries may be useful in establishing *guanxi*. For example, if person A wants to make a request of person C with whom A has no *guanxi*, A may seek out a member of C's *guanxi* network, person B. If B provides A with an introduction to C, a *guanxi* relationship may begin between A and C. Developing such a network may involve performing favours or the giving of gifts. For example, a business person may participate in a public ceremonial function or a professor could send books to a Chinese university. Favours are 'banked' and there is a reciprocal obligation to return a favour. Three important elements of *guanxi* are *ganqing* (feelings or affection), *renquing* (reciprocation and favour) and *xinren* (trust). All three elements are important in fostering good buyer–seller relationships.

An important aspect of Chinese culture is the avoidance of loss of face. This can occur when a Chinese person finds him/herself embarrassed by, for example, displaying lack of knowledge or understanding. Chinese people like to gather as much information as possible before revealing their thoughts to avoid losing face and displaying ignorance. They also value modesty and reasoning. They also regard the signing of a contract to be only the beginning of a business relationship.

Questions

1. What are the implications of *guanxi* networks for selling in China?
2. An important Chinese cultural issue is the avoidance of loss of face. Discuss its implications for selling in China.
3. Explain the concept of self-reference criteria and its implications for selling in China.

This case study was prepared by David Jobber, Emeritus Professor of Marketing, University of Bradford.

References

Based on: Barnes, B. R., D. Yen and L. Zhou (2011) Investigating guanxi dimensions and relationship outcomes: Insights from Sino-Anglo business relationships, Industrial Marketing Management, 40(4), 510–21; Leung, T. K. P., R. Y.-K.Chan, K. H. Lai and E. W. T. Ngai (2011) An examination of the influence of guanxi and xinyong (utilization of personal trust) on negotiation outcome in China: An old friend approach, Industrial Marketing Management, 40, 1193–1205.

CASE 30
JCPenney and Direct Marketing

Using Something Old to Improve Something New?

There is nothing more outdated or far removed from the digital age of social media and online communication than a paper catalogue that you receive by (snail) mail. Surprisingly, after a five-year hiatus, US clothing and home goods retailer JCPenney announced the resurrection of its mailing catalogue. Is this a sign of marketing communication desperation or marketing communication genius on the part of the struggling company? First, some background.

JCPenney is one of the biggest retailers in the USA, with almost 1,100 stores selling a mixed selection of clothing and home products under its own in-house label, as well as those of national brands. Once a primary destination for middle class shoppers, the company has fallen on hard times, still trying to recover from the recession of 2008 and a series of missteps by top management.

In 2011, Ron Johnson was hired to run a poorly performing JCPenney. Previously, he was senior vice president of retail at Apple, and it was hoped that he would bring with him some of his Silicon Valley hi-tech magic and turn the company around. This was not to be. He was fired in April of 2013 after the company lost a reported $1 billion over the previous 12 months—one of worst losses in the history of retailing. What went wrong?

Traditionally, the key market segment that JCPenney appealed to most was middle aged women looking for savings as well as good value and quality. They were attracted mainly by the frequent sales and promotions that the store ran (a reported 600 a year). These were all done away with under Mr. Johnson's tenure in favour of what were called 'fair and square' prices, similar to Walmart's promotion of 'everyday low prices'. Instead of using discounts and coupons, the company used promotions which were, confusingly, limited to the first and third Friday of each month. As a result, sales at stores, as well as online, fell. The company grossly underestimated people's love for coupons and discounts and their desire to be seen as getting a great deal. 'We

have work to do to educate the customer on our pricing strategy and to drive more traffic to our stores,' said the former Apple wunderkind. Unfortunately, JCPenney shoppers did not get the lesson, and the CEO was out. The situation was so bad that after Mr. Johnson's departure, the company started running ads apologizing for the mistakes that were made and thanked customers for 'coming back'. Some analysts at the time said that it might be better for JCPenney to wait for the customers to actually come back before thanking them.

In the aftermath of the turmoil, the company was seen as returning to its marketing roots, putting a greater emphasis on sales and promotions, and running up to three times as many online specials in 2013 as it had done in the previous year. JCPenney also began communicating discounts to the almost 4 million fans that it had on Facebook, albeit after some of its competitors had started doing the same thing several months before it. More recently, the company has made efforts to better target teenagers and their parents through a multichannel marketing communication campaign based on trends in social media. In a 'Back to School' promotion, JCPenney combined televisions ads with an interactive online site that invited people to create their very own emoji (a graphic smiley face). Users could then personalize it with different hair styles and accessories, and post a selfie right next to it. JCPenney then offered customers personalized suggestions about what they should buy based on how they customized their emoji.

However, the company is still trying to undo the damage caused by previous strategic and marketing initiatives that were poorly thought out and implemented. One of the latest ways is with the reintroduction of its catalogue. JCPenney's old-school marketing communication strategy of going back to ink and paper might strike some as counterintuitive at best, folly at worst, but there is a certain logic to the company's decision. While almost all consumers in developed countries (and many in developing countries) use the Internet as a key shopping tool when choosing what to buy and where to buy it, it appears that many of these decisions are still influenced by something that people first saw in print.

The use of catalogues as a direct marketing communication tool is not dead, but it is definitely in critical condition and on life support. An industry trade group, the Direct Marketing Association (DMA), says that catalogue usage peaked in 2007 with 19.6 billion mailings. In 2013, the number of mailings grew for the first time in almost six years, coming in at almost 12 billion. JCPenney's Chief Executive Officer, Myron Ullman, was the one who took the decision to end the catalogue after getting the top job at the company back in 2013 (he also ran the company before Mr. Johnson took over). Now, in retrospect, that decision appears to have been a mistake. Originally, it was believed that shoppers who used catalogues would eventually migrate to the store's online website. However, market research showed that what JCPenney thought were authentic and unique online sales were in fact sales that had originated from someone looking in a catalogue. Mr. Ullman said that by getting rid of the catalogue he lost a lot of customers.

While it is easy to criticize JCPenney for getting rid of its catalogue, the reasons for why Mr. Ullman took his decision are fairly clear. The company had been using catalogues since 1963, publishing three 'big books' a year, sometimes running to 1,000 pages each. These were supplemented by several smaller catalogues focusing on specialized or seasonal items. Unfortunately, the printing and distribution costs associated with this communication method can be enormous. In 1993, one of JCPenney's direct competitors, Sears, stopped issuing its flagship catalogue. This left JCPenney as one of the last large retailers still putting out a main catalogue. With the growing use of the Internet and social media platforms as a mode of communication, as well as the continued pressure to cut costs as a result of a somewhat weak economy, using a catalogue to reach customers seemed outdated. Plus, many environmentally conscious people complained that it was needless waste. As a result, in 2009 JCPenney ceased putting out its big book, followed by the gradual phasing out of supplemental catalogues the following year.

However, this trend appears to be reversing, with more and more retailers seeing a value to using printed advertising material and direct mailings to customers' homes. Strategy consulting firm Kurt Salmon believes that about 31 per cent of people have a catalogue next to them when they buy something online. One marketing expert said that catalogues allowed his company to 'tell a fuller narrative about the brand and our products in a way that we were struggling to do online'. Also, customers who use catalogues tend to be more loyal and spend more money. Customers who still visit a physical store appear to be the best of all. JCPenney, in the latest iteration of its catalogue, plans to focus on home furnishings, since this category accounts for about 40 per cent of online sales. Mr. Ullman says the company is trying to get back those lapsed customers that were lost due to its unexpected failure to migrate online.

The fact that JCPenney still exists is somewhat of a victory. A financial news tracking service known as 24/7 Wall St voted JCPenney as one of the 10 brands most likely to disappear. In the future, the company may have the last laugh; sales during the holiday season at the end of 2014 were fairly strong, but the stock price is still down substantially from previous highs. Going forwards, in an effort to better reach and better communicate with its customers, the company reportedly spends over $400 million a year on media and marketing (it is thought that this figure does not include online spending). The ideal customer is believed to be multicultural, with 'two little kids, too little time and too little money'. Hopefully, JCPenney's catalogue will have just what they are looking for.

Questions

1. What marketing mistakes did Mr. Johnson make when he took over JCPenney? After he was fired, what did the company do to get its customers back and what is it doing now to keep those customers?

2. Why is the marketing tool—the catalogue—important to JCPenney, what are the advantages and disadvantages of the tool and how can it be used to increase sales?

3. Why are retailers, including JCPenney, moving back to direct marketing communication tools?

This case study was written by Tom McNamara and Asha Moore-Mangin, the ESC Rennes School of Business.

References

Based on: Kapner, S. (2015) JCPenney brings back its catalogue to drive web sales, *The Wall Street Journal*, through *The Australian Business Review*, 21 January, http://www.theaustralian.com.au/business/wall-street-journal/jcpenney-brings-back-its-catalogue-to-drive-web-sales/story-fnay3ubk-1227191237867?nk=20cb10905c6c6c6718a3983cab03a83e; Hoffmann, M. (2013) JCPenney One of 10 Brands Predicted to Die in Next Year, *AdWeek*, 24 May, http://www.adweek.com/news/advertising-branding/martha-stewart-living-one-10-brands-predicted-die-year-149798; Heine, C. (2013) JCPenney Returns to Sales Strategy Online, but Struggles Persist, *AdWeek*, 8 May, http://www.adweek.com/news/advertising-branding/jcpenney-returns-sales-strategy-online-struggles-persist-149258; Gianatasio, D. (2013) JCPenney Says Thanks for Coming Back, but Isn't It a Little Soon for a Victory Dance?, 14 May, http://www.adweek.com/adfreak/jcpenney-says-thanks-coming-back-isnt-it-little-soon-victory-dance-149496; Maytom, T. (2014) JCPenney Targets Teens with 'Express Yourselfie' Campaign by im Mobile Marketing, 19 August, http://mobilemarketingmagazine.com/jcpenney-express-yourselfie-campaign#zxGOTx2tMuvFiYbx.99; JCPenney to review US $450m Media Business, Portada, 28 October 2014, http://www.portada-online.com/2014/10/28/jcpenney-to-review-us-450m-media-business/#ixzz3PkPl3EPH; Nudd, T. (2013) JCPenney's Brutally Honest New Ad: 'It's No Secret' That You Hate Us Please like us again, though!, *AdWeek*, 1 May, http://www.adweek.com/adfreak/jcpenneys-brutally-honest-new-ad-its-no-secret-you-hate-us-149073; Johnson, R. (2013) The man from Apple: Why J.C. Penney dumped The Economist, 13 April, http://www.economist.com/news/business/21576138-why-jc-penney-dumped-ron-johnson-man-apple; Tuttle, B. (2012) Why JCPenney's 'No More Coupons' Experiment Is Failing, *Time*, 17 May, http://business.time.com/2012/05/17/why-jcpenneys-no-more-coupons-experiment-is-failing

CHAPTER 16
Digital Marketing and Social Media

In the digital world. . .customers no longer follow a linear path from awareness to action.

P. THOROGOOD (2015)

LEARNING OBJECTIVES

After reading this chapter, you should be able to:

1. explain the concept of digital marketing
2. explain the meaning of the term 'social media'
3. identify the dimension of the digital marketing environment
4. discuss the implications of digital marketing and social media for marketing planning
5. identify and explain different digital communication tools
6. discuss social media and networking
7. discuss ethical issues in marketing (including digital marketing)

D igital technologies are becoming increasingly important in most sectors of economic activity. Due to high levels of interconnectivity, the Internet has been likened to the wheel and the airplane in terms of its ability to affect the future development of business and society. Consequently, the Internet has provided the impetus for many companies to rethink the role of technology, and evidence already indicates the extent of its global impact. Research on major trends in the dispersion of Internet technologies found that approximately 90 per cent of UK businesses have access to the Internet and, in companies with over 50 employees, the percentage is approaching 100 per cent (DTI, 2004). The situation was found to be very similar in Australia, Canada, France, Germany, Italy, Japan, the Republic of Ireland, South Korea, Sweden and the USA. Interestingly, the report also concluded that the key measure of information and communication technologies (ICT) adoption is no longer just about connectivity and access to the Internet but rather the degree to which digital technology is being used to deliver real value for businesses. Increasingly, business adoption of technologies focuses on an expanding range of digital devices and platforms (e.g. mobile phones, wireless, and digital television). Indeed, global system for mobile communications (GMS) has become the fastest-growing communications technology of all time. Consequently, adoption of digital technologies has profound implications for marketing planning and implementation.

The Internet is a major communications channel, providing an arena for multi-faceted communications. Vast numbers of people spend hours each day online engaging with business and each other, but Internet penetration still varies significantly around the world: in Europe it is approximately 70 per cent, whereas the world average is 42.3 per cent. Figure 16.1 shows the variation in levels of Internet penetration between countries in Europe. With the exception of Russia, levels of adoption in northern Europe are higher than in southern Europe.

The Internet exploded into commercial life in the 1990s. During the same period network technology was also undergoing significant change, switching from analogue to digital circuits, and mobile phone networks and handsets were rapidly developing both in terms of sophistication and number of users. By 2000 further changes had occurred in the world of digital communications infrastructure. Suddenly there were more mobile phone subscribers than fixed-line phone users, Internet traffic exceeded voice traffic on fixed-line telephone networks at night, and wireless technologies began to be developed. Mobile phones have increased facilities for receiving multimedia content, and online television has become widely available.

For its users the Internet and digital technologies have not only provided the means to find, buy and sell products but they have also created an environment for building communities, where like-minded people can network, socialize and be entertained. The emergence of successful social networking sites such as Facebook, LinkedIn and Google+ and **microblogging** sites like Twitter and Tumblr have had a significant impact on global society. Social networking has become pervasive throughout the world, even in China where Facebook was banned. Digital and social media have given a voice to masses of individuals, businesses and communities around the world, and adoption rates have been rapid. For example, at the turn of the century there were approximately 1.5 million Internet users in China (Chaffey et al., 2000); now there are over 640 million (Internet World Stats, 2015), and reportedly 91 per cent of users have accounts with social media platforms like Renren (the Chinese equivalent of Facebook), Weibo (microblogging site) and Twitter.

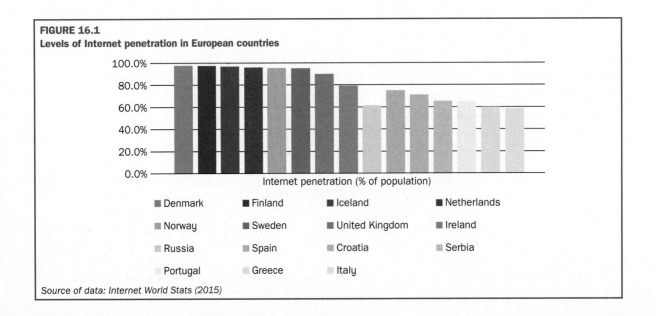

FIGURE 16.1
Levels of Internet penetration in European countries

Internet penetration (% of population)

■ Denmark   ■ Finland   ■ Iceland   ■ Netherlands

■ Norway   ■ Sweden   ■ United Kingdom   ■ Ireland

■ Russia   ■ Spain   ■ Croatia   ■ Serbia

■ Portugal   ■ Greece   ■ Italy

Source of data: Internet World Stats (2015)

The trend for exponential growth in Internet users spread from the USA, where the Internet's commercial use began early in the 1990s, throughout Europe to Oceania, Asia, the Middle East and Africa. As the use of the Internet, the web and social media grows, a major challenge for marketers is to determine how to make the best use of what the technology offers. The rapid pace of innovation and change in the digital environment means there are many challenges for marketers to manage. There is also a growing debate about how *digital* is affecting the concept of marketing. On one side, it is suggested that the *marketing funnel* approach to planning, whereby marketers use a limited number of channels to engage their target audiences, is no longer appropriate. It is suggested that 'The proliferation of digital platforms has forever changed consumer engagement with businesses' and that accessing target audiences can only be achieved through digital-driven data analysis of customer conversion rates to determine the most appropriate channels to use (Thorogood, 2015). But on the other side of the debate, the focus is more of a traditional one, where the marketing concept remains central, and it is business as usual in what has been referred to as the '*post-digital world*' (Friedlein, 2015). In this world, *digital* is merely a new set of tools and platforms that should be applied creatively to support marketing and communication objectives.

In this chapter, we adhere to the more traditional viewpoint and focus on how this technology can be used in the integrated marketing communications (IMC) context. We use the terms *digital marketing* and *social media* to frame our discussions, and consider digital promotional tools and social media. We begin by defining these terms, and then we explore the key dimensions of the digital communications environment, and planning and types of digital communications; social media is then examined in detail. The chapter concludes by considering the ethical and social issues raised by digital marketing and social media.

What is Digital Marketing?

Digital technologies are able to emulate almost every aspect of marketing communications and traditional media channels and, in doing so, span the marketing mix. However, **digital marketing** is more specific and is an element of the marketing communication mix. Nevertheless, the boundaries are less than clear, because digital technology is not only a means of communication but also a method of distribution. The flexibility afforded by the technology means it is highly complex. Marketers are faced with learning how to use and understand emerging technologies (e.g. social media), determining how to make strategic decisions that enable them to make the best use of the technology and implementing digital marketing plans which benefit their businesses. Due to the expansive use of 'all things digital', many terms have been used to describe marketers' use of the technology. In this text, digital marketing includes digitally enabled communication tools—websites, email marketing, **blogging**, and the supporting media. See Marketing in Action 16.1 to find out more about the meaning of digital marketing at Gucci.

Digital marketing can be defined as the application of digital technologies that form channels to market and achieve corporate goals through meeting and exceeding customer needs better than the competition does. Even though *digital platforms* offer a fundamentally different environment for marketing activities—insofar as the technology has unique properties that facilitate many-to-many interactive communications—the goals of the digital communication activities remain the same as those guiding the application of more traditional communication tools.

But it is important to understand the importance of digital technologies and the way they are increasingly being used to interact with target audiences. Furthermore, the widening application of digital technologies suggests that marketers should extend their thinking beyond the Internet to encompass all the platforms—for example mobile, web—that permit a company to do business electronically.

Social media

Later in the chapter we discuss **social media** in more detail and explore how it is used in marketing. However, to begin with we need a working definition—and, like digital marketing, social media (in the digital world) is another complicated phenomenon that means different things to different people. There are three separate elements to consider: *social*, *media* and *network*. According to Tuten and Solomon (2013: 33–41), the social element involves thinking:

> 'about social media as the way digital natives live a social life . . . it is all about a culture of participations; a belief in democracy, the ability to freely interact with other people, companies and organizations; open access to venues that allows users to share content from simple comments to reviews, ratings, photos, stories and more' (Tuten and Solomon, 2013: 3).

In other words, being part of a social media network means that individuals and companies share ideas, interact with one another, work together, learn, enjoy group entertainment and even buy and sell.

MARKETING IN ACTION 16.1
Gucci goes Digital in Style

Gucci is seen as being the embodiment of Italian luxury (in spite of being owned by a French company). Less well known is how the company has been able to combine old-world tradition with a deep understanding of modern technology and marketing techniques. Research named Gucci a 'fashion genius' due to its online capabilities regarding the use of e-commerce, social media, digital marketing and the integration of smartphone apps.

Unlike other luxury retailers, Gucci believes in providing a broad selection of products both in its boutiques and on its website. The reason for this is to ensure that customers have the same Gucci 'experience' in both the real world and the virtual one as well. In the early days of the web, many luxury brands struggled to move online,

but Gucci led the way by having a well defined and well branded digital presence. The brand was an early adopter of Flipboard, a social network and social news aggregator that combines 'the beauty and ease of print with the power of social media.' Gucci also invested in an e-commerce infrastructure so the company was well positioned to take advantage of the anticipated growth in online luxury markets.

Gucci's digital marketing strategy involves a multi-faceted approach using a variety of social media platforms. The company uses elaborate store window displays in conjunction with superbly designed online video ads. Gucci has also cleverly tied promotional campaigns to the anniversaries of some of its iconic products, one example being the 60th anniversary of its famous Horsebit loafers in which famous fashion bloggers were asked to show off the celebrated shoes. Gucci also invited fans to get involved, and simultaneously generated even more interest, by asking them to post their favourite pictures on Instagram. The success of these efforts can be seen in the size of Gucci's online community, with the company having almost 1 million followers on Instagram and well over 11 million fans on Facebook in 2014.

Another example of Gucci's digital skills is its recent 'Made to Measure' campaign. Here, the company tied the promotion of a new cologne to an existing line of men's suits using Hollywood actor James Franco. The company ingeniously used Facebook, hashtags and social media postings in a coordinated effort to arouse interest in its new fragrance. In previous promotional campaigns, Gucci has used Facebook pages that included videos and apps for locating stores that carry a particular product.

Source: Prepared from various published sources

Use of the word media also deserves separate attention because it has further meanings in the social context than those discussed in Chapter 13 (broadcast, print). In this context the technology is used to create an environment which facilitates different forms of online activity. For example:

- *social community media*, like Facebook and LinkedIn, which enable sharing of ideas, interests, socializing and having conversations
- *social publishing media* like YouTube, Pinterest, Flickr which enable signed-up members to publish and distribute editorial content, movies, audio, photos
- *social commerce media* like TripAdvisor, Groupon and Facebook, which enable buying and selling, trading, building relationships
- *social entertainment media* like *Candy Crush, Clash of the Clans, Pet Rescue Saga*, which enable game playing and entertainment across communities

The final element is network, which in one sense can be defined by the underlying technology which makes everything possible. For example, if you are a member of the Facebook social community, the network element is the message boards, forums and wikis, which facilitate communication and conversation. In a social publishing environment, a **blog** (online diary) often forms the underlying technology. In the commerce arena the technology can be: deal sites, deal aggregators and social shopping markets. Finally, virtual worlds and avatars are at the heart of social entertainment media.

However, in another sense, networks are the interconnections between the members of the community. The greater the number of members and interactions the more interesting the network becomes to all involved. In other words, social (life), media (environment) and network (interconnections—technology and human) are three elements which have come together to create the latest and fastest-growing online phenomenon.

Key Dimensions of the Digital Communication Environment

Since 1982, *digitization* has taken place and there has been a steady increase in the use of digital technologies. Products such as televisions, telephones, watches, cameras and music have changed to digital formats. As digitization spreads, the level of *connectivity* across devices, people and locations increases. For example, photographs can be shown on computer screens, shared on social networks and stored remotely in the computing cloud. The Internet connects billions of people and organizations around the world, allowing fast transfer of information. Intranets connect people within a company, facilitating communications, and extranets connect a company with its trading partners, such as suppliers and distributors. In this chapter we are concerned with four dimensions of the digital age that have implications for marketing: 1) technology, 2) marketing, 3) applications, 4) audiences (see Figure 16.2).

Technology

The *Internet* is at the heart of the digital age; it has facilitated the creation of a global network of computer networks, which creates the infrastructure for all online activity. Wireless networks are a growing part of the Internet and are enabling users to access the Internet remotely. *Mobile and satellite technologies* are revolutionizing the communication industry. They are widely used in logistics from the transportation industry and air traffic control to the individual shopper at home. Tesco, for example, uses mobile and satellite technology throughout the supply chain; at the shopper end there is a Tesco app that lets you add your shopping list to a smartphone and then it will create a map to show you the shortest route to your product selection (Martin, 2011). In store, Tesco's best-selling product is bananas, and there are technology systems in place to make sure the fruit is readily available on the shelves to meet customer demand. On the road there is a satellite grid system which updates managers on the distance from the store of the next bunch of bananas (Fenwick, 2010).

One of the main drivers of this expansion of the use of digital technology is convergence, which means the bringing together into one device of the functions that were previously performed by several. For example, smartphones perform the functions of telephones, cameras, computers, audio systems and televisions.

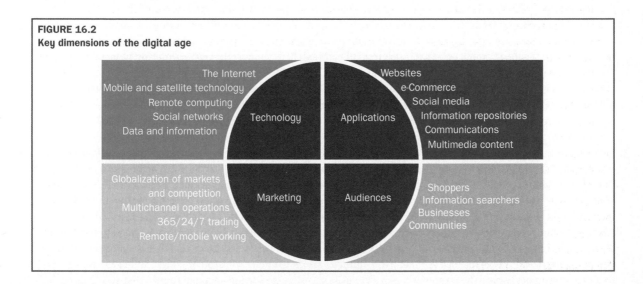

FIGURE 16.2
Key dimensions of the digital age

Technology
- The Internet
- Mobile and satellite technology
- Remote computing
- Social networks
- Data and information

Applications
- Websites
- e-Commerce
- Social media
- Information repositories
- Communications
- Multimedia content

Marketing
- Globalization of markets and competition
- Multichannel operations
- 365/24/7 trading
- Remote/mobile working

Audiences
- Shoppers
- Information searchers
- Businesses
- Communities

Convergence brings the convenience of being able to carry out several tasks using just one device. Platforms are switching from analogue to digital (e.g. television) and also from fixed to wireless (e.g. telephones and computers); services are offered over multiple platforms (e.g. online television—BBC iPlayer; television over broadband—iTV by Apple). Convergence is creating many opportunities for developing new ways to provide access to multimedia content and a range of additional services. Convergence has also prompted the development of *remote computing* and given rise to the concept of cloud computing.

We probably all have many documents, spreadsheets, business and personal files and photographs which we are saving on an increasing array of storage devices. But the problem can be finding a particular document in its latest version. Cloud computing offers a solution to this problem as all documents can be stored in a single secure remote location. Google and Apple offer different ways to access cloud computing, but both are aiming to make these services more accessible. Steve Jobs said 'keeping these devices in sync is driving us crazy' when he launched Apple's iCloud service (Nuttall, 2011). *Social networks* are the underlying technology which facilitate community developments and the sharing of information. This topic is covered in detail later in the chapter.

Data and information: data are the building blocks on which many of the applications are built; information is the 'intelligence' that can be gleaned from the data. We covered these topics earlier (see Chapter 6).

Marketing

The development of digital technologies and subsequent widespread adoption has significant implications for marketing.

Globalization of markets and competition

According to research, the Internet's 'global connectivity opens up new avenues for business in a manner that traditional commerce conduits cannot match' (Pyle, 1996) and it has also been suggested that a company based anywhere in the world can launch a website to compete on a global basis, as long as its products are easily transportable or downloadable (Doherty and Ellis-Chadwick, 2010a). Many established brands are successfully taking advantage of these online opportunities to expand globally (e.g. Tesco, Zara, Apple). However, they inevitably face stiff competition from *virtual merchants*—global online players like Amazon, ASOS, Netflix, and '*disintermediators*' that have cannabilized the supply chain by going straight from manufacturer to the end consumer (e.g. Dell.com, and the Alibaba Chinese e-commerce platform, which serves all markets via its websites). Retailers and consumer brands are likely to face growing pressure from a variety of new businesses that are keen to get their share of the electronic market. One thing that has become very clear during the last years of online trading is that there is always the opportunity for the innovative and dynamic company that has read the market well and has an effective business model to make a strong impact, and in so doing, grow very big and powerful, very quickly, as in the case of Google, Facebook and eBay. The experiences of these organizations demonstrate that the Internet can be a very fertile environment for global expansion if organizations have good ideas, supported by an appropriate set of core competences and capabilities (Doherty and Ellis-Chadwick, 2010a). These discussions link to the later chapters on competition (Chapter 19) and global strategy (Chapter 21).

Multichannel is becoming the de-facto approach to managing online and offline operations. Many retailers have harnessed the Internet's capacity to provide information, facilitate two-way communication with customers, collect market research data, promote goods and services and ultimately to support the online ordering of merchandise, as an extremely rich and flexible new channel (Basu and Muylle, 2003). The Internet has given retailers a mechanism for broadening target markets, improving customer communications, extending product lines, improving cost efficiency, enhancing customer relationships and delivering customized offers (Srinivasan, Anderson and Kishore, 2002) through their cross operations (Doherty and Ellis-Chadwick, 2010a). Dixon Carphone Warehouse is an example of a European retailer that is using the web and mobile technology to provide multichannel assistance and drive customers to their stores. To begin with they developed a multichannel service by building a mobile-optimized website incorporating a 'click to call' feature, which allowed users to contact the call centre and make a purchase. Then they also promoted the service through mobile and web channels and also included a link on the Carphone Warehouse main website store finder page. This enabled customers in the high street who were thinking about buying a new mobile phone to be instantly directed to the nearest store (Jones, 2011). Indeed many retailers are finding that they are achieving a much higher return on investment (ROI) if they use their website, and mobile apps as an integral part of their businesses (Barnett, 2011). A multichannel strategy brings together the different routes a company uses to access its market. Arguably, the ultimate aim is to create a customer journey that seamlessly links together every point where the customer touches a business, to create a single-channel (**omni-channel**) approach.

This includes traditional and digital communications and distribution channels operating together. These discussions link to further issues associated with channel development and management in Chapter 17.

Continuous trading

The Internet never closes; 365, 24/7 trading is a reality, and companies are being pressurised to manage their interface with the customers on an 'open all hours basis'. Many companies provide self-help information on their websites, which customers can access around the clock. But they also provide call centres, customer services and returns departments which provide real-time support, via the phone or online.

Remote and mobile working

Many more people are now working remotely than in the past. In the UK 13.6 per cent of the working population are working on a remote basis. A surprisingly large proportion do so from their home premises (37.5 per cent). However, the biggest group of 62.5 per cent work remotely away from home (e.g. transport drivers, sales representatives) (Frary, 2012). New technology is facilitating this process and making more things possible. For home workers, there are many advantages and disadvantages to consider. On the plus side, travel costs are reduced, workers can have more control over how they plan their working day. On the negative side, there can be an increase in family conflict, lack of understanding from family members about the tasks the worker has to complete, and pressure on the space needed to successfully carry out a job at home. There is also the loss of interaction with other members of the workforce, and managerial support is only available on a remote basis. However, research has found that if there is increased social support from the workplace for remote workers, many of the negatives of working at home are reduced (Wylie et al., 2010). Social media has been found to offer support and boost employee satisfaction, trust and productivity (Snoad, 2011). Leeds Beckett University introduced MyWellbeing to tackle absenteeism among university staff, and it estimates the portal has saved the university £75,000 a year in salary costs. Aviva World (available to over 36,000 staff worldwide) is very popular and regularly receives over 7 million hits a month. Aviva encourages its staff to get involved with the business at various different levels through social media and in doing so it is enabling remote workers to feel more involved in the business. These are not isolated examples: companies from Coca-Cola, the BBC and Unilever to Sainsbury's are using social media networks and intranets to communicate, interact and ultimately improve job satisfaction and productivity.

Applications

In the early days, the Internet was viewed primarily as a means to facilitate two-way communications between companies and their customers. However, very quickly the underlying technology and widespread adoption of websites became far more sophisticated and enabled more applications and uses to be introduced (see Chapter 13 for further detailed discussion of the use of digital communication in IMC strategies and Chapter 15 for discussion of direct marketing). E-commerce enabled websites to be added to the extent that they could be used to: purchase and pay for merchandise, sell and promote goods and services, collect market research data, and track orders (Basu and Muylle, 2003; Doherty and Ellis-Chadwick, 2009). Currently, the Internet provides business with a highly effective mechanism for broadening target markets, improving customer communications, extending product lines, improving cost efficiency, enhancing customer relationships and delivering customized offers (Srinivasan, Anderson and Kishore, 2002). Indeed, target audiences have taken to the new technology, and whether companies are trading in business to business or business to consumer markets there is an increasing range of applications being used—e-commerce, information repositories, social media, interactive communications and multimedia content delivery.

Given the Internet's potential to radically reconfigure underlying business processes and because of the highly dynamic and innovative nature of the online marketplace, it is not surprising that there has been a rapid expansion in the application of these relatively new technologies. Furthermore, it should be remembered that commercial exploitation of the Internet has far-reaching implications: technical, logistical, strategic, behavioural, social and legal. Companies wishing to take advantage of the opportunities created by the Internet need to make sure they are integrated into their wider strategic goals if they are to garner the best advantage from digital applications (Doherty and Ellis-Chadwick, 2010b). (See Chapter 18 for further discussion of marketing strategy and planning.)

Audiences

Across the world, many *shoppers, information searchers, businesses* and *communities members* are now happy to use Internet technology as part of their daily lives. For marketing managers it is, however, increasingly important to understand the target audiences, as there are significant changes taking place resulting from more and more interactions between organizations and their audiences via digital technology. (For more detailed discussion of target audiences and related segmentation strategies see Chapter 7.) For instance, in the consumer services sector there is an increasingly intense struggle for power between the consumer and the service provider. Sites like TripAdvisor freely allow visitors to hotels, restaurants and other places of entertainment to air their views of the service they received. However, while service providers need to take heed and be aware of what their customers are saying online, they too make use of highly sophisticated customer databases, to track and trace their customers, so that they can implement highly targeted 'one-to-one' marketing campaigns (Arora et al., 2008) and other initiatives which build strong customer relationships and deliver even more value (Kim, Zhao and Yang, 2008). So, on the one hand, consumer audiences have access to tools which can help them disseminate their levels of satisfaction and dissatisfaction far and wide. On the other hand, consumer service providers have a wealth of consumer-oriented data that could enable them better to predict their customers' needs (Kaufman-Scarborough et al., 2006) and requirements, and in doing so create more effective IMC campaigns. For example, Britvic set out to create a 'light touch' communication strategy that would engage the interest of parents of 10-year-olds. So, the soft drinks company monitored online behaviour when it launched its Fruit shoot website. Once the site was established, Britvic launched its 'parents for playgrounds' campaign and monitored what people were responding to, then tailored the content to suit their interests. This is a very different approach to planning an eight-week advertising campaign with fixed content and messages (Nutley, 2011).

The Internet allows advertisements to be targeted on an individual basis. *Behavioural targeting* (or personalized digital advertising) is a method of directing advertisements at consumers based on their previous online behaviour. At its most basic, it is the Amazon 'you've bought this so you might like to buy this' approach. However, more sophisticated behavioural techniques log where Internet users have been surfing online, using 'cookies'. Once this is known, advertisements on other sites appear based on that information. For example, an online user could be browsing cinema listings when a banner advertisement for bargain breaks in Rome appears—something the user had been researching a few days previously (Grant, 2008). There is some evidence that consumers object to this kind of tracking of their Internet activity, with a survey revealing that 77 per cent objected to behavioural targeting (Murphy, 2008).

A word of warning: the EU Privacy and Electronic Communication Directive is bringing in a new set of legislation to control the use of data. For digital marketers this means rethinking how they use 'cookies'. In the past cookies (text-files that recognize users) have been seen as digital mechanisms which remember log-in details and store individual preferences. However, the EU sees cookies as a means of tracking online behaviour and potentially represents an intrusion of privacy. As a result the new legislation is being implemented to ensure that website visitors explicitly agree to the use of cookies when browsing websites.

A huge amount of research has been conducted to try to understand typical online buyer behaviour. In Chapter 3 we learnt how pre-family man uses online technology depending on lifecycle stages, cultural differences and personal priorities. Other influences identified from a body of academic research carried out during the past 20 years (Doherty and Ellis-Chadwick, 2010) are:

1 *Demographic variables*: personal attributes that tend to remain static throughout an individual's life time, or evolve slowly over time—such as age, gender, race, etc.—can be defined as 'demographic variables'. Key elements of a customer's demographic profile that have been found to influence their online behaviour include such variables as income, education, race, age, gender and lifestyle (Hoffman and Novak, 1997).

2 *Psychographic and behavioural variables*: any aspect of a person's perceptions, beliefs and attitudes that might influence their online behaviour, and in particular their intention to shop. Indeed, behavioural characteristics—such as knowledge, attitude, innovativeness, risk aversion etc.—can also affect a person's intention to shop. For example, it has been found that consumers who are primarily motivated by convenience were more likely to make purchases online, while those who value social interactions were found to be less interested (Swaminathan, Lepkowska-White and Rao, 1999).

3 *Personal profiles*: age, gender, education, salary. Indeed, it is important to note that Internet shoppers are no longer likely to be greatly different from their offline counterparts (Jayawardhena, Wright and Dennis, 2007). However, it is perhaps useful to differentiate between the most enthusiastic and profitable Internet shoppers. For example, it has recently been found that the Internet is a favourite channel for the compulsive shopper, as consumers are able to 'buy unobserved', 'without contact with other shoppers', and in so doing, 'experience strong positive feelings during the purchase episode' (Kukar-Kinney, Ridgway and Monroe, 2009). This study, which looked at the behaviour of Internet shoppers from six countries, including both developing and developed countries, found a surprisingly high degree of homogeneity in their characteristics and habits

(Brashear, Kashyap, Musante and Donthu, 2009). Internet shoppers were found to share their desire for convenience, were more impulsive, have more favourable attitudes towards direct marketing and advertising, were wealthier and were heavier users of both email and the Internet.

For marketing managers the importance is to understand the nature and behaviour of the target audience. Read Marketing in Action 16.2 to find out more about how behaviours are being translated into action.

MARKETING IN ACTION 16.2
Know your Customers and the Importance of Understanding Where and When They Shop

Arguably, real-world relationships have been replicated in a digital form: online almost every dimension of the human existence has been replicated in one form or another. Perhaps one of the most compelling reasons for consumers to go online is that there is a wealth of information that can improve the efficiency of their shopping behaviour and reduce their risk. Information in the digital world is enhanced by user participation. Product descriptions and price comparisons and reviews, generated by sellers and buyers, abound and provide a rich tapestry of information. Ranking systems exist to help reduce the guesswork; for example, Feefo, the global feedback engine, produces product ratings for buyers and customer experience insight for sellers. Marketers have become interested *not* in whether customers are using digital sources as part of their decision-making, but in what types of information customers are they signing up to. Research has shown that digital and social media platforms have become increasingly important in the purchasing decision-making process.

SHOPPING ONLINE MORE OFTEN MAKES CUSTOMERS LESS ENGAGED

'The more customers shop online, the more likely they'll become disenchanted with a brand. Overall, 25% of retail customers are actively disengaged, while 58% are indifferent and 17% are not fully engaged. In contrast, 32% who shopped online more often and shopped the same or less offline are actively disengaged, while 53% are indifferent and 16% are not fully engaged.

RETAIL CUSTOMERS OVERALL

17% ARE FULLY ENGAGED   **58**% ARE INDIFFERENT   **25**% ARE ACTIVELY DISENGAGED

RETAIL CUSTOMERS WHO SHOPPED ONLINE MORE OFTEN AND THE SAME OR LESS OFFLINE

16% ARE FULLY ENGAGED   **53**% ARE INDIFFERENT   **32**% ARE ACTIVELY DISENGAGED

GALLUP®

© 2015 Gallup, Inc. All Rights Reserved. Gallup panel web study completed by 12,055 adults conducted Nov. 14–Dec 1. 2014. The maximum magin of sampling error is ±1

Where consumers are making their purchases is changing, but online is not necessarily the first choice. According to a recent survey by Gallup, the number of online shoppers is increasing; for example, in the USA approximately a third of the population buy online, and this number has grown year on year. But the study also found that some shoppers are increasingly going to physical stores, attracted by the service offer from their favourite retailers. Indeed, if the online experience does match up to customers' expectations, they are likely to become disengaged with the digital offer. Furthermore the digital experience, if repeated frequently, can lead to customers becoming *agnostic* towards a brand, if they become frustrated with the technology associated with websites and mobile apps.

When consumers shop is changing too. Research suggests that shopping online and via mobile apps can occur when consumers are at work, watching television or even in bed. Shop Direct, the UK's leading digital retailer, discovered that laptops and PCs are still the principal shopping devices, but more people are going mobile. This flexibility in purchasing methods means that the times we buy are changing. For example on Black Friday, Cyber Monday and other peak online shopping days we buy throughout the day and night, and eBay sellers in the UK know that Sunday evening is a peak buying time. Nevertheless, if you go to Oxford Street a few days before Christmas, the streets will still be crammed with people and the tills ringing at a cumulative rate of nearly a £1 million a minute.

Based on: Feefo (2015); Borges and Veríssimo (2014); Deneen and Yu (2015); Shop Direct (2014)

The dimensions of the digital age have far-reaching implications for marketers. The technology has led to the development of new routes and channels to market, and there are a myriad of new applications which are used to entice growing audiences to live part of their lives online. Existing and new companies are continually in competition for market share. To succeed, online companies should plan carefully how they are using digital technology.

Digital Marketing and Social Media Planning

This section explores the implications of digital marketing and social media for marketing planning. Digital technologies are reshaping business models, choice of promotional tools and media. In a recent study it was found digital is the 'central plank' which all communication agencies must be able to deliver. As a consequence there has been a significant shift away from more traditional communication tools and media (Singh, 2011) and battles are being fought over which service providers are the most adept at delivering digital communication plans. This shift in emphasis means marketers need to be aware of what they expect and how the technology can deliver their marketing objectives.

Deciding how to plan, resource, integrate, implement and monitor digital marketing activities can be guided by applying established marketing management principles and planning activities (as discussed in detail in Chapters 2 and 18). Digital technologies can be used to meet a range of different business objectives: sales, communications, or focus on the development and maintenance of mutually satisfying long-term relationships with customers by using digital technologies (Chaffey and Smith, 2008). Therefore, the type of activities will determine the strategic significance of the plan and give focus to the operational context.

The formulation of the digital marketing plan is likely to be informed by four significant and interdependent elements (Doherty and Ellis-Chadwick, 2004).

1 *Strategic alignment* of digital marketing activities with corporate marketing and marketing communication strategies is important as it should ensure development of a potentially successful digital marketing plan. This process should also help define the purpose of the digital marketing activities.

2 *Integration* of digital marketing and social media with traditional tools and techniques is essential. This means that planning is required to consider all of the touchpoints in a customer's journey and ensure that customers receive a consistent message. But integration also requires a cross-company approach, bringing together cross-company teams to achieve unified strategic-level corporate and marketing goals as well as tactical communication goals (Chaffey and Ellis-Chadwick, 2016).

3 The *value proposition* should emphasize the unique advantages created by the use of digital technologies, for example *choice* (amazon.com offers the world's widest and deepest range of books at very low prices), *convenience* (tesco.com offers round-the-clock shopping), *community* (Facebook brings people together around the world). The value proposition created through the relative advantage afforded by digital technologies should reinforce core brand values and be clearly articulated to target audiences. It will also determine the extent to which organizational change is required.

4 *Organizational change* is likely if the digital marketing plan is to be delivered successfully. A good example to consider is how retailers like Tesco and Sainsbury's have developed unique logistical solutions to support online ordering. E-commerce initiatives can involve applying a wide range of digital technologies: Internet, EDI, email, electronic payment systems, advanced telephone systems, mobile and handheld digital appliances, interactive television, self-service kiosks and smart cards. Consequently, the integration of such technologies may require significant changes to operations and working practices in order to ensure that the right skill sets (capabilities) and resources are available when required.

5 *Implementation* of the plan should be executed in a timely manner. Additionally, the success of the digital marketing plan is likely to be affected by senior management commitment, availability of appropriate resources and the appropriateness of the strategic vision that is guiding the implementation. The significance of the digital marketing plan for a company's overall strategy will also largely be dependent upon levels of technology adoption, investment and integration.

Scan the QR code to view eBay's value proposition.

In addition, analysis of the environment should take place in order to determine the likely relevance of digital marketing. When assessing a target audience the following information will be useful (Chaffey and Ellis-Chadwick, 2012).

1 *Customer connectivity*: the proportion of the target markets that has access to relevant technologies.
2 *Customer channel usage*: how often target market participants use online channels and how they use the particular digital channel/platform (e.g. purchase or research?). For instance, for each customer segment and digital channel (e.g. web, digital television, social media or mobile), a company should know the proportion of the target market that:
   • *makes use* of and has access to a particular channel
   • *browses* and, as a result, is influenced by using the channel for pre-purchase research and evaluation
   • *buys* through the particular channel.
3 *Online media consumption*: how many hours each week are spent using the web, social media and mobile in comparison with traditional media such as watching television, reading newspapers or magazines, or listening to the radio?

In addition, marketers should also consider the competition and be able to answer the following questions.
   • What specific strategic resources, capabilities and competences are required for successful digital marketing?
   • How well are the expectations of consumers being fulfilled by our digital marketing activities? For example, is our website easy to use? Are our email or mobile campaigns well received or regarded as intrusive?
   • What is the number of visitors to our website per month? How many viewers watch our interactive television (iTV) commercials?
   • What is the average length of time visitors spend on our site?
   • What are the most popular pages and products? What are the least popular?
   • Which product categories generate most sales?
   • Conversion rates: what is the proportion of visitors who place an order? What is the proportion of recipients of email or mobile campaigns, or iTV viewers who place an order?
   • Click-through rates: how many visitors arrive at our site from banner advertisements or web links from other sites?

Findings of the internal and external analysis should feed into marketing objectives, the creation of competitive advantage and communication plans.

Implications for Marketing Planning in a Digital World

The degree to which digital marketing objectives will be defined can vary tremendously depending on the extent and time in which digital technologies have been utilized (for example, mobile phone operator EE may set objectives that focus on customer retention, whereas Britvic sets objectives designed to foster the engagement of their target audience of parents). In general, digital marketing objectives fall within some or all of five categories (Chaffey and Smith, 2008). Marketers must decide whether all or only some are going to drive their marketing plan.

1 *Grow sales*: through cheaper prices, wider distribution or greater product range.
2 *Add value*: through greater convenience (home shopping), improved 24/7 access, and/or more information (e.g. track orders, receive advice, read customer reviews, compare product features and benefits), deliver extra benefits.
3 *Get closer to customers*: inbound by conducting online marketing research, monitoring chatrooms, blogs and social network sites, and tracking visits to sites; outbound by search engine marketing, online public relations and advertising, and email and viral marketing campaigns.
4 *Save costs*: by replacing sales and telemarketing staff with online sales, order confirmation by email rather than post, online purchasing, and replacing hard copy catalogues, manuals and reports with online versions.
5 *Extend the brand online*: by raising awareness, enhance brand image and extend the brand experience.

Creating competitive advantage

Marketers have long accepted that success demands identification of some form of *competitive advantage* capable of distinguishing an organization from other firms operating in the same market sector. The unique properties of digital technologies offer opportunities to establish new forms of competitive advantage. These include highly tailored communication campaigns which can be designed to meet very specific communication objectives. The secret of the success of most digital operations is that they have exploited digital market advantages and new technologies, in order to deliver a value proposition superior to that of their competitors. Once a company has developed an understanding of the environment, competition and target market, it can then begin to decide which digital tools are likely to be most effective.

Evaluation and performance control

Evaluation and control systems need to be created that permit management to rapidly identify variance in actual performance versus forecast for all aspects of the digital marketing mix. Management also requires mechanisms that generate diagnostic guidance on the cause of any variance. To achieve this aim, control systems should focus on the measurement of key variables within the plan, such as targeted market share, customer attitudes, awareness objectives for digital marketing and distribution targets.

Digital analytics is a catch-all term for the methods used to evaluate the success of digital marketing programmes. Such techniques allow the checking of whether objectives have been achieved, by recording traffic volume, website visitor numbers, the most popular pages and products, how long visitors spend on site, which pages they visit (clickstreams), referrals, sales, and the individual sites or search terms used by visitors to find digital content (Chaffey and Ellis-Chadwick, 2016). For example, Google Analytics is an excellent analytical tool which offers some basic-level analysis for free.

Analytics tools and techniques offer various solutions for measuring the performance of online different digital channels. Determining which to use will be dependent on the goals set for a particular campaign. Figure 16.3 shows how different objectives might be measured using digital analytics.

Research has shown that marketing managers often measure digital effectiveness using measures like brand awareness, word of mouth, customer satisfaction, and popular measures such as page views, cost per thousand impressions and click-throughs. However, Chaffey (2015) suggests that it is important to use appropriate key performance indicators in a planned manner to consider more than just the volume of traffic. He recommends that for the best results, it is important to determine the quality of the traffic and the value. For example, if a company is seeking to build a new customer base, it should be determining the value of unique visitors. It should then be considering how extensively visitors navigate around the site (the bounce rate), which helps to determine the quality of the online customers. To determine the value, the revenue per visit needs to be monitored. Finally, the company should evaluate the number of searches the brand is attracting.

Evaluation of digital marketing activities is also important, and so a planner should decide which tactics might be the most effective and then optimize (focus on) the use of specific tools and techniques. For example, a

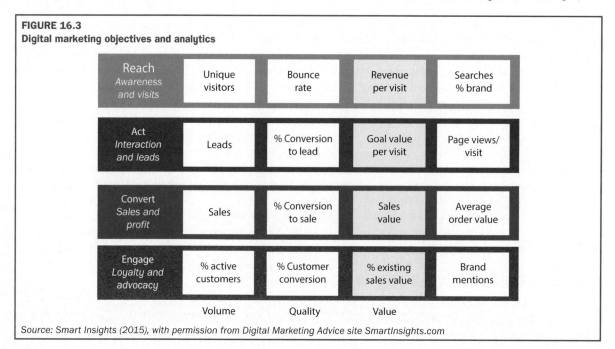

FIGURE 16.3
Digital marketing objectives and analytics

Reach *Awareness and visits*	Unique visitors	Bounce rate	Revenue per visit	Searches % brand
Act *Interaction and leads*	Leads	% Conversion to lead	Goal value per visit	Page views/ visit
Convert *Sales and profit*	Sales	% Conversion to sale	Sales value	Average order value
Engage *Loyalty and advocacy*	% active customers	% Customer conversion	% existing sales value	Brand mentions
	Volume	Quality	Value	

Source: Smart Insights (2015), with permission from Digital Marketing Advice site SmartInsights.com

fashion retailer like Net-a-Porter might be pursuing engagement objectives (for its Net Set app). If this were the case, according to Chaffey (2015), it would need to optimize its content management strategy, e-contact strategy, customer service and support, mobile market campaigns and social customer relationship management (CRM). However, if a company were following a customer acquisition strategy, it would need to optimize its search engine optimization (SEO), pay per click (PPC) advertising, affiliate and partner marketing, online public relations (PR) and social media marketing (Chaffey, 2015).

As the complexity of the digital world increases, so do the number of tools and techniques that can be used to monitor and evaluate digital performance. This has become a growing subject, which goes beyond the remit of this chapter. Analytics have been discussed in Chapter 6, and recommended further reading on this topic is provided at the end of the chapter.

Digital marketing tools

Once the environmental analysis is complete and the objectives set, consideration of the mix of digital marketing tools should be carried out. The Internet and the web provide innovative options for the digital marketer: communications can be interactive, animated, personalized and instantaneous. However, the marketer needs to understand how the target customers will respond if he/she is to use this media successfully. For instance, sending personalized email marketing messages can help to build customer relationships, but the level of personalization should be appropriate to the stage of the relationship. If a company is too familiar too early in the relationship, the customer is likely to feel the company is being intrusive (White, Zahay, Thorbjørnsen and Shavitt, 2008). Nevertheless, use of digital marketing tools is on the increase (Miller, 2012). In the UK, spend on online advertising is now the most popular media for advertisers having overtaken the spend on television advertising. This includes social media, **mobile marketing**, video and online display advertising, all of which are increasing in terms of spend year on year (Sweney, 2012). Types of digital marketing include the following:

Online advertising and search engine marketing

Online display advertising aims to get a target customer to act immediately by clicking on the advert or watching a video. Display adverts include banner adverts, skyscrapers and pop-ups. They may be used to elicit various responses and meet a range of communications objectives, for example increase action, change opinions, increase recall. Since the first banner adverts were used in 1994, the percentage rate of click-throughs to the adverts has dropped significantly. However, mobile devices have created opportunities for more creative forms of display advertising, and currently have created a renaissance for display advertising. Recently, Google, Facebook and Twitter have seen an increase in the spend on this form of advertising.

 Scan the QR code to hear what the Internet Advertising Bureau (IAB) has to say about digital advertising spend.

Affiliate marketing was a popular form of online advertising in which one business rewards another for placing advertising on its website. Each time a potential customer clicks on the link through to the originator of the advert website, the third party earns revenue. However, while sophisticated new SEO techniques are increasingly being favoured for brand building over this technique, it should not be completely dismissed as an option (Olenski, 2014).

Search engine marketing involves optimization of search listings and keyword searching. For instance, if searching Yahoo! using key words such as 'jewellery shop', the search engine will provide a list of companies offering such services. Yahoo! provides its Keyword Selector to help advertisers choose the best search term. Search engines like Yahoo! and Google generate revenue by charging each time an individual clicks on a sponsored link. The higher up the listing, the higher the price for click-through. Google sells a product called AdWords and claims that it can enable users to attract more customers, help messages reach the *right* target audience, and be used on a local and global scale (Google AdWords, 2015).

AdWords adverts connect you with new customers at the precise moment the customers are looking for your products or services. With Google AdWords you create your own ads, choose keywords to help Google match your adverts to your audience and you pay only when someone clicks on them (Google AdWords, 2006).

It has been argued that it is very important for advertisers to appear in the optimum position on the computer screen if they are to attract the greatest number of visitors to their online offering. By paying for a sponsored link, an advertiser gains a prominent position on the search engine's listings. The amount a company pays depends on how much it bids for keywords that Internet users seeking a particular product are likely to enter: the higher the keyword bid compared to rivals, the higher the listing. While the average cost per click is 10–20p, in some competitive industries, such as financial services, it can be as high as £3 (Chaffey, 2008).

A second method of traffic building to a particular website is known as *search engine optimization* (SEO). This involves the achievement of the highest position in the natural listings on the search engine results pages after a keyword or phrase has been entered. The position depends on a calculation made by a search engine (e.g. Google) that matches the relevant site page content with the keyword (phrase) that is typed in. Unlike sponsored search (pay-per-click) SEO does not involve payment to a search engine to achieve high rankings. What a digital marketer needs is an understanding of how to achieve high natural rankings. Search engines use 'spiders' to identify the titles, links and headings that are employed to assess relevance to keywords and phrases. It is therefore important to ensure that the website includes the keywords (phrases) that a potential visitor might use to search for a particular type of company. For example, Ragdale Hall Spa Hotel's website includes terms such as 'weekend spa break', 'spa resort' and 'health spa', because they are key phrases used by consumers when searching for that type of hotel. This has achieved high ranking for the hotel on search engine listings (Chaffey, 2008).

However, SEO has become more of an exercise in behavioural segmentation than a technical website development exercise, and so driving the *right* type of person to a site might be more important than where it ranks for a key phrase. Google suggest that there are more than 200 separate variables that can have an effect on the where and how a website finds itself in a search result. Google has set in place changes that might see website owners 'penalized' for overzealous SEO activity. There are clearly some organizations that play the SEO game with consummate success. A search for almost any consumer product will often find Amazon and eBay returned within the first few results, a virtue of their size and authority as sites, their high-level linking, involvement in advertising programs and sophisticated automation of the SEO process. Within the hotel sector, many specialists admire Laterooms.com for its ability to perform highly against hotel brands and other booking services. Highly competitive industries, such as the insurance business, expend huge resources to compete with other firms on Google. However, some brand names, such as GoCompare, prefer to spend that resource in pay-per-click campaigns than on SEO activity—perhaps an indication that brand awareness and a large PPC budget might be more important in some verticals than SEO.

Online video and interactive television advertising

Media-sharing sites have become increasingly popular and provide organizations and individuals with a platform on which to share visual, video and audio content. Popular platforms like YouTube, Flickr and Vimeo enable sharing of such content in an online environment. There are different types of content being produced depending on whether it is an individual or a business.

 Scan the QR code to learn how Volvo Trucks won a creative effectiveness award for its 'live test' series.

The growth of digital television has given rise to an increase in *interactive television (iTV) advertising*, where viewers are invited to 'press the red button' on their remote control handset to see more information about an advertised product. This form of advertising has a number of advantages from being highly measurable, which means advertisers can track the success of adverts displayed on different channels and at different times of the day. It also allows the targeting of niche audiences through specialist digital channels that focus on leisure activities such as sport, music and motoring and the provision of more in-depth information than a single television or press advertisement. For the user it is a convenient means of buying a product without having to use a telephone or computer.

 Scan the QR code to see how Amazon Prime positions its instant video service.

Permission-based emails are in use because of widespread consumer complaints about unsolicited emails (known as 'spam'). Generally, permission marketing messages are sent when the receiver has given their consent to receive direct emails (in some countries, this is a legal requirement). Marketers using this form of communication find ways to encourage target audiences to 'opt in' to a firm's emailing list and in return they will receive materials that match their interests as recipients are more likely to open and read such messages.

Email marketing has been found to be most widely used as a call to action or for sales promotion offers. There are many techniques and tactics that can be used to ensure the best performance for email marketing campaigns.

Content marketing

According to Chaffey and Ellis-Chadwick (2016), this form of marketing is central to digital campaigns. The reason for this is that content drives engagement with target audiences through searches and social media. Ultimately, having the *right* content will affect customer conversion rates, help a brand to increase its visibility on the web, mobile and social media platforms, aid customer motivation and engagement, and eventually help develop sales.

Effective content can vary depending on the goals of a digital campaign. Campaigns that seek to raise awareness and foster engagement and customer retention are more likely to succeed with a content marketing approach than those that seek to stimulate action through sales promotions. In the latter case, the customer is likely to engage in a swift purchase rather than interact with content. While content should be engaging for the audience, it should also be designed to meet communication campaign objectives. To be effective, the content that conveys a brand's stories must be interesting, communicate brand values and reflect customer needs. This is a challenge, and content marketing efforts can have a negative effect if they are too *editorial* in tone and fall into the trap of becoming 'the creation of vague and generic brand visions' (Ritson, 2015). However, at Hertz Europe they have found a way to inspire customer engagement using thousands of pieces of local content at each of their car hire locations, and their 'Hertz in 60 seconds' video provides lots of local information, including how to find a parking space in central London (Hemsley, 2015), (See Exhibit 16.1).

EXHIBIT 16.1
Hertz Europe engages its digital audiences using value-added content marketing

Another example of a company that knows how to use and manage content is Net-a-Porter, the fashion retailer. It values content highly and has taken the use of content to a new level with its Net Set social shopping offer. Natalie Massenet, founder of Net-a-Porter, got the inspiration for this shopping innovation when she saw an increase in mobile sales to 40 per cent of sales. The Net Set app brings together the online retailer's e-commerce capabilities and knowledge of social media, and in doing so creates a value-added offer for millennials, who form the majority of its target audience (O'Connor, 2015). Members of the Net Set can buy with confidence using shared recommendations from friends and '*shoppable live feeds of items trending on Net-a-Porter worldwide*', and follow guidance from the in-house 'Style Council'. See Exhibit 16.2 and find out more about how fashionistas everywhere can join the Net Set.

EXHIBIT 16.2
Fashionistas everywhere join the Net Set

 Scan the QR code to see how to join the Net Set.

Given the current importance placed on content marketing, many companies develop a content marketing strategy as part of their digital marketing planning. As with all strategies, this will involve review of the current approach, setting specific objectives and developing strategies to create and share content. Here are two simple models that can help businesses review which content to deploy and then share (Chaffey and Ellis-Chadwick 2016).

Online newsletters, magazines and user-generated content (UGC). This form of digital marketing tends to focus on a specific set of issues or interests. The items can be sent at different frequencies and serve different communication objectives. Online newsletters and magazines form an important element of content marketing strategies, and often include user-generated content, depending on whether a company is telling its customers about a brand or conversing with them. For example, Notcutts Garden Centres often include real customer reviews in their magazine contributions. Cineworld invited users of its app to post photos and comments on its Facebook page to promote the launch of the superhero movie *Marvel's Avengers Assemble*.

UGC can be highly effective, as it creates a tone of authenticity that cannot be achieved by even the most creative marketers. Ikea found when it launched Ikeafamilylive.com, enabling its customer to upload pictures and stories of their homes, that this was an excellent source of indirect marketing material, as 'Alongside Ikea's own roomsets, you can now browse shelving arrangements created by Monika in Poland or Eline in Belgium on a Pinterest-style mood board.' The value of this approach is that if used appropriately, UGC can create loyalty and customer engagement (Handley, 2013).

Mobile marketing refers to the creation and delivery of marketing communications messages through mobile devices (phones, smartphones or tablet computers). Early examples of mobile marketing involved sending text messages containing advertising to willing recipients. However, widespread adoption of smartphones and wireless tablet computers have increased capacity for visual content as well as text-based content. Mobile marketing is becoming increasingly popular, but not all consumers are keen to receive marketing messages via their phones. Research found that 75 per cent of consumers in the UK were happy to get offers via their handsets compared to 72 per cent in the USA, 50 per cent in France and 46 per cent in Germany (Akhtar, 2012). Nevertheless, one of the most rapidly growing forms of mobile marketing is smartphone applications (apps). (See Marketing in Action 16. 3, which discusses how Shazam is partnering with Office Depot to create a whole new retail experience.)

MARKETING IN ACTION 16.3
Shazam Joins with Retailers and Expands the Future of Mobile Marketing

Shazam has over 100 million users every month, who enjoy being able to identify songs and audio messages. The value proposition for Shazam's customers is that it connects users to the world around them through music, adverts, cinema, television and radio. Shazam has now extended the offer to retail. Shazam In-Store is a location-based mobile marketing app that allows users to create a personalized mobile shopping experience by linking together loyalty programmes, social media and the latest deals and offers. Retailers are able to target shoppers using in-store music, and once the shopper's smartphone recognizes the signal he or she can receive a Shazam song along with a tailored offer from the retailer. For example, Shazam and Office Depot

have joined forces to create an innovative shopping experience using the app's music-based digital signature and iBeacons. An iBeacon is a digital innovation that is very flexible and can be used to communicate with any smartphone. Designed by Apple, iBeacons work on a localized basis, and many retailers, bars, restaurants and transport companies have adopted this technology to give customers information on the latest deals and offers.

Arguably, iBeacons are bridging the gap between the digital and physical world by seamlessly linking together communication devices, creating opportunities for peer-to-peer sharing of coupons and vouchers, and creating Retail 2.0, whereby companies can push content to their customers depending where they are in a store.

Based on: Vanhemert (2014); Shazam (n.d.); Bold (2014)

Scan the QR code to find out how the Shazam In-Store app creates a personalized shopping experience.

Mobile marketing has several advantages. It is:

- *cost effective*. The cost per message is between 15p and 25p, compared with 50p to 75p per direct mail shot, including print production and postage.
- *targeted and personalized*. For example, operators like Vodafone, Virgin Mobile and Blyk offer free texts and voice calls to customers if they sign up to receive some advertising. In signing up, customers have to fill out questionnaires on their hobbies and interests.
- *interactive*. The receiver can respond to the text message, setting up the opportunity for two-way communication.
- *personal*. It enables dialogues and relationship development. Retailers like DixonCarphone are developing ongoing 'conversations' with their customers across a range of mobile and digital media.
- *time-flexible*. Text messages can be sent at any time, giving greater flexibility when trying to reach the recipient.
- able to *engage the audience*. This is becoming known as *proximity marketing*. Messages can be sent to mobile users at nightclubs, shopping centres, festivals and universities, indeed wherever recipients are at any time of the day or night.
- *immediately available*. For example, the US consumer electronics retailer, Best Buy, sends special offers and deals to customer smartphones using a technology that pinpoints when they are entering a Best Buy store.
- *immediate and measurable*. It can assist in database development.
- the *gateway to other channels*. For example, while the majority of marketers spend less than 5 per cent of their marketing budgets on mobile marketing, smartphones are increasingly replacing other devices as the means by which users download music, films and other multimedia content, access the web, answer their emails and navigate (e.g. satnav apps). **QR codes** may increasingly be linked to an app store, where coupons can be downloaded for instant use.

Viral marketing is defined as the passing of information about products and services by verbal or electronic means in an informal, person-to-person manner. It is also about identifying triggers that will prompt new conversations from target audiences. For example, Red Bull wanted to drive awareness for its Stratos mission, which aimed to test the limits of human capabilities and to contribute to scientific understanding. So it set up a team of medical and aerospace experts, and using a helium-filled balloon took Felix Baumgartner to the edge of the stratosphere, where he jumped back to earth. To engage a global audience for this event, Red Bull created a destination website and a social media site, and created a game with a prize of £12,000 for the person who guessed most accurately (on an interactive map) where Felix would land. The viral part of the campaign attracted over 250,000 followers on Twitter after one day. This turned out to be one of the biggest events on the Internet; 9 million people watched the jump online; 8 million streamed the video on YouTube; there were 26 million unique visits to the website; and on the day of the event there were 29,000 shares on Facebook of Felix on the ground, in just 40 minutes (Ryan, 2014).

The spread of messages through viral marketing is usually driven by personal interests, which will determine which messages are successfully shared. However, this can lead to unpredictable trends emerging. For example, Shabani, a gorilla at the Hiashiyama Zoo, captured the imagination (and hearts) of Japanese women, who referred to him with similar words they would use for actors like George Clooney and Hugh Jackman: 'dark and brooding', 'hunky', 'heart throb'. Shabani went viral as pictures and comments were widely shared on social media. This has also sent visitors flocking to the zoo to get a closer look at this primate (Murphy, 2015).

 Scan the QR code to see viral content of Shabani the gorilla.

Buzz marketing is similar to viral marketing and more traditional word-of-mouth marketing, long recognized as one of the most powerful forms of marketing, but it has enjoyed a renaissance due to advances in technology such as email, websites and mobile phones.

The first step in a buzz marketing campaign involves identifying and targeting 'alphas'—that is, the trendsetters that adopt new ideas and technologies early on—and the 'bees', who are the early adopters. Brand awareness then passes from these customers to others, who seek to emulate the trendsetters. In many instances, the alphas are celebrities who either directly or indirectly push certain brands . Once the target audience has been identified, the next key decisions, like those for all forms of promotion, are the message and the medium. The message may take many forms, such as a funny video clip or email attachment, a blog or story, an event such as a one-off concert, and so on. But, as with all aspects of buzz marketing, the only limitation is the imagination. For example, many individuals have used parts of their bodies or their private cars to carry commercial messages. Finally, given its novelty, evaluating the effectiveness of buzz marketing is difficult. Numbers are available regarding how many times a video clip is viewed but marketers will not be able to determine by whom. For example, when a nearly naked image of model and reality television star Kim Kardashian appeared on the cover of *Paper* magazine, it created an instantaneous buzz and went viral on a global scale. Jean-Paul Goude aimed to #BreakTheInternet with his controversial image of Kim. And in just two hours, the image had been re-tweeted over 70,000 times, and within a day nearly 1 per cent of the US browsing traffic had seen the story (Hershkovits, 2014).

Websites are an important part of an organization's communication strategy. The web offers a high degree of flexibility in terms of what can be created in a website, along with supporting digital technologies, which have revolutionized how organizations communicate.

Some organizations have developed highly sophisticated websites that target various global audiences with an extensive range of product. However, others have been far more timid, developing small-scale experimental applications: for example, the stark contrast between the reach and sophistication of Tesco.com compared to Morrison.co.uk (Doherty and Ellis-Chadwick, 2009). Websites are potentially much more than a form of advertising as they can be used as an online store, an information repository, a portal or gateway for many different services. Two examples of website types are:

1 *Intermediaries websites*—which act as a portal or gateway to a variety of content. Examples are:
   - *Mainstream news media sites or portals.* These include traditional, for example, FT.com, Times, Guardian, Pureplay, Google news.
   - *Social networks*, for example, Facebook, Twitter, LinkedIn, Renren, Google+
   - *Price comparison sites* (also known as aggregators), for example, Moneysupermarket, Kelkoo, Shopping.com, confused.com, mysupermarket.com.

- *Superaffiliates*. Affiliates gain revenue from a merchant they refer traffic to by being paid commission based on a proportion of the sale or a fixed amount. They are important in e-retail markets, accounting for significant sales.
- *Niche affiliates or bloggers*. These are often individuals but they may be important, for example, in the UK Martin Lewis of Moneysavingexpert.com receives millions of visits every month. Smaller affiliates and bloggers can be important collectively.

2 *Destination sites*. These are the sites that the marketer is trying to generate visitors for and which may be transactional sites: for example, retailers—John Lewis Partnership; financial services—Aviva.com; travel companies—ryanair.com, manufacturer's brands—Procter & Gamble.

Social Media and Social Networking

Social media and social networking are relatively new phenomena, which are shaping the way some sectors of society communicate. Digital natives (Prensky, 2001), keyboard warriors and serial bloggers live out parts of their lives online, in communities created at virtual meeting places like Facebook, Biip, Habbo, Pinterest or Weibo. The Internet has given us a virtual environment which has wrapped its way around the planet and created a platform for a multitude of activities. Social networking is the most pervasive so far; it has overtaken porn as the number 1 online activity, and consequently is proving to be of great interest to marketers as a potential communication and sales channel. In comparison, it took radio nearly 40 years to reach 50 million listeners and television 13 years to reach the same number, but in just four years 50 million users had Internet access and in less than one year over 100 million people had a Facebook account (Tuten and Solomon, 2013: 3). Table 16.1 shows the examples of social media sites, their country of origin and key community users. There are many online communities, which focus on various interests from art to education, but by far the most compelling driver of community growth is socializing, and sharing information, pictures, music and video.

TABLE 16.1 Social media sites, their origin and users				
Social network	**Country of origin**	**User community**	**Number of members**	**Geographical scope**
Facebook	USA	Youth 13+	1.4 billion	Global
Renren	China	College students	223 million	China, Asia
QQ	China	Business and professionals	829 million	China, Asia
LinkedIn	USA		347 million	Europe, Asia, South Africa
Badoo	Europe	Place to meet with friends	252 million	Europe and Latin America
Tagged	USA	Youth 13+ Mature users 35+	300 million	North America
Instagram	USA	Under 35, predominantly female	300 million	USA
Google+	USA	Male-dominated community of users	300 million	USA, Europe
Pinterest	USA	Tablet users, young adults, mainly female	73 million	USA, Europe
Twitter	USA	Mainly under-30s	675 million	Global

Source: http://en.wikipedia.org/wiki/List_of_social_networking_websites (accessed June 2015)

In reality, social networks are nothing new and certainly were not invented by Tom Anderson (Myspace), Mark Zuckerberg (Facebook) or Joseph Chen (Renren). Social networks have existed almost since the beginning of human kind. They consist of people (for the purpose of this text) who are connected together by relationships, friendships or interests. In 1975, Burke and Weir (1975) found that individuals prefer to turn to friends and family in times of need, and being part of a social community gives individuals a sense of purpose (Argyle and Henderson, 1985). Sociologists suggested that a great deal of our daily lives involves relationships between *helpers* and *recipients* (of help) (Amato and Saunders, 1990) and the nature of these relationships is at the heart of the creation of social networks.

Online social networks have spread through global societies and research provides insight into this rapid diffusion (Katona, Zubcsek and Sarvary, 2010). It has been found that a potential adopter of a social network that is connected to many adopters (already members of a social network) is predisposed toward becoming an adopter him/ herself. In other words, if you know many people who are, say, connected to Facebook, you are more likely to become a member than if very few of your friends, family, work colleagues are members. You are also more likely to join a network that already has many members than one that is new with few members. The purpose of a social network is to enable an online community to use the functionality tools of the site (e.g. Pinterest, enable the sharing of pictures and images; YouTube, the sharing of video) to share messages, ideas and content with an online community of *friends* (term used by Facebook).

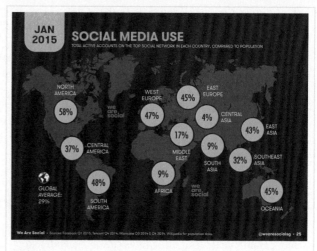

EXHIBIT 16.3
The global spread of social media. Find out more and get the latest statistics: http://wearesocial.net/tag/sdmw

So, now we understand a little about why more people than ever before are connected to each other via the Internet. But who are these people, what are they actually doing online, what is the impact of virtual communities on marketing? The rest of this section explores who social media consumers are and what they are doing online. How are social media used in marketing? What is the impact of social media on social behaviour?

Social networks are a well-established part of the digital world, and even though user communities differ in terms of the value proposition to members and the demographic profile, it is important for marketers to understand the nature and reach of the platforms they might use as part of their digital campaigns. See Mini Case 16.1 to discover how crowdsourcing can be used to develop advertising campaigns (see Exhibit 16.3).

Who are social media consumers?

What do Eminem, Lady Gaga, Van Diesel and Megan Fox have in common? Nearly 20 million Facebook users say they like them. As well as saying who they like, every hour Facebook users share 3 million links, tag 4 million photos, upload almost 9 million pictures and post over 30 million comments (Kiss, 2011). But who are the members of social network communities and which businesses are seeking to target online communities?

Research has found that over 9 per cent of marketers use social media and over three-quarters feel this environment is important to their business (Miller, 2012).

By 2015, 29 per cent of the world's population that had access to the Internet used social networking sites, and nearly 50 per cent had mobile phones. Their users are most likely to be aged between 18 and 49, as almost three-quarters of all adults in these age bands say they use one or more social networking sites. They are most likely to have some form of post-16 education and are slightly more likely to be female than male.

Age has been a key differentiator of the users of social networks since their inception. Although the number of users over the age of 65 is increasing, those under 30 are more likely to use a social networking site than any other age group. Social media are increasingly being added to campaigns targeting younger audiences and for commercial and non-commercial marketing campaigns. For example, a partnership between World Animal Protection and Netherlands advertising agency FVV BBDO used a 3D printer and social media to raise awareness of the harm done by tourists riding elephants when they go on holiday. Each time someone in the Netherlands (or a visitor to Schiphol airport) made a pledge online, another section of the elephant was printed (Oakes, 2015). See Exhibit 16.4.

How social media are used in marketing

Developing a plan for using social media is much the same as any other marketing planning exercise in so far as there is a requirement to understand the situation in which social media are going to be used, the needs of the target audience and their behaviour. It is also equally important to set clear objectives. This is perhaps where the planning process becomes more complicated. In order to state objectives, a company must be clear about the types of objectives that can be achieved through social media. According to Tuten and Solomon (2015), companies using social media can be at different stages, which can have implications for the types of objectives they are likely to pursue:

Trial phase—at this level, a company has just begun using social media and is testing what it can deliver. There is a tendency to 'play' and experiment. At this stage, there is little consideration of longer-term strategic objectives, as the focus is on making use of social media platforms like Facebook, Twitter and YouTube. The types of objectives typically pursued at the level are: increasing website traffic and improving public relations.

Transition phase—this occurs when companies are making more significant use of social media. This can be considered as a mature phase. Beall's, a US department store, began using Internet advertising in the early days to drive

EXHIBIT 16.4
World Animal Protection crosses the boundary between the digital and physical world to raise awareness of the plight of elephants used in the tourism industry

traffic to its website and promote sales, etc. Currently, the company makes extensive use of social media in order to engage its target audiences in conversation. The company's Facebook pages are updated several times a day and commercial fan coupons are released so they can be shared among the community. At this phase, the use of social media becomes more sophisticated and more integrated with the IMC and marketing strategy. At this level examples of objectives are: improving public relations and increasing product awareness.

Strategic phase—this occurs when an organization enters the final level. At this point the use of social media will be fully integrated across the business activities and incorporated into all levels of planning. At this level, the majority of adopters are pursuing objectives such as: increasing brand awareness, improving brand reputation and increasing website traffic.

Across all of the phases limited attention is given to objectives associated with increasing sales or reducing costs.

Once objectives have been set, the next stage in planning social media initiatives is to gather insight into target audiences by finding out which segments to target and which type of social media is the most appropriate. It is especially important to find out about their media habits, interests and online behaviour. This analysis should help to focus on the type of social media area (as discussed earlier in the chapter), for example *social community media*, *social publishing media*, *social commerce media* or *social entertainment media*.

Each area has implications for the types of social media that the organization might employ to achieve its objectives. Figure 16.4 shows the different zones.

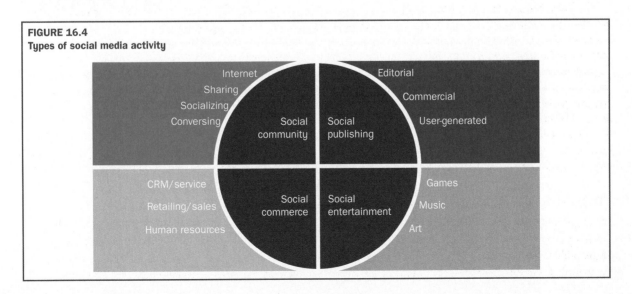

FIGURE 16.4
Types of social media activity

MINI CASE 16.1
Crowdsourcing of Advertising

Marketing is increasingly using the Internet in more innovative ways. One of these is crowdsourcing as a means of exploiting user-generated content (UGC) as part of an advertising campaign.

One great example of crowdsourcing is the 'Crash the Super Bowl' campaign from Doritos. This annual competition is run to unearth a television advert that Doritos will air live on one of its prestigious and hugely expensive television slots during the NFL Super Bowl in the USA. Since its launch in 2006, thousands of adverts have been submitted. The winner not only gets to see the advert shown live during one of the world's largest sports events, but also wins $1 million and a job at Universal Pictures. Perhaps one of the most interesting aspects of this competition is that the public decides who the winner is from a shortlist of eight finalists whose 30-second videos are uploaded to YouTube a month before the Super Bowl is played. This innovative and hugely engaging campaign puts crowdsourcing at the centre of not only the production but also the decision-making behind which advert will be shown.

The impact of this competition is that it generates great PR and also uncovers a talented mix of video producers who can be used by the company for more standard promotional work. The real positive for Doritos is that it is able to create a narrative that runs alongside the sporting event. The public are engaged in the process, and the impact and brand awareness of the company grows as interest in the potential winner increases. The narrative is also enhanced by the fact that official odds are given as to the likely winner and people are able to place bets not only on the winner of the Super Bowl but also on who will win the Dorito's advert competition. This type of organized crowdsourcing, although appearing to give control to the general public, can legitimately be included as part of a conventional media execution.

It can be argued that crowdsourcing is still in its infancy and has the potential to grow using other platforms. One that has attracted a large amount of interest is the crowdsourcing content of the 'Our Stories' feature on Snapchat. When at an event, anyone using the app with the location setting turned on and posting their pictures to 'Our Stories' may have their post collated into an 'official' collection of snaps for that event. These are uploaded by Snapchat in near real-time (after a moderating process) and appear as part of the timeline of the event. The timeline can be viewed by anybody. Snapchat often utilizes the 'Our Stories' feature for NCAA College Football matches, and the timeline regularly features snaps taken from not only the fans but also players, giving a unique view not offered anywhere else. These 'Our Stories' include pre-event, in-event and post-event content, with the added interest of the sportsmen/musicians and so on also snapping behind-the-scenes action. The rise of this type of activity is particularly powerful in the area of event marketing, where new perspectives can be generated that would not be possible using conventional media.

Questions:

1. A big factor in crowdsourcing is that it enables the public to influence a marketing communication. What are the pros and cons of this type of influence?
2. To what extent do you think that crowdsourcing and conventional marketing approaches are compatible?
3. Organizational structures have adapted to the rapid rise of the World Wide Web. To what extent do you expect crowdsourced marketing campaigns, such as the Doritos Crash the Super Bowl campaign, to continue to be popular, and what are the consequences of this to a marketing organization?

Social community: in this type of community individuals build personal profiles and these form the basis of what other community members can see and engage with. In addition there are indicators as to the type of presence an individual wishes to portray. For example, they can use availability indicators, mood icons, friend lists, status updates and news feeds, which can be shared with other community members (e.g. Facebook).

Social publishing: in this type of community the focus is on producing content: written, video, audio, and in the form of blogs, microblogs, reviews, press releases, webinars, podcasts. Site examples are Twitter, YouTube and Pinterest.

Social commerce: in this type of site the community interest is shopping, developing relationships and providing support. The aim of the community is to enhance the shopping experience through referrals, ratings, reviews and sharing opinions of levels of service. Retailers are part of these communities and they seek to educate shoppers about their products and services. Site examples are Groupon, Etsy, Facebook.

Social entertainment: involves communities of like-minded individuals who play games and enjoy online entertainment. Social games include games platforms such as Sony Playstation3 and Microsoft Xbox which enable multiplayer games. Other genres of games are *simulation games* (e.g. Farmville), *action games* (e.g. Epic goal, Paradise Paint Ball), *role playing games* (e.g. Dungeons and Dragons, Tennis Mania) and *strategy games* (e.g. Word Cube, Kingdoms of Camelot). Game-based marketing means that brands take part and offer social games which have promotional marketing elements. In-game advertising is also popular as well as product placement.

A key benefit of digital technology is that it allows companies to target very specific markets, even a market of one. This means developing plans to operate as 'micronichers', customizing communications to the needs of an individual. Broadly speaking, at this highly customized level it is crucial to know which variables are most important for the target customer. A digital marketing manager should know the key triggers for individual (targeted) customer decisions (best price, best quality, best delivery, best service, best image, best environment) as this will help to determine which form of digital marketing is the most significant.

The rise of microblogging

In the early part of the 21st century, blogging platforms appeared on a regular basis allowing individuals and (perhaps more importantly) the non-technical participants of business to publish content on the Internet for others to see and share. Many commentators, such as Robert Scoble, identified the blog as a key platform that businesses could use to engage directly with customers, sharing news and views and communicating values through what appeared to be a more human and organic approach.

With the growth of other participatory content-creation platforms, including Facebook, the question has to be asked whether blogs have simply blurred into mainstream media production—or is there still a place for something special called 'a blog'? Many corporate blogs have become part of the normal production of everyday marketing communications. Too many blogs are not written by the CEO, but by a ghost writer, and they seem less of an insight and a direct communication with customers and more of a channel to broadcast news. Celebrity bloggers seem to have moved channels, with many transforming their content into written literature or working with traditional media news outlets. Other blogs have increased in size (e.g. Mashable and BoingBoing), in terms of followers.

However, platforms such as Twitter (described as a 'micro-blogging' tool) have become increasingly popular. Successful blogs have become social networks in their own right—which establishes 'the blog' as potentially the digital heart of a community. Marketers who identify this may find they are able to access customers directly in their channel of preference. As for the small business, a blog becomes a valuable and simple communication tool. Micro-blogging platforms now regard themselves as content-management systems that are easy to use. The name may be changing as a result of evolution, but there are still elements that will persist for the foreseeable future.

Once the focus of the social media campaign is decided then the messages need to be shaped and the experience decided on. This is challenging for many brands and organizations as they have to determine how to engage their customers in an online social space. In the final stages of the planning activity an activation plan is defined and suggestions on how to measure performance are offered.

Measurement of social media involves looking at levels of:

- *activity*—frequency and number of blogs, and posts
- *interaction*—frequency of registrations, downloads, time spent on the site
- *performance*—customer lifetime value, lead conversion rates, ROI (Tuten and Solomon, 2013: 209).

However, engaging with a target audience through microblogging sites requires just as much attention to detail and planning as using any other form of digital marketing. But the real-time nature of this form of communication can present many challenges. See Marketing in Action 16.4 for further discussion of how microblogging has been used in digital campaigns.

MARKETING IN ACTION 16.4
Microblogging Winners and Losers

Digital and social media are pushing the boundaries of marketing activities in many ways, but they are not always successful. Here are two extreme examples.

Winners: Greggs the bakers

One day Google made a marketing faux pas when its search engine optimization algorithm automatically displayed the tagline 'Providing s**t to scum for over 70 years' to accompany Greggs' online adverts. The slogan should have read 'Always fresh and always tasty', as it is part of the company's logo. What happened next was a Twitter storm that engaged and amused a nation of tweeters. The social media team at Greggs were quick to respond to Google's mistake, and rapidly took control of the situation. They set up the hashtag #FixGreggs and responded to tweets with humorous replies.

Google then quickly joined the conversation and followed the humorous tone set by Greggs by using an image of Homer Simpson eating doughnuts and the following tweet:

'Sorry @GreggstheBakers, we're on it. Throw in a sausage roll and we'll get it done ASAP. #fixgreggs'

The dialogue between Greggs and Google continued in a light-hearted fashion, and somewhat surprisingly no legal action ensued. Once the issue was fixed, the mistake was drawn to a close by Greggs.

The lessons learned from this example are that brands need to be able to respond quickly and appropriately. Brands should ensure they have a social media team that are trained in media crisis management.

Losers: Mastercard sponsors the Brit Awards but finds trying to bribe journalist is a dangerous game

When Mastercard's PR agency tried to tempt *Telegraph* journalist Tim Walker with a pass to the Brit Awards in return for mentioning #PricelessSurprises, the agency didn't quite get what it bargained for. Mastercard was a sponsor of the Brit Awards and it required Walker to publish tweets that included the hashtag and URL before, during and after the event. He refused, but shared a message that elicited some very negative tweets from other journalists in the press community. For example, Felicity Morse, social media editor for the *Independent*, tweeted with a pun on the credit card's own brand slogan: '*Good press coverage is hard to bribe. For everything else there's Mastercard. #PricelessSurprises*' (Morse, 2014).

The lessons learned in this case are that ethical and moral principles should not be sidelined, and brands need to maintain a standard of behaviour fitting of the brand, both online and offline.

Based on: Bold (2014); Haggerty (2014); Ponsford (2014); Smith (2014)

Ethical Issues in Digital Marketing

Increased adoption of digital technologies within marketing has had many beneficial effects, such as increasing customer choice and convenience, and enabling smaller companies to compete in global markets across a range of digital platforms. However, there are some key ethical issues emerging as a result of increased usage of digital technologies.

The digital divide and social exclusion

The historical timeline of the development of Internet technologies reveals that, in the early days, it served highly specialized purposes and was used by expert technologists. Expansion and changes in the development of the World Wide Web have made Internet technology more accessible to a greater number of people, but there remains a virtual divide between the technology's 'haves' and 'have nots'. Hoffman and Novak (1999) examined the extent to which the Internet has become indispensable, and found significant differences in usage based on race and educational attainment. They concluded that educational attainment is crucial if the digital divide is to be closed, and that efforts should be made to improve access for Hispanic and black populations in North America (Hoffman, Novak and Venkatesh, 2004).

Public and private organizations around the globe need to find creative solutions to improve Internet access for all citizens, regardless of their demographic background, as they should not be deprived of Internet access due to financial restrictions, a poor education and/or a lack of computer skills. From a commercial perspective it is also important to acknowledge that while the networks forming the Internet reach around the globe, access is far from equal and equitable.

However, mobile phones and digital television (DTV) have been more widely adopted and reach into the community. For example, mobile phone ownership is currently nearing 95 per cent of the adult population and DTV reaches 63 per cent of households (Ofcom, 2005). The digital divide in computing might also be on the point of being bridged, with a £7 laptop being launched in India (Ramesh, 2009).

Recent research suggests that there is a new form of digital divide forming (Office of Communications, 2005). As digital technologies become more widespread it is specific aspects of the technologies that form divisions. For example, Londoners prefer to talk rather than text, whereas in Northern Ireland more texts are sent per week than anywhere else in the UK; rural Internet users are stuck with slow connections in comparison with their urban neighbours, and three hours more television is watched per week in Scotland than anywhere else in the UK.

Another ethical consideration is the fear of technological exclusion of the poorest members of society who cannot afford a computer, broadband connection, interactive television, digital radio or 4G network connection and smartphone and therefore cannot benefit from the vast array of products and services available, or access to information sources.

However, there is also evidence of technology delivering advantages to socially deprived sectors of society. Mobile phones have aided homeless people by allowing them to avoid the embarrassment of not having a permanent address by giving a mobile number on job applications (Office of the Deputy Prime Minister, 2005). Additionally, mobile phones are reportedly popular with people who are deaf and hard of hearing, as using the short messaging service (SMS) functions on mobiles helps people with hearing difficulties to communicate freely by sending text messages (*BBC News*, 2002).

When you have read this chapter

Discover further resources and test your understanding: McGraw-Hill **Connect**™ is a digital teaching and learning environment that improves performance over a variety of critical outcomes; it can be tailored, is easy to use and is proven effective. **LearnSmart**™ is the most widely used and intelligent adaptive learning resource that is proven to strengthen memory recall, improve course retention and boost grades. Fuelled by **LearnSmart**™, **SmartBook**™ is the first and only adaptive reading experience available today.

Review

1 **The concept of digital marketing**
   - The application of digital technologies that form channels to market (the Internet, mobile, wireless, and digital television) to achieve corporate goals through meeting and exceeding customer needs better than the competition.

2 **The concept of social media**
   - Online social communities which facilitate the sharing of ideas, information, publishing documents and video content. The concept is increasingly being used by marketing managers as part of their digital marketing campaigns.

3 **Dimensions of the digital communication environment**
- There are four key dimensions to consider: technology, applications, marketing, and audiences.

4 **Digital marketing and social media planning**
- Deciding how to plan, resource, integrate, implement and monitor digital marketing activities can be guided by applying established marketing management principles and planning activities (as discussed in detail in Chapters 2 and 3). New technologies can be used to meet a range of different business objectives: sales, communications, or focus on the development and maintenance of mutually satisfying long-term relationships with customers by using digital technologies.

5 **Digital marketing objectives**
- Fall into five categories; grow sales, add value, get closer to customers, save costs, and extend the brand online. Marketing managers need to select objectives which meet their needs.

6 **Digital marketing tools**
- Types of digital marketing include online advertising, online video and interactive television advertising, mobile marketing, buzz marketing, websites and social media.

7 **Social media and social networking**
- A term used to refer to online community websites, with individuals who can become members, share ideas and interests, for example Facebook; publish and distribute articles and video and other multimedia content, for example YouTube; carry out social commerce activities like writing reviews, buying and selling, for example TripAdvisor; play games across communities, for example Zynga.

8 **Ethical issues in digital marketing**
- These are the potentially harmful effects of creating a digital divide between those with digital access and those without. The possible outcome is social exclusion of those who cannot afford digital devices.

Key Terms

blog short for weblog; a personal diary/journal on the web; information can easily be uploaded on to a website and is then available for general consumption by web users

buzz marketing the passing between individuals of information about products and services that is sufficiently interesting to act as a trigger for the individuals to share the information with others

digital marketing the application of digital technologies that form channels to market (the Internet, mobile communications, interactive television and wireless) to achieve corporate goals through meeting and exceeding customer needs better than the competition

microblogging involves the posting of short messages on social media sites like Twitter and Reddit

mobile marketing the sending of text messages to mobile phones to promote products and build relationships with consumers

multichannel involves an organization that is using different channels—physical retailer stores, the web and mobile, to enable its customers to buy, communicate, gain access to information or pay for goods and services. The organization in return provides consistent levels of service and marketing mix across all of the channels

omni channel the bringing together of all of the customer touchpoints into a seamless shopping journey, which means that every time the customer 'touches' or interacts with a company, for example by store, by phone, by the web by mobile

QR codes a form of barcode which, once scanned, can link the user directly to web content, digital adverts and other available content. They are easy to use and smartphones can read the codes

social media online community websites with individuals who can become members, share ideas and interests, for example Facebook; publish and distribute articles and video and other multimedia content, for example YouTube; carry out social commerce activities like writing reviews, buying and selling, for example TripAdvisor; or play games across communities, for example Zynga

Study Questions

1. Explain the meaning of the terms digital marketing and social media.

2. Identify the key dimensions of the digital communication environment.

3. Is digital the death knell for marketing? Discuss how marketing might be affected by the dimensions of the digital communication environment.

4. Suggest how a business-to-consumer organization might use a multichannel approach. Give examples of companies using a multichannel approach.

5. Consumer behaviour is highly variable and complex. Suggest what variables a marketing manager might use to help him gain a better understanding of the company's online target audiences.

6. Discuss the key considerations when developing a digital and social media campaign.

7. Identify and explain the different types of digital marketing tools.

8. Explain social media and suggest how this growing phenomenon might be used by marketing managers.

9. Discuss the key ethical issues a marketing manager might consider when planning a social media campaign.

Recommended Reading

Chaffey (2015), The state of digital marketing http://www. slideshare.net/Smart-Insights

Chaffey, D. (2015, June 24). *Introducing RACE: a practical framework to improve your digital marketing*. Retrieved from Smart Insights: http://www. smartinsights.com/digital-marketing-strategy/race-a -practical-framework-to-improve-your-digital -marketing/

Chaffey, D. and F. Ellis-Chadwick (2016) *Digital Marketing: Strategy, Implementation and Practice.* Harlow, Essex: Pearson 6th Edition

Ellis-Chadwick, F. and N. F. Doherty (2012), Web Advertising: The role of e-mail marketing *Journal of Business Research* 65 (6), 843-848

Tiago, M. T. P. M. B. and J. M. C. Veríssimo (2014) Digital marketing and social media: Why bother? *Business Horizons* 57(6), 703–8.

Tuten, T. and M. Solomon (2015) *Social Media Marketing*, 2nd edn., LA, USA: Sage.

References

Akhtar, T. (2012) Brands search for higher level of reception, *Marketing Week*, 5 January, 18–20.

Amato, R. and J. Saunders (1990) Personality and social network involvement as predictors of helping behaviour in everyday life, *Social Psychology Quarterly* 53(1), 31–43.

Argyle, M. and M. Henderson (1985) *The Anatomy of Relationships and the Rules and Skills Needed to Manage Them Successfully*, London: Heinemann.

Arora, N., X. Dreze, A. Ghose, J. D. Hess, R. Iyengar, B. Jing, Y. Joshi, V. Kumar, N. Lurie, S. Neslin, S. Sajeesh, M. Su, N. Syam, J. Thomas and Z. J. Zhang (2008) Putting One-to-One Marketing to Work: Personalization, Customization, and Choice, *Marketing Letters* 19, 305–21.

Barnett, M. (2011) Why websites generate much more than sales, *Marketing Week*, 16 June, 22–3.

Basu, A. and S. Muylle (2003) Online support for commerce processes by web retailers, *Decision Support Systems* 34(4), 379–95.

BBC News (2002) Deaf Go Mobile Phone Crazy, at http://news.bbc. co.uk/1/hi/sci/tech/1808872.stm.

Bold, B. (2014) Greggs gives lesson in Twitter crisis management after fake logo debacle, *Marketing Week*, 20 August, Greggs twitter campaign (accessed 20 June 2015).

Borges, T. M. T. P. M. and Veríssimo, J. M. C. (2014) Digital marketing and social media: Why bother? *Business Horizons* 57(6), 703–8.

Brashear, T. G., V. Kashyap, M. D. Musante and N. Donthu (2009) A profile of the Internet shopper: evidence from six countries, *Journal of Marketing Theory and Practice* 17(3), 267–281.

Burke, R. J. and T. Weir (1975) Receiving and giving help with work and non-work related problems, *Journal of Business Administration* 6, 59–78.

Chaffey (2008) Rise Through the Ranks, *The Marketer*, November, 51–3.

Chaffey, D. (2015) Introducing RACE: a practical framework to improve your digital marketing, Smart Insights, 24 June. http://www.smartinsights.com/digital-marketing-strategy/ race-a-practical-framework-to-improve-your-digital-marketing

Chaffey, D. and Ellis-Chadwick (2016) *Digital Marketing: Strategy, Implementation and Practice*, 6th edn, Harlow, Essex, UK: Pearson.

Chaffey, D. and F. E. Ellis-Chadwick (2012) *Digital Marketing: Strategy, Implementation and Practice*, 5th edn, Harlow: Pearson, 8.

Chaffey, D. and P. R. Smith (2008) *eMarketing Excellence: Planning and Optimizing your Digital Marketing*, Oxford: Butterworth Heinemann; Payne, A. F. T. and P. Frow (2005) A Strategic Framework for Customer Relationship Marketing, *Journal of Marketing* 69(4), 161–76.

Chaffey, D., K. Johnston, R. Mayer and F. Ellis-Chadwick (eds.) (2000) *Internet Marketing: strategy, implementation and practice*, Harlow: Prentice Hall/Financial Times, 411.

Deneen, K. and D. Yu (2015) Online Shopping Is Making Many Customers Antagonistic, Gallup.com/Business Journal, 17 March. http://www.gallup.com/businessjournal/182006/online-shopping-making-customers-antagonistic.aspx

Doherty, N. and F. Ellis-Chadwick (2004) Strategic Thinking in the Internet Era, *British Rail Consortium [BRC] Consortium Solutions* 3, 59–63.

Doherty, N. F. and F. Ellis-Chadwick (2009) Exploring the drivers, scope and perceived success of e-commerce strategies in the UK retail sector, *European Journal of Marketing* 43(9/10), 1246–62.

Doherty, N. F. and F. Ellis-Chadwick (2010a) Internet retailing: the past, the present and the future, *International Journal of Retail & Distribution Management* 38(11/12), 943–65.

Doherty, N. F. and F. Ellis-Chadwick (2010b) Evaluating the role of electronic commerce in transforming the retail sector, *The International Review of Retail, Distribution and Consumer Research*, 20(4), 375–78.

DTI (2004) *Business in the Information Age: The International Benchmarking Study 2004*.

Feefo (2015) http://www.feefo.com/web/en

Fenwick, T. (2010) *Bar Code Technology, Retail Management and Marketing*, The Open University, iTunes.

Frary, M. (2012) Staff may be remote but they're not out of touch, *The Times*, 1 May.

Friedlein, A. (2015) Are we witnessing a reverse takeover of marketing by digital? *Marketing Week*, 18 May. http://www.marketingweek.com/2015/05/18/our-modern-marketing-manifesto-revisited (accessed 28 May 2015).

Google AdWords (2006) https://adwords.google.co.uk/select/Login?sourceid=AWO&subid=UK-ET-ADS&hl-en_GB, accessed 30 April 2006.

Google AdWords (2015) How it works. https://www.google.co.uk/adwords/how-it-works

Grant, J. (2008) Timesaver or Digital Foot in the Door?, *The Guardian*, Special Report on Internet Advertising, 3 November, 4.

Haggerty, A. (2014) Mastercard's #PricelessSurprises Brit Awards nightmare unfolds after House PR demands rile the nation's journalists, *The Drum*, 19 February. http://www.thedrum.com/news/2014/02/19/mastercards-pricelesssurprises-pr-nightmare-unfolds-after-house-pr-riled-nations (accessed 20 June 2015).

Handley, L. (2013) For the best user-generated content, look to the newsstand, *Marketing Week*, 20 March. http://www.marketingweek.com/2013/03/20/for-the-best-user-generated-content-look-to-the-newsstand (accessed 20 June 2015).

Hemsley, S. (2015) How to create content relevant to your business, *Marketing Week*, 12 June. http://www.marketingweek.com/2015/06/12/how-to-create-content-relevant-to-your-business

Hershkovits, D. (2014) How Kim Kardashian broke the internet with her butt, *The Guardian*, 17 December. http://www.theguardian.com/lifeandstyle/2014/dec/17/kim-kardashian-butt-break-the-internet-paper-magazine (accessed 25 June 2015).

Hoffman, D. and T. Novak (1999) *The Growing Digital Divide: Implications for an Open Research Agenda*, eLab Owen Graduate School of Management Vanderbilt University (http://ecommerce.vanderbilt.edu/).

Hoffman, D. L., T. P. Novak and A. Venkatesh (2004) Has the Internet Become Indispensable? *Communications of the ACM* 47(7), 37–42.

Hoffman, L. and T. P. Novak (1997) A New Marketing Paradigm for Electronic commerce, *The Information Society* 13, 43–54.

Internet World Stats (2015) Internet Stats and Facebook Usage in Europe, Internet World Stats, 21 June. http://www.internetworldstats.com/stats4.htm

Jayawardhena, C., L. T. Wright and C. Dennis (2007) Consumers online: intentions, orientations and segmentation, *International Journal of Retail & Distribution Management* 35(6), 512–26.

Jones, G. (2011) The Carphone Warehouse harnesses the power of the mobile medium to facilitate multi-channel assistance and drive sales, *Marketing Week*, May, 43.

Katona, Z., P. P. Zubcsek and M. Sarvary (2010) Network effects and personal influence: the diffusion of an online social network, *Journal of Marketing Research* 48(3), 425–43.

Kaufman-Scarborough, C., M. Morrin, G. Petro and E. T. Bradlow (2006) Improving the Crystal Ball: Consumer Consensus and Retail Prediction Markets, Working Paper: The Wharton School of the University of Pennsylvania, April.

Kim, C. S., W. H. Zhao and K. H. Yang (2008) An Empirical Study on the Integrated Framework of e-CRM in Online Shopping: Evaluating the Relationships Among Perceived Value, Satisfaction, and Trust Based on Customers' Perspectives, *Journal of Electronic Commerce in Organizations* 6(3), 1–19.

Kiss, J. (2011) Facebook began as a geeks hobby now it's more popular than google, *The Guardian*, 4 January, 23.

Kukar-Kinney, M., N. M. Ridgway and K. B. Monroe (2009) The relationship between consumers' tendencies to buy compulsively and their motivations to shop and buy on the Internet, *Journal of Retailing* 85(3), 298.

Martin, Arlene (2011) Want a 'sat nav' app to get round Tesco? Um, no thanks, *Which?*, 27 May.

Miller, M. (2012) The 5 Ws of social media marketing: Industry survey & insights, Search Engine Watch, http://searchenginewatch.com/article/2166552/The-5-Ws-of-Social-Media-Marketing-Industry-Survey-Insights-Study, 9 April.

Morse, F. (2014) via Twitter. https://twitter.com/felicitymorse/status/436089974941691904

Murphy, C. (2008) Campaigns Get Smart, *The Guardian*, Media Guardian Report on Changing Advertising, 22 September, 1.

Murphy, F. (2015) Japanese women go ape over 'handsome' gorilla named Shabani, *The Telegraph*, 26 June. http://www.telegraph.co.uk/news/worldnews/asia/japan/11700427/Japanese-women-go-ape-over-handsome-gorilla-named-Shabani.html

Nutley, M. (2011) Constant communication takes marketers down a beta channel, *Marketing Week*, 1 September.

Nuttall, C. (2011) Our future is up in the clouds, *Financial Times*, 17 June, 14.

O'Connor, C. (2015) Net-a-Porter's New Social Shopping App Might Be Fashion's Smartest Data Play, *Forbes*, 13 May. http://www.forbes.com/sites/clareoconnor/2015/05/13/net-a-porters-new-social-shopping-app-might-be-fashions-smartest-data-play (accessed 10 June 2015).

Oakes, O. (2015) Can data really be creative? Campaign, 19 June. http://www.campaignlive.co.uk/news/1352173

Ofcom (2005) Digital Television UK Household Penetration, www.ofcom.org.uk/media/news/2005/09/nr_20050915#content.

Office of Communications (2005) http://www.ofcom.org.uk/.

Office of the Deputy Prime Minister (2005) Digital Solutions to Social Exclusion, at http://egovmonitor.com/node/3362.

Olenski, S. (2014) 4 Myths About Affiliate Marketing You Need To Know, *Forbes*, 8 July. http://www.forbes.com/sites/steveolenski/2014/07/08/4-myths-about-affiliate-marketing-you-need-to-know

Ponsford, D. (2014) Journalist seeking accreditation for Brit Awards asked to agree to coverage of sponsor MasterCard, *Press Gazette*, 19 February. 2015, from http://www.pressgazette.co.uk/journalists-seeking-accreditation-brit-awards-asked-gaurantee-coverage-sponsor-mastercard (accessed 20 June 2015).

Prensky, M. (2001) Digital natives digital immigrants, *On the horizon* 9(5), 1–6.

Pyle, R. (1996) Electronic Commerce and the Internet, *Communications of the ACM* 39(6), 22–4.

Ramesh, R. (2009) After the World's Cheapest Car, India Launches £7 Laptop, *The Guardian*, 3 February, 19.

Ritson, M. (2015) Brands' inane 'visions' have lost touch with what consumers really use them for, *Marketing Week*, 20 May. https://www.marketingweek.com/2015/05/20/mark-ritson-brands-inane-visions-have-lost-touch-with-what-consumers-really-use-them-for

Ryan, D. (2014) *The Best Digital Marketing Campaigns in the World*, London: Kogan Page.

Shazam (n.d.) About Us, http://www.shazam.com/company

Shop Direct (2014) Shop Direct Celebrates 20 years of online Shopping, Shop Direct, 1 August. https://www.shopdirect.com/shop-direct-celebrates-20-years-online-shopping

Singh, S. (2011) Pitch, *Marketing Week*, http://pitch.marketingweek.co.uk.

Smart Insights (2015) http://www.smartinsights.com/digital-marketing-strategy/race-a-practical-framework-to-improve-your-digital-marketing

Smith, P. (2014) Offensive Greggs logo debacle: what are the lessons for other retailers? *The Guardian*, August 20. http://www.theguardian.com/media-network/media-network-blog/2014/aug/20/offensive-greggs-logo-lessons-retailers (accessed 25 June 2015).

Snoad, L. (2011) The vital connection between staff and the bottom line, *Marketing Week*, 10 November, 14–18.

Srinivasan, S., R. Anderson and P. Kishore (2002) Customer Loyalty in e-commerce: an Exploration of its Antecedents and Consequences, *Journal of Retailing* 78(1), 41–50.

Swaminathan, V., E. Lepkowska-White and B. P. Rao (1999) Browsers or buyers in cyberspace? An investigation of factors influencing electronic exchange, *Journal of Computer-Mediated Communication* 5(2), 1–19.

Sweney, M. (2012) UK advertising spending to hit £5 billion, *The Guardian* http://www.guardian.co.uk/media/2012/apr/03/uk-webadvertising-spend, 3 April.

Thorogood, P. (2015) Let's Split the Funnel, American Marketing Association, 10 June. http://ama-academics.communityzero.com/elmar?go=6097918

Tuten, T. and Solomon, M. (2015) *Social Media Marketing*, London: Sage Publications Ltd.

Tuten, T. L. and M. R. Solomon (2013) *Social Media Marketing*, Upper Saddle River NJ: Pearson, 3.

Vanhemert, K. (2014) 4 REASONS WHY APPLE'S IBEACON IS ABOUT TO DISRUPT INTERACTION DESIGN, *Wired*, 11 November. http://www.wired.com/2013/12/4-use-cases-for-ibeacon-the-most-exciting-tech-you-havent-heard-of (accessed 20 June 2015).

White, T. B., D. L. Zahay, H. Thorbj rnsen and S. Shavitt (2008) Getting too Personal: Reactance to Highly Personalized Email Solicitations, *Marketing Letters* 19(1), 39–50.

Wylie, E., S. Moore, L. Grunberg, E. Greenberg and P. Sikora (2010) What Influences Work-Family Conflict? The Function of Work Support and Working from Home, *Curr. Psychol.* 29, 104–120, DOI 10.1007/s12144-010-9075-9.

CASE 31
To Google or not to Google, that is the Question

Google helps the world to answer questions and solve problems by using its search engine, and now also offers a host of other virtual services. This case looks at how Google has created competitive advantage by using virtual information to create new products and services.

Graduate students Larry Page and Sergey Brin began developing their search technology in 1996, and Google.com was launched in September 1998. By 2014, the company had grown rapidly and Google had become a top global brand. Its rapid rise to being 'the world's biggest and best-loved search engine' can in part be attributed to the smart algorithms (mathematical instructions that computers can understand) devised by Larry and Sergey. But equally important is the value proposition (the benefits to the user) the search engine provides. Google enables its users to find relevant information quickly and easily, and delivers search results in an uncluttered format, which improves usability and increases user enjoyment online. However, in return, users of the search engine provide valuable information about their interests, lifestyles and behaviour. Indeed, Google gathers information every step of the way from when we search and browse the Web, to sending and receiving Gmail communications, to using maps to find directions. By gathering this data from its users Google is able to sell highly targeted advertising space, which enables advertisers to reach the customers they need.

But having access to personal data has not been without problems for Google. In 2014, the European minister of justice ruled that Google must allow citizens the right to request removal of links about them if they were out of date or irrelevant. This ruling came about because previously Google made some changes to make it easier for users to sign up for its additional services (e.g. Google+), which gave it access to more sources of customer data and raised questions about security of data and personal privacy because the new joining process also meant that Google could pool data about signed-up users across over 60 different services including Google search, YouTube, Gmail, Google Maps, web browsing and Blogger. The debate about access to, uses of and management of personal data continues; meanwhile Google carries on (within legal parameters) using its unique access to data

sources to provide highly targeted advertising services, through services like AdWords.

Google Technology

Data is only part of the story; the technology infrastructure is also key to Google's leadership in the search engine marketplace. Google has developed sophisticated IT resources that offer distinctively better functionality and services than its competitors, and part of the company's success comes from its network of data centres based around Santa Clara, USA. It uses thousands of computer servers to provide a search capacity much greater than its competitors.

Google's search principle is straightforward: by focusing on page rankings rather than just indexing contents, the search engine is able to provide more relevant search results than its competitors (e.g. Yahoo!, AltaVista, Excite). Search tools crawl the Web, checking the content of pages without needing to understand the meaning of the content. As a result, such 'web crawlers' are unable to differentiate between relevant and irrelevant web pages when delivering search results. However, adopting a rank-ordering system, logging pages according to the number of links from other Web pages and the structure of these connections, has enabled Google to develop a quasi-intelligent search tool. To assist the ranking process, Google also checks font sizes, whether a word appears in the page title, the position on the page in which a word appears, and a range of other page characteristics, in order to give an indication of the significance of the search term within a given page.

By making creative use of information technology resources to enhance the capabilities of its search engine, Google created a search service that was quickly perceived by its users as superior to the competition. The Google brand differentiated itself from the competition by introducing the customer benefit of 'relevance' to online searching. The business continued to grow as consumers and business users increasingly turned to the Internet as a primary source of information (searching is the second most common function of the web).

In addition to its effective and efficient use of technology resources and capabilities, Google's strong market position was supported by its financial success. This was generated by the application of an e-business model that provided free-to-user search services, highly targeted and yet discreet advertising and licensing the search technology to third parties (Google currently provides search services for a number of leading search engines). It should be noted that Google continues to generate the majority of its income from advertising. Advertisers pay per click for referrals to their web pages via the Google interface using AdWords, which are search terms chosen by the advertisers and paid for at a rate determined by the popularity of the term. The cost per click varies according to the level of competition from advertisers for a particular keyword.

Competitive Markets

Larry and Sergey had a good idea and implemented it in a manner that enabled the company to differentiate itself from the competition, while protecting itself by raising market entry barriers through innovative applications of its resources and capabilities. However, the marketplace is constantly changing as technologies advance and new entrants join the market. Google has responded by diversifying and providing niche search services—news, maps, alerts, blogs, videos for specific target audiences; Scholar (for academics) and Mobile (for remote users)—and the company continues to explore how new technologies can be used to provide innovative search services and products.

Google has entered new markets:

- Web browsers—Chrome, Google's first attempt at developing a web browser, was released in September 2008; the browser was designed to be more robust than its competitors. Since then, Chrome has increased its share of the browser market, and by 2015 accounted for just under 50 per cent global market share, overtaking Internet Explorer (18 per cent), Firefox (17 per cent) and Safari (10 per cent).

- Email—Gmail (Google email), a free email service, became available to the general public in 2007 and has become very popular, and by 2015, approaching 1 billion users worldwide, with a large percentage of accounts being accessed via mobile devices.
- Mobile Internet—Google's Android mobile phone operating system enables its users to call their friends, surf the web and find their way around through a touch-screen interface. A built-in compass enables locations of users to be pinpointed, so they can find local services such as restaurants, entertainment venues and shops. The Android operating system dominates in the global mobile smartphone market.
- Social media—in 2011, Google+ was introduced as a social network linking with Gmail, YouTube and Google search. Google+ is a follower in this market behind market leaders Facebook and Twitter.
- Apps—Google Play was launched in 2012, bringing together Android market, Google music, the ebook store and many more applications. Currently, there are over 1.4 million apps on offer through this service, and new services and products are continually being developed to meet market demand. For example, Google has launched Android pay, which is a mobile payment service, to be a contender against its competitors' mobile payment services, for example Samsung Pay and Apple Pay.

Since it was established, Google has used technology resources creatively and, in so doing, has developed superior technology-based capabilities that have enabled the company to become financially successful and stay ahead of the competition. In terms of the search market advertising revenues, Google dominates with around 55 per cent share; followed by Baidu (China), which has just under 9 per cent of the market and Microsoft with just over 4 per cent. Baidu benefits from the ban on Google in China and from the rapid growth in Internet users in this part of the world. However, Google's share of searches worldwide rises to 88.4 per cent, with Yahoo! accounting for just 3.7 per cent, Bing 4.5 per cent and Baidu 0.6 per cent.

Postscript: Who Will be the Number 1 Choice in the Future?

Google and Apple vie for being number 1 most valuable global brand. According to David Roth of WWP (global communications services), 'We're at the threshold of a new normal and a changing consumer,' and technology is a key feature in the leading brands' markets.

Google is a dynamic technology company, which has created markets and been a market challenger. The company has not always anticipated changes in the marketplace but seems to find an effective

»

»

response when its markets are threatened. One of the advantages that Google can always rely on is access to unique market information from users of its products and services. The cross-platform analytics give valuable insights into market behaviour, and this is a real strength of the business. But Microsoft, Facebook, Amazon, Baidu and Twitter and all contenders in the digital marketplace have the potential to anticipate the 'new normal' and take a lead. There have been many brands in the digital space that have led the market and then either completely disappeared or been reduced to small niche markets, for example Netscape (once the dominant web browser), Alta Vista (first natural language search engine) and Myspace (social network).

Questions

1. **How does Google differentiate itself from the competition and, in doing so, create competitive advantage?**

This case study was written by Fiona Ellis-Chadwick, Senior Lecturer in Marketing and Retailing, Loughborough University.

References

Based on: Barney, J. B. (1991) From Resources and Sustained Competitive Advantage, Journal of Management 17(1), 99–120; Forbes (2015) The world's most valuable brands, http://www.forbes.com/companies/google (accessed July 2015); Brit, B. (2005) Google Moves Beyond Search, Marketing, September, 19; Gallup, S (2015) It's closing in on a billion users, http://fortune.com/2015/05/29/gmail-users (accessed July 2015); Griffin, A (2015), Google Play Music goes free, days before launch of Apple's streaming service, *The Independent*, 24 June (accessed July 2015); Hitwise (2006) http://www.hitwise.com/news/us200508.html (accessed May 2006); Kiss, J. (2015) Dear Google: open letter from 80 academics on 'right to be forgotten, *The Guardian*, 14 May (accessed July 2015); McHugh, J. (2003) Google vs Evil, Wired 11(1), 130–5; Naughton, J. (2002) Web Masters, Observer, 15 December, 27; Reisinger, D. (2015) For Google and search ad revenue, it's a glass half full, CNET http://www.cnet.com/uk/news/all-google-all-the-time-in-search-ad-biz-new-data-shows (accessed July 2015); Rose, F. (2006) Are You Ready for Googlevision?, Wired 14(5), www.wired.com/wired/archive/14.05/google_pr.html; Statista (2015) Global market share held by the leading internet browsers from January 2012 to March 2015, http://www.statista.com/statistics/268254/market-share-of-internet-browsers-worldwide-since-2009 (accessed July 2015); Statista (2015) Which social media platforms used by marketeers worldwide http://www.statista.com/statistics/268254/market-share-of-internet-browsers-worldwide-since-2009 (accessed July 2015); Vogelstein, F. (2002) Looking for a Dotcom Winner? Search no Further, *Fortune* 145(11), 65–8; WWP (2015), Apple overtakes Google for the top spot in the 10th annual BrandZ Top 100 brands, http://www.wpp.com/wpp/press/2015/may/27/apple-overtakes-google-for-the-top-spot-in-the-10th-annual-brandz-top-100-brands-ranking/# (accessed July 2015).

Social Media and Real-Time Marketing

Over the past decade, social media has exploded onto the marketing scene, with brands' budgets and organisational structures attempting to respond to the opportunities that this form of communication offers. With Facebook passing 1.35 billion active monthly users and Twitter having 13 million active monthly members, companies are fighting to gain a dominant presence in the social media space. With such a large audience and widespread connectivity, social media platforms are now seen to rival conventional broadcast news channels in the speed that a message can be posted or news communicated. This has led to the rise of real-time content becoming part of an organisation's marketing activity. Real-time marketing is a reactive piece of content posted during a live event. It relies on the 'second screen experience' where a person is online on another device or has opened up a split screen while watching something else. Sporting events tend to attract this two-screen approach, as the viewer is often a fan who is emotionally engaged with the event and is seeking additional information as the match or game progresses. Real-time marketing has become increasingly prevalent at big sporting events when a brand attempts to 'own' a key moment in the sporting encounter. By placing the brand message at a key moment in the event, the aim is for the consumer to recall both the incident and the brand.

The 'Oreo—You Can Still Dunk In The Dark' moment is widely regarded as the first successful piece of real-time marketing content. It came in 2013 when there was a power outage during the NFL Super Bowl XLVII between the Baltimore Ravens and the San Francisco 49ers. With a Super Bowl commercial costing millions of dollars, social media gave the opportunity to own a moment of the match online, with the only cost being staff time. When the power cut happened, the Oreo social media team produced this post in a matter of minutes. Due to the second-screen nature of the sports event, spectators all over the globe saw this clear call-to-action by Oreo, and it gained 10,000+ retweets and 18,000+ likes on Facebook in just one hour, earning 525 million impressions worldwide for a grand total of zero media dollars being spent.

Since then, real-time marketing via social media has continued to develop. Another famous sporting incident occurred during the 2014 Football World Cup when Luis Suarez, while playing for Uruguay against Italy, bit the

Kia Motors America @Kia · Follow

Hey @jcpenney need a designated driver?

RETWEETS 3,086   LIKES 2,446

4:32 PM - 2 Feb 2014

Italian defender Giorgio Chellini. Almost immediately, a number of companies posted brand messages relating to the incident. Most were light-hearted and poked fun at the incident.

However, real-time marketing does not have to be specifically around the event itself, but can also comment on the outcome. Andy Murray, the British tennis player, is well known for not having the most charismatic of personalities on the ATP tennis circuit. When in 2014 he won the BBC Sports Personality of the Year Award, his main sponsor Adidas posted on social media that this was 'not bad for a man with no personality'.

Part of the attraction of this type of activity is the ad hoc 'on the fly' type of feel to both the content as well as the timing. It gives the impression of spontaneity and that the company or brand is sharing the experience with you. They are part of the event itself. Although this may be the perception over the last three years, there has been a radical change in the way real-time marketing happens. Brand teams are now setting up reactive social media centres. These centres often have an array of copywriters, a design team and a community manager to manage the social media aspect of the job. It takes months to organise, and many brainstorms take place to maximise the efficiency of the copy being inserted onto the relevant imagery that will be posted ideally in seconds but more likely within a couple of minutes of an incident taking place.

Real-time marketing also offers the opportunity for brands to work together. JC Penny during the 2014 Super Bowl produced a series of tweets that appeared to be either from someone who was drunk or someone who had hacked into JC Penny's account. The activity created a lot of interest but was deliberately designed to create JC Penny's own narrative running alongside the game. This was done by other brands joining in the conversation, with Kia offering a designated driver. After an hour, JC

»

»

Penny admitted that someone was supposedly 'tweeting with mittens on', therefore promoting the retailer's Team USA mittens ahead of the Winter Olympics.

Social media, and specifically real-time content, has opened up many opportunities for brands, especially in the area of ambush marketing. Owing to the lack of legislation around sponsorship rights on social media, the social media platform sees innovative, and often humorous ambush marketers make a connection to an event that would not have been previously possible. Therefore, this arguably devalues the paid rights of an official sponsor.

Social media have swung open a new door for marketers to maximise their brand reach. However, since the Oreo moment, this space has become saturated with brands trying to catch the eye of the consumer with real-time content. This has put pressure on the recruitment of high-quality staff in a new type of industry that did not exist 15 years ago. Also, social media platforms have realised the potential for income through paid promotions, therefore this previously inexpensive marketing tool now requires more budget if it is to be well staffed, along with media spend to maximise the impact of a real-time intervention. As it grows, the challenge will be to integrate real-time marketing into the overall marketing strategy of an organization.

Questions

1. What are the pros and cons of using real time marketing?

2. Who do you feel will be the audience for two screen viewing? What implications will this have for its use?

3. A lot of discussion is taking place regarding the integration of social media and other forms of marketing activity. To what extent does 'real time marketing' lead to the possible fragmentation of marketing activity?

This case study was written by James Saker, Synergy Sponsorship London, and Jim Saker, Ford Professor in Retail Management, Loughborough University.

References

The material in the case has been drawn from a variety of published sources.

CHAPTER 17
Distribution

LEARNING OBJECTIVES

After reading this chapter, you should be able to:

1 describe the functions and types of channels of distribution

2 explain how to determine channel strategy

3 discuss the three components of channel strategy: channel selection, intensity and integration

4 discuss the five key channel management issues: member selection, motivation, training, evaluation and conflict management

5 explain the cost–service trade-off in physical distribution

6 discuss the components of a physical distribution system: customer service, order processing, inventory control, warehousing, transportation and materials handling

7 explain how to improve customer service standards in physical distribution

8 discuss retailing and retail marketing

9 discuss ethical issues in distribution

D istribution, along with location of services, makes up the place element of the marketing mix. Products need to be available in adequate quantities, in convenient locations and at times when customers want to buy them. In this chapter we examine the functions and types of distribution channels, the key decisions that determine channel strategy, how to manage channels, and issues relating to the physical flow of goods through distribution channels (physical distribution management). We also explore the relevance of place in terms of where goods are purchased by looking at the retail industry.

Producers should consider not only the needs of their ultimate customer but also the requirement of **channel intermediaries** (the organizations which facilitate the distribution of products to customers). For example, success for Müller yoghurt in the UK was dependent on convincing a powerful retailer group (Tesco) to stock the brand. The high margins the brand supported were a key influence in Tesco's decision. Without retailer support Müller would have found it uneconomic to supply consumers with its brand. Clearly, establishing a supply chain that is efficient and meets customers' needs is vital to marketing success. The supply chain is often referred to as a **channel of distribution**, and is the means by which products are moved from producer to the final customer. Logistics is a related term, which is used to refer to the movement of goods through the supply chain; this function has become increasingly complex as retailers offer their customers multiple collection points. Management of the supply chain is also important, as it is often the criterion considered by decision-making units when choosing suppliers. (See Chapter 4 for further discussion of influences on buying decisions.) To be successful, manufacturers and suppliers need to get access to their end customers and gain distribution outlets. Advertising to channel intermediaries is sometimes used to explain the benefits of the brand to encourage channel members to stock products. For example, Chupa Chups encourages retailers to stock its sugar-free products using promotional discounts to drive sales.

Choosing the most effective channel of distribution is an important aspect of marketing strategy. Supermarkets effectively shortened the distribution channel between producer and consumer by eliminating the wholesaler. Prior to their introduction the typical distribution channel for products like food, drink, tobacco and toiletries was producer to wholesaler to retailer. The wholesaler would buy in bulk from the producer and sell smaller quantities to the retailer (typically a small grocery shop). By building up buying power, supermarkets could shorten this chain by buying direct from producers. This meant lower costs to the supermarket chain and lower prices to the consumer. The competitive effect was to drastically reduce the numbers of small grocers and wholesalers in this market. By being more efficient and meeting customers' needs better, supermarkets had created a competitive advantage for themselves.

Digital technologies are making further changes to distribution channels. In some cases from physical to virtual: for example, the distribution of music and video (downloads), airline booking (electronic ticketing), hotel reservations (electronic booking). In other cases the shift is from store to home and office purchasing—for example groceries (home shopping). Mobile networks permit the distribution of such products as music, video and ringtones (Bunwell, 2005). Increasingly, retailers are adopting a multichannel approach, which means they supply products and communicate with their customers, in store, online, via mobile and through social media. In business-to-business markets customers can place orders, receive quotes and track deliveries over the Internet.

Next, we explore the functions of channel intermediaries and then examine the different types of channels that manufacturers can use to supply their products to customers.

Functions of Channel Intermediaries

The most basic question to ask when deciding channel strategy is whether to sell directly to the ultimate customer or to use channel intermediaries such as retailers and/or wholesalers. To answer this question we need to understand the functions of channel intermediaries—that is, what benefits might producers and consumers derive from their use. Channel intermediaries add value by providing useful functions for producers and consumers. These functions are: to reconcile the needs of producers and customers, to improve efficiency by reducing the number of transactions or creating bulk, to improve accessibility by lowering location and time gaps between producers and consumers, and to provide specialist services to customers. Each of these functions is now examined in more detail.

Reconciling the needs of producers and consumers

Manufacturers typically produce a large quantity of a limited range of goods, whereas consumers and businesses usually want only a limited quantity of a wide range of goods (Coughlan et al., 2005). The role of channel intermediaries is to reconcile these conflicting situations. For example, a manufacturer of tables sells to retailers, each of which buys from a range of manufacturers of furniture. The manufacturer can gain economies of scale by producing large quantities of tables, and selling to many companies further along the supply chain—for example, retailers like DFS, Harvey's, Furniture Village. Each retailer can then offer its customers a wide assortment of products offering its customers considerable choice under one roof. It is important to remember the key function of channel intermediaries is *breaking bulk*. A wholesaler may buy large quantities from a manufacturer (perhaps a container load) and then sell smaller quantities (such as by the case) to retailers. Alternatively, large retailers such as supermarkets buy large quantities from producers, and break bulk by splitting the order between outlets. In this way, producers make large quantities while consumers are offered limited quantities at the point of purchase.

Improving efficiency

Channel intermediaries can improve distribution efficiency by *reducing the number of transactions* and *creating bulk for transportation*. Figure 17.1 shows how the number of transactions between three producers and three customers is reduced by using one intermediary. Direct distribution to customers results in nine transactions, whereas the use of an intermediary cuts the number of transactions to six. Distribution (and selling) costs and effort, therefore, are reduced.

Small producers can benefit by selling to intermediaries, which then combine a large number of small purchases into bulk for transportation. Without the intermediary it may prove too costly for each small producer to meet transportation costs to the consumer. Agricultural products such as fruit and vegetables—for example, green beans from Kenya, pineapples and bananas from Central America—are grown by small producers, who sometimes benefit from this arrangement.

Improving accessibility

Two major divides that need to be bridged between producers and consumers are the location and time gaps. The *location gap* derives from the geographic separation of producers from the customers they serve. Many of the

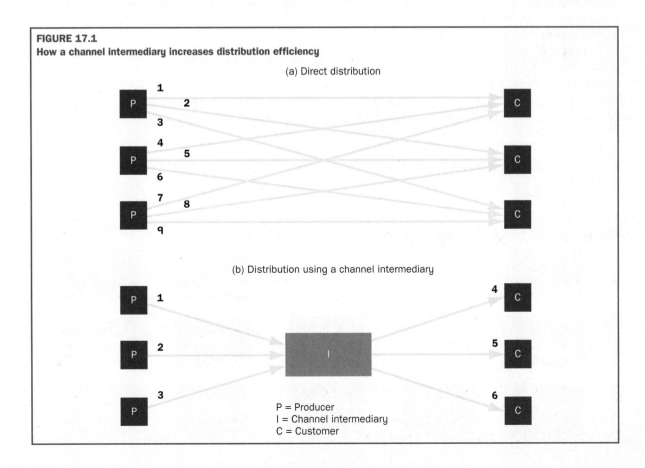

FIGURE 17.1
How a channel intermediary increases distribution efficiency

(a) Direct distribution

(b) Distribution using a channel intermediary

P = Producer
I = Channel intermediary
C = Customer

cars produced in the UK by Nissan and Toyota are exported to Europe. Car dealers in Europe provide customer access to these cars in the form of display and test drive facilities, and the opportunity to purchase locally rather than deal direct with the producer thousands of miles away. The Internet is reducing the location gap, allowing buyers to purchase without the need to visit a producer or distributor. Producers can play their part in improving accessibility by making consumers aware of the location of their distributors.

The *time gap* results from discrepancies between when a manufacturer wants to produce goods and when consumers wish to buy. For example, manufacturers of spare parts for cars may wish to run their manufacturing processes from Monday to Friday but shoppers may wish to purchase goods every day of the week. By opening at the weekend, car accessory outlets bridge the time gap between production and consumption. The Internet has facilitated 365/24/7 buying, which is streamlining communications throughout global supply chains. This is also very popular in consumer markets.

Providing specialist services

Channel intermediaries can perform specialist customer services that manufacturers may feel ill-equipped to provide themselves. Distributors may have long-standing expertise in such areas as selling, servicing and installation to customers. Producers may feel that these functions are better handled by channel intermediaries so that they can specialize in other aspects of manufacturing and marketing activity.

Types of Distribution Channel

Everything we buy, whether they are consumer goods, business-to-business goods or services, requires a channel of distribution. Business channels tend to be shorter than consumer channels because of the small number of ultimate customers, the greater geographic concentration of customers, and the greater complexity of the products that require close producer–customer liaison. Service channels also tend to be short because of the intangibility of services and the need for personal contact between the service provider and consumer.

Consumer channels

Figure 17.2 shows four alternative consumer channels. Each one is described briefly below.

Producer direct to consumer

Cutting out distributor profit margin may make this option attractive to producers as they can sell directly to consumers. Many companies—from men's outfitters such as Charles Tyrwhitt, to iTunes and Dell Computers—have

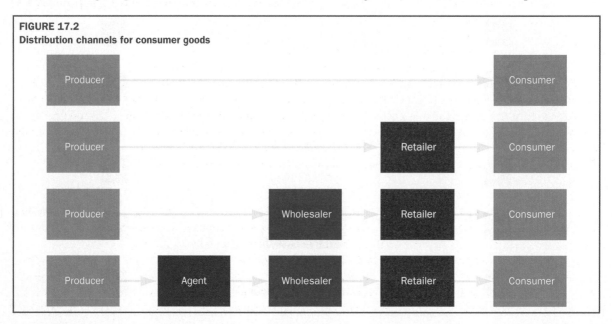

FIGURE 17.2
Distribution channels for consumer goods

adopted this approach. The Internet has provided the technology infrastructure to supply consumers direct rather than through retailers. Manufacturers of digital products such as music, films and software have benefited from these types of distribution channel as their products are readily downloadable via a customer's computer.

Eliminating a layer of intermediaries from a distribution channel is called **disintermediation** (Mills and Camek, 2004). This is a term coined in the banking industry with the advent of retail banking. The basic idea is that the 'middleman' is removed and manufacturers sell directly to consumers. Examples in other industries include airlines such as easyJet and Ryanair who have moved towards Internet bookings, eliminating the need to go through a travel agent. Dell Computers has largely eliminated retailers from the traditional PC distribution channel. A broader definition of disintermediation includes the displacement of traditional channel intermediaries with new forms of distribution. For example, iTunes music stores are replacing specialist record shops in the distribution of music. Disintermediation occurs when a new type of channel intermediary or structure serves customers better than the old channels. Spotify and Last.fm provide access to almost limitless musical choice through streaming technology for a small monthly fee. YouTube provides a distribution platform for new recording artists.

At the opposite end of the spectrum is **reintermediation**. In this case, retailers use the Internet for different purposes ranging from a simple poster website advertising the company to a fully integrated online business operation that facilitates online sales, builds customer relationships, and acts as a portal for new business opportunities. Research has found that in general retailers tend to lack the skills and technical resources required to develop their online presence. A solution is to use web service providers that act as 'cyber intermediaries' for designing, developing, hosting and managing their websites. Adding this extra level in the supply chain enables retailers to exploit the potential of the Internet by using third-party web service providers, who have the technical expertise and knowledge necessary for all of the retailer's online business requirements. Many retailers are taking this action in an attempt to protect their investment in increasingly competitive and challenging online trading environments. They also try to build strong collaborative relationships with their web service providers (Vize et al., 2010; Doherty and Ellis-Chadwick, 2010).

Producer to retailer to consumer

The growth in retailer size has meant that it becomes economic for producers to supply retailers directly rather than through wholesalers. Consumers then have the convenience of viewing and/or testing the product at the retail outlet. Supermarket chains such as Sainsbury's exercise considerable power over manufacturers because of their enormous buying capabilities. However, technology has created new channels to consumers. Internet retailers such as Amazon (books and consumer goods), ASOS (fashion) and Expedia (travel and hotel bookings) compete with store-based retailers supplying directly from their websites. Apple has created its own online retail store, iTunes, to supply music downloads for the iPod, and the App Store to distribute software applications to owners of the iPhone. Store-based retailers have responded by developing their own sophisticated websites selling a wide range of goods. Increasingly, these types of retailer are developing a multichannel approach that means they can serve customer needs in store, online and on the move via mobile communications. See Marketing in Action 17.1 which describes how Costco shortens its distribution channel to keep costs low.

Producer to wholesaler to retailer to consumer

For small retailers (e.g. confectionery, tobacco and news (CTNs), convenience stores) with limited order quantities, the use of wholesalers makes economic sense. Wholesalers can buy in bulk from producers, and sell smaller quantities to numerous retailers. The danger is that large retailers in the same market have the power to buy directly from producers and thus cut out the wholesaler. In certain cases the buying power of large retailers has meant that they can sell products to their customers cheaper than a small retailer can buy from the wholesaler. In Europe long channels involving wholesalers are common in France and Italy. In France, for example, the distribution of vehicle spare parts is dominated by small independent wholesalers (Dudley, 1990).

Producer to agent to wholesaler to retailer to consumer

This long channel is sometimes used by companies entering foreign markets. They may delegate the task of selling the product to an agent (who does not take title to the goods). The agent contacts wholesalers (or retailers) and receives commission on sales. Overseas sales of books are sometimes generated in this way.

Some companies use multiple channels to distribute their products. Grocery products, for example, use both producer to wholesaler to retailer (small grocers), and producer to retailer (supermarkets). The Internet has also encouraged the use of multiple channels. For example, in the tourist industry, package holidays can be booked through travel agencies or via the Internet, and hotels and flights can be booked over the telephone or by using

MARKETING IN ACTION 17.1
Fingerprinting the Supply Chain Leads to Success for Costco

Costco is a leading global retailer, with sales over $110 billion, 195,000 employees, and warehouses in important strategic locations around the world. The operational structure is organized to support the movement of goods, and Costco's global supply chain is important to the firm's success. Costco spans the boundary between business and consumer by operating a membership model that encourages both business buyers and individual shoppers to use its warehouses. All buyers become members of Costco, and this allows them to enjoy different levels of discounts. The prices and benefits of membership programmes vary depending on the type of customer, their spending patterns and whether they are businesses or

individuals. The club membership fee, paid annually in advance, is another important factor in the company's success. The level of loyalty among Costco's members is very high, which supports its global purchasing strategy. Costco is a low-cost operator, and its spend on servicing the supply chain, administration cost and costs associated with generating sales is lower than that of other global retailers, for example Walmart and Amazon.

How Costco achieves this low-cost position, even when its buyers are constantly looking for new products to tempt its customers, is by reducing the 'fingerprints' on its products. In other words, it reduces the number of times products are *touched* as they move through the distribution chain, because each touchpoint generates a handling cost which has to be attributed to the products. Following the traditional distribution model, goods would pass from the manufacturers to distributors, then to retailers. Costco buys most of its products from manufacturers, and this approach to distribution reduces the number of handling points using cross-dock distribution depots, which is where manufactured goods are sorted, gathered together and allocated to individual stores. The result is that Costco is able to maximize the efficiency of its distribution chain. Ultimately, this approach shortens the distribution channel for both business and consumers.

Based on: Wulfratt (2014); Costco (2015)

---

the Internet. Such multichannel strategies allow companies to differentiate their services to take advantage of the inherent strengths of each channel (Wikström, 2005). Multiple channels also provide wide market coverage. For example, Sony achieves wide distribution coverage by using multiple channels, including its own Sony Centres, electrical goods chain stores such as Currys/PC World, catalogue shops such as Argos and online retailers such as Amazon. In Japan, distribution channels to consumers tend to be long and complex, with close relationships between channel members, a fact that has acted as a barrier to entry for foreign companies.

Business-to-business channels

Common business-to-business distribution channels are illustrated in Figure 17.3. Usually a maximum of one channel intermediary is used.

Producer to business customer

Supplying business customers directly is common for expensive industrial products such as gas turbines, diesel locomotives and aero-engines. There needs to be close liaison between supplier and customer to solve technical problems, and the size of the order makes direct selling and distribution economic.

Producer to agent to business customer

Instead of selling to business customers using their own salesforce, a business-to-business goods company could employ the services of an agent who may sell a range of goods from several suppliers (on a commission basis). This spreads selling costs and may be attractive to companies without the reserves to set up their own

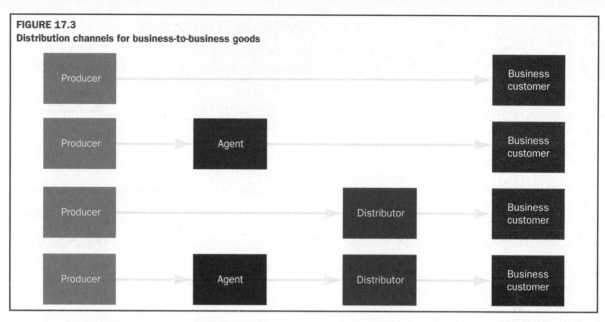

FIGURE 17.3
Distribution channels for business-to-business goods

sales operation. The disadvantage is that there is little control over the agent, who is unlikely to devote the same amount of time selling on products compared with a dedicated sales team.

Producer to distributor to business customer

For less expensive, more frequently bought business-to-business products, distributors are used. These may have both internal and field sales staff (Narus and Anderson, 1986). Internal staff deal with customer-generated enquiries and order placing, order follow-up (often using the Internet) and checking inventory levels. For many goods that are routinely purchased, fully automated digital systems are used. Outside sales staff are more proactive: their practical responsibilities are to find new customers, get products specified, distribute catalogues and gather market information. The advantage to customers of using distributors is that they can buy small quantities locally.

Producer to agent to distributor to business customer

Where business customers prefer to call upon distributors, the agent's job will require selling into these intermediaries. The reason why a producer may employ an agent rather than a dedicated salesforce is usually cost based (as previously discussed).

Services channels

Distribution channels for services are usually short: either direct or using an agent. While in many situations stocks are not held, the role of the wholesaler, retailer or industrial distributor is different in service supply chains. For example in the fast food industry and beauty industries products are purchased to use in the 'production' of service deliverables, like a Big Mac burger or a manicure and painted nails. Figure 17.4 shows the two alternatives whether they be to consumer or business customers. Service organizations look for innovative ways to reach customers as Marketing in Action 17.2 describes.

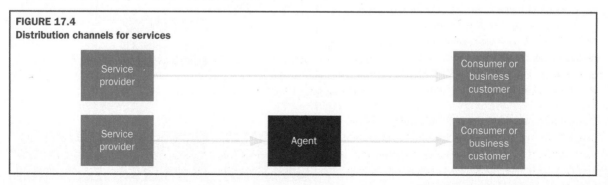

FIGURE 17.4
Distribution channels for services

Service provider to consumer or business customer

The close personal relationships between service providers and customers often mean that service supply is direct. Examples include healthcare, office cleaning, accountancy, marketing research and law. See Exhibit 17.1 for how global accountancy firm KPMG is using digital technology to stay close to its customers.

Service provider to agent to consumer or business customer

A channel intermediary for a service company usually takes the form of an agent. Agents are used when the service provider is geographically distant from customers, and where it is not economical for the provider to establish its own local sales team. Examples include insurance, travel, secretarial and theatrical agents.

EXHIBIT 17.1
KPMG helps its customers understand their tax liabilities

Channel Strategy

Channel strategy decisions involve the selection of the most effective distribution channel, the most appropriate level of distribution intensity and the degree of channel integration (see Figure 17.5). Each of these decisions will now be discussed.

Channel selection

Why does Procter & Gamble sell its brands through supermarkets rather than selling direct? Why does General Electric sell its locomotives direct to train operating companies rather than use a distributor? The answers are to be found by examining the following factors that influence *channel selection*. These influences can be grouped under market, producer, product and competitive factors.

Market factors

An important market factor is buyer behaviour: buyer expectations may dictate that the product be sold in a certain way. Buyers may prefer to buy locally and in a particular type of shop. Failure to match these expectations can have serious consequences.

Buyer needs regarding product information, installation and technical assistance also have to be considered. A judgement needs to be made about whether the producer or channel intermediary can best meet these needs in terms of expertise, commitment and cost. For example, products that require facilities for local servicing, such as cars, often use intermediaries to carry out the task. Where the service requirement does not involve large capital investment the producer may carry out the service. For example, supplier of pest control Rentokil trains its staff to conduct annual inspections and servicing as well as fulfilling their sales roles. See Exhibit 17.2 for how Rentokil invites people from around the world to try alternative foods in its Pestaurants.

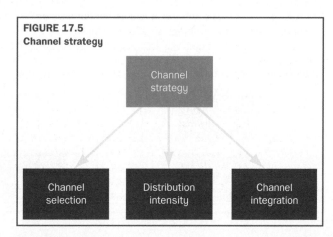

FIGURE 17.5
Channel strategy

Channel strategy

Channel selection | Distribution intensity | Channel integration

The willingness of channel intermediaries to market a product is also a market-based factor that influences channel decisions. Direct distribution may be the only option if distributors refuse to handle the product. For industrial products, this may mean the recruitment of salespeople, and for consumer products direct mail may be employed to communicate to and supply customers. The profit margins demanded by wholesalers and retailers, and the commission rates expected by sales agents also affect their attractiveness as channel intermediaries. These costs need to be assessed in comparison with those of a salesforce.

The location and geographical concentration of customers also affects channel selection. The more local and clustered the customer base, the more likely direct distribution is feasible. Direct distribution is also more prevalent when buyers are few in number and buy large quantities. A large number of small customers may mean that using channel intermediaries is the only economical way of reaching them (hence supermarkets).

EXHIBIT 17.2
Rentokil invites people from around the world to try alternative foods in its Pestaurants

---

MARKETING IN ACTION 17.2
Sotheby's—Bidding on a New Distribution Channel

'Going once . . . going twice . . . and gone! Sold to . . .' is sometimes a relief to buyers, and at other times a bigger relief to sellers of auction lots. A print by the American photographer Berenive Abbot, *New York at Night*, was sold to the highest bidder for $6,000. Yet, the buyer, although quite involved with the process, was not present to bid for the item at the Sotheby's New York salesroom. The sale was in fact conducted by a click of a mouse (or a tap with a quick finger) by a 'virtual bidder', yet with real money. The buyer had placed her bids in Sotheby's first 'live' auction on eBay on 1 April 2015.

The collaboration between Sotheby's and eBay represents the coupling of two seemingly different worlds. Sotheby's, established in 1744 by London bookseller Samuel Baker, is the world's oldest fine art auctioneer. Traditional auction houses such as Sotheby's and Christie's are often seen as intimidating places that are the exclusive domain of the wealthy elite. eBay, on the other hand, is a mass online marketplace founded in Pieer Omidyar's living room in Silicon Valley in 1995. The online auction and shopping website, which has won over 155 million customers in 190 countries, sells basically anything from toys to screwdrivers to cars.

It has never been easier for art aficionados or casual collectors to purchase art, whether a print, painting or sculpture. However, the new live auction platform of eBay.com and Sotheby's is like being there in person. Live video of the auctioneer and images of the item being sold appear on the screen, attempting to replicate the real-time saleroom bidding experience. It even provides a 'museum view' that simulates the experience of walking through a museum or gallery. Registered users (upon registration for each sale, users receive a unique paddle number associated with their eBay account) can place a bid with a click of the blue 'bid' button. This real-time bidding is sensitive to the millisecond. Following the bids can be quite dramatic, and the sound of the auctioneer's gavel has a lasting impact. However, buying at auction is not for the faint-hearted. Some works can be bought at below $5,000, but a number of evaluations are in excess of $500,000. All bidders are notified that, 'By bidding, you agree to buy this item if you win.'

Sotheby's new online strategy has seized on a fresh growth opportunity. According to the TEFAF Art Market Report 2015, global sales of art and antiques reached their highest ever recorded level: a total of just over 51 billion euros worldwide. Online sales were estimated to account for only 6 per cent of global sales, but are expected to grow at least 25 per cent annually. Sotheby's collaboration with eBay will allow it to expand beyond the showroom to eBay's 155 million buyers worldwide. It will also bring the 'auction house appeal' to a younger generation that are not only technologically savvy, but also have an increasing interest in art, antiques and collectibles. These consumers are likely to be the biggest winners, assuming their good taste translates into bids that prove to be wise investments.

Source: Prepared from various published sources

Producer factors

A constraint on the channel decision is when the producer lacks adequate resources to perform the functions of the channel. Producers may lack the financial and managerial resources to take on channel operations. Lack of financial resources may mean that a salesforce cannot be recruited, and sales agents and/or distributors are used instead. Producers may feel that they do not possess the customer-based skills to distribute their products and prefer to rely on intermediaries.

The product mix offered by a producer may also affect channel strategy. A wide mix of products may make direct distribution (and selling) cost-effective. Narrow or single product companies, on the other hand, may find the cost of direct distribution prohibitive unless the product is extremely expensive.

The final product influence is the desired degree of control of channel operations. The use of independent channel intermediaries reduces producer control. For example, by distributing their products through supermarkets, manufacturers lose total control of the price charged to consumers. Furthermore, there is no guarantee that new products will be stocked. Direct distribution gives producers control over such issues.

Product factors

Large, complex products are often supplied direct to customers. The need for close personal contact between producer and customer, and the high prices charged, mean that direct distribution and selling is both necessary and feasible. Perishable products such as frozen food, meat and bread require relatively short channels to supply the customer with fresh stock. Finally, bulky or difficult to handle products may require direct distribution because distributors may refuse to carry them if storage or display problems arise (Rosenbloom, 1987). The increase in online shopping in Europe has encouraged retailers to explore increasingly innovative ways to get goods to their customers and add collection points to the end of the distribution chain. See Marketing in Action 17.3 to find out more.

MARKETING IN ACTION 17.3
Online Order Delivery

The delivery side of online shopping presents many challenges for retailers as they aim to create seamless shopping experiences for their customers when they buy online. As a result, an array of different collection solutions have been developed.

Click and collect: this is a simple concept: customers buy online and then choose where they would like to collect the goods—for example, at petrol stations, local corner shops and Royal Mail post offices. The concept has proved so popular for retailers like John Lewis that it is predicted that soon over three-quarters of online purchases will be delivery through click-and-collect schemes. eBay has even set up a collection scheme by partnering with Argos so that its sellers can offer this delivery option.

Remote click-and-collect locker: this delivery solution enables shoppers to pick up their goods from secure lockers. Amazon first used this method so that London commuters could get their orders from tube stations. The service has been extended to supermarkets, universities and libraries across the UK.

Temperature-controlled lockers: grocery retailers such as Asda and Waitrose have developed collection lockers that are sited in convenient locations for customers who do not want to visit the retailer's store. The locations of the lockers are carefully chosen to give consumers maximum convenience—for example, in car parks, near rail stations.

Based on: Felsted (2013); Planet Retail (2014); Dodds (2014); Vincent (2014)

Competitive factors

If the competition controls traditional channels of distribution—for example, through franchise or exclusive dealing arrangements—an innovative approach to distribution may be required. Two alternatives are to recruit a salesforce to sell direct or to set up a producer-owned distribution network (see the section on vertical marketing systems, under 'Conventional marketing channels', below). Producers should not accept that the channels of distribution used by competitors are the only ways to reach target customers. Direct marketing provides opportunities to supply products in new ways. Traditional channels of distribution for personal computers through high-street retailers are being circumvented by direct marketers, who use direct response advertising to reach buyers. The emergence of the more computer-aware and experienced buyer, and the higher reliability of these products as the market reaches maturity, has meant that a local source of supply (and advice) is less important. Digitization of product not only changes the mode but also changes timings, access and availability.

Distribution intensity

The second channel strategy decision is the choice of *distribution intensity*. The three broad options are intensive, selective and exclusive distribution.

Intensive distribution

Intensive distribution aims to achieve saturation coverage of the market by using all available outlets. With many mass-market products, such as soft drinks, foods, toiletries, alcohol and newspapers, sales are a direct function of the number of outlets penetrated. This is because consumers have a range of acceptable brands from which they can choose. If a brand is not available in an outlet, an alternative is bought. The convenience aspect of purchase is paramount. New outlets may be sought that hitherto had not stocked the products, such as the sale of confectionery and grocery items at petrol stations: for example, Esso has introduced 380 On the Run stores in 13 European countries (Exxon Mobil, 2012). In the UK, this trend has also encouraged supermarkets to locate convenience stores with a wide range of products at motorway service station; for example, Marks & Spencer's Simply Food stores in Moto service stations, and Waitrose became Welcome Break's latest food brand in its service stations (see Exhibit 17.3) (Motorway Services Online, 2015).

Selective distribution

Market coverage may also be achieved through **selective distribution**, in which a producer uses a limited number of outlets in a geographical area to sell its products. The advantages to the producer are the opportunity to select only the best outlets to focus its efforts to build close working relationships and to train distributor staff on fewer outlets than with intensive distribution, and, if selling and distribution is direct, to reduce costs. Upmarket aspirational brands are often sold in carefully selected outlets. Retail outlets and industrial distributors like this arrangement since it reduces competition. Selective distribution is more likely to be used when buyers are willing to shop around when choosing products. This means that it is not necessary for a company to have its products available in all outlets—for example, Jaguar Land Rover (vehicles), Louise Vuitton and Chanel (luxury apparel), Moët Hennessy (fine champagne and cognac)—and brands can restrict where their products can be sold.

Problems can arise when a retailer demands distribution rights but is refused by producers, as in the case of Jaguar Land Rover refusing to allow Auto 24, an authorized car dealership, to sell Land Rover vehicles in Perigueux, France (Court of Justice of the European Union, 2012).

EXHIBIT 17.3
Waitrose became Welcome Break's latest food brand in its service stations

Exclusive distribution

This is an extreme form of selective distribution in which only one wholesaler, retailer or industrial distributor is used in a geographic area. Cars are often sold on this basis with only one dealer operating in each town or city. This reduces a purchaser's power to negotiate prices for the same model between dealers since to buy in a neighbouring town may be inconvenient when servicing or repairs are required. It also allows very close cooperation between producer and retailer over servicing, pricing and promotion. Initially, Apple's iPhone was also subject to exclusive distribution in the UK through the mobile phone operator O₂ and retailer Carphone Warehouse (Ritson, 2008). The right to **exclusive distribution** may be demanded by distributors as a condition for stocking a manufacturer's product line. Similarly, producers may wish for exclusive dealing where the distributor agrees not to stock competing lines. The selection of an exclusive set of distributors can provide the basis for excellent customer service. For example, Caterpillar, the tractor manufacturer, is renowned for the quality of its exclusive dealer network. Dealers undergo rigorous selection procedures but, once accepted, are treated royally in order to make them feel part of the Caterpillar family. This is because Caterpillar recognizes the importance of dealer service in backing up its reputation for highly reliable machines (Nagle and Hogan, 2006).

Exclusive dealing can reduce competition in ways that may be considered contrary to consumers' interests. The European Court of Justice rejected an appeal by Unilever over the issue of exclusive outlets in Germany. By supplying freezer cabinets Unilever maintained exclusivity by refusing to allow other competing ice creams into them. Also, Coca-Cola, Schweppes Beverages and Britvic's exclusive ties with the leisure trade (such as sports clubs) were broken by the Office of Fair Trading, making competitive entry easier (Meller, 1992).

However, the European Court rejected an appeal by the French Leclerc supermarket group over the issue of the selective distribution system used by Yves St Laurent perfumes. The judges found that the use of selective distribution for luxury cosmetic products increased competition and that it was in the consumer's and manufacturer's interest to preserve the image of such luxury products.

Channel integration

Channel integration can range from conventional marketing channels, comprising an independent producer and channel intermediaries, through a franchise operation, to channel ownership by a producer. Producers need to consider the strengths and weaknesses of each system when setting channel strategies.

Conventional marketing channels

The independence of channel intermediaries means that the producer has little or no control over them. Arrangements such as exclusive dealing may provide a degree of control, but separation of ownership means that each party will look after its own interests. Conventional marketing channels are characterized by hard bargaining and, occasionally, conflict. For example, a retailer may believe that cutting the price of a brand is necessary to move stock, even though the producer objects because of brand image considerations.

However, separation of ownership means that each party can specialize in the function in which it has strengths: manufacturers produce, intermediaries distribute. Care needs to be taken by manufacturers to stay in touch with customers and not abdicate this responsibility to retailers.

A manufacturer that dominates a market through its size and strong brands may exercise considerable power over intermediaries even though they are independent. This power may result in an **administered vertical marketing system** where the manufacturer can command considerable cooperation from wholesalers and retailers. Major brand builders such as Procter & Gamble and Lever Brothers had traditionally held great leverage over distribution but, more recently, power has moved towards the large dominant supermarket chains through their purchasing and market power. Marks & Spencer is a clear example of a retailer controlling an administered vertical marketing system. Through its dominant market position it is capable of exerting considerable authority over its suppliers.

Franchising

A **franchise** is a legal contract in which a producer and channel intermediaries agree each member's rights and obligations. Usually, the intermediary receives marketing, managerial, technical and financial services in return for a fee. Franchise organizations such as McDonald's, Benetton, Hertz, the Body Shop and Avis combine the strengths of a large sophisticated marketing-orientated organization with the energy and motivation of a locally owned outlet. Franchising is also commonplace in the car industry, where dealers agree exclusive deals with manufacturers in return for marketing and financial backing. Although a franchise operation gives a degree of producer control, there are still areas of potential conflict. For example, the producer may be dissatisfied with the standards of service provided by the outlet, or the franchisee may believe that the franchising organization provides inadequate promotional support. Goal conflict can also arise. For example, some McDonald's franchisees were displeased with the company's rapid expansion programme which meant that new restaurants opened within a mile of existing outlets. This led to complaints about lower profits and falling franchise resale values (Helmore, 1997). Also, compared with ownership, the franchise organization lacks total control over franchisees. For example, Marriott, which franchises many of its hotels, had to rely on persuasion rather than control when it asked its franchisees to spend more than $1 billion worldwide on its new bedding design (Lambert, 2005).

A franchise agreement provides a **contractual vertical marketing system** through the formal coordination and integration of marketing and distribution activities. Some franchise organizations exert a considerable degree of control over financial and marketing operations. For example, to become a KFC franchisee, there is a licence fee of $43,600, a monthly royalty of 6 per cent, a 5 per cent contribution to advertising plus the cost of buying and fitting out the restaurant, which can be in excess of $100,000. Additional funding is required for purchasing stock, paying for training, wages, utility bills and insurance premiums (KFC, 2012).

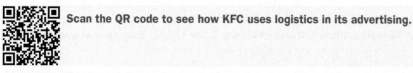 **Scan the QR code to see how KFC uses logistics in its advertising.**

Despite the cost of setting up and running a franchise there are compelling reasons why a producer might choose franchising as a means of distribution. Franchising allows the producer to overcome internal resource constraints by providing access to the franchisee's resources as can be seen in the KFC example. The franchisee not only pays a set-up fee but also makes an ongoing contribution through regular royalty payments. Using this method, companies can gain access to geographically dispersed areas. KFC dominates the fast food franchise market in China, beating McDonald's to highly sought-after locations in major Chinese cities. Read Marketing in Action 17.4 to find out more about franchising Yum! and its successful franchise operations.

MARKETING IN ACTION 17.4
Alone We're Delicious, Together We're Yum!

Yum! Brands Inc. (http://www.yum.com) is based in Louisville, Kentucky, USA, and has three highly successful brands in its portfolio: KFC, Pizza Hut and Taco Bell, which makes it one of the world's largest restaurant companies, with over 41,000 outlets in over 125 countries. Yum! operates 3,700 fast-food restaurants in China of which KFC is currently the most profitable. Initially, Yum! took care to recruit managers who understood the local area and was also careful to select the right joint-venture partners: Beijing Corp. of animal production, processing, industry and commerce, and Beijing Travel & Tourism Corp. The reasons for not using the franchise model to expand in the early days

were because of stringent Chinese rules and legislation. Changing economic conditions favour franchising, and there is plenty of demand from the 600-million-strong middle class.

Yum! aims to expand the number of outlets in this area to 20,000. The franchise approach has enabled the company to become the most successful foreign company operating in China. The business has been so successful because it has used local foods and management teams to build partnerships and drive expansion. If you visit a KFC in China, you can not only buy a bucket of fried chicken, you can also have a bowl of rice porridge, with pork, pickles, mushrooms and preserved egg.

Yum! has also moved into Africa with its highly successful franchise approach. There is a Pizza Hut in Johannesburg, South Africa.

Based on: Mellor (2011); Hernandez (2011) Yum! (2015)

In such situations, producers may value the notion of the owner-manager who has a vested interest in the success of the business. Although some control may still be necessary, the franchisee benefits directly from increases in sales and profits and so has a financial incentive to manage the business well. Finally, franchising may be a way for a producer to access the local knowledge of the franchisee. Franchising may therefore be attractive when a producer is expanding into new markets and where potential franchisees have access to information that is important in penetrating such markets.

The three most common levels where franchising is used in the distribution chain are:

1   *Manufacturer and retailer*: the car industry is dominated by this arrangement. The manufacturer gains retail outlets for its cars and repair facilities without the capital outlay required by ownership.

2   *Manufacturer and wholesaler*: this is commonly used in the soft drinks industry. Manufacturers such as Schweppes, Coca-Cola and Pepsi grant wholesalers the right to make up and bottle their concentrate in line with their instructions, and to distribute the products within a defined geographic area.

3   *Retailer and retailer*: a frequently used method that often has its roots in a successful retailing operation seeking to expand geographically by means of a franchise operation, often with great success. Examples include McDonald's, Benetton, Pizza Hut and KFC. See Table 17.1 for examples of some of the top franchises.

TABLE 17.1 Examples of top franchises in Europe

Rank	Franchise name	Number of units in Europe	Industry	Origin
1.	7-Eleven	47,298	Food convenience stores	USA
2.	Subway	37,000	Food sandwich bars	USA
3.	McDonald's	33,427	Food restaurants	USA
4.	Kumon Institution of Education	25,431	Education	Japan
5.	KFC (Yum! restaurants)	22,000	Food restaurants	USA
6.	Spar	13,600	Food convenience stores	Netherlands
7.	Europcar	13,000	Auto leasing and rental	France
8.	Pizza Hut	12,700	Food restaurants	USA
9.	Burger King	12,000	Food restaurants	USA
10.	Mexx	11,000	Retail clothing	Netherlands

Source: Franchise Europe (2015) http://www.franchiseeurope.com/top500

Channel ownership

Total control over distributor activities comes with channel ownership. This establishes a **corporate vertical marketing system**. By purchasing retail outlets, producers control their purchasing, production and marketing activities. In particular, control over purchasing means a captive outlet for the manufacturer's products. For example, channel ownership is common in the clothing industry, with companies such as Zara and H&M owning their own chains of retail outlets.

The advantages of control have to be weighed against the high price of acquisition and the danger that the move into retailing will spread managerial activities too widely. Nevertheless, corporate vertical marketing systems have operated successfully for many years in the oil industry where companies such as Shell and BP own not only considerable numbers of petrol stations but also the means of production.

Channel Management

Once the key channel strategy decisions have been made, effective implementation is required. Specifically, a number of channel management issues must be addressed (see Figure 17.6). These are the selection, motivation, training and evaluation of channel members, and managing conflict between producers and channel members.

FIGURE 17.6
Channel management

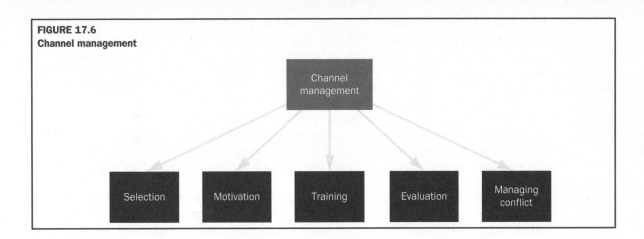

Selection

For some producers the distribution problem is not so much channel selection as channel acceptance. The selection decision can vary depending on the size of the producer: for example, very small companies face difficulties when trying to persuade large retailers to stock their products. Selection then involves identifying candidates and developing *selection criteria*.

Identifying sources

Sources for identifying candidates include trade sources, reseller enquiries, customers of distributors and the field salesforce. *Trade sources* include trade associations, exhibitions and trade publications. Talking to trade associations can lead to the supply of names of prospective distributors. Exhibitions provide a useful means of meeting and talking to possible distributors. Sometimes channel members may be proactive in contacting a producer to express an interest in handling their products. Such *reseller enquiries* show that the possible distributor is enthusiastic about the possibility of a link. *Customers of distributors* are a useful source since they can comment on their merits and limitations. Finally, if a producer already has a *field salesforce* calling on intermediaries, salespeople are in a good position to seek out possible new distributors in their own territory.

Developing selection criteria

Common selection criteria include market, product and customer knowledge, market coverage, quality and size of the salesforce (if applicable), reputation among customers, financial standing, the extent to which competitive and complementary products are carried, managerial competence, and the degree of enthusiasm for handling the producer's lines. In practice, selection may be complex because large, well-established distributors may carry many competing lines and lack enthusiasm for more, whereas smaller distributors may be more enthusiastic and hungry for success. The top selection criteria of overseas distributors are market knowledge, enthusiasm for the contract, hunger for success, customer knowledge, and the fact that the distributor does not carry competitors' products.

Motivation

Once selected, channel members need to be motivated to agree to act as a distributor, and allocate adequate commitment and resources to the producer's lines. The key to effective motivation is to understand the needs and problems of distributors as they are linked. For example, a distributor that values financial incentives may respond more readily to high commission than one that is more concerned with having an exclusive territory. Possible motivators include financial rewards, territorial exclusivity, providing resource support (e.g. sales training, field sales assistance, provision of marketing research information, advertising and promotion support, financial assistance and management training) and developing *strong work relationships* (e.g. joint planning, assurance of long-term commitment, appreciation of effort and success, frequent interchange of views and arranging distributor conferences).

Producers should seek to develop strong long-term relationships with their distributors based on a recognition of their performance and integrated planning and operations. Jointly determined sales targets can motivate salespeople, who might receive a bonus on achievement. Targets are also useful for monitoring performance.

At the outset, establishing a long-term commitment is important, especially with international partners as this can foster trust. The most popular methods cited by export managers and directors to motivate their overseas distributors were territorial exclusivity, provision of up-to-date product and company information, regular personal contact, appreciation of effort and understanding of the distributors' problems, attractive financial incentives, and provision of salespeople to support the distributors' salesforce (Shipley, Cook and Barnett, 1989). Given overseas distributors' fears that they may be replaced, it was disappointing to note that only 40 per cent of these exporters provided assurances of a long-term business commitment to their distributors as a major motivator.

Mutual commitment between channel members is central to successful relationship marketing. Two types of commitment are affective commitment that expresses the extent to which channel members like to maintain their relationship with their partners, and calculative commitment where channel members need to maintain a relationship. Commitment is highly dependent on interdependence and trust between the parties (Kumar, Scheer and Steenkamp, 1995).

Training

The need to train channel members obviously depends on their internal competences. Large-market supermarket chains, for example, may regard an invitation by a manufacturer to provide marketing training as an insult. However, many smaller distributors have been found to be weak on sales management, marketing, financial management, stock control and personnel management, and may welcome producer initiatives on training (see Shipley and Prinja, 1988; Webster, 1976). From the producer's perspective, training can provide the necessary technical knowledge about a supplier company and its products, and help to build a spirit of partnership and commitment.

However, the training of overseas distributors by British exporters appears to be the exception rather than the rule (Shipley, Cook and Barnett, 1989). When training is provided, it usually takes the form of product and company knowledge. Nevertheless when such knowledge is given it can help to build strong personal relationships and give distributors the confidence to sell those products.

Evaluation

The evaluation of channel members has an important bearing on distributor retention, training and motivation decisions. Evaluation provides the information necessary to decide which channel members to retain and which to drop. Shortfalls in distributor skills and competences may be identified through evaluation, and appropriate training programmes organized by producers. Where a lack of motivation is recognized as a problem, producers can implement plans designed to deal with the root causes of demotivation (e.g. financial incentives and/or fostering a partnership approach to business) (see Pegram, 1965; Shipley, Cook and Barnett, 1989).

However, the scope and frequency of evaluation may be limited where power lies with the channel member. If producers have relatively little power because they are more dependent on channel members for distribution than channel members are on individual producers for supply, in-depth evaluation and remedial action will be restricted. Channel members may be reluctant to spend time providing the producers with comprehensive information on which to base evaluation. Remedial action may be limited to tentative suggestions when producers suspect there is room for improvement.

Where manufacturer power is high, through having strong brands and many distributors from which to choose, evaluation may be more frequent and wider in scope. Channel members are more likely to comply with the manufacturer's demands for performance information and agree for their sales and marketing efforts to be monitored by the manufacturer.

Evaluation criteria include sales volume and value, profitability, level of stocks, quality and position of display, new accounts opened, selling and marketing capabilities, quality of service provided to customers, market information feedback, ability and willingness to meet commitments, attitudes and personal capability.

Although the evaluation of overseas distributors and agents is more difficult than that for their domestic counterparts, research has shown that over 90 per cent of producers carry out evaluation, usually at least once a year (Philpot, 1975; Shipley, Cook and Barnett, 1989).

Managing conflict

When producers and channel members are independent, conflict inevitably occurs from time to time. The intensity of conflict can range from occasional, minor disagreements that are quickly forgotten, to major disputes that fuel continuous bitter relationships (Magrath and Hardy, 1989).

Sources of channel conflict

The major sources of *channel conflict* are differences in goals, differences in views on the desired product lines carried by channel members, multiple distribution channels, and inadequacies in performance.

- *Differences in goals*: most resellers attempt to maximize their own profit. This can be accomplished by improving profit margin, reducing inventory levels, increasing sales, lowering expenses and receiving greater allowances from suppliers. In contrast, producers might benefit from lower margins, greater channel inventories, higher promotional expenses and fewer allowances given to channel members. These inherent conflicts of interest mean that there are many potential areas of disagreement between producers and their channel members.
- *Differences in desired product line*: resellers that grow by adding product lines may be regarded as disloyal by their original suppliers and can cause resentment. For example, WHSmith, a UK retailer, originally specialized in books, magazines and newspapers but has grown by adding new product lines such as computer games, DVDs and PC accessories. In Europe the growth of speciality shops selling sportswear and trainers is another source of potential conflict as the retailers with a narrow product range have a deep assortment on offer, selling a wide variety of branded sports shoes, for example. The increased competition can cause conflict with its original suppliers of these product lines since the addition of competitors' brands makes the retailer appear disloyal (Magrath and Hardy, 1989).
- *Multiple distribution channels*: in trying to achieve market coverage, a producer may use multiple distribution channels. For example, a producer may decide to sell directly to key accounts because their size warrants a key account salesforce, and use channel intermediaries to give wide market coverage. Conflict can arise when a channel member is denied access to a lucrative order from a key account because it is being serviced directly by the producer. Disagreements can also occur when the producer owns retail outlets that compete with independent retailers that also sell the producer's brands. For example, Clarks, a footwear manufacturer, owns a chain of outlets that compete with other shoe outlets that sell Clarks' shoes (Magrath and Hardy, 1989).
- *Inadequacies in performance*: an obvious source of conflict is when parties in the supply chain do not perform to expectations. For example, a channel member may underperform in terms of sales, level of inventory carried, customer service, standards of display and salesperson effectiveness. Producers may give poor delivery, inadequate promotional support, low profit margins, poor-quality goods and incomplete shipments. These can all be potential areas of conflict.

Avoiding and resolving conflict

How can producers and channel members avoid and resolve conflict? There are several ways of managing conflict.

- *Developing a partnership approach*: this calls for frequent interaction between producer and resellers to develop a spirit of mutual understanding and cooperation. Producers can help channel members with training, financial help and promotional support. Distributors, in turn, may agree to mutually agreed sales targets and provide extra sales resources. The objective is to build confidence in the manufacturer's products and relationships based on trust. When conflicts arise there is more chance they will be resolved in a spirit of cooperation. Organizing staff exchange programmes can be useful in allowing each party to understand the problems and tensions of the other to avoid giving rise to animosity.
- *Training in conflict handling*: staff who handle disputes need to be trained in negotiation and communication skills. They need to be able to handle high-pressure conflict situations without resorting to emotion and *blaming behaviour*. Instead, they should be able to handle such situations calmly and be able to handle concession analysis, in particular the identification of *win-win situations*. These are situations where both the producer and reseller benefit from an agreement.
- *Market partitioning*: to reduce or eliminate conflict from multiple distribution channels, producers can try to partition markets on some logical basis, such as customer size or type. This can work if channel members accept the basis for the partitioning. Alternatively, different channels can be supplied with different product lines.

- *Improving performance*: many conflicts occur for genuine reasons. For example, poor delivery by manufacturers or inadequate sales effort by distributors can provoke frustration and anger. Rather than attempt to placate the aggrieved partner, the most effective solution is to improve performance so that the source of conflict disappears. This is the most effective way of dealing with such problems.
- *Channel ownership*: an effective but expensive way of resolving conflicting goals is to buy the other party. Since producer and channel member are under common ownership, the common objective is to maximize joint profits. Conflicts can still occur but the dominant partner is in a position to resolve them quickly. Some producers in Europe have integrated with channel intermediaries successfully. For example, over 40 per cent of household furniture is sold through producer-owned retail outlets in Italy (Magrath and Hardy, 1989).
- *Coercion*: In some situations, conflict resolution may be dependent on coercion, where one party induces compliance through the use of force. For example, producers can threaten to withdraw supply, deliver late or withdraw financial support; channel members, on the other hand, can threaten to delist the manufacturer's products, promote competitive products and develop own-label brands.

Physical Distribution and Retailing

In the first part of this chapter we examined channel strategy, focusing on the key areas of channel management decisions. In this section we examine physical distribution decisions, and the implications for channel management and for retailing.

Physical distribution is defined as a 'set of activities concerned with the physical flows of materials, components and finished goods from producer to channel intermediaries and consumers'. The combination of channels used by retailers is becoming increasingly diverse as they try to provide customers with non-stop access to goods and services. For retailers the aim is to provide customers with the right products, in the right quantities, in the right locations, at the right time. Physical distribution activities have been the subject of managerial attention for some time because of the potential for cost savings and improving customer service levels. Cost savings can be achieved by reducing inventory levels, using cheaper forms of transport and shipping in bulk rather than small quantities. Customer service levels can be improved by fast and reliable delivery, including just-in-time delivery, holding high inventory levels so that customers have a wide choice and the chances of stockouts are reduced, fast order processing, and ensuring products arrive in the right quantities and quality. But now channel selection has become a means of adding customer value. Zara uses the distribution channel as a source of competitive advantage (see Exhibit 17.4).

In the clothing industry, fast-changing fashion demands mean that companies such as H&M and Zara use extremely short lead times to create a competitive advantage over their slower, more cumbersome, rivals. Such methods used are discussed in Mini Case 17.1.

Physical distribution management concerns the balance between cost reduction and meeting customer service requirements. Trade-offs are often necessary. For example, low inventory and slow, cheaper transportation methods reduce costs but lower customer service levels and satisfaction. Determining this balance is a key marketing decision as physical distribution can be a source of competitive advantage. A useful approach is to analyse the market in terms of customer service needs and price sensitivity. The result may be the discovery of two segments:

- segment 1—low service needs, high price sensitivity
- segment 2—high service needs, low price sensitivity.

Unipart was first to exploit segment 2 in the do-it-yourself car repair and servicing market. It gave excellent customer service but charged

EXHIBIT 17.4
Zara uses open-plan work spaces to encourage collaboration in its manufacturing units in Spain

MINI CASE 17.1
Managing the Supply Chain the Zara Way

Zara, the Spanish clothing company owned by Inditex, has revolutionized the fashion industry by becoming the first global retailer to sell fashion lines designed especially for seasons in the southern as well as the northern hemisphere. Zara has a successful business model that has enabled the retail chain to expand to over 5,000 outlets and stores in Europe, South America, Oceania and Africa, so developing ranges to suit the seasons is an important part of the expansion strategy. Its key competitive advantage lies in its ability to match fashion trends that change quickly. This in turn relies on an extremely fast and responsive supply chain. While other retailers moved production to the Far East to save money, Zara knew that it could make its best-selling clothes faster in Spain; (see Exhibit 17.4).

Zara uses its stores to find out what consumers want, what styles are selling, what colours are in demand, and which items are hot sellers and which are failures. The data are fed back to Zara headquarters through a sophisticated marketing information system. At the end of each day Zara sales assistants report to the store manager using wireless headsets to communicate inventory levels. The store managers then inform the Zara design and distribution departments at headquarters about what consumers are buying, asking for and avoiding. Top-selling items are requested and low-selling items are withdrawn from shops within a week. There is a big incentive for the store managers to get it right, as up to 70 per cent of their salary is based on commission.

Garments are made in small production runs to avoid overexposure, and no item stays in the shops for more than four weeks, which encourages Zara shoppers to make repeat visits. Whereas the average high-street store in Spain expects shoppers to visit on average three times a year, Zara shoppers visit up to 17 times.

The company's designers use the feedback from the stores when preparing new designs. The fabrics are cut and dyed at Zara's own highly automated manufacturing facilities, which gives it control over this part of the supply chain. Seamstresses in 350 independently owned workshops in Spain and Portugal stitch about half of the pre-cut pieces into garments; the other half are stitched in-house. Only basic items such as T-shirts are bought from low-cost regions such as eastern Europe, Africa and Asia. Although wages are higher in Spain, Zara saves time and money on shipping.

The finished garments are sent back to Zara's headquarters with its state-of-the-art logistics centre where they are electronically tagged, quality checked and sorted into distribution lots for shipping to their destinations. Although Zara supplies every market from warehouses in Spain, it manages to get new merchandise to European stores within 24 hours, and, by flying goods via commercial airlines, to stores in the Americas and Asia in 48 hours or less.

So efficient are Zara's production and distribution systems that the average turnaround time from design to delivery is 10 to 15 days, with around 12,000 garments being marketed each year. In this way, Zara stays on top of fashion trends rather than being outpaced by the market. And, by producing smaller batches of clothing, it adds an air of exclusivity that encourages customers to shop often. As a result, the chain does not have to slash prices by 50 per cent, as rivals often do, to move mass quantities of out-of-season stock. Since Zara is more in tune with current looks, it can also charge slightly more than, for example, Gap, which it has now overtaken to become the world's largest clothing retailer.

Questions:

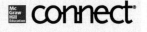

1 Discuss the implications of shorter product life-cycles for a clothing manufacturer like Zara and H&M.
2 Suggest why Zara doesn't just use the garment ranges developed in the winter for the northern hemisphere and then sell them on in the southern hemisphere.
3 At the opposite end of the spectrum is the 'slow fashion' movement, which advocates buying fewer clothes of better quality that will last longer and help to save the environment. Do you think this growing trend will affect the demand for fast fashion and do fast fashion brands only appeal to the young?

Based on: The Economist (2002); Roux (2002); BBC (2003); Mitchell (2003); Fahy and Jobber (2015); Capell (2008); Johnson and Falstead (2011)

a high price. This analysis, therefore, defined the market segment to target and the appropriate marketing mix. Alternatively, both segments could be targeted with different marketing mixes. In business-to-business markets, large companies may possess their own service facilities while smaller firms require producer or distributor service as part of the product offering and are willing to pay a higher price.

Not only are there trade-offs between physical distribution costs and customer service levels, but there are also possible conflicts between elements of the physical distribution system itself. For example, an inventory manager may favour low stocks to reduce costs, but if this leads to stock-outs this may raise costs elsewhere: the freight manager may have to accept higher costs resulting from fast freight deliveries in order to guarantee the safety of the products. A key role that the physical distribution manager would perform would be to reconcile the conflicts inherent in the system so that total costs are minimized subject to required customer service levels.

The Physical Distribution System

A system is a set of connected parts managed in such a way that overall objectives are achieved. The physical distribution system contains the following parts (see Figure 17.7).

- *Customer service*: What level of customer service should be provided?
- *Order processing*: How should the orders be handled?
- *Inventory control*: How much inventory should be held?
- *Warehousing*: Where should the inventory be located? How many warehouses should be used?
- *Transportation*: How will the products be transported?
- *Materials handling*: How will the products be handled during transportation?

Companies like DHL, Fedex and Norbert Dentressangle provide specialist expertise in these areas. Each of the above questions will now be explored.

Customer service

Customer service standards need to be set. For example, a customer service standard might be that 90 per cent of orders are delivered within 24 hours of receipt and 100 per cent are delivered within 48 hours.

Higher customer service standards normally mean higher costs as inventory levels need to be higher. Since inventory ties up working capital, the higher the inventory level the higher the working capital charge. The physical distribution manager needs to be aware of the costs of fulfilling various customer service standards (e.g. 80, 90 and 100 per cent of orders delivered within 48 hours) and the extra customer satisfaction that results from raising standards.

In some cases, customers value consistency in delivery time rather than speed. For example, a customer service standard of guaranteed delivery within five working days may be valued more than that of 60 per cent within two, 80 per cent within five or 100 per cent within seven days. Since the latter standard requires delivery at 60 per cent within two days it may require higher inventory levels than the former. Therefore, by understanding customer requirements, it may be possible to increase satisfaction while lowering costs.

Customer service standards should be given considerable attention because they may be the differentiating factor between suppliers: they may be used as a key customer choice criterion. Methods of improving customer service standards in physical distribution are listed in Table 17.2. By examining ways of improving product availability and order cycle time, and raising information levels and flexibility, considerable goodwill and customer loyalty can be created. The advertisement for DHL explains how it provides excellent service, versatility and a portfolio of shipping solutions.

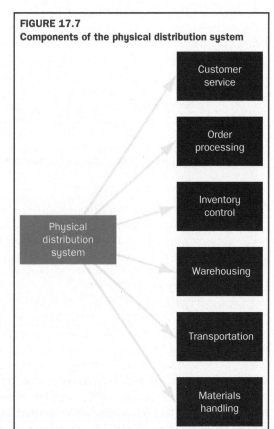

FIGURE 17.7
Components of the physical distribution system

TABLE 17.2 Methods of improving customer service standards in physical distribution
Improve product availability
Raise in-stock levels
Improve accuracy, speed and reliability of deliveries
Improve order cycle time
Shorten time between order and delivery
Improve consistency between order and delivery time
Raise information levels
Improve salesperson information on inventory
Raise information levels on order status
Be proactive in notifying customer of delays
Raise flexibility
Develop contingency plans for urgent orders
Ensure fast reaction time to unforeseen problems (e.g. stolen goods, damage in transit)

The Internet is providing the means of improving customer service for some distribution companies. For example, if a customer of Federal Express wants to track a package they can do so via the Internet. Creating a user-friendly way to track parcels is a win-win situation as the customer instantly knows where his parcel is and FedEx saves money as it is no longer handling as many customer telephone enquiries. The main logistical companies—FedEx, UPS and DHL—take a significant percentage of their business-to-business transactions via the Internet; (see Exhibit 17.5).

Technology has also enabled logistics to become more efficient and effective through satellite-based distribution systems. Everything from the clothes we wear to the fresh fish we eat can now be tracked from its point of manufacture to the point of delivery.

Order processing

Reducing time between a customer placing an order and receiving the goods may be achieved through careful analysis of the components that contribute to the order-processing time. Automated digital ordering systems and modern electronic data interchange (EDI) systems via the Internet speed up order-processing, validating customers, checking availability, issuing an order to the warehouse, invoicing the customer and updating the inventory records.

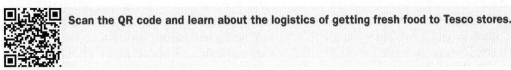 **Scan the QR code and learn about the logistics of getting fresh food to Tesco stores.**

Grocery deliveries which fulfil online orders present the greatest logistical challenges. Typically, online orders for tesco.com involve picking an order comprising 60–80 items, across three temperature regimes from a total range of 10–25,000 products within 12–24 hours for delivery to customers within one- to two-hour time-slots.

Inventory control

Inventory levels can be a source of conflict between finance and marketing management. Since inventory represents costs, financial managers seek stock minimization; marketing management, acutely aware of the customer problems caused by stock-outs, want large inventories. In reality, a balance has to be found, particularly as inventory cost rises at an increasing rate as customer service standards near 100 per cent. This means that to always have in stock every conceivable item that a customer might order would normally be prohibitively expensive for companies marketing many items. One solution to this problem is to separate items into those that are in demand and those that are slower-moving. This is sometimes called the '80:20 rule', since for many companies 80 per cent of sales are achieved by 20 per cent of products. A high customer service standard is then set for the high-demand 20 per cent (e.g. in stock 95 per cent of the time) but a much lower standard used for those items less in demand (e.g. in stock 70 per cent of the time).

Two related *inventory decisions* are knowing when and how much to order so that stocks are replenished. As inventory for an item falls, a point is reached when new stock is required. Unless a stock-out is tolerated the *order point* will be before inventory reaches zero. This is because there will be a *lead time* between ordering and receiving inventory. The *just-in-time inventory system* (discussed in Chapter 4) is designed to reduce lead times so that the order point (the stock level at which reordering takes place), and overall inventory levels for production items, are low. The key to the just-in-time system is the maintenance of a fast and reliable lead time so that deliveries of supplies arrive shortly before they are needed.

The order point depends on three factors: the viability of the order lead time, fluctuation in customer demand, and the customer service standard. The more variable

EXHIBIT 17.5
DHL communicates its excellent service and versatility

the lead time between ordering and receiving stock, and the greater the fluctuation in customer demand, the higher the order point. This is because of the uncertainty caused by the variability, leading to the need for **safety (buffer) stocks** in case lead times are unpredictably long or customer demand unusually high. Suppliers can build strong relationships with their customers through automated inventory restocking systems, as Mini Case 17.1, on Zara, describes.

Warehousing

Warehousing involves all the activities required in the storing of goods between the time they are produced and the time they are transported to the customer. These activities include breaking bulk, making up product assortments for delivery to customers, storage and loading. *Storage warehouses* hold goods for moderate or long time periods whereas *distribution centres* operate as central locations for the fast movement of goods. Retailing organizations use distribution centres where suppliers bring products in bulk. These shipments are broken down into loads, which are then quickly transported to retail outlets. Distribution centres are usually highly automated with computer-controlled machinery facilitating the movement of goods. Mobile and wireless technology is increasingly being used to manage modern warehousing and distribution systems. Online shopping has added a layer of complexity, as there are an increasing number of separate orders to manage. For retailers, the solution is often to pass the responsibility for handling the goods supplied through e-commerce orders to third-party logistic companies (Keifer, 2015) to benefit from their specialist expertise, up-to-date technology and infinite scalability—for example DHL, Excel, Hermes.

Transportation

Customer service ultimately depends on the ability of the physical distribution system to transport products on time and without damage. Timely delivery is even more important with wider use of the just-in-time system, distribution centres and quick response systems. Goods are moved around the world with amazing efficiency. In the UK and parts of Europe goods are sourced and delivered from over 125 different countries. Movement of goods, especially perishable goods, relies on the transportation network spanning the globe. Road, rail, air and sea transport systems are interlinked to provide streamlined and efficient logistics solutions. Companies like Maersk (one of the world's largest shipping companies), FedEx, Kuehne Nagel, Deutche Logistics SCM (logistics and supply chain management) work together to move goods on different forms of transport. Key forms of transport include water, air, road and rail.

Water transport—moving goods by sea is an important part of the goods 'super-highway'. At any one time there are approximately 6 million containers, full of goods, being transported from one part of the world to another. Water transportation is slower but less costly. A large proportion of long-haul deliveries between Europe and the Pacific Rim is by sea transport.

Air transport—this moves goods quickly and is a solution which offers speed and long-distance capabilities. Furthermore, in a period when companies are seeking to reduce inventories, air freight can be used to supply inventories under just-in-time systems. With the growth in international trade, air freight is predicted to be a growth activity. Its major disadvantages are high cost and the need to transport goods by road to and from air terminals.

Road transport—this provides more flexibility than rail, when moving goods from supplier to, say, retailer. Furthermore, the speed of road transport in Europe has increased since the advent of the EU, with the removal of cross-border restrictions (Samiee, 1990). However, the growth of road transport in Europe, and particularly the UK, has received considerable criticism because of increased traffic congestion and the damage done to roads by heavy juggernauts. Nevertheless, the quote at the beginning of the chapter is about Eddie Stobart, a man who 'humanized transport' and built his small family business (started in Cumbria) into one of Britain's most popular brands (Childs, 2011). Eddie built up the business on a reputation of having good-looking trucks and well-dressed drivers, who acknowledge the public when a Stobart lorry is 'spotted'.

Rail transport—this is efficient at transporting large, bulky freight on land over large distances. Rail is often used to transport coal, chemicals, oil, aggregates and nuclear flasks. A problem, though, is lack of flexibility. For many companies the use of rail would mean transport by lorry to and from a rail depot. Furthermore, for small quantities the use of rail may prove uneconomic. Nevertheless, rail is more environmentally friendly than road and can be an ideal solution, especially when long, regular journeys carrying large quantities are needed.

There are some industry specific issues which distributors must adhere to when moving foodstuffs and perishables. Health authorities set rules for the movement of these products at controlled temperatures, which apply to all forms of transport. One of the biggest issues for food producers to deal with is that the moment that fresh produce is picked it is deteriorating. Some exotic foodstuffs are grown in equatorial regions, picked, processed, packaged and transported thousands of miles within a very short time frame—for example, chopped mango and pineapple from equatorial regions are flown to the northern hemisphere.

Materials handling

Materials handling involves the activities related to the moving of products in the producer's plant, warehouses and transportation depots. Modern storage facilities are designed to allow a high level of automation. At the Dixons Carphone distribution centre in Newark, a large part of goods processing is automated. In-bound goods enter on pallets and are identified and documented using scanners. At any time the logistics team know where every product is, from the smallest memory card to the largest flat-screen television. Out-bound goods are processed and picked using part automation. Individual team members responsible for picking have digital headsets which enable speedy and efficient selection of orders for stores and individual customers.

Two key developments in materials handling are unit handling and containerization. *Unit handling* achieves efficiency by combining multiple packages on to pallets that can be moved by forklift trucks. *Containerization* involves the combining of many quantities of goods (e.g. car components) into a single large container; once sealed, they can easily be transferred from one form of transport to another. For example, a container could be loaded on to a lorry and taken to a rail freight terminal to form part of a trainload of containers destined for the docks. There the container can easily be transferred to a ship for transportation to a destination thousands of miles away. Since individual items are not handled, damage in transit is reduced.

An important element in materials handling is the quality of packaging. It is necessary to evaluate not only the appearance and cost of packaging, but also the ability to repackage into larger quantities for transportation. Packages must be sturdy enough to withstand the rigours of physical distribution, such as harsh handling and stacking.

Retailing

Traditionally, retailing was considered a rather passive activity, with goods passing from the manufacturer to the wholesaler then to the retailer and, finally, to individual customers. Retailers would display available products and attempt to sell them to their customers with limited regard for what the customers wanted. However, eventually, retailers discovered that understanding what was important to the customer meant they could stock the right products, sell at the right price and ultimately *increase profits*, rather than having to *push* the products they had in stock, often at reduced prices. The era of 'stack them high and sell them cheap' ended. Retailers had discovered the importance of *understanding and satisfying customer needs* and this represented an important landmark in the development and definition of modern retailing (Ellis-Chadwick, 2011). The implication of this shift towards a customer-centric operation is at the heart of many of the channel management decisions we have discussed so far in this chapter.

Retail marketing decisions

Like any modern business retailers must understand the environment they trade in and anticipate and adapt to changing environmental circumstances. We shall now explore some of the key retailing decisions necessary to prosper in today's competitive climate. These decisions are retail positioning, store location, product assortment and services, price and store atmosphere. These call for decisions to be taken against a background of rapid change in information technology.

Retailers are no strangers to information technology developments, with electronic point of sale (EPOS) systems allowing the counting of products sold, money taken and faster service at checkouts. Barcodes, UPC codes, scanners and associated technology have revolutionized retail supply chains, stock management and retail operations. A further technological innovation is using the Internet to shop. Online shopping is growing as more people become accustomed to electronic payment, have broadband access to the Internet and are prepared to shop via a mobile phone. See Exhibit 17.6 to find out how virtual retailer Yihaodian became the number one retailer in China.

As with all marketing decisions, **retail positioning** involves the choice of target market and differential advantage. Targeting allows retailers to tailor their marketing mix, which includes product assortment, service levels, store location, prices and promotion, to the needs of their chosen customer segment. Differentiation provides a reason to shop at one store rather than another. For some retailers, the low-cost strategic option remains viable—Aldi, Costco, Asda Walmart, Amazon—and for others, the high-quality differentiated route—for example Waitrose, John Lewis Partnership, Harrods. But many retailers find themselves 'stuck in the middle', falling between low cost and high quality (Berman, 2010). Often this occurs when retailers attempt to be all things to all people. The outcome can be that the retailer needs to respond rapidly if it is to survive. For example, in 2015, leading UK supermarket retailer Tesco was facing falling profits and market share, and in response cut its prices in order to compete with limited range discounters Aldi and Lidl.

Many of the changes occurring in retail are as a result of the effect of the Internet on traditional models. Retailers are left facing challenging decisions about which market positions to inhabit, which locations to utilize, how to communicate with their customers, and the extent to which their products can be augmented by additional services. Consequently, the way retailers are using the marketing mix to differentiate their brands has changed (Verhoef, Kannan and Inman, 2015). The rest of this section explores how retailers seek to differentiate their offer.

Place: store location

Multichannel retailing, whereby retailers add new channels to their existing offer, is becoming increasingly important. For example, traditional store-based retailers have introduced online and mobile digital stores, for example Dixons Carphone, John Lewis Partnership. Alternatively, online-only retailers have moved onto the physical high street, for example eBay, Amazon.

EXHIBIT 17.6
Yihaodian, number 1 retailer in China

But the discussion of the channels retailers might choose to serve their customers does not end here. As the journey that customers take to purchase becomes more complex, crossing over from the physical to the virtual, they may encounter many touchpoints. For example, a shopper likes a product in a magazine and may then go to the web to find out about the product, actually visit a store to see what the product looks like, then make a purchase online and finally go to a social media site to review the product. The decision for the retailer ceases to be which channels, but how to create a seamless journey for the customer.

The solution is to adopt an omni-channel approach whereby, regardless of where shoppers interact with the retailer, their experience is the same. This means that a retailer should ensure that products, prices, customer service and communication messages are consistent. The increasing use of digital, mobile and social media channels, giving rise to new types of customer journey—for example: reserve online, collect from store; order in store, delivered to home; buy online, return unwanted goods to store—should be addressed alongside sales performance and marketing strategy.

As channel decisions become more complex, it is increasingly important to understand the target customers. However, convenience remains an important issue for many shoppers, and so store location can still have a major bearing on sales performance. Also, given that approximately 90 per cent of retail sales take place in physical stores, retailers have to decide on regional coverage, the towns and cities to target within regions, and the precise location within a given town or city. Location for Ted Baker, the clothes and home furnishings fashion retailer, is absolutely key, as the company does not advertise. Ted Baker is at Gatwick and Heathrow airports, Bluewater and Glasgow, but also in Miami, Paris and New York's Bloomingdale's. Its London store sits opposite Paul Smith, the designer clothes store, in one of the city's trendiest enclaves (Ryle, 2002). Many retailers begin life as regional suppliers and grow by expanding geographically. In the UK, for example, the Asda supermarket chain expanded from the north of England, while the original base for Sainsbury's was in the south of England.

The location of stores can be greatly aided by geographic information systems (GISs), which profile geographical areas according to such variables as disposable income, family size, age and birth rates. We saw in Chapter 7, on market segmentation and positioning, how such systems can be used to segment markets. GISs allow marketers to understand the profiles of people living in specific geographic areas. Asda, the UK supermarket chain, uses GIS data as a method of finding new store locations. By understanding the number and profile of consumers living in different geographical areas, it can plan its stores (and product assortment) to be located in the right areas to serve its target market (Hayward, 2002).

Product assortment and services

Retailers have to decide upon the breadth of their product assortment and its depth. A supermarket, for example, may decide to widen its product assortment from food, drink and toiletries to include clothes, electrical goods and toys; this is called *scrambled merchandising*. Within each product line it can choose to stock a deep or shallow product range. Some retailers specialize in particular product rages, like Rymans the stationery retailer. Department stores like Debenhams and House of Fraser offer a much broader range of products including toys, cosmetics, jewellery, clothes, electrical goods and household accessories. Some retailers begin with one product line and gradually broaden their product assortment to maximize revenue per customer. For example, petrol stations broadened their product range to include motor accessories, confectionery, drinks, flowers and newspapers. A by-product of this may be to reduce customers' price sensitivity since selection of petrol station may be based on the ability to buy other products rather than the lowest price.

The choice of product assortment will be dependent on the positioning strategy of the retailer, customer expectations and, ultimately, on the profitability of each product line. Another product decision concerns own-label branding. Large retailers may decide to sell a range of own-label products to complement national brands. Often the purchasing power of large retail chains means that prices can be lower and yet profit margins higher than for competing national brands. This makes the activity an attractive proposition for many retailers. Consumers also find own-label brands attractive, with many of them in the grocery field being regarded as being at least equal to, if not better than, established manufacturer brands (Burt, 2000). Finally, retailers need to consider the nature and degree of *customer service*. Discount stores traditionally provided little service but, as price differentials have narrowed, some have sought differentiation through service. For example, many electrical goods retailers provide a comprehensive after-sales service package for their customers. Superior customer service may make customers more tolerant of higher prices and, even where the product is standardized (as in fast-food restaurants), training employees to give individual attention to each customer can increase loyalty to the outlet (Bloemer, de Ruyter and Wetzels, 1999).

Price

For some market segments price is a key factor in store choice. Consequently, some retailers use price as their differential advantage. This requires vigilant cost control and significant buying power. Where price is a key choice criterion, retailers who lose price competitiveness can suffer. For example, Carrefour, the world's second largest retailer after Walmart, lost its reputation for low prices in France because of its focus on profit margins rather than volume. Market share plummeted in the face of intense competition from its domestic rivals Leclerc and Auchan and discounters such as Germany's Aldi and Lidl (*The Economist*, 2005). The popular trend is towards *everyday low prices* favoured by retailers rather than higher prices supplemented by promotions supported by manufacturers. Retailers such as Aldi, Lidl and Asda maintain that customers prefer predictable low prices rather than occasional money-off deals, three-for-the-price-of two offers and free gifts. Supermarket chains are also pressurizing suppliers to provide consistently low prices rather than temporary promotions. This action is consistent with the desire to position themselves on a low-price platform.

Store atmosphere

This is created by the design, colour and layout of a store. Both exterior and interior design affect atmosphere. External factors include architectural design, signs, window display and use of colour, which together create an identity for a retailer and attract customers. Retailers aim to create a welcoming rather than an intimidating mood. The image that is projected should be consonant with the ethos of the shop. The Body Shop, for example, projects its environmentally caring image through the green exterior of its shops, and window displays that feature environmental issues.

Interior design also has a major impact on atmosphere. Store lighting, fixtures and fittings, and layout are important considerations. Supermarkets that have narrow aisles hat contribute to congestion can project a negative image, and poorly lit showrooms can feel intimidating. Colour, sound and smell can affect mood. Sometimes red-toned lighting is used in areas of impulse purchasing. For example, one stationer uses red tones at the front of its stores for impulse buys such as pens and stationery. Supermarkets often use music to create a relaxed atmosphere, whereas some boutiques use contemporary music to attract their target customers. Departmental stores often place perfume counters near the entrance, and supermarkets may use the smell of baking bread to attract their customers.

Ethical Issues in Distribution

The final section in this chapter discusses ethical issues associated with distribution. Ethical issues in distribution include the use of slotting allowances, exclusive dealing, restrictions on supply, grey markets and fair trading.

Slotting allowances, exclusive dealing and restrictions to supply

Food is big business, and the majority of products find their way to supermarket shelves rather than the local corner shop. The retail grocery business therefore tends to be dominated by mega brands, for example Walmart, Carrefour, Tesco. The power shift from manufacturers to retailers in this industry has meant that slotting allowances are often demanded by large retailers. A *slotting allowance* is a fee paid in exchange for an agreement to place a product in a preferential space on the retailer's shelves. Retailers say they are simply charging rent for a valuable, scarce commodity: shelf space (Stanton and Herbst, 2006). Tesco got into a row over slotting allowances, and the dispute was blamed for destabilizing the power they exerted over suppliers (Meville, 2014). Critics argue that these charges represent an abuse of power and work against small manufacturers who cannot afford to pay the fee. Research in the grocery sector found that nearly 40 per cent of manufacturers complained of being asked to pay fees for the retailer to stock their produce (Butler, 2015).

Another concern of small suppliers is that the power of large manufacturers and retailers will mean that they are squeezed out of the supply chain. In the UK, farmers and small grocery suppliers have joined forces to demand better treatment from large supermarket chains, which are forging exclusive deals with major manufacturers. They claim the problem is made worse by the growth of category management, where retailers appoint 'category captains' from their suppliers, who act to improve the standing of the whole product category, such as breakfast cereals or confectionery. The small suppliers believe this forces them out of the category altogether, as category captains look after their own interests. They would like to see a system similar to that in France, where about 10 per cent of shelf space is by law given to small suppliers (McCawley, 2000).

Grey markets

These occur when a product is sold through an unauthorized distribution channel. When this occurs in international marketing, the practice is called parallel importing. Usually, a distributor buys goods in one country (where prices are low) and sells them in another (where prices are high) at below the going market price. This causes anger among members of the authorized distribution channel, who see their prices being undercut. Furthermore, the products may well be sold in downmarket outlets that discredit the image of the product, or be sold cheaply online. Quality fashion brands such as Burberry, Armani and Abercrombie & Fitch have experienced the 'grey market effect' on their brands. Nevertheless, supporters of grey markets argue that they encourage price competition, increase consumer choice and promote the lowering of price differentials between countries.

Fair trading

One problem of free market forces is that when small commodity producers are faced with large powerful buyers the result can be very low prices. This can bring severe economic hardship to the producers, who may be situated in countries of the developing world. In the face of a collapse in world coffee prices, a fair trading brand, Cafédirect, was launched. Fair trade business models provide benefits to small producers by helping them to achieve higher prices and retain access to important markets, training and improvements to working practices. But there are drawbacks; for example, prices may be fixed at a commodity level rather than at a country level, and certified Fairtrade coffee producers can be made to pay the cost of marketing of the Fairtrade brand, through licensing fees as a proportion of their sales (Macatonia, 2013).

When you have read this chapter

Discover further resources and test your understanding: McGraw-Hill **Connect**™ is a digital teaching and learning environment that improves performance over a variety of critical outcomes; it can be tailored, is easy to use and is proven effective. **LearnSmart**™ is the most widely used and intelligent adaptive learning resource that is proven to strengthen memory recall, improve course retention and boost grades. Fuelled by **LearnSmart**™, **SmartBook**™ is the first and only adaptive reading experience available today.

Review

1 **The functions and types of channels of distribution**
   - The functions are to reconcile the needs of producers and consumers, improving efficiency, improving accessibility and providing specialist services.
   - Four types of consumer channel are producer direct to consumer, producer to retailer to consumer, producer to wholesaler to retailer to consumer, and producer to agent to wholesaler to retailer to consumer.

- Four types of industrial channels are producer to industrial customer, producer to agent to industrial customer, producer to distributor to industrial customer, and producer to agent to distributor to industrial customer.
- Two types of service channel are service provider to consumer or industrial customer, and service provider to agent to consumer or industrial customer.

2 How to determine channel strategy

- Channel strategy should be determined by making decisions concerning the selection of the most effective distribution channel, the most appropriate level of distribution intensity and the correct degree of channel integration.

3 The three components of channel strategy: channel selection, intensity and integration

- Channel selection is influenced by market factors (buyer behaviour, ability to meet buyer needs, the willingness of channel intermediaries to market a product, the profit margins required by distributors and agents compared with the costs of direct distribution, and the location and geographic concentration of customers), producer factors (lack of resources, the width and depth of the product mix offered by a producer, and the desired level of control of channel operations), product factors (complexity, perishability, extent of bulkiness and difficulty of handling), and competitive factors (need to choose innovative channels because traditional channels are controlled by the competition or because a competitive advantage is likely to result).
- Channel intensity options are intensive distribution to achieve saturated coverage of the market by using all available outlets, selective distribution, where a limited number of outlets in a geographical area are used, and exclusive distribution, which is an extreme form of selective distribution where only one wholesaler, retailer or industrial distributor is used in a geographic area.
- Channel integration can range from conventional marketing channels (where there is separation of ownership between producer and distributor, although the manufacturer power of channel intermediaries may result in an administered vertical marketing system), franchising and channel ownership.

4 The five key channel management issues: member selection, motivation, training, evaluation and conflict management

- Selection of members involves identifying sources and establishing selection criteria.
- Motivation of distributors involves understanding the needs and problems of distributors, and methods include financial rewards, territorial exclusivity, providing resource support, the development of strong work relationships.
- Training may be provided where appropriate. It can provide the necessary technical knowledge about a supplier company and its products, and help to build a spirit of partnership and commitment.
- Evaluation criteria include sales volume and value, profitability, level of stocks, quality and position of display, new accounts opened, selling and marketing capabilities, quality of service, market information feedback, willingness and ability to meet commitments, attitudes and personal capability. Evaluation should be based on mutually agreed objectives.
- Conflict management sources are differences in goals, differences in desired product lines, the use of multiple distribution channels by producers, and inadequacies in performance. Conflict-handling approaches are developing a partnership approach, training in conflict handling, market partitioning, improving performance, channel ownership and coercion.

5 The cost–customer service trade-off in physical distribution

- Physical distribution management concerns the balance between cost reduction and meeting customer service requirements. An example of a trade-off is incompatibility between low inventory and slow, cheaper transportation methods that reduce costs, and the lower customer service levels and satisfaction that results.

6 The components of a physical distribution system: customer service, order processing, inventory control, warehousing, transportation and materials handling

- The system should be managed so that its components combine to achieve overall objectives. Management needs to answer a series of questions related to each component: customer service, order processing, inventory control, warehousing, transportation, materials.

7 How to improve customer service standards in physical distribution

- Customer service standards can be raised by improving product availability (e.g. by increasing inventory levels), improving order cycle time (e.g. faster order processing), raising information levels (e.g. information on order status) and raising flexibility (e.g. fast reaction time to problems).

8 Retailing and retail marketing

- Retailing fulfils an essential role in the supply chain insofar as breaking bulk and enabling goods manufactured in very large quantities to be supplied to consumers in very small quantities. This process has many implications for channel management. Furthermore, marketing mix decisions, positioning and other marketing concepts have particular meaning when applied to retailing.
- Retail positioning involves the choice of target marketing and use of the marketing mix to develop differential advantage.
- Store location decisions are made using a number of variables from convenience to disposable income of a particular catchment area.
- Product assortment decisions focus on the breadth and depth of range, which enables retailers to tailor their product mix to suit particular audiences.
- Pricing is important in retailing and retailers need to ensure they manage cost control and levels of pricing effectively.
- Store atmosphere—the internal and external design, colour and store layout can all impact on consumer buying behaviour.

9 Ethical issues in distribution

- There are potential problems relating to slotting allowances, exclusive dealing, restrictions on supply, grey markets and fair trading.

Key Terms

administered vertical marketing system a channel situation where a manufacturer that dominates a market through its size and strong brands may exercise considerable power over intermediaries even though they are independent

channel integration the way in which the players in the channel are linked

channel intermediaries organizations that facilitate the distribution of products to customers

channel of distribution the means by which products are moved from the producer to the ultimate consumer

channel strategy the selection of the most effective distribution channel, the most appropriate level of distribution intensity and the degree of channel integration

contractual vertical marketing system a franchise arrangement (e.g. a franchise) that ties together producers and resellers

corporate vertical marketing system a channel situation where an organization gains control of distribution through ownership

disintermediation the removal of channel partners by bypassing intermediaries and going directly from manufacturer to consumer via the Internet

exclusive distribution an extreme form of selective distribution where only one wholesaler, retailer or industrial distributor is used in a geographical area to sell the products of a supplier

franchise a legal contract in which a producer and channel intermediaries agree each other's rights and obligations; usually the intermediary receives marketing, managerial, technical and financial services in return for a fee

intensive distribution the aim of this is to provide saturation coverage of the market by using all available outlets

reintermediation the introduction of new forms of channel intermediary that provide services which link members of the supply chain, for example web service providers and retailers

retail positioning the choice of target market and differential advantage for a retail outlet

safety (buffer) stocks stocks or inventory held to cover against uncertainty about resupply lead times

selective distribution the use of a limited number of outlets in a geographical area to sell the products of a supplier

Study Questions

1. What is the difference between channel decisions and physical distribution management? In what ways are they linked?

2. The best way of distributing an industrial product is direct from manufacturer to customer. Discuss.

3. Why is channel selection an important decision? What factors influence choice?

4. What is meant by the partnership approach to managing distributors? What can manufacturers do to help build partnerships?

5. Describe situations that can lead to conflict between channel members. What can be done to avoid and resolve conflict?

6. Why is there usually a trade-off between customer service and physical distribution costs? What can be done to improve customer service standards in physical distribution?

7. What are the considerations a retailer might make when planning its channel strategy?

Recommended Reading

Doherty, N. F. and F. Ellis-Chadwick, F. (2010) Internet retailing: the past, the present and the future, *International Journal of Retail & Distribution Management* 38(11/12), 943–65.

Digital High Street Report (2015) http://thegreatbritishhighstreet.co.uk/pdf/Digital_High_Street_Report/The-Digital-High-Street-Report-2020.pdf

Fernie J., L. Sparks and A. C. McKinnon (2010) Retail logistics in the UK: past, present and future',

International Journal of Retail & Distribution Management 38(11/12), 894–914.

Myerson, P. (2014) *Lean Wholesale and Retail*, London: McGraw Hill Higher Education.

Palmiatier, R., L. Stern and A. El-Ansary (2015) *Marketing channel strategy*, USA: Prentice Hall.

Statistica (2015) Distribution channels. http://www.statista.com/statistics/406667/b2b-marketing-content-distribution-channels

References

Barford, V. (2011) How did Eddie Stobart become so famous? http://www.bbc.co.uk/news/magazine-12925163, 1 April.

BBC (2003) Store Wars: Fast Fashion, *The Money Programme*, 19 February.

Berman, B. (2010) *Competing in Tough Times*, London: FT Press.

Bloemer, S., K. de Ruyter and M. Wetzels (1999) Linking Perceived Service Quality and Service Loyalty: A Multi-Dimensional Perspective, *European Journal of Marketing* 33(11/12), 1082–106.

Bunwell, S. (2005) One Channel, Many Paths, *The Mobile Channel*, supplement to *Marketing Week*, 7 June, 5.

Burt, S. (2000) The Strategic Role of Retail Brands in British Grocery Retailing, *European Journal of Marketing* 34(8), 875–90.

Butler, S. (2015) Suppliers scared to blow the whistle on big retailers, *The Observer*, 8 February, 41.

Capell, K. (2008) Zara Thrives By Breaking All the Rules, *Business Week*, 20 October, 66.

Childs, M. (2011) Edward Stobart, *Independent* 5 April, 8.

Costco (2015) *Investor Relations*, www.costco.com, 2 May. http://phx.corporate-ir.net/phoenix.zhtml?c=83830&p=irol-news&nyo=0

Coughlan, A., E. Anderson, L. W. Stern and A. I. El-Ansary (2005) *Marketing Channels*, Englewood Cliffs, NJ: Prentice-Hall, 6.

Court of Justice of the European Union (2012) PRESS RELEASE No 80/12 Luxembourg, 14 June, Judgment in Case C-158/11 Auto

24 SARL v Jaguar Land Rover France SAS. http://curia.europa.eu/jcms/upload/docs/application/pdf/2012-06/cp120080en.pdf (accessed May 2015).

Dodds, L. (2014) eBay and Argos' click-and-collect deal goes nationwide, *The Telegraph*, 20 July. http://www.telegraph.co.uk/finance/newsbysector/retailandconsumer/10943206/eBay-and-Argos-click-and-collect-deal-goes-nationwide.html (accessed 20 April 2015).

Doherty, N. and F. Ellis-Chadwick (2010) Internet Retailing: the past, the present and the future, *International Journal of Retail & Distribution Management* 38(11/12), 943–65.

Dudley, J. W. (1990) *1992 Strategies for the Single Market*, London: Kogan Page, 327.

Ellis-Chadwick, F. (2011) An introdution to retail management and marketing, *The Open University*, block 1, 8–9.

Exxon Mobil (2012) Downstream, http://www.exxonmobileurope.com/Europe-English/about_what_downstream.aspx, 22 April.

Fahy, J. and Jobber (2009) *Foundations of Marketing*, Maidenhead: McGraw-Hill.

Felsted, A. (2013) Waitrose to open remote click-and-collect food lockers, *The Financial Times*, 11 July. http://www.ft.com/cms/s/0/b1f3598a-ea43-11e2-b2f4-00144feabdc0.html#axzz3Z06RP4x2 (accessed 2 May 2015).

Hayward, C. (2002) Who, Where, Win, *Marketing Week*, 12 September, 43.

Helmore, E. (1997) Restaurant Kings or Just Silly Burgers, *Observer*, 8 June, 5.

Hernandez, H. (2011) Franchising in China, http://www. businessforum-china.com/article_detail.html?articleid 333, December.

Johnson, M. and A. Falstead (2011) Inditex breaks new ground for season in the south, *Financial Times*, May, p. 17.

Keifer, S. (2015) Why the internet is forcing retailers to rethink their supply chains, *Computer Weekly*. http://www.computerweekly.com/opinion/Why-the-internet-is-forcing-retailers-to-rethink-their-supply-chains

KFC (2012) Want to open a KFC? http://www.kfc.co.uk/our-restaurants/franchise.

Kumar, N., L. K. Scheer and J.-B. E. M. Steenkamp (1995) The Effects of Perceived Interdependence on Dealer Attitudes, *Journal of Marketing Research* 32 (August), 248–56.

Lambert, K. (2005) Marriott Hip? Well, It's Trying, *Business Week*, 26 September, 79.

Macatonia, S. (2013) Going beyond fair trade: the benefits and challenges of direct trade, *The Guardian*, 13 March, 42.

Magrath, A. J. and K. G. Hardy (1989) A Strategic Paradigm for Predicting Manufacturer–Reseller Conflict, *European Journal of Marketing* 23(2), 94–108.

McCawley, I. (2000) Small Suppliers Seek Broader Shelf Access, *Marketing Week*, 17 February, 20.

Meller, P. (1992) Isostar Enters the Lucozade League, *Marketing*, 2 July, 9.

Mellor, W. (2011) McDonald's no match for KFC in China as Colonel rules fast food, http://www.bloomberg.com/news/2011-01-26/mcdonald-s-no-match-for-kfc-in-china-where-colonel-sanders-rulesfast-food.html, 26 January.

Meville, S (2014) Tesco share price: What analysts are saying, *The Independent*, 10 December. http://www.independent.co.uk/news/business/news/tesco-share-price-what-analysts-are-saying-9916346.html (accessed May 2015).

Mills, J. F. and V. Camek (2004) The Risks, Threats and Opportunities of Disintermediation: A Distributor's View, *International Journal of Physical Distribution and Logistics Management* 34(9), 714–27.

Mitchell, A. (2003) When Push Comes to Shove, It's All About Pull, *Marketing Week*, 9 January, 26–7.

Motorway Services Online (2015) Waitrose. http://motorwayservicesonline.co.uk/Waitrose.

Nagle, T. T. and J. E. Hogan (2006) *The Strategy and Tactics of Pricing*, Upper Saddle River, NJ: Pearson.

Narus, J. A. and J. C. Anderson (1986) Industrial Distributor Selling: The Roles of Outside and Inside Sales, *Industrial Marketing Management* 15, 55–62.

Pegram, R. (1965) *Selecting and Evaluating Distributors*, New York: National Industrial Conference Board, 109–25.

Philpot, N. (1975) Managing the Export Function: Policies and Practice in Small and Medium Companies, *Management Survey Report No. 16*, British Institute of Management.

Planet Retail. (2014) 76% of online shoppers to use click & collect by 2017. http://www1.planetretail.net/news-and-events/press-release/76-online-shoppers-use-click-collect-2017 (accessed 2 April 2015).

Ritson, M. (2008) iPhone Strategy: No Longer a Grey Area, *Marketing*, 11 June, 21.

Rosenbloom, B. (1987) *Marketing Channels: A Management View*, Hinsdale, IL: Dryden, 160.

Roux, C. (2002) The Reign of Spain, *The Guardian*, 28 October, 6–7.

Ryle, S. (2002) How to Get Ahead in Advertising at No Cost, *Observer*, 1 December, 8.

Samiee, S. (1990) Strategic Considerations of the EC 1992 Plan for Small Exporters, *Business Horizons*, March–April, 48–56.

Shipley, D. D. and S. Prinja (1988) The Services and Supplier Choice Influences of Industrial Distributors, *Service Industries Journal* 8(2), 176–87.

Shipley, D. D., D. Cook and E. Barnett (1989) Recruitment, Motivation, Training and Evaluation of Overseas Distributors, *European Journal of Marketing* 23(2), 79–93.

Stanton, J. and K. Herbst (2006) Slotting allowances: short-term gains and long-term negative effects on retailers and consumers, *International Journal of Retail & Distribution Management* 34(3), 187–97.

The Economist (2002) Chain Reaction, 2 February, 1–3.

The Economist (2005) Carrefour at the Crossroads, 22 October, 79.

Verhoef, P., P. Kannan and J. Inman (2015) From Multi-Channel Retailing to Omni-Channel Retailing, *Journal of Retailing*, 8. http://ac.els-cdn.com/S0022435915000214/1-s2.0-S0022435915000214-main.pdf?_tid=a237e420-f19e-11e4-b844-00000aab0f27&acdnat=1430662615_9950500b09ba86261ca27172443b4bf5

Vincent, J. (2014) Shop during your commute and pick it up at the station–Amazon Lockers arrive on the Tube. *The Independent*, 25 June. http://www.independent.co.uk/life-style/gadgets-and-tech/shop-during-your-commute-and-pick-it-up-at-the-station–amazon-lockers-arrive-on-the-tube-9562079.html (accessed 2 May 2015).

Vize, R., J. Coughlan, A. Kennedy and F. Ellis-Chadwick (2010) B2B Relationship Quality: Do Trust and Commitment lead to Loyalty? Exploring the Factors that Influence Retailers' Loyalty with Web Solution Providers, 17th Recent Advances in Services Science Conference, European Institute of Retailing and Services Science, 2–5 July.

Webster, F. E. (1976) The Role of the Industrial Distributor in Marketing Strategy, *Journal of Marketing* 40, 10–16.

Wikström, S. (2005) From E-channel to Channel Mix and Channel Integration, *Journal of Marketing Management* 21, 725–53.

Wulfratt, M. (2014) The secret to Costco's success lies in supply chain efficiency, *Canadian Grocer*, 13 May. http://www.canadiangrocer.com/blog/the-secret-to-costcos-success-lies-in-supply-chain-efficiency-40691 (accessed 2 May 2015).

Yum! (2015) *Building and defining global company that feeds the world*. Yum! 28 April. http://www.yum.com/company

CASE 33
ASOS

Setting the Pace in Online Fashion

ASOS is the UK's largest online-only fashion retailer. The company has experienced phenomenal growth based on showing young shoppers how to emulate the designer looks of such celebrity magazine favourites as Kate Moss, Alexa Chung and Sienna Miller at a fraction of the cost.

ASOS was founded in 2000 by Nick Robertson. In 1996 he set up a business called Entertainment Marketing to place products in films and television programmes. By 2000 he was running a website called AsSeenOnScreen showing and selling brands that were used in films and on TV—from a pair of Oakley sunglasses worn by Tom Cruise in *Mission Impossible* to a pestle and mortar used by Jamie Oliver the *TV Chef*. But it was fashion that proved the biggest success and Robertson decided to focus on that. ASOS was born.

The company offers 50,000 branded and own-label product lines including womenswear, menswear, footwear, accessories, jewellery and beauty—a much wider range than that offered by other online rivals such as Topshop and New Look. Its key target market is women aged 18–34, with half of the online retailer's customers aged under 25. They demand new items to choose from, and ASOS provides this. Stock turnover (the speed at which items are replaced) is nine weeks, ensuring that visitors to the site are rewarded with new items on offer.

The company has its own design team and prefers to use suppliers based in Europe rather than the Far East. Between 60 and 70 per cent of its stock is made in Europe. This means that from spotting a celebrity wearing a new style of dress ASOS designers and buyers are in a position to have similar ones made and ready to sell in four weeks.

The ASOS Website

A major factor in the success of ASOS is its website. Visitors to the site can click on their favourite celebrity or pop star and view clothes they have been seen in. Perhaps a shopper prefers the style of

Kate Moss. The cheapest way is not to visit ASOS's bricks-and-mortar competitor Topshop, but to choose a £6 ASOS Lurex vest 'in the style of' the London supermodel. At any one time on the website there are over 400 styles of dresses plus mountains of tops, trousers, shoes, bags, lingerie, swimwear and jewellery and an entire men's section, all of which is modelled by people walking on a catwalk. At the ASOS headquarters in North London, there are four studios where a pool of 30 models attempt to bring the clothes to life and transmit the excitement of the catwalk to the consumer.

The range of brands has expanded from own-label celebrity look-a-like items to include its own luxury brand together with well-established labels such as Nike, Levi's, Calvin Klein and Tommy Hilfiger. The website attracts 22 million visitors a month and 7 million active customers (those who have bought within the past six months), who place orders worth on average £60. Women's fashion items make up the vast majority of sales. Menswear accounts for 20 per cent of sales with beauty and cosmetics a further 3 per cent.

One problem with buying online rather than in a traditional retail outlet is that returns are higher. An average catalogue company experiences about 40 per cent returns but ASOS achieves the much lower figure of 22 per cent. A key feature of ASOS's marketing tactics is to offer free delivery anywhere in the world and free returns in the UK.

Customer Service

ASOS aims for fast speed of delivery and when a delay is foreseeable every effort is made to contact the customer. For example, when snow was forecast emails were sent warning customers of probable delays. When it did snow, an apology email was sent offering a delivery refund and 10 per cent off next orders. The customer care team is available 24 hours a day. They are required to reply to customer enquiries within an hour and are assessed by the speed and quality of their reply.

Promotion

ASOS's success has provided many opportunities for PR activity in newspapers, including quarterly reports on record profits and sales, and features on the reasons for its success. ASOS prefers digital to traditional media, although the latter is sometimes used. Search engine optimization and pay-per-click advertising on women's magazine sites such as *Look* and *Grazia* help to generate traffic to ASOS's site. Social networking also plays a part in raising awareness. ASOS has the second largest UK fan group for any fashion retailer on Facebook (behind H&M). In 2011 ASOS launched a Facebook application that allows customers to make purchases from the store without having to leave the social networking site.

ASOS's largest marketing expenditure is on a print magazine which is carefully targeted to reach 500,000 active customers. It showcases well-known brands as well as its own brands, and photos are blended with editorial content to rival the standards of news-stand glossies. It is also available online. This is supplemented by 24-page supplements in magazines such as *Glamour* and *Cosmopolitan*, and sponsorship of the Sky Living show *America's Next Top Model*. ASOS achieves 60 per cent awareness among its target market.

New Ventures

A major source of sales and profit growth has been overseas expansion with new websites being established in the USA, Germany, France, Spain, Denmark, Russia, Italy and Australia. The company also supplies goods to an additional 240 countries.

ASOS has also launched a number of extensions from the core brand including:

- ASOS Marketplace: this allows customers to sell their own clothes and accessories on the ASOS site—whether they are recycling their clothes for cash or opening a boutique to sell their own designs. ASOS receives commission on sales.
- Little ASOS: this site caters for babies and children aged two to six years. As well as stocking ranges from high-fashion brands such as Diesel and Tommy Hilfiger, Little ASOS offers a number of boutique and independent labels such as Cath Kidston and No Added Sugar.
- ASOS Outlet: this is the discount arm of ASOS offering end-of-line and previous season products at discounts of up to 75 per cent.
- ASOS Life: this allows customers to create their own profiles and communicate through forums, blogs and groups. The site includes a help forum that allows customers to answer each other's questions and an ideas section that lets customers submit suggestions for site improvements.
- ASOS Fashion Finder: showcases fashion trends and allows customers to research outfit building and creation. Visitors to the site are redirected to rival retailers if the product the shopper wants is not available at ASOS.

ASOS is not alone in selling online fashion worldwide. For example, boohoo.com dispatches to 100 countries, and is differentiated from ASOS as all its clothes are own brand and sell at lower price points. Its target market is 16- to 24-year-olds who are looking for inexpensive fashion items.

Questions

1. **Discuss the advantages and disadvantages of marketing fashion items online rather than through traditional retail stores.**
2. **To what extent does ASOS operate an integrated distribution channel system?**
3. **Perform a strengths, weaknesses, opportunities and threats (SWOT) analysis on ASOS.**
4. **On the basis of the SWOT analysis, what are your recommendations for ASOS?**

This case study was prepared by David Jobber, Emeritus Professor of Marketing, University of Bradford.

References

Based on: Finch, J. (2008) Nick Robertson: Wannabe Celebs Provide The Silver On Screen, *The Guardian*, 18 April, 31; Kollewe, J. (2008) Asos Defies Shopping Gloom by Reaching Height of Online Fashion, *The Guardian*, 18 November, 32; Barda, T. (2009) Winning Looks, *Marketer*, April, 24–7; Armstrong, L. (2009) Asos.com: As Seen On The Screens of The Fashion Savvy, *The Times*, 21 January, 26; Asos. com http://en. wikipedia.org/w/index; Costa, M. (2011) Fashion Leader Maps Out an International Future, *Marketing Week*, 16 June, 17–20; Treanor, J. (2012) Asos Managers Share £66m Bonus Pot, *The Guardian*, 25 May, 33; Butler, S. and S. Farrell (2014) Soaring Asos Is Latest Online Success Story, *The Guardian*, 15 January, 20.

From 'Clicks to Bricks'

We are definitely a nation of shoppers, and more and more of us are multichannel shoppers. In response to this, multichannel retailing, where retailers use two or more integrated channels to sell products and services, has become a strategic issue for most retailers. Over the last decade, more retailers have extended the number of channels used to reach customers, adding online and mobile to the distribution mix. However, while attention to date has focused on how traditional bricks-and-mortar retailers have *added* an Internet channel to implement a multichannel retail strategy, Screwfix, Oak Furniture Land and Simply Be are examples of three retailers who have been extending their multichannel strategies by opening stores to complement their *existing* Internet and catalogue channels. Table C34.1 gives an overview of these retailers.

The Move to Multichannel Retailing

The main impetus behind Screwfix opening stores was to meet customer needs. Customers told Screwfix that while they wanted to be able to shop via the retailer's website and customer contact centre, there were times when they wanted to be able to go to a store to purchase a product and receive it instantaneously. Andrew Livingstone, the current Chief Executive of Screwfix, commented, 'we had tradesmen turning up at our main warehouse in Somerset asking for things that day—our next day Internet delivery service was not soon enough.' The main driver behind Oak Furniture Land's decision to open the company's first outlet also appears to have been customer led. Almost from the day the website was launched, Jason Bannister, the Managing Director of Oak Furniture Land, was constantly being asked if there was an Oak Furniture Land shop. 'People were ringing us up asking if we had a showroom and we were telling them, no, we're an online business, that's how we keep the prices down,' he said. He had initially held back from opening a bricks and mortar store, fearing that it would take business away from his Internet operation. However, after enough people got in touch, Mr. Bannister and his colleagues decided to take some space on an airfield that had units going spare. 'It wasn't even a real shop, but after a few weeks it was turning over the equivalent of £5 million a year. At first we thought it would be £5 million taken from the website, but the online business was still going up, so we opened a proper shop in Cheltenham.' The store in Cheltenham opened its doors in 2009, and the bricks and mortar side of the business has expanded dramatically ever since.

In contrast, Simply Be tested the addition of a store channel because the parent company had acquired a chain with a retail store presence (High & Mighty). It saw the opportunity to build on this expertise for its leading clothing brand, Simply Be. At the time of the first store opening, N Brown Group Development Director, Paul Kendrick, for Simply Be commented that a reason why the retailer had added a store channel was because it believed that 'the multichannel approach is the future and to get real brand cut through then high street stores need to be part of that mix . . . The stores will provide us with plenty of opportunities that we can explore in 12 months' time, by which point we will be able to review the performances of the stores, see if the formats work well and how we can improve.' Likewise, Oak Furniture Land and Screwfix have also explored other diversification opportunities through opening stores; for example, Oak Furniture Land has recently opened SofaStore concessions in its stores.

TABLE C34.1 Overview of Screwfix, Oak Furniture Land and Simply Be

Retailer	Sector	Target market	Size	Ownership	Culture	Multichannel evolution
Screwfix	DIY	Professional tradespeople and DIY enthusiasts	Turnover £665m Employs around 5,500 staff	Part of the Kingfisher Group	Entrepreneurial, fast-paced and dynamic	- 1979 started as a niche retailer, the Woodscrew Company, selling screws to tradespeople via a one page catalogue under the name of Screwfix Direct - 1999 opened its customer contact centre and added an Internet channel to sell products and services to customers - 2005 extended its multichannel strategy through embarking on an ambitious store opening programme, - Today has circa 350 stores and opened Plumbfix and Electricfix stores within existing B&Q network
Simply Be	Fashion	Women, in their 30s and 40s, who embrace their size and enjoy stylish clothes.	Group turnover £834.9m Employs around 3,000 staff	Part of the N Brown Group	Acquisition orientated	- 1989 began selling products to customers via catalogues in 1989 - 2000 launched its Internet channel - 2013 opened its first store, and today the retailer has 9 stores with plans to open up to 25 - Jacamo for men concessions are in 8 of the Simply Be stores
Oak Furniture Land	Furniture	Value-seeking furniture buyers	Turnover of £194m around 620 employees	Part of the JB Global Group; an owner managed business	Entrepreneurial leadership	- 2006 Oak Furniture Land started trading by selling its products to customers via eBay - 2006 launched its own website, and started selling its products via websites such as Amazon - 2010 opened its first Oak Furniture Land store; now has around 53 stores - December 2014 opened four standalone SofaStore outlets and 53 concessions in its existing Oak Furniture Land stores

≫

The Multichannel Journey

Screwfix has implemented a number of initiatives to support its store openings and to enable customers to shop seamlessly across multiple channels. In 2011, the retailer rolled out its innovative 'Fusion Platform'—a large-scale initiative developed to transform the company's multichannel ordering process. 'Fusion' enables store staff, at the point of purchase, to view a customer's purchase history across all the retailer's channels. It also automatically generates product recommendations for staff to use to up-sell and cross-sell products to customers. In other words, the customer receives product recommendations at the point of purchase in store in the same way as if shopping online. Opening a high number of stores in a short period of time has also involved the retailer making major financial investment. In fact, in 2008 the level of investment in the store-opening programme caused the retailer's profit to fall by £8 million from the previous year, to £22 million. Luckily, by the following year the retailer's profit had returned back to healthy levels, and in 2012–13 the retailer's profit was £47 million.

Adding a store channel has meant that all the retailers have had to recruit new staff to work in their stores and reshape the skillset of existing staff. Oak Furniture Land, for example, currently employs more than 600 staff to deal with every aspect of the business from design to aftersales care. The majority of these staff are employed in store (34 per cent), with the remainder in IT (31 per cent), other support services such as transport (22 per cent) and in the warehouse (13 per cent). Simply Be has also needed to make sure it has head office staff with the necessary store expertise to, for example, select appropriate store locations and create a suitable store design and atmosphere. The retailer has selected store locations for easy access to its target market, and stores have been configured to reflect the needs of the plus-sized customer. There are larger changing rooms, for example, and mannequins that enable larger garments to hang accurately. Other facilities include magic mirrors allowing photos to be taken and emailed to friends for a second opinion, and online ordering facilities available in store for customers and staff. For Screwfix, the Fusion platform, which arms staff with tailored customer product recommendations, calls for staff to be able to use the technology in a customer service and sales minded way.

The Future

Simply Be opened stores as part of a trial to evaluate the benefits of full multichannel capability. Early reports suggest the trial has been successful, and up to 25 stores are planned. Likewise, Oak Furniture Land appears to be having success with its store-opening programme, with reports that 65 per cent of the retailer's sales are generated through its store network, with the remainder of its sales coming from its e-commerce sites. Further, Screwfix has experienced phenomenal growth over recent years, with a key driver being its 'click and collect' initiative, whereby customers order via the Internet, tablet or mobile and collect in store. The retailer has also embarked on a store-opening programme in Germany.

Arguably, this is a reversal of the approach taken by physical store retailers moving online. It will be interesting to see if the knowledge of managing online channels enables these retailers to move ahead of their more established high street counterparts in the race to provide seamless omni-channel experiences for customers.

Questions

1. What factors might have stimulated these three organisations to adopt a 'clicks to bricks' channel strategy?

2. What problems did the three case retailers experience?

3. Which of the three organisations do you think will have the greatest chance of success with this channel strategy? Justify your choice with evidence from the case and other secondary data sources you can find.

This case study was written by Kim Cassidy, Julie Lewis and Sheilagh Resnick, Nottingham Trent University.

References

Based on: Avery, J., T. J. Steenburgh, J. Deighton and M. Caravella (2012) Adding Bricks to Clicks: Predicting the Patterns of Cross-Channel Elasticities Over Time, *Journal of Marketing*, 76 (May), 96–111.

PART 4
MARKETING PLANNING AND STRATEGY

A number of videos featuring CEOs, CMOs, brand and PR managers related to the Chapters in this Part are available to lecturers for presentation and class discussion.

CHAPTER 18
Marketing Planning: An Overview of Strategic Analysis and Decision-making

Fact is, inventing an innovative business model is often mostly a matter of serendipity.

GARY HAMEL (VAN VLIET, 2011)

LEARNING OBJECTIVES

After reading this chapter, you should be able to:

1 describe the role of marketing planning within businesses
2 identify the key planning questions
3 discuss the process of marketing planning
4 describe the concept of the business mission
5 explain the marketing audit and SWOT analysis
6 discuss the nature of marketing objectives
7 identify the components of core strategy and how to test its effectiveness
8 explain marketing mix decisions in relation to the planning process
9 discuss implementation and control in the marketing planning process
10 describe the rewards and problems associated with marketing planning
11 discuss recommendations to overcoming marketing planning problems

Part 1 explores the fundamentals of marketing, which inform the development of a marketing plan; Part 2 considers how core elements of marketing can be used to create value for customers; Part 3 studies how to communicate and deliver customer value. In Part 4, our attention turns to how to bring all these elements of marketing theory and practice together in a cohesive and coherent manner. The focus is on managing, planning and applying strategic thinking within the framework of marketing.

Specifically, this chapter presents the marketing planning framework and discusses ways to develop a manageable approach towards implementing the marketing concept (as discussed in Chapter 1). Chapter 19 focuses on specific strategic notions—competitor analysis—and in doing so presents ways of creating competitive advantage. Chapter 20 examines product strategy and looks at ways products can be used for growth. Chapter 21 investigates what is involved in developing global marketing strategies. Chapter 22 discusses implementation and many issues at the heart of the application of the principles and practice of marketing.

Marketing planning and strategy comprises a complex and resource-intensive set of processes that can deliver great rewards if fully embraced. However, the marketing environment is in flux: digital technologies are proving to be a source of disruptive innovations that are re-shaping the marketing landscape and speeding up the rate of change. So no longer does it take years to evolve and introduce a new product; for example, Twitter emerged within less than 18 months from concept to global adoption as a marketing tool. Arguably, this situation makes Gary Hamel's notion of serendipitous business planning (in the quotation above) seem quite compelling. But for marketing to function effectively across an organization, it should act as a guiding business philosophy for improving performance. Therefore, to gain the potential advantages that marketing might bring, managers must make and communicate many marketing planning decisions, for example which customer groups to serve, how to create value-added products and services, which technology to use and which marketing strategies are most likely to deliver competitive advantages. Managers must also consider the impact of the environment and determine how to get the best strategic fit between their organization's capabilities and resources and the market opportunities.

This chapter presents the **marketing planning** framework, which addresses many of the key questions and decisions a manager might encounter and provides a straightforward structured framework for handling all the complexities marketers must accommodate. We begin the chapter by considering the marketing planning context. Then we delve into the key functions of marketing planning, before exploring the stages in the marketing planning process. The chapter concludes by looking at the rewards and problems of marketing planning.

Marketing Planning Context

Marketing planning is part of a broader concept of *corporate strategic planning* which involves all business functions: marketing, operations, finance, human resources, information management, distribution and the trading environment. The aim of corporate strategic planning is to provide direction for a company so its activities constantly meet high-level corporate objectives, for example being market leader, improving profitability. Marketing links to this high level of strategic planning by managing the interface between a company and its environment; for example, a corporate objective to be market leader will take account of the economic forces and their impact on a particular market. So the marketing planning team carrying out a marketing audit, for example, should produce sufficient knowledge to enable the corporate management team to make long-term strategic decisions, thereby creating a link between strategy and marketing planning.

In reality, the role of marketing planning in strategy development is complex and can vary considerably in terms of what is involved. At the simplest level, a company may market only one product in one market. In this case, the role of marketing planning is to ensure the marketing plan for the product matches its customers' needs. Also the company can use all available resources to achieve its marketing objectives— for example, to sell more products. This should also enable the marketing plan to feed into the corporate objective of becoming market leader. However, this is rarely the case, as companies tend to offer many products and/or services to many different target markets. In this situation decisions have to be made about the allocation of resources to each product and/or service. This is far from a straightforward process as resource allocation is dependent on the attractiveness of the market for each product, and the capabilities and resources of the company.

EXHIBIT 18.1
Virgin is a disruptive and innovative brand that aims to stand out; see how StartJG's graphic captures the essence of the Virgin brand

To add to the complexity, a company may comprise a number of discrete but connected divisions (or totally separate companies) each of which serves distinct groups of customers and has a distinct set of competitors (Day, 1984). For example: the Virgin Group operates many companies in different activity sectors, such as media (Virgin Media); music (Virgin Megastore); travel (Virgin Atlantic Airways). Each business may be strategically autonomous and thus form a **strategic business unit** (SBU). For example, the Virgin Group is made up of a *community* of independently operating companies, (see Exhibit 18.1). A major component of a strategic plan—at the corporate level—is allocation of resources to each SBU. Strategic decisions at the corporate level are normally concerned with acquisition, divestment and diversification (Weitz and Wensley, 1988). In the Virgin Group example, each company contributes to the overarching aims of the group—that is, Virgin Media was created through mergers with NTL, Telewest and Virgin Mobile. The decisions to add or release a business are taken at the corporate and strategic planning level. Richard Branson, the founder of the Virgin empire, expanded the business's reach by entering markets as diverse as cosmetics, weddings and hotels. Marketing feeds into such corporate decision-making by identifying opportunities and threats in the environment. So, the opportunity to develop the travel arm of the Virgin group by adding Virgin hotels is likely to have emerged from marketing planning actions.

 Scan the QR code to see why Sky allows its competitor Virgin Media to provide viewers with Sky channels.

In summary, marketing planning is part of the overarching corporate strategic planning process and provides a range of insights from the trading environment to target markets and customer needs. Thinking about where marketing planning fits in the wider business planning process is only part of the challenge managers encounter. There are two other aspects of marketing planning to consider: the core functions and key planning processes of marketing planning, which are discussed in more detail in the following sections.

The Functions of Marketing Planning

Arguably, the core function of a marketing plan is to answer the following questions:

1   Where are we now?
2   Where would we like to be?
3   How do we get there?
4   Are we on course?

For the marketing planning team at Virgin answering these questions means considering:

*   Where are we now? Looking at the current position of the business in terms of its past performance, considering the effectiveness of previous marketing plans and questioning what might happen if there were no changes in current practice. In 2014 Virgin Atlantic performed well against its objectives, managing its resources effectively through continuing tough economic conditions and against strong competition in the airline industry (Topham, 2015; Virgin Atlantic, 2015).
*   Where would we like to be? The future direction of the business is defined by its marketing objectives. Virgin's corporate objective is to 'offer *the best business product* in the air', so the implications for the marketing planning team are setting suitable objectives which ensure improved customer service of its *business* products.
*   How do we get there? This can be answered in the case of Virgin Atlantic by looking at the needs of business travellers, considering their expectations and experiences. Virgin has won industry awards for its Upper Class Suite, which is designed to be a first-class product for a business-class fare. The marketing planning team looked at this key target audience (business travellers) and devised a marketing mix strategy that it could implement to achieve its marketing objectives.
*   Are we on course? This question is answered by looking at performance measures. Like many companies, Virgin measures sales and profitability but it uses other measures such as increase in fuel efficiency and reduction in carbon emissions, targeting the use of sustainable products and renewable resources.

The core functions of marketing planning addressed by these questions link into specific stages in the marketing planning process (see Table 18.1). 'Where are we now?' is forecast by reference to the marketing audit and SWOT analysis. 'Where would we like to be?' is determined by the setting of marketing objectives. 'How do we get there?' refers to core strategy, marketing mix decisions, organization and implementation. Finally 'Are we on course?' is answered by the establishment of a control system.

TABLE 18.1 Key questions and the process of marketing planning	
Key questions	**Stages in marketing planning**
Where are we now?	Business mission, marketing audit, SWOT analysis
Where would we like to be?	Marketing objectives
How do we get there?	Core strategy, marketing mix decisions, organization, implementation
Are we on course?	Control

The next section discusses the process of marketing planning in detail.

The Process of Marketing Planning

In reality, planning is rarely straightforward. Different people are involved at various stages of the planning process. The key marketing planning process can broadly be divided into distinct areas:

*   the business unit level—e.g. Virgin Atlantic
*   the product level—e.g. Virgin flights to America.

The process of marketing planning is outlined in Figure 18.1. This overview of the framework provides a systematic way for understanding the analysis and the decision-making processes involved in marketing planning. Additionally, the framework shows how key elements of marketing—discussed in subsequent chapters—relate to each other and fit into the planning process.

FIGURE 18.1
The marketing planning process

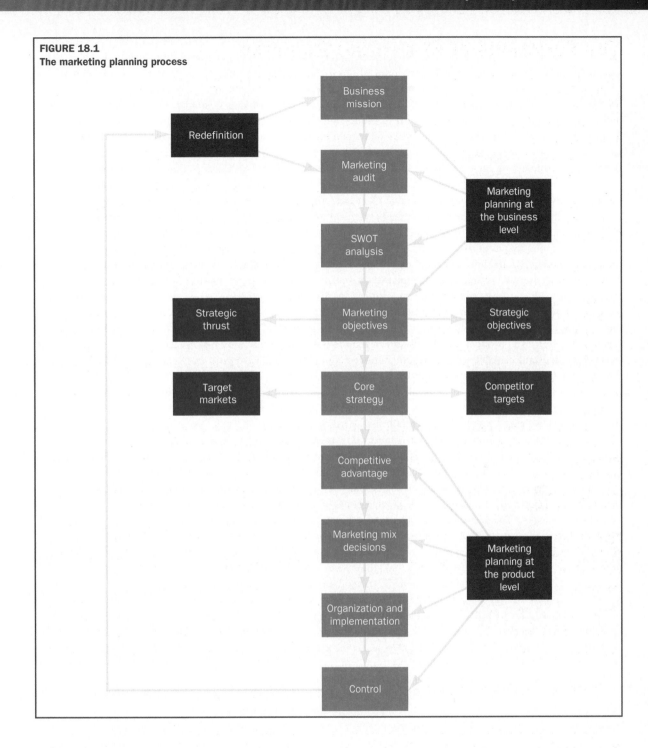

Business mission

Russell Ackoff, an American organizational theorist defined **business mission** as:

A broadly defined, enduring statement of purpose that distinguishes a business from others of its type (Ackoff, 1987).

This definition captures two essential ingredients in mission statements: they are enduring and specific to the individual organization (Hooley, Cox and Adams, 1992). Two fundamental questions that need to be addressed are 'What business are we in?' and 'What business do we want to be in?' The answers define the scope and activities of the company. The business mission explains the reason for its existence and focuses on the present. The mission statement should not be confused with a vision statement, which looks to the future: for example, Samsung's 2020 vision statement for the coming decade is 'Inspire the World, Create the Future' (Samsung, n.d.), whereas Google's mission statement is 'to organize the world's information and make it universally accessible and useful' (Google, n.d.). Consider how each statement has different implications for marketing planning (Samsung, n.d.; Google, n.d.).

A mission statement can take many forms, but it should reflect the customer groups being served (the market), refer to the customer needs being satisfied, and describe the process by which a customer need can be satisfied. The inclusion of market and needs ensures that the business definition is market focused rather than product based. Thus, the purpose of a company such as Apple Inc. is not to manufacture computers but to solve customers' information problems. The reason for ensuring that a business definition is market focused is that products are transient, but basic needs such as transportation, entertainment and eating are lasting. Thus, Levitt argued that a business should be viewed as a customer-satisfying process, not a goods-producing process (Levitt, 1960). Through adopting a customer perspective, new opportunities are more likely to be revealed. In Apple's case this has led to streamlining its product ranges and focusing its innovations on customers' needs for mobile computing, through the iPod, iPhone and iPad.

While this advice has merit in advocating the avoidance of a narrow business definition, management must be wary of a definition that is too wide. Theodore Levitt, a leading American economist, suggested that railroad companies would have survived had they defined their business as transportation and moved into the airline business. But this is to ignore the limits of the business competence of the railroads. Did they possess the necessary skills and resources to run an airline? Clearly a key constraint on a business definition can be the competences (both actual and potential) of management, and the resources at their disposal. Conversely, competences can act as the motivator for widening a business mission. Asda (Associated Dairies) redefined its business mission as a producer and distributor of milk to a retailer of fast-moving consumer goods partly on the basis of its distribution skills, which it rightly believed could be extended to products beyond milk. The Virgin Group is another example of a company that has adapted to changing market demands. Founded by Richard Branson in 1970 in the music business with Virgin records, the group has developed into a multi-faceted global business with over 300 successful companies in sectors ranging from mobile telephony through to transportation, travel, financial services, media, music and fitness (Virgin Group, n.d.).

A second influence on business mission is **macroenvironmental** change. Change provides opportunities and threats that influence mission definition. Asda saw that changes in retail practice from corner shops to high-volume supermarkets presented an opportunity that could be exploited by its skills. Its move redefined its business.

A third influence on business mission is the background of the company and the personalities of its senior management. The personalities and beliefs of the people who run businesses also shape the business mission and influence its success. This last factor emphasizes the judgemental nature of business definition and indicates there is no right or wrong way to write a business mission statement. However, the mission should be based on the vision that top management and its subordinates have of the future of the business. This vision is a coherent and powerful statement of what the business should aim to become (Wilson, 1992).

Additionally, an effective mission statement should be based on:

- *a solid understanding of the business* and the forces acting on its operations, which might change in the future. For example, PayPal is a business that had a clear mission, which it has been able to adapt to take advantage of market opportunities. PayPal has not always provided one-touch payment solutions to everyone. Originally, Confinity Inc. created PayPal as a service that would allow funds to be transferred between Palm Pilots (handheld personal digital devices). But it was not long before the company signed an agreement with eBay to enable instantaneous payments for the millions of auction transactions (Davis, 2014). Then, mobile commerce proved to be another tipping point for PayPal as it extended its offer beyond eBay's auction platform to offer a truly one-touch financial payment solution (Hazan, 2014).
- *strong personal conviction and motivation of the leader*, who has the ability to make his or her vision contagious. For example, Walt Disney wrote his company's mission statement, 'To make people happy', which is both contagious and motivating for staff (Sanghera, 2005). Jeff Bezos's vision and mission for Amazon is 'to be the earth's most customer-centric company, to build a place where people can come to find and discover anything they might want to buy online' (Gapper and Jopson, 2011). His passion and commitment has led the company through challenging times to become the world's leading consumer e-commerce company. See Marketing in Action 18.1 to find out more about the passion that drives Jeff Bezos's leadership style.
- *creating strategic intent of winning throughout the organization*. This helps to build a sense of common purpose, and stresses the need to create competitive advantages rather than settle for imitative moves.
- *enabling success*. Managers must believe they have the latitude to make decisions about strategy without being second-guessed by top management.

MARKETING IN ACTION 18.1
Jeff Bezos and the Two-pizza Rule

Jeff Bezos is passionate about customers, and he wants his employees to share his level of commitment in everything they do. His leadership style is said to be full of quirks, and he has exacting standards. Standards at Amazon include a set of leadership principles which demands that all employees: share Jeff's obsession with customers; are frugal and don't spend company resources on things that are not customer centric; and are vocally self-critical and always seeking ways to innovate and simplify the way the company operates. For example, Amazon was one of the first e-commerce websites to allow negative customer reviews. But this initiative gave the company an opportunity to identify the things it needed to get right in order to improve customer service.

When it comes to innovation, Jeff has an unusual rule for building teams: the two-pizza rule. This rule means that a team can have no more members than can be fed by two pizzas (approximately five to seven). There is a logic behind this rule, which is that active teams are small and can all communicate with one another in a meaningful way. Jeff's leadership style relies on empowering his teams to act fast and innovate, so the pizza rule reduces complexity within a group, *and* increases in-group communication and overall productivity.

Based on: Sanghani (2013); Amazon (2015)

In summary, the mission statement provides the framework within which managers decide which opportunities and threats to address, and which to disregard. A well-defined mission statement is a key element in the marketing planning process, as it defines boundaries within which new opportunities are sought and motivates staff to succeed in the implementation of marketing strategy.

Marketing Audit

The **marketing audit** is a systematic examination of a business's marketing environment, objectives, strategies and activities, with a view to identifying key strategic issues, problem areas and opportunities. The marketing audit provides the basis for developing a plan of action to improve marketing performance and in doing so should provide answers to the question: where are we now? And the supplemental issues of: how did we get here? where are we heading?

Answers to these questions depend upon an analysis of the internal and external environment of a business. This analysis benefits from a clear mission statement, since the latter defines the boundaries of the environmental scan and helps decisions regarding which strategic issues and opportunities are important.

The internal audit focuses on those areas that are under the control of marketing management, whereas the external audit is concerned with those forces over which management has no control. The results of the marketing audit are a key determinant of the future direction of the business and may give rise to a redefined business mission statement. Alongside the marketing audit, a business may conduct audits of other functional areas such as production, finance and personnel. The coordination and integration of these audits produces a composite business plan in which marketing issues play a central role, since they concern decisions about which products to manufacture for which markets. These decisions clearly have production, financial and personnel implications, and successful implementation depends upon each functional area acting in concert.

A checklist of issues that may be examined in a marketing audit is given in Tables 18.2 (external) and 18.3 (internal). External analysis covers the **macroenvironment** and the microenvironment. The macroenvironment consists of broad environmental issues that may affect business performance. These are political/legal, economic, ecological/physical, social/cultural and technological forces. Auditing these issues is known by the acronym PEEST analysis. Originally, Francis J. Aguilar alerted managers to the importance of scanning the business environment, and he is credited with inventing the PEST acronym, a structured method of analysis that assisted an organization's future planning (Aguilar, 1967). (PEST analysis does not include the influence of changes in the physical environment.) Since then, various acronyms have been used in management literature, for example STEP, STEEP, PESTLE (Gillespie, 2007). The key point to remember is that scanning the business environment in a systematic manner is crucially important for all organizations, as changes in the environment can have dramatic effects on long-term success.

TABLE 18.2 External marketing audit checklist	
Forces	**Key topics / Trends**
Macroenvironment	
Political/legal	EU and national laws; codes of practice; political instability
Economic	Economic growth; unemployment; interest and exchange rates; global economic trends (e.g. the growth of the BRICS economies—Brazil, Russia, India, China and South Africa)
Ecological/physical environmental	Global warming; pollution; energy and other scarce resources; environmentally friendly ingredients and components; recycling and non-wasteful packaging
Social/cultural	Changes in world population, age distribution and household structure; attitude and lifestyle changes; subcultures within and across national boundaries; consumerism
Technological	Innovations; communications; technology infrastructures; bio-technology
Microenvironment	
Market	Size; growth rates
Customers	Who they are, their choice criteria, how, when and where they buy; how they rate the competition on product, promotion, price and distribution; how customers group (market segmentation), and what benefits each group seeks
Competitors	Who are the major competitors (actual and potential); their objectives and strategies; strengths and weaknesses; size, market share and profitability; entry barriers to new competitors
Distributors	Channel attractiveness; distributor decision-making unit, decision-making process and choice criteria; strengths and weaknesses; power changes; physical distribution methods
Suppliers	Who they are and location; strengths and weaknesses; power changes

Table 18.2 lists the forces and key topics that fall within each area. Chapter 2 explores the marketing environment in depth.

The **microenvironment** consists of the actors in the firm's immediate environment that affect its capabilities to operate effectively in its chosen markets. The key actors are customers, distributors, suppliers and competitors and microenvironmental analysis will consist of an analysis of issues relating to these actors and an overall analysis of market size, growth rates and trends (see Table 18.2).

More specifically, microenvironmental analysis consists of:

- **market analysis**, which involves the statistical analysis of market size, growth rates and trends
- **customer analysis** of buyer behaviour—how they rate competitive offerings, and how they segment
- **competitor analysis**, which examines the nature of actual and potential competitors, and their objectives and strategies. It also seeks to identify their strengths and weaknesses, size, market share and profitability. Finally, entry barrier analysis identifies the key financial and non-financial barriers that protect the industry from competitor attack

- **distribution analysis**, which covers an examination of the attractiveness of different distribution channels, distributor buyer behaviour, their strengths and weaknesses, movements in power bases, and alternative methods of physical distribution
- **supplier analysis** examines who and where they are located, their strengths and weaknesses, power changes and trends in the supply chain.

The internal audit allows the performance and activities of the business to be assessed in the light of environmental developments. Operating results form a basis of assessment through analysis of sales, market share, profit margins and costs. **Strategic issues analysis** examines the suitability of marketing objectives and segmentation bases in the light of changes in the marketplace. Competitive advantages and the core competences on which they are based would be reassessed and the positioning of products in the market critically reviewed. Core competences are the principal distinctive capabilities possessed by a company, which define what it really is good at.

TABLE 18.3 Internal marketing audit checklist	
Operating results (by product, customer, geographic region)	**Marketing mix effectiveness**
Sales	Product
Market share	Price
Profit margins	Promotion
Costs	Distribution
Strategic issues analysis	**Marketing structures**
Marketing objectives	Marketing organization
Market segmentation	Marketing training
Competitive advantage	Intra- and interdepartmental communication
Core competences	**Marketing systems**
Positioning	Marketing information systems
Portfolio analysis	Marketing planning system
	Marketing control system

An example of a company that has invested in its core competences is Eddie Stobart Ltd (see Exhibit 18.2). When Eddie set about transforming his dad's haulage business he knew that customers 'hated slovenly drivers and old dirty lorries' and so focusing on dress code and cleanliness helped him to transform not only his own company but the whole of the haulage industry in the UK. Other core competencies included just-in-time stock management and highly effective logistics solutions (Madden, 2011). Zara is another example of a company that has utilized its supply-side competencies to build a global fashion brand.

One danger that companies face is moving away from their core competences into areas where their skills and capabilities do not provide a competitive advantage. Management can become distracted, leading to poor performance. For example, IBM suffered as demand for its computing hardware and IT solutions declined and competition from Hewlett Packard and other more agile competitors increased. For several years, IBM seemed to be searching for markets where the business could leverage its expertise. Eventually, the focus of the business has shifted from selling hardware to big data, business analytics and cloud computing.

Finally, **product portfolios** should be analysed to determine future strategic objectives.

EXHIBIT 18.2
Eddie Stobart transformed the image of his dad's haulage company by focusing on presenting the company as smart and clean

Each element of the marketing mix is reviewed in the light of changing customer requirements and competitor activity. The **marketing structures** on which marketing activities are based should be analysed. Marketing structure consists of the marketing organization, training, and intra- and interdepartmental communication that takes place within an organization. Marketing organization is reviewed to determine fit with strategy and the market, and marketing training requirements are examined. Finally, communications and the relationship within the marketing department and between marketing and other functions (e.g. R&D, engineering, production) need to be appraised.

Marketing systems are audited for effectiveness. These consist of the marketing information, planning and control systems that support marketing activities. Shortfalls in information provision are analysed; the marketing planning system is critically appraised for cost-effectiveness; and the marketing control system is assessed in the light of accuracy, timeliness (does it provide evaluations when managers require them?) and coverage (does the system evaluate the key variables affecting company performance?).

Marketing systems can be vital assets. For example, marketing information systems at British Airways, Qantas and Singapore Airlines provide knowledge regarding repeat passengers' preferred seats, newspapers, food and drinks, allowing customization of their offerings.

This checklist provides the basis for deciding on the topics to be included in the marketing audit. However, to give the same amount of attention and detailed analysis to every item would grind the audit to a halt under a mass of data and issues. In practice, the judgement of those conducting the audit is critical in deciding the key items to focus upon. Those factors that are considered of crucial importance to the company's performance will merit most attention. One by-product of the marketing audit may be a realization that information about key environmental issues is lacking.

All assumptions should be made explicit as an ongoing part of the marketing audit: for example, key assumptions might be:

- inflation will average 3 per cent during the planning period
- VAT levels will not be changed
- worldwide overcapacity will remain at 150 per cent
- no new entrants into the market will emerge.

The marketing audit should be an ongoing activity, not a desperate attempt to turn round an ailing business. Some companies conduct an annual audit as part of their annual planning system; others operating in less turbulent environments may consider two or three years an adequate period between audits. Others might consider the use of an outside consultant to coordinate activities and provide an objective, outside view to be beneficial, while some may believe that their own managers are best equipped to conduct the analyses. Clearly there is no set formula for deciding when and by whom the audit is conducted. The decision ultimately rests on the preferences and situation facing the management team.

SWOT analysis

A **SWOT analysis** is a structured approach to evaluating the strategic position of a business by identifying its strengths, weaknesses, opportunities and threats. It provides a simple method of synthesizing the results of the marketing audit. Internal strengths and weaknesses are summarized as they relate to external opportunities and threats (see Figure 18.2).

When evaluating strengths and weaknesses, only those resources or capabilities that would be valued by the customer should be included (Piercy, 2008). Thus strengths such as 'We are an old established firm', 'We are a large supplier' and 'We are technologically advanced' should be questioned for their impact on customer satisfaction. It is conceivable that such bland generalizations confer as many weaknesses as strengths. Also, opportunities and threats should be listed as anticipated events or trends *outside* the business that have implications for performance. Figure 18.3 shows an example of a SWOT chart for a specialist low-volume US sports car manufacturer.

Once a SWOT analysis has been completed, thought can be given to how to turn weaknesses into strengths and

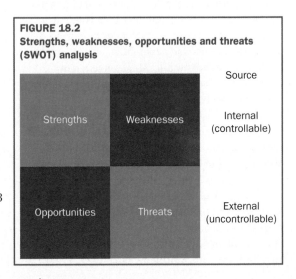

FIGURE 18.2
Strengths, weaknesses, opportunities and threats (SWOT) analysis

Source

| Strengths | Weaknesses | Internal (controllable) |
| Opportunities | Threats | External (uncontrollable) |

threats into opportunities. For example, a perceived weakness in customer care might suggest the need for staff training to create a new strength. A threat posed by a new entrant might call for a strategic alliance to combine the strengths of both parties to exploit a new opportunity. Because these activities are designed to convert weaknesses into strengths and threats into opportunities, they are called *conversion strategies* (see Figure 18.4). Another way to use a SWOT analysis is to match strengths with opportunities. An example of a company that successfully matched strengths with opportunities is Charles Tyrwhitt, the men's clothing retailer, whose founder Nick Wheeler saw an opportunity in the growing demand for online sales. One of the company's strengths was the fact that it had run its own catalogue business for more than a decade to service its existing home shopping operation. The result is that Charles Tyrwhitt has created a highly profitable online business, outselling its rivals Thomas Pink and TM Lewin in terms of online sales.

Using the SWOT chart for the specialist sports car manufacturer (Figure 18.3), conversion strategies might include building a new manufacturing facility to raise production levels to 50 cars per week and to incorporate more modern production methods, establishing a marketing function and (if marketing research supports it) raising price levels. The company could also seek to eliminate the threat of tougher European standards on exhaust emissions by redesigning its engines to meet them. Marketing strategies might include building on the company's strengths in producing reliable products and possessing a well-respected global brand name to establish distribution in Germany, France, Benelux and Scandinavia, while building sales in the USA and UK (opportunities). Given the company's lack of marketing expertise, the geographic expansion would need to be carefully planned (with full input from the newly created marketing department) at a rate of growth compatible with its managerial capabilities and production capacity. International marketing research would be conducted to establish the relative attractiveness of the new European markets to decide the order of entry. Such a phased entry strategy would enable the company to learn progressively about what is needed to market successfully in Europe.

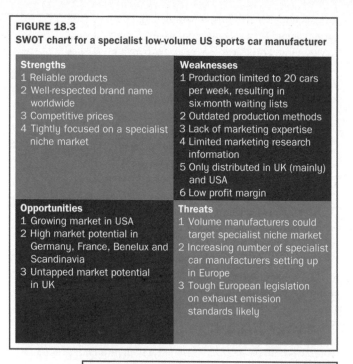

FIGURE 18.3
SWOT chart for a specialist low-volume US sports car manufacturer

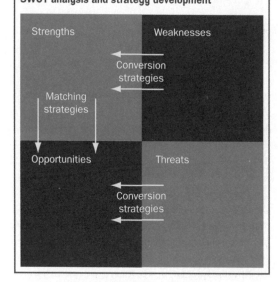

FIGURE 18.4
SWOT analysis and strategy development

Marketing Objectives

The results of the marketing audit and SWOT analysis lead to the definition of **marketing objectives**. These objectives also link through the business mission to corporate objectives. Imagine you are responsible for managing Danone's yoghurt portfolio, which includes Activia, Shape and Actimel product ranges. The corporate objective is to become number one in the yoghurt markets, overtaking Muller, the existing market leader. You will need to develop a marketing plan, which contributes to this corporate objective. How you do this involves deciding on which markets to target with which products and then setting specific objectives for individual products. There are two levels of objective used in marketing planning:

1 *Strategic thrust objectives* which shape the direction of the plan and involve deciding on which markets to target and which products/service to sell. So, in the Danone case you might decide to target new customers (Muller yoghurt eaters) with existing products (Activia fruit yoghurts).

2 *Strategic objectives* set specific objectives for individual products. So, to implement your plan you will need to build market share of (Activia fruit yoghurts).

Each type of objectives is now discussed in more detail.

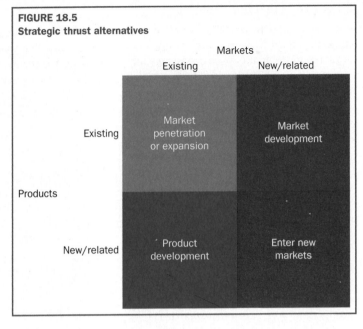

FIGURE 18.5
Strategic thrust alternatives

Strategic thrust

Objectives should be set in terms of which products to sell in which markets (McDonald, 2007). This describes the **strategic thrust** of the business. The strategic thrust defines the future direction and areas of potential growth for a business. The alternatives (see Figure 18.5) comprise:

- existing products in existing markets (market penetration or expansion)
- new/related products for existing markets (product development)
- existing products in new/related markets (market development)
- new/related products for new/related markets (entry into new markets).

Market penetration

This strategy is to take the existing product in the existing market and to attempt increased penetration. Existing customers may become more brand loyal (brand-switch less often) and/ or new customers in the same market may begin to buy the brand. Other tactics to increase penetration include getting existing customers to use the brand more often (e.g. wash their hair more frequently) and to use a greater quantity when they use it (e.g. two spoonfuls of tea instead of one). The latter tactic would also have the effect of expanding the market; for example, Glasses Direct, the online reseller of spectacles and sunglasses, launched a 2-for-1 offer encouraging existing customers to buy several pairs of glasses at a time (Glasses Direct, n.d.). They also use incentives to encourage existing customers to introduce their friends and seek and encourage new customers in the same market to switch to their brand. See Exhibit 18.3.

EXHIBIT 18.3
Glasses Direct 'share with a friend'

Product development

This strategy involves increasing sales by improving present products or developing new products for current markets. New product replacements that fail to provide additional benefits are unlikely to succeed. Google Glass, smart glasses that linked to the Internet and allowed wearers to take photos and videos, were withdrawn as usability, privacy and safety issues created problems for the product's early adopters (Cellan-Jones, 2015). Product development may take the form of brand extensions (Cadbury's Dairy Milk Caramel bars and Caramel Nibbles, Cadbury's Crunchie bars and Crunchie Rocks) that provide slightly modified features for target customers. See Mini Case 18.1 to find out more about how jewellery maker Pandora used its products to develop markets.

Market development

This strategy is used when current products are sold in new markets. This may involve moving into new geographical markets. Many consumer durable brands, such as cars, consumer electronics and household appliance brands, are sold in overseas markets with no or only very minor modifications to those sold at home. An alternative market development strategy is to move into new market segments. For example, BSkyB has expanded its market share through the acquisition of Virgin Media's TV channel. This has enabled BSkyB to gain access to Virgin's customers by providing Sky's existing content. Santander, one of the world's largest banking groups, has also developed markets for its existing financial products in both Latin America and the UK (*The Economist*, 2010).

Entry into new markets

This strategy occurs when new products are developed for new markets. This is the most risky strategy but may be necessary when a company's current products and markets offer few prospects for future growth. When there

---

MINI CASE 18.1
Pandora: Wherever Life Takes You, Take it With You

Pandora developed its markets from a single store in Copenhagen, Denmark, into an international jewellery brand. Having established a manufacturing base in Thailand, Per and Winne Enevoldsen—who founded the company—concentrated on building their business through wholesale jewellery markets. They focused on the products and introduced the Pandora charm bracelet into Denmark, where it was a great success, and then moved on to Germany, Austria and the USA. The innovativeness of the product, positioned at affordable prices, enabled Pandora to develop these markets quickly. More factories were opened in Thailand, and a vertically integrated system—in-house designers, the company's own factories and retail stores and franchises—was used to service the increased demand.

The company continued to use its products to reinforce the brand's market position. Its 'Wherever life takes you, take it with you' campaign aimed to encourage loyalty from existing customers, who were targeted to build up their collection of Pandora products as keepsakes of the special moments in their lives.

For the future, Pandora has a strategic vision, which is 'to become the world's most recognised jewellery brand'. Its marketing plan involves continuing to position the brand as affordable, good quality jewellery, but to develop the product portfolio beyond the bracelets and charms into rings, earrings and necklaces.

Questions:

1 Suggest how Pandora's strategic vision could be operationalized into a guiding mission statement.
2 Explain why Pandora concentrates on its products to leverage market growth.
3 Propose a marketing plan that might enable Pandora to achieve its strategic aim of becoming the world's most recognised jewellery brand.

Based on: Pandora (2015); West (2014); Pandora Group (2015)

is synergy between the existing and new products, this strategy is more likely to work. For example, Apple's experience and competences in computer electronics provided the platform for designing a new product, the iPod, targeting a different market: young people who want downloadable music on a portable music player (Helmore, 2005). This, in turn, has been followed by the launch of the iPhone, which has placed Apple in a strong position in the market for smartphones (Allison, 2008) and the development of the tablet computer market with the iPad. Intel also believes it has the core competence required to move into smartphones, netbooks and tablet computing. Companies in technology markets are constantly investing in new developments and looking for markets for their offers.

Strategic objectives

Alongside objectives for product/market direction, **strategic objectives** for each product need to be agreed. This begins the process of planning at the product level. There are four options:

1 build
2 hold
3 harvest
4 divest

For new products, the strategic objective will inevitably be to build sales and market share. For existing products, the appropriate strategic objective will depend on the particular situation associated with the product. This will be determined in the marketing audit, SWOT analysis and evaluation of the strategic options outlined earlier. In particular, product portfolio planning tools such as the Boston Consulting Group Growth–Share Matrix, the General Electric Market Attractiveness–Competitive Position Model. These will be discussed in detail in Chapter 20, which deals with managing products.

The important point to remember at this stage is that *building* sales and market share is not the only sensible strategic objective for a product. As we shall see, *holding* sales and market share may make commercial sense under certain conditions; *harvesting*, where sales and market share are allowed to fall but profit margins are maximized, may also be preferable to building; finally, *divestment*, where the product is dropped or sold, can be the logical outcome of the situation analysis.

Together, strategic thrust and strategic objectives define where the business and its products intend to go in the future.

Core Marketing Strategy

Once objectives have been set, the next stage in the plan involves deciding how to meet the objectives and answer the question: how do we get there? The **core marketing strategy** focuses on how objectives can be accomplished. There are three key elements to consider: target markets, competitor targets and establishing a competitive advantage. Each element is interlinked and together they form the key aspects of **competitive positioning** (Hooley, Piercy and Nicoulaud, 2012). We will consider each of the three elements in turn.

Target markets

A central plank of core strategy is the choice of **target market(s)**. Marketing is not about chasing any customer at any price. Decisions should be taken about which groups of customers (segments) are most attractive to the business and best fit with its capabilities. The *Economist* targets business professionals who wish to be regarded as well-informed about business matters. This periodical is able to 'offer authoritative insight and opinion on international news, politics, business, finance, science and technology'. It is able to achieve high standards of journalism across a wide range of subject as it attracts many writers who wish to work together to produce thought-provoking articles. This is an example of a company which has a clear target market and it is able to use its capabilities and resources to produce a product which satisfies the needs of its customers. See Exhibit 18.4.

EXHIBIT 18.4
The Economist is positioned as an authoritative information source

MARKETING IN ACTION 18.2
Birds Eye Presents 'The food for life' as Part of its Target Marketing Strategy

Birds Eye devised a new marketing strategy that aimed to double its market share by 2020. Arguably, the reasoning driving this plan was missed opportunities, because when the brand assessed its marketing situation it found (in the UK market) that whilst over 80 per cent of households were aware of and used the brand, only 2 per cent used it at all meal times. In fact, its analysis revealed that many customers perceived Birds Eye as just a '*teatime fish fingers and peas brand*'. This was also a cause for concern, as adults represented 65 per cent of customers but fish fingers were perceived as food for 'kids'.

At the heart of the marketing strategy was a £16 million pan-European marketing communications campaign designed to reposition the brand in the minds of its customers. The aim was to get existing customers to consider the brand as a 'food' rather than a frozen alternative. The aim was to penetrate the large market of customers who trust the brand in both the UK and the rest of Europe, by encouraging them to change the way they use Birds Eye products.

Based on: Tesseras (2014)

The choice of target market can result from the SWOT analysis and the setting of marketing objectives (strategic thrust). For existing products, marketing management should consider its current target markets and their changing needs. Consequently, Samsung should focus on customers' needs across its established product ranges. For example, smart televisions are constantly evolving in response to technology innovations and changing customer needs, and in order to retain its market share Samsung should make changes to the marketing mix to adapt to new requirements. In other cases, current target markets may have decreased in attractiveness, so products will need to be repositioned to target different market segments. The process of market segmentation and targeting is examined in depth in Chapter 7. See Marketing in Action 18.2 for discussion of how Birds Eye, leading European frozen brand adapted its target marketing strategy.

 Scan the QR code to find out how Birds Eye is positioning its brands against the competition by making meal times something special.

Competitor targets

Competitor targets are the organizations against which a company chooses to compete directly. Samsung competes directly with Apple in the tablet computer market. Weak competitors may be viewed as easy prey, and resources channelled to attack them. The importance of understanding competitors and strategies for attacking and defending against competitors are discussed in Chapter 19, which examines in detail the areas of competitor analysis and competitive strategy.

Competitive advantage

The link between target markets and competitor targets is the establishment of a competitive advantage. A competitive advantage is the achievement of superior performance through differentiation to provide superior customer value, or by managing to achieve lowest delivered cost. For major success, businesses need to achieve a clear performance differential over the competition on factors that are important to target customers. The most successful methods are built upon some combination of three advantages (Day, 1984):

1   *being better*—providing superior quality or service (e.g. Mercedes-Benz, Dulux paints, Singapore Airlines)
2   *being faster*—anticipating or responding to customer needs faster than the competition does (e.g. Zara)
3   *being closer*—establishing close long-term relationships with customers (e.g. Amazon).

Another route to competitive advantage is achieving the lowest relative rate cost position of all competitors (Porter, 1980). Lowest cost can be translated into a competitive advantage through low prices, or by producing standard items at price parity when comparative success may be achieved through higher profit margins than those of competitors. Achieving a highly differentiated product is not incompatible with a low cost position, however (Phillips, Chang and Buzzell, 1983). Inasmuch as high-quality products suffer lower rejection rates through quality control and lower repair costs through their warranty period, they may incur lower total costs than their inferior rivals. Methods of achieving competitive advantages and their sources are analysed in Chapter 19.

Tests of an effective core strategy

Figure 18.6 shows six key considerations that can be used to test a core strategy. The six considerations are that the strategy should:

1 be based upon a *clear definition of target customers and their needs*.
2 show understanding of competitors and be able to create *competitive advantage*.
3 *incur acceptable risk*. Challenging a strong competitor with a weak competitive advantage and a low resource base would not incur acceptable risk.
4 be *resourced and managerially supportable*. The strategy should match the resources, capabilities and managerial competences of the business.
5 be derived from the *product and marketing objectives* established as part of the planning process. Extensive use of promotions that makes commercial logic when following a build objective may make no sense when following a harvesting objective.
6 be *internally consistent*. Each of the elements of the core strategy should be consistent with the rest of the marketing plan.

Marketing mix decisions

At this stage in the planning process, managers consider the marketing mix. The tools they use and the choices they make will be informed by the core strategy. Decisions about use of each of the elements of the mix will vary depending on whether the focus is on a product or service. Nevertheless, decisions will consist of judgements about how to select and blend each of the relevant elements of the mix. Such decisions will not be taken in isolation, as they will also consider how their close competitors use the mix. For example, major supermarkets Asda, Sainsbury's, Morrisons and Tesco constantly vie for market share. As there is limited growth in the overall size of the grocery market, so each of these major players grows its share of the market by attracting its competitors' customers. This is achieved through the marketing mix and each of these supermarket brands uses the mix differently. At a basic level, Asda creates its competitive advantage by focusing on keeping prices very

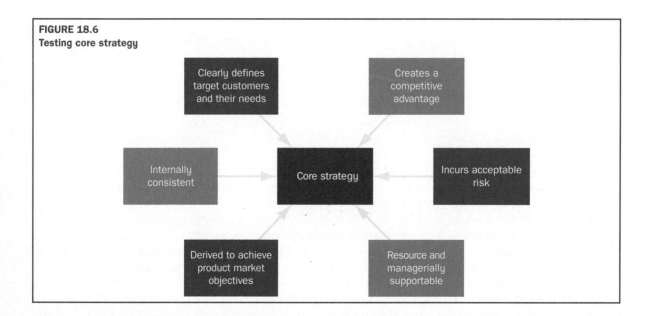

FIGURE 18.6
Testing core strategy

low. Sainsbury's creates competitive advantage through the quality of its products. Morrisons differentiates itself through the freshness of its products and its store destinations, and Tesco positions its brand on offering the greatest value across the widest product range.

As with all of the other stages of the marketing plan, there are many complex choices involved in selecting an effective marketing mix. Part 3 of the book devotes several chapters to exploring each of elements of the mix in detail: product (Chapters 8, 11 and 20), services (Chapter 9), price (Chapter 12), promotion (Chapters 13, 14, 15, 16) and place (Chapter 17).

Organization and implementation

No marketing plan will succeed unless it 'degenerates into work' (Drucker, 1993). Consequently, the business must design an organization that has the capability of implementing the plan. Indeed, organizational weaknesses discovered as part of the SWOT analysis may restrict the feasible range of strategic options. Reorganization could mean the establishment of a new marketing organization or department in the business. In the past many manufacturing organizations did not have a marketing department (Piercy, 1986). In some cases marketing was done by the chief executive, or the sales department dealt with customer enquiries so there was no further need for other marketing input. In other situations environmental change caused strategy change and subsequent reorganization of marketing and sales business functions. More recently, the growth of large corporate customers with enormous buying power has resulted in businesses focusing their resources more firmly on meeting their needs (strategy change), which in turn has led to dedicated marketing and sales teams being organized to service these accounts (reorganization). Implementation and organizational issues are explored in Chapter 22.

Because strategy change and reorganization affect the balance of power in businesses, and the daily life and workloads of people, resistance may occur. Consequently marketing personnel need to understand the barriers to change, the process of change management and the techniques of persuasion that can be used to effect the implementation of the marketing plan. These issues are dealt with in Chapter 22.

Control

The final stage in the marketing planning process is **control**. The aim of control systems is to evaluate the results of the marketing plan so that corrective action can be taken if performance does not match objectives. Short-term control systems can plot results against objectives on a weekly, monthly, quarterly and/or annual basis. Measures include sales, profits, costs and cash flow. There is a growing need for marketing managers to assess the payoff from their investments and justify them. This has resulted in the use of marketing metrics, which are quantitative measures of the outcomes of marketing activities and expenditures. There is extensive coverage of them in Chapter 22, and in the Online Learning Centre that accompanies this book. Strategic control systems are more long term. Managers need to stand back from week-by-week and month-by-month results to reassess critically whether their plans are in line with their capabilities and the environment.

Lack of this long-term control perspective may result in the pursuit of plans that have lost strategic credibility. New competition, changes in technology and moving customer requirements may have rendered old plans obsolete. This, of course, returns the planning process to the beginning, since this kind of fundamental review is conducted in the marketing audit. It is the activity of assessing internal capabilities and external opportunities and threats that result in a SWOT analysis. This outcome may be a redefinition of the business mission, and, as we have seen, changes in marketing objectives and strategies to realign the business with its environment.

So how do the stages of marketing planning relate to the fundamental planning questions stated earlier in this chapter? Table 18.1 illustrates this relationship. The question 'Where are we now?' is answered by the business mission definition, the marketing audit and SWOT analysis.

Rewards of Marketing Planning

Many authors have suggested there is a positive relationship between market-orientated business and performance (Jaworski and Kohli, 1993; Narver and Slater, 1998; Kumar, Subramaniam and Yauger, 1998), and companies with a highly developed market orientation tend to derive greater benefits from marketing planning (Pulendran, Speed and Widing, 2003). Moreover, various authors have attributed the following benefits to marketing planning (Leppard and McDonald, 1991; Greenley, 1986; Terpstra and Sarathy, 1991).

1 *Consistency*: the plan provides a focal point for decisions and actions. By reference to a common plan, management decisions should be more consistent and actions better coordinated.

2 *Encourages the monitoring of change*: the planning process forces managers to step away from day-to-day problems and review the impact of change on the business from a strategic perspective.

3 *Encourages organizational adaptation*: the underlying premise of planning is that the organization should adapt to match its environment. Marketing planning, therefore, promotes the necessity to accept the inevitability of change. This is important as the capability to adapt has been linked to superior performance (Oktemgil and Greenley, 1997).

4 *Stimulates achievement*: the planning process focuses on objectives, strategies and results. It encourages people to ask, 'What can we achieve given our capabilities?' As such it motivates people to set new horizons for objectives when they otherwise might be content to accept much lower standards of performance.

5 *Resource allocation*: the planning process asks fundamental questions about resource allocation. For example, which products should receive high investment (build), which should be maintained (hold), which should have resources withdrawn slowly (harvest) and which should have resources withdrawn immediately (divest)?

6 *Competitive advantage*: planning promotes the search for sources of competitive advantage.

However, it is important to realize that this logical planning process (sometimes called *synoptic planning*) may conflict with the culture of the business, which may plan effectively using an *incremental approach* (Raimond and Eden, 1990). The style of planning should match business culture (Driver, 1990). Saker and Speed (1992) argue that the considerable demands on managers in terms of time and effort implied by the synoptic marketing planning process may mean that alternative planning schemes are more appropriate, particularly for small companies. (For information on marketing and planning in small and medium-sized firms, see: Carson, 1990; Fuller, 1994.)

Incremental planning is more problem-focused in that the process begins with the realization of a problem (for example, a fall-off in orders) and continues with an attempt to identify a solution. As solutions to problems form, so strategy emerges. However, little attempt is made to integrate consciously the individual decisions that could possibly affect one another. Strategy is viewed as a loosely linked group of decisions that are handled individually. Nevertheless, its effect may be to attune the business to its environment through its problem-solving nature. Its drawback is the lack of a broad situation analysis and strategy option generation, which renders the incremental approach less comprehensive. For some companies, however, its inherent practicality may support its use rather than its rationality (O'Shaughnessy, 1995).

Problems in Making Planning Work

Empirical work into the marketing planning practices has found that most commercial companies did not practise the kinds of systematic planning procedures described in this chapter and, of those that did, many did not enjoy the rewards described in the previous section (Greenley, 1987). However, others have shown that there is a relationship between planning and commercial success. See, for example, Armstrong (1982) and McDonald (1984). A more recent study (Pulendran, Speed and Wildin II, 2003) also confirmed that marketing planning is linked to commercial success. The problem is that the *contextual difficulties* associated with the process of marketing planning are substantial and need to be understood. Inasmuch as forewarned is forearmed, the following is a checklist of potential problems that have to be faced by those charged with making marketing planning work.

Political

Marketing planning is a resource allocation process. The outcome of the process is an allocation of more funds to some products and departments, the same or less to others. Since power bases, career opportunities and salaries are often tied to whether an area is fast or slow growing, it is not surprising that managers view planning as a highly political activity. An example is a European bank, whose planning process resulted in the decision to insist that its retail branch managers divert certain types of loan application to the industrial/ merchant banking arm of the group where the return was greater. This was required because the plan was designed to optimize the return to the group as a whole. However, the consequence was considerable friction between the divisions concerned because the decision lowered the performance of the retail branch.

In another European bank the introduction of a series of market-based products was blocked by managers of existing product-orientated offerings who feared their launch would mean, for them, losing their jobs. Both these

MARKETING IN ACTION 18.3
Sweden Offers Solutions for Uber's Setback in European Roll-out

European taxi drivers came out in force against Uber, as shown in the photo above.

Marketing planning can hit problems. Great ideas that fulfil customer needs do not necessarily succeed, as unforeseen barriers and resistance can arise. This is why it is essential to understand *contextual difficulties* that might get in the way of a marketing strategy. For example, Uber's ride-sharing concept is popular and is based on customer needs, but the company has come up against strong political resistance when moving into European markets.

Politically, drink-driving is a big issue; globally, around a third of road deaths are alcohol related. In many countries, it is legal to have at least one drink and then drive, but often a night out, lunch with friends or even a business meeting can involve more than one drink and going over legal limits. This behaviour creates a problem: how to get home when the party is over? Public transport services may have stopped running—especially late in the evening—and taxi services are often limited to urban boundaries, can be expensive and on a busy Saturday night difficult to find. Uber offers solutions to the problem and has actually started making a difference to the drink-driving statistics in the USA by making it easier to 'get a ride home'.

The idea was born out of a very simple need: two guys looking for a taxi in Paris after attending a business conference. These two people were Travis Kalanick and Garrett Camp, who were already successful technology entrepreneurs, so developing the Uber mobile app got off to a good start. Launched in San Francisco, the UberCab idea is based on carpooling. Uber is a mini-cab service that is accessed via mobile phone. Drivers and riders sign up through the Uber app and are then connected together based on the riders' needs and the drivers' availability. The idea proved to be very popular in California and soon spread to other parts of the USA. Market expansion to Europe was the next step.

Globally, there are over 160,000 active Uber drivers, but the launch of Uber in Europe has been far from straightforward. A German court banned Uber from offering its ride-sharing services countrywide. The German taxi association claimed Uber was involved in illegal practices by providing unlicensed drivers; similar problems in the Netherlands, Spain and France have been tarnishing Uber's image and halting expansion into European markets.

However, in Sweden the Uber roll-out has been successful. Arguably, Uber has turned threats into opportunities in this market. Consequently, initial resistance has been overcome, as the benefits of Uber have been conveyed to the Swedish Government and the people. Issues and questions include suggestions of tax avoidance by Uber, but this has created an opportunity for the company to show how its digital systems are superior to those of many other transport companies. The Uber principle has been embraced as an innovative approach to transportation that delivers benefits to its riders and has the potential to improve the industry. Taxi Stockholm has already responded to competition from Uber by improving and extending its services. And Taxi Stockholm's head of marketing is quoted as saying, '*Uber is good for the market by pushing the industry to use a different technique, a new platform.*'

So Uber is learning how to manage contextual difficulties, and Sweden's innovative and forward-thinking culture is providing ideas about how Uber's marketing team might counter resistance in other parts of Europe.

Based on: Ewing (2015); Alert Driving (2010); Benson Strategy Group (2015); Frizell (2015); CBS Money Watch (2015)

examples demonstrate how political factors can be a barrier to marketing planning initiatives. See Marketing in Action 18.3 to find out how Uber is encountering and overcoming political resistance as it moves into European markets.

Opportunity cost

Some busy managers view marketing planning as a time-wasting ritual that conflicts with the need to deal with day-to-day problems. They view the opportunity cost of spending two or three days away at a hotel thrashing out long-term plans as too high. This difficulty may be compounded by the fact that people who are attracted to the hectic pace of managerial life may be the type who prefer to live that way (Mintzberg, 1975). Hence, they may be ill at ease with the thought of a long period of sedate contemplation.

Reward systems

The reward systems of many businesses are geared to the short term. Incentives and bonuses may be linked to quarterly or annual results. Managers may thus overweight short-term issues and underweight medium- and long-term concerns if there is a conflict of time. Thus marketing planning may be viewed as of secondary importance.

Information

To function effectively, a systematic marketing planning system needs informational inputs. Market share, size and growth rates are basic inputs into the marketing audit but may be unavailable. More perversely, information may be wilfully withheld by vested interests who, recognizing that knowledge is power, distort the true situation to protect their position in the planning process.

Culture

The establishment of a systematic marketing planning process may be at variance with the culture of the organization. As has already been stated, businesses may 'plan' by making incremental decisions. Hence, the strategic planning system may challenge the status quo and be seen as a threat. In other cases, the values and beliefs of some managers may be hostile to a planning system altogether.

Personalities

Marketing planning usually involves a discussion between managers about the strategic choices facing the business and the likely outcomes. This can be a highly charged affair where personality clashes and pent-up antagonisms can surface. The result can be that the process degenerates into abusive argument and sets up deep chasms within the management team.

Lack of knowledge and skills

Another problem that can arise when setting up a marketing planning system is that the management team does not have the knowledge and skills to perform the tasks adequately (McDonald, 1989). Basic marketing knowledge about market segmentation, competitive advantage and the nature of strategic objectives may be lacking. Similarly, skills in analysing competitive situations and defining core strategies may be inadequate.

How to Handle Marketing Planning Problems

Some of the problems revealed during the market planning process may be deep-seated managerial inadequacies rather than being intrinsic to the planning process itself. As such, the attempt to establish the planning system may be seen as a benefit to the business by revealing the nature of these problems. However, various authors have proposed recommendations for minimizing the impact of such problems (McDonald, 1984; Abell and Hammond, 1979).

1 *Senior management support*: top management must be committed to planning and be seen by middle management to give it total support. This should be ongoing support, not a short-term fad.
2 *Match the planning system to the culture of the business*: how the marketing planning process is managed should be consistent with the culture of the organization. For example, in some organizations the top-down/bottom-up balance will move towards top-down; in other less directive cultures the balance will move towards a more bottom-up planning style.
3 *The reward system*: this should reward the achievement of longer-term objectives rather than focus exclusively on short-term results.
4 *Depoliticize outcomes*: less emphasis should be placed on rewarding managers associated with build (growth) strategies. Recognition of the skills involved in defending share and harvesting products should be made. At General Electric managers are classified as 'growers', 'caretakers' and 'undertakers', and matched to products

that are being built, defended or harvested in recognition of the fact that the skills involved differ according to the strategic objective. No stigma is attached to caretaking or undertaking; each is acknowledged as contributing to the success of the organization.

5 *Clear communication*: plans should be communicated to those charged with implementation.
6 *Training*: marketing personnel should be trained in the necessary marketing knowledge and skills to perform the planning job. Ideally the management team should attend the same training course so that they each share a common understanding of the concepts and tools involved and can communicate using the same terminology.

When you have read this chapter

Discover further resources and test your understanding: McGraw-Hill **Connect**™ is a digital teaching and learning environment that improves performance over a variety of critical outcomes; it can be tailored, is easy to use and is proven effective. **LearnSmart**™ is the most widely used and intelligent adaptive learning resource that is proven to strengthen memory recall, improve course retention and boost grades. Fuelled by **LearnSmart**™, **SmartBook**™ is the first and only adaptive reading experience available today.

Review

1 **The role of marketing planning within business**
   • Marketing planning is part of a broader concept known as strategic planning.
   • For one-product companies, its role is to ensure that the product continues to meet customers' needs as well as seeking new opportunities.
   • For companies marketing a range of products in a number of markets, marketing planning's role is as above plus the allocation of resources to each product.
   • For companies comprising a number of businesses (SBUs), marketing planning's role is as above plus a contribution to the allocation of resources to each business.

2 **The key planning questions**
   • These are: 'Where are we now?', 'How did we get there?', 'Where are we heading?', 'Where would we like to be?', 'How do we get there?' and 'Are we on course?'

3 **The process of marketing planning**
   • The steps in the process are: deciding the business mission, conducting a marketing audit, producing a SWOT analysis, setting marketing objectives (strategic thrust and strategic objectives), deciding core strategy (target markets, competitive advantage and competitor targets), making marketing mix decisions, organizing and implementing, and control.

4 **The concept of the business mission**
   • A business mission is a broadly defined, enduring statement of purpose that distinguishes a business from others of its type.
   • A business mission should answer two questions: 'What business are we in?' and 'What business do we want to be in?'

5 The nature of the marketing audit and SWOT analysis
- The marketing audit is a systematic examination of a business's marketing environment, objectives, strategies and activities, with a view to identifying key strategic issues, problem areas and opportunities.
- It consists of an examination of a company's external and internal environments. The external environment is made up of the macroenvironment, the market and competition. The internal environmental audit consists of operating results, strategic issues analysis, marketing mix effectiveness, marketing structures and systems.
- A SWOT analysis provides a simple method of summarizing the results of the marketing audit. Internal issues are summarized under strengths and weaknesses, and external issues are summarized under opportunities and threats.

6 The nature of marketing objectives
- There are two types of marketing objective: i) strategic thrust, which defines the future direction of the business in terms of which products to sell in which markets; and ii) strategic objectives, which are product-level objectives relating to the decision to build, hold, harvest or divest products.

7 The components of core strategy and the criteria for testing its effectiveness
- The components are target markets, competitor targets and competitive advantage.
- The criteria for testing its effectiveness are that core strategy clearly defines target customers and their needs, creates a competitive advantage, incurs acceptable risk, is resource and managerially supportable, is derived to achieve product–market objectives and is internally consistent.
  Each element is interlinked. and together they form the core aspects of competitive positioning.

8 Where marketing mix decisions are placed within the marketing planning process
- Marketing mix decisions follow those of core strategy as they are based on an understanding of target customers' needs and the competition so that a competitive advantage can be created.

9 The importance of organization, implementation and control within the marketing planning process
- Organization is needed to support the strategies decided upon. Strategies are unlikely to be effective without attention to implementation issues. For example, techniques to overcome resistance to change and the training of staff who are required to implement strategic decisions are likely to be required.
- Control systems are important so that the results of the marketing plan can be evaluated and corrective action taken if performance does not match objectives.

10 The rewards and problems associated with marketing planning
- The rewards are consistency of decision-making, encouragement of the monitoring of change, encouragement of organizational adaptation, stimulation of achievement, aiding resource allocation and promotion of the creation of a competitive advantage.
- The potential problems with marketing planning revolve around the context in which it takes place and are political, high opportunity cost, lack of reward systems tied to longer-term results, lack of relevant information, cultural and personality clashes, and lack of managerial knowledge and skills.

11 Recommendations for overcoming marketing planning problems
- Recommendations for minimizing the impact of marketing planning problems are: attaining senior management support, matching the planning system to the culture of the business, creating a reward system that is focused on longer-term performance, depoliticizing outcomes, communicating clearly to those responsible for implementation, and training in the necessary marketing knowledge and skills to conduct marketing planning.

Key Terms

business mission the organization's purpose, usually setting out its competitive domain, which distinguishes the business from others of its type

competitive positioning consists of three key elements: target markets, competitor targets and establishing a competitive advantage

competitor analysis an examination of the nature of actual and potential competitors, and their objectives and strategies

competitor targets the organizations against which a company chooses to compete directly

control the stage in the marketing planning process or cycle when the performance against plan is monitored so that corrective action, if necessary, can be taken

core marketing strategy the means of achieving marketing objectives, including target markets, competitor targets and competitive advantage

customer analysis a survey of who the customers are, what choice criteria they use, how they rate competitive offerings and on what variables they can be segmented

distribution analysis an examination of movements in power bases, channel attractiveness, physical distribution and distribution behaviour

macroenvironment a number of broader forces that affect not only the company but the other actors in the environment, for example social, political, technological and economic

market analysis the statistical analysis of market size, growth rates and trends

marketing audit a systematic examination of a business's marketing environment, objectives, strategies and activities with a view to identifying key strategic issues, problem areas and opportunities

marketing objectives there are two types of marketing objective: strategic thrust, which dictates which products should be sold in which markets, and strategic objectives—that is, product-level objectives such as build, hold, harvest and divest

marketing planning the process by which businesses analyse the environment and their capabilities, decide upon courses of marketing action and implement those decisions

marketing structures the marketing frameworks (organization, training and internal communications) upon which marketing activities are based

marketing systems sets of connected parts (information, planning and control) that support the marketing function

microenvironment the actors in the firm's immediate environment that affect its capability to operate effectively in its chosen markets—namely, suppliers, distributors, customers and competitors

product portfolio the total range of products offered by the company

strategic business unit a business or company division serving a distinct group of customers and with a distinct set of competitors, usually strategically autonomous

strategic issues analysis an examination of the suitability of marketing objectives and segmentation bases in the light of changes in the marketplace

strategic objectives product-level objectives relating to the decision to build, hold, harvest or divest products

strategic thrust the decision concerning which products to sell in which markets

supplier analysis an examination of who and where suppliers are located, their competences and shortcomings, the trends affecting them and the future outlook for them

SWOT analysis a structured approach to evaluating the strategic position of a business by identifying its strengths, weaknesses, opportunities and threats

target market a market segment that has been selected as a focus for the company's offering or communications

Study Questions

1. **Discuss how to carry out a situation analysis and explain why it is an important part of marketing planning.**

2. **Discuss how macro and micro level influences might influence marketing planning decisions.**

3. **Explain how each stage of the marketing planning process links with the fundamental planning questions identified in Table 18.1.**

4. **The quote at the beginning of the chapter by business guru Gary Hamel suggests that marketing planning is somewhat irrelevant. Discuss the extent to which you agree with this comment.**

5. **Evaluate the extent to which the marketing planning process is a true reflection of how businesses plan their marketing strategies.**

6. Explain the extent to which a clear business mission statement is a help to marketing planners?

7. What is meant by core marketing strategy? What role does it play in the process of marketing planning?

8. Discuss the key decision marketing planners should make when setting marketing objectives.

9. Discuss the importance of digital technology in the marketing planning process.

Recommended Reading

Craven, D. and N. Piercy (2012) *Strategic Marketing*, London: McGraw-Hill Education.

Dawar, N. (2013) When marketing is strategy, *Harvard Business Review*. 91(12), 101–8.

Ellis, N., J. Fitchett, M. Higgins, G. Jack, M. Lim, M. Saren and M. Tadajewski (2010) *Marketing: A Critical Textbook*, London: Sage Publications Ltd.

Joshi, A. and E. Gimenez (2014) Decision-driven data, *Harvard Business Review*, July 2014, https://hbr.

org/2014/07/decision-driven-marketing (accessed July 2015).

Morgan, N. A. (2012), Marketing and business performance, *Journal of the Academy of Marketing Science* 40(1), 102–19.

Varadarajan, R. (2010) Strategic marketing and marketing strategy: domain, definition, fundamental issues and foundational premises, *Journal of the Academy of Marketing Science* 38, 119–40.

References

Abell, D. F. and J. S. Hammond (1979) *Strategic Market Planning*, Englewood Cliffs, NJ: Prentice-Hall.

Ackoff, R. I. (1987) Mission Statements, *Planning Review* 15(4), 30–2.

Aguilar, F. J. (1967) *Scanning the Business Environment*, New York, NY: Macmillan.

Alert Driving (2010) DRUNK DRIVING INCREASING CONCERN WORLDWIDE. Retrieved from Alertdriving.com: http://www.alertdriving.com/home/fleet-alert-magazine/international/drunk-driving-increasing-concern-worldwide (accessed 2 June 2015).

Allison, K. (2008) Apple Unveils iPhone Grand Plan, *Financial Times*, 10 March, 23.

Amazon (2015) Leadership Principles, Amazon, April. http://www.amazon.com/Values-Careers-Homepage/b?tag=skim0x680-20&ie=UTF8&node=239365011

Armstrong, J. S. (1982) The Value of Formal Planning for Strategic Decisions: Review of Empirical Research, *Strategic Management Journal* 3(3), 197–213.

Benson Strategy Group (2015) More Options, Shifting Mindsets, Driving Better Choices, Uber and MADD. https://newsroom.uber.com/wp-content/uploads/2015/01/UberMADD-Report.pdf (accessed 2 June 2015).

Carson, D. (1990) Some Exploratory Models for Assessing Small Firms' Marketing Performance: A Qualitative Approach, *European Journal of Marketing* 24(11), 8–51.

CBS Money Watch (2015) Uber faces another setback in Europe, CBS Money Watch, 18 March. http://www.cbsnews.com/news/uber-faces-another-setback-in-europe

Cellan-Jones, R. (2015) Google Glass sales halted but firm says kit is not dead, BBC, 15 January. http://www.bbc.co.uk/news/technology-30831128

Davis, M. (2014) Six Companies That Changed Direction And Found Success, The richest.com, 10 February. http://www.therichest.com/business/companies-business/six-companies-that-changed-direction-and-found-success (accessed 28 March 2015).

Day, G. S. (1984) *Strategic Marketing Planning: The Pursuit of Competitive Advantage*, St Paul, MN: West, 41.

Driver, J. C. (1990) Marketing Planning in Style, *Quarterly Review of Marketing* 15(4), 16–21.

Drucker, P. F. (1993) *Management Tasks, Responsibilities, Practices*, New York: Harper and Row, 128.

Ewing, Adam (2015), 'Uber draws Teslas, Therapy Out of Taxi Rivals in Sweden. http://www.bloomberg.com/news/articles/2015-01-26/uber-draws-teslas-therapy-out-of-swedish-rivals-unfazed-by-apps

Frizell, S. (2015) Uber Just Answered Everything You Want to Know About Your Driver, *Time*, 22 January. http://time.com/3678507/uber-driver-questions (accessed 2 June 2015).

Fuller, P. B. (1994) Assessing Marketing in Small and Medium-Sized Enterprises, *European Journal of Marketing* 28(12), 34–9.

Gapper, J. and B. Jopson (2011) An inventor with fire in his belly and Jobs in his sights, *Financial Times*, 30 September.

Gillespie, A. (2007) Foundation of Economics, *Oxford University Press*, 12: http://www.oup.com/uk/orc/bin/9780199296378/01student/additional/page_12.htm.

Glasses Direct (n.d.) http://www.glassesdirect.co.uk/about/story/#os2006 (accessed 15 January 2012).

Google (n.d.) http://www.google.com/about/corporate/company (accessed 15 January 2012).

Greenley, G. (1987) An Exposition into Empirical Research into Marketing Planning, *Journal of Marketing Management* 3(1), 83–102.

Greenley, G. E. (1986) *The Strategic and Operational Planning of Marketing*, Maidenhead: McGraw-Hill, 185–7.

Hazan, E. (2014) Paypal's vision for a global market place, McKinsey & Company, August. http://www.mckinsey.com/insights/high_tech_telecoms_internet/paypals_vision_for_a_global_marketplace (accessed 4 April 2015).

Helmore, E. (2005) Big Apple, *Observer*, 16 January, 3.

Hooley, G. J., A. J. Cox and A. Adams (1992) Our Five Year Mission: To Boldly Go Where No Man Has Been Before . . . , *Journal of Marketing Management* 8(1), 35–48.

Hooley, G., N. F. Piercy and B. Nicoulaud (2012) *Marketing Strategy & Competitive Positioning*, Harlow: FT Prentice Hall, 32.

Jaworski, B. J. and A. K. Kohli (1993) Market orientation: antecedents and consequences, *Journal of Marketing* 57, 53–70.

Kumar, K., R. Subramaniam and C. Yauger (1998) Examining the market orientation performance relationship: a context-specific study, *Journal of Management* 24(2), 201–33.

Leppard, J. W. and M. H. B. McDonald (1991) Marketing Planning and Corporate Culture: A Conceptual Framework which Examines Management Attitudes in the Context of Marketing Planning, *Journal of Marketing Management* 7(3), 213–36.

Levitt, T. (1960) Marketing Myopia, *Harvard Business Review*, July–August, 45–6.

Madden, R. (2011) The best form of innovation is simply doing things better, *Marketing Week*, 5 May, 12.

McDonald, M. H. B. (1984) The Theory and Practice of Marketing Planning for Industrial Goods in International Markets, Cranfield Institute of Technology, PhD thesis.

McDonald, M. H. B. (1989) The Barriers to Marketing Planning, *Journal of Marketing Management* 5(1), 1–18.

McDonald, M. H. B. (2007) *Marketing Plans*, London: Butterworth-Heinemann, 2nd edn.

Mintzberg, H. (1975) The Manager's Job: Folklore and Fact, *Harvard Business Review*, July–August, 49–61.

Narver, J. C. and S. F. Slater (1998) Additional thoughts on the measurement of market orientation: a comment on Deshpande and Farley, *Journal of Market-Focused Management* 2(1), 233-6.

O'Shaughnessy, J. (1995) *Competitive Marketing*, Boston, Mass: Allen & Unwin.

Oktemgil, M. and G. Greenley (1997) Consequences of High and Low Adaptive Capability in UK Companies, *European Journal of Marketing* 31(7), 445–66.

Pandora (2015) The Pandora story, Pandora, 4 April. http://www.pandora.net/en-gb/pandora-company/about-pandora/the-pandora-story

Pandora Group (2015) *BUSINESS STRATEGY*, Pandora Group, 2 April. http://pandoragroup.com/About-Pandora/Business-Strategy

Phillips, L. W., D. R. Chang and R. D. Buzzell (1983) Product Quality, Cost Position and Business Performance: A Test of Some Key Hypotheses, *Journal of Marketing* 47(Spring), 26–43.

Piercy, N. (1986) The Role and Function of the Chief Marketing Executive and the Marketing Department, *Journal of Marketing Management* 1(3), 265–90.

Piercy, N. (2008) *Market-led Strategic Change: Transforming the Process of Going to Market*, Oxford: Butterworth-Heinemann, 259.

Porter, M. E. (1980) *Competitive Strategy: Techniques for Analysing Industries and Competitors*, New York: Free Press, Ch. 2.

Pulendran, S., R. Speed and R. Widing (2003) Marketing planning, market orientation and business performance, *European Journal of Marketing* 37(3/4), 476–97.

Raimond, P. and C. Eden (1990) Making Strategy Work, *Long Range Planning* 23(5), 97–105.

Saker, J. and R. Speed (1992) Corporate Culture: Is it Really a Barrier to Marketing Planning? *Journal of Marketing Management* 8(2), 177–82.

Samsung (n.d.) http://www.samsung.com/uk/aboutsamsung/corporateprofile/vision.html (accessed 15 January 2012).

Sanghani, R. (2013) How Jeff Bezos rules his Amazonian empire, *The Telegraph*, 15 October. http://www.telegraph.co.uk/technology/amazon/10379912/How-Jeff-Bezos-rules-his-Amazonian-empire.html (accessed 28 March 2015).

Sanghera, S. (2005) Why So Many Mission Statements are Mission Impossible, *Financial Times*, 22 July, 13.

Terpstra, V. and R. Sarathy (1991) *International Marketing*, Orlando, FL: Dryden, Ch. 17.

Tesseras, L. (2014) Birds Eye readies £16m marketing campaign to reveal new brand positioning, *Marketing Week*, 28 February. https://www.marketingweek.com/2014/02/28/birds-eye-readies-16m-marketing-campaign-to-reveal-new-brand-positioning (accessed 28 February 2015).

The Economist (2010) Breaking and entering: Why it is hard to copy Santander, 13 May: http://www.economist.com/node/16078452 (accessed January 2012).

Topham, G. (2015) Virgin Atlantic soars back into profit, *The Guardian*, 10 March. http://www.theguardian.com/business/2015/mar/10/virgin-atlantic-soars-back-into-profit

Van Vliet, V. (2011) *Gary Hamel*, ToolsHero. http://www.toolshero.com/gary-hamel

Virgin Atlantic (2015) Virgin Atlantic 2014 financial results, Virgin Atlantic, 10 March. http://www.virgin-atlantic.com/gb/en/footer/media-centre/press-releases/financial-results-2014.html

Virgin Group (n.d.) http://www.virgin.com/about-us (accessed January 2012).

Weitz, B. A. and R. Wensley (1988) *Readings in Strategic Marketing*, New York: Dryden, 4.

West, G. (2014) Pandora put life's unforgettable moments centre stage in 'Wherever life takes you, take it with you' campaign, *The Drum*, 14 November. http://www.thedrum.com/news/2014/11/14/pandora-put-lifes-unforgettable-moments-centre-stage-wherever-life-takes-you-take-it (accessed 2 April 2015).

Wilson, I. (1992) Realizing the Power of Strategic Vision, *Long Range Planning* 25(5), 18–28.

CASE 35
Adopting a Marketing Orientation Really Makes a Difference at Dixons Carphone

Dixons Carphone is Europe's leading specialist electrical and telecoms retailer, with over 40,000 employees, operating in 14 countries, and with 3,000 retail stores and online operations (Dixons Carphone, 2015). The company has grown from a one-man band into this fully orchestrated international retail and service operation, which attracts over 100 million shoppers, who spend over £10 billion in its stores and online businesses. How did the company get started and then develop into this successful company? This case explores the significance of adopting a market-orientated approach to planning in developing a *family* of successful international retail brands.

Background: Start-up to Market Leader

Dixons started out in the photography business during challenging trading times in the early 1940s (first store opened in 1937). By the 1960s the original photographic studio had developed into a relatively large public limited company, with an expanding mail order business and high street retail operation. The business continued to grow in the UK, by opening high street stores selling photographic equipment, computers and other high-tech gadgetry. In the 1990s, the acquisition of PC World, opening tax-free travel stores in airports (Dixons Travel) and expansion into European markets with the acquisition of Elkjóp, a leading Nordic retailer, enabled the business to grow further and more rapidly. More acquisitions in Italy (UniEuro), Russia and the Ukraine (in Russia it explored

a joint venture with an existing retailer ElDorado but decided not to pursue it) and expansion into Ireland, Greece and the Czech Republic enabled Dixons Retail plc to become Europe's largest specialist electrical retailer and services company, which employs over 38,000 people spread over 26 countries. (see Table C35.1 for details of Dixons Carphone brands).

Products to Markets: 'stack-em high—sell-em cheap' to 'bringing life to technology'

Clearly, over its history, Dixons has developed a robust business model but the customer has not always been at the heart of business planning. In the past the Group's competitive position largely revolved around a product-focused approach and the strategy was 'stack-em high—sell-em cheap' in brightly coloured

TABLE C35.1 Dixons Retail plc Pan-European brands			
Location	**UK and Ireland**	**Nordics**	**Other international**
Brands	Currys, PC World, Dixons Travel, Carphone Warehouse	Elkjøp, Gigantti, El Giganten, Lefdal	Kotsovolos (Greece), Phone House (Spain, Portugal, Germany and Slovakia)
Sales	£4 billion	£2.8 billion	£1 billion
Market position	No. 1	No. 1	No. 1 in Greece

stores, which attracted customers by being packed with new and exciting electrical goods. However, customer satisfaction was often overlooked as it was not central to this strategic approach—something which had not been missed by some of the brand's competitors.

Change was needed and the condition of the marketing environment and the behaviour of competitors prompted Dixons to consider where the company was heading. In 2006 economic forces were threatening to affect market performance. Signs of trouble in global financial markets and recession were looming large. As a result the competition for market share intensified. Dixons and other UK retailers like Kesa (owner of Comet Plc until 2012) set about developing strategies to secure their future. Global players also showed interest in UK markets. Best Buy, the leading US retailer, believed it had spotted an opportunity in the UK consumer electronics market. The company thought consumers in the UK were getting a bad deal in terms of the service they received from electronic goods retailers like Currys and Comet. So Best Buy committed to an expansion strategy based on building market share, providing better customer service and supply-chain improvements. However, Best Buy was slow to roll out its strategy and waited until summer 2009 to enter the UK. By this time Dixons Retail had revolutionized its approach, moving into a transformation strategy, which put the customers at the heart of the business, and its approach to planning was guided by a new positioning statement 'bringing life to technology'.

A Transformation Strategy

Faced with intensified competition, global recession and poorly performing retail markets, the senior management team at Dixons, headed by then CEO John Browett, devised a service-led business model which transformed every aspect of the business (see Figure C35.1). This strategy gave the company the competitive edge not only to survive and grow during the severest economic collapse since the Great Depression of the 1930s, but also to fend off the competition and become an international market leader in specialist consumer electronics.

Every area of the business had to contribute to the implementation of the new strategy. At an operational level, stores were remodelled so they became 'easy to shop'; channels were extended to a fully integrated multichannel approach; products were selected based on giving the widest, best and most exclusive product choice based on customer needs. After-sales service and support were completely restructured and rebranded in accordance with the strategic plan.

The strategic plan had five clear objectives.
1 Focus on the customer.
2 Focus the portfolio on winning positions.
3 Transform the business.
4 Win in the Internet market.
5 Reduce costs.

At the corporate level, decisions were taken to 'clean up' the business. This meant exiting poorly performing

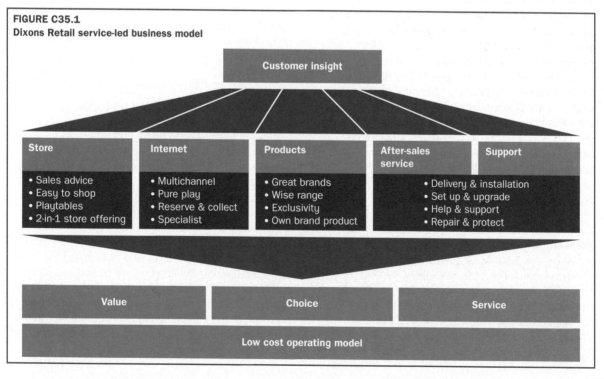

FIGURE C35.1
Dixons Retail service-led business model

Customer insight

Store	Internet	Products	After-sales service	Support
• Sales advice • Easy to shop • Playtables • 2-in-1 store offering	• Multichannel • Pure play • Reserve & collect • Specialist	• Great brands • Wise range • Exclusivity • Own brand product	• Delivery & installation • Set up & upgrade • Help & support • Repair & protect	

Value   Choice   Service

Low cost operating model

»

areas, identifying process improvements and reducing costs. From a marketing perspective the core strategy focused on customer needs and how to get the voice of the customer heard throughout the business, and at the same time making cost efficiencies. Every part of the business made a contribution to the success of the strategy. Since its launch the marketing strategy has been evolving but the concepts of value range and service remain central. In order to make the strategy happen, the marketing team had to get the range right by reviewing all the product ranges and target markets. The review identified that ranges were too narrow, and there was a need for more price points in order to satisfy all customers' needs. The segmentation strategy changed as a result and Dixons began to target seven or eight segments in the UK, based on lifestyle, lifecycle and income.

Making the Plan Work Took an Integrated Effort

Getting the plan to work involved all areas of the business. Each area of the business contributed to the implementation of the plan.

Customer service

A key element in the marketing plan was an overhaul of the customer service provision. The KNOWHOW brand (see Figure C35.2) was created in 2010, with the aim of consolidating sales and after-service elements of the business. The management team believed that where they could make a difference was around service. So they chose to put all the existing brands (e.g. Tech Guys, Partmaster) together under one service umbrella brand, and so created KNOWHOW. After-sales service is hugely important for the customer of complex electrical goods. What the introduction of KNOWHOW did was to help differentiate Dixons as a brand and increase the customer value by never leaving a customer with a problem unsolved (Niall O'Keefe, KnowHow Development Director, 2011).

Human resources

The transformation strategy put the customers at the heart of everything the company does. The key challenge (for skills training) was to ensure that employees throughout the company were able to deliver the service promise. So the company made investment in training to ensure everyone across the business understood the importance of customer service and how this new focus could help develop market share. New methods of staff training were used to ensure delivery of appropriate cost-effective training. All the investment (in training) was evaluated in order to measure the benefits (Boyd Glover, Head of Skills Training, 2011).

Store operations

Dixons focused on building a multichannel operation. This created challenges, as there were many legacy systems and processes that needed to be replaced to enable all parts of the company to operate seamlessly. But it was felt this was a necessary investment, especially as industry predictions were for the majority of retail growth in the coming years to be from multichannel retail. The blend of online and offline retail operations was deemed to be the growth engine for sales.

The key to the success of the multichannel approach is understanding that there are multiple touch points for the customers to engage with the brands. This means getting the communications *right* at every point at which customers touch the company. For example, 70 per cent of the people who shop in store have been on the website prior to coming in. This shows that people are researching away from the stores before they come to buy. Shoppers are increasingly reading reviews, using social media sites and picking up opinions from other people, which creates a challenge. Multichannel is 'the understanding of where the customers are doing their research and where the customers are doing their shopping, because even at the point of purchase customers aren't making a decision between stores and the Internet; they are quite often using both channels combined. Forty per cent of the sales at Dixons made on the Internet are collected at the store' (Jeremy Fennel, E-Commerce Director, 2011).

Distribution and logistics

Dixons Carphone's distribution hub in Newark, Nottinghamshire, is the UK's largest distribution warehouse. This facility serves the stores and manages the flow of products. According to the UK Logistics Director (Tim Allinson, 2011) people are key—from operators to leaders—as they make the processes work and enable the company to meet customers' key performance indicators, for example delivering on time and in full and picking accurately. 'We measure how many orders we picked and how many errors we've made. Without this link in the chain the products don't get to the customers' homes and don't get to the stores. Agility is also important to this part of the operation as we have to be able to respond to changing demand in a timely fashion.'

Each aspect of the business has taken on board the importance of the new strategy and the role that this part of the company has to play in delivering the transformation strategy.

The Marketing Mix and Implementation

The mix was adapted to reflect the strategic initiatives and this had implications for implementation.

- *Place*: store formats were redesigned and the 2-in-1 Currys and PC World store format was rolled out. Other changes in-store included the introduction of play tables to allow customers to explore products, and storyboards to help with selecting complex television and satellite products (interesting to note that this initiative was suggested by a member of staff, and then applied across the business). Distribution and supply were streamlined and made more efficient and cost-effective through the development of a high-tech distribution centre in Nottinghamshire.
- *Service*: KNOWHOW was launched replacing a myriad of different customer case and support services. The new after-sales service and support brand offers a multiple touch-point approach to customer care from the 'cradle to the grave' customer experience. KNOWHOW services provide delivery and installation; help with setting up and upgrading complex technology products; help and support online, on the phone and in-store; and repair and protection to give peace of mind when things go wrong. Additionally, the Fives training scheme was introduced to ensure that staff in-store and throughout the business have the *right* knowledge and behaviour to respond to all customer needs regardless of where they 'touched' the business.
- *Product*: The product portfolio was revised to offer wider product choice from brand leaders like Apple, but also to include own-brands; Currys and PC World Essentials range included televisions, DVD, white goods, computers, keyboards, printers and other peripheral devices.
- *Promotion*: significant investment was made in repositioning of the brand aims to engage the interest of consumers in different target markets. And customer service rather than products feature strongly in advertising campaigns.
- *Price*: rapid innovation of high-tech products drives up volumes of purchasing and this means pricing was tailored to follow market demand.

Success was measured by monitoring customer satisfaction, customer advocacy (recommendations and referrals), profitability, sales, tracking store transformations.

Debrief

Dixons Retail has confounded its critics by succeeding in transforming its business model by shifting from a product-led to a service-led model that puts the customer at the heart of the business. Being informed by the marketing environment, the needs of the customers, the behaviour of the competitors and the contribution of the staff, the company has built a strong new competitive positioning.

The transformation strategy applied by Dixons is a solid example of how the marketing concept can help a business succeed. This case has highlighted the benefits of setting corporate goals that acknowledge the importance of meeting and exceeding customer needs better than the competition. Furthermore, it has emphasized the importance of an integrated effort across the business; the strategy reinforces the need for everyone in the business to be involved with creating customer satisfaction. Nevertheless, the business environment is constantly changing; major competitors, such as Best Buy, have made a strategic withdrawal because, although their 'big box stores . . . delivered exceptional customer satisfaction scores', they did not have the national reach to offer this experience to customers on a national scale in the UK. Additionally, Comet was sold off for £2 with a massive debt burden, which leaves the market open for Dixons. However, even in this climate the biggest challenge for Dixons is to ensure that its transformation strategy continues to gather momentum and drive the business forward.

Dixons has continued to develop its operation and find new ways to stay ahead of the competition. Online it has fought off the challenge of other competitors by improving price perceptions. The multichannel operation enables costs to be kept low, and so it can compete with Amazon and other online discounters operating in the consumer electronics market. A merger with Carphone Warehouse in 2014 helped to expand the depth and breadth of product ranges, especially in the telecoms markets. This increased the brand's store base in the UK but also opened up other opportunities, for example to extend services into the provision of domestic heating, lighting and security services, through the use of mobile phones. The move also increased buying power and created further market growth opportunities. Sebastian James, Chief Executive, said, 'This is a genuine merger of equals founded on core strategic principles rather than straight cost cuts.' He also confirmed one of the drivers of this move to be changing external market circumstances. By this he meant that products are converging and so it made sense for the leading electrical and telecoms firms to do the same (Garside and Farrell, 2014).

Questions

1. Consider the extent to which Dixons Carphone has applied a formal marketing planning process, when devising its marketing strategy. Illustrate your answer with specific examples.

2. Discuss how each of the business functions explored in this case have contributed to the success of Dixons' marketing strategy plan.

3. Explain how the KNOWHOW customer service brand has contributed to the performance of the marketing strategy.

4. Debate the extent to which the adopting of the marketing philosophy has transformed Dixons Carphone.

5. Find current evidence from the external marketing environment which is likely to have implications for the future direction of Dixons Carphone's marketing strategy.

This case study was prepared by Fiona Ellis-Chadwick, Senior Lecturer, Loughborough University.

References

Based on: Baker, R. (2011) Best Buy to withdraw from UK, Marketing Week, 7 November, http://www.marketingweek.co.uk/bestbuy-to -withdraw-from-uk/3031624.article; Black Book (2010) Dixons Retail: Ambitious self-help in the midst of structural pressure, Bernstein Research, 77–93; Dixons Carphone (2015) Corporate profile, http:// www.dixonscarphone.com/investors/understanding-dixons-carphone/ corporate-profile; Dixons Retail PLC group Presentation, September 2011; Dixons Retail PLC (2007) Press Releases Extra Colleagues for the Newark Distributions centre, http://www.dixonsretail.com/dixons/ en/mediacentre/mediapressreleases?id=413.

Garside, J. and S. Farrell (2014) Carphone Warehouse and Dixons agree £3.8bn merger, The Guardian, 15 May, http://www.theguardian.com/ business/2014/may/15/carphone-warehouse-dixons-agree-merger; Kesa Electricals (2012) Sale of Comet, http://kesaelectricals.com/ index.php?cID=304&cType=news; Lawson, A (2013), Dixons powers ahead with renewal and transformation plan, Retail week, 28 June.

CASE 36
Proudly Made in Africa—The Value Added in Africa (VAA) Branding Story

" Delivering beautiful, ethical goods from Africa to the world, reliably. "

(CEO VAA, CONALL O'CAOIMH, 2014)

The idea of finding a way to provide African producers with access to markets where they could export shelf-ready products came to the CEO and co-founder of VAA when he was on a trip to Mozambique in 1996. Conall O'Caoimh saw large 50 kilogram bags of cashew nuts being exported and thought that there must be a way to allow producers to trade in value-added goods—supporting them to export products in ready-to-export packets.

However, it would be over a decade before his idea came to fruition. After years of working in development charities he became further convinced of the need to support African producers in overcoming cultural and institutional barriers to penetrating markets with value-added goods. While working in policy and advocacy roles within these charities, the 'cashew nut' idea was always at the back of his mind, and in 2005–06 he, along with two other co-founders who shared his passion and belief in the idea, prepared a business plan and set about putting the idea into action. With initial funds coming from family and friends, the organisation was registered as a company in October 2008; Value Added in Africa (VAA) was open for business. Table C36.1 gives an overview of VAA.

At the start-up stage, the founders were working from a charitable model where they believed that retail businesses would support them because of the 'good work' they were doing, but they soon realised that businesses need to make profits and would only engage with VAA if what it was offering made business sense. Creating social value alone was not enough. They moved to a social enterprise model enabling better engagement with businesses, offering services that businesses would want to take on and moving towards becoming self-financing. VAA acted as 'sales reps for producers' and spent time trying to engage buyers; however, it did not achieve significant sales—it was waiting for 'better products' to offer retailers. VAA knew the benefits of the manufactured African-made retail-ready products, but also recognised the outstanding challenges it had to overcome in order to advance its mission (see Table C36.2).

Addressing the Challenges

Understanding these challenges, VAA continued to work with African producers, building their capacity and organising meetings throughout Europe, but in a more focused way than before through the packaging design programme, which involved top-level Irish and British design companies who worked with African producers to

TABLE C36.1 Overview of VAA	
Category	**Non-profit social enterprise**
Established	In 2008, by Co-Founders Conall O'Caoimh, Michelle Hardiman and Professor Matt Murphy
Mission	To open channels for African businesses into international markets
Purpose/role	VAA was formed to act as a 'trade facilitator' between African producers with retail-ready products and European businesses
Objectives	• To alleviate poverty among communities in Africa through helping the development of sustainable livelihoods and raising awareness through corporate and social responsibility • To make it 'normal' for retailers and brands to source sustainable products from Africa • To make it 'normal' for African countries to process their resources before they export them

TABLE C36.2 The benefits and challenges for manufactured goods from Africa	
Benefits	**Challenges**
• Security of supply	• Understanding of the marketplace
• New and different products	• Product consistency and volume
• Cost advantages	• Infrastructural and institutional barriers
• Preferential tariff rates	• Finding appropriate products
• Traceability and transparency	• Capacity and skills
• A good story	• Distance from the marketplace
• Less wastage	
• Income and community development	
• Creation of jobs and a boost to the regional economies	

Source: Brouder and Tulej (2015)

redesign their brand identities for the European market, as well as the networking programme, whose aim was to create a forum for African business leaders to network and exchange business ideas. However, one of the main challenges faced by VAA was in addressing the retail buyer's poor comprehension of African produce and an uneducated bias against African finished goods. VAA decided to focus on its marketing communications strategy in an attempt to educate and inform buyers and consumers alike of the quality African produce and the consistency of this produce for the marketplace. As a result, VAA embarked on a process facilitated by Brand Led Growth (www.brandledgrowth.com)

through which it revisited its core values and vision and rethought the VAA strategy.

'Our concern at the time was that there was potentially a lot of African brands whose reputation we would need to build with consumers, and this would be a challenge, given limited marketing resources . . . So a big impetus for us was to build a strong reputation for a single brand entity'. (Donogh Lane, CEO Brand Led Growth)

A number of stakeholders were invited to participate in that process (producers, advertisers, buyers, customers, VAA board, and creatives), in which they identified the core values of the brand (see Figure C36.1).

FIGURE C36.1
VAA brand values

Quality
• Relevant international industry standard for specific sector: Has certification (e.g. ISO 22,000, BRC, etc).
• For smaller companies a 'robust quality system' is accepted and VAA have criteria for identifying that.

Origin: Africa
• Minimum 65% inputs African sourced, before packaging – may vary depending on how well the supply sector has developed in that country.

Ethically Made
• Social compliace or Certification or Transparency process by a reputable independent standards body, (e.g. Ethical Trading Initiative, SEDEX, Better Work, Aim Process, GSCP, etc)
• For smaller companies a 'robust system of management' for quality and social responsibility is accepted –with conditions of timed steps towards external compliance systems
• Fair Trade ingredients used if available

Source: www.proudlymadeinafrica.org

Proudly Made In Africa Brand was Born

The new concept was tested with stakeholders and revised a number of times. Up to this point, there was no visual identity. Once agreed on the concept, they engaged a company called Dynamo to help build the brand identity, the look and feel, and to create the visual that is the Proudly Made in Africa (PMIA) brand (see Figure C36.2). After thorough testing and research, VAA launched the PMIA brand in 2012 as a mechanism by which buyers and consumers could recognise authentic African products. PMIA is a standard that African producers can aim to achieve through stringent procedures, as the brand ensures that products are quality assured, ethically sourced, manufactured from locally grown materials and socially beneficial.

African businesses engaging with VAA wanted to ensure that they met the standards as required by the PMIA brand as a form of certification (see Table C36.3).

Brett Beach, Co-CEO and Co-founder of Madécasse Chocolate, was keen to get the PMIA brand on its products to reinforce the quality of the product offering.

'PMIA embodies what we stand for, which is adding value in Madagascar, as a way to create jobs there . . . it's not only a way to improve prosperity, it's also about the quality of the product. We want to demonstrate to the market that the continent that produces the best ingredients can also introduce the best products'.

FIGURE C36.2
Proudly Made in Africa (PMIA) brand

PROUDLY MADE IN AFRICA

PRODUCTS THAT BUILD COMMUNITIES

VAA verified the Madécasse value chain and in 2014 granted Madécasse a licence to use the Proudly Made in Africa brand on its packaging. Madécasse, with the PMIA certification, is now available in 240 Waitrose stores in the UK, 2,100 stores throughout the USA, and in selected gourmet stores in Ireland.

The Future for VAA

Value Added in Africa emerged as a result of the passion of a small group of people who believed that change could be made. It is a relatively young organisation that has achieved much with limited resources in a competitive market environment and has stayed true to its mission. It had to adapt its business model and review organisational strategies on an ongoing basis, learning as it developed, and continuing to learn from each opportunity and risk it takes. The PMIA brand and standard has contributed to the development of the business, providing recognition

TABLE C36.3 Sample of Businesses working with VAA		
Company	**Product offering**	**Relationship with VAA**
Meru Herbs, Kenya	Produces a range of organic herbal teas, gourmet fruit jams and tomato based sauces.	• 90% of its produce is exported to Europe and Japan, and 10% is sold to the local market. Helped connect with potential new international buyers, formulation of a marketing strategy and product packaging. • Facilitated in gaining new wholesale customers in England and Scotland.
Black Mamba, Swaziland	Produces a range of chilli sauces.	• Supported in fulfilling EU compliance standards in the labelling of its products. • Facilitated in gaining a new wholesale customer in England.
Madécasse, Madagascar	Gourmet chocolate made from bean to bar in Madagascar.	• VAA verified the Madécasse value chain and granted Madécasse a licence to use the PMIA brand. • Available in Waitrose stores in the UK, speciality stores in 10 European countries, and selected stores in Ireland, the USA and Australia.
Iriaini Tea Coop, Kenya	Tea cooperative.	• Supported own brand and packaging development, under the name of 'Single Garden'.

Source: Conall O'Caoimh and Siobhan McGee (2015)

>>

and an integral identity between African produce and quality. It is hoped that over time this brand will be as recognisable as other brands such as Fairtrade.

Questions

1. Based on your own experience and awareness, what are your perceptions of African-produced goods on your supermarket shelf?

2. What do you consider are the top three main challenges for Value Added in Africa?

3. Based on your understanding of this case, what do perceive is/are the significance of the PMIA brand image from a consumer and retail buyer's perspective?

4. Review the strength of the PMIA brand's position in the marketplace using the six elements of brand positioning.

This case study was written by Christina O'Connor, Lecturer in Marketing, Maynooth University and Siobhán McGee, Proudly Made in Africa Fellow of Business and Development, University College Dublin

References

Based on: Brouder, A.-M. and S. Tulej (2015) Africa: Making it#- A UK Business Perspective, http://www.proudlymadeinafrica.org/images/uploads/docs/VAA-FFF_Africa_Making_It_-_A_UK_Business_Perspective_report.pdf, 22–4; www.proudlymadeinafrica.org; www.brandledgrowth.com; www.africacashewalliance.com; www.madecasse.com

CHAPTER 19

Analysing Competitors and Creating a Competitive Advantage

If you don't have a competitive advantage, don't compete.

JACK WELCH, FORMER CHIEF EXECUTIVE OF GENERAL ELECTRIC

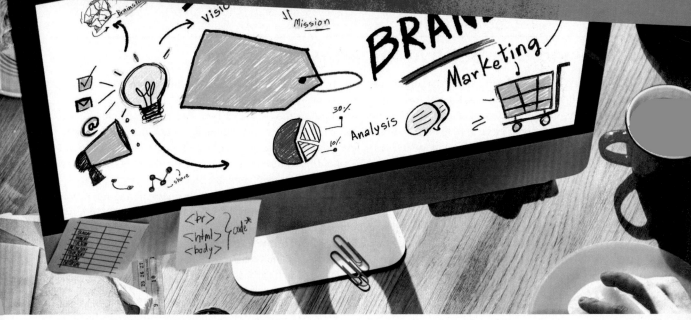

LEARNING OBJECTIVES

After reading this chapter, you should be able to:

1 describe the determinants of industry attractiveness
2 explain how to analyse competitors
3 distinguish between differentiation and cost leader strategies
4 discuss the sources of competitive advantage
5 discuss the value chain
6 explain how to create and maintain a differential advantage
7 explain how to create and maintain a cost leadership position
8 discuss the nature of competitive behaviour
9 explain the key elements of a competitive marketing strategy

S atisfying customers is central to the marketing concept, but it is not enough to guarantee success. The real question is whether a company can satisfy customers better than the competition. For example, many car manufacturers market cars that give customer satisfaction in terms of appearance, reliability and performance. They meet the basic requirements necessary to compete. Customer choice, however, will depend on creating more value than the competition. Extra value is brought about by establishing a competitive advantage—a topic that will be examined later in this chapter.

Since corporate performance depends on both customer satisfaction and creating greater value than the competition, companies need to understand their competitors as well as their customers. By understanding its competitors, a firm can better predict their reactions to any marketing initiative that the firm might make, and exploit any weaknesses. Competitor analysis is thus crucial to the successful implementation of marketing strategy. Our discussion of competitors in this chapter begins by examining competitive industry structure, then explains how to create competitive and differential advantage, then cost leadership. Finally we explore the key elements associated with developing a competitive marketing strategy.

Analysing Competitive Industry Structure

An **industry** is a group of companies that market products that are close substitutes for each other. There is more to understanding an 'industry' and how it works than the core product or service being sold. Commonly we refer to the oil, computer or retail industry. Some industries are more profitable than others. In the past the car, steel, coal and textile industries have been highly profitable, but in more recent years they have had poor profitability records, whereas recently the creative industries, (e.g. television, publishing, web development), pharmaceuticals and soft drinks industries have enjoyed high profits. Not all of this difference can be explained by the fact that one industry provides better customer satisfaction than another. Other determinants of industry attractiveness and long-run profitability shape the rules of competition. These are the threat of entry of new competitors, the threat of substitutes, the bargaining power of buyers and of suppliers, and the rivalry between the existing competitors (Porter, 1980). The intensity of these forces shapes an industry and its levels of performance. Their influence is shown diagrammatically in Figure 19.1, which shows what is known as the Porter model of competitive industry structure. Each of the 'five forces' in turn comprises a number of elements that, together, combine to determine the strength of each force and its effect on the degree of competition. Each force is discussed below.

The threat of new entrants

New entrants can raise the level of competition in an industry, which may ultimately reduce its attractiveness. For example, Starbucks is entering the 'coffee capsules market' to take on market leaders Nespresso. Nestlé owns the Nespresso brand and has made significant investment in building the market for this product in Europe using an extensive advertising campaign fronted by Hollywood actor George Clooney, which led to a 20 per cent rise in sales. Nespresso's high levels of profitability have attracted many new entrants including Green Mountain, Côte D'Or, and Kenco (see Exhibit 19.1) (Simonian and Lucas, 2012). The threat of new entrants depends on the barriers to entry. High entry barriers exist in some industries (e.g. pharmaceuticals), whereas other industries are much easier to enter (e.g. restaurants).

 Scan the QR code to see how Nespresso uses Celebrity endorsement to differentiate the brand from the competition.

Key **entry barriers** include:
- economies of scale
- capital requirements
- switching costs
- access to distribution
- expected retaliation.

For present competitors, industry attractiveness can be increased by raising entry barriers. High promotional and R&D expenditures, and clearly communicated retaliatory actions to entry are some methods of raising

FIGURE 19.1
The Porter model of competitive industry structure

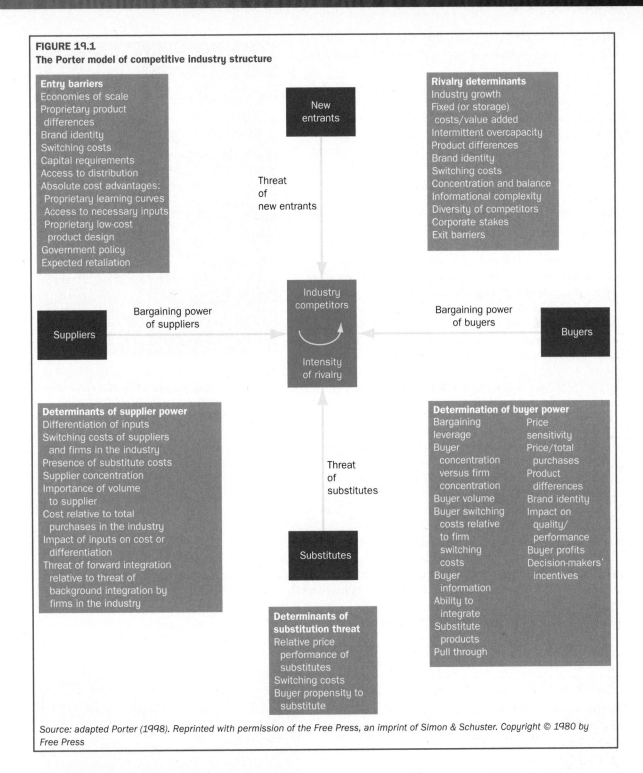

Source: adapted Porter (1998). Reprinted with permission of the Free Press, an imprint of Simon & Schuster. Copyright © 1980 by
Free Press

barriers as in the situation with the Nespresso coffee pods. Nestlé continues to make a significant investments
in these areas. Other ways of raising barriers are by taking out patents and developing strong relationships/
partnerships with suppliers and/or distributors. Some managerial actions can unwittingly lower barriers. For
example, new product designs that dramatically lower manufacturing costs can ease entry for newcomers.

The bargaining power of suppliers

The cost of raw materials, components and intellectual skills can have a major bearing on a company's
profitability. The higher the bargaining power of suppliers, the higher these costs. For example when Apple

decided to adopt Intel processors there were lengthy extensive negotiations. The bargaining power of suppliers will be high when:

- there are many buyers and few dominant suppliers
- there are differentiated highly valued products
- suppliers threaten to integrate forward into the industry
- buyers do not threaten to integrate backward into supply
- the industry is not a key customer group to the suppliers.

A company can reduce the bargaining power of suppliers by seeking new sources of supply, threatening to integrate backward into supply, and designing standardized components so that many suppliers are capable of producing them.

Backwards integration means that a buyer (like Apple) purchases the supplier and a form of vertical integration takes place. Currently, there is speculation that Apple might switch from using Intel chips and replace them with ARM (processor chips made by Apple, through an acquisition of PA Semi), but this move has far-reaching implications that would mean popular Apple apps such as iTunes, TextEdit and Logic Pro would need to be rewritten (Gruman, 2015).

EXHIBIT 19.1
Nespresso aims to retain its competitive advantage in the coffee capsule market by using celebrity endorsement of the brand

The bargaining power of buyers

The concentration of buyers can lower manufacturers' bargaining power. For example, the large retailers in Europe (e.g. Dixons Carphone, Carrefour and Bauhaus GMbH) buy from many suppliers in large volumes and this has increased the bargaining power. The bargaining power of buyers is greater when:

- there are few dominant buyers and many sellers
- products are standardized
- buyers threaten to integrate backwards into the industry
- suppliers do not threaten to integrate forwards into the buyer's industry
- the industry is not a key supplying group for buyers.

Manufacturing companies in the industry can attempt to lower buyer power by increasing the number of buyers they sell to, threatening to integrate forwards into the buyer's industry and producing highly valued, differentiated products. Apple has become a leading retailer around the world with its dedicated, high-tech, Apple product stores, see Exhibit 19.2.

Threat of substitutes

The presence of substitute products can lower industry attractiveness and profitability because these put a constraint on price levels. For example, tea and coffee are fairly close substitutes in many European countries. Raising the price of coffee, therefore, would make tea more attractive. The threat of substitute products depends on:

- buyers' willingness to substitute
- the relative price and performance of substitutes
- the costs of switching to substitutes.

The threat of substitute products can be lowered by building up switching costs, or for example, by creating a strong distinctive brand and maintaining a price differential in line with perceived customer values. If these tactics fail to deter a rival from launching a substitute product, the incumbent is faced with the following options: copy the substitute; copy but build

EXHIBIT 19.2
The design of Apple's Store in Shanghai reflects the innovativeness of its products

in a differential advantage; form a strategic alliance with the rival; buy the rival; or move to a new market. For example, BlackBerry products manufacturer Research in Motion (RIM) saw its market share plummet as adopters switch to faster touchscreen smartphones like iPhone and Samsung Galaxy (Garside, 2012). MySpace was a pioneer in the world of social media: it introduced the concept of friends' social networks on a large scale. But once Facebook was launched and started to grow, it provided people with more reasons to belong to its network than to that of its rival MySpace (Dredge, 2015).

Industry competitors

The intensity of rivalry between competitors in an industry will depend on the following factors.

- *Structure of the competition*: there is more intense rivalry when there are a large number of small competitors or a few equally balanced competitors, and less rivalry when a clear market leader exists with a large cost advantage.
- *Structure of costs*: high fixed costs encourage price-cutting to fill capacity.
- *Degree of differentiation*: basic commodity products encourage rivalry, while highly differentiated products that are hard to copy are associated with less intense rivalry.
- *Switching costs*: rivalry is reduced when switching costs are high because the product is specialized, the customer has invested a lot of resources in learning how to use the product or has made tailor-made investments that are worthless with other products and suppliers. For example, a product might be customized, production, logistical or marketing operations might be geared to using the equipment of a particular supplier (e.g. computer systems), or retraining may be required as a result of a switch to another supplier.
- *Strategic objectives*: when competitors are pursuing build strategies, competition is likely to be more intense than when playing **hold** or **harvesting objectives**.
- *Exit barriers*: when barriers to leaving an industry are high due to such factors as lack of opportunities elsewhere, high vertical integration, emotional barriers or the high cost of closing down plant, rivalry will be more intense than when exit barriers are low.

Companies need to be careful not to spoil a situation of competitive stability. They need to balance their own position against the well-being of the industry as a whole. For example, an intense price or promotional war may gain a few percentage points in market share but lead to an overall fall in long-run industry profitability as competitors respond to these moves. It is sometimes better to protect industry structure than follow short-term self-interest.

A major threat to favourable industry structure is the use of a no-frills, low-price strategy by a minor player seeking positional advantage. For example, the launch of generic products in the pharmaceutical and airline industries has lowered overall profitability.

Despite meeting customers' needs with high-quality, good-value products, companies can 'compete away' the rewards. An intensive competitive environment means that the value created by companies in satisfying customer needs is given away to buyers through lower prices, dissipated through costly marketing battles (e.g. advertising wars) or passed on to powerful suppliers through higher prices for raw materials and components.

In Europe, the competitive structure of industries was fundamentally changed with the advent of the single European market. The lifting of barriers to trade between countries has radically altered industry structures by affecting the underlying determinants. For example, the threat of new entrants and the growth in buyer/supplier power through acquisition or merger are fundamentally changing the competitive climate of many industries. See Marketing in Action 19.1 to find out more about the world's most competitive industry.

MARKETING IN ACTION 19.1
Rovio and Supercell Battle for Market Share in the Intensely Competitive Apps Market

There are more mobile devices in the world than there are people, according to the US Census Bureau. So it is perhaps no surprise that the competitive pressure for mobile app developers is intense. What also makes this such a highly competitive industry are the low entry barriers, the large number of competitors with similar capabilities, low switching costs for the customers, and many competitors trying to build market share. As a result there are apps for almost every aspect of modern life, for example games, photo editors, magic pianos, healthy living.

»

The app industry is reliant on downloads and revenues, but the increase in the quality of freely downloadable games has succeeded in getting customers to switch to new products. The industry has been affected by this change in pricing structure, and free downloads have come to dominate. So, companies competing in this market must find different ways to ensure a strong revenue stream and create competitive advantage. Some examples follow.

Rovio, a Finnish developer of *Angry Birds*, a highly successful mobile game app, regularly tops the charts in the app market. In 2014, *Angry Birds* was downloaded by 600 million mobile gamers. Despite the popularity of this game, the company has seen its profits fall. Part of the reason for this was a reduction in sales from associated merchandise, for example soft toys, clothing, gifts. So the company had to find other ways to extend the franchise around this game title, for example the *Angry Birds Movie*. It is also developing new apps for the games market, for example Nibblers.

Supercell is also a Finnish developer and one of the fastest growing technology companies in Europe. The company is known for producing successful game apps, for example *Clash of the Clans*, *Hay Day* and *Boom Beach*. Supercell has managed to take market share from market-leading app developers like Electronic Arts. The key to its success has been its ability to successfully enter Asian markets, something that other developers have failed to achieve.

These are just two examples of successful app companies. Finnish app developers seem to have been able to garner competitive advantage from a number of sources to ensure their success in this highly competitive industry—for example, distinctive graphics that have global appeal, successful targeting of Apple's iPad and smartphone platforms with high-quality apps that have been through extensive product testing prior to launch, and by developing creative pricing strategies.

Based on: Boren (2014); Sinclair (2015); Rovio (2015); Kuittinen (2013, 2014); Reisinger (2015); Cellan-Jones (2015)

Competitor Analysis

The analysis of how industry structure affects long-run profitability has shown the need to understand and monitor competitors. Their actions can spoil an otherwise attractive industry, their weaknesses can be a target for exploitation, and their response to a firm's marketing initiatives can have a major impact on their success. Indeed, companies that focus on competitors' actions have been found to achieve better business performance than those who pay less attention to their competitors (Noble, Sinha and Kumar, 2002). Competitive information can be obtained from marketing research surveys, secondary sources (e.g. the web, trade magazines, newspaper articles), analyzing competitors' products and gathering competitors' sales literature.

Competitor analysis seeks to answer five key questions.

1 Who are our competitors?
2 What are their strengths and weaknesses?
3 What are their strategic objectives and thrust?
4 What are their strategies?
5 What are their response patterns?

These issues are summarized in Figure 19.2. Each question will now be examined.

Who are our competitors?

We need to take a wide view of potential competition. If only those companies that are producing technically similar products are considered to be the competition, (e.g. paint companies) it is possible to miss other sources of competition. For example, by ignoring companies that produce substitute products that perform a similar function (e.g. polyurethane varnish companies) and those that solve a problem or eliminate it in a dissimilar way (e.g. PVC double-glazing companies). The actions of all of these types of competitors can affect the performance of a company and therefore should be monitored. Their responses also need to be assessed as they will determine the outcome of any competitive move that the company may wish to make, which can result in loss of market share or being made irrelevant. Making the competition irrelevant is a strategic option discussed later in the chapter.

The marketing environment needs to be scanned for potential entrants into the industry. These can take two forms: entrants with technically similar products and those invading the market with substitute products. Companies with similar core competences to the present incumbents may pose the threat of entering with technically similar products. For example, Apple's skills in computer electronics provided the springboard for it to become market leader in several key technology markets, for example the portable music player market with its iPod brand, tablet computers with its iPad, and mobile phone with its iPhone. The source of companies entering with substitute products may be more difficult to locate, however. A technological breakthrough may transform an industry by rendering the old product obsolete, for example the computer replacing the typewriter. In such instances it is difficult to locate the source of the substitute product well in advance. Figure 19.3 illustrates this competitive arena.

What are their strengths and weaknesses?

Having identified our competitors the next stage is to complete a **competitor audit** in order to assess their relative strengths and weaknesses. Understanding competitor strengths and weaknesses is an important prerequisite for developing a competitor strategy and identifying a competitor's vulnerabilities.

The process of assessing competitors' strengths and weaknesses may take place as part of a marketing audit (see Chapter 18). As much internal, market and customer information should be gathered as is needed. For example, financial data concerning profitability, profit margins, sales and investment levels, market data relating to price levels, market share and distribution channels used, and customer data concerning awareness of brand names, and perceptions of brand and company image, product and service quality, and selling ability may be relevant.

Not all of this information will be easily accessible. Management needs to decide the extent to which each element of information is worth pursuing. For example, a decision is required regarding how much expenditure is to be allocated to measuring customer awareness and perceptions through marketing research.

This process of data gathering needs to be managed so that information is available to compare our company with its competitors on the *key factors for success* in the industry. A three-stage process can then be used.

1   Identify key factors for success in the industry

These should be restricted to about six to eight factors otherwise the analysis becomes too diffuse (Macdonald and Wilson, 2011). Which factors to use is a matter of managerial judgement. They may be functional (such as financial strength or flexible production) or generic (for example, the ability to respond quickly to customer needs, innovativeness, or the capability to provide other sales services). Since these factors are critical for success they should be used to compare our company with its competitors.

2   Rate our company and competitors on each key success factor using a rating scale

Each company is given a score on each success factor using a rating device. This may be a scale ranging from 1 (very poor) to 5 (very good); this results in a set of company capability profiles (an example is given in Figure 19.4). Our company is rated alongside two competitors on six key success factors. Compared with our company, competitor 1 is relatively strong regarding technical assistance to customers and access to international distribution channels, but relatively weak on product quality. Competitor 2 is relatively strong on international distribution channels but relatively weak on innovativeness, financial strength and having a well-qualified workforce.

3   Consider the implications for competitive strategy

The competitive profile analysis helps to identify possible competitive strategies. This analysis would suggest that our company should consider taking steps to improve technical assistance to customers to

---

FIGURE 19.2
Competitor analysis

Identifying competitors
• Product form • Product substitutes • Generics
• New entrants

Audit competitor capabilities
• Financial • Technical • Managerial
• Marketing assets • Strengths and weaknesses

Infer competitor objectives and strategic thrust
• Build • Hold • Harvest
• Growth directions

Deduce competitor strategies
• Target segments • Differential advantages
• Competitive scope • Cost leadership

Estimate competitor response patterns
• Retaliator • Complacent • Hemmed-in
• Selective • Unpredictable

match or exceed competitor 1's capability on this factor. At the moment, our company enjoys a differential advantage over competitor 1 on product quality. Our strength in innovativeness should be used to maintain this differential advantage and competitor 1's moves to improve product quality should be monitored carefully.

Competitor 2 is weaker overall than competitor 1 and our company. However, it has considerable strengths in having access to international distribution channels. Given our company's weakness in this area, a strategic alliance with or take-over of competitor 2 might be sensible if our company's objective is to expand internationally. Our company's financial strength and competitor 2's financial weakness suggests that a take-over might be feasible.

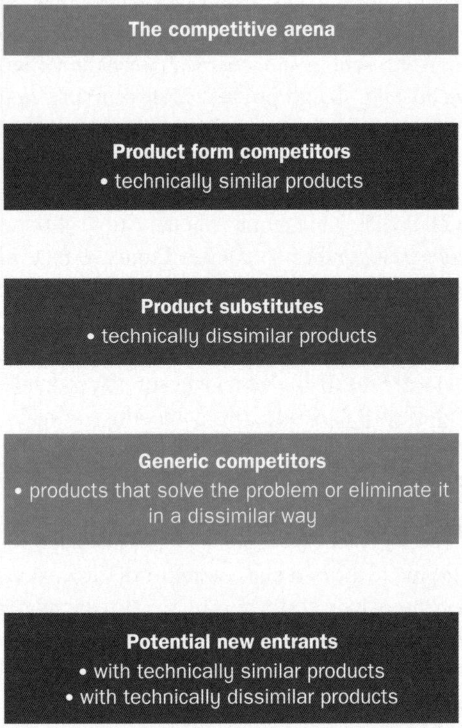

What are their strategic objectives and thrust?

The third part of competitor analysis is to infer their *strategic objectives*. In Chapter 18, we discussed how companies might determine their broader strategic aims by deciding which products they need to sell into particular markets. Likewise, knowing the strategic thrust of competitors can help with strategic marketing planning decision-making and also set the overall direction which defines the target market (Varadarajan, 2010). Equally, it is useful to know which strategic objectives are being pursued by competitors, because their response pattern and marketing strategies may depend upon their objectives. Knowing whether a competitor is planning to build, hold, harvest or **divest** particular products and/or strategic business units is also important for planning.

Determining a competitor's objectives can be difficult, as information of a strategic nature can be hard to come by. However, by studying market conditions it is possible to garner insight into what objectives a competitor might be seeking to achieve, and then infer the possible implementation actions it might pursue in order to succeed. Table 19.1 summarizes the market conditions and implementation actions that might occur when a competitor starts to pursue a particular strategic marketing objective.

FIGURE 19.3
Competitor identification

> The competitive arena

> **Product form competitors**
> • technically similar products

> **Product substitutes**
> • technically dissimilar products

> **Generic competitors**
> • products that solve the problem or eliminate it in a dissimilar way

> **Potential new entrants**
> • with technically similar products
> • with technically dissimilar products

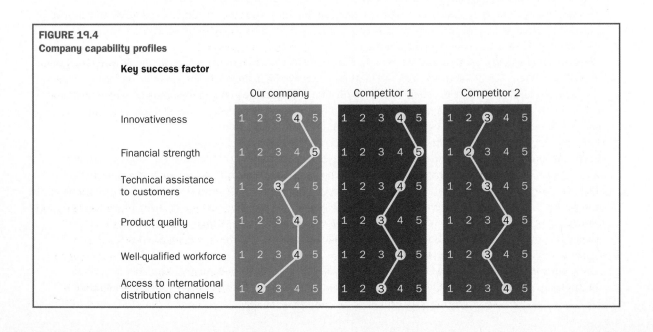

FIGURE 19.4
Company capability profiles

Key success factor

TABLE 19.1 Market conditions and implementation actions related to different marketing objectives

Strategic objectives	Market conditions	Implementation actions
Build	Growth markets Exploitable competitor weaknesses Firm has exploitable strengths, capabilities & resources	**Market expansion** e.g., attracting new customers; finding ways to develop new uses for the goods; increasing the frequency of use **Winning marketing** share through innovative application of the marketing mix e.g., exploiting new channels to market; new products **Mergers and acquisition** **Forming strategic alliances**
Hold	Firm is market leader in a mature or declining state Costs exceed the possible benefits of building market share	**Continually monitoring the competition** e.g., in a market characterized by competitive stability where no one is willing to destabilize the industry structure. Monitoring is necessary to check that there are no significant changes in competitor behaviour **Confronting the competition** e.g., where rivalry is intense and strategic action may be required to defend market share from aggressive challenges
Harvest	Market in decline Core of loyal customers exist Firm has future new products	**Eliminate R&D expenditure** e.g., reduce investment in the products **Reformulation of product** e.g., to reduce costs **Rationalize of product lines** e.g., cutting product variants, keeping best sellers **Reduce marketing spend** e.g., cutting promotional budgets & spend on advertising **Increase prices** as loyal customer will continue to buy
Divest	Low market share in declining markets Too expensive to revive products Removal will not impact on other products	**Exit the market** e.g., get out quickly to minimize costs and potential future losses
Niche	Niche market opportunities Small budget available Opportunities to create competitive advantage	**Market segmentation** e.g. survey market, apply segmentation strategies to identify underserved market opportunities. **Focused R&D** e.g. focus on developing sustainable differential advantage **Differential advantage** e.g. understanding the needs of the customer group & satisfying their needs better than the competition **Thinking small** e.g. emphasis is on high margins not high volume

What are their strategies?

At the product service level, competitor analysis will attempt to deduce positioning strategy. This involves assessing a competitor's target market and differential advantage of its product and/or service. The marketing mix strategies (e.g. price levels, media used for promotion, and distribution channels) may indicate target market, and marketing research into customer perceptions can be used to assess relative differential advantages.

Companies and competitors should be monitored continuously for changes in positioning strategy. For example, Volvo's traditional positioning strategy, based on safety, has been modified to give more emphasis to performance and style enabling the company to compete with other high performance cars.

Strategies can also be defined in terms of competitive scope. For example, are competitors attempting to service the whole market or a few segments of a particular **niche**? If a niche player, is it likely that they will be content to stay in that segment or will they use it as a beachhead to move into other segments in the future? Japanese companies are renowned for their use of small niche markets as springboards for market segment expansion (e.g. the small car segments in the USA and Europe).

Competitors may use cost-leadership, focusing on cost-reducing measures rather than expensive product development and promotional strategies. (Cost leadership will be discussed in more detail later in this chapter.) If competitors are following this strategy it is more likely that they will be focusing research and development expenditure on process rather than product development in a bid to reduce manufacturing costs.

What are their response patterns?

A key consideration in making a strategic or tactical move is the likely response of competitors. Indeed, it is a major objective of competitor analysis to be able to predict competitor response to market and competitive changes. A competitor's past behaviour is also a guide to what they might do in the future. Market leaders often try to control competitor response by retaliatory action. These are called *retaliatory* competitors because they can be relied on to respond aggressively to competitive challenges. For example, Amazon bought out LoveFilm, which offered streaming video and DVD rentals, in a competitive move against US rival Netflix. Amazon Instant video service provides a service for consumers in the UK and Germany. Amazon planned to challenge Netflix as market leader in the UK with this move (Sweney, 2014).

By punishing competitor moves, market leaders can condition competitors to behave in predicted ways— for example, by not taking advantage of a price rise by the leader. It is not only market leaders that retaliate aggressively. Where management is known to be assertive, and our move is likely to have a major impact on their performance, a strong response is usual.

The history, traditions and managerial personalities of competitors also have an influence on competitive response. Some markets are characterized by years of competitive stability with little serious strategic challenge to any of the incumbents. This can breed complacency, with predictably slow reaction times to new challenges. For example, innovation that offers superior customer value may be dismissed as a fad and unworthy of serious attention.

Another situation where competitors are unlikely to respond is where their previous strategies have restricted their scope for retaliation. An example of such a *hemmed-in competitor* was a major manufacturer of car number plates that were sold to car dealerships. A new company was started by an ex-employee who focused on one geographical area, supplying the same quality product but with extra discount. The national supplier could not respond since to give discount in that particular region would have meant granting the discount nationwide.

A fourth type of competitor may respond *selectively*. Because of tradition or beliefs about the relative effectiveness of marketing instruments, a competitor may respond to some competitive moves but not others. For example, extra sales promotion expenditures may be matched but advertising increases to, say, build brand awareness may be ignored. Another reason for selective response is the varying degree of visibility of marketing actions. For example, giving extra price discounts may be highly visible, but providing distributors with extra support (e.g. training, sales literature, loans) may be less discernible.

A final type of competitor is totally *unpredictable* in its response pattern. Sometimes there is a response and, at other times, there is no response. Some moves are countered aggressively; with others reaction is weak. No factors explain these differences adequately; they appear to be at the whim of management.

Interestingly, research has shown that managers tend to over-react more frequently than they under-react to competitors' marketing activities (Leeflang and Wittink, 1996).

Competitive Advantage

The key to superior performance is to gain and hold a *competitive advantage*. Companies can gain a competitive advantage through *differentiation* of their product offering to provide superior customer value, or by managing for *lowest delivered cost*.

Competitive strategies

These two means of competitive advantage, when combined with the **competitive scope** of activities (broad vs narrow), result in four generic strategies: differentiation, cost leadership, differentiation focus, and cost focus.

The differentiation and cost leadership strategies seek competitive advantage in a broad range of market or industry segments, whereas differentiation focus and cost focus strategies are confined to a narrow segment (Porter, 1980).

Differentiation

Differentiation strategy involves the selection of one or more choice criteria that are used by many buyers in an industry. The firm then uniquely positions itself to meet these criteria. Differentiation strategies are usually associated with a premium price, and higher than average costs for the industry as the extra value to customers (e.g. higher performance) often raises costs. The aim is to differentiate in a way that leads to a price premium in excess of the cost of differentiating. Differentiation gives customers a reason to prefer one product over another and thus is central to strategic marketing thinking. Here are some examples of brands that have achieved success using a differentiation strategy.

- Nissan produced the Leaf, a battery electric car, which met the needs of customers looking for a *greener* solution. The innovations incorporated into the car enabled it to become the best-selling electronic vehicle in Europe.
- Toyota has built its success and reputation by targeting a broad market with highly reliable, high build quality, stylish and environmentally friendly cars, which differentiate the brand from its competitors, such as GM, Ford and Fiat.
- Dyson differentiated its vacuum cleaners by inventing a bagless version that outperformed its rivals by providing greater suction and convenience, and by eliminating the need to buy and install dust bags. Its vacuum cleaners are also differentiated from other brands by their distinctive design.
- Google created a differential advantage over its search engine rivals by enabling the most relevant websites to be ranked at the top of listings.

Cost leadership

This strategy involves the achievement of the lowest cost position in an industry. Many segments in the industry are served and great importance is attached to minimizing costs throughout the business so long as the price achievable for its products is around the industry average, cost leadership should result in superior performance. Thus, cost leaders often market standard products that are believed to be acceptable to customers. Heinz and United Biscuits are believed to be cost leaders in their industries. They market acceptable products at reasonable prices, which means that their low costs result in above-average profits. Walmart is also a cost leader, which allows the company the option of charging lower prices than its rivals to achieve higher sales and yet achieve comparable profit margins, or to match competitors' prices and attain higher profit margins. Zara, owned by Inditex, has an extremely efficient supply chain that not only enables the brand to produce very low-cost fashion garments, but also to get products to market faster than its competitors.

Differentiation focus

With this strategy, a firm aims to differentiate within one or a small number of target market segments. The special needs of the segment mean that there is an opportunity to differentiate the product offering from that of the competition, which may be targeting a broader group of customers. For example, some small speciality chemical companies thrive on taking orders that are too small or specialized to be of interest to their larger competitors. Differentiation focusers must be clear that the needs of their target group differ from those of the broader market (otherwise there will be no basis for differentiation) and that existing competitors are underperforming. Examples of differentiation focusers are Burberry, Bang & Olufsen, Mercedes and Ferrari; each of these markets differentiated products to one or a small number of target market segments. Not all attempts to differentiate succeed as Marketing in Action 19.2 explains.

Cost focus

With this strategy a firm seeks a cost advantage with one or a small number of target market segments. By dedicating itself to the segment, the cost focuser can seek economies that may be ignored or missed by broadly targeted competitors. In some instances, the competition, by trying to achieve wide market acceptance, may be over-performing (for example, by providing unwanted services) to one segment of customers. By providing a basic product offering, a cost advantage will be gained that may exceed the price discount necessary to sell it. Examples of cost focusers are easyJet and Ryanair, who focus on short-haul flights with a basic product trimmed to reduce costs. Lidl is also a cost focuser, targeting price-sensitive consumers with a narrow product line (around 300 items in stock) but with large buying power. Ibis, the no-frills hotel brand in the Accor Hotels portfolio, is another example with its focus on one market segment: price-conscious consumers.

MARKETING IN ACTION 19.2
Maybach: The Rise, Fall and (Possible) Rise Again of a Luxury Icon

In 2002, Mercedes-Benz announced, with great fanfare, that after a 60-year hiatus it was reviving the storied Maybach brand. The expectation was that the Maybach would successfully compete against both Rolls-Royce and Bentley in the exclusive arena known as the ultra-luxury car market. But sadly for Mercedes-Benz, it was not to be. Less than 10 years after its glorious return, it was announced that the Maybach division would be closing, with final production ceasing by 2013. Analysts believed the main reason for the brand's demise was years of disappointing sales. What happened? How could a company like Mercedes-Benz, so well known for the luxury and high performance of its cars, mess up so badly with the revival and introduction of an 'ultra-luxury' car brand?

The attractiveness of the ultra-luxury car market is its proven resistance to the effects of recession, and Mercedes-Benz believed that the Maybach had what it took to compete head on with the old-world masters of luxury. Each car was a work of art, being built by hand and incorporating only the finest materials. Available options were dizzying. Customers could have a 'movie-theatre-like' experience thanks to high-resolution television screens placed in the rear, as well as leather seats similar to those found in a private business jet. For the paranoid, it was even possible to get steel- and Kevlar-reinforced armour plating.

But with luxury features came a luxury price tag. Prices for the Maybach started at around $343,000 for the 'basic' Maybach 57, but could go up to well over $1 million for the 'luxury' 62S Landaulet model.

Mercedes-Benz is recognized as a world-class leader in luxury. But the problem was that it just wasn't seen in the same class as Rolls-Royce and Bentley. A common complaint was that the power-train and interior were both a bit 'stale.' Some cynics said that Mercedes-Benz tried to get by on the cheap, basing its new ultra-luxury car's chassis on the previously designed W140 platform, which was used in the 1991–99 S-Class. Critics also argued that Maybach suffered from flawed and poorly executed strategic marketing, with the message of the car's 'purpose' or how it was preferentially differentiated from a Rolls-Royce Phantom, for example, never being made clear. In the end, Mercedes-Benz lost an estimated $1 billion on the Maybach.

In November 2014, Mercedes-Benz announced (for a second time) the triumphant return of the Maybach brand, but this time plans appeared to be far less ambitious than previous ones. The revived brand is being targeted at what is called the 'super-premium' market. In Goldilocks fashion, Mercedes-Benz is trying to provide not too much luxury, not too little luxury, but just the right amount of luxury with the new version of the Maybach. The car is not a stand-alone brand this time. Rather, it is called the 'Mercedes-Maybach' and is based on an elongated version of the successful S-series.

Choosing a competitive strategy

The essence of corporate success is to choose a generic strategy and pursue it with gusto. Below-average performance is associated with the failure to achieve any of these generic strategies. The result is no competitive advantage: a *stuck-in-the-middle position* that results in lower performance than that of the cost leaders, differentiators or focusers in any market segment. An example of a company that made the mistake of moving to a stuck-in-the-middle position is Fiat. The Fiat 500 was sold in the US through a stand-alone dealership network. Dealers were required to make a heavy investment in creating an Italian feel in their showrooms. This was in preference to launching the car through the 500-strong Chrysler dealers (Chrysler acquired a stake in Fiat in 2009). The advantages of the first option were an image of exclusivity, but heavy investment was required—for example, $3 million for the showroom makeover. In the second option leveraging (Wunker, 2012) advantage from Chrysler could have meant making use of existing sales and service infrastructures. One of the downsides was that the Fiat 500 had a higher ticket price than similar performing cars like the Nissan Versa or Toyota Yaris and being sold in the same location could have had a negative impact on sales. So, the Fiat 500 was, arguably, stuck in the middle and its strategy did not lead to the coverage needed to establish the brand as rapidly as it would have liked.

Companies need to understand the generic basis for their success and resist the temptation to blur strategy by making inconsistent moves. For example, a no-frills cost leader or focuser should beware the pitfalls of moving to a higher cost base (perhaps by adding expensive services). A focus strategy involves limiting sales volume. Once domination of the target segment has been achieved there may be a temptation to move into other segments in order to achieve growth with the same competitive advantage. This can be a mistake if the new segments do not value the firm's competitive advantage in the same way.

In most situations differentiation and cost leadership strategies are incompatible: differentiation is achieved through higher costs. However, there are circumstances when both can be achieved simultaneously. For example, a differentiation strategy may lead to market share domination, which lowers costs through economies of scale and learning effects; or a highly differentiated firm may pioneer a major process innovation that significantly reduces manufacturing costs leading to a cost-leadership position. When differentiation and cost leadership coincide, performance is exceptional since a premium price can be charged for a low-cost product.

Sources of competitive advantage

In order to create a differentiated or lowest cost position, a firm needs to understand the nature and location of the potential *sources of competitive advantage*. The nature of these sources are the superior skills and resources of a firm. Management benefits by analyzing the superior skills and resources that are contributing, or could contribute, to competitive advantage (i.e. differentiation or lowest cost position). Their location can be aided by value chain analysis. A **value chain** is the discrete activities a firm carries out in order to perform its business.

Superior skills

Superior skills are the distinctive capabilities of key personnel that set them apart from the personnel of competing companies (Day and Wensley, 1988). The benefit of superior skills is the resulting ability to perform functions more effectively than other companies. For example, Sergey Brin and Larry Page worked together to produce a search engine that outperformed its rivals. Their technical know-how enabled them to use their superior skills not only to create Google, but also to lead the company to become the world's most influential Internet search tool.

Superior resources

Superior resources are the tangible requirements for advantage that enable a firm to exercise its skills. Examples of superior resources include:
* the number of salespeople in a market
* expenditure on advertising and sales promotion
* distribution infrastructure
* expenditure on R&D
* scale of and type of production facilities
* financial resources
* brand equity
* knowledge.

Core competences

The distinctive nature of these skills and resources makes up a company's **core competences**. For example, Google is able to use its technical skills and vast resources to enable the company to operate a global search engine. Google's operation has grown thanks to its innovative use of technology and its data centres in the USA, Northern Europe and Asia.

Value chain

A useful method for locating superior skills and resources is the value chain (Porter, 1985). All companies consist of a set of activities that are conducted to design, manufacture, market, distribute and service its products. The value chain categorizes these into primary and support activities (see Figure 19.5). This enables the sources of costs and differentiation to be understood and located.

Primary activities include inbound physical distribution (e.g. materials handling, warehousing, inventory control), operations (e.g. manufacturing, packaging, reselling), outbound physical distribution (e.g. delivery, order processing), marketing (e.g. advertising, selling) and service (e.g. installation, repair, customer training). A key skill of Walmart is its inbound logistics, which are based on real-time information systems and lets customers decide what appears in its stores. The Internet is used to inform suppliers what was sold the day before. In this way, it buys only what sells. Zara's competitive advantage relies on its marketing skills, which relate product design to fashion trends, and operational and logistical skills that get new clothing designs in stores faster than competitors.

Support activities are found within all of these primary activities, and consist of purchased inputs, technology, human resource management and the firm's infrastructure. These are not defined within a given primary activity because they can be found in all of them. Purchasing can take place within each primary activity, not just in the purchasing department; technology is relevant to all primary activities, as is human resource management;

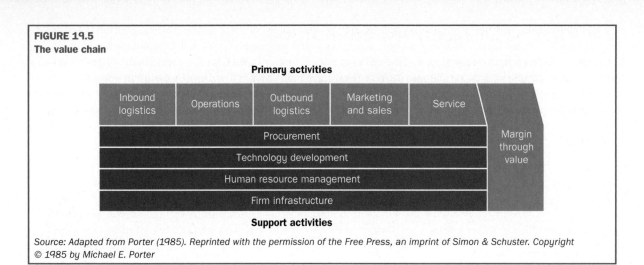

FIGURE 19.5
The value chain

Primary activities

Inbound logistics	Operations	Outbound logistics	Marketing and sales	Service	Margin through value

Procurement

Technology development

Human resource management

Firm infrastructure

Support activities

Source: Adapted from Porter (1985). Reprinted with the permission of the Free Press, an imprint of Simon & Schuster. Copyright © 1985 by Michael E. Porter

and the firm's infrastructure, which consists of general management, planning, finance, accounting and quality management, supports the entire value chain.

By examining each value-creating activity, management can look for the skills and resources that may form the basis for low cost or differentiated positions.

To the extent that skills and resources exceed (or could be developed to exceed) those of the competition, they form the key sources of competitive advantage. Not only should the skills and resources within value-creating activities be examined, the *linkages* between them should be examined too. For example, greater coordination between operations and inbound physical distribution may give rise to reduced costs through lower inventory levels.

Value chain analysis can extend to the value chains of suppliers and customers. For example, just-in-time supply could lower inventory costs; providing salesforce support to distributors could foster closer relations. Thus, by looking at the linkages between a firm's value chain and those of suppliers and customers, improvements in performance can result that can lower costs or contribute to the creation of a differentiated position.

Overall, the contribution of the value chain is in providing a framework for understanding the nature and location of the skills and resources that provide the basis for competitive advantage. Furthermore, the value chain provides the framework for cost analysis. Assigning operating costs and assets to value activities is the starting point of cost analysis so that improvement can be made, and cost advantages defended. For example, if a firm discovers that its cost advantage is based on superior production facilities, it should be vigilant in upgrading those facilities to maintain its position against competitors. Similarly, by understanding the sources of differentiation, a company can build on these sources and defend against competitive attack. For example, if differentiation is based on skills in product design, then management knows that sufficient investment in maintaining design superiority is required to maintain the firm's differentiated position. Also, the identification of specific sources of advantage can lead to their exploitation in new markets where customers place a similar high value on the resultant outcome. For example, Marks & Spencer's skills developed in clothing retailing were successfully extended to provide differentiation in food retailing. Finally, analysis of the value chain can lead to its reconfiguration to fundamentally change the way a market is served. Figure 19.6 provides some examples.

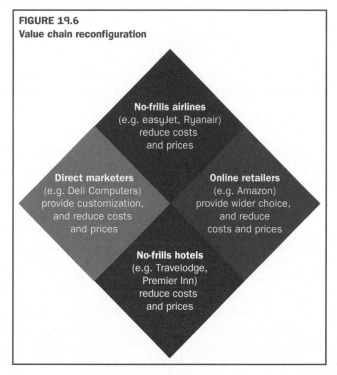

FIGURE 19.6
Value chain reconfiguration

No-frills airlines (e.g. easyJet, Ryanair) reduce costs and prices

Direct marketers (e.g. Dell Computers) provide customization, and reduce costs and prices

Online retailers (e.g. Amazon) provide wider choice, and reduce costs and prices

No-frills hotels (e.g. Travelodge, Premier Inn) reduce costs and prices

Creating a Differential Advantage

Although skills and resources are the sources of competitive advantage, they are translated into a **differential advantage** only when the customer perceives that the firm is providing value above that of the competition. (For methods of calculating value in organizational markets, see Anderson and Narus (1998).) The creation of a differential advantage, then, comes from linking skills and resources with the key attributes (choice criteria) that customers are looking for in a product offering. However, it should be recognized that the distinguishing competing attributes in a market are not always the most important ones. For example, if customers were asked to rank safety, punctuality and onboard service in order of importance when flying, safety would undoubtedly be ranked at the top. Nevertheless, when choosing an airline, safety would rank low because most airlines are assumed to be safe. This is why airlines look to less important ways of differentiating their offerings (e.g. by giving superior onboard service).

A differential advantage can be created with any aspect of the marketing mix. Product, distribution, promotion and price are all capable of creating added customer value (see Figure 19.7).

The key to knowing whether improving an aspect of marketing is worthwhile is to know whether the potential benefit provides value to the customer. Table 19.2 lists ways of creating differential advantages and their potential impact on customer value.

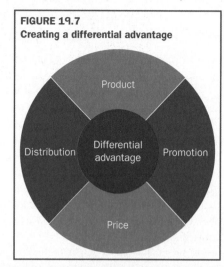

FIGURE 19.7
Creating a differential advantage

Marketing mix	Differential advantage	Value to the customer
TABLE 19.2 Creating a differential advantage using the marketing mix		
Product	Performance	Lower costs; higher revenue; safety; pleasure; status; service; added functions
	Durability	Longer life; lower costs
	Reliability	Lower maintenance and production costs; higher revenue; fewer problems
	Style	Good looks; status
	Upgradability	Lower costs; prestige
	Technical assistance	Better-quality products; closer supplier–buyer relationships
	Installation	Fewer problems
Distribution	Location	Convenience; lower costs
	Quick/reliable delivery	Lower costs; fewer problems
	Distributor support	More effective selling/marketing; close buyer–seller relationships
	Delivery guarantees	Peace of mind
	Computerized reordering	Less work; lower costs
Promotion	Creative/more advertising	Superior brand personality
	Creative/more sales promotion	Direct added value
	Cooperative promotions	Lower costs
	Well-trained salesforce	Superior problem-solving and building close relationships
	Dual selling	Sales assistance; higher sales
	Fast, accurate quotes	Lower costs; fewer problems
	Free demonstrations	Lower risk of purchase
	Free or low-cost trial	Lower risk of purchase
	Fast complaint handling	Fewer problems; lower costs

»

Marketing mix	Differential advantage	Value to the customer
Price	Lower price	Lower cost of purchase
	Credit facilities	Lower costs; better cash flow
	Low-interest loans	Lower costs; better cash flow
	Higher price	Price–quality match

Product

Product performance can be enhanced by, say, raising speed, comfort and safety levels, capacity and ease of use, or improving taste or smell. For example, improving comfort levels (e.g. of a car), taste (e.g. of food), or smell (e.g. of cosmetics) can give added pleasure to consumption. There are many ways to enhance performance. For example, Apple has enhanced the performance of its iPhone with the creation of its App Store, which allows users to access software applications from independent developers. This creates additional functions that the iPhone can carry out, such as Foursquare, which allows users to find the location, price range and reviews of restaurants nearby. For further discussion on marketing apps, see Marketing in Action 19.1.

Exclusive designs and style are another way products can be used to differentiate a brand. Bang & Olufsen and Audi are two companies that have used style as a way to compete in highly competitive markets. Bang & Olufsen has long been regarded as the style leader in audio and television equipment, and Audi has become one of the car industry's most successful luxury brands, producing some of the world's most coveted and copied cars.

Apple has become a world-leading brand by continually introducing innovative products, the latest being the iWatch. However, currently, the small battery means the watch has to be charged regularly; so while the iWatch may be a desired high-status product, its performance might create an opportunity for competitors to enter this market. Performance can also be improved by added functions that create extra benefits for customers.

 Scan the QR code to discover how Vodafone differentiates its products from the competition by encouraging its customers to live life to the full.

The *durability* of a product has a bearing on costs since greater durability means a longer operating life. Improving product *reliability* (i.e. lowering malfunctions or defects) can lower maintenance and production costs, raise revenues through lower downtime and reduce the hassle of using the product. Product *styling* can also give customer value through the improved looks that good style brings. This can confer status to the buyer and allow the supplier to charge premium prices, for example Bridgestone (Japanese), Michelin (French) and Pirelli (Italian).

The capacity to *upgrade* a product (to take advantage of technological advances) or to meet changing needs (e.g. extra storage space in a computer) can lower costs, and confer prestige by maintaining state-of-the-art features. The Apple MacBook Pro and MacBook Air computers demonstrate how style can be used to create a differential advantage.

Products can be augmented by the provision of *guarantees* that give customers peace of mind and lower costs should the product need repair, as well as giving *technical assistance* to customers, so that they are provided with better-quality products. Both parties benefit from closer relationships and from the provision of product *installation*, which means that customers do not incur problems in properly installing a complex piece of equipment.

Distribution

Wide distribution coverage and/or careful selection of distributor *locations* can provide convenient purchasing for customers. *Quick and/or reliable delivery* can lower buyer costs by reducing production downtime and lowering inventory levels. Reliable delivery, in particular, reduces the frustration of waiting for late delivery. Providing distributors with *support* in the form of training and financial help can bring about more effective selling and marketing, and offers both parties the advantage of closer relationships. FedEx has continued to prosper by giving *delivery guarantees* of critical documents 'down to the hour' (*Business Week*, 2006). Working with organizational customers to introduce *computerized reordering* systems can lower their costs, reduce their workload and increase the cost for them of switching to other suppliers.

Promotion

A differential advantage can be created by the *creative use of advertising*. For example, *spending more on advertising* can also aid differentiation by creating a stronger brand personality than competitive brands. For example, Twinings tea's 'get back to where you belong' campaign targeted women using new emotive techniques and animations to significantly grow market share (Owen, 2012). Similarly, using *more creative sales promotional methods* or simply *spending more on sales incentives* can give direct added value to customers. By engaging in *cooperative promotions* with distributors, producers can lower their costs and build goodwill.

The salesforce can also offer a means of creating a differential advantage. Particularly when products are similar, a *well-trained salesforce* can provide superior problem-solving skills for their customers.

EXHIBIT 19.3
Bang & Olufsen's stylish audio and television equipment

Scan the QR code to see how Twinings tea used emotional appeals to differentiate its brand and increase sales.

Price

Using low price as a means of gaining differential advantage can fail unless the firm enjoys a cost advantage and has the resources to fight a price war. For example, Acer has successfully challenged Dell and Hewlett-Packard in the computer market by launching a very low-cost desktop PC. Its strategy is to exploit its lowest cost position, allowing it to become extremely aggressive on price (Einhorn, 2009). Budget airlines such as Ryanair and easyJet have challenged more traditional airlines by charging low prices based on low costs.

A less obvious means of lowering the effective price to the customer is to offer *credit facilities* or *low-interest loans*. Both serve to lower the cost of purchase and improve cash flow for customers. Finally, a *high price* can be used as part of a premium positioning strategy to support brand image. Where a brand has distinct product, promotional or distributional advantages, a premium price provides consistency within the marketing mix.

This analysis of how the marketing mix can be used to develop a differential advantage has focused on how each action can be translated into value to the customer. Remember, however, that for a differential advantage to be realized, a firm needs to provide not only customer value but also value that is superior to that offered by the competition. If all companies provide distributor support in equal measure, for example, distributors may gain value, but no differential advantage will have been achieved.

EXHIBIT 19.4
TK Maxx uses price and quality to differentiate from its competitors with its 'Big labels small prices' campaign

Fast reaction times

In addition to using the marketing mix to create a differential advantage, many companies are recognizing the need to create *fast reaction times* to changes in marketing trends. For example, H&M and Zara have developed fast-reaction systems so that new designs can be delivered to stores within three weeks, and top-selling items are requested and poor sellers withdrawn from shops within a week. This is made possible by sophisticated marketing information systems that feed data from stores to headquarters every day.

Scale of operations

Companies can also create a differential advantage when the scale of their operations creates value for their customers. For example, eBay has built a sustainable differential advantage by building a large participant base. As the customer value of an auction site is directly related to the size of the participant base, once eBay gained a large user base advantage it became extremely difficult for any competitor to duplicate the value that it offers (Nagle and Hogan, 2006).

Sustaining a differential advantage

When searching for ways to achieve a differential advantage, management should pay close attention to factors that cannot easily be copied by the competition. The aim is to achieve a *sustainable differential advantage*. Competing on low price can often be copied by the competition, meaning that any advantage is short-lived. Other attempts at creating a differential advantage may also be copied by the competition. For example, when DHL challenged FedEx and UPS in the US postal delivery market, all its attempts at gaining a competitive edge were copied by its rivals. When DHL hired the US Postal Service to carry out its domestic deliveries, a move that was popular with customers, FedEx and UPS followed suit. The result was that DHL could not find a way of creating a differential advantage and was forced to exit the US market (*The Economist*, 2008). The key to achieving a long-term advantage is to focus on areas that the competition find impossible or, at the very least, very difficult to copy, including:
- patent-protected products
- strong brand personality
- close relationships with customers
- high service levels achieved by well-trained personnel
- innovative product upgrading
- creating high entry barriers (e.g. R&D or promotional expenditures)
- strong and distinctive internal processes that deliver the above and are difficult to copy
- scale (where the scale of operations provides value to the customer, for example eBay) (De Chernatony, Harris and Dall'Olmo Riley, 2000).

Eroding a differential advantage

However, many advantages are contestable. For example, IBM's stronghold on personal computers was undermined by cheaper clones. Three mechanisms are at work that can erode a differential advantage (Day, 1999).

1 technological and environment changes that create opportunities for competitors by eroding the protective barriers (e.g. long-standing television companies are being challenged by satellite television)
2 competitors learn how to imitate the sources of the differential advantage (e.g. competitors engage in a training programme to improve service capabilities)
3 complacency leads to lack of protection of the differential advantage. Read Marketing in Action 19.3 to discover how IBM invented an artificial intelligence computer and in doing so acquired a new source of competitive advantage.

Creating Cost Leadership

Creating a cost-leadership position requires an understanding of the factors that affect costs. Porter has identified 10 major *cost drivers* that determine the behaviour of costs in the value chain (see Figure 19.8) (Porter, 1985).

Economies of scale

Scale economies can arise from the use of more efficient methods of production at higher volumes. For example, United Biscuits benefits from more efficient machinery that can produce biscuits more cheaply than that used by

MARKETING IN ACTION 19.3
Want to Know How to Beat the Competition? Ask Watson

Watson is an artificial intelligence computer system that can answer *spoken* questions, using natural language rather than computer code. The machine, devised by IBM, has won the television quiz show *Jeopardy* in the USA by outperforming human opponents in answering questions. Watson's advantage comes from its vast memory store and the speed at which information can be retrieved.

But IBM is not intending to use Watson for playing games; it is being used in various commercial settings in the health industry as a diagnostic tool for use with cancer patients. Watson has been fed information relating to oncology (lung, prostate and breast cancers) which has provided a knowledge base that the machine can interpret. This information includes more than 2 million pages of information from medical journals and 1.5 million patient records. Wellpoint's Samuel Nessbaum claims that Watson can interrogate the knowledge base and produce a diagnosis that is correct 90 per cent of the time, which once again outperforms humans; doctors found to be correct only 50 per cent of the time.

IBM has now launched Watson Health, which is a cloud-computing-based supercomputer for analyzing healthcare data on a global basis. The company has also entered into partnership with Apple and Johnson & Johnson (leading pharmaceutical product manufacturer) to develop consumer and medical devices. At Apple, Watson Health Cloud services will be linked to the Apple Health Kit, which will enable Apple iWatch wearers to take part in a huge health data study.

At Johnson & Johnson, the focus will be on creating intelligent healthcare coaching systems, including for joint replacement and spinal surgery. It also intends to launch new apps for targeting chronic conditions such as diabetes and obesity.

Based on: IBM (2015); Steadman (2013); Mearian (2015)

Fox's Biscuits, which operates at much lower volume. Scale economies also arise from the less-than-proportional increase in overheads as production volume increases. For example, a factory with twice the floor area of another factory is less than twice the price to build. A third scale economy results from the capacity to spread the cost of R&D and promotion over a greater sales volume. Such scale economies mean that companies such as Coca-Cola, General Electric, Intel, Microsoft and Walmart have a huge advantage over their competitors. However, economies of scale do not proceed indefinitely. At some point, diseconomies of scale are likely to arise as size gives rise to over-complexity and, possibly, personnel difficulties.

Learning

Costs can also fall as a result of the effects of learning. For example, people learn how to assemble more quickly, pack more efficiently, design products that are easier to manufacture, lay out warehouses more effectively, cut driving time and reduce inventories. The combined effect of economies of scale and learning as

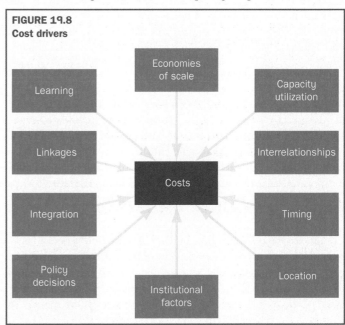

FIGURE 19.8 Cost drivers

cumulative output increases has been termed the **experience curve**. The Boston Consulting Group has estimated that costs are reduced by approximately 15–20 per cent on average each time cumulative output doubles. This suggests that companies with greater market share will have a cost advantage through the experience curve effect, assuming all companies are operating on the same curve. However, a move towards a new manufacturing technology can lower the experience curve for adopting companies, allowing them to leap-frog more traditional companies and thereby gain a cost advantage even though cumulative output may be lower.

Capacity utilization

Since fixed costs must be paid whether a plant is manufacturing at full or zero capacity, underutilization incurs costs. The effect is to push up the cost per unit for production. The impact of capacity utilization on profitability was established by the PIMS (profit impact of marketing strategy) studies, which have shown a positive association between utilization and return on investment (Buzzell and Gale, 1987). Changes in capacity utilization can also raise costs (e.g. through the extra costs of hiring and laying off workers). Careful production planning is required for seasonal products such as ice cream and fireworks, in order to smooth output.

Linkages

These describe how the costs of activities are affected by how other activities are performed. For example, improving quality-assurance activities can reduce after-sales service costs. In the car industry, the reduction in the number of faults on a new car reduces warranty costs. The activities of suppliers and distributors also link to affect the costs of a firm. For example, the introduction of a just-in-time delivery system by a supplier reduces the inventory costs of a firm. Distributors can influence a company's physical distribution costs through their warehouse location decision. To exploit such linkages, though, the firm may need considerable bargaining power. In some instances it can pay a firm to increase distributor margins or pay a fee in order to exploit linkages.

Interrelationships

Sharing costs with other business units is another potential cost driver. Sharing the costs of R&D, transportation, marketing and purchasing means lower costs. Know-how can also be shared to reduce costs by improving the efficiency of an activity. Car manufacturers share engineering platforms and components to reduce costs. For example, Volkswagen does this across its VW, Skoda, Seat and Audi cars. Care has to be taken that the cars appearing under different brand names do not appear too similar, however, or this may detract from the appeal of the more expensive marques (MacKintosh, 2005).

Integration

Both integration and forms of integration can affect costs. For example, owning the means of physical distribution rather than using outside contractors could lower costs. Ownership may allow a producer to avoid suppliers or customers with sizeable bargaining power. De-integration can lower costs and raise flexibility. For example, by using many small clothing suppliers, Benetton is in a powerful position to keep costs low while maintaining a high degree of production flexibility.

Timing

Both first movers and late entrants have potential opportunities for lowering costs. First movers in a market can gain cost advantages: it is usually cheaper to establish a brand name in the minds of customers if there is no competition. Also, they have prime access to cheap or high-quality raw materials and locations. However, late entrants to a market have the opportunity to buy the latest technology and avoid high market development costs.

Policy decisions

Companies have a wide range of discretionary policy decisions that affect costs. Product width, level of service, channel decisions (e.g. small number of large dealers vs large number of small dealers), salesforce decisions (e.g. in-company salesforce vs sales agents) and wage levels are some of the decision areas that have a direct impact on costs. Southwest Airlines, for example, cuts costs by refusing to waste time assigning seats and does not wait for late arrivals. The overriding concern is to get the aeroplane in and out of the gate quickly so that it is in the air earning money. Southwest flies only one kind of aircraft, which also keeps costs down (McNulty, 2001).

Companies can also collaborate to reduce costs. For example, Vodafone has teamed up with O₂'s parent company, Telefónica, to share mobile network infrastructure (e.g. masts, equipment and power supply), following a similar deal between T-Mobile and 3 (Kollewe, 2008).

 Scan the QR code to analyse how Quaker Oats supports its parent company's (PepsiCo) corporate strategy.

Ryanair accepts bookings only over the Internet, thus eliminating the need for an inbound telemarketing team and allowing e-ticketing, which cuts postage and paper costs. Other sectors, such as insurance, rail, banking, package holidays and hotels, encourage transactions over the Internet in order to reduce costs. Care must be taken, however, not to reduce costs with regard to activities that have a major bearing on customer value. For example, moving from a company-employed salesforce to sales agents may not only cut costs but at the same time also destroy supplier–customer relationships.

Location

The location of plant and warehouses affects costs through different wage, physical distribution and energy costs. Dyson, for example, manufactures its vacuum cleaners in Malaysia to take advantage of low wage costs (Marsh, 2002). Car manufacturers such as VW, Peugeot, Skoda and Mercedes have moved production to eastern Europe to take advantage of low costs (Milne and Williamson, 2005). Locating near customers can lower outbound distributional costs, while locating near suppliers reduces inbound distributional costs.

Institutional factors

These include government regulations, tariffs and local content rules. For example, regulations regarding the maximum size of lorries affect distribution costs.

Companies employing a cost leadership strategy will be vigilant in pruning costs. This analysis of cost drivers provides a framework for searching out new avenues for cost reduction.

Once a company has identified a strategic direction and developed an understanding of the nature of the competition and how it might compete, it then has to decide on developing a competitive marketing strategy.

Competitive Marketing Strategy

When developing marketing strategy, companies need to be aware of their own strengths and weaknesses, customer needs, and the competition. This three-pronged approach to strategy development has been termed the 'strategic triangle' and is shown in Figure 19.9. This framework recognizes that to be successful it is no longer sufficient to be good at satisfying customers' needs: companies need to be better than the competition. So far, we have considered creating and sustaining competitive advantage; now we explore the development of marketing strategies in the face of competitive activity and challenges, by looking at alternative modes of competitive behaviour and then examining when and how to achieve strategic marketing objectives.

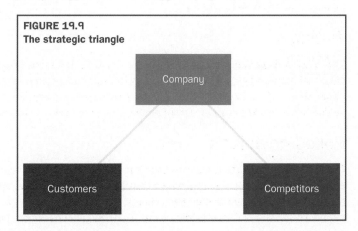

FIGURE 19.9
The strategic triangle

Competitive Behaviour

Rivalry between companies does not always lead to conflict and aggressive marketing battles. **Competitive behaviour** can take five forms: conflict, competition, co-existence, cooperation and collusion (Easton and Araujo, 1986).

Conflict

Conflict is characterized by aggressive competition, where the objective is to drive competitors out of the marketplace. The retail industry is highly competitive. Compounded by the global economic recession, many businesses have been forced to close as a result of competitive conflict or devise ways of strengthening their market position. Dixons Retail changed the face of its business in the UK by merging with Carphone Warehouse. The move created a very large retailer with over 3,000 physical stores and additional product ranges, strengthened the company's buying power, and created opportunities for growth and costs savings on operational costs (Garside and Farrrell, 2014).

Competition

The objective of competition is not to eliminate competitors from the marketplace, but to perform better than them. This may take the form of trying to achieve faster sales and/or profit growth, larger size or higher market share. Competitive behaviour recognizes the limits of aggression. Competitor reaction will be an important consideration when setting strategy. Players will avoid spoiling the underlying industry structure, which is an important influence on overall profitability. For example, price wars will be avoided if competitors believe that their long-term effect will be to reduce industry profitability.

Co-existence

Three types of co-existence can occur. First, co-existence may arise because companies do not recognize their competitors, owing to difficulties in defining market boundaries. For example, Waterman and Mont Blanc, makers of fine-quality and luxury writing instruments, fountain pens and propelling pencils, may ignore competition from jewellery companies, since their definition may be product-based rather than market-centred (i.e. the gift market). Second, companies may not recognize other companies they believe are operating in a separate market segment. For example, Mont Blanc and Waterman are likely to ignore the actions of Mitsubishi Pencil Company, which manufactures Uniball rollerball pens, as they are operating in different market segments. Third, companies may choose to acknowledge the territories of their competitors (for example, geography, brand personality, market segment or product technology) in order to avoid harmful head-to-head competition.

Cooperation

This involves the pooling of the skills and resources of two or more companies to overcome problems and take advantage of new opportunities. A growing trend is towards **strategic alliances**, where companies join together through a joint venture, licensing agreement, long-term purchasing and supply arrangements, or joint research and development contract to build a long-term competitive advantage. For example, Shell International Petroleum, Rolls-Royce and Airbus have worked in collaboration to develop alternative fuels for the A380, which has led to the use of cleaner aviation fuels. In today's global marketplace, where size is a key source of advantage, cooperation is a major type of competitive behaviour (Airbus, 2012). See Mini Case 19.1 to find out more about the Diageo way of growing markets.

 Scan the QR code to see how Diageo's 'Keep Walking' creative campaign has maintained the position of its world-beating Johnnie Walker whisky for over a decade.

Collusion

The final form of competitive behaviour is collusion, whereby companies come to some arrangement that inhibits competition in a market. Collusion is more likely where there are a small number of suppliers in each national market, the price of the product is a small proportion of buyer costs, cross-national trade is restricted by tariff barriers or prohibitive transportation costs, and buyers are able to pass on high prices to their customers. For example, Apple joined forces with five major book publishers (Hachette Book Group, HarperCollins, Penguin,

MINI CASE 19.1
Growing Markets the Diageo Way

Diageo is a company that owns over a quarter of the world's leading brands of spirits, for example Smirnoff vodka, Johnnie Walker whisky and Guinness, which is a leading global beer brand. In addition, Diageo also owns local brands, which are used to broaden market penetration in particular parts of the world. For Diageo, growth opportunities are in new markets in Asia Pacific, Latin America and Africa, and the company is making acquisitions of strong local brands that appeal to its target customers.

Diageo's strategies for winning market share make use of the company's marketing knowledge and expertise. Elements of the marketing mix are used innovatively to differentiate its brands—for example the global Johnnie Walker 'Keep Walking' marketing communications campaign, which has increased sales and market share for over a decade. This creative idea has grown and been reinvented for a new generation of digital consumers. Products also undergo regular reinventions, and new flavours, packaging and formats are introduced to ensure the interest of new and existing customers, for example the 'From the bar' premixed drinks range using Gordon's, Pimm's and Smirnoff.

Collaboration with partners is another method used by Diageo to build market share. The company's 'Diageo Way of Selling' programme aims to help retailers and other trade partners achieve high levels of sales through education and sharing best practices, which creates value for all involved in the collaboration. It has made a significant investment in facilitating partnerships. The European Customer Collaboration Centre provides a state-of-the-art facility for Diageo to bring together customers, retailers, trade partners and distributors to aid brand development, integrated planning and research and development for new products and services. This investment not only helps Diageo show support to its business partners and customers, but also to foster constant brand development and innovation, which ultimately increases sales and growth of market share.

Questions:

1 Explain the actions Diageo has used to build market share.
2 Discuss the difference between strategic thrust and strategic objectives, using examples from Diageo.
3 Discuss the importance of setting marketing objectives as part of the marketing planning process.

Based on: BBH (2015); Diageo (2015)

Simon & Schuster and Macmillan) to raise the price of e-books. The US Justice Department and the European Commission decided that Apple's decision to side with the publishers was tantamount to collusion and an example of anti-competitive behaviour. The publishers settled, but Apple went to trial and was found guilty of price fixing and collusion (Hughes, 2014).

Developing Competitive Marketing Strategies

Researchers Ries and Trout (2005), and Kotler and Singh (1981) have drawn attention to the relationship between military and marketing 'warfare'. Their work has stressed the need to develop strategies that are more than customer based. They placed the emphasis on attacking and defending against the competition, and used military analogies to guide strategic thinking. They saw competition as the enemy and thus recognized the relevance to business of the principles of military warfare as put forward by such writers as Sun Tzu (1963) and von Clausewitz (1908). As von Clausewitz wrote:

> 'Military warfare is a clash between major interests that is resolved by bloodshed—that is the only way in which it differs from other conflicts. Rather than comparing it to an art we could more accurately compare it to commerce, which is also a conflict of human interests and activities.'

Earlier in the chapter we discussed analyzing competitors and their marketing objectives, which shape their direction in terms of products and markets and, more specifically, objectives for individual products and services. We now consider the marketing strategies that companies might apply when pursuing particular strategic marketing objectives.

Attack strategies

If a market cannot be expanded, a build strategy implies gaining marketing success at the expense of the competition. Winning market share is an important goal, as market share has been found to be related to profitability in many studies (see Chapter 11). There are several reasons why this should be. Market leaders are often high-price brands (e.g. Coca-Cola, Kellogg's, Heinz, Nestlé, and Nike). They are also in a stronger position to resist distributor demands for trade discounts. Because of economies of scale and experience curve effects, their costs are likely to be lower than those of their smaller-volume rivals. Therefore, their profit margins should be greater than those of their competitors. Since they are market leaders, by definition the unit sales volume is higher and consequently their overall profits (profit margin × sales volume) should be higher than those of their rivals. This is why companies such as GE, Unilever, Procter & Gamble and Heinz are willing to compete only in those markets where they can reach number one or two position.

Companies seek to win market share through product, distribution, promotional innovation and penetration pricing. Kotler and Singh (1981) have identified five competitor confrontation strategies designed to win sales and market share. See Table 19.3.

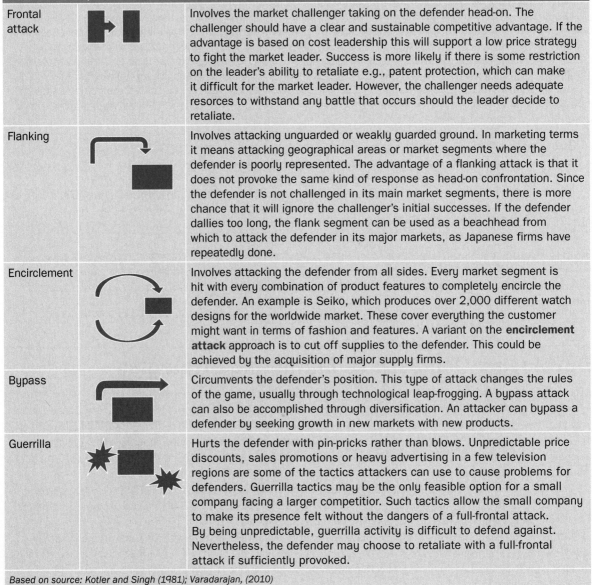

TABLE 19.3 Competitor confrontation strategies designed to win sales and market share		
Frontal attack		Involves the market challenger taking on the defender head-on. The challenger should have a clear and sustainable competitive advantage. If the advantage is based on cost leadership this will support a low price strategy to fight the market leader. Success is more likely if there is some restriction on the leader's ability to retaliate e.g., patent protection, which can make it difficult for the market leader. However, the challenger needs adequate resorces to withstand any battle that occurs should the leader decide to retaliate.
Flanking		Involves attacking unguarded or weakly guarded ground. In marketing terms it means attacking geographical areas or market segments where the defender is poorly represented. The advantage of a flanking attack is that it does not provoke the same kind of response as head-on confrontation. Since the defender is not challenged in its main market segments, there is more chance that it will ignore the challenger's initial successes. If the defender dallies too long, the flank segment can be used as a beachhead from which to attack the defender in its major markets, as Japanese firms have repeatedly done.
Encirclement		Involves attacking the defender from all sides. Every market segment is hit with every combination of product features to completely encircle the defender. An example is Seiko, which produces over 2,000 different watch designs for the worldwide market. These cover everything the customer might want in terms of fashion and features. A variant on the **encirclement attack** approach is to cut off supplies to the defender. This could be achieved by the acquisition of major supply firms.
Bypass		Circumvents the defender's position. This type of attack changes the rules of the game, usually through technological leap-frogging. A bypass attack can also be accomplished through diversification. An attacker can bypass a defender by seeking growth in new markets with new products.
Guerrilla		Hurts the defender with pin-pricks rather than blows. Unpredictable price discounts, sales promotions or heavy advertising in a few television regions are some of the tactics attackers can use to cause problems for defenders. Guerrilla tactics may be the only feasible option for a small company facing a larger competitior. Such tactics allow the small company to make its presence felt without the dangers of a full-frontal attack. By being unpredictable, guerrilla activity is difficult to defend against. Nevertheless, the defender may choose to retaliate with a full-frontal attack if sufficiently provoked.

Based on source: Kotler and Singh (1981); Varadarajan, (2010)

Table 19.4 shows examples of companies that are regularly in head-to-head competitive confrontation.

TABLE 19.4 Major marketing head-on battles	
Companies	**Competitive area**
Nike vs. Adidas	Footwear
Coca-Cola vs. Pepsi	Soft drinks
McDonald's vs. Burger King	Fast-food restaurants
Unilever vs. Procter & Gamble	Fast-moving consumer goods
Apple (iPhone) vs. Samsung Galaxy	Smartphones
iPad vs. Samsung Galaxy Tab	Tablet computers
Apple vs. Dell	Computers
Google vs. Yahoo!	Search engines
Intel vs. Advanced Micro Devices	Microchips
Boeing vs. Airbus	Aircraft
Google Plus vs. Facebook	Social networks

Defence strategies

In circumstances where there is rivalry among competitors, strategic action may be required to defend sales and market share from aggressive challenges. The principles of defensive warfare provide a framework for identifying strategic alternatives that can be used in this situation. Table 19.5 illustrates six methods of defence derived from military strategy.

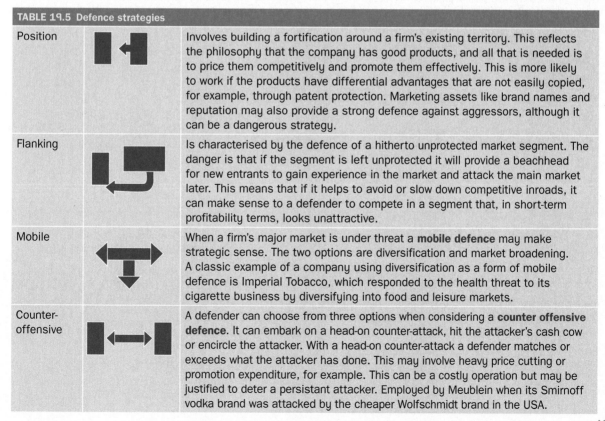

TABLE 19.5 Defence strategies		
Position		Involves building a fortification around a firm's existing territory. This reflects the philosophy that the company has good products, and all that is needed is to price them competitively and promote them effectively. This is more likely to work if the products have differential advantages that are not easily copied, for example, through patent protection. Marketing assets like brand names and reputation may also provide a strong defence against aggressors, although it can be a dangerous strategy.
Flanking		Is characterised by the defence of a hitherto unprotected market segment. The danger is that if the segment is left unprotected it will provide a beachhead for new entrants to gain experience in the market and attack the main market later. This means that if it helps to avoid or slow down competitive inroads, it can make sense to a defender to compete in a segment that, in short-term profitability terms, looks unattractive.
Mobile		When a firm's major market is under threat a **mobile defence** may make strategic sense. The two options are diversification and market broadening. A classic example of a company using diversification as a form of mobile defence is Imperial Tobacco, which responded to the health threat to its cigarette business by diversifying into food and leisure markets.
Counter-offensive		A defender can choose from three options when considering a **counter offensive defence**. It can embark on a head-on counter-attack, hit the attacker's cash cow or encircle the attacker. With a head-on counter-attack a defender matches or exceeds what the attacker has done. This may involve heavy price cutting or promotion expenditure, for example. This can be a costly operation but may be justified to deter a persistant attacker. Employed by Meublein when its Smirnoff vodka brand was attacked by the cheaper Wolfschmidt brand in the USA.

»

| Pre-emptive | 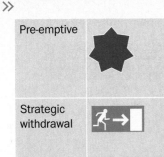 | Follows the philosophy that the best form of defence is to attack first. This may involve continuous innovation and new product development e.g., Apple inc. invests heavily in design and innovation. Failure to maintain the ability to lead the market could result in loss of market share and eventual collapse of the brand. |
| Strategic withdrawal | | Market exit strategy requires a company to define its strengths and weaknesses, and then to hold on to its strengths while divesting its weaknesses. This results in the company concentrating on its core business. An example is Diageo, which withdrew from the fast-food business by selling Burger King, and from food by selling Pillsbury to concentrate on premium drinks. |

Based on source: Kotler and Singh (1981); Varadarajan (2010)

Working together in competitive markets

When companies are trading in intensely competitive markets, there is a likelihood that they will interact through attacking and defending market territories. However, in increasingly turbulent and changing markets, collaboration and cooperation often occur. Marketing managers can find themselves considering whether to compete or cooperate with companies that operate in similar market territories. Collaborative networks of competing companies can develop based on shared interests, with the aim of solving common problems (Meng and Layton, 2011). For example, Nissan, BMW and Tesla are rivals in the electronic car market, but they have agreed to collaborate and share patents in order to speed up development of electric cars. Growth in this relatively new industry has been slow, so by cooperating there is potential for all partners to benefit. Table 19.6 shows examples of strategic alliances and other collaborative partnerships

TABLE 19.6 Examples of strategic alliances and collaborative partnerships	
Companies	**Competitive area**
Apple/IBM	Health monitoring/smart watches
British Airways/American Airlines	Transatlantic air travel
Accenture/General Electric	Big data
BP/Schlumberger	Oil drilling processes
Nissan/BMW/Tesla	Electric cars
Warner Group/Shazam	Discovering new acts and signing them to new labels
Volvo/Dongfeng Motor Group	Commercial vehicles

When you have read this chapter

Discover further resources and test your understanding: McGraw-Hill **Connect**™ is a digital teaching and learning environment that improves performance over a variety of critical outcomes; it can be tailored, is easy to use and is proven effective **LearnSmart**™ is the most widely used and intelligent adaptive learning resource that is proven to strengthen memory recall, improve course retention and boost grades. Fuelled by **LearnSmart**™, **SmartBook**™ is the first and only adaptive reading experience available today.

Review

1   The determinants of industry attractiveness

- Industry attractiveness is determined by the degree of rivalry between competitors, the threat of new entrants, the bargaining power of suppliers and buyers, and the threat of substitute products.

2   How to analyze competitors

- Competitor analysis should identify competitors (product from competitors, product substitutes, generic competitors and potential new entrants); audit their capabilities; analyze their objectives, strategic thrust and strategies; and estimate competitor response patterns.

3   The difference between differentiation and cost leadership strategies

- Differentiation strategy involves the selection of one or more choice criteria used by buyers to select suppliers/brands and uniquely positioning the supplier/brand to meet those criteria better than the competition.
- Cost leadership involves the achievement of the lowest cost position in an industry.

4   The sources of competitive advantage

- Competitive advantage can be achieved by creating a differential advantage or achieving the lowest cost position.
- Its sources are superior skills, superior resources, and core competences. A useful method of locating superior skills and resources is value chain analysis.

5   The value chain

- The value chain categorizes the value-creating activities of a company. The value chain divides these into primary and support activities. Primary activities are in-bound physical distribution, operations, outbound physical distribution, marketing and service. Support activities are found within all of these primary activities, and consist of purchased inputs, technology, human resource management and the company's infrastructure.
- By examining each value-creating activity, management can search for the skills and resources (and linkages) that may form the basis for low cost or differentiated positions.

6   How to create and maintain a differential advantage

- A differential advantage is created when the customer perceives that the company is providing value above that of the competition.
- A differential advantage can be created using any element in the marketing mix: superior product, more effective distribution, better promotion and better value for money by lower prices. A differential advantage can also be created by developing fast reaction times to changes in marketing trends.
- A differential advantage can be maintained (sustained) through the use of patent protection, strong brand personality, close relationships with customers, high service levels based on well-trained staff, innovative product upgrading, the creation of high entry barriers (e.g. R&D or promotional expenditures), and strong and distinctive internal processes that deliver the earlier points and are difficult to copy.

7   How to create and maintain a cost leadership position

- Cost leadership can be created and maintained by managing cost drivers, which are economies of scale, learning effects, capacity utilization, linkages (e.g. improvements in quality assurance can reduce after-sales service costs), interrelationships (e.g. sharing costs), integration (e.g. owning the means of distribution), timing (both first movers and late entrants can have low costs), policy decisions (e.g. controlling labour costs), location, and institutional factors (e.g. government regulations).

8   The nature of competitive behaviour

- Competitive behaviour can take five forms: conflict, competition, co-existence, cooperation and collusion.

9 Competitive marketing strategy can appear as a military initiative

- Military analogies have been used in the past to guide strategic thinking, because of the need to attack and defend against competition. While the underlying thinking remains important, the language of war appears less in modern business-speak.
- Attack strategies are the **frontal attack**, the **flanking attack**, **encirclement**, the bypass attack and the **guerrilla attack**.
- Defence strategies are the **position defence**, the **flanking defence**, the **pre-emptive defence**, the **counter-offensive defence**, the **mobile defence**, and **strategic withdrawal**.

Key Terms

competitive behaviour the activities of rival companies with respect to each other; this can take five forms—conflict, competition, co-existence, cooperation and collusion

competitive scope the breadth of a company's competitive challenge, for example broad or narrow

competitor audit a precise analysis of competitor strengths and weaknesses, objectives and strategies

core competences the principal distinctive capabilities possessed by a company—what it is really good at

counter-offensive defence a counter-attack that takes the form of a head-on counter-attack, an attack on the attacker's cash cow or an encirclement of the attacker

differential advantage a clear performance differential over the competition on factors that are important to target customers

differentiation strategy the selection of one or more customer choice criteria and positioning the offering accordingly to achieve superior customer value

divest to improve short-term cash yield by dropping or selling off a product

entry barriers that act to prevent new companies from entering a market, for example the high level of investment required

encirclement attack attacking the defender from all sides; i.e. every market segment is hit with every combination of product features

experience curve the combined effect of economies of scale and learning as cumulative output increases

flanking attack attacking geographical areas or market segments where the defender is poorly represented

flanking defence the defence of a hitherto unprotected market segment

frontal attack a competitive strategy where the challenger takes on the defender head on

guerrilla attack making life uncomfortable for stronger rivals through, for example, unpredictable price discounts, sales promotions or heavy advertising in a few selected regions

harvest objective the improvement of profit margins to improve cash flow even if the longer-term result is falling sales

hold objective a strategy of defending a product in order to maintain market share

industry a group of companies that market products that are close substitutes for each other

mobile defence involves diversification or broadening the market by redefining the business

niche a small market segment

position defence building a fortification around existing products, usually through keen pricing and improved promotion

pre-emptive defence usually involves continuous innovation and new product development, recognizing that attack is the best form of defence

strategic alliance collaboration between two or more organizations through, for example, joint ventures, licensing agreements, long-term purchasing and supply arrangement, or a joint R&D contract to build a competitive advantage

strategic focus the strategies that can be employed to achieve an objective

strategic withdrawal holding onto the company's strengths while getting rid of its weaknesses

value chain the set of a company's activities that are conducted to design, manufacture, market, distribute and service its products

Study Questions

1. Using Porter's 'five forces' framework, suggest why there is intense rivalry between leading European supermarket brands.

2. For any product of your choice identify the competition using the four-layer approach discussed in this chapter.

3. Why is competitor analysis essential in today's turbulent environment? How far is it possible to predict competitor response to marketing actions?

4. Distinguish between differentiation and cost-leadership strategies. Is it possible to achieve both positions simultaneously?

5. How might Google use differential advantage to stand out from its rivals?

6. How can value chain analysis lead to superior corporate performance?

7. What are cost drivers? Should marketing management be concerned with them, or is their significance solely the prerogative of the accountant?

8. Discuss the favourable conditions for pursuing build and hold marketing strategic objectives.

9. Explain the attack and defence strategies a company might need to use if they are the market leader.

Recommended Reading

Day, G. S. and R. Wensley (1988) Assessing advantage: A framework for diagnosing competitive superiority, *Journal of Marketing* 52, April, 1–20

Fleisher, C. and B. Bensoussan (2015) *Competitive Analysis: Effective Application of New and classic Methods*, Upper Saddle River, NJ, USA: Pearson Education.

Institute for Strategy & Competitiveness (2015) Creating Shared Value. http://www.isc.hbs.edu/about-michael -porter/Pages/default.aspx (accessed July 2015).

Noble, C.H., R. K. Sinha and A. Kumar, A. (2002) Market orientation and alternative strategic orientations: A longitudinal assessment of performance implications, *Journal of Marketing* 66 (4), 25–40

Porter, M. E. and J. E. Heppelmann, J.E. (2014) How Smart, Connected Products Are Transforming Competition, *Harvard Business Review* 92(11) 64–88.

Porter, M. E. (2008) On Competition. Boston, USA: Harvard Business School Publishing.

References

Airbus (2012) Alternative Fuel Sources http://www.airbus.com/ innovation/eco-efficiency/operations/alternative-fuels

Anderson, J. C. and J. A. Narus (1998) Business Marketing: Understand What Customers Value, *Harvard Business Review*, Nov.–Dec., 53–65.

BBH (2015) Case Study: Johnnie Walker, CreativeBrief.com, April. http://www.creativebrief.com/agency/work/686/12/johnnie-walker -advertising-keep-walking-by-bartle-bogle-hegarty-bbh-london

Boren, Z. (2014) There are officially more mobile devices than people in the world, *The Independent*, 7 October. http://www.independent. co.uk/life-style/gadgets-and-tech/news/there-are-officially-more- mobile-devices-than-people-in-the-world-9780518.html

Business Week (2006) Business Week Top 50 US Firms, 3 April, 82–100.

Buzzell, R. D. and B. T. Gale (1987) *The PIMS Principles*, New York: Free Press.

Cellan-Jones, R. (2015) Supercell: Europe's supercharged games success, BBC.co.uk, 15 October. http://www.bbc.co.uk/news/ technology-24541073

Day, G. S. (1999) *Market Driven Strategy: Processes for Creating Value*, New York: Free Press.

Day, G. S. and R. Wensley (1988) Assessing Advantage: A Framework for Diagnosing Competitive Superiority, *Journal of Marketing* 52, April, 1–20.

De Chernatony, L., F. Harris and F. Dall'Olmo Riley (2000) Added Value: Its Nature, Roles and Sustainability, *European Journal of Marketing* 34(1/2), 39–56.

Diageo (2015) Our Strategy, Diageo, April. http://www.diageo.com/ EN-SC/OURBUSINESS/ABOUTUS/Pages/our-strategy.aspx

Dredge, S. (2015) MySpace—what went wrong: 'The site was a massive spaghetti-ball mess', *The Guardian*, 6 March. http://www.

theguardian.com/technology/2015/mar/06/myspace-what-went-wrong-sean-percival-spotify (accessed 20 March 2015).

Easton, G. and L. Araujo (1986) Networks, Bonding and Relationships in Industrial Markets, *Industrial Marketing and Purchasing* 1(1), 8–25.

Einhorn, B. (2009) Acer's Game-Changing PC Offensive, *Business Week*, 20 April, 65.

Garside, J. (2012) BlackBerry creators pay price for failing to keep up with Apple, *The Guardian*. 23 January, 23.

Garside, J. and S. Farrrell (2014) Carphone Warehouse and Dixons agree £3.8bn merger, *The Guardian*, 15 May. http://www.theguardian.com/business/2014/may/15/carphone-warehouse-dixons-agree-merger (accessed 20 April 2015).

Gruman, G. (2015) InfoWorld, InfoWorld, 20 January: http://www.infoworld.com/article/2868766/macs/will-the-mac-dump-intel-for-the-same-chip-as-the-ipad.html

Hughes, N. (2014) Apple agrees to pay $450 million to settle ebook price fixing lawsuit, appleinsider, 16 July. http://appleinsider.com/articles/14/07/16/apple-settles-ebook-price-fixing-complaint-with-states-consumers-could-pay-450m

IBM (2015) What is Watson? http://www.ibm.com/smarterplanet/us/en/ibmwatson/what-is-watson.html

Kollewe, J. (2008) Vodafone Cuts Costs by Sharing Networks with Telefónica, *The Guardian*, 24 March, 26.

Kotler, P. and R. Singh (1981) Marketing Warfare in the 1980s, *Journal of Business Strategy*, Winter, 30–41.

Kuittinen, T. (2013) 5 Reasons Why Finnish Apps Are Beating American Rivals On US iPad Market, *Forbes*, 22 November. http://www.forbes.com/sites/terokuittinen/2013/11/22/5-reasons-why-finnish-apps-are-beating-american-rivals-on-us-ipad-market/ (accessed 20 April 2015).

Kuittinen, T. (2014) Rovio's Revenue Crisis and the App Market Evolution, *Forbes*, 6 March. http://www.forbes.com/sites/terokuittinen/2013/03/06/rovios-revenue-crisis-and-the-app-market-evolution (accessed 20 April 2015).

Leeflang, P. H. S. and D. R. Wittink (1996) Competitive Reaction versus Consumer Response: Do Managers Over-react? *International Journal of Research in Marketing* 13, 103–19.

Macdonald, M. H. B. and H. Wilson (2011) *Marketing Plans*, Oxford: Butterworth Heinemann.

MacKintosh, J. (2005) Car Design in a Generalist Market, *Financial Times*, 6 December, 20.

Marsh, P. (2002) Dismay at Job Losses as Dyson Shifts Production to Malaysia, *Financial Times*, 6 February, 3.

McNulty, S. (2001) Short on Frills, Big on Morale, *Financial Times*, 31 October, 14.

Mearian, L. (2015) IBM launches Watson Health global analytics cloud, *Computerworld*, 14 April. http://www.computerworld.com/article/2909534/ibm-launches-watson-health-global-analytics-cloud.html (accessed 20 April 2015).

Meng, J. and R. Layton (2011) Understanding managers' marketing strategy choice in a collaborative competition industry, *European Business Review* 23(5), 477–501.

Milne, R. and H. Williamson (2005) BMW Ignores Signals and Puts its Faith in Germany, *Financial Times*, 13 May, 20.

Nagle, T. T. and J. E. Hogan (2006) *The Strategy and Tactics of Pricing*, Upper Saddle River, NJ: Pearson.

Noble, C. H., R. K. Sinha and A. Kumar (2002) Market Orientation and Alternative Strategic Orientations: A Longitudinal Assessment of Performance Implications, *Journal of Marketing*, 66, October, 25–39.

Owen, E. (2012) Twinings to build on Gets You Back To You campaign, *Campaign*, 29 February. http://www.campaignlive.co.uk/news/1119572 (accessed 20 April 2015).

Porter, M. E. (1980) *Competitive Strategy: Techniques for Analysing Industries and Competitors*, New York: Free Press.

Porter, M. E. (1985) *Competitive Advantage*, New York: Free Press.

Porter, M. E. (1998) *Competitive Strategy*, New York: Free Press, 4.

Reisinger, D. (2015) Angry Birds maker's earnings fall while games rise, Cnet, 19 March. http://www.cnet.com/uk/news/angry-birds-maker-rovio-revenue-earnings-fall-but-games-rise

Ries, A. and J. Trout (2005) *Marketing Warfare*, New York: McGraw-Hill.

Rovio (2015) *RAND NEW GAME OUT - NIBBLERS SOFT LAUNCHES IN CANADA, FINLAND, NEW ZEALAND AND AUSTRALIA!* Rovio, 24 April. http://www.rovio.com/en/news/blog/651/brand-new-game-out-nibblers-soft-launches-in-canada-finland-new-zealand-and-australia

Simonian, H. and L. Lucas (2012) Starbucks takes coffee wars to Nespresso, *Financial Times* http://www.ft.com/cms/s/0/d90109a4-66ec-11e1-9e53-00144feabdc0.html, 5 March.

Sinclair, B. (2015) Apps are the most competitive market ever - Rovio exec, gamesindustry.biz, 16 April. http://www.gamesindustry.biz/articles/2015-04-16-apps-are-the-most-competitive-market-ever-rovio-exec

Steadman, I. (2013) IBM's Watson is better at diagnosing cancer than human doctors, *Wired*, 11 February. http://www.wired.co.uk/news/archive/2013-02/11/ibm-watson-medical-doctor (accessed 20 April 2015).

Sun Tzu (1963) *The Art of War*, London: Oxford University Press.

Sweney, M. (2014) Amazon takes on Netflix with rebrand of LoveFilm video-on-demand service, *The Guardian*, 21 February. http://www.theguardian.com/technology/2014/feb/21/amazon-lovefilm-revamp-film-tv-rental (accessed 18 April 2015).

The Economist (2008) Failure to Deliver, 15 November, 80.

Varadarajan, R. (2010) Strategic marketing and marketing strategy: domain, definition, fundamental issues and foundational premises, *Journal of Academy of Marketing Science* 38, 119–40. doi:10.1007/s11747-009-0176-7

Von Clausewitz, C. (1908) *On War*, London: Routledge & Kegan Paul.

Wunker, S. (2012) Fiat's Smart US launch strategy—really, HBR Blog Network http://blogs.hbr.org/cs/2012/02/fiats_smart_us_launch_strategy_really.html, 1 February.

CASE 37
General Motors

Back from the Brink

On 1 June 2009, General Motors (www.gm.com) filed for bankruptcy protection, a historic landmark event. GM has been leading the automotive business for over a century. The company owns several internationally known automotive brands, which it markets around the world. It builds nearly 9.9 million vehicles a year, making it an industry colossus. It is seen as the heartbeat of the American manufacturing industry. For decades it was viewed as an exemplar in the effective management, strategic thinking and organization of a modern corporation. Yet, it faced the perfect storm in 2009, as sales fell by a staggering 30 per cent. Most alarmingly, the company had over $176 billion in liabilities and lost a staggering $30 billion in 2008. Low-cost competition was eroding its market share. It had lost its mantle as the world's largest car manufacturer to Toyota in 2007. Now even the German VW group has eased itself into the number 2 position above GM.

General Motors was once the iconoclast of the American multinational corporation. The contribution of GM to American industry is gargantuan, spending $50 billion dollars a year on parts, and with a wage bill of $476 million a month. However, it had lost a colossal $88 billion since 2004—an untenable situation. At the height of the financial crisis, GM had to be bailed out by the US government due to bankruptcy. The US government invested over $862 billion into the motor vehicle industry. The company then offloaded several brands so that it could concentrate on core car models, and shed thousands of dealerships to make it leaner. The bankruptcy meant that original investors lost everything as the share price collapsed. Backed by the US and Canadian governments, the company had undergone radical change. The company's sheer size and impact on American economic life meant that it was too big to countenance failure.

GM slowly emerged from this traumatic period. In November 2010, it completed the world's largest initial public offering on the stock exchange, with the US government selling its stake in the business. The company now employs 212,000 staff based in 396 facilities, producing vehicles for over 120 countries. In 2014, the company had shaken off its shackles, earning net income of $2.8 billion on revenue of $155.9

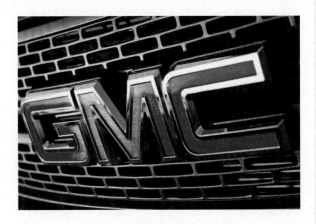

billion. Under its new leadership of CEO Mary T. Barra, the company expected to sell a colossal 1,000 new cars globally, every hour in 2015. The company now has a global network of 20,512 authorized dealerships around the globe. Yet global markets experience peaks and troughs; for example, sales in Russia have been decimated due to political and economic uncertainty. In 2015, sales of GM brands rose by 9 per cent.

General Motors had a huge product portfolio, where its sells cars in nearly every single market. Under its eight different car brands it manufactures over 89 different car models. The company had a truly international manufacturing presence with 11 assembly plants in Europe, 3 in Asia, 8 in South America, and 29 in North America. The company has set up a number of manufacturing centres in low-cost countries such as Mexico, India, South Africa and China. The company had hoped to grow through a series of acquisitions and alliances, designed to strengthen the brand portfolio even further. In 2000, GM gained 100 per cent control of Swedish luxury carmaker Saab. However, the luxury car brand ceased manufacturing cars in 2011, due to the accumulation of huge losses. In 2002, it took over troubled South Korean car maker Daewoo. The firm produces low-cost cars under the Chevrolet brand in 10 different international markets, using low-cost manufacturing bases. The company dropped the Daewoo brand in 2004, using the Chevrolet brand, with the aim of turning it into a global brand and moving it away from the firm's over-reliance on the North American market. However, this strategy of a global automotive car brand has failed, with the firm pulling the

»

Chevrolet brand out of Europe, citing difficult economic conditions. Its grand vision of a global car brand failed to materialize. The brand even sponsors the football team Manchester United for £47 million a year.

It is attempting to strengthen its international presence by focusing on growth areas such as China and developing countries. Growth there has been stellar, achieving 10 per cent quarterly sales growth. In China it operates 11 joint ventures with local companies, and employs over 35,000, selling international brands like Chevrolet, Buick and Opel, coupled with domestic Chinese automotive brands like Baojun and Wuling. In 2002, it formed a three-way strategic alliance with two domestic Chinese partners, SAIC and Liuzhou Wuling, to form SGMW, selling over 10 million cars. To see a synopsis of GM's eight main automotive brands, see Table C37.1. The company uses these different brands to target different segments of the market, and in different countries. In the USA, its uses four different car brands—Chevrolet, GMC, Buick and Cadillac—while in Europe it sells Opel and Vauxhall. In Australia, it sells GM car marques under the Holden brand.

One of the biggest difficulties for the GM stable of car brands was the lack of distinction between the various car marques. Car buyers view many of the models launched by GM as very similar to other cars in its range. GM adopted a 'euthanasia' policy on several of its underperforming brands in an effort to quell costs and create a stronger brand proposition. It argues that the cars sold under the various brands confuse

TABLE C37.1 General Motors' main automotive brands

Current GM brands				
Chevrolet	**Cadillac**	**Buick**	**Opel/Vauxhall**	**GMC**
The Chevrolet brand is the third biggest car brand in the world. GM's most important brand. Has offering in nearly every sector of market. GM sells this brand in Asian markets, focusing on small/medium size cars that are value for money. Sales up 3.4 per cent.	The luxury car brand in the GM stable. The quintessential luxury American car brand, with an emphasis on luxury, comfort, performance and technology. Aims to hold on to its premium brand. Sales up 13.7% in USA.	A mid-tier brand, with several luxury saloon cars and SUV offerings. Criticized for lacking distinction and rationalizing its current car model portfolio. Focuses on safety, quality and premium interiors at attainable prices. Brand has been successful in China. Sales down 5.2% in USA.	The Vauxhall and Opel brands are sold in the UK, Germany and other parts of Europe. There are a wide range of cars and vans in product ranges. Strong demand for cars in Europe. Market rose by 6.9%, with Opel/Vauxhall rising only by 1.7%.	It focuses on producing SUVs, pickup trucks and a range of commercial vehicles. Formerly known as GMC Truck. Sales up 20%, strong demand for SUVs due to cheap petrol. Sales up 20%.
GM brands sold or defunct				
Pontiac	**Saab**	**Hummer**	**Saturn**	
Pontiac is a mid-level brand, aimed typically at a young market. Focuses on projecting an image of performance, sport and youth. Only available in North America. Sells roadsters, saloons and SUVs. Brand was phased out, as part of restructuring.	Focused on premium market with sporty designs. Small niche brand. Sold to Swedish super luxury car maker, with support from the Swedish government. Now in receivership. Production stopped in 2011.	The former military vehicle jeep has been transformed into a highly popular and ridiculously expensive 4 × 4 vehicle. Launched in 1999, has earned a cache for cool. Sold for $100 million to Chinese manufacturer. Stopped production in 2010.	Created Saturn brand in 1990 in response to low cost Japanese imports in the sub-compact sector, using plastic body styling. Saturn is now repositioning in several different sectors such as saloons, SUV, roadsters and minivans. GM shut Saturn factories in 2009.	
GM Brands Sold in China (SGMW)				
Wuling Motors		**Baojun Motors**		
Wuling's brand orientation is called 'Quality Drives Life'. The Chinese brand produces a range of mini-vans, MPVs and small pickup trucks. The focus is low cost, yet high value.		Baojun Motors was launched in 2011. Sells a range of sedans and MPVs.		

customers, and that better returns could be gained by a coordinated branding strategy that communicated the true brand essence of each of the brands. For example, you could have bought a similar saloon car under the Pontiac, Buick and Chevrolet brand names with little or no discernable differences. GM suffers from the curse of sameness. Other companies have developed stronger reputations with a smaller repertoire of vehicles. Originally each of the GM brands had a strong distinctive image, with various brands focusing on different tiers of the market. For instance, Chevrolet focused on the value end, while Cadillac focused on the premium spectrum of the market. It has culled its line-up in the past in an effort to rationalize its product portfolio; it scrapped the Oldsmobile brand in 2000. This famous US car brand suffered perennially a decline in its revenue, due to a poor product offering and the brand's lack of differentiation. Now the company has culled its Pontiac, Saab, Saturn and Hummer brands from its portfolio.

To put the malaise into perspective, in the USA the four different brands had four different slogans.

- GMC—We are professional grade
- Chevrolet—Find new roads
- Buick—That's not a Buick
- Cadillac—Dare greatly

One of the key challenges for its brand stable is the production of eco-friendly cars, in response to oil prices and growing environmental concerns. It launched the Chevrolet Volt in 2011, which is an electric hybrid car. However, this is not its first foray into green energy as it launched the EV11 car, an innovative electric car, in 1999. This car was immortalized in a documentary called *Who Killed the Electric Car?*, which accused oil companies, car dealers, and the car companies themselves of helping to accelerate the project's downfall. This green initiative failed to be capitalized upon by General Motors, whereas Toyota's Prius hybrid car became an instant hit. GM let this innovative technology languish, while driving ahead with its traditional product portfolio. GM focused on hydrogen-powered technology as the future for the car industry. However, this technology is years from providing a viable alternative to oil, leaving GM without any foothold in this sector. Hybrid technology, ethanol or electricity were seen as viable technologies. Sales of new rival Tesla for its luxury range of electric cars have proved positive. The sales of the Volt, however, have failed to electrify industry pundits, despite receiving very positive reviews and awards. It has high hopes for selling electric cars projecting to sell 500,000 electric vehicles by 2017; however, only 180,000 have been sold.

The Credit Crisis

The company has been prone to difficulties throughout its history. It managed to stave off bankruptcy by

40 minutes in 1992 during a credit crunch. During that turbulent period it bounced back by slashing 21 plants and cutting 70,000 jobs, eliminating corporate bureaucracy and improving productivity and quality. GM is heavily reliant on the North America market, where most of its problems resided. Excess capacity, diminishing margins, a rigid sales channel structure, confusing brand propositions, falling market share, labour problems and exorbitant legacy costs have all made a serious impact. The majority of its revenue still comes from North America, making it very susceptible to market shocks within the US market. Sales in key western European markets are still falling. It has the number 1 market share in the Americas, the number 2 position in Asia, whilst languishing at number 6 in Europe.

In recent years, the firm had focused on churning out gas-guzzling SUVs (large Sports Utility Vehicles) and pick-up trucks, diverting its attention from normal saloon cars. These vehicles at the time were much sought after by the market and yielded higher margins. The company lost sight of developing a solid car range, while foreign competitors developed strong reputations in the sector. In the wake of rising oil prices, demand for these expensive-to-run SUVs has slumped, and consumers have turned to more fuel-efficient cars. So much of GM's portfolio is focused on large cars. Consumers swapped their gas guzzlers for smaller cars, which destroyed the residual value of second-hand GM cars. This led to losses for GM Finance division, as cars returning from a lease were depreciating at a calamitous rate. The price of oil has serious ramifications on GM's success. The oil price decline in 2015 has proved serendipitous for the firm.

Its US market share is continuing to slide: where it once garnered 41 per cent of the market in 1985, it now accounts for only 17.6 per cent. In an effort to stave off the decline, the company has deployed an aggressive price-discounting strategy, which has devalued many of GM's venerable brands. It offered its cars at 'employee discount for everyone'. Sales drop when a promotion ends and consumers wait for the latest rebate or promotional offer. The company shifted away from price promotions and focused on building brands through lower advertised prices, more advertising expenditure and extra equipment as standard.

Key to the future survival is the efficiency and effectiveness of GM's manufacturing capabilities. GM factories have won several awards for quality processes: however, this is not reflected in the market, where consumers have poor-quality perceptions toward GM brands. Continued improvement in its manufacturing capabilities is vital, focusing on quality, efficiency and costs. For instance, it takes 34 hours to build a typical GM car, while a Toyota takes 28 hours. The company

»

»

has only recently focused on harmonizing production and sharing parts and car platforms. The new GM company has formed a partnership, with its powerful trade unions now owning 17.5 per cent of the new company and agreeing to profit-sharing incentives.

GM has been criticized for launching numerous new models under different brands, then subsequently ditching them if not proved to be a stellar success, thus creating huge levels of product churn. This is a substantial investment in terms of marketing expenditure, constantly investing in brand recognition campaigns for these new brands. Other car-makers have several cornerstone car marques, which they frequently update with the latest technology and revamp with subtle stylistic changes. GM has increased the level of new product launches to unprecedented levels, placing the emphasis on getting newer models out to market very quickly. Also, GM had too many dealers. GM had five times more dealers than Toyota. Now it has cut nearly a half of its dealer network. Dealer margins have slipped to 1.6 per cent. The dealership structure needs to be consolidated and to become more sustainable. Continued efforts to alter GM sales channels have been restricted due to franchised dealers' rights under US law. However, bankruptcy enabled the company to make radical changes that would normally be impossible. The only way to change a dealership contract is through expensive compensation to the franchise. Over 1100 GM dealers were culled in 2009, with the subsequent sizable job losses.

Its Rebirth and Turnaround Strategy

Between 2009 and the end of 2010, GM had a total of four different CEOs. This highlights the extent of the calamity at the company. On 18 November 2010 GM emerged from bankruptcy a very different company, free from the shackles that potentially obliterated it. The group has launched several initiatives in order to reverse its declining fortunes: namely, reducing exorbitant fixed costs, maximizing manufacturing capacity and revitalizing a weak product offering through improved R&D. Manufacturing plants that are not operating at full capacity really hurt the business, especially in high-cost manufacturing countries. Previously the company had allowed autonomous R&D within divisions, but now the firm is seeking to leverage engineering expertise across its global operations. This it is hoped will improve design, reduce costs and avoid fruitless duplication of activities. It is spending nearly $8 billion on R&D every year, which equates to approximately 5 per cent of its revenue. It also hopes to eliminate look-alike products from its portfolio, developing best in segment cars. It has culled a swath of middle managers, in a bid to

eliminate bureaucracy. The company wants to radically overhaul its cost base, rationalizing powertrains, trim options and the sheer variety of models. All of which cost money. In addition it has formed strategic alliances with rivals like French-based Peugeot-Citroën to develop cost-saving initiatives like shared vehicle platforms and shared purchasing costs. From a marketing perspective, it has placed a renewed focus on customer satisfaction, earning customers for life. It has initiated programmes to improve the customer experience through all touchpoints, measuring customers' net promotor scores, in an effort to delight the customer.

GM is now attempting to amalgamate several brands into one sales channel. For instance, in the US it is creating dealerships where Buick and GMC are sold under the same dealership, creating strong sales propositions. Obviously developing markets like China and Brazil are the big hope for the automotive trade. This burgeoning market is a key priority for the firm. In Europe, Opel/Vauxhall is still struggling. Developing cars that Chinese consumers want is critical, leveraging their relationships with local partners to achieve success. The company has to have a truly global perspective. GM is developing an array of cross-over cars, supermini cars and fuel-efficient electric cars. In 2015, GM earned over $155 billion. The new GM vision is to design, build and sell the world's best vehicles. Can it maintain the positive momentum?

Questions

Mc Graw Hill Education **connect**

1. **Using Porter's 'five forces' framework, discuss the competitiveness of the global automobile market.**

2. **Identify and discuss the weaknesses associated with General Motors' marketing strategy. (Visit its affiliated sites: www.gm.com, www.opel.com, www.vauxhall.co.uk, www.chevrolet.com.)**

3. **What are GM's sources of competitive advantage? Discuss how GM could achieve a differential advantage over competitors.**

This case was written by Conor Carroll, Lecturer in Marketing, University of Limerick. The material in the case has been drawn from a variety of published sources and research reports.

References

The material in the case has been drawn from a variety of published sources.

CASE 38
Walmart and Asda

Battling for Retail Success

Enter any Walmart store in the USA and you are struck by the sheer scale of the operation. These are stores of over 200,000 square feet in which seven UK superstores could be accommodated. Next come the 'greeters', who welcome customers into the stores, give them their card in case they need help and put a smiley sticker on them. Then come the prices where, for example, a cotton T-shirt that would sell for the equivalent of around $15 (£9.40/€13.5) in a UK department store sells for $1 (£0.60/€0.90) in Walmart. The choice of products is wide ranging, from clothes via groceries and pharmaceuticals to electrical goods. Stores are well organized with the right goods always available, kept neat and clean in appearance and with goods helpfully displayed.

At the heart of the Walmart operation are its systems and information technology: 1,000 information technologists run a massive database; its information collection, which comprises over 65 million transactions (by item, time, price and store), drives most aspects of its business. Within 90 minutes of an item being sold, Walmart's distribution centres are organizing its replacement. Distribution is facilitated by state-of-the-art delivery tracking systems. So effective is the system that when a flu epidemic hit the USA, Walmart followed its spread by monitoring flu remedy sales in its stores. It then predicted its movement from east to west so that Walmart stores were adequately stocked in time for the rise in demand.

Walmart also uses real-time information systems to let consumers decide what appears in its stores. The Internet is used to inform suppliers what was sold the day before. In this way, it only buys what sells.

Its relationship with its suppliers is unusual in that they are only paid when an item is sold in its stores. Not only does this help cash flow, it also ensures that the interests of manufacturer and Walmart coincide. Instead of the traditional system where once the retailer had purchased stock it was essentially the retailer's problem to sell it, if the product does not sell it hurts the manufacturer's cash flow more than Walmart's. Consequently, at a stroke, the supplier's and retailer's interests are focused on the same

measures and rewards. There is no incentive for the supplier to try to sell Walmart under-performing brands since they will suffer in the same way as the retailer if they fail to sell in the store.

Walmart staff are called 'associates' and are encouraged to tell top management what they believe is wrong with their stores. They are offered share options and encouraged to put the customer first.

Walmart has enjoyed phenomenal success in the USA, but faced a tough challenge by its rival, Target, which has built its business by selling similar basic consumable goods like soap at low prices, but also higher-margin, design-based items such as clothing and furnishings. The problem Walmart faced was that consumers were buying groceries and toiletries at its stores but not its clothing, furnishing or electronics ranges. Target was stealing customers by positioning itself as an up-market discounter using designers such as Isaac Mizraki and stylish lifestyle advertising to attract consumers to its clothing and furnishings. Walmart, by contrast, was using mundane in-store advertising focusing on low prices.

Walmart's response was to commission, for the first time, a marketing research survey. Hitherto it had believed marketing research was the province of its suppliers. The survey of its customers revealed that Walmart's clothing was considered dull. This led to the launch in 2005 of a more up-market fashion brand, Metro 7, targeted at the group Walmart called

»

'selective shoppers'—those who buy groceries and toiletries but who previously would not have bought clothing. The new clothing range was backed by a change in advertising, including a spread in *Vogue* magazine and a move to lifestyle advertising, designed to appeal to what the retailer termed 'fashion-savvy' female customers with an urban lifestyle. However, Metro 7 failed, as the line was not 'hip' enough to attract fashion buyers or cheap enough to appeal to traditional Walmart customers.

Walmart also redesigned its electronics and furnishings departments and improved the product ranges to appeal to wealthier customers. In consumer electrics, for example, it added high-end products from Sony LCD televisions and Toshiba laptops to Apple iPods, and backed the new ranges with aggressive advertising campaigns. Departments were redesigned with wider aisles and lower shelves. Walmart revamped all its stores to make them appear less dull and appeal to middle-income shoppers trading down in the recent recession.

The retailer also employed what it termed its 'win, play or show' strategy. 'Win' product categories are those where Walmart can out-manoeuvre rivals with low prices on high demand products such as flat-screen TVs, including higher-end models. This has increased Walmart's share of TVs while increasing margins. 'Play' applies to areas like clothing where Walmart can be a player but is unlikely to dominate. Here product lines are pruned to top sellers like $20 Levi jeans while cutting back on higher-end items. 'Show' are the one-stop-shopping essentials such as hardware, which are necessary to compete in the USA with rivals like Home Depot. Here, product lines like hammers and tape measures are restricted to one or two brands.

-However, Walmart has been criticized for being slow to fully embrace the opportunities provided by online shopping. In response, the company embarked on a major investment programme to rectify this weakness.

Walmart's Overseas Operations

Since 1992, Walmart has moved into 16 countries, and this strategy has been the engine for most of its sales and profit growth in recent years. In Canada and Mexico it is already market leader in discount retailing. In Canada it bought Woolco in 1994, quickly added outlets, and by 1997 became market leader with 45 per cent of the discount store market—a remarkable achievement. In countries such as China and Argentina it has been surprisingly successful and international sales have grown to around 25 per cent of total revenue.

In 1998, it entered Europe with the buying of Germany's Wertkauf warehouse chain, quickly followed by the acquisition of 74 Interspar hypermarkets. It

immediately closed stores, then reopened them with price cuts on 1,100 items, making them 10 per cent below competitors' prices. Walmart's German operation was not a success, however, because of the presence of more aggressive discounters such as Aldi. In 2006, it admitted failure by selling its 85 stores to a local rival, Metro, at a loss of £530 million (€740 million).

Walmart's entry into the UK was the next step in its move into the European market. Asda was a natural target since it shared Walmart's 'everyday low prices' culture. It was mainly a grocery supermarket, but also sold clothing. Its information technology systems lagged badly behind those of its UK supermarket competitors, but it has acted as 'consumer champion' by selling cosmetics and over-the-counter pharmaceuticals for cheaper prices than those charged by traditional outlets. Walmart decided to keep the Asda store name rather than rebranding it as Walmart. Most of Asda's stores are located in the north of the UK.

The early signs were that the acquisition was a success with sales and profits rising. A major move was to create a speciality division that operates pharmacy, optical, jewellery, photography and shoe departments. The aim was to make store space work harder (i.e. improve sales revenue and profits per square metre). Asda has also benefited from the introduction of thousands of non-food items across a wide range of home and leisure categories. Space has been made for these extra products in existing food-dominated supermarkets by decreasing the amount of shelf space devoted to food and reducing pack sizes.

The George line of clothing was a huge success and was expanded to include a lower-priced version of the brand called Essentially George. So impressed were Walmart management with the success of George clothing, that they introduced the range in their own stores. Asda took the George brand to the high street by launching standalone 10,000-square-foot clothing stores branded George. The stores carried the complete line of George-brand men's, women's and children's clothing at prices the same as those offered in the George departments in Asda supermarkets. However, in the face of competition from Primark and New Look they were only moderately successful.

Besides expanding its product lines, Asda has also focused on cutting prices, aided by its inclusion in the Walmart stable, which brings it enormous buying power. For example, since the takeover, it has made 60 per cent savings on fabrics and 15 per cent on buttons. This has meant price reductions on such clothing items as jeans, ladies' tailored trousers, skirts, silk ties and baby pyjamas. In four years, the price of George jeans fell from £15 (€21.6) to £6 (€8.6).

Change of Fortune

Asda's initial success was reflected in its overtaking of Sainsbury's to become the UK's number two supermarket chain behind Tesco in 2004. Shortly afterwards, however, Asda's fortunes changed. Faced with a rampant Tesco and a resurgent Sainsbury's, the company lost market share. When Walmart bought Asda, the intention was to build huge, US-style hypermarkets. Unfortunately, shortly after the acquisition, UK planning rules tightened to prevent out-of-town shopping developments. Tesco, and to a lesser extent Sainsbury's, entered the smaller store market, opening outlets in town and city centres and petrol stations where planning restrictions were much less severe. Asda kept its focus on large supermarkets.

In 2005, Andy Bond was promoted internally to replace Tony de Nunzio, who left to join Dutch non-food retailer Vendex. Faced with a dominant Tesco with over 30 per cent market share, and a more aggressive Sainsbury's under the leadership of Justin King, Bond faced an enormous challenge. Helped by Asda's positioning as a cut-price, full-range supermarket Bond met with early success. Some of his key actions were as follows.

- Removed 1,400 managers: 200 jobs at Asda's head office and 1,200 junior managerial positions in stores were cut. Part of the savings were invested in front-line customer service staff in stores.
- Opened 17 more Asda Living stores to bring the total to 22 and developed the Living range online: these are non-food stores offering such products as homeware, electrical goods, George clothing, music and video, health and beauty, and toys and baby products. It was planned that by 2015, 150 Asda Living stores would have been opened.
- Slowed the growth of George fashion store openings and in 2010 closed all of them, citing high rental costs.
- Trialled two Asda Essentials stores: these were small-format stores to challenge Tesco Express and Sainsbury's Local convenience stores. They stocked a limited range of products, including fresh food, and were based on the French Leader Price chain, which sells fresh fruit, vegetables, meat, grocery products and cosmetics. The stores sold almost entirely Asda own-label products. After less than a year one of these trial stores was closed and Asda announced it had no plans to open any more.
- Improved the product line: healthier food sourced from local producers, and sold new products online such as contact lenses and airline tickets.

- Urged the Office of Fair Trading to open an inquiry into Tesco's land bank of 185 development sites with a view to preventing it buying land and opening stores close to existing outlets without reference to the OFT. And if an existing store was sold by one supermarket chain to another, the deal had to be scrutinized by the competition authority.
- Responded to the recent recession by selling hundreds of products for £1, offering 50p bargains, including 400g of mince, two pints of milk, a white loaf, six eggs and 2kgs of carrots, and launching a TV campaign (supported by evidence from the price comparison website moneysupermarket.com) showing how Asda was cheaper than Tesco.
- Adopted the 'less is more' strategy, which includes dropping secondary brands to concentrate on the biggest brand names.

Mr Bond Resigns

In 2010, Mr. Bond resigned from his post as chief executive to take up the role of part-time chairman. He was replaced by Andy Clarke, formerly Asda's chief operating officer. One of his first moves was to buy the 193 UK stores off Danish discount retailer Netto. Netto stores averaged only 750 square metres compared with Asda's average superstore of 4,300 square metres.

Mr. Clarke soon faced an onslaught from the discount chains Aldi and Lidl, which competed by offering lower prices than Asda and smaller local stores. He responded by slashing prices, revamping Asda's 170 medium stores, giving more space to fresh food, hot food, and health and beauty products, while taking out a fifth of the space devoted to goods now bought mainly online, such as televisions, DVDs and CDs. Asda has also grown its online grocery business, including expanding click-and-collect locations from 250 in 2013 to 1,000 by 2018. In 2015, Asda trialled collection points at tube station car parks. Further, unlike Tesco, which has retrenched, Mr. Clarke is opening more stores, particularly small and medium-sized supermarkets and outlets at petrol outlets. However, he has decided to avoid expansion into the convenience store sector, which is dominated by Tesco and Sainsbury's. 'Online and click and collect is our convenience solution,' he said.

Questions

1. What are Walmart's sources of competitive advantage? How do these sources manifest themselves in creating competitive advantage for Walmart customers?

≫

2. **Did Walmart's acquisition of Asda make competitive sense?**

3. **Why did Asda's fortunes worsen around 2004?**

4. **Assess the actions taken by Andy Bond and Andy Clarke to revive Asda.**

This case was written by David Jobber, Emeritus Professor of Marketing, University of Bradford.

References

Based on: Merrilees, B. and D. Miller (1999) Defensive Segmentation Against a Market Spoiler Rival, *Proceedings of the Academy of Marketing Conference*, Stirling, July, 1–10; Teather, D. (2003) Asda's £360m Plan Will Create 3,900 Jobs, *The Guardian*, 19 February, 23; Troy, M. (2003) 'Buy' George! Wal-Mart's Asda Takes Fashion to UK's High Street, *DSN Retailing Today*, 23 June, 1; Finch, J. (2005) Asda to Open Hundreds of Discount Shops, *The Guardian*, 10 December, 22; Finch, J. (2005) Asda Cuts 1400 Managers in Fight to Stay No 2 Grocer, *The Guardian*, 6 July, 16; Birchall, J. (2005) What Wal-Mart Women Really Want, *Financial Times*, 10 October, 11; Birchall, J. (2005) Supermarket Sweep, *The Financial Times*, 10 November, 17; Anonymous (2006) Wal-Mart Admits Defeat in Germany and Sells Stores, *The Guardian*, 24 July, 32; Palmeri, C. (2008) Wal-Mart Is Up For This Downturn, Businessweek, 30 October, 42; Finch, J. and A. Clark (2008) 70,000 Extra Customers a Week Head For Asda, *The Guardian*, 10 July, 27; Finch, J. (2009) Asda Sales Continue To Soar As 'Intelligent Offers' Pull in Record 18m Shoppers a Week, *The Guardian*, 14 August, 23; Wood, Z. and G. Wearden (2010) Asda Boss Andy Bond Stuns City by Quitting, *The Guardian*, 13 April, 24; Finch, J. and Z. Wood (2010) Asda Buys Netto for £778m in Attempt to Close Gap on Tesco, *The Guardian* 28 May, 33; Boyle, M. and D. MacMillan (2011) Wal-Mart's Rocky Path From Bricks to Clicks, *Bloomberg Business Week*, 25–31 July, 31–3; Felsted, A. (2012) Asda Goes for Growth but Tesco Pulls Back, *The Financial Times*, 24 January, 18; Butler, s. Asda Launches Tube Station Grocery Collections, Guardian, 20 November, 31; Butler, S. (2015) Tesco Is Having Heart Surgery, Says Asda Boss, Guardian, 6 February, 28; Butler, S. (2015) Asda Reveals Plans to Open More Stores As Sales Slip, Guardian, 20 February, 27; Butler S. (2015) Asda Sales Slump Worst of the Big Four, *The Guardian*, 20 May, 19.

CHAPTER 20

Product Strategy: Product Lifecycle, Portfolio Planning and Product Growth Strategies

Innovation distinguishes between a leader and a follower.

STEVE JOBS, APPLE INC.

LEARNING OBJECTIVES

After reading this chapter, you should be able to:

1 describe the concept of the product lifecycle
2 discuss the uses and limitations of the product lifecycle
3 describe the concept of product portfolio planning
4 explain the Boston Consulting Group Growth-Share Matrix, its uses and the criticisms of it
5 explain the General Electric Market Attractiveness–Competitive Position Model, its uses and the criticisms of it
6 discuss the contribution of product portfolio management
7 discuss product strategies for growth

T his chapter examines the application of analytical tools used in the area of strategic product planning beginning with the product lifecycle. This section also considers the implication for managing brands over a period of time. The next key topic area is managing brand and product line portfolios. Many companies handle numerous products and serve multiple markets segments. Consequently, managers need to address the question of where to place investment for product growth and where and when to withdraw resources. Such questions are considered in the second part of this chapter. Finally, the topic of product strategies for growth is explored.

Managing Product Lines and Brands over Time: the Product Lifecycle

No matter how wide the product mix, both product lines and individual brands need to be managed over time. A useful tool for conceptualizing the changes that may take place during the time that a product is on the market is called the **product lifecycle**. It is quite flexible and can be applied to both brands and product lines (Polli and Cook, 1969). For simplicity, in the rest of this chapter, brands and product lines will be referred to as products. We shall now look at the product lifecycle, before discussing its uses and limitations.

The classic product lifecycle has four stages (see Figure 20.1): introduction, growth, maturity and decline.

Introduction

When first introduced on to the market a product's sales growth is typically low, and losses are incurred because of heavy development and promotional costs. Companies will be monitoring the speed of product adoption and, if this is disappointing, may terminate the product at this stage.

All leading companies, such as Samsung, IBM, Mercedes, Toyota and Apple, invest heavily in new product development to create products that confer new features and benefits for consumers. Because of this heavy investment, high promotional expenditures and low sales, losses are often suffered during product introduction. Nokian Tyres has made a long-term investment in product research and innovations. The company's expertise in heavy-tyre manufacturing has made it a world-leading specialist manufacturer. It also invests in communicating the benefits of its products (Nokian, 2015).

 Scan the QR code to see how Nokian Tyres uses its features in its advertising.

Growth

This stage is characterized by a period of faster sales and profit growth. Sales growth is fuelled by rapid market acceptance and, for many products, repeat purchasing. Profits may begin to decline towards the latter stages of

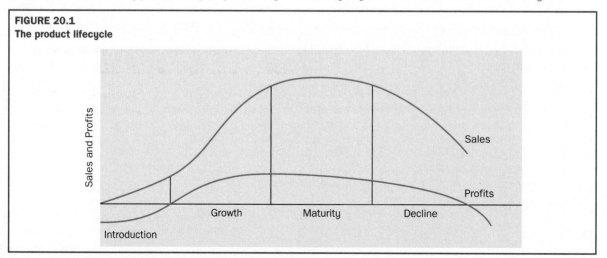

FIGURE 20.1
The product lifecycle

growth as new rivals enter the market, attracted by fast sales growth and high profit potential. The tablet computer market is an example of this. Apple introduced the iPad in 2010 and the rapid sales growth was mirrored by a vast increase in competitors such as Samsung Galaxy Tab and Hewlett-Packard TouchPad (see Exhibit 20.1). The smartphone market developed as technology innovation enabled mobile computing to be integrated into modern handsets. During the growth stage many rival technology companies entered the market with operating systems for the new type of phones, including Apple iOS, Google Android and Microsoft Windows. The end of the growth period is often associated with *competitive shakeout*, when weaker suppliers cease production. Technology markets are particularly susceptible. Read Marketing in Action 20.1 to find out about the winners and losers in the dot-com bubble.

MARKETING IN ACTION 20.1
The Dot-Com Bubble Winners and Losers

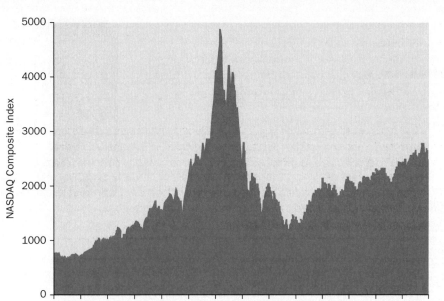

The size of the Internet economy started to grow rapidly from 1996. Between 1999 and 2001 there was a period of intense growth in the value of technology stocks. Forrester Research estimated the total Internet economy was worth US$15 billion, and by 2000 revenues from online consumer spending in the USA alone were estimated at US$45 billion (Boston Consulting Group, 2001). Predictions about the growth of online markets and the rapidly rising share prices got everyone excited. This was a rapid growth market. But there were very few Internet-savvy businesses offering stocks for sale. Investors scrambled to buy Internet stocks. The high demand and low level of supply created a trading frenzy, which stimulated exponential market growth (see image). In the retail sector, predictions suggested that 'by the year 2005 it (the Internet) would capture between 8 and 30 per cent of the UK retail market', leaving high streets looking like ghost towns. Extreme examples of increases in valuations and personal gains for the entrepreneurs (dot-com millionaires) helped to drive the growth even more. For example, Xcelera.com, developed by Norwegian Alexander Vik saw its stock soar from a few pennies to over $200 a share in less than a year, giving the company a market capitalization of $3.8 billion. Indeed, in 2000 there were 63 dot-com millionaires on the *Sunday Times* rich list but by 2001 this was down to just 26. The bubble burst and many innovative companies—which had rushed to move online—collapsed almost overnight. There were some notable winners and losers.

Winners:
- Google
- Amazon
- Lastminute.com
- eBay.

»

»

Losers:

- Boo.com (spent $180 million in six months trying to create a global fashion store, but went into bankruptcy in 2000)
- America Online (AOL) (merged with Time Warner)
- Geocities.com (bought out by Yahoo!)
- Webvan (filed for bankruptcy in 2001)
- Startups.com (failed in 2002)
- FreeInternet.com (filed for bankruptcy in October 2000)
- Pets.com (pet supplies retailer filed for bankruptcy in 2000).

Based on: Doherty, Ellis-Chadwick and Hart (2003); Ellis-Chadwick, Doherty and Hart (2002); Boston Consulting Group (2001); Pavitt (1997); Wikipedia (n.d.); Virzi (2000); Hudson (2010)

Maturity

Eventually sales peak and flatten as saturation occurs, hastening competitive shakeout. The survivors battle for market share by employing product improvements, advertising and sales promotional offers, dealer discounts and price cutting; the result is a strain on profit margins particularly for follower brands. The need for effective brand building is acutely recognized during maturity as brand leaders are in the strongest position to resist the pressure on profit margins (Doyle, 1989). Heinz has been advertising its brand of beans for over 40 years. The manufacturer differentiated the brand using the slogan 'Beanz Meanz Heinz'. Investment in this iconic advertising campaign enabled Heinz to fend off competitors and stimulate sales in a mature market.

Decline

Sales and profits fall during the decline stage as new technology or changes in consumer tastes work to reduce demand for the product. For example, Sony lost out when the market for cathode-ray TVs went into decline following the development of flat-screen TVs. The technological advance resulted in Samsung and Panasonic overtaking Sony in sales of televisions (Gapper, 2006). Suppliers may decide to cease production completely or reduce product depth. Promotional and product development budgets may be slashed and marginal distributors dropped as suppliers seek to maintain (or increase) profit margins. Advertising may be used to defend against rivals and prevent the sales of a brand from falling into decline.

EXHIBIT 20.1
Samsung reminds its customers there are no limits with new products in its Galaxy range

Uses of the Product Lifecycle

The product lifecycle (PLC) concept is useful for product management in several ways.

Product termination

First, the PLC emphasizes the fact that nothing lasts for ever. There is a danger that management may fall in love with certain products. Maybe a company was founded on the success of a particular product; perhaps the product champion of a past success is now the chief executive. Under such circumstances there can be emotional ties with the product that can transcend normal commercial considerations. The PLC underlines the fact that companies have to face the fact that products need to be terminated and new products developed to replace them. Without this sequence a company may find itself with a group of products all in the decline stage of their PLC.

Growth projections

The second use of the PLC concept is to warn against the dangers of assuming that growth will continue for ever. Swept along by growing order books, management can fall into the trap of believing that the heady days of rising sales and profits will continue for ever. The PLC reminds managers that growth will end, and suggests a need for caution when planning investment in new production facilities.

Marketing objectives and strategies over the PLC

The PLC emphasizes the need to review marketing objectives and strategies as products pass through the various stages. Changes in market and competitive conditions between the PLC stages suggest that marketing strategies should be adapted to meet them. Table 20.1 shows a set of stylized marketing responses to each stage. Note these are broad generalizations and serve to emphasize the need to review marketing objectives and strategies in the light of environmental change.

TABLE 20.1 Marketing objectives and strategies over the product lifecycle

	Introduction	Growth	Maturity	Decline
Strategic marketing objective	Build	Build	Hold	Harvest/manage for cash/divest
Strategic focus	Expand market	Penetration	Protect share/innovation	Productivity
Brand objective	Product awareness/trial	Brand preference	Brand loyalty	Brand exploitation
Products	Basic	Differentiated	Differentiated	Rationalized
Promotion	Creating awareness/trial	Creating awareness/ trial/ repeat purchase	Maintaining awareness/ repeat purchase	Cut/eliminated
Price	High	Lower	Lowest	Rising
Distribution	Patchy	Wider	Intensive	Selective

The strategic marketing objective is to build sales by expanding the market for the product. The brand objective will be to create product (as well as brand) awareness so that customers will become familiar with generic product benefits.

The product is likely to be fairly basic, with an emphasis on reliability and functionality rather than special features to appeal to different customer groups. For example, the introduction of the netbook when desktop computers were the de facto machine for all our computing needs. Then the laptop arrived which was a mobile equivalent. Generally, these machines were expensive, heavy and suffered from poor battery life. So there was a gap in the market for target audiences which wanted lighter machines to last longer while on the move. The netbook was able to fill this gap. Fairly basic models were offered, providing mobile computing and Internet access at affordable prices (e.g. Asus, Acer, Samsung). The functionality was basic, and the processor speed and memory fairly limited compared to their desktop and laptop counterparts. This lack of benefits eventually enabled other faster devices with a greater range of benefits to supersede the netbook—for example, tablet computers like the iPad and Microsoft Surface Pro, and smartphones like the Apple iPhone and Samsung Galaxy.

Promotion will support the brand objectives by gaining awareness for the brand and product type, and stimulating trial. Advertising has been found to be more effective in the beginning of the life of a product than in later stages (Vakratsas and Ambler, 1999). Typically price will be high because of the heavy development costs and the low level of competition. Distribution will be patchy as some dealers are wary of stocking the new product until it has proved to be successful in the marketplace.

Growth

The strategic marketing objective during the growth phase is to build sales and market share. The strategic focus will be to penetrate the market by building brand preference. To accomplish this task the product will be redesigned to create differentiation, and promotion will stress the functional and/or psychological benefits that accrue from the differentiation. Awareness and trial to acquire new customers are still important, but promotion will begin to focus on repeat purchasers. As development costs are defrayed and competition increases, prices will fall. Rising consumer demand and increased salesforce effort will widen distribution.

Maturity

As sales peak and stabilize, the strategic marketing objective will be to hold on to profits and sales by protecting market share rather than embarking on costly competitive challenges. Since sales gains can only be at the expense of competition, strong challenges are likely to be resisted and lead to costly promotional or price wars. Brand objectives now focus on maintaining brand loyalty and customer retention, and promotion will defend the brand, stimulating repeat purchase by maintaining brand awareness and values. For all but the brand leader, competition may erode prices and profit margins, while distribution will peak in line with sales.

A key focus will be innovation to extend the maturity stage or, preferably, inject growth. This may take the form of innovative promotional campaigns, product improvements, and extensions and technological innovation. Ways of increasing usage and reducing repeat purchase periods of the product will also be sought.

Decline

The conventional advice to companies managing products in the decline stage of the product lifecycle is to harvest or divest. A harvest strategy would result in the raising of prices while slashing marketing expenditures in an effort to boost profit margins. The strategic focus, therefore, is to improve marketing productivity rather than holding or building sales. The brand loyalty that has been built up over the years is in effect being exploited to create profits that can be used elsewhere in the company (e.g. new products). Product development will cease, the product line will be cut to the bare minimum of brands and promotional expenditure cut, possibly to zero. Distribution costs will be analyzed with a view to selecting only the most profitable outlets. The Internet will be examined to explore its potential as a low-cost promotional and distribution vehicle.

Divestment may take the form of selling products to other companies, or, if there are no willing buyers, product elimination. The strategy is to extract any residual value in the products where possible, and to free up managerial time and resources to be redirected at more attractive products and opportunities. Occasionally, products are harvested and then divested. For example, Nokia sold off its mobile phone business when it lost significant market share to rivals Apple and Samsung, so that it could focus its attention in other areas, for example mobile phone networks and mapping and location devices.

Two other strategies that can be applied at the decline stage are: 1) industry revitalization, and 2) pursuit of a profitable survivor strategy.

Industry revitalization: some products go into decline not because they are inherently unpopular but because of lack of investment. For example, years of under-investment in cinemas meant the facilities were often dilapidated and the programming offered limited choice of films. However, one company saw this scenario as a marketing opportunity. Showcase Cinemas was launched, offering a choice of around 12 films in modern purpose-built premises near large conurbations. This completely changed the experience of going to the cinema, resulting in revitalization of the industry and growth in cinema attendances and profits. Thus, the classic PLC prescription of harvesting in the decline stage was rejected by a company that was willing to invest in order to reposition cinemas as an attractive means of offering evening entertainment.

Profitable survivor strategy: another alternative to harvesting or divestment is called the profitable *survivor strategy* (Aaker, 2007). This involves deciding to become the sole survivor in a declining market. This may involve being willing to incur losses while competitors drop out, or if it is thought that this process is likely to be lengthy and slow, to accelerate it by:

- further reducing the attractiveness of the market by such actions as price cuts or increases in promotional expenditures
- buying competitors (which may be offered at a low price due to the unattractive markets they operate in) or their product lines that compete in the same market
- agreeing to take over competitors' contracts (e.g. supplying spare parts or service contracts) in exchange for their agreement to drop out of the market.

Once in the position of sole supplier, the survivor can reap the rewards of a monopolist by raising prices and resuming profitable operations.

Product planning

The PLC emphasizes the need for *product planning*. We have already discussed the need to replace old products with new. The PLC also stresses the need to analyse the balance of products that a company markets from the point of view of the PLC stages. A company with all of its products in the mature stage may be generating profits today, but as it enters the decline stage, profits may fall and the company become unprofitable. A balanced range of product is better, i.e. some products in the mature stage, some in the growth stage, and prospects of new product launches in the near future. The growth products would replace the mature products as the latter enter decline, and the new product successes would eventually become the growth products of the future. The PLC is, then, a stimulus to thinking about products as an interrelated set of profit-bearing assets that need to be managed as a group. We shall return to this theme when discussing product portfolio analysis later in this chapter.

The dangers of overpowering

The PLC concept highlights the dangers of overpowering. A company that introduces a new-to-the-world product may find itself in a very powerful position early in its PLC. Assuming that the new product confers unique benefits to customers there is an opportunity to charge a very high price during this period of monopoly supply. However, unless the product is patent-protected this strategy can turn sour when competition enters during the growth phase (as predicted by the PLC concept). This situation arose for the small components manufacturer that was the first to solve the technical problems associated with developing a seal in an exhaust recirculation valve used to reduce pollution in car emissions. The company took advantage of its monopoly supply position to charge very high prices to Ford. The strategy rebounded when competition entered and Ford discovered it had been overcharged (Cline and Shapiro, 1979). Had the small manufacturer been aware of the predictions of the PLC concept it may have anticipated competitive entry during the growth phase, and charged a lower price during introduction and early growth. This would have enabled it to begin a relationship-building exercise with Ford, possibly leading to greater returns in the long run.

Limitations of the Product Lifecycle

The product lifecycle is an aid to thinking about marketing decisions, but it needs to be handled with care. Management needs to be aware of the limitations of the PLC so that it is not misled by its prescriptions.

Fads and classics

Not all products follow the classic S-shaped curve. The sales of some products 'rise like a rocket then fall like a stick'. This is normal for *fad* products such as hula hoops (popularized in the 1950s), 'pet rocks' (1970s), Pokemon cards (1990s), and Zumba classes and superfoods such as quinoa (2010s).

Other products (and brands) appear to defy entering the decline stage. For example, classic confectionery products and brands such as Mars bars, Cadbury's Milk Tray and Toblerone have survived for decades in the mature stage of the PLC. Nevertheless, research has shown that the classic S-shaped curve does apply to a wide range of products, including grocery food products, and pharmaceuticals (Polli and Cook, 1969).

Marketing effects

The PLC is the *result* of marketing activities not the cause. One school of thought argues that the PLC is not simply a fact of life—unlike living organisms—but is simply a pattern of sales that reflects marketing activity (Dhalia and Yuspeh, 1976). Clearly, sales of a product may flatten or fall simply because it has not received enough marketing attention, or has had insufficient product redesign or promotional support. Using the PLC, argue the critics, may lead to inappropriate action (e.g. harvesting or dropping the product) when the correct response should be increased marketing support (e.g. product replacement, positioning reinforcement or repositioning).

Unpredictability

The duration of the PLC stages is unpredictable. The PLC outlines the four stages that a product passes through without defining their duration.

EXHIBIT 20.2
Toblerone uses magic and fantasy to maintain its position as a classic chocolate brand

Clearly this limits its use as a forecasting tool since it is not possible to predict when maturity or decline will begin. The exception to this problem is when it is possible to identify a comparator product that serves as a template for predicting the length of each stage. Two sources of comparator products exist: first, countries where the same product has already been on the market for some time; second, where similar products are in the mature or decline stages of their lifecycle but are thought to resemble the new product in terms of consumer acceptance. In practice, the use of comparator products is fraught with problems. For example, the economic and social conditions of countries may be so different that simplistic exploitation of the PLC from one country to another may be invalid; the use of similar products may offer inaccurate predictions in the face of ever-shortening product lifecycles.

Misleading objective and strategy prescriptions

The stylized marketing objectives and strategy prescriptions may be misleading. Even if a product could accurately be classified as being in a PLC stage, and sales are not simply a result of marketing activities, critics argue that the stylized marketing objectives and strategy prescriptions can be misleading. For example, there can be circumstances where the appropriate marketing objective in the growth stage is to harvest (e.g. in the face of intense competition), in the mature stage to build (e.g. when a distinct, defensive differential advantage can be developed), and in the decline stage to build (e.g. when there is an opportunity to dominate).

As was discussed earlier, the classic PLC advice concerning strategy in the decline stage is to harvest or divest, but other strategies—industry revitalization or the profitable survivor strategy—can be employed if the right conditions apply.

MARKETING IN ACTION 20.2
The Permanent Beta

Companies finding the traditional product development lifecycle is taking too long before a product can reach market have now adopted the 'Permanent Beta'. While some traditional products still require a formal development process, particularly where safety, warranty or legality is concerned (e.g. cars, airplanes, electrical goods), services and digital products can be released ahead of their final version.

There are potential advantages to early product release:

- *Encourages evangelism*—early adopters can experience early versions of software or services and then provide feedback and reviews on design and performance. Evangelist users often communicate with other potential adopters, and this can spread excitement, which encourages wider adoption.
- *Allows for errors*—in a freemium economy model (products are provided free of charge—e.g. Google Search, Internet Explorer web browser) mistakes can be made and customers are far more forgiving of a service that does not work—as expected—if they are not paying. Again users are more inclined to provide feedback—passively in the form of usage statistics and data and actively as engaged users who want to contribute to the production of something special. Companies can then experience an early-to-market introduction of a service and respond early to the feedback. Companies such as Dropbox do this regularly for new features in their Cloud storage service to see how they work for a broad range of customers. Because many businesses regard their products as constantly evolving, it makes sense for them to be described as in a state of permanent beta.

However, there are also drawbacks to the permanent beta concept:

- *Questionable reliability*—in the early days, Google found that it could not convince businesses to take its Gmail and Google Docs services seriously, because businesses did not know how reliable those services were for mission-critical and key operation. In fact, Google's history for ending the lifecycle of products in permanent beta made many suspicious and reluctant to commit to a particular product, and it was only when Google took many products 'out of permanent beta' that there was increased uptake by business users.
- *Lack of permanence*—while there may be benefits from continual developments, this can also be troublesome as continual investment in training of how to use products might be required.

Arguably, permanent beta is *work in progress*, and this has implications for product management insofar as the whole concept of product development becomes highly fluid and constantly evolving. For the marketing manager this means changing planning horizons between pre-launch activity, launch and eventual divestment.

Based on: Rowan (2012)

A Summary of the Usefulness of the Product Lifecycle Concept

Like many marketing tools, the product lifecycle should not be viewed as a panacea to marketing thinking and decision-making but as an aid to managerial judgement. By emphasizing the changes that are likely to occur as a product is marketed over time, the concept is a valuable stimulus to strategic thinking. Yet as a prescriptive tool it is blunt. Marketing management must monitor the real-life changes that are happening in the marketplace before setting precise objectives and strategies. Marketing in Action 20.2 offers insight into the digital world and the PLC.

Managing Brand and Product Line Portfolios

So far in this chapter we have treated the management of products as distinct and independent entities. However, many companies are multi-product, serving multiple markets and segments. Some of these products will be strong, others weak. Some will require investment to finance their growth, others will generate more cash than they need. Somehow companies must decide how to distribute their limited resources among the competing needs of products so as to achieve the best performance for the company as a whole. Specifically within a product line, management needs to decide which brands to invest in or hold, or from which to withdraw support. Similarly within the product mix, decisions regarding which product lines to build or hold, or from which to withdraw support, need to be taken. Canon, for example, took the strategic decision to focus on its profitable products—mainly copiers, printers and cameras—while divesting personal computers, typewriters and liquid crystal displays (Rowley and Tashiro, 2005). Managers who focus on individual products often miss the bigger picture that helps ensure the company's entire portfolio of products fits together coherently rather than being a loose confederation of offerings that has emerged out of a series of uncoordinated historical decisions (Shah, 2002). Philips found itself in this position, marketing a sprawling set of products, namely semiconductors, consumer electronics, medical equipment, lighting and small electrical appliances (Marsh and Bickerton, 2005). In an attempt to bring coherence to its product lines, Philips has responded by selling its semiconductor business to focus on consumer lifestyle (consumer electronics and domestic appliances), healthcare and lighting. See Exhibit 20.3.

EXHIBIT 20.3
Phillips' innovations in LED lighting products

MARKETING IN ACTION 20.3
Portfolio Planning to the Core

The composition of a company's product portfolio is a vital strategic issue for marketers. Few companies have the luxury of starting with a clean sheet and creating a well-balanced set of products. An assessment of the strengths and weaknesses of the current portfolio is, therefore, necessary before taking the strategic decisions of which ones to build, hold, harvest or divest.

Major multinationals, like Nestlé, Mondelez Foods, Procter & Gamble, GE and Unilever, constantly review their product portfolios to achieve their strategic objectives. The trend has been to focus on core brands and product categories, and to divest minor, peripheral brands.

Nestlé is the world's largest producer of packaged foods and constantly strives to manage its product portfolio. Nestlé sold Crosse & Blackwell and Davigel frozen and chilled foods to focus on key product categories and maintain market leadership. The focus is on the core categories of beverages, confectionery, chilled dairy, milks and nutrition. In line with this strategy, Nestlé has acquired the Ski and Munch Bunch dairy brands from Northern Foods, propelling it into the number-two position behind Müller in the chilled dairy market.

Mondelez Foods has many globally recognized food brands in its product portfolio, for example Oreo, Nabisco, Trident and Tang. It has a mixed portfolio, with 49 per cent of its business in North America, 23 per cent in Europe and 28 per cent in developing markets. Of these businesses, the largest concentration are in the confectionery sector (28 per cent), followed by biscuits (22 per cent), beverages (18 per cent), cheese (14 per cent), convenience meals (10 per cent) and grocery (8 per cent). These holdings in its portfolio make Mondelez Foods the second largest food company in the world and in order to maintain this position, the product portfolio is constantly reviewed, as 80 per cent of its revenues come from products that are market leaders in their categories. In 2008, Mondelez acquired LU, a global biscuit business, but got rid of Post, its cereal food operation. In 2010, Cadbury was added to the portfolio to help build its dominance in the confectionery sector in Europe, while DiGiono, its pizza business, was divested as convenience foods account for only a small part of the portfolio.

This trend is not confined to the grocery business, however. For example, Adidas sold its ski and surf equipment firm Salomon to Amer Sports Corporation so that it could focus on its core strength in the athletic footwear and apparel market as well as the growing golf category. IBM sold its PC division to Lenovo to concentrate on software and services.

Philips rationalized its product portfolio, selling its semiconductor business to focus on consumer lifestyle, healthcare and lighting. Its mission is to centre on health and well-being, and it has invested in healthcare, moving away from its medical imaging business and into patient monitoring and home healthcare. One example is its acquisition of Respironics, a medical equipment maker specialising in sleep therapy. It sees healthcare as a growth market as people live longer.

One advantage of this strategy is to enable maximum firepower to be put behind core brands.

Based on: Costello (2015); Mondelez Foods (n.d.); Mason (2002); Tomlinson (2005); Milner (2006); Steen (2008)

Clearly, these are strategic decisions since they shape where and with what brands/product lines a company competes and how its resources should be deployed. Furthermore these decisions are complex because many factors (e.g. current and future sales and profit potential, cash flow) can affect the outcome. The process of managing groups of brands and product lines is called **portfolio planning**.

Key decisions regarding portfolio planning involve decisions regarding the choice of which brands/product lines to build, hold, harvest or divest. Marketing in Action 20.3 discusses several companies' approach to portfolio planning.

 Scan the QR code to consider the iWatch, the development of its product features and how the features are used in the iWatch's advertising.

Two methods for managing products are widely discussed in management literature: 1) Boston Consulting Group Growth-Share Matrix, and 2) General Electric Market Attractiveness– Competitive Position portfolio-evaluation models. Like the product lifecycle these are very flexible tools and can be used at both the brand and product line levels. Indeed, corporate planners can also use them when making resource allocation decisions at the strategic business unit level.

The Boston Consulting Group Growth-Share Matrix

A leading management consultancy, the Boston Consulting Group (BCG), developed the well-known BCG Growth-Share Matrix (see Figure 20.2). The matrix allows portfolios of products to be depicted in a 2 × 2 box, the axes of which are based on market growth rate and relative market share. The analysis is based upon cash flow (rather than profits) and its key assumptions are:

- market growth has an adverse effect on cash flow because of the investment in such assets as manufacturing facilities, equipment and marketing needed to finance growth
- market share has a positive effect on cash flow as profits are related to market share.

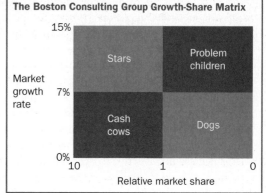

FIGURE 20.2
The Boston Consulting Group Growth-Share Matrix

The following discussion will be based on an analysis at the product line level.

Market growth rate forms the vertical axis and indicates the annual growth rate of the market in which each product line operates. In Figure 20.2, it is shown as 0–15 per cent, although a different range could be used, depending on economic conditions, for example. In this example the dividing line between high and low growth rates is considered to be 7 per cent. Market growth rate is used as a proxy for market attractiveness.

Relative market share is shown on the horizontal axis and refers to the market share of each product relative to its largest competitor. It acts as a proxy for competitive strength. The division between high and low market share is 1. Above this figure a product line has a market share greater than its largest competitor. For example, if our product had a market share of 40 per cent and our largest competitor's share was 30 per cent this would be indicated as 1.33 on the horizontal axis. Below 1 we have a share less than the largest competitor. For example, if our share was 20 per cent and the largest competitor had a share of 40 per cent our score would be 0.5.

The Boston Consulting Group argued that cash flow is dependent on the box in which a product falls. Note that cash flow is not the same as profitability. Profits add to cash flow but heavy investment in such assets as manufacturing facilities, equipment and marketing expenditure can mean that a company can make profits and yet have a negative cash flow.

Stars are likely to be profitable because they are market leaders but require substantial investment to finance growth (e.g. new production facilities) and to meet competitive challenges. Overall cash flow is therefore likely to be roughly in balance. *Problem children* are products in high-growth markets, which cause a drain on cash flow, but these are low-share products; consequently they are unlikely to be profitable. Overall, then, they are big cash users. *Cash cows* are market leaders in mature (low-growth) markets. High market share leads to high profitability and low market growth means that investment in new production facilities is minimal. This leads to a large positive cash flow.

Dogs also operate in low-growth markets but have low market share. Except for some products near the dividing line between cash cows and dogs (sometimes called *cash dogs*) most dogs produce low or negative cash flows. Relating to their position in the product lifecycle, they are the also-rans in mature or declining markets.

What are the strategic implications of the BCG analysis? It can be used for setting strategic objectives and for maintaining a balanced product portfolio.

Guidelines for setting strategic objectives

Having plotted the position of each product on the matrix, a company can begin to think about setting the appropriate strategic

FIGURE 20.3
Strategic objectives and the 'Boston box'

Stars	**Problem children**
Build sales and/or market share	*Build* selectively
Invest to maintain/increase leadership position	Focus on defendable *niche* where dominance can be achieved
Repel competitive challenges	*Harvest* or *divest* the rest

Cash cows	**Dogs**
Hold sales and/or market share	*Harvest* or
Defend position	*Divest* or
Use excess cash to support stars, selected problem children and new product development	Focus on defendable niche

objective for each line. As you may recall from Chapter 18, there are four possible strategic objectives: build, hold, harvest and divest. Figure 20.3 shows how each relates to the star, problem children, cash cow and dog categories. However, it should be emphasized that the BCG Matrix provides guidelines for strategic thinking and should not be seen as a replacement for managerial judgement.

- *Stars*: these are the market leaders in high-growth markets. They are already successful and the prospects for further growth are good. As we have seen when discussing brand building, market leaders tend to have the highest profitability so the appropriate strategic objective is to build sales and/or market share. Resources should be invested to maintain/ increase the leadership position. Competitive challenges should be repelled. These are the cash cows of the future and need to be protected.
- *Problem children*: as we have seen these are cash drains because they have low profitability and need investment to keep up with market growth. They are called problem children because management has to consider whether it is sensible to continue the required investment. The company faces a fundamental choice: to increase investment (*build*) to attempt to turn the problem child into a star, or to withdraw support by either *harvesting* (raising price while lowering marketing expenditure) or *divesting* (dropping or selling it). In a few cases, a third option may be viable: to find a small market segment (*niche*) where dominance can be achieved. Unilever, for example, identified its speciality chemicals business as a problem child. It realized that it had to invest heavily or exit. Its decision was to sell and invest the billions raised in predicted future winners such as personal care, dental products and fragrances (Brierley, 1997).
- *Cash cows*: the high profitability and low investment associated with high market share in low-growth markets mean that cash cows should be defended. Consequently the appropriate strategic objective is to *hold* sales and market share. The excess cash that is generated should be used to fund stars, problem children that are being built, and research and development for new products.
- *Dogs*: dogs are weak products that compete in low-growth markets. They are the also-rans that have failed to achieve market dominance during the growth phase and are floundering in maturity. For those products that achieve second or third position in the marketplace (*cash dogs*) a small positive cash flow may result, and for a few others it may be possible to reposition the product into a defendable *niche*. But for the bulk of dogs the appropriate strategic objective is to *harvest* to generate a positive cash flow for a time, or to *divest*, which allows resources and managerial time to be focused elsewhere.

Maintaining a balanced product portfolio

Once all of the company's products have been plotted, it is easy to see how many stars, problem children, cash cows and dogs are in the portfolio. Figure 20.4 shows a product portfolio that is unbalanced. The company possesses only one star and the small circle indicates that sales revenue generated from the star is small. Similarly the two cash cows are also low revenue earners. In contrast, the company owns four dogs and four problem children. The portfolio is unbalanced because there are too many problem children and dogs, and not enough stars and cash cows. What many companies in this situation do is to spread what little surplus cash is available equally between the products in the growth markets (Hedley, 1977). To do so would leave each with barely enough money to maintain market share, leading to a vicious circle of decline.

The BCG remedy would be to conduct a detailed competitive assessment of the four problem children and select one or two for investment. The rest should be harvested (and the cash channelled to those that are being built) or divested. The aim is to build the existing star (which will be the cash cow of the future) and to build the market share of the chosen problem children so that they attain star status.

The dogs also need to be analyzed. One of them (the large circle) is a large revenue earner, which despite low profits may be making a substantial contribution to overheads. Another product (on the left) appears to be in the cash dog situation. But for the other two, the most sensible strategic objective may be to harvest or divest.

Criticisms of the BCG Growth-Share Matrix

The simplicity, ease of use and importance of the issues tackled by the BCG Matrix saw its adoption by a host of

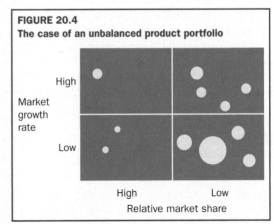

FIGURE 20.4
The case of an unbalanced product portfolio

Market growth rate — High / Low

Relative market share — High / Low

North American and European companies that wanted to get a handle on the complexities of strategic resource allocation. But the tool has also attracted a litany of criticism (see, for example, Day and Wensley, 1983; Haspslagh, 1982; Wensley, 1981). The following list draws together many of the points raised by its critics.

1 The assumption that cash flow will be determined by a product's position in the matrix is weak. For example, some stars will show a healthy positive cash flow (e.g. IBM PCs during the growth phase of the PC market) as will some dogs in markets where competitive activity is low.

2 The preoccupation of focusing on market share and market growth rates distracts managerial attention from the fundamental principle in marketing: attaining a sustainable competitive advantage.

3 Treating the market growth rate as a proxy for market attractiveness, and market share as an indicator of competitive strength is over-simplistic. There are many other factors that have to be taken into account when measuring market attractiveness (e.g. market size, strengths and weaknesses of competitors) and competitive strengths (e.g. exploitable marketing assets, potential cost advantages), besides market growth rates and market share.

4 Since the position of a product in the matrix depends on market share, this can lead to an unhealthy preoccupation with market share gain. In some circumstances this objective makes sense (for example, brand building) but when competitive retaliation is likely the costs of share building may outweigh the gains.

5 The matrix ignores interdependencies between products. For example, a dog may need to be marketed because it complements a star or a cash cow. For example, the dog may be a spare part for a star or a cash cow. Alternatively, customers and distributors may value dealing with a company that supplies a full product line. For these reasons, dropping products because they fall into a particular box may be naive.

6 The classic BCG Matrix prescription is to build stars because they will become the cash cows of the future. However, some products have a very short product lifecycle, in which case the appropriate strategy should be to maximize profits and cash flow while in the star category (e.g. fashion goods).

7 Marketing objectives and strategy are heavily dependent on an assessment of what competitors are likely to do. How will they react if we lower or raise prices when implementing a build or harvest strategy, for example? This is not considered in the matrix.

8 The matrix assumes that products are self-funding. For example, selected problem children are built using cash generated by cash cows. But this ignores capital markets, which may mean that a wider range of projects can be undertaken so long as they have positive net present values of their future cash flows.

9 The matrix is vague regarding the definition of 'market'. Should we take the whole market (e.g. for confectionery) or just the market segment that we operate in (e.g. expensive boxed chocolates)? The matrix is also vague when defining the dividing line between high- and low-growth markets. A chemical company that tends to generate in lower-growth markets might use 3 per cent, whereas a leisure goods company whose markets on average experience much higher rates of growth might use 10 per cent. Also, over what period do we define market growth? These issues question the theoretical soundness of the underlying concepts, and allow managers to manipulate the figures so that their products fall in the right boxes.

10 The matrix was based on cash flow but perhaps profitability (e.g. return on investment) is a better criterion for allocating resources.

11 The matrix lacks precision in identifying which problem children to build, harvest or drop.

General Electric Market Attractiveness–Competitive Position model

As we have already noted, the BCG Matrix enjoyed tremendous success as management grappled with the complex issue of strategic resource allocation. Stimulated by this success and some of the weaknesses of the model (particularly the criticism of its over-simplicity) McKinsey & Co developed a more wide-ranging market attractiveness–competitive position (MA–CP) model in conjunction with General Electric (GE) in the USA.

Market attractiveness criteria

Instead of market growth alone, a range of market attractiveness criteria were used, such as:

- market size
- market growth rate
- beatable rivals
- market entry barriers
- social, political and legal factors.

Competitive strength criteria

Similarly, instead of using only market share as a measure of competitive strength, a number of factors were used, such as:

- market share
- reputation
- distribution capability
- market knowledge
- service quality
- innovation capability
- cost advantages.

Assessing market attractiveness and competitive strength

Management is allowed to decide which criteria are applicable for their products. This gives the MA–CP Model flexibility. Having decided the criteria, management's next task is to agree upon a weighting system for each set of criteria, with those factors that are more important having a higher weighting. Table 20.2 shows a set of weights for market attractiveness. Management has decided that the key factors that should be used to assess market attractiveness are market size, market growth rate, beatable rivals and market entry barriers. Ten points are then shared between these four factors depending on their relative importance in assessing market attractiveness. Market size (weighting = 4.0) is considered the most important factor and market entry barriers (1.5) the least important of the four factors.

TABLE 20.2 An example of market attractiveness assessment

Market factors	Relative importance weightings (10 points shared)	Factor ratings (scale 1–10)	Factor scores (weightings × ratings)
Market size	4.0	9.0	36
Market growth rate	2.0	7.0	14
Beatable rivals	2.5	8.0	20
Market entry barriers	1.5	6.0	9
			79%

Next, management assesses the particular market for the product under examination on each of the four factors on a scale of 1 to 10. The market is rated very highly on size (rating = 9.0), it possesses beatable rivals (8.0), its growth rate is also rated highly (7.0) and there are some market barriers, although they are not particularly high (6.0). By multiplying each weighting by its corresponding rating, and then summing, a total score indicating the overall attractiveness of the particular market for the product under examination is obtained. In this case, the market attractiveness for the product achieves an overall score of 79 per cent.

Competitive strength assessment begins by selecting the strengths that are needed to compete in the market. Table 20.3 shows that market share, distribution capability, service quality, innovation capability, and cost advantages were the factors considered to be needed for success. Management then assigns a weight by sharing 10 points between each of these strengths according to their relative importance in achieving success. Innovation capability (weighting = 3.0) is regarded as the most important strength required to compete effectively. Distribution capability (1.0) is considered the least important of the five factors. The company's capabilities on each of the required strengths are rated on a scale of 1 to 10. Company capabilities are rated very highly on innovation capability (rating = 9.0), market share (8.0) and cost advantages (8.0), highly on distribution capability (7.0) but service quality (5.0) is mediocre. By multiplying each weighting by its corresponding rating, and then summing, a total score indicating the overall competitive strength of the company is obtained. In this example, the competitive strength of the company achieves an overall score of 76 per cent.

TABLE 20.3 An example of competitive strength assessment

Strengths needed for success	Relative importance weightings (10 points shared)	Factor ratings (scale 1–10)	Factor scores (weightings × ratings)
Market share	2.5	8.0	20
Distribution capability	1.0	7.0	7
Service quality	2.0	5.0	10
Innovation capability	3.0	9.0	27
Cost advantages	1.5	8.0	12
			76%

The market attractiveness and competitive strength scores for the product under appraisal can now be plotted on the MA–CP matrix (see Figure 20.5). The process is repeated for each product under investigation so that their relative positions on the MA–CP Matrix can be established. Each product position is given by a circle, the size of which is in proportion to its sales.

Setting strategic objectives

The model is shown in Figure 20.5. Like the BCG Matrix, the recommendations for setting strategic objectives are dependent on the product's position on the grid. Five zones are shown in Figure 20.5. The strategic objectives associated with each zone are as follows (Hofer and Schendel, 1978).

- *Zone 1*: build—manage for sales and market share growth as the market is attractive and competitive strengths are high (equivalent to star products).
- *Zone 2*: hold—manage for profits consistent with maintaining market share as the market is not particularly attractive but competitive strengths are high (equivalent to cash cows).
- *Zone 3*: build/hold/harvest—this is the question-mark zone. Where competitors are weak or passive, a build strategy will be used. In the face of strong competitors a hold strategy may be appropriate, or harvesting where commitment to the product/market is lower (similar to problem children).
- *Zone 4*: harvest—manage for cash as both market attractiveness and competitive strengths are fairly low.
- *Zone 5*: divest—improve short-term cash yield by dropping or selling the product (equivalent to dog products).

In the example shown in Figure 20.5, the circle labelled A indicates the position of the product, which shows that it falls within zone 1 as it operates in an attractive market and its competitive strengths are high. This would suggest a build strategy that probably involves investing in raising service quality levels, which were found to be relatively weak.

Criticisms of the GE portfolio model

The proponents of the GE portfolio model argue that the analysis is much richer than BCG analysis—thanks to more factors being taken into account—and flexible. These are substantial advantages and the model is widely used, with companies such as BP, IBM, Honda, Nissan, Philips, Centrica, Mitsubishi and GE employing it to aid their strategic thinking. Critics argue, however, that it is harder to use than the BCG Matrix since it requires managerial agreement on which factors to use, their weightings and scoring. Furthermore, its flexibility provides a lot of opportunity for managerial bias to enter the analysis whereby product managers argue for factors and weightings that show their products in a good light (zone 1). This last point suggests that the analysis should be conducted at a managerial level higher than that being assessed. For example, decisions on which product lines to be built, held, and so on, should be taken at the strategic business unit level, and allocations of resources to brands should be decided at the group product manager level.

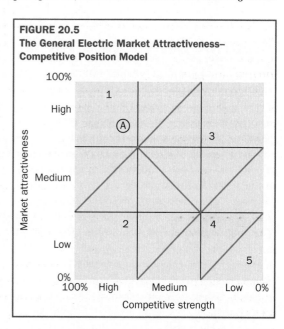

FIGURE 20.5
The General Electric Market Attractiveness–Competitive Position Model

The contribution of product portfolio planning

Despite the limitations of the BCG and the GE portfolio evaluation models, both have made a contribution to the practice of portfolio planning. We shall now discuss this contribution and suggest how the models can usefully be incorporated into product strategy.

Different products and different roles

The models emphasize the important strategic point that *different products should have different roles* in the product portfolio. Hedley points out that some companies believe that all product lines and brands should be treated equally—that is, set the same profit requirements (Hedley, 1977). The portfolio planning models stress that this should not necessarily be the case, and may be harmful in many situations. For example, to ask for a 20 per cent return on investment (ROI) for a star may result in under-investment in an attempt to meet the profit requirement. On the other hand, 20 per cent ROI for a cash cow or a harvested product may be too low. The implication is that products should be set profitability objectives in line with the strategic objective decisions.

Different reward systems and types of manager

By stressing the need to set different strategic objectives for different products, the models, by implication, support the notion that *different reward systems and types of manager* should be linked to them. For example, managers of products being built should be marketing led, and rewarded for improving sales and market share. Conversely, managers of harvested (and to some extent cash cow) products should be more cost orientated, and rewarded by profit and cash flow achievement (see Figure 20.6).

Aid to managerial judgement

Managers may find it useful to plot their products on both the BCG and GE portfolio grids as an initial step in pulling together the complex issues involved in product portfolio planning. This can help them get a handle on the situation and issues to be resolved. The models can then act as an *aid to managerial judgement* without in any way supplanting that judgement. Managers should feel free to bring into the discussion any other factors they feel are not adequately covered by the models. The models can therefore be seen as an aid to strategic thinking in multi-product, multi-market companies.

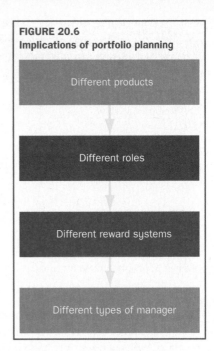

FIGURE 20.6
Implications of portfolio planning

Different products

Different roles

Different reward systems

Different types of manager

Product Strategies for Growth

The emphasis in product portfolio analysis is on managing an *existing* set of products in such a way as to maximize their strengths, but companies also need to look to new products and markets for future growth. The Dyson DC08 vacuum cleaner is an example of a new product that is an addition to an existing line.

A useful way of looking at growth opportunities is the Ansoff Matrix, as shown in Figure 20.7 (Ansoff, 1957). By combining present and new products, and present and new markets into a 2 × 2 matrix, four product strategies for growth are revealed. Although the Ansoff Matrix does not prescribe when each strategy should be employed, it is a useful framework for thinking about the ways in which growth can be achieved through product strategy.

Figure 20.8 shows how the Ansoff Matrix can be used to implement a growth strategy. The most basic method of gaining **market penetration** in existing markets with current products is by *winning competitors' customers*. This may be achieved by more effective use of promotion or distribution, or by cutting prices. Increasing

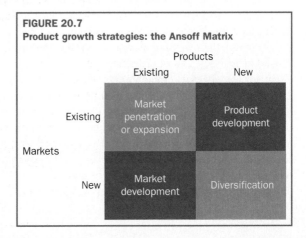

FIGURE 20.7
Product growth strategies: the Ansoff Matrix

		Products	
		Existing	New
Markets	Existing	Market penetration or expansion	Product development
	New	Market development	Diversification

promotional expenditure is a method of winning competitors' customers and market penetration. Greggs, the UK's largest retail food brand, with more shops than McDonald's and Subway, made a significant investment in digital promotion by using Facebook to find out what its 20,000 customers thought about the brand. Eleven thousand replied and the information gathered from this promotional initiative was used to deliver a 7.5 per cent increase in annual turnover (Handley, 2012). Another way of gaining market penetration is to *buy competitors*. An example is the Morrisons supermarket chain, which bought Safeway, a competitor, in order to gain market penetration. This achieves an immediate increase in market share and sales volume. To protect the penetration already gained in a market, a business may consider methods of *discouraging competitive entry. Barriers* can be created by cost advantages (lower labour costs, access to raw materials, economies of scale), highly differentiated products, high switching costs (the costs of changing from existing supplier to a new supplier, for example), high marketing expenditures and displaying aggressive tendencies to retaliate.

A company may attempt **market expansion** in a market that it already serves by converting *non-users to users* of its product. This can be an attractive option in new markets when non-users form a sizeable segment and may be willing to try the product given suitable inducements. Lapsed users can also be targeted. Kellogg's has targeted

FIGURE 20.8
Strategic options for increasing sales volume

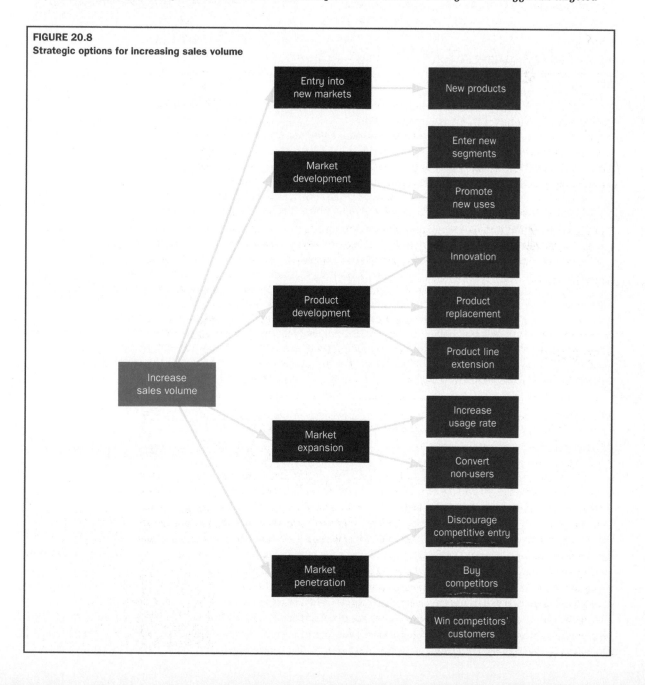

MINI CASE 20.1
Domyos Product Growth Strategies

Created in 1998 by Decathlon, Domyos is the group's brand dedicated to fitness. As the Top 10 global fitness brand in 2014, its intention was to make fitness sports accessible to as many people as possible, with a vision of fitness that places pleasure at the heart of sport. Originally, Domyos designed and sold, in all Decathlon stores, a complete range of products including textiles, materials, accessories, shoes and so on.

Ten years after its creation, however, in order to expand its market, Domyos extended its activity and transformed into a service provider. In November 2008, Domyos created an original concept, unique in the world: a new type of brand experience, with shopping and sports facilities in one location. It set up its international headquarters within a sports complex—the Domyos Centre, an 8-hectare wooded site with:

- a fitness centre, the Domyos Club
- the largest European speciality store dedicated to fitness sports, offering a wide range of Domyos products
- the World Centre for Domyos product design
- a restaurant, *Pause Forme*, in which to relax and enjoy healthy, balanced meals
- a 2-kilometre external track
- a car park with 600 spaces.

Based on its success,[1] a second Domyos Club opened in 2010. At the end of 2014, on average 1,500 athletes were crossing the threshold of Domyos on a daily basis. Domyos's price approach was novel among fitness clubs: users could pay €5 for a one and a half hour class without a subscription.

In 2014, the brand also developed an exclusive free service for its customers: Domyos Live. To give everyone the chance to enjoy their favourite activity, Domyos fitted out two of its rooms in order to broadcast around 50 live fitness classes per week. The same service was rolled out in China, followed by the rest of Europe.

If the fitness industry has gained new members over the last decade, it is thanks to new sports that are more 'fun', like Zumba, which in 2001 revolutionized fitness by providing an activity half way between dance and fitness, with a Latino ambiance. Could Domyos in its turn launch a new sports discipline that would enable the extension of the fitness market while creating new business opportunities for the brand? To penetrate and gain a share of the Chinese market, in July 2013 Domyos came up with the original idea of 'Tai-Chip-Hop', a new discipline that fuses Tai-Chi (the most popular form of exercise in China) with western hip-hop moves. At the end of 2014, 18 months later, the idea had broken through in China and sales of the clothing brand had increased by 10 per cent, a rate faster than that of the Chinese sports market.

---

[1] In 2009, 245,000 hours of classes were sold.

Questions:

1 What strategies do Domyos brand managers use to increase their sales volume?
2 How does product development nourish market development and market expansion?

Based on: Ruaud, Boulocher and Daly (2015)

---

lapsed breakfast cereal users (fathers) who rediscover the pleasure of eating cornflakes when feeding their children. Market expansion can also be achieved by *increasing usage rate*. Kellogg's has also tried to increase the usage (eating) rate of its cornflakes by promoting eating in the evening as well as at breakfast. Affordability and improving sustainability market expansion have also been found to aid market expansion (Banga and Joshib, 2010).

The **product development** option involves the development of new products for existing markets (Ansoff, 1957). One variant is to *extend existing product lines* to give current customers greater choice. For example, the original iPod has been followed by the launches of the iPod nano, shuffle and touch, giving its target market

MARKETING IN ACTION 20.4
Sweden is the Land of Innovation

Sweden is a small country with a population of 9.5 million, but it is home to many of the world's most successful innovations, which have had an impact on the lives of individuals. The three-point seat belt, safety matches and Spotify are among the many innovations to have been designed and developed in Sweden. The country ranks very highly on the Innovative Capacity Index (Harvard Business School) and the Global Innovation Index (INSEAD Business School). Sweden's success is attributed to: continual investment in research and design; its focus on specific areas in which to achieve excellence, for example medicine, bioscience, technology and the climate; and encouraging young people to become interested in technology and entrepreneurship at a young age.

In the field of medicine, the very first battery-run heart pacemaker that was small enough to be implanted under a patient's skin was developed by a surgeon and the Karolinska University Hospital in Stockholm. Over half a million patients every year are fitted with a pacemaker to ensure the heart keeps beating regularly, and subsequently benefit from normalized heart rhythms.

The TetraPak is a revolution in paper-based packaging that allows billions of shoppers to take home their milk and other liquids in a carton instead of a glass bottle. Erik Wallenberg came up with the idea and it was then produced by Ruben Raising, who was instrumental in setting up the first specialized packaging company in Sweden. Since then, the company has grown and it now supplies more than 8.5 billion packs a year, which can be recycled. The company has won many awards for being an environmentally responsible manufacturer.

Skype is another globally recognized application to emerge from Scandinavia. Niklas Zennstrom (from Sweden) worked with Janus Friis (from Denmark) with Estonian developers to produce this innovative software application that enables Internet users to make free voice calls via the web.

The Swedish government has a strategy that aims to continue to foster the right conditions for the development of many more innovations. The strategy aims to meet global societal challenges by focusing on sustainability, increasing competitiveness and creating jobs in the knowledge economy, and increasing the efficiency of public services. The innovation strategy focuses on creating the best possible conditions for innovation by enabling people to be innovative, investing in research and higher education, and creating an infrastructure that provides solid foundations for the future.

Based on: Swedish Institute (2015); Tetrapak (2015); Swedish Ministry of Enterprise, Energy and Communications (2015)

of young music lovers greater choice in terms of size, capacity and price. When new features are added (with an accompanying price rise) trading up may occur, with customers buying the enhanced-value product on repurchase. However, when the new products are cheaper than the original (as is the case with the iPod) the danger is cannibalization of sales of the core product. *Product replacement* activities involve the replacement of old brands/models with new ones. This is common in the car market and often involves an upgrading of the old model with a new (more expensive) replacement. For Skoda, the third oldest car manufacturer in the world, product replacement has been essential to its survival, and in recent years the introduction of new models—Fabia, Superb, Citigo and Rapid—has enabled the brand to retain and develop its market share, selling more than a million vehicles in 2014. A final option is the replacement of an old product with a fundamentally different one, often based on technology change. The business thus replaces an old product with an *innovation* (although both may be marketed side by side for a time). Microsoft operating systems are a classic example of replacement products being introduced, but the older products continue to be marketed and supported: for example, Windows Vista (released in 2006) was superseded by Windows 7 in 2009 (Microsoft, 2013), Windows 8 in 2012, and Windows 10 in 2015. See Marketing in Action 20.4 to find out about the innovative products and technology applications that have helped Sweden become Europe's third most innovative nation.

Scan the QR code to take the Skoda attention test to see how alert you are to the brand's advertising messages.

Market development entails the promotion of *new uses of existing products to new customers*, or the marketing of *existing products (and their current uses) to new market segments*. The promotion of new uses accounted for the growth in sales of nylon, which was first marketed as a replacement for silk in parachutes but expanded into shirts, carpets, tyres, etc. Tesco, the UK supermarket chain, practised market development by marketing existing grocery products, which were sold in large out-of-town supermarkets and superstores, to a new market segment—convenience shoppers—by opening smaller grocery shops in town centres and next to petrol stations. Market development through entering new segments could involve the search for overseas opportunities. Andy Thornton Ltd, an interior design business, successfully increased sales by entering Scandinavia and Germany, two geographic segments that provided new expansion opportunities for its services. The growth of overseas markets in China, India, Russia and eastern Europe is providing major market development opportunities for companies such as BP, Vodafone, Walmart and Carrefour (*The Economist*, 2008). When Wagner, the German manufacturer of spray guns for painting, expanded to the USA in search of market development it found that it had to refocus on an entirely different market segment. In Europe it sells its products to professional painters but in the USA its products are bought by people who use spray guns in their own homes to paint interiors and outside surfaces such as fences (Bolfo, 2005).

The **entry into new markets (diversification)** option concerns the development of *new products for new markets*. This is the most risky option, especially when the entry strategy is not based on the *core competences* of the business. However, it can also be the most rewarding, as exemplified by Honda's move from motorcycles to cars (based on its core competences in engines), and Apple Computer's launch of the iPod mobile music player, which can download music via a computer (based on its core competences in computer electronics). This was followed by its highly successful diversification into smartphones (the iPhone) based on its new-found competences in mobile communication and tablet computers with the iPad. It is the lure of such rewards that has tempted the Internet networking equipment maker Cisco to venture into consumer electronics, and Intel, which manufactures microprocessors that power personal computers, to diversify into platforms combining silicon and software, which has led to new devices and technologies in consumer electronics, wireless communications and healthcare (see Palmer, 2006; Edwards, 2006).

Ethical Issues and Products

The final section in this chapter considers the three major ethical issues relating to products.

1   *Product safety* is a major concern, particularly in relation to consumables. Genetically modified (GM) products have attracted the attention of pressure groups such as Greenpeace, who have spoken out about the dangers of genetic modification. People are sharply divided as to whether GM products are safe. Although plant breeders have for thousands of years been tampering with the genes of plants through traditional cross-pollination of plants of the same species, genetic modification goes one step further as it allows scientists to cross the species barrier.

Concerns about product safety also relate to tobacco (lung cancer), the levels of fat, sugar and salt in foods (obesity and heart problems), and sugar in soft drinks (obesity and tooth decay). Such issues have led to bans on tobacco advertising, the setting up of independent bodies to protect consumers' interests in the food and drinks industries, and reductions in the levels of fat, sugar and salt in many food and drink brands, particularly the level of sugar in food and soft drinks consumed by children. For example, Nestlé has reduced the level of sugar in its cereals targeted at children and reformulated its Rowntree range of children's sweets to make them free from artificial flavours and colours.

2   *Planned obsolescence.* Many products are not designed to last a long time. From the producer's point of view this is sensible, as it creates a repeat purchase situation. Hence cars rust, clothes wear out and fashion items are replaced by the latest styles. Consumers accept that nothing lasts forever, but the issue concerns what is an acceptable length of time before replacement is necessary. One driving force is competition. To quell the Japanese invasion, car manufacturers such as Ford and Volkswagen have made the body shells of their cars

much more rust-resistant than before. Furthermore, it has to be recognized that many consumers welcome the chance to buy new clothes, new appliances with the latest features, and the latest models of car. Critics argue that planned obsolescence reduces consumers' 'right to choose', since some consumers may be quite content to drive an old car so long as its body shell is free from rust and the car functions well. As we have noted, the forces of competition may act to deter the excesses of planned obsolescence.

3 *Deceptive packaging.* This can occur when a product appears in an oversized package to create the impression that the consumer is buying more than is the case. This is known as 'slack' packaging and has the potential to deceive when the packaging is opaque. Products such as soap powder and breakfast cereals have the potential to suffer from 'slack' packaging. A second area where packaging may be deceptive is through misleading labelling, for example the failure of a package to state that the product contains genetically modified soya beans. This relates to the consumer's 'right to be informed', which can include stating ingredients (including flavouring and colourants), nutritional contents and country of origin on labels. Nevertheless, labelling can be misleading. For example, in the UK, 'country of origin' is only the last country where the product was 'significantly changed'. So oil pressed from Greek olives in France can be labelled 'French', and foreign imports that are packed in the UK can be labelled 'produce of the UK'. Consumers should be wary of loose terminology. For example, smoked bacon may well have received its 'smoked' flavour from a synthetic liquid solution, 'farm fresh eggs' are likely to be un-date-marked eggs of indeterminate age laid by battery hens, and 'farmhouse cheese' may not come from farmhouses but from industrial factories.

The use of loose language and meaningless terms in the UK food and drink industry has been criticized by the Food Standards Agency (FSA). A list of offending words has been drawn up, which includes 'fresh', 'natural', 'pure', 'traditional' and 'original'.

Recommendations regarding when it is reasonable to use certain words have been drawn up. For example, 'authentic' should only be used to emphasize the geographic origin of a product, and 'homemade' should be restricted to the preparation of the recipe on the premises, and must involve 'some degree of fundamental culinary preparation'. The FSA has also expressed concern about the use of meaningless phrases such as 'natural goodness' and 'country style', and recommended that they should not be used.

When you have read this chapter

Discover further resources and test your understanding: McGraw-Hill **Connect**™ is a digital teaching and learning environment that improves performance over a variety of critical outcomes; it can be tailored, is easy to use and is proven effective. **LearnSmart**™ is the most widely used and intelligent adaptive learning resource that is proven to strengthen memory recall, improve course retention and boost grades. Fuelled by **LearnSmart**™, **SmartBook**™ is the first and only adaptive reading experience available today.

Review

1 The concept of the product lifecycle

- A four-stage cycle in the life of a product illustrated as sales and profit curves, the four stages being introduction, growth, maturity and decline. It is quite flexible and can be applied to both brands and product lines.

2 The uses and limitations of the product lifecycle

- Its uses are that it emphasizes the need to terminate old and develop new products, warns against the danger of assuming growth will last forever, stresses the need to review marketing objectives and strategies as products pass through the four stages, emphasizes the need to maintain a balanced set of products across the four stages, and warns against the damages of overpowering (setting too high prices early in the cycle when competition is low).

- The limitations are that it is wrong to assume that all products follow the classic S-shaped curve and it is misleading to believe that the product lifecycle sales curve is a fact of life; it depends on marketing activity. The duration of the stages are unpredictable, limiting its use as a forecasting tool, and the stylized marketing objectives and strategy prescriptions associated with each stage may be misleading in particular cases.

- Overall, it is a valuable stimulus to strategic thinking but as a prescriptive tool it is blunt.

3 The concept of product portfolio planning

- This is the process of managing products as groups (portfolios) rather than separate, distinct and independent entities.
- The emphasis is on deciding which products to build, hold, harvest and divest (i.e. resource allocation).

4 The Boston Consulting Group Growth-Share Matrix, its uses and associated criticisms

- The matrix allows portfolios of products to be depicted in a 2 × 2 box, the axes of which are based on market growth rate (proxy for market attractiveness) and relative market share (proxy for competitive strength).
- Cash flow from a product is assumed to depend on the box in which a product falls.
- Stars are likely to have cash flow balance; problem children cause a drain on cash flow; cash cows generate large positive cash flow; and dogs usually produce low or negative cash flow.
- Its uses are that the matrix provides guidelines for setting strategic objectives (for example, stars should be built; problem children built selectively, harvested or divested; cash cows held; and dogs harvested or divested), and emphasizes the need to maintain a balanced portfolio with the cash generated by the cash cows being used to fund those being built.
- The criticisms are: the assumption that cash flow is determined by a product's position in the matrix is weak; it distracts management from focusing on sustainable competitive advantage; treating market growth rate and market share as proxies for market attractiveness and competitive strength is over-simplistic; it can lead to an unhealthy preoccupation with market share; it ignores interdependencies between products; building stars may be inappropriate; competitor reactions are ignored; the assumption that products are self-funding ignores capital markets; the theoretical soundness of some of the underlying concepts (e.g. market definition) is questionable; cash flow may not be the best criteria for allocating resources; and the matrix lacks precision in identifying which problem children to build, harvest or divest.

5 The General Electric market attractiveness–competitive position model, its uses and associated criticisms

- The model is based on market attractiveness (e.g. market size, market growth rate, strength of competition) and competitive strength (e.g. market share, potential to develop a differential advantage, cost advantages). By weighting the criteria and scoring products, these can be positioned on a matrix.
- Its advantages over the 'Boston Box' are that more criteria than just market growth rate and market share are used to determine the position of products in the matrix, and it is more flexible.
- Its uses are that the matrix provides guidelines for setting strategic objectives based upon a product's position in the matrix, and that the analysis is much richer than that of the Boston Box because more factors are being taken into account, leading to better resource allocation decisions.
- The criticisms are that it is harder to use than the Boston Box, and its flexibility can provide an opportunity for managerial bias.

6 The contribution of portfolio planning

- The models emphasize the important strategic point that different products should have different roles in a product portfolio, and different reward systems and managers should be linked to them.
- The models can be useful as an aid to managerial judgement and strategic thinking, but should not supplant that judgement and thinking.

7 Product strategies for growth

- A useful way of looking at growth opportunities is offered by the Ansoff Matrix as it is a practical framework for thinking about how growth can be achieved through product strategy.

- It comprises four general approaches to sales growth: market penetration/expansion, product development, market development and diversification.
- Market penetration and expansion are strategies relating to growing existing products in existing markets. Market penetration depends on winning competitors' customers or buying competitors (thereby increasing market share). Defence of increased penetration may be through discouraging competitive entry. Market expansion may be through converting non-users to users or increasing usage rate. Although market share may not increase, sales growth is achieved through increasing market size.
- Product development is a strategy for developing new products for existing markets. It has three variants: extending existing product lines (brand extensions) to give current customers greater choice; product replacement (updates of old products); and innovation (developing fundamentally different products).
- Market development is a strategy for taking existing products and marketing them in new markets. This may be through the promotion of new uses of existing products to new customers, or the marketing of existing products to new market segments (e.g. overseas markets).
- Diversification (entry into new markets) is a strategy for developing new products for new markets. It is the most risky of the four growth strategies but also potentially the most rewarding.

8   Ethical issues
- Ethical issues associated with products fall into three main categories: 1) product safety, 2) planned obsolescence, 3) deceptive packaging.

Key Terms

entry into new markets (diversification) the entry into new markets by new products

market development to take current products and market them in new markets

market expansion the attempt to increase the size of a market by converting non-users to users of the product and by increasing usage rates

market penetration to continue to grow sales by marketing an existing product in an existing market

portfolio planning managing groups of brands and product lines

product development increasing sales by improving present products or developing new products for current markets

product lifecycle a four-stage cycle in the life of a product illustrated as sales and profits curves, the four stages being introduction, growth, maturity and decline

Study Questions

1. To what extent can the product lifecycle help to inform marketing management decision-making? Discuss.

2. Evaluate the usefulness of the BCG Matrix. Do you believe that it has a role to play in portfolio planning?

3. What is the difference between product and market development in the Ansoff Matrix? Give examples of each form of product growth strategy.

4. How does the GE Matrix differ from the BCG Matrix? What are the strengths and weaknesses of the GE Matrix?

5. Evaluate the contribution of product portfolio planning models to product strategy.

6. Suggest possible advantages of actively managing a company's product portfolios.

7. Suggest how product portfolio planning might be affected by changing forces in the marketing environment.

Recommended Reading

Aaker, D. (2013) *Strategic Market Management*, New York, Wiley

Hill, S., Ettenson, R. & Tyson, D. (2005) Achieving the ideal brand portfolio, *Sloan Management Review*, 46 (2), 85–91

Moon, Y. (2005) Break free from the product life cycle, *Harvard Business Review*, 83 (5), 86–95

Morgan, N. A., & Rego, L.L. (*2009*) Brand Portfolio Strategy and Firm Performance. *Journal of Marketing*: 73) (1), 59–74

Qiu, T. (*2014*) Product Diversification and Market Value of Large International Firms: A Macroenvironmental Perspective. *Journal of International Marketing*: 22, (4), 86–107

Reeves, M., Love, C., & Tilmans, P. (2012) Your Strategy Needs a Strategy, BCG Perspectives https://www.bcgperspectives.com/content/articles/strategic_planning_vision_mission_your_strategy_needs_a_strategy (accessed July 2015).

References

Aaker, D. (2007) *Strategic Marketing Management*, New York: Wiley.

Ansoff, I. (1957) Strategies for Diversification, *Harvard Business Review*, Sept.–Oct., 113–24.

Banga, V. V. and S. L. Joshib (2010) Market expansion strategy–performance relationship, *Journal of Strategic Marketing* 18(1), 57–75.

Bolfo, B. (2005) The Art of Selling One Product to Two Markets, *Financial Times*, 10 August, 11.

Boston Consulting Group (2001) On-line Retail Market in North America to reach $65 billion in 2001, http://www.beg.com.

Brierley, D. (1997) Spring-Cleaning a Statistical Wonderland, *European*, 20–26 February, 28.

Cline, C. E. and B. P. Shapiro (1979) *Cumberland Metal Industries (A): Case Study*, Cambridge, Mass: Harvard Business School.

Costello, M. (2015) Nestlé to shed frozen and chilled goods brand Davigel, *The Times*, 16 April. http://www.thetimes.co.uk/tto/business/industries/consumer/article4412839.ece

Day, G. S. and R. Wensley (1983) Marketing Theory with a Strategic Orientation, *Journal of Marketing*, Fall, 79–89.

Dhalia, N. K. and S. Yuspeh (1976) Forget the Product Life Cycle Concept, *Harvard Business Review*, Jan.–Feb., 102–12.

Doherty, N. F., F. E. Ellis-Chadwick and C. A. Hart (2003) An analysis of the factors affecting the adoption of the Internet in the UK retail sector, *Journal of Business Research* 56, 887–97.

Doyle, P. (1989) Building Successful Brands: The Strategic Options, *Journal of Marketing Management* 5(1), 77–95.

Edwards, C. (2006) Inside Intel, *Business Week*, 9 January, 43.

Ellis-Chadwick, F., N. Doherty and C. Hart (2002) Signs of change? A longitudinal study of Internet adoption in the UK retail sector, *Journal of Retailing and Consumer Services* 9, 71–80.

Gapper, J. (2006) Sony is Scoring Low at its Close Game, *Financial Times*, 6 November, 17.

Handley, L. (2012) Greggs finds ingredient for growth on Facebook, *Marketing Week*, 1 March, 15–18.

Haspslagh, P. (1982) Portfolio Planning: Uses and Limits, *Harvard Business Review*, Jan.–Feb., 58–73.

Hedley, B. (1977) Boston Consulting Group Approach to the Business Portfolio, *Long Range Planning*, February, 9–15.

Hofer, C. and D. Schendel (1978) *Strategy Formulation: Analytical Concepts*, St Paul, MN: West.

Hudson, A. (2010) Whatever happened to the dotcom millionaires? http://news.bbc.co.uk/1/hi/technology/8505260.stm.

Marsh, P. and I. Bickerton (2005) Stewardship of a Sprawling Empire, *Financial Times*, 18 November, 13.

Mason, T. (2002) Nestlé Sells Big Brands in Core Strategy Focus, *Marketing*, 7 February, 5.

Microsoft (2013) A history of Windows, http://windows.microsoft.com/en-US/windows/history

Milner, M. (2006) £1.2bn Sale of Schweppes' European Drinks Business Agreed, *Guardian*, 22 November, 26.

Mondelez Foods (n.d.) About Us. http://www.Mondelezfoodscompany.com

Nokian (n.d.) http://www.nokianheavytyres.com/en/innovation/tailored-special-expertise

Palmer, M. (2006) Cisco Lays Plans to Expand into Home Electronics, *Financial Times*, 16 January, 21.

Pavitt, D. (1997) Retailing and the super highway: the future of the electronic home shopping industry, *International Journal of Retail & Distribution Management*, 25(1), 38–43.

Polli, R. and V. Cook (1969) Validity of the Product Life Cycle, *Journal of Business*, October, 385–400.

Rowan, D. (2012) Reid Hoffman: The network philosopher, *Wired*, April. http://www.wired.co.uk/magazine/archive/2012/04/features/reid-hoffman-network-philosopher (accessed 20 April 2015).

Rowley, I. and H. Tashiro (2005) Can Canon Keep Printing Money? *Business Week*, 5/12 September, 18–20.

Ruaud, S., V. Boulocher and P. Daly (2015) Domyos or the Fitness Revolution: Service Innovation, case study, Paris: CCMP.

Shah, R. (2002) Managing a Portfolio to Unlock Real Potential, *Financial Times*, 21 August, 13.

Steen, M. (2008) Reinventing the Philips Brand, *Financial Times*, 27 March, 18.

Swedish Institute (2015) Innovation in Sweden, Sweden.Se, https://sweden.se/business/innovation-in-sweden (accessed 20 April 2015).

Swedish Ministry of Enterprise, Energy and Communications (2015) The Swedish Innovation Strategy, Swedish Ministry of Enterprise, Energy and Communications. http://www.government.se/content/1/c6/20/25/58/ace0cef0.pdf (accessed 20 April 2015).

Tetrapak (2015) About Tetrapak, Tetrapak. http://www.tetrapak.com/uk/about-tetra-pak/the-company/history/ourfounder (accessed 20 April 2015).

The Economist (2008) Face Value, 31 May, 86.

Tomlinson, H. (2005) Adidas Sells Ski and Surf Group for £329m, *Guardian*, 3 May, 5.

Vakratsas, D. and T. Ambler (1999) How Advertising Works: What Do We Really Know? *Journal of Marketing* 63, January, 26–43.

Virzi, A. M. (2000) Billionaire builds wealth at Internet speed, *Forbes.com*, http://www.forbes.com/2000/06/30/feat.html.

Wensley, R. (1981) Strategic Marketing: Betas, Boxes and Basics, *Journal of Marketing*, Summer, 173–83.

Wikipedia (n.d.) Dot-com bubble. http://en.wikipedia.org/wiki/Dot-com_bubble

Growth Strategies at Unilever

In February 2000, when Niall FitzGerald, chairman of Unilever, rose in front of his shareholders to reveal his plans for the most comprehensive restructuring and strategy review to hit the company in over a hundred years, there was a sharp intake of breath. His four-year 'Path to Growth' strategy was to see 1,200 of its 1,600 consumer brands axed to concentrate marketing muscle behind 400 high-growth brands. All brands that were not among the top two sellers in their market segment would be dropped either immediately or over a period of time.

Buyers would be sought for those that were to be divested immediately, the rest would be harvested (milked) and the cash generated ploughed into support for the 400 big brands. This would mean £450 million (€648 million) of extra marketing expenditure put behind such global brands as Magnum ice cream, Dove soap, Knorr soup and Lipton's tea. Local successes such as Persil washing powder and Colman's mustard in the UK would also be supported heavily. The promise was to increase profit margins from 11 to 16 per cent and to achieve target annual growth rates of between 4.5 and 5 per cent from its 400 top brands. Brands scheduled to be harvested or divested included Timotei shampoo, Brut deodorant, Radion washing powder, Harmony hairspray, Pear's soap and Jif lemon.

The analysis that Unilever had done revealed that only a quarter of Unilever's brands provided 90 per cent of its turnover and that disposing of the other three-quarters would lead to a more efficient supply chain and reduced costs of £1 billion (€1.44 billion) over three years. As FitzGerald explained, 'We were doing too many things. We had too many brands in too many places. Many were just not big enough to move the needle so we had to focus and simplify. That simplification would allow us to take cost out of the business.'

Not everyone was convinced. There were £3.5 billion (€5 billion) of restructuring costs (bigger than most companies' market capitalizations) and the prospect of 25,000 jobs going. The exercise would require a highly effective internal communications programme to obtain buy-in from Unilever staff.

By the end of 2002, FitzGerald could claim considerable achievements. Cost savings of over £450 million (€648 million) had already been banked and margins had moved from 11 to 15 per cent. The top 400 leading brands accounted for 88 per cent of sales and achieved an average growth rate of 4.5 per cent. Three businesses had also been bought. Bestfoods, the US foods giant, brought the Hellman's mayonnaise, Knorr soups and Skippy peanut butter brands into the Unilever portfolio; the acquisition of Ben & Jerry's gave the company one of two major brands in the premium ice cream sector; and Slimfast provided major penetration of the diet food market.

Unilever was also busy dropping or selling off Elizabeth Arden, Batchelor's soups, Oxo, Knight's Castille soap, Frish toilet cleaner and Stergene handwashing liquid. Some of Unilever's unwanted brands were bought by small companies. For example, Buck UK bought Unilever's Sqezy—the washing-up liquid formerly marketed as 'easy, peasy, lemon Sqezy'. Also, Unilever sold its Harmony hairspray and Stergene fabric conditioner brands to Lornamead. Others such as Oxo and Bachelors were sold to larger companies—in this case Campbell Grocery Products.

A number of brand extensions were also planned in 2002, most notably in the Bertolli olive oil, Dove soap, Knorr soup, Lynx (Axe) male grooming and Slimfast diet food brands. The Lynx (Axe) men's deodorant was launched in the USA, and three new flavours of Hellman's mayonnaise and an Asian side-dishes range were introduced.

»

The result of all this activity was that Unilever posted a 16 per cent increase in 2002 profits: that is, £1.5 billion compared to £1.3 billion (€2.1 billion compared to €1.9 billion) in 2001. Sales of its top 400 brands grew 5.4 per cent, above the company's target of 4.5 and 5 per cent. The company invested £5.1 billion (€7.3 billion) in advertising and promotion, up 8.5 per cent on the 2001 level.

During 2003 Unilever earmarked an additional 20 per cent of marketing investment in its global ice cream portfolio over the next three years. The ice cream group has a remarkable global brand portfolio. For example, in the UK Unilever owns Walls; in France, it bought Miko; in Portugal it owns Ola; and in Sweden it owns GB Glace. Over Europe as a whole Unilever owns and operates more than 12 different ice cream brands, each with its own strong heritage and relationships with customers. Unilever has retained the names of its national brands while replacing original brand symbols with a single heart-shaped logo.

Unfortunately the successes of the early years were followed by two years of performance below expectations leading to the departure of Mr. FitzGerald in May 2004. Poor sales and profit performance was blamed on poor organizational structure, lack of innovation and poor advertising. Poor structure stemmed from Unilever's Anglo-Dutch heritage which resulted in joint chairmen—one for the Dutch arm and one for the UK—and no chief executive. The company was run by two boards and separate headquarters in London and Rotterdam. Consequently, decision-making was cumbersome and slow with the ever-present threat of conflict between the two groups compounding the problems. The group was also divided into divisions: health and personal products, food, and frozen foods. These were regarded as fiefdoms under which separate management teams managed their products separately in each country.

Following Mr. FitzGerald's departure, Unilever carried out a strategic review under its joint chairmen, Patrick Cescau in the UK and Antony Burgmans in the Netherlands. Mr. Cescau, the driving force behind the review, became Unilever's chief executive with Mr. Burgmans becoming non-executive chairman. The board was unified and headquarters were centralized in London. These changes gave Mr. Cescau the autonomy to push through the reform needed to get Unilever back on track. Under the slogan 'One Unilever' he dismantled the fiefdoms which were merged to form one executive team covering all divisions and nationalities, resulting in the loss of almost a fifth of senior management. A cull of about 30,000 jobs took place and some loss-making factories were closed to cut costs.

Mr. Cescau also changed focus from Path to Growth's fixation on profit margins to boosting market share. This meant price reductions and the introduction of cheaper product ranges to complement the premium priced brands. The Magnum ice cream brand was complemented in this way, for example.

He also sold Unilever's cosmetics and fragrances arm Unilever Cosmetics International to Coty International for £438 million (€613 million) in a move which allowed it to focus on its core categories of food, cleaning and personal care brands such as Ben & Jerry's ice cream, Knorr soups, Flora margarine, Cif cleaning products, Persil detergents, Dove personal care products, Sunsilk shampoos and Lynx (Axe) men's deodorants. This was quickly followed by the sale of its frozen-food division (Birds Eye) to Permira, a venture capitalist, for £1.2 billion (€1.7 billion). At the time of the sale, Birds Eye was the number one food brand in the UK with a turnover of £500 million (€700 million) a year and profits of around £50 million (€70 million). It was also the UK's second-biggest supermarket brand after Walker's crisps. Unilever also sold its North American detergents business in 2008 to a private equity firm.

A greater emphasis was placed on emerging markets such as China, India, Brazil, Russia, Africa, and central and eastern Europe. Advertising budgets in western Europe were tightened to fund extra investment in these growth markets. In line with this strategy, Inmarko, Russia's largest ice cream brand, was acquired in 2008. By 2009 emerging markets accounted for around 50 per cent of Unilever's sales revenue.

Another change in strategy was to adopt a more standardized approach to global marketing. The company moved from autonomous localized initiatives to the roll-out of innovation and marketing programmes on a global basis. Power was taken away from country managers and given to global marketing teams to oversee the development and marketing of new products. Brand marketing was split into two divisions: the brand development team and brand building. The brand development team devise a global strategy for each brand including innovation. A package of recommendations is then created, usually in conjunction with two key countries. This is then sent to brand building teams in each country and they 'make it happen' within local markets.

Mr. Cescau has also invested in 'healthy living' brands to capitalize on the trend towards health and well-being. For example, a number of 'healthy' sauces and soups under the Knorr brand were launched with no artificial flavours or colourings, reflecting Unilever's 'vitality' positioning.

In 2008, Mr. Cescau stepped down as chief executive after achieving what most commentators regard as a fairly successful period at the helm, transforming the company from a lumbering, regionally driven bureaucracy into a more streamlined, globally managed business. However, Unilever's performance did not match that of Reckitt Benckiser, maker of the Cillit Bang cleaner, whose strategy was to launch brands such as stain removers targeting niche markets that avoided direct head-to-head competition with Procter & Gamble and Unilever.

His successor was Paul Polman, a former P&G and Nestlé man, breaking with an 80-year-old tradition of appointing insiders. Faced with a recession, Mr. Polman embarked on a cost-cutting programme, including a freeze on management salaries and travel budget cuts of 30 per cent (replacing travel with teleconferencing), designed to achieve £45 million (€50 million) savings. A job-cutting and factory closure programme that began in 2007 was accelerated, and a global procurement officer was recruited to seek savings by using the company's vast scale to obtain better prices. Acquisitions were also made, including the purchase of Toni & Guy and Alberto Culver (both haircare), and Sara Lee's personal care business. The Russian personal care group Kalina was also bought in 2011. By 2012, emerging markets accounted for over half of Unilever's sales revenue. The impact of its brand portfolio strategy is reflected in the fact that 75 per cent of sales are now made from its top 25 brands.

Mr. Polman has continued his quest for cost efficiencies and constantly reviews his product portfolio. For example, in 2014 he sold the troubled Slimfast brand, which was hit by the Atkins diet craze in the USA. Unilever also sold its Peperami, Ragu and Bifi brands as it focuses on its health and beauty businesses.

His third focus is on product 'premiumization'. By developing premium brands, such as Regenerate toothpaste priced at £10 (€14) and Maille mustard with wine and truffles, costing £29 (€41), together with a constant drive towards lower costs, Unilever has achieved improved profits margins from 12.8 per cent in 2010 to 14.8 per cent in 2014.

Questions

1. What were the advantages to Unilever of reducing the size of its brand portfolio? What were the risks?

2. To what extent does it appear that Unilever followed (i) the BCG Growth-Share Matrix, and (ii) the General Electric Market Attractiveness-Competitive Position Model approaches to portfolio planning during the FitzGerald era?

3. What are the attractions to small companies of buying marginal Unilever brands? What are the dangers of doing so?

4. Comment on Unilever's approach to the global marketing of its brands.

5. Why did the sale of Birds Eye and its North American detergent business make strategic sense for Unilever?

This case study was prepared by David Jobber, Emeritus Professor of Marketing, University of Bradford.

References

Based on: Farrell, S. (2014) Unilever to Revamp Products to Lure Back cash-Strapped Customers, theguardian.com/business, 23 October; Jack, L. (2009) The Soaps, the Glory and the Universal Truths in Marketing, *Marketing Week*, 23 April, 20–4; Kilby, N. (2005) Coty Scents Growth Potential in Unilever Cosmetics, *Marketing Week*, 26 May, 11; Kilby, N. (2006) Permira Aims to Make Birds Eye Cooler than Chilled, *Marketing Week*, 7 September, 10; Kollewe, J. (2014) Unilever Puts Slimfast and US Pasta Sauce Range up for Sale, the guardian.com/business, 24 April; Lucas, L. (2011) Unilever 'On Front Foot' but Full-Year Margins Disappoint, *Financial Times*, 4 November, 22; Mortished, C. (2009) Unilever Chief Paul Polman Ditches Pay Rises and Targets, *The Times*, 6 February, 18; Pratley, N. (2015) Unilever's Weak Results Show It's a Low Growth, Low Inflation World, theguardian.com/business, 21 January; Ritson, M. (2003) Unilever Goes with its 'Heart' to Make Global Brand of Local Ices, *Marketing*, 1 May, 18; Ritson, M. (2012) Bereft of Stars, Premier's Plan Will Flop, *Marketing Week*, 26 January, 58; Vizard, S. (2014) Unilever Eyes More 'Agile' Marketing for Spreads Brands as Bisiness Splits into Standalone Unit, thegurdian.com/business, 4 December; Wiggins, J. (2008) Unilever Hangs on to European Laundry List, *Financial Times*, 29 July, 18; Wiggins, J. (2008) Unilever Buys Russia's Inmarko Ice Cream, *Financial Times*, 5 February, 21; Wiggins, J. (2009) Unilever Looks to the Silver Lining, *Financial Times*, 6 February, 19.

Intel Inside

The Search for Growth in Technology Markets

Intel is one of the most famous business-to-business brand names in the world, and with sales of over $55 billion, profits of $12 billion and 75 per cent share of the market for microprocessors that power PCs and laptops, it is also one of the most successful. The foundation for its success was the development and marketing of microprocessors for PCs and servers. By investing billions in ever-faster processors Intel has become the dominant force in this industry, with efficient plants that can produce more processors in a day than some rivals can in a year. The combination of low-cost production and ever faster chips was a powerful concoction that none of its rivals could match.

Much of the credit for Intel's success goes to Andy Grove, its former chief executive, who took the decision to leave the unprofitable memory chip business in order to focus on microprocessors for the fast-growing personal computer market, a move that enabled Intel to bury the competition. Intel's products were supported by powerful branding using the Pentium brand name and 'Intel inside' strapline, bringing consumer awareness of a product hidden from sight in the heart of a computer. Intel's strategy was to work with Microsoft to appeal to PC industry giants such as Dell, HP, IBM and Compaq to be the first choice for microprocessors.

Under Grove, engineers dominated and the culture at Intel was summarized by his motto: 'Only the paranoid survive'. Managers often engaged in 'constructive confrontation', otherwise known as shouting at each other. Under Grove's successor, Craig R. Barrett, the company continued its successful path to ever greater sales and profits.

Times They are a 'Changin'

By 2005, the market for microprocessors was changing. Growth in PC demand was slowing as markets became saturated. No longer could Intel rely on double-digit market growth to fuel its sales and profit trajectory. Another change was occurring within Intel itself. A new chief executive, Paul Otellini, was at the helm. A non-engineer, Otellini joined Intel in 1974 straight

out of business school at the University of California at Berkeley. A close working associate of Grove, who continued as chairman until 2005 after his departure as CEO in 1998, Otellini has a marketing background. Among his successes was the Centrino brand. When Otellini was head of product planning, he decided, against the wishes of Intel engineers, that rather than launch yet another fast processor, he would bundle it with a relatively new wireless Internet technology called WiFi. The combination enabled consumers to connect from their laptop to the Internet from such places as airport lounges and coffee shops. Supported by a $300 million marketing campaign, Centrino laptops caught on, revitalizing the PC market while encouraging consumers to purchase higher margin products. Since launch, over $6 billion worth of Centrino chips have been sold.

Intel was also faced with an energetic British competitor, Advanced Micro Devices, which had slowly been gaining ground in the battle of the microchip. A major competitive weapon of AMD was price, which prompted Intel to develop the low-priced Celeron microprocessor. AMD stole a march on Intel by being the first to design a 64-bit chip, which held the competitive advantages of having greater power and lower power consumption. ARM does not manufacture chips but designs chip technology that others—for example, Apple, Samsung, and Qualcomm—license and then build on. By 2005, AMD had increased its market share to 15 per cent of the PC microprocessor market and held 26 per cent of the market for the microprocessors that drive servers, where lower power consumption is highly valued. Even more impressive was its 48 per cent share of the growing multi-core processor market, where two or more chips are put onto a single sliver of silicon. Such products consume less power, enabling laptops to run longer before recharge, and enhance performance without generating more heat, which was a problem with single chips. Using less power is especially important for business-to-business customers. For example, Google claimed that it cost more to run its computers than to buy them. A landmark came in 2005 when Dell, hitherto an Intel stronghold, moved to AMD chips for its servers. Its decision was influenced by the competitive advantage its rivals HP, Toshiba and Gateway were getting by using the more powerful AMD chips in their consumer and business systems, particularly servers.

A Change of Strategy

The promotion of Otellini to chief executive heralded a change in strategic direction for Intel. The changing technological, competitive and market landscape was reflected in his desire to move the company away from its dependence on single microprocessor chips for the PC market. First, Intel developed new dual-core chips for laptops (using the Core brand name), which place two microprocessors on one sliver of silicon. This allowed laptops to run for five to ten hours rather than three to four, which was typical before.

Second, Intel focused on 'complete technology platforms' rather than individual microprocessors. *Platformization*, as Intel calls it, means bundling a range of chips and the software needed to tie them all together, offering different features such as security, video, audio and wireless capabilities in a combination to suit a particular target market. This is recognition of the fact that computer manufacturers value the opportunity to buy a complete package of chips from one manufacturer rather than assemble components from several suppliers. It also means that Intel sells more components, and so takes a larger slice of the selling price of each PC. Whereas Intel can handle the process in-house, AMD requires partners to develop platforms.

Otellini also announced plans to broaden Intel's target markets. Rather than focus only on PC manufacturers, Intel intended to be a major technological player in home entertainment, wireless communications and healthcare. In home entertainment, Otellini's vision was for the PC to be the central connection to individual entertainment devices. The company developed the Viiv multicore chip, which allowed PCs to connect to DVD players, TVs, stereo systems, and so on, so that consumers could move digital content around the home. This meant that Viiv computers could act as an all-in-one DVD player, games console, CD player and television, and enable downloads of movies, music and games, which could then be moved around the home. Viiv was chosen as the chip to power Windows Media Centre PCs.

In targeting wireless communications, Intel was hoping to make a breakthrough in an area where it has traditionally been weak. Hitherto, Intel's focus on PC microprocessors meant that investment in chips for mobile communications was considered secondary. Intel launched in 2008 the Atom, an ultra-small energy-efficient chip. The Atom allowed Intel to compete in the market for mobile internet devices (MIDs, bigger than smartphones), netbooks (very small laptops) and nettops (cheap, stripped-down desktop PCs). By 2009, the Atom chip was found at the heart of most netbooks. However, the market for netbooks has faded with the rise of tablets, most notably the Apple iPad. In response Intel championed a new category of mobile computers called Ultrabooks. Powered by second-generation Core chips these ultra-thin, ultra-responsive devices were designed to take over from netbooks and challenge tablets.

Despite its successes in the PC and server markets, Intel's impact in the growing smartphone and tablets markets has been poor with AMD the market leader. In an attempt to make inroads into this market, Intel and Google signed an alliance so that Android-based smartphones and tablets could be powered by Intel chips. Intel also developed a chip based on 3D technology aimed to generate the power efficiency needed with these devices. Already Intel chips are powering Motorola (which is Google-owned) and Lenovo smartphones. Otellini also hoped for breakthrough innovations in healthcare. His vision was for digital technology to help healthcare professionals. Ethnographers were employed to understand the problems of the elderly and people with specific diseases such as Alzheimer's. Intel developed sensors that could communicate with computer networks, enabling caregivers to monitor the health of the elderly remotely. One benefit of this would be to allow elderly people to remain in their own homes.

In line with his strategy, Otellini reorganized Intel into platform-specific divisions: digital home (for consumer PCs and home entertainment), corporate (business PCs and servers), mobility (laptops and mobile devices) and healthcare, and scattered the processor engineers among them. New product development was also reorganized. In the past engineers worked on ever faster chips and marketers were asked to sell them. Now new products are developed by teams of people: chip engineers, software developers and marketers all work together to design attractive new products. The type of person Intel hires has changed too. They include ethnographers, sociologists and software developers. Ethnographers, for example, are researching how people in emerging markets like China and India use technology.

Eric Kim, chief marketing officer, was recruited from Samsung and was widely credited with raising its brand awareness and image as a leading consumer electronics company. Among his first marketing

»

initiatives was the rebranding of the Core family of microprocessors to simplify a range that had become too unwieldy and confusing. The names—the Core i3, Core i5 and Core i7—described the basic, mid-range and high-end features of the Core line, respectively. Intel has also become corporate technological partner with BMW, which sees its chips powering operations across BMW dealerships, the company and its cars.

Not everyone at Intel was happy about the reorganization and the increased emphasis on marketing, however. Before Otellini's elevation to CEO anyone not working for the core PC business was considered a second-class citizen, and many high-level engineers working on PC products felt they had lost their star status. Some regarded marketing as little more than gloss and glitz, and others left to join rivals such as AMD. The competition is also critical of Intel's practice of offering volume-based rebates to computer manufacturers, which they claim acts as a barrier to entry. This led to a record £950m (€1.03m) fine imposed by the European Commission for anticompetitive behaviour.

In 2013, Otellini retired after eight years as chief executive. Shortly before his departure, he confessed that Apple had offered Intel the chance to supply the processor for the first iPhone.

'At the end of the day, there was a chip that they were interested in that they wanted to pay a certain price for, and not a nickel more, and that price was below our forecast cost. I couldn't see it. It wasn't one of these things you make up on volume. And in hindsight, the forecast cost was wrong and the volume was 100x what anyone thought.'

Brian Krzanich replaced Otellini as chief executive, and the company is still the major player in the PC, server and laptop markets, and is increasing its share in tablets. However, despite an R&D spend of over $13 billion a year (6.4 percent of revenue), Intel remains a minor player in the market for microprocessors for mobile devices. It also does not provide the processors that power the Apple smartwatch. Instead, it formed a partnership with Tag Heur and Google to launch an Android smartwatch in 2015.

Questions

1. Interpret Intel's move from its reliance on microprocessors for PCs into home entertainment, healthcare and mobile communications using (i) the product lifecycle, (ii) the BCG, and (iii) the General Electric Market Attractiveness–Competitive Position models.

2. Locate each of Intel's moves (products and markets) since Otellini became CEO in the Ansoff product growth matrix. Justify your answer.

3. How has the corporate culture changed since Otellini became CEO? Support your answer with examples.

4. What challenges does Intel face as it moves into home entertainment, healthcare and mobile communications?

This case study was prepared by David Jobber, Emeritus Professor of Marketing, University of Bradford.

References

Based on: Edwards, C. (2006) AMD: Chipping Away at Intel's Lead, *Business Week*, 12 June, 72–3; *The Economist* (2008) Battlechips, 7 June, 76–7; Nuttall, C. (2011) Intel Raises Stakes for Rivals as it Hails Revolution in 3D chips, *Financial Times*, 5 May, 1; Nuttall, C. (2011) Intel and Google Sign Android Alliance, *The Financial Times*, 14 September, 26; Nuttall, C. and R. Kwong (2011) Intel Unveils Vision for Laptops as it Fends off Tablet Rivals, *The Financial Times*, 1 June, 21; Garside, J. and C. Arthur (2012) Intel Chips Away at ARM's Control of Mobile Market, *The Guardian*, 12 January, 30; Anonymous (2013) Intel Appoints Brian Krzanich as New Chief Executive, theguardian.com/business,2 May; Gassee, J.-L. (2013) Intel Is Under New Management—And It's Already Starting to Show, theguardian.com/business, 4 November; Cassey, M. and R. Hackett (2014) The 10 Biggest R & D Spenders Worldwide, fortune.com, 17 November; Fletcher, N. (2015) ARM Falls Back on Intel Competition Worries, theguardian.com/business, 16 January.

CHAPTER 21
Global Marketing Strategy

> *I want to be a good Frenchman in France and a good Italian in Italy. My strategy is to go global when I can and stay local when I must.*
>
> **ERIC JOHANNSON, FORMER PRESIDENT OF ELECTROLUX**

LEARNING OBJECTIVES

After reading this chapter, you should be able to:

1. explain why companies seek foreign markets
2. discuss the factors that influence which foreign market to enter
3. identify and discuss the range of foreign market entry strategies
4. identify the factors influencing foreign market entry strategies
5. discuss the influences on the degree of standardization or adaptation
6. discuss the special considerations involved in designing a marketing mix for foreign markets
7. explain how to organize for global marketing operations

From a marketing perspective, the world is becoming more accessible; as a result, global brands like Apple, Nike, Coca-Cola, Google and Samsung are widely recognized. But not all brands have such reach, and trading overseas raises many challenges for companies wishing to export their goods. While new technologies are making it easier to communicate with a global audience, many internal and external factors need to be considered if new market entry is to be successful. Consequently, managers need the *right* marketing skills to be able to compete in this increasingly global marketplace. Companies require the capabilities to identify and seize opportunities that arise across the world. Failure to do so could bring stagnation and decline, not only to individual companies but also to whole regions.

Global expansion and exports are important to all nations and all sectors, but the contribution to the economy varies by sector; for example, in China exporting electrical goods and apparel is important, whereas in the EU key sectors are machinery, motor vehicles, and in the UK manufactured goods, fuels and chemicals (CIA, 2015).

The importance of international trade is reflected in the support given by governmental bodies set up to encourage and aid export activities. For example, UK Trade & Investment (UKTI) is a government body that works with UK-based businesses to help them succeed in overseas markets, whether they are trying to establish a new business or exporting to a new country. UKTI offers various services, including: expert advice on international trade and export; taking part in trade fairs and outward trade missions; providing market intelligence; identifying international business opportunities; and helping to develop international business relationships (UKTI, 2012).

This chapter explores the challenges of global marketing. The chapter is organized around the key issues associated with developing global marketing strategies: 1) whether to go global or stay domestic; 2) the factors that impact on the selection of countries in which to market; 3) foreign market-entry strategies; and 4) the options available for companies developing global marketing strategies. It also builds on earlier chapters and considers how the principles of marketing might be applied in a global marketplace.

Deciding Whether to Go Global or Stay Local

Some companies do not look to compete internationally. They know their domestic markets well, and if they chose to go global they would have to come to terms with the customs, language, tariff regulations and transport systems of other countries and with trading in foreign currencies. Furthermore, their products might require significant modifications to meet foreign regulations and different customer preferences. So, why do companies choose to market abroad? There are seven triggers for global expansion (see Figure 21.1).

Saturated domestic markets

The pressure to raise sales and profits, coupled with few opportunities to expand in current domestic markets, provide one condition for international expansion. This has been a major driving force behind Tesco's expansion into Europe and Asia. In 1997, less than 2 per cent of the group's profits were generated by international trade; by 2014, this figure had risen to over 30 per cent (Tesco PLC, 2014). Many of the foreign expansion plans of European supermarket chains are fuelled by the desire to take a proven retailing formula out of their saturated domestic market into new overseas markets. Currently, many retailers, including Carrefour, Walmart and Tesco, are focusing on emerging markets in India, Brazil and China and looking at expansion opportunities with existing formats or new offerings.

Small domestic markets

In some industries survival means broadening scope beyond small national markets to the international arena. For example, Philips and Electrolux (electrical goods) could not compete against the strength of global competitors by servicing their small domestic market alone. For them, internationalization was not an option: it was a fundamental condition for survival.

Low-growth domestic markets

Often recession at home provides the spur to seek new marketing opportunities in more buoyant overseas economies. BMW exploited demand for luxury cars in China while its home markets in Europe were experiencing slow growth. In China sales rose by 76 per cent compared with 13 per cent in Europe, although

FIGURE 21.1
Triggers for expansion to global markets

Saturated domestic markets
Small domestic markets
Low-growth domestic markets
Customer drivers
Competitive forces
Cost factors
Portfolio balance

globalization

EXHIBIT 21.1
New Porsche Boxter, which was launched at the Beijing Motor Show.

more recently this rate has begun to slow as the *super-rich* reconsider the amounts they spend on luxury purchases (Bryant, 2015). VW has also announced a significant increase in profits thanks to an increase in demand in these overseas markets for its luxury brands, Porsche, Audi and Bentley (see Exhibit 21.1). Indeed, growth in Chinese markets has boosted VW's aspirations to become the world's largest car manufacturer by 2018 (BBC News, 2014).

Customer drivers

Customer-driven factors may also affect the decision to go global. In some industries customers may expect their suppliers to have an international presence. This is increasingly common in advertising, with clients requiring their agencies to coordinate worldwide campaigns. A second customer-orientated factor is the need to internationalize operations in response to customers expanding abroad.

Competitive forces

There is a substantial body of research which suggests that when several companies in an industry go abroad, others feel obliged to follow suit to maintain their relative size and growth rate. (See Aharoni, 1966; Agarwal and Ramaswami, 1992; Knickerbocker, 1973.) This is particularly true in oligopolistic industries. A second competitive factor may be the desire to attack, in their own home market, an overseas competitor that has entered our domestic market. This may make strategic sense if the competitor is funding its overseas expansion from a relatively attractive home base.

Cost factors

High national labour costs, shortages of skilled workers, and rising energy charges can raise domestic costs to uneconomic levels. These factors may stimulate moves towards foreign direct investment in lower-cost areas such as China, Taiwan, South Korea, and central and eastern Europe. Expanding into foreign markets can also reduce costs by gaining economies of scale through an enlarged customer base.

Portfolio balance

Marketing in a variety of regions provides the opportunity to achieve portfolio balance as each region may be experiencing different growth rates. At any one time, the USA, Japan, individual European and Far Eastern countries will be enjoying varying growth rates. By marketing in a selection of countries, the problems of recession in some countries can be balanced by the opportunities for growth in others.

Deciding Which Markets to Enter

Having made the commitment to enter international territories, marketing managers require the analytical skills necessary to pick those countries and regions that are most attractive for overseas operations. There are various factors that govern this decision to enter a foreign market. These are shown in Figure 21.2.

Macroenvironmental issues

These consist of *economic, socio-cultural* and *political-legal technological influences* on market choice.

Economic influences

A country's size, per capita income, stage of economic development, infrastructure, and exchange rate stability and conversion affect its attractiveness for international business expansion. Small markets may not justify setting up a distribution and marketing system to supply goods and services. Low per capita income will affect the type of product that may sell in that country. The market may be very unattractive for car manufacturers but feasible for bicycle producers. Less developed countries, in the early stages of economic development, may demand inexpensive agricultural tools but not computers. Research into the decision to enter a new foreign market found that the issue that had the greatest impact was that the country had a developed economy, emphasizing the importance of economic considerations in this decision (Whitelock and Jobber, 2004).

The economic changes that have taken place globally have had varying effects on each country's attractiveness. For example, China has become the world's largest economy; it has shifted from being a centrally planned to a market-based economy, and this has aided both economic and social development. Direct foreign investment is on the increase as cumbersome administrative procedures have been relaxed and financial controls liberalized.

Another economic consideration is a nation's infrastructure. This comprises the transportation structures (roads, railways, airports), communication systems (telephone, television, the press, radio) and energy supplies (electricity, gas, nuclear). A poor infrastructure may limit the ability to manufacture, advertise and distribute goods, and provide adequate service back-up. Some central and eastern European countries suffer because of this. In other areas of Europe, infrastructure improvements are enhancing movement of goods—for example, the Eurotunnel linking the UK with mainland Europe, and the Øresund Bridge and Drogden Tunnel that connect Sweden and Denmark.

Finally, exchange rate stability and conversion may affect market choice. A country that has an unstable exchange rate or one that is difficult to convert to hard currencies such as the dollar or euro may be considered too risky

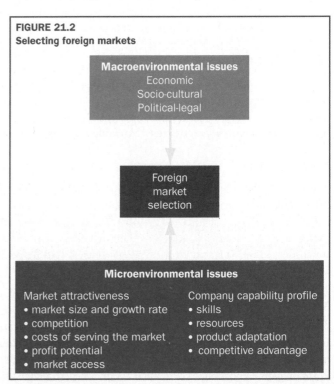

FIGURE 21.2
Selecting foreign markets

Macroenvironmental issues
Economic
Socio-cultural
Political-legal

Foreign
market
selection

Microenvironmental issues

Market attractiveness
• market size and growth rate
• competition
• costs of serving the market
• profit potential
• market access

Company capability profile
• skills
• resources
• product adaptation
• competitive advantage

to enter. Equally important are exchange rates, as countries can find their goods become too expensive in export markets if their currency rates are high.

Socio-cultural influences

Differences in socio-cultural factors between countries are often termed *psychic distance*. These are the barriers created by cultural disparities between the home country and the host country, and the problems of communication resulting from differences in social perspectives, attitudes and language (Litvak and Banting, 1968). This can have an important effect on selection. International marketers sometimes choose countries that are psychically similar to begin their overseas operations. This has a rationale in that barriers of language, customs and values are lower. It also means that less time and effort is required to develop successful business relationships (Conway and Swiff, 2000). Research looking at Swedish manufacturing companies showed that they often begin by entering new markets that are psychically close—that is, both culturally and geographically—and gained experience in these countries before expanding operations abroad into more distant markets (Johanson and Vahlne, 1977). This has also been found to be the case for service companies that move from culturally similar foreign markets into less familiar markets as their experience grows (Erramilli, 1991). Language, in particular, has caused many well-documented problems for marketing communications in foreign markets. Classic communication faux pas resulting from translation errors in brand names include: General Motors car called Nova which means 'doesn't go' in Spanish; Mitsubishi had to change the name Pajero in Spanish-speaking countries because it is a slang word meaning masturbator; Toyota's MR2 is pronounced 'merde' in French which translates to excrement, while Nissan's Moco means mucus in Spanish. In addition, history, religion and culture have also been found to influence the attractiveness of a global market and competitive positioning (Prasad, 2011). Greater knowledge of the history of a country and the resulting culture and economic performance can assist marketing managers in developing a better understanding of the social fabric of a new market. For example, in Indian supermarkets they do not display as many varieties of individual products, such as bread, as western supermarkets do. Careful analysis of the history of a nation and its cultural heritage can offer an insight into its business behaviour. See Marketing in Action 21.1.

 Scan the QR code to consider how Tommy Hilfiger uses an irreverent attitude to appeal to its global customers.

Political–legal influences

Political factors which have implications for global marketing are: the general attitudes of foreign governments to imports and foreign direct investment; political stability; governmental policies; and trade barriers. Negative attitudes towards foreign companies may also discourage imports and investment because of the threat of protectionism and expropriation of assets. Positive governmental attitudes can be reflected in the willingness to grant subsidies to overseas companies to invest in a country and a willingness to cut through bureaucratic procedures to assist foreign companies and their imports. The willingness of the UK government to grant investment incentives to Japanese companies was a factor in Nissan, Honda and Toyota setting up production facilities there.

Countries with a history of political instability may be avoided because of the inevitable uncertainty regarding their future. Countries such as Iraq and Lebanon have undoubtedly suffered because of their respective political situations.

Government policies can also influence market entry. For example, the Chinese government still operates censorship of information, which can act as a barrier to entry especially for media and information-based web companies. As of 2015, YouTube, Twitter and Facebook are blocked from accessing Chinese consumers (Stone, 2014).

Finally, a major consideration when deciding which countries to enter will be the level of tariff barriers. Undoubtedly the threat of tariff barriers to imports to the countries of the EU has encouraged US and Japanese foreign direct investment into Europe. Within the single market the removal of trade barriers is making international trade in Europe more attractive, as not only do tariffs fall but, in addition, the need to modify products to cater for national regulations and restrictions is reduced. See Mini Case 21.1 to find out more about how Amazon helps sellers reach customers in the worldwide marketplace.

MARKETING IN ACTION 21.1
Cultural Differences and Leadership Styles in the Global Marketplace

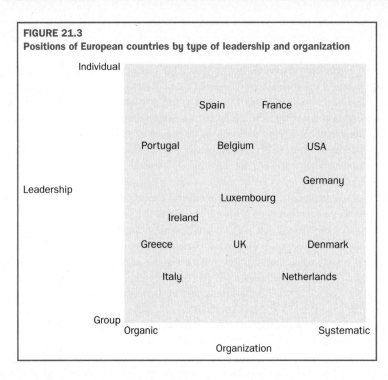

FIGURE 21.3
Positions of European countries by type of leadership and organization

As more companies operate on a global scale, there is a greater need for cross-cultural understanding. Leadership styles need to recognize that leading a global team requires the ability to operate with eastern and western cultures in order to achieve the best outcomes, as successful leadership in developed economies is very different from the approaches used in emerging economies. According to research, American and Chinese approaches often appear incompatible; for example, Americans tend to view Chinese negotiators as inefficient and indirect, while the Chinese see American negotiators as aggressive and impersonal. Therefore, it is important to develop ways that enable both sides to move forwards. So when negotiations take place between US and Chinese companies, they should seek to find ways to cooperate, for example build relationships, shape attitudes towards each other that foster win–win situations, strike a balance of emotions and set mutually acceptable timeframes.

Research also examined business culture and management styles in Europe using two dimensions: type of leadership and organization. Figure 21.3 shows the position of each of the 13 nations according to these two characteristics. Individual leadership (autocratic, directive) is found in Spain and France, whereas an organic leadership style (democratic, equalitarian) tends to be found in Italy and the Netherlands. Systematic organization (formal, mechanistic) is found in Germany, Denmark and the Netherlands, while organic companies (informal, social) are more likely to exist in Spain, Italy, Portugal and Greece.

Studies have also shown that business life in Italy, Spain and the Netherlands is very different.

Italian organizations tend to be informal, with democratic leadership. Decisions are taken informally, usually after considerable personal contact and discussion. Italian managers are flexible improvisers who have a temperamental aversion to forecasting and planning. Interpersonal contact with deciders and influencers in the decision-making unit (DMU) is crucial for suppliers. Finding the correct person to talk to is not easy, since DMUs tend to be complex, with authority vested in trusted individuals outside the apparent organizational structure. Suppliers must demonstrate commitment to a common purpose with their Italian customers.

In Spain, business is typified by the family firm where the leadership style is autocratic and the organizational system informal. Communications tend to be vertical with little real teamwork. Important purchasing decisions are likely to be passed to top management for final approval, but good personal relationships are vital to prevent middle management blocking approaches.

Leadership in the Netherlands is more democratic, although the organizational style tends to be systematic, with rigorous management systems designed to involve multilevel consensus decision-making. Buying is, therefore, characterized by large DMUs and long decision-making processes as members attempt to reach agreement without conflict or one-sided outcomes.

Ultimately, it is important to understand how management and leadership styles vary and then to develop market strategies that can facilitate collaborative relationships. In India and China, this means focusing on developing strong skillsets and effective implementation. In Benelux and Nordic countries, leaders focus on planning and communications. In the USA and UK, there tend to be *hybrid leadership models* with leaders adopting a *push-orientation towards change*.

Based on: Mole (1990); Wolfe (1991); Salacuse (2004); Bersin (2012)

Technological influences

The Internet has had a profound influence on global market expansion and we have discussed many examples throughout the book of how companies have used the Internet and associated technologies to grow market share both nationally and internationally. However, when considering the influence of technology on market entry, it is important to understand the information and communication technology (ICT) infrastructure of a nation as it is essential particularly in emerging economies to understand the quality infrastructure that is in place. ICT is particularly important for the coordination of the movement of goods, transportation, global production and for cross-border investment (Ngwenyama and Morawczynski, 2009).

MINI CASE 21.1
Amazon Helps Companies Grow their Businesses Around the Globe

Online companies like eBay and Amazon pioneered the development of global markets. Together they have approaching 500 million active accounts for buyers and sellers, which generates revenues in excess of $74 billion. These marketplaces have also enabled more companies (and even individuals) to trade in foreign markets than ever before and have fostered the development of other trading platforms, for example La Redoute (France), Rakuten (Japan) and Alibaba (China).

Amazon takes a very proactive role in encouraging and helping its sellers to trade around the world. While developing its global digital marketplace, it has accumulated knowledge about how to succeed in distance selling, especially when crossing national boundaries. Amazon now shares this information to help its own customers trade in foreign markets.

The Amazon marketplaces operate on a global scale, and the company provides advice to its sellers—large and small—about what is required when trading in different parts of the world. Amazon has a five-step plan that guides sellers through the international selling process. This plan involves:

1 *Deciding what and where to sell.* Amazon operates country-specific marketplaces in three broad regions: North America, Europe and Asia. Each region has country-specific domains, for example Amazon.ca (Canada), Amazon.de (Germany), Amazon.co.jp (Japan). A seller simply chooses a region in which to sell, and registers with the particular marketplace; the seller then has access to customers in that region. Consideration should be given to the type of products that are to be sold to ensure they comply with country-specific laws and standards. Amazon even provides its sellers with help with languages and coaching in how to maximize selling opportunities.
2 *Exploring taxes and regulations.* Amazon provides some country-specific guidance on tax laws, duties and selling restrictions, but also advises that sellers must ensure they are fully aware of legal and industry requirements.

≫

>>

3 *Setting up and registering an account.* Once steps 1 and 2 are complete, a seller is then almost ready to begin trading in foreign markets. The seller then sets up a *seller central* account, establishes payment methods and begins listing products for sale. The Amazon marketplace then acts as a gateway to the global market, making it easier for sellers that are new to international trade to access these markets.

4 *Shipping and fulfilment.* No matter where in the world buyers live, they will want to receive the goods they purchase in a timely and secure fashion. Amazon marketplace sellers can arrange their own methods of delivery or use Amazon's fulfilment service. With this service, Amazon helps sellers with the complexities of exporting and importing around the globe.

5 *Customer support and returns.* Amazon is a highly customer-centric company and so insists that sellers provide high-quality aftersales support and return policies and procedures.

Arguably, Amazon and similar international digital marketplaces are lowering the entry barriers for international trade by providing access to global markets. But political and legal barriers remain and must be recognized by all companies wishing to trade in global markets.

Questions:

1 Visit Amazon services at http://services.amazon.com/global-selling and then, using the information provided, select a region—a country-specific domain—and suggest a range of products you might sell to a new market in this region.

2 Suggest what difficulties you might encounter when deciding which marketplace to enter.

3 Based on your answers to questions 1 and 2, devise your own set of priorities that companies should consider when selecting and entering foreign markets.

Based on: Amazon.com Inc. (2015); Raconteur (2013)

Microenvironmental issues

While the macroenvironmental analysis provides indications of how attractive each country is to an international marketer, microenvironmental analysis focuses on the attractiveness of the particular market being considered, and the company capability profile.

Market attractiveness

Market attractiveness can be assessed by determining market size and growth rate, competition, costs of serving the market, profit potential and market access.

- *Market size and growth rate*: large, growing markets (other things being equal) provide attractive conditions for market entry. Research supports the notion that market growth is a more important consideration than market size (Knickerbocker, 1973). It is expectations about future demand rather than existing demand that are important, particularly for foreign direct investment. It is China's enormous market size and growth rate that is attracting many European companies, for example Tesco, Carrefour, Louis Vuitton, Metro and Tengelmann (Birchall and Parkers, 2006). Russia's technology boom, subsidies and tax cuts for foreign investors have stimulated growth, but recent political unrest has also been a limiting factor (Henni, 2012).

- *Competition*: markets that are already served by strong, well-entrenched competitors may dampen enthusiasm for foreign market entry. However, when a competitive weakness is identified a decision to enter may be taken. For example, in China there is growing demand for *clean* energy, and while local producers of solar energy dominate this market, there are opportunities for foreign exporters that are able to supply specialized niche services, for example engineering and environmental consultancy. Volatility of competition also appears to reduce the attractiveness of overseas markets. Highly volatile markets, with many competitors entering and leaving the market and where market concentration is high, are particularly unattractive (Whitelock and Jobber, 1994). Dixons Carphone sold off its Electro World operations in Central Europe and Turkey to enable it to focus on its core business, allowing more specialist national retailers to flourish (Jarvis, 2014).

- *Costs of serving the market*: two major costs of servicing foreign markets are distribution and control. As geographic distance increases, so these two costs rise. Many countries' major export markets are in neighbouring countries—such as the USA, whose largest market is Canada. Costs are also dependent on the form of market entry. Obviously, foreign direct investment is initially more expensive than using distributors. Some countries may not possess suitable low-cost entry options, making entry less attractive and more risky. Long internal distribution channels (e.g. as in Japan) can also raise costs as middlemen demand their profit margins. If direct investment is being contemplated, labour costs and the supply of skilled labour will also be a consideration. Finally, some markets may prove unattractive because of the high marketing expenditures necessary to compete in them.
- *Profit potential*: some markets may be unattractive because industry structure leaves them with poor profit potential. For example, the existence of powerful buying groups may reduce profit potential through their ability to negotiate low prices.
- *Market access*: some foreign markets may prove difficult to penetrate because of informal ties between existing suppliers and distributors. Without the capability of setting up a new distribution chain, this would mean that market access would effectively be barred. Links between suppliers and customers in organizational markets would also form a barrier. In some countries and markets, national suppliers are given preferential treatment. China is said to be moving away from using foreign technology companies for its banks, military and key government agencies, in favour of Chinese suppliers (Yang, 2014).

Company capability profile

Company capability to serve a foreign market also needs to be assessed: this depends on skills, resources, product adaptation and competitive advantage.

- *Skills*: does the company have the necessary skills to market abroad? If not, can sales agents or distributors compensate for any shortfalls? Does the company have the necessary skills to understand the requirements of each market? For example, when VW established Volkswagen Financial Services in Milton Keynes one of the biggest concerns about locating in this operation in the UK was the availability of a workforce with the right skills. The operation is now based in Milton Keynes and employs 400 people which serve 250,000 customers.
- *Resources*: different countries may have varying market servicing costs. Does the company have the necessary financial resources to compete effectively in them? Human resources also need to be considered as some markets may demand domestically supplied personnel.
- *Product adaptation*: for some foreign markets, local preferences and regulations may require the product to be modified. Does the company have the motivation and capability to redesign the product?
- *Competitive advantage*: a key consideration in any market is the ability to create a competitive advantage. Each foreign market needs to be studied in the light of the company's current and future ability to create and sustain a competitive advantage.

Deciding How to Enter a Foreign Market

Once a firm has decided to enter a foreign market, it must choose a mode of entry—that is, select an institutional arrangement for organizing and conducting marketing activities.

 Scan the QR code to learn more about how government agencies and agents can help with entering and buying in foreign markets.

The choice of foreign market entry strategy is likely to have a major impact on a company's performance overseas (Young et al., 1989). Each mode of entry has its own associated levels of commitment, risks, control and profit potential. The major options are indirect exporting, direct exporting, licensing, joint ventures, and direct investment either in new facilities or through acquisition (see Figure 21.4).

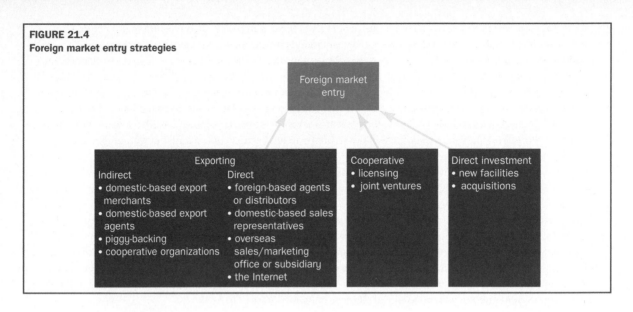

FIGURE 21.4
Foreign market entry strategies

Indirect exporting

Indirect exporting involves the use of independent organizations within the exporter's domestic market; these include the following:

1 *Domestic-based export merchants* who take title to the products and sell them abroad.
2 *Domestic-based export agents* who sell on behalf of the exporter but do not take title to the products; agents are usually paid by commission.
3 *Piggy-backing*, whereby the exporter uses the overseas distribution facilities of another producer.
4 *Cooperative organizations*, which act on behalf of a number of producers and are partly controlled by them; many producers of primary products, such as fruit and nuts, export through cooperative organizations.

Indirect exporting has three advantages. First, the exporting organization is domestically based, making communication easier than using foreign intermediaries. Second, investment and risk are lower than setting up one's own sales and marketing facility. Third, use can be made of the exporting organization's knowledge of selling abroad.

Direct exporting

As exporters grow more confident, they may decide to undertake their own exporting task. This will involve building up overseas contracts, undertaking marketing research, handling documentation and transportation, and designing marketing-mix strategies. **Direct exporting** modes include export through foreign-based agents or distributors (independent middlemen), a domestic-based salesforce, an overseas sales/marketing office or subsidiary, and via the Internet.

Foreign-based agents or distributors

Most companies use specialist agents or distributors in some or all of their exporting abroad. Over 60 per cent of US companies use them for some or all of their export activity, and for European companies the figure rises to over 70 per cent (West, 1987). Agents may be *exclusive*, where the agreement is between the exporter and the agent alone; *semi-exclusive*, where the agent handles the exporter's goods along with other non-competing goods from other companies; or *non-exclusive*, where the agent handles a variety of goods, including some that may compete with the exporter's products.

Distributors, unlike agents, take title to the goods, and are paid according to the difference between the buying and selling prices rather than commission. Distributors are often appointed when after-sales service is required as they are more likely to possess the necessary resources than agents.

The advantages of both agents and distributors are that they are familiar with the local market, customs and conventions, have existing business contracts and employ foreign nationals. They have a direct incentive to sell through either commission or profit margin, but, since their remuneration is tied to sales, they may be reluctant to devote much time and effort to developing a market for a new product. Also, the amount of market feedback may be limited as the agent or distributor may see themselves as a purchasing agent for their customers rather than a selling agent for the exporter.

Overall, exporting through independent middlemen is a low-investment method of market entry although significant expenditure in marketing may be necessary. Also, it can be difficult and costly to terminate an agreement with them, which suggests that this option should be viewed with care and not seen as an easy method of market entry.

Domestic-based sales representatives

As the sales representative is a company employee, greater control of activities compared to that when using independent middlemen can be expected. A company has no control over the attention an agent or distributor gives to its products or the amount of market feedback provided, whereas it can insist that various activities be performed by its sales representatives.

Also, the use of company employees shows a commitment to the customer that the use of agents or distributors may lack. Consequently, they are often used in industrial markets, where there are only a few large customers who require close contact with suppliers, and where the size of orders justifies the expense of foreign travel. This method of market servicing is also found when selling to government buyers and retail chains, for similar reasons.

Overseas sales/marketing office or subsidiary

This option displays even greater customer commitment than using domestic-based sales representatives, although the establishment of a local office requires a greater investment. However, the exporter may be perceived as an indigenous supplier, improving its chances of market success. In some markets, where access to distribution channels is limited, selling direct through an overseas sales office may be the only feasible way of breaking into a new market. The sales office or subsidiary acts as a centre for foreign-based sales representatives, handles sales distribution and promotion, and can act as a customer service centre.

The Internet

The global reach of the Internet means that companies can now engage in exporting activities direct to customers. (See Mini Case 21.1 to learn how Amazon and other digital companies are helping.) By creating a website, overseas customers can be made aware of a company's products and ordering can be direct. Products can be supplied straight to the customer without the need for an intermediary. The Internet is not only a channel to market but also a useful research tool.

Licensing

Licensing refers to contracts in which a foreign licensor provides a local licensee with access to one or a set of technologies or know-how in exchange for financial compensation (Young et al., 1989). The licensee will normally have exclusive rights to produce and market the product within an agreed area for a specific period of time in return for a *royalty* based on sales volume. A licence may relate to the use of a patent for either a product or process, copyright, trademarks and trade secrets (e.g. designs and software), and know-how (e.g. product and process specifications).

Licensing agreements allow the exporter to enter markets that otherwise may be closed for exports or other forms of market entry, without the need to make substantial capital investments in the host country. However, control of production is lost and the reputation of the licensor is dependent on the performance of the licensee. A grave danger of licensing is the loss of product and process know-how to third parties, which may become competitors once the agreement is at an end.

The need to exploit new technology simultaneously in many markets has stimulated the growth in licensing by small high-tech companies that lack the resources to set up their own sales and market offices, engage in joint ventures or conduct direct investment abroad. Licensing is also popular in R&D-intensive industries such as pharmaceuticals, chemicals and synthetic fibres, where rising research and development costs have encouraged licensing as a form of reciprocal technology exchange.

Sometimes the licensed product has to be adapted to suit local culture. For example, packaging that uses red and yellow, the colours of the Spanish flag, is seen as an offence to Spanish patriotism; in Greece purple should be avoided as it has funereal associations; and the licensing of a movie, TV show or book whose star is a cute little pig will have no prospect of success in Muslim countries, where the pig is considered an unclean animal (Bloomgarden, 2000).

In Europe licensing is encouraged by the European Union (EU), which sees the mechanism as a way of offering access to new technologies to companies lacking the resources to innovate; this provides a means of technology sharing on a pan-European scale. Licensing activities have been given exemption in EU competition law (which means that companies engaged in licensing cannot be accused of anti-competitive practices), and *tied purchase* agreements, whereby licensees must buy components from the licensor, have not been ruled anti-competitive since they allow the innovating firm protection from loss of know-how to other component suppliers.

Franchising

Franchising is a form of licensing where a package of services is offered by the franchisor to the franchisee in return for payment. The two types of franchising are *product* and *trade name franchising*, the classic case of which is Coca-Cola selling its syrup together with the right to use its trademark and name to independent bottlers, and *business format franchising* where marketing approaches, operating procedures and quality control are included in the franchise package as well as the product and trade name. Business-format franchising is mainly used in service industries such as restaurants, hotels and retailing, where the franchisor exerts a high level of control in the overseas market since quality-control procedures can be established as part of the agreement. For example, McDonald's specifies precisely who should supply the ingredients for its fast-food products wherever they are sold to ensure consistency of quality in its franchise outlets.

The benefits to the franchisor are that franchising may be a way of overcoming resource constraints, as an efficient system to overcome producer–distributor management problems and as a way of gaining knowledge of new markets (Hopkinson and Hogarth-Scott, 1999). Franchising provides access to the franchisee's resources. For example, if the franchisor has limited financial resources, access to additional finance may be supplied by the franchisee.

Franchising may overcome producer–distributor management problems in managing geographically dispersed operations through the advantages of having owner-managers that have vested interests in the success of the business. Gaining knowledge of new markets by tapping into the franchisee's local knowledge is especially important in international markets where local culture may differ considerably between regions.

There are risks, however. Although the franchisor will attempt to gain some control of operations, the existence of multiple, geographically dispersed owner-managers makes control difficult. Service delivery may be inconsistent because of this. Conflicts can arise through dissatisfaction with the standard of service, lack of promotional support and the opening of new franchises close to existing ones, for example. This can lead to a breakdown of relationships and deteriorating performance. Also, initial financial outlays can be considerable because of expenditures on training, development, promotional and support activities.

The franchisee benefits by gaining access to the resources of the franchisor, its expertise (sometimes global) and buying power. The risks are that it may face conflicts (as discussed above) that render the relationship unviable.

Franchising is also exempt from EU competition law as it is seen as a means of achieving increased competition and efficient distribution without the need for major investment. It promotes standardization, which reaps scale economies with the possibility of some adaptation to local tastes. For example, in India McDonald's uses goat and lamb rather than pork or beef in its burgers, and Benetton allows a degree of freedom to its franchisees to stock products suitable to their particular customers (Welford and Prescott, 2000).

Joint ventures

Two types of joint venture are *contractual* and *equity* joint ventures. In **contractual joint ventures** no joint enterprise with a separate personality is formed. Two or more companies form a partnership to share the cost of an investment, the risks and long-term profits. The partnership may be to complete a particular project or for a longer-term cooperative effort (Wright, 1981). They are found in the oil exploration, aerospace and car industries, and in co-publishing agreements (Young et al., 1989). An **equity joint venture** involves the creation of a new company in which foreign and local investors share ownership and control.

Joint ventures are sometimes set up in response to government conditions for market entry or because the foreign firm lacks the resources to set up production facilities alone. Also, the danger of expropriation is less when a company has a national partner than when the foreign firm is the sole owner (Terpstra and Sarathy, 1999). Finding a national partner may be the only way to invest in some markets that are too competitive and saturated to leave room for a completely new operation. Many of the Japanese/US joint ventures in the USA were set up for this reason. The foreign investor benefits from the local management talent, and knowledge of local markets and regulations. Also, joint ventures allow partners to specialize in their particular areas of technological expertise in a given project. They may also be the only means of entering a country because of national laws. For example, in India overseas supermarket chains are not allowed to operate as retailers unless they can find a local partner to own and operate the store Rigby and Leaky, 2008). For this reason, Marks & Spencer's stores are operated by Indian retailer Reliance Retail, and the firm aims to make India its largest overseas market (Butler, 2013). Finally, the host firm benefits by acquiring resources from its foreign partners. For example, in Hungary host companies have gained through the rapid acquisition of marketing resources, which has enabled them to create positions of competitive advantage (Hooley et al., 1996).

There are potential problems, however. The national partner's interests relate to the local operation, while the foreign firm's concerns relate to the totality of its international operations. Particular areas of conflict can be the use made of profits (pay-out vs plough-back), product line and market coverage of the joint venture, and transfer pricing.

Equity joint ventures are common between companies from western European and eastern European countries. Western European companies gain from low-cost production and raw materials, while former eastern bloc companies acquire western technology and know-how. Eastern European governments are keen to promote joint ventures rather than wholly owned foreign direct investment in an attempt to prevent the exploitation of low-cost labour by western companies. A joint research project between French car makers and British designers led to the Renault Clio winning European Car of the Year Award.

Direct investment

This method of market entry involves investment in foreign-based assembly or manufacturing facilities. It carries the greatest commitment of capital and managerial effort. Wholly owned **direct investment** can be through the acquisition of a foreign producer (or by buying out a joint venture partner) or by building *new facilities*. Acquisition offers a quicker way into the market and usually means gaining access to a qualified labour force, national management, local knowledge, and contacts with the local market and government. Acquisition also is a means of getting ownership of global brands. But such investments do not always deliver immediate profits; for example, when Tata Motors bought Jaguar and Land Rover, it took several years before significant profits were declared. This was a risky investment, as it took Tata Motors into the luxury car market and away from its trucks and small cars, which were the mainstay of its business at the time of the investment (Gribeben, 2013). In saturated markets, acquisition may be the only feasible way of establishing a production presence in the host country (*The Economist*, 2008). However, coordination and styles of management between the foreign investor and the local management team may cause problems. Whirlpool, the US white goods (washing machines, refrigerators, etc.) manufacturer, is an example of a company that has successfully entered new international markets using acquisition. The company has successfully entered European markets through its acquisition of Philips' white goods business and its ability to develop new products that serve cross-national Euro-segments. European companies have also gained access to North American markets through acquisition. For example, ABN-Amro has built up market presence in the USA through a series of acquisitions to become the largest foreign bank in that country (Smit, 1996). One company that has built a global brand through acquisitions is Vodafone, as Marketing in Action 21.2 explains.

Central and eastern Europe have been the recipients of high levels of direct investment as companies have sought to take advantage of low labour costs. Car companies, in particular, have opened production facilities there, notably VW in the Czech Republic and Slovakia; Renault in Romania, Slovakia and Turkey; and Fiat in Poland.

Wholly owned direct investment offers a greater degree of control than licensing or joint ventures, and maintains the internalization of proprietary information for manufacturers. It accomplishes the circumvention of tariff and non-tariff barriers, and lowers distribution costs compared with domestic production. A local presence means that sensitivity to customers' tastes and preferences is enhanced, and links with distributors

MARKETING IN ACTION 21.2
M-Pesa the Mobile Money Service: Vodafone's Market in Africa

Arguably, the M-Pesa makes it easier to pay for a taxi ride in Nairobi than almost anywhere else in the world. This is due to the revolutionary mobile money system developed by Nick Hughes, Head of Global Payments at Vodafone, with various partners. Nick believed that access to finance facilitated entrepreneurial activity, thus creating wealth through economic growth, job creation and trade. He was aware that in emerging markets, transferring money is challenging due to poor infrastructure and the fact that very few people hold bank accounts. Moving cash in Kenya was risky, costly and slow. People had limited choices: they could use expensive services such as MoneyGram, Postapay or Western Union, ferry money via 'letter parcels' with bus companies, or travel long distances themselves with cash on public buses and at the risk of being robbed.

M-Pesa was a project that aimed to solve some of the problems of money exchange and enable small-scale financial transactions to take place via a mobile phone. The key to accessing the market in Kenya was the partnerships created between Vodafone, a local Kenyan micro-finance institute (Faulu) and the Commercial Bank of Kenya. This was considered a highly innovative approach, as such partnerships were rare, especially as, the telecoms sector was viewed as young, entrepreneurial and fast moving, whereas the financial services sector was often seen as traditional, cautious and conservative. While the use of technology in banking was not new, the concept of using existing SMS mobile technology to allow people without bank accounts to carry out money transactions was ground-breaking. Consequently, the partnership approach had to overcome many challenges, and this was done in a series of stages.

First, there was a pilot phase in 2005 that identified a number of key considerations: the need for extensive training for customers on phone familiarity and task complexity; the scope of the project; and the extent to which it could be broadened to include more types of money transaction. For example, the pilot was established with the aim of allowing customers of Faulu to repay small business loans, but the M-Pesa could be used to include payments for trading between businesses, purchasing airtime for relations in rural areas, and depositing cash to be withdrawn at some other destination. Vodafone now realized where the scale opportunity was for M-Pesa. The pilot also highlighted the usefulness of M-Pesa for helping customers manage their personal finances, but was not really suitable for institutions like monetary financial institutions—further modifications would be required for back-office management systems (an obstacle to scale).

The next phase was a country-wide rollout. Traditionally in Kenya, many people work a long distance from home and send money to family members around the country, so the key marketing message was 'send money home'. The marketing strategy focused on three core features: the ability to deposit or withdraw cash at agent shops, to transfer money person-to-person, and to buy prepaid airtime. One of the key challenges facing Vodafone at this stage was the issue of financial regulation. The M-Pesa team also worked with a strategic consultancy group that specialised in secure electronic transactions and with lawyers in Kenya and the UK to ensure that M-Pesa would meet the requirements of the financial sector. The success of the product was phenomenal, and within two years, M-Pesa had approximately 6.5 million registered users making 2 million transactions per day.

Based on: Anon (2013)

and the host nation's government can be forged. Foreign direct investments can act as a powerful catalyst for economic change in the transition from a centrally planned economy. Foreign companies bring technology, management know-how and access to foreign markets (Ghauri and Holstius, 1996). Direct investment is an expensive option, though, and the consequent risks are greater. If the venture fails, more money is lost and there is always the risk of expropriation. Furthermore, closure of plant may mean substantial redundancy payments.

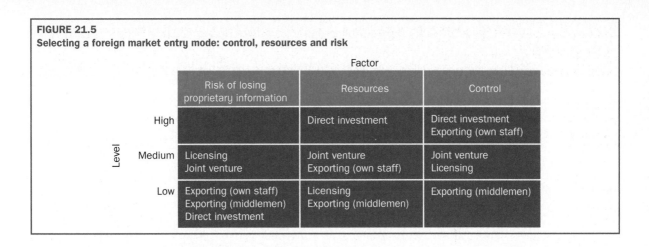

FIGURE 21.5
Selecting a foreign market entry mode: control, resources and risk

The creation of the single European market allows free movement of capital across the EU, removing restrictions on direct investment using greenfield sites. Foreign direct investment through acquisition, however, may be subject to investigation under EC competition policy. American companies, in particular, sought to acquire European companies prior to 1992 in an attempt to secure a strong position in the face of the threat of 'Fortress Europe'.

The selection of international market entry mode is dependent on the trade-offs between the levels of control, resources and risk of losing proprietary information and technology. Figure 21.5 summarizes the levels associated with exporting using middlemen, exporting using company staff, licensing, joint ventures and direct investment.

Considerable research has gone into trying to understand the factors that have been shown to have an impact on selection of market entry method. Both external (country environment and buyer behaviour) and internal (company issues) factors have been shown to influence choice. A summary of these research findings is given in Table 21.1.

TABLE 21.1 Factors affecting choice of market-entry method

External variables

Country environment

- Large market size and market growth encourage direct investment
- Barriers to imports encourage direct investment (Buckley, Mirza and Sparkes, 1987)
- The more the country's characteristics are rated favourable, the greater the propensity for direct investment (Goodnow and Hansz, 1972)
- The higher the country's level of economic development, the greater the use of direct investment
- Government incentives encourage direct investment
- The higher the receiving company's technical capabilities, the greater the use of licensing
- Government intervention in foreign trade encourages licensing (Contractor, 1984)
- Geocultural distance encourages independent modes, for example agents, distributors (Anderson and Coughlan, 1987)
- Psychical distance does not favour integrated modes, for example own salesforce, overseas sales/ marketing offices (Klein and Roth, 1990)
- Low market potential does not necessarily preclude direct investment for larger companies (see Agarwal and Ramaswami, 1992; Knickerbocker, 1973)

Buyer behaviour

- Piecemeal buying favours independent modes
- Project and protectionist buying encourages cooperative entry, for example licensing and joint ventures (Sharma, 1988)

»

»

Internal variables

Company issues

- Lack of market information, uncertainty and perception of high investment risk lead to the use of agents and distributors (Johanson and Vahlne, 1977)
- Large firm size or resources encourage higher level of commitment (Johanson and Vahlne, 1990)
- Perception of high investment risk encourages joint ventures (Buckley, Mirza and Sparkes, 1987)
- Small firm size or resources encourages reactive exporting (Sharma, 1988)
- Limited experience favours integrated entry modes (Klein and Roth, 1990)
- Service companies with little or no experience of foreign markets tend to prefer full control modes, for example own staff, overseas sales/marketing offices
- Service companies that expand abroad by following their clients' expansion plans tend to favour integrated modes (Erramilli, 1991)
- When investment rather than exporting is preferred, lack of market information leads to a preference for cooperative rather than integrated modes (Buckley, Mirza and Sparkes, 1987)

Source: Whitelock and Jobber (1994)

Developing Global Marketing Strategy

Standardization or adaptation

A fundamental decision that managers have to make regarding their global marketing strategy is the degree to which they standardize or adapt their marketing mix around the world (these are referred to, respectively, as the **adapted marketing mix** and the **standardized marketing mix**). Many writers on the subject discuss standardization and adaptation as two distinct options but the literature on the subject is full of contradictions (Hise and Choi, 2010). Pure standardization means that a company keeps the same marketing mix in all countries to which it markets. Such an approach is in line with Levitt's view that world markets are being driven 'towards a converging commonality' (Levitt, 1983). However, the world has moved on since Levitt made this comment. There are compelling arguments for and against standardization. The commercial reality is that few marketing mixes are totally standardized. Some brands that are most often quoted as being standardized are Coca-Cola, McDonald's and Levi Strauss. It is true that many elements of their marketing mixes are identical in a wide range of countries, but even here adaptation is found (Exhibit 21.2).

First, in Coca-Cola the sweetness and carbonization vary between countries. For example, sweetness is lowered in Greece and carbonization lowered in eastern Europe. Diet Coke's artificial sweetener and packaging differ between countries (Quelch and Hoff, 1986).

Second, Levi Strauss uses different domestic and international advertising strategies (Banerjee, 1994). As Dan Chow Len, Levi's US advertising manager, commented:

'The markets are different. In the US, Levi's is both highly functional and fashionable. But in the UK, its strength is as a fashion garment. We've tested UK ads in American markets. Our primary target market at home is 16–20-year-olds, and they hate these ads, won't tolerate them, they're too sexy. Believe it or not, American 16–20-year-olds don't want to be sexy. . . . When you ask people about Levi's here, it's quality, comfort, style, affordability. In Japan, it's the romance of America' (Mayer, 1991).

EXHIBIT 21.2
McDonald's: a truly global brand

FIGURE 21.6
An example of a grid to aid thinking about standardization and adaptation of the marketing mix

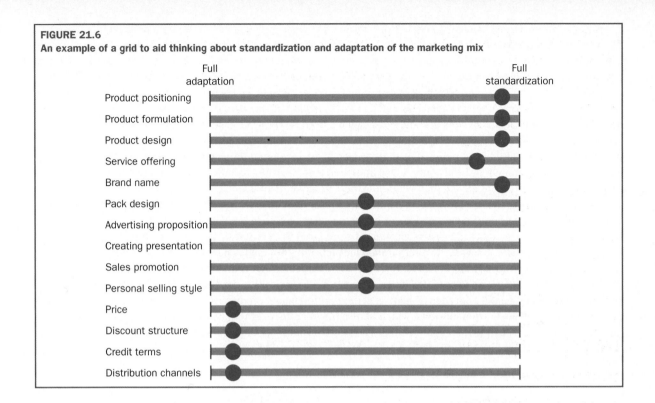

Third, in McDonald's, menus are changed to account for different customer preferences. For example, in France, McDonald's offers 'Croque McDo', its version of the French favourite the *croque monsieur*. It also works with French companies to offer local products such as yoghurts from Danone and coffee from Carte Noire, and buys 80 per cent of its products from French farmers. The proportion of meat in the hamburgers also varies between countries.

Most global brands adapt to meet local requirements. Even high-tech electronic products have to conform to national technical standards and may be positioned differently in various countries.

How do marketers tackle the standardization–adaptation issue? A useful rule of thumb was cited at the start of this chapter: go global (standardize) when you can; stay local (adapt) when you must.

Figure 21.6 provides a grid for thinking about the areas where standardization may be possible and where adaptation may be necessary. The example shows a highly standardized approach to the product and service elements and brand name, some adaptation of advertising, packaging, selling and sales promotion, and an adapted approach towards pricing, finance and distribution.

There are many variations in which elements are standardized and which are adapted. For example, IKEA's product offering and stores are largely standardized, but advertising is varied between countries. SEAT's car models are standardized, but its positioning alters; for example, it is positioned as a more upmarket brand in Spain than in the UK. Also, the Kronenbourg product is standardized, but it is positioned as more of a premium beer in the UK than in Germany. Occasionally the brand name changes for the same product. For example, Unilever's male toiletries brand is marketed as Lynx in the UK and Ireland, because of trademark problems, and as Axe across the rest of the world (Lewis, 2006) (see Exhibit 21.3).

EXHIBIT 21.3
Unilever's male toiletry brand is marketed as Axe across the rest of the world

Standardization is an attractive option because it can create massive economies of scale. For example, lower manufacturing, advertising and packaging costs can be realized. Also, the logistical benefit of being able to move stock from one country to another to meet low-stock situations should not be underestimated. This has led to the call to focus on similarities rather than differences between consumers across Europe, and the rest of the world. Procter & Gamble, for example, standardizes most of its products across Europe, so Pampers nappies and Pringles crisps are the same in all western European countries, although P&G's detergent Daz does differ (Mazur, 2002). However, there are a number of barriers to developing standardized global brands. These are discussed in Marketing in Action 21.3

Developing global and regional brands requires commitment from management to a coherent marketing programme. The sensitivities of national managers need to be accounted for as they may perceive a loss of status associated with greater centralized control. One approach is to have mechanisms that ensure the involvement of national managers in planning, and that encourage them to make recommendations. The key is to balance this local involvement with the need to look for similarities rather than differences across markets. It is the essential differences in consumer preferences and buyer behaviour that need to be recognized in marketing mix adaptation, rather than the minor nuances. Managers must also be prepared to invest heavily and over a long time period to achieve brand penetration. Success in international markets does not come cheaply or quickly. Market research should be used to identify the required positioning in each global market segment (De Chernatony, 1993).

This discussion has outlined the difficulties in achieving a totally standardized marketing mix package. Rather, the tried-and-tested approach of market segmentation based on understanding consumer behaviour and identifying international target markets, which allows the benefits of standardization to be combined with the advantages of customization, is recommended. The two contrasting approaches are summarized in Figure 21.7.

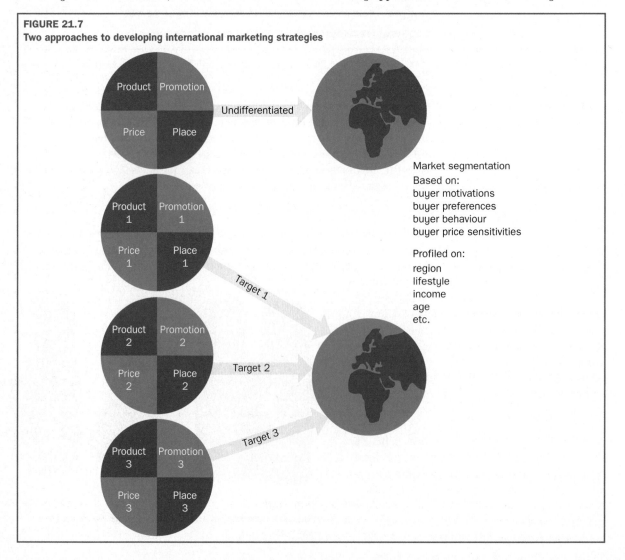

FIGURE 21.7
Two approaches to developing international marketing strategies

┌───

MARKETING IN ACTION 21.3
Barriers to Developing Standardized Global Brands

The cost of the logistical advantages of developing standardized global marketing approaches has meant that many companies have looked carefully at standardizing their approach to the European market. Mars, for example, changed the name of its chocolate bar Marathon in the UK to conform to its European brand name Snickers. Full standardization of the marketing mix is difficult, however, because of five problems.

1 *Culture and consumption patterns*: different cultures demand different types of product in every aspect of people's lives, such as washing, eating, drinking. For example, people wash clothes at different temperatures and so need laundry products that perform differently. In Europe, where adoption of sophisticated washing machines is high, along with interest in reducing carbon emissions there is strong demand for low-temperature laundry products, for example Ariel gel with Actilift, whereas in India the demand is for hot-water products. In the USA, it is not the temperature/performance of the laundry products but the floral fragrance that is most important.

UK consumers like their chocolate to be sweeter than people in mainland Europe do. Also, in South America hot chocolate is a revitalizing drink to have at breakfast, whereas in the UK it is a comfort drink to have just before going to bed. In some countries, Marmite, Unilever's savoury spread, is promoted as a cooking ingredient (India) rather than a spread for a slice of bread (UK). In South America, there are two female beer drinkers to every three males, while in the USA one in four women drink beer. Yet in the UK, only 10 per cent of women drink beer. In China, a fashionable drink is red wine with a dash of Coca-Cola, and in Singapore Guinness is drunk out of shared jugs as though it were Sangria. The failure of KFC in India is believed to be due to its standardized offering of plain fried chicken, while McDonald's succeeded by adapting its offering to the Indian palate; for example, the Maharajah Mac made from chicken and local spices. Coca-Cola also had to change its Minute Maid orange juice for the UK market. After spending almost two years trying to understand what the British consumer wanted, Coca-Cola changed its US formulation of concentrate and water to fresh orange juice without concentrate. Consumer electrical products are less affected, though.

2 *Language*: brand names and advertising may have to change because of language differences. For example, PSCHITT is a soft drink developed by Perrier in the mid-1950s. If it were to be launched in the UK, the name might have to be adapted because of the English pronunciation.

3 *Regulations*: while national regulations are being harmonized in the single market, differences still exist—for example, with colourings and added vitamins in food.

4 *Media availability and promotional preferences*: varying media practices also affect standardization. For example, wine cannot be advertised on television in Denmark, but in the Netherlands this is allowed. Beer cannot be advertised on television in France, but this is allowed in most other European countries. In Italy levels of nudity in advertising that would be banned in some other countries are accepted.

5 *Organizational structure and culture*: the changes necessary for a standardized approach may be difficult to implement where subsidiaries have, historically, enjoyed considerable power. Also where growth had been achieved through acquisition, strong cultural differences may lead to differing views about pan-European brand strategy.

As discussed, standardization is rarely possible. Even brands that are regarded as global, such as Sony, Nike, Visa, IBM, Disney, Heineken, McDonald's and Pringles, are not as globally identical as they may first appear. For example, Visa uses different logos in some countries, Heineken is positioned as a mainstream beer in some countries but as a premium beer in others, Pringles uses different flavours and advertising executions in different countries and, although McDonald's core food items are consistent across countries, some products are customized to local tastes. Setting the objective as being to develop a standardized global brand should not be the priority; instead, global brand leadership—strong brands in all markets backed by effective global brand management—should be the goal.

Based on: De Chernatony (1993); Kirby (2000); Aaker and Joachimsthaler (2002); Luce (2002); Benady (2003); Charles (2008); Lovell (2008); Neff (2010)

International marketing mix decisions

When developing an international marketing mix, marketers need to avoid falling into the trap of applying national stereotypes to country targets. As with domestic markets, overseas countries contain market segments that need to be understood in order to design a tailored marketing mix.

Before entering an overseas market a firm should develop an understanding of its target customers. This is to avoid the danger of using self-reference criteria where there is an assumption that the choice criteria, motivations and behaviour that are important to overseas customers are the same as those used by domestic customers.

For example, although Audi adopts a standardized approach to product design, it still researches overseas customers. For example, it sent members of its design team to California and China for eight weeks each, to live with families and better understand how they live and drive. Its research in the USA persuaded Audi to put cup and bottle holders on its car doors. Also, Chinese drivers' liking of tea led to the installation of a cup holder in its A8 that can be heated or cooled. Rather than incur the expense of changing designs for specific countries, Audi has made these features standard globally.

The cup holder used by Chinese drivers for green tea is promoted for use as a baby bottle holder elsewhere.

Expanding into overseas markets is notoriously difficult. Marks & Spencer failed in continental Europe, B&Q withdrew from South Korea and Tesco itself pulled out of France and the USA when its convenience supermarket, Fresh & Easy, failed to secure sufficient trade. Nevertheless, marketing research can provide dividends, with Tesco's in-depth study of overseas markets being the platform that has led it to build over half of its retailing space overseas, with 700 stores in Europe and over 1,000 in Asia.

Once a thorough understanding of the target market has been achieved, marketing managers can then tailor a marketing mix to fit those requirements. We will now explore some of the special considerations associated with developing an effective *marketing mix* for global markets.

Product

Some companies rely on global markets to provide the potential necessary to justify their huge research and development costs. For example, in the pharmaceutical industry GlaxoSmithKline's Zantac and Zovirax could not have been developed (R&D costs exceeded £30 million in both cases) without a worldwide market. Canon's huge research and development budget is also justified by the potential of global markets. For example, the bubble-jet and laser-beam computer printers it invented formed the basis upon which it has built world market shares of 30 and 65 per cent, respectively (Dawkins, 1996). Once developed, the company can offer a standardized product to generate huge positive cash flow as the benefits that these products provide span national boundaries. Many car companies also standardize as much of their car models as possible, particularly those parts that are not visible to drivers, such as the air-conditioning system, suspension and steering column.

A second situation that supports a standardized product is where the brand concept is based on *authentic national heritage* across the globe: Scotch whisky, Belgian chocolate and French wine are relevant examples. Clearly, there are sound marketing reasons for a standard product. A third basis for standardization is where a global market segment of like-minded people can be exploited. This is the basis for the success of such products as Swatch and Rolex watches, Gucci fashion accessories and Chanel perfume. Where brands make statements about people, the *worldwide properties* of the brand add significantly to its appeal.

In other cases, products need to be modified. Product adaptations come in two forms: permanent and temporary (Dudley, 1989). A company may make a fairly standard product worldwide, but make adaptations for particular markets. For example, Mattel's Barbie doll is a standardized product for most countries, but in Japan, following market research, the doll was redesigned by making it smaller, with darker hair colour. This was a *permanent adaptation*.

Sometimes, a change is only a *temporary adaptation* to see if the local consumer needs time to adjust gradually to a new product. This often occurs with food products. For example, when McDonald's entered Japan it had to alter the red meat content of its hamburgers because Japanese consumers preferred fat to be mixed with beef. Over time, the red meat content has been increased, making it almost as high as it is in the USA. Also, when Mister Donut was introduced in Japan, the cinnamon content was reduced as market research had shown that the Japanese customers did not like the taste. Over time, the cinnamon content was increased to US levels (Ohmae, 1985).

Many products that appear to be the same are modified to suit differing tastes. For example, the ubiquitous Mars bar has different formulations in northern and southern Europe, with northern Europeans favouring a sweeter taste. Also, the movement of large multinational companies to seek global brand winners can provide opportunities for smaller companies to exploit emerging market segments. For example, in the Netherlands, a small company took the initiative to sell environmentally friendly products, and captured one-quarter of the household cleaning market (Mitchell, 1993).

Brand names may require modification because of linguistic idiosyncrasies. Many companies are alive to this type of problem now. Mars, for example, changed the name of its Magnum ice cream in Greece to Magic. However, in France McVitie's had problems trying to convince consumers that the word 'digestive' has nothing to do with stomach disorders. Brand name changes also occur in the UK with Brooke Bond PG Tips being called Scottish Blend in Scotland and coming in distinctive Scottish packaging (Harris and McDonald, 1994).

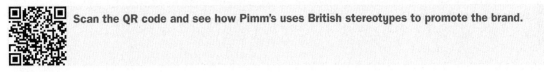

Scan the QR code and see how Pimm's uses British stereotypes to promote the brand.

Promotion

A survey of agency practitioners found that the use of standardized advertising campaigns is set to increase in the future (Duncan and Ramaprasad, 1993). Standard campaigns can realize cost economies and a cohesive positioning statement in a world of increasing worldwide travel. Standardization allows the multinational corporation to maintain a consistent image identity throughout the world, and minimizes confusion among consumers who travel frequently (Papavassiliou and Stathakopoulos, 1997). As with all standardization–adaptation debates, the real issue is one of degree. Rarely can a campaign be transferred from one country to another without any modifications because of language difference. The clever use of pop music (arguably a universal language) in Levi's advertising was one exception. Coca-Cola is also close to the full standardization position with its one-sound, one-sight, one-appeal philosophy. Audi has successfully used the strap-line '*Vorsprung durch Technik*' globally. Other examples of the same copy being used globally are McDonald's ('I'm Lovin' It'), Johnnie Walker ('Keep Walking') and HSBC ('The World's Local Bank'). Yet research has found that full standardization of advertising is rare (Harris and Attour, 2003).

Other companies find it necessary to adopt different positions in various countries, resulting in the need for advertising adaptation. In Mexico, Nestlé managed to position the drinking of instant coffee as an upmarket activity. It is actually smarter to offer guests a cup of instant coffee than ground coffee. This affects the content of its advertising. When brands are used differently in various countries, the advertising may need to be changed accordingly. For example, Schweppes tonic water is very much a mixer (e.g. drunk with gin) in the UK and Ireland, but is drunk on its own in Spain and France. An analysis of the extent of advertising adaptation that is necessary can be assisted by separating the advertising proposition from the creative presentation of that proposition. The advertising platform is the aspect of the seller's product that is most persuasive and relevant to the potential customer: it is the fundamental proposition that is being communicated. The *creative presentation* is the way in which that proposition is translated into visual and verbal statements (Killough, 1978). Advertising platforms, being broad statements of appeal, are more likely to be transferable than creative presentations. If this is the case, the solution is to keep the platform across markets but change the creative presentation to suit local demands. In other cases both platform and presentation can be used globally, as is the case with the McDonald's 'I'm Lovin' It' campaign.

Advertising can be used to position brands using one of three strategies, as outlined below (Alden, Steenkamp and Batra, 1998).

1 **Global consumer culture positioning**: this strategy defines the brand as a symbol of a given global culture. For example, Benetton, whose slogan ('The United Colours of Benetton') emphasizes the unity of humankind and promotes the idea that people all over the world consume the brand. Fresh Intelligence developed a measure of global brands to identify the closeness between brand and country values; the Glocalization score has been found to be important to the success of brand development in foreign markets (Sandler and Churkina, 2011).

2 **Foreign consumer culture positioning**: with this strategy the brand is associated with a specific foreign culture. It becomes symbolic of that culture so that the brand's personality, use occasion and/or user group are associated with a foreign culture. For example, Gucci in the USA is positioned as a prestigious and fashionable Italian product; Singapore Airlines' use of the 'Singapore Girl' in its global advertising campaign, and the positioning of Louis Vuitton as representing French style and gracious living are two further examples (Wachman, 2004).

3 **Local consumer culture positioning**: this involves the association of the brand with local consumer culture. The brand is associated with local cultural meanings, reflects the local culture's norms and identities, is portrayed as consumed by local people in the national culture and/or depicted as locally produced for local

people. For example, Dr Pepper soft drink is positioned in the USA as part of the 'American' way of life. Irn-Bru also has a strong brand personality influenced by its powerful Scottish heritage. This soft drink is manufactured under licence in Russia, Canada, Australia and Norway and is exported to Spain, Netherlands, Germany and other parts of Europe, as well as Africa and Asia.

 Scan the QR code to see how Irn-Bru uses its powerful Scottish heritage to emphasize the personality of the brand.

Selling styles may also require adaptation because of cultural imperatives. Various cultures have different *time values*: in Latin American cultures, salespeople are often kept waiting a long time for a business appointment, and in Spain delay in answering correspondence does not mean the matter has low priority but may reflect the fact that close family relatives take absolute priority and, no matter how important other business is, all other people are kept waiting. In the West deadlines are common in business but in many Middle Eastern countries a deadline is taken as an insult and may well lose the overseas salesperson business.

The concept of space has different meanings in different cultures too. In the West the size of an executive's office is often taken to indicate status. In the Arab world this is not the case: a managing director may share the same office with clerks. In western cultures business is often conducted at a distance, say six feet or more. In the Middle East and Latin America, business discussions are often carried out in close proximity, involving physical contact to which the western salesperson needs to get accustomed.

The unwritten rules of doing business are often at variance too. In the West business may be discussed over lunch or at dinner in the businessperson's home. In India this would violate hospitality rules. Western business relies on the law of contract for sales agreements, but in Muslim culture a person's word is just as binding. In fact, a written contract may be seen as a challenge to his or her honour (Jobber and Lancaster, 2015). Salespeople need to adapt their behaviour to accommodate the expectations of customers abroad. For example, in Japan sales presentations should be low key with the use of a moderate, deliberate style reflecting their preferred manner of doing business. Salespeople should not push for a close of sale; instead they should plan to cultivate relationships through sales calls, courtesy visits, the occasional lunch and other social events.

The Internet is creating opportunities for companies to advertise globally by setting up a website. Using electronic media as a promotional tool may be hampered by the need to set price lists, however. Where prices are currently very different across national borders, some companies may decide that the risks of establishing a global Internet presence outweigh the advantages.

Country images may have a role to play in the selection of goods in overseas markets. For example, a negative image of a country may influence a consumer's attitudes towards products originating from that country. Country of origin is sometimes used to promote products abroad when associations are believed to be favourable and the extent to which the national image is considered suitable for the specific type of product being marketed. For example, the product categories most often promoted by means of the Danish image are foodstuffs and dairy produce, design goods and products related to agriculture (Niss, 1996).

Germany is highly regarded for its engineering excellence, which is a major asset for companies such as Audi, BMW and Volkswagen. So strong is this image that Citroën ran an advertising campaign for its C5 claiming German engineering excellence even though the car is made in France (Whitehead, 2008).

A trend in organizing global advertising campaigns is for consolidation. Advertisers are either using an agency network where the agency has a global presence, or a holding group that contains many agencies spread worldwide; both routes provide the opportunity for greater coordination than employing different agencies in different countries. This also provides the client with the likelihood of negotiating a reduction in fees because of the large budgets involved.

Price

Price setting is a key marketing decision because price is the revenue-generating element of the marketing mix. Poor pricing decisions can undermine previous cost saving strategies.

In the face of more intense global competition, marketers need to consider six issues when considering cross-national pricing decisions:

1   calculating extra costs and making price quotations
2   understanding the competition and customers

3   using pricing tactics to undermine competitor actions
4   parallel importing
5   transfer pricing
6   counter-trade.

Each of these special considerations will now be explored.

Calculating extra costs and making price quotations: the extra costs of doing business in a foreign market must be taken into account if a profit is to be made. *Middlemen and transportation costs* need to be estimated. Distributors may demand different mark-ups and agents may require varying commission levels in different countries. The length of the distribution channel also needs to be understood, as do the margins required at each level before a price to the consumer can be set. These can sometimes almost double the price in an overseas market compared to at home. Overseas transportation may incur the additional costs of insurance, packaging and shipping. *Taxes and tariffs* also vary from country to country. A tariff is a fee charged when goods are brought into a country from another country. Although tariff barriers have fallen among the member states of Europe, they can still be formidable between other countries. Companies active in non-domestic business need to protect themselves against the costs of *exchange rate fluctuations*. Nestlé, for example, lost $1 million in six months due to adverse exchange rate moves (Cateora, Graham and Ghauri, 2006). Companies are increasingly asking that transactions be written in terms of the vendor company's national currency, and *forward hedging* (which effectively allows future payments to be settled at around the exchange rate in question when the deal was made) is commonly practised.

Care should be taken when *quoting a price* to an overseas customer. The contract may include such items as credit terms, currency of exchange, quality standards, quantities, responsibilities for the goods in transit, and who pays insurance and transportation charges and specify the currency. The price quoted can vary considerably depending on these factors.

Understanding the competition and customers: as with any pricing decision these factors play a major role. The difference is that information is often more difficult to acquire for exporters because of the distances involved. When making pricing moves, companies need to be aware of the present *competitors' strategic degrees of freedom*, how much room they have to react, and the possibility of the price being used as a weapon by companies entering the market from a different industry. Where prices are high and barriers to entry low, incumbent companies are especially vulnerable.

Companies also need to be wary of using **self-reference criteria** when evaluating overseas customers' perceptions. This occurs when an exporter assumes that the choice criteria, motivations and behaviour that are important to overseas customers are the same as those used by domestic customers. The viewpoints of domestic and foreign consumers to the same product can be very different. For example, a small Renault car is viewed as a luxury model in Spain but utilitarian in Germany. This can affect the price position vis-à-vis competitors in overseas markets.

Marketers entering products into foreign markets need to understand how to use appropriate pricing tactics in the face of increasingly fierce global competition.

Parallel importing: a major consideration in foreign markets is the threat of parallel imports. These occur when importers buy products from distributors in one country and sell them in another to distributors who are not part of the manufacturer's normal distribution system. The motivation for this practice occurs when there are large price differences between countries, and the free movement of goods between member states means that it is likely to grow. Companies protect themselves by:

- lowering price differentials
- offering non-transferable service/product packages
- changing the packaging—for example, a beer producer by offering differently shaped bottles in various countries ensured that the required recyclability of the product was guaranteed only in the intended country of sale (Leszinski, 1992).

Another means of parallel importing (or 'grey market' trading as it is sometimes called) is by supermarkets buying products from abroad to sell in their stores at reduced prices. A landmark legal battle was won by Levi Strauss to prevent Tesco, the UK supermarket chain, from selling Levi's jeans imported cheaply from outside Europe.

Transfer pricing: this is the price charged between profit centres (e.g. manufacturing company to foreign subsidiary) of a single company. Transfer prices are sometimes set to take advantage of lower taxation in some countries than others. For example, a low price is charged to a subsidiary in a low-tax country and a high price in one where taxes are high. Similarly, low transfer prices may be set for high-tariff countries. Transfer prices should not be based solely on taxation and tariff considerations, however. For example, transfer pricing rules can cause subsidiaries to sell products at higher prices than the competition even though their true costs of manufacture are no different.

Counter-trade: not all transactions are concluded in cash; goods may be included as part of the asking price. Four major forms of counter-trade are as follows.

1 *Barter*: payment for goods with other goods, with no direct use of money; the vendor then has the problem of selling the goods that have been exchanged.
2 *Compensation deals*: payment using goods and cash. For example, General Motors sold $12 million worth of locomotives and diesel engines to former Yugoslavia and received $8 million in cash plus $4 million worth of cutting tools (Cateora, Graham and Ghauri, 2006).
3 *Counter-purchase*: the seller agrees to sell a product to a buyer and receives cash. The deal is dependent on the original seller buying goods from the original buyer for all or part of the original amount.
4 *Buy-backs*: these occur when the initial sale involves production plant, equipment or technology. Part or all of the initial sale is financed by selling back some of the final product. For example, Levi Strauss set up a jeans factory in Hungary that was financed by the supply of jeans back to the company.

A key issue in setting the counter-trade 'price' is valuing the products received in exchange for the original goods, and estimating the cost of selling on the bartered goods. However, according to Shipley and Neale, this forms 20–30 per cent of world trade with yearly value exceeding $100 billion (Shipley and Neale, 1988).

Place

A key market decision when trading abroad is whether to use importers/distributors or the company's own personnel to distribute a product in a foreign market. Initial costs are often lower with the former method, so it is often used as an early method of market entry. For example, Sony and Panasonic originally entered the US market by using importers. As sales increased they entered into exclusive agreements with distributors, before handling their own distribution arrangements by selling directly to retailers (Darlin, 1989).

Marketers must not assume that overseas distribution systems should resemble their own. As we have mentioned, Japan is renowned for its long, complex distribution channels; in Africa the physical landscape and the underdeveloped transport infrastructure create many challenges. Nonetheless, Kenyan growers have established distribution networks that enable beans, mangoes and other fresh produce to be picked, processed, packed and transported to markets in Northern Europe and the USA within a few short days. An important consideration when evaluating a distribution channel is the power of its members. Selling directly to large powerful distributors such as supermarkets may seem attractive logistically but their ability to negotiate low prices needs to be taken into account.

Customer expectations are another factor that has a bearing on the channel decision. For many years in Spain yoghurt was sold through pharmacies (as a health product). As customers expected to buy yoghurt in pharmacies, suppliers had to use them as an outlet. Regulations also affect the choice of distribution channel. For example, over-the-counter (OTC) pharmaceuticals are sold only in pharmacies in Belgium, France, Spain and Italy, whereas in Denmark, the UK and Germany, other channels (notably grocery outlets) also sell them.

Nevertheless, there can be opportunities to standardize at least part of the distribution system. For example, BMW standardizes its dealerships so that customers have the same experience when they enter their showrooms around the world (*Campaign*, 2005). Fiat adopted a similar approach when launching the Fiat 500 in the US. The Italian car manufacturer insisted that all dealerships invested heavily to convert showrooms to create an 'Italian' feel to the customer experience.

As with domestic marketing, the marketing mix in a foreign market needs to be blended into a consistent package that provides a clear position for the product in the marketplace. Furthermore, managers need to display high levels of commitment to their overseas activities as this has been shown to be a strong determinant of performance (Chadee and Mattsson, 1998).

Organizing for Global Operations

The starting point for organizing trade that goes beyond domestic boundaries is, for many companies, to establish an export department. As sales, the number of global markets and the complexity of activities increase, the export department may be replaced by a more complex structure. Bartlett and Ghoshal (2002) describe four types of structure for managing a worldwide business enterprise: international, global, multinational and transnational organization.

International organization

The philosophy of management is that overseas operations are appendages to a central domestic operation. Subsidiaries form a coordinated federation with many assets, resources, responsibilities and decisions decentralized, but overall control is in the hands of headquarters. Formal management planning and control systems permit fairly tight headquarters–subsidiary links.

Global organization

The management philosophy is that overseas operations should be viewed as 'delivery pipelines' to a unified global market. The key organizational unit is the centralized hub that controls most strategic assets, resources, responsibilities and decisions. The centre enforces tight operational control of decisions, resources and information.

Multinational organization

A multinational mentality is characterized by a regard for overseas operations as a portfolio of independent businesses. Many key assets, responsibilities and decisions are decentralized. Control is through informal headquarters–subsidiary relationships supported by simple financial controls.

Transnational organization

This organizational form may be described as a complex process of coordination and cooperation in an environment of shared decision-making. Organizational units are integrated with large flows of components, products, resources, people and information among interdependent units. The transnational organization attempts to respond to an environment that is characterized by strong simultaneous forces for both global integration and national responsiveness (Ghoshal and Nohria, 1993).

Centralization Versus Decentralization

A key determinant of the way global operations are organized is the degree to which the environment calls for global integration (centralization) versus regional responsiveness (decentralization). **Centralization** reaps economies of scale and provides an integrated marketing profile to channel intermediaries that, themselves, may be international, and customers that are increasingly geographically mobile. Confusion over product formulations, advertising approaches, packaging design and labelling, and pricing is eliminated by a coordinated approach. However, too much centralization can lead to the *not invented here syndrome*, where managers in one country are slow to introduce products that have been successful in others, or fail to fully support advertising campaigns that have been conceived elsewhere.

Decentralization maximizes customization of products to regional tastes and preferences. Since decentralized decision-making is closer to customers, speed of response to new opportunities is quicker than with a centralized organizational structure. Relationships with the trade and government are facilitated by local decision-making.

Many companies feel the pressure of both sets of forces, hence the development of the transnational corporation. European integration has led many companies to review their overseas operations with the objective of realizing global economies wherever possible. European centralized marketing teams carry the responsibility for looking at the longer-term strategic picture alongside national marketing staff who deal less with advertising theme development and brand positioning, and more with handling retailer relationships (Mazur, 1993). The result is loss of responsibility and power for national marketing managers. This is a sensitive issue, and many companies are experimenting with the right blend of centralization and national power (Ohbora, Parsons and Riesenbeck, 1992). The fact that national marketing managers often lose responsibility and power in moves to a more centralized marketing approach means that simply preaching the virtues of globalization will not gain their commitment. Neither is compelling business logic likely to remove their opposition.

One approach to developing support is through the creation of *taskforces*. A business area is selected where the urgency of need is most clear; and where positive early results can begin a 'ripple effect', creating champions for change within the company. Procter & Gamble, for example, created a taskforce of national product managers to decide upon common brand requirements. A freight company, under intense pressure from foreign buying groups, set up a pricing taskforce to thrash out a coordinated European pricing strategy. One by-product of the taskforce approach is that it provides top management with a forum for identifying potential Euro-managers.

Companies such as Coca-Cola, McDonald's, Shell and HSBC employ a global marketing director to coordinate worldwide operations. Such a role is not for the faint-hearted: much of their time is spent travelling and they have to combine an ability to digest reams of consumer research with the talent to persuade, through powerful argument, local marketing executives to adopt a strategy. HSBC's global marketing chief managed to achieve the right balance between the need to create a global positioning statement for its advertising and local demands for a bank by the use of the tag-line 'HSBC—the world's local bank'.

To minimize conflict, some companies are trying to build tiered systems where the marketing decisions that are centrally determined and those that are subject to local control are clearly defined. For example, the brand positioning and advertising theme issues may be determined centrally but the creative interpretation of them is decided locally.

Whichever approach is used, a system that shares insights, methods and best practice should be established. The system should provide a global mechanism to identify first-hand observations of best practice, communicate them to those who would benefit from them, and allow access to a store of best-practice information when required. To do this, companies need to nurture a culture where these ideas are communicated. This can be helped by rewarding the people who contribute. Tracking employees who post insights and examples of best practice, and rewarding them during annual performance reviews is one method. Regular meetings can also aid communication, especially when they include workshops that engage the participants in action-orientated learning. Sometimes the sharing of information at these meetings is less important than the establishment of personal relationships that foster subsequent communications and interactions.

Technological developments can also make communication easier and quicker, such as the formation of intranets that allow global communication of best practice news, competitor actions and technological change. Of more lasting use, however, is the sending of teams to see best practice at first hand to facilitate the depth of understanding not usually achieved by descriptive accounts.

When you have read this chapter

Discover further resources and test your understanding: McGraw-Hill **Connect**™ is a digital teaching and learning environment that improves performance over a variety of critical outcomes; it can be tailored, is easy to use and is proven effective. **LearnSmart**™ is the most widely used and intelligent adaptive learning resource that is proven to strengthen memory recall, improve course retention and boost grades. Fuelled by **LearnSmart**™, **SmartBook**™ is the first and only adaptive reading experience available today.

Review

1 The reasons why companies seek foreign markets

- The reasons are to find opportunities beyond saturated domestic markets; to seek expansion beyond small, low-growth domestic markets; to meet customer expectations; to respond to competitive forces (e.g. the desire to attack an overseas competitor); to act on cost factors (e.g. to gain economies of scale); and to achieve a portfolio balance where problems of economic recession in some countries can be balanced by growth in others.

2 The factors that influence which foreign markets to enter

- The factors are macroenvironmental issues (economic, socio-cultural and political-legal) and microenvironmental issues (market attractiveness, which can be assessed by analyzing market size and growth rate, degree of competition, the costs of serving the market, profit potential and market accessibility) and company capability profile (skills, resources, product adaptability and the ability to create a competitive advantage).

3 The range of foreign market entry strategies

- Foreign market entry strategies are indirect exporting (using, for example, domestic-based export agents), direct exporting (using, for example, foreign-based distributors); licensing (using, for example, a local licensee with access to a set of technologies or know-how); joint venture (where, for example, two or more companies form a partnership to share the risks, costs and profits) and direct investment (where, for example, a foreign producer is bought or new facilities built).

4 The factors influencing foreign market entry strategies

- The factors are the risk of losing proprietary information (for example, direct investment may be used to avoid this risk), resources (for example, when resources are low, exporting using agents or distributors may be favoured) and the desired level of control (for example, when high control is desired direct investment or exporting using the company's staff may be preferred).

5 The influences on the degree of standardization or adaptation

- A useful rule of thumb is to go global (standardize) when you can and stay local (adapt) when you must.
- The key influences are cost; the need to meet local regulations, language and needs; the sensitivities of local managers, who may perceive a loss of status associated with greater centralized control; media availability and promotional preferences; and organizational structure and culture (for example, where subsidiaries hold considerable power).

6 The special considerations involved in designing a marketing mix for global markets

- The special considerations are huge research and development costs, where a brand concept is based on an authentic national heritage that transcends global boundaries, where a global segment of like-minded people can be exploited, and where a cohesive positioning statement makes sense because of increasing global travel. All of these considerations favour a standardized marketing mix. Where there are strong local differences an adapted marketing mix is required.

7 How to organize for global marketing operations

- Many companies begin with an export department but this may be replaced later by more complex structures.
- Four types of structure for managing a worldwide business enterprise are: international (where overseas operations are appendages to a central domestic operation); global (where overseas operations are delivery pipelines to a unified global market); multinational (where overseas operations are managed as a portfolio of independent businesses); and transnational organizations (which are characterized by a complex process of coordination and cooperation in an environment of shared decision-making).

Key Terms

adapted marketing mix an international marketing strategy for changing the marketing mix for each foreign target market

centralization is the global integration of marketing operations

contractual joint venture two or more companies form a partnership but no joint enterprise with a separate identity is formed

counter-trade a method of exchange where not all transactions are concluded in cash; goods may be included as part of the asking price

decentralization is the delegation of marketing operations to individual countries or regions

direct exporting the handling of exporting activities by the exporting organization rather than by a domestically based independent organization

direct investment market entry that involves investment in foreign-based assembly or manufacturing facilities

equity joint venture where two or more companies form a partnership that involves the creation of a new company

foreign consumer culture positioning positioning a brand as associated with a specific foreign culture (e.g. Italian fashion)

franchising a form of licensing where a package

of services is offered by the franchisor to the franchisee in return for payment

global consumer culture positioning positioning a brand as a symbol of a given global culture (e.g. young cosmopolitan men)

indirect exporting the use of independent organizations within the exporter's domestic market to facilitate export

licensing a contractual arrangement in which a licensor provides a licensee with certain rights, for example to technology access or production rights

local consumer culture positioning positioning a brand as associated with a local culture (e.g. local production and consumption of a good)

self-reference criteria the use of one's own perceptions and choice criteria to judge what is important to consumers. In global marketing the perceptions and choice criteria of domestic consumers may be used to judge what is important to foreign consumers

standardized marketing mix a marketing strategy for using essentially the same product, promotion, distribution, and pricing in all the company's global markets

transfer pricing the price charged between the profit centres of the same company, sometimes used to take advantage of lower taxes in another country

Study Questions

1. What are the factors that drive companies to enter global markets?

2. Discuss possible entry methods for markets in Europe.

3. For a company of your choice, research its reasons for expanding into new foreign markets, and describe the moves that have been made.

4. Using information in this chapter and from Chapter 17, on distribution, describe how you would go about selecting and motivating overseas distributors.

5. Why are so many companies trying to standardize their global marketing mixes? With examples, show the limitations to this approach.

6. What are the factors that influence the choice of market entry strategy?

7. Select a familiar advertising campaign in your country and examine the extent to which it is likely to need adaptation for another country of your choice.

8. Describe the problems of pricing in overseas markets and the skills required to price effectively in the global marketplace.

Recommended Reading

Cadogan, J. (2012) International marketing, strategic orientations and business success: Reflections on the path ahead, *International Marketing Review* 29(4), 340–8.

Chang, J., X. Bai and J. J. Li (2015) The Influence of Institutional Forces on International Joint Ventures' Foreign Parents' Opportunism and Relationship Extendedness, *Journal of International Marketing* 23(2), 73–93.

Ghauari, P. and P. Cateora (2014) *International Marketing*, London: McGraw Hill Higher Education.

Holt, D. B., J. A. Quelch and E. L. Taylor (2004) How global brands compete, *Harvard Business Review*, September, 69–75.

Nemkova, E., A. Souchon and P. Hughes (2012) Export decision-making orientation: an exploratory study, *International Marketing Review* 29(4), 349–78.

Piercy, N. (2015) *Export Strategy: Markets and Competition*, Oxford, UK: Routledge.

References

Aaker, D. A. and E. Joachimsthaler (2002) *Brand Leadership*, New York: Free Press, 303–9.

Agarwal, S. and S. N. Ramaswami (1992) Choice of Foreign Market Entry Mode: Impact of Ownership, Location and Internalisation Factors, *Journal of International Business Studies*, Spring, 1–27.

Aharoni, S. (1966) *The Foreign Investment Decision Process*, Boston, Mass: Harvard University Press.

Alden, D. L., J.-B. E. M. Steenkamp and R. Batra (1998) Brand Positioning Through Advertising in Asia, North America, and Europe: The Role of Global Consumer Culture, *Journal of Marketing*, 63, January, 75–87.

Amazon.com Inc. (2015) *Amazon Services Europe*, amazon.co.uk, 10 May. http://services.amazon.co.uk/services/global-selling/overview.html

Anderson, E. and A. T. Coughlan (1987) International Market Entry and Expansion via Independent or Integrated Channels of Distribution, *Journal of Marketing* 51, January, 71–82.

Anon (2013) Why does Kenya lead the world in mobile money? *The Economist*, 27 May. http://www.economist.com/blogs/economist-explains/2013/05/economist-explains-18 (accessed 4 June 2015).

Banerjee, A. (1994) Transnational Advertising Development and Management: An Account Planning Approach and a Process Framework, *International Journal of Advertising* 13, 95–124.

Bartlett, C. and S. Ghoshal (2002) *Managing Across Borders: The Transnational Solution*, Cambridge, MA: Harvard Business School Press.

BBC News (2014) Volkswagen's luxury car brands post record sales, BBC News, 10 January. http://www.bbc.co.uk/news/business-25663549

Benady, D. (2003) Uncontrolled Immigration, *Marketing Week*, 20 February, 24–7.

Bersin, J. (2012) How Does Leadership Vary Across the Globe? *Forbes*, 31 October. http://www.forbes.com/sites/joshbersin/2012/10/31/are-expat-programs-dead (accessed 10 May 2015).

Birchall, J. and C. Parkers (2006) Assault on West Coast Market, *Financial Times*, 10 February, 21.

Bloomgarden, K. (2000) Branching Out, *Marketing Business*, April, 12–13.

Bryant, C. (2015) BMW warns earnings growth will slow as China car market cools, *The Financial Times*, 18 March. http://www.ft.com/cms/s/0/3446253c-cd66-11e4-9144-00144feab7de.html#axzz3abkp6PRp

Buckley, P. J., H. Mirza and J. R. Sparkes (1987) Foreign Direct Investment in Japan as a Means of Market Entry: The Case of European Companies, *Journal of Marketing Management* 2(3), 241–58.

Butler, S. (2013) M&S aims to make India its second largest market, *The Guardian*, 11 November. http://www.theguardian.com/business/2013/nov/11/m-s-india-market-marks-spencer-stores (accessed 10 May 2015).

Campaign (2005) When the World is your Market, 27 May, 46–7.

Cateora, P. R., J. L. Graham and P. J. Ghauri (2006) *International Marketing*, London: McGraw-Hill, 376.

Chadee, D. D. and J. Mattsson (1998) Do Service and Merchandise Exporters Behave and Perform Differently?, *European Journal of Marketing* 32(9/10), 830–42.

Charles, C. (2008) Coors Seeks Feminine Touch, *Marketing*, 27 August, 16.

CIA (2015) The World Factbook. https://www.cia.gov/library/publications/the-world-factbook/rankorder/2078rank.html

Contractor, F. J. (1984) Choosing between Direct Investment and Licensing: Theoretical Considerations and Empirical Tests, *Journal of International Business Studies* 15(3), 167–88.

Conway, T. and J. S. Swift (2000) International Relationship Marketing, *European Journal of Marketing* 34(1/2), 1391–413.

Darlin, D. (1989) Myth and Marketing in Japan, *Wall Street Journal*, 6 April, B1.

Dawkins, W. (1996) Time to Pull Back the Screen, *Financial Times*, 19 November, 14.

De Chernatony, L. (1993) Ten Hints for EC-wide Brands, *Marketing*, 11 February, 16.

Dudley, J. W. (1989) *1992: Strategies for the Single Market*, London: Kogan Page.

Duncan, T. and J. Ramaprasad (1993) Ad Agency Views of Standardised Campaigns for Multinational Clients, Conference of the American Academy of Advertising, Chicago, IL, 17 April.

Erramilli, M. K. (1991) Entry Mode Choice in Service Industries, *International Marketing Review* 7(5), 50–62.

Ghauri, P. N. and K. Holstius (1996) The Role of Matching in the Foreign Market Entry Process in the Baltic States, *European Journal of Marketing* 30(2), 75–88.

Ghoshal, S. and N. Nohria (1993) Horses for Courses: Organizational Forms of Multinational Corporations, *Sloan Management Review*, Winter, 23–35.

Goodnow, J. D. and J. E. Hansz (1972) Environmental Determinants of Overseas Market Entry Strategies, *Journal of International Business Studies* 3(1), 33–50.

Gribeben, R. (2013) Jaguar Land Rover: £1.3bn Tata gamble pays off as big cat purrs at last, *The Telegraph*, 15 September. http://www.telegraph.co.uk/finance/newsbysector/transport/10310725/Jaguar-Land-Rover-1.3bn-Tata-gamble-pays-off-as-big-cat-purrs-at-last.html (accessed 10 May 2015).

Harris, G. and S. Attour (2003) The International Advertising Practices of Multinational Companies: A Content Analysis Study, *European Journal of Marketing* 37(1/2), 154–68.

Harris, P. and F. McDonald (1994) *European Business and Marketing: Strategic Issues*, London: Chapman.

Henni, A. (2012) Russia's technology boom attracts foreign investment, *The Telegraph*, 3 April. http://www.telegraph.co.uk/sponsored/rbth/technology/9183881/Russia-technology-foreign-investors.html (accessed 2 May 2015).

Hise, R. and Y.-T. Choi (2010) Are US companies employing standardization or adaptation strategies in their international markets? *Journal of Business and Cultural Studies* 4, 1–29.

Hooley, G., T. Cox, D. Shipley, J. Fahy, J. Beracs and K. Kolos (1996) Foreign Direct Investment in Hungary: Resource Acquisition and Domestic Competitive Advantage, *Journal of International Business Studies* 4, 683–709.

Hopkinson, G. C. and S. Hogarth-Scott (1999) Franchise Relationship Quality: Microeconomic Explanations, *European Journal of Marketing* 33(9/10), 827–43.

Jarvis, M. (2014) Dixons Retail to sell off European Electroworld business, *PCR*, 19 May. http://www.pcr-online.biz/news/read/dixons-retail-to-sell-off-european-electroworld-business/033978 (accessed 10 May 2015).

Jobber, D. and G. Lancaster (2015) *Selling and Sales Management*, London: Pitman.

Johanson, J. and J.-E. Vahlne (1977) The Internationalisation Process of the Firm: A Model of Knowledge Development and Increasing Foreign Market Commitments, *Journal of International Business Studies* 8(1), 23–32.

Johanson, J. and J.-E. Vahlne (1990) The Mechanisms of Internationalisation, *International Marketing Review* 7(4), 11–24.

Killough, J. (1978) Improved Pay-offs from Transnational Advertising, *Harvard Business Review*, July–Aug., 58–70.

Kirby, K. (2000) Globally Led, Locally Driven, *Marketing Business*, May, 26–7.

Klein, S. and J. R. Roth (1990) Determinants of Export Channel Structure: The Effects of Experience and Psychic Distance Reconsidered, *International Marketing Review* 7(5), 27–38.

Knickerbocker, F. T. (1973) *Oligopolistic Reaction and Multinational Enterprise*, Boston, Mass: Harvard University Press.

Leszinski (1992) Pricing for the Single Market, *McKinsey Quarterly* 3, 86–94.

Levitt, T. (1983) The Globalization of Markets, *Harvard Business Review*, May/June, 92–102.

Lewis, E. (2006) Going Global, *The Marketer*, June (Issue 25), 7–9.

Litvak, I. A. and P. M. Banting (1968) A Conceptual Framework for International Business Arrangements, in King, R. L. (ed.) *Marketing and the New Science of Planning*, Chicago: American Marketing Association, 460–7.

Lovell, C. (2008) Universal Truths Cross Booze Borders, *Campaign*, 15 August, 8.

Luce, E. (2002) Hard Sell to a Billion Consumers, *Financial Times*, 15 April, 14.

Mayer, M. (1991) *Whatever Happened to Madison Avenue? Advertising in the '90s*, Boston, MA: Little, Brown, 186–7.

Mazur, L. (1993) Brands sans Frontières, *Observer*, 28 November, 8.

Mazur, L. (2002) No Pain, No Gain, *Marketing Business*, September, 10–13.

Mitchell, A. (1993) Can branding take on global proportions? *Marketing*, 29 April, 20–1.

Mole, J. (1990) *Mind Your Manners*, London: Industrial Society.

Neff, J. (2010) The Dirt on Laundry Trends Around the World Unilever, P&G, Henkel Adjust Products to Suit Cultural Preferences—and Washing Temperatures, *Advertising Age*, 14 June. http://adage.com/article/global-news/global-marketing-dirt-laundry-trends-world/144398

Ngwenyama, O. and O. Morawczynski (2009) Factors affecting ICT expansion in emerging economies: an analysis of ICT infrastructure expansion in five Latin American countries, *Information Technology for Development*, 15(4), 237–58.

Niss, N. (1996) Country of Origin Marketing Over the Product Life Cycle: A Danish Case Study, *European Journal of Marketing* 30(3), 6–22.

Ohbora, T., A. Parsons and H. Riesenbeck (1992) Alternative Routes to Global Marketing, *McKinsey Quarterly* 3, 52–74.

Ohmae, K. (1985) *Triad Power*, New York: Free Press.

Papavassiliou, N. and V. Stathakopoulos (1997) Standardisation versus Adaptation of International Advertising Strategies: Towards a Framework, *European Journal of Marketing* 31(7), 504–27.

Prasad, A. (2011) The Impact of Non-Market forces on Competitive Positioning Understanding Global Industry Attractiveness through the Eyes of M. E. Porter, *Journal of Management Research*, 11(3), 131–7.

Quelch, J. A. and E. J. Hoff (1986) Customizing Global Marketing, *Harvard Business Review*, May–June, 59–68.

Raconteur (2013) *MARKETPLACES: UNDERPINNING THE GROWTH IN E-COMMERCE*, Raconteur.net, 24 September. http://raconteur.net/business/marketplaces-underpinning-the-growth-in-e-commerce

Rigby, E. and J. Leaky (2008) Tesco Finds its Passage to India, *The Guardian*, 13 August, 17.

Salacuse, J.W. (2004) Negotiating: The Top Ten Ways That Culture Can Affect Your Negotiation, IBJ.

Sandler, C. and O. Churkina (2011) *GLOCALIZATION - A MEASURE OF GLOBAL BRANDS.* ESOMAR.

Sharma, D. D. (1988) Overseas Market Entry Strategy: The Technical Consultancy Companies, *Journal of Global Marketing* 2(2), 89–110.

Shipley, D. and B. Neale (1988) Countertrade: Reactive or Proactive, *Journal of Business Research*, June, 327–35.

Smit, B. (1996) Dutch Bank Moves Deeper into the Mid West, *European*, 28 November–4 December, 25.

Stone, M. (2014) The Great Firewall Blocking Facebook In China, Sky News, 4 February. http://news.sky.com/story/1206329/the-great-firewall-blocking-facebook-in-china

Terpstra, V. and R. Sarathy (1999) *International Marketing*, Fort Worth, Texas: Dryden.

Tesco PLC (2014) Annual Report and Financial Statement 2014. http://www.tescoplc.com/files/pdf/reports/ar14/download_strategic_report.pdf (accessed 2 May 2015).

The Economist (2008) The Challengers, 12 January, 61–3.

UKTI (2012) About UKTI, http://www.ukti.gov.uk/uktihome/aboutukti.html, April 2012.

Wachman, R. (2004) Papa of the Branded Bags, *Observer*, 25 July, 16.

Welford, R. and K. Prescott (2000) *European Business*, London: Pitman.

West, A. (1987) *Marketing Overseas*, London: Pitman.

Whitehead, J. (2008) More to Citroën Campaign than Stereotypes, *The Guardian*, 22 September, 7.

Whitelock, J. and D. Jobber (1994) The Impact of Competitor Environment on Initial Market Entry in a New, Global market, *Proceedings of the Marketing Education Group Conference*, Coleraine, July, 1008–17.

Whitelock, J. and D. Jobber (2004) An Evaluation of External Factors in the Decision of UK Industrial Companies to Enter a New Nondomestic Market: an Exploratory Study, *European Journal of Marketing* 38(1/2), 1437–56.

Wolfe, A. (1991) The 'Eurobuyer', How European Businesses Buy, *Market Intelligence and Planning* 9(5), 9–15.

Wright, R. W. (1981) Evolving International Business Arrangements, in Dhawan, K. C., H. Etemad and R. W. Wright (eds) *International Business: A Canadian Perspective*, Reading, MA: Addison Wesley.

Yang, S. (2014) China Said to Plan Sweeping Shift From Foreign Technology to Own. *BloombergBusiness*, 17 December. http://www.bloomberg.com/news/articles/2014-12-17/china-said-to-plan-sweeping-shift-from-foreign-technology-to-own (accessed 2 May 2015).

Young, S., J. Hamill, C. Wheeler and J. R. Davies (1989) *International Market Entry and Development*, Englewood Cliffs, NJ: Prentice-Hall.

CASE 41
IKEA

Building a Cult Global Brand

IKEA is a state of mind that revolves around contemporary design, low prices, wacky promotions and an enthusiasm that few organizations can match. Perhaps more than any other company in the world, IKEA has become a curator of people's lifestyles, if not their lives. At a time when consumers face so many choices for everything they buy, IKEA provides a one-stop sanctuary for coolness. It is a trusted safe zone that people can enter and immediately be part of a like-minded cost/design/environmentally sensitive global tribe.

If the Swedish retailer has its way, you too will live in a BoKlok home and sleep in a Leksvik bed under a Brunskära quilt. Beds are named after Norwegian cities; bedding after flowers and plants. IKEA wants to supply the food in your fridge, it also sells the fridge, and the soap in your shower.

The IKEA concept has plenty of room to run: the retailer accounts for just 5 to 10 per cent of the furniture market in each country in which it operates. It is, however, a global phenomenon. That is because IKEA is far more than a furniture merchant. It sells a lifestyle that consumers around the world embrace as a signal that they've arrived, that they have good taste and recognize value. 'If it wasn't for IKEA,' writes British design magazine *Icon*, 'most people would have no access to affordable contemporary design.' The magazine even voted IKEA founder Ingvar Kamprad the most influential taste master in the world today.

As long as consumers from Moscow to Beijing and beyond keep striving to enter the middle class, there will be a need for IKEA. Think about it. What mass-market retailer has had more success globally? Not Walmart Stores Inc., which despite vast strengths has stumbled in Brazil, Germany and Japan. Not France's Carrefour, which has never made it in the USA. IKEA has had its slip-ups, too. But right now its 301 stores mainly in Europe, Asia, Australia and the USA are thriving, hosting over 500 million shoppers a year.

Why the Uproar?

IKEA is the quintessential global cult brand. Just take those stunts. Before an Atlanta opening, IKEA

managers invited locals to apply for the post of Ambassador of Kul (Swedish for fun). The five winners wrote an essay on why they deserved $2,000 in vouchers. There was one catch. They would have to live in the store for three days before the opening, take part in contests and sleep in the bedding department. 'I got about eight hours of sleep total because of all the drilling and banging going on,' says winner Jordan Leopold, a manager at Costco Wholesale.

Leopold got his bedroom set. And IKEA got to craft another story about itself—a story picked up in the press that drew even more shoppers. More shoppers, more traffic. More traffic, more sales. More sales, more buzz. Such buzz has kept IKEA's sales growing at a healthy rate: for the fiscal year ending 31 August 2014, sales revenues were a colossal $32.8 billion, with profits of $3.8 billion. IKEA maintains these profits even while it cuts prices steadily. 'IKEA's operating margins of approximately 10 per cent are among the best in home furnishing,' says Mattias Karlkjell of Stockholm's ABG Sundal Collier. They also compare well with margins of 5 per cent at Pier 1 Imports and 7.7 per cent at Target, both competitors of IKEA in the USA.

To keep growing at that pace, IKEA has continued its new store openings around the world with up to 20 per year (although that number was reduced in recent years). IKEA has boosted its profile in three of its fastest-growing markets: the USA, Russia (where IKEA is already a huge hit—today's Russian yuppies are called 'the IKEA generation', and China (now worth

»

»

TABLE C41.1 IKEA at a glance
Privately owned home products retailer that markets flat-pack furniture, accessories, and bathroom and kitchen items globally.
Ikea is the world's largest furniture manufacturer.
Sales of $32.8 billion (2014).
Estimated profits of $3.8 billion (2014).
Number of stores in 2014: 301 in 37 countries, mainly in Europe, USA, Canada, Asia and Australia. The largest number of stores are in Germany (46) and USA (38). Ikea owns 267 stores and 34 are franchises.

over $ 1 billion in sales). In the USA the number of stores has grown from 25 in 2005 to 38 in 2014. IKEA is also investing in emerging markets such as the Czech Republic and Slovakia. In the UK, IKEA has built smaller, multi-level, city stores in Coventry and Southampton in response to restrictions on the building of out-of-town retail establishments.

The key to these roll-outs is to preserve the strong enthusiasm IKEA evokes—an enthusiasm that has inspired endless shopper comment on the Internet. Examples: 'IKEA makes me free to become what I want to be' (from Romania). Or this: 'Half my house is from IKEA—and the nearest store is six hours away' (the USA). Or this: 'Every time, it's trendy for less money' (Germany).

The Shopping Experience

What enthralls shoppers and scholars alike is the store visit—a similar experience the world over. The blue-and-yellow buildings average 28,000 square metres in size, about equal to five football fields. The sheer number of items—7,000, from kitchen cabinets to candlesticks—is a decisive advantage. 'Others offer affordable furniture,' says Bryan Roberts, research manager at Planet Retail, a consultancy in London. 'But there's no one else who offers the whole concept in the big shed.'

The global middle class, which IKEA targets, shares buying habits. The $50 Billy bookcase, $13 Lack side table and $190 Ivar storage system are best-sellers worldwide. Even spending per customer is similar. According to IKEA, the figure in Russia is $85 per store visit—exactly the same as in affluent Sweden.

Wherever they are, customers tend to think of the store visit as more of an outing than a chore. That's intentional. IKEA practises a form of 'gentle coercion' to keep you as long as possible. Right at the entrance, for example, you can drop off your kids at the playroom, an amenity that encourages more leisurely shopping.

Then, clutching your dog-eared catalogue (the print run is over 160 million—more than the Bible, IKEA claims), you proceed along a marked path through the warren of showrooms. 'Because the store is designed as a circle, I can see everything as long as I keep walking in one direction,' says Krystyna Gavora, an architect who frequents IKEA in Schaumburg, Illinois. Wide aisles let you inspect merchandise without holding up traffic. The furniture itself is arranged in fully accessorized displays, down to the picture frames on the nightstand, to inspire customers and get them to spend more. The settings are so lifelike that one writer staged a play at IKEA in Renton, Washington.

Along the way, one touch after another seduces the shopper, from the paper measuring tapes and pencils to strategically placed bins with items like pink plastic watering cans, scented candles and picture frames. These are things you never knew you needed but at less than $2 each you load up on them anyway. You set out to buy a $40 coffee table but end up spending $500 on everything from storage units to glassware. 'They have this way of making you believe nothing is expensive,' says Bertille Faroult, a shopper at IKEA on the outskirts of Paris. The bins and shelves constantly surprise. IKEA replaces a third of its product line every year.

Then, there's the stop at the restaurant, usually placed at the centre of the store, to give shoppers a breather and encourage them to keep going. You proceed to the warehouse, where the full genius of founder Kamprad is on display. Nearly all the big items are flat-packed, which not only saves IKEA millions in shipping costs from suppliers but also enables shoppers to haul their own stuff home—another saving. Finally, you have the fun, or agony, of assembling at home, equipped with nothing but an Allen key and those cryptic instructions.

A vocal minority rails at IKEA for its long queues, crowded car parks, exasperating assembly experiences and furniture that's hardly built to last. The running joke is that IKEA is Swedish for particle board. But the converts outnumber the critics. And for every fan who shops at IKEA, there seems to be one working at the store itself. The fanaticism stems from founder Ingvar Kamprad, 86, a figure as important to global retailing as Wal-Mart's Sam Walton. Kamprad started the company in 1943 at the age of 17, selling pens, Christmas cards and seeds from a shed on his family's farm in southern Sweden. In 1951 the first catalogue appeared. Kamprad penned all the text himself until 1963. His credo of creating 'a better life for many' is enshrined in his almost evangelical 1976 tract, *A Furniture Dealer's Testament*. Peppered with folksy titbits—'divide your life into 10-minute units and sacrifice as few as possible in meaningless activity', 'wasting resources is a mortal sin' (that's for sure: employees are the catalogue models) or the more revealing 'it is our duty to expand'—the pamphlet is given to all employees the day they start. Employees at IKEA will never get rich but they do get to enjoy autonomy, very little hierarchy and a family-friendly culture. In return they buy into the culture of frugality and style that drives the whole company.

Kamprad, though officially retired, is still the cheerleader for the practices that define IKEA culture. One is egalitarianism. IKEA regularly stages Anti-bureaucracy Weeks, during which executives work on the shop floor or tend the checkouts.

Prices and Costs

A feature of IKEA is its steely competitiveness. You get a sense of that at one of IKEA's main offices, in Helsingborg, Sweden. At the doorway, a massive bulletin board tracks weekly sales growth, names the best-performing country markets and identifies the best-selling furniture. The other message that comes across loud and clear: cut prices. IKEA designers found a way to pack the Ektorp three-seater sofa more compactly, doubling the amount of sofa they could get into a given space. The cost saving meant that $135 could be shaved from its price.

The montage vividly illustrates IKEA's relentless cost cutting. The retailer aims to lower prices across its entire offering by an average of 2 per cent to 3 per cent each year. It goes deeper when it wants to hit rivals in certain segments. 'We look at the competition, take their price and then slash it in half,' says Mark McCaslin, manager of IKEA Long Island, in Hicksville, NY.

It helps that frugality is as deeply ingrained in the corporate DNA as the obsession with design. Managers fly economy, even top brass. Steen Kanter, who left IKEA in 1994 and now heads his own retail consultancy in Philadelphia, Kanter International, recalls that while flying with founder Ingvar Kamprad once, the boss handed him a coupon for a car rental he had ripped out from an in-flight magazine.

This cost obsession fuses with the design culture. 'Designing beautiful-but-expensive products is easy,' says Josephine Rydberg-Dumont, president of IKEA of Sweden. 'Designing beautiful products that are inexpensive and functional is a huge challenge.'

No design—no matter how inspired—finds its way into the showroom if it cannot be made affordable. To achieve that goal, the company's 12 full-time designers at Almhult, Sweden, along with 80 freelances, work hand in hand with in-house production teams to identify the appropriate materials and least costly suppliers, a trial-and-error process that can take as long as three years. Example: for the PS Ellan, a $39.99 dining chair that can rock back on its hind legs without tipping over, designer Chris Martin worked with production staff for a year and a half to adapt a woodfibre composite, an inexpensive blend of wood chips and plastic resin used in highway noise barriers, for use in furnishings. Martin also had to design the chair to break down into six pieces, so it could be flat-packed and snapped together without screws.

With a network of 2,000 suppliers in over 50 countries, IKEA works overtime to find the right manufacturer for the right product. It once contracted with ski makers—experts in bent wood—to manufacture its Poang armchairs, and it has tapped makers of supermarket carts to turn out durable sofas. Simplicity, a tenet of Swedish design, helps keep costs down. The 50c Trofé mug came only in blue and white, the least expensive pigments. IKEA's conservation drive extends naturally from this cost cutting. For its PS line, it challenged 28 designers to find innovative uses for discarded and unusual materials. The results: a table fashioned from reddish-brown birch heartwood (furniture makers prefer the pale exterior wood) and a storage system made from recycled milk cartons.

Adaptation to Local Tastes

Adding to the challenge, the suppliers and designers have to customize some IKEA products to make them sell better in local markets. In China, the 250,000 plastic placemats IKEA produced to commemorate the year of the rooster sold out in just three weeks. Julie Desrosiers, the bedroom line manager at IKEA of Sweden, visited people's houses in the USA and Europe to peek into their closets, learning that 'Americans prefer to store most of their clothes folded, and Italians like to hang'. The result was a wardrobe that features deeper drawers for US customers.

The US market poses special challenges for IKEA because of the huge differences inside the USA. 'It's so easy to forget the reality of how people live,' says IKEA's US interior design director, Mats Nilsson. For example, IKEA realized it might not be reaching California's Hispanics, so its designers visited the homes of Hispanic staff. They soon realized they had set up the store's displays all wrong. Large Hispanic families need dining tables and sofas that fit more than two people, the Swedish norm. They prefer bold colours to the more subdued Scandinavian palette and display tons of pictures in elaborate frames. Nilsson warmed up the showrooms' colours, adding more seating and throwing in numerous picture frames.

»

»

IKEA is particularly concerned about the USA since it is key to expansion—and since IKEA came close to blowing it. 'We got our clocks cleaned in the early 1990s because we really didn't listen to the consumer,' says Kanter. Stores weren't big enough to offer the full IKEA experience, and many were in poor locations. Prices were too high. Beds were measured in centimetres, not king, queen and twin. Sofas weren't deep enough, curtains were too short and kitchens didn't fit US-size appliances. 'American customers were buying vases to drink from because the glasses were too small,' recalls Goran Carstedt, the former head of IKEA North America, who helped engineer a turnaround. Parts of the product line were adapted (no more metric measurements), new and bigger store locations chosen, prices slashed and service improved. Now US managers are paying close attention to the tiniest details. 'Americans want more comfortable sofas, higher-quality textiles, bigger glasses, more spacious entertainment units,' says Pernille Spiers-Lopez, head of IKEA North America.

The Future

Can the cult keep thriving? IKEA has stumbled badly before. A foray into Japan 30 years ago was a disaster (the Japanese wanted high quality and great materials, not low price and particle board). The company returned to Japan in 2006. IKEA is also seeing more competition than ever. In the USA, Target Corp. recruited top designer Thomas O'Brien to develop a range of low-priced furnishings. An IKEA-like chain called Fly is popular in France. In Japan, Nitori Co. is the major player in low-cost furniture. ILVA is successfully selling upmarket furniture in Denmark and Sweden although its foray into the UK market was unsuccessful.

Perhaps the bigger issue is what happens inside IKEA. 'The great challenge of any organization as it becomes larger and more diverse is how to keep the core founding values alive,' says Harvard Business School Professor Christopher A. Bartlett. IKEA is still run by managers who were trained and groomed by Kamprad himself—and who are personally devoted to the founder. As the direct links with Kamprad disappear, the culture may start to fade.

For now, the fans keep clamouring for more. At least once a year, Jen Segrest, a 36-year-old freelance web designer, and her husband make a 10-hour round-trip from their home in Middletown, Ohio, to IKEA in Schaumburg, Illinois, near Chicago. 'Every piece of furniture in my living room is IKEA—except for an end table, which I hate. And next time I go to IKEA I'll replace it,' says Segrest. To lure the retailer to Ohio, Segrest has even started a blog called OH! IKEA. The banner on the home page reads 'IKEA in Ohio— Because man cannot live on Target alone.'

Questions

Mc Graw Hill Education **connect**

1. IKEA has chosen to enter new markets mainly by direct investment. What advantages does this form of entry give it? Why doesn't IKEA use franchising like McDonald's and Benetton as its main method of entering new markets?

2. How would you categorize IKEA's approach to developing an international marketing strategy in terms of standardization and adaptation?

3. What are the factors that have helped IKEA to build a successful global brand?

This case study was written by David Jobber, Emeritus Professor of Marketing, University of Bradford.

References

Based on: Sains, A., C. Lindblad, A. T. Palmer, J. Bush, D. Roberts and K. Hall (2005) IKEA: How The Swedish Retailer Became a Golbal Cult Brand, *Business Week*, 14 November, 45–54; Wearden, G. (2009) IKEA to Cut More Jobs, *The Guardian*, 8 July, 22; Clark, N. (2008) ILVA, Marketing, 30 January, 20; Boyle, C. (2009) IKEA to Cut More Staff as Demand Falls Falls, www.business.timesonline.co.uk/tol/business; Anonymous (2011) The Secret of Ikea's Success, Economist, 26 February, 634; BBC News (2012) Ikea Profits Rise Ten Per Cent as Emerging Markets Boost Sales, www. bbc.co.uk/news/business; Anonymous (2015) Ikea Repeats Flat Profits Despite Rising Sales, www.bbc.co.uk/news/business, 28 January; Anonymous (2015) About Ikea, www.ikea.com/ms/en_GB/about ikea/factsand figures.

CASE 42
Frozen: A Global Hit in Any Language

Introduction

If you don't know your Elsa from your elbow and the words from 'Let It Go', then you have probably been hiding under a rock for the last two years. The Disney movie *Frozen* rapidly achieved worldwide domination and has led to *Frozen*-mania across the globe. Inspired by the Hans Christian Andersen's fairy tale 'The Snow Queen', the film tells the story of a fearless princess (Anna), who sets off on an epic journey alongside a rugged mountain man (Kristoff), his loyal pet reindeer (Sven) and a naive snowman (Olaf) to find her estranged sister (Elsa), whose icy powers have inadvertently trapped the Kingdom of Arendelle in eternal winter.

The film has met with strongly positive reviews from critics and audiences and has been a massive commercial success, accumulating nearly $1.3 billion in worldwide box office revenues. The movie ranks as the highest-grossing animated film of all time and won two Academy Awards for Best Animated Feature and Best Original Song ('Let It Go'). But what has contributed to this phenomenal global success?

A Global Success

Disney's *Frozen* was always expected to be big, but it surpassed all expectations. Its global success is due to a number of factors. It is universally acceptable, as it is driven by sibling love rather than romantic infatuation (Thedrum.com, 2015). A strong point of appeal in the movie is that the story keeps the audience engaged and subverts expected stereotypes (Konnikova, 2014). It is not a typical princess movie: the handsome prince is evil and the person with the magical powers is good. In addition, both leads are female and strong characters, and it is the women and not the men who save the day with their selfless act of sacrifice, rather than a 'kiss of true love' (Konnikova, 2014). While the relationship between Anna and Elsa was central to the film, the 'princess' theme was downplayed in Disney's marketing of the film as it carefully picked a gender-unspecific title and chose group images of the animated cast in its promotional posters. This helped ensure the movie appealed to both boys and girls. According to Mike Stagg, Vice President and General Manager of Retail for the

Frozen character Elsa

Walt Disney Company in the UK and Ireland, '*Frozen* has universal appeal. Its successful "four-quadrant" strategy [meaning it pulled in boys, girls, over 25s and under 25s] has helped it become the highest grossing animated movie of all time' (Slattery, 2014).

In addition, the movie characters were ones that a lot of people could identify with. Elsa wasn't a typical princess or Disney character. She was flawed and her flaws resulted in real mistakes and consequences. Everyone could interpret her in their own way and her story resonated with many. For some, it was about emotional repression, for others about gender and identity, and for others about broader social acceptance and depression (Konnikova, 2014). Olaf also provided some light relief in the movie, and his adorable nature and dim antics endeared him to audiences (Ebiri, 2014). The witty and catchy musical numbers in the movie were also at the core of its critical and box-office success. *Frozen* has yielded a chart-topping soundtrack and thousands of fan-made singing videos on YouTube (Keegan, 2014). Finally, social media helped create a huge buzz online. There were endless blogs, videos and articles by and about *Frozen*-loving fans online, YouTube tutorials for recreating the princesses' hairstyles, and on Twitter the hashtag #TheColdNeverBotheredMeAnyway (a pivotal line from 'Let It Go') was used as a badge of devotion by hardcore *Frozen* fans (Everett, 2014).

A Localized Strategy

Disney invested a huge amount in attempting to make the animated film *Frozen* accessible worldwide (Kang,

»

»

2014). Like other Disney movies, which are often localized, the *Frozen* movie and songs were translated and dubbed into 41 languages. The localization of the movie's music posed a special challenge for Disney, as it needed to mimic the vocal tone and texture of soprano Idina Menzel, who sang the original award-winning song 'Let It Go'. Disney auditioned women from all over the globe to sing the title role of Elsa in their native tongues (NPR, 2014)—Disney auditioned approximately 200 singers to fill the slots for Elsa alone! The Idina Menzel English-language version was used as a blueprint, but Disney sought to understand local idioms in various countries to ensure that each language version of the song was a local interpretation. According to Rick Dempsey, Senior Vice President of Creative for Disney Character Voice International, 'At the end of the day, we really want audiences to feel like this film was made for them in their own country, even animated in their country—we want the lip-sync to be that good' (NPR, 2014).

In a lot of cases, Disney was able to fool people into thinking that it was Idina Menzel's voice used in all the various language versions created. The goal was to ensure that there was character consistency and that the voices were very similar around the world, and Disney seems to have been able to find talent and pull it off (NPR, 2014). That talent included women who were divas in their own countries, such as Spanish pop singer Gisela, who voiced the Castillian and Catalan versions, and pop singer Takako Matsu, who sang the Japanese version (Keegan, 2014).

The localization of the movie's soundtrack involved 'a difficult juggling act. . . . to get the right intent of the lyrics and also have it match rhythmically to the music. And then you have to go back and adjust for lip sync. . . It requires a lot of patience,' noted Rick Dempsey, the man responsible for the translation process. After casting all other roles for all 41 languages, the international cast ended up including more than 900 people, who voiced roles through approximately 1,300 recording sessions (Kang, 2014).

The *Frozen* Franchise

Since the film's release in November 2013, the *Frozen* franchise has expanded very rapidly. *Frozen* is no longer a movie; it has now become a global brand and is a larger-than-life franchise built around products. The movie was released for digital download on 25 February 2014, and was subsequently released on Blu-ray disc and DVD on 18 March 2014 (Sims, 2014). On the first day of its release on Blu-ray and DVD, it sold 3.2 million units, becoming one of the biggest

home video sellers in the last decade (Lang, 2014). In addition to the movie and DVD release, *Frozen* has been promoted heavily at several Disneyland parks, where people are offered the opportunity to meet and greet the two main characters, Anna and Elsa (Sudock, 2014). The franchise now also includes an ice-skating show, 'Frozen on Ice', and a 'Frozen-inspired' tour of Norway, the country that served as visual inspiration for the film.

Frozen has become one of the most profitable animated Disney movies of all time, and is continuing to rake in staggering amounts of money beyond its initial release, thanks in large part to the sell-out success of the movie's merchandise (Hoyle and Lankston, 2014). In November 2013, Disney Consumer Products began releasing a line of toys and other merchandise relating to the film in Disney Stores and other retailers (Disney, 2013). Just about everything in the film became fodder for merchandising (Husband, n.d.). In the lead-up to Christmas 2013 and 2014, stores across the world sold out of Frozen products as parents desperately tried to get hold of the latest Anna or Elsa doll for their child. Many Anna and Elsa dolls actually sold out months before Christmas, as parents attempted to get ahead of the Christmas rush. *Fortune* reported that Frozen merchandise sales were on the verge of surpassing $1 billion, and *Frozen* has now been named in Disney's top five franchises (Husband, n.d.).

Conclusion

Frozen's success has changed the way Disney and other studios think about the production of their films. According to *Frozen* Producer, John Del Vecho, 'for international success, we need to make sure we have universal stories, with universal characters that are relatable to today's audience' (Kang, 2014). It's no surprise that Disney has long-term plans for extending *Frozen*'s life and overall popularity even more. In the follow-up to *Frozen*'s success, an animated short sequel premiered on 13 March 2015, alongside Disney Pictures' *Cinderella* (Graser, 2014). Disney Theatrical is also working on a stage adaptation of the animated film, which is due to premier on Broadway in 2017 (McPhee, 2015). Disney has also announced plans to produce a sequel to *Frozen*. The sequel doesn't come as much of a surprise, considering how the first film has continued to be a major moneymaking force for Disney since its introduction and helped reinvigorate Walt Disney Animation Studios. However, it remains to be seen if the sequel will achieve the same global success enjoyed by the original movie (Graser, 2015).

Questions

1. **What are the factors that have led to** *Frozen* **becoming a successful global brand?**

2. **Comment on how Disney has balanced standardization and adaptation to achieve worldwide appeal for the** *Frozen* **movie.**

3. **Discuss the importance of the** *Frozen* **franchise to the brand's success.**

This case study was written by Marie O'Dwyer, Lecturer in Marketing, Waterford Institute of Technology

References

Based on: http://en.wikipedia.org/wiki/Frozen_%282013_film%29; http://www.imdb.com/title/tt2294629; Thedrum.com (2015) The Frozen frenzy: Marketing lessons from Disney's unstoppable franchise, Thedrum.com. Available at: http://www.thedrum.com/opinion/2015/02/03/frozen-frenzy-marketing-lessons-disneys-unstoppable-franchise; Konnikova, M. (2014) How 'Frozen' took over the world, New Yorker, http://www.newyorker.com/science/maria-konnikova/how-frozen-took-over-the-world; Slattery, L. (2014) More than just pink to marketing princesses, Irish Times, http://www.irishtimes.com/business/media-and-marketing/more-than-just-pink-to-marketing-princesses-1.1755848; Ebiri, B. (2014) The eight reasons Frozen is unstoppable, vulture.com, http://www.vulture.com/2014/01/why-is-frozen-such-a-big-hit.html; Keegan, R. (2014) 'Frozen': Finding a diva in 41 languages, LA Times, http://articles.latimes.com/2014/jan/24/entertainment/la-et-mn-frozen-how-disney-makes-a-musical-in-41-languages-20140124; Everett, L. (2014) Frozen: inside Disney's billion-dollar social media hit, The Telegraph, http://www.telegraph.co.uk/culture/film/10668942/Frozen-inside-Disneys-billion-dollar-social-media-hit.html; Kang, C. (2014) Disney's global success with 'Frozen' took lots of translation, investment, The Washington Post, http://www.washingtonpost.com/news/business/wp/2014/11/20/disneys-global-success-with-frozen-took-lots-of-translation-investment; NPR (2014) 'Let It Go': A Global Hit In Any Language, NPR.org, http://www.npr.org/2014/02/24/282081061/let-it-go-a-global-hit-in-any-language; Doty, M. (2014) How These Singers Around the Globe Pushed 'Frozen' Over the Top, Yahoo, https://www.yahoo.com/movies/bp/how-these-singers-around-the-globe-pushed--frozen--over-the-top-063739448.html; Sims, A. (2014) 'Frozen' now available for digital download—win a copy! http://www.hypable.com/frozen-now-available-for-digital-download-win-a-copy; Lang, B. (2014) 'Frozen' Sells Massive 3.2 Million Discs in One Day, thewrap.com, http://www.thewrap.com/frozen-heats-home-entertainment-market-sells-massive-3-2-million-units; Sudock, J. (2014) 'Frozen' characters draw unprecedented lines at Disneyland, OC Register, http://www.ocregister.com/articles/line-602644-wait-minutes.html; Hoyle, A. and Lankston, C (2014) $1 billion Frozen fever: Animated movie is the most lucrative Disney cartoon ever - and what your kids will be pestering you for this Christmas, Daily Mail, http://www.dailymail.co.uk/femail/article-2856095/1-billion-Frozen-fever-Animated-movie-lucrative-Disney-cartoon-thanks-blizzard-spin-merchandise.html; Disney (2013) Disney Celebrates Family Bonds and Epic Storytelling in New Frozen Product Collection Available at Retail Now, Disney press release, https://www.disneyconsumerproducts.com/Home/display.jsp?contentId=dcp_home_pressroom_pressreleases_dcp_home_pr_us_dcp_frozen_products_110613&forPrint=false&language=en&preview=false&imageShow=0&pressRoom=US&translationOf=null&region=0&ccPK=dcp_home_pressroom_press_room_all_US; Husband, H. (n.d.) 11 Examples that show how hugely successful 'Frozen' still is, allday.com, http://allday.com/post/2400-11-examples-that-show-just-how-hugely-successful-frozen-still-is; Graser, M. (2014) 'Frozen Fever' Short to Debut in Front of Disney's 'Cinderella', Variety, http://variety.com/2014/film/news/frozen-fever-short-to-debut-in-front-of-disney-cinderella-1201369889; McPhee, R. (2015) Frozen Aims to Cast a Spell on Broadway in 2017 with New Songs! Alex Timbers May Direct, Broadway.com, http://www.broadway.com/buzz/179575/frozen-aims-to-cast-a-spell-on-broadway-in-2017-with-new-songs-alex-timbers-may-direct; Graser, M. (2015) Disney announces 'Frozen 2', Variety, http://variety.com/2015/film/news/disney-announces-frozen-2-1201451480

CHAPTER 22
Managing Marketing Implementation, Organization and Control

"There is nothing more difficult than to take the lead in the introduction of a new order of things."
MACHIAVELLI

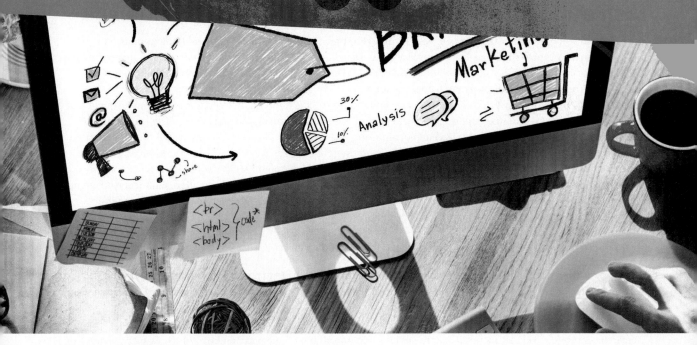

LEARNING OBJECTIVES

After reading this chapter, you should be able to:

1 describe the relationship between marketing strategy, implementation and performance
2 identify the stages that people pass through when they experience disruptive change
3 describe the objectives of marketing implementation and change
4 discuss the barriers to the implementation of the marketing concept
5 discuss the forms of resistance to marketing implementation and change
6 explain how to develop effective implementation strategies
7 describe the elements of an internal marketing programme
8 discuss the skills and tactics that can be used to overcome resistance to the implementation of the marketing concept and plan
9 discuss marketing organizational structures
10 explain the nature of a marketing control system

Designing marketing strategies and positioning plans that meet today's and tomorrow's market requirements is a necessary but not a sufficient condition for corporate success. They need to be translated into action through effective implementation. Throughout this book, we explore the theoretical principles and business practices that are key to understanding this dynamic and complex subject. In this chapter, we explore the following issues: the importance of implementation for business outcomes; the relationship between strategy, implementation and performance; how people react to change; and the objectives of implementation. We also explore resistance to change that might result from implementing the marketing strategy, and the skills and tactics marketing managers can use to bring about marketing implementation and change. Finally, we examine how companies organize their marketing activities and establish control procedures to check that objectives have been achieved.

Marketing Strategy, Implementation and Performance

Marketing strategy concerns the issues of *what* should happen and *why* it should happen. Implementation focuses on actions: *who* is responsible for various activities, *how* the strategy should be carried out, *where* things will happen and *when* action will take place. Managers devise marketing strategies to meet new opportunities, counter environmental threats and match core competences. The framework for strategy development was discussed in Chapter 18, as part of the marketing planning process. Although implementation is a consequence of strategy, it also affects planning and is an integral part of the strategy development process. The proposition is straightforward: without a well-organized implementation, even the best strategy is likely to fail. Implementation capability is an integral part of strategy formulation and the link between the two is shown in Figure 22.1. Implementation affects marketing strategy choice. For example, a company that traditionally has been a low-cost, low-price operator may have a culture that finds it difficult to implement a value-added, high-price strategy. Strategy also determines implementation requirements: for example, a value-added, high-price strategy may require the salesforce to refrain from price discounting.

Combining strategies and implementation

Bonoma has argued that combinations of appropriate/inappropriate strategy and good/poor implementation will lead to various business outcomes (Bonoma, 1985). Figure 22.2 shows the four-cell matrix, with predicted performances.

Appropriate strategy—good implementation

This is the combination most likely to lead to success. No guarantee of success can be made, however, because of the vagaries of the marketplace, including competitor actions and reactions, new technological breakthroughs and plain bad luck; but with strong implementation backing sound strategy, marketing management has done all it can to build success.

Appropriate strategy—bad implementation

This combination is likely to lead to trouble if sub-standard performance is attributed to poor strategy. Management's tendency to look for strategy change in response to poor results will result in a less appropriate strategy being grafted on to an already wayward implementation system.

Inappropriate strategy—good implementation

Two effects of this combination can be predicted. First, the effective implementation of a poor strategy can hasten failure. For example, very

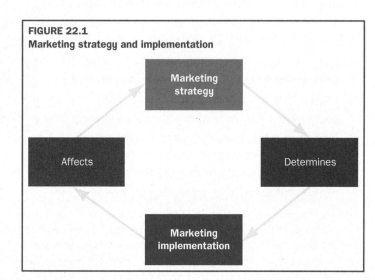

FIGURE 22.1
Marketing strategy and implementation

Marketing strategy

Determines

Affects

Marketing implementation

effectively communicating a price rise (which is part of an inappropriate repositioning strategy) to customers may accelerate a fall in sales. Second, if good implementation takes the form of correcting a fault in strategy, then the outcome will be favourable. For example, if strategy implies an increase in sales effort to push a low margin *dog* product to the detriment of a new *star* product in a growing market (perhaps for political reasons), modification at the implementation level may correct the bias. The reality of marketing life is that managers spend many hours supplementing, subverting, overcoming or otherwise correcting shortcomings in strategic plans.

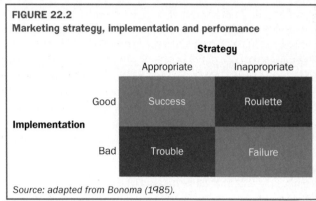

FIGURE 22.2
Marketing strategy, implementation and performance

		Strategy	
		Appropriate	Inappropriate
Implementation	Good	Success	Roulette
	Bad	Trouble	Failure

Source: adapted from Bonoma (1985).

Inappropriate strategy—bad implementation

This obviously leads to failure, which is difficult to correct because so much is wrong. An example might be a situation where a product holds a premium price position without a competitive advantage to support the price differential. The situation is made worse by an advertising campaign that is unbelievable, and a salesforce that makes misleading claims leading to customer annoyance and confusion.

Implications

So what should managers do when faced with poor performance? First, strategic issues should be separated from implementation activities and the problem diagnosed. Second, when in doubt about whether the problem is rooted in strategy or implementation, implementation problems should be addressed first so that strategic adequacy can be assessed more easily. Read Mini Case 22.1 to find out how Abercrombie & Fitch is struggling to find an appropriate strategy to revive the brand.

MINI CASE 22.1
Is Abercrombie & Fitch playing roulette?

Abercrombie & Fitch has been said to be *the best-run fashion brand on the planet*, but declining sales and falling share prices in recent years have led to doubts about whether this iconic fashion brand can survive in the digital age.

Mike Jeffries became CEO of Abercrombie & Fitch in 1992. He had a vision for developing the brand that would turn it into an *'exclusive club for teenagers'*. His implementation of the vision was striking: he alienated and offended the parents of his target audience—teenagers—but this approach appealed to the young people. In his first two years in control the turnover doubled, and within five years the brand had reached $1 billion in sales.

However, the dimly lit stores—which were designed to have the look and feel of an exclusive night club, with loud music and perfumed air, and to give the target audience (*cool kids . . . . with attitude and a lot of friends*) a feeling of belonging to an exclusive, high-status echelon of youth society—began to alienate the more mainstream customers. Ordinary teenagers who dared to venture into a store, passing by the slender assistants with highly toned bodies and polished looks, were disappointed if they were looking for a size XL or larger. The brand's policy of only selling smaller sizes was part of its controversial positioning of only selling to *beautiful people*. Other alienated groups were potential gift buyers—parents, relatives and older friends

>>

of the target teenagers—who found Abercrombie & Fitch stores unpleasant to visit and highly over-priced. Feminist groups were outraged by its provocative slogans on T-shirts; Hispanic, black and Asian groups sued the company over its employment policies.

Arguably, the highly proficient implementation of Mike Jeffries' vision, brand positioning and exceedingly focused targeting strategy were responsible for the brand's success and failure. The factors that made the brand strong also exposed its weaknesses. Abercrombie & Fitch's positioning was out of kilter with the expectations of the newly emerging generation of teenagers, and the brand was also losing touch with its ageing core market.

In 2015, Jeff Gomez replaced Mike Jeffries and set about implementing a new strategy to revive the brand. Larger sizes have been introduced, the lights have been turned up and the music turned down. The new leadership has announced it will stop hiring the 'beautiful' people and put an end to 'its overtly sexualised marketing with the iconic images of half-naked teenagers'. Finally, the athletic door-keepers have been retired. But the new strategy raises many questions. What does this implementation mean for the brand? What has happened the edgy, provocative heritage of the brand, and what are today's anarchic teenagers expected to latch onto? Is Gomez playing roulette by implementing this revitalization strategy, and will the brand be completely eradicated?

Questions:

1   How have the key strategic issues facing Abercrombie & Fitch changed since Jeff Gomez took over?
2   What problems is the change strategy trying to address, and how might they be addressed by the implementation of recent changes?
3   Imagine you replaced Mike Jeffries. Suggest where you would take the brand and how you would implement your new strategy.

Based on: Ritson (2015); Saner (2012); Trefis Team (2014)

Implementation and the Management of Change

A key factor in implementing a change programme is top management support. Without its clear, visible and consistent backing a major change programme is likely to falter under the inertia created by vested interests (Johannessen, Olaisen and Havan, 1993). It is important for companies to monitor change and ensure that systems are in place to gather and disseminate information throughout the organization. For example, Cisco invites key clients to discussions, workshops and collaboration meetings, using a combination of face-to-face and technology-driven approaches such as video and WebEx cloud conferencing to enhance customer relationships. The objectives are to analyze how the company can develop to better serve the customers. Cisco's partnership approaches not only enable it to gain first-hand knowledge of customer preferences, but also to ensure the entire organization is immediately aware of customers' experiences and demands, which helps build stronger and closer customer relationships (Cisco, 2015).

The implementation of a new strategy may have profound effects on people in organizations. Brand managers who discover their product is to receive fewer resources (harvested) may feel bitter and demoralized; a salesperson who loses as a result of a change in the payment system may feel equally aggrieved. The implementation of a strategy move is usually associated with the need for people to adapt to *change*. The cultivation of change, therefore, is an essential ingredient in effective implementation.

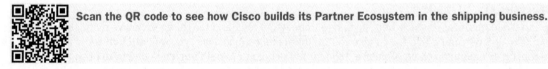

Scan the QR code to see how Cisco builds its Partner Ecosystem in the shipping business.

It is helpful to understand the emotional stages that people pass through when confronted with an adverse change. These stages are known as the **transition curve** and are shown in Figure 22.3 (Wilson, 1993).

FIGURE 22.3
The transition curve

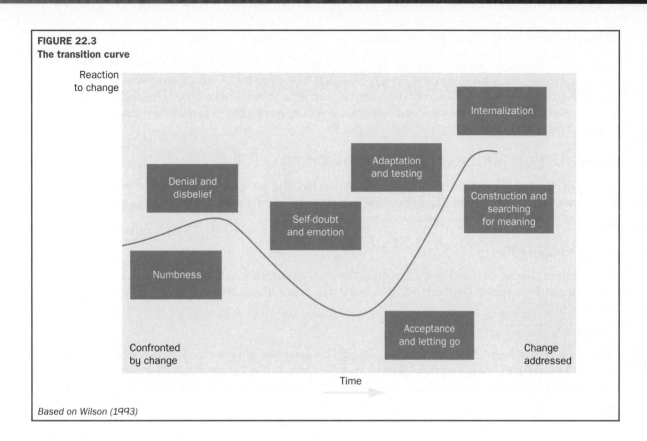

Based on Wilson (1993)

Numbness

The first reaction is usually shock. The enormity of the consequences leads to feelings of being overwhelmed, despair and numbness. The outward symptoms include silence and lack of overt response. The news that a field salesforce is to be replaced by a telemarketing team is likely to provoke numbness in the field salespeople.

Denial and disbelief

Denial and disbelief may follow numbness, leading to trivializing the news, denying it or joking about it. The aim is to minimize the psychological impact of the change. News of the abandonment of the field salesforce may be met by utter disbelief, and sentiments such as 'They would never do that to us'.

Self-doubt and emotion

As the certainty of the change dawns, so personal feelings of uncertainty may arise. The feeling is one of powerlessness, of being out of control: the situation has taken over the individual. The likely reaction is one of anger: both as individuals and as a group, salesforce staff are likely to vent their anger and frustration on management.

Acceptance and letting go

Acceptance is characterized by tolerating the new reality and letting go of the past. This is likely to occur at an emotional low point but is the beginning of an upward surge as comfortable attitudes and behaviours are severed, and the need to cope with the change is accepted. In the salesforce example, salespeople would become accustomed to the fact that they would no longer be calling upon certain customers and receiving a particular salary.

Adaptation and testing

As people adapt to the changes they become more energetic, and they begin testing new behaviours and approaches to life. Alternatives are explored and evaluated. The classic case is the divorcee who begins dating again. This stage is fraught with personal risk, as in the case of the divorcee who is let down once more, leading to anger and frustration. Salespeople may consider another sales job, becoming part of the telemarketing team or moving out of selling altogether.

Construction and searching for meaning

As people's emotions become much more positive and they feel they have got to grips with the change, they seek a clear understanding of the new. The salespeople may come to the conclusion that there is much more to life than working as a salesperson for their previous company.

Internalization

The final stage is where feelings reach a new high. The change is fully accepted, adaptation is complete and behaviour alters too. Sometimes this is reflected in statements like 'That was the best thing that could have happened to me'.

Implications

Most people pass through all the above stages, although the movement from one stage to the next is rarely smooth. The implication for managing marketing implementation is that the acceptance of fundamental change such as the reprioritizing of products, jobs or strategic business units will take time for people to accept and come to terms with. The venting of anger and frustration is an accompanying behaviour to this transition from the old to the new, and should be accepted as such. Some people will leave as part of the fifth stage—the testing of new behaviours—but others will see meaning in and internalize the changes that have resulted from strategic redirection. See Marketing in Action 22.1 to find out how large companies find it hard to adapt to change.

MARKETING IN ACTION 22.1
How the Mighty Fall—Is this the End for Nokia?

A senior management team should provide leadership and ensure that a company provides goods and services in accordance with market demand. As the pace of change increases and competition intensifies, companies have to become more agile and the senior management teams more responsive. So why do market leaders fail? For example, Nokia dominated the mobile phone market but lost out to its competitors, Apple and Samsung.

Entrenched management processes—budgeting, planning performance reviews, succession planning—the processes that drive a business—are often not adapted in line with new trading environments and conditions. Sometimes, these processes are so deeply engrained in the company that they are rarely challenged. So companies should regularly review their processes and be prepared to change any that no longer add value.

Failure to monitor the competition. As markets change and develop, the key success factors on which companies compete can change rapidly too, particularly for those companies operating in high-tech markets. For example, Nokia was not benchmarking carefully enough against competitors like Apple. Nokia's problems were not due to lack of technological invention, as it had a smartphone prototype, or because it hadn't recognized the market changing. The problem for Nokia was it failed to successfully implement changes and did not make decisive, timely decisions—which ultimately meant it was not able to compete effectively in the emerging smartphone market.

Lack of management diversity. Senior management teams that have been successful over time tend to become homogeneous, made up of people with similar world views. Consequently, there is a propensity for events, opportunities and marketplace changes to be missed. This was an issue for Nokia as the top executives were all very similar in outlook, age and culture. In contrast, successful technology company Infosys proactively sought to avoid this situation by implementing a programme—the Voice of Youth programme—that gave the under-30s an opportunity to influence senior management decisions.

Intolerance of failure. Large companies can become risk-averse, as they perceive there is more to lose if they make mistakes. Therefore it is important to ensure that there is an innovative culture that tolerates failure if a company is to remain vital. Google, Amazon and Netflix all actively encourage an entrepreneurial and innovative culture.

In the mobile phone handset market Nokia has paid a heavy price, as the brand largely disappeared when it became Microsoft Mobile in April 2015. Microsoft also took over Nokia's social media presence, as the new owner did not want any confusion over the positioning of the new brand. Those who remain on Nokia's team— satellite telecoms networks—will have to watch the gradual disappearance of what was once an innovative market leader and iconic brand.

Based on: Burke et al. (2007); Birkinshaw (2013); Chang (2012); Gokey (2015); Nokia (2015)

Objectives of Marketing Implementation and Change

The overriding objective of marketing implementation and change from a strategic standpoint is the successful execution of the marketing plan. This may include:

- gaining the support of key decision-makers in the company for the proposed plan (and overcoming the opposition of others)
- gaining the required resources (e.g. people and money) to be able to implement the plan
- gaining the commitment of individuals and departments in the company who are involved in frontline implementation (e.g. marketing, sales, service and distribution staff)
- gaining the cooperation of other departments needed to implement the plan (e.g. production and R&D).

FIGURE 22.4
The ladder of support

For some people, the objectives and execution of the plan are consistent with their objectives, interests and viewpoints; gaining support from them is easy. But there are likely to be others who are involved with implementation who are less willing to support the planned change. They are the losers and neutrals. Loss may be in the form of lower status, a harder life or a reduction in salary. Neutrals may be left untouched overall with gains being balanced by losses. For some losers, support will never be forthcoming, for others they may be responsive to persuasion, whereas neutrals may be more willing to support change. Read Marketing in Action 22.2 to see how SAS gained support for its new marketing strategy.

The ladder of support

What does support mean? Figure 22.4 illustrates the degree of support that may be achieved; this can range from outright opposition to full commitment.

Opposition

The stance of direct opposition is taken by those with much to lose from the implementation of the marketing strategy, and who believe they have the political strength to stop the proposed change. Opposition is overt, direct and forceful.

Resistance

With resistance, opposition is less overt and may take a more passive form such as delaying tactics. Perhaps because of the lack of a strong power base, people are not willing to display open hostility but, nevertheless, their intention is to hamper the implementation process.

MARKETING IN ACTION 22.2
SAS and Marketing Strategy: Success is in the Details

Scandinavian Airlines (SAS) is one of Scandinavia's most popular carriers, providing over 28 million passengers a year with service to cities in 193 countries around the world. The company's business model is to efficiently serve its core customer group—frequent fliers in Scandinavia who want ease and convenience when they travel.

Compared to the rest of Europe, the Nordic market for air travel is considered to be fairly large, with Scandinavians usually preferring short haul flights. These are the types of trips that SAS is well placed to provide and which are at the centre of its business strategy. But like many other airlines, SAS is facing the challenge of continued economic weakness in Europe. This has caused the company to reemphasize improving operating efficiencies as well as refocus its marketing strategy in order to better control its brand and communication efforts (especially digital ones). This last part is not surprising given that SAS has an estimated 700,000 fans on Facebook and 50,000 followers on Twitter, along with 100 million hits to its website every year.

The new marketing strategy is called 'We Are Travelers', and a key component is an innovative editorial concept called Scandinavian Traveler. The platform will incorporate and integrate 'a new onboard magazine, website, web TV, social media content, and newsletters' in an attempt to better serve passengers and fans. SAS believes its marketing strategy will promote 'the idea of travel as part of our way of life' while celebrating 'the joy and anticipation we feel before a flight.' While the strategy might sound a bit idealistic, the company says that it arose from a clear analysis and deep understanding of its customers and the markets that it serves (the initial target audience is Sweden, Norway and Denmark). This provided senior management with some indication that implementation capabilities were already in place at SAS.

Stefan Hedelius, Vice President of Marketing and Brand at SAS, was sure to make the objectives of the new marketing strategy clear from the very beginning, and take efforts to communicate them effectively throughout the organization in order to ensure 'buy in' from the over 13,000 people who work for the airline. These actions were critical if the implementation of the new strategy was to have any chance of success. The main focus of the We Are Travelers campaign will be to build its brand and improve the overall experience that customers have with it, while at the same time trying to create a sense of community for the 80,000 people who fly SAS every day. Mr. Hedelius has also made it clear that SAS will track the campaign's performance through the detailed recording and measurement of data, another key element with regard to successful marketing strategy implementation.

Along with the new strategy came a change in the way SAS allocated its marketing and communication resources. Previously, the company spent over 90 per cent of its budget on traditional paid media and advertising. Mr. Hedelius says that he now plans on using more of that money to develop SAS' own marketing and communication channels.

Compliance

Compliance means that people act in accordance with the plan but without much enthusiasm or zest. They yield to the need to conform but lack conviction that the plan is the best way to proceed. These reservations limit the lengths to which they are prepared to go to achieve its successful implementation. Staff feel valued when included in key organizational practices/activities.

Acceptance

A higher level of support is achieved when people accept the worth of the plan and actively seek to realize its goals. Their minds may be won but their hearts are not set on fire, limiting the extent of their motivation.

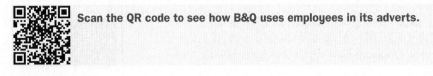 **Scan the QR code to see how B&Q uses employees in its adverts.**

Commitment

Commitment is the ultimate goal of an effective implementation programme. People not only accept the worth of the plan but also pledge themselves to secure its success. Both hearts and minds are won, leading to strong conviction, enthusiasm and zeal. This can be encouraged by making people feel valued. B&Q, a market-leading

EXHIBIT 22.1
Autoglass features its staff in TV adverts and online

DIY chain in the UK, for example, uses members of staff in its television advertising to promote its garden products. Pizza Hut followed a similar approach using YouTube for an open casting call to find eight employees to feature in their ad campaigns. In this way they were able to involve many hundreds of employees. The Chief Marketing Officer said 'There is no better way to express the emotional side of the brand than through the employees that actually deliver the brand experience every day' (Bruno Ken, 2010).

Barriers to the Implementation of the Marketing Concept

In this section we discuss forms of opposition and resistance towards implementation, and examine the skills and tactics which can be used to get over any such barriers. Increasingly, marketing managers need to be adept at managing the internal environment of the company as well as the external. First we shall examine barriers to the implementation of the marketing concept discussed in Chapter 1. Acceptance of marketing as a philosophy in a company is a necessary prerequisite for the successful development of marketing strategy and implementation.

The marketing concept states that business success will result from creating greater customer satisfaction than the competition. So why do so many companies score so badly at marketing effectiveness? The fact is that there are inherent *personal and organizational barriers* that make the achievement of marketing implementation difficult in practice. These are summarized in Figure 22.5.

High-cost solutions

Often giving what the customer wants involves extra costs. In highly competitive environments most companies will meet customers' low-cost solutions. Therefore many marketing recommendations to beat competition will involve higher costs. Travelworld, a travel agency, was founded on giving better service to its customers. The chief executive recognized that the competition often required customers to queue at peak periods when booking a holiday. This he felt was unacceptable when customers were involved in a major transaction: a

holiday is one of the highest-expenditure items for families each year. The solution was to hire enough staff at his outlets to ensure that queuing was not a problem. He came from a marketing background and accepted the higher costs involved.

Meeting customer requirements can also conflict with production's desire to gain cost economies of scale, and the finance director's objective of inventory reduction. Customers invariably differ in their requirements—they have different personalities, experiences and lifestyles—and to meet individual requirements is clearly not feasible. A solution to this problem is to group customers into segments that have similar needs and to target one product or service offering to each group. This allows the production manager to reap some economies of scale, and marketing to tailor offerings to the marketplace, whilst working within the finance director's parameters.

Unquantifiable benefits

A problem with marketing recommendations is that they are often unquantifiable and it is difficult to measure the exact increase in revenue (and profits) that will result from their implementation. For example, a business school faced a customer problem: the student car park was regularly being raided by thieves who stole radios and cars. One marketing solution was to employ at least one security guard. The extra cost could easily be quantified, not so the economic benefits to the business school, however. On a purely commercial basis, it is impossible to say what the marginal revenue would be. On a similar theme, what is likely to be the reduced revenue from removing one platform attendant from a railway station? The cost saving is immediate and quantifiable; the reduced customer satisfaction through not having someone to answer queries is not.

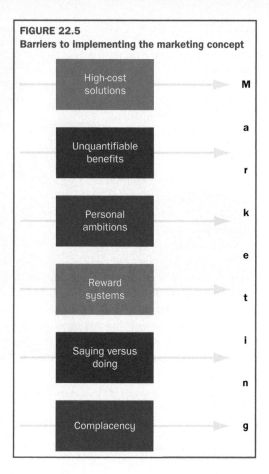

FIGURE 22.5
Barriers to implementing the marketing concept

High-cost solutions

Unquantifiable benefits

Personal ambitions

Reward systems

Saying versus doing

Complacency

Marketing

Personal ambitions

Personal ambitions can also hinder the progress of marketing in an organization. The R&D director may enjoy working on challenging, complex technical problems at the cutting edge of scientific knowledge. Customers may simply want products that work. Staff may want an easy life, which means that the customer is neglected.

Reward systems

It is a basic tenet of motivation theory that behaviour is influenced by reward systems (Stanton, Buskirk and Spiro, 2002). Sometimes, organizations reward individuals in ways that conflict with marketing-orientated action. An example is the situation that occurred between a supplier of motor oil and a supermarket chain. The supplier delivered 200 litres of motor oil in cans to each supermarket petrol station at a time. The supermarket asked if it would be possible to deliver smaller quantities more often as it did not have sufficient storage space. The marketing manager, anxious to please a major customer, asked the logistics manager to meet this request. The logistics manager refused on the grounds that it would raise delivery costs: he was measured and rewarded on the basis of efficiency. A classic case of a reward system (and efficiency) being in conflict with effectiveness. Sales staff who are rewarded by incentives based on sales revenue may be tempted to give heavy discounts, which secures easy sales in the short term but may ruin positioning strategies and profits. Webster argued that the key to developing a market-driven, customer-orientated business lies in how managers are evaluated and rewarded (Webster, 1988). If managers are evaluated on the basis of short-term profitability and sales, they are likely to pay heed to these criteria and neglect market factors such as customer satisfaction that ensure the long-term health of an organization.

Saying versus doing

Another force that blocks the implementation of the marketing concept is the gap between what senior managers say and what they do. Webster suggests that senior management must give clear signals and establish clear values and beliefs about serving the customer (Webster, 1988). However, Argyris (1966) found that senior executives' behaviour often conflicted with what they said—for example, they might say 'Be customer orientated' and then cut back on marketing research funds. This resulted in staff not really believing that management was serious about achieving a customer focus.

For those companies preaching an ethical stance, their words need to be backed up by deeds. For example, the Accor Hotel chain, which operates over 3,700 hotels and employs 170,000

EXHIBIT 22.2
BMW's efficient dynamics

staff worldwide, has recently launched its new sustainable development programme—Planet 21. The group, which includes brands Novotel, Ibis, Mercure, Adagio and Sofitel, develops about 48,000 new rooms every year. Their plan is to combine growth with respect for the environment and local communities, by involving all of its hotels and customers. Through Planet 21 Accor is making 21 commitments and goals: for example, employees trained in disease prevention in 95 per cent of hotels; 80 per cent of properties promoting balanced meals; 85 per cent of hotels using eco-labelled products; a 15 per cent reduction in water consumption; and a 10 per cent decrease in energy use.

In order to avoid 'saying rather than doing' and being accused of green washing, Accor plan to guarantee the credibility of this programme by only allowing hotels to use the Planet 21 messages if they achieve a certain agreed level of performance (Hasek, 2012).

Complacency

A final barrier to the implementation of marketing change is complacency, which can be fuelled by past success. For example, at BMW, whose engineers had been used to success based on building powerful gas-guzzling cars, there was strong resistance to the introduction of a new fuel-efficiency programme called Efficient Dynamics. Their argument was that there was no need for efficient dynamics. Given their past success they believed that dynamics was enough. To drive through the change required to meet new market requirements, BMW's chief executive had to successfully change this mindset (Reed and Schäfer, 2008). See Exhibit 22.2.

Implications

The implications are that marketing managers have to face the fact that some people in the organization will have a vested interest in blocking the introduction and growth of marketing in the organization, and will have some ammunition (e.g. the extra costs, unquantifiable benefits) to achieve their aims. Marketing implementation, then, depends on being able to overcome the opposition and resistance that may well surface as a result of developing market-driven plans. The following sections discuss the nature of such resistance, and ways of dealing with it.

Forms of Resistance to Marketing Implementation and Change

Opposition to the acceptance of marketing and the implementation of marketing plans is direct, open and conflict driven. Often, arguments such as the lack of tangible benefits and the extra expense of marketing proposals will be used to cast doubt on their worth. Equally likely, however, is the more passive type of *resistance*. Kanter and Piercy suggest 10 forms of resistance (Kanter, 1997; Piercy, 2008):

1 criticism of specific details of the plan
2 foot-dragging
3 slow response to requests
4 unavailability
5 suggestions that, despite the merits of the plan, resources should be channelled elsewhere
6 arguments that the proposals are too ambitious
7 hassle and aggravation created to wear the proposer down
8 attempts to delay the decision, hoping the proposer will lose interest
9 attacks on the credibility of the proposer with rumour and innuendo
10 deflation of any excitement surrounding the plan by pointing out the risks.

Market research reports supporting marketing action can also be attacked. Johnson (1987) describes the reaction of senior managers to the first marketing research report commissioned by a new marketing director.

'As a diagnostic statement the research was full, powerful, prescriptive. The immediate result of this analysis was that the report was rubbished by senior management and directors. The analysis may have been perceived by its initiator as diagnostic but it was received by its audience as a politically threatening statement.'

Ansoff and McDonnell (1990) argue that the level of resistance will depend on how much the proposed change is likely to disrupt the culture and power structure of the organization and the speed at which the change is introduced. The latter point is in line with the previous discussion about how people adapt to adverse change, requiring time to come to terms with disruptions. The greatest level of opposition and resistance will come when the proposed change is implemented quickly and is a threat to the culture and politics of the organization; the least opposition and resistance will be found when the change is consonant with the existing culture and political structure, and is introduced over a period of time. Further, Pettigrew states that resistance is likely to be low when a company is faced with a crisis, arguing that a common perception among people that the organization is threatened with extinction also acts to overcome inertia against change (Pettigrew, 1985).

Developing Implementation Strategies

Faced with the likelihood of resistance from vested interests, a **change master** should develop an implementation strategy that can deliver the required change (Kanter, 1997). For example, when Anne Mulcahy was CEO at Xerox, the company was in trouble and she had to act as a change master. She began by talking to customers and employees, to gain an understanding of what was wrong. She ran meetings differently, forcing people to face the tough decisions that were necessary, and used the severity of the crisis at Xerox to gain acceptance for the required changes, which included cutting $1 billion of overheads and closing unprofitable businesses (London and Hill, 2002). The workforce was cut by almost 40 per cent, while gaps in Xerox's product portfolio were filled with lower-priced products. This gave the company its largest product portfolio and has made it more competitive. Mulcahy was succeeded in 2009 by Ursula Burns, who was instrumental in pulling Xerox back from the brink of bankruptcy (McGregor, 2009). A change master is a person who is responsible for driving through change within an organization. This necessitates a structure for thinking about the problems to be tackled and the way to deal with them. Figure 22.6 illustrates such a framework. The process starts with a definition of objectives.

FIGURE 22.6
Managing implementation

Objectives	Strategy	Execution	Evaluation
• Would-like objectives • Must-have objectives	• Internal marketing	• Persuasion • Negotiation • Politics • Tactics	• Who wins? • What can be learned?

Implementation objectives

These are formulated at two levels: what we would like to achieve (*would-like objectives*) and what we must achieve (*must-have objectives*). Framing objectives in this way recognizes that we may not be able to achieve all that we desire. Would-like objectives are our preferred solution: they define the maximum that the implementer can reasonably expect (Kennedy, Benson and MacMillan, 1987). Must-have objectives define our minimum requirements: if we cannot achieve these then we have lost and the plan or strategy will not succeed. Between the two points there is an area for negotiation, but beyond our must-have objective there is no room for compromise.

By clearly defining objectives at the start, we know what we would like, the scope for bargaining, and the point where we have to be firm and resist further concessions. For example, suppose our marketing plan calls for a move from a salary-only payment system for salespeople to salary plus commission. This is predicted to lead to strong resistance from salespeople and some sales managers, who favour the security element of fixed salary. Our would-like objective might be a 60:40 split between salary and commission. This would define our starting point in attempting to get this change implemented. But in order to allow room for allowances, our must-have objective would be somewhat lower, perhaps an 80:20 ratio between salary and commission. Beyond this point we refuse to bargain: we either win or lose on the issue. In some situations, however, would-like and must-have objectives coincide: here there is no room for negotiation, and persuasive and political skills are needed to drive through the issue.

Internal marketing strategy

All worthwhile plans and strategies necessitate substantial human and organizational change inside companies (Piercy, 1990). Marketing managers, therefore, need a practical mechanism for thinking through strategies to drive change. One such framework is known as internal marketing, and is widely seen as an important element of value creation (Shyh-Rong et al., 2014).

Originally the idea of internal marketing was developed within services marketing and it applied to the development, training, motivation and retention of employees, in retailing, catering and financial services (see Grönroos, 1985; Gummesson, 1987; Mudie, 1987). However, the concept can be expanded to include marketing to all employees with the aim of achieving successful marketing implementation. The framework is appealing as it draws an analogy with external marketing structures such as market segmentation, target marketing and the marketing mix. The people inside the organization to whom the plan must be marketed are considered *internal customers*. We need to gain the support, commitment and participation of sufficient of these to achieve acceptance and implementation of the plan. For those people where we fail to do this we need to minimize the effectiveness of their resistance. They become, in effect, our competitors in the internal marketplace.

Internal market segmentation

As with external marketing, analysis of customers begins with market segmentation. One obvious method of grouping internal customers is into three categories.

1 *Supporters*: those who are likely to gain from the change or are committed to it.
2 *Neutrals*: those whose gains and losses are in approximate balance.
3 *Opposers*: those who are likely to lose from the change or are traditional opponents.

These three market segments form distinct *target groups* for which specific *marketing mix* programmes can be developed (see Figure 22.7).

Internal marketing mix programmes

Product is the marketing plan and strategies that are being proposed, together with the values, attitudes and actions that are needed to make the plan successful. Features of the product may include increased marketing budgets, extra staff, different ways of handling customers, different pricing, distribution and advertising, and new product development strategies. The product will reflect our would-like objectives; however, it may have to be modified slightly to gain acceptance from our opponents. Hence the need for must-have objectives.

The *price* element of the marketing mix is what we are asking our internal customers to pay as a result of accepting the marketing plan. The price they pay may be lost resources, lower status, fear of the unknown, harder work and rejection of their pet projects because of lack of funds. Clearly, price sensitivity is a key segmentation variable that differentiates supporters, neutrals and opposers.

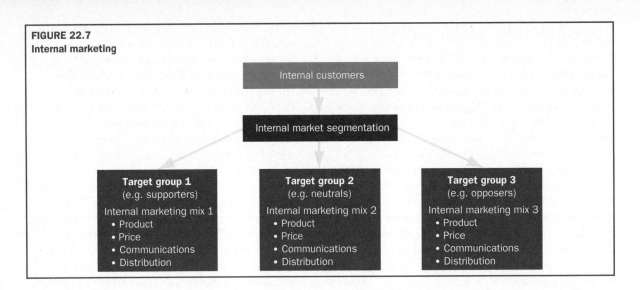

FIGURE 22.7
Internal marketing

Communications is a major element of the internal marketing mix and covers the communications media and messages used to influence the attitudes of key players. A combination of personal (presentations, discussion groups) and non-personal (the full report, executive summaries) can be used to inform and persuade. Communication should be two-way: we should listen as well as inform. We should also be prepared to adapt the product (the plan) if necessary in response to our internal customers' demands. It may also be necessary to fine-tune the language of marketing (e.g. eliminating jargon) to fit the corporate culture and background of the key players (research conducted by Oxford Strategic Marketing and Hunter Miller Executive Search and reported in *Marketing Business*, 2005).

Communication objectives will differ according to the target group, as follows.

* *Supporters*: to reinforce existing positive attitudes and behaviour, mobilize support from key players (e.g. chief executive).
* *Neutrals*: the use of influence strategies to build up perception of rewards and downgrade perceived losses; display key supporters and explain the benefits of joining 'the team'; negotiate to gain commitment.
* *Opposers*: disarm and discredit; anticipate objections and create convincing counterarguments; position them as 'stuck in their old ways'; bypass by gaining support of opinion and political leaders; negotiate to lower resistance.

Opposition to the proposals may stem from a misunderstanding on the part of staff of the meaning of marketing. Some people may equate marketing with advertising and selling rather than the placing of customer satisfaction as central to corporate success. An objective of communications, therefore, may be to clarify the real meaning of marketing, or to use terms that are more readily acceptable such as 'improving service quality' (Laing and McKee, 2001).

Distribution describes the places where the product and communications are delivered to the internal customers such as meetings, committees, seminars, informal conversations and away-days. Consideration should be given to whether presentations should be direct (proponents to customers) or indirect (using third parties such as consultants). Given the conflicting viewpoints of the three target segments, thought should be given to the advisability of using different distribution channels for each group. For example, a meeting may be arranged with only supporters and neutrals present. If opponents tend to be found in a particular department, judicious selection of which departments to invite may accomplish this aim.

Execution

In order to execute an implementation strategy successfully, certain skills are required, and particular tactics need to be employed. Internal marketing has provided a framework to structure thinking about implementation strategies. Within that framework, the main skills are persuasion, negotiation and politics.

Persuasion

The starting point of persuasion is to try to understand the situation from the internal customer's standpoint. The new plan may have high profit potential, the chance of real sales growth and be popular among external customers but if it is perceived to cause grief to individuals and/or internal departments resistance is likely to occur. As with personal selling, the proponents of the plan must understand the needs, motivations and problems of their customers before they can hope to develop effective messages. For example, appealing to a production manager's sense of customer welfare will fail if that person is interested only in smooth production runs. In such a situation the proponent of the plan needs to show how smooth production will not be affected by the new proposals, or how disruption will be marginal or temporary.

The implementer also needs to understand how the features of the plan (e.g. new payment structure) confer customer benefits (e.g. the opportunity to earn more money). Whenever possible, evidence should be provided to support claims. Objectives should be anticipated and convincing counter-arguments produced. Care should be taken not to bruise egos unnecessarily.

Negotiation

Implementers have to recognize that they may not get all they want during this process. By setting would-like and must-have objectives (see earlier in this chapter) they are clear about what they want and have given themselves negotiating room wherever possible. Two key aspects of negotiation will be considered next: concession analysis and proposal analysis.

The key to **concession analysis** is to value the concessions the implementer might be prepared to make from the viewpoint of the opponent. By doing this it may be possible to identify concessions that cost the implementer very little and yet are highly valued by the opponent. For example, if the must-have objective is to move from a fixed salary to a salary plus commission, a salesperson's compensation plan conceding that the proportions should be 80:20 rather than 70:30 may be trivial to the implementer (an incentive to sell is still there) and yet highly valued by the salesperson as they will gain more income security and value the psychological bonus of winning a concession from management. By trading concessions that are highly valued by the opponent and yet cost the implementer little, painless agreement can be reached.

Proposal analysis: another sensible activity is to try to predict the proposals and demands that opponents are likely to make during the process of implementation. This provides time to prepare a response to them rather than relying on quick decisions during the heat of negotiation. By anticipating the kinds of proposals opponents are likely to make, implementers can plan the types of counter-proposal they are prepared to make.

Politics

Success in managing implementation and change also depends on the understanding and execution of political skills. Understanding the sources of power is the starting point from which an assessment of where power lies and who holds the balance can be made. The five sources are reward, expert, referent, legitimate and coercive power (French and Raven, 1959).

Reward power derives from the implementer's ability to provide benefits to members in the organization. The recommendations of the plan may confer natural benefits in the form of increased status or salary for some people. In other cases, the implementer may create rewards for support—for example, promises of reciprocal support when required, or backing for promotion. The implementer needs to assess what each target individual values and whether the natural rewards match those values, or whether created rewards are necessary. A limit on the use of reward power is the danger that people may come to expect rewards in return for support. Created rewards, therefore, should be used sparingly.

Expert power is based on the belief that implementers have special knowledge and expertise that renders their proposals more credible. For example, a plan outlining major change is more likely to be accepted if produced by someone who has a history of success rather than a novice. Implementers should not be reluctant to display their credentials as part of the change process.

Referent power occurs when people identify with and respect the architect of change. That is why charismatic leadership is often thought to be an advantage to those who wish to see change implemented.

Legitimate power is wielded when the implementer insists on an action from a subordinate as a result of their hierarchical relationship and contract. For example, a sales manager may demand compliance with a request for a salesperson to go on a training course or a board of directors may exercise its legitimate right to cut costs.

The strength of **coercive power** lies with the implementer's ability to punish those who resist or oppose the implementation of the plan. Major organizational change is often accompanied by staff losses. This may be a required cost-cutting exercise but it also sends messages to those not directly affected that they may be next if further change is resisted. The problem with using coercive power is that, at best, it results in compliance rather than commitment.

Applications of power

The balance of power will depend on who holds the sources of power and how well they are applied. Implementers should pause to consider any sources of power they hold, and also the sources and degree of power held by supporters, neutrals and opposers. Power held by supporters should be mobilized, those neutrals who wield power should be cultivated, and tactics should be developed to minimize the influence of powerful opposers. The tactics that can be deployed will be discussed shortly, but two applications of power will be discussed first: overt and covert power plays.

Overt power plays are the visible, open kind of power plays that can be used by implementers to push through their proposals. Unconcealed use of the five sources of power is used to influence key players. The use of overt power by localized interests, who battle to secure their own interests in the process of change, has been well documented (see Hickson et al., 1971; Hinings et al., 1974).

Covert power plays are a more disguised form of influence. Their use is more subtle and devious than that of overt power plays. Their application can take many forms including agenda setting, limiting participation in decisions to a few select individuals/departments, and defining what is and what is not open to decision for others in the organization (Wilson, 1992).

Tactics

The discussion of overt and covert power plays has introduced some of the means by which implementers and change agents can gain acceptance of their proposals and overcome opposition. Now we examine in more detail the tactics and skills needed to win implementation battles and how they can be applied in the face of some hostile reaction within the organization. These can be grouped into tactics of persuasion, politics, time and negotiation (see Figure 22.8), and are based on the work of a number of authorities (see Kanter, Stein and Jick, 1992; Kanter, 1983; Piercy, 2008; Ansoff and McDonnell (1990). They provide a wide-ranging checklist of approaches to mobilizing support and overcoming resistance.

Persuasion

- *Articulate a shared vision*: the vision of where the organization is heading and the desired results of the change need to be clearly stated to key players in the organization. For example, if the marketing plan calls for a reduction in staffing levels, the vision that this is required to reposition the company for greater competitiveness needs to be articulated. Without an understanding of the wider picture, people may regard the exercise as 'just another cost drive' (Kanter, Stein and Jick, 1992). Since most change involves risk and discomfort, a clear vision of its purpose and consequences can make the risk acceptable and the discomfort endurable.
- *Communicate and train*: implementation of the marketing concept or a fundamentally different marketing plan means that many individuals have to reorientate and engage in new activities. To achieve this requires a major commitment to communicating the nature and purpose of the change, as well as to training staff in

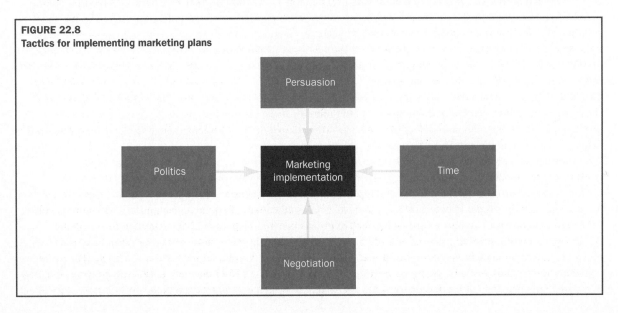

FIGURE 22.8
Tactics for implementing marketing plans

the new skills to be mastered. Major changes require face-to-face communication at discussion sessions and management education seminars. Formal training programmes are needed to upgrade skills and introduce new procedures.

- *Eliminate misconceptions*: a major part of the communication programme will be designed to eliminate misconceptions about the consequences of the change. Unfounded fears and anxieties should be allayed. Certain individuals will exaggerate the negative consequences of the proposed changes, and their concerns need to be addressed.

- *Sell the benefits*: the needs of key players have to be identified and the benefits of the change sold to them on that basis. The benefits may be economic (e.g. increased salary) or psychological (e.g. increased status, enhanced power). Whereas shared vision provides evidence of a wider general benefit (e.g. increased competitiveness) personal benefits should also be sold. This recognizes the fact that individuals seek to achieve not only organizational goals but also personal ambitions.

- *Gain acceptance by association*: position the plan against some well-accepted organizational doctrine such as *customer service or quality management*. Because the doctrine is heavily backed, the chances of the plan being accepted and implemented are enhanced. Another positioning strategy is to associate the plan with a powerful individual (e.g. the chief executive). The objective is to create the viewpoint that if the boss wants the plan, there is no point in opposing it.

- *Leave room for local control over details*: leaving some local options or local control over details of the plan creates a sense of ownership on the part of those responsible for implementation, and encourages adaptation to different situations. Thought should be given to the extent of uniformity in execution, and the areas where local adoption is both practical and advisable.

- *Support words with action*: when implementation involves establishing a more marketing orientated culture, it is vital to support words with corresponding action. As we saw when discussing resistance to the marketing concept, it is easy for managers to contradict their words with inappropriate actions (e.g. stressing the need to understand customers and then cutting the marketing research budget). An illustrative case of how management actions supported the culture they were trying to create is the story of a regional manager of US company United Parcel Service (UPS), who used his initiative to untangle a misdirected shipment of Christmas presents by hiring an entire train and diverting two UPS-owned 727s from their flight plans (Bonoma, 1984). Despite the enormous cost (which far exceeded the value of the business), when senior management learned what he had done they praised and rewarded him: their actions supported and reinforced the culture they wanted to foster. As this story became folklore at UPS, its staff knew that senior management meant business when they said that the customer had to come first.

- *Establish two-way communication*: it is important that the people who are responsible for implementation feel that they can put their viewpoints to senior management, otherwise the feeling of top-down control will spread and resistance will build up through the belief that 'no one ever listens to us'. It is usually well worth listening to people lower down the management hierarchy and especially those who come face to face with customers. One way of implementing this approach is through staff suggestion schemes, but these need to be managed so that staff believe it is worth bothering to take part.

Asda, the UK supermarket chain acquired by Walmart, is well known for its policy of tapping into the collective wisdom of its 85,000 staff. It encourages them to put forward suggestions for improved customer service and the best ideas are presented at an annual meeting called the National Circle. It also invites staff to write directly to its chief executive officer, with the most promising ideas being rewarded with 'star points' that staff can redeem against a catalogue of offers including clothes and holidays.

See Marketing in Action 22.3 to find out more about how Unilever is chatting with its employees on a global scale.

Politics

- *Build coalitions*: the process of creating allies for the proposed measures is a crucial step in the implementation process. Two groups have special significance: power sources that control the resources needed for implementation such as information (expertise or data), finance and support (legitimacy, opinion leadership and political backing); and stakeholders, who are those people likely to gain or lose from the change (Kanter, Stein and Jick, 1992). Discussion with potential losers may reveal ways of sharing some rewards with them ('Invite the opposition in'). At the very least, talking to them will reveal their grievances and so allow thought to be given to how these may be handled. Another product of these discussions with both potential allies and foes is that the original proposals may be improved by accepting some of their suggestions.

MARKETING IN ACTION 22.3
Unilever Creates Virtual Jams while Chatting with its Employees

Unilever has over 400 brands, 170,000 employees and is number one in fast-moving consumer goods markets in 26 countries, so managing internal communications creates many challenges. However, in order to ensure that it can maintain its record of excellent customer service and high product quality, the company is always looking at innovative ways to interact with its customers and employees around the globe. More specifically, in 2013 it looked for ways to bring internal teams together more effectively, improve morale and inspire and motivate personal and professional development.

The image above shows Unilever's global brands.

The solution was a 'virtual jam lobby'—a virtual conference that enabled employees working across the globe to communicate and take part in a scheduled event using a digital communications hub. The event created an opportunity to share live content, cut the costs of employees having to travel to a single location, enabled multiple collaborations and delivered very effective internal communications.

Based on: WorkCast (2014); Unilever (2015)

- *Display support*: having recruited powerful allies these should be asked for a visible demonstration of support. This will confirm any statements that implementers have made about the strength of their backing ('gain acceptance by association'). Allies should be invited to meetings, presentations and seminars so that stakeholders can see the forces behind the change.

- *Invite the opposition in*: thought should be given to creating ways of sharing the rewards of the change with the opposition. This may mean modifying the plan and how it is to be implemented to take account of the needs of key players. So long as the main objectives of the plan remain intact, this may be a necessary step towards removing some opposition.

- *Warn the opposition*: critics of the plan should be left in no doubt as to the adverse consequences of opposition. This has been called *selling the negatives*. However, the tactic should be used with care because statements that are perceived as threats may stiffen rather than dilute resistance, particularly when the source does not have a strong power base.

- *Use of language*: in the political arena the potency of language in endorsing a preferred action and discrediting the opposition has long been apparent. Language can be used effectively in the implementation battle. For example, critics of the new plan may be being labelled 'outdated', 'backward looking' and 'set in their ways'. In meetings, implementers need to avoid the temptation to *overpower* in their use of language. For people without a strong power base (such as young newcomers to a company) using phrases like 'We must take this action' or 'This is the way we have to move' to people in a more senior position (e.g. a board of directors) will provoke psychological resistance even to praiseworthy plans. Phrases like 'I suggest' or 'I have a proposal for you to consider' recognize the inevitable desire on the part of more senior management to feel involved in the decision-making rather than being treated like a rubber stamp.

- *Decision control*: this may be achieved by agenda setting (i.e. controlling what is and is not discussed in meetings), limiting participation in decision-making to a small number of allies, controlling which decisions are open for debate in the organization, and timing important meetings when it is known that a key critic is absent (e.g. on holiday, or abroad on business).

- *The either/or alternative*: finally, when an implementation proposal is floundering, a powerful proponent may decide to use the either/or tactic in which the key decision-maker is required to choose between two documents placed on the desk: one asks for approval of the implementation plan, the other tenders the implementer's resignation.

Time

- *Incremental steps*: people need time to adjust to change, therefore consideration should be given to how quickly change is introduced. Where resistance to the full implementation package is likely to be strong, one option is to submit the strategy in incremental steps. A small, less controversial strategy is implemented first. Its success provides the impetus for the next implementation proposals, and so on.

- *Persistence*: this tactic requires the resubmission of the strategy until it is accepted. Modifications to the strategy may be necessary on the way but the objective is to wear down the opposition by resolute and persistent force. Implementation can be a battle of wills, and requires the capability of the implementer to accept rejection without loss of motivation.
- *Leave insufficient time for alternatives*: a different way of using time is to present plans at the last possible minute so that there is insufficient time for anyone to present or implement an alternative. The proposition is basically 'We must move with this plan as there is no alternative'.
- *Wait for the opposition to leave*: for those prepared to play a waiting game, withdrawing proposals until a key opposition member leaves the company or loses power may be feasible. Implementers should be alert to changes in the power structure in these ways as they may present a window of opportunity to resubmit hitherto rejected proposals.

Negotiation

- *Make the opening stance high*: when the implementer suspects that a proposal in the plan is likely to require negotiation, the correct opening stance is to start high but be realistic. There are two strong reasons for this. First, the opponent may accept the proposal without modification; second, it provides room for negotiation. When deciding how high to go, the limiting factor is the need to avoid unnecessary conflict. For example, asking for a move from a fixed salary to a commission-only system with a view to compromising with salary plus commission is likely to be unrealistic and to provoke unnecessary antagonism among the salesforce.
- *Trade concessions*: sometimes it may be possible to grant a concession simply to secure agreement to the basics of the plan. Indeed, if the implementer has created negotiating room, this may be perfectly acceptable. In other circumstances, however, the implementer may be able to trade concession for concession with the opponent. For example, a demand from the salesforce to reduce list price may be met by a counter-proposal to reduce discount levels. A useful way of trading concessions is by means of the *if . . . then* technique: 'If you are prepared to reduce your discount levels from 10 to 5 per cent, I am then prepared to reduce list price by 5 per cent' (Kennedy, Benson and McMillan, 1980). This is a valuable tool in negotiation because it promotes movement towards agreement and yet ensures that concessions given to the opponent are matched by concessions in return. Whenever possible, an attempt to create win-win situations should be made where concessions that cost the giver very little are highly valued by the receiver.

Evaluation

Finally, during and after the implementation process, evaluation should be made to consider what has been achieved and what has been learned. Evaluation may be in terms of the degree of support gained from key players, how well the plan and strategy have been implemented in the marketplace (e.g. by the use of customer surveys), the residual goodwill between opposing factions, and any changes in the balance of power between the implementers and other key parties in the company.

Marketing Organization

Marketing organization provides the context in which marketing implementation takes place: companies may have no marketing departments; those that do may have functional, product-based market-centred or matrix organizational structures.

No marketing department

As we have seen this is a common situation. Small companies that cannot afford the luxury of managerial specialism, or production- or financially driven organizations that do not see the value of a marketing department. In small companies, the owner-manager may carry out some of the functions of marketing, such as developing customer relationships, and product development. In larger companies, which may use the traditional production, finance, personnel and sales functional division, the same task may be undertaken by those departments, especially sales (e.g. customer feedback, sales forecasting).

It should be noted that not all companies that do not have a marketing department are poor at marketing; nor does the existence of a marketing department guarantee marketing orientation. Nevertheless, marketing should be seen as a company-wide phenomenon, not something that should be delegated exclusively to the marketing department.

Functional organization

As small companies grow, a formal marketing structure might emerge as a section within the sales department. As the importance of marketing is realized and the company grows, a marketing manager could be appointed with equivalent status to the sales manager who reports to a marketing director (see Figure 22.9). If the marketing director title is held by the previous sales director, little may change in terms of company philosophy: marketing may subsume a sales support role. This is the case in many companies where a more appropriate name for the person given the title 'marketing manager' would be 'communications manager'. An alternative route is to set up a *functional structure* under a sales director and a marketing director (see Figure 22.9b). Both have equal status, and the priorities of each job may lead to conflict (Dewsnap and Jobber, 2009) (see Table 22.1).

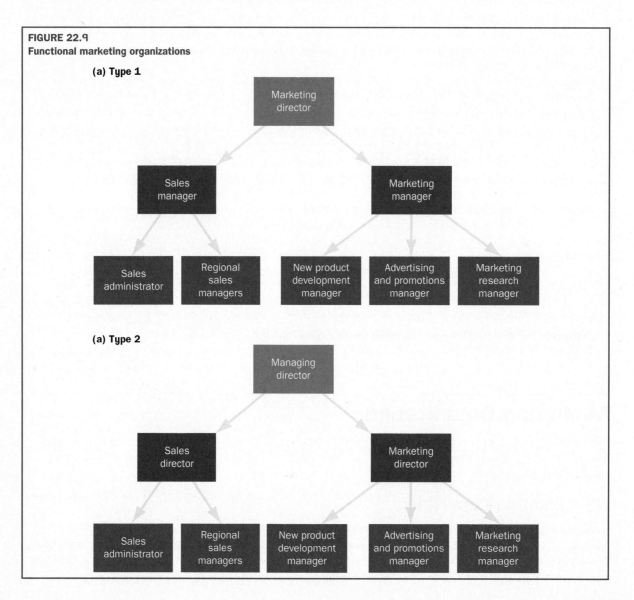

FIGURE 22.9
Functional marketing organizations

There are two sources of friction between sales and marketing:

1 Economic—wrangles over budget allocations. For example, the salesforce tends to blame marketers for the way they spend money on promotions, and the marketers look to the salesforce to achieve the highest possible prices; friction is rife between the two groups.

2 Cultural—the two job roles attract different types of individual: marketers tend to be analytical and project focused, whereas salespeople are skilled relationship builders and have an acute insight into which products will sell (Kotler, Rackham and Krishnaswamy, 2006).

Table 22.1 adds to this discussion, identifying more sources of conflict. Therefore it is important to appoint a marketing director who understands the relationship between sales and marketing and has the power to implement marketing strategies that recognize sales as a key element of the marketing mix.

TABLE 22.1 Potential areas of conflict between marketing and sales		
Area	**Sales**	**Marketing**
Objectives	Short-term sales	Long-term brand/market building
Focus	Distributors/retail trade	Consumers
Marketing research	Personal experience with customers/ trade	Market research reports
Pricing	Low prices to maximize sales volume. Discount structure in the hands of the salesforce	Price set consistent with positioning strategy. Discount structure built in to the marketing implementation plan
Marketing expenditure	Maximize resources channelled to the salesforce	Develop a balanced marketing mix using a variety of communication tools
Promotion	Sales literature, free customer give-aways, samples, business entertainment, sales promotions	Design a well-blended promotional mix including advertising, promotion and public relations

Functionalisms bring the benefit of specialization of task and a clear definition of responsibilities, and is still the most common form of marketing organization (Workman, Homburg and Gruner, 1998). However, as the product range widens and the number of markets served increases, the structure may become unwieldy with insufficient attention being paid to specific products and markets since no one has full responsibility for a particular product or market.

Product-based organization

The need to give sufficient care and attention to individual products has led many companies (particularly in the fast-moving consumer goods field) to move to a product-based structure. For example, Nestlé has moved from a functional to a product management system. A common structure is for a product manager to oversee a group of brands within a product field (e.g. bottled water, shampoos) supported by brand managers who manage specific brands (see Figure 22.10). Their role is to coordinate the business management of their brands. This involves dealing with advertising, promotion and marketing research agencies, and function areas within the firm. Their dilemma stems from the fact that they have responsibility for the commercial success of their brands without the power to force through their decisions as they have no authority over other functional areas such as sales, production and R&D. They act as ambassadors for their brands, attempting to ensure adequate support from the salesforce, and sufficient marketing funds to communicate to customers and the trade through advertising and promotion.

The advantages of a *product-based organization* are that adequate attention is given to developing a coordinated marketing mix for each brand. Furthermore, assigning specific responsibility means that speed of response to market or technological developments is quicker than relying on a committee of functional specialists. A by-product of the system is it provides excellent training for young business people as they come into contact with a wide range of business activities.

The drawbacks with this approach are:

- Healthy rivalry between product managers can become counter-productive, negatively competitive and cause conflict.

- The system can lead to new layers of management, which can be costly—brand managers might be supplemented by assistants—as brands increase and additional brand managers are recruited. Companies like Procter & Gamble and Unilever are eliminating layers of management in the face of increasing demands from supermarkets to trim prices (and thus increase efficiency).

FIGURE 22.10
Product-based organization

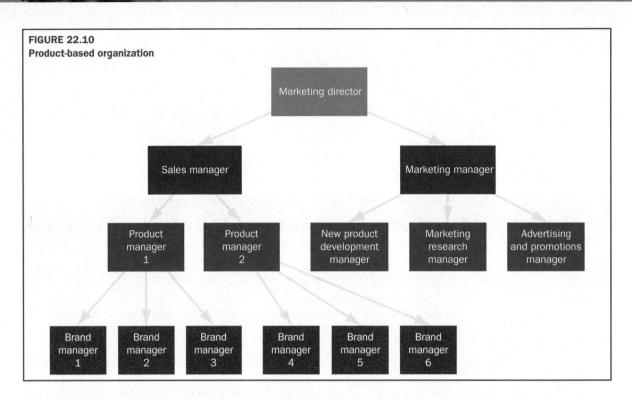

- Brand managers can be criticized for spending too much time coordinating in-company activities and too little time talking to customers. **Category management** can be an effective solution; it involves management of brands in a group, or *category* with specific emphasis on the retail trade's requirements. Suppliers such as Unilever, Heinz and L'Oréal have moved to category management to provide greater clarity in strategy across brands in an age where retailers themselves are managing brands as categories. (For further insights into category management, see: Aaker, 2009; Ambler, 2001.) See Exhibit 22.3.

Market-centred organization

Where companies sell their products to diverse markets, *market-centred organizations* should be considered. Instead of managers focusing on brands, *market managers* concentrate their energies on understanding and satisfying the needs of particular markets. The salesforce, too, may be similarly focused. For example, Figure 22.11 shows a market-centred organization for a hypothetical computer manufacturer. The specialist needs and computer applications in manufacturing, education and financial services justify a sales and marketing organization based on these market segments.

Occasionally, hybrid product/market-centred organizations based on distribution channels are appropriate. For example, at Philips, old organizational structures based on brands or products have been downgraded, replacing them with a new focus on distribution channels. Product managers who ensure that product designs fit market requirements still exist. However, under a new combined sales and marketing director the emphasis has moved to markets. Previously, different

EXHIBIT 22.3
Heinz brand categories

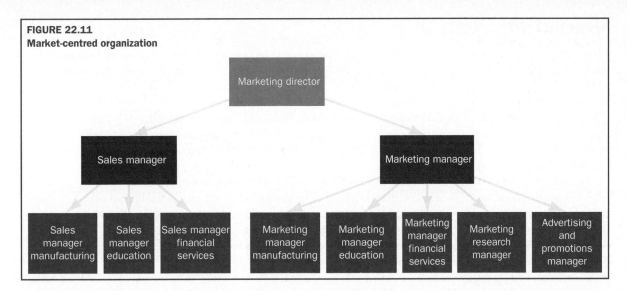

FIGURE 22.11
Market-centred organization

salespeople would visit retailers selling different products from the Philips range. This has been replaced by dedicated sales teams concentrating on channels such as the multiples, the independents and mail order (Mitchell, 1994).

The enormous influence of the trade in many consumer markets has forced other companies besides Philips to rethink their marketing organization. This has led to the establishment of **trade marketing** teams, which serve the needs of large retailers.

The advantage of the market-centred approach is the focus it provides on the specific customer requirements of new opportunities, and developing new products that meet their customer needs. By organizing around customers, it embodies the essence of the marketing concept. However, for companies competing in many sectors it can be resource-hungry.

Matrix organization

For companies with a wide product range selling in diverse markets, a *matrix structure* may be necessary. Both product and market managers are employed to give due attention to both facets of marketing activity. The organizational structure resembles a grid, as shown in Figure 22.12, again using a hypothetical computer company. Product managers are responsible for their group of products' sales and profit performance, and monitor technological developments that impact on their products. Market managers focus on the needs of customers in each market segment.

For the system to work effectively, clear lines of decision-making authority need to be drawn up because of the possible areas of conflict. For example, who decides the price of the product? If a market manager requires an addition to the product line to meet the special needs of some customers, who has the authority to decide if the extra costs are justified? How should the salesforce be organized: along product or market lines? Also, it is a resource-hungry method of organization. Nevertheless, the dual specialism does promote the careful analysis of both product and markets so that customer needs are met.

Marketing organization and implementation are inevitably intertwined as the former affects the day-to-day activities of marketing managers. It is important that we understand the organizational world as marketing managers have come to understand it, in particular the activities that constitute their job (Brownlie and Saren, 1997).

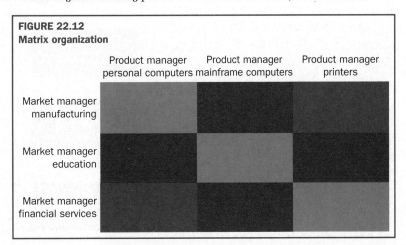

FIGURE 22.12
Matrix organization

Marketing Control

Marketing control is an essential element of the marketing planning process because it provides a review of how well marketing objectives have been achieved. A framework for controlling marketing activities is given in Figure 22.13. The process begins by deciding marketing objectives, leading to the setting of performance standards. For example, a marketing objective of 'widening the customer base' might lead to the setting of the performance standard of 'generating 20 new accounts within 12 months'. Similarly the marketing objective of 'improving market share' might translate into a performance standard of 'improving market share from 20 per cent to 25 per cent'. Some companies set quantitative marketing objectives, in which case performance standards are automatically derived.

The next step is to locate responsibility. In some cases responsibility ultimately falls on one person (e.g. the brand manager), in others it is shared (e.g. the sales manager and salesforce). It is important to consider this issue since corrective or supportive action may need to focus on those responsible for the success of marketing activity.

Performance is then evaluated against standards, which relies on an efficient information system, and a judgement has to be made about the degree of success and/or failure achieved, and what corrective or supportive action is to be taken. This can take various forms.

- First, failure that is attributed to poor performance of individuals may result in the giving of advice regarding future attitudes and actions, training and/or punishment (e.g. criticism, lower pay, demotion, termination of employment). Success, on the other hand, should be rewarded through praise, promotion and/or higher pay.
- Second, failure that is attributed to unrealistic marketing objectives and performance standards may cause them to be lowered for the subsequent period. Success that is thought to reflect unambitious objectives and standards may cause them to be raised next period.
- Third, the attainment of marketing objectives and standards may also mean modification next period. For example, if the marketing objective and performance standard of opening 20 new accounts is achieved, this may mean the focus for the next period may change. The next objective may focus on customer retention, for instance.
- Finally, the failure of one achieved objective to bring about another may also require corrective action. For example, if a marketing objective of increasing calls to new accounts does not result in extra sales, the original objective may be dropped in favour of another (e.g. improving product awareness through advertising).

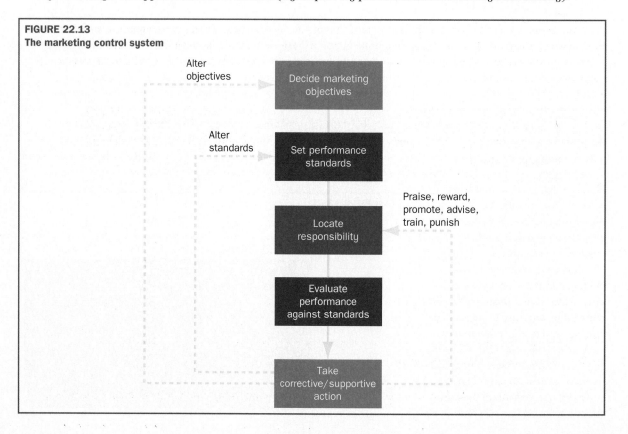

FIGURE 22.13
The marketing control system

Strategic Control

Two types of control system may be used. The first concerns major strategic issues and answers the question 'Are we doing the right thing?' It focuses on company strengths, weaknesses, opportunities and threats, and the process of control is through a marketing audit. This was discussed in depth in Chapter 18 under the heading 'The process of marketing planning'.

Operational Control and the Use of Marketing Metrics

The second control system concerns tactical ongoing marketing activities, and is called operational control. An array of measures (often referred to as **marketing metrics**) are available to marketing managers who wish to measure the effectiveness of their activities (Faris et al., 2006). However, it is often difficult to determine the exact contribution of marketing efforts because outcomes are usually dependent on several factors. For example, higher sales may be caused by increased (or better) advertising, a more motivated salesforce, weaker competition, more favourable economic conditions, and so on. This makes it difficult to justify, for example, increased advertising expenditure, because it is hard to quantify the past effects of advertising. This contrasts with production, where the effects of the introduction of a new machine can be calculated by measuring output; or finance, where a cost-cutting programme's effect on costs is easily calculated.

Despite these problems, there are now demands on marketing to become accountable for its activities. In order to be accountable, marketing managers are using *marketing metrics*, which are quantitative measures of the outcomes of marketing activities and expenditures. No longer can marketing executives attend budget meetings expecting to spend more money on advertising, promotion, direct marketing and other marketing activities without quantitative justification of these expenditures. The new mantra is **marketing accountability**: the requirement to justify marketing investment by using marketing metrics. Without such justification it is hardly surprising that marketing budgets are often the first to be cut in an economic downturn.

A research study has identified the kinds of marketing metrics being employed by companies, and the 10 most used metrics are shown in Table 22.2, together with an importance measure (Ambler, Kokkinaki and Puntoni, 2004). Although discussed under operational issues, the information can also usefully be fed into the marketing audit for strategic purposes.

Rank	Metric	% using measure	% rating it as important
\ TABLE 22.2 The use of marketing metrics in UK companies			

Rank	Metric	% using measure	% rating it as important
1	Profit/profitability	92	80
2	Sales: value and/or volume	91	71
3	Gross margin	81	66
4	Awareness	78	28
5	Market share (value/volume)	78	37
6	Number of new products	73	18
7	Relative price	70	36
8	Customer dissatisfaction	69	45
9	Customer satisfaction	68	48
10	Distribution/availability	66	18

Source: Ambler, Kokkinaki and Puntoni (2004)

Each of these metrics—as shown in Figure 22.14—will now be assessed, and specific measures identified, together with their calculation.

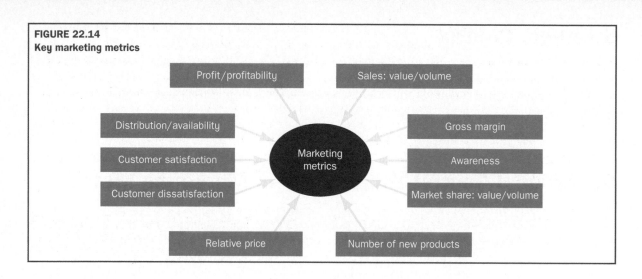

FIGURE 22.14
Key marketing metrics

Profit/profitability

Table 22.3 shows some typical profit metrics.

TABLE 22.3 Some typical profit metrics

Typical metrics	Calculation
Profit	Profit = total revenue − total costs
Return on investment (ROI)	$ROI = \dfrac{\text{net profit}}{\text{investment}}$

Profit is the financial objective of most organizations so it is the most used metric. Similarly, profitability, which measures the profit return on investments such as products or advertising campaigns, is a popular metric since it relates to the financial objectives of companies. It is usually measured as return on investment (ROI) and, increasingly, marketers are attempting to measure return on marketing investment, although, as discussed earlier, accounting for marketing contribution to a sales (and hence profit) increase is sometimes difficult. What is required is a baseline figure (i.e. what would have happened without the marketing expenditure). Apart from direct marketing, where experiments can be conducted to test effects, such baseline figures can be difficult to establish. Also ROI is usually measured over a short time period (e.g. a year) and so such calculations can underestimate the full effects of marketing investments, which, through brand building, often have positive long-term effects (Ambler and Roberts, 2008).

For operational control, **profitability analysis** can provide useful information on the profit performance of key aspects of marketing, such as products, customers or distribution channels. The example given focuses on products. The hypothetical company sells three types of product: paper products, printers and copiers. The first step is to measure marketing inputs to each of these products. These are shown in Table 22.4. Allocation of sales calls to products is facilitated by separate sales teams for each group.

TABLE 22.4 Allocating functional costs to products

Products	Salesforce (number of sales calls per year)	Advertising (number of one-page ads placed)	Order processing (number of orders placed)
Paper products	500	20	1,000
Printers	400	20	800
Copiers	250	10	200
Total	1,150	50	2,000
Total cost	£190,000	£130,000	£80,000
Functional cost per unit	£165 per call	£2,600 per ad	£40 per order

If the sales teams were organized on purely geographic lines, an estimate of how much time was devoted to each product, on average, at each call would need to be made. Table 22.4 shows how the costs of an average sales call, advertising insertion and order are calculated. This provides vital information to calculate profitability for each product.

Table 22.5 shows how the net profit before tax is calculated. The results show how copiers are losing money. Before deciding to drop this line the company would have to take into account the extent to which customers expect copiers to be sold alongside paper products and printers, the effect on paper sales of dropping copiers, the possible annoyance caused to customers that already own one of its copiers, the extent to which copiers cover overheads that otherwise would need to be paid for from paper products and printer sales, the scope for pruning costs and increasing sales, and the degree to which the arbitrary nature of some of the cost allocations has unfairly treated copier products.

TABLE 22.5 Profitability statement for products (£)			
	Paper products	**Printers**	**Copiers**
Sales	1,000,000	700,000	300,000
Cost of goods sold	500,000	250,000	250,000
Gross margin	500,000	450,000	50,000
Marketing costs			
Salesforce (at £165 per call)	82,500	66,000	41,250
Advertising (at £2,600 per advertisement)	52,000	52,000	26,000
Order processing (at £40 per order)	40,000	32,000	8,000
Total cost	174,500	150,000	72,250
Net profit (or loss) before tax	325,500	300,000	(25,250)

Sales

Table 22.6 shows some typical sales metrics.

TABLE 22.6 Some typical sales metrics	
Typical metrics	**Calculation**
Sales revenue	Sales revenue = unit sales × price
Sales volume	Sales volume = unit sales
Sales revenue against target	Variance = sales revenue − target sales revenue

Processing sales revenue and sales volume is easy and the metrics are important determinants of marketing investments. Sales increases are normally sought to justify higher marketing expenditures, but without corresponding profit metrics can be misleading. This is because sales can be bought with excessive discounting, leading to higher sales but lower profit. For this reason, rewarding salesforces for higher sales without also measuring profits can be harmful.

Despite these dangers, **sales analysis** of actual against target sales revenue can be useful for operational control. Negative variance may be due to lower sales volume or lower prices. Product, customer and regional analysis will be carried out to discover where the shortfall arose. A change in the product mix could account for a sales fall, with more lower-priced products being sold. The loss of a major customer may also account for a sales decline. Regional analysis may identify a poorly performing area sales manager or salesperson. These findings would point the direction of further investigations to uncover the reasons for such outcomes.

Gross margin

Table 22.7 shows some typical gross margin metrics.

TABLE 22.7 Some typical gross margin metrics	
Typical metrics	**Calculation**
Gross margin per unit (GMU)	GMU = price—cost of goods sold (material plus labour)
Gross margin percentage (GMP)	$GMP = \dfrac{GMU \times 100}{price}$

The third most popular metric is gross margin. Different industries can achieve widely varying gross margins. For example, high-volume, low-price supermarkets achieve low single-digit margins, while traditional jewellers typically require and achieve 50 per cent or more gross margins because their business is lower volume. Calculated as a percentage, gross margin is an indication of the percentage of the selling price that is a contribution to profit. It is not necessarily actual profit, as other expenses such as sales, marketing, distribution and administrative costs have not been deducted. A problem with using gross margin as a marketing metric is that it can be misleading if these other expenses are high. The answer is to calculate unit margin, where all costs are included.

Awareness

Table 22.8 shows some typical awareness metrics.

TABLE 22.8 Some typical awareness metrics	
Typical metrics	**Calculation**
Recall	Survey respondents are asked to name all the brands in a product category that they can think of
Recognition	Survey respondents are shown a list of brands and asked to name those that they have heard of

Awareness is an important metric because it measures whether a marketing communications campaign is entering target consumers' minds. Awareness measures before and after a campaign are particularly useful. However, awareness does not necessarily raise purchase levels if the brand is not liked. It is therefore best used alongside other communications-orientated metrics such as measures of beliefs, liking, willingness to recommend, and purchase intention.

Market share

Table 22.9 shows some typical market share metrics.

TABLE 22.9 Some typical market share metrics	
Typical metrics	**Calculation**
Market share (value)	$\text{Market share (value)} = \dfrac{\text{sales revenue}}{\text{total market revenue}}$
Market share (unit)	$\text{Market share (unit)} = \dfrac{\text{unit sales}}{\text{total market unit sales}}$
Relative market share	$\text{Relative market share} = \dfrac{\text{brand's market share}}{\text{largest competitor's share}}$

Market share analysis evaluates a company's performance in comparison to that of its competitors. Sales analysis may show a healthy increase in revenues but this may be due to market growth rather than an improved performance over competitors. An accompanying decline in market share would sound warning bells regarding relative performance. This would stimulate further investigation to root out the causes.

It should be recognized that a market share decline is not always a symptom of poor performance. This is why outcomes should always be compared to marketing objectives and performance standards. If the marketing objective was to harvest a product, leading to a performance standard of a 5 per cent increase in profits, its achievement may be accompanied by a market share decline (through the effect of a price rise). This would be a perfectly satisfactory outcome given the desired objective. Conversely, a market share gain may not signal improved performance if it was brought about by price reductions that reduced profits.

The relative market share metric (percentage) was used when calculating a brand's position on the Boston Consulting Group Matrix (see Chapter 20). When a brand is a market leader, relative market share has a value greater than one.

Number of new products

Table 22.10 shows some typical new product metrics.

TABLE 22.10 Some typical new product metrics	
Typical metrics	**Calculation**
Number of new products	Number of new products launched per year
Number of successful new products	Number of new products achieving objectives
Proportion of sales attributable to new products (PSANP)	$PSANP = \dfrac{\text{sales revenue of product on the market for less than n years}}{\text{total sales revenue}}$

Innovation is the lifeblood of success and as a consequence it is not surprising that an important marketing metric is the number of new products. However, simply counting the number of new products launched per year does not take into account their success rate. Two other metrics can be used to indicate success: the number (and proportion) of successful launches, where success is recognized when objectives are achieved, can be measured; also the proportion of sales revenue (and profits) attributable to new products within a given time period can be used. For example, 3M measures the proportion of sales attributable to new products launched within six years as a check on their innovative capability.

Care needs to be taken when defining what is a new product. As we saw in Chapter 11, there are many categories of new product, stretching from brand extensions to radical innovation (new-to-the-world products). Therefore it can be sensible to categorize each of the metrics according to type of new product.

Relative price

Table 22.11 shows some typical relative price metrics.

TABLE 22.11 Some typical relative price metrics	
Typical metrics	**Calculation**
Ratio of brand A's price to the average price charged in the product category (RPAP)	$RPAP = \dfrac{\text{brand A's price}}{\text{average price in the product category}}$
Ratio of brand A's price to the price of its main competitor (RPPM)	$RPPM = \dfrac{\text{brand A's price}}{\text{price of its main competitor}}$

The relative price metric indicates the extent to which a brand is operating at a price premium or discount in a product category. A benchmark is required, which is usually the average price charged or the price of the brand's main competitor or the market leader. If brand A was priced at £4 and the average price charged was £3, the RPAP would be 1.33, demonstrating that the brand was charging a price premium (over the market average) of 33 per cent. If this metric was supported by market leadership (indicated by using a market share metric), this would suggest a strong differential advantage for the brand: not only does the brand outsell its rivals but it does so with a higher price. Therefore, when used with other metrics, relative price measures can be indicative of the strength of a brand (brand equity).

Customer dissatisfaction

Table 22.12 shows some typical customer dissatisfaction metrics.

TABLE 22.12 Some typical customer dissatisfaction metrics

Typical metrics	Calculation
Number of customer complaints	Number of complaints per period
Number of lost customers	Number of lost customers per period
Proportion of lost customers (PLC)	$PLC = \dfrac{\text{number of lost customers per period}}{\text{total number of customers at the start of the period}}$

Companies measure customer dissatisfaction because it is associated with losing customers. Companies monitor customer complaints to assess weaknesses in the product offering, including service levels. The outcomes of customer complaints should also be measured as research has shown that the successful resolution of a complaint can cause customers to feel more positive about the company than before the service failure (Maxham and Netemeyer, 2002). The number and proportion of lost customers are also useful metrics. These can be measured for consumer packaged goods by consumer panels and for business-to-business accounts directly from sales data.

Customer satisfaction

Table 22.13 shows some typical customer satisfaction metrics.

TABLE 22.13 Some typical customer satisfaction metrics

Typical metrics	Calculation
Satisfaction rating scales	Responses to 'Very dissatisfied' to 'Very satisfied' rating scales
Satisfaction compared to expectations	Responses to 'Worse than expected' to 'Better than expected' rating scales
Willingness to recommend	Responses to 'Would you recommend brand X to a friend or colleague?' question

An increasingly common barometer of marketing success is **customer satisfaction measurement**, which is encouraging as customer satisfaction is at the heart of the marketing concept. Although this measure does not appear directly on a company's profit and loss account, it is a fundamental condition for corporate success. The process involves the setting of customer satisfaction criteria, the design of a questionnaire to measure satisfaction on those criteria, the choice of which customers to interview, and the analysis and interpretation of results. The use of a market research agency is advised, to take advantage of its skills and unbiased viewpoint. A potential problem is that its measurement can lead to harmful behaviour on the part of the employees whose performance is being measured. For example, in one company salespeople gave price concessions to customers simply to build up goodwill that they hoped would improve their scores on a customer satisfaction questionnaire (Piercy and Morgan, 1995).

One business-to-business marketing research agency advocates interviewing three customer groups to give a valid picture of customer satisfaction and marketing effectiveness.

1 Ten current customers
2 Ten lapsed customers (who bought from us in the past but do not now)
3 Ten non-customers (who are in the market for the product but hitherto have not bought from us).

Invaluable information can be gained concerning customer satisfaction, how effective the salesforce is, why customers have switched to other suppliers, and why some potential customers have never done business with our company.

A powerful question to ask customers is 'Would you recommend brand X to a friend or colleague?' It provides insight into the strength of customer relationships and, therefore, likely future performance. Research by Reichheld into 14 companies in six industries in the USA showed that the answers to this question provided the first or second best predictor of future customer behaviour in 11 out of 14 tests (Reichheld, 2006). Responses are given on a scale of 1 to 10, with 9s and 10s being defined as promoters, and 6s and below as detractors. The difference between the two gives the Net Promoter Score (NPS). A major benefit of this is its simplicity, but it has been criticized because a given NPS score can arise from very different sets of responses. For example, an

NPS of 40 may arise from 70 per cent promoters and 30 per cent detractors, or one of 40 per cent promoters and zero detractors. Also the method does not allow measurement of satisfaction of particular aspects of the product offering such as product performance, service quality and salesperson satisfaction. In practice, the question is normally followed by the open-ended 'why' question, to tease out these elements. It also tends to be used alongside the normal customer satisfaction rating scales, rather than as a replacement for them (Mitchell, 2008).

Distribution/availability

Table 22.14 shows some typical distribution/availability metrics.

TABLE 22.14 Some typical distribution/availability metrics	
Typical metrics	**Calculation**
Availability ratio (AR)	$AR = \dfrac{\text{number of outlets stocking brand A}}{\text{total number of outlets}}$
Out of stock ratio (OSR)	$OSR = \dfrac{\text{number of outlets where brand A is listed but unavailable}}{\text{total number of outlets where brand A is listed}}$

The availability of a brand in distribution outlets is an important marketing metric because, if an outlet is out of stock, a consumer may be unwilling to visit another shop, preferring the convenience of buying a rival brand instead. Two important metrics are the availability ratio, which measures the proportion of outlets stocking the brand, and the out-of-stock ratio, which measures the proportion of outlets that normally stock the brand but are out of stock at a particular point in time. Poor scores on these ratios mean that the causes need to be identified and remedial action taken.

In practice, marketing managers need to decide on the set of metrics that are relevant to their business, and seek ways of gathering them, which may mean employing a marketing research agency.

When you have read this chapter

Discover further resources and test your understanding: McGraw-Hill **Connect**™ is a digital teaching and learning environment that improves performance over a variety of critical outcomes; it can be tailored, is easy to use and is proven effective. **LearnSmart**™ is the most widely used and intelligent adaptive learning resource that is proven to strengthen memory recall, improve course retention and boost grades. Fuelled by **LearnSmart**™, **SmartBook**™ is the first and only adaptive reading experience available today.

Review

1 **The relationship between marketing strategy, implementation and performance**
   - Appropriate strategy with good implementation will have the best chance of successful outcomes; appropriate strategy with bad implementation will lead to trouble, especially if the substandard implementation leads to strategy change; inappropriate strategy with good implementation may hasten failure or may lead to actions that correct strategy and therefore produce favourable outcomes; and inappropriate strategy with bad implementation will lead to failure.

2 The stages that people pass through when they experience disruptive change

- The stages are numbness, denial and disbelief, self-doubt and emotion, acceptance and letting go, adaptation and testing, construction and meaning, and internalization.

3 The objectives of marketing implementation and change

- The overall objective is the successful execution of the marketing plan.
- This may require gaining the support of key decision-makers, gaining the required resources and gaining the commitment of relevant individuals and departments.

4 The barriers to the implementation of the marketing concept

- The barriers are the fact that new marketing ideas often mean higher costs; the potential benefits are often unquantifiable; personal ambitions may conflict with the customer's desire to have simple but reliable products; reward systems may reward short-term cost savings, sales and profitability rather than long-term customer satisfaction; and there may be a gap between what managers say (e.g. 'be customer-orientated') and what they do (e.g. cut back on marketing research funds).

5 The forms of resistance to marketing implementation and change

- The 10 forms of resistance are criticisms of specific details of the plan; foot-dragging; slow response to requests; unavailability; suggestions that, despite the merits of the plan, resources should be channelled elsewhere; arguments that the proposals are too ambitious; hassle and aggravation created to wear the proposers down; attempts to delay the decision; attacks on the credibility of the proposer; and pointing out the risks of the plan.

6 How to develop effective implementation strategies

- A change master is needed to drive through change.
- Managing the implementation process requires the setting of objectives ('would like' and 'must have'), strategy (internal marketing), execution (persuasion, negotiation, politics and tactics) and evaluation (who wins, and what can be learned).

7 The elements of an internal marketing programme

- An internal marketing programme mirrors the structures used to market externally such as market segmentation, targeting and the marketing mix.
- The individuals within the organization are known as internal customers. These can be segmented into three groups: supporters, neutrals and opposers. These form distinct target markets that require different internal marketing mixes to be designed to optimize the chances of successful adoption of the plan.

8 The skills and tactics that can be used to overcome resistance to the implementation of the marketing concept and plan

- The skills are persuasion (the needs, motivations and problems of internal customers need to be understood before appealing messages can be developed), negotiation and political skills (the understanding of the sources of power, and the use of overt and covert power plays).
- The tactics are persuasion, politics, timing and negotiation.

9 Marketing organizational structures

- The options are no marketing department, functional, product-based, market-centred or matrix organizational structures.

10 The nature of a marketing control system

- There are two types of marketing control: strategic and operational control systems.
- Strategic control systems answer the question 'Are we doing the right things?' and are based on a marketing audit.
- Operational control systems concern tactical ongoing marketing activities. Marketing metrics are used for this purpose and to justify marketing investments. The most commonly used metrics are profit/profitability, sales (value and/or volume), gross margin, awareness, market share, number of new products, relative price, customer dissatisfaction, customer satisfaction, and distribution/availability.

Key Terms

category management the management of brands in a group, portfolio or category, with specific emphasis on the retail trade's requirements

change master a person that develops an implementation strategy to drive through organizational change

coercive power power inherent in the ability to punish

concession analysis the evaluation of things that can be offered to someone in negotiation valued from the viewpoint of the receiver

covert power play the use of disguised forms of power tactics

customer satisfaction measurement a process through which customer satisfaction criteria are set, customers are surveyed and the results interpreted in order to establish the level of customer satisfaction with the organization's product

expert power power that derives from an individual's expertise

legitimate power power based on legitimate authority, such as line management

market share analysis a comparison of company sales with total sales of the product, including sales of competitors

marketing accountability the requirement to justify marketing investment by using marketing metrics

marketing control the stage in the marketing planning process or cycle when performance against plan is monitored so that corrective action, if necessary, can be taken

marketing metrics quantitative measures of the outcomes of marketing activities and expenditures

overt power play the use of visible, open kinds of power tactics

profitability analysis the calculation of sales revenues and costs for the purpose of calculating the profit performance of products, customers and/or distribution channels

proposal analysis the prediction and evaluation of proposals and demands likely to be made by someone with whom one is negotiating

referent power power derived by the reference source, for example when people identify with and respect the architect of change

reward power power derived from the ability to provide benefits

sales analysis a comparison of actual with target sales

trade marketing marketing to the retail trade

transition curve the emotional stages that people pass through when confronted with an adverse change

Study Questions

1. Think of a situation when your life suffered from a dramatic change. Using Figure 22.3 for guidance, recall your feelings over time. How closely did your experiences match the stages in the figure? How did your feelings at each stage (e.g. denial and disbelief) manifest themselves?

2. Can good implementation substitute for an inappropriate strategy? Give an example of how good implementation might make the situation worse and an example of how it might improve the situation.

3. Why do some companies fail to implement the marketing concept?

4. Describe the ways in which people may resist the change that is implied in the implementation of a new marketing plan. Why should they wish to do this?

5. What is internal marketing? Does the marketing concept apply when planning internal marketing initiatives?

6. What tactics of persuasion are at the implementer's disposal? What are the advantages and limitations of each one?

7. Discuss the options available for organizing a marketing department. How well is each form likely to serve customers?

8. Discuss the problems involved in setting up and implementing a marketing control system.

Recommended Reading

Armstrong, M. (2015) *Armstrong's Handbook of Reward Management Practice*, London: Kogan Page.

Hrebiniak, L. (2013) *Making Strategy Work: Effective Execution and Change*, London: Pearson Higher Education.

Northouse, P. (2015) *Leadership*, London: Sage Publications Ltd.

Rust, R., T. Ambler, G. Carpenter, V. Kumar and R. Srivastava (2004) Measuring marketing productivity: Current knowledge and future directions, *Journal of Marketing* 68(4),76–89.

Sarin, S., G. Challagalla and A. K. Kohli (2012) Implementing Changes in Marketing Strategy: The Role of Perceived Outcome- and Process-Oriented Supervisory Actions, *Journal of Marketing Research*, 49(4), August 2012, 564–80.

Slater S.F., G. T. M. Hult and E. M. Olson (2010), Factors influencing the relative importance of marketing strategy creativity and marketing strategy implementation effectiveness, *Industrial Marketing Management* 39(4), 551–9.

References

Aaker, D. (2009) *Brand Leadership*, New York: Free Press

Ambler, T. (2001) Category Management is Best Deployed for Brand Positioning, *Marketing*, 29 November, 18.

Ambler, T. and J. H. Roberts (2008) Assessing Marketing Performance: Don't Settle For a Silver Metric, *Journal of Marketing Management* 24, 733–50.

Ambler, T., F. Kokkinaki and S. Puntoni (2004) Assessing Marketing Performance: Reasons for Metrics Selection, *Journal of Marketing Management* 20, 475–98.

Ansoff, I. and E. McDonnell (1990) *Implanting Strategic Management*, Englewood Cliffs, NJ: Prentice-Hall.

Argyris, C. (1966) Interpersonal Barriers to Decision Making, *Harvard Business Review* 44 (March–April), 84–97.

Birkinshaw, J. (2013) Why corporate giants fail to change, *Fortune*, 8 May. http://fortune.com/2013/05/08/why-corporate-giants-fail-to-change (accessed 2 May 2015).

Bonoma, T. V. (1984) Making your Marketing Strategy Work, *Harvard Business Review* 62 (March–April), 68–76.

Bonoma, T. V. (1985) *The Marketing Edge: Making Strategies Work*, New York: Free Press.

Brownlie, D. and M. Saren (1997) Beyond the One-Dimensional Marketing Manager: The Discourse of Theory, Practice and Relevance, *International Journal of Research in Marketing* 14, 147–61.

Bruno Ken (2010) Marketers turn employees into Ad stars, http://www.forbes.com/sites/marketshare/2010/09/23/marketers-advertising-employees-yum-pizza-hut-bp-cathay-pacific/.

Burke, D., C. Hajim, J. Elliot, J. Mero and C. Tkaczy (2007) Top 10 Companies for Leaders, *Fortune*.

Chang, A. (2012) Headline: 5 Reasons Why Nokia Lost Its Handset Sales Lead and Got Downgraded to 'Junk', *Wired*, 27 April. http://www.wired.com/2012/04/5-reasons-why-nokia-lost-its-handset-sales-lead-and-got-downgraded-to-junk (accessed 2 May 2015).

Cisco (2015) Cisco Collaboration Meeting Rooms, 3 May. http://www.cisco.com/c/en/us/solutions/collaboration/index.html

Dewsnap, B. and D. Jobber (2009) An exploratory study of sales-marketing integrative devices, *European Journal of Marketing* 43 (7/8), 985–1007.

Faris, P. W., N. T. Bendle, P. E. Pfeifer and D. J. Reibstein (2006) *Key Marketing Metrics*, Harlow: Pearson.

French, J. R. P. and B. Raven (1959) The Bases of Social Power, in Cartwright, D. (ed.) *Studies in Social Power*, Ann Arbor: University of Michigan Press, 150–67.

Gokey, M. (2015) It's official: Nokia to become Microsoft Mobile April 25—What happens next? *Tech Times*, 22 April. http://www.techtimes.com/articles/5872/20140422/its-official-nokia-to-become-microsoft-mobile-april-25-what-happens-next.htm (accessed 2 May 2015).

Grönroos, C. (1985) Internal Marketing: Theory and Practice, in Bloch, T. M., G. D. Upah and V. A. Zeithaml (eds) *Services Marketing in a Changing Environment*, Chicago: American Marketing Association.

Gummesson, E. (1987) Using Internal Marketing to Develop a New Culture: The Case of Ericsson Quality, *Journal of Business and Industrial Marketing* 2(3), 23–8.

Hasek, G. (2012) Accor's Planet 21 program brings sustainability to all its hotels, greenbiz.com, http://www.greenbiz.com/news/2012/04/17/accors-planet-21-program-brings-sustainability-allits-hotels, 17 April 2012.

Hickson, D. J., C. R. Hinings, C. A. Lee, R. E. Schneck and J. M. Pennings (1971) A Strategic Contingencies Theory of Intraorganizational Power, *Administrative Science Quarterly* 16(2), 216–29.

Hinings, C. R., D. J. Hickson, J. M. Pennings and R. E. Schneck (1974) Structural Conditions of Intraorganizational Power, *Administrative Science Quarterly* 19(1), 22–44.

Johannessen, J.-A., J. Olaisen and A. Havan (1993) The Challenge of Innovation in a Norwegian Shipyard Facing the Russian Market, *European Journal of Marketing* 27(3), 23–38.

Johnson, G. (1987) *Strategic Change and the Management Process*, Oxford: Basil Blackwell.

Kanter, R. M. (1983) *The Change Masters*, London: Allen and Unwin.

Kanter, R. M., B. A. Stein and T. D. Jick (1992) *The Challenge of Organizational Change*, New York: Free Press.

Kennedy, G., J. Benson and J. MacMillan (1987) *Managing Negotiations*, London: Business Books.

Kotler, P., N. Rackham and S. Krishnaswamy (2006) Ending the War Between Sales and Marketing, *Harvard Business Review*, July–August. https://hbr.org/2006/07/ending-the-war-between-sales-and-marketing

Laing, A. and L. McKee (2001) Willing Volunteers or Unwilling Conscripts? Professionals and Marketing in Service Organizations, *Journal of Marketing Management* 17(5/6), 559–76.

London, S. and A. Hill (2002) A Recovery Strategy Worth Copying, *Financial Times*, 16 October, 12.

Marketing Business (2005) 100 Days, June, 15–17.

Maxham III, J. G. and R. G. Netemeyer (2002) A Longitudinal Study of Complaining Customers' Evaluations of Multiple Service Failures and Recovery Efforts, *Journal of Marketing* 66, October, 57–71.

McGregor, J. (2009) An Historic Succession at Xerox, *Business Week*, 8 June, 18–22.

Mitchell, A. (1994) Dark Night of Marketing or a New Dawn?, *Marketing*, 17 February, 22–3.

Mitchell, A. (2008) The Only Number You Need to Know Does Not Add Up To Much, *Marketing Week*, 6 March, 15–16.

Mudie, P. (1987) Internal Marketing: Cause of Concern, *Quarterly Review of Marketing*, Spring–Summer, 21–4.

Nokia (2015) Nokia. http://company.nokia.com/en/our-businesses

Pettigrew, A. M. (1985) *The Awakening Giant: Continuity and Change in ICI*, Oxford: Basil Blackwell.

Piercy, N. (1990) Making Marketing Strategies Happen in the Real World, *Marketing Business*, February, 20–1.

Piercy, N. (2008) *Marketing-Led Strategic Change*, Oxford: Butterworth-Heinemann.

Piercy, N. and N. A. Morgan (1995) Customer Satisfaction Measurement and Management: A Processual Analysis, *Journal of Marketing Management* 11, 817–34.

Reed, J. and D. Schäfer (2008) BMW's Accelerator of Change, *Financial Times*, 6 October, 18.

Reichheld, F. (2006) *The Ultimate Question*, Boston: Harvard Business School Press.

Ritson, M. (2015) Abercrombie's new direction hasn't revitalised the brand but eradicated it, *Marketing Week*, 29 April. http://www.marketingweek.com/2015/04/29/abercrombies-new-direction-hasnt-revitalised-the-brand-but-eradicated-it (accessed 30 April 2015).

Saner, E. (2012) Abercrombie & Fitch: for beautiful people only, *The Guardian*, 28 April. http://www.theguardian.com/fashion/2012/apr/28/abercrombie-fitch-savile-row (accessed 2 May 2015).

Shyh-Rong, F., C. Enchi, C.-C. Chang and C, C.-H. (2014) Internal market orientation, market capabilities and learning orientation, *European Journal of Marketing* 48(1/2), 170–92.

Stanton, W. J., R. H. Buskirk and R. Spiro (2002) *Management of a Sales Force*, Boston, Mass: Irwin.

Trefis Team (2014) Abercrombie and Fitch's CEO Mike Jeffries To Step Down Immediately, *Forbes*, 10 December. http://www.forbes.com/sites/greatspeculations/2014/12/10/abercrombie-and-fitchs-ceo-mike-jeffries-to-step-down-immediately (accessed 2 May 2015).

Unilever (2015) About us, www.unilever.com (accessed June 2015).

Webster, F. E. Jr. (1988) Rediscovering the Marketing Concept, *Business Horizons* 31 (May–June), 29–39.

Wilson, D. C. (1992) *A Strategy of Change: Concepts and Controversies in the Management of Change*, London: Routledge.

Wilson, G. (1993) *Making Change Happen*, London: Pitman.

WorkCast (2014) Top 3 Takeaways from Unilever's Virtual Event, Workcast, 13 October. http://www.workcast.com/uk/blog/showcasing-unilevers-virtual-event

Workman J. P. Jr, C. Homburg and K. Gruner (1998) Marketing Organisation: an Integrative Framework of Dimensions and Determinants, *Journal of Marketing* 62 July, 21–41.

CASE 43
Subway Germany: Destination Success?

The world loves fast-food.[1] And Germany is no exception. Burgers? Pizza? Kebabs? Sushi? Currywurst? There has never been a wider choice of fast-food offerings. The German fast-food market is expected to achieve a value of $6.7 billion by the end of 2016 (Fast Food in Germany, n.d.).

So what is driving fast-food consumption in Europe's largest economy? First, the increase in the number of fast-food outlets means that a quick bite is within easy reach. Second, aggressive pricing strategies; for example, a cheeseburger at McDonald's costs just €1.20, which has created new snacking opportunities. Third, consumers are attracted to the convenience of fast food. Hectic lifestyles means that time has become a scarce commodity. Fast-food saves all the time and hassle of cooking at home— particularly in single-person households. Next, fast-food outlets have become a social space to spend quality time with family and friends. The 'Starbucks experience' has been extended to other settings such as McCafé where consumers are trading up to enjoy a latté with a muffin or cupcake. Finally, the fast-food industry has responded to consumer health concerns with the introduction of healthier options. For example, a choice of salads and wraps are now ubiquitous at McDonald's.

Subway: The Winding Track to Global Success . . .

This should all seem like good news for the restaurant chain Subway, which has been positioned as the 'healthier' fast-food alternative. It is claimed that the sandwich was invented by John Montagu, the fourth Earl of Sandwich in 1762. Fast forward more than three hundred years to 1965, when Fred DeLuca and Peter Buck opened the first Subway store in the US state of Connecticut; consumers discovered a new way to eat sandwiches. The submarine sandwich (known as a 'sub') was born. Growth in the USA has

surpassed 27,060 outlets. The advertising slogan 'Eat Fresh' explains how every sandwich is made to order— prepared by so-called 'sandwich artists' right in front of the customer using a variety of baked breads, fillings, toppings and sauces.

The Subway sub may not be a major product innovation breakthrough, but it has just the same become an exponential success in the global market. Subway opened its first international restaurant in Bahrain in 1984. This was the start of an aggressive global expansion plan. The franchise format ensured Subway's expansion, not only rapidly, but with limited capital investment required by the franchisee and the franchisor.

Subway has since overtaken McDonald's as the world's largest restaurant chain. Subway has currently 43,825 outlets (at the time of writing) in 110 countries with outlets from Afghanistan to Zambia. Subway claims on its website that 'We've become the leading choice for people seeking quick, nutritious meals that the whole family can enjoy.'

Subway Germany: Side-tracked or Sunk?

Subway continues to open new stores across the globe with one curious exception—Germany. The first Subway restaurant opened in Berlin in 1999 and was able to expand as in other international markets

---

[1]Marketline defines the fast-food market as the sale of food and drinks for immediate consumption either on the premises or in designated eating areas shared with other foodservice operators, or for consumption elsewhere.

with their franchise model which emphasises small, low-cost outlets. Franchisees at Subway pay a fee of 12.5 per cent of their monthly sales turnover to the franchiser from which 4.5 per cent is put aside for advertising support. The franchisee is also able to benefit from Subway's franchise support system that includes employee training, product development, advertising, as well as a purchasing cooperative and field support.

By 2009, the German Subway chain had grown to 798 outlets. However, while Subway was able to sustain the growth in fast food in other European markets, German consumers were voting with their mouths. The result was that 190 Subway outlets there have already been sunk—closed for business since 2009.

There remain only 608 Subway restaurants in Germany. To make things worse, it seems that lending institutions have lost confidence in the Subway franchise. In April 2010, it was reported that Deutsche Bank would no longer offer loans to prospective Subway franchise holders (Wirtschafts Woche, 2010). This anomaly of Subway Germany's market performance is more pronounced given that Germans not only eat the most bread in Europe, but are collectively striving to follow healthier lifestyles, driven by the recognition that one in two adults are deemed as being overweight or obese.

So why are Germans jumping ship regarding Subway? William Walker was appointed the new area development manager for Germany, Austria, Luxembourg and Switzerland in May 2012. With almost 25 years' experience at McDonald's, it was hoped that Walker's fast-food industry expertise would help put the company on the right track in a market that has reached near maturity. Many Subway franchise holders are looking towards the franchiser for an action plan to revive their business fortunes—a recipe for success or failure?

Can the 'Subs' Engage under Pressure?

McDonald's is undoubtedly the giant of the German fast-food market. However, the fast-food market in

Germany remains fairly fragmented and diverse, giving the consumer greater choice. It is estimated that there are about 16,000 independent doner kebab outlets generating an annual turnover of €2.5–3 billion. Moreover, Subway is not the only quick service restaurant chain to offer so-called 'better-for-you' meals. The increasing popularity of gourmet burger chains (e.g. Hans-im-Glück) and sushi restaurant chains (e.g. Sushi Circle) are offering a premium fast-food alternative.

Moreover, Subway is subject to direct competition from approximately 14,500 master bakeries, with over 40,000 sales outlets in Germany that can be found on any High Street. For instance, the bakery chains Kamps and Wiener Feinbäcker have over 700 outlets in Germany. These bakeries sell bread rolls (*Brötchen*) that are freshly prepared with conventional fillings such as ham and cheese with a slice of pickle, using traditional German bread. Lunchtime queues are not uncommon as consumers seek the convenience of consistent home style quality closer to their workplace.

So has Subway underestimated the aggressive intensity of the German market? Is Subway's ultra-customized offering that also includes ultra-healthy options such as 6 grams or less of fat per sub a relevant product offering in this market? With 2 million different combinations available, there is something for everyone (!). . . is this actually a disadvantage?

Refloating the Value Proposition

'Icon Added Value & Brand Rating' reported in a 2007 survey that Subway is perceived as being too expensive by German consumers. This might well be a critical factor, as Germans are regarded as being particularly value-conscious consumers. A Subway 'meal deal' consisting typically of a sandwich, drink and cookie, sells for €5.19. Subway has, however, attempted to boost sales and increase restaurant frequency with the promotion of 'sub of the day' (*'Sub des Tages'*). Customers can enjoy a different sandwich each day for a set price of €2.69.

TABLE C43.1 Fast-food key players in Germany						
	Turnover in millions of euros			Number of outlets		
Year:	2014	2013	2012	2014	2013	2012
McDonald's, McCafé	3,000	3,100	3,200	1,477	1,468	1,440
Burger King	800	870	820	688	685	684
Nordsee	298	292	291	332	334	336
KFC, Pizza Hut	248	233,5	199	172	163	157

Source: Bundesverband der Systemgastronie (BdS)

>>

However, the recent success of low-cost discount bakery chains that also sell filled rolls has created new competitive price pressures. Backwerk, for example, has over 300 outlets in Germany, Austria and Switzerland, and offers a wide selection of traditional filled rolls at competitive low prices. Is Subway able to offer a competitive value proposition in order to compete simultaneously on quality and price?

TABLE C43.2 Sub of the day (*Sub des Tages*)	
Monday	Italian B.M.T
Tuesday	Salami
Wednesday	Turkey
Thursday	Chicken fajita
Friday	Tuna
Saturday	Turkey and ham
Sunday	Roasted chicken

Local Taste Buds . . . Do they Choke 'Exotic' Tastes?

Germans' passion for bread may have actually been turning them off the Subway sandwich. There are more than 300 different varieties of bread in Germany, and it may be that Germans do not wish to accept imposed quality and taste. Product localization, which has been the forefront of McDonald's global strategy, has now subtly been adopted by Subway to adapt to the culinary expectations of the German market. The introduction of locally inspired breads such as wholemeal bread, familiar to the average German, is one example. Similarly, fillings such as barbecue ribs and meatballs, considered too strange and foreign to the German palate, have since been dropped from the menu. Can Subway find the balance between global and local differences to appeal to collective German culinary preferences?

Laying New Communication Tracks

Often, executives take advantage of having informal meetings in a local Starbucks. Regularly, families choose to celebrate children's birthdays in McDonald's. Brands are appealing to the emotions and behaviours of the fast-food consumer to win over their hearts and minds, and wallets and purses.

Television advertising, which was once seen as a key advertising medium for Subway in Germany, has since been abandoned. Subway is now investing much more in social media to connect more efficiently and effectively with its customer base. Subway

Germany has over 800,000 likes on Facebook, and it recently launched a digital storytelling campaign (http://alles-fuer-dein-sub.subway-sandwiches.de) which showcases behind-the-scene stories of Subway employees.

It has also followed McDonald's with promotional tie-ups with Disney, such as *Muppets Most Wanted*, to promote its Kids Pak™ and build a stronger relationship with younger customers. Moreover, Subway was the first fast-food player in Germany to launch an electronic loyalty card. The SUBCARD™, which is also available as an app, encourages customers to collect points for purchases made at Subway that can be redeemed for Subway products.

According to YouGov Brand Index 2013, the most popular fast-food brands in Germany that year were Nordsee and McCafé, followed by Subway. Can Subway continue to compete against the huge media budgets of its international competitors?

Back on Track or Just Staying Afloat?

The German market has, however, been traditionally difficult for many foreign retailers. Walmart, Virgin and GAP have all exited from the Germany. Will Subway become another casualty of the German market? Latest data suggest that Subway Germany may have indeed weathered the storm and may be heading in the right direction. According to internal data, Subway reported a sales turnover increase of 5.6 per cent per store and an increase of 1.5 per cent in the number of customers for January to September 2014 (Subway Newsroom, 2014).

However, Subway cannot rest on its laurels. The fast-food industry remains fiercely competitive, as the battles still wage to win over the fast-food customer with new and innovative marketing initiatives. For example, McDonald's is testing 'Create Your Taste' made-to-order burgers in the USA, and has even introduced table service in some restaurant outlets in Germany. Can Subway Germany do better than just stay afloat?

Questions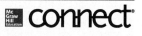

1. Using additional data from Internet sources, such as from company websites and media reports, conduct a competitor analysis of the German fast-food market.

2. Conduct a SWOT analysis of Subway Germany. Prioritize your key findings and discuss options for Subway Germany to deal with them.

3. Critically evaluate Subway Germany's competitive and marketing strategies.

4. What specific actions can Subway take to become more competitive in the German market?

5. What future consumer trends should Subway consider in its long-term marketing strategies?

This case study was prepared by Glyn Atwal, Professor in Marketing, Burgundy School of Business and Douglas Bryson, the ESC Rennes School of Business

References

Based on: Fast Food in Germany, http://www.spi-reports.com/productpdf.php?params=71779; Wirtschafts Woche (2010) Probleme bei Subway spitzen sich zu, 1 April, http://www.wiwo. de/unternehmen-maerkte/probleme-bei-subwayspitzen-sich-zu-426518; Storytelling campaign, http://alles-fuer-dein-sub.subway-sandwiches.de; YouGov BrandIndex Top-Performer 2013, https://yougov.de/loesungen/ueber-yougov/presse/presse-2014/pressemeldung-yougov-topperformer-brandindex-2013; Subway Newsroom (2014) Dem Wettbewerb voraus Subway Sandwiches trotzt dem Markttrend, 18 December, http://newsroom.subway-sandwiches.de/news_detail?id=40

CASE 44
The Good, The Bad and the Not So Ugly: Implementation in the Digital Music Industry

The music business is a fickle and challenging industry. Digital platforms have added to the complexity but also opened up opportunities in the marketplace. Streaming music from online sources has many advantages: instant access to a global resource of music, and opportunities to share music, search for new artists, and enjoy music on the go, anywhere in the world from a mobile device. This has quickly become a very popular way to access music, which many millions of music lovers around the world have been keen to adopt. The aim of this case is to explore different approaches towards implementation in the digital music industry.

According to the British Phonographic Industry (BPI), music streaming continues to be a booming business, with over 14.8 billion music tracks being downloaded in 2014 in the UK (which is double the number in the previous year). By 2019, predictions suggest the market for digital music will be worth approaching $14 billion. There are many companies seeking to take advantage of the growth market opportunities, but they have to contend with the demands of the consumer and work out how to offer a service that is better than the competition. This is challenging, as the key driver for 70 per cent of adopters is that the service is free, and 48 per cent enjoy streaming music because they can listen to music without having to purchase every song. This means that companies entering this market have to create innovative revenue streams in order to generate sufficient profits. However, there are some consumer benefits, which are not related to free access to products: customers enjoy the legitimacy of streamed music from legal providers and see this as a way to access new music.

Companies seeking to develop marketing strategies and clearly defined positioning propositions need to plan carefully and have an awareness of the current and future market requirements. Ultimately, it is how the market entrant presents their offer to the target market that is likely to define the level of success.

The Music Streaming Market

Spotify

Daniel Ek is the co-founder and CEO of Spotify, which was launched in 2008 from its base in Stockholm, Sweden. He claims, 'We started Spotify because we love music and piracy was killing it.' After a financially troubled start and a few problems with security, Spotify began to attract investment and implement its marketing strategy. Spotify was aiming to create a legal and safe digital environment for music streaming. Sean Parker, a US entrepreneur and co-founder of Napster, was recruited to 'win over the labels of the world's largest music market'. Sean brought his knowledge and experience and set about developing relationships with the big players in the music industry. Spotify developed a revenue model that overcame the issues of music being free at the point of consumption, in order to satisfy customer needs. This involved using two modes of access to the music: 1) a freemium model—a free advertising-supported streaming service—and 2) a premium subscription service, which offered access to millions of music tracks, free from advertising. This revenue model successfully supports a distinct value proposition, which encourages users to sign up to the service. By 2015, Spotify had 15 million paying customers and 45 million free users. Recording artists receive payment for each streamed track.

However, some have questioned the value of this, and notable artists like Taylor Swift and the band AC/DC have withdrawn some of their music from the platform. Spotify's response is that any value lost through the free service can be recouped through the premium service and the access to new listeners through the sharing of individuals' playlists.

Currently, Spotify is doing well, but it also faces competition from establish streaming brands such as iTunes and new market entrants including Google's YouTube Music Key and Amazon's Prime Music subscription service.

Napster

In the early days of Internet adoption, peer-to-peer music sharing (P2P) posed a significant threat to the music industry, and it was technologically a challenge for users. Napster introduced a system that allowed music fans to share music via the Internet for free. This was a popular idea. Music fans enjoyed widespread free access to music and for recording artists, this was a new way to access their listening audiences without being tied into music industry recording deals and business models. Napster created a global community, which had a profound influence on the music industry; it created a market, it broke down established business models, affected global record sales and changed the way music is consumed and paid for.

Some might think that Napster should have been closed down sooner, other mourn its loss. Founder Shawn Fanning wrote the code which changed the music industry. His idea was simple: enable users to swap music files via the Internet, without going through a middle man (centralized server). He'd been motivated to develop this service, as many people were complaining they could not find good music on the Internet. His idea succeeded, but arguably

his implementation failed. The service worked, and there was excessive demand in the marketplace, but Shawn was a technology trailblazer and he came up against five major media companies that were seeing their revenues fall. The Recording Industry Association of America sued Napster, arguing that it was facilitating the theft of intellectual property. Despite the fact that Napster only facilitated the sharing of music files and never held the music files on its server, the law suit was successful and the court order shut down the operation. At its height, Napster had 57 million users. When Napster was shut down, there was no strong management team to drive the business forward. There were failed attempts to reinstate the company through collaborations with UK electrical retailer Dixons, and then the Post Office created a market opportunity for other technology firms.

Tidal

Tidal was founded in 2014 by Aspiro, and relaunched in 2015 on a large scale following its acquisition by Jay Z, a US rapper, record producer and entrepreneur. This streaming music service set out to be artist-friendly, taking a market position that was anti its competitors, for example Spotify and Pandora Internet radio. Tidal's stance on launch was that the competing companies were not paying their artists sufficiently well, and it adopted an aggressive implementation strategy. An act of aggression against Spotify was to secure the streaming rights for Taylor Swift.

Branded as a high-fidelity service, Tidal offers a high quality sound, which is argued to be better than the competition, and uses images of recording artists in high fashion clothing as part of its positioning statement. As a result, its aggressive marketing strategy appears to have had limited traction in the marketplace, as it is out of the top 700 iTunes apps and is not attracting the number of subscribers its management anticipated. Also, its advertising strategy has failed to deliver. The company, largely managed by recording artists, developed a social media campaign using the hashtag #TIDALforALL, supported by a YouTube video explaining how this service is different (see video at https://www.youtube.com/watch?t=84&v=cYYGdcLbFkw). However, apart from the quality of the sound, Tidal is very similar to Spotify and Pandora; the breadth and depth of its play list is similar. Moreover, the management team failed to show sufficient understanding of the target audience, and people began flocking to the hashtag

»

≫

#TIDALforNOONE, which trended on Twitter. Tidal needs to focus more on its customers and start building relationships if it is to compete in the streaming music marketplace.

Questions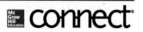

1. For each of the companies in this case, identify the barriers and opportunities of their approaches to bringing the offer to market.

2. Using Bonoma's appropriate–inappropriate strategy matrix as guide, suggest which of the companies in this case apply to quadrants of the matrix.

3. Choose one of the companies above and suggest ways to improve or develop the implementation of its marketing strategy.

4. Imagine you have an innovative business idea. From an implementation viewpoint, make a list of the problems you might encounter in bringing your idea to market.

This case was written by Fiona Ellis-Chadwick, Senior Lecturer, Loughborough University.

References

Based on: Arthur, C. (2015) Streaming: the future of the music industry, or its nightmare? *The Guardian*, 2 January http://www.theguardian.com/technology/2015/jan/02/streaming-music-industry-apple-google (accessed July 2015); Bradshaw, T. and J. Menn (2010) Spotify—MOG battle heats up, The Financial Times, 28th February http://www.ft.com/cms/s/2/7a289b4e-249b-11df-8be0-00144feab49a.html#axzz1U5W8Lyq9 (accessed July 2015); Chaffey, D. (2015) How Spotify built a $5 billion business with more than 50 million subscribers, Smartmarketing Insights http://www.smartinsights.com/digital-marketing-strategy/online-business-revenue-models/spotify-case-study (accessed July 2015); Dredge, S. (2014) Spotify CEO speaks out on Taylor Swift albums removal: 'I'm really frustrated', *The Guardian*, 11 November, http://www.theguardian.com/technology/2014/nov/11/spotify-ceo-taylor-swift-albums-daniel-ek (accessed July 2015); Geigner, T. (2015) Tidal's Failure: A Reminder To Musicians That It's Not Easy To Build A Successful Streaming Service, 1 May, https://www.techdirt.com/blog/casestudies/articles/20150422/10201730756/tidals-failure-reminder-to-musicians-that-not-easy-to-build-successful-streaming-service.shtml (accessed July 2015); Lamont, T. (2013) Napster: the day the music was set free, *The Guardian*, 24 February, http://www.theguardian.com/music/2013/feb/24/napster-music-free-file-sharing (accessed July 2015); Taro, K. (2000) Meet the Napster, *Time Magazine*, 2 October, http://content.time.com/time/world/article/0,8599,2053826,00.html (accessed July 2015); Statista (2015) digital music industry revenue, worldwide in 2014 and 2019, http://www.statista.com/statistics/267730/global-digital-music-industry-revenue (accessed July 2015); Wilhelm, P. (2015) This is why Tidal sounds better than iTunes or Spotify, 5 May, http://www.techradar.com/news/audio/this-is-why-tidal-sounds-better-than-itunes-or-spotify-1292918 (accessed July 2015)

Glossary

ad-hoc research a research project that focuses on a specific problem, collecting data at one point in time with one sample of respondents

adapted marketing mix an international marketing strategy for changing the marketing mix for each foreign target market

administered vertical marketing system a channel situation where a manufacturer that dominates a market through its size and strong brands may exercise considerable power over intermediaries even though they are independent

advertising agency an organization that specializes in providing services such as media selection, creative work, production and campaign planning to clients

advertising any paid form of non-personal communication of ideas or products in the prime media, i.e. television, the press, posters, cinema and radio, the Internet and direct marketing

advertising any paid form of non-personal communication of ideas or products in the prime media: i.e. television, the press, posters, cinema and radio, the Internet and direct marketing

advertising message the use of words, symbols and illustrations to communicate to a target audience using prime media

agency an organization that specializes in providing services such as media selection, creative work, production and campaign planning to clients

attitude the degree to which a customer or prospect likes or dislikes a brand

augmented product the core product plus extra functional and/or emotional values combined in a unique way to form a brand

awareness set the set of brands that the consumer is aware may provide a solution to the problem

beliefs descriptive thoughts that a person holds about something

benefit segmentation the grouping of people based on the different benefits they seek from a product

blog short for weblog; a personal diary/journal on the web; information can easily be uploaded on to a website and is then available for general consumption by web users

bonus pack giving a customer extra quantity at no additional cost

brainstorming the technique where a group of people generate ideas without initial evaluation; only when the list of ideas is complete is each idea then evaluated

brand a distinctive product offering created by the use of a name, symbol, design, packaging, or some combination of these, intended to differentiate it from its competitors

brand assets the distinctive features of a brand

brand domain the brand's target market

brand equity a measure of the strength of a brand in the marketplace by adding tangible value to a company through the resulting sales and profits

brand extension the use of an established brand name on a new brand within the same broad market or product category

brand heritage the background to the brand and its culture

brand personality the character of a brand described in terms of other entities such as people, animals and objects

brand reflection the relationship of the brand to self-identity

brand stretching the use of an established brand name for brands in unrelated markets or product categories

brand valuation the process of estimating the financial value of an individual or corporate brand

brand values the core values and characteristics of a brand

broadcast sponsorship a form of sponsorship where a television or radio programme is the focus

business analysis a review of the projected sales, costs and profits for a new product to establish whether these factors satisfy company objectives

business ethics the moral principles and values that guide a firm's behaviour

business intelligence the actionable knowledge produced by the analysis of 'big data' (very large data sets)

business mission the organization's purpose, usually setting out its competitive domain, which distinguishes the business from others of its type

buyers generally refers to professionals in procurement. A buyer makes business decisions on purchasing

buying centre a group that is involved in the buying decision (also known as a *decision-making unit*)

buying signals statements by a buyer that indicates/he is interested in buying

buzz marketing the passing between individuals of information about products and services that is sufficiently interesting to act as a trigger for the individuals to share the information with others

C

campaign objectives goals set by an organization in terms of, for example, sales, profits, customers won or retained, or awareness creation

category management the management of brands in a group, portfolio or category, with specific emphasis on the retail trade's requirements

cause-related marketing a commercial activity by which businesses and charities or causes form a partnership with each other to market an image or product for mutual benefit

centralization is the global integration of marketing operations

change master a person that develops an implementation strategy to drive through organizational change

channel integration the way in which the players in the channel are linked

channel intermediaries organizations that facilitate the distribution of products to customers

channel of distribution the means by which products are moved from the producer to the ultimate consumer

channel strategy the selection of the most effective distribution channel, the most appropriate level of distribution intensity and the degree of channel integration

choice criteria the various attributes (and benefits) people use when evaluating products and services

classical conditioning the process of using an established relationship between a stimulus and a response to cause the learning of the same response to a different stimulus

coercive power power inherent in the ability to punish

cognitive dissonance post-purchase concerns of a consumer arising from uncertainty as to whether a decision to purchase was the correct one

cognitive learning the learning of knowledge and development of beliefs and attitudes without direct reinforcement

combination brand name a combination of family and individual brand names

commitment a process whereby individuals (and companies) establish a bond to reduce negative aspects of a relationship

communications-based co-branding the linking of two or more existing brands from different companies or business units for the purposes of joint communication

competitive advantage the achievement of superior performance through differentiation to provide superior customer value or by managing to achieve lowest delivered cost

competitive behaviour the activities of rival companies with respect to each other; this can take five forms—conflict, competition, co-existence, cooperation and collusion

competitive bidding drawing up detailed specifications for a product and putting the contract out to tender

competitive positioning consists of three key elements: target markets, competitor targets and establishing a competitive advantage

competitive scope the breadth of a company's competitive challenge, for example broad or narrow

competitor analysis an examination of the nature of actual and potential competitors, and their objectives and strategies

competitor audit a precise analysis of competitor strengths and weaknesses, objectives and strategies

competitor targets the organizations against which a company chooses to compete directly

concept testing testing new product ideas with potential customers

concession analysis the evaluation of things that can be offered to someone in negotiation valued from the viewpoint of the receiver

consumer a person who buys goods and services for personal use

consumer decision-making process the stages a consumer goes through when buying something—namely, problem awareness, information search, evaluation of alternatives, purchase and post-purchase evaluation

consumerism organized action against business practices that are not in the interests ofconsumers

consumer movement an organized collection of groups and organizations whose objective it is to protect the rights of consumers

consumer panel household consumers who provide information on their purchases over time

consumer pull the targeting of consumers with communications (e.g. promotions) designed to create demand that will pull the product into the distribution chain

continuous research repeated interviewing of the same sample of people

contractual joint venture two or more companies form a partnership but no joint enterprise with a separate identity is formed

contractual vertical marketing system a franchise arrangement (e.g. a franchise) that ties together producers and resellers

control the stage in the marketing planning process or cycle when the performance against plan is monitored so that corrective action, if necessary, can be taken

core competences the principal distinctive capabilities possessed by a company—what it is really good at

core marketing strategy the means of achieving marketing objectives, including target markets, competitor targets and competitive advantage

core product anything that provides the central benefits required by customers

corporate social responsibility the ethical principle that an organization should be accountable for how its behaviour might affect society and the environment

corporate vertical marketing system a channel situation where an organization gains control of distribution through ownership

counter-offensive defence a counter-attack that takes the form of a head-on counter-attack, an attack on the attacker's cash cow or an encirclement of the attacker

counter-trade a method of exchange where not all transactions are concluded in cash; goods may be included as part of the asking price

covert power play the use of disguised forms of power tactics

culture the combination of traditions, taboos, values and attitudes of the society in which an individual lives

customer analysis a survey of who the customers are, what choice criteria they use, how they rate competitive offerings and on what variables they can be segmented

customer-based brand equity the differential effect that brand knowledge has on consumer response to the marketing of that brand

customer benefits those things that a customer values in a product; customer benefits derive from product features

customer relationship management (CRM) a term for the methodologies, technologies and e-commerce capabilities used by companies to manage customer relationships

customer satisfaction measurement a process through which customer satisfaction criteria are set, customers are surveyed and the results interpreted in order to establish the level of customer satisfaction with the organization's product

customer satisfaction the fulfilment of customers' requirements or needs

customer value perceived benefits minus perceived sacrifice

customers a term used in both consumer and organizational purchasing situations. These are individuals and companies that have an established relationship with a seller (e.g. retailers, producers, manufacturers)

customized marketing the market coverage strategy where a company decides to target individual customers and develops separate marketing mixes for each

D

data the most basic form of knowledge, the result of observations

decentralization is the delegation of marketing operations to individual countries or regions

decision-making process the stages that organizations and people pass through when purchasing a physical product or service

decision-making unit (DMU) a group of people within an organization who are involved in the buying decision (also known as the buying centre)

demography changes in the population in terms of its size and characteristics

descriptive research research undertaken to describe customers' beliefs, attitudes, preferences and behaviour

differential advantage a clear performance differential over the competition on factors that are important to target customers

differential marketing strategies market coverage strategies where a company decides to target several market segments and develops separate marketing mixes for each

differentiated marketing a market coverage strategy where a company decides to target several market segments and develops separate marketing mixes for each

differentiation strategy the selection of one or more customer choice criteria and positioning the offering accordingly to achieve superior customer value

diffusion of innovation process the process by which a new product spreads throughout a market over time

digital marketing the application of digital technologies that form channels to market (the Internet, mobile communications, interactive television and wireless) to achieve corporate goals through meeting and exceeding customer needs better than the competition

digital promotion the promotion of products to consumers and businesses through electronic media

digital surveys various methods of gathering qualitative (and in some cases quantitative) data using email or web-based surveys

direct-cost pricing the calculation of only those costs that are likely to rise as output increases

direct exporting the handling of exporting activities by the exporting organization rather than by a domestically based independent organization

direct investment market entry that involves investment in foreign-based assembly or manufacturing facilities

direct mail material sent through the postal service to the recipient's house or business address promoting a product and/or maintaining an ongoing relationship

direct marketing (1) acquiring and retaining customers without the use of an intermediary; (2) the distribution of products, information and promotional benefits to target consumers through interactive communication in a way that allows response to be measured

direct response advertising the use of the prime advertising media such as television, newspapers and magazines to elicit an order, enquiry or request for a visit

disintermediation the removal of channel partners by bypassing intermediaries and going directly from manufacturer to consumer via the Internet

distribution analysis an examination of movements in power bases, channel attractiveness, physical distribution and distribution behaviour

distribution push the targeting of channel intermediaries with communications(e.g. promotions) to push the product into the distribution chain

divest to improve short-term cash yield by dropping or selling off a product

E

ecology the study of living things within their environment

e-commerce involves all electronically mediated transactions between an organization and any third party it deals with, including exchange of information

economic value to the customer (EVC) the amount a customer would have to pay to make the total lifecycle costs of a new and a reference product the same

effectiveness doing the right thing, making the correct strategic choice

efficiency a way of managing business processes to a high standard, usually concerned with cost reduction; also called 'doing things right'

encirclement attack attacking the defender from all sides; i.e. every market segment is hit with every combination of product features

entry barriers that act to prevent new companies from entering a market, for example the high level of investment required

entry into new markets (diversification) the entry into new markets by new products

environmentalism the organized movement of groups and organizations to protect and improve the physical environment

environmental scanning the process of monitoring and analyzing the marketing environment of a company

e-procurement digital systems that facilitate the management of the procurement process; often integrates with e-commerce systems

equity joint venture where two or more companies form a partnership that involves the creation of a new company

ethical consumption the taking of purchase decisions not only on the basis of personal interests but also on the basis of the interests of society and the environment

ethics the moral principles and values that govern the actions and decisions of an individual or group

ethnography a form of qualitative research which involves detailed and prolonged observation of consumers in the situations which inform their buying behaviour

event sponsorship sponsorship of a sporting or other event

evoked set the set of brands that the consumer seriously evaluates before making a purchase

exaggerated promises barrier a barrier to the matching of expected and perceived service levels caused by the unwarranted building up of expectations by exaggerated promises

exchange the act or process of receiving something from someone by giving something in return

exclusive distribution an extreme form of selective distribution where only one wholesaler, retailer or industrial distributor is used in a geographical area to sell the products of a supplier

exhibition an event that brings buyers and sellers together in a commercial setting

experience curve the combined effect of economies of scale and learning as cumulative output increases

experimental research research undertaken in order to establish cause and effect

expert power power that derives from an individual's expertise

exploratory research the preliminary exploration of a research area prior to the main data-collection stage

F

fair trade marketing the development, promotion and selling of fair trade brands and the positioning of organizations on the basis of a fair trade ethos

family brand name a brand name used for all products in a range

fighter brands low-cost manufacturers' brands introduced to combat own-label brands

flanking attack attacking geographical areas or market segments where the defender is poorly represented

flanking defence the defence of a hitherto unprotected market segment

focused marketing a market coverage strategy where a company decides to target one market segment with a single marketing mix

focus group a group normally of six to twelve consumers brought together for a discussion focusing on an aspect of a company's marketing

foreign consumer culture positioning positioning a brand as associated with a specific foreign culture (e.g. Italian fashion)

franchise a legal contract in which a producer and channel intermediaries agree each other's rights and obligations; usually the intermediary receives marketing, managerial, technical and financial services in return for a fee

franchising a form of licensing where a package of services is offered by the franchisor to the franchisee in return for payment

frontal attack a competitive strategy where the challenger takes on the defender head on

full-cost pricing pricing so as to include all costs and based on certain sales volume assumptions

G

geodemographics the process of grouping households into geographic clusters based on information such as type of accommodation, occupation, number and age of children, and ethnic background

global account management (GAM) the process of coordinating and developing mutually beneficial long-term relationships with a select group of strategically important customers (accounts) operating in globalized industries

global branding achievement of brand penetration worldwide

global consumer culture positioning positioning a brand as a symbol of a given global culture (e.g. young cosmopolitan men)

going-rate pricing pricing at the rate generally applicable in the market, focusing on competitors' offerings rather than on company costs

guerrilla attack making life uncomfortable for stronger rivals through, for example, unpredictable price discounts, sales promotions or heavy advertising in a few selected regions

H

halo customers customers that are not directly targeted but may find the product attractive

harvest objective the improvement of profit margins to improve cash flow even if the longer-term result is falling sales

hold objective a strategy of defending a product in order to maintain market share

I

inadequate delivery barrier a barrier to the matching of expected and perceived service levels caused by the failure of the service provider to select, train and reward staff adequately, resulting in poor or inconsistent delivery of service

inadequate resources barrier a barrier to the matching of expected and perceived service levels caused by the unwillingness of service providers to provide the necessary resources

in-depth interviews the interviewing of consumers individually for perhaps one or two hours, with the aim of understanding their attitudes, values, behaviour and/or beliefs

indirect exporting the use of independent organizations within the exporter's domestic market to facilitate export

individual brand name a brand name that does not identify a brand with a particular company

industry a group of companies that market products that are close substitutes for each other

information combinations of data that provide decision-relevant knowledge

information framing the way in which information is presented to people

information processing the process by which a stimulus is received, interpreted, stored in memory and later retrieved

information search the identification of alternative ways of problem-solving

ingredient co-branding the explicit positioning of a supplier's brand as an ingredient of a product

innovation the commercialization of an invention by bringing it to market

inseparability a characteristic of services, namely that their production cannot be separated from their consumption

intangibility a characteristic of services, namely that they cannot be touched, seen, tasted or smelled

integrated marketing communications (IMC) the concept that companies coordinate their marketing communications tools to deliver a clear, consistent, credible and competitive message about the organization and its products

intensive distribution the aim of this is to provide saturation coverage of the market by using all available outlets

internal marketing training, motivating and communicating with staff to cause them to work effectively in providing customer satisfaction; more recently the term has been expanded to include marketing to all staff, with the aim of

achieving the acceptance of marketing ideas and plans

invention the discovery of new methods and ideas

J

just-in-time (JIT) this concept aims to minimize stocks by organizing a supply system that provides materials and components as they are required

K

key account management (KAM) an approach to selling that focuses resources on major customers and uses a team selling approach

L

learning any change in the content or organization of long-term memory as the result of information processing

legitimate power power based on legitimate authority, such as line management

licensing a contractual arrangement in which a licensor provides a licensee with certain rights, for example to technology access or production rights

lifecycle costs all the components of costs associated with buying, owning and using a physical product or service

lifestyle segmentation the grouping of people according to their pattern of living as expressed in their activities, interests and opinions

lifestyle the pattern of living as expressed in a person's activities, interests and opinions

local consumer culture positioning positioning a brand as associated with a local culture (e.g. local production and consumption of a good)

loyalty a term used to explain repeated purchasing behaviour

M

macroenvironment a number of broader forces that affect not only the company but the other actors in the environment, for example social, political, technological and economic

macrosegmentation the segmentation of organizational markets by size, industry and location

manufacturer brands brands that are created by producers and bear their chosen brand name

market analysis the statistical analysis of market size, growth rates and trends

market development to take current products and market them in new markets

market expansion the attempt to increase the size of a market by converting non-users to users of the product and by increasing usage rates

marketing accountability the requirement to justify marketing investment by using marketing metrics

marketing audit a systematic examination of a business's marketing environment, objectives, strategies and activities with a view to identifying key strategic issues, problem areas and opportunities

marketing concept the achievement of corporate goals through meeting and exceeding customer needs better than the competition

marketing control the stage in the marketing planning process or cycle when performance against plan is monitored so that corrective action, if necessary, can be taken

marketing database an interactive approach to marketing that uses individually addressable marketing media and channels to provide information to a target audience, stimulate demand and stay close to customers

marketing environment the actors and forces that affect a company's capability to operate effectively in providing products and services to its customers

marketing ethics the moral principles and values that guide behaviour within the field of marketing

marketing information system a system in which marketing information is formally gathered, stored, analyzed and distributed to managers in accordance with their informational needs on a regular, planned basis

marketing metrics quantitative measures of the outcomes of marketing activities and expenditures

marketing mix a framework for the tactical management of the customer relationship, including product, place, price, promotion (the 4-Ps); in the case of services, three other elements to be taken into account are process, people and physical evidence

marketing objectives there are two types of marketing objective: strategic thrust, which dictates which products should be sold in which markets, and strategic objectives—that is, product-level objectives such as build, hold, harvest and divest

marketing planning the process by which businesses analyse the environment and their capabilities, decide upon courses of marketing action and implement those decisions

marketing research the gathering of data and information on the market and consumer reactions to product, pricing, promotional and distribution decisions

marketing structures the marketing frameworks (organization, training and internal communications) upon which marketing activities are based

marketing systems sets of connected parts (information, planning and control) that support the marketing function

market-orientated pricing an approach to pricing that takes a range of marketing factors into account when setting prices

market orientation companies with a market orientation focus on customer needs as the primary drivers of organizational performance

market penetration to continue to grow sales by marketing an existing product in an existing market

market segmentation the process of identifying individuals or organizations with similar characteristics that have significant implications for the determination of marketing strategy

market share analysis a comparison of company sales with total sales of the product, including sales of competitors

market testing the limited launch of a new product to test sales potential

media channel the means used to transmit a message, including spoken words, print, radio, television or the Internet. Also called the *medium*

media class the press, cinema, television, posters, radio, or some combination of these

media planning an advertising strategy most commonly employed to target consumers using a variety of informational outlets. Media planning is generally conducted by a professional media planning or advertising agency and typically finds the most appropriate media outlets to reach the target market

media relations the communication of a product or business by placing information about it in the media without paying for time or space directly

media type (also referred to as a *content type*) is a general category of data content, such as: application (executable program), audio content, an image, a text message, a video stream, and so forth

media vehicle the choice of the particular newspaper, magazine, television spot, poster site, etc.

media vehicle decision the choice of the particular newspaper, magazine, television spot, poster site, etc.

message the use of words, symbols and illustrations to communicate to a target audience using prime media

microblogging involves the posting of short messages on social media sites like Twitter and Reddit

microenvironment the actors in the firm's immediate environment that affect its capability to operate effectively in its chosen markets—namely, suppliers, distributors, customers and competitors

microsegmentation segmentation according to choice criteria, DMU structure, decision-making process, buy class, purchasing structure and organizational innovativeness

misconception barrier a failure by marketers to understand what customers really value about their service

mobile defence involves diversification or broadening the market by redefining the business

mobile marketing the sending of text messages to mobile phones to promote products and build relationships with consumers

modified rebuy where a regular requirement for the type of product exists and the buying alternatives are known but sufficient change (e.g. a delivery problem) has occurred to require some alteration to the normal supply procedure

money-off promotions sales promotions that discount the normal price

motivation the process involving needs that set drives in motion to accomplish goals

multichannel involves an organization that is using different channels—physical retailer stores, the web and mobile, to enable its customers to buy, communicate, gain access to information or pay for goods and services. The organization in return provides consistent levels of service and marketing mix across all of the channels

N

new task refers to the first-time purchase of a product or input by an organization

niche a small market segment

not-for-profit marketing involves the use of marketing frameworks, concepts and ideas used by an organization that operates on a not-for-profit basis; this type of organization often employs a volunteer workforce and relies on donations and external funding

O

omnibus survey a regular survey, usually operated by a marketing research specialist company, which asks questions of respondents for several clients on the same questionnaire

omni channel the bringing together of all of the customer touchpoints into a seamless shopping journey, which means that every time the customer 'touches' or interacts with a company, for example by store, by phone, by the web by mobile

operant conditioning the use of rewards to generate reinforcement of response

overt power play the use of visible, open kinds of power tactics

own-label brands brands created and owned by distributors or retailers

P

parallel co-branding the joining of two or more independent brands to produce a combined brand

PEEST analysis the analysis of the political/legal, economic, ecological/physical, social/cultural and technological environments

perception the process by which people select, organize and interpret sensory stimulation into a meaningful picture of the world

perishability a characteristic of services, namely that the capacity of a service business, such as a hotel room, cannot be stored—if it is not occupied, this is lost income that cannot be recovered

personality the inner psychological characteristics of individuals that lead to consistent responses to their environment

personal selling oral communication with prospective purchasers with the intention of making a sale

place the distribution channels to be used, outlet locations, methods of transportation

portfolio planning managing groups of brands and product lines

position defence building a fortification around existing products, usually through keen pricing and improved promotion

positioning strategy the choice of target market (*where* the company wishes to compete) and differential advantage (*how* the company wishes to compete)

positioning the choice of target market (where the company wishes to compete) and differential advantage (how the company wishes to compete)

pre-emptive defence usually involves continuous innovation and new product development, recognizing that attack is the best form of defence

premiums any merchandise offered free or at low cost as an incentive to purchase

price (1) the amount of money paid for a product; (2) the agreed value placed on the exchange by buyer and seller

price unbundling pricing each element in the offering so that the price of the total product package is raised

price waterfall the difference between list price and realized or transaction price

product a good or service offered or performed by an organization or individual, which is capable of satisfying customer needs

product-based co-branding the linking of two or more existing brands from different companies or business units to form a product in which the brand names are visible to consumers

product churning a continuous and rapid spiral of new product introductions

product development increasing sales by improving present products or developing new products for current markets

product features the characteristics of a product that may or may not convey a customer benefit

product lifecycle a four-stage cycle in the life of a product illustrated as sales and profits curves, the four stages being introduction, growth, maturity and decline

product line a group of brands that are closely related in terms of the functions and benefits they provide

product mix the total set of products marketed by a company

product placement the deliberate placing of products and/or their logos in movies and television, usually in return for money

product portfolio the total range of products offered by the company

production orientation a business approach that is inwardly focused either on costs or on a definition of a company in terms of its production facilities

profile segmentation the grouping of people in terms of profile variables, such as age and socio-economic group, so that marketers can communicate to them

profitability analysis the calculation of sales revenues and costs for the purpose of calculating the profit performance of products, customers and/or distribution channels

project teams the bringing together of staff from such areas as R&D, engineering, manufacturing, finance and marketing to work on a project such as new product development

promotional mix advertising, personal selling, sales promotions, public relations, direct marketing, and Internet and online promotion

proposal analysis the prediction and evaluation of proposals and demands likely to be made by someone with whom one is negotiating

proprietary-based brand equity is derived from company attributes that deliver value to the brand

psychographic segmentation the grouping of people according to their lifestyle and personality characteristics

public relations (PR) the management of communications and relationships to establish goodwill and mutual understanding between an organization and its public

Q

QR codes a form of barcode which, once scanned, can link the user directly to web content, digital adverts and other available content. They are easy to use and smartphones can read the codes

qualitative research exploratory research that aims to understand consumers' attitudes, values, behaviour and beliefs

quantitative research a structured study of small or large samples using a predetermined list of questions or criteria

R

reasoning a more complex form of cognitive learning where conclusions are reached by connected thought

rebranding the changing of a brand or corporate name

reference group a group of people that influences an individual's attitude or behaviour

referent power power derived by the reference source, for example when people identify with and respect the architect of change

reintermediation the introduction of new forms of channel intermediary that provide services which link members of the supply chain, for example web service providers and retailers

relationship marketing the process of creating, maintaining and enhancing strong relationships with customers and other stakeholders

repositioning changing the target market or differential advantage, or both

research brief a written document stating the client's requirements

research proposal a document defining what the marketing research agency promises to do for its client and how much it will cost

retail audit a type of continuous research tracking the sales of products through retail outlets

retail positioning the choice of target market and differential advantage for a retail outlet

reverse marketing the process whereby the buyer attempts to persuade the supplier to provide exactly what the organization wants

reward power power derived from the ability to provide benefits

rote learning the learning of two or more concepts without conditioning

S

safety (buffer) stocks stocks or inventory held to cover against uncertainty about resupply lead times

sales analysis a comparison of actual with target sales

sales promotion incentives to customers or the trade that are designed to stimulate purchase

salesforce evaluation the measurement of salesperson performance so that strengths and weaknesses can be identified

sampling process a term used in research to denote the selection of a sub-set of the total population in order to interview them

satisfaction an indicator of the extent to which customer expectations have been met. As a concept it is important to long-term relationship building

secondary research data that have already been collected by another researcher for another purpose

selective attention the process by which people screen out those stimuli that are neither meaningful to them nor consistent with their experiences and beliefs

selective distortion the distortion of information received by people according to their existing beliefs and attitudes

selective distribution the use of a limited number of outlets in a geographical area to sell the products of a supplier

selective retention the process by which people only retain a selection of messages in memory

self-reference criteria the use of one's own perceptions and choice criteria to judge what is important to consumers. In global marketing the perceptions and choice criteria of domestic consumers may be used to judge what is important to foreign consumers

service any deed, performance or effort carried out for the customer

service quality involves the experience a customer has of a company's offer. Services vary in complexity and the investment and risk a customer makes in the purchase

services marketing mix product, place, price, promotion, people, process and physical evidence (the '7-Ps')

simultaneous engineering the involvement of manufacturing and product development engineers in the same development team in an effort to reduce development time

social marketing seeks to change behaviour for the benefit of the individual and society and its applications come in many different guises.

social media online community websites with individuals who can become members, share ideas and interests, for example Facebook; publish and distribute articles and video and other multimedia content, for example YouTube; carry out social commerce activities like writing reviews, buying and selling, for example TripAdvisor; or play games across communities, for example Zynga

societal marketing focuses on consumers' needs and long-term welfare as keys to satisfying organizational objectives and responsibilities by taking into account consumers' and societies' wider interests rather than just their short-term consumption

sponsorship a business relationship between a provider of funds, resources or services and an individual, event or organization that offers in return some rights and association that may be used for commercial advantage

stakeholder an individual or group that either (i) is harmed by or benefits from the company, or (ii) whose rights can be violated or have to be respected by the company

stakeholder theory this contends that companies are not managed purely in the interests of their shareholders alone but a broader group including communities associated with the company, employees, customers and suppliers

standardized marketing mix a marketing strategy for using essentially the same product, promotion, distribution, and pricing in all the company's global markets

straight rebuy refers to a purchase by an organization from a previously approved supplier of a previously purchased item

strategic alliance collaboration between two or more organizations through, for example, joint ventures, licensing agreements, long-term purchasing and supply arrangement, or a joint R&D contract to build a competitive advantage

strategic business unit a business or company division serving a distinct group of customers and with a distinct set of competitors, usually strategically autonomous

strategic focus the strategies that can be employed to achieve an objective

strategic issues analysis an examination of the suitability of marketing objectives and segmentation bases in the light of changes in the marketplace

strategic objectives product-level objectives relating to the decision to build, hold, harvest or divest products

strategic thrust the decision concerning which products to sell in which markets

strategic withdrawal holding onto the company's strengths while getting rid of its weaknesses

strong theory of advertising the notion that advertising can change people's attitudes sufficiently to persuade people who have not previously bought a brand to buy it; desire and conviction precede purchase

supplier analysis an examination of who and where suppliers are located, their competences and shortcomings, the trends affecting them and the future outlook for them

sustainable marketing focuses on reducing environmental damage by creating, producing and delivering sustainable solutions while continuing to satisfy customers and other stakeholders

SWOT analysis a structured approach to evaluating the strategic position of a business by identifying its strengths, weaknesses, opportunities and threats

T

target accounts organizations or individuals whose custom the company wishes to obtain

target audience the group of people at which an advertisement or message is aimed

target market a market segment that has been selected as a focus for the company's offering or communications

target marketing the choice of which market segment(s) to serve with a tailored marketing mix

team sponsorship sponsorship of a team—for example, a football, cricket or motor racing team

telemarketing a marketing communications system whereby trained specialists use telecommunications and information technologies to conduct marketing and sales activities

test marketing the launch of a new product in one or a few geographic areas chosen to be representative of the intended market

total quality management the set of programmes designed to constantly improve the quality of physical products, services and processes

touchpoints points at which a customer interacts with a company across a customer journey and where data can be collected

trade marketing marketing to the retail trade

trade-off analysis a measure of the trade-off customers make between price and other product features so that their effects on product preference can be established

trade show similar to an exhibition as it brings together buyers, sellers and competitors under one roof, but is not open to the public

transfer pricing the price charged between the profit centres of the same company, sometimes used to take advantage of lower taxes in another country

transition curve the emotional stages that people pass through when confronted with an adverse change

trust a customer's level of confidence in a company's ability to supply the required goods, its reliability and integrity

U

undifferentiated marketing a market coverage strategy where a company decides to ignore market segment differences and develops a single marketing mix for the whole market

V

value analysis a method of cost reduction in which components are examined to see if they can be made more cheaply

value chain the set of a company's activities that are conducted to design, manufacture, market, distribute and service its products

variability a characteristic of services, namely that, being delivered by people, the standard of their performance is open to variation

vicarious learning learning from others without direct experience or reward

W

weak theory of advertising the notion that advertising can first arouse awareness and interest, nudge some consumers towards a doubting first trial purchase and then provide some reassurance and reinforcement; desire and conviction do not precede purchase

Companies and Brands Index

Subjects And Authors Index